The Illustrated

A to Z Encyclopedia

of Garden Plants

The Illustrated
A to Z Encyclopedia
of Garden Plants

A Guide to Choosing the Best Plants

for Your Garden

TIME-LIFE BOOKS

ALEXANDRIA, VIRGINIA

Time-Life Books is a division of Time Life Inc.
Time-Life is a trademark of Time Warner Inc. and affiliated companies.

Time Life Inc.
Chairman and Chief Executive Officer: Jim Nelson
President and Chief Operating Officer: Steven Janas
Senior Executive Vice President and Chief Operations Officer:
   Mary Davis Holt
Senior Vice President and Chief Financial Officer: Christopher Hearing

Time-Life Books
President: Larry Jellen
Senior Vice President, New Markets: Bridget Boel
Vice President, Home and Hearth Markets: Nicholas M. DiMarco
Vice President, Content Development: Jennifer L. Pearce

Time-Life Trade Publishing
Vice President and Publisher: Neil S. Levin
Senior Sales Director: Richard J. Vreeland
Director, Marketing and Publicity: Inger Forland
Director of Trade Sales: Dana Hobson
Director of Custom Publishing: John Lalor
Director of Rights and Licensing: Olga Vezeris

The Illustrated A to Z Encyclopedia of Garden Plants
Director of New Product Development: Carolyn M. Clark
New Product Development Manager: Lori A. Woehrle
Executive Editor: Linda Bellamy
Director of Design: Kate L. McConnell
Director of Production: Carolyn Bounds
Quality Assurance: Jim King and Stacy L. Eddy

Project Manager: Lynn McGowan
Book Design: Kathleen Mallow-Sager
Writers: Lisa Leicht, Gisela McBride, Lynn McGowan
Technical Specialist: Monika Lynde
Proofreader: Celia Beattie
Indexer: Lina B. Burton

Editorial Staff for The Time-Life Complete Gardener
Editor: Janet Cave
Administrative Editor: Roxie France-Nuriddin
Art Directors: Cindy Morgan-Jaffe, Kathleen Mallow-Sager,
   Alan Pitts, Sue Pratt
Picture Editors: Jane Jordan, Jane A. Martin
Text Editors: Sarah Brash, Darcie Conner Johnston, Paul Mathless
Associate Editors/Research and Writing: Megan Barnett, Constance
   Contreras, Sharon Kurtz, Katya Sharpe, Robert Speziale, Karen Sweet,
   Mary-Sherman Willis
Senior Copyeditors: Anne Farr (principal), Donna D. Carey,
   Colette Stockum
Picture Coordinators: David Cheatham, Ruth Goldberg,
   Kimberly Grandcolas, David A. Herod, Betty H. Weatherley
Editorial Assistant: Donna Fountain

Contributors: Jennifer Clark, Catherine Harper Parrott (picture research);
   Vilasini Balakrishnan, Linda Bellamy, Cyndi Bemel, Susan S. Blair,
   Dena Crosson, Meg Dennison, Catriona Tudor Erler, Catherine
   Hackett, Adrian Higgins, Marie Hofer, Jamie R. Holland, Ann Kelsall,
   Bonnie Kreitler, Jocelyn G. Lindsay, Peter Loewer, Carole Ottesen,
   Rita Pelczar, Ann Perry, Warren Schultz, Roseanne Scott, Margaret
   Stevens, Marianna Tait-Durbin, Susan Gregory Thomas, André
   Viette, Cheryl Weber, Olwen Woodier (research and writing);
   Margery duMond, Marfé Ferguson-Delano, Jim Hicks, Bonnie
   Kreitler, Joyce B. Marshall, Gerry Shremp, Lynn Yorke (editing);
   John Drummond (art); Anne Sinderman (consultant).

Correspondents: Christine Hinze (London), Christina Lieberman
   (New York). Valuable assistance was also provided by Liz Brown
   (New York) and Judy Aspinall (London).

© 2001 Time Life Inc. All rights reserved. No part of this book may be reproduced
in any form or by any electronic or mechanical means, including information storage
and retrieval devices or systems, without prior written permission from the publisher,
except that brief passages may be quoted for reviews.

Printed in U.S.A.
10 9 8 7 6 5 4 3 2 1

School and library distribution by Time-Life Education
P.O. Box 85026, Richmond, Virginia 23285-5026

ISBN 0-7370-0632-3

CIP data available upon application:
Librarian, Time-Life Books
2000 Duke Street
Alexandria, VA 22314

For information on and a full description of any of the Time-Life Books series listed above,
please call 1-800-621-7026 or write:

Reader Information
Time-Life Customer Service
P.O. Box C-32068
Richmond, Virginia 23261-2068

Contents

Introduction

When it comes time to choose plants for your garden, you may be tempted to pick anything that looks interesting or appealing. But your chances of success will be greater if you first consider which plants best suit your needs and growing conditions. And learning all about your options *before* you visit the nursery can be every bit as rewarding as selecting plants and watching them flourish in your garden.

To help you make your selections, presented on the following pages are some of the most popular and readily available garden plants in the United States. The plants are organized into nine different categories or sections for easy reference. In some cases, plants are listed under more than one category—for instance, *Lavandula* is found under Perennials, Herbs, and Trees and Shrubs. Within each of these sections, the plants are listed alphabetically by their Latin botanical names; common names appear in bold type beneath the Latin. (Plants in the Roses and Vegetables sections are listed alphabetically by cultivar or common name.) If you are looking for a plant and only know it by its common name, check the index.

Generally, a botanical name consists of the genus (such as *Iris*) and a species (as in *Iris ensata*), both printed in italics. Many species contain one or more cultivars, which are set off by single quotation marks (for example, *Iris ensata* 'Pink Lady'). An "x" preceding the name—as in *Iris* x 'Louisiana'— indicates a hybrid.

PLANT TYPES

Although plant categories are not always clear-cut, they're an important factor in the plant selection process. Following are brief explanations of a few horticultural terms you'll find in the entries throughout this book.

Annuals, Biennials, and Perennials Strictly speaking, a true annual such as marigold or petunia completes its entire life cycle—from seed germination through flowering, setting seed, and death—in just one season. From a practical standpoint, however, an annual is any plant that is going to flower for only a single season or year in your garden, regardless of its potential for greater longevity. The definition of "annual," then, expands to include biennials and tender perennials.

A typical biennial, left to its own devices, usually requires two growing seasons to complete its life cycle. Sprouting from seed and producing a leafy rosette in the first year, it then flowers in the second, sets seed, and dies. Biennials can be started in the open garden in late spring or seeded in flats and moved to the garden in late summer or early fall for blooms the next spring. But if you start seeds early indoors, some biennials will flower late in the first season.

Whether a biennial can complete its cycle in one season depends on the variety and your climate. Most foxgloves, for example, take up to 300 days to flower and set seed, and in cooler climates will have to overwinter. If you plant biennial seedlings in their permanent home and plan for blooms the next spring, make sure the variety is hardy enough for your zone *(map, page 466)*. If it's not, overwinter the young plants in a cold frame for protection.

Tender perennials—which include the popular wax begonias—may live out several seasons in semitropical climates. But these plants can't tolerate the winter cold of more northerly zones, so they die with the frost. Since they flower in their first season, tender perennials are treated as annuals in most climates.

In contrast, perennials that aren't too tender to survive the winter, such as daylilies, go through a cycle of growth that repeats each year. Sprouting from seed in the spring, the plant develops roots and foliage, and may flower as well during the first summer. By winter the foliage dies back and the roots go dormant. The following spring the plant reawakens, and during the summer and into the fall, both roots and foliage renew their growth while the plant blossoms. Each year the plant repeats the process, producing more roots, foliage, and flowers.

Hardy, Half-Hardy, and Tender With perennials and shrubs, "hardiness" refers to a plant's ability to survive degrees of winter cold, usually in terms of geographical zones. When applied to annuals, however, "hardy" and "tender" signify the minimum temperature required for the seeds to germinate. With annuals, the terms also indicate the frost tolerance of the plants once they are in the ground.

Hardy annuals are those whose seeds can withstand temperatures below freezing (32° F); they may even require such frigid conditions to break dormancy and sprout. Once they germinate, hardy annuals easily weather any number of late-winter and early-spring freezes and thaws. If planted directly outdoors, the seeds are typically sown as soon as the soil can be worked in the spring or a couple of weeks past the first frost in fall. As mature plants, hardy annuals are able to tolerate hard frosts. Ornamental cabbage, for example, easily stands up to cold temperatures and is a favorite in the winter garden.

Tender annuals such as New Guinea impatiens originate in tropical climates, and to flourish they require equally warm conditions. These annuals can't be sown outdoors—or transplanted—until all danger of frost has passed and the soil has warmed completely. A few months later, they usually die with the first fall frost.

A third group—half-hardy annuals—is a catch-all class composed of annuals that fall anywhere between the two extremes; some tolerate a surprising number of frosts, others just a few. Typically, they can be sown or transplanted to the garden after the last spring frost even if the soil has not warmed thoroughly. Although they aren't impervious to hard freezes, half-hardy seedlings willingly accept the extended cold, damp periods that often accompany mid- to late-spring weather.

Cool- and Warm-Season Vegetables Cool-season vegetables include annuals that can be sown or transplanted outdoors when the soil is cool and that can withstand spring or fall frosts. In addition to true annuals, this category includes biennials such as Brussels sprouts and carrots that are commonly grown as annuals.

Warm-season vegetables germinate best when soil temperatures reach 65° to 70° F and will tolerate light frost. Hot-season crops require very warm soil temperatures to germinate and both warm days and warm nights to develop and ripen.

Winter-hardy vegetables are perennials in some climate zones, where they can be allowed to remain in the same garden spot from one year to the next. Some of these perennials can also be cultivated as cool-season annuals. Use the frost maps on page 467 as a guide in determining when you can expect the last hard spring frost and the first hard fall frost in your area.

Bulbs The four major types of bulbs—corms, true bulbs, rhizomes, and tubers—all consist of fleshy tissue where nutrients and moisture are stored.

Corms such as crocuses are actually modified stems packed with nutrients; shoots emerge from the bud at the top, and the corm itself is protected by a layer of dried leaf bases. True bulbs also have a modified stem, but in addition they contain an embryonic flower attached to the base. Some true bulbs, such as daffodils, have a papery protective outer cover, or tunic. Inside are fleshy leaves called scales; shoots emerge from the top, and roots from the base. Other bulbs—lilies, for example—have no tunic. A rhizome, such as canna, is a thickened stem growing horizontally and functioning as the food reserve. The dried, flaky vertical tip is what remains of last season's stalk and leaves. The shoots grow from the eye at the rhizome's side, with new roots emerging around and beneath the eye.

Tubers vary in their structure. For example, the swollen part of the potato-like begonia is a stem; it produces shoots from eyes at the top and projects thin roots from its bottom surface. Dahlias, on the other hand, are thickened roots that store food; the smaller roots take up water and nutrients. Growth buds cluster on the old stem, called the crown.

Some bulbs—crocus, tulip, daffodil, and iris, for instance—are winter-hardy. In contrast, tender bulbs can survive winter in the ground only in warm regions; elsewhere, they must be dug up in fall for winter storage or grown in pots. This group includes amaryllis, dahlia, and gladiolus.

GROWING CONDITIONS

No matter how appealing a plant may look displayed in a catalog or nursery, it won't grow well in your yard if you can't provide the right conditions. When selecting plants, you'll need to consider such factors as local climate and the amount of light your garden receives.

The USDA Hardiness Zone Map The climate in your region—especially your lowest average winter temperature—is probably the single most important factor in determining what you can grow successfully.

The United States Department of Agriculture has produced the most widely used hardiness map, which divides North America into 11 zones. The warmest of these regions, Zone 11 on the map, rarely experiences temperatures below freezing and includes tropical and subtropical climates. The coldest region, Zone 1, is north of the Arctic Circle in central Alaska and northern Canada, where temperatures can plunge to 50° below zero. Between these extremes lie the remaining nine climate zones. Use the map on page 466 to find your growing zone, then select the plants that will thrive where you live. The hardiness zone range assigned to each plant in the encyclopedia entries indicates where it will grow best; plants grown outside the recommended zones may do poorly or die.

Sun versus Shade In addition to climatic elements such as winter cold, summer heat, and rainfall, you'll need to consider the light or shade your garden receives. The common measures of light are amount and intensity, both of which vary depending on the time of day, the season, and the latitude. For example, sunlight is least intense in early morning and most intense at noon. And the South enjoys more intense sunshine year round than do the northern states.

The term "full sun" is generally used to mean a total of 6 hours or more of direct, unobstructed sunlight between 9:00 a.m. and 4:00 p.m. If a site receives *less* than 6 hours of direct sunlight per day—with 4 of those hours occurring in the morning—then it is considered shady.

Shade is created by trees, shrubs, and other plants, and by physical features such as walls, fences, and hills. The atmosphere—for example, clouds, fog, and even pollution—can also block sunlight. These different sources produce various types of shade:

Partial shade—This is the sunniest shade, in which an area receives up to 6 hours of direct sun, including 4 or more hours in the morning, but lies in shadow the rest of the day. Many plants listed as requiring full shade will tolerate partial shade if the soil is kept moist, especially in cooler climates. And many sun-loving plants adapt well to partial shade. Keep in mind, however, that if 4 or more of those 6 hours of sun occur in the afternoon instead of the morning, the area is considered to be in full sun.

Filtered, dappled, or light shade—The sun's light is screened through the open foliage of high-branched trees or through latticework structures, creating shifting patterns all day. Most plants will thrive in dappled shade, though sun lovers may produce fewer flowers than they would in full sun.

Full shade—Direct sunlight never reaches an area in full shade. Some full shade may be deep and dense, and few plants will survive there. But an area in full shade can also experience considerable ambient or reflected light (what is sometimes referred to as "bright full shade"). These conditions often occur on the north side of a building, fence, hedge, or tree. Shade-tolerant plants will grow in this kind of full shade if they have enough air circulation and moisture.

Annuals

TO MOST GARDENERS, ANNUALS MEAN DRAMATIC color—and lots of it. From the simplest display in a window box to the most lavish design in a formal garden, these short-lived plants enhance any landscape with their exuberance.

Annuals have many other virtues as well. Dependable performers, they require little in the way of nutrients, space, and maintenance. Even under less-than-ideal conditions, these remarkable plants rarely let you down. And they race to maturity and flower in a matter of weeks, gratifying the most impatient gardener with both a prolific and long-lasting display.

The sheer variety of annuals is also hard to beat. Cultivated varieties number in the thousands, and each year hybridizers produce still more. On the following pages you'll find a sampling of the many colorful species and cultivars currently available to home gardeners.

Abelmoschus (a-bel-MOS-kus)

ABELMOSCHUS

Abelmoschus moschatus

PLANT TYPE:	tender perennial
HEIGHT:	15 inches to 6 feet
INTEREST:	flowers, foliage
SOIL:	moist, well-drained, fertile
LIGHT:	full sun to partial shade

Originally from tropical Asia, the hibiscus-like flowers and deeply lobed leaves of abelmoschus add a bold texture and an exotic appearance to borders.

Selected species and varieties
A. manihot (sunset hibiscus) grows 5 to 6 feet tall and is a good choice for the back of a border or a fast-growing summer hedge. Its 6-inch flowers appear in late summer; the five overlapping petals are pale yellow to cream with a brown or maroon eye. Dark green leaves are up to a foot long. 'Golden Bowl' bears yellow flowers with maroon centers. *A. moschatus* (musk mallow) grows 15 to 24 inches tall with a mounded habit well suited to the front of a border. From midsummer until frost, showy 3- to 4-inch blooms appear continuously. Colors range from yellow to scarlet with blends of pink and orange; petals fade to white near the center.

Growing conditions and maintenance
Start seed indoors 6 to 8 weeks prior to the last frost. Seed can be sown directly in the garden, but flowering may be delayed. Plants thrive in hot weather, performing well up to Zone 6. Space *A. manihot* 2 to 3 feet apart; *A. moschatus* 12 to 18 inches apart.

Adonis (a-DOE-nis)

PHEASANT'S-EYE

Adonis aestivalis

PLANT TYPE:	annual
HEIGHT:	12 to 18 inches
INTEREST:	flowers, foliage
SOIL:	moist, well-drained, rich
LIGHT:	full sun to partial shade

Pheasant's-eye produces a large mound of feathery leaves topped with intensely colored blooms in early to midsummer. Plants are most effective planted in drifts in a mixed border.

Selected species and varieties
A. aestivalis is a European wildflower with lacy leaves that bend to the ground, forming attractive fernlike mounds. Cup-shaped flowers consist of brilliant crimson petals surrounding black stamens. The prolifically borne flowers are about 1½ inches in diameter.

Growing conditions and maintenance
For earliest flowers, sow seed directly in the garden in late fall, before the ground freezes, thinning plants to stand 6 inches apart after germination. In spring, thin plants to stand 12 inches apart. Seed can also be sown in early spring as soon as the soil can be worked, but flowering will commence somewhat later. This hardy annual performs best in cool coastal or mountainous regions and prefers a soil rich in humus; it does not tolerate extreme heat.

Ageratum (aj-er-AY-tum)

FLOSSFLOWER

Ageratum houstonianum 'Blue Horizon'

PLANT TYPE:	annual
HEIGHT:	6 to 30 inches
INTEREST:	flowers, foliage
SOIL:	moist, well-drained
LIGHT:	full sun

A profusion of fluffy flowers with thread-like petals crown flossflower's clumps of heart-shaped leaves. With soft colors and a compact mounding habit, dwarf varieties create excellent garden edgings. Taller varieties combine well with other flowers in the middle or back of a border and are good candidates for indoor arrangements.

Selected species and varieties
A. houstonianum bears tiny blue or bluish purple flowers in dense, fuzzy clusters from summer through fall; white- and pink-flowered varieties are available; 'Blue Horizon' grows to 30 inches with deep blue flowers that are excellent for cutting; 'Capri' grows to a uniform 12 inches, producing bicolored flowers that are medium blue with white centers, and it is heat tolerant; 'Summer Snow' grows 6 to 8 inches tall with pure white flowers that begin early and continue to frost.

Growing conditions and maintenance
Sow seed indoors 6 to 8 weeks before the last expected frost. Space plants 6 to 12 inches apart. Pinching early growth will promote compactness, and removing spent blooms will encourage continuous production of flowers.

Agrostemma (ag-roe-STEM-a)

CORN COCKLE

Agrostemma githago

PLANT TYPE: annual or biennial

HEIGHT: 1 to 4 feet

INTEREST: flowers, foliage

SOIL: poor, well-drained

LIGHT: full sun

Corn cockles are troublefree plants from Europe that have naturalized throughout the eastern United States. They provide a long season of bright blooms for borders. Abundant 1- to 2-inch flowers in shades of pink, lilac, cherry red, or magenta top their stems throughout the summer. Their old-fashioned appearance is effective massed or in combination with other flowers in a cottage garden. Blooms are excellent for cutting.

Selected species and varieties
A. githago is a hardy annual with willowy stems up to 4 feet tall and narrow leaves covered with a silvery down; each flower has five petals that sport delicate stripes or spots seeming to radiate from the center; the black seeds are plentiful—and poisonous.

Growing conditions and maintenance
Corn cockle is easy to grow. Sow seed in place in late fall or early spring. Thin plants to stand 6 to 12 inches apart. They tolerate dry conditions and almost any soil. Deadhead to encourage reblooming and prevent excessive self-seeding.

Alcea (al-SEE-a)

HOLLYHOCK

Alcea rosea

PLANT TYPE: biennial

HEIGHT: 2 to 9 feet

INTEREST: flowers

SOIL: well-drained, fertile

LIGHT: full sun

The bell-shaped flowers of hollyhock are borne on sturdy, erect stems. The lower flowers open first, and new blossoms appear from midsummer to early fall. It is useful for the back of a border or as a colorful accent against fences or walls.

Selected species and varieties
A. ficifolia (Antwerp hollyhock) grows 4 to 7 feet tall with bold foliage and large 3- to 5-inch flowers, usually in shades of yellow or orange; 'Country Garden Mix' is a blend of single-flowered types with a wide color range including mahogany, rose, pink, salmon, and ivory. *A. rosea* grows to 9 feet with 2- to 4-inch flowers; 'Marjorette' bears double flowers in a wide range of colors on plants that are only 24 inches tall; 'Pinafore Mixed' is a blend of single and semidouble flower types in shades of pink, yellow, and white, growing to 3½ feet.

Growing conditions and maintenance
Plant seed indoors in winter for spring transplanting. Some varieties will bloom their first summer. Seed sown outdoors in spring will usually bloom its second year. Space plants 18 to 24 inches apart. Once they become established, hollyhocks will self-seed in Zones 3 to 9.

Amaranthus (am-a-RAN-thus)

AMARANTH

Amaranthus caudatus

PLANT TYPE: annual

HEIGHT: 18 inches to 6 feet

INTEREST: flowers, foliage

SOIL: dry to well-drained

LIGHT: full sun

Amaranths are large, brilliantly colored plants that hail from the tropics of the Far East. They add a bold touch to borders with their long-lasting tasseled flowers and colorful leaves. Tall types are effective as accents, while shorter selections are suited to beds or containers. Flowers are suitable for both fresh and dried arrangements.

Selected species and varieties
A. caudatus (love-lies-bleeding) grows 3 to 5 feet tall with green or red leaves and huge drooping tassels of red flowers that may reach 2 feet in length; 'Viridis' grows 2 to 3½ feet with greenish yellow flower tassels. *A. cruentus* (purple amaranth, prince's-feather) produces huge 12-inch leaves along erect 6-foot stems, and drooping red or purple flower spikes. *A. tricolor* (Joseph's-coat amaranth, tampala) grows from 1½ to 5 feet tall with variegated leaves up to 6 inches long that sport shades of green, red, and gold.

Growing conditions and maintenance
Seed requires very warm temperatures and can be started indoors 4 to 6 weeks prior to the last frost. In warm areas sow seed directly. Thin to allow 1 to 2 feet between plants. Water sparingly.

Ammi (AM-mi)

BISHOP'S FLOWER

Ammi majus

PLANT TYPE: annual

HEIGHT: 2 to 3 feet

INTEREST: flowers

SOIL: moist, fertile

LIGHT: full sun to partial shade

The delicate flower heads of bishop's flower resemble Queen Anne's lace in appearance, but the plant is far more manageable in the garden. Originally from Eurasia, it has naturalized in many parts of North America. It is well suited to flower borders, where it provides fine-textured contrast with coarser and more colorful plants. It can be sprinkled among annuals and perennials or planted in drifts. The flowers are highly valued for indoor arrangements; wear gloves when cutting as sap can irritate skin.

Selected species and varieties

A. majus develops thin, well-branched stems up to 3 feet tall with sharply serrated leaves. In summer, stems are topped with 5- to 6-inch umbels, each containing numerous delicate white flowers that tremble with the slightest wind or touch.

Growing conditions and maintenance

Start seed about 6 weeks indoors—or 2 weeks outdoors—before the last frost. Thin or transplant to allow 6 to 12 inches between plants. Plants transplant easily at nearly any stage and, once established, are free flowering. They thrive in cooler regions but may be stressed by high temperatures and humidity.

Ammobium (a-MOE-bee-um)

WINGED EVERLASTING

Ammobium alatum

PLANT TYPE: tender perennial

HEIGHT: 2 to 3 feet

INTEREST: flowers, foliage, stems

SOIL: well-drained, sandy

LIGHT: full sun

This Australian native produces its solitary flower heads continuously from early to late summer. The flowers have a papery texture with yellow centers surrounded by silvery white bracts. They are attractive massed in a bed, and are excellent for both fresh and dried arrangements.

Selected species and varieties

A. alatum develops a tuft of 6- to 8-inch basal leaves that are covered with fine white woolly hairs. In summer, erect, branched stems rise 3 feet high from the clump. Each stem is topped with a solitary 1- to 2-inch flower head. The common name refers to the unusual wings along the length of the stems.

Growing conditions and maintenance

Start seed indoors 6 to 8 weeks before the last frost, or sow directly in the garden after the last hard frost. In warm regions, seed can be sown in the fall. Thin to allow 8 to 12 inches between plants. Plants self-seed from Zone 7 south and are perennial in Zones 10 and 11. Avoid overwatering. To use in winter arrangements, cut stems before flowers are fully open and hang upside down in an airy room until dry.

Antirrhinum (an-tir-RYE-num)

SNAPDRAGON

Antirrhinum majus 'White Sonnet'

PLANT TYPE: tender perennial

HEIGHT: 6 inches to 4 feet

INTEREST: flowers

SOIL: well-drained, fertile

LIGHT: full sun to partial shade

Snapdragons, with their wide range of heights and flower colors and long season of bloom, have been cultivated since ancient times. Short varieties add color to rock gardens and edgings, while taller types are well suited to the middle and rear of mixed borders, where they provide a vertical accent. They are outstanding in fresh arrangements.

Selected species and varieties

A. majus bears terminal clusters of flowers that open from the bottom up. Each bloom has five lobes, divided into an upper and a lower lip. Varieties are classified by height: small (6-12 inches), intermediate (12-24 inches), and tall (2-4 feet); 'Black Prince' is 18 inches with deep crimson flowers and bronze foliage; 'Madame Butterfly' grows to 3 feet with flaring blossoms in a range of colors; 'White Sonnet' is 22 inches with white flowers that are superb for cutting.

Growing conditions and maintenance

Start seed indoors in late winter for transplanting in mid- to late spring. Space plants 6 to 18 inches apart. Deadhead to encourage continuous flowering. Taller types may need staking. Perennial in Zones 8 to 11.

Arctotis (ark-TOE-tis)

AFRICAN DAISY

Arctotis stoechadifolia

PLANT TYPE: tender perennial

HEIGHT: 2 to 3 feet

INTEREST: flowers, foliage

SOIL: well-drained to dry, sandy

LIGHT: full sun

This native of South Africa produces a steady supply of 3-inch daisy-type flowers from summer until frost. Brightly colored blooms stand out against woolly gray leaves. They are a good choice for beds and borders, and even though flowers close at night, they are cheerful additions to fresh arrangements.

Selected species and varieties

A. stoechadifolia has a bushy habit with velvety lobed leaves and slender stems. Flower petals are typically silvery white with a lavender band at their base where they surround a violet center. The reverse of the petals is lavender. Yellow, orange, red, and pink varieties are also available.

Growing conditions and maintenance

For earliest flowers start seed indoors about 8 weeks before the last frost; plant seedlings outside, 8 to 12 inches apart, after all danger of frost has past. In Zones 7 and warmer, seed can also be sown directly in the garden. African daisy tolerates both drought and coastal conditions and is perennial in Zones 9 and 10.

Argemone (ar-JEM-o-nee)

PRICKLY POPPY

Argemone munita

PLANT TYPE: annual or tender perennial

HEIGHT: 1 to 3 feet

INTEREST: flowers, foliage

SOIL: dry, well-drained

LIGHT: full sun

The crinkled, spiny foliage and large flowers of prickly poppies make a bold statement at the back of borders and beds. The flowers, which come in shades of white, yellow, and orange, have a unique crepe-paper texture and a mass of yellow stamens in the center. The fruit is composed of small, spiny capsules filled with tiny seeds.

Selected species and varieties

A. grandiflora is an annual or short-lived perennial with 2-inch bright yellow or white summer flowers atop 2- to 3-foot stems. The sparsely spined blue-green foliage is veined with white. *A. mexicana* (Mexican poppy) is an annual with 1- to 2-foot spiny stems bearing 2-inch yellow or orange flowers in summer above green leaves often spotted with white. *A. munita* (white prickly poppy) is an annual or perennial to 3 feet tall, with many 2- to 5-inch showy white summer flowers surrounding yellow stamens and a purple stigma.

Growing conditions and maintenance

Start seed indoors in late winter and transplant after danger of frost has passed. Space plants 1 to 2 feet apart. Prickly poppies can be grown as perennials in Zone 10.

Asclepias (as-KLEE-pee-as)

MILKWEED

Asclepias curassavica

PLANT TYPE: tender perennial

HEIGHT: 2 to 6 feet

INTEREST: flowers, seedpods

SOIL: moist to dry

LIGHT: full sun

Often referred to as weeds in South America, *Asclepias* species are suited to the rear of a herbaceous border, where their clusters of flowers put on a fine display from summer until frost. Flowers are followed by attractive seedpods that are useful in dried arrangements.

Selected species and varieties

A. curassavica (bloodflower) develops sturdy branched stems 2 to 4 feet tall and narrow 5-inch dark green leaves that clasp the stems in pairs. The 6-inch flower clusters arise from branch tips and axils and are made up of many tiny purplish red and orange flowers. Flowers are followed by 4-inch brown seedpods. *A. fruticosa* (gomphocarpus) grows 3 to 6 feet tall and bears creamy white flowers and spiny silvery green pods.

Growing conditions and maintenance

Start seed indoors in midwinter for transplanting to the garden after all danger of frost has past. Space plants 15 to 18 inches apart and pinch when they reach 4 to 6 inches to promote branching. Plants thrive in warm weather and can be grown as perennials from Zone 8 south.

Atriplex (AT-ri-plex)

ORACH

Atriplex hortensis

PLANT TYPE: annual

HEIGHT: 3 to 6 feet

INTEREST: foliage

SOIL: well-drained, fertile

LIGHT: full sun

Orach is grown for its ornamental foliage, which is powdery white when young and green, yellow-green, or purplish red when mature. Native to Asia, this fast-growing annual makes an effective summer hedge or screen, or it can be used as a backdrop for shorter annuals. Stems are often cut for fresh indoor arrangements. Leaves can be eaten as salad greens.

Selected species and varieties
A. hortensis (mountain spinach) has an erect habit with somewhat triangular or arrow-shaped leaves. Young leaves are covered with a white bloom. Flowers are insignificant. 'Rubra' (red orach) grows 4 to 5 feet tall with blood red leaves and stems.

Growing conditions and maintenance
Start seed indoors 4 to 6 weeks before the last frost for transplanting to the garden in late spring, or sow directly outdoors after all danger of frost has past. Space or thin plants to stand 12 inches apart. Orach is easy to grow and tolerates wind and coastal conditions.

Begonia (be-GO-nee-a)

WAX BEGONIA

Begonia 'Cocktail Series'

PLANT TYPE: tender perennial

HEIGHT: 5 to 16 inches

INTEREST: flowers, foliage

SOIL: moist, fertile

LIGHT: partial shade to shade

Wax begonias add color to the shady garden with both their perpetual clusters of delicate flowers and their glossy rounded leaves. Flowers range from white to pink to red, and leaves may be green, bronze, or variegated green and white. They are useful for edging, massing, and growing in containers both indoors and outside.

Selected species and varieties
B. x *semperflorens-cultorum* (bedding begonia) has a mounding habit and produces flowers nonstop from spring until frost. In Zones 9 and 10 they bloom almost year round. Selections vary in both flower and leaf color, flower size, and height; 'Cocktail Series' offers white, pink, rose, salmon, and red flowers on dwarf 5- to 6-inch plants with glossy bronze foliage; 'Pizzazz Mixed' grows to 10 inches with large red, pink, or white flowers and glossy green leaves.

Growing conditions and maintenance
Start seed 4 to 6 months prior to the last frost, or purchase bedding plants in spring. Plants can also be propagated by cuttings. Space 8 to 12 inches apart. Although the ideal site is filtered shade, plants will tolerate full sun if given sufficient water, especially in cooler regions.

Borago (bor-RAY-go)

BORAGE

Borago officinalis

PLANT TYPE: annual

HEIGHT: 2 to 3 feet

INTEREST: flowers, foliage

SOIL: well-drained

LIGHT: full sun to light shade

This European native makes an attractive addition to flower or herb gardens, fresh flower arrangements, and summer salads. Both leaves and flowers are edible, with a refreshing cucumber-like flavor, and can be used to garnish salads or fruit cups. It has a somewhat sprawling habit that is best suited to an informal garden, where its soft-textured leaves and sky blue flowers add a cool, gentle touch.

Selected species and varieties
B. officinalis (talewort, cool-tankard) is a hardy annual with a rounded, sprawling habit, bristly gray-green foliage, and succulent stems. Flowers are arranged in drooping clusters. Each is ¾ inch across and star shaped, with five petals. Though usually clear blue, they are sometimes light purple. Flower buds are covered with fine hairs.

Growing conditions and maintenance
Sow seed directly in the garden at monthly intervals beginning 2 to 3 weeks prior to the last frost for continuous summer bloom. Once established, plant will self-seed. Allow 12 to 18 inches between plants. Where summers are very hot, afternoon shade is recommended. Borage tolerates drought.

Brachycome *(bra-KIK-o-me)*

SWAN RIVER DAISY

Brachycome iberidifolia

PLANT TYPE: annual

HEIGHT: 9 to 14 inches

INTEREST: flowers

SOIL: moist, well-drained, fertile

LIGHT: full sun

The Swan River daisy is a tender annual from Australia with a neat, mounding habit and colorful daisylike flowers. Although small, the brightly colored flowers are produced in masses, making this plant a good choice for rock gardens, edgings, and containers, including hanging baskets.

Selected species and varieties
B. iberidifolia grows to 14 inches tall with a compact habit and a 12-inch spread. The delicate pale green leaves are 3 inches long and are borne on slender stems. Flowers are about 1 inch across and appear for 4 to 6 weeks in the summer, tapering off toward the end of the season. Colors include white, pink, lavender, and blue.

Growing conditions and maintenance
Start seed indoors 5 to 6 weeks prior to the last frost, or sow directly in the garden when the soil has warmed. Successive plantings will lengthen the flowering season. Allow 6 to 12 inches between plants. Water during dry spells.

Brassica *(BRASS-i-ka)*

ORNAMENTAL CABBAGE

Brassica oleracea

PLANT TYPE: biennial

HEIGHT: 10 to 15 inches

INTEREST: foliage

SOIL: moist, well-drained

LIGHT: full sun

This ornamental cousin of the familiar vegetable side dish is highly valued for the splash of color it provides in the fall and winter landscape. A biennial, it is grown as an annual for its brightly colored and intricately curled foliage, which grows in a flowerlike rosette.

Selected species and varieties
B. oleracea, Acephala group (ornamental kale) does not form heads but produces an open rosette of leaves that typically spreads 12 inches across. Foliage colors include lavender-blue, white, green, red, purple, pink, and assorted variegations. Color improves in cool weather. Leaves of 'Cherry Sundae' are a blend of carmine and cream; 'Color Up' displays a center of red, pink, cream, white, and green surrounded by green margins; 'Peacock' series has feathery notched and serrated leaves in a variety of colors.

Growing conditions and maintenance
For spring planting, start seed indoors 4 to 6 weeks prior to the last frost. For fall gardens, start seed 6 to 8 weeks prior to the first anticipated frost. Space plants 18 to 24 inches apart. Plants will last all winter in Zones 8 to 10.

Browallia *(bro-WALL-ee-a)*

BUSH VIOLET

Browallia speciosa

PLANT TYPE: tender perennial

HEIGHT: 8 to 16 inches

INTEREST: flowers

SOIL: moist, well-drained

LIGHT: partial to full shade

A good choice for the shady border, bush violet bears clusters of blue, violet, or white flowers from early to late summer. It has a low-growing rounded habit that is well suited for use as an edging, and it's an outstanding choice for window boxes or hanging baskets, where it cascades gracefully over the edge. In fall, plants can be cut back severely and potted to be grown as flowering houseplants through winter.

Selected species and varieties
B. speciosa has a rounded to sprawling habit with 1½- to 2-inch-long throated, star-shaped flowers; 'Blue Bells' bears blue-violet flowers with prominent white centers; 'Jingle Bells' bears flowers in a mixture of colors including shades of blue, white, and lavender; 'Silver Bells' bears large white blooms.

Growing conditions and maintenance
Start seeds indoors about 8 weeks prior to the last frost. Plant in the garden after all danger of frost is past, spacing plants 8 inches apart. Avoid overwatering and overfertilizing.

Caladium (ka-LAY-dee-um)

ELEPHANT'S-EAR

Caladium bicolor 'White Queen'

PLANT TYPE: annual or tender perennial

HEIGHT: 1 to 2 feet

INTEREST: foliage

SOIL: moist, well-drained

LIGHT: partial to full shade

Caladium's large leaves, shaped like arrowheads and 6 to 18 inches long, are colorfully patterned in various combinations of red, pink, white, and green. A good container plant, caladium is also excellent for mass plantings in shady borders.

Selected species and varieties

C. bicolor [formerly *C. x hortulanum*]—shieldlike leaves may be flat, wavy, or ruffled; 'Fannie Munson' has pink leaves with narrow green margins; 'Frieda Hempel', solid red leaves with green margins; 'Pink Beauty', soft pink leaves with rose-colored veins on a deep green background; 'White Queen' is 18 inches tall with red-veined, green-edged, whitish leaves 8 to 12 inches long.

Growing conditions and maintenance

Caladiums need ample water in the growing season and do poorly in low humidity. Feed with an all-purpose fertilizer during the growing season. Tender plants with tropical origins, they can be treated as perennials and naturalized only in the southern tip of Florida and in southwestern California. Elsewhere, however, they can be dug in the fall and stored during winter; divide before replanting.

Calendula (ka-LEN-dew-la)

POT MARIGOLD

Calendula officinalis

PLANT TYPE: annual

HEIGHT: 12 to 24 inches

INTEREST: flowers

SOIL: moist, well-drained

LIGHT: full sun

The long-lasting blooms of pot marigolds are daisylike with flattened, wide-spreading rays ranging in color from deep orange to yellow or cream. They are a good choice for mixed beds, containers, or indoor arrangements. Native to the Mediterranean, this hardy annual has long been grown as an ornamental and used as a flavoring for puddings and cakes.

Selected species and varieties

C. officinalis has a neat, mounding habit and grows 1 to 2 feet tall with a similar spread. Leaves are 2 to 6 inches long, blue-green, and aromatic. The solitary 2½- to 4½-inch flower heads close at night; 'Bon-Bon' grows 12 inches tall with a compact, early-blooming habit and a mixture of flower colors.

Growing conditions and maintenance

Start seed indoors 6 to 8 weeks prior to the last frost, for transplanting to the garden after the last hard frost. In areas with mild winters it can be sown directly outdoors in fall or early spring. Space plants 12 to 18 inches apart. Deadhead to increase flowering. Calendulas thrive in cool conditions and tolerate poor soils if they have adequate water.

Callistephus (kal-LIS-tee-fus)

CHINA ASTER

Callistephus chinensis

PLANT TYPE: annual

HEIGHT: 6 to 36 inches

INTEREST: flowers

SOIL: well-drained, fertile

LIGHT: full sun to light shade

The China aster, as its name implies, is native to Asia. Its flowers display a remarkable range of colors, sizes, and shapes. Dwarf and intermediate-sized selections are good choices for the border, while tall varieties are outstanding for cutting.

Selected species and varieties

C. chinensis has an upright, branching habit with 3½-inch irregularly toothed dark green basal leaves and flower heads up to 5 inches across. Flowers may be single, semi-double, or double, and are available in many colors including red, white, pink, blue, purple, and yellow; 'Blue Skies' is a 6-inch dwarf that covers itself with pale lavender-blue double flowers; 'Giant Princess' grows to 2½ feet with large, long-stemmed flowers in many colors.

Growing conditions and maintenance

Start seed indoors in late winter for transplanting into the garden after all danger of frost has passed, or sow directly in the garden. Space plants 12 inches apart. Make successive plantings for continuous flowers. To avoid disease, do not overwater or plant in the same location in successive years.

Campanula (kam-PAN-yew-la)

BELLFLOWER

Campanula medium

PLANT TYPE: biennial

HEIGHT: 1 to 4 feet

INTEREST: flowers

SOIL: moist, well-drained

LIGHT: full sun to partial shade

This native of southern Europe is an old-fashioned garden favorite. In late spring and early summer, sturdy flower stalks appear, bearing numerous bell-shaped blossoms, each 2 inches long. Flowers may be blue, violet, white, or pink, and are long-lasting both in a mixed border and in fresh indoor arrangements.

Selected species and varieties
C. medium (Canterbury bells) has an erect habit and usually grows 2 to 4 feet tall, although dwarf varieties have a compact habit and reach only 12 inches in height. Leaves are narrow and up to 10 inches long, and bell-shaped flowers are born singly or in pairs along an open raceme; 'Calycanthema' (cup-and-saucer) bears a 3-inch-wide saucerlike, flattened calyx beneath the flower "cup" and is available in blue, white, and rose.

Growing conditions and maintenance
Sow seed outdoors in late spring or summer to bloom the following year. Plants are hardy to Zone 4 but require some winter protection. Some varieties will flower 6 months after seeding and can be started indoors. Transplant in early spring, spacing plants 12 to 18 inches apart. Water during dry periods.

Canna (CAN-ah)

CANNA

Canna x generalis 'Lerape'

PLANT TYPE: tender perennial

HEIGHT: 18 inches to 6 feet

INTEREST: flowers

SOIL: moist, well-drained

LIGHT: full sun

Cannas produce 4- to 5-inch flowers with a tousled arrangement of petal-like stamens from summer through frost. Bold leaves provide a dramatic backdrop to the flowers. They are well suited to the back of borders and to massing. Grow dwarf cultivars as edgings or in patio containers.

Selected species and varieties
C. x *generalis* (canna lily) is available in standard varieties that grow 4 to 6 feet tall or dwarfs that are less than 3 feet. The flowers are carried on stiff, erect stems; colors include red, orange, salmon, yellow, pink, white, and bicolors. The broad leaves, up to 24 inches long, are usually a deep glossy green but are sometimes bronzy red or striped or veined in white or pink; 'Lerape' bears yellow flowers with bright orange spots; 'Seven Dwarfs Mixed' grows to 18 inches with a wide range of flower colors.

Growing conditions and maintenance
Soak seed prior to planting indoors in midwinter, or start rhizomes indoors 4 weeks before the last frost and move them to the garden when night temperatures reach 60°F. In Zones 9 and 10, plant directly in the garden in spring, spaced 1 to 2 feet apart.

Capsicum (KAP-si-kum)

PEPPER

Capsicum annuum 'Treasure Red'

PLANT TYPE: tender perennial

HEIGHT: 6 to 20 inches

INTEREST: fruit

SOIL: moist, well-drained, fertile

LIGHT: full sun

Bushy, rounded pepper plants produce brightly colored fruit that is well displayed against dark green leaves. In its native environment of tropical North and South America, peppers are woody perennials, but in temperate climates they are treated as annuals. Ornamental varieties make tidy and colorful edgings for beds and are superb for containers.

Selected species and varieties
C. annuum (ornamental pepper) has a bushy, compact habit with evergreen leaves from 1 to 5 inches long. Flowers are white and small. Fruit ranges from ¾ to 2 inches long and may be red, purple, yellow, green, black, cream, or variegated; 'Holiday Cheer' grows to 8 inches with round 1-inch fruit that turns from cream to red; 'Red Missile' grows to 10 inches with tapered 2-inch fruit; 'Treasure Red' grows 8 inches tall with conical fruit that turns from white to bright red.

Growing conditions and maintenance
Start seed indoors in late winter to transplant to the garden after all danger of frost has past. Space plants to stand 8 to 15 inches apart. Dig and pot plants in the fall to grow as houseplants; perennial in Zones 10 and 11.

Carthamus (KAR-tha-mus)

SAFFLOWER

Carthamus tinctorius

PLANT TYPE: annual

HEIGHT: 1 to 3 feet

INTEREST: flowers

SOIL: well-drained

LIGHT: full sun

Native to Eurasia and Egypt, where it has been used since ancient times to produce a bright yellow dye, safflower is at home in wildflower and herb gardens, informal borders, and cutting gardens. Its fluffy bright orange flowers are valued for their use in dried arrangements and have been used as a substitute for saffron in flavoring food. Seeds are the source of safflower oil.

Selected species and varieties
C. tinctorius (false saffron) has an erect, branched habit with 2½-inch spiny, thistle-like leaves along straight stems. The 1-inch flower heads are surrounded by spiny bracts and are typically orange, but varieties offer a wider range of colors, including yellow, gold, cream, and white; 'Lasting Orange' is an early-blooming selection with 1½-inch clear orange flowers; 'Lasting Yellow' is similar in habit with yellow flowers.

Growing conditions and maintenance
Start seed indoors in late winter in peat pots to minimize transplant shock, or sow directly in garden after danger of frost has past. Space plants 8 to 10 inches apart.

Catharanthus (kath-ah-RAN-thus)

PERIWINKLE

Catharanthus roseus

PLANT TYPE: tender perennial

HEIGHT: 3 to 18 inches

INTEREST: flowers, foliage

SOIL: moist, well-drained

LIGHT: sun to partial shade

Periwinkle provides summer-to-fall color for temperate gardens. Its flowers resemble those of *Vinca,* and it is available in both creeping and upright varieties. Use it as a summer ground cover or in mass plantings, annual borders, or containers.

Selected species and varieties
C. roseus [sometimes listed as *Vinca rosea*] (Madagascar periwinkle) produces glossy oblong leaves, 1 to 3 inches long. Creeping varieties grow 3 inches tall, spreading 18 to 24 inches across. Erect strains grow 8 to 18 inches tall. Flowers are 1½ inches wide and cover the plant throughout the summer; colors range from shades of pink or mauve to white; 'Parasol' produces large 1½- to 2-inch white flowers with pink eyes on 12- to 18-inch plants; 'Tropicana' grows to 12 inches and produces flowers in several shades of pink from pale blush to deep rose, with contrasting eyes.

Growing conditions and maintenance
Start seed indoors 10 to 12 weeks prior to the last frost for late-spring transplanting to the garden; space 1 to 2 feet apart. Plants can also be started from cuttings. They thrive in warm, humid conditions and are perennial in Zones 9 to 11.

Celosia (sel-OH-see-a)

CELOSIA

Celosia cristata 'Pink Tassels'

PLANT TYPE: annual

HEIGHT: 6 to 24 inches

INTEREST: flowers, foliage

SOIL: moist to dry, well-drained

LIGHT: full sun

These vibrant annuals are native to the tropics of Asia. Their crested or plumed flowers are extremely long-lasting, making them ideal for bedding and cutting for both fresh and dried arrangements.

Selected species and varieties
C. cristata displays a range of heights and flower types. Leaves may be green, purple, or variegated. Flowers appear from mid-summer to fall and are usually deep shades of red, orange, yellow, or gold. The species is divided according to flower type: Childsii group (crested cockscomb) produces crested or convoluted flower heads that resemble lumps of coral. Plumosa group (feather amaranth) bears feathery 6- to 12-inch flower heads. Spicata group bears flowers in slender spikes; 'Pink Tassels' bears long pale pink spikes with bright pink tips.

Growing conditions and maintenance
Start seed indoors 4 to 6 weeks before transplanting to the garden after all danger of frost has passed. In warm areas, sow directly outside. Space plants 6 to 18 inches apart. Celosias thrive in warm weather and tolerate dry soils. For use in winter arrangements, cut flowers at their peak and hang them upside down to dry.

Celsia (SEL-see-a)

CRETAN CELSIA

Celsia cretica

PLANT TYPE: biennial

HEIGHT: 4 to 6 feet

INTEREST: flowers

SOIL: well-drained

LIGHT: full sun

This half-hardy biennial is native to the Mediterranean region. It is similar to the more familiar *Verbascum* mulleins, differing mainly in number of stamens: *Celsia* has four, *Verbascum* five. Its yellow flowers are borne on tall, open racemes and appear over a long period in the summer. They are extraordinarily fragrant. The plant's statuesque habit and coarse leaves combine well with other, more delicate flowers in the rear of a mixed border.

Selected species and varieties
C. cretica (Cretan mullein) has a stout, erect habit with large, hairy leaves and stems. From the clump of leaves rises a 5- to 6-foot flower stalk bearing yellow flowers. Individual blossoms are 1½ inches across and display purple filaments and two brown or rust-colored spots on their upper petal.

Growing conditions and maintenance
Sow seed directly in the garden. In Zones 6 and south, seed can be sown in fall or early spring; in cooler areas plant in spring. Cover the seed very lightly with soil. Plants tolerate a wide range of soils, provided they are well drained.

Centaurea (sen-TOR-ee-a)

KNAPWEED

Centaurea cyanus

PLANT TYPE: annual

HEIGHT: 1 to 6 feet

INTEREST: flowers

SOIL: well-drained

LIGHT: full sun

The tufted blooms of these popular annuals come in shades of pink, blue, lavender, yellow, and white. Sprinkle them liberally in informal borders, wildflower gardens, and the cutting garden. They can be used for both fresh and dried arrangements.

Selected species and varieties
C. americana (basket flower) grows up to 6 feet tall with sturdy stems and 4- to 5-inch pink flowers with cream centers and a fringe of thistlelike bracts. *C. cyanus* (bachelor's-button, cornflower) produces gray-green leaves on erect stems to 3 feet; perky 1-inch flowers appear from early summer until frost and are available in many colors. *C. moschata* (sweet-sultan) grows 2 to 3 feet with 2- to 3-inch musk-scented flowers; the hybrid 'Imperialis' grows to 4 feet with pink, purple, or white flowers.

Growing conditions and maintenance
Sow seed in place in late winter or early spring; in areas with mild winters it can also be sown in fall. Space 6 to 12 inches apart. Once established plants often self-seed. For continuous bloom, make successive plantings 2 weeks apart throughout the season.

Chamaecrista (kam-ee-KRIS-ta)

SENNA

Chamaecrista fasciculata

PLANT TYPE: annual

HEIGHT: 1 to 2 feet

INTEREST: flowers

SOIL: sandy, wet to dry

LIGHT: full sun to partial shade

This genus, which is also listed as *Cassia*, includes both annuals and perennials that inhabit open woods and prairies in the eastern and central United States. Their bright yellow flowers are attractive in borders or as a transition between lawn and woodlands.

Selected species and varieties
C. fasciculata (partridge pea) and *C. nictitans* (sensitive plant)—annuals that grow to 2 feet and 12 inches respectively with yellow flowers arising from leaf axils and light green, pinnately compound leaves that fold together when touched.

Growing conditions and maintenance
Chamaecristas thrive in full sun. Both species grow well in well-drained to dry sandy soil, and *C. nictitans* also tolerates wet conditions. They benefit from soil inoculation with nitrogen-fixing bacteria, available from wildflower nurseries. Propagate by seed.

Cheiranthus (ky-RAN-thus)

WALLFLOWER

Cheiranthus cheiri 'Bowles' Mauve'

PLANT TYPE: tender perennial

HEIGHT: 6 to 24 inches

INTEREST: flowers

SOIL: well-drained, fertile

LIGHT: full sun

This Eurasian native bridges the flowering season between early bulbs and bedding plants. Fragrant 1-inch flowers are borne in clusters resembling stock; colors include deep shades of yellow, orange, red, purple, and brown. Dwarf varieties are perfect for rock gardens or growing in gaps of stone walls. Plant taller types in borders.

Selected species and varieties
C. cheiri (English wallflower) has a low, erect habit; dwarf varieties grow 6 to 9 inches, while tall varieties may reach 2 feet. Early-flowering strains often bloom their first year from seed, but most varieties are treated as biennials; 'Bowles' Mauve' produces large clusters of deep pink flowers.

Growing conditions and maintenance
Sow seed outdoors in spring or fall for bloom the following season. Provide winter protection in areas with severe winters. Early-flowering varieties can be started indoors in midwinter, hardened in a cold frame, and transplanted to the garden as soon as the soil can be worked in spring. Space plants about 12 inches apart. Wallflowers thrive in cool climates and do well in coastal and mountainous areas such as the Pacific Northwest.

Chrysanthemum (kri-SAN-the-mum)

CHRYSANTHEMUM

Chrysanthemum coronarium 'Primrose Gem'

PLANT TYPE: annual

HEIGHT: 1 to 3 feet

INTEREST: flowers

SOIL: well-drained

LIGHT: full sun to partial shade

Annual chrysanthemums, which hail from the Mediterranean region, supply the summer and fall border with a nonstop production of colorful daisylike flowers. They make excellent cut flowers.

Selected species and varieties
C. carinatum (tricolor chrysanthemum) grows 2 to 3 feet tall and bears toothed, dark green leaves. It derives its common name from its 2½-inch flower heads that are white with a yellow band surrounding a purple or chocolate brown central disk; 'Court Jesters' produces red, pink, orange, yellow, maroon, and white flowers with either red or orange bands. *C. coronarium* (crown daisy, garland chrysanthemum) grows 1 to 2½ feet tall with coarsely cut leaves and yellow and white flowers, 1 to 2 inches across, which may be single, semidouble, or double; 'Primrose Gem' bears semidouble soft yellow blooms with darker yellow centers.

Growing conditions and maintenance
These plants are easily grown from seed planted directly in the garden as soon as soil can be worked in the spring. Thin plants to stand 12 to 18 inches apart. Once established they will self-seed.

Cirsium (SIR-see-um)

THISTLE

Cirsium japonicum

PLANT TYPE: biennial

HEIGHT: 18 to 30 inches

INTEREST: flowers

SOIL: light, well-drained

LIGHT: full sun to partial shade

Solitary or small clusters of rose or magenta flower heads top the erect stems of this somewhat coarse Japanese native. The dark green spiny leaves provide a dramatic foil for the intensely colored flowers. This plant adds a bold texture to the mixed border and is excellent for both fresh and dried arrangements.

Selected species and varieties
C. japonicum (rose thistle) produces an erect, branched stem with deeply lobed 4-inch leaves. The leaves are deep green with spiny edges and often display silvery veins. Flower heads top each stem in summer. The buds are covered with silvery overlapping scales, and the opened flower heads are 1 to 2 inches across. Each head consists of a mass of tiny tubular flowers.

Growing conditions and maintenance:
Sow seed directly in the garden as soon as soil can be worked in spring for late-summer flowers. Once established, plants will self-seed. Space plants 1 to 2 feet apart. They are adaptable to a wide range of soils as long as drainage is good.

Clarkia (KLAR-kee-a)

GODETIA

Clarkia amoena

PLANT TYPE: annual

HEIGHT: 1 to 3 feet

INTEREST: flowers

SOIL: dry, sandy

LIGHT: full sun to partial shade

Clarkias are free-flowering annuals from the coastal ranges of the western United States. They are named after the explorer William Clark, who collected their seed during the Lewis and Clark expedition. These species are also listed under the genus *Godetia*.

Selected species and varieties
C. amoena (farewell-to-spring, satin-flower) grows 1 to 3 feet tall. Throughout summer, 2- to 4-inch cup-shaped flowers appear in the axils of the upper leaves. Petals number four and are pink to lavender with a bright red or pink splash at the base; the four sepals are red. *C. concinna* (red-ribbons) grows 1 to 2 feet tall and bears rose-purple flowers with deeply cut fan-shaped petals in late spring and early summer. *C. purpurea* grows to 3 feet tall with 1-inch flowers in shades of purple, lavender, red, and pink.

Growing conditions and maintenance
Sow seed outdoors in fall where winters are mild, and elsewhere in spring as soon as the soil can be worked. Sow fairly heavily since crowding will encourage flowering. Plants perform best where nights are cool.

Cleome (klee-O-me)

SPIDER FLOWER

Cleome hasslerana 'Helen Campbell'

PLANT TYPE: annual

HEIGHT: 3 to 4 feet

INTEREST: flowers, seedpods

SOIL: moist, well-drained

LIGHT: full sun to light shade

Enormous clusters of 1-inch flowers top the stems of cleome continuously from summer until frost. Pink, lavender, or white flower petals surround 2- to 3-inch-long stamens that protrude from the center, creating a spiderlike effect further enhanced by the slender, conspicuous seedpods that follow the flowers. Cleome makes a graceful summer hedge, accent, or border plant.

Selected species and varieties
C. hasslerana [also known as *C. spinosa*] has an erect habit with dark green palmately compound leaves and airy, ball-shaped flower heads. While flowers are short-lived, new ones are produced continuously at the top of the stem; 'Cherry Queen' bears rose red flowers; 'Helen Campbell' has white blooms; 'Pink Queen' bears clear pink blossoms; the flowers of 'Violet Queen' are purple, and leaves display a purple tint at their edges.

Growing conditions and maintenance
Start seed indoors 4 to 6 weeks prior to the last frost, or plant directly in the garden in early spring. Plants often self-seed. Space plants about 24 inches apart. Cleome thrives in warm weather and responds well to abundant moisture.

Coleus (KO-lee-us)

FLAME NETTLE

Coleus x hybridus

PLANT TYPE: tender perennial

HEIGHT: 8 to 24 inches

INTEREST: foliage

SOIL: moist, well-drained

LIGHT: partial shade

The exuberantly colored heart-shaped leaves of coleus provide a long season of color to borders and planters in partially shaded sites. Leaves sport attractive patterns, and their colors include chartreuse, green, orange, red, pink, bronze, and white.

Selected species and varieties
C. x hybridus is available in a very wide range of foliage colors and patterns. Leaves grow opposite each other on square stems, and usually are 3 to 8 inches long with scalloped edges. Plants often grow as wide as they are tall. Dwarf strains grow 8 to 10 inches tall, while taller types may reach 2 feet. Small pale blue flowers bloom on upright spikes but are often removed to encourage leaf growth.

Growing conditions and maintenance
Start seed indoors 8 to 10 weeks prior to the last frost, or grow from leaf-stem cuttings. Transplant outdoors after soil has warmed, allowing 8 to 12 inches between plants. Most varieties grow best in light or partial shade, although some will do fine in full sun if adequate water is supplied. Plants survive as perennials in Zones 10 and 11.

Collinsia (ko-LIN-see-a)

PAGODA COLLINSIA

Collinsia heterophylla

PLANT TYPE: annual

HEIGHT: 1 to 2 feet

INTEREST: flowers

SOIL: moist, well-drained

LIGHT: partial shade

Collinsias are native to the western United States. Their clusters of two-toned flowers resemble snapdragons and appear continuously from early summer to early autumn in tiers on stems that reach to 24 inches. They are at home in a shady mixed border, rock garden, or woodland garden, and are also effective in containers.

Selected species and varieties
C. heterophylla (Chinese houses) bears bright green leaves in opposite pairs along the stem with loose clusters of flowers. Each flower is two lipped; the upper is pale lilac or white, and the lower is rose-purple or violet. The entire plant is often covered with velvety hairs.

Growing conditions and maintenance
Sow seed outdoors in fall where winters are mild; and in colder climates, in early spring as soon as the ground can be worked. Successive seedings and removal of faded blooms will provide a longer flowering season. Thin seedlings to allow 6 inches between plants. They thrive in filtered sun or dappled shade where night temperatures remain relatively cool.

Consolida (kon-SO-li-da)

LARKSPUR

Consolida ambigua

PLANT TYPE: annual

HEIGHT: 1 to 4 feet

INTEREST: flowers

SOIL: well-drained, fertile

LIGHT: full sun to light shade

This native of southern Europe produces dense clusters of flowers upon stately, erect spikes. The flowers are available in shades of blue, lilac, pink, red, purple, and white and are quite long-lasting. Plant tall types toward the rear of a border, where they provide a graceful vertical accent and a fine source of fresh-cut flowers. Shorter varieties can be placed in the mid- or foreground of a mixed border.

Selected species and varieties
C. ambigua (rocket larkspur) produces lacy, deeply cut leaves. Spurred flowers in many pastel shades are borne in dense, graceful spikes throughout the summer; 'Imperial Blue Bell' grows to 4 feet with double blue flowers; 'Imperial White King' is similar with double white flowers.

Growing conditions and maintenance
Start seed indoors in peat pots 6 to 8 weeks prior to the last frost. Seed can be sown directly outdoors in fall from Zone 7 south and or in early spring elsewhere. Space plants to stand 8 to 15 inches apart. Tall varieties often require staking. Plants thrive in cool conditions, and where summers are warm will benefit from light shade. Keep soil evenly moist throughout the growing season.

Convolvulus (kon-VOL-view-lus)

DWARF MORNING GLORY

Convolvulus tricolor

PLANT TYPE: annual

HEIGHT: 6 to 18 inches

INTEREST: flowers

SOIL: well-drained to dry, sandy

LIGHT: full sun

The dwarf morning glory hails from southern Europe, and unlike the vining morning glory (*Ipomoea* species), has a bushy, spreading habit. Plants grow about a foot tall and 2 feet wide, producing bright flowers in shades of pink, blue, or purple with yellow centers banded by a white stripe. Although each flower lasts but a single day, plants are constantly in bloom from midsummer to early fall and are a good choice for a border edging, window box, or hanging basket.

Selected species and varieties
C. tricolor produces small, narrow leaves on well-branched, semitrailing stems. Flowers are funnel shaped and are 1 to 2 inches across; 'Royal Ensign' grows 12 to 18 inches tall and bears 2-inch flowers that are a vivid blue with white throats and yellow centers.

Growing conditions and maintenance
Dwarf morning glories thrive in nearly any well-drained soil. Start seed indoors in individual peat pots 6 weeks before the last frost by first nicking the seed coat and soaking the seed overnight in warm water. Transplant to the garden in late spring, allowing 9 to 15 inches between plants. Plants tolerate heat and dry soils.

Coreopsis (ko-ree-OP-sis)

TICKSEED

Coreopsis tinctoria

PLANT TYPE: annual

HEIGHT: 2 to 3 feet

INTEREST: flowers

SOIL: well-drained to dry

LIGHT: full sun

This easy-to-grow annual is native to the eastern United States and is a common component of wildflower mixtures. Daisylike flower heads are borne on wiry stems and appear throughout the summer to early fall. Colors include yellow, orange, red, mahogany, and bicolors. Plant them in mixed borders and wildflower gardens, and cut them for fresh arrangements.

Selected species and varieties
C. tinctoria (calliopsis) produces wiry, multiply branched stems with opposite-lobed or dissected leaves. Flower heads may be solitary or appear in branched clusters. Ray flowers are notched and often banded, surrounding a dark red or purple center. Double-flowered and dwarf varieties are available.

Growing conditions and maintenance
Start seed indoors 6 to 8 weeks before the last frost or sow directly in the garden in early spring. Space plants 6 to 8 inches apart. Make a second sowing in midsummer for fall flowers. Deadhead to prolong flowering. Plants tolerate hot weather and drought.

Cosmos (KOS-mos)

COSMOS

Cosmos bipinnatus 'Sonata White'

PLANT TYPE: annual

HEIGHT: 10 inches to 6 feet

INTEREST: flowers

SOIL: well-drained to dry

LIGHT: full sun to light shade

Daisylike flowers crown the wiry stems of this tropical American native. Its showy, delicate blossoms appear singly or in long-stalked loose clusters from midsummer until frost. Cosmos makes a graceful addition to mixed borders, where it will attract numerous butterflies, and is an excellent source of long-lasting cut flowers.

Selected species and varieties
C. bipinnatus grows to 6 feet with delicate, finely cut leaves and flowers in shades of red, pink, and white; 'Candy Stripe' grows 30 inches tall with white flowers with crimson markings; 'Seashells Mixture' grows 3 to 3½ feet with fluted petals of white, pink, or crimson surrounding a yellow center; 'Sonata White' grows 24 inches tall with snowy white blooms; 'Versailles Pink' develops strong, tall stems and pink flowers and is recommended for cutting. *C. sulphureus* grows to 6 feet—and cultivars to 18 to 36 inches—with yellow, orange, or scarlet flowers.

Growing conditions and maintenance
Sow seed directly in the garden after the last frost in spring. Thin to allow 12 to 18 inches between plants. Do not fertilize. Taller types are subject to lodging and may need staking. Plants often self-seed.

Crepis (KREEP-is)

HAWKSBEARD

Crepis rubra

PLANT TYPE: annual

HEIGHT: 8 to 18 inches

INTEREST: flowers

SOIL: well-drained to dry, sandy

LIGHT: full sun

This late-summer and fall bloomer produces fluffy flower heads that look like pink dandelions. It is native to eastern Europe and is very easy to grow. It makes an effective edging for a border and is a good rock-garden specimen.

Selected species and varieties
C. rubra produces a clump of slender pale green basal leaves. Beginning in late summer, flower stems rise about 12 inches above the leaves. Each stem is topped by a feathery pink flower head, often with a darker pink or red center. Because the flowers close in the afternoon, they are not good for cutting. 'Alba' produces white flowers.

Growing conditions and maintenance
Sow seed directly in the garden in fall or spring. Space plants 4 to 6 inches apart. Plants tolerate exposed sites and dry, infertile soils. They thrive in coastal regions. Remove spent flowers to prevent self-seeding or they may become weedy.

Cuphea (KYOO-fee-a)

CIGAR PLANT

Cuphea ignea

PLANT TYPE: tender perennial

HEIGHT: 8 to 18 inches

INTEREST: flowers, foliage

SOIL: well-drained

LIGHT: full sun to light shade

These brightly flowered plants with their rounded, shrubby appearance are perfect candidates for an edging, a planter, or a rock garden. Grown as perennials from Zone 9 south, where they may reach 3 feet, they are treated as annuals elsewhere, where they bloom from midsummer to fall and rarely top 18 inches.

Selected species and varieties

C. ignea (Mexican cigar pant, firecracker plant), grows to 12 inches with an equal spread and narrow dark green leaves. Its scarlet tubular flowers are 1 inch long with a black-and-white tip. *C. llavea* 'Bunny Ears Mixed' grows to 18 inches with a neat, uniform habit and bright red flowers with two protruding stamens bearded with violet hairs. *C. x purpurea* grows to 18 inches with hairy 3-inch leaves and bright rose red flowers tinged with purple and borne in terminal clusters.

Growing conditions and maintenance

Start seed indoors in midwinter and transplant seedlings to the garden after soil has warmed. Plants can also be started from cuttings. Allow 12 to 18 inches between plants. They adapt to any well-drained soil and thrive in warm weather.

Cynara (SIN-ah-ra)

CYNARA

Cynara cardunculus

PLANT TYPE: tender perennial

HEIGHT: 4 to 6 feet

INTEREST: flowers, foliage

SOIL: moist, well-drained, fertile

LIGHT: full sun

Related to the edible artichoke, this species forms clumps of thick stems lined with spiny, lacy silver-gray leaves with woolly undersides that provide a bold accent in a border or form a fast-growing summer hedge. Fuzzy thistlelike flower globes tip each stem from summer through fall. Both leaves and flowers are prized by floral designers for fresh and dried arrangements. It is native to southern Europe.

Selected species and varieties

C. cardunculus (cardoon) will grow up to 6 feet tall in warm climates, though it often reaches only 4 feet in cooler regions. Leaves grow to 3 feet long. Both the leaf-stalks and the roots are edible. Flower heads are purplish, up to 3 inches across, and are surrounded by spiny bracts.

Growing conditions and maintenance

Start seed indoors in late winter, transplanting to successively larger pots as needed before moving to the garden in midspring. Allow 3 feet between plants. Cardoon can be grown as a perennial from Zone 8 south.

Cynoglossum (sin-o-GLOSS-um)

HOUND'S-TONGUE

Cynoglossum amabile

PLANT TYPE: biennial

HEIGHT: 18 inches to 2 feet

INTEREST: flowers

SOIL: moist to dry, well-drained

LIGHT: full sun to light shade

This Asian biennial produces tiny clear blue flowers throughout summer and into fall. It puts on a fine show in borders or beds and is excellent for massing and fresh flower arrangements.

Selected species and varieties

C. amabile (Chinese forget-me-not) has an irregular to rounded habit with a clump of erect stems with somewhat coarse leaves. Each stem is topped with an arching cluster of brilliant blue blossoms. Individual flowers are ¼ inch across and have five petals. Pink- and white-flowered forms are also available.

Growing conditions and maintenance

Though biennial, this species usually flowers the first year from seed. Start seed indoors 6 to 8 weeks before the last frost, or sow directly outside as soon as the soil can be worked in spring. Allow 9 to 12 inches between plants. It thrives in a wide range of soils and will often self-seed. When cutting for arrangements, submerge the stems three-quarters of their length in water to keep flowers from collapsing.

DAHLIA

Dahlia 'Mickey'

PLANT TYPE: tender perennial

HEIGHT: 12 inches to 8 feet

INTEREST: flowers

SOIL: moist, well-drained, fertile

LIGHT: full sun

Dahlias brighten the border over a long season with diverse blooms whose sizes range from a few inches across to the diameter of a dinner plate. Their tightly packed disk flowers are surrounded by one or more rows of petal-like ray flowers that may be doubled, curved, twisted, cupped, or rolled into tiny tubes. Colors range widely; some are bicolored or variegated. The more than 20,000 cultivars available today descend from a few wild species cultivated by Aztec botanists. Dwarf dahlias are cultivated in beds or borders as low-growing bushy edgings; standard dahlias are grown as medium to tall fillers in beds and borders or as specimens. All make long-lasting cut flowers.

Selected species and varieties

Anemone-flowered dahlias—a central disk obscured by a fluffy ball of short, tubular petals and rimmed by one or more rows of longer, flat petals. *Ball dahlias*—cupped, doubled petals crowding spirally into round domes or slightly flattened globes. *Cactus dahlias*—straight or twisted petals rolled like quills or straws over half their length to a pointed tip. *Chrysanthemum-type dahlias*—double rows of petals curving inward and hiding the central disk. *Col-larette dahlias*—central disks surrounded by a collar of short petals backed by a second collar of broader, flat petals; 'Mickey' bears neat yellow-centered blooms with red and yellow ruffles surrounded by red outer petals. *Formal decorative dahlias*—double rows of flat, evenly spaced petals covering the central disk; 'Audacity' produces lavender-pink petals that fade to white at the base. *Informal decorative dahlias*—double rows of randomly spaced flat petals hiding the central disk. *Peony-flowered dahlias*—two or three overlapping layers of ray petals surrounding a central disk. *Pompom dahlias*—small, round balls of tightly rolled petals less than 2 inches in diameter. *Semicactus dahlias*—flat petals curling over less than half their length into tubes at their tips. *Single dahlias*—one or two rows of flat petals surrounding a flat central disk. *Star dahlias*—two or three rows of short petals curving inward. *Waterlily-flowered dahlias*—short petals tightly clasped over the central disk like a waterlily bud, surrounded by several rows of broad, flat petals. Dahlias are further categorized by the size of their flowers.

Growing conditions and maintenance

Start seed indoors in very early spring, or plant tubers directly in the garden in spring, spacing them 1 to 4 feet apart, depending on their type. Provide abundant water and mulch. Remove faded blooms to extend bloom period. Taller types require staking. Dahlias are perennial in Zones 9 to 11; elsewhere tubers may be dug up in fall and stored in a dry, cool location until planting time the next spring.

Dahlia 'Audacity'

ANGEL'S-TRUMPET

Datura inoxia

PLANT TYPE: annual or tender perennial

HEIGHT: 2 to 5 feet

INTEREST: flowers

SOIL: moist, well-drained

LIGHT: full sun to light shade

Datura's large flower trumpets bloom above coarse, oval leaves on shrubby plants that are useful as fillers or as backdrops in a border. Each summer-blooming flower opens at sunset and lasts only a day. Though flowers are sometimes fragrant, the leaves are unpleasantly scented, and most plant parts are extremely poisonous. Plant them only in places where they are completely out of the reach of children and pets.

Selected species and varieties

D. inoxia (angel's-trumpet, thorn apple) grows to 3 feet with 10-inch leaves and pendant pink, white, or lavender flowers 8 inches long and 5 inches wide. *D. metel* (Hindu datura) grows 3 to 5 feet tall with 8-inch leaves and 7-inch white or yellow- or purple-tinged flowers. *D. stramonium* (jimson weed) grows to 5 feet with 8-inch leaves and white or purple 2- to 5-inch flowers; it is extremely poisonous.

Growing conditions and maintenance

Start seed indoors 6 to 8 weeks prior to moving outdoors to warmed soil. Space plants 1½ to 2 feet apart. Provide shelter from wind. *D. inoxia* may survive as a short-lived perennial in Zones 9 and 10.

Daucus *(DAW-kus)*

DAUCUS

Daucus carota var. *carota*

PLANT TYPE: biennial

HEIGHT: 3 to 4 feet

INTEREST: flowers

SOIL: average to poor, well-drained

LIGHT: full sun

This native of Eurasia has naturalized in the United States along roadsides and in abandoned fields. It is very closely related to the garden carrot but is grown for its dainty 4-inch flower heads, called umbels, which appear in late spring to midsummer. The flat-topped umbels consist of tiny white flowers with, often, a single dark red flower at the center. Its lacy appearance serves as a nice filler in a sunny border, and it naturalizes easily in wildflower meadows, attracting butterflies and bees. Flowers are valued for both fresh and dried arrangements.

Selected species and varieties

D. carota var. *carota* (Queen Anne's lace, Queen's lace, wild carrot) produces a prominent rosette of fernlike leaves in early spring, from which grows a 3- to 4-foot branched flowering stem. Each branch is topped by a 3- to 4-inch umbel.

Growing conditions and maintenance

Sow seed outdoors in late spring for flowers the following year. Once established, plant will vigorously self-seed. To prevent unwanted plants, remove flowers before seeds mature. Plants are easy to grow and thrive in nearly any well-drained soil.

Dianthus *(dy-AN-thus)*

PINK

Dianthus chinensis 'Telestar Picotee'

PLANT TYPE: annual, biennial, or tender perennial

HEIGHT: 4 to 30 inches

INTEREST: flowers, foliage

SOIL: moist, well-drained, slightly alkaline

LIGHT: full sun to partial shade

Pinks form mats of grassy foliage with white, pink, red, and bicolored flowers with fringed petals. Low-growing types make delightful edgings or rock-garden or container specimens, while taller selections are useful in the foreground or middle of a border, and as cut flowers.

Selected species and varieties

D. barbatus (sweet William) is a biennial that self-seeds freely; dwarf varieties grow 4 to 10 inches tall, while tall varieties may reach 2 feet. Flowers are borne in dense, flat-topped clusters from late spring to early summer. *D. chinensis* (China pink, rainbow pink) is an annual, biennial, or short-lived perennial that grows 6 to 30 inches tall with a dense, mounded habit; 1- to 2-inch flowers, often fragrant, are borne singly or in loose clusters from early summer to fall; 'Telestar Picotee' has a compact habit with deep pink flowers fringed with white.

Growing conditions and maintenance

Sow seed outdoors in late spring for flowers the following year. Start seed of China pinks indoors 6 to 8 weeks prior to the last frost for transplanting in midspring. Space plants 8 to 18 inches apart.

Diascia *(dy-ASS-ee-a)*

TWINSPUR

Diascia barberae 'Ruby Fields'

PLANT TYPE: annual

HEIGHT: 8 to 12 inches

INTEREST: flowers

SOIL: light, well-drained

LIGHT: full sun

A native of South Africa, twinspur is a slender plant with glossy dark green leaves and five-petaled pink flowers with a pair of spurs at the back. It adds a touch of elegance to the front of beds or borders or to a rock garden. It also makes a charming container plant, suitable for window boxes and hanging baskets.

Selected species and varieties

D. barberae has a mounding habit with slender stems bearing loose clusters of rosy pink flowers from early summer to early fall; 'Pink Queen' grows to 12 inches and bears pink flowers with yellow throats in 6-inch clusters; 'Ruby Fields' produces deep rose pink flowers over an exceptionally long period.

Growing conditions and maintenance

Start seed indoors 6 to 8 weeks prior to the last frost. Transplant to the garden after the soil has warmed, spacing plants 8 inches apart. Plants can also be seeded directly in the garden in early spring. Flowering begins about 14 weeks after seeding. Pinch young plants to encourage bushiness, and after flowering cut flower stems back to the base of the plant to stimulate production of more flowers.

Digitalis (di-ji-TAL-us)

FOXGLOVE

Digitalis purpurea 'Excelsior'

PLANT TYPE: biennial

HEIGHT: 2 to 6 feet

INTEREST: flowers, foliage

SOIL: moist, well-drained, acid

LIGHT: partial shade

Foxglove's striking summer-blooming flower trumpets line the tips of stiff stalks above clumps of coarse, hairy leaves. Most are native to Europe and North Africa but have been grown in the Americas since Colonial times. They add an old-fashioned look and a vertical accent to borders. They also fit well into naturalized plantings such as a woodland garden, and bees love their flowers. Though most bloom their second season, some varieties flower the first year from seed. Because foxglove self-seeds easily, new plants appear each year, giving it a perennial quality. Leaves contain digitalis and are poisonous if eaten.

Selected species and varieties
D. ferruginea (rusty foxglove) produces a basal clump of narrow, deeply veined dark green leaves, each up to 9 inches long. A leafy 5- to 6-foot flower stalk rises from the clump, bearing dense clusters of small yellowish blooms that open from mid- to late summer. Each flower is ½ to 1¼ inches long, yellow-brown, and netted with a rusty red. Tiny hairs fringe the flower lip. *D. purpurea* (common foxglove) produces a broad clump of large rough-textured woolly leaves from which an erect flower stem with smaller leaves emerges in early summer. The flower stalk ranges in size from 2 to 5 feet. The 2- to 3-inch pendulous flowers are borne in a one-sided cluster up to 2 feet long. Their colors include purple, pink, white, rust, or yellow, and their throats are often spotted; 'Alba' grows to 4 feet with white flowers; 'Apricot' grows to 3½ feet with flowers ranging from pale pink to bold apricot; 'Excelsior' grows to 5 feet with blooms borne all around the stem rather than on one side, in colors of purple, pink, white, cream, and yellow; 'Foxy' grows 2½ to 3 feet with flowers in pastel shades from rose pink to white appearing the first year from seed; 'Giant Shirley' grows 5 feet or more, producing strong stems with large mottled blooms in shades of pink.

Growing conditions and maintenance
Start seed outdoors in spring or summer, thinning to stand 6 inches apart. Transplant seedlings to their flowering location in fall or early spring. Types that bloom their first year from seed should be started indoors about 10 weeks, and transplanted to the garden 2 weeks, before the last frost. Space plants 18 to 24 inches apart. Foxgloves thrive in a rich, loose soil and benefit from the addition of compost. Provide water during dry periods and mulch after the ground freezes in fall.

Digitalis purpurea 'Foxy'

Dimorphotheca (dy-mor-foe-THEE-ka)

CAPE MARIGOLD

Dimorphotheca sinuata

PLANT TYPE: annual

HEIGHT: 12 to 16 inches

INTEREST: flowers

SOIL: well-drained to dry

LIGHT: full sun

These South African daisies come in a wide range of bright colors and appear over a very long season, from late spring until fall. Given the right growing conditions, they add a festive touch to the front of beds or borders and are a good choice for rock gardens. The flowers close at night.

Selected species and varieties
D. pluvialis (rain Cape marigold) grows to 16 inches with showy 2½-inch flower heads with yellow centers, often marked with violet, surrounded by white petal-like ray flowers with a purple to violet reverse. *D. sinuata* (winter Cape marigold) grows 12 to 15 inches with a compact, mounded habit, producing 1½-inch flower heads composed of white, yellow, pink, or orange rays surrounding golden centers.

Growing conditions and maintenance
Start seed indoors 4 to 6 weeks prior to the last frost or sow directly in the garden after all danger of frost has passed. Space plants 6 to 9 inches apart. Plants thrive in light, dry soils and tolerate heat and drought.

Dyssodia (dis-OH-dee-ah)

DAHLBERG DAISY

Dyssodia tenuiloba

PLANT TYPE: annual or tender perennial

HEIGHT: 4 to 8 inches

INTEREST: flowers, foliage

SOIL: well-drained to dry

LIGHT: full sun

Their dainty blooms lavishly sprinkled on a dense carpet of finely divided foliage, Dahlberg daisies (also called golden-fleece) constantly flower throughout the summer. They are perfect for bedding and edging, in rock gardens, and in hanging baskets. They can be planted between stepping-stones to add color to a sunny garden path.

Selected species and varieties
D. tenuiloba grows to 8 inches tall but spreads up to 18 inches wide. Its slender stems produce threadlike, bristle-tipped leaves that are aromatic. Flower heads are ½ to 1 inch across with orange-yellow ray flowers surrounding a yellow center.

Growing conditions and maintenance
Start seed indoors 6 to 8 weeks prior to the last frost to transplant to the garden after all danger of frost has passed. In warm areas they can be planted directly in the garden and will self-seed. Allow 6 to 12 inches between plants. Water sparingly and do not fertilize. Plants thrive in sunny, dry locations and tolerate heat, drought, and coastal conditions.

Echium (EK-ee-um)

VIPER'S BUGLOSS

Echium candicans

PLANT TYPE: biennial

HEIGHT: 1 to 10 feet

INTEREST: flowers, foliage

SOIL: dry, poor

LIGHT: full sun

These tropical natives provide a striking accent to borders and rock gardens with their brightly colored and closely packed tubular flowers, which appear from early to late summer. Plants often flower their first year from seed. They are especially useful in sunny, dry locations where the soil is poor.

Selected species and varieties
E. candicans (pride-of-Madeira) grows 3 to 6 feet tall with narrow gray-green leaves covered with silvery hairs and an erect 20-inch cluster of white or purple ½-inch flowers held well above the leaves. *E. lycopsis* (viper's bugloss) grows 1 to 3 feet tall with a bushy habit; flowers are blue, lavender, purple, pink, or white and appear on dense 10-inch spikes. *E. wildpretii* (tower-of-jewels) grows to a showstopping 10 feet, with pale red blooms.

Growing conditions and maintenance
Start seed indoors 6 to 8 weeks before the last frost or outdoors as soon as soil can be worked in spring. In Zones 9 and south, seed can be sown in fall for earlier bloom. Space plants 12 to 18 inches apart. They thrive in poor soils and will produce few flowers on a fertile site. Water sparingly.

Emilia (ee-MILL-ee-a)

TASSEL FLOWER

Emilia javanica

PLANT TYPE: annual

HEIGHT: 18 inches to 2 feet

INTEREST: flowers

SOIL: dry, well-drained

LIGHT: full sun

Tassel flower (also called Emilia's paintbrush) is native to the tropics of both the Eastern and the Western Hemisphere. Throughout summer, it produces small, brilliantly colored flowers on wiry stalks that rise well above a cluster of gray-green leaves. Plant it among other annuals in a border. Flowers can be cut for both fresh and dried arrangements.

Selected species and varieties
E. javanica [also known as *E. coccinea* and *Cacalia coccinea*] develops a clump of oblong leaves 6 inches high. Erect stems up to 2 feet tall are topped with 1-inch clusters of flowers in various shades of red, orange, and yellow.

Growing conditions and maintenance
Start seeds indoors 6 to 8 weeks prior to the last frost for earliest bloom, or sow directly in the garden after the soil has warmed. Space plants 6 to 9 inches apart. They thrive in coastal conditions and tolerate hot, dry locations.

Erysimum (e-RISS-i-mum)

WALLFLOWER

Erysimum perofskianum

PLANT TYPE: biennial

HEIGHT: 9 to 24 inches

INTEREST: flowers

SOIL: well-drained, slightly alkaline

LIGHT: full sun

This native of the mountains of Afghanistan and Pakistan is closely related to *Cheiranthus* species, with which it is sometimes confused. From spring to early summer, yellow and orange spicy-scented flowers appear in dense spikes. It is a good choice for rock gardens, beds, or window boxes.

Selected species and varieties
E. perofskianum [also listed as *Cheiranthus allionii*] (fairy wallflower) produces a rosette of narrow 3-inch leaves and erect 9- to 24-inch flower stems crowded with yellow, orange, or red-orange blossoms. Each flower is ½ inch long and is composed of four petals and four sepals.

Growing conditions and maintenance
In areas with mild winters, sow seed outdoors in fall; elsewhere, sow in early spring as soon as soil can be worked. Seed can also be started indoors, 6 weeks prior to the last frost. Space plants 6 inches apart.

Eschscholzia (es-SHOL-zee-a)

CALIFORNIA POPPY

Eschscholzia californica

PLANT TYPE: annual or tender perennial

HEIGHT: 4 to 24 inches

INTEREST: flowers

SOIL: dry

LIGHT: full sun

This genus includes both annuals and tender perennials native to the grasslands of California and the Southwest. Flowers open during the day and close at night and in cloudy weather. They are effective for massing in beds and borders and compete well in wildflower meadows.

Selected species and varieties
E. caespitosa (tufted California poppy, pastel poppy) is an annual with pale yellow flowers on 4- to 12-inch stalks above finely cut basal foliage. *E. californica* is a 1- to 2-foot tender perennial from Zone 8 south but is grown as an annual elsewhere, with 1- to 3-inch yellow or orange flowers from spring to fall and feathery blue-green foliage; 'Aurantiaca' is an old variety with rich orange single blooms; 'Monarch Mixed' bears single and semidouble flowers in yellow, orange, red, and pink; 'Orange King' bears translucent orange flowers.

Growing conditions and maintenance
Plant seed outdoors in early spring; seedlings do not transplant well. Once established, plants self-seed freely. Space them 6 inches apart. Though they tolerate most soils, they prefer a poor, sandy one.

Euphorbia (yew-FOR-bee-a)

EUPHORBIA

Euphorbia marginata

PLANT TYPE: annual

HEIGHT: 18 inches to 2 feet

INTEREST: flowers, foliage

SOIL: dry to wet

LIGHT: full sun

This hardy annual is native to many parts of the United States and is grown as much for its neatly variegated leaves as for its tiny green flowers surrounded by white bracts. It is an effective accent for annual beds, especially planted in groups of three or five among plants with dark leaves or brightly colored flowers. The sap may cause skin irritation.

Selected species and varieties
E. marginata (snow-on-the-mountain, ghostweed) produces erect, stout, branched stems bearing gray-green oval leaves attractively striped and margined with white. Though the late-summer flowers are small, they are surrounded by showy white leaf-like bracts.

Growing conditions and maintenance
Sow seed directly in the garden in late fall or early spring. Allow 10 to 12 inches between plants. Moisture is needed for seed to germinate and for the plants to become established, but they become very drought tolerant as they mature. They self-seed easily and may become invasive. Use gloves when handling stems to avoid contact with the sap.

Eustoma (yew-STO-ma)

TULIP GENTIAN

Eustoma grandiflorum 'Lion Mixed'

PLANT TYPE: biennial	
HEIGHT: 2 to 3 feet	
INTEREST: flowers	
SOIL: moist, well-drained	
LIGHT: full sun to partial shade	

This native American wildflower produces waxy blue-green leaves on a thick stem with upturned flowers that resemble small roses. Though exacting in their requirements, they are well worth the effort. When grown well, they are exquisite border or container plants and make superb cut flowers, lasting up to 2 weeks.

Selected species and varieties
E. grandiflorum [also known as *Lisianthus russellianus*] (prairie gentian) has an erect habit with sturdy stems and 3-inch oblong leaves. Flowers may be single or double, are 2 inches wide and are usually purple, although pink, blue, and white varieties are available; 'Lion Mixed' is a double-flowered strain with colors from white to deep purple.

Growing conditions and maintenance
Start seed indoors about 3 months prior to the last frost, barely covering them with soil. Move them to the garden after the soil warms, handling seedlings with care. Space plants 6 to 10 inches apart. Keep the soil evenly moist but not too wet. They are slow growers and need a long growing season to perform well. Once they have developed their taproot, plants tolerate drought and heat.

Exacum (EKS-a-kum)

GERMAN VIOLET

Exacum affine

PLANT TYPE: biennial	
HEIGHT: 8 to 24 inches	
INTEREST: flowers	
SOIL: moist, well-drained	
LIGHT: partial to full shade	

The German violet hails from the island of Socotra in the South Indian Ocean. It has an attractive bushy habit and produces abundant sweet-smelling flowers that cover the plant from summer to early fall. It is an excellent choice for edging a shady border or walkway and is often used as a container plant.

Selected species and varieties
E. affine (Persian violet) has a compact, rounded habit with neat, glossy, oval leaves. Each ½-inch lavender-blue flower is star shaped with five pointed petals surrounding prominent yellow anthers. Varieties are available with white, purple, or blue flowers.

Growing conditions and maintenance
Start seed indoors 8 weeks prior to the last frost. Do not cover the seed; it needs light to germinate. Transplant to the garden after all danger of frost has passed, spacing plants 8 to 16 inches apart. Keep soil evenly moist. Plants thrive in warm weather but need some shade.

Foeniculum (fee-NIK-you-lum)

FENNEL

Foeniculum vulgare 'Purpureum'

PLANT TYPE: tender perennial	
HEIGHT: 3 to 5 feet	
INTEREST: flowers, foliage	
SOIL: light, well-drained	
LIGHT: full sun	

The fine-textured, threadlike leaves of fennel are attractive from summer to frost and provide an attractive background for the flat clusters of small yellow flowers. Fennel combines well with bold-textured plants in the middle or back of a mixed border. Leaves, stems, and seed have an anise flavor and are used in cooking.

Selected species and varieties
F. vulgare produces multiply compound leaves and numerous yellow-green flowers in disklike umbels 3 to 4 inches across; 'Purpureum' (bronze fennel) is somewhat smaller in size and produces attractive bronze-red foliage that is particularly appealing combined with plants with gray or silver foliage.

Growing conditions and maintenance
Sow seed directly in the garden in late fall or early spring. Thin seedlings to stand 1 to 2 feet apart. Fennel is not particular about soil and tolerates drought. Though perennial in many areas, it is generally treated as an annual because it is so fast and is easy to grow from seed.

Fuchsia (FEW-sha)

FUCHSIA

Fuchsia x hybrida

PLANT TYPE: annual

HEIGHT: 1½ to 3 feet

INTEREST: flowers

SOIL: moist, well-drained

LIGHT: partial shade

Though technically a tender shrub, fuchsia is most commonly grown as an annual. The pendulous blooms resemble brightly colored earrings dangling from stems up to 3 feet long. Fuchsia is especially attractive in a hanging basket or container, which shows its trailing habit to best advantage.

Selected species and varieties
F. x *hybrida* grows 1½ to 3 feet tall, with a rounded to trailing habit and 2- to 5-inch-long, pointed leaves. The pendant flowers have a 2- to 3-inch-long calyx tube and four sepals; the ½-inch-long petals, often in a contrasting shade, surround protruding stamens and styles; 'Swingtime' bears large double flowers with red tubes and sepals and red-veined white petals.

Growing conditions and maintenance
Grow fuchsia in a moisture-retentive, well-drained potting medium. Provide even moisture and good indirect light or partial shade. Protect plants from midday sun, which causes flowers to fade. In Zones 9 and 10 they may be grown as perennials.

Gaillardia (gay-LAR-dee-a)

BLANKET-FLOWER

Gaillardia pulchella

PLANT TYPE: annual

HEIGHT: 1 to 2 feet

INTEREST: flowers

SOIL: well-drained, sandy

LIGHT: full sun

Gaillardias are native to the southern and western United States. They are easy to grow, producing their brightly colored flowers freely from midsummer to frost, and are most effective when planted in groups of five or more in beds, borders, or along walkways. Their lively colors are attractive in fresh flower arrangements.

Selected species and varieties
G. pulchella (Indian blanket) grows to 2 feet with woolly oblong leaves and daisy-like flowers 2 to 3 inches wide. The petal-like rays may be dark red with yellow tips, yellow with red tips, or solid red or yellow, surrounding a reddish purple disk. Dwarf and double-flowered varieties are also available.

Growing conditions and maintenance
Start seed indoors 6 weeks before the last frost, or outdoors in early spring. Space plants 6 to 12 inches apart. Plants will tolerate most soils as long as they are well drained, but thrive in sandy, open sites. They withstand heat, wind, and drought.

Gazania (ga-ZAY-nee-a)

GAZANIA

Gazania rigens 'Fiesta Red'

PLANT TYPE: tender perennial

HEIGHT: 6 to 16 inches

INTEREST: flowers

SOIL: well-drained to dry

LIGHT: full sun

This tender perennial from South Africa produces daisylike flowers from midsummer to frost. Blossoms open when the sun is out, and close at night and on overcast days. They provide a colorful show in beds or containers.

Selected species and varieties
G. linearis grows to 16 inches with narrow leaves and 2¾-inch flower heads with golden rays and orange-brown disks. *G. rigens* (treasure flower) grows 6 to 12 inches tall with 3-inch flower heads, borne on long stalks, that may be yellow, orange, pink, or red; 'Chansonette' grows to 10 inches with a compact habit and flowers in a wide range of colors; 'Fiesta Red' bears deep burnt orange flowers with a dark ring surrounding a yellow disk; 'Harlequin Hybrids' bear flowers in many shades with a brown zone around the central disk; 'Sunshine' grows to 8 inches with 4-inch multicolored flowers.

Growing conditions and maintenance
Sow seeds indoors in early spring to transplant to the garden after all danger of frost has passed. Space plants 12 inches apart. Do not overwater. They thrive in sunny, dry locations, and tolerate wind and coastal conditions.

Gilia *(GIL-ee-a)*

BIRD'S-EYES

Gilia tricolor

PLANT TYPE: annual

HEIGHT: 1 to 2½ feet

INTEREST: flowers

SOIL: loose, well-drained

LIGHT: full sun

The following gilias are annuals native to coastal areas of California and the nearby mountain ranges. They are vigorous plants that are suitable for a sunny meadow garden.

Selected species and varieties

G. achilleifolia (showy gilia, yarrow gilia)—erect stems 1 to 1½ feet tall with doubly compound leaves. In late spring, deep blue funnel-shaped flowers appear in dense, terminal clusters. *G. capitata* (globe gilia)—1 to 2½ feet tall with finely divided leaves on slender stems. Powder blue globe-shaped flower heads appear in late spring and early summer. *G. tricolor* (bird's-eyes)—1 foot tall with multiple branches and dissected leaves. Flowers are blue with a yellow throat and a dark purple ring at the top.

Growing conditions and maintenance

Gilias are adaptable to most well-drained soils. They are strong self-seeders, but they do not transplant easily. Sow seed where it is to grow.

Gomphrena *(gom-FREE-na)*

GLOBE AMARANTH

Gomphrena globosa

PLANT TYPE: annual

HEIGHT: 8 to 24 inches

INTEREST: flowers

SOIL: well-drained

LIGHT: full sun

Colorful cloverlike flower heads of gomphrena top upright stems from summer to frost. A native of India, this half-hardy annual is easy to grow and imparts a cheerful, informal appearance to beds and borders. Plants perform well in patio planters and window boxes. Flowers, which have a papery texture even when fresh, are excellent for both fresh and dried arrangements.

Selected species and varieties

G. globosa produces erect, branched stems and somewhat coarse, hairy leaves. The 1-inch-long globular flower heads may be pink, white, magenta, orange, or red.

Growing conditions and maintenance

Start seed indoors 8 to 10 weeks before the last frost and transplant outdoors after all danger of frost has passed. Seed can be sown directly outside in late spring. Allow 8 to 15 inches between plants. Though slow to start, plants are easy to grow once established, and they thrive in warm weather. To use in dried arrangements, cut before the flowers are fully open and hang them upside down in an airy room until completely dry.

Gypsophila *(jip-SOFF-il-a)*

BABY'S-BREATH

Gypsophila elegans

PLANT TYPE: annual

HEIGHT: 8 to 24 inches

INTEREST: flowers

SOIL: well-drained, alkaline

LIGHT: full sun

This hardy annual from Europe and northern Asia produces a cloud of delicate, tiny flowers on sprawling, branched stems from midspring to early fall. It is beautiful as a filler between more brightly colored and boldly textured plants in flower borders or rock gardens and in indoor arrangements both fresh and dried.

Selected species and varieties

G. elegans has a mounded habit with thin, multibranched stems bearing pairs of narrow gray-green leaves and airy clusters of white, pink, red, or purple flowers. Each flower is ¼ to ¾ inch across.

Growing conditions and maintenance

Sow seed directly in the garden in midspring. Supplement acid soils with limestone. Plants are short-lived, so make successive sowings every 2 to 3 weeks for continuous bloom. Thin plants to stand 9 to 12 inches apart. Taller varieties may need staking. In Zone 9 and south, provide afternoon shade.

Helianthus (hee-lee-AN-thus)

SUNFLOWER

Helianthus annuus 'Inca Jewels'

PLANT TYPE: annual

HEIGHT: 2 to 10 feet

INTEREST: flowers

SOIL: moist, well-drained

LIGHT: full sun

The sunflower's daisylike blooms in yellow, cream, mahogany, crimson, and assorted blends appear from midsummer to frost on erect stalks. The flowers make a bold statement in mixed borders, and a row them of makes a delightful temporary screen. Flowers are great for cutting. The seeds are a favorite food of many wild birds.

Selected species and varieties

H. annuus (common sunflower) has an erect habit and a coarse texture, producing sturdy stems with broad, bristly leaves and flowers composed of petal-like, often yellow rays surrounding brown or purple disk flowers; 'Inca Jewels' has a multibranched habit with yellow-tipped orange rays; 'Italian White' grows to 4 feet with multibranched stems and 4-inch cream-colored flowers with a brown center; 'Sunbeam' grows 5 feet tall with 5-inch pollenless flowers ideal for cutting; 'Teddy Bear' produces single and double yellow flowers on 2-foot plants.

Growing conditions and maintenance

Sow seed directly outdoors after the last frost. Thin seedlings to allow 1 to 2 feet between plants. Plants thrive in hot, dry weather conditions.

Helichrysum (hel-i-KRY-sum)

EVERLASTING

Helichrysum bracteatum

PLANT TYPE: tender perennial

HEIGHT: 1 to 3 feet

INTEREST: flowers

SOIL: light, well-drained

LIGHT: full sun

This Australian native, also known as immortelle, produces papery-textured flowers in shades of white, yellow, orange, salmon, red, and pink. What appear to be the flower's petals are actually colorful bracts; the true flowers are at the center of the flower head. Use dwarf types for adding color to a rock garden or the edge of a border. Taller varieties are highly valued for cutting, especially for winter arrangements. Flowers retain their colors very well when dried.

Selected species and varieties

H. bracteatum (strawflower) produces narrow, coarsely toothed leaves on wiry, branching stems. Flower heads appear from midsummer to early fall and are 1 to 2½ inches across.

Growing conditions and maintenance

Start seed indoors 6 to 8 weeks prior to the last frost. In warm climates, seed can be sown directly in the garden. Allow 12 inches between plants. Once established, plants thrive in dry soil and often self-seed. They do not perform well in areas with very high humidity. For winter arrangements, cut flowers when they are about half open and hang them upside down in an airy room to dry.

Heliotropium (hee-lee-oh-TRO-pee-um)

HELIOTROPE

Heliotropium arborescens 'Marine'

PLANT TYPE: tender perennial

HEIGHT: 1 to 3 feet

INTEREST: flowers

SOIL: well-drained, fertile

LIGHT: full sun to partial shade

Heliotrope is a tender perennial from Peru grown as an annual in temperate zones. Large clusters of summer flowers range from deep purple to white and bear a lovely vanilla fragrance. Site plants in the foreground of a mixed border; they are especially effective in groups located where their fragrance will be appreciated. They are ideal container plants, and flowers can be cut for fresh arrangements.

Selected species and varieties

H. arborescens (cherry pie) grows 1 to 3 feet in the garden, though plants grown in a greenhouse or in their native range may reach 6 feet. Foliage is dark green and wrinkled. Five-petaled flowers are ¼ inch across, occurring in clusters as large as a foot across; 'Marine', a compact variety reaching 2 feet, has large deep purple flowers and is excellent for bedding, although it lacks intense fragrance.

Growing conditions and maintenance

Start seed indoors 10 to 12 weeks prior to the last frost, or buy young plants in spring. Plants can also be started from cuttings. Do not transplant to the garden until soil has warmed, as plants are very frost sensitive. Allow 12 inches between plants and keep them well watered.

MALLOW, ROSE MALLOW

Hibiscus acetosella

PLANT TYPE: tender perennial

HEIGHT: 18 inches to 8 feet

INTEREST: flowers, foliage

SOIL: moist, well-drained

LIGHT: full sun to light shade

These shrubby tender perennials are attractively grown as annuals in many temperate gardens. Some are grown for their ornamental foliage, while others produce large funnel-shaped five-petaled flowers with prominent stamens that add a tropical flavor to a border. You will find many uses for these bold-textured plants. Plant them individually as specimens or in groups as a fast-growing summer hedge. Tall types are effective as a background for mixed borders or as the centerpiece of an island bed. Shorter ones are useful for fronting shrub borders or planting in the foreground of annual beds. Both large and small types are excellent choices for patio containers.

Selected species and varieties

H. acetosella hails from Africa and is grown primarily for its attractive foliage. Purple flowers form so late in the season in most areas that they fail to open before frost. The plant grows to 5 feet tall, with glossy red leaves and stems. Leaves may be smooth in outline or deeply lobed. This plant makes a bold accent mixed with other annuals, or a stunning summer hedge; the variety 'Red Shield' produces burgundy leaves with a metallic sheen that resemble maple leaves in shape. *H. moscheutos* (common rose mallow, swamp rose mallow, wild cotton) grows 3 to 8 feet tall with a shrubby habit. It is native to marshlands of the eastern United States and can be grown as a perennial in Zones 7 and south, but is often grown as a half-hardy annual. The large gray-green leaves provide a soft foil for the huge white, pink, rose, or red summer flowers that are often 8 inches across; 'Southern Belle' grows 4 to 6 feet tall with red, pink, or white flowers with a distinct red eye, up to 10 inches across. *H. trionum* (flower-of-an-hour) grows 18 to 36 inches with a bushy habit and dark green three- or five-lobed leaves. Flowers are 2 inches across and are creamy yellow with a deep maroon throat. Though flowers are short-lived, they appear in abundance from midsummer to late fall.

Growing conditions and maintenance

Start seed of *H. acetosella* and *H. moscheutos* indoors about 8 weeks prior to the last frost and transplant outdoors after all danger of frost has passed. Space *H. acetosella* 12 to 14 inches apart, *H. moscheutos* 3 feet apart. Because *H. trionum* is difficult to transplant, seed should be sown directly in the garden after all danger of frost has passed, allowing 12 inches between plants. Plants tolerate heat as long as abundant moisture is supplied.

Hibiscus trionum

CANDYTUFT

Iberis umbellata

PLANT TYPE: annual

HEIGHT: 6 to 18 inches

INTEREST: flowers

SOIL: well-drained

LIGHT: full sun

These European wildflowers are easy to grow and free flowering. Like the perennial species [*I. sempervirens*], annual candytufts produce clusters of tiny four-petaled flowers above dark green leaves. They flower throughout the summer and are effective in rock gardens and borders, or as an edging or in a planter, where their sweet fragrance will be noticed.

Selected species and varieties

I. amara (rocket candytuft) grows 12 to 18 inches tall with fragrant white flowers in cone-shaped spikes that can be cut for fresh arrangements. *I. odorata* (fragrant candytuft) grows 6 to 12 inches with flat clusters of white flowers. *I. umbellata* (globe candytuft) grows 8 to 16 inches with clusters of pink, red, lilac, or violet flowers that are not fragrant.

Growing conditions and maintenance

Sow seed in the garden in fall or as soon as soil can be worked in the spring, thinning to allow 6 to 9 inches between seedlings. Make successive sowings to extend the flowering season. Cut back lightly after bloom to stimulate growth. Plants thrive in city conditions.

Impatiens *(im-PAY-shens)*

BALSAM, JEWELWEED

Impatiens wallerana 'Super Elfin Twilight'

PLANT TYPE: annual

HEIGHT: 6 inches to 8 feet

INTEREST: flowers, foliage

SOIL: moist, well-drained

LIGHT: full sun to full shade

Massed as edgings or ground covers, impatiens brighten a shady garden with flowers in jeweled hues from summer through frost. Low-growing types are ideal for planters and hanging baskets.

Selected species and varieties
I. balsamina (garden balsam, rose balsam) grows to 3 feet, producing 1- to 2-inch flowers in mixed colors. *I. glandulifera* (Himalayan jewelweed) grows to 8 feet with 2-inch purple, pink, or white flowers in mid- to late summer. *I. x New Guinea* (New Guinea impatiens) grows to 2 feet with showy, often variegated leaves with flowers up to 3 inches across. *I. wallerana* (busy Lizzie) grows 6 to 18 inches tall with a compact, mounded habit and 1- to 2-inch flat-faced flowers available in many colors; 'Super Elfin Twilight' bears deep pink flowers on spreading plants.

Growing conditions and maintenance
Plant *I. glandulifera* seed outdoors in fall. Start impatiens indoors 3 to 4 months prior to the last frost, or purchase bedding plants to transplant to the garden after all danger of frost has passed. Space *I. glandulifera* 2 feet apart, others 12 to 18 inches apart. Most species prefer some shade and abundant water.

Kochia *(KOE-kee-a)*

BURNING BUSH

Kochia scoparia f. trichophylla

PLANT TYPE: annual

HEIGHT: 2 to 4 feet

INTEREST: foliage

SOIL: moist, well-drained

LIGHT: full sun

This Eurasian annual has naturalized in some parts of the United States. Its fine-textured foliage and neat, symmetrical form make it an attractive summer hedge, screen, or background for a flower border.

Selected species and varieties
K. scoparia f. trichophylla (summer cypress, firebush) has an erect, uniform habit with dense, feathery foliage that is light green in summer, turning bright red in fall, while flowers are insignificant; 'Acapulco Silver' produces variegated silver-tipped leaves.

Growing conditions and maintenance
Start seed indoors in individual peat pots 6 to 8 weeks prior to the last frost or plant directly in the garden after all danger of frost has passed. Do not cover the seed; it needs light for germination. Plants often self-seed and may become invasive. Allow 1½ to 2 feet between plants. Plants can be sheared to maintain their shape or size, and they tolerate heat. Avoid overwatering. In windy locations, plants may require staking.

Lathyrus *(LATH-er-us)*

LATHYRUS

Lathyrus odoratus

PLANT TYPE: annual

HEIGHT: 6 inches to 6 feet

INTEREST: flowers

SOIL: moist, well-drained

LIGHT: full sun to partial shade

The sweet pea is a hardy annual from southern Europe that bears puffy flowers on branching flowering stalks. It can be used as a trailing ground cover, a climbing vine for a screen or backdrop, or a bushy accent among bulbs.

Selected species and varieties
L. odoratus (sweet pea) produces fragrant spring or summer flowers up to 2 inches wide on compact 6-inch- to 2½-foot-tall annual bushes, or on a twining vine 5 to 6 feet long. Flower colors include deep rose, blue, purple, scarlet, white, cream, salmon, pink, and bicolors; 'Bijou Mixed' is a bush type that grows to 12 inches with a full range of colors; 'Royal Family' is a vining type that comes in a wide range of colors, grows to 6 feet, and is heat resistant.

Growing conditions and maintenance
Sow seed 2 inches deep in well-prepared soil in late fall or early spring. Provide climbing types with support. Mulch to keep soil cool, and provide abundant water. Remove faded blooms to prolong flowering.

Lavatera (lav-a-TEER-a)

TREE MALLOW

Lavatera trimestris

PLANT TYPE: annual

HEIGHT: 2 to 6 feet

INTEREST: flowers

SOIL: well-drained

LIGHT: full sun

Native to the Mediterranean region, lavatera is a hardy annual with a bushy habit and cup-shaped summer flowers that resemble hollyhocks. Their long blooming season makes these plants a good choice for the mixed border. They are also useful as a summer hedge, and flowers can be cut for fresh arrangements.

Selected species and varieties
L. trimestris produces pale green rounded leaves on branched stems that may reach 6 feet, although most varieties are between 2 and 3 feet; both leaves and stems are hairy. Solitary 2½- to 4-inch flowers, each with five wide petals, are borne in great numbers throughout the summer. Colors include shades of pink, red, and white; 'Mont Blanc' grows only 2 feet tall and bears pure white flowers; 'Silver Cup' also grows to 2 feet, bearing salmon pink flowers with darker veins.

Growing conditions and maintenance
Sow seed outdoors in midspring, thinning to allow plants to stand 1½ to 2 feet apart. Young plants require abundant water and should be mulched. Once established, plants are drought resistant. Deadhead to prolong flowering.

Layia (LAY-ee-ah)

TIDYTIPS

Layia platyglossa

PLANT TYPE: annual

HEIGHT: 1 to 2 feet

INTEREST: flowers

SOIL: well-drained

LIGHT: full sun

Layia is a member of the sunflower family and is native to California, where it grows as a wildflower. Its common name refers to the showy white-tipped ray petals that surround a golden disk. It is a good choice for beds, borders, rock gardens, and sunny banks. Flowers are excellent for fresh arrangements.

Selected species and varieties
L. platyglossa has a neat habit and coarsely toothed gray-green leaves covered with dense hairs. Flowers appear from spring to early summer; they are bright yellow, single, 2 inches across, and daisylike. This species is often included in wildflower mixes.

Growing conditions and maintenance
Start seed indoors 6 to 8 weeks prior to the last frost, or sow outdoors in early spring. In Zone 9 and warmer, seed can be sown in fall. Space plants 9 to 12 inches apart, and provide abundant moisture to seedlings. Once plants are established, they are quite drought tolerant. Remove flowers as they fade to prolong blooming period.

Limonium (ly-MO-nee-um)

STATICE

Limonium sinuatum

PLANT TYPE: annual or biennial

HEIGHT: 10 to 24 inches

INTEREST: flowers

SOIL: well-drained, sandy, slightly alkaline

LIGHT: full sun

Statice, also called sea lavender, is native to the Mediterranean region and bears clusters of brightly colored flowers surrounded by a papery calyx that remains after the rest of the flower drops. This long-lasting display is useful both in beds and for cutting. Because flowers dry easily and retain their color well, they are often used in dried arrangements.

Selected species and varieties
L. sinuatum (notchleaf statice) grows 18 to 24 inches with a clump of 4- to 8-inch basal leaves and branched, winged flower stems. The papery-textured flowers are borne in short one-sided clusters; colors include pink, blue, lavender, yellow, and white. *L. suworowii* [also known as *Psylliostachys suworowii*] (Russian statice) grows 10 to 20 inches tall with large basal leaves and spikes of lavender and green flowers from summer to frost.

Growing conditions and maintenance
Start seed indoors in individual peat pots 8 weeks prior to the last frost, or sow directly outdoors in midspring in warm climates. Allow 9 to 18 inches between plants. They tolerate drought and seaside conditions but will rot in soil that remains wet.

Linaria (ly-NAY-ree-a)

TOADFLAX

Linaria maroccana 'Fairy Bouquet'

PLANT TYPE: annual

HEIGHT: 10 to 18 inches

INTEREST: flowers

SOIL: moist, well-drained

LIGHT: full sun to partial shade

This hardy annual from Morocco, also called spurred snapdragon, has become naturalized in much of the northeastern United States. Its dainty spikes of bicolored flowers resemble small snapdragons and are at home in mixed borders and rock gardens. Flowers can be cut for indoor arrangements.

Selected species and varieties
L. maroccana (Moroccan toadflax) has an erect, bushy habit with narrow light green leaves and slender spikes of ½-inch flowers in shades of pink, purple, yellow, and white, usually with a contrasting throat; 'Fairy Bouquet' grows to 10 inches and bears flowers in shades of pink, rose, coppery orange, purple, white, and pale yellow, all with a deeper yellow throat, and are suitable for an edging or a window box.

Growing conditions and maintenance
Sow seed directly in the garden in early spring, thinning seedlings to stand 6 inches apart. Although it prefers cool weather, linaria will grow well in warm areas if provided with abundant water.

Lobelia (lo-BEE-lee-a)

LOBELIA

Lobelia erinus 'Sapphire'

PLANT TYPE: annual or tender perennial

HEIGHT: 4 to 8 inches

INTEREST: flowers

SOIL: moist, well-drained

LIGHT: full sun to partial shade

Lobelia hails from South Africa and is grown for its profusion of dainty, brightly colored blooms, which appear from early summer to frost on airy plants. Both trailing and compact, erect forms are available. Trailing types are well suited to hanging baskets and window boxes or for use as a ground cover. Compact varieties fit well into the foreground of borders and make colorful edgings.

Selected species and varieties
L. erinus develops a rounded and compact or a trailing and spreading habit, with narrow to oblong serrated leaves. Flowers are ¾ inch long and are typically blue, although violet, pink, purple, and white varieties are available. Flowers generally display a yellow or white throat; 'Sapphire' bears deep blue flowers with white eyes.

Growing conditions and maintenance
Start seed indoors 10 to 12 weeks prior to the last frost for transplanting to the garden after the danger of frost has passed. New plants can also be started from cuttings. Allow 6 to 10 inches between plants. Lobelia thrives in cool regions; in areas with warm summers, grow in partial shade. Plants may be sheared to encourage compact growth.

Lobularia (lob-yew-LAIR-ee-a)

SWEET ALYSSUM

Lobularia maritima

PLANT TYPE: tender perennial

HEIGHT: 4 to 12 inches

INTEREST: flowers

SOIL: well-drained

LIGHT: full sun to partial shade

This Mediterranean native spreads to nearly twice its height, producing tiny fragrant flowers from late spring to frost. It makes a good choice for an edging, for a rock garden, along dry walls, or for window boxes. In the front of a mixed border, it neatly covers the dying foliage of spring-flowering bulbs.

Selected species and varieties
L. maritima is a fine-textured plant with alternate narrow leaves 1 to 2 inches long. It has a low-branching and spreading habit. Four-petaled flowers are borne in clusters and bear a honeylike scent; colors include white, lilac, pink, and purple.

Growing conditions and maintenance
Start seed indoors 6 to 8 weeks prior to the last frost, or sow directly in the garden in early spring. Avoid overwatering seedlings. Space plants 6 inches apart; they tolerate crowding. In warm areas, they will self-seed. They thrive in cool weather; flowering may stop in hot temperatures. Cutting back plants will encourage more flowering.

Lonas (LO-nas)

YELLOW AGERATUM

Lonas annua

PLANT TYPE: annual

HEIGHT: 10 to 18 inches

INTEREST: flowers

SOIL: light, well-drained

LIGHT: full sun

This native of Italy and northwestern Africa produces showy yellow flower clusters all summer. It adds color to an informal border and is long-lasting when cut for fresh or dried flower arrangements.

Selected species and varieties
L. annua is a vigorous grower with an open, rounded habit. It develops finely divided leaves along erect, multibranched stems and tiny yellow flowers borne in dense clusters 1 to 2 inches across.

Growing conditions and maintenance
Start seed indoors 6 to 8 weeks prior to the last frost or sow directly in the garden when danger of frost has passed. Thin seedlings to 10 inches apart. Plants thrive in light, infertile soil and tolerate seaside conditions. To use for winter arrangements, cut flowers when they reach full color, tie in bunches, and hang upside down in an airy room until dry.

Lunaria (loo-NAY-ree-a)

HONESTY, MONEY PLANT

Lunaria annua

PLANT TYPE: biennial

HEIGHT: 2 to 3 feet

INTEREST: fruit

SOIL: well-drained

LIGHT: full sun to partial shade

This old-fashioned biennial is native to southern Europe. It is grown primarily for its fruit, a flat, oval, translucent seedpod. Plants are best suited to the cutting garden, an informal border, or a wildflower meadow. Their papery seedpods are highly valued for dried arrangements.

Selected species and varieties
L. annua (silver-dollar, bolbonac) has an erect habit with broad, coarsely toothed leaves and fragrant pink or purple flowers, each with four petals, borne in terminal clusters in late spring. Flowers are followed by the seedpods, which fall apart, revealing a thin, silvery white disk, 1 to 2 inches across, to which the seeds cling; 'Alba' produces white flowers well displayed when grown against a dark background.

Growing conditions and maintenance
Lunaria can be grown as an annual or a biennial. For flowers and seedpods the first year, sow seed outdoors in very early spring, or plant in midsummer to early fall for flowers and seedpods the following year. Once established they will reseed through Zone 4. Space plants 8 to 12 inches apart. They tolerate wet and dry conditions and are not fussy about soil quality, as long as it is well drained.

Machaeranthera (mak-e-RAN-ther-a)

TAHOKA DAISY

Machaeranthera tanacetifolia

PLANT TYPE: annual

HEIGHT: 6 to 12 inches

INTEREST: flowers

SOIL: well-drained, sandy to rocky

LIGHT: full sun

Native to the sunny, open spaces from southern Canada through the Great Plains to the southwestern United States, this low-spreading annual blooms profusely over a long period.

Selected species
M. tanacetifolia (Tahoka daisy)—clusters of 2-inch asterlike lavender flowers with yellow centers and dense mounds of deeply cut, sharply pointed foliage 6 to 12 inches tall. Plants readily seed themselves and will make a pretty and colorful ground cover on a favorable site.

Growing conditions and maintenance
Tahoka daisy requires full sun and is tolerant of most soils as long as it has excellent drainage. Propagate by seed. Plants may begin to flower 6 weeks after sowing, and a succession of sowings can extend the blooming period to 6 months.

Matthiola (ma-THY-o-la)

STOCK

Matthiola incana

PLANT TYPE: annual or biennial

HEIGHT: 12 to 30 inches

INTEREST: flowers

SOIL: well-drained, fertile

LIGHT: full sun to light shade

The blossoms of stock perfume a garden throughout summer. Plant them in beds, window boxes, or patio containers where their fragrance can be appreciated. Flowers add a dainty appearance and sweet scent to fresh indoor arrangements.

Selected species and varieties

M. bicornis [also known as *M. longipetala* ssp. *bicornis*] (night-scented stock, evening stock, perfume plant) has a bushy habit and grows 12 to 18 inches tall. It bears single ¾-inch flowers in shades of lilac and pink that open at night from mid- to late summer and are extremely fragrant. *M. incana* (common stock, gillyflower) grows 12 to 30 inches with gray-green oblong leaves and terminal clusters of 1-inch-long flowers that may be single or double and bear a spicy fragrance; colors include pink, purple, white, and blue.

Growing conditions and maintenance

Start seed indoors 6 to 8 weeks prior to the last frost, or sow directly in the garden in early spring. Space plants to stand 6 to 12 inches apart; they tolerate crowding. Plants thrive in cool weather and may stop flowering when temperatures rise. *M. bicornis* will tolerate poorer soil and drier conditions than will *M. incana*.

Mentzelia (ment-ZEE-lee-a)

MENTZELIA

Mentzelia lindleyi

PLANT TYPE: annual or biennial

HEIGHT: 1 to 4 feet

INTEREST: flowers

SOIL: well-drained to dry

LIGHT: full sun

These natives of the western United States bear fragrant yellow or white flowers that brighten borders and beds from summer until frost.

Selected species and varieties

M. decapetala (petal mentzelia) is a biennial that grows 2 to 4 feet with 3- to 5-inch starburst-shaped flowers opening in the evening. *M. laevicaulis* (blazing star, evening star) is a biennial or short-lived perennial that grows to 3½ feet with narrow leaves and pale yellow 4-inch flowers, also opening at night. *M. lindleyi* [also known as *Bartonia aurea*] is an annual species that usually grows 1 to 2½ feet with fragrant bright yellow flowers displaying a colorful orange-red center with a buss of yellow stamens.

Growing conditions and maintenance

Sow seed of the biennial species in fall, or stratify the seed and sow it in spring, directly in the garden. Sow *M. lindleyi* outdoors in midspring. This genus does not transplant well. Thin to allow 6 to 10 inches between plants. Keep seedlings moist, but once established keep plants on the dry side. Plants tolerate heat, wind, poor soil, and drought.

Mimulus (MIM-yew-lus)

MONKEY FLOWER

Mimulus x hybridus

PLANT TYPE: tender perennial

HEIGHT: 10 to 14 inches

INTEREST: flowers

SOIL: moist, well-drained, fertile

LIGHT: partial to full shade

Blooming from midsummer to fall, this native of both North and South America provides bright color to shady beds and borders. It fits well alongside a garden pond or stream and also makes an attractive container plant. Funnel-shaped, two-lipped flowers are thought to resemble monkeys' faces.

Selected species and varieties

M. x hybridus has a mounded habit with glossy 2- to 2½-inch leaves and 2-inch tubular flowers in shades of red, yellow, orange, rose, and brown, usually with brown or maroon spotting or mottling.

Growing conditions and maintenance

Start seed indoors 10 to 12 weeks prior to the last frost for transplanting to the garden after all danger of frost has passed. Space plants 6 inches apart. Plants benefit from the addition of organic matter to the soil. They require some shade and ample moisture. In fall, plants can be dug and potted to continue flowering indoors over the winter.

Mirabilis (mi-RAB-i-lis)

FOUR-O'CLOCK

Mirabilis jalapa

PLANT TYPE: tender perennial

HEIGHT: 18 to 36 inches

INTEREST: flowers

SOIL: well-drained to dry, sandy

LIGHT: full sun to partial shade

This native of the American tropics produces a fresh crop of fragrant blossoms in a wide variety of colors every evening throughout the summer and into fall. Plants fit well into beds and borders and provide a dense, shrubby edging for walkways and vegetable gardens.

Selected species and varieties
M. jalapa (marvel-of-Peru, beauty-of-the-night) has a bushy, shrublike habit with broad deep green leaves up to 6 inches long that provide a perfect foil for colorful 1- to 2-inch-long trumpet-shaped flowers; colors include white, red, yellow, pink, violet, and bicolors. The flowers open in late afternoon and remain open until the following morning.

Growing conditions and maintenance
For earliest blooms start seed indoors 6 to 8 weeks prior to the last frost or sow seed directly in the garden in spring. Allow 1 to 2 feet between plants. Once established, plants often self-seed. They grow equally well in sun or partial shade, and are tolerant of heat and pollution.

Moluccella (mol-lew-SELL-a)

BELLS OF IRELAND

Moluccella laevis

PLANT TYPE: annual

HEIGHT: 2 to 3 feet

INTEREST: flowers

SOIL: moist, well-drained

LIGHT: full sun

This native of the eastern Mediterranean region provides a lovely vertical accent to beds, borders, and indoor arrangements both fresh and dried. It is grown for its showy calyxes, which surround the bases of tiny flowers in late summer and fall.

Selected species and varieties
M. laevis has an erect habit and grows to 3 feet tall and 18 inches wide. Its rounded leaves are about an inch across with rounded teeth along each margin. Flowers are fragrant, pink or white, and rather inconspicuous but are surrounded by a 1- to 2-inch white-veined, light green calyx that resembles a bell. These are borne close to the stem, giving the plant a graceful, vertical form.

Growing conditions and maintenance
Start seed indoors 6 to 8 weeks prior to the last frost; do not cover seed with soil as it needs light to germinate. Seed can also be sown directly in the garden in early spring. Space plants 9 to 12 inches apart. In areas exposed to wind and rain they may require staking.

Myosotis (my-oh-SO-tis)

FORGET-ME-NOT

Myosotis sylvatica 'Ultramarine'

PLANT TYPE: annual or biennial

HEIGHT: 6 to 10 inches

INTEREST: flowers, foliage

SOIL: moist, well-drained

LIGHT: full sun to partial shade

Airy clusters of dainty flowers with prominent eyes open above the forget-me-not's low mounds of delicate foliage. Forget-me-nots provide a soft filler or a delicate border edging. They are particularly attractive in combination with spring-flowering bulbs such as tulips.

Selected species and varieties
M. sylvatica (woodland forget-me-not, garden forget-me-not) produces 8- to 10-inch stems in clumps almost as wide, lined with soft, elongated leaves and tipped with loose clusters of ¼-inch yellow-centered blue flowers from spring through early summer; 'Ultramarine' is very dwarf, growing to 6 inches, with dark blue flowers; 'Victoria Blue' grows 6 to 8 inches, forming neat mounds and producing early flowers of gentian blue.

Growing conditions and maintenance
Start seed outdoors in late summer to early fall for flowers the following spring. Once established, forget-me-nots self-seed readily, performing like a perennial. Enrich the soil with organic matter. Allow 6 to 12 inches between plants, and water during dry periods.

Nemesia (ne-ME-see-a)

NEMESIA

Nemesia strumosa 'Carnival Mixed'

PLANT TYPE: annual

HEIGHT: 9 to 24 inches

INTEREST: flowers

SOIL: moist, well-drained

LIGHT: full sun to partial shade

These brightly colored annuals from South Africa bear pouched, orchidlike flowers from early summer to fall, and are perfect for massing in beds and borders or for growing in containers in areas where summers are cool. They also make effective edgings and provide an attractive cover for the dying foliage of spring bulbs.

Selected species and varieties
N. strumosa has an attractive bushy, mounded habit with narrow bright green toothed leaves and spurred five-lobed flowers in clusters 4 inches long. Flower colors include yellow, white, red, purple, orange, pink, and bicolors; 'Carnival Mixed' is a dwarf variety that grows to 9 inches with brightly colored flowers.

Growing conditions and maintenance
Start seed indoors 4 to 6 weeks prior to the last frost and transplant to the garden after danger of frost has passed, or sow directly outdoors in late spring. Allow 6 inches between plants. Plants require a long, cool growing season to perform well. Pinch young plants to encourage bushiness, and provide water during dry periods.

Nemophila (nem-OFF-i-la)

BABY-BLUE-EYES

Nemophila menziesii

PLANT TYPE: annual

HEIGHT: 6 to 10 inches

INTEREST: flowers

SOIL: moist, well-drained

LIGHT: full sun to partial shade

Baby-blue-eyes hails from California and Oregon, where it grows as a wildflower. In the garden its low, mounded habit and dainty flowers make good edgings, rock-garden specimens, and companions for spring-flowering bulbs. They are also attractive when planted so that their trailing stems spill over the edge of a wall.

Selected species and varieties
N. menziesii produces trailing stems to form a mounding plant, usually about 6 inches tall and 12 inches across, with deeply cut light green leaves. Flowers are tubular, 1 to 1½ inches across, and sky blue in color with white centers; 'Pennie Black' has deep purple ¾-inch blooms edged with silvery white.

Growing conditions and maintenance
Sow seed directly in the garden in early spring, thinning the seedlings to stand 6 inches apart. Enrich the soil with organic matter and provide abundant moisture. Plants thrive in areas with cool summers and self-seed under ideal conditions.

Nicotiana (ni-ko-she-AN-a)

TOBACCO

Nicotiana sylvestris

PLANT TYPE: annual

HEIGHT: 1 to 6 feet

INTEREST: flowers, foliage

SOIL: moist, well-drained

LIGHT: full sun to partial shade

Flowering tobacco produces clusters of fragrant, flat-faced flowers with elongated tubular throats growing at the tips of soft stems, and clumps of large leaves. Plants are useful as border fillers or specimens. Flowers of some varieties close in sunlight but open on cloudy days or in the evening. Leaf juices are poisonous.

Selected species and varieties
N. alata (jasmine tobacco) produces 1- to 2-foot-tall clumps with flowers that bloom from spring to fall; 'Domino Hybrids' have compact cushions of foliage to 15 inches and early-spring flowers in mixed colors; 'Nikki' grows to 18 inches tall with pink, red, white, yellow, or lime green flowers; 'Sensation Mixed' grows 2 to 2½ feet tall with red, pink, purple, white, and yellow blooms. *N. langsdorffii* produces nodding green flowers with turquoise anthers at the tips of 5-foot stems. *N. sylvestris* (woodland tobacco) produces drooping white flowers tinged pink or purple on branching plants 3 to 6 feet tall.

Growing conditions and maintenance
Start seed indoors 6 to 8 weeks prior to the last frost, or sow directly outdoors in late spring. Space plants about 12 inches apart. Deadhead spent blooms.

Nigella (nye-JEL-a)

LOVE-IN-A-MIST

Nigella damascena

PLANT TYPE: annual

HEIGHT: 18 to 24 inches

INTEREST: flowers, seed heads

SOIL: well-drained

LIGHT: full sun

Love-in-a-mist adds a delicate, fine texture to any border or flower arrangement in which it is used. Its fernlike leaves are light green, and solitary flowers are nestled in a mist of foliage at the ends of stems throughout the summer. Interesting seed capsules replace the flowers and are attractive in dried flower arrangements. This annual is native to southern Europe and North Africa.

Selected species and varieties
N. damascena has an erect multibranched habit with delicate leaves divided into threadlike segments. Flowers are 1 to 1½ inches across with blue, white, or pink notched petals. The papery 1-inch seed capsules are pale green with reddish brown markings.

Growing conditions and maintenance
Start seed directly outdoors in early spring, and make additional sowings every 2 or 3 weeks until early summer to extend the flowering season. Plants are not easily transplanted. Thin to allow 6 to 10 inches between plants. Water during dry periods. If pods are allowed to remain on plants, they will self-seed.

Ocimum (OS-si-mum)

BASIL

Ocimum basilicum

PLANT TYPE: annual

HEIGHT: 1 to 2 feet

INTEREST: foliage

SOIL: moist, well-drained

LIGHT: full sun

This annual native of Asia and Africa has been cultivated for centuries as a culinary and medicinal herb. Its lush, fragrant foliage and mounded form make it an exceptional edging for borders and beds. Basil can also be effectively combined with flowering plants in window boxes and patio containers. Plant enough to allow for snipping leaves for seasoning.

Selected species and varieties
O. basilicum (common basil, sweet basil) has a rounded growth habit and square stems typical of the mint family to which it belongs. Green or purple leaves are opposite, oval, and slightly crinkled. Flowers are tiny, white or purple, and borne in terminal clusters, but are often removed to promote leafy growth; 'Dark Opal' grows 1 to 1½ feet with dark purple leaves and lavender-pink flowers, and makes an outstanding accent plant in a bed or border.

Growing conditions and maintenance
Start seed indoors 8 weeks prior to the last frost to transplant outdoors after all danger of frost has passed. Allow 10 to 12 inches between plants. Pinch out flowers as they appear to promote leaf growth.

Oenothera (ee-no-THEE-ra)

EVENING PRIMROSE

Oenothera biennis

PLANT TYPE: biennial

HEIGHT: 2 to 8 feet

INTEREST: flowers

SOIL: well-drained to dry

LIGHT: full sun to partial shade

Among this genus of mostly perennial plants are a few hardy biennials that can be treated as annuals. Their pale yellow funnel-shaped blooms appear from early summer to midfall, opening in the evening atop tall, erect stems. They are suitable for massing at the rear of a border or for use in a wildflower garden.

Selected species and varieties
O. biennis produces a clump of coarse basal leaves from which a stout, erect flower stem rises. Stems may reach 6 feet and bear 1- to 2-inch flowers that open pale yellow and turn gold. *O. erythrosepala* [also called *O. glazioviana*] grows 2 to 8 feet tall with yellow flowers that turn orange or red; 'Tina James' grows 3 to 4 feet with showy yellow flowers that burst open in 1 to 2 minutes and are pleasantly fragrant.

Growing conditions and maintenance
Start seed indoors 8 to 12 weeks prior to the last frost, or outdoors in early spring. Where winters are mild, seed can be sown outdoors in fall. Once established, plants often self-seed, and may become invasive. Space plants 12 inches apart. They thrive in warm weather and tolerate poor soil.

Omphalodes (om-fa-LO-dez)

NAVELWORT, NAVELSEED

Omphalodes linifolia

PLANT TYPE: annual

HEIGHT: 6 to 12 inches

INTEREST: flowers, foliage

SOIL: moist, well-drained, acid

LIGHT: full sun to partial shade

This dainty little annual is native to Spain and Portugal. It produces loose one-sided spikes of white flowers set among silvery gray leaves. Appearing from summer to fall, the flowers are slightly fragrant and excellent for cutting. Plants are well suited to growing in a rock garden or along a stone wall.

Selected species and varieties

O. linifolia produces narrow gray-green lance-shaped leaves and sprays of ½-inch-wide five-petaled flowers. Each petal displays a prominent vein running from its tip to its base, giving it a starlike appearance. Seeds resemble navels.

Growing conditions and maintenance

Start seed indoors 4 to 6 weeks prior to the last frost, or sow directly outdoors in mid-spring. Allow 4 to 6 inches between plants. They prefer a somewhat acid soil and benefit from the addition of peat moss. Water plants during dry periods.

Onopordum (o-no-POR-dum)

THISTLE

Onopordum acanthium

PLANT TYPE: annual or biennial

HEIGHT: 6 to 9 feet

INTEREST: flowers, foliage

SOIL: well-drained to dry

LIGHT: full sun

Scotch thistle produces fuzzy, globular flower heads on tall, stiffly erect branching stems lined with spiny gray-green leaves. The unusual flowers and foliage add both color and texture as vertical accents in a border.

Selected species and varieties

O. acanthium (Scotch thistle, cotton thistle, silver thistle) produces stiff, downy leaves to 2 feet long, deeply lobed and scalloped into spiny segments on branching stems 6 to 9 feet tall. In late spring to summer, stems are tipped with purple or white round, prickly flowers that have flat, fuzzy tops up to 2 inches in diameter.

Growing conditions and maintenance

Start seed indoors 6 to 8 weeks prior to the last frost, or sow directly in the garden after all danger of frost has passed. Space plants 3 feet apart. Once established they will self-seed and may become invasive. To avoid self-seeding, remove faded flowers. Plants thrive in hot, dry locations.

Orthocarpus (or-tho-KAR-pus)

OWL'S CLOVER

Orthocarpus purpurascens

PLANT TYPE: annual

HEIGHT: 12 to 15 inches

INTEREST: flowers

SOIL: light, well-drained

LIGHT: full sun

Owl's clover is native to the southwestern United States, where it covers entire hillsides with rose-purple blooms set off by red-tinged bracts. Individual flowers resemble snapdragons and are tipped with yellow or white on their lower lip. These annuals are useful in wildflower meadows and informal borders, where they provide a long season of color. They are also effective for massing.

Selected species and varieties

O. purpurascens (escobita) grows to 15 inches with linear leaves often tinged with brown and either cut or smooth margins, and red-tipped bracts. The two-lipped rose-purple or crimson flowers are about 1 inch long and appear from early to midsummer.

Growing conditions and maintenance

Sow seed directly outdoors as soon as the soil can be worked in early spring. Thin plants to stand 6 to 8 inches apart. Plants thrive in warm weather. Water during dry periods.

Oxypetalum *(ox-y-PET-a-lum)*

BLUE MILKWEED

Oxypetalum caeruleum

PLANT TYPE: tender perennial

HEIGHT: 15 to 36 inches

INTEREST: flowers

SOIL: well-drained, fertile

LIGHT: full sun

This elegant tender perennial from South America produces its exquisite star-shaped flowers the first year from seed. Flowers are borne in graceful sprays of pink buds that open to reveal baby blue flowers, which mature to lilac-purple. Plant it where its long-lasting flowers can be viewed up close: at the edge of a border, or in a patio planter or hanging basket.

Selected species and varieties

O. caeruleum has a weakly twining habit, and though it becomes a 3-foot shrub in Zones 10 and 11, where it is perennial, it rarely exceeds 18 inches when grown elsewhere as an annual. Leaves are heart shaped and covered with downy hairs. The ½- to 1-inch flowers are borne in open clusters from summer to early fall.

Growing conditions and maintenance

Start seed indoors 6 to 8 weeks prior to the last frost, and transplant to the garden after all danger of frost has passed. Space plants 8 to 12 inches apart. Plants thrive in cool weather and tolerate dry soil. They can be dug and potted in the fall for growing indoors in winter.

Papaver *(pa-PAY-ver)*

POPPY

Papaver nudicaule

PLANT TYPE: annual or tender perennial

HEIGHT: 1 to 4 feet

INTEREST: flowers

SOIL: well-drained to dry

LIGHT: full sun to light shade

Poppy's showy spring flowers surround prominent centers above clumps of coarse, hairy, deeply lobed leaves. The brightly colored flower petals are extremely delicate in appearance, with a tissuelike texture. Flowers may be single, with four overlapping petals, or double, with many petals forming a rounded bloom. They are borne on solitary stems, and are suitable for mixed borders and good for cutting.

Selected species and varieties

P. nudicaule (Iceland poppy, Arctic poppy) produces a fernlike clump of 6-inch lobed gray-green leaves from which 12- to 18-inch leafless flower stems rise from spring to early summer. Flowers are fragrant, 2 to 4 inches across, and saucer shaped; colors include white, yellow, orange, salmon, pink, and scarlet. *P. rhoeas* (corn poppy, Flanders poppy, Shirley poppy, field poppy) grows to 3 feet with wiry, branching stems and pale green deeply lobed leaves. Flowers may be single or double, and are borne from late spring to early summer in colors of red, purple, pink, and white; 'Fairy Wings' produces flowers in soft shades of blue, lilac, dusty pink, and white with faint blue margins; 'Mother of Pearl' bears flowers in shades of blue, lavender,

pink, gray, white, and peach, and the flowers may be solid or speckled. *P. somniferum* (opium poppy) grows 3 to 4 feet tall with large white, red, pink, or mauve flowers that appear throughout summer and are often double or fringed; 'Alba' bears white blooms; 'Pink Chiffon' produces double bright pink flowers; 'White Cloud' bears large double white blooms on sturdy stems.

Growing conditions and maintenance

P. nudicaule can be started indoors 10 weeks prior to the last frost for transplanting in late spring. Handle seedlings carefully because they are difficult to transplant. You can also sow directly in the garden in late fall or early spring. Other species are so difficult to transplant that they are best sown in place. Papaver seed is very small and can be mixed with sand for easier handling. Thin *P. nudicaule* to stand 8 to 10 inches apart, *P. rhoeas* about 12 inches apart, and *P. somniferum* 4 to 8 inches apart. Double-flowered varieties of *P. somniferum* often require staking. Poppies will often self-seed. Deadhead plants to prolong flowering season. For use in indoor arrangements, cut the flowers as the buds straighten on their nodding stems but before the flowers actually open.

Papaver rhoeas

Pelargonium (pel-ar-GO-nee-um)

GERANIUM

Pelargonium x hortorum 'Freckles'

PLANT TYPE: annual or tender perennial

HEIGHT: 10 to 36 inches

INTEREST: flowers, foliage

SOIL: moist, well-drained

LIGHT: full sun

These tender perennials are primarily hybrids of South African natives, and since their introduction over 100 years ago they have become some of the most popular bedding plants grown. Geraniums have a shrubby habit with showy leaves and clusters of vividly colored flowers. They have many uses in the garden: Their reliable and long-lasting flowers are well suited to formal beds, they provide nonstop color for hanging baskets and window boxes, and trailing types make good ground covers.

Selected species and varieties
P. x *domesticum* (show geranium, regal geranium, Martha Washington geranium) has a shrubby habit and usually grows 1 to 1½ feet tall, although in Zone 9 and warmer it may reach 3 feet. Plants bear light green deeply lobed, serrated leaves and huge, dense clusters of red, white, or pink flowers that are often blotched or veined with a darker color. *P.* x *hortorum* (zonal geranium, house geranium, bedding geranium) typically grows 10 inches to 3 feet tall, with a rounded habit; in frost-free areas, it may grow considerably taller. Plants produce rounded, pale to medium green leaves that have scalloped edges and are usually marked with a

brown or maroon horseshoe-shaped zone. Flowers are single, semidouble, or double; appear in 5-inch dense, long-stemmed clusters; and include shades of red, pink, white, and salmon; 'Freckles' has a compact habit and pink flowers with a dark rose spot at the base of each petal. *P. peltatum* (ivy-leaved geranium, hanging geranium) has a vinelike habit with gracefully trailing stems up to 3 feet long and medium green leathery leaves. Flowers are borne in loose clusters and range from single to very double; colors include pink, white, lavender, and cherry red. These are particularly attractive in hanging baskets or in planters where their stems are allowed to trail over the edge.

Growing conditions and maintenance
Start seed indoors 12 to 16 weeks prior to last frost. Geraniums can also be started indoors from cuttings taken from overwintered plants. Transplant after all danger of frost has passed. Space plants 8 to 15 inches apart. Geraniums, especially regal types, prefer cool climates and may die out during the heat of summer in southern zones. Water during dry periods. Remove faded flowers to encourage blooming. Geraniums may be dug and potted in the fall for growing indoors.

Pelargonium x domesticum

Perilla (per-RILL-a)

BEEFSTEAK PLANT

Perilla frutescens 'Crispa'

PLANT TYPE: annual

HEIGHT: 2 to 3 feet

INTEREST: foliage

SOIL: well-drained to dry

LIGHT: full sun to partial shade

This Asian native is grown for its attractive foliage, which resembles that of coleus or purple basil. Plants are useful as accents in borders, especially toward the back, where the dark leaves contrast well with brightly colored flowers. Leaves are used as a seasoning in oriental cooking.

Selected species and varieties
P. frutescens has an upright habit with the square stems and opposite leaves typical of the mint family. Leaves are up to 5 inches long, have a quilted texture, and are purple-bronze, green, or variegated in color; 'Crispa' develops bronze leaves with wrinkled margins; 'Atropurpurea' has very dark purple leaves.

Growing conditions and maintenance
Start seed indoors 6 weeks prior to the last frost, or sow directly in the garden after the soil has warmed. Space plants 15 to 18 inches apart. Once established, perilla will self-seed and may become invasive; to avoid this problem, remove flowers as they develop. Plants will tolerate poor soil.

Petunia (pe-TOO-nya)

PETUNIA

Petunia x hybrida 'Fluffy Ruffles'

PLANT TYPE: annual

HEIGHT: 8 to 18 inches

INTEREST: flowers

SOIL: well-drained

LIGHT: full sun

Open flower trumpets bloom in profusion from summer until frost along petunia's trailing or upright stems amid small, hairy, pointed leaves. Petunias are effective cascading over walls or banks or when massed as bedding plants. Their nonstop flower display is ideal for window boxes and hanging baskets.

Selected species and varieties
P. x hybrida (common garden petunia) produces white, yellow, pink, red, purple, blue-purple, or lavender blooms that may be speckled, splotched, veined, or striped in a contrasting color on compact, bushy, or trailing plants; 'Fantasy Pink Morn' bears small light pink flowers with a creamy white center on plants that reach 10 to 12 inches in height and spread up to 18 inches; 'Fluffy Ruffles' produces 5- to 6-inch flowers that are often tricolored with contrasting veins and throats; 'Heavenly Lavender' produces 2½- to 3-inch double lavender blooms on compact plants 8 to 12 inches tall.

Growing conditions and maintenance
Start seed indoors 10 to 12 weeks before the last frost date. Pinch to develop bushy plants; remove dead blooms to encourage further flowering.

Phacelia (fa-SEEL-ee-a)

HAREBELL PHACELIA

Phacelia campanularia

PLANT TYPE: annual

HEIGHT: 6 to 20 inches

INTEREST: flowers

SOIL: well-drained to dry, sandy

LIGHT: full sun

This annual, also called scorpion weed, is native to the southwestern United States, where it grows on dry, rocky slopes and in deserts. Bell-shaped flowers appear in clusters along one side of a curved stem in spring and midsummer. The plants are useful for massing and creating low borders, and are also well suited to rock gardens. Some people develop a skin rash from handling the leaves.

Selected species and varieties
P. campanularia (California bluebell) has a creeping habit with 1-inch hairy, round or heart-shaped leaves and ¾- to 1-inch bright blue bell-shaped flowers borne in loose clusters.

Growing conditions and maintenance
Sow seed directly in the garden in fall in Zones 9 and warmer; elsewhere sow in midspring. Plants are difficult to transplant. Thin young plants to stand 6 to 8 inches apart. They thrive in dry conditions and poor soil. Make successive sowings at 3- to 4-week intervals to extend the flowering period.

Phlox (flox)

PHLOX

Phlox drummondii 'Palona Rose with Eye'

PLANT TYPE: annual

HEIGHT: 6 to 20 inches

INTEREST: flowers

SOIL: dry, sandy

LIGHT: full sun to partial shade

This Texas native provides a long season of colorful blooms on low, spreading plants that are useful as edgings, in rock gardens, massed in beds, and in containers. Flowers are also good for cutting. Their colors include white, pink, red, purple, yellow, and bicolors.

Selected species and varieties
P. drummondii (annual phlox, Drummond phlox) grows to 20 inches with a spreading, mounded habit, hairy leaves and stems, and five-lobed flowers that are 1 inch across; 'Palona Rose with Eye' is compact, 6 to 8 inches tall, with rose flowers with contrasting white eyes; 'Petticoat' series are compact 6-inch plants that come in a mix of colors with good drought and heat tolerance; 'Twinkle' series are 8 inches with small, early, star-shaped flowers in mixed colors.

Growing conditions and maintenance
Start seed indoors 8 weeks prior to the last frost. In Zone 8 and warmer, seed can also be sown in fall. Remove spent flowers to extend bloom, and provide water when dry. Flowering often declines in midsummer but will resume in fall.

Portulaca (por-tew-LAK-a)

MOSS ROSE

Portulaca grandiflora 'Sundance'

PLANT TYPE: annual

HEIGHT: 6 to 8 inches

INTEREST: flowers, foliage

SOIL: well-drained to dry

LIGHT: full sun

This spreading, low-growing annual is native to South America. Its succulent leaves cover the ground like a carpet and set off its brightly colored blooms. Flowers appear from early summer to frost, opening in the morning and closing late in the day. Portulaca is a fine choice for a rock garden, an edging, a ground cover, or containers, especially in hot, dry sites where few other flowers will thrive.

Selected species and varieties
P. grandiflora (sun plant, eleven-o'clock) produces sprawling succulent stems that bear fleshy, narrow leaves and showy bowl-shaped flowers. Blooms may be single, semidouble, or double, and may be red, pink, white, yellow, orange, magenta, or striped; 'Sundance' bears semidouble flowers in a mixture of red, orange, yellow, cream, and white; 'Sundial' blooms early with double flowers.

Growing conditions and maintenance
Start seed indoors about 6 weeks prior to the last frost for transplanting to the garden after the soil has warmed. Seed can also be sown directly in the garden after danger of frost is past. Space plants 6 to 8 inches apart. Moss rose often self-seeds. Do not fertilize; it likes poor, dry soils.

Proboscidea (pro-bo-SID-ee-a)

DEVIL'S-CLAW

Proboscidea louisianica

PLANT TYPE: annual

HEIGHT: 1 to 2 feet

INTEREST: flowers, fruit

SOIL: well-drained, sandy

LIGHT: full sun

This annual native of North America bears tubular flowers followed by very unusual fruit: a fleshy 4- to 6-inch pod that splits into two clawlike, curved ends as it dries. The green pods can be pickled and eaten, while the dried pods are outstanding for dried arrangements.

Selected species and varieties
P. louisianica (ram's horn, proboscis flower) grows to 2 feet with a bushy, spreading habit. The wavy-margined leaves are 7 to 10 inches across with long petioles and are covered with sticky hairs. Flowers have five lobes and are yellow, white, or pink with purple markings; they commonly appear right after a rain, and have an unpleasant odor. The unique fruits appear after the blooms have faded.

Growing conditions and maintenance
Start seed indoors 6 to 8 weeks before the last frost. In Zone 8 and warmer, seed can be sown directly in the garden in mid-spring. Plants may self-seed and become invasive in warm climates. Space them 6 to 12 inches apart and at least 5 feet away from other plants so that their odor does not overpower more delicate or appealing scents.

Reseda (re-ZEE-da)

MIGNONETTE

Reseda odorata

PLANT TYPE: annual

HEIGHT: 6 to 18 inches

INTEREST: flowers

SOIL: well-drained, fertile

LIGHT: full sun to partial shade

This native of northern Africa produces thick spikes of small, deliciously fragrant flowers from late summer through fall. Star-shaped flowers are creamy white to greenish yellow with bright orange stamens. Use plants at the edge of a border or in a patio planter or window box where their fragrance can be appreciated. Flowers are long-lasting and excellent for cutting.

Selected species and varieties
R. odorata develops thick stems and small oval leaves. Flowers are ⅓ inch across with four to seven fringed petals. Although not extremely showy, the flowers are so fragrant as to be well worth growing.

Growing conditions and maintenance
Plants are difficult to transplant, so sow seed directly in the garden in early spring. Seeds require light to germinate; do not cover. A second planting a month later will extend the flowering season. In Zones 9 and 10 seed can be planted in fall for earlier flowers. Thin seedlings to stand 6 to 12 inches apart. Water and mulch to keep soil evenly moist and cool.

Ricinus (RISS-i-nus)

CASTOR-OIL PLANT

Ricinus communis

PLANT TYPE: tender perennial

HEIGHT: 8 to 10 feet

INTEREST: foliage

SOIL: well-drained

LIGHT: full sun

Ricinus's clumps of large, glossy leaves make an effective coarse-textured backdrop in sunny borders, and because the plants grow rapidly, they are also used as screens. Flowers, which are insignificant, are followed by prickly husks filled with tiny brown seeds. These are extremely poisonous—and a particular danger to children, who find them attractive; care must be taken to locate plants appropriately.

Selected species and varieties
R. communis (castor bean) produces leaves until frost on plants that grow up to 10 feet tall and 3 to 4 feet wide; leaves emerge tinged with red and turn glossy green and are broad, up to 3 feet across, with narrow, pointed segments; 'Carmencita' produces early-blooming bright red flowers and deep brown leaves.

Growing conditions and maintenance
Plant seed indoors 6 to 8 weeks prior to the last frost. Plants grow best in hot, humid climates. Provide ample water and fertilizer; they may survive as perennials in warm climates.

Rudbeckia (rood-BEK-ee-a)

CONEFLOWER

Rudbeckia hirta 'Double Gold'

PLANT TYPE: annual, biennial, or tender perennial

HEIGHT: 1 to 3 feet

INTEREST: flowers

SOIL: moist to dry, well-drained

LIGHT: full sun to partial shade

Rudbeckias have prominent dark centers fringed with petal-like ray flowers. The yellow summer flowers bloom on stems lined with large, hairy leaves. They are useful as a filler or backdrop in a border or sunny meadow garden.

Selected species and varieties
R. hirta (black-eyed Susan) may be an annual, a biennial, or a short-lived perennial with single or double 2- to 3-inch flower heads whose drooping yellow rays surround dark centers; 'Double Gold' produces spectacular double yellow blooms; 'Gloriosa Daisy' bears flowers in shades of yellow with mahogany centers, and other bicolors; 'Goldilocks' grows to 15 inches with 3- to 4-inch double flowers; 'Green Eyes' (also called 'Irish Eyes') grows to 30 inches and bears 5-inch flowers with golden rays around a green eye.

Growing conditions and maintenance
Start seed indoors 8 to 10 weeks prior to the last frost, or sow directly outdoors in fall or early spring. Allow 9 to 24 inches between plants. Once established they may self-seed. They tolerate a wide range of soils and drought.

Salpiglossis (sal-pi-GLOSS-is)

PAINTED TONGUE

Salpiglossis sinuata 'Bolero'

PLANT TYPE: annual

HEIGHT: 2 to 3 feet

INTEREST: flowers

SOIL: well-drained, fertile

LIGHT: full sun

The flowers of salpiglossis come in an incredible range of colors, including red, pink, purple, blue, white, yellow, and brown. Blooms are typically veined or spotted with a contrasting color. Plants add a cheerful accent to beds and borders, and are excellent for cutting.

Selected species and varieties
S. sinuata has an erect, bushy habit with narrow 4-inch leaves. Both leaves and stems are slightly hairy and sticky. Flowers resemble petunias, are 2 to 2½ inches wide, have a velvety texture, and appear in terminal clusters; 'Bolero' is 18 to 24 inches tall with flower colors that include gold, rose, red, and blue.

Growing conditions and maintenance
Start seed indoors 6 to 8 weeks prior to the last frost for transplanting to the garden after all danger of frost has passed, or plant directly outdoors in late spring. Space plants 10 to 12 inches apart. Prepare soil deeply to provide excellent drainage. Taller varieties may need staking. Plants thrive in cool weather and die in high heat and humidity.

Salvia (SAL-vee-a)

SAGE

Salvia coccinea 'Lady in Red'

PLANT TYPE: annual or tender perennial

HEIGHT: 8 inches to 4 feet

INTEREST: flowers, foliage

SOIL: sandy, dry to well-drained

LIGHT: full sun to partial shade

Whorled spikes of tiny hooded summer- to fall-blooming flowers line the tips of salvia's erect stems above soft, sometimes downy leaves. Salvias are particularly effective in masses that multiply the impact of their flowers. Tender perennial salvias that cannot withstand frost are grown as annuals in Zone 8 and colder.

Selected species and varieties

S. argentea (silver sage) produces branching clusters of white flowers tinged yellow or pink on 3-foot stems above rosettes of woolly gray-green 6- to 8-inch leaves. *S. coccinea* (Texas sage) produces heart-shaped leaves on 1- to 2-foot branching stems; 'Lady in Red' has slender clusters of bright red flowers. *S. farinacea* (mealycup sage) grows 2 to 3 feet tall with gray-green leaves and spikes of small blue flowers; 'Silver White' grows 18 to 20 inches tall with silvery white flowers; 'Strata' reaches 16 to 24 inches with 6- to 10-inch spikes of bicolored flowers in blue and white that are useful in both fresh and dried arrangements; 'Victoria' grows to 18 inches with a uniform habit and a 14-inch spread with violet-blue flowers. *S. greggii* (autumn sage) grows 2 to 4 feet tall with an erect, shrubby habit, medium green leaves, and

red, pink, yellow, or white flowers that bloom from midsummer through fall and attract hummingbirds. *S. leucantha* (Mexican bush sage) grows 2 to 4 feet with gracefully arching stems, gray-green leaves, and arching spikes of purple and white flowers in summer and fall. *S. officinalis* (common sage, garden sage, culinary sage) bears whorls of tiny white, blue, or purple flowers above hairy, aromatic gray-green leaves used for cooking; 'Icterina' grows 18 inches tall with variegated leaves of golden yellow and green; 'Tricolor' grows to 18 inches and produces leaves that are white and purple with pink margins. *S. splendens* (scarlet sage) grows 8 to 30 inches with bright green 2- to 4-inch leaves and terminal clusters of red, pink, purple, lavender, or white flowers up to 1½ inches long; 'Blaze of Fire' grows 12 to 14 inches with bright red blooms; 'Laser Purple' bears deep purple flowers that resist fading; 'Rodeo' grows to 10 inches with early red flowers. *S. viridis* (clary sage, painted sage) grows to 18 inches with white and blue flowers with showy pink to purple bracts throughout summer and fall, and is superb for fresh and dried arrangements.

Growing conditions and maintenance

Start seed indoors 6 to 8 weeks prior to the last frost. Space smaller types 12 to 18 inches apart, larger types 2 to 3 feet apart. Salvias are generally drought tolerant. Remove faded flowers to extend bloom.

Salvia farinacea 'Victoria'

Sanvitalia (san-vi-TAY-lee-a)

CREEPING ZINNIA

Sanvitalia procumbens

PLANT TYPE: annual

HEIGHT: 5 to 6 inches

INTEREST: flowers

SOIL: well-drained to dry

LIGHT: full sun

This low-growing annual from Mexico produces a nonstop display of flowers from early summer to frost. Flowers resemble zinnias, but each head is only ¾ inch across. Sanvitalia makes a superb edging or ground cover, and it is well suited to a sunny rock garden.

Selected species and varieties

S. procumbens (trailing sanvitalia) grows to a height of 6 inches, although its trailing stems spread to 18 inches, with pointed, oval leaves that are ½ to 1 inch long. Flowers are composed of yellow or orange rays surrounding a dark purple center and may be single, semidouble, or double; 'Gold Braid' produces double yellow blooms; 'Mandarin Orange' bears semidouble orange flowers.

Growing conditions and maintenance

Start seed indoors 4 to 6 weeks prior to the last frost, or sow directly outdoors in late spring. Allow 6 to 12 inches between plants. Sanvitalia thrives in hot, humid weather and is drought tolerant.

Scabiosa (skab-ee-O-sa)

SCABIOUS

Scabiosa atropurpurea

PLANT TYPE: annual

HEIGHT: 18 inches to 3 feet

INTEREST: flowers

SOIL: well-drained, fertile

LIGHT: full sun

Scabiosa is easy to grow and produces long-lasting flowers that are well suited to borders, massing, and both fresh and dried arrangements. Flower heads are 1 to 2 inches across with prominent stamens that resemble pins stuck in a pincushion; colors include lavender, pink, purple, maroon, red, and white.

Selected species and varieties
S. atropurpurea grows 2 to 3 feet tall with an erect habit and showy, domed flower heads on long stems. *S. stellata* (paper moon) grows 1½ to 2½ feet with pale blue flowers that become papery when dry and are highly valued for dry arrangements; 'Drumstick' bears faded blue flowers that quickly mature to bronze; 'Ping-Pong' bears white flowers on heads the size of a ping-pong ball.

Growing conditions and maintenance
Start seed indoors 4 to 6 weeks prior to the last frost and transplant to the garden after danger of frost has passed, or sow directly outdoors in late spring. Space plants 8 to 12 inches apart. Water during dry periods.

Schizanthus (ski-ZAN-thus)

BUTTERFLY FLOWER

Schizanthus pinnatus

PLANT TYPE: annual

HEIGHT: 1 to 4 feet

INTEREST: flowers

SOIL: moist, well-drained, fertile

LIGHT: full sun to partial shade

Schizanthus is a native of Chile that produces exotic flowers resembling orchids. Borne in loose clusters, the two-tone flowers, which come in many colors, are pleasantly displayed against fernlike foliage. They are useful in beds or containers and are excellent for cutting.

Selected species and varieties
S. pinnatus grows to 4 feet with light green finely cut leaves and 1½-inch flowers produced in open clusters from early summer to early fall. Flowers have a tropical appearance, and colors include pink, rose, salmon, vivid red, lavender, violet, and cream. Each displays contrasting markings on the throat.

Growing conditions and maintenance
Start seed indoors 8 weeks before the last frost, or plant directly outdoors in midspring. Make successive plantings to extend the blooming season. Space plants 12 inches apart. Provide abundant moisture in a soil with excellent drainage. Grow in light shade where summers are hot. Tall varieties require staking; shorter types are better for borders.

Senecio (sen-EE-see-o)

GROUNDSEL, RAGWORT

Senecio cineraria

PLANT TYPE: tender perennial

HEIGHT: 6 to 30 inches

INTEREST: foliage

SOIL: well-drained

LIGHT: full sun to light shade

Woolly white to silvery gray leaves combine well with brightly colored flowers in borders and beds. Native to the Mediterranean region, the species commonly known as dusty-miller is perennial from Zone 9 south but is grown as an annual elsewhere. It makes an attractive edging, rock-garden specimen, or container plant.

Selected species and varieties
S. cineraria (dusty-miller, silver groundsel) has a rounded, branched habit. Leaves are thick, up to 8 inches long, and deeply cut into rounded lobes; they are covered with dense woolly hairs, giving the foliage a feltlike texture. Flowers are yellow or cream, appearing in small terminal clusters in late summer, but are best removed to encourage foliage growth.

Growing conditions and maintenance
Start seed indoors 8 to 10 weeks prior to the last frost. Do not cover the seed; light is necessary for germination. Transplant outdoors when danger of frost has passed, spacing plants 10 inches apart. Avoid soils that are too fertile, and do not overwater as this will result in weak growth and susceptibility to disease. Plants tolerate drought.

Silene (sy-LEE-ne)

CAMPION, CATCHFLY

Silene coeli-rosa

PLANT TYPE: annual or biennial

HEIGHT: 6 to 24 inches

INTEREST: flowers

SOIL: well-drained

LIGHT: full sun to light shade

Silene is robust and easy to grow and provides an abundance of summer flowers for borders and beds. Low-growing types are well suited to rock gardens or for use as edgings, and taller types are attractive when cut for fresh arrangements.

Selected species and varieties
S. armeria (sweet William catchfly) grows 12 to 18 inches tall with blue-gray leaves and 3-inch clusters of pink or red flowers. It is often included in wildflower mixes and is suitable for naturalizing. *S. coeli-rosa* [also known as *Lychnis coeli-rosa* and *Viscaria coeli-rosa*] usually grows to about 12 inches with narrow, pointed leaves and blue, lavender, pink, or white flowers that often sport a contrasting eye; each single, saucer-shaped flower is 1 inch across. *S. pendula* (drooping catchfly) grows 6 to 16 inches tall with a compact habit, hairy medium green leaves, and loose clusters of pale pink flowers.

Growing conditions and maintenance
Sow seed directly outdoors in early spring as soon as the soil can be worked. Established plants often self-seed. Allow 8 inches between plants. They perform best in well-drained, sunny locations but will tolerate light shade.

Silybum (sil-LY-bum)

BLESSED THISTLE

Silybum marianum

PLANT TYPE: annual or biennial

HEIGHT: to 4 feet

INTEREST: flowers, foliage

SOIL: well-drained

LIGHT: full sun

Silybum is grown primarily for its spiny, glossy foliage, which is dark green with silvery white spots. The 12- to 14-inch deeply lobed basal leaves form an attractive wide-spreading rosette from which 2-inch thistlelike flowers rise in late summer. It is useful as a ground cover in dry, sunny sites. The roots, leaves, and flower heads can be eaten as a vegetable.

Selected species and varieties
S. marianum grows to 4 feet with coarse, prominently veined and spotted leaves and solitary nodding flower heads ranging in color from rose to purple. Flowers are surrounded by curved, spiny bracts.

Growing conditions and maintenance
Sow seed directly outdoors in early spring. Once established, plants often self-seed and may become weedy. Space plants 2 feet apart. They tolerate poor soil and dry conditions.

Tagetes (ta-JEE-tez)

MARIGOLD

Tagetes erecta 'Primrose Lady'

PLANT TYPE: annual or tender perennial

HEIGHT: 6 inches to 3 feet

INTEREST: flowers, foliage

SOIL: well-drained

LIGHT: full sun

Marigolds are among the most popular bedding plants in the United States. They are easy to grow, provide a reliable display, and are available in a wide range of heights. Their flowers typically range from pale yellow to bright orange and burgundy and are produced nonstop from early summer to frost in many varieties. Some species are grown for their fernlike foliage, which is often quite aromatic. Marigolds are suited to many uses, depending on their size: They can be placed in the background of a border, used as an edging, or massed in a bed. They are suitable for cutting for fresh arrangements and can be effectively grown in patio planters and window boxes. Despite some of their common names, marigolds are native to Mexico and Central and South America.

Selected species and varieties
T. erecta (American marigold, African marigold, Aztec marigold) has an erect to rounded habit and a wide range of heights, categorized as dwarf—10 to 14 inches, medium—15 to 20 inches, or tall—to 36 inches; flower heads are solitary, single to double, and 2 to 5 inches across; 'Primrose Lady' is 15 to 18 inches with a compact habit and double yellow carnation-like

flowers. *T. filifolia* (Irish lace) is grown primarily for its finely divided fernlike foliage; it grows 6 to 12 inches tall and wide and produces small white blooms in late summer. *T. lucida* (Mexican tarragon, sweet-scented marigold) grows 2 to 2½ feet tall with dark green tarragon-scented leaves and small, single yellow flowers in clusters; it may be perennial in warm climates. *T. patula* (French marigold, sweet mace) grows 6 to 18 inches tall with a neat, rounded habit and deeply serrated bright green leaves; flower heads are solitary, up to 2½ inches across, and may be single or double; double flowers often display a crest of raised petals at their center; colors include yellow, orange, maroon, and bicolors. *T. tenuifolia* (dwarf marigold, signet marigold) grows 6 to 12 inches tall with compact mounds of fernlike foliage and single yellow or orange 1-inch flowers that are so profuse they almost completely cover the leaves; excellent for edgings and window boxes.

Growing conditions and maintenance

Start seed indoors 6 to 8 weeks prior to the last frost, or sow directly outdoors 2 weeks before that date. Space plants 6 to 18 inches apart, depending on the variety, and pinch the seedlings to promote bushiness. Marigolds thrive in a moist, well-drained soil but tolerate dry conditions. Remove dead blossoms to encourage continuous flowering. Avoid overwatering the plants.

Tagetes tenuifolia

Tithonia   (ti-THO-nee-a)

MEXICAN SUNFLOWER

Tithonia rotundifolia

PLANT TYPE:	annual
HEIGHT:	2 to 6 feet
INTEREST:	flowers
SOIL:	well-drained
LIGHT:	full sun

This native of Mexico and Central America is exceptional in its ability to withstand heat and dry conditions. Its daisylike flowers range in color from yellow to red and are borne atop erect stems with coarse-textured leaves. Plants are suitable for the background of borders and for cutting; they can also be used as a fast-growing summer screen.

Selected species and varieties

T. rotundifolia has a vigorous, erect habit with broadly oval, velvety, serrated leaves that may reach 10 inches in length. Flower heads consist of orange, yellow, or scarlet raylike petals surrounding an orange-yellow disk; 'Goldfinger' grows 2 to 3 feet with 3-inch orange-scarlet blooms.

Growing conditions and maintenance

Start seed indoors 6 to 8 weeks prior to the last frost, or sow directly outdoors after all danger of frost has passed. Do not cover seed. Space plants 24 to 30 inches apart. Plants tolerate poor soil, heat, and drought. When cutting flowers for arrangements, cut in the bud stage and sear the stem.

Torenia   (to-REE-nee-a)

WISHBONE FLOWER

Torenia fournieri

PLANT TYPE:	annual
HEIGHT:	6 to 12 inches
INTEREST:	flowers
SOIL:	moist, well-drained
LIGHT:	partial to full shade

The blossoms of wishbone flower, also called blued torenia, have upper and lower lobed lips and are borne above a mound of foliage from midsummer to early fall. Because they thrive in shady locations, they are the perfect choice for a woodland bed or shady border. They are also well suited to hanging baskets and patio planters.

Selected species and varieties

T. fournieri (bluewings) has a rounded, compact habit with neat, oval leaves 1½ to 2 inches long. The 1-inch flowers appear in stalked clusters; each bloom displays a pale violet tube with a yellow blotch and flaring lower petal edges marked with deep purple-blue. A pair of fused yellow stamens resemble a poultry wishbone, hence the common name.

Growing conditions and maintenance

Start seeds indoors 10 to 12 weeks prior to the last frost; in Zone 9 and warmer, seed can be sown directly outdoors in early spring. Space seedlings 6 to 8 inches apart. Plants thrive in humid areas, and they tolerate full sun only in cool climates.

Tropaeolum (tro-PEE-o-lum)

NASTURTIUM

Tropaeolum majus

PLANT TYPE: annual

HEIGHT: 6 inches to 8 feet

INTEREST: flowers, foliage

SOIL: poor, well-drained to dry

LIGHT: full sun

Nasturtiums' bright flowers and attractive shieldlike leaves make them excellent fast-growing screens or bedding plants. Blooms appear from summer through frost. Young leaves and flowers are edible, and flowers are ideal for cutting.

Selected species and varieties
T. majus (common nasturtium) may be bushy, about 1 foot tall and twice as wide, or climbing, reaching 6 to 8 feet; leaves are round, 2 to 7 inches across, with long stems, and the showy 2- to 3-inch flowers are red, yellow, white, or orange and may be spotted or streaked. *T. minus* (dwarf nasturtium) reaches 6 to 12 inches in height, with a bushy habit suitable for edgings or massing; 'Alaska Mixed' grows 8 to 15 inches with variegated leaves and a wide range of flower colors. *T. peregrinum* (canary creeper, canarybird vine) is a climbing vine up to 8 feet long with pale yellow fringed flowers and deeply lobed leaves that resemble those of a fig.

Growing conditions and maintenance
Sow seed directly outdoors after danger of frost has passed. Nasturtiums do not transplant well. Space dwarf types 12 inches apart, vines 2 to 3 feet apart. Do not fertilize plants.

Verbascum (ver-BAS-cum)

MULLEIN

Verbascum bombyciferum

PLANT TYPE: biennial

HEIGHT: 2 to 8 feet

INTEREST: flowers, foliage

SOIL: well-drained

LIGHT: full sun

Mulleins develop a rosette of coarse leaves and tall, sturdy spikes of long-lasting summer flowers followed by attractive dried seedpods. Plant them in the rear of a border or in a wildflower garden.

Selected species and varieties
V. blattaria (moth mullein) grows 2 to 6 feet with dark green glossy leaves and slender spikes of pale yellow flowers with a lavender throat. *V. bombyciferum* (silver mullein) produces rosettes of oval leaves covered with silvery, silky hairs and 4- to 6-foot spikes of sulfur yellow flowers; 'Arctic Summer' is a heavy-flowering form with powdery white stems and leaves; 'Silver Candelabra' grows to 8 feet, with silver leaves and pale yellow blooms; 'Silver Lining' produces cool yellow flowers and metallic silver leaves and stems. *V. thapsus* (flannel mullein) bears felt-textured leaves and 3-foot spikes of yellow flowers, and may be found growing wild along the roadside.

Growing conditions and maintenance
Sow seed directly outdoors in spring to bloom the following year. Established plants will self-seed. Space 1 to 2 feet apart. Plants tolerate dry conditions.

Verbena (ver-BEE-na)

VERVAIN

Verbena bonariensis

PLANT TYPE: annual or tender perennial

HEIGHT: 6 inches to 4 feet

INTEREST: flowers

SOIL: moist, well-drained

LIGHT: full sun

From summer through frost, small, vividly colored flowers bloom in clusters on wiry stems with soft green foliage. Verbenas are useful as ground covers or as fillers in a border; smaller types are a good choice for containers, while taller types are excellent for cutting.

Selected species and varieties
V. bonariensis (Brazilian verbena) grows to 4 feet tall with slender, multibranched stems; wrinkled, toothed leaves grow primarily on the lowest 12 inches of the stem so that the fragrant rosy violet flower clusters seem nearly to float in the air. *V. x hybrida* (garden verbena) grows 6 to 12 inches tall and spreads to 2 feet, with wrinkled leaves and small flowers in loose, rounded heads to 2 inches across in shades of pink, red, blue, purple, and white; 'Peaches and Cream' bears flowers in shades of apricot, orange, yellow, and cream; flowers of 'Silver Ann' open bright pink and fade to blended pink and white.

Growing conditions and maintenance
Start seed indoors 12 weeks prior to the last frost and transplant outdoors after all danger of frost has passed. Allow 12 inches between plants of common verbena and 2 feet between Brazilian verbenas.

PANSY

Viola tricolor

PLANT TYPE: annual

HEIGHT: 3 to 12 inches

INTEREST: flowers

SOIL: moist, well-drained, fertile

LIGHT: full sun to partial shade

Although many pansies are technically short-lived perennials, they are considered annuals because they bloom their first year from seed and their flowers decline in quality afterward, regardless of region. They may also be treated as biennials, sown in late summer for bloom early the following spring. Their vividly colored and interestingly marked flowers are borne over a long season, often beginning with the first signs of spring and lasting until the summer heat causes them to fade, although a bit of shade and water may encourage the blossoms to continue throughout most of the summer. The rounded flower petals overlap, and their patterns often resemble a face. Pansies are a good choice for planting with bulbs, combining well with the flower forms and providing cover for fading foliage. They are attractive when massed in beds and useful as edgings or combined with other annuals in patio planters or window boxes.

Selected species and varieties

V. rafinesquii (field pansy) is a true annual that is native to much of the United States and grows 3 to 12 inches tall. Its ½-inch flowers are pale blue to cream, often with purple veins and a yellow throat. *V. tricolor* (Johnny-jump-up, miniature pansy) is a European native that has naturalized in much of the United States. It typically grows to 8 inches with a low, mounded habit and small, colorful flowers that have been favorites in the garden since Elizabethan times. The 1-inch flowers are fragrant, and colors include deep violet, blue, lavender, mauve, yellow, cream, white, and bicolors; flowers are edible and are often used as a garnish; 'Bowles' Black' bears blue-black flowers. *V.* x *wittrockiana* (common pansy) grows 4 to 8 inches tall and spreads to 12 inches. The 1- to 2-inch flowers are usually three-tone in shades of purple, blue, dark red, rose, pink, brown, yellow, and white. Many varieties are available; 'Melody Purple and White' bears flowers with white and purple petals marked with deep violet-blue.

Growing conditions and maintenance

Sow seed outdoors in late summer for earliest spring blooms or purchase transplants. Pansies started in late summer should be protected over the winter in a cold frame or by covering plants after the first hard frost with a light mulch or branches. They can also be started indoors in midwinter to transplant to the garden in midspring. Germination can be enhanced by moistening and chilling the seed (between 40° and 45°F) for 1 week prior to planting. Space plants about 4 inches apart. Pansies prefer a cool soil. Remove faded blooms and keep plants well watered to extend flowering.

Viola 'Melody Purple and White'

EVERLASTING

Xeranthemum annuum

PLANT TYPE: annual

HEIGHT: 18 inches to 3 feet

INTEREST: flowers

SOIL: moist, well-drained to average

LIGHT: full sun

Xeranthemum's fluffy flower heads in purple, pink, and white are displayed on long stems from summer to early fall. This Mediterranean native is a good choice for the midground of a mixed border and is exceptional for cutting, for both fresh and dried arrangements.

Selected species and varieties

X. annuum has an erect habit and gray-green leaves that are concentrated toward the bottom of the wiry stems. The 1½-inch flowers may be single or double, and they are surrounded by papery bracts that are the same color as the true flowers at the center of the head.

Growing conditions and maintenance

In colder zones, start seed indoors in individual peat pots 6 to 8 weeks prior to the last frost, but handle carefully because they are difficult to transplant. In warmer climates, sow seed directly in the garden in spring after all danger of frost has passed. Allow 6 to 9 inches between plants. They adapt to most soils. For use in winter arrangements, cut flowers when they are fully open and hang them upside down in a well-ventilated room until dry.

Zea (ZEE-a)

CORN

Zea mays

PLANT TYPE: annual

HEIGHT: 2 to 15 feet

INTEREST: seed heads

SOIL: moist, well-drained, fertile

LIGHT: full sun

Corn is native to the American tropics and is one of the most important cereal crops in the world. Several varieties are grown for their ornamental appeal; they provide a vertical accent in the garden and kernels that can be enjoyed in the garden or harvested for fall decoration.

Selected species and varieties

Z. mays grows to 15 feet with an erect habit and broad, grasslike blades to 3 feet long and 4 inches wide. Male flowers (tassels) form in spreading terminal panicles, while the female flowers (silks) are found in the leaf axils where the ear forms; 'Indian Corn' produces multicolored kernels that can be harvested for fall decoration as the husks begin to dry; var. *japonica* grows 5 to 6 feet with leaves attractively striped green, white, pink, and yellow; var. *rugosa* bears 1½-inch rounded ears with red kernels useful for both decoration and popcorn.

Growing conditions and maintenance

Sow seed directly in the garden after soil warms in spring. Incorporate organic matter and fertilizer into soil prior to planting. For proper pollination, plant in blocks with rows 18 to 30 inches apart; allow 8 to 12 inches between plants.

Zinnia (ZIN-ee-a)

ZINNIA

Zinnia elegans

PLANT TYPE: annual

HEIGHT: 8 to 36 inches

INTEREST: flowers

SOIL: well-drained

LIGHT: full sun

Zinnias brighten the border with pompom or daisylike blooms whose petal-like rays may be flat and rounded, or rolled into fringes, or crowded around yellow or green centers that are actually the true flowers. Hues range from riotous yellows, oranges, and reds to subdued pinks, roses, salmons, and creams, and maroon and purple. Flowers bloom from summer through frost and are best massed for effect as edgings or in the border. Low, spreading types are at home in window boxes and patio planters, while taller forms are excellent for fresh summer arrangements.

Selected species and varieties

Z. angustifolia (narrowleaf zinnia) has a compact, spreading habit, grows 8 to 16 inches in height with narrow, pointed leaves and 1-inch-wide single orange flowers, and is excellent as an edging or ground cover; 'White Star' bears abundant 2-inch flowers consisting of white rays surrounding orange-yellow centers. *Z. elegans* (common zinnia) grows 1 to 3 feet with an erect habit, rough-textured, clasping leaves up to 4 inches long, and showy flowers in many colors up to 6 inches across; 'Big Red' bears blood red 5- to 6-inch blooms on vigorous plants that reach 3 feet in height; 'Cut and Come Again' is a mildew-resistant variety that grows 2 feet tall and bears abundant 2½-inch flowers in a wide range of colors on long, sturdy stems that are suitable for cutting; 'Peter Pan' is an early bloomer with a uniform habit reaching 10 to 12 inches tall and 3- to 4-inch flowers in a wide range of colors. *Z. haageana* (Mexican zinnia) grows 1 to 2 feet tall with narrow leaves and 1½- to 2½-inch single or double flowers in colors that include red, mahogany, yellow, orange, and bicolors; 'Persian Carpet' has a bushy habit and 2-inch, mostly bicolored flowers with pointed petals and crested centers in shades from maroon through chocolate to gold and cream.

Growing conditions and maintenance

Zinnias are among the easiest annuals to grow. Start seed indoors 6 weeks prior to the last frost, or sow directly outdoors after all danger of frost has passed. Space seedlings 6 to 12 inches apart and pinch young plants to encourage bushiness. Remove spent blooms to keep plants attractive and to encourage flowering. Zinnias thrive in hot weather but benefit from regular watering. *Z. angustifolia* tolerates dry conditions well.

Zinnia angustifolia 'White Star'

Perennials

THE IMMENSE POPULARITY OF PERENNIALS HAS changed the face of American gardens. In an age when people want beauty and color in their garden but have little time to nurture it, perennials provide the perfect solution. These hardy herbaceous plants live at least three years and usually much longer. Diverse as well as versatile, they can be used in virtually any landscape setting. And they can withstand climatic extremes, pests, and diseases better than many other plants in the garden.

If you don't have gardening friends or relatives eager to divide mature plants, your initial investment in perennials can be high. But you'll have the chance to create landscapes full of color and vitality using plants that require relatively little care. You'll also save the money you would spend on replacing annuals year after year.

Choosing plants to fit your garden style is the most challenging and rewarding aspect of perennial gardening. Presented here is a selection of the most popular and readily available perennials in the United States.

Acanthus (a-KAN-thus)

BEAR'S-BREECH

Acanthus spinosus

HARDINESS: Zones 7-10

FLOWERING SEASON: summer

HEIGHT: 3 to 4 feet

FLOWER COLOR: mauve, white

SOIL: well-drained, acid

LIGHT: full sun to partial shade

Valued for its bold sculptural effects, bear's-breech forms spreading clumps of broad, shiny, deeply lobed leaves up to 2 feet long that arise from the base of the plant and tall, stiff spikes of tubular flowers borne well above the foliage in summer. The flowers and seed heads are effective in arrangements.

Selected species and varieties
A. spinosus (spiny bear's-breech)—dense flower spikes, usually mauve but sometimes white, bloom on 3- to 4-foot stalks over arching, deeply cut, thistlelike leaves.

Growing conditions and maintenance
Give bear's-breech the full sun it loves except where summers are hot, when some shade is advisable. Plant 3 feet apart, and propagate by seed or by division in early spring or fall after the plant has bloomed at least 3 years. Tolerant of moderate drought, bear's-breech abhors wet winter soil. Once established, this plant is difficult to remove from a site, as bits of fleshy roots inadvertently left behind easily grow into new plants.

Achillea (ak-il-EE-a)

YARROW

Achillea 'Coronation Gold'

HARDINESS: Zones 4-8

FLOWERING SEASON: summer

HEIGHT: 6 inches to 4½ feet

FLOWER COLOR: white, yellow, pink

SOIL: well-drained, poor

LIGHT: full sun

Flat-topped flower clusters grown above green or gray-green fernlike foliage. Long-lasting when cut, the flowers also dry well.

Selected species and varieties
A. filipendulina (fernleaf yarrow)—yellow flower clusters up to 5 inches across; 'Gold Plate', 6-inch yellow flower heads on 4½-foot stems. *A.* 'Coronation Gold', a hybrid with 3-inch-deep yellow flower clusters on 3-foot stems. *A.* x *lewisii* 'King Edward'—small yellow flowers on 4-inch stalks. *A. millefolium* (common yarrow)—2-inch white flowers with cultivars in shades from pink to red; 'Red Beauty' has broad crimson flower clusters.

Growing conditions and maintenance
Plant taller species 2 feet apart and dwarfs 1 foot apart. Propagate by division every 2 to 4 years in spring or fall or from midsummer stem cuttings.

Aconitum (ak-o-NY-tum)

MONKSHOOD

Aconitum napellus

HARDINESS: Zones 3-8

FLOWERING SEASON: mid- to late summer

HEIGHT: 2 to 4 feet

FLOWER COLOR: blue, purple

SOIL: fertile, moist, well-drained, acid

LIGHT: partial shade

Monkshood produces lush, glossy green foliage that remains attractive throughout the growing season. Tall, upright stems of blue or purple helmet-shaped flowers appear from mid to late summer.

Selected species and varieties
A. carmichaelii—2 to 4 feet tall, with leathery, dark green leaves and deep blue flowers that bloom in late summer on strong stems. *A. napellus*—3 to 4 feet, with finely divided leaves and blue to violet flowers from mid to late summer. *A.* x *bicolor*—a hybrid between *A. napellus* and *A. variegatum* that has given rise to many attractive garden hybrids, including 'Spark's Variety', with deep violet-blue flowers.

Growing conditions and maintenance
Though it prefers partial shade, monkshood will tolerate full sun if it receives ample water. Plants should not be allowed to dry out. Taller types may need staking. They can remain undisturbed indefinitely. The leaves and roots are poisonous, so do not plant near a vegetable garden.

Aeonium (ee-OH-nee-um)

AEONIUM

Aeonium arboreum 'Schwartzkopf'

HARDINESS: Zones 9-10

FLOWERING SEASON: spring

HEIGHT: 1 to 3 feet

FLOWER COLOR: yellow

SOIL: light, well-drained

LIGHT: full sun

Aeoniums bear fleshy leaves in attractive rosettes on succulent stems. Flowers in shades of yellow develop in terminal pyramidal clusters. Aeoniums are prized for their long season of interest in West Coast gardens, where they are often used as accents in rock gardens, dry borders, and containers.

Selected species and varieties
A. arboreum 'Schwartzkopf'—2 to 3 feet tall, upright and shrubby, with golden yellow flowers and dark, shiny, purple-black leaves appearing in 6- to 8-inch rosettes on branched stems. *A. tabuliforme*—12 inches, with leaves forming saucer-shaped, stemless rosettes 3 to 10 inches across, and pale yellow flowers.

Growing conditions and maintenance
Aeoniums thrive in California coastal conditions, where their soil and light needs are best met and they enjoy high humidity and mild temperatures. They can be grown farther inland, but may require some shade for protection from midday heat. They do not tolerate frost.

Agapanthus (ag-a-PAN-thus)

AFRICAN LILY

Agapanthus africanus

HARDINESS: Zones 8-10

FLOWERING SEASON: summer

HEIGHT: 1½ to 4 feet

FLOWER COLOR: blue

SOIL: moist, well-drained

LIGHT: full sun

Massive clusters of trumpet-shaped flowers bloom above clumps of arching, sometimes evergreen, straplike leaves.

Selected species and varieties
A. africanus (blue African lily)—profuse blue flowers above narrow, curving leaves on stems to 2 feet tall. *A. campanulatus* (bell agapanthus)—pale blue summer-blooming flowers on stems to 4 feet. *A.* 'Headborne Hybrids'—pale to dark to gray-blue summer flowers up to 8 inches across on 2½-foot stalks. *A.* 'Peter Pan'—a dwarf variety with 1½-foot-tall summer flower stalks above 12-inch clumps of evergreen leaves. *A. praecox* ssp. *orientalis* [also listed as *A. umbellatus*] (oriental agapanthus)—rich blue summer flowers on 4-foot-tall stalks above evergreen leaves.

Growing conditions and maintenance
Plant African lilies in containers or 2 feet apart in gardens in soil enriched with organic matter. Water well during the growing season; allow to dry out during dormancy. Flower stalks tend to lean toward the sun. Propagate by dividing the fleshy roots.

Agastache (a-GAH-sta-kee)

GIANT HYSSOP

Agastache foeniculum

HARDINESS: Zones 3-8

FLOWERING SEASON: mid- to late summer

HEIGHT: 2 to 5 feet

FLOWER COLOR: purplish red, blue, white

SOIL: rich, moist to sandy, well-drained

LIGHT: full sun to shade

The giant hyssops are aromatic perennials of the mint family. They provide a long season of bloom in a mixed herbaceous planting.

Selected species and varieties
A. foeniculum (fragrant giant hyssop, anise hyssop)—2 to 4 feet tall, with neat, oval toothed leaves and fat terminal spikes of blue flowers. Both leaves and flowers have a distinct anise scent when crushed. The variety 'Alba' has white flowers. *A. scrophulariifolia* (purple giant hyssop)—2 to 5 feet tall with erect purplish stems bearing oval toothed leaves. It produces terminal spikes of purple-red flowers with purple bracts.

Growing conditions and maintenance
A. foeniculum prefers a dry, open site in full sun or partial shade. It is well suited to sandy soils and tolerates summer heat. *A. scrophulariifolia* prefers a shady site with rich, moist soil. Propagate giant hyssops by seed or by cuttings taken from nonflowering lateral shoots in the summer.

Agave (a-GAH-vay)

CENTURY PLANT

Agave parryi

HARDINESS: Zones 9-10

FLOWERING SEASON: summer

HEIGHT: 18 inches to 40 feet

FLOWER COLOR: yellow-green, yellow

SOIL: well-drained to dry, sandy

LIGHT: full sun

Century plant's rosettes of coarse, wickedly spiny evergreen leaves are accentuated—generally at the end of the plant's long life—by erect, often extremely tall stalks bearing heavy spikes of fragrant flower bells. Grown for the strapping, pointed leaves, century plants are impressive accents to mix with finer-textured plants.

Selected species and varieties
A. americana (American aloe)—arching, blue-green leaves in mounds 6 feet wide. *A. attenuata* (foxtail agave)—rosettes of waxy, pale green leaves up to 5 feet across. *A. parryi*—rosettes of powdery gray-green leaves up to 3 feet across.

Growing conditions and maintenance
Protect young plants from frost and winter moisture. *A. americana* can be very hazardous to handle, even after it dies; be certain about the choice of plant and location before starting one. Propagate by transplanting offsets.

Ajuga (a-JOO-ga)

BUGLEWEED

Ajuga reptans

HARDINESS: Zones 3-9

FLOWERING SEASON: late spring to summer

HEIGHT: to 12 inches

FLOWER COLOR: white, pink, violet, blue

SOIL: well-drained, acid loam

LIGHT: full sun to light shade

An excellent ground cover, ajuga spreads by stolons in or on top of the soil, creating dense mats of attractive foliage that suppress weeds; very vigorous and sometimes invasive. The foliage, growing in shades of green, deep purple, bronze, or creamy white mottled dark pink, is topped by whorled flowers.

Selected species and varieties
A. genevensis (Geneva bugleweed)—blue, pink, or white summer flowers on erect stems 6 to 12 inches tall; Zones 4-9. *A. pyramidalis* (upright bugleweed)—blue late-spring flowers on 4- to 6-inch spikes; less invasive than other species; Zones 3-9. *A. reptans* (common bugleweed)—violet flowers ¼ inch long in late spring on 3- to 6-inch prostrate stems. 'Alba' offers white flowers; 'Atropurpurea' bronze leaves; 'Rubra' dark purple leaves; and 'Metallica Crispa' curled metallic leaves and blue flowers. Zones 3-9.

Growing conditions and maintenance
Grows equally well in sun or shade. Sow seed in late summer or fall. Divide in spring or fall.

Alchemilla (al-kem-ILL-a)

LADY'S-MANTLE

Alchemilla mollis

HARDINESS: Zones 3-8

FLOWERING SEASON: late spring to early summer

HEIGHT: 12 to 18 inches

FLOWER COLOR: green, yellow-green

SOIL: moist, well-drained loam

LIGHT: full sun to light shade

Lady's-mantle's sprays of tiny blossoms rise from low mats of attractive deeply lobed foliage that make it a good ground cover. The flowers are an excellent filler in arrangements and also dry well.

Selected species and varieties
A. conjuncta—pale green ⅛-inch flowers and star-shaped green leaves edged with silver; Zones 4-8. *A. mollis*—2- to 3-inch clusters of chartreuse blossoms above crinkled, velvety leaves; Zones 4-7.

Growing conditions and maintenance
Space lady's-mantle plants 1½ feet apart. In hot climates, select locations with partial shade. Propagate by digging up and replanting self-sown seedlings or by division in early spring or fall.

Allium (AL-lee-um)

FLOWERING ONION

Allium sphaerocephalum

HARDINESS: Zones 3-9

FLOWERING SEASON: late spring to early summer

HEIGHT: 6 inches to 5 feet

FLOWER COLOR: blue, purple, red, pink, white

SOIL: moist, well-drained

LIGHT: full sun to partial shade

Flowering onion bears unique globes of tiny blossoms on stiff stalks above leaf clumps that fade after bloom. They make excellent cut flowers.

Selected species and varieties

A. aflatunense (Persian onion)—4-inch lilac-purple flowers on 2- to 4-foot stems; Zones 3-8. *A. christophii* (stars-of-Persia)—10-inch violet spheres on 24-inch stems; Zones 4-8. *A. giganteum* (giant onion)—6-inch reddish purple flower clusters on 5-foot stalks; Zones 5-8. *A. sphaerocephalum* (drumstick chives)—green to purple flower clusters atop 2- to 3-foot stalks; Zones 4-8.

Growing conditions and maintenance

Some species form bulbils; others form small bulbs at base of main bulb. Plant bulbs in the fall. Propagate by seed and division. Some species, including *A. aflatunense,* may take 2 years to germinate. Resistant to pests.

Aloe (AL-oh)

ALOE

Aloe striata

HARDINESS: Zones 9-10

FLOWERING SEASON: spring to fall, winter to spring

HEIGHT: 1½ to 3 feet

FLOWER COLOR: pink, orange

SOIL: well-drained to dry

LIGHT: full sun

Aloe's rosettes of sword-shaped, fleshy evergreen leaves make striking specimens among finer-textured plantings. Branched clusters of long-lasting flowers rise from their centers on stiff stalks.

Selected species and varieties

A. saponaria (soap aloe)—stubby, green-and-white-variegated leaves 8 inches long and coral pink to orange spring-to-fall-blooming flowers on stalks up to 3 feet tall. *A. striata* (coral aloe)—pink-edged green leaves up to 20 inches long and coral pink to orange winter-to-spring flowers on 3-foot-tall stalks.

Growing conditions and maintenance

Aloes tolerate seaside conditions, poor soil, and drought; excess water promotes root rot. They prefer a frost-free location and suffer serious injury at temperatures below 25° F. Once aloes are established, the only care they require is occasional deep watering. Propagate by transplanting suckered offsets.

Amsonia (am-SO-nee-a)

BLUESTAR

Amsonia tabernaemontana

HARDINESS: Zones 3-9

FLOWERING SEASON: late spring to early summer

HEIGHT: 2 to 3 feet

FLOWER COLOR: blue

SOIL: moderately fertile, well-drained

LIGHT: full sun to partial shade

Amsonia produces pale blue star-shaped blossoms. Blooming in late spring and early summer, they are particularly effective combined with more brightly colored flowers. The densely mounded willowlike leaves remain attractive throughout the growing season, providing a lovely foil for later-blooming perennials.

Selected species and varietie

A. tabernaemontana—produces blue flowers in terminal clusters on 2- to 3-foot-tall stiff, erect stems with densely occurring leaves 3 to 6 inches long that turn yellow in fall; *A. tabernaemontana* var. *salicifolia* has longer and thinner leaves and blooms later than the species.

Growing conditions and maintenance

Amsonias grown in shade will have a more open habit than those grown in sun. In poor to moderately fertile soil, amsonia stems rarely need staking; avoid highly fertile soil, which produces rank, floppy growth. Other than for propagating, division is usually not necessary.

Anaphalis (an-AFF-al-is)

PEARLY EVERLASTING

Anaphalis triplinervis

HARDINESS: Zones 3-9

FLOWERING SEASON: late summer to early fall

HEIGHT: 1 to 3 feet

FLOWER COLOR: white

SOIL: moist, well-drained loam

LIGHT: full sun to light shade

Anaphalis bears flat clusters of fluffy ¼-inch flower buttons atop erect stems with narrow silvery leaves. It provides a gray-white accent in borders and is excellent for drying.

Selected species and varieties

A. margaritacea (common pearly everlasting)—2½ feet tall with slender leaves that are green on top and woolly gray underneath. *A. triplinervis*—pearly flowers above silvery gray leaves that turn a soft gray-green toward the end of summer; 'Summer Snow' is more compact, with clear white flowers.

Growing conditions and maintenance

Plant pearly everlasting 1 foot apart. *A. margaritacea* tolerates drought. Propagate by division in spring.

Anchusa (an-KOO-sa)

BUGLOSS

Anchusa azurea

HARDINESS: Zones 3-8

FLOWERING SEASON: late spring to midsummer

HEIGHT: 3½ to 5 feet

FLOWER COLOR: blue, pink, white

SOIL: very well-drained loam

LIGHT: full sun to light shade

Branching clusters of small trumpetlike flowers rise above hairy, tongue-shaped leaves. Blossoms persist a month or more, and a second bloom sequence is possible.

Selected species and varieties

A. azurea (Italian bugloss)—bright blue ¾-inch flowers bloom abundantly on 3- to 5-foot stems; 'Little John' is a dwarf cultivar growing to 18 inches with deep blue flowers; 'Loddon Royalist' grows 3 feet tall with royal blue flowers.

Growing conditions and maintenance

Plant anchusas 1½ to 3 feet apart. Tall varieties require staking. Cutting plants to the ground after flowers fade forces a second show of blossoms and prevents foliage from becoming lank. Provide good drainage, as standing moisture will rot roots in winter. Propagate by division every 2 to 3 years or from root cuttings.

Anemone (a-NEM-o-ne)

WINDFLOWER

Anemone pulsatilla

HARDINESS: Zones 2-9

FLOWERING SEASON: spring through fall

HEIGHT: 3 inches to 2 feet

FLOWER COLOR: white, cream, red, purple, blue

SOIL: well-drained, fertile loam

LIGHT: partial shade to full sun

This diverse genus carries sprightly 1- to 3-inch-wide flowers with single or double rows of petals shaped like shallow cups surrounding prominent stamens and pistils. The flowers are held on branched stems above mounds of handsome deeply cut foliage. Many species brighten the garden during periods when few other plants with similar flowers are in bloom. Native to North America, anemone species can be found in moist woodlands, meadows, and dry prairies.

Selected species and varieties

A. canadensis (meadow anemone)—1 to 2 feet tall with deeply lobed basal leaves and 1½-inch white flowers with golden centers on leafy flower stems in late spring; Zones 2-6. *A. caroliniana* (Carolina anemone)—6 to 12 inches tall with numerous 1½-inch white flowers with yellow centers in spring; Zones 6-8. *A.* x *hybrida* (Japanese anemone)—white or pink flowers with a silky sheen on their undersides above dark green foliage from late summer to midfall; Zones 6-8; 'Alba' cultivar grows 2 to 3 feet tall with large clear white flowers; 'Honorine Jobert' has white flowers with yellow centers on 3-foot stems; 'Prince Henry', deep rose flowers on 3-foot stems; 'Queen Charlotte', full, semidouble pink flowers; 'September Charm', single-petaled silvery pink flowers; 'September Sprite', single pink flowers on 15-inch stems. *A. magellanica*—cream-colored flowers bloom from late spring through summer atop 18-inch stems; Zones 2-8. *A. multifida* (early thimbleweed)—loose clump of silky-haired stems up to 20 inches tall with deeply divided leaves on long stalks; sepals of the ⅜-inch flowers that appear from late spring to summer are usually yellowish white but occasionally bright red; Zones 3-9. *A. pulsatilla* [also classified as *Pulsatilla vulgaris*] (pasqueflower)—2-inch-wide blue or purple bell-shaped spring flowers on 1-foot stems above hairy leaves; Zones 5-8. *A. sylvestris* 'Snowdrops' (snowdrops windflower)—1 to 1½ feet tall, with light green foliage topped by dainty, fragrant 2-inch spring flowers. *A. vitifolia* 'Robustissima' (grapeleaf anemone)—branching clusters of pink flowers from late summer to fall on 1- to 3-foot stalks; an invasive variety good for naturalizing; Zones 3-8.

Growing conditions and maintenance

Plant small anemones 1 foot apart, taller varieties 2 feet apart. The latter may require staking. Meadow anemone prefers a moist, sandy soil and needs frequent division to prevent overcrowding. Pasqueflowers need full sun and a neutral to alkaline soil in a cool location. Snowdrops windflowers prefer moist soil; grapeleaf anemones tolerate dry conditions. Protect all anemones from afternoon sun and do not allow to dry out completely. Propagate cultivars of Japanese anemone by root cuttings or division, others from seed. Divide Japanese and grapeleaf anemones in spring every 3 years to maintain robustness. Other species grow slowly and division is rarely needed.

Anthemis (AN-them-is)

CHAMOMILE

Anthemis tinctoria

HARDINESS: Zones 3-8

FLOWERING SEASON: midsummer through early fall

HEIGHT: 2 to 3 feet

FLOWER COLOR: yellow, orange

SOIL: well-drained to dry, poor

LIGHT: full sun

Anthemis has daisylike blossoms 2 to 3 inches across. The blossoms grow amid shrubby, aromatic, gray-green foliage and are excellent as cut flowers.

Selected species and varieties

A. sancti-johannis (St. John's chamomile)—2-inch bright orange flowers on evergreen shrubs; Zones 5-8. *A. tinctoria* (golden marguerite)—2-inch, upturned gold-yellow flowers above finely cut, aromatic foliage; 'Kelwayi' has bright yellow flowers; 'Moonlight', pale yellow; 'E.C. Buxton', creamy white; Zones 3-8.

Growing conditions and maintenance

Plant anthemis 1½ feet apart. Remove spent flowers for continuous bloom over several months. Propagate by division every 2 years, from seed, or from stem cuttings in spring.

Aquilegia (ak-wil-EE-jee-a)

COLUMBINE

Aquilegia canadensis

HARDINESS: Zones 3-9

FLOWERING SEASON: spring to early summer

HEIGHT: 8 inches to 3 feet

FLOWER COLOR: white, yellow, pink, red, blue

SOIL: moist, well-drained, acid loam

LIGHT: full sun to shade

The flowers of this beautiful and delicate wildflower come in many colors and bicolors, appearing in spring on erect stems; they are nodding or upright and consist of a short tube surrounded by five petals and backward-projecting spurs of varying lengths. The blue-green compound leaves fade early. Many species have a life span of only 3 to 4 years.

Selected species and varieties

A. caerulea (Rocky Mountain columbine)—2- to 3-inch blue-and-white flowers. *A. canadensis* (Canadian columbine)—1 to 3 feet tall, with nodding flowers consisting of yellow sepals, short red spurs, and yellow stamens that project below the sepals. *A. flabellata* 'Nana Alba' (fan columbine)—8 to 12 inches tall, with pure white nodding flowers 2 inches wide with spurs to 1 inch long. *A. x hybrida* 'Crimson Star'—30 to 36 inches tall, bearing bright red and white upright flowers with long spurs.

Growing conditions and maintenance

Columbines require good drainage; for heavy soils, work pebbles in before planting. Plant 1½ feet apart. Propagate from seed or by careful division in the fall.

Arabis (AR-a-bis)

ROCK CRESS

Arabis caucasica

HARDINESS: Zones 3-7

FLOWERING SEASON: spring

HEIGHT: 6 to 12 inches

FLOWER COLOR: pink, white

SOIL: well-drained loam

LIGHT: full sun

Low-growing rock cress, with its flat-faced single- or double-petaled ½-inch flowers, makes an excellent creeping ground cover for the border or rock garden.

Selected species and varieties
A. alpina—'Flore Pleno' has white, fragrant double-petaled flowers. *A. caucasica* (wall rock cress)—'Rosabella' is a compact 5-inch plant with rosy pink flowers; 'Snow Cap' has pure white single flowers. *A. procurrens*—sprays of white flowers above mats of glossy evergreen leaves.

Growing conditions and maintenance
Rock cress is easily grown, but humid weather and standing water will cause rot. Prune after flowering to keep the plants compact. *A. procurrens* thrives in light shade as well as full sun. Propagate from seeds sown in spring or by division in fall.

Aralia (a-RAY-lee-a)

WILD SARSAPARILLA

Aralia racemosa

HARDINESS: Zones 3-10

FLOWERING SEASON: spring, summer

HEIGHT: 1 to 6 feet

FLOWER COLOR: greenish white, white

SOIL: dry to moist, acid, fertile

LIGHT: partial to full shade

Aralias are perennials that grow in open woods over much of the United States. Their large compound leaves impart a lush appearance to a garden, and their berries attract birds to the garden.

Selected species and varieties
A. nudicaulis (wild sarsaparilla)—up to 1 foot in height with 6-inch doubly compound leaves, greenish white flowers from late spring to early summer, and purplish fall berries; use as a woodland ground cover; Zones 3-7. *A. racemosa* (spikenard)—6 feet tall with leaves up to 2½ feet long and large clusters of tiny white flowers tinged with yellow or green in early to midsummer followed by purple berries in fall; Zones 4-10.

Growing conditions and maintenance
Aralias thrive in open woods and require little care once they have become established. Wild sarsaparilla prefers a dryish soil, while spikenard prefers a moist, fertile one. Mulch for winter protection. Propagate by seed or division in fall.

Arenaria (a-ren-AIR-ee-a)

SANDWORT

Arenaria montana

HARDINESS: Zones 5-9

FLOWERING SEASON: spring

HEIGHT: 2 to 8 inches

FLOWER COLOR: white

SOIL: moist but well-drained, sandy

LIGHT: full sun to partial shade

Sandwort forms mats of small, dainty evergreen foliage crowned with tiny white flowers. This low, spreading perennial is ideal tucked into wall crevices and between pavers.

Selected species and varieties
A. montana—trailing stems up to 12 inches long with grasslike leaves and topped by 1-inch star-shaped white flowers with yellow centers. *A. verna caespitosa* [now formally listed as *Minuartia verna* ssp. *caespitosa*] (Irish moss)—narrow mosslike leaves and ⅜-inch star-shaped white flowers in dainty 2-inch clumps that grow rapidly and withstand heavy foot traffic.

Growing conditions and maintenance
Plant sandwort 6 to 12 inches apart. Water well during dry spells in the growing season. Propagate by division in late summer or early fall.

Armeria (ar-MEER-ee-a)

THRIFT, SEA PINK

Armeria maritima 'Laucheana'

HARDINESS: Zones 3-8

FLOWERING SEASON: spring or summer

HEIGHT: 6 inches to 2 feet

FLOWER COLOR: white, pink, rose

SOIL: well-drained, sandy loam

LIGHT: full sun

Thrifts produce spherical clusters of flowers on stiff stems above tufts of grassy evergreen leaves.

Selected species and varieties

A. alliacea [also called *A. plantaginea*] (plantain thrift)—1¾-inch rosy pink or white flower clusters on 2-foot stems; 'Bee's Ruby' cultivar has intense ruby red flower clusters. *A. maritima* (common thrift)—white to deep pink flowers on 1-foot stems; 'Alba' is a dwarf cultivar with white flowers on 5-inch stems; 'Bloodstone' has brilliant bright red flowers on 9-inch stems; 'Laucheana', rose pink flowers on 6-inch stems.

Growing conditions and maintenance

Plant thrifts 9 to 12 inches apart. Older clumps die out in the middle. Rejuvenate and propagate plants by division every 3 or 4 years.

Artemisia (ar-tem-IS-ee-a)

WORMWOOD

Artemisia x 'Powis Castle'

HARDINESS: Zones 3-9

FLOWERING SEASON: summer to fall

HEIGHT: 4 inches to 6 feet

FLOWER COLOR: white, yellow

SOIL: poor, well-drained to dry

LIGHT: full sun

Wormwood's finely textured gray-green leaves—a few varieties are evergreen—complement the more dramatic hues in a border. Its form ranges from low and mounding to tall and erect, in most cases with inconspicuous flowers.

Selected species and varieties

A. absinthium—aromatic foliage to 4 feet tall; 'Lambrook Silver' has silvery gray evergreen leaves. *A. lactiflora* (white mugwort)—sprays of creamy summer flowers above dark green foliage on stems to 6 feet. *A. ludoviciana* (white sage)—silvery willowlike leaves on 2- to 4-foot plants; 'Silver Queen' has divided leaves. *A.* x 'Powis Castle'—2- to 3-foot-high mounds of lacy, silvery green leaves. *A. schmidtiana* (silvermound artemisia)—compact 2-foot-high mounds of filigreed silvery leaves; 'Nana' grows to only a few inches. *A. stellerana* (dusty miller)—deeply lobed silver-gray leaves on 1- to 2-foot plants.

Growing conditions and maintenance

Space smaller plants 1 foot apart, taller ones 2 feet apart. Most artemisias rot in hot and humid conditions. Propagate from seed or by division.

Aruncus (a-RUNK-us)

GOATSBEARD

Aruncus dioicus

HARDINESS: Zones 3-9

FLOWERING SEASON: early summer

HEIGHT: 1 to 6 feet

FLOWER COLOR: white

SOIL: moist, rich loam

LIGHT: partial shade

Goatsbeard carries dramatic, long-lasting 6- to 10-inch plumes of tiny cream-colored blossoms on tall stalks of light green ferny foliage.

Selected species and varieties

A. aethusifolius (miniature goatsbeard)—dark green 12-inch foliage and long, creamy white flower spires lasting 6 weeks; Zones 3-8. *A. dioicus*—handsome shrubby foliage that grows up to 4 feet tall, with flower stalks up to 6 feet; 'Kneiffii' is more compact, with finely divided leaves to 3 feet tall; Zones 4-9.

Growing conditions and maintenance

Plant goatsbeard 4 to 5 feet apart, miniature goatsbeard 12 to 15 inches apart. Thrives in full sun where summers are cool. Propagate by division in spring or autumn.

Asarum (a-SAR-um)

WILD GINGER

Asarum caudatum

HARDINESS: Zones 3-10

FLOWERING SEASON: spring

HEIGHT: 2 to 12 inches

FLOWER COLOR: purple, brown

SOIL: moist, acid, fertile

LIGHT: shade

The handsome, rich green leaves of these ground-hugging perennials make beautiful carpets for the woodland garden. The dusky 1- to 2-inch spring flowers are often hidden by the leaves.

Selected species and varieties
A. arifolium (wild ginger)—2 to 4 inches high with triangular evergreen leaves up to 5 inches long, mottled with paler green; native to eastern North America; Zones 6-10. *A. canadense* (wild ginger, snakeroot) —hairy, deciduous heart-shaped leaves 3 to 6 inches wide on 12-inch arching petioles, or leafstalks; eastern North America; Zones 3-8. *A. caudatum* (British Columbia wild ginger)—glossy heart-shaped evergreen leaves 2 to 6 inches wide on petioles 7 or 8 inches long; Zones 4-8.

Growing conditions and maintenance
Wild gingers require shade and ample moisture. They benefit from the addition of organic matter to soil. Propagate by division, rhizome cuttings, or seed.

Asclepias (as-KLEE-pee-as)

MILKWEED

Asclepias tuberosa

HARDINESS: Zones 3-9

FLOWERING SEASON: summer to fall

HEIGHT: 2 to 4 feet

FLOWER COLOR: rose, orange, yellow

SOIL: well-drained sandy, or moist and deep

LIGHT: full sun

Milkweed's thick stalks bear brilliantly colored clusters of flowers followed by canoe-shaped pods, which burst to release silky seeds. The flowers are excellent for cutting, and the decorative pods dry well. Some species may be weedy.

Selected species and varieties
A. incarnata (swamp milkweed)—clusters of fragrant, pink to rose ¼-inch flowers on 2- to 4-foot stems. *A. tuberosa* (butterfly weed)—showy, vibrant orange flower clusters on 2- to 3-foot stems; the leaves and stems are poisonous.

Growing conditions and maintenance
Plant asclepias 12 inches apart. Swamp milkweed prefers moist conditions; butterfly weed does best in dry soils, where its long taproot makes plants drought tolerant. Propagate from seed sown in spring to blossom in 2 years.

Aster (AS-ter)

ASTER

Aster novae-angliae 'Harrington's Pink'

HARDINESS: Zones 3-9

FLOWERING SEASON: early summer to fall

HEIGHT: 6 inches to 8 feet

FLOWER COLOR: white, blue, purple, pink

SOIL: moist, well-drained, fertile

LIGHT: full sun

Asters are prized for their large, showy, daisylike flowers that appear over weeks and even months. Most varieties are subject to mildew.

Selected species and varieties
A. alpinus—a low-growing species forming 6- to 12-inch-high clumps topped by violet-blue 1- to 3-inch flowers with yellow centers; 'Dark Beauty' produces deep blue flowers; 'Goliath' grows a few inches taller than the species, with pale blue flowers; 'Happy End' has semidouble lavender flowers. *A. x frikartii* (Frikart's aster)—2- to 3-foot-tall plants topped by fragrant 2½-inch lavender-blue flowers with yellow centers blooming in summer and lasting 2 months or longer; 'Mönch' has profuse blue-mauve flowers and is resistant to mildew. *A. novae-angliae* (New England aster)—3 to 5 feet tall with 4- to 5-inch leaves and 2-inch violet-purple flowers; less important than its many cultivars, most of which are quite tall and require staking; 'Alma Potschke' has vivid rose-colored blossoms from late summer to fall; 'Harrington's Pink' grows to 4 feet tall with large salmon pink flowers in fall; 'Purple Dome' is a dwarf variety, growing

18 inches tall and spreading 3 feet wide, with profuse deep purple fall flowers. *A. novi-belgii* (New York aster, Michaelmas daisy)—cultivars from 10 inches to 4 feet tall, blooming in white, pink, red, blue, and purple-violet from late summer through fall; 'Eventide' has violet-blue semidouble flowers on 3-foot stems; 'Professor Kippenburg' is compact and bushy, 12 to 15 inches tall with lavender-blue flowers; 'Royal Ruby' is a compact cultivar with large crimson fall flowers; 'Winston S. Churchill' grows violet-red flowers on 2-foot stems.

Growing conditions and maintenance

Choose sites for asters carefully to avoid mildew problems. Good air circulation is essential; well-drained soils deter rot. Space dwarf asters 1 foot apart, taller ones 2 to 3 feet apart, and thin out young plants to improve air circulation. Taller varieties may require staking. Prompt deadheading encourages a second flowering in early summer bloomers. *A.* x *frikartii* in Zone 5 or colder must be mulched over the winter and should not be cut back or divided in fall; otherwise, divide asters in early spring or fall every 2 years or so when a plant's center begins to die out. Asters can also be propagated by stem cuttings in spring and early summer. Cultivars seldom grow true from seed.

Aster x frikartii 'Mönch'

Astilbe (a-STIL-bee)

PERENNIAL SPIREA

Astilbe chinensis var. taquetii 'Purple Lance'

HARDINESS: Zones 3-9

FLOWERING SEASON: summer to early fall

HEIGHT: 8 inches to 4 feet

FLOWER COLOR: white, pink, red, lavender

SOIL: moist, well-drained, fertile

LIGHT: bright full shade to full sun

Feathery plumes in many colors make astilbe one of the treasures of a shade garden. Depending on variety, blooms appear through summer and into early fall atop 1- to 4-foot stalks. The 6- to 18-inch-high foliage, consisting of finely divided fernlike leaves, adds a medium-fine texture to the landscape. Some varieties are nearly as ornamental in seed as they are in flower. Astilbe can be used as a background accent to shorter perennials, or to grace water features. The dwarf forms work well tucked into rock gardens and border fronts.

Selected species and varieties

A. x *arendsii* (false spirea)—a hybrid group, 2 to 4 feet tall, with pink, salmon, red, white, and lavender varieties; 'Bridal Veil' blooms early, with elegant creamy white flower spikes to 30 inches; 'Fanal' has carmine red flowers on 2-foot stems with bronzy leaves in early to midsummer; 'Cattleya' has 36-inch rose flower spikes at midseason; 'Feuer' ('Fire') bears coral red flowers on 30-inch stems in late summer; 'Red Sentinel', 3-foot-tall brilliant red flowers and reddish green leaves in midsummer; 'White Gloria' ('Weisse Gloria'), with white plumes to 2 feet in late sum-mer. *A. chinensis* (Chinese astilbe)—to 2 feet tall, with white, rose-tinged, or purplish blooms; 'Finale' grows 18 inches tall with light pink blooms; 'Pumila' (dwarf Chinese astilbe), a drought-tolerant variety that produces mauve-pink flowers in narrow plumes on 8- to 12-inch stems in late summer and spreads by stolons for a good ground cover; var. *taquetii* 'Purple Lance' ('Purpulanze') (fall astilbe) grows 4 feet tall with purple-red flowers; 'Superba', 3 to 4 feet tall with lavender-pink or reddish purple spikes that bloom from late summer to fall over bronze-green, somewhat coarse foliage. *A. simplicifolia* (star astilbe)—a compact species with simple leaves having several cultivars from 12 to 20 inches tall in white and several shades of pink; Zones 4-8. *A. thunbergii* 'Ostrich Plume' ('Straussenfeder')—salmon-pink plumes to 3 feet in midsummer.

Growing conditions and maintenance

Plant astilbes 1½ to 2 feet apart. In hot climates, they require shade, where the soil does not dry out; in cooler climates, partial or full sun is acceptable if the soil is moisture retentive. Select an area that has good drainage, and enrich the soil with compost, peat moss, or leaf mold. Astilbe is a heavy feeder, so take care not to plant under shallow-rooted trees. Allow soil to dry out in the winter. Apply a high-phosphorus fertilizer such as 5-10-5 each spring. Plants will multiply quickly and lose vigor as they become crowded. Divide clumps every 2 or 3 years to rejuvenate. Leave dried flower spikes on plants through the winter for ornamental effect.

Astilbe chinensis 'Pumila'

Astrantia (as-TRAN-tee-a)

MASTERWORT

Astrantia major

HARDINESS: Zones 4-8

FLOWERING SEASON: spring through summer

HEIGHT: 2 to 3 feet

FLOWER COLOR: white tinged with green, pink

SOIL: well-drained, fertile loam

LIGHT: partial shade

Masterwort bears unique blossoms composed of a colorful collar of bracts supporting jagged petals.

Selected species and varieties
A. major (great masterwort)—unusual creamy white 2- to 3-inch blossoms tinged pink by the collar of purple bracts below the petals; 'Rosea' has rosy pink blooms suitable for drying and pressing; 'Sunningdale Variegated', stripes of cream and yellow on lobed green leaves.

Growing conditions and maintenance
Plant masterwort 18 inches apart. They will grow in full sun given adequate moisture. Propagate by division in spring or from seed sown in fall.

Aurinia (o-RIN-ee-a)

BASKET-OF-GOLD

Aurinia saxatilis

HARDINESS: Zones 4-10

FLOWERING SEASON: late spring to early summer

HEIGHT: 6 to 12 inches

FLOWER COLOR: yellow, gold

SOIL: well-drained, sandy

LIGHT: full sun

One of the most widely used rock garden plants, basket-of-gold's tiny flowers mass in frothy clusters on low-growing mats of silver-gray foliage.

Selected species and varieties
A. saxatilis [formerly listed as *Alyssum saxatile*]—golden yellow flowers in open clusters; 'Citrina' has pale yellow flowers and gray-green, hairy foliage; 'Compacta' is dense and slow spreading, with vivid yellow blossoms; 'Dudley Neville' grows light apricot blooms.

Growing conditions and maintenance
Space aurinia plants 9 to 12 inches apart. Plants become leggy if overfertilized. Cut plants back by one-third after flowering. Remove and replace plants when they become woody after a few years. Propagate from seed sown in spring or fall or from cuttings. Aurinia plants grow and bloom best in full sun.

Balsamorhiza (bawl-sa-mo-RI-za)

BALSAMROOT

Balsamorhiza sagittata

HARDINESS: Zones 4-10

FLOWERING SEASON: spring to summer

HEIGHT: 24 to 32 inches

FLOWER COLOR: yellow

SOIL: sandy or gravelly, moderately dry

LIGHT: full sun

A perennial native to mountain grasslands and prairies of the West, balsamroot produces bright sunflower-like blossoms in late spring and early summer.

Selected species and varieties
B. sagittata (balsamroot, Oregon sunflower)—low clump of arrow- or heart-shaped leaves covered with silvery hairs and measuring up to 6 inches wide and 12 inches long; may be undivided or deeply divided into fernlike segments; flower stems up to 32 inches tall bear a single 2½- to 4-inch yellow flower.

Growing conditions and maintenance
Balsamroot thrives in full sun and deep, sandy soil, but it will tolerate poor, infertile soil. Because of its deep woody taproot, it does not transplant well. Propagate from seed sown in fall where you want the plants to grow. Balsamroot generally requires 2 years of growth before it begins flowering.

Baptisia (bap-TIZ-ee-a)

WILD INDIGO

Baptisia australis

HARDINESS: Zones 3-9

FLOWERING SEASON: midspring to early summer

HEIGHT: 3 to 4 feet

FLOWER COLOR: blue

SOIL: well-drained to dry, sandy

LIGHT: full sun

Wild (false) indigo produces dainty blue pealike flowers from midspring to early summer. Its blue-green leaves are an attractive foil for both its own blooms and those of surrounding plants. The leaves remain handsome throughout the growing season. The plant is useful for the background of a border or as a specimen; its pods are used in dried arrangements.

Selected species and varieties

B. australis—erect stems to 4 feet in height, producing compound leaves with three leaflets, each 1½ to 3 inches long, and indigo blue flowers in long, terminal racemes, good for cutting. *B. alba*—to 3 feet tall with white flowers; Zones 5-8.

Growing conditions and maintenance

Wild indigo adapts to almost any well-drained soil. It is slow growing and non-invasive. Tall selections may require staking. Remove faded flowers to extend the blooming season.

Begonia (be-GO-nee-a)

HARDY BEGONIA

Begonia grandis

HARDINESS: Zones 6-9

FLOWERING SEASON: early summer to frost

HEIGHT: 2 feet

FLOWER COLOR: pink, white

SOIL: moist, rich loam

LIGHT: full sun to partial shade

The popular hardy begonia bears 1-inch flowers at the tips of reddish branched stems. Leaves are hairy, with red-tinted undersides and veins.

Selected species and varieties

B. grandis—the hardiest of the begonia genus, with sprays of pink flowers surrounded by heart-shaped leaves; the variety 'Alba' has white flowers.

Growing conditions and maintenance

Plant hardy begonias 1½ feet apart. They tolerate full sun in cooler climates but require partial shade where summers are hot and dry. Propagate by digging and transplanting the sprouts that emerge from the small bulbils that form in leaf junctions, then fall to the ground to root.

Bergenia (ber-JEN-ee-a)

BERGENIA

Bergenia cordifolia 'Purpurea'

HARDINESS: Zones 3-8

FLOWERING SEASON: spring

HEIGHT: 12 to 18 inches

FLOWER COLOR: white, pink, red, magenta

SOIL: moist, well-drained, poor

LIGHT: full sun to light shade

Bergenia bears flowers resembling tiny open trumpets in clusters 3 to 6 inches across. Blooms are held above handsome fleshy leaves that are evergreen in milder climates.

Selected species and varieties

B. cordifolia (heartleaf bergenia)—pink flower clusters; 'Purpurea' has magenta flowers above leaves that turn purplish in winter. *B. crassifolia* (leather bergenia)—reddish pink blossoms above leaves turning bronze in winter. *B. hybrids*—'Abendglut' ('Evening Glow') has magenta flowers on 1½-foot stems; 'Bressingham White', early-spring white flowers maturing to pale pink; 'Sunningdale', crimson flowers.

Growing conditions and maintenance

Plant bergenias 1 foot apart. Propagate by division after flowering.

Boltonia (bowl-TO-nee-a)

BOLTONIA

Boltonia asteroides 'Snowbank'

HARDINESS: Zones 4-8

FLOWERING SEASON: midsummer through fall

HEIGHT: 3 to 4 feet

FLOWER COLOR: white

SOIL: moist, well-drained

LIGHT: full sun

Boltonia offers flowers from midsummer through fall, providing an extended display for the back of a mixed border or center of an island bed. Its daisylike blossoms appear above tall stems with narrow, gray-green willowlike leaves.

Selected species and varieties
B. asteroides 'Snowbank'—3 to 4 feet tall, with a compact, self-supporting habit; it produces white flowers ¾ to 1 inch across, borne profusely on branched stems.

Growing conditions and maintenance
Boltonia is adaptable to most sunny sites. In loose, moist soil it tends to spread more rapidly than in dry soil, but it is not generally invasive. Pinching off the tops of plants in late spring encourages bushy, compact growth. Divide in spring or fall.

Brunnera (BRUN-er-a)

BRUNNERA

Brunnera macrophylla

HARDINESS: Zones 4-9

FLOWERING SEASON: spring

HEIGHT: 1 to 2 feet

FLOWER COLOR: blue

SOIL: moist, well-drained loam

LIGHT: full sun to light shade

Brunnera produces airy sprays of dainty azure blue flowers resembling forget-me-nots above large dark green, heart-shaped foliage that grows in loose, spreading mounds. The stems of the plants are slightly hairy.

Selected species and varieties
B. macrophylla (Siberian bugloss)—boldly textured leaves up to 8 inches across and dainty bright blue flowers; 'Hadspen Cream' has light green leaves edged in cream; 'Langtrees', spots of silvery gray in the center of the leaves; 'Variegata', striking creamy white leaf variegations.

Growing conditions and maintenance
Plant brunneras 1 foot apart. Propagate from seed, by transplanting the self-sown seedlings, or by division in spring.

Campanula (cam-PAN-ew-la)

BELLFLOWER

Campanula glomerata

HARDINESS: Zones 3-9

FLOWERING SEASON: early summer to late fall

HEIGHT: 6 inches to 5 feet

FLOWER COLOR: blue, violet, purple, white

SOIL: well-drained loam

LIGHT: full sun to light shade

With spikes or clusters of showy, bell- or star-shaped flowers on stems rising from deep green foliage, bellflowers offer a long season of bloom. Dwarf and trailing varieties enhance a rock garden, wall, or border edge. Taller species form neat tufts or clumps in a perennial border or cutting garden.

Selected species and varieties
C. carpatica (Carpathian harebell)—2-inch-wide, bell-shaped, upturned blue flowers bloom on plants up to 1 foot tall; 'Blaue Clips' ('Blue Clips') has 3-inch-wide blue flowers on 6- to 8-inch stems; 'China Doll', lavender flowers on 8-inch stems; 'Wedgewood White' is compact, with white flowers; Zones 3-8. *C. glomerata* (clustered bellflower)—1- to 2-foot stems, with clusters of 1-inch white, blue, or purple flowers; 'Joan Elliott' grows deep violet blooms atop stems 18 inches tall; 'Schneekrone' ('Crown of Snow'), white flowers; 'Superba' grows to 2½ feet, with violet flowers; Zones 3-8. *C. latifolia* (great bellflower)—purplish blue flowers 1½ inches long on spikes, tipping 4- to 5-foot stems; 'Alba' is similar to the species but with white flowers; 'Brantwood' has large

violet-blue trumpet-shaped flowers; Zones 4-8. *C. persicifolia* (peachleaf bellflower)—spikes of 1½-inch blue or white cup-shaped blossoms on stems to 3 feet; 'Alba' has white flowers; 'Telham Beauty', 2- to 3-inch lavender-blue blooms lining the upper half of 4-foot flower stalks; Zones 3-7. *C. portenschlagiana* (Dalmatian bell-flower)—a 6- to 8-inch dwarf species with blue flower clusters; Zones 5-7. *C. poscharskyana* (Serbian bellflower)—a mat-forming, creeping dwarf with abundant 1-inch lilac blossoms; Zones 3-8. *C. rotundifolia* (Scottish bluebell)—profuse, nodding, 1-inch-wide blue-violet blooms; 'Olympica' cultivar has bright blue flowers; Zones 3-7.

Growing conditions and maintenance
Plant small bellflowers 12 to 18 inches apart, larger ones 2 feet apart. Clip faded flowers to encourage further bloom. 'Superba' and Serbian bellflower are heat tolerant. Great bellflower thrives in moist shade. Dalmatian and Serbian bellflowers do well in sandy or gritty soil. Dig up and divide every 3 or 4 years to maintain plant vigor. Propagate from seed or by division every 3 or 4 years.

Campanula portenschlagiana

Centaurea (sen-TOR-ee-a)

KNAPWEED

Centaurea montana

HARDINESS: Zones 3-8

FLOWERING SEASON: spring to summer

HEIGHT: 1 to 3 feet

FLOWER COLOR: lavender, pink, blue, yellow

SOIL: well-drained loam

LIGHT: full sun

Excellent plants for a flower garden, centaurea's fringed, thistlelike flowers bloom at the tips of erect stems that are lined with distinctive gray-green foliage.

Selected species and varieties
C. dealbata (Persian centaurea)—feathery, lavender to pink 2-inch flowers on stems to 3 feet with coarsely cut, pinnately lobed leaves. *C. hypoleuca* 'John Coutts' (John Coutts' knapweed)—2- to 3-inch pink-and-white flowers on stems to 3 feet tall. *C. macrocephala* (globe centaurea)—yellow flowers up to 3 inches across on erect stems up to 4 feet tall. Globe centaurea is generally planted as a specimen, not in groups. *C. montana* (mountain bluet, cornflower)—2-inch-deep cornflower-blue blooms on 1- to 2-foot stems; *C. ruthenica* (ruthenian centaurea)—2- inch pale yellow flowers on stems 3 feet tall with pinnately divided leaves.

Growing conditions and maintenance
Space centaureas 1 to 2 feet apart. Taller species will need staking. Propagate by transplanting self-sown seedlings, by division, or from seed.

Centranthus (sen-TRAN-thus)

RED VALERIAN

Centranthus ruber

HARDINESS: Zones 4-9

FLOWERING SEASON: summer

HEIGHT: 1 to 3 feet

FLOWER COLOR: pink, red, white

SOIL: well-drained, neutral to slightly alkaline loam

LIGHT: full sun

Dense, round flower clusters tip each of red valerian's erect stems, which grow in vigorous clumps. They make excellent cut flowers.

Selected species and varieties
C. ruber (Jupiter's-beard)—bushy plants to 3 feet tall with fragrant ½-inch spurred flowers in rounded terminal clusters above paired blue-green leaves; 'Atrococcineus' has deep red flowers; 'Coccineus', scarlet flowers; 'Albus', white flowers.

Growing conditions and maintenance
Plant red valerian 12 to 18 inches apart. It can thrive in sterile limestone soil. Propagate by transplanting self-sown seedlings, from seed, or by division in spring.

Ceratostigma (ser-at-o-STIG-ma)

PLUMBAGO, LEADWORT

Ceratostigma plumbaginoides

HARDINESS: Zones 5-10

FLOWERING SEASON: summer to late fall

HEIGHT: 8 to 48 inches

FLOWER COLOR: blue

SOIL: well-drained

LIGHT: full sun to partial shade

Plumbago develops shiny leaves and blue flowers that bloom late in the season. Low-growing species are effectively used as a ground cover for shrub borders, an edging for a garden walk, or creeping among stones in a rock garden. Taller types are attractive in a mixed-shrub border.

Selected species and varieties

C. plumbaginoides—8 to 12 inches tall and 18 inches wide, with leaves to 3 inches, turning bronze in fall in cool climates, and dark blue, saucer-shaped flowers in summer to late fall; hardy to Zone 6. *C. willmottianum*—to 4 feet, upright, deciduous; has 2-inch leaves and bears 1-inch bright blue flowers continuously from midsummer through fall; hardy to Zone 8.

Growing conditions and maintenance

Plumbago requires good drainage but is otherwise tolerant of most soils. It will die out in soils that remain wet over the winter, and it does not compete well with tree roots. Mark the location of *C. plumbaginoides* because it is slow to emerge in spring.

Chelone (kee-LO-nee)

TURTLEHEAD

Chelone lyonii

HARDINESS: Zones 3-9

FLOWERING SEASON: summer, early fall

HEIGHT: 1 to 4 feet

FLOWER COLOR: white, pink, purple

SOIL: moist, rich

LIGHT: partial shade to full sun

Turtleheads are perennials native to marshes, stream banks, low meadows, and moist woodlands in much of eastern North America. Their distinctively shaped flowers, which somewhat resemble a turtle's head, appear in terminal racemes on erect stems. They are well suited to bog gardens or the edges of garden pools.

Selected species and varieties

C. glabra (white turtlehead)—1 to 4 feet tall with 6-inch, lance-shaped leaves; clusters of white or pale pink 1½-inch flowers at the tops of the stems in summer; Zones 3-8. *C. lyonii* (pink turtlehead)—2 to 3 feet tall with dark green foliage and clusters of pinkish purple flowers beginning in late summer; Zones 3-9.

Growing conditions and maintenance

Turtleheads thrive in moist soils in partial shade but will tolerate a sunny location if abundant water is supplied. Place them among stout plants to provide support for their slender stems. Propagate by seed, division, or cuttings.

Chrysanthemum (kri-SAN-the-mum)

CHRYSANTHEMUM

Chrysanthemum x morifolium 'Pink Daisy'

HARDINESS: Zones 4-10

FLOWERING SEASON: spring to fall

HEIGHT: 1 to 3 feet

FLOWER COLOR: all colors but blue

SOIL: well-drained, fertile loam

LIGHT: full sun to partial shade

Chrysanthemum flower forms vary widely but generally consist of tiny central disk flowers surrounded by petal-like ray flowers. Reliable performers in the garden, often blooming throughout summer, they are also valued as cut flowers.

Selected species and varieties

C. coccineum (painted daisy)—white, pink, lilac, crimson, and dark red single radiating flowers 2 to 4 inches wide, blooming from late spring to early summer on stems 2 to 3 feet tall; 'Eileen May Robinson' produces salmon pink flowers atop 30-inch stems; 'James Kelway', scarlet flowers with bright yellow centers on 18-inch stems; 'Robinson's Pink', 2-foot-tall plants with medium pink flowers; Zones 3-7. *C. frutescens* (marguerite)—single or double daisylike flowers in pink, white, or pale yellow colors throughout the summer on shrubby plants that grow up to 3 feet tall; perennial in Zones 9 and 10, annual elsewhere. *C. leucanthemum* (oxeye daisy)—solitary flowers 1½ inches across with white rays surrounding yellow disks on stems to 2 feet tall in spring and summer. *C.* x *morifolium* (hardy chrysanthemum, florist's chrysanthemum)—rounded plants up to 3 feet tall with aromatic gray-green lobed leaves and 1- to 6-inch flowers in all colors but blue and in a wide range of forms; button chrysanthemums are usually under 18 inches tall with small double flowers less than an inch across; cushion mums usually grow less than 20 inches tall in rounded, compact mounds with numerous double blossoms; daisy chrysanthemums have pronounced yellow centers surrounded by a single row of ray flowers on 2-foot stems, the 'Pink Daisy' cultivar having 2-inch rose pink flowers; decorative chrysanthemums have semidouble or double 2- to 4-inch flowers on loose, open plants to 3 feet tall; pompom chrysanthemums, ball-shaped flowers on 18-inch plants; spider chrysanthemums, rolled petals of irregular lengths; spoon chrysanthemums, petals rolled so that open tips resemble spoons. *C. nipponicum* (Nippon daisy)—solitary 1½- to 3½-inch blossoms with single white ray flowers and greenish yellow disk flowers in the fall on erect, branching stems to 2 feet tall over shrubby mounds. *C. parthenium* (feverfew)—pungently scented ¼-inch white flower buttons with yellow centers, growing from early summer through fall on plants 1 to 3 feet tall; 'Golden Ball' is a dwarf cultivar with yellow flowers; 'White Star', a dwarf with white flowers. *C. x superbum* (Shasta daisy)—white flowers with yellow centers up to 3 inches across from early summer to frost on 3-foot stems with narrow, toothed leaves up to a foot long; 'Alaska' cultivar has large single pure white flowers on 2- to 3-foot stems; 'Little Miss Muffet' is a 12-inch dwarf with semidouble white flowers. Double varieties include 'Horace Read', with 4-inch, ball-

like blooms if grown in a cool climate, and 'Marconi', with 6-inch blooms.

Growing conditions and maintenance
Space chrysanthemums 1 to 2 feet apart. Their shallow root systems demand frequent watering and fertilizing. In cooler climates, apply winter mulch to prevent frost heaving. Divide *C*. x *morifolium* and *C*. x *superbum* every 2 years to prevent overcrowding, which can lead to disease and fewer flowers. Cut back *C. morifolium* and Nippon daisies two or three times in spring and early summer to develop compact, bushy plants and abundant flowers. Feverfew and oxeye daisies self-sow. Shasta, feverfew, and oxeye daisies are easily propagated from seed. Propagate all chrysanthemums by division or from spring cuttings.

Chrysanthemum x superbum

Chrysanthemum nipponicum

Chrysogonum virginianum var. virginianum

GOLDENSTAR

HARDINESS: Zones 5-9

FLOWERING SEASON: late spring to summer

HEIGHT: 4 to 9 inches

FLOWER COLOR: yellow

SOIL: well-drained

LIGHT: full sun to full shade

The deep green foliage of goldenstar provides a lush background for its bright yellow, star-shaped flowers, which appear from late spring into summer. Its low-growing, spreading habit makes it useful as a ground cover, for edging at the front of a border, or in a rock garden.

Selected species and varieties
C. virginianum var. *virginianum*—6 to 9 inches, with dark green, bluntly serrated leaves along upright spreading stems, and 1½-inch flowers that bloom throughout the spring in warm areas, well into summer in cooler zones; var. *australe* is similar to var. *virginianum* but more prostrate.

Growing conditions and maintenance
Goldenstar grows well in most soils with average fertility. For use as a ground cover, space plants 12 inches apart. Divide every other year in spring.

Chrysopsis (kri-SOP-sis)

GOLDEN ASTER

Chrysopsis mariana

HARDINESS: Zones 4-10

FLOWERING SEASON: summer to fall

HEIGHT: 6 inches to 5 feet

FLOWER COLOR: yellow

SOIL: wet to dry, sandy

LIGHT: full sun

The perennial golden asters are tough, vigorous plants that punctuate the landscape with long-lasting clusters of bright daisy-like blossoms.

Selected species and varieties

C. graminifolia [also called *Pityopsis graminifolia*] (grass-leaved golden aster)—12-inch grasslike leaves and clusters of bright yellow flowers on 2½-foot stems; makes a good evergreen ground cover; Zones 5-10. *C. mariana* (Maryland golden aster)—18 to 30 inches tall with showy clusters of flowers on sturdy stems; Zones 4-9. *C. villosa* (golden aster)—as little as 6 inches to as much as 5 feet in height with flowers near the tips of stems that may be upright or trailing; Zones 4-9.

Growing conditions and maintenance

C. graminifolia and *C. villosa* are easy to grow on sunny, dry sites; they may do poorly in too rich a soil. *C. mariana* requires wet to moist soil. Propagate by seed.

Cimicifuga (si-mi-SIFF-yew-ga)

BUGBANE

Cimicifuga ramosa 'Brunette'

HARDINESS: Zones 3-8

FLOWERING SEASON: late summer to fall

HEIGHT: 3 to 7 feet

FLOWER COLOR: white

SOIL: moist, well-drained, fertile

LIGHT: full sun to partial shade

Bugbane's lacy leaflets create airy columns of foliage topped by long wands of tiny, frilled flowers. Use it as an accent specimen, naturalized in a woodland garden, or massed at the edge of a stream or pond.

Selected species and varieties

C. americana (American bugbane) dense spikes of creamy blossoms on branched 2- to 6-foot-tall flower stalks in late summer to fall. *C. ramosa* (branched bugbane)—3-foot wands of fragrant white flowers on reddish stalks in fall; 'Atropurpurea' grows to 7 feet with bronzy purple leaves; 'Brunette' has purplish black foliage and pink-tinged flowers on 3- to 4-foot stalks. *C. simplex* 'White Pearl'—2-foot wands of white flowers on branching, arched 3- to 4-foot flower stalks followed by round, lime green fruits.

Growing conditions and maintenance

Plant bugbane in cooler areas of the garden in soil enriched with organic matter. Propagate by division in spring.

Claytonia (klay-TOH-nee-a)

SPRING BEAUTY

Claytonia virginica

HARDINESS: Zones 4-9

FLOWERING SEASON: spring

HEIGHT: 4 to 12 inches

FLOWER COLOR: pink, white

SOIL: moist, rich

LIGHT: shade to partial shade

Spring beauties are low-growing perennials found in rich woodlands throughout much of the eastern and central United States. Their dainty flowers are pink or white with darker pink stripes on the petals and dark pink stamens. They are lovely planted in large drifts or scattered among other woodland flowers. The plants disappear shortly after flowering.

Selected species and varieties

C. caroliniana (broad-leaved spring beauty) grows from corms to produce two oval leaves, each 2 inches long. Throughout spring flowers are borne in loose clusters along the upper portion of the 4- to 12-inch stems. *C. virginica* (narrow-leaved spring beauty) is similar to the above species except that its leaves are slender and grasslike.

Growing conditions and maintenance

Claytonias will thrive and spread rapidly in a moist soil with high humus content. Incorporate generous amounts of organic matter into the soil prior to planting. Propagate by corms or seed.

Clematis (KLEM-a-tis)

CLEMATIS

Clematis integrifolia

HARDINESS: Zones 3-8

FLOWERING SEASON: summer

HEIGHT: 1½ to 5 feet

FLOWER COLOR: blue, white, pink, purple

SOIL: moist, well-drained, fertile loam

LIGHT: full sun

Clematis produces delicate summer flowers singly or in clusters, followed by feathery seed heads.

Selected species and varieties

C. heracleifolia 'Davidiana' (tube clematis)—fragrant blue flower bells in hyacinth-like clusters on 2- to 3-foot plants. *C. integrifolia* (solitary clematis)—solitary blue, urn-shaped flowers appear at the ends of 1½- to 2-foot-tall stems. *C. recta* (ground clematis)—fragrant white flowers in clusters at the ends of 3- to 5-foot trailing stems; 'Purpurea' has purple foliage.

Growing conditions and maintenance

Space clematis 2 to 4 feet apart. Stake to grow erect border plants or allow to trail. Propagate from seed or from stem cuttings taken in summer.

Clintonia (klin-TOH-nee-a)

BEAD LILY

Clintonia andrewsiana

HARDINESS: Zones 2-9

FLOWERING SEASON: spring to summer

HEIGHT: 4 to 20 inches

FLOWER COLOR: white, rose, yellow

SOIL: moist, rich

LIGHT: shade

Different species of these low-growing perennials are found in woodlands of the West and the East. All have broad, glossy leaves, delicate flowers, and marble-sized berries.

Selected species and varieties

C. andrewsiana (bead lily)—10- to 20-inch stalks of deep rose bell-shaped flowers followed by steel blue berries; native to California and Oregon; Zones 8-9. *C. borealis* (blue bead lily)—greenish yellow flowers on 8- to 15-inch stalks followed by bright blue berries; eastern Canada and United States; Zones 2-7. *C. umbellulata* (speckled wood lily, white bead lily)—white flowers with green and purple specks on 6- to 20-inch stalks followed by black berries. *C. uniflora* (bride's bonnet)—4 to 8 inches tall with white flowers and amethyst-blue berries; grows wild from California to Alaska; Zones 4-8.

Growing conditions and maintenance

Clintonias require cool, damp, shady locations, where they make excellent ground covers. Mulch in winter. Propagate by division in the fall or early spring, or by seed.

Coreopsis (ko-ree-OP-sis)

COREOPSIS, TICKSEED

Coreopsis grandiflora

HARDINESS: Zones 4-9

FLOWERING SEASON: spring to summer

HEIGHT: 6 inches to 3 feet

FLOWER COLOR: yellow, orange, pink

SOIL: well-drained loam

LIGHT: full sun

Coreopsis bears single- or double-petaled daisylike, predominantly yellow flowers on wiry, sometimes branching stems over a long season of bloom. The blossoms are excellent for indoor arrangements.

Selected species and varieties

C. auriculata (mouse-ear coreopsis)—bears 1- to 2-inch flowers in late spring and early summer above fuzzy leaves with lobed bases lining 1- to 2-foot stems; 'Nana' is a creeping variety 4 to 6 inches tall. *C. grandiflora*—yellow or orange single, semidouble, and double flowers 1 to 1½ inches across, blooming from early to late summer on 1- to 2-foot stems; 'Sunburst' grows to 2 feet tall, with large semidouble golden flowers; 'Sunray', 2 feet tall, with 2-inch double yellow flowers. *C. lanceolata* (lance coreopsis)—yellow flowers 1½ to 2½ inches across, with yellow or brown centers, blooming from late spring through summer on stems up to 3 feet tall; 'Brown Eyes' has maroon rings near the center of yellow flowers; 'Goldfink' is a 10- to 12-inch-tall dwarf that blooms prolifically from summer to fall. *C. maritima* (sea dahlia)—1- to 3-foot stems with long yellow-green leaves and yellow flowers 2½ to

4 inches wide from early spring to summer; suited to the hot, dry summers of southern California. *C. rosea* (pink coreopsis)—delicate pink flowers with yellow centers on stems 15 to 24 inches tall lined with needlelike leaves; can be invasive. *C. verticillata* (threadleaf coreopsis)—yellow flowers 1 to 2 inches across from late spring to late summer grow atop stems that are 2 to 3 feet tall lined with finely cut, delicate leaves 2 to 3 inches long to form dense clumps about 2 feet wide; 'Zagreb' is a 12- to 18-inch-tall dwarf with bright yellow flowers; 'Moonbeam' is a warm-climate variety that grows 18 to 24 inches tall with a prolific output of creamy yellow flowers; 'Golden Showers', 2 to 3 feet tall with 2½-inch-wide star-shaped flowers.

Growing conditions and maintenance
Space coreopsis 12 to 18 inches apart. Remove spent flowers to extend bloom time. Transplant the self-sown seedlings of threadleaf coreopsis. Propagate *C. maritima* from seed, all other coreopsis from seed or by division in the spring.

Coreopsis verticillata

Corydalis (ko-RID-a-lis)

FUMEWORT

Corydalis flexuosa 'Blue Panda'

HARDINESS:	Zones 5-8
FLOWERING SEASON:	midspring through summer
HEIGHT:	8 to 15 inches
FLOWER COLOR:	blue, yellow
SOIL:	moist, well-drained
LIGHT:	dappled to bright full shade

Corydalis is useful for edgings, rock gardens, and perennial beds. Spikes of small trumpet-shaped flowers bloom from midspring through summer. The fernlike foliage remains attractive throughout the growing season.

Selected species and varieties
C. flexuosa 'Blue Panda'—8- to 12-inch-tall mounds bearing bright blue flower spikes from late spring until frost. *C. lutea* (yellow corydalis, yellow bleeding heart)—a bushy, multistemmed plant 12 to 15 inches tall with ¾-inch-long yellow flowers flaring out from spikes above the foliage.

Growing conditions and maintenance
Corydalis grows best in light or dappled shade but will tolerate deep shade. For increased vigor, work organic matter such as compost, leaf mold, or peat moss into the soil before planting. Good drainage is essential. Apply an all-purpose fertilizer in spring. After 2 or 3 years, divide plants in early spring. Propagate by seeds or stem cuttings. Yellow corydalis self-seeds freely.

Crambe (KRAM-bee)

CRAMBE

Crambe cordifolia

HARDINESS:	Zones 5-9
FLOWERING SEASON:	late spring to early summer
HEIGHT:	2 to 6 feet
FLOWER COLOR:	white
SOIL:	well-drained, slightly alkaline
LIGHT:	full sun

Crambe forms broad mounds of wrinkly, gray-green, heart-shaped leaves with deep lobes attractive as edgings or fillers. In late spring or early summer, stout stems carry an enormous branching cloud of tiny, strongly scented white flowers above the fleshy leaves to create an unusual accent in a border.

Selected species and varieties
C. cordifolia (colewort)—leafy mounds 4 feet across crowned by an equally wide froth of flowers on stalks to 6 feet tall. *C. maritima* (sea kale)—2-foot-wide mounds of blue-green leaves with a powdery coating topped by a billow of tiny white flowers on a stalk up to 3 feet tall.

Growing conditions and maintenance
Plant colewort and sea kale at least 4 feet apart. Sea kale tolerates the sandy, salty conditions in seaside gardens. Propagate from fresh seed sown immediately after ripening or from 4- to 6-inch-long root cuttings.

Delphinium (del-FIN-ee-um)

DELPHINIUM

Delphinium 'Blue Fountains'

HARDINESS: Zones 3-7

FLOWERING SEASON: summer

HEIGHT: 2 to 8 feet

FLOWER COLOR: blue, white, purple, pink

SOIL: moist, well-drained, fertile

LIGHT: full sun

Enormous showy spikes of 2-inch flowers on stiff stalks bloom atop delphinium's clumps of finely cut, lobed leaves. The spurred flowers often have deeply contrasting centers. Delphiniums make impressive specimens in a border.

Selected species and varieties

D. x *belladonna* (belladonna delphinium)—blue or white flowers on branching 3- to 4-foot-tall stems. *D.* 'Blue Fountains'—dwarf delphinium 2½ to 3 feet tall with flowers in shades of blue. *D. elatum* Pacific Hybrids—blue, violet, lavender, pink, or white mostly double flowers on stalks usually 4 to 6 feet tall.

Growing conditions and maintenance

Plant delphiniums in slightly alkaline soil enriched with organic matter. Remove dead flowers after bloom and cut foliage back as it yellows to encourage a second blooming. Stake tall varieties. Propagate from seed.

Dentaria (den-TAR-ee-a)

TOOTHWORT

Dentaria diphylla

HARDINESS: Zones 4-9

FLOWERING SEASON: spring

HEIGHT: 6 to 16 inches

FLOWER COLOR: white, pink

SOIL: moist, rich

LIGHT: partial to full shade

Toothworts are low-growing perennials native to rich woods and bottom lands in the eastern and central United States. They grow from rhizomes, producing loose clusters of small bell-shaped flowers in the spring. After these shade-loving plants flower, they disappear.

Selected species and varieties

D. diphylla (toothwort, crinkleroot)—8 to 16 inches tall with deeply dissected leaves and loose clusters of white or pale pink four-petaled flowers from early to late spring; Zones 4-7. *D. laciniata* (cut-leaved toothwort)—6 to 12 inches tall with a whorl of deeply divided and coarsely toothed leaves halfway up each stem; clusters of pink or white flowers above the foliage in spring; Zones 4-9.

Growing conditions and maintenance

Toothworts do not tolerate direct sun. Mulch lightly with leaves in winter. Propagate by seed sown immediately after collection or by division when the plant is dormant.

Dianthus (dy-AN-thus)

PINKS, CARNATIONS

Dianthus gratianopolitanus 'Karlik'

HARDINESS: Zones 4-8

FLOWERING SEASON: spring to summer

HEIGHT: 3 inches to 2 feet

FLOWER COLOR: pink, red, white

SOIL: moist, well-drained, slightly alkaline loam

LIGHT: full sun to partial shade

Pinks are perennials whose fragrant flowers with fringed petals are borne singly or in clusters above attractive grassy foliage that is evergreen in mild climates.

Selected species and varieties

D. x *allwoodii* (Allwood pinks)—single or double flowers in a wide range of colors grow for 2 months above gray-green leaves in compact mounds 12 to 24 inches tall; 'Aqua' grows white double blooms atop 12-inch stems. *D.* x *a. alpinus* (Alpine pinks)—dwarf varieties of Allwood pinks; 'Doris' grows very fragrant, double salmon-colored flowers with darker pink centers on 12-inch stems; 'Robin', coral red flowers. *D. barbatus* (sweet William)—a biennial species that self-seeds so reliably that it performs like a perennial; unlike other pinks, it produces flowers in flat clusters and without fragrance; 'Harlequin' grows ball-shaped pink-and-white flowers; 'Indian Carpet', single flowers in a mix of colors on 10-inch stems. *D. deltoides* (maiden pinks)—¾-inch red or pink flowers on 12-inch stems above 6- to 12-inch-high mats of small bright green leaves; 'Brilliant' has scarlet flowers; 'Flashing

Light' ('Leuchtfunk'), ruby red flowers. *D. gratianopolitanus* (cheddar pinks)—1-inch-wide flowers in shades of pink and rose on compact mounds of blue-green foliage 9 to 12 inches high; 'Karlik' has deep pink, fringed, fragrant flowers; 'Tiny Rubies', dark pink double blooms on plants just 4 inches tall. *D. plumarius* (cottage pinks)—fragrant single or semidouble flowers 1½ inches across in shades of pink and white or bicolors above 12- to 18-inch-high mats of evergreen leaves; 'Essex Witch' produces fragrant salmon, pink, or white flowers.

Growing conditions and maintenance

Space pinks 12 to 18 inches apart. Cut stems back after bloom and shear mat-forming types in the fall to promote dense growth. Maintain vigor by division every 2 to 3 years. Propagate from seed, from cuttings taken in early summer, or by division in the spring.

Dianthus plumarius 'Essex Witch'

Dicentra (dy-SEN-tra)

BLEEDING HEART

Dicentra spectabilis

HARDINESS: Zones 3-8

FLOWERING SEASON: spring to summer

HEIGHT: 1 to 3 feet

FLOWER COLOR: pink, white, purple

SOIL: moist, well-drained loam

LIGHT: partial shade

Bleeding heart's unusual puffy, heart-shaped flowers dangle beneath arched stems above mounds of lacy leaves.

Selected species and varieties

D. eximia (fringed bleeding heart)—pink to purple flowers above 12-inch mounds of blue-green leaves; 'Alba' has white flowers. *D. formosa* (Pacific bleeding heart)—deep pink flowers on 12- to 18-inch stems; 'Luxuriant', cherry pink flowers; 'Sweetheart', white flowers on 12-inch stems. *D. spectabilis* (common bleeding heart)—pink, purple, or white flowers on arching 3-foot stems.

Growing conditions and maintenance

Space fringed and Pacific bleeding hearts 1 to 2 feet apart, common bleeding heart 2 to 3 feet. Propagate from seed or by division in the early spring.

Dictamnus (dik-TAM-nus)

GAS PLANT, DITTANY

Dictamnus albus 'Purpureus'

HARDINESS: Zones 3-8

FLOWERING SEASON: early summer

HEIGHT: 2 to 3 feet

FLOWER COLOR: white, purple

SOIL: moist, well-drained

LIGHT: full sun to light shade

Gas plant is easy to grow and long-lived, with soft-colored blossoms and shiny, aromatic, dark green leaves. It adds lasting charm to a perennial border. The common name refers to the flammable gas that is secreted by the plant's leaves, stems, and roots.

Selected species and varieties

D. albus—produces leathery, lemon-scented leaves, white flowers 1½ to 2 inches across that bloom in early summer on erect stems held a foot above the foliage, and seed pods that are attractive and useful in dried arrangements; *D. a.* 'Purpureus' has pale mauve-purple flowers with darker purple veins.

Growing conditions and maintenance

Select your site for gas plants carefully, because once planted, they do not like to be disturbed. Add organic matter to the soil prior to planting. It often takes a full season or more before the plants bloom, but once established, they are reliable garden performers.

Digitalis (di-ji-TAL-us)

FOXGLOVE

Digitalis purpurea 'Foxy'

HARDINESS: Zones 3-9

FLOWERING SEASON: summer

HEIGHT: 2 to 5 feet

FLOWER COLOR: purple, white, yellow, pink

SOIL: moist, well-drained, acid

LIGHT: partial shade

Foxglove's striking summer-blooming flower trumpets line the tips of stiff stalks above clumps of coarse, hairy leaves.

Selected species and varieties
D. grandiflora (yellow foxglove)—yellow flowers with spotted throats on stalks to 3 feet tall. *D.* x *mertonensis* (strawberry foxglove)—coppery pink flowers on plants to 4 feet. *D. purpurea* (common foxglove)—purple, sometimes pink, white, or brownish red flowers with spotted throats on plants to 5 feet; foliage may be poisonous to pets; 'Alba' grows white flowers; 'Apricot', peach blooms; 'Excelsior Hybrids', pink, mauve, yellow, or white blooms that encircle the stalks; 'Foxy' produces blooms in mixed colors from seed the first year; 'Shirley Hybrids', profuse flowers on stalks to 5 feet.

Growing conditions and maintenance
Plant foxgloves 12 to 18 inches apart in organically rich soil. Propagate from seed, by transplanting self-sown seedlings, or by division in fall.

Doronicum (do-RON-i-kum)

LEOPARD'S-BANE

Doronicum cordatum

HARDINESS: Zones 4-8

FLOWERING SEASON: spring

HEIGHT: 1½ to 2 feet

FLOWER COLOR: yellow

SOIL: moist loam

LIGHT: full sun to partial shade

The daisylike flowers of leopard's-bane stand brightly above mounds of heart-shaped dark green leaves.

Selected species and varieties
D. cordatum (Caucasian leopard's-bane)—yellow flowers 2 to 3 inches across on 12- to 18-inch stems above mounds of leaves up to 24 inches across. *D.* 'Miss Mason'—compact 18-inch-tall plants with long-lasting, attractive foliage. *D.* 'Spring Beauty'—double-petaled yellow flowers.

Growing conditions and maintenance
Space leopard's-bane 1 to 2 feet apart in full sun but in cool locations where its shallow roots will receive constant moisture. Foliage dies out after flowers bloom. Propagate from seed or by division every 2 to 3 years.

Echeveria (ek-e-VEER-ee-a)

HENS AND CHICKS

Echeveria agavoides

HARDINESS: Zones 9-11

FLOWERING SEASON: spring to early summer, winter

HEIGHT: 3 inches to 3 feet

FLOWER COLOR: red, orange, yellow

SOIL: well-drained to dry

LIGHT: full sun

Hens and chicks makes an interesting, attractive ground cover or rock-garden plant for warm, dry climates. It is grown primarily for the beauty of its fleshy, succulent, often colorful leaves that form compact rosettes. Bell-shaped nodding flowers develop on slender stems that rise well above the foliage.

Selected species and varieties
E. agavoides—6- to 8-inch rosettes of bright green leaves with reddish margins, topped in summer by red-and-yellow flowers. *E. crenulata*—loose rosettes of pale green leaves with wavy margins, growing up to 1 foot long and covered with white powder, and red to orange flowers on stems up to 3 feet tall. *E. imbricata*—4- to 6-inch rosettes of gray-green leaves and loose stems of orange, red, and yellow flowers; develops many offsets around the base.

Growing conditions and maintenance
Hens and chicks thrives in warm locations and is quite tolerant of drought and coastal conditions. It is easily propagated from offsets.

Echinacea (ek-i-NAY-see-a)

PURPLE CONEFLOWER

Echinacea purpurea

HARDINESS: Zones 3-9

FLOWERING SEASON: summer

HEIGHT: 2 to 4 feet

FLOWER COLOR: pink, purple, white

SOIL: well-drained loam

LIGHT: full sun to light shade

Drooping petals surrounding dark brown, cone-shaped centers bloom on purple coneflower's stiff stems over many weeks.

Selected species and varieties
E. pallida (pale coneflower)—rosy purple or white flowers up to 3½ inches long on 3- to 4-foot stems. *E. purpurea*—pink, purple, or white flowers up to 3 inches in diameter on stems 2 to 4 feet tall; 'Bright Star' has rosy pink petals surrounding maroon centers; 'Robert Bloom', reddish purple blooms with orange centers on 2- to 3-foot stems; 'White Lustre', abundant white flowers with bronze centers.

Growing conditions and maintenance
Space plants 2 feet apart. Transplant self-sown seedlings or propagate from seeds or by division.

Echinops (EK-in-ops)

GLOBE THISTLE

Echinops ritro 'Taplow Blue'

HARDINESS: Zones 3-9

FLOWERING SEASON: summer

HEIGHT: 3 to 4 feet

FLOWER COLOR: blue

SOIL: well-drained, acid loam

LIGHT: full sun

The round, spiny, steel blue flowers of globe thistle are held well above coarse, bristly foliage on stiff, erect stems. Several stout stems emerge from a thick, branching taproot. Flowers are excellent for both cutting and drying.

Selected species and varieties
E. exaltatus (Russian globe thistle)—spiny flowers grow on stems up to 5 feet tall above deep green foliage. *E. ritro* (small globe thistle)—bright blue flower globes up to 2 inches across on stems 3 to 4 feet tall; 'Taplow Blue' has medium blue flowers 3 inches in diameter.

Growing conditions and maintenance
Space globe thistles 2 feet apart. Once established, the plant is drought tolerant. Propagate from seed or by division in the spring.

Epimedium (ep-i-MEE-dee-um)

BARRENWORT

Epimedium grandiflorum 'Rose Queen'

HARDINESS: Zones 5-8

FLOWERING SEASON: spring

HEIGHT: 6 to 12 inches

FLOWER COLOR: red, pink, yellow, white

SOIL: moist, well-drained

LIGHT: partial to full shade

The small, heart-shaped leaves of barrenwort are reddish bronze when they first emerge in spring. They soon turn deep green, providing a lush ground cover for shady gardens before turning bronze again in fall. Red, pink, yellow, or white flowers rise above the foliage on delicate, wiry stems in spring.

Selected species and varieties
E. grandiflorum—9 to 12 inches tall, forming dense clumps; 'Rose Queen' has deep pink flowers with white-tipped spurs. *E. x rubrum*—6 to 12 inches tall, with very showy, bright red flowers flushed with white or yellow. *E. x youngianum* 'Niveum'—7 to 8 inches tall, compact, with white flowers.

Growing conditions and maintenance
Barrenwort is a rugged plant that grows in a clump and increases in size without becoming invasive. It can be left undisturbed indefinitely, or can be easily divided to increase the number of plants. Cut it back to the ground in late winter.

Erigeron *(e-RIJ-er-on)*

FLEABANE

Erigeron speciosus 'Pink Jewel'

HARDINESS: Zones 3-8

FLOWERING SEASON: summer

HEIGHT: 1½ to 2 feet

FLOWER COLOR: blue, lavender, pink

SOIL: well-drained loam

LIGHT: full sun

Fleabane's asterlike blossoms grow singly or in branched clusters with a fringe of petal-like ray flowers surrounding a yellow center. Flowers sit atop leafy stems above basal rosettes of fuzzy swordlike or oval leaves.

Selected species and varieties
E. pulchellus (Poor Robin's plantain)—pink, lavender, or white flowers 1½ inches across on plants up to 2 feet tall. *E. speciosus* (Oregon fleabane)—the most popular species in the genus, *E. speciosus* bears purple flowers 1 to 2 inches across on stems to 30 inches; 'Azure Fairy' has semidouble lavender flowers; 'Double Beauty', double blue-violet flowers; 'Foerster's Liebling', deep pink semidouble flowers; 'Pink Jewel', single lavender-pink flowers; 'Sincerity', single lavender flowers.

Growing conditions and maintenance
Plant fleabane 18 inches apart. Propagate by transplanting self-sown seedlings or by division in spring.

Eryngium *(e-RIN-jee-um)*

SEA HOLLY

Eryngium bourgatii

HARDINESS: Zones 4-9

FLOWERING SEASON: summer to fall

HEIGHT: 1 to 6 feet

FLOWER COLOR: blue, white

SOIL: dry, sandy

LIGHT: full sun

Ruffs of spiny bracts cradle sea holly's conical flower heads with tiny, tightly packed florets. The long-lasting summer-blooming flowers rise on stiff stalks above crisp, leathery, often wavy leaves with deeply cut, spiny margins.

Selected species and varieties
E. alpinum (bluetop sea holly)—frilled bracts on 1- to 2-foot-tall plants. *E. bourgatii* (Mediterranean sea holly)—narrow, pointed bracts and wavy, gray-green leaves with prominent white veins on plants to 2 feet. *E. giganteum* (stout sea holly)—wide bracts like silvery holly leaves on plants 4 to 6 feet tall. *E. planum* (flat-leaved eryngium)—light blue flower heads with blue-green bracts on plants to 3 feet. *E. yuccifolium* (rattlesnake master)—has narrow, drooping gray-green leaves with spiny edges on 4-foot stalks.

Growing conditions and maintenance
Plant sea hollies 12 to 18 inches apart. Plants may need staking in fertile soils. Propagate by separating and transplanting plantlets that appear at the base of mature plants.

Eupatorium *(yew-pa-TOR-ee-um)*

BONESET

Eupatorium coelestinum

HARDINESS: Zones 5-10

FLOWERING SEASON: summer to frost

HEIGHT: 1 to 6 feet

FLOWER COLOR: blue, mauve, purple

SOIL: moist, well-drained loam

LIGHT: full sun to partial shade

Boneset produces flat, dense clusters of fluffy, frizzy ½-inch flowers on erect stems lined with hairy, triangular leaves. The sturdy clumps will naturalize in marshy areas at the edges of meadows or in wild gardens. The flowers provide a fall foil for yellow or white flowers such as chrysanthemums and are excellent for cutting.

Selected species and varieties
E. coelestinum (mist flower, hardy ageratum, blue boneset)—bluish purple to violet ½-inch flowers crowded in clusters at the tips of 1- to 2-foot-tall stalks in late summer to fall. *E. fistulosum* (hollow Joe-Pye weed)—large flat clusters of mauve flowers on hollow purple stems to 6 feet in late summer through fall. *E. maculatum* (Joe-Pye weed, smokeweed)—large flattened clusters of reddish purple or white flowers on 6- to 10-foot stems.

Growing conditions and maintenance
Plant boneset 18 to 24 inches apart (allow 3 feet between taller species) in soil enriched with organic matter. Cut foliage back several times through the summer for bushier plants. Propagate from seed or by division in spring.

Euphorbia (yew-FOR-bee-a)

SPURGE

Euphorbia griffithii 'Fireglow'

HARDINESS: Zones 3-10

FLOWERING SEASON: spring or summer

HEIGHT: 6 inches to 3 feet

FLOWER COLOR: white, green, red, yellow

SOIL: light, well-drained

LIGHT: full sun to partial shade

Euphorbia is a large, diverse genus that includes many interesting low-maintenance perennials well suited for rock gardens, dry herbaceous borders, south-facing slopes, and dry walls. As with another member of this genus, the poinsettia, spurge produces flowers that are actually quite small but are surrounded by showy bracts that create colorful effects both in the garden and in indoor arrangements. Many species produce attractive foliage with intense color in autumn.

Selected species and varieties

E. corollata (flowering spurge)—1 to 3 feet tall, with slender green leaves 1 to 2 inches in length that turn red in the fall. In mid to late summer, it bears clusters of flowers surrounded by small white bracts that resemble baby's-breath and impart an airy, lacy quality to a mixed border or indoor arrangement; hardy in Zones 3-10. *E. epithymoides* (cushion spurge)—forms a neat, very symmetrical mound 12 to 18 inches high, with green leaves that turn dark red in fall. In spring it produces numerous small green flowers that are surrounded by showy, inch-wide, chartreuse-yellow bracts. Cushion spurge should be

planted in partial shade in the South. It performs best in soil that is on the dry side; in moist, fertile soil it may become invasive. A long-lived plant, cushion spurge should be allowed to grow undisturbed, since it may not respond well to transplanting; hardy to Zones 4-8. *E. griffithii* 'Fireglow'—2 to 3 feet tall, with green leaves that turn yellow and red in fall and brick red flower bracts in late spring and early summer; Zones 4-8. *E. myrsinites* (myrtle euphorbia)—6 to 8 inches high, with 12- to 18-inch-long trailing stems and closely set, fleshy, evergreen, blue-green leaves, ½ inch long, that grow in a dense spiral around the stem and remain handsome throughout winter if the plant is sheltered from wind and sun. Small spring-blooming green flowers surrounded by attractive pale yellow bracts measuring 2 to 4 inches across appear in clusters at the ends of the stems. Performing well in the hot, humid summers of the southeastern states, myrtle euphorbia is hardy to Zones 5-9.

Growing conditions and maintenance

Spurges require a sunny, dry location and soil that is not too rich. In moist, fertile locations, growth may become rank, unattractive, and invasive. These plants do not like to be transplanted. Use gloves when handling them, as they exude a milky sap that can cause skin irritation. When cutting for indoor arrangements, put a flame to the cut end of the stem.

Euphorbia epithymoides

Filipendula (fil-i-PEN-dew-la)

MEADOWSWEET

Filipendula rubra 'Venusta'

HARDINESS: Zones 3-9

FLOWERING SEASON: spring to summer

HEIGHT: 1 to 7 feet

FLOWER COLOR: white, pink

SOIL: moist loam

LIGHT: partial shade

The long-lasting, feathery flower plumes of meadowsweet bloom above loose mounds of fine-textured foliage.

Selected species and varieties

F. rubra (queen-of-the-prairie)—fluffy pink summer flower clusters on 4- to 7-foot stems that require no staking; 'Venusta' has deep pink flowers. *F. ulmaria* (queen-of-the-meadow)—fluffy, creamy white summer flowers on 3- to 4-foot-tall stems. *F. vulgaris* (dropwort)—white flowers in spring and early summer, sometimes tinged with red, in loose clusters on 1- to 3-foot stems; 'Flore Pleno' grows to 15 inches tall with double flowers; 'Grandiflora' has fragrant, yellow-tinted flowers.

Growing conditions and maintenance

Space meadowsweet 2 feet apart in sites with moist, even soggy, soils. Dropwort self-sows. Propagate by seed or division.

Gaillardia (gay-LAR-dee-a)

BLANKET-FLOWER

Gaillardia x grandiflora 'Goblin'

HARDINESS: Zones 3-8

FLOWERING SEASON: early summer to frost

HEIGHT: 1 to 3 feet

FLOWER COLOR: yellow, red, purple

SOIL: well-drained to dry

LIGHT: full sun

Gaillardia produce cheerful daisylike flowers in bright color combinations from early summer until frost, above attractive mounds of hairy leaves. They provide a long season of color in the sunny perennial border and make fine cut flowers.

Selected species and varieties
G. x *grandiflora*—yellow ray flowers surround yellow or purplish red disk flowers in a 3- to 4-inch daisy on stems up to 3 feet with large, hairy, gray-green leaves at the base; 'Goblin' bears red flowers with yellow margins on stems to 12 inches; 'Monarch Strain', flowers in varying combinations of red and yellow on 30-inch stems.

Growing conditions and maintenance
Space plants 18 inches apart. They tolerate hot, dry locations, poor soil, and seaside conditions. Crowns may die out in heavier soils, but roots will send out new plants, which can be dug and replanted in spring. Propagate by seed or division.

Gaura (GAW-ra)

GAURA

Gaura lindheimeri

HARDINESS: Zones 3-9

FLOWERING SEASON: spring, summer, fall

HEIGHT: 1 to 5 feet

FLOWER COLOR: white, pink, red

SOIL: dry, sandy to well-drained

LIGHT: full sun to partial shade

Native to prairies, roadsides, and pond edges in the central and western United States, these perennials have an extended bloom season and a tolerance for summer heat that make them valuable in herbaceous borders and meadow gardens.

Selected species and varieties
G. coccinea (scarlet gaura)—branched stems 1 to 2 feet tall with narrow, oblong leaves. Fragrant flowers that resemble honeysuckle are clustered on a spikelike inflorescence from late spring and through summer. The flowers open white, fade to pink, and finally turn red; Zones 3-9. *G. lindheimeri* (white gaura)—2 to 5 feet with a vase-shaped open habit. Flowering begins in early summer and lasts until frost; the delicate four-petaled flowers are white when young and fade to pink as they age; Zones 6-9.

Growing conditions and maintenance
Gaura thrives in dry to well-drained soil and tolerates both heat and drought. Propagate from seed. Scarlet gaura can also be divided.

Gazania (ga-ZAY-nee-a)

GAZANIA

Gazania x hybrida 'Aztec Red'

HARDINESS: Zones 8-10

FLOWERING SEASON: early spring to early summer

HEIGHT: 6 to 12 inches

FLOWER COLOR: white, yellow, orange, red, lavender, pink

SOIL: well-drained

LIGHT: full sun

Gazanias are valued for their daisylike blooms in shades of white, yellow, orange, red, lavender, and pink. Their main season of bloom is early spring to early summer, but they often flower year round in mild climates.

Selected species and varieties
Gazanias fall into two distinct types—clumping and trailing. Both types have been extensively hybridized. Clumping gazanias grow 6 to 12 inches high with a 12- to 18-inch spread; *G.* x *hybrida* 'Aztec Red' and 'Fiesta Red' are two outstanding clumping varieties. Trailing gazanias have long, spreading stems and are well suited for growing on banks as a ground cover; varieties include *G.* x *hybrida* 'Sunburst' and 'Sunrise Yellow'.

Growing conditions and maintenance
Although gazanias require good drainage and full sun to look their best, they tolerate drought, coastal conditions, and poor soil. Too much water and fertilizer will weaken them. They spread naturally, and after several years may require thinning.

Gentiana (jen-shee-AH-na)

GENTIAN

Gentiana saponaria

HARDINESS: Zones 3-8

FLOWERING SEASON: summer to fall

HEIGHT: 6 to 30 inches

FLOWER COLOR: blue, purple, violet

SOIL: moist, well-drained, rich

LIGHT: full sun to partial shade

Several perennial gentians inhabit low woodlands, alpine meadows, and damp prairies over much of eastern North America. Their flowers are generally shades of blue or purple, providing contrast to the predominately yellow flowers of late summer and fall.

Selected species and varieties
G. andrewsii (bottle gentian, closed gentian)—2 feet tall with clusters of deep blue 1½-inch bottle-shaped flowers with vertical white bands; petals remain closed; Zones 3-7. *G. puberulenta* (downy gentian)—clusters of funnel-shaped purplish blue blossoms atop a single upright 6- to 24-inch flower stalk; Zones 3-8. *G. saponaria* (soapwort gentian)—to 2½ feet tall with clusters of blue-violet flowers whose petals open partially; Zones 4-7.

Growing conditions and maintenance
Gentians require cool temperatures and rich, well-drained soil with ample moisture throughout the growing season. Propagate by seed or division.

Geranium (jer-AY-nee-um)

CRANESBILL

Geranium endressii

HARDINESS: Zones 4-8

FLOWERING SEASON: spring to summer

HEIGHT: 4 inches to 4 feet

FLOWER COLOR: pink, purple, blue, white

SOIL: moist, well-drained loam

LIGHT: full sun to partial shade

Cranesbill is valued for both its dainty flat, five-petaled flowers and its neat mounds of lobed or toothed leaves that turn red or yellow in the fall. The plants are sometimes called hardy geraniums to distinguish them from annual geraniums, which belong to the genus *Pelargonium*.

Selected species and varieties
G. cinereum (grayleaf cranesbill)—summer-long pink flowers with reddish veins above 6- to 12-inch-high mounds of deeply lobed, dark green leaves with a whitish cast. *G. dalmaticum* (Dalmatian cranesbill)—clusters of rosy pink inch-wide spring flowers on 4- to 6-inch trailing stems. *G. endressii* (Pyrenean cranesbill)—pink flowers ½ inch across in spring and summer above spreading 12- to 18-inch-high mounds of sometimes evergreen leaves; 'A.T. Johnson' has silver-pink flowers; 'Wargrave Pink', deep pink flowers. *G. 'Johnson's Blue'*—1½- to 2-inch blue flowers from spring to summer on plants up to 18 inches tall. *G. macrorrhizum* (bigroot cranesbill)—clusters of magenta or pink flowers with prominent stamens in spring and summer on spreading mounds of aromatic leaves turning red and yellow in fall;

'Ingersen's Variety' has lilac-pink flowers; 'Spessart', pink flowers. *G. maculatum* (wild geranium)—loose clusters of rose-purple or lavender-pink flowers in spring on 1- to 2-foot stems. *G. psilostemon* (Armenian cranesbill)—vivid purplish red flowers up to 2 inches across with darker centers on plants 2 to 4 feet tall and equally wide. *G. sanguineum* (bloody cranesbill)—solitary magenta flowers 1 to 1½ inches across in spring and summer on 9- to 12-inch-high spreading mounds of leaves turning deep red in fall; 'Album' has white flowers; *G. sanguineum* var. *striatum* [also listed as var. lancastriense], with dark red veins tracing light pink flowers.

Growing conditions and maintenance
Space Dalmatian cranesbill 12 inches apart, Armenian cranesbill 3 to 4 feet apart, and other species about 1½ to 2 feet apart. Cranesbill grows in full sun to partial shade in cool areas but needs partial shade in warmer zones. Taller species may need staking. Propagate from seed, summer cuttings, or by division. Divide in spring when clumps show signs of crowding—approximately every 4 years.

Geranium psilostemon

Gerbera (GER-ber-a)

TRANSVAAL DAISY

Gerbera jamesonii

HARDINESS: Zones 8-11

FLOWERING SEASON: late spring to late summer

HEIGHT: 12 to 18 inches

FLOWER COLOR: orange, yellow, red, pink

SOIL: well-drained

LIGHT: full sun to partial shade

Transvaal daisies produce spectacular 4-inch flowers on sturdy stems, providing a fine display in the garden, in containers, or as cut flowers for indoor arrangements. Although they are hardy only to Zone 8, in cooler areas they can be planted as annuals or dug up in the fall and planted in containers to grow indoors as houseplants.

Selected species and varieties

G. jamesonii—has gray-green, deeply lobed leaves 5 to 10 inches long that grow in the form of a basal rosette, erect flower stems 12 to 18 inches tall, and flowers 2 to 4 inches across with strap-shaped petals in yellow, salmon, cream, pink, rose, or red.

Growing conditions and maintenance

Incorporate organic matter into the soil before planting Transvaal daisies, and fertilize regularly. For massing, space plants 2 feet apart. Water deeply, allowing the soil to dry before watering again. Protect plants over the winter in Zone 8 with a loose mulch.

Geum (JEE-um)

GEUM, AVENS

Geum x borisii

HARDINESS: Zones 5-8

FLOWERING SEASON: spring to summer

HEIGHT: 8 to 30 inches

FLOWER COLOR: red, orange, yellow

SOIL: well-drained, fertile loam

LIGHT: full sun to light shade

Geums produce flat-faced flowers in single or double blooms. The flowers, which resemble wild roses with ruffled petals surrounding frilly centers and growing singly on slender stems, make excellent cut flowers. The bright green, hairy leaves, which are lobed and frilled at their edges, form attractive mounds of foliage ideal for the front of a border or for the rock garden.

Selected species and varieties

G. coccineum [also called *G. borisii*, which is different from *G.* x *borisii*](scarlet avens)—early-summer-blooming ½-inch bright orange flowers ride above bright green toothed leaves on 12-inch-tall stems; 'Red Wings' has semidouble scarlet flowers atop 2-foot stems. *G. quellyon* (Chilean avens)—scarlet flowers 1 to 1½ inches wide on plants 18 to 24 inches tall; needs winter protection in the North. 'Fire Opal' grows reddish bronze flowers that are up to 3 inches across; 'Mrs. Bradshaw' bears semidouble red-orange blossoms; 'Lady Stratheden' produces semidouble deep yellow flowers; 'Princess Juliana', semidouble orange-bronze blooms; 'Starker's Magnificent', double-petaled deep orange flowers. *G. reptans* (creeping avens)— yellow or orange flowers on plants 6 to 9 inches tall that spread by runners; Zones 4-7. *G. rivale* (water avens)—tiny, nodding, bell-shaped pink flowers on 12-inch stems above low clumps of dark green, hairy leaves; 'Leonard's Variety' produces copper-rose flowers on slightly taller stems than the species; Zones 3-8. *G. triflorum* 'Prairie Smoke'—nodding purple to straw-colored flowers on 6- to 18-inch-tall plants; Zones 5-10. *G.* x *borisii*—orange-scarlet flowers on 12-inch plants. G. 'Georgenberg'—orange flowers on 10- to 12-inch stems.

Growing conditions and maintenance

Space geums 12 to 18 inches apart in soil enriched with organic matter. They grow best in moist but well-drained sites in cooler climates and will not survive wet winter soil. Most species dislike high temperatures; protect the plants from hot afternoon sun in warmer zones. *G. reptans* requires full sun and alkaline soil. Keep geums robust by dividing annually. Propagate by division in late summer for plants that will be ready to flower the following year, or from seed sown outdoors in fall; *G. rivale* may be sown in early spring.

Gillenia (gil-LEE-nee-a)

BOWMAN'S ROOT

Gillenia trifoliata

HARDINESS: Zones 4-8

FLOWERING SEASON: spring to summer

HEIGHT: 2 to 4 feet

FLOWER COLOR: white

SOIL: moist, well-drained loam

LIGHT: light to moderate shade

Gillenia is a tall, delicate, woodland perennial with white, star-shaped flowers, often blushed with pink. The flowers emerge from wine-colored sepals, which remain as ornaments after the petals drop. It is native to the eastern United States.

Selected species and varieties

G. trifoliata [formerly *Porteranthus trifoliata*] (bowman's root)—five-petaled flowers 1 inch wide, growing in loose, airy clusters on wiry, branching stems 2 to 4 feet tall above lacy leaves with toothed edges.

Growing conditions and maintenance

Space gillenia 2 to 3 feet apart in sites with abundant moisture and light to moderate shade. Incorporate organic matter into soil to help retain water. Plants often require staking. Propagate from seed or by division in spring or fall.

Gypsophila (jip-SOFF-il-a)

BABY'S-BREATH

Gypsophila repens 'Rosea'

HARDINESS: Zones 4-9

FLOWERING SEASON: summer

HEIGHT: 3 to 4 feet

FLOWER COLOR: white, pink

SOIL: moist, well-drained, alkaline loam

LIGHT: full sun

Clouds of tiny flowers on widely branching stems rise above fine-textured foliage.

Selected species and varieties

G. paniculata (perennial baby's-breath)—airy clusters on stems to 4 feet tall; 'Bristol Fairy' has double white flowers; 'Perfecta' is similar to 'Bristol Fairy', with larger flowers; 'Pink Fairy' has pink double flowers on 18-inch stems. *G. repens* (creeping baby's-breath)—trailing stems 6 to 8 inches long; 'Alba' has white flowers; 'Rosea', pink flowers; 'Dorothy Teacher', dark pink flowers.

Growing conditions and maintenance

Space perennial baby's-breath plants 3 feet apart and stake; space creeping baby's-breath 18 inches apart. Established plants are difficult to divide or transplant. Propagate from seed.

Helenium (hel-EE-nee-um)

SNEEZEWEED

Helenium autumnale 'Bruno'

HARDINESS: Zones 3-8

FLOWERING SEASON: summer through fall

HEIGHT: 2½ to 6 feet

FLOWER COLOR: yellow, brown

SOIL: moist, well-drained

LIGHT: full sun

Sneezeweed's clumps of erect stems lined with willowy leaves form a backdrop for shorter border plantings or provide a fall-blooming filler among plants that bloom earlier in the season. Daisylike flowers with fan-shaped petals and prominent centers bloom at the ends of sneezeweed's branching tips.

Selected species and varieties

H. autumnale (common sneezeweed)—flowers up to 2 inches wide bloom in summer and persist through frost on 5- to 6-foot-tall stems; 'Brilliant' has profuse bronze blossoms; 'Bruno', mahogany flowers on 4-foot plants; 'Butterpat', clear yellow petals surrounding bronze centers on 4- to 5-foot plants; 'Moerheim Beauty', reddish bronze blossoms on 4-foot stems.

Growing conditions and maintenance

Plant sneezeweed 18 to 24 inches apart. Plants may need staking. Divide every 3 to 4 years to prevent crowding and to propagate.

Helianthus (hee-lee-AN-thus)

SUNFLOWER

Helianthus angustifolius

HARDINESS: Zones 3-9

FLOWERING SEASON: summer through fall

HEIGHT: 5 to 12 feet

FLOWER COLOR: yellow

SOIL: moist, well-drained

LIGHT: full sun

Perennial sunflowers are tall, stately plants that put on a dramatic flower show in late summer and fall. They are well suited to the back of a sunny border or the center of an island bed. Their flowers are excellent for indoor arrangements.

Selected species and varieties

H. angustifolius—5 to 7 feet tall, 4 feet wide, with yellow petals around dark brown or purple centers forming flowers 2 to 3 inches across in midsummer to late fall; Zones 6-9. *H. maximiliani*—3 to 12 feet tall, with yellow flowers growing in leaf axils along the entire length of the stems, emerging in midsummer in the warmer zones, late summer in the cooler areas, and continuing through the fall; Zones 3-9.

Growing conditions and maintenance

Plant sunflowers in soil rich in organic matter. The plants will grow in shade but will develop a more open habit than in sun and will require staking. Cutting back stems by a third in late spring produces bushier plants. *H. maximiliani* tolerates dry conditions.

Heliopsis (hee-li-OP-sis)

FALSE SUNFLOWER

Heliopsis helianthoides

HARDINESS: Zones 4-9

FLOWERING SEASON: summer to fall

HEIGHT: 3 to 5 feet

FLOWER COLOR: yellow, orange

SOIL: moist, well-drained loam

LIGHT: full sun

False sunflower bears bright flowers in shades of yellow and gold with single or double rows of petals surrounding prominent centers on bushy plants. They make excellent cut flowers.

Selected species and varieties

H. helianthoides var. *scabra*—single, semi-double, or double flowers 2 to 3 inches across on plants 3 to 5 feet tall; 'Golden Plume' grows double yellow flowers; 'Incomparabilis', semidouble yellow flowers with dark centers; 'Summer Sun', semi-double golden yellow flowers; 'Karat', large single yellow flowers.

Growing conditions and maintenance

Space false sunflowers 2 feet apart and stake taller plants. Propagate from seed or by division.

Helleborus (hell-e-BOR-us)

HELLEBORE

Helleborus orientalis

HARDINESS: Zones 3-9

FLOWERING SEASON: winter to spring

HEIGHT: 1 to 3 feet

FLOWER COLOR: white, green, purple, pink

SOIL: moist, well-drained, fertile

LIGHT: partial shade to bright full shade

The cuplike flowers of hellebores offer such subtle variation in rich coloration that every plant carries a distinctive look. Most species are long-lived, consistent bloomers for borders and perennial beds. Depending on the species, hellebores are stemmed or stemless plants with deeply lobed leaves that may remain evergreen if given winter protection. *Caution:* All parts of the plant are poisonous.

Selected species and varieties

H. argutifolius [also listed as *H. corsicus* and *H. lividus* ssp. *corsicus*] (Corsican hellebore)—shrubby growth 1 to 2 feet tall without rhizomes, with glossy, heavily toothed leaves having ivory veins and, sometimes, red margins and producing clusters of yellowish green cups in spring; Zones 6-8. *H. atrorubens*—produces dark red, brownish, or plum-colored flowers on 1½-foot stems in winter or early spring followed by deciduous leaves; hardy to Zone 6. *H. foetidus* (stinking hellebore)—2 feet tall and bearing small green bells edged with maroon over lobed, glossy black-green leaves that form rosettes around the flowers; some hybrids are well scented; hardy to Zone 6. *H. lividus*—12 to 18 inches tall, similar to Corsican hellebore, but the 2-inch-wide greenish yellow cups are brushed with pink and gray and borne in clusters of 15 to 20 in spring over deeply toothed, purple-toned leaves; hardy to Zone 8. *H. niger* (Christmas rose)—highly variable in size and bloom time and color, but generally 12 to 15 inches tall, each stalk bearing a seminodding, white or pinkish green flower almost 3 inches across in late fall to early spring; Zones 5-8; ssp. *macranthus* has unusually large flowers in winter and pale blue-green foliage; hardy to Zone 5. *H. orientalis* (Lenten rose)—bears cream, pale to deep pink, plum, brownish purple, chocolate brown, or nearly black flowers 2 inches wide in early to midspring on 18-inch plants; Zones 4-9.

Growing conditions and maintenance
Hellebores are adaptable to most garden soils, but they do best when leaf mold or peat moss has been added to the soil. Although near neutral or alkaline soils are considered ideal, many hellebores seem to do just as well under acid conditions. Space smaller species 1 foot apart, larger ones up to 2 feet apart. Hellebores form clumps and self-seed under suitable conditions. Most species develop rhizomes; the exception is Corsican hellebore, which cannot be cut back because of its unusual habit. Christmas rose appears to thrive and flower best when it receives ample water from spring to midsummer, followed by a dry period in late summer. Stinking hellebores are especially tolerant of dry shade. Hellebore roots are brittle; take special care when dividing, which is best done in early summer.

Helleborus niger

Hemerocallis (hem-er-o-KAL-lis)

DAYLILY

Hemerocallis 'Stella de Oro'

HARDINESS: Zones 3-10

FLOWERING SEASON: summer to fall

HEIGHT: 1 to 4 feet

FLOWER COLOR: all shades but blue

SOIL: moist, well-drained loam

LIGHT: full sun to partial shade

Daylilies produce dainty to bold flower trumpets with petals resembling those of true lilies. Their colors span the rainbow, with the exception of blue and pure white, and blooms are often bi- or tricolored. Sometimes with ruffled edges or double or even triple rows of petals, and occasionally fragrant, the flowers rise above mounds of grasslike, arching leaves on branched stems called scapes. Each flower lasts only one day, but each scape supports many buds that continue to open in succession for weeks, even months. Daylilies have been extensively hybridized, offering a wide choice of plant sizes, flower colors and styles, and periods of bloom. In some hybrids, the normal number of chromosomes has been doubled, giving rise to tetraploid daylilies with larger, more substantial flowers on more robust plants. Miniature varieties with smaller flowers on shortened scapes have also been bred.

Selected species and varieties
H. fulva (tawny daylily)—the common orange daylily found along roadsides; 6 to 12 orange flower trumpets per scape on vigorous, robust plants in large clumps; 'Kwanso Variegata' is a larger plant than

the species and produces double blooms; 'Rosea' has rose-colored flowers. *H. lilioasphodelus* (lemon daylily) [also known as *H. flava*]—lemon yellow 4-inch flowers on 2- to 3-foot scapes over clumps of slender dark green leaves up to 2 feet long; spreads rapidly by rhizomatous roots; 'Major' grows taller than the species and produces larger, deep yellow flowers. *H. hybrids*—yellow-gold hybrids include 'Golden Chimes', a miniature variety with gold-yellow flowers; 'Stella de Oro', another gold-yellow miniature that blooms from late spring until frost; 'Happy Returns', a hybrid offspring of 'Stella de Oro' with abundant, ruffled lemon yellow blooms and a similarly long flowering season; 'Little Cherub', 3½-inch light yellow flowers on 22-inch scapes over evergreen foliage; 'Alice in Wonderland', with 5½-inch ruffled lemon yellow flowers on 3-foot scapes and beautiful deep green foliage; 'Bountiful Valley', with 6-inch yellow blooms sporting lime green throats; 'Hyperion', an older variety still very popular for its fragrant, late-blooming yellow flowers on 4-foot scapes; 'Fall Glow', a shorter alternative with late, golden orange blooms.

Among red hybrids are 'Artist's Dream', a midseason tetraploid bearing red blooms with yellow midribs above a yellow-green throat; 'Anzac', true red blooms with yellow-green throats, 6 inches wide on 28-inch scapes; 'Cherry Cheeks', with cherry red petals lined by white midribs; 'Pardon Me', prolific producer of cerise flowers 2¾ inches across with green throats on 18-inch scapes; 'Autumn Red', sporting late-season red flowers with yellow-green throats.

Hemerocallis 'Grapeade'

Pink to purple hybrids include 'Country Club' and 'Peach Fairy', with pink-peach flowers; 'Joyful Occasion', 6-inch medium pink flowers with green throats and ruffled petals over evergreen foliage; 'Flower Basket', with coral pink double flowers; 'Catherine Woodbury', with pale lilac-pink flowers; and 'Grapeade', with green-throated purple blossoms.

Growing conditions and maintenance

Daylilies are among the least demanding of perennials, providing spectacular results with minimal care. Planted in groups, they spread to create a rugged ground cover that will suppress most weeds. Plant daylilies in spring or fall, spacing miniature varieties 18 to 24 inches apart, taller varieties 2 to 3 feet apart. Daylilies prefer sunny locations but adapt well to light shade. Light-colored flowers that fade in bright sun often show up better with some shade. Fertilize with an organic blend, if necessary, but do not overfeed, as this will cause rank growth and reduce flowering. Propagate by dividing clumps every 3 to 6 years.

Hemerocallis 'Artist's Dream'

Heuchera (HEW-ker-a)

ALUMROOT

Heuchera sanguinea

HARDINESS: Zones 4-8

FLOWERING SEASON: spring to summer

HEIGHT: 12 to 24 inches

FLOWER COLOR: white, pink, red

SOIL: moist, well-drained, rich loam

LIGHT: partial shade to full sun

The delicate, bell-shaped flowers of alumroot line slender upright stalks held above neat mounds of attractive evergreen leaves that can be rounded, triangular, or heart shaped.

Selected species and varieties

H. micrantha (small-flowered alumroot) —white flowers above gray-green heart-shaped leaves; 'Palace Purple' has dramatic, deep bronze leaves. *H. sanguinea* (coral bells)—the showiest of the genus, with red flowers persisting 4 to 8 weeks; 'Red Spangles' grows scarlet flowers on short stems; 'Chatterbox', rose pink flowers; 'Snowflakes', white flowers.

Growing conditions and maintenance

Space heuchera 1 to 1½ feet apart. Water well during dry spells. Plants tolerate full sun in cooler climates but prefer partial shade in warmer zones. Propagate from seed or by division every 3 years.

Hibiscus (hy-BIS-kus)

MALLOW, ROSE MALLOW

Hibiscus coccineus

HARDINESS: Zones 5-9

FLOWERING SEASON: summer

HEIGHT: 3 to 8 feet

FLOWER COLOR: pink, white, red

SOIL: moist to wet

LIGHT: full sun to partial shade

Found naturally in low meadows, swamps, and marshes, all of these perennial species bear very large bell-shaped flowers.

Selected species and varieties

H. coccineus (wild red mallow)—4 to 7 feet tall with blue-green leaves and scarlet flowers 6 inches across; Zones 7-9. *H. grandiflorus* (great rose mallow)—grows up to 6 feet tall and bears pale pink to purplish rose flowers, sometimes with crimson centers; Zones 7-9. *H. lasiocarpus* (woolly mallow)—3 to 5 feet tall with terminal clusters of 5- to 8-inch pink or white flowers that sometimes have purple centers; Zones 5-9. *H. moscheutos* (swamp rose mallow, wild cotton)—3 to 8 feet tall with a shrubby habit; gray-green leaves and white, pink, or rose flowers 8 inches across, often with red or purple centers; Zones 7-9.

Growing conditions and maintenance

Plant mallows in a moist spot where they will receive at least half a day's sun. Allow plenty of room between plants, which may spread to 5 feet in width. Propagate by seed or early summer cuttings.

PLANTAIN LILY

Hosta 'Krossa Regal'

HARDINESS: Zones 3-9

FLOWERING SEASON: summer

HEIGHT: 5 inches to 3 feet

FLOWER COLOR: white, lavender, violet

SOIL: moist, rich, acid loam

LIGHT: partial to bright full shade

Hostas are valued chiefly for their foliage—mounds of oval or heart-shaped green, blue, or gold leaves in a variety of sizes—but also produce tall, graceful spires of pale lilylike flowers during the summer. They are useful as edging or border plants, as ground covers, and in mass plantings. The variegated and light green forms make beautiful accent plants and brighten shady corners.

Selected species and varieties

H. decorata (blunt plantain lily)—1 to 2 feet tall, with white-edged leaves 3 to 8 inches long and dark blue flowers. *H. fortunei* (Fortune's hosta, giant plantain lily)—to 2 feet tall, with 5-inch-long oval leaves and pale lilac to violet flowers; 'Albomarginata' forms a 15- to 24-inch-high clump with white margins on 5-inch leaves. *H. lancifolia* (narrow-leaved plantain lily)—a 2-foot-high cascading mound of 4- to 6-inch-long leaf blades and 1- to 1½-inch blue-purple flowers in late summer; hardy to Zone 3. *H. plantaginea* (fragrant plantain lily)—fragrant pure white flowers 2½ inches wide open in late summer on 2½-foot stems above bright green heart-shaped foliage; Zones 3-8. *H. sie-*

boldiana (Siebold plantain lily)—2½ to 3 feet tall with 10- to 15-inch-long glaucous, gray to blue-green puckered leaves and lavender flowers that bloom amid the leaves in midsummer; hardy to Zone 3; 'Big Mama' has blue leaves and pale lavender flowers; 'Blue Umbrellas' grows 3 feet tall and 5 feet wide, with blue to blue-green leaves; 'Frances Williams', 32 inches tall and 40 inches wide with round, puckered, blue-green leaves having wide, irregular gold margins; var. *elegans* [also classified as *H. sieboldiana* 'Elegans'], 36 inches tall with lavender-white flowers and large, dark blue puckered leaves. *H. tardiflora* (autumn plantain lily)—glossy dark green medium-size leaves and large purple flowers on 1-foot scapes in fall. *H. tokudama*—18 inches tall and 40 inches wide, with puckered bluish leaves and white flowers in midsummer; 'Flavo-circinalis' grows to 18 inches tall and 50 inches wide with round, heavily puckered blue-green leaves that have irregular cream-and-yellow margins and white

Hosta 'Golden Tiara'

flowers in early summer. *H. undulata* var. *univittata* [also classified as *H. undulata* 'Univittata'] (wavy-leaf shade lily, snow feather funkia)—2 to 3 feet tall and 3 feet wide, with broad white centers in medium green leaves and lavender flowers. *H. venusta* (dwarf plantain lily, pretty plantain lily)—5 inches tall and 8 inches wide with medium green leaves and light purple flowers. *H.* hybrids—'August Moon', to 12 inches tall, with small yellow puckered leaves and midsummer white flowers; 'Fringe Benefit', 36 inches tall and 42 inches wide, with broad cream-colored margins on green heart-shaped leaves and pale

lavender flowers in early summer; 'Ginko Craig', an excellent ground cover, 10 inches tall with narrow, white-edged, dark green lance-shaped leaves and lavender flowers in midsummer; hardy to Zone 4; 'Golden Tiara', a low, compact mound 6 inches high and 16 to 20 inches wide bearing yellow-edged medium green heart-shaped leaves and purple flowers on 15-inch scapes in midsummer; 'Gold Standard', 15 inches tall with dark green margins on greenish gold leaves and lavender flowers on 3-foot scapes in mid- to late summer; 'Halcyon', 12 inches tall and 16 inches wide, with grayish blue heart-shaped leaves having wavy margins and distinct parallel veins and lilac-blue flowers blooming in late summer; 'Honeybells', fragrant lavender flowers and light green leaves to 2 feet tall; 'Krossa Regal', to 3 feet tall, with silvery blue leaves and 2- to 3-inch-long lavender flowers in late summer on 5-foot scapes; hardy to Zone 4; 'Royal Standard', full-sun-tolerant plant with fragrant white flowers on 30-inch stems in late summer to early fall; 'Shade Fanfare', lavender blooms on 2-foot scapes in midsummer above leaves with broad cream-colored margins.

Growing conditions and maintenance

Plant smaller hostas 1 foot apart, larger species 2 to 3 feet apart, in a moist but well-drained soil; wet soil in winter often damages plants. Water during dry spells. The blue forms need bright shade in order to hold color. *H. plantaginea* is tender until established; in the northern part of its range, mulch or cover during the first winter. Once established, hostas are long-lasting and need little attention.

Hosta sieboldiana 'Frances Williams'

Iberis (eye-BEER-is)

CANDYTUFT

Iberis sempervirens 'Snowmantle'

HARDINESS: Zones 4-8

FLOWERING SEASON: spring

HEIGHT: 6 to 12 inches

FLOWER COLOR: white

SOIL: moist, well-drained loam

LIGHT: full sun

The dark green leaves of candytuft are effective year round covering the ground before a perennial border, edging a walkway, or cascading over a stone wall. The delicate white flowers that cover the plant in spring are a delightful bonus.

Selected species and varieties
I. sempervirens—to 12 inches high and 24 inches wide, with a low, mounded habit, linear evergreen leaves 1 inch long, semi-woody stems, and very showy white flowers in dense clusters 1 inch across; 'Snowflake' grows 10 inches high, with 2- to 3-inch flower clusters; 'Snowmantle', 8 inches high, with a dense, compact habit.

Growing conditions and maintenance
Incorporate organic matter into the soil before planting candytuft. Space plants 12 to 15 inches apart. Protect the plant from severe winter weather with a loose mulch in colder zones. Cut it back at least 2 inches after it flowers to maintain vigorous growth.

Inula (IN-yew-la)

INULA

Inula ensifolia

HARDINESS: Zones 4-9

FLOWERING SEASON: summer

HEIGHT: 6 to 12 inches

FLOWER COLOR: yellow

SOIL: well-drained, average fertility

LIGHT: full sun to partial shade

Inula produces cheerful, bright yellow, daisylike flowers at the tips of wiry stems that form mounds.

Selected species and varieties
I. acaulis (stemless inula)—single yellow flowers borne on 6-inch stems in midsummer, over tufts of spatulate leaves 2 inches tall. *I. ensifolia* (swordleaf inula)—dense clumps, 12 inches tall and wide, of wiry, erect stems lined with narrow, pointed 4-inch leaves and tipped with 1- to 2-inch flowers. The blooms last 2 to 3 weeks in warmer zones, or up to 6 weeks in cooler areas.

Growing conditions and maintenance
Space inulas 1 foot apart in massed plantings. Propagate from seed or by division in spring or fall.

Kniphofia (ny-FO-fee-a)

TORCH LILY, TRITOMA

Kniphofia uvaria 'Robin Hood'

HARDINESS: Zones 5-9

FLOWERING SEASON: summer to fall

HEIGHT: 2 to 4 feet

FLOWER COLOR: red, orange, yellow, cream

SOIL: well-drained, sandy loam

LIGHT: full sun

Torch lily's stiff clusters of tubular flowers on bare stems held above tufts of stiff, gray-green leaves are a bold accent in a mixed border and a favorite visiting place of hummingbirds.

Selected species and varieties
K. uvaria (red-hot poker)—individual 1- to 2-inch flowers clustered along the top several inches of stem like a bristly bottle brush open a bright red then turn yellow as they mature.

Growing conditions and maintenance
Plant torch lilies 1½ to 2 feet apart in locations protected from strong winds. Propagate from seed, by division in spring, or by removing and transplanting the small offsets that develop at the base of plants. Plants grown from seed require 2 to 3 years to flower.

Lamium *(LAY-mee-um)*

DEAD NETTLE

Lamium maculatum 'White Nancy'

HARDINESS: Zones 4-8

FLOWERING SEASON: late spring to summer

HEIGHT: 8 to 24 inches

FLOWER COLOR: yellow, pink, violet, white

SOIL: moist, well-drained, average

LIGHT: partial to full shade

Dead nettle, so called because it does not sting like other nettles, is a vigorous, colorful ground cover with silvery foliage and flowers that bloom from late spring to summer. Several cultivars have been bred to be less weedy than the genus.

Selected species and varieties
L. galeobdolon [also listed as *Lamiastrum galeobdolon*] (yellow archangel)—to 2 feet tall with coarse-toothed 3-inch-long leaves and bright yellow blooms with brown marks; 'Herman's Pride' is 12 inches tall with green-and-silver leaves and yellow flowers; 'Variegata' has variegated green-and-silver leaves and yellow flowers. *L. maculatum* (spotted dead nettle)—to 18 inches high, with small, crinkled, spreading leaves that cover the ground; 'Beacon Silver' has greenish silver leaves with green margins and pink flowers; 'Chequers' is a heat-tolerant cultivar with dark green leaves bearing a silver center stripe and violet flowers; 'White Nancy' has greenish silver leaves and white flowers.

Growing conditions and maintenance
Dead nettle needs little care. *L. galeobdolon* tolerates deep to bright shade. *L. maculatum* needs bright to partial shade.

Lavandula *(lav-AN-dew-la)*

LAVENDER

Lavandula stoechas

HARDINESS: Zones 5-9

FLOWERING SEASON: summer

HEIGHT: 1 to 3 feet

FLOWER COLOR: lavender, purple, pink

SOIL: well-drained loam

LIGHT: full sun

Lavender forms neat cushions of erect stems lined with fragrant, willowy, gray or gray-green leaves tipped with spikes of tiny flowers. Lavender's attractive evergreen foliage blends into rock gardens or at the edges of borders and can be clipped into a low hedge.

Selected species and varieties
L. angustifolia (true lavender, English lavender)—whorls of lavender-to-purple ¼-inch flowers in summer on compact, round plants 1 to 2 feet tall; 'Hidcote' produces deep violet-blue flowers and silvery gray foliage. *L. latifolia* (spike lavender)—branched stalks of lavender-to-purple summer flowers above broader leaves than true lavender on plants to 2 feet tall. *L. stoechas* (French lavender)—dense whorls of tufted purple flowers in summer on plants to 3 feet tall.

Growing conditions and maintenance
Plant lavender 12 to 18 inches apart in soil that is not overly rich. Cut stems back to 8 inches in early spring to encourage compact growth and to remove old woody stems that produce few flowers. Propagate from seed or by division.

Lewisia *(loo-ISS-ee-a)*

BITTERROOT, LEWISIA

Lewisia cotyledon

HARDINESS: Zones 3-8

FLOWERING SEASON: spring, summer

HEIGHT: 4 to 12 inches

FLOWER COLOR: white, pink

SOIL: dry, rocky

LIGHT: partial shade

Lewisias are low-growing perennials that inhabit rocky slopes and open woods of the western United States. They are excellent choices for rock gardens.

Selected species and varieties
L. columbiana (bitterroot)—evergreen rosette of flat, dark green leaves with branched clusters of pink-veined white or pink flowers on 4- to 12-inch stalks in spring; Zones 4-8. *L. cotyledon* (broadleaf lewisia)—neat rosettes of spoon-shaped leaves and loose clusters of white or pink striped flowers on 12-inch stalks in early summer; Zones 6-8. *L. rediviva* (bitterroot)—rosette of cylindrical leaves appears in late summer and remains green over winter. In early spring showy rose-colored flowers up to 2 inches across are borne on short stems. After flowering the plant goes dormant; Zones 4-8.

Growing conditions and maintenance
Lewisias prefer partial shade and must have excellent drainage. A 1- to 2-inch mulch of gravel or stone chips is beneficial. Propagate by seed.

Liatris (ly-AY-tris)

SPIKE GAY-FEATHER

Liatris spicata 'Kobold'

HARDINESS: Zones 3-9

FLOWERING SEASON: summer to fall

HEIGHT: 18 inches to 5 feet

FLOWER COLOR: purple, pink, lavender, white

SOIL: sandy, well-drained

LIGHT: full sun to light shade

The flowers of spike gay-feather are borne on erect stems, and unlike most spike flowers the top buds open first and proceed downward. The effect is that of a feathery bottle brush. It provides a striking vertical accent in both the garden and indoor arrangements.

Selected species and varieties

L. pycnostachya (Kansas gay-feather)—bright purple flower spikes on 4- to 6-foot stems. *L. spicata*—usually 2 to 3 feet tall and 2 feet wide but may reach 5 feet tall. Leaves are narrow and tapered, up to 5 inches long, on erect, stout stems; flowers are purple or rose, borne closely along top of stem in mid to late summer; 'Kobold'—18- to 24-inch dwarf form, bright purple flowers, good for the front or middle of the herbaceous border.

Growing conditions and maintenance

Space gay-feathers 1 foot apart. Spike gay-feather prefers a light, well-drained soil and full sun but adapts to light shade and tolerates wet conditions better than other species of liatris. Tall types often need support; however, 'Kobold', with its stout habit, rarely requires staking.

Ligularia (lig-yew-LAY-ree-a)

GOLDEN-RAY

Ligularia dentata 'Desdemona'

HARDINESS: Zones 4-8

FLOWERING SEASON: summer

HEIGHT: 3 to 6 feet

FLOWER COLOR: yellow, orange

SOIL: moist loam or bog

LIGHT: full sun to partial shade

These coarse-textured plants develop into showy clumps of attractive, often variegated leaves up to 4 feet tall and as wide. Several species are also prized for their eye-catching flowers, some on stalks up to 6 feet tall.

Selected species and varieties

L. dentata (bigleaf golden-ray)—leathery, kidney-shaped leaves 20 inches wide forming lush mounds 3 to 4 feet high with yellow daisylike flowers on branched stalks; 'Desdemona' is more compact than the species, with leaf stems and undersides a striking mahogany red; 'Othello' is similar in color but less compact. *L.* 'Gregynog Gold'—heart-shaped leaves and bright orange flowers in conical spikes on stalks up to 6 feet tall. *L. stenocephala* 'The Rocket' [often listed under *L. przewalskii* or as a hybrid of the two species] (rocket ligularia)—light green leaves 8 to 12 inches wide with coarse-toothed edges in soft mounds punctuated by 4- to 6-foot stalks tipped with bright yellow flower spikes. *L. tussilaginea*—leathery leaves on woolly white stalks growing in clumps 2 feet tall, with clusters of pale yellow flowers on branched stems; 'Argentea' has leaves mottled gray-green, dark green, and cream; 'Aureomaculata' has leaves with yellow spots; Zones 7-10.

Growing conditions and maintenance

Plant ligularia 2 to 3 feet apart in cool, sunny, moist locations, a microclimate often best achieved alongside a pond or stream. Full sun may wilt leaves, but too much shade causes flowers to lean toward the light. Propagate both species and varieties by division in spring or fall; species can also be propagated from seed.

Ligularia przewalskii

Limonium (ly-MO-nee-um)

SEA LAVENDER

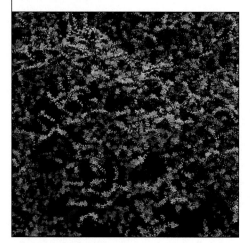

Limonium latifolium

HARDINESS: Zones 4-9

FLOWERING SEASON: summer

HEIGHT: 18 to 30 inches

FLOWER COLOR: lavender-blue to violet

SOIL: well-drained, slightly acid loam

LIGHT: full sun

Small, lacy flowers of sea lavender spread over the top of the plant like a cloud and persist for several weeks. The long-lasting flowers are outstanding in either fresh or dried arrangements.

Selected species and varieties

L. latifolium—branching flower stems carry an airy, rounded crown of lavender-blue blossoms above a tuft of leathery, oblong evergreen leaves; 'Blue Cloud' produces soft, light blue flowers; 'Violetta', deep violet.

Growing conditions and maintenance

Space plants 18 inches apart. Sea lavender tolerates seaside conditions. Extremely fertile soils produce weak branches that require staking. Propagate from seed or by division in the spring.

Linum (LY-num)

FLAX

Linum perenne

HARDINESS: Zones 5-9

FLOWERING SEASON: spring to summer

HEIGHT: 12 to 24 inches

FLOWER COLOR: blue, white, yellow

SOIL: well-drained, sandy loam

LIGHT: full sun to light shade

Delicate flax blooms prolifically with inch-wide, cup-shaped flowers held aloft on soft stems. Though blossoms last only one day, new buds open continuously for 6 weeks or more.

Selected species and varieties

L. flavum (golden flax)—bright yellow blossoms on stalks 1 to 1½ feet tall. *L. perenne* (perennial flax)—sky blue, saucer-shaped flowers on stems up to 2 feet tall; 'Diamant White' has abundant white blossoms on 12- to 18-inch stems.

Growing conditions and maintenance

Space flax plants 18 inches apart in groups of 6 or more for an effective display. Flax is a short-lived perennial but often reseeds itself. Propagate from seed or from stem cuttings taken in late spring or summer, after new growth hardens.

Liriope (li-RYE-o-pee)

LILYTURF

Liriope muscari 'Christmas Tree'

HARDINESS: Zones 4-10

FLOWERING SEASON: summer

HEIGHT: 18 inches

FLOWER COLOR: blue, purple, white

SOIL: moist to dry, well-drained, fertile

LIGHT: full sun to full shade

Tidy tufts of evergreen, grassy lilyturf leaves create dense ground covers or border edgings. Spikes of ¼-inch flowers in whorls lining erect flower stalks held above the leaves are followed by attractive blue-black berries.

Selected species and varieties

L. muscari (big blue lilyturf)—grasslike leaves ½ inch wide and up to 18 inches long with deep blue summer flowers; 'Christmas Tree' has conical spikes of lilac flowers; 'Majestic', large violet-blue blossoms in heavy clusters; 'Monroe's White', white flowers; 'Variegata', yellow-edged new foliage.

Growing conditions and maintenance

Plant lilyturf in any light conditions; a sunny spot will produce more flowers. Foliage may suffer winter burn in colder areas; shear to the ground as new growth begins in the spring. Propagate by division in spring.

Lobelia (lo-BEE-lee-a)

CARDINAL FLOWER

Lobelia cardinalis

HARDINESS: Zones 3-9

FLOWERING SEASON: summer

HEIGHT: 2 to 4 feet

FLOWER COLOR: red, pink, white, blue

SOIL: moist, fertile loam

LIGHT: light shade

Cardinal flower bears spires of intensely colored tubular blossoms with drooping lips on stiff stems rising from rosettes of dark green leaves. Opening in mid- to late summer, the flowers last 2 to 3 weeks; they are followed by seed capsules shaped like buttons.

Selected species and varieties
L. cardinalis (red lobelia)—1½-inch scarlet blossoms on 3-foot-tall flower stalks; pink and white varieties available. *L. siphilitica* (great blue lobelia)—1-inch-long blue flowers persist a month or more. 'Alba' has white flowers.

Growing conditions and maintenance
Plant lobelia 12 inches apart in locations with adequate moisture and in soil with ample organic matter. Lobelia will grow in full sun with sufficient moisture. Though short-lived, it self-sows freely. It can also be propagated by division in early fall. Lobelias are suited to moist-soil gardens, and do well alongside ponds and streams.

Lupinus (loo-PY-nus)

LUPINE

Lupinus 'Russell Hybrids'

HARDINESS: Zones 4-6

FLOWERING SEASON: summer

HEIGHT: 3 to 4 feet

FLOWER COLOR: all shades

SOIL: moist, well-drained, acid

LIGHT: full sun to light shade

Lupine's elongated spikes of small, butterfly-shaped flowers at the tips of stiff stalks lined with whorls of narrow leaves dramatically embellish the flower border. The stalks grow in clumps that can be used as accents or massed effectively.

Selected species and varieties
L. 'Russell Hybrids'—plants to 4 feet tall with showy 18- to 24-inch-long summer-blooming flower spires that open from the bottom up in a multitude of colors and combinations; dwarf strains 1½ feet tall include 'Little Lulu' and 'Minarette'.

Growing conditions and maintenance
Plant lupines in acidic soil enriched with organic matter. Lupines will not tolerate hot summers. Plants may require staking. Propagate from seed or from root cuttings taken with a small piece of crown in early spring.

Lychnis (LIK-nis)

CATCHFLY, CAMPION

Lychnis chalcedonica

HARDINESS: Zones 4-9

FLOWERING SEASON: summer

HEIGHT: 1 to 3 feet

FLOWER COLOR: red, pink, purple, white

SOIL: moist, well-drained, fertile loam

LIGHT: full sun to partial shade

Lychnis bears intensely colored flowers singly or in clusters on slender stems with airy foliage.

Selected species and varieties
L. x *arkwrightii* (Arkwright campion)—orange-red flowers contrast with bronze foliage. *L. chalcedonica* (Maltese cross)—4-inch clusters of scarlet flowers on 3- to 4-foot stems. *L. coronaria* (rose campion)—cerise flowers amid woolly gray-green leaves. *L. viscaria* (German catchfly)—magenta flowers on sticky 12-inch stems above tufts of grasslike leaves; 'Flore Pleno' grows deep pink to magenta double flowers; 'Splendens Plena', double rose pink flowers; 'Zulu', red blooms.

Growing conditions and maintenance
Plant lychnis 1 to 1½ feet apart. Rose campion self-sows. Other lychnises can be propagated from seed or by division.

Lysimachia (ly-sim-MAK-ee-a)

LOOSESTRIFE

Lysimachia clethroides

HARDINESS: Zones 4-8

FLOWERING SEASON: spring to summer

HEIGHT: 2 inches to 3 feet

FLOWER COLOR: white, yellow

SOIL: moist, fertile loam

LIGHT: full sun to partial shade

Loosestrife varies in habit from low-growing ground covers to medium-tall, erect clumps. Flowers bloom singly or in small spikes amid attractive foliage. [NOTE: Most species are quite invasive and should be contained when planted.]

Selected species and varieties

L. clethroides (gooseneck loosestrife)—white, arched flower spikes on 3-foot stems. *L. nummularia* (moneywort, creeping Jenny)—2- to 4-inch-tall creeper with ¾-inch yellow flowers amid small round leaves; 'Aurea' has yellow leaves. *L. punctata* (yellow loosestrife)—clusters of bright yellow ¾-inch flowers in the leaf axils along 18- to 30-inch stems.

Growing conditions and maintenance

Plant 2 feet apart. Loosestrife naturalizes easily, particularly alongside streams or in swampy areas. Propagate from seed or by division.

Macleaya (mak-LAY-a)

PLUME POPPY

Macleaya cordata

HARDINESS: Zones 3-8

FLOWERING SEASON: summer

HEIGHT: 6 to 10 feet

FLOWER COLOR: cream

SOIL: moist, well-drained

LIGHT: full sun

Plume poppy's massive clumps of foliage, growing almost as wide as high, develop into imposing, shrubby specimens at the back of a border, as temporary screens, or as an anchor in the center of an island bed. Feathery clusters of tiny flowers bloom at the tips of erect stems lined with broad, deeply lobed leaves that cover the plants, producing a frothy effect.

Selected species and varieties

M. cordata (tree celandine)—creamy ½-inch flowers above gray-green leaves up to 1 foot across with wavy edges and silvery undersides.

Growing conditions and maintenance

Plant plume poppies 3 to 4 feet apart. Shady conditions and fertile soils will accentuate their invasive tendencies. Propagate from seed, by division in spring, or by transplanting plantlets that develop along the roots.

Malva (MAL-va)

MALLOW

Malva alcea

HARDINESS: Zones 4-8

FLOWERING SEASON: summer to fall

HEIGHT: 1 to 4 feet

FLOWER COLOR: pink, white

SOIL: dry to moist, well-drained loam

LIGHT: full sun to partial shade

Mallows produce a profusion of satiny flowers with notched petals, growing throughout the summer and often into the fall above finely cut, bushy foliage.

Selected species and varieties

M. alcea 'Fastigiata' (hollyhock mallow)—2-inch pink blossoms on 3- to 4-foot-tall stems. *M. moschata* (musk mallow)—white or rose flowers on plants 1 to 3 feet tall; 'Alba' has white blossoms; 'Rosea', mauve-pink.

Growing conditions and maintenance

Plant mallows 2 feet apart. Although these drought-tolerant plants are short-lived, they often self-sow. Propagate by division in spring or fall.

Mertensia (mer-TEN-see-a)

BLUEBELLS

Mertensia virginica

HARDINESS: Zones 3-8

FLOWERING SEASON: spring to summer

HEIGHT: 1 to 3 feet

FLOWER COLOR: blue

SOIL: moist, acid, rich

LIGHT: full sun to full shade

Mertensias are perennials native to stream banks, moist woods, and damp meadows. Their bell-shaped blue flowers hang in clusters from the ends of leafy stems.

Selected species and varieties
M. ciliata (mountain bluebells)—1 to 3 feet tall with loose clusters of pink buds opening to sky blue, lightly fragrant flowers from late spring through summer; produces a clump of stems with smooth, succulent 2- to 6-inch leaves; native to western mountains; Zones 3-8. *M. virginica* (Virginia bluebells)—up to 2 feet tall with clusters of lavender-blue flowers in spring and attractive gray-green oval leaves 2 to 5 inches long. The plant disappears after flowering; Zones 3-7.

Growing conditions and maintenance
Mertensias thrive in acid soil with abundant moisture. Add organic matter to the soil before planting. *M. ciliata* adapts to full sun to partial shade, and *M. virginica* requires partial to full shade. Propagate by seed or division.

Mimulus (MIM-yew-lus)

MONKEY FLOWER

Mimulus lewisii

HARDINESS: Zones 3-10

FLOWERING SEASON: spring, summer, fall

HEIGHT: 1 to 4 feet

FLOWER COLOR: red, yellow, pink

SOIL: moist

LIGHT: full sun to partial shade

Among the monkey flowers are several perennials that grow along stream banks and in moist meadows in the West. Their brightly colored funnel-shaped flowers have a two-lobed upper lip and a three-lobed lower lip.

Selected species and varieties
M. cardinalis (scarlet monkey flower)—2 to 4 feet tall with brilliant orange-red flowers from spring through fall. The lower lip of the flower is swept backward and has a patch of yellow; Zones 7-10. *M. guttatus* (golden monkey flower)—2 to 3 feet tall with yellow snapdragon-like flowers spotted with purple on the lower lip in spring and summer; Zones 6-10. *M. lewisii* (Lewis monkey flower)—1 to 2½ feet tall with pink to rose red flowers often marked with darker lines or maroon blotches in the throat; Zones 3-9.

Growing conditions and maintenance
Monkey flowers thrive in partial shade in moist soil. Golden monkey flower also grows in full sun, though its flowers last longer with afternoon shade. It can be grown as an annual in cooler climates. Propagate from seed or by dividing the clumps.

Mirabilis (my-RAB-i-lis)

WILD FOUR-O'CLOCK

Mirabilis multiflora

HARDINESS: Zones 5-10

FLOWERING SEASON: spring to summer

HEIGHT: 1½ to 3 feet

FLOWER COLOR: pink, purple, magenta

SOIL: dry, rocky

LIGHT: full sun

Among the four-o'clocks are several perennials native to dry areas of the western United States. The tubular flowers open in the afternoon and close the following morning. They are lovely massed as a ground cover or trailing over a wall.

Selected species and varieties
M. froebelii (wild four-o'clock, wishbone plant)—numerous clusters of 1½- to 2¼-inch-long deep rose pink to reddish purple flowers at the ends of much-branched stems up to 3 feet; Zones 7-10. *M. multiflora* (wild four-o'clock)—up to 18 inches with magenta tubular flowers about 2 inches long and leaves that are dark green; Zones 5-10.

Growing conditions and maintenance
Four-o'clocks are easily grown, long-lived drought-tolerant perennials. Supplemental watering during dry periods will extend the flowering season. Propagate by seed or divide roots in the fall.

Monarda (mo-NAR-da)

BEE BALM

Monarda didyma

HARDINESS: Zones 4-9

FLOWERING SEASON: summer

HEIGHT: 2 to 4 feet

FLOWER COLOR: red, purple, pink, white

SOIL: moist or dry loam

LIGHT: full sun to light shade

Bee balm has fragrant leaves and shaggy clusters of tiny tubular flowers growing on square stems. Attractive to bees, butterflies, and hummingbirds, these plants are easily cultivated.

Selected species and varieties

M. didyma—scarlet flowers on 3- to 4-foot stems; 'Cambridge Scarlet', wine red flowers; 'Croftway Pink', rose pink; 'Mahogany', dark red; 'Marshall's Delight', mildew resistant, with pink flowers on 2-foot stems; 'Blue Stocking', violet-blue; 'Snow Queen', white. *M. fistulosa* (wild bergamot)—lilac to pink flower clusters on plants up to 4 feet tall. *M. punctata* (spotted bee balm)—yellow blossoms with purple spots.

Growing conditions and maintenance

Allow 1½ to 2 feet between plants. They thrive in moist areas, although wild bergamot and spotted bee balm tolerate dry conditions. Propagate from seed or from cuttings; divide every two to three years in the spring to maintain vigor. Thin plant occasionally for air circulation and to avoid mildew.

Nepeta (NEP-e-ta)

CATMINT

Nepeta mussinii 'Blue Wonder'

HARDINESS: Zones 3-9

FLOWERING SEASON: summer

HEIGHT: 1 to 3 feet

FLOWER COLOR: lavender-blue, white

SOIL: average, well-drained loam

LIGHT: full sun

Catmint forms loose cushions of fragrant stems lined with soft, oval, pointed leaves and tipped with spikes of tiny white, mauve, or blue flower whorls that form a haze of color above the foliage. The plant is effective massed as a ground cover.

Selected species and varieties

N. x faassenii (blue catmint)—18- to 36-inch-high mounds of silvery gray foliage with lavender-blue spring-to-summer-blooming flowers; 'Six Hills Giant' grows taller and is more robust than the species. *N. mussinii* (Persian catmint)—sprawling 1-foot-high mounds with lavender summer flowers; 'Blue Wonder' has deep blue blossoms on compact plants to 15 inches.

Growing conditions and maintenance

Plant catmint 1 to 1½ feet apart in any well-drained soil. It can be invasive. Shearing plants after flowering may produce a second season of bloom. Propagate blue catmint from cuttings, Persian catmint from seed, and either species by division.

Oenothera (ee-no-THEE-ra)

SUNDROP

Oenothera fruticosa

HARDINESS: Zones 4-8

FLOWERING SEASON: summer

HEIGHT: 6 to 24 inches

FLOWER COLOR: yellow, pink, white

SOIL: well-drained loam

LIGHT: full sun

Showy, saucer-shaped flowers bloom on sundrops during the day and on evening primroses (night-blooming oenothera) at night.

Selected species and varieties

O. fruticosa (common sundrop)—prolific clusters of 1- to 2-inch bright yellow flowers at the tips of 18- to 24-inch stems. *O. missouriensis* (Ozark sundrop)—large 5-inch yellow flowers on 6- to 12-inch plants. *O. speciosa* (showy evening primrose)—white or pink blossoms on spreading stems that grow 6 to 18 inches tall. *O. tetragona*—yellow flowers similar to those of *O. fruticosa* but with young buds and stems tinted red.

Growing conditions and maintenance

Plant Ozark sundrops 2 feet apart, other species 12 to 18 inches apart. Propagate Ozark sundrops from seed, other species either from seed or by division.

Ophiopogon (o-fi-o-PO-gon)

DWARF MONDO GRASS

Ophiopogon japonicus

HARDINESS: Zones 7-9

FLOWERING SEASON: summer

HEIGHT: 6 to 12 inches

FLOWER COLOR: blue

SOIL: moist, well-drained

LIGHT: full sun to partial shade

Dense clumps of grasslike leaves make dwarf mondo grass an excellent ground cover or edging for a bed. It is similar in appearance to liriope but smaller and less hardy. Stems of light blue flowers are produced in the summer, followed by metallic blue berries, though both flowers and fruit are somewhat hidden among the leaves.

Selected species and varieties
O. japonicus—6 to 12 inches tall, leaves are dark, evergreen, arching, 8 to 16 inches long, plant spreads by underground runners, tiny individual flowers are lilac-blue and grow in clusters on short stems, steel blue fruit is pea size.

Growing conditions and maintenance
Dwarf mondo grass is adaptable to sun or partial shade, though it prefers some protection from hot afternoon sun. It can be grown under trees and is useful for controlling erosion on slopes. Cut back foliage in early spring before new growth begins. Propagate by dividing the clumps.

Osteospermum (os-tee-o-SPER-mum)

AFRICAN DAISY

Osteospermum fruticosum

HARDINESS: Zones 9-10

FLOWERING SEASON: early spring and intermittently throughout the year

HEIGHT: 6 to 12 inches

FLOWER COLOR: purple, white

SOIL: well-drained

LIGHT: full sun

The African daisy is a flowering ground cover for warm zones. It has a trailing habit and spreads rapidly to create a dense mat. Flowers bloom most heavily in late winter and early spring, and intermittently throughout the rest of the year. It makes a lovely show in containers or behind stone walls where it can spill over the edges.

Selected species and varieties
O. fruticosum—6 to 12 inches tall with 3-foot spread, stems root where they touch the ground, oval leaves are 1 to 2 inches long, flowers are lavender with purple centers, fading to white, 2 inches across; 'Hybrid White'—more upright habit, white flowers; 'African Queen'—purple blooms.

Growing conditions and maintenance
Because the stems root as they grow along the ground, the African daisy is well suited to covering large areas. It thrives in full sun and, once established, tolerates drought. Cut back old plants occasionally to encourage branching and to prevent stems from becoming straggly.

Pachysandra (pak-i-SAN-dra)

PACHYSANDRA

Pachysandra terminalis

HARDINESS: Zones 5-9

FLOWERING SEASON: early spring

HEIGHT: 6 to 12 inches

FLOWER COLOR: white, pink

SOIL: moist, well-drained, acid

LIGHT: partial to full shade

Pachysandra is a spreading ground cover whose dark green leaves provide a lush carpet beneath trees and shrubs. In early spring, short flower spikes rise from the center of each whorl of leaves.

Selected species and varieties
P. procumbens (Allegheny pachysandra, Allegheny spurge)—6 to 12 inches tall, 12 inches wide, leaves are deciduous in cooler zones and semievergreen to evergreen in mild areas, 2 to 4 inches long, prominently toothed, blue-green, often with gray or purple mottling, flowers are white or pink on 2- to 4-inch spikes. *P. terminalis* (Japanese pachysandra)—6 to 8 inches tall, 12 to 18 inches wide, leaves are evergreen, dark, 2 to 4 inches long, flowers are white on 1- to 2-inch spikes.

Growing conditions and maintenance
Pachysandra thrives in the shade; given too much sun, leaves will yellow. It grows well beneath trees. Incorporate organic matter into the soil prior to planting. Space plants 8 to 10 inches apart for a ground cover, and keep new plantings uniformly moist.

Paeonia (pee-O-nee-a)

PEONY

Paeonia lactiflora

HARDINESS: Zones 3-8

FLOWERING SEASON: spring to summer

HEIGHT: 18 to 36 inches

FLOWER COLOR: white, pink, red

SOIL: well-drained, fertile loam

LIGHT: full sun to light shade

Peonies are long-lived perennials beloved for their large, showy flowers and attractive foliage. Dramatic in the garden, they are stunning in bouquets. Peony flowers are classified by their form. Single-flower peonies have a single row of five or more petals surrounding a center of bright yellow stamens. Japanese and anemone peonies have a single row of petals surrounding modified stamens that resemble finely cut petals. Semidouble peonies have several rows of petals surrounding conspicuous stamens. Double-flowered peonies have multiple rows of petals crowded into ruffly hemispheres.

Selected species and varieties
P. lactiflora (garden or Chinese peony)—white, pink, or red flowers on 3-foot stems. *P. mlokosewitschii* (Caucasian peony)—very early blooming, 2-inch single lemon yellow flowers on 2-foot-tall stems with soft gray-green foliage. *P. officinalis* (common peony)—hundreds of varieties with 3- to 6-inch blooms in various forms and colors from red to light pink to white on 2-foot stems. *P. tenuifolia* (fern-leaf peony)—single deep red flowers and finely divided, fernlike leaves on 18- to 24-inch stems; 'Flore Pleno' has double flowers.

Hundreds of peony hybrids are available. 'Lobata' (red-pink), 'Lotus Bloom' (pink), and 'Krinkled White' are outstanding singles. 'Isani-Gidui' (white) and 'Nippon Beauty' (dark red) are lovely Japanese types. 'Gay Paree' (pink with white-blush center) grows anemone-type blossoms. Semidouble varieties include 'Ludovica' (salmon pink) and 'Lowell Thomas' (deep red). Among the double-flowered varieties, 'Festiva Maxima' (white with red marking), 'Red Charm' (deep true red, early blooming), 'Mons. Jules Elie' (early, pink), 'Karl Rosenfeld' (deep red), and 'Nick Shaylor' (pink) are all exceptional.

Growing conditions and maintenance
Plant peonies 3 feet apart in soil containing some organic matter. Set the buds (eyes) 2 inches below the soil surface; setting them deeper delays flowering. Propagate by dividing clumps in late summer-early fall into sections containing three to five eyes each.

Paeonia mlokosewitschii

Papaver (pap-AY-ver)

POPPY

Papaver orientale

HARDINESS: Zones 3-9

FLOWERING SEASON: spring to summer

HEIGHT: 1 to 4 feet

FLOWER COLOR: red, pink, orange, yellow, white

SOIL: well-drained loam

LIGHT: full sun to partial shade

Poppies bear large, brilliantly colored, silky-textured blossoms on wiry stems above finely cut leaves. The blooms open from nodding buds and last several weeks.

Selected species and varieties
P. nudicaule (Iceland poppy)—fragrant flowers up to 3 inches across on 12- to 24-inch stems. *P. orientale* (Oriental poppy)—blossoms up to 8 inches across composed of tissue-thin petals on wiry stems rising from mounds of coarse, hairy leaves; 'Glowing Embers' has orange-red ruffled petals; 'Mrs. Perry', clear pink flowers; 'Beauty of Livermore', deep red petals spotted black at the base; 'Princess Victoria Louise', bright salmon-pink flowers.

Growing conditions and maintenance
Space poppies 1½ feet apart. Propagate Oriental poppies, which are tough, long-lived plants, from seed or from root cuttings. Grow Iceland poppies from seed to flower in their first year; sow in late summer in the North and in fall in southern climates.

Patrinia (pat-RIN-ee-a)

PATRINIA

Patrinia scabiosifolia

HARDINESS: Zones 5-9

FLOWERING SEASON: late summer and fall

HEIGHT: 2 to 6 feet

FLOWER COLOR: yellow

SOIL: moist, well-drained

LIGHT: full sun to light shade

Patrinia produces large, airy sprays of flowers late in the summer and fall. These are followed by bright yellow seed pods on orange stems. It is well suited to the middle or rear of a perennial border or a natural garden, where it combines particularly well with ornamental grasses. Patrinia flowers can be cut for long-lasting indoor arrangements.

Selected species and varieties

P. scabiosifolia—3 to 6 feet tall, leaves are ruffled, pinnately divided, 6 to 10 inches, and form a large, basal mound, yellow flowers form 2-inch clusters held well above foliage, long-lasting, late summer and fall bloom; 'Nagoya'—2 to 3 feet, compact habit, flowers are almost fluorescent yellow.

Growing conditions and maintenance

Plant patrinias in moist, well-drained soil in sun or light shade. Taller types often require staking. Once established, patrinias are long-lived perennials. They self-sow; to avoid an excess of plants, remove fading flowers before seed is released. They rarely need to be divided.

Penstemon (pen-STEE-mon)

BEARDTONGUE

Penstemon digitalis

HARDINESS: Zones 3-10

FLOWERING SEASON: spring, summer, fall

HEIGHT: 1 to 5 feet

FLOWER COLOR: white, pink, lavender, blue, purple

SOIL: well-drained, sandy

LIGHT: full sun to partial shade

Penstemons are perennials with showy terminal clusters of brightly colored two-lipped flowers. Most species are natives of the sunny plains and prairies of the Midwest. Good drainage is essential for all penstemons.

Selected species and varieties

P. ambiguus (sand penstemon)—1-inch white to pink flowers on a symmetrical mounded plant 1 to 4 feet tall and up to 3 feet wide. Blooms most heavily in late spring, with sporadic flowers through fall; Zones 5-9. *P. canescens* (gray beardtongue)—pale lavender to white flowers in early summer on erect stems to 2 feet tall; Zones 5-7. *P. cobaea* (cobaea penstemon, giant foxglove)—flowers 2 to 3 inches long on 1- to 2-foot stems rising from a rosette of leaves. Flower color ranges from white to pale pink, lavender, and purple, with dark purple markings in the throats; Zones 5-8. *P. digitalis* (beardtongue, white penstemon)—3 to 5 feet tall with white or pinkish flowers on erect purplish stems in early summer; eastern to central United States; Zones 3-8. *P. grandiflorus* (large-flowered penstemon)—pink to lavender flowers on stout unbranched 2- to 4-foot stems with waxy blue-green leaves in late spring and summer; Zones 3-9. *P. heterophyllus* (foothill penstemon)—a profusion of 1-inch blue or violet flowers in late spring and early summer on a neat, shrubby plant to 1½ feet in height that is evergreen in mild climates and can tolerate drought and heat; California; Zones 8-10. *P. smallii* (Small's beardtongue)—rose to dark pink white-throated flowers in spring on branching stems 1½ to 2½ feet tall above a rosette of shiny dark-veined leaves that turn reddish in fall; southern Appalachian Mountains; Zones 7-9. *P. strictus* (Rocky Mountain penstemon)—deep blue to purple flowers from late spring to early summer on 1- to 3-foot stems above a mat of evergreen foliage; Zones 4-5.

Growing conditions and maintenance

Plant these species in sandy, well-drained soil. All are adapted to full sun, and *P. smallii* also thrives in partial shade. Since penstemons are usually short-lived, leave some fading flowers in place to produce seed so the plants can self-sow. Propagate from seed after moist-stratification.

Penstemon smallii

Perovskia (per-OV-skee-a)

RUSSIAN SAGE

Perovskia atriplicifolia

HARDINESS: Zones 5-9

FLOWERING SEASON: summer

HEIGHT: 3 to 4 feet

FLOWER COLOR: lavender-blue

SOIL: well-drained loam

LIGHT: full sun

Russian sage's shrubby mounds of fine-textured, deeply toothed aromatic gray foliage are an effective filler in the border and remain attractive through winter. In summer, spires of tiny lavender flowers tip each stem. They combine particularly well with ornamental grasses. Planted in a mass, Russian sage develops into a summer hedge, and the stems remain attractive through the winter.

Selected species and varieties
P. atriplicifolia (azure sage)—tubular, two-lipped lavender flowers growing in whorls, spaced along 12-inch flower spikes above downy gray, finely divided leaves. Clumps of woody stems grow to 4 feet tall and as wide. 'Blue Spire' is upright with violet-blue flowers.

Growing conditions and maintenance
Space Russian sage plants 2 to 3 feet apart in full sun; shade causes floppy, sprawling growth. Soil should not be overly rich. Cut woody stems to the ground in spring before new growth begins. Propagate by seed or from summer cuttings.

Phlox (flox)

PHLOX

Phlox divaricata 'Fuller's White'

HARDINESS: Zones 3-9

FLOWERING SEASON: spring, summer, or fall

HEIGHT: 3 inches to 4 feet

FLOWER COLOR: pink, purple, red, blue, white

SOIL: sandy and dry to moist, fertile loam

LIGHT: full sun to full shade

Versatile phlox produces flat, five-petaled flowers, either singly or in clusters, many with a conspicuous eye at the center. There is a species suitable for nearly every combination of soil and light, as well as for nearly any landscape use, from 3-inch creepers to upright border plants that grow up to 4 feet tall.

Selected species and varieties
P. divaricata (wild blue phlox)—blue blossoms on 12-inch-tall creepers; 'Fuller's White' has creamy white flowers. *P. maculata* (wild sweet William)—elegant, cylindrical flower heads in shades of pink to white on 3-foot plants; 'Miss Lingard' [sometimes listed as a variety of *P. carolina*] has 6-inch trusses of pure white blossoms; 'Omega', white petals surrounding a lilac-colored eye; 'Alpha', rose pink petals around a darker pink eye. *P. paniculata* (summer phlox, garden phlox)—magnificent pyramidal clusters of white, pink, red, lavender, or purple flowers on 2- to 4-foot stems; 'Fujiyama' has white flower heads 12 to 15 inches long; 'Bright Eyes', pale pink petals surrounding a crimson eye; 'Orange Perfection', salmon orange blossoms; 'Starfire', cherry red. *P. stolonifera*

(creeping phlox)—blue, white, or pink flowers on creeping 6- to 12-inch stems with evergreen leaves that form a dense ground cover; 'Blue Ridge' produces clear blue flowers; 'Bruce's White', white flowers with yellow eyes. *P. subulata* (moss phlox, moss pink)—bears white, pink, blue, lavender, or red flowers above dense clumps of evergreen foliage 3 to 6 inches tall and 2 feet wide.

Growing conditions and maintenance
Space lower-growing phlox 1 to 1½ feet apart, taller species up to 2 feet apart. Wild blue phlox grows well in shady, moist sites; moss phlox thrives in sunny, dry spots. Creeping phlox grows in sun or shade. Both moss phlox and creeping phlox form lush mats of evergreen foliage and make wonderful ground covers. Wild sweet William and summer phlox thrive in full sun, provided they receive ample moisture during the growing season. Space summer phlox for good air circulation to avoid powdery mildew. Propagate phlox by division. Promote dense growth and reblooming by cutting plants back after flowering.

Phlox subulata

Phormium (FOR-mee-um)

FLAX LILY

Phormium tenax

HARDINESS: Zones 9-10

FLOWERING SEASON: summer

HEIGHT: 7 to 15 feet

FLOWER COLOR: red

SOIL: moist, well-drained

LIGHT: full sun

Dramatic fans of stiff, evergreen leaves, sometimes split at their ends or edged with red, make phormium a bold specimen or an effective screen. Tall flower stalks lined with dull red 2-inch flowers rise above the foliage.

Selected species and varieties

P. tenax (New Zealand flax)—leathery leaves 6 to 10 feet tall with flower stalks to 15 feet; 'Atropurpureum' produces rich purple leaves; 'Bronze', deep red-brown leaves; 'Maori Sunrise' bears bronze leaves striped pink and cream; 'Tiny Tim' is a semidwarf cultivar with yellow-striped bronze leaves; 'Variegatum' has creamy white striping on green leaves.

Growing conditions and maintenance

Plant New Zealand flax in soil enriched with organic matter. Plants tolerate seaside conditions and pollution. Propagate from seed or by division.

Physostegia (fy-so-STEE-gee-a)

FALSE DRAGONHEAD

Physostegia virginiana

HARDINESS: Zones 4-8

FLOWERING SEASON: late summer to fall

HEIGHT: 2 to 4 feet

FLOWER COLOR: pink, purple, white

SOIL: moist or dry acid loam

LIGHT: full sun to partial shade

False dragonhead produces unusual 8- to 10-inch flower spikes with four evenly spaced vertical rows of blossoms resembling snapdragons.

Selected species and varieties

P. virginiana—pink flowers tipping each stem in clumps of 4-foot stalks; 'Variegata' has pink flowers above green-and-white variegated leaves; 'Vivid', rosy pink blossoms on compact plants only 20 inches tall; 'Summer Snow', early-blooming white flowers.

Growing conditions and maintenance

Plant false dragonhead 1½ to 2 feet apart. It is so tolerant of varying growing conditions that it can become invasive. Propagate the plants from seed or by division every 2 years.

Platycodon (plat-i-KO-don)

BALLOON FLOWER

Platycodon grandiflorus

HARDINESS: Zones 4-9

FLOWERING SEASON: summer

HEIGHT: 10 to 36 inches

FLOWER COLOR: blue, white, pink

SOIL: well-drained, acid loam

LIGHT: full sun to partial shade

The balloon flower derives its common name from the fat, inflated flower buds it produces. These pop open into spectacular cup-shaped 2- to 3-inch-wide blossoms with pointed petals.

Selected species and varieties

P. grandiflorus—deep blue flowers on slender stems above neat clumps of blue-green leaves; 'Album' has white flowers; 'Shell Pink', pale pink flowers; 'Mariesii' is a compact variety 18 inches tall with bright blue flowers. 'Double Blue' has bright blue double flowers on 2-foot stems.

Growing conditions and maintenance

Space balloon flowers 18 inches apart. Pink varieties develop the best color when they are grown in partial shade. Propagate from seed to flower the second year or by division.

Podophyllum (po-doh-FIL-um)

MAY APPLE

Podophyllum peltatum

HARDINESS: Zones 3-9

FLOWERING SEASON: spring

HEIGHT: 12 to 18 inches

FLOWER COLOR: white, whitish pink

SOIL: moist, well-drained, slightly acid, fertile

LIGHT: full to dappled shade

This woodland wildflower bears huge, deeply lobed leaves up to 1 foot wide and nodding six- to nine-petaled, 2-inch-wide white flowers that arise in spring at the joint between two leaves. Flowers mature into 1- to 2-inch berries. The common May apple quickly spreads to form large colonies that may be invasive. The foliage dies down in summer. The seeds, stem, and root are poisonous, but the fruits are said to be edible, though not palatable.

Selected species and varieties

P. hexandrum (Himalayan May apple)—clumped stems 12 to 18 inches tall, with six-petaled white to pink flowers that bloom before the three- to five-lobed 10-inch leaves unfurl. *P. peltatum* (common May apple, wild mandrake, raccoon berry) —leaves start developing before the flowers, which are often hidden by the foliage and are followed by yellow fruit.

Growing conditions and maintenance

Often found in boggy, low-lying areas near woodland streams, May apple thrives in constantly moist soil to which leaf mold has been added. Propagate by dividing in late summer or fall. Mulch with leaf litter in winter.

Polemonium (po-le-MO-nee-um)

JACOB'S-LADDER

Polemonium viscosum

HARDINESS: Zones 2-9

FLOWERING SEASON: spring, summer

HEIGHT: 4 to 36 inches

FLOWER COLOR: pink, purple, blue, white

SOIL: moist to rocky, well-drained, rich

LIGHT: full sun to partial shade

The polemoniums are natives of meadows, open woodlands, and stream banks. Their dark green compound leaves provide an attractive foil for their upward-facing, cup-shaped flowers.

Selected species and varieties

P. carneum (royal polemonium)—1 to 2 feet tall with clusters of purple, pink, or salmon flowers 1½ inches across from spring through summer; California and Oregon; Zones 7-9. *P. occidentale* [also called *P. caeruleum* ssp. *amygdalinum*] (western polemonium)—to 3 feet with clusters of pale blue summer flowers; Alaska to Colorado; Zones 3-9. *P. reptans* (creeping polemonium)—to 2 feet with large clusters of blue or pink flowers from spring to summer; eastern United States; Zones 2-9. *P. viscosum* (sky pilot)— 4 to 20 inches tall with light blue or white flower clusters in spring and summer; western mountains; Zones 3-7.

Growing conditions and maintenance

P. viscosum grows in full sun and well-drained rocky soil. The other species prefer partial shade and moist soil; for *P. reptans*, provide ample organic matter. Propagate by seed or division.

Polygonatum (po-lig-o-NAY-tum)

SOLOMON'S-SEAL

Polygonatum biflorum

HARDINESS: Zones 3-9

FLOWERING SEASON: late spring

HEIGHT: 1 to 6 feet

FLOWER COLOR: greenish white

SOIL: moist, acid, rich

LIGHT: partial to full shade

These woodland perennials native to the eastern half of the United States bear drooping greenish white flowers suspended from the undersides of gracefully arching stems in late spring. Blue berries follow the flowers.

Selected species and varieties

P. biflorum (small Solomon's-seal)—small, ½- to 1-inch bell-shaped greenish white flowers in pairs on zigzag stems 1 to 3 feet long. The prominently veined leaves are 2 to 6 inches long. Blue berries follow the flowers. *P. commutatum* (great Solomon's-seal)—grows to 6 feet with flowers similar to those of *P. biflorum* in clusters of two to 10 and leaves to 7 inches long.

Growing conditions and maintenance

Solomon's-seals are easily grown in light to dense shade and a rich, moist, acid soil, where they will spread to form dense colonies. They benefit from organic matter added to the soil before planting. Propagate by seed or by division of rhizomes.

Polygonum (po-LIG-o-num)

SMARTWEED, KNOTWEED

Polygonum bistorta 'Superbum'

HARDINESS: Zones 4-9

FLOWERING SEASON: summer

HEIGHT: 6 inches to 3 feet

FLOWER COLOR: pink, white, red

SOIL: moist loam

LIGHT: full sun to light shade

Although the genus *Polygonum* contains many weeds familiar to gardeners, it also boasts a few highly ornamental species with colorful flower spikes held above neat mats of foliage.

Selected species and varieties

P. affine (Himalayan fleeceflower)—spikes of rose pink flowers 6 to 9 inches tall above dark green leaves turning bronze in fall; 'Superbum' produces crimson flowers. *P. bistorta* (snakeweed)—pink flowers like bottle brushes on 2-foot stems above striking clumps of 4- to 6-inch-long wavy green leaves with a white midrib; 'Superbum' grows to 3 feet.

Growing conditions and maintenance

Space polygonums 1 foot apart. Himalayan fleeceflower thrives in full sun; snakeweed prefers some shade. Propagate by division in spring. Use *P. bistorta* wherever you need a spreading ground cover; plant *P. affine* alongside a path or at the front of a border.

Potentilla (po-ten-TILL-a)

CINQUEFOIL

Potentilla nepalensis 'Miss Wilmott'

HARDINESS: Zones 5-8

FLOWERING SEASON: spring to summer

HEIGHT: 2 to 18 inches

FLOWER COLOR: white, yellow, pink, red

SOIL: well-drained, sandy loam

LIGHT: full sun to light shade

Cinquefoil's neat, compound leaves, with three to five leaflets arranged like fingers on a hand, grow in spreading clumps of foliage. The open-faced flowers, which have five petals arranged around a ring of fuzzy stamens, resemble wild roses. Cinquefoils are effective creeping between stones in the rock garden and as a ground cover on dry slopes.

Selected species and varieties

P. atrosanguinea (Himalayan or ruby cinquefoil)—dark red 1-inch-wide flowers and five-fingered 8-inch green leaves with silvery undersides on plants 12 to 18 inches tall; 'Fire Dance' flowers have a scarlet center and a yellow border on 15-inch stems; 'Gibson's Scarlet' has bright scarlet flowers on 15-inch stems; 'William Rollinson' grows to 18 inches with deep orange and yellow semidouble flowers; 'Yellow Queen' grows bright yellow flowers with a red center on 12-inch stems above silvery foliage. *P. nepalensis* (Nepal cinquefoil)—a bushy species with cup-shaped flowers in shades of salmon, rose, red, orange, and purple, often flowering throughout the summer; 'Miss Wilmott' is a dwarf variety 10 to 12 inches tall with cherry red flowers;

'Roxana' has coppery orange petals surrounding red centers on 15-inch stems. *P. x tonguei* (staghorn cinquefoil)—apricot-colored flowers with red centers on trailing stems 8 to 12 inches long above evergreen foliage. *P. tridentata* (wineleaf cinquefoil) [also classified as *Sibbaldiopsis tridentata*] —clusters of tiny white flowers blooming late spring to midsummer on 2- to 6-inch plants with shiny, leathery evergreen leaves that turn wine red in the fall; 'Minima' is a low-growing cultivar (3 inches high) that performs well as a ground cover. *P. verna* (spring cinquefoil)—a prostrate, fast-spreading plant that grows 2 to 3 inches high and produces golden yellow flowers ½ inch wide; 'Nana' has larger flowers than the species and grows slightly higher.

Growing conditions and maintenance

Plant smaller cinquefoils 1 foot apart and larger species 2 feet apart. Potentillas prefer a poor soil; they will produce excess leafy growth if raised in fertile soil. Wineleaf cinquefoil develops its best fall color in acid soils. Cinquefoils are generally short-lived perennials and grow best in areas with mild winters and summers. *P. verna* can be invasive; its stems may root, forming a broad mat. Propagate from seed or by division every 3 years in spring or fall.

PRIMROSE

Primula japonica 'Postford White'

HARDINESS: Zones 3-8

FLOWERING SEASON: spring

HEIGHT: 2 to 24 inches

FLOWER COLOR: wide spectrum

SOIL: moist loam

LIGHT: partial shade

Neat, colorful primroses produce clusters of five-petaled blossoms on leafless stems above rosettes of tongue-shaped leaves, which are evergreen in milder climates. More than 400 species of primroses in nearly every color of the rainbow offer the gardener a multitude of choices in height and hardiness.

Selected species and varieties

P. auricula (auricula primrose)—fragrant, bell-shaped flowers in yellow, white, or other hues on plants 2 to 8 inches tall; hardy to Zone 3. *P. denticulata* (Himalayan primrose)—globe-shaped clusters of purple flowers with a yellow eye on 8- to 12-inch stalks; varieties are available in strong red, pink, and white flower tones; to Zone 6. *P. helodoxa* (amber primrose)— soft yellow flowers on 24-inch stems; to Zone 6. *P. japonica* (Japanese primrose)— whorls of white, red, pink, or purple flowers on 2-foot stalks; 'Miller's Crimson' has deep red blossoms; 'Postford White', white flowers; to Zone 6. *P.* x *polyantha* (polyanthus primrose)—flowers singly or in clusters on 6- to 12-inch stems in a wide choice of colors; to Zone 4. *P. sieboldii* (Japanese star primrose)—nodding heads of pink, purple, or white flowers on 12-inch stalks. *P. vulgaris* (English primrose)—fragrant single flowers in yellow and other colors on 6- to 9-inch stems.

Growing conditions and maintenance

Space primroses 1 foot apart in moisture-retentive soil. Water deeply during dry periods. Himalayan, amber, and Japanese primroses require a boglike soil. English and polyanthus primroses tolerate drier conditions, while other species mentioned fall somewhere in between. Polyanthus primroses are short-lived and often treated as annuals. Japanese star primroses go dormant after flowering. Propagate primroses from seed or by division every 3 to 4 years in spring. Auricula and Japanese star primroses can also be propagated from stem cuttings, Himalayan primroses from root cuttings. Plant primroses in masses with spring bulbs, or use as border plants.

Primula x polyantha

LUNGWORT

Pulmonaria saccharata 'Sissinghurst White'

HARDINESS: Zones 4-8

FLOWERING SEASON: spring

HEIGHT: 6 to 18 inches

FLOWER COLOR: blue, purple, pink, white, red

SOIL: moist, well-drained

LIGHT: bright full shade

Small mounds or clumps of oval leaves follow bell-shaped flowers that nod on arching stems in spring.

Selected species and varieties

P. longifolia (long-leaved lungwort, Joseph and Mary, spotted dog)—tight clump with leaves more than a foot long; 'Ankum' has blue flowers; 'Roy Davidson' has silver-and-green foliage. *P. montana* [also known as *P. rubra*] (red lungwort)—1 to 2 feet tall with bright red spring flowers; 'Barfield Pink' has pale green leaves and pink flowers; 'Bowles' Red', medium green leaves, often slightly spotted, and red flowers. *P. officinalis* 'Rubra' (blue lungwort, Jerusalem sage, Jerusalem cowslip) white-spotted leaves and flowers that turn mottled violet. *P. saccharata* (Bethlehem sage)— white-spotted 6-inch leaves and funnel-shaped flowers on stems to 18 inches; 'Janet Fisk' has silver-splotched foliage and lavender-pink flowers in spring; 'Sissinghurst White' has large white flowers and spotted foliage.

Growing conditions and maintenance

Plant 12 to 18 inches apart. Cut foliage back severely after flowering and feed with an all-purpose fertilizer.

Rodgersia (ro-JER-zee-a)

RODGERSIA

Rodgersia podophylla

HARDINESS: Zones 5-7

FLOWERING SEASON: summer

HEIGHT: 3 to 6 feet

FLOWER COLOR: white, pink

SOIL: boggy loam

LIGHT: full sun to light shade

Rodgersia's large leaves make them dramatic foliage plants and excellent fillers massed in marshy bog or woodland gardens. In summer, huge frothy pyramids of flowers rise on stout stalks followed by reddish seeds in fall.

Selected species and varieties

R. aesculifolia (fingerleaf rodgersia)—clumps to 5 feet across of 1-foot-wide leaves formed of leaflets arranged like fingers and creamy 2-foot flower clusters on 5-foot-tall stalks. *R. pinnata* 'Superba'—pink flowers in 10-inch clusters above bronze-tinged foliage on plants to 4 feet tall and as wide. *R. podophylla*—bronze-green, 1-foot-wide leaves shaped like a duck's foot and creamy white flowers on 3-foot stalks. *R. tabularis* (shieldleaf rodgersia)—round leaves up to 3 feet across with scalloped edges and white flower clusters on 4-foot stalks.

Growing conditions and maintenance

Plant rodgersia 3 feet apart in constantly moist soil, as at the edge of a stream or pond. Propagate by division in spring.

Romneya (RAHM-nee-a)

CALIFORNIA TREE POPPY

Romneya coulteri

HARDINESS: Zones 7-10

FLOWERING SEASON: summer

HEIGHT: 4 to 8 feet

FLOWER COLOR: white

SOIL: dry, infertile

LIGHT: full sun

The California tree poppy produces fragrant 3- to 6-inch flowers with silky white petals surrounding a bright golden center. They bloom throughout the summer, and though each flower lasts only a few days, they make a handsome show in both the garden and indoor arrangements.

Selected species and varieties

R. coulteri—up to 8 feet tall, 3 feet wide, multiple branched stems, spreading by suckers from roots, leaves are gray-green and deeply cut, fragrant summer flowers are very large with 5 or 6 crinkled white petals that resemble crepe paper surrounding golden stamens, useful for naturalizing on dry banks, may become invasive in a border.

Growing conditions and maintenance

Plant California tree poppies in poor, dry soil in full sun where invasive roots will not cause a problem. They are most successfully grown in Zones 8 to 10 but can survive in Zone 7 with a heavy winter mulch. Cut them back nearly to the ground in late fall.

Rudbeckia (rood-BEK-ee-a)

CONEFLOWER

Rudbeckia fulgida 'Goldstrum'

HARDINESS: Zones 3-9

FLOWERING SEASON: summer

HEIGHT: 1 to 4 feet

FLOWER COLOR: yellow

SOIL: moist to dry

LIGHT: full sun to partial shade

Rudbeckias are annuals, biennials, and perennials from open woodlands and meadows throughout most of the United States. Their gay yellow daisylike flowers, with a fringe of narrow petals surrounding a prominent center, are favorites among wildflower gardeners. These plants bloom prolifically on wiry stems above vigorous clumps of deeply cut foliage.

Selected species and varieties

R. fulgida 'Goldstrum'—bright yellow flowers with brown centers, growing from midsummer to frost on compact 2-foot plants. *R. grandiflora* (large coneflower)—1½ to 3 feet tall. Flowers up to 6 inches or more across have drooping petals and a brown cone-shaped center. *R. nitida*—bright yellow petals surrounding extremely large 2-inch centers on 2- to 7-foot-tall stems. *R. subtomentosa* (sweet coneflower)—1 to 4 feet tall with 3-inch flowers with dark centers.

Growing conditions and maintenance

Plant coneflowers 1½ to 2 feet apart. Propagate from seed or by division every 2 years in spring. Coneflowers are a good choice for southern gardens.

RUELLIA

Ruellia caroliniensis

HARDINESS: Zones 4-9

FLOWERING SEASON: summer, fall

HEIGHT: 1 to 3 feet

FLOWER COLOR: lavender, purple

SOIL: dry, sandy

LIGHT: full sun to partial shade

Ruellias are perennials found growing wild in open woods and prairies in the eastern United States. Their loose clusters of funnel-shaped flowers add a delicate touch to wildflower meadows, herbaceous borders, and woodland edges.

Selected species and varieties

R. caroliniensis (ruellia)—clusters of two to four light purple flowers near the tops of unbranched stems 2 to 3 feet tall throughout summer; Zones 6-9. *R. humilis* (wild petunia)—showy lavender to purple 2-inch flowers on compact bushy plants 1 to 2 feet tall throughout summer and fall; Zones 4-9.

Growing conditions and maintenance

Ruellias prefer dry soils that are sandy or rocky but will adapt to other types of soil as long as they are not too moist. Propagate by seed or cuttings taken in summer.

SAGE

Salvia farinacea 'Victoria'

HARDINESS: tender or Zones 4-10

FLOWERING SEASON: spring to fall

HEIGHT: 1 to 6 feet

FLOWER COLOR: blue, purple, white, red

SOIL: well-drained loam

LIGHT: full sun

Whorled spikes of tiny, hooded, summer-to-fall-blooming flowers line the tips of salvia's erect stems above soft, sometimes downy leaves. Salvias are particularly effective in masses that multiply the impact of their flowers. Tender perennial salvias that cannot withstand frost are grown as annuals in Zone 8 and colder.

Selected species and varieties

S. argentea (silver sage)—branching clusters of white flowers tinged yellow or pink on 3-foot stems above rosettes of woolly, gray-green, 8-inch leaves. *S. azurea* ssp. *pitcheri* var. *grandiflora* (blue sage)—large, deep blue flowers on stems to 5 feet lined with gray-green leaves. *S. farinacea* (mealy-cup sage)—violet-blue or white flowers from midsummer to frost on 2- to 3-foot stems; 'Blue Bedder' has deep blue flowers on 8-inch clusters on compact plants to 2 feet tall. *S. haematodes* (meadow sage)—airy sprays of lavender-blue flowers from early to midsummer on plants to 3 feet tall. *S. jurisicii* (Jurisici's sage)—dangling lilac or white flowers on stems 12 to 18 inches tall. *S. officinalis* (common sage)—whorls of tiny white, blue, or purple flowers above wrinkled, hairy, and aromatic, gray-green

leaves, which can be used as a seasoning for food; 'Purpurascens' has purple-tinged leaves; 'Tricolor', leaf veins turning from cream to pink and red as foliage ages. *S. sclarea* 'Turkestanica' [also called *S. sclarea* var. *turkestana* or var. *turkestaniana*]—rosy pink flower spikes tipping 3-foot stems above wrinkled, hairy leaves. *S. x superba* (perennial salvia)—violet-purple flowers in dense whorls around 4- to 8-inch spikes from late spring to early summer on rounded plants to 3 feet tall; 'Blue Queen' grows 18 to 24 inches tall; 'East Friesland' has deep purple blossoms on 18- to 24-inch plants; 'May Night' grows to 24 inches with intense violet-blue flowers.

Growing conditions and maintenance

Sage grows best in dry soils; its roots should not stay wet over winter. Because they vary in hardiness, particular care must be given to selection of species. Garden sage is hardy to Zone 4; Pitcher's salvia and perennial salvia, to Zone 5; meadow sage and Jurisici's sage, to Zone 6; mealy-cup sage, to Zone 8 and evergreen in Zone 9. Plant smaller salvia varieties 18 inches apart and larger ones 2 to 3 feet apart. Remove spent flowers to encourage reblooming. Propagate by division, cuttings, or, except for perennial salvia, seed.

Salvia officinalis 'Purpurascens'

Santolina (san-to-LEE-na)

LAVENDER COTTON

Santolina chamaecyparissus

HARDINESS: Zones 6-8

FLOWERING SEASON: summer

HEIGHT: 18 to 24 inches

FLOWER COLOR: yellow

SOIL: well-drained to dry

LIGHT: full sun

Lavender cotton forms a broad, spreading clump of aromatic leaves. It makes an attractive edging for a bed or walkway, or can be used as a low-growing specimen in a rock garden. It can also be sheared to form a tight, low hedge.

Selected species and varieties

S. chamaecyparissus—up to 24 inches tall with equal or greater spread, forms a broad, cushionlike, evergreen mound, aromatic leaves are silvery gray-green and ½ to 1½ inches long, yellow flowers are button-shaped in summer and are often removed to maintain a clipped hedge.

Growing conditions and maintenance

Lavender cotton is a tough plant, well suited to adverse conditions such as drought and salt spray. It prefers dry soils of low fertility and becomes unattractive and open in fertile soils. Avoid excess moisture, especially in winter. Prune after flowering to promote dense growth, or shear anytime for a formal, low hedge.

Saponaria (sap-o-NAR-ee-a)

SOAPWORT

Saponaria ocymoides

HARDINESS: Zones 4-9

FLOWERING SEASON: spring and summer

HEIGHT: 6 inches to 3 feet

FLOWER COLOR: pink

SOIL: well-drained loam

LIGHT: full sun

Saponarias bear clusters of tiny pink flowers at the tips of either erect or trailing stems.

Selected species and varieties

S. ocymoides (rock soapwort)—has loose sprays of deep pink ½-inch flowers on trailing 6- to 12-inch reddish stems with semi-evergreen leaves in broad mounds. *S. officinalis* (bouncing Bet)—clusters of pale pink or white 1-inch flowers on erect 3-foot stems.

Growing conditions and maintenance

Plant rock soapwort 1 foot apart, *S. officinalis* 2 to 3 feet apart. Propagate from seed or by division in spring or fall.

Saxifraga (Saks-IF-ra-ga)

SAXIFRAGE, ROCKFOIL

Saxifraga pensylvanica

HARDINESS: Zones 2-8

FLOWERING SEASON: spring to summer

HEIGHT: 4 inches to 3 feet

FLOWER COLOR: white, purple, yellow, greenish

SOIL: dry, rocky to moist, well-drained

LIGHT: full sun to shade

The saxifrages described here include two western perennials well suited to rock gardens and containers and an eastern perennial for boggy or moist gardens.

Selected species and varieties

S. californica (California saxifrage)—clusters of white flowers on 4- to 12-inch stalks in spring and low rosettes of broad fuzzy leaves; mountains from California to Oregon; Zones 6-8. *S. oppositifolia* (purple saxifrage)—showy flowers with crimped purple petals and brownish orange anthers in summer above a dense 2-inch mat of narrow pointed leaves; Canada, Alaska, and western mountains; Zones 2-6. *S. pensylvanica* (swamp saxifrage)—clusters of greenish, yellow, or purple flowers on stems 1 to 3 feet tall in spring above a rosette of 1-foot leaves; Maine to Missouri; Zones 5-8.

Growing conditions and maintenance

Grow *S. oppositifolia* in dry, rocky soil in full sun to partial shade. *S. californica* requires a moist, well-drained location and partial to full shade. *S. pensylvanica* grows in wet to moist soils in full sun to partial shade. Propagate by seed.

Scabiosa (skab-i-O-sa)

PINCUSHION FLOWER

Scabiosa caucasica 'Clive Greaves'

HARDINESS: Zones 4-9

FLOWERING SEASON: summer

HEIGHT: 18 to 24 inches

FLOWER COLOR: blue, lavender, white

SOIL: well-drained, neutral loam

LIGHT: full sun

Pincushion flowers produce blooms up to 3 inches across with prominent stamens resembling a dome of pinheads surrounded by a ruffle of petals. Tipping slender stems above low tufts of leaves, the blossoms offer rare blue color in a summer border.

Selected species and varieties

S. caucasica (pincushion flower, Caucasian scabiosa)—3-inch flowers on long stems; 'Clive Greaves' has lavender-blue flowers; 'Fama', deep blue petals encircling silver centers on 18-inch stems. *S. columbaria* 'Butterfly Blue' is a prolific compact form with small flowers on 15-inch stems.

Growing conditions and maintenance

Space pincushion flowers 18 to 24 inches apart. Remove faded flowers for continuous bloom. Propagate from seed or by division in spring.

Sedum (SEE-dum)

STONECROP

Sedum 'Autumn Joy'

HARDINESS: Zones 3-10

FLOWERING SEASON: spring to fall

HEIGHT: 3 inches to 2 feet

FLOWER COLOR: white, yellow, orange, red, pink

SOIL: well-drained loam

LIGHT: full sun to light shade

Stonecrops are valued for both their flowers and their foliage, which add color and rich texture to a garden over a long season. Their thick, succulent leaves vary in color from bright green to blue-green to reddish green. Individual flowers are small and star-shaped, with 5 petals. Generally borne in dense clusters that cover the plant, they attract butterflies to the garden. The blooming season varies among species from spring to fall, with some flowers even persisting into winter. Sedums are easy to grow and tolerate drought, making them well suited to rock gardens and dry borders. They can be used as individual specimens, in groupings of three or more, or massed as a succulent ground cover.

Selected species and varieties

S. aizoon (Aizoon stonecrop)—yellow flowers above bright green leaves on stems 12 to 18 inches tall, blooming from spring to summer; 'Auranticum' has deep yellow flowers and red-tinted stems. *S.* 'Autumn Joy'—rosy pink flower buds that form above gray-green leaves on 2-foot stems in midsummer, turn red before opening bronze-red in fall, and turn golden brown

if left in place for the winter. *S. kamtschaticum* (orange stonecrop)—6 to 9 inches tall with a wide-spreading habit, excellent for rock gardens, grows small orange-yellow flowers in summer; 'Variegatum' produces deep orange flowers and green leaves with a broad white margin blushed with pink. *S. maximum* (great stonecrop)—greenish yellow, star-shaped flowers in late summer above oval, gray-green leaves on stems up to 2 feet tall; 'Atropurpureum' has red flowers and maroon leaves. *S. rosea* (roseroot)—tiny yellow or purple flowers atop clumps of 12-inch stems with small toothed leaves; *S. rosea integrifolium* has pink to red-purple flowers. *S.* 'Ruby Glow'—ruby red fall flowers above purple-gray foliage on compact plants 8 inches tall; a good choice for the front of a border. *S. sieboldii* (Siebold stonecrop)—dense heads of pink flowers effective throughout fall above nearly triangular blue-gray leaves on 6- to 9-inch somewhat trailing stems. *S. spectabile* (showy stonecrop)—a heat-tolerant species with bright pink flowers that bloom from late summer till frost on 18-inch stems; 'Brilliant' has raspberry red flowers; 'Carmen', rose pink flowers; 'Variegatum', bright pink flowers atop leaves variegated yellow and green; 'Meteor', large wine red blooms; 'Stardust', white flowers that stand out against blue-green leaves; Zones 3-10. *S. spurium* (two-row stonecrop)—pink, red, or white summer flowers on vigorously spreading evergreen stems 3 to 6 inches tall that make a tough evergreen ground cover; 'Bronze Carpet' has pink flowers and red-brown foliage;

Sedum kamtschaticum

'Coccineum' has scarlet blooms; 'Dragon's Blood' produces purple-bronze leaves and deep crimson star-shaped flowers; 'Red Carpet' has bronze leaves and red flowers; 'Variegatum' has green leaves with pink margins. S. 'Vera Jameson'—a slightly larger hybrid of S. 'Ruby Glow' at 12 inches tall, with bronze foliage and magenta flowers.

Growing conditions and maintenance

Stonecrops are tough plants that spread without becoming invasive. Space *S. sieboldii* 1 foot apart, other species 1½ to 2 feet apart. They tolerate almost any well-drained soil, even if it is dry and sterile. Stonecrops can be left undivided for many years, but can be propagated by division in spring or from stem cuttings taken in summer.

Sedum spurium

GROUNDSEL, SENECIO

Senecio aureus

HARDINESS: Zones 4-10

FLOWERING SEASON: spring, summer, fall

HEIGHT: 1 to 5 feet

FLOWER COLOR: yellow

SOIL: moist to dry, sandy

LIGHT: full sun to partial shade

The daisylike flowers of the perennial groundsels described here add a golden glow to their native grasslands or wooded areas for several weeks.

Selected species and varieties

S. aureus (golden groundsel, golden ragwort)—1 to 3 feet tall with clusters of deep golden yellow flowers in late spring and summer above the heart-shaped dark green basal foliage. It spreads rapidly by horizontal offshoots to form an attractive ground cover; eastern North America; Zones 4-8. *S. douglasii* (shrubby senecio) —shrubby perennial up to 5 feet tall with yellow flowers in summer and fall and fuzzy white foliage; California; Zones 6-10.

Growing conditions and maintenance

Grow *S. aureus* in moist, acid soil and full sun to partial shade. *S. douglasii* grows in full sun and prefers a well-drained sandy or rocky soil. Propagate by seed, division, or cuttings.

CHECKERMALLOW

Sidalcea malviflora

HARDINESS: Zones 4-10

FLOWERING SEASON: spring to summer

HEIGHT: 2 to 4 feet

FLOWER COLOR: pink, purple, mauve

SOIL: wet to dry

LIGHT: full sun to partial shade

Perennials from the western United States, the checkermallows have showy flowers resembling hollyhocks and provide a colorful vertical accent in mixed herbaceous borders or meadow plantings.

Selected species and varieties

S. malviflora (checkermallow, checkerbloom)—up to 4 feet tall with pink or purple flowers on erect stems in spring and summer and dark green lobed leaves. The flowers open in the morning and close up in the evening; Zones 5-10. *S. neomexicana* (prairie mallow)—up to 3 feet tall with mauve flowers in spring and early summer; Zones 4-10.

Growing conditions and maintenance

S. malviflora prefers soil that is moist in winter and well drained to dry in summer and grows in full sun to partial shade. *S. neomexicana* grows in moist, well-drained to wet soils in full sun. Remove faded flowers or cut back spent flower stems to prolong blooming. Propagate from seed or by division.

Silene (sy-LEE-ne)

CAMPION, CATCHFLY

Silene schafta

HARDINESS: Zones 4-8

FLOWERING SEASON: summer to fall

HEIGHT: 4 inches to 2 feet

FLOWER COLOR: white, pink, red

SOIL: well-drained, sandy loam

LIGHT: full sun to light shade

Campions have star-shaped, five-petaled flowers that appear on branching stems for several weeks during the growing season. The plant's tufts of low-growing, narrow foliage sometimes spread.

Selected species and varieties
S. schafta (moss campion)—rose pink or purple flowers on 12-inch stems above 6-inch rosettes of hairy, oblong, light green leaves. *S.* 'Robin's White Breast'—white flower bells above dense 8-inch mounds of silvery gray leaves. *S. virginica* (fire-pink catchfly)—clusters of pink to red flowers on sticky 2-foot stems above flat rosettes of evergreen leaves.

Growing conditions and maintenance
Space campions 12 inches apart. Propagate from seed or by division in spring.

Sisyrinchium (sis-i-RINK-ee-um)

BLUE-EYED GRASS

Sisyrinchium bellum

HARDINESS: Zones 3-10

FLOWERING SEASON: spring, summer

HEIGHT: 3 to 18 inches

FLOWER COLOR: blue, white, purple

SOIL: moist to seasonally dry

LIGHT: full sun to partial shade

Sisyrinchiums are dainty-looking perennials with starry six-petaled flowers and clumps of grasslike leaves. They are especially pretty planted in naturalistic drifts in the dappled shade of deciduous trees.

Selected species and varieties
S. angustifolium (narrow-leaved blue-eyed grass)—bears light blue flowers on twisted stalks that rise just above the 12- to 18-inch clump of foliage from spring to summer; eastern Canada and United States; Zones 3-10. *S. bellum* (California blue-eyed grass)—3 to 18 inches high with great numbers of blue, violet, or white flowers in spring. The foliage may be evergreen; Zones 8-10. *S. douglasii* (Douglas blue-eyed grass)—6 to 12 inches high with reddish purple flowers up to an inch across in spring; British Columbia to California and Nevada; Zones 4-9.

Growing conditions and maintenance
Sisyrinchiums thrive in full sun or light shade. *S. angustifolium* needs a poor to average, evenly moist soil. *S. bellum* and *S. douglasii* need soil that is moist in spring and dry in summer. Propagate by seed or division.

Smilacina (smy-la-SEE-na)

FALSE SOLOMON'S-SEAL

Smilacina racemosa

HARDINESS: Zones 2-8

FLOWERING SEASON: spring

HEIGHT: 1 to 3 feet

FLOWER COLOR: white

SOIL: moist, deep, rich

LIGHT: partial to full shade

These perennial woodland natives are found throughout much of the United States and Canada. Their graceful arching stems, spring flowers, and fall berries make them an outstanding choice for a shady garden.

Selected species and varieties
S. racemosa (false Solomon's-seal, false spikenard)—stems up to 3 feet tall with conical flower clusters at the tips and 3- to 6-inch elliptical leaves. The berries that follow the flowers are green in summer, turning pinkish red in fall; Zones 4-8. *S. stellata* (starry false Solomon's-seal)—arching zigzag stems 1 to 2 feet tall with terminal clusters of star-shaped flowers and dark green leaves. The berries are dark red in fall; Zones 2-7.

Growing conditions and maintenance
Smilacinas grow best in moist, deep, humus-rich soil in shade. *S. stellata* tolerates somewhat drier soil and more sun, but its growth will be stunted. Propagate by seed or division.

Solidago (sol-i-DAY-go)

GOLDENROD

Solidago canadensis

HARDINESS: Zones 3-10

FLOWERING SEASON: summer, fall

HEIGHT: 1 to 10 feet

FLOWER COLOR: yellow

SOIL: moist, well-drained to dry

LIGHT: full sun to partial shade

The upright stems of goldenrods are tipped with eye-catching clusters of yellow flowers in summer and fall. These tough, dependable perennials are native to meadows and prairies in Canada and throughout most of the United States. They make excellent cut flowers, and butterflies feed on their nectar.

Selected species and varieties

S. caesia (blue-stemmed goldenrod, wreath goldenrod)—has slender, 1- to 3-foot-tall blue- or purple-tinged stems with small arching sprays of yellow flowers in late summer and fall; Zones 4-8. *S. canadensis* (Canada goldenrod)—2 to 4 feet tall with branching flower clusters in late summer; Zones 3-10. *S. juncea* (early goldenrod)—up to 6 feet or more in height with arching clusters of flowers from mid- to late summer; Zones 3-7. *S. missouriensis* (Missouri goldenrod)—an early-blooming goldenrod with nodding flower clusters on reddish stems 1 to 2 feet tall from mid- to late summer; Zones 4-8. *S. nemoralis* (gray goldenrod)—up to 2 feet high with plume-shaped flower clusters in late summer and fall; Zones 3-9. *S. odora* (sweet goldenrod)—2 to 5 feet tall with large flower clusters from midsummer through fall and neat, bright green foliage that smells like anise when crushed; Zones 3-9. *S. rugosa* (rough-leaved goldenrod)—2 to 5 feet tall with flower sprays composed of thin, arching stems for 3 to 4 weeks in fall; Zones 3-8. *S. sempervirens* (seaside goldenrod)—large branching clusters of flowers on stems to 8 feet tall in late summer and fall above a clump of narrow evergreen leaves up to 16 inches long; Zones 4-8.

Growing conditions and maintenance

Space goldenrods 18 to 24 inches apart. These plants thrive in full sun in soils of average fertility. *S. caesia* also tolerates partial shade. *S. sempervirens* tolerates salt spray and can be pinched in early summer to encourage compact growth. Most goldenrods are aggressive growers and may need dividing every 2 to 3 years. *S. caesia*, *S. odora*, and *S. sempervirens* are less vigorous growers than the others and easier to keep within bounds. Propagate goldenrods by seed or division. Propagate hybrids by division.

Solidago odora

Sphaeralcea (sfee-RAL-see-a)

GLOBE MALLOW

Sphaeralcea coccinea

HARDINESS: Zones 3-10

FLOWERING SEASON: spring, summer, fall

HEIGHT: 2 to 3 feet

FLOWER COLOR: orange, pink, red

SOIL: dry, rocky

LIGHT: full sun

Globe mallows are drought-resistant perennials native to dry, rocky slopes and desert plains of the western United States. They bear brightly colored cupped flowers and are an excellent choice for sunny rock gardens.

Selected species and varieties

S. ambigua (desert mallow)—3-foot stems bearing wandlike clusters of apricot-orange flowers up to 2 inches across in spring; Zones 6-10. *S. coccinea* (prairie mallow, scarlet globe mallow)—3 feet tall with orange-pink flowers surrounded by red bracts in spring, summer, or fall and hairy gray-green leaves; Zones 3-10. *S. munroana* (Munro's globe mallow)—2 to 3 feet tall with spikes of numerous bright pink to deep apricot flowers and gray-green foliage; Zones 4-10. *S. parvifolia* (globe mallow)—2 to 3 feet tall with clusters of orange-red flowers and whitish gray leaves from spring to summer; Zones 5-10.

Growing conditions and maintenance

Plant sphaeralceas in full sun and dry, rocky soil. They tolerate drought. Though individual plants are often short-lived, they usually self-sow. Propagate by seed or cuttings.

Spigelia (spy-JEE-lee-a)

PINKROOT, INDIAN PINK

Spigelia marilandica

HARDINESS: Zones 5-9

FLOWERING SEASON: late spring to early summer

HEIGHT: 1 to 2 feet

FLOWER COLOR: pinkish red

SOIL: moist, well-drained, acid

LIGHT: partial shade

Pinkroot bears interesting trumpet-shaped flowers along one side of an arching stem. The 2-inch flowers are red with yellow throats, and all face upward, creating an unusual and pleasing effect. This is a nice selection for the front of a shady border or along a garden path, where its flower display can be viewed at close range.

Selected species and varieties
S. marilandica—1 to 2 feet tall, 18 inches wide, erect stems, 3- to 4-inch-long leaves, flowers are pinkish red with yellow throats and trumpet-shaped in elongated clusters at ends of stems, blooming late spring to early summer.

Growing conditions and maintenance
Plant pinkroot in a well-drained, slightly acid soil amended with organic matter. It thrives in partial shade, especially in warmer climates, but tolerates full sun if adequate moisture is supplied. It does not compete well with surface tree roots. Division of the clumps is an easy way to increase plants.

Stachys (STAY-kis)

LAMB'S EARS

Stachys 'Helene Von Stein'

HARDINESS: Zones 4-9

FLOWERING SEASON: summer

HEIGHT: 6 to 18 inches

FLOWER COLOR: pink, purple

SOIL: well-drained

LIGHT: full sun to light shade

Lamb's ears is a low-growing, spreading perennial that adds soft color and texture to the front of a perennial border, alongside a path, or as a ground cover. Its gray-green leaves are covered with white hairs, giving them the appearance and feel of velvet. Nonflowering varieties eliminate the need for removing flowers that are often considered unattractive.

Selected species and varieties
S. byzantina 'Silver Carpet'—12 to 15 inches tall with 18- to 24-inch spread, leaves and stems densely covered with white hairs, leaves up to 4 inches long, no flowers; 'Helene Von Stein'—larger leaves, few flowers, tolerates hot, humid weather.

Growing conditions and maintenance
Plant lamb's ears in well-drained soil that is not too fertile. Excess moisture encourages leaf rot. For use as a ground cover, space plants 12 to 18 inches apart. Remove old leaves before new growth begins in spring.

Stokesia (sto-KEE-zi-a)

STOKES' ASTER

Stokesia laevis 'Blue Danube'

HARDINESS: Zones 5-9

FLOWERING SEASON: summer

HEIGHT: 12 to 18 inches

FLOWER COLOR: lavender, blue, white

SOIL: well-drained, sandy loam

LIGHT: full sun

The showy, fringed flowers of Stokes' aster bloom on branched flowerstalks rising from neat rosettes of shiny, narrow, straplike leathery leaves that are evergreen in warmer climates. Stokes' aster is excellent in bouquets.

Selected species and varieties
S. laevis—solitary flower heads 2 to 5 inches across, blooming over a 4-week season in summer; 'Blue Danube' has 5-inch clear blue flowers; 'Blue Moon', lilac flowers; 'Jelitto' has 4-inch-deep blue blossoms; 'Silver Moon' blooms white.

Growing conditions and maintenance
Space *Stokesia* 18 inches apart. Mulch over winter in colder climates. Propagate the species from seed, and the species and its hybrids by division in the spring.

Thalictrum (thal-IK-trum)

MEADOW RUE

Thalictrum dasycarpum

HARDINESS: Zones 3-10

FLOWERING SEASON: spring to summer

HEIGHT: 8 inches to 8 feet

FLOWER COLOR: green, purple, cream

SOIL: moist, rich

LIGHT: full sun to full shade

Meadow rues, native to the woodlands, meadows, and prairies in southern Canada, on the West Coast, and in much of the eastern United States, are prized for their finely cut leaves and delicate flowers.

Selected species and varieties

T. dasycarpum (purple meadow rue)—to 6 feet tall with purplish stems and green flowers in loose terminal clusters; Zones 3-6. *T. dioicum* (early meadow rue)—8 to 28 inches tall with beautiful long-stalked foliage divided into many rounded segments. Female flowers have purple petals. Male flowers lack petals but produce a tassel of yellow stamens; Zones 4-9. *T. polycarpum* (meadow rue)—2 feet tall; grown mainly for its attractive foliage divided into rounded segments. Tiny green flowers bloom in spring; Zones 6-10. *T. polygamum* (tall meadow rue)—to 8 feet tall with showy cream-colored flowers in summer and feathery blue-green foliage; Zones 4-7.

Growing conditions and maintenance

T. dasycarpum, T. dioicum, and *T. polycarpum* grow in partial to full shade. *T. polygamum* grows in full sun to partial shade. Mulch in spring to keep soil moist. Propagate by seed.

Tiarella (ty-a-REL-a)

FALSE MITERWORT

Tiarella cordifolia 'Slick Rock'

HARDINESS: Zones 3-8

FLOWERING SEASON: spring to summer

HEIGHT: 6 to 12 inches

FLOWER COLOR: white, pinkish white

SOIL: moist, well-drained, slightly acid, fertile

LIGHT: medium to bright full shade

Sweeps of frothy tiarella plumes blooming above rich green heart-shaped foliage lend an airy texture to the woodland garden. Good for massings, rock gardens, and wildflower areas, tiarella also provides fall color when its long-lasting leaves turn reddish to dark purple. Foamflower makes a good ground cover.

Selected species and varieties

T. cordifolia (foamflower)—downy, bright green, lobed leaves arise from creeping stolons to form a 6-inch-high mat and stems up to 1 foot long that bear white 1- to 4-inch flower racemes in spring; 'Eco Red Heart' has medium green leaves with red hearts in the center and pinkish flowers; 'Slick Rock', deeply cut, maplelike leaves and pinkish flowers. *T. wherryi* (lakela, Wherry's foamflower)—fragrant, very showy, pinkish white flower plumes bloom from late spring to early summer on 1-foot-tall white stems above nonstoloniferous clumps of rich green heart-shaped leaves.

Growing conditions and maintenance

Space plants 12 to 18 inches apart. Foamflowers do not tolerate drought. Propagate by division in fall.

Tradescantia (trad-e-SKAN-shee-a)

SPIDERWORT

Tradescantia ohiensis

HARDINESS: Zones 3-10

FLOWERING SEASON: spring, summer

HEIGHT: 10 to 36 inches

FLOWER COLOR: blue-violet, blue

SOIL: well-drained, humus-rich

LIGHT: full sun to partial shade

Found in open woods and on prairies, spiderworts are upright or trailing perennials whose flowers have three wide petals and showy stamens.

Selected species and varieties

T. bracteata (bracted spiderwort)—clusters of blue-violet flowers surrounded by leaflike bracts on erect 10- to 16-inch stems with grasslike foliage in late spring to early summer; Zones 3-8. *T. ohiensis* (Ohio spiderwort)—blue flowers clustered at the tops of erect, branching stems 2 to 3 feet tall from spring to summer in warm climates and summer in cooler zones; Zones 4-10. *T. virginiana* (Virginia spiderwort)—blue to blue-violet flowers 1½ to 3 inches wide from spring to summer on a dense clump of branching stems up to 3 feet tall with narrow bright green leaves 12 inches long; Zones 4-10.

Growing conditions and maintenance

Plant spiderworts in full sun or partial shade in well-drained, humus-rich soil. Propagate by seed, stem cuttings taken at any time, or division.

Tricyrtis (try-SER-tis)

TOAD LILY

Tricyrtis hirta

HARDINESS: Zones 4-8

FLOWERING SEASON: summer or fall

HEIGHT: 2 to 3 feet

FLOWER COLOR: white, yellow, purple

SOIL: moist, well-drained, slightly acid, fertile

LIGHT: bright full shade

Toad lilies bloom in summer or fall, producing flared, trumpet-shaped, spotted flowers either in clusters or singly in the leaf axils on tall stems. The foliage is often hairy. They are best used in perennial borders and rock gardens.

Selected species and varieties

T. hirta (hairy toad lily)—1-inch-wide white, cream, or pale purple waxy flowers spotted with dark purple appear singly or clustered in leaf axils at the top of 2- to 3-foot stems in fall. *T. latifolia*—yellow flowers with purple or brown spots bloom in clusters in early summer on 3-foot stems with mottled foliage. *T. macrantha*—nodding, soft to deep yellow shuttlecock-style flowers with reddish brown spots blooming in fall on hairy 3-foot stems.

Growing conditions and maintenance

Space rhizomes 12 to 18 inches apart in peaty garden loam. Remove dead leaves in late fall. Propagate by dividing in spring or fall. Toad lilies are half-hardy perennials; in the northern limits of their hardiness, dig up the roots, dry them, and store over the winter, or mulch heavily to overwinter in the ground.

Trillium (TRIL-ee-um)

TRILLIUM, WAKE-ROBIN

Trillium grandiflorum

HARDINESS: Zones 2-9

FLOWERING SEASON: late spring

HEIGHT: 6 to 18 inches

FLOWER COLOR: white, pink, maroon

SOIL: moist, acid, rich

LIGHT: partial shade to shade

Trilliums are woodland perennials whose solitary flowers consist of three broad petals and three greenish sepals. Below each flower is a whorl of three leaves.

Selected species and varieties

T. cernuum (nodding trillium)—12 to 18 inches tall with nodding white flowers 1½ inches across with deep rose anthers; Zones 3-7. *T. erectum* (purple trillium, squawroot)—to 18 inches tall with upward-facing maroon flowers 2½ inches across that have an unpleasant scent detectable at close range; Zones 2-6. *T. grandiflorum* (large-flowered trillium, white wake-robin)—up to 15 inches tall with upward-facing, long-lasting white flowers 3 to 4 inches across that turn pink with age; Zones 3-8. *T. sessile* (red trillium, toadshade)—to 12 inches tall with upward-facing maroon flowers; Zones 4-9.

Growing conditions and maintenance

Trilliums require at least partial shade and moist, humus-rich soil. Propagate from seed, or by dividing rhizomes in fall. It may take 5 years for seed-grown trilliums to bloom.

Trollius (TROL-ee-us)

GLOBEFLOWER

Trollius ledebourii 'Golden Queen'

HARDINESS: Zones 4-8

FLOWERING SEASON: spring to summer

HEIGHT: 18 inches to 3 feet

FLOWER COLOR: yellow, orange

SOIL: continuously moist loam

LIGHT: full sun to partial shade

Globeflower's brightly colored 2- to 4-inch blossoms, consisting of waxy curved petals in dense balls, bloom on erect stems above clumps of deeply lobed leaves.

Selected species and varieties

T. europaeus (common globeflower)—lemon yellow flowers on stems up to 24 inches tall; 'Superbus' has light yellow flowers in spring and often again in late summer or fall. *T. ledebourii* (Ledebour globeflower)—orange flowers on 3-foot stems; 'Golden Queen' has golden orange blossoms. *T. x cultorum* (hybrid globeflower)—yellow to orange flowers.

Growing conditions and maintenance

Space globeflowers 18 inches apart in soil containing generous amounts of organic matter. Propagate from seed or by division in fall.

Verbascum (ver-BAS-cum)

MULLEIN

Verbascum chaixii 'Album'

HARDINESS: Zones 5-9

FLOWERING SEASON: summer

HEIGHT: 3 feet

FLOWER COLOR: yellow-and-purple, white

SOIL: well-drained, sandy loam

LIGHT: full sun to partial shade

Branched spikes of small, flat-faced blossoms rise from mullein's rosettes of fuzzy gray leaves. Mullein offers a stately vertical form for a mixed border.

Selected species and varieties

V. chaixii (chaix mullein)—½- to 1-inch-wide yellow flowers with fuzzy purple stamens creating a prominent eye; 'Album' has white flowers complementing the gray foliage.

Growing conditions and maintenance

Space plants 18 to 24 inches apart. Propagate species from seed or from root cuttings taken in early spring. Propagate named varieties from root cuttings only.

Verbena (ver-BEE-na)

VERVAIN, VERBENA

Verbena stricta

HARDINESS: Zones 3-10

FLOWERING SEASON: spring, summer, fall

HEIGHT: 8 inches to 5 feet

FLOWER COLOR: pink, purple, blue, violet

SOIL: dry, sandy to moist, well-drained

LIGHT: full sun

The perennial verbenas described below are native to meadows, prairies, and open woods.

Selected species and varieties

V. canadensis (rose verbena)—fragrant ¾-inch pink flowers in rounded clusters in summer and fall on a mat of creeping stems 8 to 12 inches tall and 3 feet across. Native from the Southeast west to Colorado; Zones 6-10. *V. gooddingii* (pink verbena)—18-inch-tall mat of purplish stems and deeply divided leaves with bright purple flowers in rounded clusters in spring. Southwest to California; Zones 5-10. *V. hastata* (blue verbena)—2 to 5 feet with spikes of blue-purple flowers in late spring and summer; widely found in moist sites in the United States and Canada; Zones 4-10. *V. stricta* (woolly verbena, hoary vervain)—1 to 4 feet tall with dense 12-inch spikes of blue to violet flowers in summer and fall; large woolly leaves. Ontario south to Texas and west to Idaho; Zones 3-10.

Growing conditions and maintenance

V. canadensis and *V. hastata* adapt to partial shade. *V. hastata* likes moist soil; the others dry, sandy soil. Propagate by seed.

Veronica (ve-RON-i-ka)

SPEEDWELL

Veronica 'Sunny Border Blue'

HARDINESS: Zones 4-8

FLOWERING SEASON: spring to summer

HEIGHT: 6 inches to 4 feet

FLOWER COLOR: blue, pink, white

SOIL: well-drained loam

LIGHT: full sun to light shade

Clumps of spreading stems lined with soft-textured, narrow leaves and tipped with long spikes of tiny, spring to summer flowers make speedwell a good choice for fillers or naturalizing.

Selected species and varieties

V. x hybrids—plants 12 to 24 inches tall; 'Sunny Border Blue' produces blue flowers. *V. incana* (silver speedwell, woolly speedwell)—pale lilac-blue flowers above low clumps of silver-gray foliage; 'Minuet' has pink flowers and gray-green leaves; 'Saraband', 12- to 18-inch plants with violet-blue flowers. *V. longifolia* (long-leaf speedwell)—plants to 4 feet; 'Icicle' has white flowers; var. *subsessilis*, lilac blooms. *V. spicata* (spike speedwell)—18-inch plants; 'Blue Fox' has lavender-blue flower spikes; 'Red Fox', rose-to-pink blooms. *V. teucrium* [also called *V. austriaca* ssp. *teucrium*] 'Crater Lake Blue'—compact 12- to 18-inch plants with wide spikes of deep blue flowers.

Growing conditions and maintenance

Plant speedwell 1 to 2 feet apart. Remove spent flowers to extend bloom. Propagate from seed or cuttings or by division in spring or fall.

Veronicastrum (ve-ro-ni-KAS-trum)

CULVER'S ROOT

Veronicastrum virginicum

HARDINESS: Zones 4-8

FLOWERING SEASON: summer

HEIGHT: 3 to 6 feet

FLOWER COLOR: white, pale lavender, pink

SOIL: well-drained, acid loam

LIGHT: full sun to partial shade

Veronicastrum produces branched clusters of tiny flower spikes on tall, erect stems. Its leaves are arranged in tiered whorls that ascend the stem.

Selected species and varieties
V. virginicum (blackroot)—tiny tubular flowers packed densely along 6- to 9-inch flower spikes on stems 6 feet tall in clumps 18 to 24 inches wide; 'Roseum' grows pink flowers; 'Album', white flowers. Veronicastrum is a good background plant for the garden.

Growing conditions and maintenance
Space veronicastrum 18 to 24 inches apart in moderately acid soil. Plants that are grown in shade may require staking for support. Propagate plants by division in the fall.

Vinca (VING-ka)

PERIWINKLE

Vinca major 'Variegata'

HARDINESS: Zones 4-8

FLOWERING SEASON: spring through summer

HEIGHT: 6 to 12 inches

FLOWER COLOR: blue, lilac, white

SOIL: average, well-drained

LIGHT: deep full to partial shade

A workhorse for difficult shady areas, *Vinca* provides a mat of glossy dark green evergreen foliage on interlaced vines that bear blue, lilac, or white five-petaled flowers, 1 to 2 inches across, in spring and sporadically throughout the summer. Useful on slopes and under trees.

Selected species and varieties
V. major (greater periwinkle)—creeping or trailing vines to 12 inches high bear leathery leaves to 2 inches long and blue flowers in spring; Zone 7; 'Variegata' has white-and-dark-green leaves. *V. minor* (common periwinkle)—glossy leaves to 1½ inches long on prostrate stems that crisscross to form a mat 8 inches high, flowering in spring; 'Alba' has white flowers; 'Bowles Variety' [also called 'La Grave'], a clump-forming habit with light blue flowers; 'Gertrude Jekyll' is a prolific bloomer with white flowers, smaller leaves, and dense but very slow growth.

Growing conditions and maintenance
Grows best in moist, rich garden soil but is widely tolerant. Once established, common periwinkle weathers drought, poor soil, and competing tree roots. Greater periwinkle is less drought tolerant.

Viola (Vy-O-la)

VIOLET

Viola canadensis var. rugulosa

HARDINESS: Zones 3-9

FLOWERING SEASON: spring and fall

HEIGHT: 3 to 12 inches

FLOWER COLOR: yellow, white, rose, violet

SOIL: moist, well-drained loam

LIGHT: partial shade

Violets produce dainty blossoms that have 2 upper petals and 3 lower petals joined into a short spur on thin stems. Leaves are heart shaped.

Selected species and varieties
V. canadensis (Canada violet)—white flowers with a yellow eye; *V. canadensis* var. *rugulosa* has narrower, wrinkled leaves with hairy undersides. *V. cornuta* (horned violet)—pansylike flowers on plants with evergreen leaves; 'Lord Nelson' has deep violet flowers. *V. cucullata* (marsh blue violet)—white flowers with purple veins; 'Royal Robe' has deep blue flowers. *V. odorata* (sweet violet)—fragrant flowers in shades of violet, rose, and white; 'Alba' has white blossoms; 'Czar', deep violet flowers. *V. tricolor* (Johnny-jump-up)—tricolored violet blue- and-yellow flowers.

Growing conditions and maintenance
Space violets 8 to 12 inches apart. Propagate from seed or by division.

Yucca (YUK-a)

YUCCA

Yucca filamentosa

HARDINESS: Zones 4-10

FLOWERING SEASON: summer

HEIGHT: 4½ to 12 feet

FLOWER COLOR: white, greenish white

SOIL: dry, well-drained

LIGHT: full sun

Yuccas have bold, stiff, sword-shaped basal leaves with a sharply pointed tip. Their flowers are borne on a stalk that rises high above the leaves. These drought-tolerant perennials are native to dry plains, sand hills, and prairies.

Selected species and varieties

Y. filamentosa (Adam's-needle)—native of southeastern United States with a rosette of blue-green leaves 2 to 3 feet long. The leaf margins have long curly threads. The 2-inch white flowers bloom on a stalk as much as 12 feet high and are followed by tan seed pods; Zones 5-10. *Y. glauca* (soapweed)—western native with a 3-foot clump of slender pale green leaves edged with white and threads along the margins. Fragrant greenish white flowers bloom on a 4½-foot stalk and are followed by cream-colored pods; Zones 4-8.

Growing conditions and maintenance

Grow yuccas in full sun in light, well-drained soil. They tolerate drought exceptionally well. Propagate by seed, offsets, or rhizome cuttings.

Zantedeschia (zan-tee-DES-kee-a)

CALLA LILY, ARUM LILY

Zantedeschia aethiopica

HARDINESS: Zones 9-10

FLOWERING SEASON: late spring to early summer

HEIGHT: 24 to 36 inches

FLOWER COLOR: white

SOIL: moist, humus-rich

LIGHT: full sun to partial shade

Calla lilies produce bold, arrow-shaped leaves and flowers composed of a gently flaring, white spathe surrounding a central golden spadix. They grow from tender rhizomes and survive winters only in mild climates, unless they are dug up in the fall for indoor storage. They are well suited to growing at the edge of a pond or stream, where the soil is constantly moist. They can also be planted in a moist perennial border or in a container.

Selected species and varieties

Z. aethiopica 'Crowborough'—24 to 36 inches tall, 24 inches wide, leaves arise from base and form a dense, erect cluster, white flowers are 6 to 10 inches on leafless stalk, spathe wraps around fragrant yellow spadix, blooming from late spring to early summer.

Growing conditions and maintenance

Plant calla lily rhizomes 4 inches deep in soil that is constantly moist. They thrive in bogs and near water. To maintain adequate moisture in garden soil, add generous amounts of organic matter prior to planting.

Zinnia (ZIN-ee-a)

ZINNIA

Zinnia grandiflora

HARDINESS: Zones 4-10

FLOWERING SEASON: spring through fall

HEIGHT: 6 to 8 inches

FLOWER COLOR: yellow, white

SOIL: well-drained to dry

LIGHT: full sun to partial shade

Most gardeners are familiar only with annual zinnias. The two perennial species described here are native to the central and southwestern United States, where they are commonly found along roadsides and on dry slopes. Both of these wildflowers bloom profusely for months and are attractive in rock gardens and on dry banks, where they help control erosion.

Selected species and varieties

Z. acerosa (dwarf white zinnia)—much-branched, shrubby plant 6 inches tall with ¾-inch white flowers with yellow centers. The narrow, silvery leaves are less than an inch long; Zones 8-10. *Z. grandiflora* (little golden zinnia, prairie zinnia, Rocky Mountain zinnia)—1½-inch yellow flowers with red or green centers on an 8-inch mound of needlelike, nearly evergreen, foliage; Zones 4-10.

Growing conditions and maintenance

Both species require well-drained to dry average soil and tolerate drought and heat. Propagate by seed sown in spring or fall. Young plants can also be divided in spring.

Bulbs

WHETHER MASSED TOGETHER OR MIXED WITH other flowers, bulbs hold no end of delights for gardeners. These adaptable plants—with their unique ability to store nutrients—usher in the garden's first colors in spring and are among the last blooms of fall. Bulbs are amenable to every planting scheme imaginable, from the spacious informality of a woodland plot to the cozy confines of a window box.

Ninety percent of the bulbs we grow for flowers belong to just six genera: *Lilium, Iris, Tulipa, Hyacinthus, Narcissus,* and *Gladiolus.* But within these six are hundreds of species and thousands of varieties. Gardeners can also choose from an array of other bulb genera.

In this section you'll find descriptions of some of the most common bulbs in the home landscape. Keep in mind that those selections designated as "tender" can survive winter in the ground only in warm zones; elsewhere, they must be dug up in fall for winter storage or grown in pots.

Achimenes (a-kim-EE-neez)

ORCHID PANSY

Achimenes longiflora

HARDINESS: tender or Zones 10-11

TYPE OF BULB: tuber or rhizome

FLOWERING SEASON: summer to fall

HEIGHT: 12 to 24 inches

SOIL: moist, well-drained

LIGHT: partial to full shade

Clusters of flat-faced flowers up to 2½ inches across with long, tubular necks bloom in masses amid fleshy, downy leaves on slender arching or trailing stems. Blossom throats are often splashed or veined in a contrasting color. New flowers appear over a long season of bloom. Excellent as houseplants, orchid pansies can also be used outdoors in containers and hanging baskets on shady patios in locations with mild temperatures. Their graceful mounded, sometimes cascading habit shows to good advantage in this setting.

Selected species and varieties

A. erecta—deep red late-summer-to-fall-blooming flowers on stems to 18 inches tall. *A. heterophylla* (yellow mist)—red-orange blossoms with yellow throats on 12-inch stems in late summer. *A. longiflora* (trumpet achimenes)—white, pink, red, lavender, or violet flowers, sometimes with contrasting throats, in midsummer amid whorls of extremely hairy leaves on stems to 12 inches; 'Paul Arnold' has blue-violet blossoms; 'Ambroise Verschaffelt' is white with a deep purple throat. *A. tubiflora* [also classified as *Sinningia tubiflora*]—fragrant white waxy summer flowers on 24-inch

stems. *A.* hybrids—'Cascade Cockade' has deep pink petals surrounding a white eye; 'Cascade Evening Glow', deep salmon flowers; 'Cascade Fairy Pink', pink petals and white centers; 'Cascade Fashionable Pink', pink blossoms; 'Cascade Great Rosy Red', rose blooms; 'Cascade Violet Night', blue-violet petals and a white throat; 'Elke Michelssen', red-orange flowers; 'English Waltz', salmon petals; 'India', deep blue flowers; 'Quick Step', blue flowers; 'Viola Michelssen', rose red blooms.

Growing conditions and maintenance

Plant achimenes in spring, setting tubers 1 inch deep and 3 to 4 inches apart. Flowers appear 12 to 14 weeks after planting; staggering plantings over several weeks provides a continuous show of blossoms for several months. For earliest bloom, start tubers indoors 6 to 8 weeks shortly before nighttime temperatures warm to 50° F. Plants grow best in a 24-hour temperature range of 60° to 80° F. Keep soil moist but not soggy, and fertilize while the plants are blooming. Gradually withhold water after flowering ceases. Store potted tubers over the winter in dry soil, or lift and dry tubers in fall for replanting in spring. Tubers do best stored at 50° to 60° F. Propagate by dividing dormant tubers into ½-inch pieces before repotting in spring or by removing and potting tiny rhizomes, which sometimes appear in leaf joints. Achimenes can also be grown from seed, but hybrids may revert to parent species.

Achimenes 'Ambroise Verschaffelt'

Agapanthus (ag-a-PAN-thus)

LILY-OF-THE-NILE

Agapanthus africanus

HARDINESS: tender or Zones 8-10

TYPE OF BULB: rhizome

FLOWERING SEASON: summer

HEIGHT: 18 inches to 5 feet

SOIL: moist, well-drained

LIGHT: full sun

Domed clusters of five-petaled, star-shaped flowers with prominent stamens rise on leafless, hollow stalks from graceful clumps of straplike evergreen leaves that persist after the flowers fade. Agapanthus makes dramatic border specimens or pot plants and can be used as long-lasting cut flowers. Its seedpods add interest to dried arrangements.

Selected species and varieties

A. africanus 'Albus' (African lily)—clusters of 30 or more 1½-inch white flower stars on stems to 3 feet tall. *A. praecox* ssp. *orientalis* (Oriental agapanthus)—up to 100 white or blue flowers clustered on stems to 5 feet tall above 3-foot-long leaves that are up to 3 inches wide and sometimes striped yellow; 'Peter Pan' is an 18-inch dwarf cultivar with blue blossoms.

Growing conditions and maintenance

Plant rhizomes 24 inches apart in spring for summer bloom, setting the tops of the bulbs just below the soil line. In colder areas, grow plants in pots, moving them indoors before frost. They bloom best when slightly potbound. Cut stems back after flowers fade. Propagate by dividing rhizomes every 4 or 5 years in spring.

FLOWERING ONION

Allium cernuum

HARDINESS: Zones 3-9

TYPE OF BULB: true bulb

FLOWERING SEASON: spring to summer

HEIGHT: 6 inches to 5 feet

SOIL: moist, well-drained

LIGHT: full sun to partial shade

Related to edible culinary species, flowering onions produce showy 2- to 12-inch flower clusters, usually in dense spheres or ovals composed of hundreds of tiny blooms packed tightly together, but sometimes in loose, dangling or upright airy domes of larger flowers. Each stout, leafless hollow stem holds a single flower well above a low rosette of grassy or straplike leaves that die back after the bulbs produce their blooms. Many species smell faintly like onion or garlic when cut or bruised, but a few are sweetly fragrant. Mass alliums for effect in spring or summer beds or borders; strategically site larger flowering onions as dramatic garden accents; and interplant smaller species with ground covers or in a rock garden. Alliums are striking as cut flowers or in dried bouquets. Some flowering onion species will naturalize, and a few are suitable for forcing. Rodent pests find flowering onion bulbs unappealing.

Selected species and varieties

A. aflatunense (ornamental onion, Persian onion)—4-inch purple flower globes in late spring on 2- to 4-foot-tall stems above 4-inch-wide foliage; Zones 4-8. *A. atro-* *purpureum*—2-inch wine red spheres on 2- to 3-foot stems in late spring above narrow 18-inch leaves; Zones 3-9. *A. caeruleum* (blue garlic, blue globe onion)—deep blue blossoms in dense 2-inch globes on 2-foot stems in late spring above narrow 10- to 18-inch-long leaves; Zones 3-9. *A. carinatum* ssp. *pulchellum* (keeled garlic)—carmine flower clusters on stems to 2 feet in summer; 'Album' has white flowers; Zones 3-9. *A. cernuum* (nodding wild onion)—loose clusters of 30 to 40 delicate pink flowers dangle atop 8- to 18-inch stems in late spring above rosettes of grassy 10-inch leaves; Zones 3-9. *A. christophii* (stars-of-Persia)—spidery late spring flowers with a metallic luster growing in lacy clusters up to 10 inches across on stout stems to 2 feet growing from rosettes of 1-inch-wide leaves up to 20 inches long; Zones 4-8. *A. flavum* (small yellow onion)—dangling 2-inch clusters of yellow bell-shaped flowers on 1-foot stems in summer; Zones 4-9. *A. giganteum* (giant ornamental onion, giant garlic)—lilac-colored summer flower globes 6 inches across on stems to 5 feet rising from clumps of leaves 2 inches wide and up to 30 inches long; Zones 5-8. *A. jesdianum*—dense clusters of deep violet flowers; Zones 4-9. *A. karataviense* (Turkestan onion)—pale rose 3-inch or larger flower clusters on 10-inch stems above broad straps of attractive, spreading blue-green foliage in late spring; Zones 4-9. *A. macleanii*—red-violet blossoms clustered at the tips of 3-foot stems in late spring above broad, shiny foliage; Zones 4-9. *A. moly* (lily leek, golden onion)—flat clusters of ¾- to 1-inch flowers; 'Jeannine' has long-lasting 2-

Allium christophii

to 3-inch vivid yellow flowers on 12-inch stems in summer above blue-green leaves with a metallic sheen; Zones 3-9. *A. neapolitanum* 'Grandiflorum' (daffodil garlic, Naples garlic)—loose, open 3-inch clusters of up to 30 fragrant 1-inch white flower stars on 12- to 18-inch stems in late spring; Zones 6-9. *A. nigrum*—white spring flowers touched with gray on 2-foot stems; Zones 4-9. *A. oreophilum*—open clusters of fragrant 2-inch rosy pink blossoms on 4-inch stems in late spring; Zones 4-9. *A. rosenbachianum* 'Album'—silvery white 4-inch flower clusters on stems to 3 feet in late spring above 2-inch-wide leaves up to 20 inches long; Zones 5-9. *A. roseum* 'Grandiflorum' (bigflower rosy onion, rosy garlic)—3-inch pinkish white flower globes in late spring on stems to 15 inches,

Allium sphaerocephalum

frequently with tiny bulbils appearing after the flowers fade; Zones 5-9. *A. schubertii*—spidery pink-violet flowers in clusters up to a foot or more across on 1- to 2-foot stems in summer above distinctively wavy, inch-wide foliage; Zones 4-9. *A. sphaerocephalum* (drumstick chive, roundheaded leek, roundheaded garlic)—has densely packed 2-inch oval heads of deep purple, bell-shaped summer flowers on 3-foot stems rising from clumps of hollow cylindrical leaves up to 24 inches long; Zones 4-8. *A. stipitatum* 'Album'—6-inch spheres of white flowers on stems to 4 feet in late spring above 2-inch-wide leaves; Zones 4-9. *A. triquetrum* (three-cornered leek, triangle onion)—dangling white flowers striped with green on unusual triangular 18-inch stems rising from clumps of deep green leaves 10 to 15 inches long throughout spring; Zones 4-9. *A. unifolium*—rose flowers on 12- to 18-inch stems in late spring; Zones 4-9. *A. ursinum* (bear's garlic, ramsons, wood garlic)—2½-inch flat-topped clusters of white flowers with a strong garlicky odor on 12- to 15-inch stems in late spring; Zones 4-9. *A. zebdanense*—white blossoms clustered on 12-inch stems in late spring; Zones 4-9. *A. hybrids*—'Globemaster' has durable large purple blooms on 2- to 3-foot stems; 'Lucy Ball', deep lilac clusters on stems to 4 feet in summer; 'Purple Sensation' bears purple flowers on 30-inch stems in spring; Zones 4-9.

Growing conditions and maintenance

Plant flowering onions in fall in northern zones, in spring or fall in warmer areas. Set bulbs at a depth two to three times their diameter, spacing smaller bulbs 4 to 6 inches apart, larger ones 12 to 18 inches. Alliums suitable for naturalizing include *A. aflatunense, A. karataviense, A. moly, A. neapolitanum, A. oreophilum, A. sphaerocephalum,* and *A. triquetrum,* although *A. triquetrum* can be invasive. Alliums may be left undisturbed in the garden for years until diminished bloom signals that bulbs are overcrowded. Both pleasantly scented *A. neapolitanum* and low-growing *A. schubertii* are suitable for forcing; plant several bulbs per 6-inch pot or bulb pan. Cut stems back after flowers fade, but allow foliage to die back before removing it. Protect bulbs with winter mulch north of Zone 5. Propagate by separating and replanting tiny bulblets that develop at the base of parent bulbs, by potting tiny bulbils that appear amid flower clusters, or by sowing seed, which will grow blooming-size bulbs in 2 years.

Alstroemeria (ahl-strum-EE-ree-a)

PERUVIAN LILY

Alstroemeria Ligtu Hybrids

HARDINESS: Zones 6-11

TYPE OF BULB: tuber

FLOWERING SEASON: summer

HEIGHT: 3 to 4 feet

SOIL: moist, well-drained

LIGHT: full sun to light shade

Peruvian lily's 2-inch flowers bloom in clusters atop stiff stems lined with narrow leaves. The intricately patterned, funnel-shaped flowers with curving stamens resemble exotic azaleas with inner petals often speckled, splotched, striped or tipped in contrasting colors. Use Peruvian lilies as border plants, container specimens, and cut flowers.

Selected species and varieties

A. aurea—clusters of up to 50 flowers on 3-foot stems; 'Dover Orange' is orange; 'Lutea', yellow. *A.* Ligtu Hybrids—inner and outer petals in contrasting shades of white to pink, salmon or orange on stems to 4 feet.

Growing conditions and maintenance

Plant Peruvian lily tubers in spring or fall setting them 6 to 9 inches deep and 12 inches apart. *A. aurea* can be invasive. Protect with winter mulch in Zones 6-8. North of Zone 6, grow Peruvian lilies in containers and bring indoors in winter. Propagate by carefully dividing in spring or fall or from seed.

Amaryllis (am-a-RIL-lis)

BELLADONNA LILY

Amaryllis belladonna

HARDINESS: tender or Zones 9-11

TYPE OF BULB: true bulb

FLOWERING SEASON: summer to fall

HEIGHT: 1½ to 3 feet

SOIL: moist, well-drained

LIGHT: full sun

Amaryllis belladonna, the sole species within this genus, produces clusters of 6 to 12 flower trumpets up to 3½ inches across. The straplike foliage, which appears in early to late spring, dies by summer. Fragrant flowers appear separately on a leafless stalk several months later. Force belladonna lilies indoors as houseplants or use as border plantings in Zones 9-11. Blossoms last a week as cut flowers.

Selected species and varieties

A. belladonna (belladonna lily)—white to pale pink or rose blossoms; 'Cape Town' has deep rose red flowers.

Growing conditions and maintenance

Pot with the neck of the bulb at the soil surface or set bulbs outdoors 4 to 6 inches deep and 12 inches apart. Begin watering when foliage appears, then withhold all water between foliage dieback and the appearance of the flower stalk; resume watering then and fertilize until flowers fade. Propagate from seed, planting the fleshy seeds as soon as they appear after flowers fade, or by removing bulblets from parent bulbs. Caution: Belladonna lily bulbs are poisonous and must be kept out of the reach of children.

WINDFLOWER

Anemone coronaria

HARDINESS: Zones 3-9

TYPE OF BULB: tuber or rhizome

FLOWERING SEASON: spring

HEIGHT: 3 to 18 inches

SOIL: moist, well-drained

LIGHT: full sun to light shade

Windflowers carpet a border with drifts of daisylike flowers held above whorls of attractively divided leaves resembling flat parsley. Single or double rows of petals surround a prominent cushion of anthers in a contrasting color, often with a halo of cream or white separating it from the main petal color. Mass windflowers for a tapestry of color beneath spring-flowering shrubs and trees or allow them to naturalize in woodland gardens. Anemones can be forced as houseplants, and the taller ones make good cut flowers.

Selected species and varieties

A. apennina 'Alba' (Apennine windflower) —inch-wide white flowers tinged blue on 6- to 12-inch stems; Zones 6-9. *A. blanda* (Grecian windflower)—2-inch single- or double-petaled flowers with prominent yellow centers on 3- to 8-inch stems; 'Blue Star' has light blue flowers; 'Blue Shades', light to dark blue blooms; 'Charmer', deep pink flowers; 'Pink Star', very large pink blossoms; 'Radar', reddish purple flowers with a white center; 'Rosea', rosy pink blooms; 'Violet Star', violet flowers with a white center; 'White Splendor', long-lasting, large white flowers; Zones 5-8. *A. coro-*

naria (poppy anemone)—'de Caen' hybrids grow 18 inches tall with single rows of petals; 'Mr. Fokker' has blue flowers; 'Sylphide', deep violet blooms; 'The Bride', pure white flowers. St. Brigid hybrids produce semidouble rows of petals; 'Lord Lieutenant' has bright blue flowers; 'Mt. Everest', white flowers; 'The Admiral', red-violet blooms; 'The Governor', deep scarlet flowers. 'Hollandia' has bright red flowers; Zones 6-9. *A. nemorosa* (wood anemone)—1-inch-wide white flowers tinged pink with yellow centers on 6- to 10-inch stems; 'Alba Plena' has double petals; Zones 4-8. *A. ranunculoides* (buttercup anemone)—yellow blossoms on 6-inch stems; 'Flore Pleno' has semidouble yellow petals giving a ruffled appearance; 'Superba', large flowers above bronzy foliage; Zones 3-9.

Growing conditions and maintenance

Plant windflowers in the fall, massing them for best effect. Soak tubers overnight before setting them out 2 inches deep and 3 to 6 inches apart. *A. apennina* and Grecian windflower can be grown north of Zone 6 by setting tubers out in spring, then lifting them for storage in fall. *A. apennina*, Grecian windflower, and poppy anemone can be forced for houseplants. *A. apennina*, Grecian windflower, wood anemone, and buttercup anemone all naturalize well, although the latter two can be invasive. Anemones need constant moisture, though not soggy conditions, to bloom at their best. Propagate windflowers from seed or by division in late summer after foliage fades.

Anemone blanda

DRAGONROOT

Arisaema triphyllum

HARDINESS: Zones 4-9

TYPE OF BULB: tuber

FLOWERING SEASON: spring

HEIGHT: 1 to 3 feet

SOIL: moist, acid

LIGHT: partial to full shade

Arisaemas produce a fleshy spike called a spadix nestled within an outer leaflike spathe, which folds over the spadix like a hood. Glossy, three-lobed leaves taller than the spathe and spadix persist throughout the summer. The spadix ripens to a cluster of attractive red fruit in fall. Use arisaemas in wildflower or woodland gardens or along stream banks, where they will slowly spread out and naturalize.

Selected species and varieties

A. dracontium (green-dragon)—green spathe enfolding a 4- to 10-inch green or yellowish green spadix on 1-foot stems. *A. sikokianum*—ivory spadix within a spathe that is deep maroon banded in green on the outside and ivory at its base on the inside, on 1-foot stems. *A. triphyllum* (jack-in-the-pulpit, Indian turnip)—green to purple spadix within a green to purple spathe striped purple, green, white, or maroon inside on 1- to 2-foot stems.

Growing conditions and maintenance

Plant arisaemas in fall, setting tubers 4 inches deep and 1 foot apart in soil that is constantly moist but not soggy. Propagate by division in early fall.

ARUM

Arum italicum

HARDINESS: Zones 6-9

TYPE OF BULB: tuber

FLOWERING SEASON: spring

HEIGHT: 12 to 18 inches

SOIL: moist, acid

LIGHT: partial shade

Italian arum (*Arum italicum*) is noteworthy for its attractively marbled, arrow-shaped leaves, which appear in fall and persist through the winter. Inconspicuous flowers appear in spring, lining a fleshy, fingerlike spadix enfolded by a leaflike hood called a spathe, which rises to a sharp point. Most gardeners grow arum for the plump cluster of glossy, brightly colored berries that follows the flowers in summer. Arum will naturalize in moist woodland or wildflower gardens.

Selected species and varieties

A. italicum 'Marmoratum' [also called 'Pictum'] (Italian arum)—narrow, waxy leaves veined in cream or silver followed by a creamy yellow or yellow-green spadix and thick clusters of brilliant orange berries.

Growing conditions and maintenance

Plant Italian arum in late summer, setting tubers 3 inches deep and 1 foot apart in soil that is moist but not soggy. Propagate from seed or by division in late summer. Caution: Both the foliage and berries of Italian arum are poisonous and must be kept out of the reach of children.

BABOON FLOWER

Babiana stricta

HARDINESS: tender or Zones 9-11

TYPE OF BULB: corm

FLOWERING SEASON: spring

HEIGHT: 8 to 12 inches

SOIL: moist, well-drained

LIGHT: full sun

Baboon flowers produce 1½-inch fragrant flowers with pointed petals surrounding a contrasting eye; the blooms last as long as 5 weeks in the garden. Flowers grow in clusters on stems rising from stiff, sword-shaped leaves. Use baboon flowers in borders or grow them in containers as patio specimens.

Selected species and varieties

B. stricta—flowers in shades of cream, blue, lilac, and crimson; 'Purple Sensation' produces white-throated purple flowers; 'White King', white petals streaked blue on their undersides surrounding a deep blue eye; 'Zwanenburg Glory', lavender to violet petals splashed with white.

Growing conditions and maintenance

Plant baboon flowers in fall, setting corms 6 inches deep and 6 inches apart. North of Zone 9, plant corms in spring and lift after foliage fades in fall for replanting the following spring. Propagate from seed or by removing and planting the cormels that develop around parent bulbs every 3 to 4 years.

TUBEROUS BEGONIA

Begonia Picotee Group

HARDINESS: tender or Zones 10-11

TYPE OF BULB: tuber

FLOWERING SEASON: summer to fall

HEIGHT: 8 to 18 inches

SOIL: moist, well-drained

LIGHT: partial to full shade

Tuberous begonias produce an abundance of large flowers over a long season of bloom with soft, waxy petals in vivid tones of red, orange, apricot, rose, pink, yellow, cream, or white, sometimes bicolored, on fleshy upright or trailing stems. Blossoms open in succession amid pointed, crenelated green to bronze foliage that is deeply veined, sometimes in contrasting colors. Their diverse flower forms have plain, frilled, or fringed petals arranged to mimic the blossoms of roses, camellias, carnations, and other garden favorites. Thousands of hybrids offer almost limitless combinations of forms and colors for varying purposes. Upright tuberous begonias are striking when massed as bedding plants or grown as specimens in patio containers, whereas cascading forms are appealing when allowed to trail gracefully from hanging baskets.

Selected species and varieties

B. x tuberhybrida—flowers to 4 inches or more across, with hundreds of hybrids classified in 12 groups according to flower form and color. *Single Group*—broad, flat-faced flowers composed of four enormous petals surrounding a central cluster of prominent stamens. *Crispa or Frilled Group*—flat-faced flowers with large petals whose edges are ruffled or fringed, surrounding a colorful cluster of stamens. *Cristata or Crested Group*—raised, frilled crests punctuating the center of each of several large tepals. *Narcissiflora or Daffodil-flowered Group*—double rows of

Begonia Camelliiflora Group

petals in an arrangement that resembles a flat-faced narcissus. *Camellia or Camelliflora Group*—smooth petals of a single color arranged in overlapping layers like camellia flowers on upright plants. *Ruffled Camellia Group*—overlapping layers of ruffled petals that conceal the stamens. *Rosiflora or Rosebud Group*—center petals tightly furled like a pointed, unopened rosebud. *Fimbriata Plena or Carnation Group*—finely fringed petals overlapping in double rows. *Picotee Group*—double rows of overlapping petals edged in a narrow or broad band of a deeper shade of the main petal color. *Marginata Group*—double rows of petals edged in a narrow or broad band of a contrasting color. *Marmorata Group*—double rows of pink or rose petals dappled with white. *Pendula or Hanging-Basket Group*—a profusion of single- or double-petaled blossoms on trailing stems. *Multiflora Group*—small single- or double-petaled blossoms on bushy plants with compact stems.

Most hybrid tuberous begonias are identified in the garden trade simply by form and color rather than by cultivar names, with the camellia-flowered, carnation-flowered, crispa marginata, picotee, and hanging basket—sometimes called cascade or pendula—types most common.

Nonstop hybrids have smaller flowers than the double hybrid begonias they resemble, but their blossoms appear throughout the summer and fall until frost.

Growing conditions and maintenance

Plant tuberous begonias outdoors in spring for summer bloom, setting tubers 1 to 2 inches deep with their concave side up and 12 to 15 inches apart. For potted plants, space three or four tubers evenly in each pot or hanging basket, with the top of the tuber at the soil line. For earliest flowering, start tuberous begonias indoors 6 to 12 weeks before planting outside. Keep soil constantly moist but not soggy. Prune small tubers to a single stem, larger ones to 3 or 4 stems, and pinch early buds to encourage more prolific flowering. Provide support for upright forms. Fertilize while blooming with a dilute balanced houseplant fertilizer. North of Zone 10, lift tubers in fall after the first light frost, allow them to dry, and store them for replanting in spring. Propagate tuberous begonias from stem cuttings taken in spring; by dividing tubers, making sure to maintain at least one growth bud in each section; or from seed sown indoors in January to bloom in June.

Begonia Pendula Group

BLACKBERRY LILY

Belamcanda chinensis

HARDINESS: Zones 5-10

TYPE OF BULB: rhizome

FLOWERING SEASON: late summer to fall

HEIGHT: 2 to 3 feet

SOIL: well-drained

LIGHT: full sun to light shade

Blackberry lilies carry sprays of lilylike flowers with narrow, curving, pointed petals on zigzag-branching flower stalks above fans of swordlike foliage. Each flower lasts only a day, but new blossoms open over several weeks. Flowers are followed by attractive seed pods, which burst open to reveal berrylike seeds. Use blackberry lilies in a sunny border or as cut flowers. Dried seed pods decorate the winter garden and can be used in dried flower arrangements.

Selected species and varieties

B. chinensis (leopard lily)—2-inch orange flowers with pointed, curving petals liberally spotted with red.

Growing conditions and maintenance

Plant blackberry lilies in spring or fall, setting rhizomes 1 inch deep and 6 to 8 inches apart. Blackberry lilies do best in full sun; in light shade, they may require staking. Propagate from seed to produce flowering plants in 2 years or by dividing rhizomes in spring or fall.

Bellevalia (bel-VAH-lee-a)

BELLEVALIA

Bellevalia pycnantha

HARDINESS: Zones 6-10

TYPE OF BULB: true bulb

FLOWERING SEASON: spring

HEIGHT: 6 to 18 inches

SOIL: well-drained

LIGHT: full sun

Bellevalia's cylindrical flower clusters composed of 20 to 30 small flower bells open from bottom to top on a single stalk rising from a clump of straplike leaves. The blooms resemble *Muscari* as they begin to open, small *Hyacinthus* when fully open. Clusters of blue-black seeds follow in fall. Use bellevalia in borders or rock gardens, where they may naturalize.

Selected species and varieties
B. pycnantha—dull blue-black flowers with yellow edges that unfold on 12-inch-tall stalks above 12-inch-long leaves. *B. romana* [also called *Hyacinthus romanus*]—gray flower buds opening into dull white, ¼-inch flowers sometimes tinged with violet, brown, or green on 6- to 18-inch flower stalks.

Growing conditions and maintenance
Plant bellevalias in fall, setting bulbs 3 inches deep and 3 inches apart. Bulbs tolerate both wet spring conditions and summer drought. Propagate by removing and replanting the small bulblets that develop at the base of parent bulbs in fall.

Bletilla (ble-TIL-la)

HARDY ORCHID

Bletilla striata

HARDINESS: Zones 5-9

TYPE OF BULB: rhizome

FLOWERING SEASON: late spring

HEIGHT: 1 to 2 feet

SOIL: moist, well-drained

LIGHT: partial shade

Hardy orchids bear up to six or more delicate flowers resembling small cattleya orchids on arching, branched stalks rising above clumps of narrow, oval, pointed leaves. Appearing over a long season of bloom, each nodding, multicolored flower has waxy petals and petal-like sepals rimming an elaborate lip with several crested ridges resembling ruffled pleats. Plant hardy orchids in woodland gardens where they can expand into handsome clumps, or pot them as houseplants.

Selected species and varieties
B. striata—inch-wide pink to purple flowers with decoratively spotted and mottled lips appearing for up to 6 weeks; 'Alba' is pure white.

Growing conditions and maintenance
Plant hardy orchids in spring or fall, placing rhizomes and the small pseudobulbs growing from them 4 inches deep and 6 inches apart in soil enriched with organic matter. In winter, mulch hardy orchids in Zones 5-7, or move potted hardy orchids to locations where they will not freeze. Propagate by division in spring or fall.

Brimeura (bri-MURE-ra)

ALPINE HYACINTH

Brimeura amethystina

HARDINESS: Zones 4-10

TYPE OF BULB: true bulb

FLOWERING SEASON: spring

HEIGHT: 6 to 12 inches

SOIL: well-drained

LIGHT: full sun to light shade

Alpine hyacinths produce up to a dozen nodding flower bells loosely spaced along one side of an arching flower stalk growing from a clump of grassy leaves. They resemble *Hyacinthus* but bloom later in the spring. Allow these dainty plants to naturalize in borders, rock gardens, or wildflower gardens. They can also be forced as houseplants.

Selected species and varieties
B. amethystina [formerly *Hyacinthus amethystinus* and *Scilla amethystina*]—up to 15 tiny ½-inch blue bells lining one side of the stalks; 'Alba' yields pure white flower bells.

Growing conditions and maintenance
Plant alpine hyacinths in fall, setting bulbs 1 to 2 inches deep and 4 to 5 inches apart. The small bulbs make the best show when planted closely and left to multiply. Save bulbs forced as potted plants to set out in the garden in fall. Propagate by removing and replanting the small bulblets that form alongside parent bulbs.

Bulbocodium (bul-bo-KO-dee-um)

BULBOCODIUM

Bulbocodium vernum

HARDINESS: Zones 3-10

TYPE OF BULB: corm

FLOWERING SEASON: late winter to spring

HEIGHT: 4 inches

SOIL: well-drained, sandy

LIGHT: full sun to light shade

One of the earliest flowers to brighten the garden, bulbocodium sends up blossoms that open into upright trumpets of narrow, ribbonlike petals. The narrow, grassy leaves appear after the flowers bloom. The plant will naturalize in a border, rock garden, or wildflower garden.

Selected species and varieties

B. vernum (spring meadow saffron)—one to three 2- to 3-inch-wide rose-violet flower trumpets on each short stalk.

Growing conditions and maintenance

Plant spring meadow saffron in late summer or fall, spacing corms 3 to 4 inches apart and setting them 3 inches deep. Locations that provide moisture in spring, when bulbs are blooming and foliage is ripening, but are slightly dry in summer are ideal. Propagate by removing and replanting the small cormels that grow at the base of each corm every 3 or 4 years after the grassy leaves die back in early summer.

Caladium (ka-LAY-dee-um)

ANGEL-WINGS

Caladium bicolor 'Aaron'

HARDINESS: tender or Zones 10-11

TYPE OF BULB: tuber

FLOWERING SEASON: summer

HEIGHT: 1 to 2 feet

SOIL: moist, well-drained

LIGHT: partial shade to shade

Exotic caladiums form clumps of intricately patterned translucent leaves that eclipse their insignificant flowers. The arrow-shaped leaves, rising continuously through out summer, are vividly marbled, shaded, slashed, veined, and flecked in contrasting colors to brighten shady borders or decorate indoor gardens.

Selected species and varieties

C. bicolor [formerly *C. x hortulanum*]—foot-long arrow- or heart-shaped leaves; 'Aaron' has green edges feathering into creamy centers; 'Candidum' is white with green veining; 'Fannie Munson', pink-veined red edged in green; 'Festiva', rose-veined green; 'Irene Dank', light green edged in deeper green; 'June Bride', greenish white edged in deep green; 'Pink Beauty', a pink dwarf spattered with green; 'White Christmas', white with green veins.

Growing conditions and maintenance

Plant in spring when night temperatures remain above 60° F, setting the tubers 2 inches deep and 8 to 12 inches apart. North of Zone 10, lift and dry tubers in fall to replant the next spring. Provide high humidity and temperatures of 60° F or more. Propagate by division in spring.

Calochortus (ka-lo-KOR-tus)

MARIPOSA LILY

Calochortus venustus

HARDINESS: Zones 6-10

TYPE OF BULB: true bulb

FLOWERING SEASON: spring

HEIGHT: 8 inches to 2 feet

SOIL: very well-drained, sandy, acid

LIGHT: full sun

The furled, overlapping petals of mariposa lilies form tuliplike, upright cups. Each erect stem rises from a small clump of shiny, fleshy, narrow leaves. Grow mariposa lilies in a rock garden or as potted plants, or use them in arrangements.

Selected species and varieties

C. splendens (lilac mariposa)—2-inch lilac flowers on 1- to 2-foot stems. *C. venustus* (white mariposa)—white, yellow, purple, or red 2-inch-wide flowers with throats splotched in darker shades or contrasting colors on 8-inch to 2-foot stems.

Growing conditions and maintenance

Plant mariposa lilies in fall, setting the bulbs 2 inches deep and 4 to 6 inches apart. The bulbs must dry out after foliage dies back; if necessary, lift them in late summer to replant in fall. Alternating freeze/thaw cycles reduce blooming; where this occurs, mulch after first frost or grow bulbs in pots to overwinter in cold frames. Avoid fertilizing. Propagate from seed or by removing and replanting bulblets growing alongside bulbs in fall.

Camassia (ka-MA-see-a)

CAMASS, QUAMASH

Camassia quamash

HARDINESS: Zones 5-9

TYPE OF BULB: true bulb

FLOWERING SEASON: spring

HEIGHT: 1 to 4 feet

SOIL: moist, well-drained, sandy

LIGHT: full sun to light shade

Camass's spires of inch-wide flowers like tiny stars with a fringe of narrow, pointed, sometimes double petals open from bottom to top over several weeks. Naturalize camass in damp wildflower gardens, alongside streams or ponds, or among other spring-blooming bulbs.

Selected species and varieties
C. cusickii (Cusick quamash)—up to 300 flowers on stalks 3 to 4 feet tall; 'Zwanenburg' has horizontal stalks upturned at their ends. *C. leichtlinii* (Leichtlin quamash)—up to 40 flowers on stems to 4 feet; 'Alba' produces white blossoms; 'Blue Danube', very dark blue; 'Sempiplena', double-petaled creamy white to yellow. *C. quamash* (common camass)—foot-long spires on 2-foot stems; 'Orion' is very deep blue. *C. scilloides* (Atlantic camass, eastern camass, wild hyacinth)—blue or white ½-inch flowers on 2½-foot stems.

Growing conditions and maintenance
Plant camass bulbs in fall, setting them 4 inches deep and 6 to 9 inches apart. Provide shade where summers are dry. Bulbs can be lifted to remove offsets but are best left undisturbed unless flowering declines. Otherwise, propagate from seed.

Canna (KAN-ah)

CANNA

Canna 'Pretoria'

HARDINESS: tender or Zones 8-11

TYPE OF BULB: rhizome

FLOWERING SEASON: summer to fall

HEIGHT: 18 inches to 6 feet

SOIL: moist, well-drained

LIGHT: full sun

Cannas produce a continuous show of bold 4- to 5-inch flowers with a tousled arrangement of petal-like stamens in strong colors from summer through frost. The flowers, which are sometimes bicolored, are carried on clumps of stiff, erect stems. The broad, bold leaves, up to 24 inches long, are usually a deep, glossy green but are sometimes bronzy red or striped or veined in white or pink. They line the stems to provide a dramatic backdrop to the flowers. Mass these coarse-textured plants at the back of borders in casual groupings or formal patterns, or grow dwarf cultivars as edgings or in patio containers.

Selected species and varieties
C. x generalis (canna lily)—standard varieties grow 4 to 6 feet tall; 'Black Knight' has deep velvet red flowers and bronze foliage; 'City of Portland', rosy salmon flowers above green leaves; 'Gaiety', yellow flowers edged in orange; 'Los Angeles', coral pink blooms above green foliage; 'The President', bright red flowers and deep green leaves; 'Red King Humbert', red flowers above bronzy foliage on very tall stems; 'Richard Wallace', canary yellow blossoms and green foliage; 'Rosamund Cole', red-and-gold bicolored blossoms; 'Stadt Fellbach', peach flowers with yellow throats fading to pink; 'Wyoming', rugged red-orange flowers and reddish bronze leaves. Dwarf varieties of this species grow to less than 3 feet tall; 'Ambrosia' has pinky orange blossoms on 18-inch stems; 'Brandywine', scarlet flowers on 3-foot stems; 'Pfitzer's Chinese Coral', rich coral pink blossoms; 'Pfitzer's Crimson Beauty', bright red flowers on 18-inch stems; 'Pfitzer's Primrose Yellow', soft yellow blooms; 'Pfitzer's Salmon', unusually large salmon pink flowers; 'Pretoria', yellow-orange flowers above deep green leaves striped with cream.

Growing conditions and maintenance
In Zones 9 and 10, set cannas out as bedding plants in spring, planting the rhizomes 4 to 6 inches deep; space standard cultivars 2 feet apart, dwarf cultivars 1 foot apart. Provide ample moisture and high humidity during the growing season. Cannas can remain in the ground year round in frost-free areas; in Zone 8, provide a protective winter mulch. North of Zone 8, start cannas for beds or containers indoors 4 weeks before night temperatures reach 60°F; in fall, cut foliage back to 6 inches and lift rhizomes for winter storage. Pinch each container-grown rhizome back to a single shoot for largest flowers. Propagate cannas from seed, soaking seeds for 48 hours before planting to loosen their tough outer coats; or by division in spring, sectioning to allow no more than two buds per piece.

Canna 'Brandywine'

Cardiocrinum (kar-dee-o-KREE-num)

GIANT LILY

Cardiocrinum giganteum

HARDINESS: Zones 6-8

TYPE OF BULB: true bulb

FLOWERING SEASON: summer

HEIGHT: 8 to 12 feet

SOIL: moist, well-drained, acid, fertile

LIGHT: light shade

Giant lilies produce clusters of fragrant, narrow flower trumpets as much as 6 inches long atop stout stems. Pencil-shaped buds open into drooping, flared funnels in tiers all around each stem. Glossy, heart-shaped leaves up to 18 inches long form a basal rosette and sparsely line each stem. Giant lilies grow best in filtered shade at the edges of moist woodlands.

Selected species and varieties
C. giganteum (heart lily)—up to 20 nodding white flowers suffused with green on the outside and striped maroon inside tipping stems to 12 feet tall.

Growing conditions and maintenance
Plant giant lily bulbs in spring or fall with their tops just at the soil line, spaced 18 inches apart. Giant lilies produce nonflowering shoots for several years before blossoming. Then bulbs die, leaving small bulblets, which will grow to flowering size in 3 to 4 years. Plant bulbs of different sizes to ensure blooms each year. Propagate by lifting and replanting bulblets after the main bulb flowers.

Chionodoxa (kee-on-o-DOKS-a)

GLORY-OF-THE-SNOW

Chionodoxa luciliae 'Pink Giant'

HARDINESS: Zones 4-9

TYPE OF BULB: true bulb

FLOWERING SEASON: spring

HEIGHT: 4 to 10 inches

SOIL: moist, well-drained

LIGHT: full sun to light shade

Glory-of-the-snow is one of the earliest bulbs to appear in spring, often before snows have completely melted. Small clusters of open-faced flower stars with narrow, gracefully curved petals are carried above grassy leaves on short stems. Glory-of-the-snow naturalizes easily in rock or wildflower gardens to create carpets of color beneath taller spring bulbs or deciduous shrubs. The plant can also be forced for indoor winter bloom.

Selected species and varieties
C. luciliae—clusters of three or more 1-inch blue flowers with centers suffused with white on 4-inch stems; 'Alba' grows pure white; 'Pink Giant' produces bright pink flowers on 3- to 6-inch stems; 'Rosea' is pink. *C. sardensis*—deep blue flowers on stems to 6 inches.

Growing conditions and maintenance
Plant glory-of-the-snow in masses for best effect, setting bulbs 3 inches deep and 3 inches apart. For forcing, allow 12 to 18 bulbs per 8-inch bulb pan. Propagate from seed or by removing and replanting bulblets growing alongside older bulbs.

Chlidanthus (klid-ANTH-us)

DELICATE LILY

Chlidanthus fragrans

HARDINESS: tender or Zones 9-11

TYPE OF BULB: true bulb

FLOWERING SEASON: summer

HEIGHT: 8 to 10 inches

SOIL: moist, well-drained, sandy

LIGHT: full sun

Lemon-scented flower funnels with six pointed petals layered like overlapping triangles grow in small clusters at the tips of the delicate lily's slender stalks. Narrow, strap-shaped, gray-green leaves appear after the flowers. Delicate lilies will slowly spread into small colonies when left in the ground in Zones 9-10 and make excellent potted plants for indoor use or patio specimens anywhere. They are also used as cut flowers.

Selected species and varieties
C. fragrans (perfumed fairy lily)—loose clusters of 3 to 4 yellow blossoms up to 3 inches across.

Growing conditions and maintenance
Plant outdoors in spring, setting bulbs 2 inches deep and 6 to 8 inches apart. North of Zone 8, lift bulbs in fall. In containers, allow one bulb per 6-inch pot, setting bulb tops at the soil line. Dry bulbs off in fall and repot in fresh soil the following spring. Propagate by removing and replanting small bulblets growing at the base of larger bulbs.

Clivia (KLY-vee-a)

NATAL LILY

Clivia miniata

HARDINESS: tender or Zones 8-11

TYPE OF BULB: tuber

FLOWERING SEASON: spring or summer

HEIGHT: 12 to 18 inches

SOIL: moist, well-drained

LIGHT: light shade

A popular houseplant in Victorian times, clivias bear domed clusters of up to 20 trumpet-shaped 3-inch flowers in dramatic hues atop a single thick stalk flanked by pairs of broad, straplike evergreen leaves up to 18 inches long. Bulbs may produce their long-lasting flowers twice a year under ideal conditions, and inch-long red berries follow the blossoms. Clivias can be grown outdoors in warm zones but bloom best as root-bound houseplants.

Selected species and varieties
C. x *cyrtanthiflora*—deep salmon pink blooms. *C. miniata*—scarlet blossoms with yellow-splashed throats; 'Aurea' grows golden yellow; 'Flame', deep red-orange; 'Grandiflora' produces larger scarlet flowers.

Growing conditions and maintenance
Plant Natal lilies outdoors in fall, setting the top of the bulbous roots at the soil line and spacing them 18 to 24 inches apart. Indoors, plant roots in 9-inch pots and leave undisturbed. Propagate from seed, or divide the fleshy rootstocks after flowering.

Colchicum (KOL-chi-kum)

AUTUMN CROCUS

Colchicum autumnale

HARDINESS: Zones 4-9

TYPE OF BULB: corm

FLOWERING SEASON: fall or spring

HEIGHT: 4 to 12 inches

SOIL: moist, well-drained, fertile

LIGHT: full sun to light shade

Actually a member of the lily family, colchicum has the common name autumn crocus because of the resemblance of its cupped, star-shaped flowers to those of the spring-flowering crocus. With the exception of one species that blooms in spring, colchicum's bare flower stems appear in fall to provide 2 to 3 weeks of color. Each corm produces multiple blossoms, so flowers carpet the ground when bulbs are planted thickly. The coarse, shiny, strap-shaped foliage appears later in winter, long after the flowers have faded. Colchicum naturalizes easily in rock gardens and lawns. The corms, which are poisonous, can also be forced as houseplants.

Selected species and varieties
C. agrippinum—flowers checkered purple and rose. *C. atropurpureum*—deep mauve 4-inch blossoms. *C. autumnale* (common autumn crocus, mysteria)—4-inch pink to lilac flowers; 'Album' is white; 'Albo-plenum', double-petaled. *C. bornmuelleri* —very large mauve blooms. *C. byzantinum*—a dozen or more pale lilac flowers followed by extremely broad foliage. *C. cilicicum* (Byzantine autumn crocus)—up to 25 bright rose 2½-inch flowers; 'Pur-

pureum' is rosy violet. *C. giganteum*—large carmine red blossoms. *C. luteum* [also called *Synsiphon luteum*]—rare spring-flowering species with 2-inch yellow flowers. *C. speciosum* (showy autumn crocus)—4-inch rose to purple flowers with white throats; 'Dick Trotter' yields early blossoms; 'Lilac Wonder', 6-inch-wide amethyst flowers; 'The Giant', 6- to 8-inch-wide rich rose flowers with white throats; 'Violet Queen', large clumps of 6- to 8-inch violet flowers with white-striped throats; 'Waterlily', double-petaled 4- to 6-inch rich lavender flowers.

Growing conditions and maintenance
Plant autumn crocus in summer, setting corms 3 to 4 inches deep and 6 to 9 inches apart. *C. luteum* is hardy only in Zones 7-9. *C. autumnale* and *C. byzantinum* tolerate light shade, but all other species prefer full sun. Where autumn crocus has naturalized in lawns, avoid mowing until foliage yellows and dies. To force as houseplants, set corms on pebbles just above water and keep the growing roots constantly moist; discard after flowering. Propagate autumn crocus by removing cormels growing alongside larger corms in early summer after foliage withers; or remove mature seed immediately when leaves wither and plant at once for corms that will reach blooming size in 3 to 4 years.

Colchicum 'The Giant'

Convallaria (kon-va-LAH-ree-a)

LILY OF THE VALLEY

Convallaria majalis 'Aureovariegata'

HARDINESS: Zones 2-7

TYPE OF BULB: rhizome

FLOWERING SEASON: spring

HEIGHT: 8 to 10 inches

SOIL: moist, acid, fertile

LIGHT: full to light shade

Lily of the valley's nodding flower bells line slender stalks nestled tightly within pairs of oval, pointed leaves that emerge from slender rhizomes called pips. The sweetly fragrant blossoms with furled edges make excellent cut flowers. Plant pips in woodland gardens or mass them to create a ground cover in shady areas. Lily of the valley can also be forced for indoor display.

Selected species and varieties
C. majalis—five to eight ¼-inch white flower bells for up to 2 weeks; 'Flore Pleno' produces ruffly, double-petaled flowers; 'Rosea' is light pink; 'Aureovariegata' grows variegated foliage.

Growing conditions and maintenance
Plant pips in spring or fall, setting them 1 inch deep and 4 to 6 inches apart. Lily of the valley competes well with shallow-rooted trees and shrubs. For forcing, buy prechilled pips or refrigerate bare pips 8 weeks or more in a plastic bag at 40°F, then pot with the top of pips just below the surface and keep in a warm room. Propagate by division in fall.

Corydalis (ko-RID-a-lis)

CORYDALIS

Corydalis solida

HARDINESS: Zones 6-10

TYPE OF BULB: tuber

FLOWERING SEASON: spring

HEIGHT: 6 to 8 inches

SOIL: moist, well-drained, fertile

LIGHT: light shade to full sun

Corydalis produces spiky clusters of up to 20 curving, tubular flowers with flared lips and a single, tiny pointed spur that dangle from stems above tufts of delicate green or blue-green foliage that resembles flat parsley. Foliage remains attractive throughout the summer. Corydalis naturalizes easily in rock or woodland gardens or borders.

Selected species and varieties
C. bulbosa—clusters of rosy lavender flowers on 8-inch stems above green leaves; 'Albiflora' is white. C. solida (fumewort)—dense 2-inch clusters of light purple flowers on 6-inch-tall stems above blue-green foliage.

Growing conditions and maintenance
Plant corydalis tubers 3 inches deep and 4 to 5 inches apart in summer or fall. Both species prefer shade, but C. solida will grow in full sun. Propagate by dividing tubers after foliage dies back in late summer or fall, or from seed, to reach blooming size in 2 to 3 years.

Crinodonna (kree-no-DON-a)

CRINODONNA

X Crinodonna corsii

HARDINESS: tender or Zones 9-11

TYPE OF BULB: true bulb

FLOWERING SEASON: late summer to fall

HEIGHT: 2½ to 3 feet

SOIL: moist, well-drained

LIGHT: full sun to light shade

Crinodonna's dense heads of oval, pointed flower buds open into large funnels with gracefully curving stamens and prominent anthers to add color and interest. The fragrant flowers unfold at the tips of sturdy, erect flower stalks. Each stalk rises from a clump of evergreen arching, narrow leaves that remain attractive year round. Crinodonna can be grown as border specimens in frost-free areas but bloom best as root-bound container plants.

Selected species and varieties
X C. corsii [also called X Amarcrinum memoriacorsii]—4- to 5-inch-wide pink flowers on stalks to 3 feet.

Growing conditions and maintenance
Outdoors, plant crinodonna bulbs at the soil line and space them 8 to 12 inches apart. Indoors, plant one 4-inch bulb per 6- to 8-inch pot. Bulbs should be left undisturbed for several years, as they bloom best when roots are crowded. Propagate by removing offsets, which grow at the base of larger bulbs.

SPIDER LILY

Crinum x powellii

HARDINESS: tender or Zones 7-11

TYPE OF BULB: true bulb

FLOWERING SEASON: spring, summer, fall

HEIGHT: 2 to 4 feet

SOIL: moist, well-drained, fertile

LIGHT: full sun to light shade

Crinums produce whorls of lilylike flowers with a spicy fragrance over a long season of bloom. Each cluster blooms atop a stout stem rising from a clump of deep green, sword-shaped, evergreen or deciduous leaves. The blossoms are either funnel shaped with thick, ridged petals curving backward, or lacy and spidery with narrow, straplike petals. Crinum's unusual bulbs, about the size of a grapefruit, have elongated necks up to 1 foot long and bloom best when they are crowded. In warmer areas, plant them where they can remain undisturbed for several years. They do especially well at the edges of ponds and streams where there is constant moisture, slowly naturalizing into large clumps. In northern areas, sink bulbs in tubs, which can be moved indoors to a greenhouse or conservatory for the winter.

Selected species and varieties

C. americanum (Florida swamp lily)—up to 6 white flower funnels in late spring or summer on 2-foot stems before leaves appear. *C. asiaticum* (grand crinum, poison bulb)—up to 50 heavily scented white flowers with straplike petals and pink stamens in summer on stalks to 4 feet. *C. bul-*

bispermum (Orange River lily)—a dozen or more pink or white flower trumpets with rose-striped petals in fall on 3-foot stems above deciduous foliage. *C. moorei* (Cape Coast lily, long-neck swamp lily)—10 to 20 rose red flower funnels in summer on 4-foot stalks rising from bold evergreen leaves. *C. x powellii* (Powell's swamp lily)—six to eight red flower trumpets touched with green at their base on 2-foot stalks rising from evergreen leaves up to 4 feet long; 'Album' has white flowers. *C.* 'Cecil Houdyshel'—profuse pink flowers. *C.* 'Ellen Bosanquet'—wine red summer flowers above evergreen foliage.

Growing conditions and maintenance

Outdoors, plant crinums so that the necks of the bulbs remain above ground and the bulbs are 2 to 3 feet apart. Keep constantly moist for best bloom. In tubs, allow no more than 1 to 2 inches of soil space between the sides of the bulbs and their container. With southern exposure and heavy mulching to protect them from frost, *C. bulbispermum* and *C. x powellii* sometimes thrive in Zones 7-8. *C. moorei* and *C.* 'Ellen Bosanquet' make excellent tub specimens. Propagate species from seeds, which sometimes begin forming roots while still on plants. Remove seeds as soon as they ripen and sow immediately to reach flowering-size bulbs in 3 years; hybrids may revert to their parent forms. Both species and hybrids can be propagated by removing and replanting the small offsets growing alongside mature bulbs in spring.

Crinum moorei

MONTBRETIA

Crocosmia 'Lucifer'

HARDINESS: Zones 5-9

TYPE OF BULB: corm

FLOWERING SEASON: summer or fall

HEIGHT: 2 to 4 feet

SOIL: moist, well-drained, fertile

LIGHT: full sun

Crocosmia's wiry stems are lined with up to 50 or more tightly clasped, inch-long flower buds that unfurl in succession from bottom to top over a long season of bloom. The vividly colored tubular flowers flare into open stars as much as 2 inches across. Emerging on either side of the stems, the combination of unopened buds and open blossoms provides interesting visual texture in the flower border. Two or more flower stems rise from sparse fans of pleated, swordlike foliage and gracefully arch with the weight of developing buds and flowers. In areas with mild winters, crocosmias will slowly spread into large clumps. Elsewhere, they make excellent container plants or can be treated as tender bulbs. Crocosmias serve well as cut flowers; sprays last up to a week in floral bouquets.

Selected species and varieties

C. aurea [also called *Tritonia aurea*](golden coppertip)—branched spikes of orange-tinged yellow flowers on arching 3½-foot stems. *C. x crocosmiiflora*—sturdy hybrids with sprays of star-shaped flowers 2 to 4 feet long in yellow, salmon, red, maroon, and bicolors. Large-flowered types produce 1½- to 3-inch blossoms; 'Citronella' is lemon yellow; 'Emily McKenzie', orange; 'James Coey', red; 'Lady Wilson', yellow-orange; 'Mars', red; 'Norwich Canary', yellow-tinged red. Small-flowered types yield 1-inch blooms; 'Bouquet Parfait' is orange to yellow; 'Venus', bicolored red and yellow. C. 'Lucifer'—deep red blooms. C. masoniorum (golden swan tritonia)—red flowers appearing very early on 2- to 4-foot stems; 'Firebird' produces orange blooms.

Growing conditions and maintenance

Plant crocosmias in spring, setting corms 3 to 5 inches deep and 6 to 8 inches apart. Where conditions are particularly favorable, they can become invasive. In Zones 7-8, choose sites sheltered from wind and protect from frost with winter mulch. North of Zone 7, lift corms in fall, cutting foliage back to 6 inches and allowing corms to dry slightly before storing at approximately 50° F for replanting in spring. Propagate by removing and repotting the small cormels that grow alongside larger corms in spring or fall, or from seed sown as soon as it ripens in fall, to flower in 3 to 4 years.

Crocosmia x crocosmiiflora 'Emily McKenzie'

CROCUS

Crocus chrysanthus 'Cream Beauty'

HARDINESS:	Zones 3-8
TYPE OF BULB:	corm
FLOWERING SEASON:	winter, spring, fall
HEIGHT:	2 to 8 inches
SOIL:	well-drained
LIGHT:	full sun

Delicate bowls of color in an otherwise drab landscape, crocus flowers hug the ground on short stems from late winter through midspring. There are also fall-blooming species, not to be confused with the flowers that are commonly known as autumn crocuses, which are actually Colchicum. Narrow, grassy crocus leaves are sometimes attractively banded down their centers in gray-green or white and may appear before, at the same time as, or after several flowers rise from each small corm. They last several weeks before dying back. Some are fragrant. Each flower has six wide petals that open into a deep, oval cup shape, then relax into a round, open bowl. Crocuses are available in a broad range of hues, and are often striped, streaked, or tinged with more than one color. Prominent yellow or orange stigmas decorate the center of each blossom. Those of C. sativus are the source of saffron for many culinary uses; it takes more than 4,000 flowers to produce an ounce of the precious herb. Mass crocuses for best effect in beds, borders, and rock gardens. They naturalize easily and are often planted as edgings and allowed to ramble in lawns. Force them for indoor winter display.

Selected species and varieties

C. ancyrensis 'Golden Bunch'—winter-to-spring-blooming flowers that are yellow outside, orange fading to yellow inside, on 2-inch stems above 12-inch leaves; Zones 6-8. C. angustifolius 'Minor'(cloth-of-gold crocus)—deep yellow flower cups flushed with mahogany outside on stems 2 inches or less in winter to spring; Zones 5-8. C. biflorus (Scotch crocus)—white or lilac flowers veined or tinged purple with yellow throats on 4-inch stems in winter to spring; ssp. alexandri is white feathered with purple; ssp. weldenii 'Fairy', white with purple blotches; Zones 5-8. C. chrysanthus (snow crocus)—late winter flowers bloom on 4-inch stems before the 12-inch leaves appear; 'Advance' produces peachy yellow flowers touched with violet; 'Ard Schenk', long-lasting white blooms; 'Blue Bird', blooms that are blue-violet outside, creamy inside; 'Blue- Pearl', petals that are lavender outside touched with bronze at their base, white inside blending to a yellow throat; 'Cream Beauty', long-lasting creamy yellow blooms; 'Dorothy', long-lasting yellow flowers feathered with bronze; 'Gipsy Girl', profuse, long-lasting yellow flowers streaked reddish brown; 'Ladykiller', petals violet-purple outside, creamy white inside; 'Miss Vain', pure white blossoms with lemon yellow throats; 'Prins Claus' is a dwarf cultivar with long-lasting white flowers blotched in blue; 'Snow Bunting' has white flowers with lilac streaking and yellow throats; 'Zwanenburg Bronze', reddish brown petals striped with yellow; Zones 4-8. C. etruscus 'Zwanenburg'—lilac flowers veined with deep purple appearing the same time as the white-

Crocus ancyrensis

Crocus chrysanthus 'Zwanenburg Bronze'

striped leaves in winter to spring; Zones 3-8. *C. flavus*—yellow to orange flowers appearing on 7-inch stems at the same time as the grassy foliage in winter to spring; 'Golden Yellow' [formerly *C. vernus* 'Yellow Giant'] has rich yellow blossoms; Zones 4-8. *C. kotschyanus* [formerly *C. zonatus*]—rose lilac flowers splashed with orange in fall; Zones 5-8. *C. medius*—lilac to purple flowers with deep purple veining on stems to 10 inches in fall; Zones 6-7. *C. minimus*—pale violet to white flowers with prominent red-orange stigmas on 2- to 3-inch stems in spring; Zones 5-8. *C. ochroleucus*—white to pale cream petals tinged with orange on 3- to 6-inch stems in fall; Zones 5-8. *C. pulchellus*—bright lilac blossoms with yellow interiors appearing the same time as the leaves in fall; 'Zephyr' is pure white; Zones 6-8. *C. sativus* (saffron crocus)—lilac or white fall flowers on 2-inch stems with prominent stamens that are dried and used for flavoring and coloring in cooking; Zones 6-8. *C. serotinus* ssp. *clusii*—fragrant, purple-veined pale lilac flowers with creamy throats on 3- to 4-inch stems appearing at the same time as sparse foliage in fall; ssp. *salzmannii* is similar but with sparser leaves and no fragrance; Zones 6-8. *C. sieberi* (Sieber crocus)—fragrant late-winter-to-spring flowers; ssp. *atticus* has white flowers streaked with purple on 2- to 3-inch stems; ssp. *sublimis* 'Tricolor', lilac blue flowers with white banding at the edge of a yellow throat; 'Firefly', white flowers touched with violet; 'Hubert Edelsten', deep purple to soft lilac flowers on 4-inch stems; 'Violet Queen', deep violet blooms on 3-inch stems; Zones 7-8. *C. spe-*

ciosus—light blue fall flowers with darker blue veining and prominent orange stigmas on 3- to 6-inch stems; 'Artabir' grows fragrant light blue flowers with conspicuous veining; 'Cassiope', lavender-blue blooms with creamy yellow throats; 'Conqueror', clear blue flowers; var. *aitchisonii*, pale lilac flowers veined with deeper lilac, the largest of all crocus blossoms; Zones 5-8. *C. tomasinianus*—lilac to purple flowers appearing at the same time as leaves in late winter to spring, reputed to be rodent resistant; 'Barr's Purple' yields large royal purple flowers; 'Ruby Giant', large violet blooms; 'Whitewell Purple' is reddish purple; Zones 5-9. *C. vernus* (Dutch crocus, common crocus)—large flowers on stems to 8 inches tall appearing at the same time as leaves in late winter to spring; 'Flower Record' is deep purple; 'Jeanne d'Arc', white; 'Paulus Potter', shiny reddish purple; 'Pickwick', white striped with lilac and splashed with purple at its base; 'Remembrance', bluish purple; 'Striped Beauty', lilac striped with white. *C. versicolor* 'Picturatus'—white flowers striped in purple with yellow throats on 5½-inch stems in late winter to spring; Zones 5-8.

Growing conditions and maintenance
Plant corms 3 to 4 inches deep and 4 to 5 inches apart in groups. They are not fussy about soil, but good drainage is essential. Space more closely in pots for forcing, allowing six to eight corms per 6-inch pot or shallow bulb pan, and setting the corms 1 inch deep. Hold potted corms at 40°F until roots form, then bring indoors at 65°F for flowering. Crocuses can also be forced in colorful bulb vases designed especially for

Crocus tomasinianus

the purpose with a pinched waist to suspend the corm just above the water line; when roots fill the vase, bring the corm into sunlight in a warm room for blooming. After forcing, allow foliage to die back, then plant corms out in the garden for reflowering the following spring. Cultivars of Dutch crocus are especially recommended for forcing. *C. ancyrensis* 'Golden Bunch', *C. speciosus* cultivars, and *C. vernus* 'Pickwick'

Crocus vernus 'Jeanne d'Arc'

are among the easiest crocuses to naturalize. To plant crocuses in lawns, cut and lift small patches of grass, place the corms, then replace the sod. Plant spring-flowering varieties from September to November, fall-flowering ones no later than August. Where crocuses have established themselves in lawns, avoid mowing in spring until the foliage of spring-flowering crocuses dies back; in fall, postpone mowing once the buds of fall-blooming species have broken through the ground until their flowers fade and foliage withers. Crocuses are easily grown from seed and self-sow freely, a characteristic that somewhat offsets the attractiveness of the corms to mice, chipmunks, and squirrels. Otherwise, propagate by lifting and dividing crowded clumps after foliage dies back, removing and replanting the smaller cormels that develop alongside mature corms. Buy *C. kotschyanus* only from reputable dealers who propagate their own bulbs, as collection in the wild has endangered this species.

Cyclamen (SIK-la-men)

PERSIAN VIOLET

Cyclamen persicum

HARDINESS: Zones 6-9

TYPE OF BULB: tuber

FLOWERING SEASON: fall, winter, spring

HEIGHT: 3 to 12 inches

SOIL: moist, well-drained, fertile

LIGHT: light shade

Cyclamen's unusual, sometimes fragrant, flowers have petals swept back from a prominent center or eye. The petals are sometimes twisted, double, ruffled, shredded, or ridged, giving the delicate, inch-long blossoms the appearance of exotic birds or butterflies. Each flower rises on a slender stem from a clump of long-lasting heart- or kidney-shaped leaves that are sometimes marbled green and gray above or reddish underneath. Multiple flower stalks appear over a long season of bloom. While the florist's cyclamen, popular as a houseplant, is a tender pot plant, other cyclamens are hardy species that will spread in wildflower gardens, rock gardens, and shady borders, naturalizing into low ground covers beneath both deciduous and evergreen plantings.

Selected species and varieties

C. africanum—rose to carmine fall flowers above large, fleshy 6-inch leaves with wavy edges; Zones 8-9. *C. cilicium* (Sicily cyclamen)—twisted pink or light rose blossoms with a dark rose eye on 3-inch stems in fall above leaves with silver centers; Zones 7-8. *C. coum*—white to carmine flowers with purple blotches blooming from winter to spring on 3- to 6-inch stems above green or marbled leaves with reddish undersides; 'Album' is white; 'Roseum', pale pink. *C. graecum*—fall-blooming rose flowers with a deep carmine eye, sometimes scented; Zones 7-9. *C. hederifolium* [also called *C. neopolitanum*] (baby cyclamen)—pink or white, sometimes fragrant, flowers with a crimson eye on 3- to 6-inch stems blooming from summer to fall above marbled leaves; 'Album' is white; Zones 6-9. *C. persicum* (florist's cyclamen, common cyclamen)—rose, pink, or white, sometimes fragrant flowers, with dark eyes on 6- to 12-inch stems above marbled leaves with toothed edges in winter; Zone 9. *C. repandum*—deep pink flowers in late spring or early summer and spotted leaves.

Growing conditions and maintenance

Plant cyclamen's flat, cormlike tubers in summer or fall, setting them ½ inch deep and 4 to 6 inches apart in soil that has a neutral to alkaline pH. Provide an annual topdressing of leaf mold. Pot florist's cyclamen's large tuber-corms individually in pots and maintain plants at temperatures of 60° to 65° F throughout the blooming period. Cyclamens do not produce offsets, but plants self-sow seed freely. Propagate from seed to reach blooming size in 3 years or by transplanting the self-sown seedlings in summer or fall.

Cyclamen hederifolium

Dahlia (DAH-lee-a)

DAHLIA

Dahlia 'Tamjoh'

HARDINESS: tender or Zones 9-11

TYPE OF BULB: tuber

FLOWERING SEASON: summer to fall

HEIGHT: 12 inches to 8 feet

SOIL: moist, well-drained, fertile

LIGHT: full sun

Dahlias reliably brighten the flower border over a long season of bloom with highly diverse blossoms varying from flat-faced, single-petaled types to round, dense mounds of petals. Dahlia sizes are as variable as petal forms, with some flowers only a few inches across and others the diameter of a dinner plate. Related to daisies, dahlias have a central disk of tightly packed disk flowers surrounded by one or more rows of petal-like ray flowers that are sometimes doubled, curved inward, twisted, cupped, or rolled into tiny tubes. Colors range widely, and some dahlias are bicolored or variegated, with petals tipped, streaked, or backed with contrasting color. The more than 20,000 cultivars available to modern gardeners descend from a few wild species cultivated by Aztec botanists. For the garden trade, dahlias are classified by the shape and arrangement of their ray flowers and coded according to flower size. Dwarf dahlias are cultivated in sunny beds or borders as low-growing bushy edgings, standard dahlias as medium to tall fillers or as exhibition-size specimens. The largest dahlias are diffilcult to use in the home garden simply because of their size—those with the largest blooms can have stems the thickness of broomsticks. Thus, the plants with smaller flowers are easier to work into a bed or border design. Regardless of their size, all dahlias make excellent, long-lasting cut flowers.

Selected species and varieties

Single dahlias—one or two rows of flat petals surrounding a flat, central disk; 'Bambino White' is a dwarf cultivar that bears 1-inch flowers on 14-inch bushes. *Anemone-flowered dahlias*—a central disk obscured by a fluffy ball of short, tubular petals and rimmed by one or more rows of longer, flat petals; 'Siemen Doorenbosch' has flat lavender petals surrounding a creamy central pincushion on 20-inch plants. *Collarette dahlias*—central disks surrounded by a collar of short, often ruffled or cupped petals, backed by a second collar of broader, flat petals; 'Jack O' Lantern' has an inner collar streaked yellow and orange and deep orange outer petals on 4-foot plants; 'Mickey' has a yellow inner collar backed by deep red outer ray flowers on 3-foot bushes. *Peony-flowered dahlias*—two or three overlapping layers of ray petals, often twisted or curled, surrounding a central disk; 'Japanese Bishop' grows dark orange flowers on 3-foot plants; 'Jescott Julie' has petals that are orange above, burgundy below, on 3-foot stems. *Formal decorative dahlias*—double rows of flat, evenly spaced petals covering the central disk; 'Duet' has crimson petals tipped with white on 3-foot plants; 'Orange Julius', orange petals edged in yellow on 4-foot stems. *Informal decorative dahlias*—double rows of randomly spaced flat petals hiding the central disk; 'Gay Princess' is pink with creamy centers on 4-foot plants. *Ball dahlias*—cupped, doubled petals crowding spirally into round domes or slightly flattened globes; 'Nijinsky' has purple flowers on 4-foot stems; 'Rothsay Superb', red blooms on 3-foot plants. *Pompom dahlias*—small round balls of tightly rolled petals less than 2 inches in diameter; 'Amber Queen' is golden amber to bronze on 4-foot stems; 'Chick-a-dee', wine red touched with pink on 3-foot plants. *Cactus dahlias*—straight or twisted petals rolled like quills or straws over half their length to a pointed tip; 'Border

Princess' is apricot bronze to yellow on 2-foot stems; 'Brookside Cheri', salmon pink on 4-foot plants; 'Juanita', ruby red on 4-foot stems. *Semicactus dahlias*—flat petals curling over less than half their length into tubes at their tips; 'Amanda Jarvis' produces rose flowers on 3-foot stems; 'Bella Bimba', apricot pink blooms on 4-foot plants. *Star dahlias*—two or three rows of short petals curving inward. *Chrysanthemum-type dahlias*—double rows of petals curving inward and hiding the central disk. *Water lily-flowered dahlias*—short petals tightly clasped over the central disk like a water lily bud, surrounded by several rows of broad, flat petals; 'Lauren Michelle' has petals that are rosy lavender

Dahlia 'Hullins Carnival'

above, purple below on 4½-foot stems; 'Gerry Hoek', shell pink flowers on 4-foot plants.

Within each of these classifications, dahlias are also coded by size: Giant or AA dahlias have flowers more than 10 inches wide; large or A, 8- to 10-inch flowers; medium or B, 6- to 8-inch flowers; small or BB, 4- to 6-inch blooms; miniature or M, flowers up to 4 inches across; pompom or P, blossoms under 2 inches.

Growing conditions and maintenance

Plant dahlia tubers in spring, placing those of taller cultivars in a hole 6 to 8 inches deep and covering them with 2 to 3 inches of soil. Space the holes 3 to 4 feet apart. As shoots develop and extend above ground level, remove all but one or two and add soil to fill the hole. Plant tubers of shorter cultivars 2 to 3 inches deep and 1 to 2 feet apart. In transplanting potted seedlings,

position them 2 inches deeper than the depth of their pot. Stake all but dwarfs, pompoms, and miniatures. Dahlias bloom 2½ to 4 months after planting. To keep plants blooming continuously, give them at least an inch of water weekly while blooming, and mulch with 2 to 3 inches of manure, compost, or ground peat moss to retain moisture and provide nutrients. To produce bushy plants, pinch out terminal leaf buds when leaves first appear and again when the first lateral branches emerge. To develop large, exhibition-size blossoms, prune all lateral side shoots and remove all but the center bud when flower buds appear. Remove faded flowers before they go to seed to prolong blooming period. For long-lasting cut flowers, pick dahlias while it is cool and stand cut stems in hot water, 100° to 160°F, in a cool, shaded location for several hours before arranging. Propagate dahlias from seed started indoors in very early spring to flower that season, from stem cuttings, or by dividing tubers in spring.

Dichelostemma (di-kel-o-STEM-a)

DICHELOSTEMMA

Dichelostemma congestum

HARDINESS: Zones 5-7

TYPE OF BULB: corm

FLOWERING SEASON: spring

HEIGHT: 1½ to 3 feet

SOIL: very well-drained, sandy

LIGHT: full sun

A native American wildflower, *Dichelostemma* produces loose, silver-dollar-size flower clusters. The flowers, which appear on slender stems above sparse, narrow, grassy leaves, are excellent in arrangements. Mass dichelostemmas in sunny borders and allow them to naturalize, or pot them in containers.

Selected species and varieties

D. congestum (ookow)—clusters of pale blue-violet flower trumpets decorated with long, split stamens.

Growing conditions and maintenance

Plant dichelostemma corms in fall, setting them 3½ to 5 inches deep and 3 inches apart. Dichelostemmas require excellent drainage, even dry conditions, in summer after blooming. In areas with wet summers, dig corms after foliage fades and replant in fall. Mulch bulbs for winter protection in northern zones. In containers, plant four or five bulbs per 6-inch container. Propagate by removing the small cormels that develop alongside mature bulbs for planting in fall.

Eranthis (e-RAN-this)

WINTER ACONITE

Eranthis hyemalis

HARDINESS: Zones 4-7

TYPE OF BULB: tuber

FLOWERING SEASON: late winter to spring

HEIGHT: 2 to 4 inches

SOIL: moist, well-drained, fertile

LIGHT: full sun to light shade

Often blooming before the snow has melted, winter aconites produce cheery buttercup-like flowers composed of waxy, curved petals cradling a loose pompom of frilly stamens. Each almost stemless blossom opens above a tiny ruff of oval, pointed leaves. The blossoms close tightly to protect themselves during cold nights, then reopen the next day with the sun's warmth. Winter aconites readily naturalize into golden ground covers in woodland or rock gardens.

Selected species and varieties

E. cilicica (Cilician winter aconite)—1½-inch-deep yellow flowers on 2½-inch stems with bronzy foliage. *E. hyemalis*—inch-wide yellow flowers on 2- to 4-inch stems.

Growing conditions and maintenance

Plant winter aconite tubers in late summer or very early fall to allow roots time to establish themselves for late-winter blooming. Soak the brittle roots overnight, then set tubers 2 to 3 inches deep and 3 inches apart where they will receive sufficient moisture. Winter aconites self-sow readily. Propagate from seed or by dividing the tiny tubers in late summer.

Eremurus (e-ray-MEW-rus)

DESERT-CANDLE

Eremurus 'Moneymaker'

HARDINESS: Zones 4-8

TYPE OF BULB: tuber

FLOWERING SEASON: spring to summer

HEIGHT: 3 to 8 feet

SOIL: well-drained, sandy, fertile

LIGHT: full sun

Desert-candles carry hundreds of tiny bell-shaped flowers in enormous, elongated spikes often 5 to 6 inches across and up to 4 feet long above rosettes of thick, fleshy leaves resembling those of yucca plants. Over a period of several weeks, the small flowers open from bottom to top along the stem so that each spike offers a range of textures and tones from lighter-colored mature flowers with prominent frothy anthers to more deeply colored, tight oval buds. Desert-candles are outstanding when grouped at the back of a border or in front of dark shrubbery. The spikes last up to 3 weeks when used as cut flowers.

Selected species and varieties

E. himalaicus (Himalayan desert-candle)—pure white flower spikes on 3- to 4-foot stems above clumps of 1-foot leaves; Zones 4-8. *E. robustus*—bright pink flowers and darker pink buds in 4-foot spikes on stems 6 to 10 feet tall above broad green foliage; 'Albus' is a white strain; Zones 7-9. *E. stenophyllus* (Afghan desert-candle)—yellow or golden yellow flowers covering the upper half or more of 2- to 3-foot stems; Zones 4-8. *E.* Ruiter and *E.* Shelford hybrids—spikes of 1-inch flowers in shades of white or cream to yellow, orange, peach pink, or rose on 3- to 4-foot stems with Ruiter hybrids flowering earlier than Shelford hybrids; 'Cleopatra' has orange flowers with a red stripe on the outside of each petal, orange anthers, and deep burnt orange buds; 'Moneymaker' is vivid yellow-orange; 'Pinokkio', softer orange; Zones 6-8.

Growing conditions and maintenance

Plant desert-candles in fall, choosing sites where plants can remain undisturbed for 10 years or more. Place the brittle, star-shaped clumps of tubers with egg-size buds at their centers on a mound of sand at the bottom of a hole 2 feet wide and deep enough to set the crowns 4 to 6 inches down. Once established, desert-candles are best left alone unless their crowns lift out of the soil. Support tall species by staking in windy sites, taking care not to disturb the tubers when setting the stakes. Foliage withers soon after blooms fade; some gardeners install stakes when they plant the tubers, not only to avoid disturbing the roots later but also to mark their location when digging other bulbs or perennials around them. Provide winter mulch in colder zones. Propagate by dividing tubers that are at least 3 years old; propagation from seed is possible but may require a wait of 5 or 6 years for bloom.

Eremurus robustus

DOGTOOTH VIOLET

Erythronium 'Kondo'

HARDINESS:	Zones 3-8
TYPE OF BULB:	corm
FLOWERING SEASON:	spring
HEIGHT:	6 inches to 2 feet
SOIL:	moist, well-drained, fertile
LIGHT:	partial to full shade

Native woodland wildflowers, dogtooth violets produce delicate, nodding lilylike blooms with petals curved back to reveal prominent stamens and anthers either singly or in small clusters. The flowers rise from pairs of oval, pointed leaves that are often marbled or mottled in gray, brown, or bronze. Mass dogtooth violets in woodland gardens or as a spring ground cover beneath deciduous shrubs, where they will naturalize into colonies.

Selected species and varieties

E. citrinum—clusters of 1½-inch white or cream flowers with pale lemon throats on 10- to 12-inch stems; Zones 6-8. *E. dens-canis* (dogtooth fawn lily, European dogtooth violet)—single white to pink or purple flowers 2 inches across with blue or purple anthers on 6- to 12-inch stems above leaves marbled brown and bluish green; 'Charmer' produces pure white flowers touched with brown at their base above leaves mottled with brown; 'Frans Hals', royal purple blooms with a green throat; 'Lilac Wonder' is soft lilac with a brownish base; 'Pink Perfection', bright pink; 'Purple King', reddish purple with a white throat above brown-spotted leaves;

'Rose Queen', rosy pink; 'Snowflake', pure white; var. *japonicum* is a miniature only 4 to 6 inches tall with violet flowers tinged purple at the base; var. *niveus* is pale pink; Zones 3-8. *E. grandiflorum* (glacier lily, avalanche lily)—golden yellow flowers with red anthers in clusters on 1- to 2-foot stems. *E. revolutum* (mahogany fawn lily, coast fawn lily)—1½-inch white to pale lavender flowers aging to purple on 16-inch stems; 'White Beauty' is a dwarf producing 2- to 3-inch white flowers with yellow throats on 7-inch stems above leaves veined in white; Zones 3-8. *E. tuolumnense* (Tuolumne fawn lily)—1¼-inch yellow flowers touched with green at the base on 12-inch stems above bright green 12-inch leaves; Zones 3-8. *E.* hybrids—'Citronella' yields lemon yellow flowers on 10-inch stems; 'Jeannine', sulfur yellow blooms; 'Kondo', greenish yellow blossoms touched with brown at the base; 'Pagoda', pale yellow flowers with a deeper yellow throat on 10-inch stems.

Growing conditions and maintenance

Plant dogtooth violets in summer or fall, placing the corms 2 to 3 inches deep and 4 to 6 inches apart. Dogtooth violets often take a year to become established before blooming. Provide adequate moisture in summer after flowers and foliage fade. Propagate from seed to bloom in 3 to 4 years or by removing and immediately replanting the small cormels that develop at the base of mature corms in late summer or fall.

Erythronium grandiflorum

Eucharis (YEW-kar-is)

AMAZON LILY

Eucharis amazonica

HARDINESS: tender or Zones 9-11

TYPE OF BULB: true bulb

FLOWERING SEASON: spring, summer, or fall

HEIGHT: 1 to 2 feet

SOIL: moist, well-drained

LIGHT: partial shade

Amazon lilies bear clusters of highly fragrant flowers with six waxy, starlike petals and flat stamens joined to resemble the corona of a daffodil. The flowers rise from clumps of broad evergreen leaves with wavy edges. Amazon lilies can be grown in beds and borders in frost-free areas where summers are hot and humid and can be forced anytime for indoor use.

Selected species and varieties
E. amazonica (Eucharist lily, star-of-Bethlehem)—drooping white flowers up to 5 inches across above leaves a foot long and 6 inches wide.

Growing conditions and maintenance
Outdoors, set bulbs with their necks at the soil line, spacing the bulbs 8 to 10 inches apart. The plants need high humidity and temperatures above 60° F to thrive, and they bloom best when crowded or potbound. Indoors, space bulbs 3 inches apart in pots, allowing three or four bulbs to each pot. To force, maintain bulbs at 80° F or higher for 4 weeks, then lower temperatures 10° F for another 12 weeks. Raise temperatures again to induce blooming. Propagate by removing and planting the bulb offsets.

Eucomis (yew-KOME-is)

PINEAPPLE LILY

Eucomis bicolor

HARDINESS: Zones 7-10

TYPE OF BULB: true bulb

FLOWERING SEASON: summer

HEIGHT: 1 to 2 feet

SOIL: well-drained, sandy

LIGHT: full sun to light shade

Pineapple lilies produce dense bottlebrush spikes of tiny flower stars topped by an arching tuft of leaflike bracts. The spikes rise from rosettes of strap-shaped leaves. Group pineapple lilies in borders, or grow them in containers as house- or patio plants. They make long-lasting cut flowers.

Selected species and varieties
E. autumnalis—spikes of ¾-inch greenish white flowers fading to yellow-green on 1- to 2-foot stems; Zones 7-10. *E. bicolor*—greenish white flowers edged with purple on 2-foot stems; Zones 8-10. *E. comosa* (pineapple flower)—has ½-inch greenish white, sometimes pinkish, blossoms with purple throats on 2-foot stems; Zones 8-10.

Growing conditions and maintenance
Plant outdoors in fall, setting bulbs 5 to 6 inches deep and 1 foot apart. Mulch bulbs in Zones 7 and 8. North of Zone 7, grow pineapple lilies as container plants, setting bulbs just below the surface and allowing three to five bulbs per 12-inch pot. Propagate by removing bulb offsets that develop at the base of mature bulbs, or from seed to flower in 5 years.

Freesia (FREEZ-ee-a)

FREESIA

Freesia 'Ballerina'

HARDINESS: tender or Zones 9-11

TYPE OF BULB: corm

FLOWERING SEASON: winter to spring

HEIGHT: 1 to 2 feet

SOIL: moist, well-drained, sandy

LIGHT: full sun to light shade

Freesias are renowned for their intense citrusy fragrance, which quickly pervades any room. Their crowded fans of flaring tubular flowers are held at right angles to branched, arching stems that rise from clumps of sword-shaped 6-inch leaves, which persist after flowers fade. The flowers open in sequence along each upright cluster for a long period of bloom. In warm zones, grow freesias in borders or rock gardens. Elsewhere, pot them for houseplants or greenhouse specimens. Freesias last 5 to 12 days as cut flowers.

Selected species and varieties
F. refracta (common freesia)—inch-wide flowers in white to greenish yellow to bright yellow, sometimes touched with mauve, on 12-inch stems. *F.* x hybrids—2-inch flowers on stems 18 to 24 inches tall; 'Ballerina' produces large white flowers touched with yellow at the throat; 'Diana', double white flowers; 'Fantasy', cream-colored doubled petals; 'Riande' is yellow-gold; 'Royal Gold', golden yellow; 'Princess Marijke', yellow-orange touched with bronze; 'Pimpernel', flaming scarlet; 'Rose Marie', double-petaled dark pink; 'Stockholm', red with a yellow throat; 'Viking',

pink; 'Romany', double-petaled bluish purple; 'Royal Blue', bright blue with a violet-striped throat.

Growing conditions and maintenance

Plant freesias outdoors in Zones 9 and 10, setting corms 2 inches deep and 2 to 4 inches apart. Corms take 10 to 12 weeks to bloom; plant in summer for winter bloom, in fall for spring bloom. Provide support for their weak stems. Left in the ground, freesias will revert to their normal late-winter to early-spring blooming cycle. North of Zone 9, plant freesias outdoors in spring for summer bloom, then dig corms for winter storage after foliage fades. Indoors, pot 6 to 8 corms per 6-inch bulb pan or 10 to 12 per 8-inch pan, setting corms barely below the surface. Water and feed freesias while growing and blooming, then withhold water after foliage fades to induce dormancy. Remove corms from pots and store in a cool, dark place for replanting. Propagate freesias from seed to bloom in 6 months to a year or by removing the tiny cormels that develop alongside mature corms.

Freesia 'Riande'

Fritillaria (fri-ti-LAH-ree-a)

FRITILLARY

Fritillaria imperialis

HARDINESS: Zones 3-8

TYPE OF BULB: true bulb

FLOWERING SEASON: spring

HEIGHT: 6 inches to 2½ feet

SOIL: moist, well-drained, sandy

LIGHT: full sun to light shade

From the imposing, musky-scented crown imperial bearing a garland of blossoms aloft on stout stalks to small, dainty woodland species with single blooms on wiry stems, fritillaries produce nodding flower bells in unusual colors and patterns in a variety of forms to accent spring gardens. The flowers have prominent, colorful stamens and are often striped, speckled, or checkered in a wide range of hues. Touching the petals sometimes produces a small "tear" from reservoirs of nectar at the base of each petal. The often glossy leaves are highly variable, sometimes appearing in whorls extending halfway up the flower stalk, sometimes alternating from one side of the stem to the other throughout its length, occasionally growing in a tuft at the stem's base. Mass fritillaries in wildflower gardens, rock gardens, or perennial borders where other plants will fill in when their foliage dies down in early summer.

Selected species and varieties

F. acmopetala—purple-striped olive green flower bells tinged lighter green inside on 18-inch stalks; Zones 3-8. *F. assyriaca*—lime-green and violet blossoms on 12- to 20-inch stems; Zones 3-8. *F. biflora*

'Martha Roderick' (mission bells, black fritillary)—four to six brownish orange flower bells with white spots in their centers on 15-inch stems; Zones 3-8. *F. camschatcensis* (Kamchatka lily, black sarana)—one to six 1-inch purple-brown-and-black flower bells on wiry 2-foot stems; Zones 3-8. *F. davisii*—plum purple blossoms on dainty plants 6 to 10 inches tall; Zones 3-8. *F. imperialis* (crown imperial)—bold 30-inch stalks, the lower half lined with whorls of glossy, pointed leaves, the tip crowned by a tuft of shorter leaves with a ring of large, 2-inch flower bells with dangling yellow stamens below it; 'Maxima Lutea' is lemon yellow; 'Rubra

Fritillaria meleagris

Maxima', dark red; Zones 4-7. *F. meleagris* (snake's-head fritillary, checkered lily, guinea hen tulip, leper lily)—1½-inch flower bells checkered dark maroon and white on 8- to 10-inch stems; 'Alba' is pure white; Zones 3-8. *F. michailovskyi*—up to five deep purplish red-and-yellow flower bells with their tips flipped daintily outward on 4- to 8-inch stems; Zones 5-8. *F. pallidiflora*—up to a dozen pale yellow and green 1- to 1½-inch flower bells flecked with brown and red, borne in the upper leaf joints along arching 18-inch stems; Zones 3-8. *F. persica*—up to 30 velvety purple blossoms lining 30-inch stems; 'Adiyaman' yields inch-wide plum flowers; Zones 4-8. *F. pudica* (yellow fritillary, yellow bell)—¾-inch yellow-orange flowers tinged purple in clusters of three on 9-inch stems; Zones 4-8. *F. purdyi* 'Tinkerbell'—six or seven dainty white flower bells striped rusty brown on the outside and spotted red inside on 6-inch stems above a low rosette of 6-inch leaves; Zones 5-8. *F. uva-vulpis*—solitary purplish gray flower bells edged in yellow on 12- to 18-inch stems; Zones 3-8. *F. verticillata*—1¼-inch cup-shaped pale yellow blossoms flecked with green outside and spotted purple inside lining 2-foot stems, the tips of the upper leaves elongating to form tendrils; Zones 6-8.

Growing conditions and maintenance
Plant fritillaries in late summer or fall, setting large bulbs 4 inches deep and 12 inches apart, smaller bulbs 2 inches deep and 8 inches apart. Bulbs may take a year to become established in new locations before they flower. Most fritillaries like full sun and very well drained soil, but *F. camschatcensis*, *F. meleagris*, and *F. pallidiflora* prefer light shade and moist soil. For all fritillaries, avoid sites with cold, wet soils, and reduce watering once foliage dies back. Both *F. imperialis* 'Rubra Maxima' and *F. persica* are endangered in the wild; buy bulbs from reputable growers selling stock propagated by themselves or other growers rather than purchased from collectors. The skunklike odor of crown imperial is said to repel mice, chipmunks, and other rodents. Propagate fritillaries by removing and replanting bulb offsets in late summer or early fall to reach flowering size in 3 to 4 years; or by removing and planting bulb scales to produce bulblets.

Fritillaria pudica

Galanthus *(ga-LANTH-us)*

SNOWDROP

Galanthus nivalis

HARDINESS:	Zones 3-8
TYPE OF BULB:	true bulb
FLOWERING SEASON:	winter to spring
HEIGHT:	6 to 12 inches
SOIL:	moist, well-drained, sandy
LIGHT:	full sun to light shade

Snowdrops produce small white flowers that often bloom before the last snow melts. Each winged blossom is composed of three longer petals almost concealing three shorter, inner petals tipped with green. A single flower dangles from a slender stem above two or three grassy leaves. Snowdrops rapidly naturalize under deciduous shrubs or on lawns, in rock gardens, and in woodland borders. They can also be potted as houseplants.

Selected species and varieties
G. elwesii (giant snowdrop)—1½-inch blossoms on flower stalks to 12 inches above blue-green leaves. *G. nivalis* (common snowdrop)—1-inch blooms on 4- to 6-inch stems; 'Flore Pleno' produces double flowers; 'Sam Arnott', large, fragrant blossoms; 'Viridi-apice' has both its outer and inner petals tipped with green.

Growing conditions and maintenance
Plant bulbs 3 inches deep and 3 inches apart in late summer or fall. For indoor bloom, pot bulbs in fall, placing four to six bulbs 1 inch deep in each 4-inch pot. Snowdrops self-sow readily and can be propagated from seed or by lifting and dividing the clumps of bulbs that form.

Galtonia *(gawl-TONE-ee-a)*

SUMMER HYACINTH

Galtonia candicans

HARDINESS:	Zones 6-10
TYPE OF BULB:	true bulb
FLOWERING SEASON:	summer to fall
HEIGHT:	2 to 4 feet
SOIL:	well-drained, sandy, fertile
LIGHT:	full sun to light shade

Summer hyacinth produces loose spires of fragrant, nodding flower bells that open from bottom to top on stout stems above clumps of fleshy, narrow, straplike leaves. The pale flowers are accented by dark stamens. Plant tall varieties at the back of flower borders where they will spread very slowly into larger clumps.

Selected species and varieties
G. candicans (giant summer hyacinth)—2-inch white blossoms tinged green along the upper third of erect stalks to 4 feet tall. *G. viridiflora*—green flowers on 2- to 3-foot stalks above broad leaves.

Growing conditions and maintenance
Plant summer hyacinths in spring or fall, placing bulbs 6 inches deep and 18 to 24 inches apart. Mulch bulbs in northern zones with 2 inches of leaf mold or compost in winter. North of Zone 6, lift bulbs in fall, allow to dry several hours, then remove tops and store for replanting the following spring. Propagate from seed to bloom in several years; or by removing and replanting the few bulblets that may develop alongside mature bulbs.

Gladiolus (glad-ee-O-lus)

CORN FLAG

Gladiolus communis ssp. byzantinus

HARDINESS: tender or Zones 4-11

TYPE OF BULB: corm

FLOWERING SEASON: spring to fall

HEIGHT: 1 to 7 feet

SOIL: well-drained, fertile

LIGHT: full sun

Gladiolus produce showy spikes of 1½- to 5½-inch flowers above fans of stiff, sword-shaped leaves. The closely spaced flowers open from bottom to top on alternate sides of the stiff flower stems. Abundant, sometimes fragrant, flowers open one at a time to provide several weeks of bloom. Use tall gladiolus in groups at the back of a border, shorter species in rock gardens or mixed in borders with spring bulbs. Gladiolus make long-lasting cut flowers; shorter species can be forced for indoor bloom.

Selected species and varieties

G. callianthus [formerly classified as *Acidanthera bicolor*] 'Murielae'—fragrant 2- to 3-inch white flowers with purple throats on 2-foot stems in summer; Zones 7-11. *G. carneus* (painted lady)—white, cream, mauve, or pink blossoms flecked purple on 2-foot stems, blooming spring to summer; Zones 9-11. *G.* x *colvillei* (Coronado hybrid)—2-inch scarlet flowers blotched yellow on branching 2-foot stems in spring; Zones 7-11. *G. communis* ssp. *byzantinus* (Byzantine gladiolus)—white-streaked burgundy flowers on 2-foot stems in spring to summer; Zones 5-11. *G.* hybrids—ruffled, waved, crimped, or frilled flowers in shades of white, yellow, red, purple, blue, or green, sometimes bicolored or multicolored, on stems to 7 feet in summer through fall; 'Nova Lux' is pure velvety yellow; 'Red Bird', flaming red; 'Priscilla', white-feathered pink with a yellow throat; 'Royal Blush' has deep rose red petals edged in white; 'White Knight' is pure white; tender. *G. nanus* [also classified as *Babiana nana*]—spring-to-summer-blooming dwarf plants 1 to 2 feet tall; 'Amanda Mahy' is salmon with violet splotches; 'Desire', cream; 'Guernsey Glory' has pink to purple petals with red edges and cream blotches; 'Impressive' is pinkish white splotched deep rose; 'Prins Claus', ivory with purple spotting; Zones 4-11.

Growing conditions and maintenance

Work well-rotted manure or other organic matter deeply into the soil a year before planting. North of Zone 8, plant hardy gladiolus in fall, tender ones in spring. Set large corms 4 to 6 inches deep and 6 to 9 inches apart, smaller ones 3 to 4 inches deep and 4 to 6 inches apart. Provide ample water while growing and blooming. North of Zone 8, tender gladiolus should be dug in fall for replanting in spring. Early-blooming hybrids flower 90 days after planting, midseason varieties in 110 days, and late midseason ones in 120 days. To avoid fungus problems, do not plant gladiolus in the same location from year to year. Pick for cut flowers as the first bloom begins to open, leaving four to five leaves to feed the corm. Propagate by removing the cormels that develop around mature corms.

Gloriosa (glo-ree-O-sa)

GLORIOSA LILY

Gloriosa superba 'Rothschildiana'

HARDINESS: tender or Zones 10-11

TYPE OF BULB: tuber

FLOWERING SEASON: year round or summer

HEIGHT: 6 to 12 feet

SOIL: moist, well-drained, fertile

LIGHT: full sun to light shade

Gloriosa lilies produce exotic flowers on climbing vines. Narrow petals with wavy or crimped edges rake backward to expose prominent stamens. The tips of the slender 4- to 6-inch-long leaves elongate into tendrils to enable the vine to scramble up fences or trellises at the back of a border. In northern zones, plant gloriosa lilies outdoors as annuals or grow them indoors as container plants. They make excellent cut flowers. Caution: All parts of these plants are poisonous.

Selected species and varieties

G. superba (Malabar gloriosa lily, crisped glory lily)—twisted yellow petals tipped with red, aging to dark red; 'Africana' has orange petals edged in yellow; 'Rothschildiana', wavy reddish purple petals edged in yellow.

Growing conditions and maintenance

In Zones 10 and 11, plant gloriosa lilies anytime, laying tubers on their sides 4 inches deep and 8 to 12 inches apart. North of Zone 10, plant in spring and lift in fall for winter storage. Indoors, pot tubers 1 to 2 inches deep in midwinter for blooms from late summer through fall. Propagate from seed or by dividing tubers.

HABRANTHUS

Habranthus robustus

HARDINESS: tender or Zones 9-11

TYPE OF BULB: true bulb

FLOWERING SEASON: summer to fall

HEIGHT: 9 to 12 inches

SOIL: moist, well-drained

LIGHT: full sun

Habranthus produces funnel-shaped flowers composed of six pointed petals curved back to reveal prominent stamens above tufts of arching, grassy leaves. The upright or slightly pendent blossoms are short-lived in rock gardens or flower beds in warmer zones. Elsewhere they are grown indoors as potted plants.

Selected species and varieties

H. brachyandrus [formerly *Hippeastrum brachyandrum*]—3-inch pink flower funnels shading to burgundy throats on 12-inch stems. *H. robustus*—drooping rosy pink to red flowers with green throats on 9- to 12-inch stems. *H. tubispathus* [formerly *Hippeastrum robustus* and *Zephyranthus robusta*]—1-inch flowers with petals yellow inside, copper outside, on 9-inch stems.

Growing conditions and maintenance

Plant habranthus outdoors anytime, setting bulbs 4 to 5 inches deep and 6 inches apart. Indoors, plant bulbs singly in 6-inch pots in spring for summer blooms. Propagate from seed; may also be grown from the few bulblets that may develop at the base of mature bulbs.

BLOOD LILY

Haemanthus katherinae

HARDINESS: tender or Zones 9-11

TYPE OF BULB: true bulb

FLOWERING SEASON: summer

HEIGHT: 12 to 18 inches

SOIL: moist, well-drained

LIGHT: full sun to light shade

Blood lilies produce frothy clusters of tubular flowers with colorful protruding stamens cradled within broad, petal-like bracts or in spherical clusters atop stout, leafless stems. While sometimes grown outdoors in warm zones, they bloom best as root-bound container specimens.

Selected species and varieties

H. albiflos (white paintbrush)—2-inch flower clusters with yellow-orange stamens within greenish white bracts on 12- to 18-inch stems. *H. coccineus* (Cape tulip)—3-inch clusters of 1-inch flowers with golden stamens within red bracts on 12-inch stems. *H. katherinae* [also known as *Scadoxus multiflorus* ssp. *katherinae*] (Catherine-wheel)—over 200 small 2½-inch pink-red flowers in 9-inch globes on 18-inch stems. *H. multiflorus* (salmon blood lily)—up to 200 inch-long coral red flowers with spiky stamens in 3- to 6-inch spheres on 18-inch stems.

Growing conditions and maintenance

Plant 6 to 8 inches apart outdoors or in pots, with the tip of the bulb at the soil surface. Start potted lilies in spring, then dry off and store over winter. Propagate from seed or from bulb offsets.

HERMODACTYLUS

Hermodactylus tuberosus

HARDINESS: Zones 6-9

TYPE OF BULB: tuber

FLOWERING SEASON: spring

HEIGHT: to 18 inches

SOIL: well-drained, fertile

LIGHT: full sun

Hermodactylus produces solitary, irislike flowers rising from unusual squared, blue-green leaves. The subtly colored blossoms have a fragrance reminiscent of roses. They are ideal in rock gardens or sunny borders, where they will slowly grow into large colonies. Hermodactylus can also be grown in containers.

Selected species and varieties

H. tuberosus (snake's-head iris, widow iris)—2-inch flowers with delicate lime green ruffled inner petals enclosed in broader, darker green outer petals tipped with purple, rising from 2-foot leaves.

Growing conditions and maintenance

Plant snake's-head iris tubers 3 inches deep and 6 to 8 inches apart in neutral to alkaline soil in late summer or fall. The tubers die after flowering but produce fingerlike offsets that will bloom the following year. Repot container-grown specimens annually while dormant in late summer or fall, discarding old tubers. Propagate from seed.

Hippeastrum (hip-ee-AS-trum)

AMARYLLIS

Hippeastrum 'Bold Leader'

HARDINESS: tender or Zones 9-11

TYPE OF BULB: true bulb

FLOWERING SEASON: spring

HEIGHT: 1 to 2 feet

SOIL: moist, well-drained, sandy

LIGHT: full sun

Spectacular amaryllis, with its flowers that can be as large as 8 inches across, is sometimes grown in sunny borders in warmer zones but is most renowned as a pot plant for indoor forcing.

Selected species and varieties
H. hybrids—'Apple Blossom' is cherry pink flushed white; 'Bold Leader', signal red; 'Double Record' has double white flowers veined and tipped red; 'Lady Jane', deep salmon orange double flowers; 'Orange Sovereign', bright orange blooms; 'Picotee', white petals rimmed red; 'Red Lion', velvety red flowers; 'Scarlet Baby' is a red miniature with two to three flower stems; 'White Christmas' is white.

Growing conditions and maintenance
Outdoors in Zones 10-11, plant in fall or spring, setting bulbs 6 inches deep and 1 foot apart. Indoors, plant the bulb with its top third out of the soil in a pot 2 inches wider than the bulb. Pot from late fall through winter; blooms in 5 to 8 weeks. Keep bulb barely moist until growth starts. After flowering, remove stem and fertilize until foliage dies. Dry bulb off for repotting. Propagate by separating offsets after foliage dies or from seed.

Hyacinthoides (hy-a-sin-THOY-deez)

HYACINTHOIDES

Hyacinthoides hispanica

HARDINESS: Zones 5-9

TYPE OF BULB: true bulb

FLOWERING SEASON: spring

HEIGHT: 15 to 20 inches

SOIL: moist, acid, fertile

LIGHT: partial to bright full shade

Tiny, sometimes fragrant flowers line the tips of hyacinthoides' erect stems above strap-shaped, fleshy leaves. Both Spanish and English bluebells naturalize in woodland gardens, borders, or rock gardens and are good for forcing.

Selected species and varieties
H. hispanica [formerly *Endymion hispanicus, Scilla hispanica,* and *Scilla campanulata*] (Spanish bluebell)—¾-inch bells on 20-inch stalks; 'Blue Queen' is pale blue; 'Dainty Maid', purple-pink; 'Danube', deep blue; 'Excelsior', blue-violet with deeper blue edges; 'Rosabella', violet pink; 'Rose Queen', pure pink; 'White City', snowy white; 'White Triumphator', white, vigorous. *H. non-scripta* [formerly *Endymion non-scripta, Scilla non-scripta,* and *Scilla nutans*] (English bluebell, wood hyacinth, harebell)—fragrant ½- to ¾-inch blue-violet to pink or white flowers lining one side of 15- to 18-inch stems.

Growing conditions and maintenance
Plant in fall, setting bulbs 3 inches deep and 3 to 6 inches apart. To force, place six or seven bulbs 1 inch deep in 6-inch pots. Propagate from seed or by dividing bulb offsets. Both species self-sow freely.

Hyacinthus (hy-a-SIN-thus)

HYACINTH

Hyacinthus 'Blue Jacket'

HARDINESS: Zones 3-7

TYPE OF BULB: true bulb

FLOWERING SEASON: spring

HEIGHT: 4 to 12 inches

SOIL: well-drained, fertile

LIGHT: full sun

With their heady fragrance, hyacinths are a classic bulb in the spring border. When first planted, most produce a single stiff, cylindrical cluster of inch-wide flower stars crowded on all sides of formally erect stems. Petal tips curve backward gracefully, giving the dense clusters a frilly appearance, an effect that is heightened when flowers are shaded in two tones of the same color. In subsequent years, flower stems grow longer and clusters become looser and more informal. The blooms last up to 2 weeks in the garden above straplike leaves at the base of the flower stalks. There are doubled cultivars with whorls of petals in graduated sizes engulfing each tiny blossom, and multiflora cultivars that produce several flower stems with widely spaced blossoms from each bulb. Mingle hyacinths with other spring bulbs in beds and borders, or force them indoors in pots or special glass hyacinth vases. They last almost a week as cut flowers.

Selected species and varieties
H. orientalis (Dutch hyacinth, common hyacinth, garden hyacinth)—clusters of star-shaped blossoms in an array of colors above foot-long leaves; 'Anne Marie' is

pastel pink aging to salmon; 'Blue Giant' has large pastel blue clusters; 'Blue Jacket' is deep purple with paler petal edges; 'Blue Magic', purple-blue with a white throat; 'Carnegie', elegant pure white; 'City of Harlem', pastel lemon yellow; 'Delft Blue', porcelain blue with paler edges; 'French Roman Blue' is a multiflora cultivar with blue blooms; 'Gipsy Queen', yellow-tinged clear orange; 'Hollyhock' has flowers with double red petals on 4-inch stalks; 'Jan Bos' is clear candy-apple red in slender spikes; 'Lady Derby', rosy pink; 'Lord Balfour' has clusters of rose purple blossoms; 'Oranje Boven' is salmon; 'Peter Stuyvesant', deep purple-blue; 'Pink Pearl', deep luminescent pink; 'Snow White' is a white multiflora variety; 'Violet Pearl' is lilac-rose aging to silver.

Growing conditions and maintenance

Outdoors, plant bulbs in fall, setting them 4 to 6 inches deep and 6 to 8 inches apart. Indoors, allow 4 or 5 bulbs per 6-inch pot. Plant indoor bulbs in fall as well; specially prechilled bulbs will bloom earlier than ordinary bulbs. Keep potted bulbs damp in a dark location below 50°F for about 12 weeks or until roots fill the pot and bulbs show 2 inches of leaf growth. Then move the pots into filtered sunlight at a temperature no higher than 65°F. If using special hyacinth vases, suspend bulb above (but not touching) the water and treat the same as potted bulbs. 'Anne Marie' and 'Blue Jacket' are particularly good cultivars for forcing. Hyacinths are hard to propagate but sometimes form offsets alongside mature bulbs that can take up to 6 years to reach blooming size.

Hyacinthus 'Anne Marie'

Hymenocallis (hy-men-o-KAL-is)

SPIDER LILY

Hymenocallis x festalis 'Zwanenburg'

HARDINESS:	tender or Zones 9-11
TYPE OF BULB:	true bulb
FLOWERING SEASON:	summer
HEIGHT:	10 inches to 3 feet
SOIL:	well-drained, fertile
LIGHT:	full sun

Spider lilies bear clusters of fragrant flowers with a funnel-shaped corona surrounded by curled, ribbonlike outer petals. Whorls of flowers bloom atop stout stems above straplike leaves. Use spider lilies in borders in warm zones or as annuals and container plants elsewhere. They last a week as cut flowers.

Selected species and varieties

H. x *festalis*—6- to 8-inch white blossoms with curly outer petals on 2-foot stems; 'Zwanenburg' is especially vigorous. *H. barrisiana*—a 10-inch-tall dwarf with white blooms. *H. longipetala*—up to 10 large flowers on 3-foot stems. *H. narcissiflora* (basket flower)—4- to 8-inch-long white blooms striped green with a fringed corona on 2-foot stems; 'Advance' is pure white; 'Sulfur Queen', yellow.

Growing conditions and maintenance

Plant spider lilies outdoors in spring, setting bulbs 4 inches deep and 1 foot apart. North of Zone 9, lift bulbs in fall for replanting the next spring. In containers, allow one bulb per 8-inch pot with the tip just breaking the surface. Propagate spider lilies from seed; the plants also produce a small number of bulblets.

Incarvillea (in-kar-VILL-ee-a)

HARDY GLOXINIA

Incarvillea delavayi

HARDINESS:	Zones 5-7
TYPE OF BULB:	tuber
FLOWERING SEASON:	summer
HEIGHT:	1 to 2 feet
SOIL:	moist, well-drained
LIGHT:	full sun

Hardy gloxinias bear funnel-shaped flowers flaring into wide, wavy-edged trumpets in clusters lining the tips of erect, leafless stems, which rise above clumps of ferny leaves. Plant them in rock gardens or sunny borders.

Selected species and varieties

I. compacta—purple flowers 2½ inches long and 1½ inches across on 1-foot stems above 8-inch leaves; 'Bee's Pink' has white to pink flowers. *I. delavayi*—purplish pink flower trumpets 3 inches long and as wide with yellow throats on 2-foot stems above 10-inch leaves.

Growing conditions and maintenance

Plant hardy gloxinias in spring, setting tubers 3 to 4 inches deep and 15 inches apart. Provide winter mulch in northern zones. Propagate from seed to bloom in 3 years or by division, although plants bloom best when undisturbed.

IPHEION

Ipheion uniflorum

HARDINESS: Zones 5-10

TYPE OF BULB: true bulb

FLOWERING SEASON: spring

HEIGHT: 4 to 6 inches

SOIL: acid, well-drained loam

LIGHT: full sun to light shade

An ipheion bulb sends up several flowering stalks, each flower rising on a single stem from clumps of grassy leaves, for a long period of bloom. The flowers have tiny pointed petals surrounding a cluster of bright orange stamens. They are faintly mint scented, whereas the leaves give off an onion odor when bruised. The leaves appear in fall, and persist all winter and through the blooming period until the bulbs go dormant in summer. Plant ipheion in woodland or rock gardens, in meadows, or among paving stones, where it will rapidly naturalize. It can also be forced indoors for midwinter bloom.

Selected species and varieties

I. uniflorum [formerly *Brodiaea uniflora* and *Tritilea uniflora*] (spring starflower)—1-inch white flowers tinged blue; 'Wisley Blue' is light blue with a white center; 'Rolf Fiedler', deep electric blue.

Growing conditions and maintenance

Plant ipheion in late summer or fall, setting bulbs 3 inches deep and 3 to 6 inches apart. Provide winter mulch in Zones 5-6. Pot bulbs 1 inch deep for forcing. Propagate spring starflowers by dividing clumps of bulb offsets.

FLAG, FLEUR-DE-LIS

Iris reticulata 'Harmony'

HARDINESS: Zones 5-9

TYPE OF BULB: rhizome; true bulb

FLOWERING SEASON: spring or summer

HEIGHT: 4 to 24 inches

SOIL: well-drained, sandy

LIGHT: full sun

Most irises, including the dramatic, tall bearded types, grow from rhizomes—although a few species, including the delicate *I. reticulata,* are bulbous. Dwarf irises, which are sometimes scented, bloom on short stems before their grassy leaves have fully emerged. The leaves continue to grow to their full length after flowers fade. Bokara and Dutch iris emerge simultaneously with their leaves and produce their flowers on tall, erect stems. All irises have complex flowers composed of three drooping outer petals known as falls and three erect inner petals called standards. The falls are marked with contrasting color at their bases and are sometimes crested with a raised ridge or punctuated by a pair of small protrusions called horns. The shorter standards, appearing in a complementary or contrasting color, may be curved, frilled, or wavy. Flowers last 1 to 3 weeks in the garden. Dwarf irises are ideal in rock gardens and at the edge of borders. Dutch irises, some of which are fragrant, naturalize easily, rapidly forming large clumps in sunny beds. Both Bokara and Dutch irises make excellent cut flowers lasting up to 2 weeks. Irises can also be forced for indoor bloom.

Selected species and varieties

Rhizomatous bearded iris hybrids are classified according to plant height as dwarf, intermediate, and tall, and are then further subdivided by flower size and season.

Dwarf bearded iris hybrids derive many of their characteristics from the parent species, *I. pumila* and *I. chamaeiris.* Miniature dwarf bearded iris—less than 10 inches tall with 1½- to 2½-inch flowers in midspring; 'Already' has wine red flowers; 'Angel Eyes', white flowers with blue spots on falls; 'Sky Baby', ruffled blue blooms. Standard dwarf bearded iris—10 to 15 inches tall with 1½- to 2½-inch blossoms that appear a week later than those of miniatures; 'Baby Snow-flake' has white flowers; 'Bingo', velvety purple flowers; 'Early Sunshine', yellow flowers; 'Red Dandy', wine red flowers.

Intermediate and border bearded iris—2- to 4-inch flowers on plants 15 to 28 inches tall, with intermediates blooming in midspring, borders in late spring to early summer; 'Little Angel' has white flowers; 'Lemonade', white falls on yellow blossoms.

Tall bearded iris—plants that grow upward of 28 inches tall with flowers to 8 inches across in late spring to summer; 'Cindy' has red-bearded white flowers; 'Charade', ruffled medium blue flowers; 'May Magic', light pink blossoms.

Reblooming bearded iris—varying heights and flower sizes, blossoming in spring and again anytime from midsummer to fall; 'Autumn Bugler' has violet flowers with dark purple falls. *I. cristata* (crested iris)—blue or white flowers with yellow or white crested ridges on 6- to 9-inch plants in early to midspring; 'Shenan-

Iris cristata

doah Sky' grows pale blue flowers; 'Summer Storm', deep blue. *I. sibirica* (Siberian iris)—deep blue, violet, or white, 2-inch flowers on 4-foot-tall stems in late spring.

Iris pseudacorus

Bulbous irises: I. bucharica (Bokara iris)—2- to 2½-inch-wide spring flowers with yellow falls touched with white on 18-inch stems; Zones 5-9. *I. danfordiae* (Danford iris)—a dwarf iris producing fragrant, spring-blooming, 4-inch single flowers with bristlelike canary yellow standards, falls splotched green and orange, and leaves growing to 12 inches; Zones 5-9. *I. hollandica* (Dutch iris)—fragrant 4-inch spring-to-summer flowers growing singly or in pairs on 15- to 24-inch stems; 'Angel's Wings' has pale blue standards and royal blue falls with white-rimmed yellow blotches; 'Blue Ideal', sky blue blooms on 20-inch stems; 'Blue Magic', deep blue-purple falls; 'Golden Harvest' is golden yellow shading to orange; 'Ideal' has dusty gray-blue falls blotched orange; 'Purple Sensation', deep violet falls with yellow blotches rimmed by royal blue; 'White Wedgewood' is pure white; Zones 6-9. *I. pseudacorus* (yellow flag)—2-inch light yellow flowers with a brown blotch on the falls, blooming in late spring to early summer on stalks to 5 feet tall. *I. reticulata*—very fragrant, spring-blooming 3- to 9-inch dwarf plants, violet purple with white-bordered orange crests on falls and leaves to 18 inches; 'Cantab' is pale turquoise blue with white-rimmed orange blotches on its falls; 'Edward', dark blue spotted in orange; 'Gordon', medium blue with yellow-ridged falls; 'Harmony', pale blue standards and royal blue falls with white-rimmed yellow splotches; 'Ida', light blue falls marked in yellow; 'Joyce', lavender blue standards and deep sky blue falls touched with yellow and green; 'J. S. Dijt', fragrant, rich purple standards and blue falls marked with yellow; 'Natashcha', snow white tinged blue with orange splashes on falls; 'Pauline', violet standards and dark purple falls marked with a blue-and-white variegated blotch; 'Purple Gem', deep violet standards and rich plum purple falls; 'Spring Time', pale blue standards and deep violet falls spotted purple and yellow and tipped with white; Zones 5-9.

Growing conditions and maintenance

Space dwarf bearded and crested irises 1 foot apart. Allow 1½ feet between taller types. Most irises grow best in full sun, but crested iris prefers partial shade. Bearded irises thrive in a well-drained neutral loam. Siberian irises need constant moisture and a soil high in organic matter. Propagate by dividing the rhizomes or clumps after flowering. Plant bulbous dwarf irises in spring, Dutch irises in spring or fall, setting bulbs 4 inches deep and 3 to 6 inches apart and massing them for best effect. *I. reticulata* prefers slightly alkaline soil. North of Zone 8, place Dutch irises in sites protected from wind and cover with winter mulch. Allow foliage to mature through summer. Both dwarf and Dutch irises do best when allowed to form thick clumps over 3 to 5 years, after which flowering will probably diminish. Lift while dormant and propagate by removing and replanting the quantities of small offsets that form alongside mature bulbs in fall.

Iris sibirica 'Harpswell Haze'

Ixia (IKS-ee-a)

CORN LILY

Ixia viridiflora

HARDINESS: tender or Zones 8-10

TYPE OF BULB: corm

FLOWERING SEASON: spring to summer

HEIGHT: 18 inches

SOIL: well-drained, sandy, fertile

LIGHT: full sun

Corn lilies produce clusters of cup- or star-shaped flowers at the tips of wiry or wand-like stems rising from clumps of sparse, grassy leaves. In warm, dry climates, their multicolored blossoms can be used to decorate beds or borders. Elsewhere, force them as indoor plants.

Selected species and varieties

I. viridiflora (green ixia)—1-inch pale green flowers with black throats and black anthers at the tips of their stamens. *I. hybrids*—flower bells in shades of white, yellow, orange, pink, red, or blue; 'Bluebird' has violet petals streaked purple outside and white inside and a black throat; 'Marquette', yellow purple-tipped blossoms.

Growing conditions and maintenance

In Zones 8-10, plant outdoors in late fall, setting corms 3 inches deep and 6 inches apart in neutral soil. North of Zone 8, plant them in late spring or early summer and lift corms in fall for storage over winter. Corms must dry out while dormant in summer. Blossoms close in any degree of shade. Indoors, plant five or six corms 1 inch deep in 6-inch pots in fall for winter-to-spring bloom. Propagate by removing cormels growing around mature bulbs.

Ixiolirion (iks-ee-o-LIR-ee-on)

SIBERIAN LILY

Ixiolirion tataricum

HARDINESS: Zones 7-10

TYPE OF BULB: true bulb

FLOWERING SEASON: spring to summer

HEIGHT: 12 to 16 inches

SOIL: well-drained, sandy

LIGHT: full sun

Siberian lilies produce small lilylike flower stars with petals curved gracefully back to reveal prominent short yellow stamens. The flowers cluster atop slender stems lined with narrow, grassy leaves. They will slowly naturalize in rock gardens where summers are hot and dry and can be grown as annuals or container plants in northern zones. Siberian lilies make excellent cut flowers.

Selected species and varieties
L. tataricum—bears up to 15 clear blue to lilac, slightly fragrant 2-inch flowers with narrow petals.

Growing conditions and maintenance
Plant Siberian lilies outdoors in fall, setting bulbs 3 inches deep and 2 to 6 inches apart. Provide winter mulch in Zone 7. In Zone 6 and north, plant bulbs in spring and lift in fall. Bulbs need hot, dry weather in summer and fall to ripen. Indoors, plant 5 or 6 bulbs per 6-inch pot. Propagate from seed.

Lachenalia (lah-shen-AHL-ee-a)

CAPE COWSLIP

Lachenalia aloides

HARDINESS: tender or Zones 9-10

TYPE OF BULB: true bulb

FLOWERING SEASON: spring

HEIGHT: 6 to 12 inches

SOIL: moist, well-drained, sandy

LIGHT: full sun

Cape cowslips bear long spikes of drooping, tubular flowers above broad, oval, pointed leaves. The waxy, inch-long flowers are often tinged and tipped in multiple colors, and the fleshy leaves and stems are marbled purple. Cape cowslips are rock-garden plants where winters are warm and are grown as container specimens elsewhere. They make long-lasting cut flowers.

Selected species and varieties
L. aloides (tricolored Cape cowslip)—yellow petals tinged green and touched with red; 'Pearsonii' is golden yellow with maroon tips; 'Aurea', bright yellow-orange. *L. bulbifera* (nodding Cape cowslip)—coral pink to red, tipped with green and purple.

Growing conditions and maintenance
Plant Cape cowslips outdoors in fall, setting bulbs 1 inch deep and 2 inches apart. Indoors, set five to six bulbs 1 inch deep in a 6-inch pot. Propagate by removing the bulblets that grow alongside mature bulbs or, for *L. bulbifera*, potting the small bulbils that develop in the plant's leaf joints.

Leucocoryne (loo-ko-KO-rin-ay)

LEUCOCORYNE

Leucocoryne ixioides

HARDINESS: tender or Zones 9-11

TYPE OF BULB: true bulb

FLOWERING SEASON: spring

HEIGHT: 10 to 20 inches

SOIL: well-drained

LIGHT: full sun

Leucocoryne produces small clusters of fragrant, star-shaped flowers on slender stems above clumps of grassy foot-long leaves. Making dainty accents in rock gardens or borders where winters are mild and summers hot and dry, they are grown as container specimens in other regions. They also make long-lasting cut flowers.

Selected species and varieties
L. ixioides (glory-of-the-sun)—up to a half-dozen white to pale blue blossoms ½ inch long and ¾ inch across.

Growing conditions and maintenance
Outdoors, plant glory-of-the-sun in fall, setting bulbs 4 to 6 inches deep and 6 to 8 inches apart. Bulbs must stay dry after foliage withers in early summer. Indoors, set bulbs 1 inch deep, allowing two to three bulbs per 6-inch pot. Propagate from seed or from offsets that develop at the base of mature bulbs.

Leucojum (loo-KO-jum)

SNOWFLAKE

Leucojum aestivum 'Gravetye Giant'

HARDINESS: Zones 3-9

TYPE OF BULB: true bulb

FLOWERING SEASON: spring

HEIGHT: 6 to 18 inches

SOIL: moist, well-drained, sandy

LIGHT: full sun to light shade

Snowflakes are delicately spotted with contrasting color in the center of each of the pointed petal tips that unite to form dainty bells. Tips are flipped gaily outward. Sometimes fragrant, the flowers dangle from thin, arching stalks fanning out from the tip of erect, hollow stems above grassy leaves. Allow snowflakes to naturalize in woodland or rock gardens.

Selected species and varieties
L. aestivum (summer snowflake, giant snowflake, Loddon lily)—small clusters of ¾-inch green-spotted white bells on 12- to 18-inch stems; 'Gravetye Giant' produces 1½-inch flowers on stems to 24 inches. *L. vernum* (spring snowflake)—green- or yellow-spotted 1-inch white flowers growing singly or in pairs on 5 to 14-inch stems.

Growing conditions and maintenance
Plant spring and summer snowflakes in fall, setting bulbs 4 inches deep and 4 inches apart. They do best when left undisturbed to form large clumps. Propagate from seed to bloom in 3 years or by removing small bulblets growing alongside mature bulbs.

Liatris (ly-AY-tris)

GAY-FEATHER

Liatris spicata 'Kobold'

HARDINESS: Zones 3-10

TYPE OF BULB: corm

FLOWERING SEASON: fall

HEIGHT: 2 to 3 feet

SOIL: moist, well-drained, poor

LIGHT: full sun

Gay-feather raises huge bottlebrush spires of tiny flowers with narrow, frilly petals crowded along the upper half of tall stems. The fat flower buds, resembling small balloons, open from top to bottom above a thick tuft of spiky, grasslike leaves that emerge in spring. Use gay-feather as a specimen planting in borders and wildflower gardens.

Selected species and varieties
L. spicata (spike gay-feather, button snakewort)—1- to 3-foot plants with deep purple flowers; 'Alba' is pure white; 'Kobold', a 2-foot dwarf.

Growing conditions and maintenance
Plant spike gay-feather corms in spring, setting them 3 to 4 inches deep and 18 to 24 inches apart. All except *L. spicata* 'Kobold' require staking, especially in fertile soils. Propagate from seed or by removing cormels growing around mature bulbs in spring.

Lilium (LIL-ee-um)

LILY

Lilium columbianum

HARDINESS: Zones 3-9

TYPE OF BULB: true bulb

FLOWERING SEASON: late spring to fall

HEIGHT: 2 to 8 feet

SOIL: moist, well-drained, fertile

LIGHT: full sun to light shade

Funnel-shaped lily flowers are composed of six overlapping pointed petals called tepals. Sometimes smooth, sometimes wavy or frilled, the tepals are flecked with raised spots, often in a contrasting shade. The flowers curve backward to varying degrees from almost flat or bowl-shaped faces to flaring trumpets to tightly rolled tiny turbans. Curling stamens carry anthers dusted with pollen in vivid colors. Lilies offer a wide range of colors and color combinations, with tepals flushed or striped in contrasting hues in addition to their spots. They bloom on flower stalks, either singly or in clusters, at the tips of stiff, erect stems lined with short, grassy leaves. Flowers may face upward or outward or may nod from arching stalks. Up to 50 often highly fragrant flowers may appear on a single stem. The wide range of choices allows fanciers to plant lilies for continuous bloom throughout the summer. Lilies attract attention when planted in borders, where they quickly develop into spreading clumps. They can also be grown in patio containers, forced for indoor bloom, or used as long-lasting cut flowers.

Selected species and varieties

L. hybrids—thousands of hybrids grouped into divisions of plants with similar flower size, height, form, and bloom time. *Division 1. Asiatic hybrids:* Early-summer-flowering compact lilies, usually 2 to 4 feet tall, divided into up-facing, outward-facing, and pendent subgroups based on the form of their 4- to 6-inch flowers, which are borne singly or in clusters; 'Avignon' is mellow orange; 'Connecticut King' has flat-faced, upright yellow blossoms with gold throats; 'Enchantment King', upright red-orange blooms with black spotting; 'Grand Cru' is yellow with tepal centers flushed maroon; 'Melon Time' has apricot-orange

Lilium 'Avignon'

upright flowers; 'Mona' is clear yellow with yellow spots; 'Montreux', lightly spotted dusty rose; 'Roma', deep cream with few spots; 'Rosefire', clear reddish gold without spotting. *Division 2. Martagon hybrids:* Late-spring-flowering plants 3 to 6 feet tall with 3- to 4-inch nodding flowers like tiny turbans; 'Mrs. R. O. Backhouse' produces yellow-orange flowers flushed with rose; 'Paisley hybrids' are yellow-orange spotted maroon. *Division 3. Candidum hybrids:* 3- to 4-foot-tall or taller plants flowering from late spring to early summer with tiered clusters of 3- to 4-inch tiny turbans; 'Cascade Strain' produces fragrant pure white flowers. *Division 4. American hybrids:* Lilies to 7 or 8 feet, flowering from late spring to midsummer with tiers of up to 30 or more tiny Turk's caps; 'Bellingham Hybrids' are 3- to 4-inch midsummer-blooming flowers in shades of yellow, orange, and red. *Division 5. Longiflorum hybrids:* Fragrant, outward-facing flower trumpets blooming in

midsummer, though the familiar Easter lily is often forced for earlier bloom; 'Casa Rosa' has 6-inch pink blossoms. *Division 6. Trumpet hybrids* [also called *Aurelian hybrids*]: Summer-flowering lilies 4 to 6 feet tall with large 6- to 10-inch flowers that are either trumpet shaped, sunburst shaped, bowl shaped, or nodding; 'Black Dragon' yields creamy 6-inch white flower trumpets flushed with purple on the outside; 'Golden Splendor', fragrant golden yellow trumpets flushed copper outside; 'Pink Perfection', large deep pink trumpets. *Division 7. Oriental hybrids:* Mid- to late-summer-blooming garden favorites from 2 to 8 feet tall bearing trumpet-shaped, flat-faced, or bowl-shaped flowers up to 12 inches across or trusses of smaller turban-shaped flowers; 'Casa Blanca' has pure white trumpets with orange anthers; 'Imperial Crimson', fragrant flat-faced white flowers blushed with pink; 'Imperial Gold', fragrant, flat-faced white flowers banded with yellow and spotted in crimson; 'Star Gazer', erect, deep carmine flowers up to 8 inches across with wavy tepals spotted dark red and rimmed in white on compact stems; 'White Mountain', upward-facing white trumpets with golden throats. *Division 8. Miscellaneous hybrids:* Reserved for future hybrids not fitting any previous division. *Division 9. Species lilies:* L. auratum (gold-banded lily, gold-rayed lily, mountain lily)—up to 30 bowl-shaped, fragrant 10-inch-wide white flowers with tepals banded in gold down their centers and spotted with crimson on 4- to 6-inch stems blooming in mid- to late summer. *L. canadense* (Canada lily, meadow lily, yellow lily)—3-inch dangling, bowl-shaped yellow to red-orange flowers

Lilium 'Rosefire'

Lilium candidum

spotted with crimson on stems to 6 feet in early to midsummer. *L. candidum* (Madonna lily, white lily)—fragrant trusses of shimmering white trumpets with yellow throats on 2- to 4-foot stems in early summer. *L. columbianum* (Columbia lily, Columbia tiger lily, Oregon lily)—tiered clusters of nodding 2-inch yellow to red turbans spotted maroon on 5-foot stalks in summer. *L. hansonii* (Japanese Turk's-cap)—loose spikes of 2½-inch yellow-orange turbans spotted purple on 2- to 5-foot stems in early summer. *L. henryi*—20 or more dangling light orange turbans with green throats on stems to 8 feet in late summer. *L. lancifolium* [also called *L. tigrinum*] (devil lily, tiger lily)—up to 25 nodding 5-inch orange or red Turk's caps spotted with purple on 6-foot plants in midsummer. *L. martagon* (Martagon lily, Turk's-cap lily, turban lily)—tiered clusters of up to 50 nodding light purple-rose flower turbans spotted with dark purple and unpleasantly scented on stems to 6 feet in midsummer; 'Album' is a pure ivory. *L. monadelphum* (Caucasian lily)—bell-shaped 5-inch yellow flowers tinged and spotted purple on 4- to 5-foot stems in early summer. *L. pumilum* (coral lily)—up to two dozen inch-wide, lacquer red nodding Turk's caps on compact 1- to 2-foot plants in early summer. *L. regale* (regal lily)—fragrant, outward-facing white flower trumpets flushed purple outside with gold throats inside, clustered like a crown atop 3- to 5-foot stems in midsummer. *L. speciosum* (showy Japanese lily)—fragrant, nodding Turk's caps rimmed in white on 4- to 5-foot stems in late summer to early fall; 'Album' is pure white; 'Rubrum', white blushed and spotted with crimson; 'Uchida', deep reddish pink with a white throat and crimson spots. *L. superbum* (American Turk's-cap lily, swamp lily, lily royal)—deep yellow-orange 3-inch flowers with maroon spots nodding in trusses on 5- to 8-foot stems in midsummer. *L. x testaceum* (Nankeen lily)—3-inch apricot turbans spotted red on 4- to 6-foot plants in midsummer.

Growing conditions and maintenance
With the exception of *L. candidum* and its *Division 3* hybrids, plant lilies in spring or fall, setting bulbs 2 to 3 times deeper than their diameter. Space bulbs 1 foot apart. Plant *L. candidum* and its hybrids with bulb tips an inch below the surface in fall. Mulch lilies to keep roots cool and moist in summer, protected from frost in winter. *L. auratum* and *L. speciosum* will not tolerate lime in the soil. *L. auratum, L. canadense,* and *L. speciosum* are susceptible to the lily mosaic virus. *L. lancifolium* is a carrier of the virus, which does not harm it but is spread to other lilies by aphids; buy only disease-free stock and plant far from other lilies. Stake taller lilies for support. For pots and patio containers, choose compact lilies and set bulbs deep enough to allow space for stem roots. Propagate lilies by removing and replanting the small bulblets that grow along the underground stem or by removing and potting the tiny black bulbils that appear in the leaf joints of some species.

Lycoris (ly-KOR-is)

SPIDER LILY

Lycoris radiata

HARDINESS: tender or Zones 7-10

TYPE OF BULB: true bulb

FLOWERING SEASON: summer to fall

HEIGHT: 18 to 24 inches

SOIL: well-drained, fertile

LIGHT: full sun to light shade

Lycoris produces whorls of frilly blossoms from late summer to fall atop stout bare stems. These are followed by clumps of narrow, strap-shaped leaves like those of narcissus, which emerge in late winter to early spring, fading as the plants enter summer dormancy. In most species, the blooms consist of ribbonlike petals that are curled or crisped, with abundant thready stamen filaments arching out beyond them in a froth of color. The flowers are less ornate in other species, forming into small funnels or trumpets of overlapping petals with stamen filaments the same length as the petals. Use lycoris in borders, woodland gardens, or rock gardens. They make good indoor container plants and excellent cut flowers.

Selected species and varieties
L. albiflora—2-inch ivory flowers with prominent filaments on 24-inch-tall stems in early fall; Zones 7-10. *L. aurea* [also called *L. africana* and *Amaryllis aurea*] (golden hurricane lily, golden spider lily)—highly crisped golden yellow petals and filaments on 12- to 24-inch stems in late summer to early fall; Zones 7-10. *L. radiata* (red spider lily)—1½-inch pink to deep red extremely crimped and frilled petals and abundant filaments on 18-inch flower stalks in early fall; Zones 7-10. *L. sanguinea*—2-inch erect, blood red frilled blossoms on 12- to 18-inch stems in late summer; Zones 7-10. *L. sprengeri*—vivid red to purple, blue, or rose 2- to 3-inch trumpets on 18-inch stems in late summer. *L. squamigera* (resurrection lily, magic lily)—extremely fragrant late-summer-blooming 3-inch rose to lilac trumpets on 2-foot stalks, differing from the other species by appearing after the foliage has died back; Zones 5-10.

Growing conditions and maintenance
Plant lycoris bulbs 3 to 5 inches deep depending on their size and 6 inches apart. They do best in areas where winters are moist while bulbs are growing and summers dry while they are dormant. North of Zone 7, treat lycoris as a container plant, placing bulb tips just at the soil surface and allowing one bulb per 6-inch pot. Pot bulbs in late summer for fall flowers, then allow foliage to develop through spring. Dry bulbs off in early summer, then resume watering in late summer for rebloom. Propagate lycoris by removing the small bulblets that grow alongside mature bulbs. Disturbing established clumps may delay rebloom for a year or more.

Lycoris squamigera

Mertensia (mer-TENZ-ee-a)

BLUEBELLS, LUNGWORT

Mertensia virginica

HARDINESS: Zones 3-8

TYPE OF BULB: rhizome

FLOWERING SEASON: spring

HEIGHT: 18 to 24 inches

SOIL: moist, well-drained, fertile

LIGHT: light shade to full sun

Mertensia produces loose clusters of nodding flower bells over several weeks. The blossoms dangle near the top of stems lined with oval, pointed, soft green leaves. Foliage dies back by midsummer. Bluebells will slowly grow into large clumps in woodland borders, rock gardens, and wildflower gardens, and provide textural contrast when interplanted with spring bulbs such as narcissus and tulip.

Selected species and varieties
M. virginica—(Virginia bluebells, Virginia cowslip, Roanoke bells)—inch-long pale dusty blue flowers with tiny curling crests at the tip of each petal.

Growing conditions and maintenance
Plant Virginia bluebells in fall, setting the tips of crowns just at the soil surface with buds facing up. Space crown sections 1½ to 3 feet apart. When purchasing Virginia bluebells, look for nursery-propagated crowns; refuse plants collected in the wild. To propagate, divide crowns in fall, making sure each section has at least one bud.

Muscari (mus-KAH-ree)

GRAPE HYACINTH

Muscari armeniacum 'Blue Spike'

HARDINESS: Zones 4-8

TYPE OF BULB: true bulb

FLOWERING SEASON: late winter to spring

HEIGHT: 6 to 12 inches

SOIL: moist, well-drained

LIGHT: full sun to light shade

Among the earliest of spring bulbs to brighten the garden, low-growing grape hyacinths rapidly spread into carpets of color. Their tiny flowers, less than ½ inch long, cluster in pyramidal tiers at the tips of slender stems above narrow, grasslike leaves. The flowers are usually tubular, with their lips turned inward so that clusters resemble small bunches of grapes, or flipped outward like those of hyacinths. The fragrant blossoms are often attractively rimmed in contrasting color. Usually nodding, the flowers are occasionally so tightly crowded that lower blossoms hold upper ones facing out or up, giving the flowers a distinctive texture. Use grape hyacinths as edging plants, in beds or borders, or in wildflower or rock gardens, where they will naturalize quickly. They can also be forced for indoor bloom or used as cut flowers.

Selected species and varieties
M. armeniacum (Armenian grape hyacinth)—dense clusters of 20 to 30 spring blooming blue flowers with flipped, white-rimmed edges nodding in overlapping tiers on 8- to 10-inch stems; 'Blue Spike' produces double-petaled, long-lasting

flowers; 'Cantab', pale blue flowers blooming later than the species; 'Christmas Pearl', violet blooms; 'Fantasy Creation', soft blue double flowers; 'Saphir', long-lasting deep blue flowers rimmed with white. *M. aucheri* 'Tubergenianium'—a 6-inch dwarf with dense spikes of clear light blue blossoms at the top shading to deep blue rimmed in white at the bottom. *M. azureum* [also called *Pseudomuscari azurea*]—20 to 40 cylindrical, open blue bells facing out and up on 8-inch stems; 'Album' is white. *M. botryoides* (common grape hyacinth, starch hyacinth)—overlapping tiers of nodding white, pink, violet, or blue flowers with white rims on 12-inch stems; 'Album' (Italian grape hyacinth) is a slightly shorter white cultivar. *M. comosum* [also called *Leopoldia comosa*] 'Plumosum' (feather hyacinth, tassel hyacinth)—dense clusters of light blue, violet, or fuchsia flowers with frilled, thread-like petals on 4- to 6-inch stems. *M. latifolium*—loose clusters of 10 to 20 flowers with flipped petals in spikes shading from light to dark blue on 12-inch stems. *M. neglectum*—dense clusters of 30 to 40 flowers with frilled white rims in spires shading from light to dark blue on 6-inch stems; 'Dark Eyes' is very dark blue; 'White Beauty', white tinged pink.

Growing conditions and maintenance
Plant grape hyacinths from late summer to fall, setting bulbs 2 to 3 inches deep and 3 to 4 inches apart. For indoor forcing, set bulbs 1 inch deep allowing 10 to 12 bulbs per 6-inch pot. Grape hyacinths self-sow freely. Propagate by removing bulblets that grow around mature bulbs or from seed.

Muscari botryoides 'Album'

DAFFODIL

Narcissus 'Dutch Master'

HARDINESS: Zones 3-10

TYPE OF BULB: true bulb

FLOWERING SEASON: late winter to late spring

HEIGHT: 4 to 18 inches

SOIL: well-drained

LIGHT: full sun to shade

Daffodil flowers, growing either singly or in small clusters, bloom atop stout, hollow stems above clumps of narrow, glossy, grasslike leaves. Mature bulbs produce two or more stems. The 1- to 4-inch-wide flowers sometimes face upward or arch downward but most often face out. Each bloom consists of an outer ring of six petals called the perianth and a raised center called a corona, which may be an almost flat small cup, a large cup of medium length, or, when it is very long, a trumpet. The edges of the corona may be ruffled, fringed, flared, frilled, or split. The petals of the perianth may be pointed or round, overlapping or separate. Colors range the spectrum. Species narcissus are renowned for their sweet, intense fragrance. Hybrids of the species number in the thousands, and the genus is grouped into 12 divisions for identification. There are miniature cultivars within almost every division. Group them in borders, beds, and woodland or rock gardens, or scatter them to naturalize on lawns and in meadows. All narcissus make excellent cut flowers, and all, particularly some species, are excellent for forcing. All parts of narcissus are poisonous.

Selected species and varieties

The 12 divisions are based on the shape of the corona, its size relationship to the perianth, and, sometimes, the species from which the plants originated. *Division 1. Trumpet daffodils:* One flower per 16- to 20-inch stem, with the corona a trumpet as long as or longer than the perianth petals; 'Arctic Gold' is deep yellow; 'Bravoure' has white petals and a yellow cup; 'Dutch Master' is all yellow, good for forcing; 'Las Vegas' has giant white petals and a yellow corona; 'Little Beauty' is a 6-inch miniature with white petals and a golden yellow trumpet; 'Little Gem' is an all-yellow miniature; 'Lunar Sea' has soft yellow petals and a white cup; 'Mount Hood', white petals with a cream trumpet; 'Spellbinder', yellow-green flowers with a corona aging white; 'Unsurpassable' is golden yellow with extremely large trumpets. *Division 2. Large-cup daffodils:* One flower on each 12- to 20-inch stem, the corona ranging in size from one-third the length of the petals to almost their length; 'Accent' has white petals and a pink corona; 'Ambergate', red corona and orange petals blushed red; 'Camelot' is a long-lasting golden yellow bloom; 'Carlton' has two shades of yellow and is vanilla scented; 'Ceylon' has yellow petals and an orange cup and grows vigorously; 'Daydream' is translucent yellow with a cup maturing to white; 'Flower Record' has white petals and a yellow corona rimmed red; 'Gigantic Star' is an extremely large pale yellow-orange bloom with a vanilla scent; 'Ice Follies' has creamy white petals and a flat yellow cup aging white; 'Kissproof', copper yellow petals, a red-orange cup; 'Pink Charm', white pet-

Narcissus 'Gigantic Star'

als, a corona banded salmon; 'Redhill', ivory petals, a deep red-orange corona; 'Salome', ivory petals, a pale yellow corona aging to salmon pink; 'St. Keverne' is all yellow; 'St. Patrick's Day', bright yellow with a flat white corona; 'White Plume', pure white. *Division 3. Small-cup daffodils:* One flower per 10- to 20-inch stem, with the corona less than a third the length of the perianth petals; 'Barrett Browning' is early flowering with a white perianth and an orange to red corona; 'Birma' has deep yellow petals with a red cup. *Division 4. Double daffodils:* One or more flowers per 12- to 16-inch stem, with either the perianth petals or the corona or both doubled, the corona sometimes a tuft of tousled petals almost as wide as the perianth instead of a cup; 'Bridal Crown' has cream petals, deep

Narcissus 'Ice Follies'

red-orange centers; 'Cheerfulness' is a single white bloom flecked yellow; 'Erlicheer' yields eight or more fragrant, white-petaled flowers with yellow-tinged centers on each stem; 'Flower Drift' is ivory with a ruffled yellow-orange center; 'Pencrebar' is a bright orange miniature cultivar less than 6 inches tall; 'Sir Winston Churchill' has fragrant white petals with orange centers; 'Tahiti' is deep yellow with a red center; 'Unique', ivory white with an extremely frilled golden center. *Division 5. Triandus hybrid daffodils:* Two or more drooping flowers per 10- to 12-inch stem, with the perianth petals flared backwards; 'Hawera' is less than 6 inches tall with clusters of tiny yellow bells; 'Liberty Bells' is soft yellow; 'Petrel' produces up to 7 fragrant white flowers per stem; 'Thalia' grows two or more fragrant white flowers, resembling

Narcissus 'Jack Snipe'

orchids, per stem. *Division 6. Cycla mineus hybrid daffodils:* One flower on each short stem—under 8 inches—with a trumpet-shaped corona and perianth petals swept backwards; 'February Gold' is yellow; 'Jack Snipe' has rounded white petals and a fringed yellow cup; 'Jenny' is pure white; 'Jet Fire' has red-orange petals with yellow cups; 'Jumblie' is a miniature, under 6 inches, with yellow petals swept back from a pencil-thin yellow-orange corolla; 'Peeping Tom' is lemon yellow; 'Tête-à-Tête' is a miniature under 6 inches with buttery yellow petals and a corona flushed orange. *Division 7. Jonquilla hybrid daffodils:* Three to 6 fragrant flowers on a round 10- to 14-inch stem with small cups; 'Baby Moon' is a miniature, under 6 inches, with fragrant yellow blooms; 'Bell Song' is fragrant, with white petals and a pink corona; 'Pipit', fragrant, with pale yellow petals and a white corona; 'Quail' is orangey yellow; 'Sun Disk', a yellow miniature, under 6 inches, with very rounded petals; 'Suzy' is fragrant, with yellow petals and a deep red-orange corona; 'Trevithian' has curled yellow petals and a frilled corona and is very fragrant. *Division 8. Tazetta hybrid daffodils:* Three to 20 fragrant flowers with almost flat coronas per 6- to 14-inch stem; 'Avalanche' has a perianth crowded with doubled white petals and a yellow corona; 'Geranium', fragrant white petals and a yellow-orange cup; 'Minnow', a miniature under 6 inches, has white petals and a bright yellow cup; 'Scarlet Gem', yellow-orange petals enfolding a deep red-orange corona with frilled edges. *Division 9. Poeticus hybrid daffodils:* One fragrant flower per 12- to 16-inch stem with rounded pure

white perianth petals and a tiny, brilliantly colored, disk-shaped, flat corona; 'Actaea' has brilliant white petals with deep green stamens tucked within a deep orange disk rimmed red. *Division 10. Species and wild forms: N. bulbocodium* var. *conspicuus* (hoop-petticoat daffodil)—petals reduced to tiny pointed projections around smooth, flaring yellow coronas like ladies' hoopskirts on 6- to 10-inch stems. *N. jonquilla* (jonquil)—2-inch golden yellow flowers with flat coronas in clusters on 12-inch stems. *N. papyraceus* (paper-white narcissus)—clusters of up to a dozen very fragrant flowers on 16-inch stems, excellent for forcing; 'Galilee' has pure white late blooms; 'Israel', creamy yellow petals and a deep yellow corona; 'Jerusalem' is pure white; 'Ziva', a very early white. *N. poeticus* var. *recurvus* (pheasant's-eye narcissus)—1½- to 3-inch blossoms with backswept white petals and a flat, disk-shaped yellow to red corona on 8- to 16-inch stems. *N. pseudonarcissus* ssp. *obvallaris* (Tenby daffodil)—rich deep yellow 2- to 3-inch flowers with ruffled and flared trumpets on 10-inch stems. *N. tazetta* (bunch-flowered narcissus, polyanthus narcissus)—4 to 8 fragrant blooms with a white perianth and yellow corona; 'Canaliculatus' has very fragrant blossoms with backswept white petals ringing a yellow cup on 6-inch stems; 'Grand Soleil d'Or', a deep yellow perianth and bright orange cup on 12-inch stems. *Division 11. Split-corona daffodils:* One upward-facing flower with a flattened corona split one-third or more of its length on each 14- to 20-inch stem; 'Cassata' has white petals and a ruffled lemon yellow cup aging to white; 'Colbanc' is pure white with

Narcissus 'Minnow'

an "eye" of deep green stamens; 'Mondragon' is golden yellow and deep orange; 'Palmares' has white petals and pink ruffled centers; 'Tricollet', white petals around an orange corolla. Plants in the Division 11 subdivision *Papillion daffodils* resemble floral butterflies; 'Sorbet' is an ivory butterfly type with a sunny yellow center. *Division 12. Miscellaneous daffodils:* All daffodils not belonging to any of the previous divisions.

Growing conditions and maintenance
Plant narcissus in fall, setting the bulbs, which can range from ¼ to 2 inches in diameter, into the ground at a depth three times the width of the bulb and spacing

Narcissus bulbocodium

them 1 to 3 inches apart, depending on their size and the effect desired in the garden. Allow foliage to sprawl and to die back for at least 6 weeks in early summer before removing it. Fragrant *N. tazetta* and its hybrids are hardy only in Zones 9 and 10 but are among the choicest daffodils for forcing because they require no chilling. To force plants into bloom, buy prechilled bulbs or chill all daffodil bulbs except those of *N. tazetta* and its hybrids before potting them 1 inch deep in containers. Propagate narcissus by removing and immediately replanting the small bulblets that develop at the base of mature bulbs as soon as foliage withers, or dry the bulbs and hold them for replanting in fall. Bulblets take several years to grow to blooming size.

NECTAROSCORDUM

Nectaroscordum siculum

HARDINESS: Zones 6-10

TYPE OF BULB: true bulb

FLOWERING SEASON: spring

HEIGHT: 4 feet

SOIL: moist, well-drained

LIGHT: full sun

Nectaroscordum produces large, loose clusters of open flower bells atop tall stems clasped by strap-shaped 2-foot leaves at their base. Pendulous in flower, the stem tips become erect as seeds form. The odor of crushed or bruised leaves confirms nectaroscordum's membership in the onion family. The plant grows slowly into clumps in borders or sunny wildflower gardens. The dried seed pods are attractive in arrangements.

Selected species and varieties
N. siculum (Sicilian honey garlic)—½-inch flowers composed of six rounded petals, overlapping at their bases and flared open at their tips, each dull buff petal tinged green to purple-green with a darker purple stripe down its center.

Growing conditions and maintenance
Plant nectaroscordum in fall, setting bulbs 2 inches deep and 18 inches apart. They bloom best when clumps are undisturbed, and they will self-sow. Propagate from seed to grow bulbs of blooming size in 2 years or by dividing clumps in fall after leaves wither.

NERINE

Nerine bowdenii

HARDINESS: tender or Zones 9-11

TYPE OF BULB: true bulb

FLOWERING SEASON: fall

HEIGHT: 8 to 24 inches

SOIL: well-drained, sandy

LIGHT: full sun

Nerines bear large clusters of star-shaped flowers with prominent stamens. The flowers appear on leafless stems in fall, followed by narrow, strap-shaped, glossy leaves from late winter to early spring. In warmer zones, use nerines in beds or borders; elsewhere, grow them as indoor plants. They make striking cut flowers.

Selected species and varieties
N. bowdenii—rose pink tufted flowers in 9-inch clusters on stems to 2 feet, appearing the same time as leaves; 'Pink Triumph' is iridescent pink; Zones 8-10. *N sarniensis* (Guernsey lily)—10-inch clusters of iridescent white to deep scarlet flowers on 18-inch stems; 'Cherry Ripe' is rosy red; 'Early Snow', pure white; 'Radiant Queen', rosy pink; 'Salmon Supreme', salmon pink; Zones 9-10. *N. undulata* (Kalahari nerine)—2-inch flowers clustered on 8- to 18-inch stems; Zones 9-10.

Growing conditions and maintenance
Plant nerine bulbs in late summer, setting them 3 to 6 inches deep and 8 inches apart. Pot with the upper half of the bulb out of the soil. Keep bulbs dry during summer dormancy. Propagate from seed or by removing bulb offsets.

ORNITHOGALUM

Ornithogalum nutans

HARDINESS: Zones 5-10

TYPE OF BULB: true bulb

FLOWERING SEASON: spring or summer

HEIGHT: 6 to 24 inches

SOIL: moist, well-drained

LIGHT: full sun to light shade

Ornithogalum bears star-shaped, often fragrant, flowers with a distinctive tight "eye" of pistils at their centers. Usually white with a green stripe down the outside of each petal, some are yellow to orange. The flowers are carried in large clusters that are sometimes pendent but more often are facing upward in flat-topped bouquets above neat clumps of shimmering green, ribbonlike leaves. Ornithogalum species vary considerably in hardiness. Allow frost-resistant species to naturalize in borders, beds, and rock gardens, where they will self-sow. Tender species can be grown outdoors in warm zones or indoors as pot plants. Some species are used for long-lasting cut flowers.

Selected species and varieties
O. arabicum (Arabian starflower)—fragrant, pure white 1-inch flowers with black centers on 1½- to 2-foot stems in spring; Zones 8-10. *O. dubium*—enormous clusters of yellow flowers tinged orange with black centers on 8- to 12-inch stems; Zones 8-10. *O. nutans* (nodding star-of-Bethlehem)—fragrant greenish white 2-inch flowers nodding along one side of 12- to 18-inch stems from late spring to early

summer; Zones 5-9. *O. saundersiae* (giant chincherinchee)—flat spikes of 1-inch white flowers with a greenish black eye on stems 3 feet or more tall above clumps of broad leaves in late spring; Zones 7-10. *O. thyrsoides* (wonder flower, chincherinchee) —¾-inch cream flowers with a greenish brown eye on 6- to 18-inch stems from late spring to summer; excellent for cutting, but all parts of the plant are poisonous; Zones 7-9. *O. umbellatum* (star-of-Bethlehem, nap-at-noon, summer snowflake)— 1-inch flowers prominently striped green on the outside opening in the afternoon on 8- to 12-inch stems in spring; an aggressive naturalizer; Zones 5-9.

Growing conditions and maintenance
Outdoors, plant ornithogalum bulbs 4 inches deep and 2 to 5 inches apart. Nodding star-of-Bethlehem prefers shade; other species will grow in sun or shade, although *O. umbellatum* only opens fully in sun. North of Zone 8, treat tender species as annuals, lifting bulbs in fall for replanting in spring, or grow as container plants. Indoors, pot 5 to 6 bulbs 1 inch deep in a 6-inch pot. Propagate from seed sown in spring or by dividing bulbs and offsets in autumn.

Ornithogalum umbellatum

Oxalis (oks-AH-lis)

WOOD SORREL

Oxalis deppei 'Iron Cross'

HARDINESS: Zones 5-9

TYPE OF BULB: tuber or true bulb

FLOWERING SEASON: summer

HEIGHT: 2 to 12 inches

SOIL: well-drained

LIGHT: full sun to light shade

Oxalis bears dainty, flat-faced flowers either singly or in clusters above lobed, cloverlike leaflets. The tiny leaves fold at night or on overcast days. Oxalis naturalizes easily, forming perfect carpets in rockeries and woodland gardens and makes fast-growing houseplants.

Selected species and varieties
O. adenophylla (Chilean oxalis)—a dwarf only 2 to 6 inches tall with tight rosettes of 1-inch pink flowers veined deeper pink above blue-green leaflets. *O. deppei* [also classified as *O. tetraphylla*] 'Iron Cross' (lucky clover, good-luck leaf)—clusters of rosy red-violet 1-inch flowers on 1-foot stems, above leaves with four leaflets arranged symmetrically and marked with deep purple to resemble an iron cross. *O. triangularis* ssp. *papilionacea*—white flowers above green leaflets.

Growing conditions and maintenance
Plant Chilean oxalis tubers in fall, 'Iron Cross' bulbs in spring, setting them 2 inches deep and 4 to 6 inches apart. To control invasiveness, plant in confined areas, such as between paving stones or in pots sunk into the garden. Propagate from seed or by dividing offsets.

Pancratium (pan-KRAT-ee-um)

PANCRATIUM

Pancratium maritimum

HARDINESS: tender or Zones 9-11

TYPE OF BULB: true bulb

FLOWERING SEASON: summer to fall

HEIGHT: 1 to 2 feet

SOIL: well-drained, sandy

LIGHT: full sun

Pancratium produces extremely fragrant flowers reminiscent of frilled daffodils above gray-green sword-shaped leaves. Where climates are reliably frost free they can he grown in borders and rock gardens. North of Zone 9, plant them in containers for patio display or indoor use.

Selected species and varieties
P. maritimum (sea daffodil, sea lily)—pure white 3-inch flowers with a deeply toothed, trumpet-shaped corona surrounded by six narrow, pointed petals in clusters at the tip of each stem.

Growing conditions and maintenance
Plant sea daffodil bulbs where they can remain undisturbed for several years, setting them 3 inches deep and 10 to 12 inches apart. Allow one large bulb per 12-inch pot to allow room for bulb offsets to develop; set the tip of the bulb level with the soil surface. Repotting or division may reduce flowering the following season. Propagate from seed to blooming-size bulbs in 5 years or by carefully removing the offsets from around mature bulbs, which tend to be fragile.

Polianthes (pol-ee-AN-theez)

POLIANTHES

Polianthes tuberosa 'The Pearl'

HARDINESS: tender or Zones 9-10

TYPE OF BULB: tuber

FLOWERING SEASON: summer to fall

HEIGHT: 2 to 4 feet

SOIL: moist, well-drained

LIGHT: full sun

The long, curving buds of polianthes open into clusters of waxy flowers with a heavy, sweet fragrance above grassy, gray-green leaves. Each bud forms a narrow trumpet whose petal ends depict a tiny star. Use polianthes outdoors in beds and borders or indoors in containers. As cut flowers, they last as long as 2 weeks.

Selected species and varieties

P. tuberosa (tuberose)—white, 2½-inch-long flowers above 12- to 18-inch leaves; 'The Pearl' has double-petaled blossoms on 2-foot stems; 'Single Mexican', single flowers on 3- to 4-foot stems.

Growing conditions and maintenance

Plant tuberoses outdoors in spring, setting the tubers 3 inches deep and 6 inches apart. Mature tubers bloom, then die, leaving behind many small offsets that reach blooming size in 1 or 2 years. North of Zone 9, start tubers indoors 4 to 6 weeks before night temperatures reach 60° F and lift for winter storage. For pot plants, allow 1 tuber per 6-inch pot, setting bulbs 1 inch deep. Propagate by removing offsets that develop around mature tubers.

Puschkinia (push-KIN-ee-a)

PUSCHKINIA

Puschkinia scilloides var. libanotica 'Alba'

HARDINESS: Zones 4-9

TYPE OF BULB: true bulb

FLOWERING SEASON: spring

HEIGHT: 4 to 6 inches

SOIL: moist, well-drained

LIGHT: full sun to light shade

Puschkinia's wands of tight, oval buds open first into loose clusters of tiny flower bells and finally into small stars on slender stems rising from tufts of narrow leaves like those of daffodils. The plants naturalize easily into drifts of blooms to carpet rockeries or beds and make an attractive border edging.

Selected species and varieties

P. scilloides var. *libanotica* (striped squill) —½-inch bluish white flowers striped darker blue above 6-inch leaves; 'Alba' is pure white.

Growing conditions and maintenance

Plant bulbs in fall, setting them 2 inches deep and 6 inches apart. Group them in small colonies for best effect. They bloom best when left undisturbed. Propagate by removing the small bulblets that grow alongside mature bulbs.

Ranunculus (ra-NUN-kew-lus)

BUTTERCUP, CROWFOOT

Ranunculus asiaticus

HARDINESS: tender or Zones 9-11

TYPE OF BULB: tuber

FLOWERING SEASON: spring and summer

HEIGHT: 10 to 18 inches

SOIL: moist, very well drained, sandy

LIGHT: full sun

Buttercups produce quantities of saucer-shaped flowers over a long season of bloom. There are many hybrids, so thickly doubled that flowers become colorful domes of whorled overlapping petals. Each tuber may produce five or six dozen flowers up to four at a time throughout the season on stems lined with ferny leaflets. Buttercups can be used in borders and rock gardens, and they excel as cut flowers.

Selected species and varieties

R. asiaticus 'Tecolote Giants' (Persian buttercup)—flowers up to 5 inches across in pastel shades of pink, rose, yellow, tangerine, and white, with bi- and tricolors.

Growing conditions and maintenance

Plant Persian buttercups in fall, soaking the tubers overnight then setting them in the soil with the claws down with the tops 1½ inches deep. Space them 8 inches apart. Crowns are subject to rot, so sites with fast drainage are essential for success. Tubers go dormant in summer. North of Zone 9, treat plants as annuals, setting them out in spring and lifting them in fall for winter storage. Propagate from seed or by dividing tubers.

Rhodohypoxis (ro-do-hi-POKS-is)

RHODOHYPOXIS

Rhodohypoxis baurii

HARDINESS: Zones 6-10

TYPE OF BULB: rhizome

FLOWERING SEASON: summer

HEIGHT: 3 to 4 inches

SOIL: well-drained, sandy

LIGHT: full sun

Rhodohypoxis sends up tufts of 3-inch, stiff, grassy leaves covered with downy hairs in spring, followed by dainty, flat-faced blossoms that appear throughout the season. Each blossom sits atop a slender stem; the plants produce several flowering stems at a time. Dwarf rhodohypoxis are excellent planted among paving stones and will form colonies in rock gardens or borders. They can also be grown as container specimens.

Selected species and varieties
R. baurii (red star)—1- to 1½-inch white, pink, rose, or red flowers with petals crowded closely together at the center, obscuring the stamens.

Growing conditions and maintenance
Plant rhodohypoxis in fall, setting rhizomes 1 to 2 inches deep and 2 to 3 inches apart. Protect rhizomes with winter mulch in Zones 5 and 6. North of Zone 6, treat rhodohypoxis as an annual, planting in spring and lifting in fall, or grow it in shallow containers, allowing 4 or 5 rhizomes per 6-inch bulb pan. They are best left undisturbed, but clumps of rhizomes can be lifted and separated for propagation in spring as leaves begin to show.

Sandersonia (sahn-der-SONE-ee-a)

SANDERSONIA

Sandersonia aurantiaca

HARDINESS: tender or Zones 9-11

TYPE OF BULB: tuber

FLOWERING SEASON: summer

HEIGHT: 2 to 3 feet

SOIL: well-drained, sandy

LIGHT: full sun

The petals of sandersonia fuse into tiny, balloon-shaped flowers that dangle from thin stalks growing in the upper leaf joints along semierect, climbing stems. Soft green, narrow pointed leaves line the stems, sometimes tapering into tendrils. Plant sandersonias along fences or walls, or grow them in containers as patio specimens. Sandersonias make excellent cut flowers.

Selected species and varieties
S. aurantiaca (Chinese lantern lily)—inch-long, golden orange, puffy blossoms resembling chubby, upside-down urns, with threadlike green spurs.

Growing conditions and maintenance
Plant Chinese lantern lilies in spring, setting the brittle tubers 4 inches deep and 8 to 12 inches apart. North of Zone 9, lift tubers in fall or grow them in containers to bring indoors in winter. Propagate from seed to bloom in 2 years or by dividing tubers in spring.

Sanguinaria (sang-gwi-NAR-ee-a)

BLOODROOT

Sanguinaria canadensis

HARDINESS: Zones 3-9

TYPE OF BULB: rhizome

FLOWERING SEASON: spring

HEIGHT: 6 to 14 inches

SOIL: moist, well-drained, rich

LIGHT: partial shade

Bloodroot is one of the loveliest spring-blooming woodland wildflowers native to eastern North America, and its large round blue-green leaves make an attractive ground cover. The plant is named for its red sap, root, and stems.

Selected species and varieties
S. canadensis (bloodroot, red puccoon)—solitary white flower to 1½ inches across with gold stamens on a 6- to 10-inch stalk. Each flower bud is surrounded by a furled leaf when it emerges. When fully expanded, the leaves are up to 1 foot across and have five or more lobes whose edges curl slightly upward.

Growing conditions and maintenance
Bloodroot thrives in rich, moist soil and benefits from added organic matter. It does best when planted beneath deciduous trees, where it receives bright sunshine before the trees leaf out and partial shade for the rest of the growing season. Mulch lightly with deciduous leaves in winter. Propagate by seed planted immediately after collection, or by dividing rhizomes in fall or early spring.

Sauromatum (sow-RO-ma-tum)

SAUROMATUM

Sauromatum venosum

HARDINESS: tender or Zones 10-11

TYPE OF BULB: tuber

FLOWERING SEASON: summer

HEIGHT: 1 to 2 feet

SOIL: moist, well-drained

LIGHT: full sun

Sauromatum's tiny, inconspicuous true flowers are carried on a pencil-shaped spadix that emerges from an exotically shaped and colored hood or spathe. The oval, pointed, curled spathe rises out of a thick, bottle-shaped stem. Blooming flowers give off a putrid odor. After the spathe withers, a finely divided leaf resembling a miniature palm tree appears. Sauromatums can be grown in beds or in containers as specimen plants.

Selected species and varieties
S. venosum [formerly *S. guttatum*] (voodoo lily, monarch-of-the-East, red calla)—12- to 20-inch spathe mottled and flecked purple, brown, green, and yellow, followed by 20- to 24-inch foliage.

Growing conditions and maintenance
In Zones 10-11 where air is humid and temperatures remain above 68° F, set tubers in a saucer of water on a sunny window sill, where they will grow without soil. Otherwise, plant them outdoors, setting tubers 4 to 6 inches deep and 12 inches apart. North of Zone 10, grow them as container plants, with the tubers set 2 inches deep in pots. Propagate by dividing offsets from the main tuber.

Schizostylis (ski-zo-STI-lis)

CRIMSON FLAG

Schizostylis coccinea 'Mrs. Hegarty'

HARDINESS: tender or Zones 6-10

TYPE OF BULB: rhizome

FLOWERING SEASON: fall

HEIGHT: 1½ to 2 feet

SOIL: moist, fertile

LIGHT: full sun

Crimson flag produces flowers with satiny pointed petals rimming curled stamens. A slender stem carries multiple blossoms above a clump of narrow, sometimes evergreen, leaves. In warm climates, crimson flag may produce sparse flowers in spring and summer as well as a full burst of fall bloom. Crimson flag thrives in bog gardens or alongside streams and ponds. In colder areas, grow crimson flag indoors in containers. It makes excellent cut flowers.

Selected species and varieties
S. coccinea (river lily)—1- to 2-inch-deep crimson flower stars; 'Major' produces larger flowers than the species; 'Mrs. Hegarty' is rose pink.

Growing conditions and maintenance
Plant crimson flag outdoors in spring or fall, setting roots 2 inches deep and 9 to 12 inches apart. For containers, start roots outdoors in spring after threat of frost has passed, then pot them to bring indoors for late-fall-to-winter bloom. Propagate by division in spring or fall, although disturbed roots may take a year or more to resume flowering.

Scilla (SIL-la)

SQUILL

Scilla peruviana

HARDINESS: tender or Zones 3-10

TYPE OF BULB: true bulb

FLOWERING SEASON: winter, spring, summer

HEIGHT: 6 to 28 inches

SOIL: moist, well-drained, fertile

LIGHT: full sun to partial shade

Squills are one of spring's classic bulbs, carpeting the ground beneath taller bulb plants and shrubbery with a haze of tiny bells that open into dainty stars. Sometimes facing upward, sometimes dangling, the blossoms appear in clusters on slender stems clasped at the base by a few narrow, ribbonlike leaves. Mass squill at the edge of borders, in rockeries, or in woodland gardens, where it will naturalize rapidly. Squill can also be forced for indoor bloom.

Selected species and varieties
S. bifolia (twinleaf squill)—loose, upright clusters of up to eight tiny ½-inch pale blue flowers on 6-inch stems above two or three leaves in early spring; 'Rosea' is rosy pink; Zones 4-8. *S. litardierei* (meadow squill)—up to 30 tiny ³⁄₁₆-inch blue flowers in a dense tuft on 8-inch stems in spring; Zones 5-8. *S. mischtschenkoana* [formerly *S. tubergeniana*] (Persian bluebell)—multiple 4- to 5-inch stems with sparse clusters of upturned 1½-inch pale blue flowers striped darker blue, and blooming late winter to early spring; Zones 5-8. *S. peruviana* (Peruvian lily, Peruvian jacinth, Cuban lily)—dense, domed 6-inch clusters of deep violet ½-inch flowers above ever-

green leaves on 18-inch stems in summer; Zones 9-10. *S. scilloides* (Chinese squill, Japanese jacinth)—12- to 18-inch leafless stems with clusters of up to 60 deep pink blossoms in summer followed by leaves in fall, sometimes persisting into spring; Zones 5-8. *S. siberica* (Siberian squill)—sparse clusters of nodding ½-inch gentian blue flowers on 4- to 6-inch stems in early spring; 'Alba' is white; 'Spring Beauty' has large, deep blue flower stars; Zones 3-8.

Growing conditions and maintenance
Select squills from reputable breeders who propagate their own bulbs, as collection has endangered many species in the wild. Plant tender Peruvian lilies outdoors in spring, setting bulbs with their necks at the soil line and 8 to 10 inches apart. North of Zone 9, grow them as container plants, starting bulbs indoors in late winter for summer bloom. Plant all other squills outdoors in fall, setting bulbs 2 to 3 inches deep and 3 to 6 inches apart. Siberian squill even succeeds under evergreens, where other bulbs fail. Squills, particularly Siberian squill, self-sow easily. They can be propagated from seed to reach blooming-size bulbs in 3 years or by dividing small bulblets produced by mature bulbs in fall.

Scilla bifolia 'Rosea'

Sparaxis (spa-RAKS-is)

WAND FLOWER

Sparaxis grandiflora

HARDINESS: tender or Zones 8-10

TYPE OF BULB: corm

FLOWERING SEASON: spring to summer

HEIGHT: 12 inches

SOIL: well-drained, fertile

LIGHT: full sun

Highly decorative wand flowers produce arching stems of up to five flowers each blooming in bold, splashy color combinations. Pointed petals form shallow saucers above stiff fans of narrow, pointed leaves. In warmer climates, wand flowers naturalize, spreading rapidly in beds, borders, or rock gardens. Elsewhere, they are grown as annuals or container specimens. Wand flowers are prized as cut flowers.

Selected species and varieties
S. grandiflora—3-inch flowers in shades of white, rose, and purple, often two-toned. *S. tricolor* (harlequin flower)—2-inch flowers with bright yellow throats rimmed with black or purple, the outer portion of the petals yellow, rose, red, or purple, and sometimes tinged brown.

Growing conditions and maintenance
Plant wand flowers in spring or fall, setting corms 2 to 3 inches deep and 1 to 1½ feet apart. North of Zone 8, plant corms in early spring and lift in fall or plant in containers for indoor forcing. Propagate from seed or by removing small cormels around the base of mature corms.

Sprekelia (spre-KEE-lee-a)

SPREKELIA

Sprekelia formosissima

HARDINESS: tender or Zones 9-11

TYPE OF BULB: true bulb

FLOWERING SEASON: summer

HEIGHT: to 12 inches

SOIL: well-drained, sandy, fertile

LIGHT: full sun

Sprekelia produces orchidlike flowers with six velvety petals, the upper petals erect, the lower ones pinched together at their bases to form a channel for long, curving stamens. Flowers grow singly on leafless stems before a sparse clump of narrow, straplike leaves appear. In warm zones, sprekelia can be grown in the border. Elsewhere, it is grown as an annual or a pot plant.

Selected species and varieties
S. formosissima (Jacobean lily, Aztec lily, St. James's lily, orchid amaryllis)—4- to 6-inch deep red-orange or deep crimson flowers with bright yellow stamens and leaves to 12 inches.

Growing conditions and maintenance
Outdoors in Zones 9 and 10, plant Jacobean lilies in any season, setting bulbs 3 to 4 inches deep and 8 to 12 inches apart for blooms in 6 weeks. North of Zone 9, plant the bulbs outdoors in spring and lift in fall for winter storage. Indoors, plant with half the bulb above the soil surface, allowing one bulb per 4-inch pot or three bulbs per 6-inch pot. Propagate by removing bulblets that develop around the base of mature bulbs.

Sternbergia (stern-BERG-ee-a)

AUTUMN DAFFODIL

Sternbergia lutea

HARDINESS: tender or Zones 6-10

TYPE OF BULB: true bulb

FLOWERING SEASON: fall

HEIGHT: 6 to 12 inches

SOIL: dry, well-drained, sandy

LIGHT: full sun

Autumn daffodils' egg-shaped buds open into deep goblets of shimmering, waxy petals reminiscent of crocuses. The flowers appear on slender stems shorter than the grassy ribbons of the foliage; each bulb commonly produces four or five flowers. Use autumn daffodils in rock gardens, tucked against walls, and in any other hot, dry location. They can also be potted for indoor forcing.

Selected species and varieties

S. lutea—1½- to 2-inch golden yellow blossoms on 4-inch stems among 6- to 12-inch leaves.

Growing conditions and maintenance

Plant autumn daffodils in summer, setting bulbs 4 inches deep and 4 to 6 inches apart. Provide a protective coat of winter mulch in Zone 6. North of Zone 6, grow as annuals or in bulb pans, placing five or six bulbs 2 inches deep in each 6-inch pan. Autumn daffodils can be propagated by removing the small bulb offsets from large clumps when flowering diminishes, but they do best when left undisturbed.

Tigridia (tye-GRID-ee-a)

PEACOCK FLOWER

Tigridia pavonia

HARDINESS: tender or Zones 7-10

TYPE OF BULB: corm

FLOWERING SEASON: summer

HEIGHT: 1 to 2 feet

SOIL: moist, well-drained, fertile

LIGHT: full sun

Peacock flower's unique blossoms are composed of three large outer petals forming a broad triangle enfolding three gaily spotted inner petals united to form a deep cup. The blossoms appear singly on erect stems rising from stiff fans of swordlike leaves. Each flower lasts only a day, but the corms produce a succession of stems over 6 to 8 weeks. Mass peacock flowers for a long show of color in borders and beds, where they will slowly naturalize, or use small clumps as accents.

Selected species and varieties

T. pavonia (tiger flower)—white or buff to yellow, orange, purple, or pink 3- to 6-inch flowers with conspicuously spotted and mottled centers; 'Alba' has white outer petals; 'Aurea' is yellow; 'Rosea', rosy pink.

Growing conditions and maintenance

Plant peacock flowers in spring, setting corms 3 to 4 inches deep and 6 to 9 inches apart. Provide a protective winter mulch in Zone 7. North of Zone 7, plant bulbs in spring and lift in fall. Propagate from seed to bloom the first year or by removing the small cormels that develop at the base of mature corms.

Triteleia (try-TEL-ee-a)

TRITELEIA

Triteleia laxa

HARDINESS: Zones 7-10

TYPE OF BULB: corm

FLOWERING SEASON: spring to summer

HEIGHT: 18 to 30 inches

SOIL: well-drained, sandy

LIGHT: full sun

Triteleias produce loose clusters of dainty flower stars on tall stems above sparse clumps of grassy leaves. They make good cut flowers and will naturalize in sunny beds, borders, or rock gardens when conditions suit them.

Selected species and varieties

T. hyacinthina (wild hyacinth)—has flat-topped clusters of up to 30 tiny white, sometimes blue or lilac, ½-inch flower stars blooming late spring to summer on 1- to 2-foot stems. *T. laxa* (grass nut, triplet lily)—loose, open spheres of 1¾-inch blue to violet, sometimes white, flowers on 30-inch stems in spring; 'Queen Fabiola' has dense spheres of pale blue blossoms.

Growing conditions and maintenance

Plant triteleias in fall, setting corms 3 inches deep and 2 to 3 inches apart. They grow best where summers are completely dry, as in the western portions of Zones 8-10. Elsewhere, lift corms after foliage withers to dry for the summer and replant in fall. Provide a protective winter mulch in Zone 7. Propagate from seed to bloom in 2 years or by removing and replanting small cormels that develop around mature bulbs.

Tritonia (try-TONE-ee-a)

BLAZING STAR

Tritonia crocata

HARDINESS: tender or Zones 7-10

TYPE OF BULB: corm

FLOWERING SEASON: spring to summer

HEIGHT: 18 inches

SOIL: moist, well-drained

LIGHT: full sun

Forming small bowls of pointed petals, tritonia's flowers open along one side of arching flower spikes in a way reminiscent of freesias. Flower stems rise from small fans of narrow pointed leaves. Use tritonia in beds, borders, or rock gardens. The stems make long-lasting cut flowers.

Selected species and varieties

T. crocata (flame freesia)—2-inch-wide flowers in a wide range of colors; 'Baby Doll' is salmon; 'Bridal Veil', white; 'Pink Sensation', pink; 'Serendipity', red; 'Tangerine', orange.

Growing conditions and maintenance

Plant tritonia in fall, setting corms 3 to 4 inches deep and 6 inches apart. From Zone 7 north, treat tritonia as an annual, planting in spring and lifting corms in fall for winter storage. Propagate from seed or by removing the small cormels growing around mature corms.

Tulipa (TOO-lip-a)

TULIP

Tulipa 'Plaisir'

HARDINESS: Zones 2-8

TYPE OF BULB: true bulb

FLOWERING SEASON: spring

HEIGHT: 6 to 28 inches

SOIL: well-drained, sandy, fertile

LIGHT: full sun

Synonymous with spring to many gardeners, tulips' egg-shaped buds unfold into a profusion of forms ranging from inverted bells to flat saucers, stars, urns, deep cups, and lilylike shapes, sometimes with the petals reduced to mere ribbons. Petals may be smooth, curled, frilled, crisped, ruffled, flared, doubled, or waved. Tulips come in every color except true blue and are often striped, edged, flecked, flushed with contrasting color, or "flamed" in a zigzag variegated pattern. The hundreds of tulip species and thousands of hybrids are sorted by botanists into groups with similar origins, shapes, and bloom times. Species tulips, also called wild tulips or botanical tulips, generally have very early flowers on strong, sturdy stems, and are the parents of the taller hybrids, which bloom at various times throughout spring. The botanical *Kaufmanniana*, *Fosteriana*, and *Greigii* tulips merited their own divisions in the latest shuffling of botanical nomenclature. Low-growing species tulips can be grown in rock gardens or as edgings for beds or borders and may naturalize where conditions are right for their growth. Plant taller hybrids in informal groupings or formal patterns where they will produce blooms

for several years before requiring renewal. Tulips can be forced for indoor bloom and make excellent cut flowers.

Selected species and varieties

Hybrids and species tulips are organized into 15 divisions used in the garden trade. *Division 1. Single early tulips:* Among the first to flower, in very early spring, on 6- to 14-inch stems with smooth petals in neat cups; 'Apricot Beauty' is salmon edged in apricot; 'Princess Irene', orange-splashed purple. *Division 2. Double early tulips:* Bowls of ruffled, doubled petals up to 4 inches across on 12-inch stems in early spring; 'Monte Carlo' is deep, clear yellow; 'Peach Blossom' has honey-scented soft rose petals edged with cream. *Division 3. Triumph tulips:* Satiny-smooth flowers in midspring on 18- to 24-inch stems; 'Attila' is pale purple-violet; 'New Design', cream flushed pink and apricot with leaves edged pinky cream. *Division 4. Darwin hybrid tulips:* Large, smooth-petaled ovals opening into flat cups up to 7 inches across in midspring on stems to 36 inches; 'Daydream' has yellow petals aging to apricot-flushed orange; 'Golden Parade', bright yellow petals edged in red; 'Pink Impression', purplish pink. *Division 5. Single late tulips* [includes Cottage and Darwin tulips]: Distinctly rectangular flower cups, some with pointed petals, in late spring on stems to 30 inches; 'Blushing Beauty' is yellow to apricot-blushed rose; 'Georgette' has clusters of butter yellow blooms with the edges aging to red; 'Halcro' is raspberry with a yellow base; 'Maureen', cool white; 'Mrs. J. T. Scheepers', pure yellow; 'Queen of the Night', deep maroon, almost black. *Division 6. Lily-flowering tulips:* Urn-

Tulipa 'Apricot Beauty'

shaped buds open in late spring into lily-like flowers with curved, pointed petals on 24-inch stems; 'Red Shine' is deep ruby red with blue center; 'White Triumphator', pure white. *Division 7. Fringed tulips:* Late-spring flowers with very finely fringed petals on 14- to 24-inch stems; 'Burgundy Lace' is deep wine; 'Fringed Elegance', yellow flecked with pink. *Division 8. Viridiflora green tulips:* Late-spring flowers with petals in varying degrees of green on 18-inch stems; 'Spring Green' is ivory white with the center of the petals slashed green. *Division 9. Rembrandt tulips:* Petal color is "broken," or variegated, with elaborately patterned stripes and blotches on 18- to 30-inch stems in midspring; 'Cordell Hull' is white streaked with red. *Division 10. Parrot tulips:* Tousled petals, exotically fringed, waved, crisped, and flared, on flowers blooming in late spring on stems to 24 inches; 'Flaming Parrot' is deep yellow flamed with crimson. *Division 11. Double late tulips* [also called *peony-flowered tulips*]: Bowls of doubled petals in late

Tulipa dasystemon

spring on 16- to 24-inch stems; 'Angelique' is deep pink shading to pale pink; 'Miranda', two shades of red with a yellow base. *Division 12. Kaufmanniana tulips:* Urn-shaped buds opening into large flowers with curved petals on stems under 12 inches in very early spring; 'Ancila' is soft rosy pink outside, white inside; 'Show Winner', deep scarlet. *Division 13. Fosteriana tulips:* Enormous blossoms in early spring on stems to 18 inches; 'Juan' is orange with a yellow base. *Division 14. Greigii tulips:* Flowers on strong, 8- to 16-inch stems above attractively purple-mot-

tled foliage; 'Czar Peter' is red rimmed with white; 'Red Riding Hood', deep red-orange with a black base. *Division 15. Species tulips:* *T. bakeri* 'Lilac Wonder'—rosy purple cups with yellow bases on 6-inch stems; Zones 5-9. *T. batalinii* 'Bright Gem'—yellow cups of pointed petals flushed orange, 6 inches tall; Zones 3-8. *T. clusiana* var. *chrysantha* (golden lady tulip)—deep saucers, yellow inside, crimson edged with yellow outside, 12 inches tall; Zones 3-9. *T. dasystemon* (Kuen Lun tulip)—clusters of white flower stars tinged bronze and green, 4 inches tall; Zones 4-8. *T. linifolia* (slimleaf tulip)—curled, pointed electric red petals and red-rimmed leaves, 6 inches tall; Zones 4-8. *T. pulchella* 'Violacea' (red crocus tulip)—tiny purple-red ovals tinged green at bases, 3½ inches tall; Zones 5-8. *T. turkestanica*—clusters of white flower stars tinged violet, 5 inches tall; Zones 5-8.

Growing conditions and maintenance
Plant tulips in late fall, at a depth equal to three times their diameter. Space according to bulb size. Plant up to 40 hybrid bulbs per square yard or up to 60 smaller species bulbs per square yard. Note, however, that the famous variegation of Rembrandt tulips is caused by a virus that does not hurt them but can be harmful if spread to lilies and other tulips by aphids. Site Rembrandts far from susceptible plants. In Zones 9 and 10, tulips must be prechilled. Buy them in that condition or prechill them yourself by placing them in a vented paper bag in the refrigerator at 40°F for 9 to 12 weeks before setting them out; in modern frost-free refrigerators, however, you run the risk of drying them out. *T. bakeri* 'Lilac Wonder', *T. clusiana* var. *chrysantha*, and the hybrids 'Burgundy Lace', 'Flaming Parrot', 'Golden Parade', 'Halcro', 'Maureen', 'Menton', and 'Mrs. J. T. Scheepers' require no prechilling and may naturalize in warm zones. Allow foliage to ripen before mowing or removing it. Tulips tend to disappear over time; either treat them as annuals or dig and replant bulbs every 2 to 3 years as flowering diminishes.

URGINEA

Urginea maritima

HARDINESS:	tender or Zones 8-10
TYPE OF BULB:	true bulb
FLOWERING SEASON:	fall
HEIGHT:	3 to 5 feet
SOIL:	dry, sandy
LIGHT:	full sun

Urgineas produce long spikes of up to 100 tiny flowers at the tips of tall stems that can be bent or twisted by the weight of the blossoms. The flower stalks appear in advance of a rosette of shiny, fleshy, narrow leaves. Plant urgineas at the back of beds and borders in areas that can provide dry summers while they are dormant. Elsewhere, plant them as pot specimens.

Selected species and varieties
U. maritima (sea onion, sea squill)—18-inch spikes of ½-inch white, yellow, or pink blossoms that open from bottom to top followed by 4-inch-wide leaves up to 18 inches long.

Growing conditions and maintenance
Plant sea onions in summer with the upper portion of the bulb out of the soil, spacing bulbs 12 to 18 inches apart. The bulb juice is irritating, and all parts of the plant are poisonous. North of Zone 9, pot bulbs in summer for fall bloom outdoors, then take foliage indoors to ripen. Propagate by removing bulb offsets in summer.

Vallota (va-LO-ta)

GEORGE LILY

Vallota speciosa

HARDINESS: tender or Zones 10-11

TYPE OF BULB: true bulb

FLOWERING SEASON: summer to fall

HEIGHT: 3 feet

SOIL: well-drained, sandy, fertile

LIGHT: full sun

Vallota [also called *Cyrtanthus*] bears whorls of amaryllis-like blossoms with pointed petals forming deep trumpets around long, prominent stamens. Clusters of up to 10 flowers grow atop sturdy stems above clumps of straplike evergreen leaves. Vallotas can be used in beds and borders in very warm regions. Elsewhere they are cultivated as pot plants.

Selected species and varieties
V. speciosa [also called *Cyrtanthus elatus*] (Scarborough lily)—3-inch-wide deep scarlet, sometimes pink or white, flower funnels above 2-foot leaves.

Growing conditions and maintenance
Plant Scarborough lilies outdoors in Zones 10 and 11 in early spring, setting bulb tips at the soil line and spacing them 15 to 18 inches apart. For pot culture, allow one bulb per 6-inch pot and place bulbs only halfway into soil. Bulbs potted in spring will bloom in fall; soil should be kept damp during winter dormancy. Repot bulbs every 5 to 6 years, removing for propagation the small bulblets growing around the base of mature bulbs.

Veltheimia (vel-TY-mee-a)

RED-HOT POKER

Veltheimia bracteata

HARDINESS: tender or Zones 10-11

TYPE OF BULB: true bulb

FLOWERING SEASON: late winter to spring

HEIGHT: 15 to 20 inches

SOIL: well-drained, sandy

LIGHT: full sun

Red-hot poker's oval clusters of up to 50 flower buds open from bottom to top into long, drooping funnels with curled lips. Clusters are carried on sturdy stems above attractive rosettes of glossy green leaves with wavy edges. Both leaves and stems are attractively mottled. Use red-hot poker outdoors in warm climates; grow as a pot plant elsewhere.

Selected species and varieties
V. bracteata—2-inch pink-red or pink-purple blossoms with green-and-white flecked lips above foliage and stems marbled green and purple.

Growing conditions and maintenance
Outdoors in Zones 10 and 11, plant red-hot poker bulbs 1 inch deep and 6 to 10 inches apart in fall. In pots, group several of the large, 6-inch bulbs together in large bulb pans for best effect. Plant them 4 to 6 inches apart with the top third of the bulb exposed and allow bulbs to dry off during summer dormancy. Propagate by removing bulb offsets after foliage withers.

Watsonia (wot-SONE-ee-a)

BUGLE LILY

Watsonia 'Pink Opal'

HARDINESS: tender or Zones 8-10

TYPE OF BULB: corm

FLOWERING SEASON: spring or summer

HEIGHT: 18 to 60 inches

SOIL: well-drained

LIGHT: full sun

Bugle lily's simple flower funnels bloom around the tips of slightly arching stems above clumps of narrow, sword-shaped leaves. The spikes of blossoms which open from bottom to top are similar to gladiolus but are daintier and less formal. Bugle lilies will slowly form clumps in gardens in warm climates. Elsewhere, they can be grown as annuals. They make long-lasting cut flowers.

Selected species and varieties
W. hybrids—2- to 3-inch flowers in pastel shades; 'Bright Eyes' is powder pink; 'Dazzle', soft orange with a purple throat; 'Humilis' has pink flowers on 18-inch dwarf stems; 'Mrs. Bullard's White' is pure white; 'Pink Opal', bright pink; 'Rubra', dusty reddish purple.

Growing conditions and maintenance
Outdoors in Zones 8-10, plant bugle lily corms 3 inches deep and 6 to 9 inches apart in fall for spring blooms. Elsewhere, plant in spring for summer blooms, then lift in fall after foliage withers. Propagate from seed, although seedlings can be difficult to transplant, or by removing cormels.

CALLA LILY

Zantedeschia aethiopica

HARDINESS: tender or Zones 9-10

TYPE OF BULB: rhizome

FLOWERING SEASON: summer or fall

HEIGHT: 2 to 3 feet

SOIL: moist to well-drained

LIGHT: full sun to partial shade

Calla lily's gracefully curved and sculpted flowers have a cool, formal elegance that few other blooms can match. Petal-like spathes curl into elongated trumpets with a flared lip pulled to a point. The waxy spathe curls around a colorful, sometimes fragrant, fingerlike spadix bearing the true flowers, which are tiny and inconspicuous. Up to 12 or more blossoms bloom at the same time amid broad, stalked, arrow-shaped leaves with wavy edges that are often heavily flecked and spotted with white for added interest. In warm zones, calla lilies are eye-catching specimens for beds or borders and will naturalize where conditions suit them. Elsewhere they are grown as annuals or as pot plants for patio or indoor use. Callas are prized as cut flowers.

Selected species and varieties

Z. aethiopica (common calla, giant white calla, arum lily, trumpet lily)—fragrant, snowy white flowers 10 inches long on 2-foot plants; 'Perle Von Stuttgart' is somewhat smaller than the species, with abundant blossoms. *Z. albomaculata* (spotted calla, black-throated calla)—5-inch white flowers with purple throats on 2-foot plants. *Z. elliottiana* (golden calla, yellow calla)—6-inch golden yellow flowers, tinged greenish yellow on the outside, on 2½-foot plants. *Z. rehmannii* (red calla, pink calla)—3-inch pink flowers on 18- to 24-inch plants. *Z.* hybrids—'Black-Eyed Beauty' produces creamy white blossoms veined green, with a black throat or eye rimming the spadix; 'Black Magic' is yellow with a black eye; 'Cameo', salmon; 'Harvest Moon' is yellow with a red eye; 'Pink Persuasion', purple-pink; 'Solfatare' is a creamy pale yellow with a black eye.

Growing conditions and maintenance

Outdoors in Zones 8-10, plant calla lilies in spring or fall, setting rhizomes 1 to 4 inches deep and spacing them 1 to 2 feet apart. Calla lilies tolerate boggy conditions and can be grown with their roots in water at the edges of ponds. North of Zone 8, start them indoors in early spring and transplant them outside after all danger of frost has passed for blooming in summer. Lift rhizomes in fall after foliage withers and store for winter. For pot culture, set growing tips of rhizomes at soil level and allow one root per 6-inch pot. Callas bloom about 2 months after planting. Golden calla lily can be propagated from seed. Propagate all calla lilies by dividing their rhizomes in spring or fall.

Zantedeschia rehmannii

ZEPHYR LILY

Zephyranthes candida

HARDINESS: tender or Zones 8-10

TYPE OF BULB: true bulb

FLOWERING SEASON: spring, summer, or fall

HEIGHT: 8 to 36 inches

SOIL: moist, well-drained, rich

LIGHT: full sun

Zephyr lilies produce open stars of pointed petals surrounding a center of short, tiny stamens. The flowers face gaily upward on hollow stems above tufts of grassy leaves. They are mildly fragrant and sometimes open at night. The atamasco lily is excellent for naturalizing in borders or lawns, although its bulbs are poisonous. The other species need warm climates or may be grown as pot plants.

Selected species and varieties

Z. atamasco (atamasco lily)—3-inch white flowers tinged purple, blooming in early spring; Zones 7-10. *Z. candida* (westwind-flower)—2-inch white flowers tinged rose in summer to fall; Zones 9-10. *Z. rosea* (Cuban zephyr lily)—1-inch rose pink fall flowers; Zones 9-10.

Growing conditions and maintenance

Plant zephyr lilies 1 to 2 inches deep and 3 to 4 inches apart in spring. North of their hardiness range, plant them in spring and dig bulbs in fall after foliage dies back for winter storage. Keep stored bulbs barely damp. Propagate from seed or by removing bulb offsets.

Roses

THE ROSE IS, WITHOUT QUESTION, THE WORLD'S favorite flower. Praised by ancient cultures from the Persian to the Chinese, roses have captivated hearts and imaginations for thousands of years. And over the millennia, this most beloved of blooms has been cultivated and crossbred so extensively that the number of varieties is now beyond counting.

The roses described on the following pages include modern and old garden varieties as well as several species. They have been chosen for their enduring appeal, availability, bloom colors, and landscape uses. Many are also notable for disease resistance, winter hardiness, or low-maintenance requirements. The American Rose Society's (ARS) evaluation of overall quality is given for each rose that has received a rating; most of the listed roses are in the excellent (8.0-8.9) or outstanding (9.0-9.9) range. Winners of the coveted All-America Rose Selections (AARS) award are also identified.

'ALBA SEMI-PLENA'

CLASSIFICATION: alba

BLOOM PERIOD: summer

HEIGHT: 6 to 8 feet

HARDINESS: Zones 4-10

ARS RATING: 8.6

DATE INTRODUCED: prior to 1600

This handsome rose is also known as the White Rose of York. Its semidouble white flowers are 2½ inches across with prominent golden stamens, and they produce a powerful old garden fragrance. Borne in clusters, flowers appear in midseason and do not repeat. Elongated orange-red hips appear in late summer and fall. The foliage is gray-green.

With sturdy, arching canes that develop a vase-shaped form, 'Alba Semi-plena' can be grown as a freestanding shrub for a specimen or for use in borders, or it can be trained as a climber on a wall, a trellis, or a fence. Like other alba roses, it tolerates some shade and is quite hardy and resistant to disease.

'ALBERIC BARBIER'

CLASSIFICATION: rambler

BLOOM PERIOD: early summer

HEIGHT: 15 to 20 feet

HARDINESS: Zones 5-10

ARS RATING: not rated

DATE INTRODUCED: 1900

Clusters of shapely yellow buds of 'Albéric Barbier' open to creamy white flowers with a yellow blush. Semidouble and double blossoms are 2 to 3 inches across and bear a moderate, fruity fragrance. Plants flower heavily in early summer and may repeat, although not reliably, in the fall. Glossy dark leaves are almost evergreen and are carried on purplish canes.

This easy-to-grow rambler requires a lot of space, since canes may grow 20 feet in a single season. It can be trained on fences or pillars, or may be used to cover a building, especially in areas where mildew is not a problem. Tied canes often produce lateral stems that arc downward for a graceful display. This rose can also be used as a ground cover. 'Albéric Barbier' is extremely disease resistant and tolerates light shade and hot, dry climates.

'ALBERTINE'

CLASSIFICATION: rambler

BLOOM PERIOD: summer

HEIGHT: 15 to 20 feet

HARDINESS: Zones 5-10

ARS RATING: not rated

DATE INTRODUCED: 1921

The buds of 'Albertine' open to bright orange-pink double blooms that are golden at the base. Produced in abundant clusters in summer, the cupped, fragrant flowers put on a spectacular show that endures for about 3 weeks. As the blooms age, they fade to a soft blush pink. Leaves are glossy green with coppery red tones. Canes bear many hooked prickles.

This vigorous rambler is fast growing and easily trained to a trellis, pergola, or arbor. It can also be grown as a freestanding shrub. It may be prone to mildew after flowering, but it is otherwise disease resistant.

'ALCHYMIST'

CLASSIFICATION: shrub

BLOOM PERIOD: early summer

HEIGHT: 6 to 12 feet

HARDINESS: Zones 5-10

ARS RATING: 8.0

DATE INTRODUCED: 1956

Although 'Alchymist' blooms only once each year, the show is long-lasting and glorious. Flowers are large, very double and quartered, and fragrant; the petals are predominantly light to egg yolk yellow, with various shades of orange, pink, and gold infusing the blossoms toward the center. Many early blooms tend to display paler colors. Foliage is rich green-bronze and glossy.

The plant is vigorous and has an upright habit. Its landscaping potential is broad, since it can be grown either as a freestanding shrub, best kept to 6 or 7 feet, in a bed or border, or as a 12-foot climber on a trellis or wall.

'ALOHA'

CLASSIFICATION: climbing hybrid tea

BLOOM PERIOD: spring to fall

HEIGHT: 6 to 10 feet

HARDINESS: Zones 5-10

ARS RATING: 7.1

DATE INTRODUCED: 1949

The cup-shaped blossoms of 'Aloha' are double or very double, 3 to 5 inches wide, and very fragrant. They appear in abundance both early in the season and again in the fall, with fairly good production in between. Petals are a clear rose pink on the inside, with a darker pink reverse; centers are shaded a warm orange-pink. Foliage is dark, glossy, and leathery.

Although it's classed as a climber, this rose can be grown as an upright shrub. Or, the nodding habit of its blooms can be shown to advantage growing over a wall, where they can be viewed from below. As a compact climber, it's a good choice for growing on a pillar. Flowers are excellent for cutting.

'ALTISSIMO'

CLASSIFICATION: large-flowered climber

BLOOM PERIOD: summer to fall

HEIGHT: 6 to 8 feet

HARDINESS: Zones 5-9

ARS RATING: 9.3

DATE INTRODUCED: 1966

The large, single flowers of 'Altissimo' are 4 to 5 inches across, with seven velvety, deep blood red petals surrounding bright yellow stamens. Blooms occur in small clusters and sometimes singly on both old and new growth, beginning in the summer and then repeating throughout the season. Although they have only a light scent, the blossoms last a long time without fading, and they make beautiful cut flowers. Leaves are large and dark green.

While generally classed as a climber that is suitable for growing on pillars, fences, and trellises, 'Altissimo' can also be grown as a tall, freestanding shrub with an upright habit. It is vigorous, heat tolerant, and disease resistant.

'AMERICA'

CLASSIFICATION: large-flowered climber

BLOOM PERIOD: summer to fall

HEIGHT: 8 to 12 feet

HARDINESS: Zones 5-10

ARS RATING: 8.8

DATE INTRODUCED: 1976

Named to honor the United States bicentennial, 'America' produces 3½- to 5-inch double blossoms in great profusion throughout the season. Flowers are coral colored with high centers and are usually borne in clusters; their fragrance is strong and spicy. Foliage is semiglossy, dark, and leathery.

Plants are both upright and bushy, and are suitable for training on pillars, fences, and walls. Flowers, produced on both new and old shoots, can be cut for long-lasting indoor arrangements. 'America' is easy to grow, disease resistant, and hardy. It's an AARS winner.

'AMERICAN PILLAR'

CLASSIFICATION: rambler

BLOOM PERIOD: summer

HEIGHT: 15 to 20 feet

HARDINESS: Zones 5-10

ARS RATING: 7.5

DATE INTRODUCED: 1902

The five-petaled single blossoms of 'American Pillar' are carmine-pink and have white centers and golden stamens. Erupting once in midsummer, they are produced in large clusters that almost cover the entire plant. Flowers have no scent. Leaves are leathery, large, and dark green; canes are green and prickly.

The plant is very vigorous, growing to 20 feet, and is best used for climbing on a fence or arbor. Like other ramblers, it may be subject to mildew.

'ANGEL FACE'

CLASSIFICATION: floribunda

BLOOM PERIOD: summer to fall

HEIGHT: 2 to 3 feet

HARDINESS: Zones 4-9

ARS RATING: 8.1

DATE INTRODUCED: 1968

The pointed buds of 'Angel Face' open to 4-inch double flowers whose ruffled, lavender-mauve petals surround golden stamens. Cup-shaped or flat, the flowers are produced almost continuously throughout the growing season in sprays that include all stages of bloom from bud to fully open. They have a strong, fruity fragrance and are well displayed against lustrous dark green foliage. They are outstanding as cut flowers.

Growing only 2 to 3 feet, 'Angel Face' is dense and compact with a somewhat spreading habit, making it useful as a low hedge or in beds and borders. Although plants are fairly disease resistant, they can be troubled by black spot and mildew in some areas. This rose is an AARS winner.

'APRICOT NECTAR'

CLASSIFICATION: floribunda

BLOOM PERIOD: summer to fall

HEIGHT: 2 to 3 feet

HARDINESS: Zones 4-10

ARS RATING: 8.2

DATE INTRODUCED: 1965

The cup-shaped flowers of 'Apricot Nectar' appear in clusters of three or more throughout the growing season. The double 4- to 4½-inch blooms are an exotic blend of apricot and pink with golden centers. Their fruity, apricot-like fragrance is intense. The leaves are dark green, leathery, and glossy.

Plants are very vigorous, bushy, and compact. Their extended flowering display makes them useful in beds or borders, singly or massed. Although resistant to some diseases, they are susceptible to black spot. 'Apricot Nectar' is an AARS winner.

'AQUARIUS'

CLASSIFICATION: grandiflora

BLOOM PERIOD: spring to fall

HEIGHT: 4 to 5 feet

HARDINESS: Zones 5-10

ARS RATING: 8.0

DATE INTRODUCED: 1971

Considered by many to be one of the very best grandifloras, 'Aquarius' flowers freely from spring until frost, producing small sprays of up to five double blooms that are lightly fragrant. Buds are dark pink, opening to blended medium-pink-and-white 4-inch flowers with high centers. Foliage is large and leathery.

Plants are urn shaped, upright, and vigorous. They are well suited to beds and borders, and flowers are ideal for cutting. This rose is extremely disease resistant. It is an AARS winner.

'ARCHDUKE CHARLES'

CLASSIFICATION: China

BLOOM PERIOD: summer to fall

HEIGHT: 2 to 5 feet

HARDINESS: Zones 6-10

ARS RATING: 7.9

DATE INTRODUCED: 1840

The 3-inch double flowers of 'Archduke Charles' open very slowly, revealing a coloration that varies with the weather from pale pink in cool, overcast conditions to deep pink or crimson under warm, sunny skies. The lightly scented flowers are produced reliably all season. New leaves are red, maturing to a glossy green. Canes are also red, as are the sparse prickles.

This rose produces moderate growth with an erect, bushy, neat form. Its continuous flowers add color to beds and borders, and the plant also makes an attractive hedge. It's moderately disease resistant and tolerates heat, humidity, and slightly alkaline soil.

'AUSBURN'

CLASSIFICATION: shrub

BLOOM PERIOD: spring

HEIGHT: 3 feet

HARDINESS: Zones 4-10

ARS RATING: 9.0

DATE INTRODUCED: 1986

'Ausburn' (also known as 'Robbie Burns') is a diminutive modern shrub rose with small, single flowers, each having five petals. Like many of the English roses bred by David Austin, it is reminiscent of older rose types, with a commanding fragrance and an old-fashioned character. The blooms are light pink with a white center, and the small leaves are a medium matte green.

The small size of this rose makes it a useful addition to beds and borders, where it can be used in the foreground. It is very effective planted in groups.

'AUTUMN DAMASK'

CLASSIFICATION: damask

BLOOM PERIOD: spring to fall

HEIGHT: 4 to 5 feet

HARDINESS: Zones 4-10

ARS RATING: 8.0

DATE INTRODUCED: ancient

This very old rose produces abundant, richly fragrant blossoms in spring followed by scattered blooms throughout summer and fall. Flowers are 3½ inches across, clear pink with deeper centers, and double. It is also known as 'Quatre Saisons' and has been used in breeding both the bourbons and the hybrid perpetuals. Foliage is light gray-green.

Plants are vigorous, of medium height, with a spreading habit. They are quite hardy and tolerate pruning better than most damasks. The long flowering season makes a valuable contribution to beds or borders, and the powerful wine fragrance of the blooms is useful for making potpourri.

'BALLERINA'

CLASSIFICATION: hybrid musk

BLOOM PERIOD: summer to fall

HEIGHT: 2 to 4 feet

HARDINESS: Zones 5-10

ARS RATING: 9.0

DATE INTRODUCED: 1937

The small (1-inch) blossoms of 'Ballerina' are soft pink with white centers and are borne in huge clusters of up to 100 blooms each. The flowers are single, each with five petals surrounding bright yellow stamens, and have a light musky scent. Foliage is medium green and dense.

Plants have a low-growing, arching habit that makes them one of the best roses for hedges, either pruned or left to their natural form. They are a good choice for containers or beds, and their flowers are long-lasting both on the plant and when cut for indoor arrangements. Plants are disease resistant and tolerant of light shade.

'BARONNE PREVOST'

CLASSIFICATION: hybrid perpetual

BLOOM PERIOD: summer to fall

HEIGHT: 4 to 6 feet

HARDINESS: Zones 5-10

ARS RATING: 8.5

DATE INTRODUCED: 1842

The elegant 3- to 4-inch-wide blooms of 'Baronne Prévost' are very double, with 100 petals that quarter and fold back on a green button-eyed center. Ranging from pale pink to deep rose pink, the recurring blooms are extremely fragrant. Buds are globular, leaves are medium green, and canes are prickly.

Best grown as a freestanding shrub, 'Baronne Prévost' grows between 4 and 6 feet high with an approximately equal spread. The plant is vigorous, and it has a less awkward form than do most hybrid perpetuals. Also, the foliage is more attractive and disease resistant than that of most of the class.

'BELINDA'

CLASSIFICATION: hybrid musk

BLOOM PERIOD: summer to fall

HEIGHT: 4 to 8 feet

HARDINESS: Zones 5-10

ARS RATING: 8.6

DATE INTRODUCED: 1936

'Belinda' produces large erect clusters of semidouble flowers almost continuously throughout the growing season. The soft medium pink blooms are 1 inch or less across, have 12 to 15 petals, and emit a light fragrance. When seen at close range, the blooms show off white centers.

Plants are vigorous, upright, and bushy, and can either be maintained as a dense hedge by pruning or be trained to a pillar. They are quite disease resistant and, like most hybrid musks, adaptable to light shade.

'BELLE POITEVINE'

CLASSIFICATION: hybrid rugosa

BLOOM PERIOD: summer to fall

HEIGHT: 3½ to 5 feet

HARDINESS: Zones 3-10

ARS RATING: 7.8

DATE INTRODUCED: 1894

The flowers of 'Belle Poitevine' are fragrant and semidouble, with twirled petals. Their coloring is somewhat dependent on weather, ranging from rose pink to magenta pink, with lighter colors more prevalent under sunny skies. In fall, the plump orange-red hips create a colorful display against the deeply veined, leathery, dark green foliage.

The vigorous plants are nicely shaped, often as broad as they are tall. This rose makes a good choice for a large hedge. Like other hybrid rugosas, it is very hardy, disease resistant, and easy to grow. It also tolerates seaside conditions.

'BELLE STORY'

CLASSIFICATION: shrub

BLOOM PERIOD: summer to fall

HEIGHT: 4 feet

HARDINESS: Zones 4-10

ARS RATING: 8.5

DATE INTRODUCED: 1984

The sweetly scented flowers of 'Belle Story' are large and semidouble, resembling peonies. A David Austin rose, this is a heavy bloomer, repeating well through the season. The wide-spreading, soft pink petals curve inward, fashioning a broad cup that accentuates golden yellow stamens. The abundant foliage is light green and semiglossy.

Plants are vigorous and healthy. They grow as broad as they do tall, forming a rounded 4-foot shrub that is well suited to a bed or border. Like many others of David Austin's English roses, this one is very hardy.

'BETTY PRIOR'

CLASSIFICATION: floribunda

BLOOM PERIOD: summer to fall

HEIGHT: 4 to 5 feet

HARDINESS: Zones 4-10

ARS RATING: 8.2

DATE INTRODUCED: 1935

The carmine-pink buds of 'Betty Prior' open to 2- to 3-inch cupped single blossoms that flatten with age and bear a light, spicy fragrance. Blossoms occur in large clusters so profuse that they can cover the entire bush. In cool weather, flowers remain carmine-pink, but as temperatures rise they become medium pink. The five petals surround yellow stamens that darken to brown. Foliage is medium green and semiglossy.

Plants are vigorous and bushy with a rounded form. One of the most popular floribundas ever, this rose is effectively used for mass plantings and hedges, in small groups, and singly in a bed. It is also very winter hardy and exceptionally resistant to black spot, but less so to mildew.

'BLANC DOUBLE DE COUBERT'

CLASSIFICATION: hybrid rugosa

BLOOM PERIOD: spring to fall

HEIGHT: 4 to 6 feet

HARDINESS: Zones 3-10

ARS RATING: 8.3

DATE INTRODUCED: 1892

This hybrid rugosa blooms heavily early in the season, with scattered blossoms in summer and fall. Flowers are semidouble, 2 to 3 inches wide, and very fragrant. Petals are pure white with a delicate tissue-paper-like texture that contrasts with the crinkled, dark, leathery leaves. Canes are gray, and in fall large orange-red hips are produced.

Plants are typically as broad as they are tall and require a lot of room. Extremely vigorous, they often send out suckers several feet from the plant base. The rose is effective as a hedge, in large beds, and as a specimen. One of the best hybrid rugosas, 'Blanc Double de Coubert' is extremely hardy, resistant to both diseases and insects, and tolerates sandy soil and salt spray, making it a good choice for seaside gardens.

'BLAZE'

CLASSIFICATION: large-flowered climber

BLOOM PERIOD: spring to fall

HEIGHT: 12 to 15 feet

HARDINESS: Zones 5-10

ARS RATING: 7.4

DATE INTRODUCED: 1932

Clusters of cup-shaped scarlet blossoms occur on both the old and new wood of 'Blaze' throughout the growing season. Flowers are semidouble, 2 to 3 inches across, lightly fragrant, and nonfading, even in hot weather. Early flowers are somewhat larger than those produced later in the season. Dark green leathery foliage contrasts nicely with the continuous show of blooms.

This easy-to-grow rose has a vigorous, upright habit, and its canes are quick to reach their height of 12 to 15 feet, making it a good choice for fences, arbors, pillars, and porches. It is quite hardy but is somewhat susceptible to powdery mildew.

'BONICA'

CLASSIFICATION: shrub

BLOOM PERIOD: summer

HEIGHT: 3 to 5 feet

HARDINESS: Zones 4-9

ARS RATING: 9.1

DATE INTRODUCED: 1981

'Bonica' (also called 'Meidomonac') is free flowering and easy to grow. Large, loose clusters of up to 20 flowers appear throughout the summer. Each spiraled bud opens to reveal a 2½- to 3½-inch double blossom with soft pink ruffled petals. The foliage is dark green and glossy. Bright orange hips appear in fall and remain attractive all winter.

The plant has a spreading habit with arching stems spanning 5 to 6 feet. This rose is not fussy about pruning; it can be maintained as a compact hedge or lightly tip pruned for a more informal appearance. 'Bonica' is an excellent choice for beds or borders, for massing, or for use as a hedge along a walk or drive. It is highly disease resistant, exceptionally hardy, and tolerant of harsh climates. This is the first shrub rose to win the AARS award.

'BOULE DE NEIGE'

CLASSIFICATION: bourbon

BLOOM PERIOD: summer to fall

HEIGHT: 4 to 5 feet

HARDINESS: Zones 5-10

ARS RATING: 7.6

DATE INTRODUCED: 1867

The rounded pink buds of 'Boule de Neige' (French word for snowball) open to reveal creamy white flowers that are at first tinted with crimson along the petal margins. As they develop, the 2- to 4-inch very double flowers turn pure white with reflexed petals that create a beautifully rounded form. They are intensely fragrant. Foliage is dark green and leathery, providing a perfect foil for the flowers; canes bear few prickles.

Plants, slender and erect in habit, are excellent for combining in beds with lower-growing, bushy plants. This rose is disease resistant.

'BRIDE'S DREAM'

CLASSIFICATION: hybrid tea

BLOOM PERIOD: summer to fall

HEIGHT: 3 to 4 feet

HARDINESS: Zones 5-10

ARS RATING: 8.0

DATE INTRODUCED: 1985

The large double flowers of 'Bride's Dream' are pale pink, high centered, and lightly fragrant. They usually occur singly on the stem and appear in great numbers during the growing season. Foliage is dark green, and stems bear brown prickles.

The plant is a strong grower with a tall, upright habit. It can be situated in beds or borders, and its flowers are ideal for both cutting and exhibition. 'Bride's Dream' is judged by some growers to be the best hybrid tea in its color class.

'BUFF BEAUTY'

CLASSIFICATION: hybrid musk

BLOOM PERIOD: summer to fall

HEIGHT: 5 to 6 feet

HARDINESS: Zones 5-10

ARS RATING: 8.3

DATE INTRODUCED: 1939

The color of the 3- to 4-inch double flowers of 'Buff Beauty' ranges from buff yellow to deep apricot, depending on weather conditions. Richly fragrant, flattened blossoms are borne in clusters. The abundant foliage emerges bronze-red, turning a glossy dark green as it matures. Canes are smooth and brown.

This rose is a very attractive plant with a graceful, arching habit and is often broader than it is tall. It requires a lot of space but makes a lovely specimen. It can also be trained to a pillar or wall, or can be used as a ground cover on banks.

'CABBAGE ROSE'

CLASSIFICATION: centifolia

BLOOM PERIOD: summer

HEIGHT: 5 to 6 feet

HARDINESS: Zones 4-10

ARS RATING: 7.9

DATE INTRODUCED: unknown

The very double flowers of 'Cabbage Rose' (also called *R. centifolia*) are clear pink and richly fragrant. This is the type of rose, with many-petaled, globular blooms, often depicted in paintings by the old European masters. The 3-inch flowers are supported by long stems and appear singly or in clusters. Though they do not repeat, they produce a stunning summer display. Foliage is gray-green and coarse, and thorns are abundant.

'Cabbage Rose' has a lax, arching habit and is moderately sized, making it useful as a garden shrub. It is very hardy.

'CAMAIEUX'

CLASSIFICATION: gallica

BLOOM PERIOD: summer

HEIGHT: 3 to 5 feet

HARDINESS: Zones 4-10

ARS RATING: 7.5

DATE INTRODUCED: 1830

Flowers of 'Camaieux' are blush mauve-pink with stripes that change from crimson to pleasing shades of purple and lavender as the blossoms mature. Flowers are double, cup shaped, 3 to 4 inches across, and spicy scented. In fall, the plant produces colorful hips. Foliage is grayish green.

The growth habit of this rose is upright and compact. Arching canes give it a rounded form that is suitable for beds and borders, where its evolving blossom colors can put on a delightful summer show. 'Camaieux' tolerates summer heat and is fairly disease resistant but can be susceptible to mildew in southern climates.

'CANDEUR LYONNAISE'

CLASSIFICATION: hybrid perpetual

BLOOM PERIOD: early spring to fall

HEIGHT: 4 feet

HARDINESS: Zones 5-10

ARS RATING: 7.1

DATE INTRODUCED: 1914

'Candeur Lyonnaise' produces a continuous succession of flowers from early spring until the first hard frost. Its buds are long and pointed, opening to very large double flowers that are 5 inches across. Blooms are white, although they sometimes take on a pale yellow tint, and the petals are delicately fringed.

The plants themselves are vigorous, stately, upright, and of moderate height. Their extended flowering season makes this an excellent shrub for nearly any garden and a good source of cut flowers.

'CARDINAL DE RICHELIEU'

CLASSIFICATION: gallica

BLOOM PERIOD: summer

HEIGHT: 2½ to 5 feet

HARDINESS: Zones 4-10

ARS RATING: 7.9

DATE INTRODUCED: 1840

The buds of 'Cardinal de Richelieu' are fat, rounded, and mauve pink, opening to become one of the deepest colored of all roses. Flowers are double and 2 to 3 inches across. Petals are a velvety purple-violet with a reverse of silvery rose, and they curve to form a ball-shaped blossom. The fragrance is strong and increases with the flower's age. Leaves are smooth and dark green, and stems are nearly smooth.

The attractive plants are compact, producing arching mounds as wide as they are tall. Unlike some gallicas, this rose responds well to heavy pruning, producing its flowers on new wood. It is extremely hardy and tolerates summer heat and humidity.

'CAREFREE BEAUTY'

CLASSIFICATION: shrub

BLOOM PERIOD: summer to fall

HEIGHT: 4 to 5 feet

HARDINESS: Zones 4-10

ARS RATING: 8.5

DATE INTRODUCED: 1977

The long, pointed buds of 'Carefree Beauty' open to semidouble medium pink flowers. Each blossom has 15 to 20 petals and bears a rich, fruity fragrance. Flowers appear in clusters of three to 20 and are produced freely all season. Foliage is a bright apple green.

This rose has a vigorous, bushy, spreading habit. It is easy to grow, as its name implies, and makes an excellent flowering hedge or garden shrub. Space plants 18 inches apart to form a dense hedge. A Dr. Buck rose, it is both disease resistant and very hardy.

'CAREFREE WONDER'

CLASSIFICATION: shrub

BLOOM PERIOD: spring to fall

HEIGHT: 4 to 5 feet

HARDINESS: Zones 4-9

ARS RATING: 8.0

DATE INTRODUCED: 1990

Borne freely all season, the fragrant, semidouble flowers of 'Carefree Wonder' are a rich pink with a creamy white to pale pink reverse. The abundant, medium green leaves provide an attractive foil for the blossoms.

This rose is upright with a bushy, rounded habit, reaching 4 to 5 feet high and 3 to 4 feet wide. 'Carefree Wonder' is an excellent choice for borders or specimen plantings. It also makes an attractive flowering hedge. Plants require little maintenance and are resistant to disease.

'CATHERINE MERMET'

CLASSIFICATION: tea

BLOOM PERIOD: summer

HEIGHT: 3 to 4 feet

HARDINESS: Zones 7-10

ARS RATING: 8.1

DATE INTRODUCED: 1869

Flowers of 'Catherine Mermet' open a blush pink with lilac edges and change to soft beige as they mature. Inner petals often display yellow at the base. The double blossoms are 3 inches across and are borne singly or in small clusters on graceful stems. Their fragrance is strong and spicy. Leaves are copper colored when young, maturing to a medium green.

This rose is somewhat delicate, requiring nothing less than a warm, sunny spot and rich, well-drained soil. It is quite tender and is frequently grown in greenhouses. With an upright, arching habit, it is well suited for beds, borders, and specimen plantings. Flowers are excellent for cutting. Pruning should be restricted to removing dead and weak, spindly canes. It is moderately disease resistant and heat tolerant.

'CECILE BRUNNER'

CLASSIFICATION: polyantha

BLOOM PERIOD: midspring to frost

HEIGHT: 2 to 4 feet

HARDINESS: Zones 4-9

ARS RATING: 8.0

DATE INTRODUCED: 1881

Although the flowers of this rose are small—only 1 to 1½ inches across—they are lovely in both form and color, earning it the nickname the sweetheart rose. The dainty spiraled buds are long and pointed. Flowers are sweetly scented and double, with delicate pink petals that become yellow toward their base; they are borne in small clusters and bloom steadily throughout the growing season. Foliage is sparse, glossy, and dark green, and canes bear few thorns.

'Cécile Brunner' is an upright shrub suitable for beds and borders and is an excellent source of cut flowers. A climbing sport that grows 15 to 25 feet was introduced in 1894; its foliage, denser than that of its parent, may hide some of the blooms. Both forms tolerate partial shade and poor soil.

'CELESTIAL'

CLASSIFICATION: alba

BLOOM PERIOD: summer

HEIGHT: 5 to 6 feet

HARDINESS: Zones 4-10

ARS RATING: 8.6

DATE INTRODUCED: prior to 1848

The 3½-inch blooms of 'Celestial' are sweetly fragrant. Borne in clusters, flowers are semidouble and pale blush pink with golden stamens, and they are particularly attractive as the delicate petals unfurl. Flowering occurs in summer with no repeat. The soft blue-gray foliage provides an exquisite contrast to the flowers.

This vigorous rose requires a large space in the garden. Usually as wide as they are tall, the shrubs make outstanding specimens with their complementary flower and foliage tones. Plants are shade tolerant and require only moderate pruning; avoid heavy pruning.

'CELINA'

CLASSIFICATION: moss

BLOOM PERIOD: summer

HEIGHT: 4 feet

HARDINESS: Zones 4-10

ARS RATING: 8.3

DATE INTRODUCED: 1855

Like others of this classification, the sepals covering the buds of 'Célina' bear a mossy growth that has a firlike scent. The buds open to large semidouble flowers in shades of mauve, pink, crimson, lavender, and purple. When fully open, the blooms reveal golden stamens. Canes are studded with long, sturdy prickles.

Suitable for beds and borders, 'Célina' has a tidy habit and a moderate height. It is a very hardy rose but has a tendency to get mildew late in the season.

'CELINE FORESTIER'

CLASSIFICATION: noisette

BLOOM PERIOD: summer to fall

HEIGHT: 6 to 10 feet

HARDINESS: Zones 6-10

ARS RATING: 7.5

DATE INTRODUCED: 1842

The flattened, very double flowers of 'Céline Forestier' are creamy yellow with darker peach or pink tones. Their petals form a quartered pattern and surround a green button eye. The intensely fragrant blooms usually occur in small clusters of three to four and are of very high quality. The plant is almost always in flower throughout the growing season. Foliage is light green.

This rose is not as vigorous or as large as most noisettes, and it takes a while to become established. It performs best in southern climates, growing against a wall or trained as a small, free-flowering climber on a pillar or fence. It tolerates summer heat and humidity.

'CELSIANA'

CLASSIFICATION: damask

BLOOM PERIOD: summer

HEIGHT: 4 to 5 feet

HARDINESS: Zones 4-10

ARS RATING: 8.8

DATE INTRODUCED: prior to 1750

The semidouble, gently nodding blooms of 'Celsiana' are 3½ to 4 inches across, cup shaped, and deliciously scented. Borne in clusters, the flowers open a clear pink and fade to a soft blush as they age. Petals are silky textured and surround bright yellow stamens. The flower colors are complemented perfectly by gray-green foliage.

The plant has an upright habit with gracefully arching canes and makes a fine choice for a bed or border, where it can put on a midseason display of color. 'Celsiana' is disease resistant and very hardy.

'CHAMPLAIN'

CLASSIFICATION: shrub

BLOOM PERIOD: summer to fall

HEIGHT: 3 to 4 feet

HARDINESS: Zones 4-10

ARS RATING: 8.1

DATE INTRODUCED: 1982

The 2- to 2½-inch-wide double blooms of 'Champlain' are a rich cherry red with darker edges. Blossoms are only slightly fragrant, but once this rose begins flowering in the summer it continues nonstop until a hard frost. Foliage is shiny and dark.

The plant is not a vigorous grower; its compact habit makes it especially well suited to beds. One of the Explorer series roses from Canada, 'Champlain' is a very hardy kordesii shrub. It is also practically immune to both black spot and mildew and appears not to be bothered by aphids.

'CHERISH'

CLASSIFICATION: floribunda

BLOOM PERIOD: summer to fall

HEIGHT: 3 feet

HARDINESS: Zones 4-9

ARS RATING: 8.3

DATE INTRODUCED: 1980

The 3- to 4-inch double blossoms of 'Cherish' put out a light cinnamon fragrance and appear over a lengthy season. Borne both singly and in clusters of up to 20, the high-centered flowers are coral-apricot with a creamy white base. The spiraled buds open slowly, and the flowers are extremely long-lasting. New leaves are bronze red, turning very dark green and glossy with age.

The compact, symmetrical habit of the bush is somewhat spreading, making 'Cherish' an appropriate choice for beds and borders. It can also be used as a low hedge. Flowers are exceptional for cutting. Added to the long list of the rose's virtues are good disease resistance and hardiness. 'Cherish' is an AARS winner.

'CHICAGO PEACE'

CLASSIFICATION: hybrid tea

BLOOM PERIOD: summer to fall

HEIGHT: 4 to 5 feet

HARDINESS: Zones 5-9

ARS RATING: 7.5

DATE INTRODUCED: 1962

A favorite of gardeners since the early '60s, 'Chicago Peace' bears stunning, fragrant double blossoms, each of which has slightly curved petals that are rose-pink at the edges, blending to golden yellow at the base. Leaves are large, glossy, and dark green.

The plants are vigorous, with an upright habit. This rose makes a lovely specimen and is also attractive when combined with other roses and shrubs in an informal border. The flowers are excellent for cutting. 'Chicago Peace' has good disease resistance.

'CHRYSLER IMPERIAL'

CLASSIFICATION: hybrid tea

BLOOM PERIOD: summer to fall

HEIGHT: 4 to 5 feet

HARDINESS: Zones 5-10

ARS RATING: 7.8

DATE INTRODUCED: 1952

The deep crimson double flowers of 'Chrysler Imperial' are 4½ to 5 inches across with 45 to 50 petals. Blooming singly on long stems, they have a rich, spicy fragrance and a velvety texture; their color fades to magenta as the blossoms age. The blossoms appear profusely in midsummer and repeat well through fall. Leaves are dark green and semiglossy.

Plants are vigorous with an upright, compact habit and perform best in climates with hot summers. They are somewhat temperamental about their conditions and are subject to mildew. Appropriate for beds and borders, this rose works especially well in a small landscape. The blooms make outstanding cut flowers. The rose is an AARS winner.

'CITY OF YORK'

CLASSIFICATION: large-flowered climber

BLOOM PERIOD: spring

HEIGHT: 15 feet

HARDINESS: Zones 5-10

ARS RATING: 8.4

DATE INTRODUCED: 1945

The semidouble cup-shaped blooms of 'City of York' are creamy white with yellow centers and are pleasantly fragrant. They appear once per season over a lengthy period in the spring in large clusters of seven to 15 flowers. Leaves are glossy and leathery.

This vigorous rose is very effective in the spring, when its abundant pale blooms create a dramatic contrast against lush, dark foliage. It is tolerant of partial shade and can be grown on a north wall. It's also a good choice for a trellis.

'COMMUNIS'

CLASSIFICATION: moss

BLOOM PERIOD: summer

HEIGHT: 4 feet

HARDINESS: Zones 4-10

ARS RATING: 7.7

DATE INTRODUCED: late 1600s

Considered by many to be the best moss rose, 'Communis' (also called 'Common Moss') produces mossy growths on its sepals, buds, and stems. Buds are rose pink, opening to pale pink, intensely fragrant double flowers that are 2 to 3 inches wide. Reflexed petals surround a green button eye. The abundant foliage is medium green.

'Communis' plants are moderate growers with an arching habit; they are usually slightly taller than they are broad. The rose is well suited to beds and borders, and is both disease resistant and hardy.

'COMPLICATA'

CLASSIFICATION: gallica

BLOOM PERIOD: early summer

HEIGHT: 5 to 10 feet

HARDINESS: Zones 4-10

ARS RATING: 8.4

DATE INTRODUCED: unknown

Although this rose blooms only in early summer, the display is spectacular. The single flowers are 5 inches across and appear along the entire length of each branch. Blooms are deep pink with a white eye and bright yellow stamens. Leaves are large and light green. Round, orange hips are produced in the fall.

Vigorous and easy to grow, this rose requires a good bit of space. It can be maintained as a shrub with a height of 5 feet and a spread of 6 to 8 feet, thanks to its arching canes. 'Complicata' makes an effective hedge and, if allowed, will reach 10 feet in height. It can also be trained as a climber. Poor soils, summer heat and humidity, and winter cold are all tolerated. The plant can become rampant.

'CONSTANCE SPRY'

CLASSIFICATION: shrub

BLOOM PERIOD: midsummer

HEIGHT: 6 to 15 feet

HARDINESS: Zones 4-10

ARS RATING: 7.8

DATE INTRODUCED: 1961

The light pink double or very double flowers of 'Constance Spry' resemble peonies. This rose blooms only once each year, but the display is dramatic, producing a wealth of 3½- to 5-inch flowers bearing a rich, myrrhlike fragrance. The flowers appear in clusters, showing up well against abundant dark green foliage. Canes bear lots of bright red prickles.

A very vigorous plant, 'Constance Spry' can be pruned to maintain a large, rounded shrub or trained to climb a fence, wall, tripod, or pillar, where it can grow as high as 15 feet.

'COUNTRY DANCER'

CLASSIFICATION: shrub

BLOOM PERIOD: summer to fall

HEIGHT: 2 to 4 feet

HARDINESS: Zones 4-10

ARS RATING: 7.5

DATE INTRODUCED: 1973

The high-centered buds of 'Country Dancer', a Dr. Buck rose, open to large, flat, double flowers that are somewhere between deep pink and rosy red in color—and quite fragrant. The petals are slightly yellow toward their base, and they surround golden stamens. Flowers occur in clusters throughout the growing season. Foliage is dark green.

This rose is usually grown as a low, spreading shrub. It can also be used as a hedge. Canes can be trained to a pillar or fence but should be trained horizontally to obtain the best flowering display; canes that grow vertically will produce all of their flowers at the tips. Although it's extremely hardy, 'Country Dancer' is somewhat susceptible to black spot.

'CRESTED MOSS'

CLASSIFICATION: moss

BLOOM PERIOD: summer

HEIGHT: 4 to 6 feet

HARDINESS: Zones 4-10

ARS RATING: 7.9

DATE INTRODUCED: 1826

The buds of 'Crested Moss' (also known as 'Cristata' and 'Chapeau de Napoleon') are uniquely beautiful, peeking through a set of large, deeply fringed, mossy-edged sepals. Open, the fragrant medium pink blooms are very double and cabbagelike, ranging from 3 to 3½ inches across. The bloom period is lengthy but not recurring. Foliage is abundant and light green.

This rose has a strong, upright form and arching canes, and can be grown as a medium-sized shrub in a bed or border or trained against a support. It is disease resistant and quite hardy.

'CRIMSON GLORY'

CLASSIFICATION: hybrid tea

BLOOM PERIOD: summer to fall

HEIGHT: 3 to 4 feet

HARDINESS: Zones 5-10

ARS RATING: 6.8

DATE INTRODUCED: 1935

'Crimson Glory' produces pointed black-red buds and deep crimson velvety flowers with purple shading. Fully opened, the 3- to 4-inch blossoms are double with 30 to 35 petals and splendidly fragrant. Flower necks tend to be weak, allowing the blooms to nod.

The plant has a spreading, asymmetrical habit suitable for a bed or border. A climbing form that grows 10 to 12 feet and has an ARS rating of 7.3 is also available; it produces blooms only on old wood and makes a fine specimen on an arbor or trellis where the nodding habit of its flowers is a viewing asset. Both forms develop leathery dark green leaves and thrive in warm climates, but should be protected from the hottest sun if purple tones are objectionable.

'DAINTY BESS'

CLASSIFICATION: hybrid tea

BLOOM PERIOD: summer

HEIGHT: 3 to 4 feet

HARDINESS: Zones 5-10

ARS RATING: 9.0

DATE INTRODUCED: 1925

The silvery pink flowers of 'Dainty Bess' are unusual for a hybrid tea in several respects: They are single, with only five large, wavy petals; the petals surround a center of stamens that are colored deep maroon; and the flowers close at night. Blooms that develop in the shade of the leaves tend to be lighter in color. They are fragrant and long-lasting, both on the stem and when cut.

Plants are sturdy, vigorous, and upright, with abundant dark green leathery foliage. This rose's constant production of flowers makes it a fine choice in a bed or border. Despite its name, it's tough, tolerant of harsh weather, and resistant to disease.

'DELICATA'

CLASSIFICATION: hybrid rugosa

BLOOM PERIOD: summer to fall

HEIGHT: 3 feet

HARDINESS: Zones 3-10

ARS RATING: 7.9

DATE INTRODUCED: 1898

The bright pink to mauve flowers of 'Delicata' are semidouble, containing 18 to 24 petals, and open to a width of 3 to 3½ inches. Scented like cloves, the blooms appear in abundance early in the season and repeat until fall. Large orange-red hips follow the blooms and are present at the same time as later flowers—which may create an objectionable color combination for some.

Plants are low growing compared with other hybrid rugosas, and they have a compact, well-branched habit. Rarely over 3 feet in height, they are useful garden shrubs. Like other members of this class, 'Delicata' is extremely hardy, disease resistant, and tolerant of seaside conditions.

'DON JUAN'

CLASSIFICATION: large-flowered climber

BLOOM PERIOD: late spring to fall

HEIGHT: 8 to 10 feet

HARDINESS: Zones 5-10

ARS RATING: 8.2

DATE INTRODUCED: 1958

This rose produces extremely large, fragrant flowers, singly or in small clusters, throughout the growing season. The dark red, nearly black buds are oval and open slowly to reveal 4- to 5-inch-wide high-centered or cupped blossoms with a deep velvety color that is among the darkest of all red roses. Flowers are borne on long stems, making them ideal for cutting. Leaves are dark and glossy.

'Don Juan' is a moderate to vigorous grower with an upright habit. Deadheading spent blossoms will encourage rebloom. The plant is very effective on a pillar, fence, wall, or trellis. Although not extremely hardy, its disease resistance is good.

'DORTMUND'

CLASSIFICATION: shrub

BLOOM PERIOD: summer to fall

HEIGHT: 7 to 15 feet

HARDINESS: Zones 4-10

ARS RATING: 9.1

DATE INTRODUCED: 1955

The single flowers of 'Dortmund' are 3 to 4 inches across, with a center of yellow stamens, and have a light, spicy scent. Each bloom's brilliant poppy red petals are white at the base. The flowers are set off by glossy, hollylike leaves. With vigorous deadheading, blooming continues throughout the growing season; if the spent blooms are allowed to remain, bright orange hips develop.

'Dortmund' is a *Rosa kordesii* hybrid, one of a race of extremely hardy and disease-resistant roses. Versatile as well, it can be grown as a freestanding shrub or a hedge, pegged as a ground cover, or trained as a climber on a pillar, fence, or trellis. It is slow to start in the garden but, once established, is a vigorous and tough plant. It thrives in full sun or partial shade.

'DOUBLE DELIGHT'

CLASSIFICATION: hybrid tea

BLOOM PERIOD: summer to fall

HEIGHT: 4 feet

HARDINESS: Zones 5-10

ARS RATING: 8.9

DATE INTRODUCED: 1977

Each blossom of 'Double Delight' is a uniquely colored combination of red and creamy white. The exact coloration depends on light and temperature, but generally the red begins at the petal tips and diffuses to a creamy center. The double flowers are 5½ inches across, borne singly on stems, and have a strong, spicy fragrance. Leaves are a medium matte green.

Its bushy form and free-flowering habit make this rose a fine choice for beds and borders. It is a superb cut flower, prized for its form, color, fragrance, and long vase life. 'Double Delight' is fairly disease resistant but is somewhat tender. It is an AARS winner.

'DREAMGLO'

CLASSIFICATION: miniature

BLOOM PERIOD: summer to fall

HEIGHT: 18 to 24 inches

HARDINESS: Zones 5-10

ARS RATING: 8.5

DATE INTRODUCED: 1978

Long and pointed, the buds of 'Dreamglo' open to double flowers. Each bloom bears about 50 white petals that are blended and tipped with red. The blooms are borne singly, appearing abundantly in mid-season and repeating well. They have the classic high-centered hybrid tea form. The 1½-inch-wide blossoms are lightly fragrant and very long lasting; leaves are small, glossy, and dark green.

This vigorous rose has a compact, upright habit and is an excellent choice for the foreground of beds and borders. It is disease resistant.

'DUBLIN BAY'

CLASSIFICATION: large-flowered climber

BLOOM PERIOD: spring to fall

HEIGHT: 7 to 10 feet

HARDINESS: Zones 5-10

ARS RATING: 8.5

DATE INTRODUCED: 1976

Produced in clusters, the 4- to 4½-inch blood red flowers of 'Dublin Bay' appear continuously from spring until frost. Blooms are double, cupped, and fragrant. They have a velvety texture and show off well against the rich green foliage.

The plant is somewhat slow growing. It can perform as a shrub during its first few seasons and then become a fine climber with an upright, well branched habit, perfect for a low fence, pillar, stone wall, or trellis. 'Dublin Bay' is disease resistant.

'DUCHESSE DE BRABANT'

CLASSIFICATION: tea

BLOOM PERIOD: early spring to fall

HEIGHT: 3 to 5 feet

HARDINESS: Zones 7-10

ARS RATING: 8.2

DATE INTRODUCED: 1857

The 2- to 3-inch double flowers of 'Duchesse de Brabant' occur freely throughout the entire growing season. Rounded and cupped blossoms open from tulip-shaped buds and range in color from soft, clear pink to bright rosy pink. They are extremely fragrant. The abundant foliage is medium green, and the canes are well supplied with prickles.

This rose has a bushy and spreading habit—it is nearly as broad as it is tall—and is suitable for a bed or border. It is vigorous, disease resistant, and heat tolerant but tender. A white sport of 'Duchesse de Brabant', 'Madame Joseph Schwartz', was introduced in 1880.

'ELINA'

CLASSIFICATION: hybrid tea

BLOOM PERIOD: summer to fall

HEIGHT: 3 to 4 feet

HARDINESS: Zones 5-10

ARS RATING: 8.6

DATE INTRODUCED: 1985

The large double blooms of 'Elina' (also known as 'Peaudouce') are a delicate pale yellow to ivory. Beautifully formed flowers appear continuously throughout the season, each bearing around 35 petals and producing a light fragrance. Leaves are large, glossy, and dark green, providing a dramatic foil for the flowers.

The plants are vigorous and upright. Blossoms are produced in abundance on long, straight stems, making this rose an excellent source for cut roses. It is hardy and resistant to black spot but somewhat susceptible to mildew.

'ERFURT'

CLASSIFICATION: hybrid musk

BLOOM PERIOD: summer to fall

HEIGHT: 5 to 6 feet

HARDINESS: Zones 5-10

ARS RATING: 8.4

DATE INTRODUCED: 1939

Buds of 'Erfurt' are rosy red, long, and pointed, opening to deep cerise-pink semidouble flowers with white centers and bright golden yellow stamens. Once plants begin to bloom, they continue nonstop until frost. The blossoms exude a pleasing musky fragrance. Foliage is leathery and wrinkled with a coppery green tone that enhances the brightly colored flowers. Stems are brown with hooked prickles.

The plants are vigorous and bushy, with arching canes that may spread outward to 6 feet. The long show of blooms and abundance of attractive foliage make 'Erfurt' an outstanding garden shrub for beds or borders. Like other hybrid musks, this rose is disease resistant and tolerates some shade and poor soil.

'ESCAPADE'

CLASSIFICATION: floribunda

BLOOM PERIOD: summer to fall

HEIGHT: 2½ to 3 feet

HARDINESS: Zones 4-10

ARS RATING: 8.8

DATE INTRODUCED: 1967

The 3-inch semidouble flowers of 'Escapade' are light mauve-pink or lilac to rosy violet with creamy white centers. They are borne in both large and small clusters, and each bloom has about 12 petals that surround amber stamens. Blooms commence in midseason, repeating consistently until a hard frost. The blooms are lightly fragrant. Leaves are light green and glossy.

'Escapade' plants have an upright, bushy habit and are vigorous growers. They are useful in beds and borders and can also be planted as a low hedge. The flowers are excellent for cutting.

'EUROPEANA'

CLASSIFICATION: floribunda

BLOOM PERIOD: summer to fall

HEIGHT: 2 to 3 feet

HARDINESS: Zones 4-10

ARS RATING: 9.0

DATE INTRODUCED: 1968

Borne in large clusters, the double blooms of 'Europeana' are 3 inches across and cup shaped. Petals are deep crimson and have a velvety texture. Beginning in midseason, flowering continues prolifically until the fall. Leaves emerge bronze red, maturing to deep, glossy green with reddish tints.

This bush is quite robust. Its enormous flower clusters can cause the stems to bend under their weight, so it should be grouped with plants that will provide support for the flower-laden stems. Because it has a bushy, spreading habit, 'Europeana' is suitable for beds, borders, and low hedges. Flowers are good for cutting, and the plants are disease resistant and very hardy. This rose is an AARS winner.

'FAIR BIANCA'

CLASSIFICATION: shrub

BLOOM PERIOD: summer to fall

HEIGHT: 3 feet

HARDINESS: Zones 4-10

ARS RATING: 8.2

DATE INTRODUCED: 1983

The very double, medium-sized blossoms of 'Fair Bianca', a David Austin rose, are shallowly cupped and bear a strong myrrh fragrance. Their small pure white petals are tightly arranged around a green button eye. As they mature, petals reflex at the edges. Blooms appear almost continuously throughout the season. Foliage is light green and semiglossy.

The plants are vigorous and compact, growing as broad as they are tall. Their neat habit and outstanding flowers make them ideally suited for beds or patio plantings. They can also be effectively used for a low hedge.

'FANTIN-LATOUR'

CLASSIFICATION: centifolia

BLOOM PERIOD: late spring

HEIGHT: 4 to 6 feet

HARDINESS: Zones 4-10

ARS RATING: 8.2

DATE INTRODUCED: unknown

Although 'Fantin-Latour' has a relatively short bloom period and does not repeat, the quality of the blossoms makes up for their short season. Each 2- to 3-inch very double flower is composed of 200 petals, giving it the full appearance typical of centifolia roses. When it first opens, the pale blush pink bloom is cupped; it then flattens as it matures. The blossoms emit a delicate fragrance. Leaves are dark green, and canes are nearly smooth.

'Fantin-Latour' plants produce arching canes that usually reach 5 feet in height and a little less in spread. They perform well in a bed or border where their late-spring flower display is breathtaking. This is a very hardy rose, but its disease resistance is only moderate.

'FELICITE PARMENTIER'

CLASSIFICATION: alba

BLOOM PERIOD: early summer

HEIGHT: 4 to 5 feet

HARDINESS: Zones 4-10

ARS RATING: 8.6

DATE INTRODUCED: 1834

The pale blush pink, very double blooms of 'Félicité Parmentier' open flat, then reflex to form a ball. As the 2- to 2½-inch flowers age, the tightly quartered petals fade to creamy white at their outer edges. Flowers are borne in clusters in profusion in early summer, but they do not repeat. Their fragrance is heady. Leaves are gray-green, and the abundant prickles are dark.

This rose has a bushy, compact habit, reaching 4 to 5 feet in height and 4 feet in width, and is less upright than most albas. The tidy form requires little pruning. It tolerates poor soil, partial shade, and climatic extremes, and is resistant to disease.

'FERDINAND PICHARD'

CLASSIFICATION: hybrid perpetual

BLOOM PERIOD: summer to fall

HEIGHT: 4 to 6 feet

HARDINESS: Zones 5-10

ARS RATING: 7.4

DATE INTRODUCED: 1921

The cupped double blooms of 'Ferdinand Pichard' are fragrant and colorful. Ranging from 2½ to 4 inches across, each flower produces pink petals splashed with white or crimson stripes, and as the blossom ages its pink fades to white and the crimson to purple. Flower clusters appear in abundance in early summer and again in the fall with sporadic blooms in between. Foliage is yellowish green, and canes are nearly thornless.

This rose has an upright, compact habit and is ideally suited to beds. It does especially well with regular fertilizing and copious watering and should be pruned heavily in winter. While fairly resistant to mildew, it is susceptible to black spot.

'FIRST EDITION'

CLASSIFICATION: floribunda

BLOOM PERIOD: summer to fall

HEIGHT: 3½ feet

HARDINESS: Zones 4-10

ARS RATING: 8.6

DATE INTRODUCED: 1976

The pointed coral-orange buds of 'First Edition' open to luminous coral-rose blossoms with orange tints. The petals surround yellow anthers. Flowers are double, 2 to 2½ inches across, and lightly fragrant, and they are borne in flat-topped clusters. Their color deepens in cool weather. Foliage is glossy and medium green.

The bushes are vigorous and upright. They are suited to many uses, including beds and borders, low hedges, and containers. Flowers are excellent for cutting and exhibition, and the plants have good disease resistance. 'First Edition' is an AARS winner.

'FIRST PRIZE'

CLASSIFICATION: hybrid tea

BLOOM PERIOD: summer to fall

HEIGHT: 5 to 8 feet

HARDINESS: Zones 5-10

ARS RATING: 8.9

DATE INTRODUCED: 1970

Gorgeous large pointed buds open to high-centered rosy pink flowers with ivory centers. Each 5- to 6-inch double blossom has 25 to 35 petals. These are borne singly or in small clusters on strong stems and are mildly fragrant. Leaves are dark and leathery.

'First Prize' has an upright habit and can be very effective in a bed or border, where it will produce abundant flowers all summer. The classical form of its huge buds and open blossoms and its long vase life make it an ideal selection for cut flowers and exhibitions. It is tender and fairly resistant to black spot. This rose is an AARS winner.

'F. J. GROOTENDORST'

CLASSIFICATION: hybrid rugosa

BLOOM PERIOD: summer to fall

HEIGHT: 5 feet

HARDINESS: Zones 3-10

ARS RATING: 7.7

DATE INTRODUCED: 1918

'F. J. Grootendorst' produces clusters of as many as 20 small, crimson flowers throughout the growing season. Individual blooms are double and have a carnation-like appearance with fringed petals. The abundant foliage is somewhat coarse, leathery, and dark green. This rose has given rise to several sports, including 'Pink Grootendorst', which has soft pink flowers; 'White Grootendorst', whose white blooms are borne on a considerably smaller plant; and 'Grootendorst Supreme', whose blossoms are lightly scented and a deeper red than those of its parent.

This rugosa hybrid is a vigorous grower with a bushy, upright habit. It is easy to grow, tolerant of seaside conditions, and disease resistant.

'FOLKLORE'

CLASSIFICATION: hybrid tea

BLOOM PERIOD: summer to fall

HEIGHT: 4 to 5 feet

HARDINESS: Zones 5-10

ARS RATING: 8.5

DATE INTRODUCED: 1977

Beautiful double blossoms of 'Folklore' appear in midseason and repeat in strong flushes until fall. The long, pointed buds open slowly to reveal 4- to 5-inch high-centered flowers that are a blend of orange tones with a yellow reverse. Blooms appear singly or in clusters and are very fragrant and long-lasting. The foliage is medium green and glossy.

Plants are vigorous and easy to grow. They have a tall, upright, and bushy habit, and make attractive additions to beds and borders, as well as being useful as screens and hedges. Flowers are excellent for cutting or exhibition. The foliage is disease resistant.

'FRAGRANT CLOUD'

CLASSIFICATION: hybrid tea

BLOOM PERIOD: summer to fall

HEIGHT: 4 to 5 feet

HARDINESS: Zones 5-10

ARS RATING: 8.3

DATE INTRODUCED: 1963

'Fragrant Cloud' is named for its scent, which is among the most powerful of all roses and is both sweet and spicy. The double flowers are 4 to 5 inches across and coral red, deepening to a purplish red as they age. Blooms are composed of 25 to 30 petals and are produced in abundance throughout the summer. The leaves are large, dark, and semiglossy.

The plant is vigorous and upright; its freely branching habit makes it well suited to a border or bed. The rose is highly valued as a cut flower both for its appearance and for its perfume. Leaves are subject to mildew.

'FRAU DAGMAR HARTOPP'

CLASSIFICATION: hybrid rugosa

BLOOM PERIOD: spring to fall

HEIGHT: 2½ to 3 feet

HARDINESS: Zones 3-10

ARS RATING: 8.5

DATE INTRODUCED: 1914

'Frau Dagmar Hartopp' flowers in spring and continues nonstop until freezing weather calls a halt to the show. The blossoms are deliciously fragrant and single, and have five silvery pink petals surrounding creamy stamens. Foliage is crinkled and deep green. In fall the leaves turn deep maroon and golden yellow with coppery tones, and the plant sets beautiful large hips that are colored deep red. Stems are exceedingly prickly.

This hybrid rugosa is compact, low growing, and wider than it is tall. Requiring little pruning, it is a neat, well-behaved shrub ideally suited to smaller gardens and is also perfect for a low hedge or for massing. The flowers last well and are wonderful for cutting. This rose is exceptionally hardy and disease resistant, and it tolerates sandy soil and salt spray.

'FRAU KARL DRUSCHKI'

CLASSIFICATION: hybrid perpetual

BLOOM PERIOD: early summer and fall

HEIGHT: 4 to 7 feet

HARDINESS: Zones 5-10

ARS RATING: 7.8

DATE INTRODUCED: 1901

This rose produces a great abundance of double blossoms from high-centered buds in early summer and repeats the show in fall. The elegant white flower is 4 to 4½ inches across with 30 to 35 rolled petals that display a touch of lemon yellow at their base. Canes are nearly smooth, supporting leathery, coarse, light green foliage.

The plant is vigorous and erect, with stout branches and long, strong stems. The color and form of its flower makes it useful in combination with other roses, both in beds and in indoor arrangements. Buds are reluctant to open in damp weather, and leaves are susceptible to mildew.

'FRENCH LACE'

CLASSIFICATION: floribunda

BLOOM PERIOD: summer to fall

HEIGHT: 3½ feet

HARDINESS: Zones 4-9

ARS RATING: 8.2

DATE INTRODUCED: 1981

Flowers of 'French Lace' are borne singly or in clusters of up to 12 and bloom continuously from early summer to frost. Buds are pointed, opening to flat, 3- to 4-inch double blossoms that are ivory with apricot tones and emit a light tea fragrance. The thorny canes produce small, dark green hollylike leaves.

Plants are well branched, bushy, and upright. Their attractive form and abundant flowering potential recommend them for use as a low hedge or in a bed or border. Flowers are long-lasting and beautiful in indoor arrangements. To top off its list of virtues, 'French Lace' is highly resistant to disease. It is an AARS winner.

'GABRIELLE PRIVAT'

CLASSIFICATION: polyantha

BLOOM PERIOD: spring to fall

HEIGHT: 2 to 4 feet

HARDINESS: Zones 5-10

ARS RATING: 8.5

DATE INTRODUCED: 1931

Large pyramidal clusters of 30 to 50 semidouble blooms are produced on the neat, low-growing plants of 'Gabrielle Privat'. Flowering begins in spring and continues in great profusion through fall. Individual blooms are carmine-pink and 1¼ inches across. They are attractively displayed against lush bright green foliage.

The bush has a full, mounding habit and requires little pruning except to thin and remove dead growth. Plants of 'Gabrielle Privat' are rugged and tolerate a wide range of soils. A good choice for small gardens or for massing, they are also pretty in containers.

'GARDEN PARTY'

CLASSIFICATION: hybrid tea

BLOOM PERIOD: summer to fall

HEIGHT: 2½ to 4 feet

HARDINESS: Zones 5-10

ARS RATING: 8.2

DATE INTRODUCED: 1959

The lightly fragrant blooms of 'Garden Party' are pale yellow fading to white, with light pink petal tips. Each flower is cup shaped and double, with petals flaring 4 to 5 inches across. Their color deepens somewhat in fall. They bloom profusely in midseason, with a good repeat. Leaves are semiglossy and dark green with reddish undersides.

The vigorous, bushy plants are valuable in the garden, where they are especially dramatic when planted in large groups. The flowers are excellent for cutting. 'Garden Party' is somewhat susceptible to mildew and may develop black spot in damp weather. This rose is an AARS winner.

'GARTENDIREKTOR OTTO LINNE'

CLASSIFICATION: shrub

BLOOM PERIOD: summer to fall

HEIGHT: 5 feet

HARDINESS: Zones 4-10

ARS RATING: 8.9

DATE INTRODUCED: 1934

The ruffled blossoms of 'Gartendirektor Otto Linne' are borne on long stems in slightly pendulous clusters of up to 30 blooms. Individual flowers are double and have a moderate, carnation-like fragrance. The carmine-pink petals are edged with a darker pink and are yellow-white at the base. Foliage is leathery and bright apple green.

This rose is vigorous and bushy. It can be used to create an elegant hedge and in mild climates can be trained as a climber. Disease resistance is very good.

'GENE BOERNER'

CLASSIFICATION: floribunda

BLOOM PERIOD: summer to fall

HEIGHT: 3½ to 5 feet

HARDINESS: Zones 4-10

ARS RATING: 8.5

DATE INTRODUCED: 1968

The blooms of 'Gene Boerner' are double, high centered, and 2½ to 3½ inches across. Petals are deep pink, and they reflex back to form points. The lightly fragrant blossoms occur singly or in clusters from midseason to autumn. Foliage is light green and glossy.

This vigorous rose is medium-sized with an upright habit. Its flowers are borne profusely and are well displayed on the plant, making it very attractive in beds, borders, and hedges. Blooms are good for cutting and exhibition. The plant is diseaseresistant. 'Gene Boerner' is an AARS winner.

'GOLDEN SHOWERS'

CLASSIFICATION: large-flowered climber

BLOOM PERIOD: summer to fall

HEIGHT: 6 to 10 feet

HARDINESS: Zones 5-9

ARS RATING: 7.1

DATE INTRODUCED: 1956

'Golden Showers' produces a profusion of lemon-scented, bright yellow flowers throughout summer and fall. These open quickly from long, pointed buds to 3½- to 4-inch double flowers with red anthers. Flowers are borne both singly and in loose clusters on strong stems and are well distributed throughout the plant. Leaves are dark and glossy.

The plants are excellent for training on pillars, trellises, walls, and fences. The sturdy stems require little support; with pruning, this rose can even be grown as a freestanding shrub. The flowers are suitable for cutting. 'Golden Showers' tolerates light shade and is somewhat disease resistant. It is an AARS winner.

'GOLDEN WINGS'

CLASSIFICATION: shrub

BLOOM PERIOD: spring to fall

HEIGHT: 4 to 5 feet

HARDINESS: Zones 4-10

ARS RATING: 7.9

DATE INTRODUCED: 1956

The sulfur yellow blooms of 'Golden Wings' are sweetly fragrant and appear abundantly throughout the season. Long, pointed buds open to single 4- to 5-inch saucer-shaped blossoms. Flowers can have as many as 10 petals, though most have five, surrounding dark amber stamens. Flowers are borne singly or in clusters. The orange hips are very showy. Leaves are intensely yellow-green.

The vigorous shrubs are about equal in height and spread. Their compact habit can be encouraged by pruning the canes back by one-third in spring. The plants are attractive in beds and borders, and the blossoms make beautiful cut flowers. This rose is hardy and disease resistant.

'GOLD MEDAL'

CLASSIFICATION: grandiflora

BLOOM PERIOD: summer to fall

HEIGHT: 4 to 5½ feet

HARDINESS: Zones 5-10

ARS RATING: 8.8

DATE INTRODUCED: 1982

The deep yellow flowers of 'Gold Medal' are flushed and edged with orange-red. High-centered double blossoms appear singly or in clusters on long stems and are 3½ to 4 inches across; they bear a fruity fragrance. Blooming in abundance throughout the season, this is one of the last roses to quit in the fall. Leaves are dark and glossy, and canes have few thorns.

Plants have a tall, bushy, and upright habit. They take well to pruning but prefer to be pruned high. The bush is suitable for beds and borders, and its flowers are excellent for cutting and exhibition. Plants are disease resistant.

'GRAHAM THOMAS'

CLASSIFICATION: shrub

BLOOM PERIOD: summer to fall

HEIGHT: 4 to 12 feet

HARDINESS: Zones 4-10

ARS RATING: 7.9

DATE INTRODUCED: 1983

The apricot-pink buds of 'Graham Thomas', one of the best known of David Austin's English roses, open to medium-sized double flowers. The recurrent blooms are loosely petaled and cup shaped, and their color is an unusual rich butter yellow that deepens toward the center. They bear a strong tea rose fragrance. Leaves are small, bright green, smooth, and glossy.

This rose is usually grown as a 4- to 6-foot shrub but in warmer climates can also be grown as a 10- to 12-foot climber. Plants are vigorous and bushy, with a graceful, slightly arching form. As a shrub it is almost as wide as it is tall.

'GRANADA'

CLASSIFICATION: hybrid tea

BLOOM PERIOD: summer to fall

HEIGHT: 5 feet

HARDINESS: Zones 5-10

ARS RATING: 8.3

DATE INTRODUCED: 1963

The 4- to 5-inch blooms of 'Granada' are extremely colorful, including shades of yellow, pink, and orange-red. Buds are spiraled, opening to high-centered double flowers that flatten with age and emit a rich, spicy fragrance. Blossoms are borne singly or in clusters continuously throughout the season. Leaves are leathery, crinkled, dark green, and distinctly serrated.

Plants are upright, vigorous, and bushy. They can be grown in beds or borders and provide a constant source of spectacular blooms for indoor flower arrangements. While resistant to black spot, plants are prone to mildew. 'Granada' is an AARS winner.

'GREAT MAIDEN'S BLUSH'

CLASSIFICATION: alba

BLOOM PERIOD: early summer

HEIGHT: 5 to 6 feet

HARDINESS: Zones 4-10

ARS RATING: 8.5

DATE INTRODUCED: prior to 1600

The 2- to 3-inch double flowers of 'Great Maiden's Blush' are white with a delicate pink blush. As a blossom matures, its outer petals reflex and fade to a pale cream, while the center remains blush pink. Borne in clusters in early summer, blooms do not repeat. They have an exceptionally sweet fragrance. Foliage is lush and blue-gray, providing a lovely foil for the flowers.

This rose is a vigorous grower, well branched and arching. It makes a fine garden shrub for large beds and an attractive informal hedge. 'Great Maiden's Blush' is very hardy.

'GRUSS AN AACHEN'

CLASSIFICATION: floribunda

BLOOM PERIOD: spring to fall

HEIGHT: 2 to 3 feet

HARDINESS: Zones 4-10

ARS RATING: 8.3

DATE INTRODUCED: 1909

Buds of 'Gruss an Aachen' are tinted with red-orange and yellow but open to reveal pale apricot-pink blooms that fade to creamy white. The flowers, reminiscent of old garden roses, are 3 inches across, double, and cup shaped, with a rich fragrance. They are borne in clusters throughout the season. The leaves are rich green and leathery.

This rose has a low growing, bushy habit and is very free blooming, even in partial shade. It is a good choice for a bed or low hedge. The plants are quite hardy and disease resistant.

'HANDEL'

CLASSIFICATION: large-flowered climber

BLOOM PERIOD: summer to fall

HEIGHT: 12 to 14 feet

HARDINESS: Zones 5-9

ARS RATING: 8.2

DATE INTRODUCED: 1965

The cream-colored double flowers of 'Handel' are edged with rosy pink. They open from shapely spiraled buds to high-centered or cupped 3½-inch blooms that produce a light fragrance. Blooms appear in abundance in early summer and repeat well through fall. Hot weather increases the pink flower color in both area and intensity. Foliage is olive green and glossy.

'Handel' grows upright and is a popular climber for pillars, walls, fences, and small structures because of its prolific flowering ability and the unusual coloring of its blooms. It tolerates light shade but is prone to black spot.

'HANNAH GORDON'

CLASSIFICATION: floribunda

BLOOM PERIOD: spring to fall

HEIGHT: 3 feet

HARDINESS: Zones 4-10

ARS RATING: 8.2

DATE INTRODUCED: 1983

The large double flowers of 'Hannah Gordon' are white with bold cerise-pink markings and petal edges. Each bloom has about 35 petals and a light fragrance. Flowers appear continuously throughout the season. The foliage is large, medium green, and semiglossy.

Plants are upright, compact, and bushy. They are useful in beds and borders, can be very effective when massed, and also do nicely when used as a low hedge.

'HANSA'

CLASSIFICATION: hybrid rugosa

BLOOM PERIOD: spring to fall

HEIGHT: 4 to 5 feet

HARDINESS: Zones 3-8

ARS RATING: 8.3

DATE INTRODUCED: 1905

'Hansa' is a prolific bloomer bearing short-stemmed clusters of rich crimson blossoms throughout the growing season. Flowers are double, cup shaped, and 3 to 3½ inches across; they bear a strong clove-like fragrance. Foliage is dark green and crinkled, and canes are gray and thorny. Large red-orange hips provide a stunning fall display.

This rose is upright and vigorous. It makes an attractive barrier hedge, providing landscape interest from spring to late fall with its succession of spicy-scented flowers followed by showy fruit. Like other hybrid rugosas, 'Hansa' tolerates sandy soil and salt spray, is extremely hardy, and resists diseases and insects.

'HENRY HUDSON'

CLASSIFICATION: hybrid rugosa

BLOOM PERIOD: spring to fall

HEIGHT: 3 to 4 feet

HARDINESS: Zones 3-10

ARS RATING: 9.1

DATE INTRODUCED: 1976

The pink-tipped buds of 'Henry Hudson' open to semi-double white blooms that are scented like cloves. Flowers consist of about 25 petals that surround bright yellow stamens. They appear continuously throughout the season and are beautifully set off by copious deep green foliage.

This rugosa hybrid, one of the Explorer series, has an extremely dense, low-growing habit, making it an excellent choice for a bed or ground cover. It produces suckers, so should be either contained or placed where its spreading tendency can be used to advantage. Remove spent flowers for best effect. The plant tolerates sandy soil and salt spray. It is also extremely hardy and disease resistant.

'HERITAGE'

CLASSIFICATION: shrub

BLOOM PERIOD: summer

HEIGHT: 4 to 5 feet

HARDINESS: Zones 4-10

ARS RATING: 8.7

DATE INTRODUCED: 1984

The blush pink double flowers of this David Austin rose are colored a bit deeper toward their centers. Their form is exquisite, with the outer petals forming a deep cup around precisely arranged and folded inner petals. Profusely borne in clusters throughout the summer, they create a cloud of rich scent that is a blend of myrrh and lemon. Foliage is dark green and semiglossy. The canes have few thorns.

The plant is a robust grower with a bushy, upright habit. It is a fine addition to beds or borders, makes a wonderful hedge, and provides a long season of cut flowers. Plants are fairly disease resistant but may be susceptible to rust.

'HONORINE DE BRABANT'

CLASSIFICATION: bourbon

BLOOM PERIOD: summer to fall

HEIGHT: 5 to 6 feet

HARDINESS: Zones 5-10

ARS RATING: 7.6

DATE INTRODUCED: unknown

The 3½- to 4-inch soft pink blooms of 'Honorine de Brabant' are striped and spotted with darker shades of violet, crimson, and mauve. Its main crop of flowers appears in midsummer, but it repeats well, and fall flowers are less prone to bleaching by the hot sun. Blossoms are double, loosely cupped, and quartered, with a raspberry scent. Foliage is light green, large, and leathery. Canes are green and bear a few large prickles.

Plants are vigorous, large, and bushy. As a shrub, it grows nearly as broad as it is tall. It can also be trained as a climber. It is more compact and blooms more continuously than most bourbons.

'HURDY GURDY'

CLASSIFICATION: miniature

BLOOM PERIOD: spring to summer

HEIGHT: 12 to 24 inches

HARDINESS: Zones 5-10

ARS RATING: 8.0

DATE INTRODUCED: 1986

The flowers of 'Hurdy Gurdy' are dark red with white stripes. Each small double bloom has 26 to 40 petals and a light fragrance. Medium green glossy leaves are also small.

This miniature has an upright habit and is a good choice for an edging. It is effective when placed in the foreground of a rose bed or incorporated into a perennial border. It can also be grown in containers or in a patio planting. Deadheading the spent blooms will encourage its flowers to repeat through the summer. It is heat tolerant and disease resistant.

'ICEBERG'

CLASSIFICATION: floribunda

BLOOM PERIOD: summer to fall

HEIGHT: 3 to 4½ feet

HARDINESS: Zones 4-9

ARS RATING: 8.7

DATE INTRODUCED: 1958

Throughout summer, 'Iceberg' produces large clusters with up to a dozen pure white blossoms that stand out beautifully against small, light green, glossy foliage. Buds are long and pointed with high centers. Each double flower is 2 to 4 inches across, somewhat flat, and sweetly scented.

'Iceberg' is an all-purpose rose in that the vigorous plant can be grown as a hedge or a border or as a container specimen, trained as a tree rose, or used for cutting flowers for indoor arrangements. It is bushy and well branched and is easily trained. A climbing version is also available, rated 8.8 by the ARS. Both forms are disease resistant.

'IMMENSEE'

CLASSIFICATION: shrub

BLOOM PERIOD: spring to fall

HEIGHT: 1½ to 3 feet

HARDINESS: Zones 4-10

ARS RATING: 9.0

DATE INTRODUCED: 1982

The small flowers of 'Immensee' are pale pink to almost white, single, and quite fragrant. The blooms appear in profusion in the spring and repeat well throughout the season. The leaves are small in proportion to the flowers and are dark green and glossy.

This rose has a low-growing, spreading habit; canes may spread as wide as 13 feet. It is useful as a flowering ground cover. Bred by Kordes of Germany using *R. wichuraiana*, 'Immensee' is very hardy and resistant to disease.

'IRRESISTIBLE'

CLASSIFICATION: miniature

BLOOM PERIOD: spring to fall

HEIGHT: 18 to 24 inches

HARDINESS: Zones 5-10

ARS RATING: 8.0

DATE INTRODUCED: 1989

The perfectly formed double flowers of 'Irresistible' are white with a pale pink center and are produced on long stems. Borne singly and in clusters, the high-centered blooms have more than 40 petals each and put off a moderate, spicy fragrance. Hips are green to yellow brown, and leaves are medium green and semiglossy.

Plants are upright and larger than most miniatures. They are well suited to growing in beds, borders, and containers. Their abundant production of long-stemmed hybrid-tea-type flowers makes them ideal for cutting and exhibiting.

'ISPAHAN'

CLASSIFICATION: damask

BLOOM PERIOD: spring to summer

HEIGHT: 4 to 6 feet

HARDINESS: Zones 4-10

ARS RATING: 8.7

DATE INTRODUCED: prior to 1832

The very fragrant, double blooms of 'Ispahan' (also called 'Pompon des Princes') appear in profusion over a 2-month period in early and midseason, but they do not repeat. Borne in clusters, the bright clear pink flowers are 2½ to 3 inches across, cup shaped, and loosely reflexing. They are long-lasting, holding both their shape and their color well. Foliage is small with a blue-green cast.

This rose is bushy and upright. With a flowering season that is remarkably long for a damask, it is valued both as a garden shrub and for cut flowers. The plant is vigorous, disease resistant, and quite hardy.

'JEAN KENNEALLY'

CLASSIFICATION: miniature

BLOOM PERIOD: summer to fall

HEIGHT: 22 to 30 inches

HARDINESS: Zones 5-10

ARS RATING: 9.7

DATE INTRODUCED: 1984

The dainty 1½-inch double blossoms of 'Jean Kenneally' are pale to medium apricot blended with yellow and pink. They appear singly or in clusters and have a hybrid tea form with high centers and petals folding back to form points. Leaves are medium green and semiglossy.

This rose is upright, well branched, and taller than most miniatures. It can be grown in beds and borders or used as an edging, and it makes a good container specimen for outside or indoors near a sunny window. It is disease resistant.

'JEANNE LAJOIE'

CLASSIFICATION: climbing miniature

BLOOM PERIOD: spring to fall

HEIGHT: 8 feet

HARDINESS: Zones 5-10

ARS RATING: 9.2

DATE INTRODUCED: 1975

'Jeanne Lajoie' produces long, pointed buds that open to miniature two-toned pink flowers. Usually borne in clusters, the flowers are most abundant during cool weather. The high-centered blooms have 20 to 25 pointed petals and are lightly fragrant. In fall, this rose produces small orange hips. Foliage is lush, glossy, and dark.

A very vigorous grower, 'Jeanne Lajoie' is upright and bushy. It can be trained as a climber, or used as a freestanding shrub or hedge rose. Deadheading after its first flush of blooms will significantly increase later flowering. Plants are disease resistant and hardy.

'JENS MUNK'

CLASSIFICATION: hybrid rugosa

BLOOM PERIOD: spring to fall

HEIGHT: 4 to 5 feet

HARDINESS: Zones 3-10

ARS RATING: 8.4

DATE INTRODUCED: 1974

The lavender-pink double flowers of 'Jens Munk' are 2 to 3 inches across and appear continuously throughout the growing season. Their 25 petals surround attractive yellow stamens. The blooms are clustered and bear a strong, spicy fragrance.

This Explorer series rose is upright, bushy, and very vigorous. In the landscape it is effective both as a large garden shrub and as a dense hedge. It is very resistant to most diseases but susceptible to stem borer, and it's extremely hardy and tolerant of sandy soil and salt spray.

'JOHN CABOT'

CLASSIFICATION: shrub

BLOOM PERIOD: summer to fall

HEIGHT: 4 to 10 feet

HARDINESS: Zones 3-10

ARS RATING: 8.2

DATE INTRODUCED: 1978

The rose pink to cherry red blooms of 'John Cabot' are produced in abundance over a 6-week period in the summer and then sporadically into the fall. Each 2½-inch double flower has 30 to 35 petals arranged in a loose cup around yellow stamens. Blossoms are borne in clusters and show up well against the medium green foliage.

A kordesii shrub in the Explorer series, 'John Cabot' can be grown as a shrub or a climber. As a shrub it can be maintained at a height of 4 to 5 feet but needs considerable room to spread. The plant is very vigorous, with an upright habit and long, arching canes. If grown as a climber, it takes about four seasons to reach its ultimate height of 8 to 10 feet. Foliage is disease resistant. This is an exceptionally hardy rose.

'JOHN FRANKLIN'

CLASSIFICATION: shrub

BLOOM PERIOD: spring to fall

HEIGHT: 3 to 4 feet

HARDINESS: Zones 5-10

ARS RATING: not rated

DATE INTRODUCED: 1980

Clusters of up to 30 medium red flowers are produced continuously on this rose. The semidouble blooms are 2½ inches across, and each has approximately 25 petals. Flowers are fragrant. Leaves are round, and canes bear yellow-green prickles tinted with purple.

The upright, bushy plants are easy to use in the landscape. Their extended bloom period make them an asset in beds and borders. An Explorer series rose, 'John Franklin' tolerates both heat and cold and is disease resistant.

'JOSEPH'S COAT'

CLASSIFICATION: large-flowered climber

BLOOM PERIOD: summer to fall

HEIGHT: 8 to 10 feet

HARDINESS: Zones 6-9

ARS RATING: 7.6

DATE INTRODUCED: 1964

The clusters of double blossoms of 'Joseph's Coat' create an amazing riot of color, with yellows, pinks, oranges, and reds all present at the same time. The red and orange tones become more prominent in autumn. Buds are urn shaped, and unlike those of numerous climbers, they occur on new wood. Flowers are 3-inch cups that are lightly fragrant, leaves are dark green and glossy, and canes are prickly.

The plant is tall and upright. It can be trained as a climber on a pillar, fence, or trellis or, because it is not very robust, can be allowed to grow as a loose, freestanding shrub. It is somewhat tender and prone to powdery mildew.

'JUST JOEY'

CLASSIFICATION: hybrid tea

BLOOM PERIOD: summer

HEIGHT: 3 feet

HARDINESS: Zones 5-10

ARS RATING: 7.7

DATE INTRODUCED: 1972

Blossoms of 'Just Joey' are 4 to 6 inches across, composed of 30 exceptionally large petals with interestingly frilly edges. Buds are large, elegantly pointed, and brandy colored, opening to double apricot blooms that lighten as they mature. Flowers bear a deep fruity scent. Both the flowers and their fragrance are long-lasting. Leaves are large and glossy, and stems are prickly.

Plants are rather squat and spreading, with a moderate growth rate. They are fairly disease resistant. The flowers are particularly outstanding for indoor arrangements because of their large size and long vase life.

'KEEPSAKE'

CLASSIFICATION: hybrid tea

BLOOM PERIOD: summer to fall

HEIGHT: 5 to 6 feet

HARDINESS: Zones 5-10

ARS RATING: 8.4

DATE INTRODUCED: 1981

Borne singly or in small clusters, the oval buds of 'Keepsake' open to 5-inch double blooms. The flowers are high centered and deep pink with lighter pink shades, and are fragrant. Foliage is dark green, large, and glossy, and canes are armed with stout prickles.

The plants are upright and bushy. They are effective in beds or borders, and the flowers are excellent for cutting and exhibition. Though somewhat tender, this rose is very disease resistant. It performs best in climates with cool summers.

'KINGIG'

CLASSIFICATION: miniature

BLOOM PERIOD: spring to fall

HEIGHT: 18 to 24 inches

HARDINESS: Zones 5-10

ARS RATING: 9.0

DATE INTRODUCED: 1987

This popular miniature produces medium-sized high-centered flowers singly or in sprays of three to five. Each double blossom has about 18 petals that are light pink with a light or dark pink reverse. As they mature, flowers fade to creamy pink. The matte leaves are medium in color and size, and canes bear slightly crooked white prickles. Hips are oval and green.

Upright 'Kingig' bushes can be combined attractively with other plants in borders and beds, or they can be used as edgings or grown as container specimens.

'KONIGIN VON DANEMARK'

CLASSIFICATION: alba

BLOOM PERIOD: summer

HEIGHT: 5 to 6 feet

HARDINESS: Zones 4-9

ARS RATING: 8.3

DATE INTRODUCED: 1826

The very double blooms of 'Königin von Dänemark' (or 'Queen of Denmark') appear in midseason and do not repeat. Short, deep pink buds open to 2½- to 3½-inch light pink flowers that are more deeply colored toward the center, where the quartered petals surround a button eye. The flowers are borne singly or in small clusters of three to five and are intensely fragrant. Foliage is an attractive blue-green.

'Königin von Dänemark' has a graceful, open habit and canes that are wide spreading. To encourage a more compact habit, shorten the canes to 2 feet in spring. Use this rose in beds or borders or train it to a trellis, wall, fence, or pillar. Flowers are good for cutting. This rose is extremely hardy and virtually immune to black spot and mildew.

'KORICOLE'

CLASSIFICATION: floribunda

BLOOM PERIOD: spring to fall

HEIGHT: 3 feet

HARDINESS: Zones 4-9

ARS RATING: 9.0

DATE INTRODUCED: 1985

Borne in clusters, the blooms of 'Koricole' are large and lightly fragrant. Each double blossom has about 35 white petals with pink edges. Flowers bloom on short stems throughout the growing season. Leaves are large, dark green, and semiglossy.

The bushy, upright plants are easy to grow and are excellent for beds and borders. Their long-lasting and prolific flower display and their low-growing habit make them ideal for placement in front of taller, leggy roses.

'KRISTIN'

CLASSIFICATION: miniature

BLOOM PERIOD: spring to fall

HEIGHT: 20 to 24 inches

HARDINESS: Zones 5-10

ARS RATING: not rated

DATE INTRODUCED: 1993

The pointed, urn-shaped buds of 'Kristin' open to display high-centered double flowers with a classic hybrid tea form. The petals are a blend of red and white. Blooms are borne singly or in small sprays on long stems; they are outstanding when halfway open and may not open further, but last for a remarkably long time at this stage. Leaves are deep green and glossy.

This vigorous miniature is exceptionally attractive as an edging in a rose garden or perennial border, and it also makes a fine container specimen. Flowers are excellent for cutting and exhibition. Plants are quite disease resistant.

'LAFTER'

CLASSIFICATION: hybrid tea

BLOOM PERIOD: summer to fall

HEIGHT: 4 to 5 feet

HARDINESS: Zones 5-10

ARS RATING: not rated

DATE INTRODUCED: 1948

This rose produces semidouble flowers that are a mixture of bright, warm colors; the salmon pink petals are yellow at the base and have an apricot reverse. Each large, fragrant flower is loosely cup shaped; petals surround visible yellow stamens. Leaves are light green and leathery, and canes have red prickles. Bloom begins late in the season and continues in waves.

The plants are vigorous and bushy, with graceful, arching canes. They can be planted in beds and borders or used as a colorful hedge. 'Lafter' is probably the most disease resistant hybrid tea, and it's also hardier than most.

'LA MARNE'

CLASSIFICATION: polyantha

BLOOM PERIOD: spring to fall

HEIGHT: 2 to 4 feet

HARDINESS: Zones 5-10

ARS RATING: 8.3

DATE INTRODUCED: 1915

The delicately fragrant, cup-shaped blooms of 'La Marne' appear continuously throughout the season; it is one of the most profusely blooming roses grown. Semidouble flowers are borne in loose clusters and are blush white with a vivid pink edge; their color deepens in cool weather. Foliage is dense and glossy.

This bushy, vigorous rose is tall for a polyantha. It is happiest in sunny, open locations. The luxuriant foliage and nonstop blooming ability make it a superb choice for a hedge or garden shrub, and it is a fine container specimen as well.

'LAMARQUE'

CLASSIFICATION: noisette

BLOOM PERIOD: summer to fall

HEIGHT: 15 feet

HARDINESS: Zones 7-10

ARS RATING: 8.6

DATE INTRODUCED: 1830

The medium-sized, very double flowers of 'Lamarque' are deliciously fragrant. The petals quarter and are colored white with a touch of lemon yellow at their base; the flowers are nodding, borne on long stems. They are well displayed against abundant light green foliage. Canes bear few prickles.

This vigorous noisette can be maintained as a large free-standing shrub or trained as a voluptuous climber. It's a good choice for warm climates, where it performs best against a sunny wall or similarly sheltered location; neither summer heat nor humidity bothers it. Flowers are perfect for cutting.

'LA REINE VICTORIA'

CLASSIFICATION: bourbon

BLOOM PERIOD: summer to fall

HEIGHT: 4½ to 6 feet

HARDINESS: Zones 6-10

ARS RATING: 7.8

DATE INTRODUCED: 1872

The double blossoms of 'La Reine Victoria' are lilac-pink to deep rose; their color is deeper in bright sun. The flowers have a silky texture and a delicate appearance; they are cupped and rounded, with overlapping, shell-shaped petals. Fragrance is strong and fruity. Flowers are held well above the lush soft green foliage. 'Madame Pierre Oger' is a color sport that bears creamy, flesh-colored blooms but is similar in all other respects.

The plants are slender, upright, and graceful. They make attractive specimens and can be used in beds or borders. Flowers are excellent for cutting. Both 'La Reine Victoria' and its sport are susceptible to black spot.

'LAVENDER LASSIE'

CLASSIFICATION: hybrid musk

BLOOM PERIOD: summer to fall

HEIGHT: 5 to 16 feet

HARDINESS: Zones 6-10

ARS RATING: 7.5

DATE INTRODUCED: 1960

The double flowers of 'Lavender Lassie' range from lilac-pink to pale lavender. They bloom in rather large clusters throughout the summer and repeat into the fall. Flowers are 3 inches across and are very fragrant. Leaves are dark and glossy.

This hybrid musk is more upright than most others in the class. It produces gracefully arching branches that bow under the weight of the abundant flower clusters. Maintain it at about 5 feet as a specimen shrub, plant several and prune them as an informal hedge, or train it as a climber. 'Lavender Lassie' is very vigorous, disease resistant, and tolerant of partial shade.

'LEANDER'

CLASSIFICATION: shrub

BLOOM PERIOD: spring to summer

HEIGHT: 6 to 8 feet

HARDINESS: Zones 4-10

ARS RATING: 8.3

DATE INTRODUCED: 1982

'Leander', a David Austin rose, produces a dizzying profusion of deep-apricot-colored flowers in spring and early summer. Borne in clusters, the blooms are small and very double, and have a fruity fragrance. Although the rose is not considered a repeat bloomer, flowers may reappear later in the season. Semiglossy leaves are medium in both size and color.

This rose has a full habit, growing nearly as wide as it is tall, and makes a fine large garden shrub. It is among the most disease resistant of the English roses.

'LEDA'

CLASSIFICATION: damask

BLOOM PERIOD: summer

HEIGHT: 3 feet

HARDINESS: Zones 4-10

ARS RATING: 7.6

DATE INTRODUCED: before 1827

Flowers of 'Léda' (also called 'Painted Damask') are double, 2½ to 4 inches across, and very fragrant. The buds are reddish brown, opening to reveal milky white to blush pink petals with crimson markings on their edges. The petals reflex to form a ball-shaped bloom. A pink sport of 'Léda' is also available. Leaves of both roses are round, downy, and gray-green.

This is a compact, rounded shrub. It has a neat habit, making it useful in beds and borders. A hardy plant, it prefers cooler climates and languishes where summers are very hot.

'LINDA CAMPBELL'

CLASSIFICATION: hybrid rugosa

BLOOM PERIOD: summer to fall

HEIGHT: 5 feet

HARDINESS: Zones 3-8

ARS RATING: 7.4

DATE INTRODUCED: 1990

This hybrid rugosa produces pointed buds that open to brilliant crimson blooms, an unusual color for this class. The semidouble flowers are slightly lighter in reverse and are borne in clusters of five to 15 blooms. They have no fragrance. Flowers repeat well with as many as six or seven flushes each season. Leaves are large, medium green, and semiglossy. Canes bear fewer prickles than most shrub roses.

Plants are full and bushy with a moderate growth rate; they may reach a height of 5 feet and a width of 8 feet. 'Linda Campbell' is suitable for beds and borders. This rose tolerates heat and seaside conditions and is extremely hardy.

'LINVILLE'

CLASSIFICATION: miniature

BLOOM PERIOD: spring to fall

HEIGHT: 18 to 24 inches

HARDINESS: Zones 5-10

ARS RATING: 7.8

DATE INTRODUCED: 1989

The pointed buds of 'Linville' open to double white flowers that have a touch of pink in them. As the blooms age, they become pure white, although in cool weather they tend to retain their pink tones. High-centered flowers are usually borne singly on long stems and produce a light, fruity fragrance. The leaves are medium green and semiglossy; stems bear straight, pink prickles.

Plants are upright and tall for a miniature, with a medium growth rate. They are useful as edgings, in beds or borders, and as container specimens in a large pot. Flowers are good for cutting and exhibiting.

'LOUISE ODIER'

CLASSIFICATION: bourbon

BLOOM PERIOD: summer to fall

HEIGHT: 4½ to 6 feet

HARDINESS: Zones 5-9

ARS RATING: 8.3

DATE INTRODUCED: 1851

The bright rose pink flowers of 'Louise Odier' are softly shaded with a hint of lilac. They appear abundantly in midseason and repeat well into fall. Blooms are very double and cup shaped, resembling camellias; petals are quartered. Their scent is deliciously rich. Borne in clusters, the heavy flowers may weigh down the branches, creating a graceful, arching effect.

Plants are vigorous and upright with slender canes. A favorite choice in Victorian gardens, 'Louise Odier' makes an elegant shrub, and it can be trained to climb a pillar or post. This rose is hardy and disease resistant.

'LOUIS PHILIPPE'

CLASSIFICATION: China

BLOOM PERIOD: spring to fall

HEIGHT: 4 to 5 feet

HARDINESS: Zones 7-10

ARS RATING: 8.5

DATE INTRODUCED: 1834

The repeating flowers of 'Louis Philippe' are deep crimson to purple with lighter-colored petal edges. Blooms are double, cup shaped, quartered, and pleasantly fragrant. The somewhat sparse foliage is distinctly rounded, and canes bear few prickles.

This rose has a compact, arching form. Rich soil is required for best performance. Its continuous flowering habit makes it a good choice for a container or patio. A tender plant, 'Louis Philippe' tolerates summer heat and humidity well and is disease resistant.

'LOVING TOUCH'

CLASSIFICATION: miniature

BLOOM PERIOD: spring to fall

HEIGHT: 22 to 30 inches

HARDINESS: Zones 5-10

ARS RATING: 8.6

DATE INTRODUCED: 1982

The apricot blooms of 'Loving Touch' are large for a miniature, especially in cool weather. Flowers are double with about 25 petals each and are produced in abundance, mostly one per stem. Each bloom is high centered with a light fragrance. Leaves are medium green and semiglossy. The rose produces pretty, globular hips.

Plants are bushy and spreading, well suited to beds and borders and for use as edgings. They also are beautiful as patio and container plants. Flowers are excellent for cutting and exhibition.

'MADAME ALFRED CARRIERE'

CLASSIFICATION: noisette

BLOOM PERIOD: summer to fall

HEIGHT: 8 to 16 feet

HARDINESS: Zones 6-9

ARS RATING: 8.3

DATE INTRODUCED: 1879

The 3- to 4-inch gardenia-like double blooms of 'Madame Alfred Carrière' are creamy blush white. Produced in clusters on upright stems, flowers are full, loosely formed, and globular, appearing in midseason and repeating well into fall. They are very fragrant. Leaves are large and light green, and canes are thorny.

Like most noisettes, this rose is a climber, and a vigorous one. The nodding habit of the blossoms makes it a good choice for viewing from below, as on a pergola, arch, or wall. It can also be trained as a shrub for a bed or border. Tolerant of partial shade, summer heat, and humidity, it's also fairly disease resistant.

'MADAME HARDY'

CLASSIFICATION: damask

BLOOM PERIOD: late spring to early summer

HEIGHT: 4 to 6 feet

HARDINESS: Zones 4-9

ARS RATING: 9.2

DATE INTRODUCED: 1832

The 2½- to 3½-inch, remarkably fragrant flowers of 'Madame Hardy' are very double and appear in large clusters. Each pale pink bud opens to a cup-shaped ivory blossom that gradually flattens, revealing some 200 intricately folded petals surrounding a green button center. Lime green leaves grow densely along the prickly canes.

The vigorous plant has a bushy, upright habit, but the weight of the flowers often causes the canes to droop. This tendency can be used to advantage by massing three or more bushes to create a billowy mound. Canes can also be tied together or staked for support. The flowers are beautiful in indoor arrangements; gather them before they have fully matured. Plants are very hardy and disease resistant.

'MADAME ISAAC PEREIRE'

CLASSIFICATION: bourbon

BLOOM PERIOD: summer to fall

HEIGHT: 5 to 7 feet

HARDINESS: Zones 5-9

ARS RATING: 8.0

DATE INTRODUCED: 1881

Although the magenta flowers of 'Madame Isaac Pereire' appear throughout summer, they do not reach their peak until fall. Each double bloom is anywhere from 3 to 6 inches across, depending on climate, with quartering petals that are rolled at their edges. The fruity-scented blossoms are possibly the most fragrant of all roses; they may be dried for potpourris. The abundant foliage is large, dark green, and semiglossy.

Plants are bushy with a somewhat spreading habit. They can be grown as free-standing shrubs or pegged; a climbing version that grows to 12 feet can be trained on a trellis or fence. Flowers are superb for cutting. Plants are vigorous, tough, and hardy, and will tolerate poor soil. A color sport of this rose, 'Madame Ernest Calvat', produces pale lavender-pink flowers.

'MADAME LEGRAS DE ST. GERMAIN'

CLASSIFICATION: alba

BLOOM PERIOD: early summer

HEIGHT: 6 to 15 feet

HARDINESS: Zones 4-9

ARS RATING: 8.6

DATE INTRODUCED: 1846

The very double, 3½-inch blooms of 'Madame Legras de St. Germain' are white with a rich, creamy center and bursting with 200 petals. The plants flower once per season and remain in bloom for several weeks, although the blooms don't stand up well to wet weather. Their sweet fragrance is very strong. Soft gray-green foliage provides a lovely foil for the flowers. Canes are nearly smooth.

This rose is a vigorous grower and can be maintained as a 6- to 7-foot shrub or trained on a support, in which case it can reach 12 to 15 feet. Its habit is upright and arching. The plant is well suited to beds, where it combines nicely with perennials. Flowers are good for cutting. It tolerates partial shade and is disease resistant.

'MADAME PLANTIER'

CLASSIFICATION: alba

BLOOM PERIOD: summer

HEIGHT: 5 to 6 feet

HARDINESS: Zones 4-10

ARS RATING: 8.1

DATE INTRODUCED: 1835

The very double blooms of 'Madame Plantier' are creamy white, with a green button eye. Borne in large clusters, the 2½- to 3-inch flowers completely cover the plant in early to midseason; they do not recur. Blooms are somewhat flattened, and they are extremely fragrant. Leaves and stems are a light gray-green.

A vigorous grower, this rose has a spreading, lax, bushy habit suitable for large gardens. As a shrub it can easily spread to 6 feet wide, and it can also be trained to climb a pillar or trellis. 'Madame Plantier' is very hardy as well as disease and shade tolerant.

'MAGIC CARROUSEL'

CLASSIFICATION: miniature

BLOOM PERIOD: summer to fall

HEIGHT: 18 to 24 inches

HARDINESS: Zones 5-10

ARS RATING: 9.0

DATE INTRODUCED: 1972

The semidouble flowers of 'Magic Carrousel' are creamy white and brightly tinged with red. This bold and attractive color combination and the fact that the rose blooms profusely have made it one of the most popular miniatures grown. Each flower is 1¾ to 2 inches across and bears a light scent. Leaves are small, leathery, and glossy.

This miniature rose has a spreading habit and should be pinched back to avoid legginess. It is useful in beds and borders, as an edging, and in containers. Plants are easy to grow and disease resistant. The flowers are frequently used by florists for boutonnieres.

'MAMAN COCHET'

CLASSIFICATION: tea

BLOOM PERIOD: summer to fall

HEIGHT: 3 to 4 feet

HARDINESS: Zones 6-10

ARS RATING: 7.2

DATE INTRODUCED: 1893

The pointed, globe-shaped buds of 'Madam Cochet' open to 4-inch high-centered blossoms. Each double flower consists of 35 to 45 petals that are colored light pink with a lemon yellow base; the flower color deepens in bright sun. Blooms are very fragrant and are nicely set off against leathery deep green foliage. Canes bear few thorns.

This old garden rose is a vigorous grower with an upright, bushy habit. Its attractive foliage and steady production of flowers make it a good choice for beds and borders. It tolerates summer heat and humidity and is disease resistant.

'MARCHESA BOCCELLA'

CLASSIFICATION: hybrid perpetual

BLOOM PERIOD: spring to fall

HEIGHT: 4 to 5 feet

HARDINESS: Zones 5-10

ARS RATING: 8.9

DATE INTRODUCED: 1842

This lovely rose (also known as 'Jacques Cartier') produces large, full flowers in repeat flushes throughout the growing season. Each very double bloom is delicate pink with blush edges. Borne in tight clusters on short, stiff stems, they are very fragrant. The petals are more numerous but smaller than those of most hybrid perpetuals. Foliage is dense and bright green.

One of the finest of the class, this rose is a robust grower with a medium to tall erect form and is somewhat spreading. Its recurring flowering habit and lush foliage are suited to large beds and borders.

'MARCHIONESS OF LONDONDERRY'

CLASSIFICATION: hybrid perpetual

BLOOM PERIOD: spring and fall

HEIGHT: 5 to 8 feet

HARDINESS: Zones 5-9

ARS RATING: 7.0

DATE INTRODUCED: 1893

The huge, fragrant flowers of 'Marchioness of Londonderry' are ivory white with a pale pink to rose pink blush. They open from high-centered buds to cup-shaped, cabbagy double blossoms 4 to 5 inches across. Though not continuous bloomers, the plants produce a fine floral display in spring and fall. Foliage is leathery; canes are nearly thornless.

This hybrid perpetual is a very vigorous grower. The plants have a sturdy, upright habit and are suitable for use in large beds and borders. They can also be trained to a fence or trellis.

'MARGO KOSTER'

CLASSIFICATION: polyantha

BLOOM PERIOD: summer to fall

HEIGHT: 1 to 2 feet

HARDINESS: Zones 5-9

ARS RATING: 8.3

DATE INTRODUCED: 1931

The double blooms of 'Margo Koster' are globular and 1 to 1½ inches across. Borne in sprays, they are somewhat variable in color, ranging from salmon pink to orange. They have little fragrance. Plants commence blooming late in the season and repeat well through fall. A climbing sport is available. Leaves are gray-green and semiglossy. Canes bear few prickles.

This rose is bushy and compact, and is often grown as a container plant for both indoors and outside. It is disease resistant.

'MARIE LOUISE'

CLASSIFICATION: damask

BLOOM PERIOD: late spring

HEIGHT: 4 feet

HARDINESS: Zones 4-10

ARS RATING: 8.0

DATE INTRODUCED: before 1813

The huge, very double blossoms of 'Marie Louise' are so heavy they weigh down the ends of the branches. Flowers are a brilliant mauve-pink with reflexed petals that quarter around a green button eye, and their rich scent hints of lemon. When fully opened, the blooms are somewhat flattened. Foliage is dense, and canes have few prickles.

Plants are bushy and compact, making this a useful shrub for beds, borders, and small gardens. It has a graceful, arching form. Like other damasks, it is quite hardy.

'MARIE PAVIE'

CLASSIFICATION: polyantha

BLOOM PERIOD: spring to fall

HEIGHT: 2 to 3 feet

HARDINESS: Zones 4-9

ARS RATING: 8.1

DATE INTRODUCED: 1888

The long, pointed pink buds of 'Marie Pavié' open to creamy white double flowers. Borne in small clusters, blossoms are 2 inches across and deliciously fragrant. Flowering is profuse throughout the season. Leaves are large and dark green. Canes have no prickles.

'Marie Pavié' is vigorous, upright, and bushy, and is adaptable to many landscape uses: It makes a fine border plant, specimen shrub, low hedge, or container plant. This rose is hardy.

'MAX GRAF'

CLASSIFICATION: hybrid rugosa

BLOOM PERIOD: late spring

HEIGHT: 2 feet

HARDINESS: Zones 3-10

ARS RATING: 7.2

DATE INTRODUCED: 1919

The single blossoms of 'Max Graf' are bright pink with white centers, surrounding prominent yellow stamens. They are borne prolifically in late spring and last for several weeks but do not recur. Blooms are sweet-ly scented, and leaves are rich green, glossy, and leathery.

The value of this hybrid rugosa is in its vigorous, low-growing, spreading habit. It makes an outstanding flowering ground cover that chokes out weeds; its stems root where they come in contact with the ground to spread even further. It is ideal for sunny banks, for cascading over walls, and in front of taller shrubs. It can also be trained to grow along a low fence. 'Max Graf' is extremely hardy.

'MINNIE PEARL'

CLASSIFICATION: miniature

BLOOM PERIOD: summer to fall

HEIGHT: 18 to 24 inches

HARDINESS: Zones 5-10

ARS RATING: 9.4

DATE INTRODUCED: 1982

The double flowers of 'Minnie Pearl' are creamy pink with a light yellow base and a deeper pink reverse. High-centered blossoms are held singly at the end of long stems, making them ideal as cut flowers; they also have a long vase life, further recommending them for this use. Leaves are small, semiglossy, and medium green.

Its small size makes this rose a good choice for edgings or foregrounds of beds and borders, and for containers. It's vigorous and disease resistant.

'MISTER LINCOLN'

CLASSIFICATION: hybrid tea

BLOOM PERIOD: summer

HEIGHT: 4 to 6 feet

HARDINESS: Zones 5-10

ARS RATING: 8.8

DATE INTRODUCED: 1964

'Mister Lincoln' produces 4½- to 6-inch deeply fragrant, cherry red flowers in abundance. Buds are red-black, high centered, and pointed. The flowers have a velvety texture and are very long lasting and nonfading, usually appearing singly on long, sturdy stems. Foliage is medium green and leathery.

This is a robust hybrid tea with an upright, vase-shaped habit. It is at home in beds or borders. The form and keeping quality of its flowers make this an excellent rose for cutting and exhibition. It has greater disease resistance than most red hybrid teas, and performs best when days are warm and nights cool. It's an AARS winner.

'MONSIEUR TILLIER'

CLASSIFICATION: tea

BLOOM PERIOD: spring to fall

HEIGHT: 3½ to 4 feet

HARDINESS: Zones 7-10

ARS RATING: 9.0

DATE INTRODUCED: 1891

The double flowers of 'Monsieur Tillier' are light red to rose pink, shaded and marked with violet-purple and salmon. Petals are intricately arranged to give the bloom a loosely full, ruffled appearance. Flowers are produced freely from early spring through late fall; they bear little fragrance. The foliage is very lush.

Plants are vigorous. Because their stems are thin, they develop a lax, wide-spreading growth habit. With their long flowering season, they add months of color to beds and borders in mild climates. They tolerate slightly alkaline soil and summer heat and humidity, and are fairly hardy for a tea rose.

'MRS. B. R. CANT'

CLASSIFICATION: tea

BLOOM PERIOD: spring to fall

HEIGHT: 4 to 8 feet

HARDINESS: Zones 7-10

ARS RATING: 8.2

DATE INTRODUCED: 1901

The cabbagelike flowers of 'Mrs. B. R. Cant' (also called 'Reine Marie Henriette') are a beautifully colored silvery rose with a deep rose reverse. The blooms are very double, cupped, and richly scented, and appear nonstop throughout the season. They are especially lovely in fall, when cooler weather brings out deep red tones at the edges of the petals. Leaves are more rounded than those of most of this class.

This rose is vigorous with a wide-spreading habit; unless it's pruned it will require a large space. It makes an attractive garden shrub or specimen, and its flowers are excellent for cutting. Summer heat and humidity don't bother it.

'MRS. DUDLEY CROSS'

CLASSIFICATION: tea

BLOOM PERIOD: spring to fall

HEIGHT: 4 to 6 feet

HARDINESS: Zones 7-10

ARS RATING: 8.7

DATE INTRODUCED: 1907

The large pointed buds of 'Mrs. Dudley Cross' open to pale yellow flowers with a pink blush. Appearing in small clusters, the flattened, pleasantly fragrant blooms are 2 to 3 inches across. In fall they often display a crimson tint. Leaves are medium green, and canes have no prickles.

'Mrs. Dudley Cross' is a vigorous grower and is best suited to drier climates. Compact and bushy, the plants are attractive in beds, borders, and hedges. The flowers, which are long-lasting, are excellent for cutting. Plants are tender but disease resistant.

'MUTABILIS'

CLASSIFICATION: China

BLOOM PERIOD: summer to fall

HEIGHT: 3 to 8 feet

HARDINESS: Zones 7-10

ARS RATING: 8.2

DATE INTRODUCED: prior to 1894

The pointed orange buds of 'Mutabilis' open into single blooms that start out sulfur yellow, change to coppery pink, and then deepen to crimson. All three colors can be present on a bush at the same time. Irregularly shaped flowers resemble butterflies, earning the plant the nickname butterfly rose. The flowers are very fragrant. Leaves emerge in an attractive shade of bronze.

If grown beneath the protection of a wall, these vigorous, robust plants are capable of reaching 8 feet in height with a 6 foot spread. In a more open site, plants usually reach only 3 feet. They benefit from regular feeding and abundant watering. 'Mutabilis' tolerates slightly alkaline soil and summer heat and humidity but is fairly tender.

'NASTARANA'

CLASSIFICATION: noisette

BLOOM PERIOD: summer to fall

HEIGHT: 3 to 4 feet

HARDINESS: Zones 6-10

ARS RATING: 8.3

DATE INTRODUCED: 1879

The semidouble blooms of 'Nastarana' are white tinged with pink and appear in large clusters on new wood. Each flower is about 2 inches across and bears a pleasant tea rose fragrance. Flowering repeats well throughout the season. Leaves are smooth, oval, and medium green.

Plants are very vigorous, with an upright habit. They prefer an open, sunny site but are tolerant of partial shade. They also tolerate poor soils, summer heat, and humidity, but may require winter protection. They may be susceptible to mildew and black spot.

'NEARLY WILD'

CLASSIFICATION: floribunda

BLOOM PERIOD: spring to summer

HEIGHT: 2 to 4 feet

HARDINESS: Zones 4-10

ARS RATING: 7.6

DATE INTRODUCED: 1941

The small, tapered buds of 'Nearly Wild' open to rose pink blooms that have five petals and are very fragrant. The flowers occur prolifically along the length of each stem. The main flowering season is spring, but some blooms appear through summer.

The plants are compact and bushy, and are often wider than tall. This rose makes an excellent ground cover for sunny banks; space plants 2½ to 3 feet apart. It can also be planted to cascade down a wall or trained to climb a low fence. Placed in front of taller shrubs, it provides good foreground color, and it makes a fine container specimen. 'Nearly Wild' tolerates slightly alkaline soil and is very hardy.

'NEW DAWN'

CLASSIFICATION: large-flowered climber

BLOOM PERIOD: summer

HEIGHT: 12 to 20 feet

HARDINESS: Zones 5-9

ARS RATING: 7.9

DATE INTRODUCED: 1930

'New Dawn' is a sport of an older climbing rose, 'Dr. W. Van Fleet,' but unlike its parent, it blooms throughout the summer. Plants produce an abundance of 3- to 4-inch semidouble flowers that are shaded a blush pink with a slightly darker center and have bright yellow stamens. They are sweetly scented and are usually borne in large clusters. Leaves are dark green and glossy on prickly canes.

This robust plant is upright and spreading. It is somewhat slow growing, but once established it produces a breathtaking display on pillars, fences, walls, and trellises that is well worth the wait. It can also be grown as a freestanding shrub. 'New Dawn' adapts to partial shade, albeit with fewer flowers, and it is extremely disease resistant.

'NOZOMI'

CLASSIFICATION: climbing miniature

BLOOM PERIOD: summer

HEIGHT: 12 to 18 inches

HARDINESS: Zones 5-10

ARS RATING: 7.9

DATE INTRODUCED: 1968

'Nozomi' produces a bounty of flat, star-shaped, pearly pink to white flowers. The small blossoms occur in clusters and are lightly fragrant. During their single bloom period in midsummer, they cover the entire plant. Leaves are small, glossy, and dense, and canes bear numerous hooked prickles.

This very versatile rose has a trailing habit, rarely exceeding a foot in height but spreading 3 to 5 feet. Planted 2½ feet apart, it can be used as a dense ground cover on a bank or in front of taller shrubs. It also makes a nice addition to a rock garden, can be situated to cascade down a wall, and is lovely when grown in a container. Finally, it can be trained as a climber, or even as a weeping standard.

'OLD BLUSH'

CLASSIFICATION: China

BLOOM PERIOD: summer to fall

HEIGHT: 3 to 5 feet

HARDINESS: Zones 6-10

ARS RATING: 8.3

DATE INTRODUCED: 1752

'Old Blush' produces clusters of dainty blush pink flowers. Each is double, cup shaped, and loosely formed with 24 to 30 petals that deepen in color with age. Their scent is reminiscent of sweet peas. Foliage is a soft green, growing on nearly smooth canes. A climbing form, rated 8.1 by the ARS, grows to 20 feet.

Its bushy, mounding habit makes this rose an attractive addition to beds or borders. It can also be used effectively as a flowering hedge, and it makes an outstanding container specimen. 'Old Blush' requires little pruning and tolerates summer heat and humidity and a range of soils. It is disease resistant as well, but tender.

'OLYMPIAD'

CLASSIFICATION: hybrid tea

BLOOM PERIOD: summer to fall

HEIGHT: 3 to 5 feet

HARDINESS: Zones 5-10

ARS RATING: 9.1

DATE INTRODUCED: 1984

The abundant 4- to 5-inch scarlet blossoms of 'Olympiad' are borne singly or in small clusters on long, sturdy stems. Buds are high centered, opening to velvety-textured double flowers with 30 to 35 petals. They are extremely long-lasting, and their bright color does not fade with age. The flowers have little fragrance. Foliage is distinctively gray-green and semiglossy; canes are prickly.

Plants are vigorous; their compact, bushy, upright habit makes them well suited to beds and borders. The flowers are outstanding for cutting and exhibition. This rose is an AARS winner.

'PAPER DOLL'

CLASSIFICATION: miniature

BLOOM PERIOD: spring to fall

HEIGHT: 18 to 24 inches

HARDINESS: Zones 5-10

ARS RATING: not rated

DATE INTRODUCED: 1992

The light apricot flowers of 'Paper Doll' have a pale pink blush that fades first to light amber and then to white. Each semidouble bloom has 15 to 25 petals and is 1¾ to 2¾ inches across. Occurring in small clusters of three to five, blooms are plentiful throughout the growing season. They have no fragrance. Leaves are small, dark green, and glossy.

Plants are low growing but upright. They can be incorporated into a perennial border, placed in the foreground of a rose bed, or used as an edging or container plant. Their disease resistance is good.

'PARADISE'

CLASSIFICATION: hybrid tea

BLOOM PERIOD: summer to fall

HEIGHT: 4 feet

HARDINESS: Zones 5-10

ARS RATING: 8.3

DATE INTRODUCED: 1978

The long, pointed buds of 'Paradise' open to 3½- to 4½-inch silvery lavender blossoms whose petals are edged with ruby red. Flowers are double and beautifully formed, with 25 to 30 petals curling to create a bull's-eye center. Their fragrance is fruity. Leaves are glossy and dark green.

Plants are medium height and have an upright, well-branched habit. They can be used in beds or borders, where they provide a continuous display of blooms. The flowers are excellent for cutting. 'Paradise' is hardy but may be prone to mildew. It's an AARS winner.

'PARTY GIRL'

CLASSIFICATION: miniature

BLOOM PERIOD: summer to fall

HEIGHT: 12 to 15 inches

HARDINESS: Zones 5-10

ARS RATING: 9.0

DATE INTRODUCED: 1979

'Party Girl' produces long, pointed buds that open into soft apricot-yellow blossoms with high centers. Borne singly or in clusters, each flower is 1 to 1½ inches across and bears a pleasant, spicy fragrance. Leaves are dark green and glossy.

This miniature is bushy and compact—and very versatile. It makes a lovely potted plant, indoors or out, and it's well suited for mixing into perennial borders or for edging a rose or shrub garden. The flowers are outstanding for cutting and exhibition. Plants are hardy and disease resistant.

'PAULII ROSEA'

CLASSIFICATION: shrub

BLOOM PERIOD: summer

HEIGHT: 3 feet

HARDINESS: Zones 4-10

ARS RATING: 8.3

DATE INTRODUCED: prior to 1912

The flowers of 'Paulii Rosea' are single and a clear pink. Their silky-textured petals are deeply notched, pleated, and white at the base, surrounding bright yellow stamens. Flowers, which are lightly fragrant, appear in summer only and do not repeat. Foliage is medium green; young wood is lime colored.

'Paulii Rosea' is low and sprawling, rarely exceeding 3 feet in height but spreading up to 10 or 12 feet. It is useful as a ground cover on sunny slopes or can be trained as a climber on fences and trellises. It prefers an open, sunny site and rich soil, and is susceptible to mildew.

'PAUL NEYRON'

CLASSIFICATION: hybrid perpetual

BLOOM PERIOD: spring and fall

HEIGHT: 3 to 6 feet

HARDINESS: Zones 5-10

ARS RATING: 8.1

DATE INTRODUCED: 1869

The huge, very double blossoms of 'Paul Neyron' are the size of small plates, measuring 4½ to 7 inches across. They are colored pink to rose pink with lilac shading, and the petals are intricately swirled. Flowers are very fragrant and appear in spring and repeat in fall. Foliage is large and matte green, and canes are nearly smooth.

This hybrid perpetual is a strong, vigorous grower with an upright habit. It's a nice choice for beds or borders, and its spectacular blooms are exceptional in indoor arrangements. 'Paul Neyron' is significantly more disease resistant than other roses in this class.

'PEACE'

CLASSIFICATION: hybrid tea

BLOOM PERIOD: summer to fall

HEIGHT: 4 to 6 feet

HARDINESS: Zones 5-10

ARS RATING: 8.6

DATE INTRODUCED: 1945

No two flowers of 'Peace' are exactly alike. Each blossom's color ranges from pale to golden yellow with a pink edging or blush. In cool weather, the pink may be missing entirely. Flowers are double, high centered, 5 to 6 inches across, and mildly fragrant. They are borne singly or in clusters. Leaves are large, glossy, and dark green. Canes are prickly.

The upright, bushy plant is extremely vigorous. It puts on an outstanding show in beds or borders, where its flower color varies pleasantly with temperature and light conditions. Strong stems keep the large flowers from drooping in indoor arrangements. 'Peace' tends to be more disease resistant than other yellow hybrid teas. It is an AARS winner.

'PENELOPE'

CLASSIFICATION: hybrid musk

BLOOM PERIOD: summer to fall

HEIGHT: 5 to 6 feet

HARDINESS: Zones 5-10

ARS RATING: 8.5

DATE INTRODUCED: 1924

The salmon-colored buds of 'Penelope' open to shell pink blooms that fade to white as they age. Borne in huge clusters, the semidouble flowers display bright yellow stamens at their centers. Fragrance is rich and musky. In fall, small coral hips decorate the canes for several weeks. Leaves are glossy, ribbed, and dark green.

Plants are vigorous and dense, and they grow equally tall and wide. This rose is a good choice for a flowering hedge or for combining with other flowering shrubs or perennials in beds. It can tolerate partial shade and is fairly disease resistant, but may be prone to mildew.

'PERLE D'OR'

CLASSIFICATION: polyantha

BLOOM PERIOD: spring to fall

HEIGHT: 3 to 4 feet

HARDINESS: Zones 4-9

ARS RATING: 8.0

DATE INTRODUCED: 1884

'Perle d'Or' produces clusters of small, perfectly formed creamy yellow-orange buds that open to very double salmon to golden pink blossoms. The flowers are fragrant and bloom over a lengthy season. Leaves are a soft, rich green, and canes bear few prickles.

Plants are vigorous, with an upright habit. They are densely leaved and often twice as tall as they are wide. This rose is seldom out of bloom during the growing season. Beautiful in beds and borders, it also makes a fine container specimen. 'Perle d'Or' is hardy.

'PETITE DE HOLLANDE'

CLASSIFICATION: centifolia

BLOOM PERIOD: summer

HEIGHT: 3 to 4 feet

HARDINESS: Zones 4-10

ARS RATING: 7.7

DATE INTRODUCED: 1800

The rose pink double blooms of 'Petite de Hollande' are borne in clusters. Flowers are 1½ inches across and cupped until fully open, when their darker centers become visible. They are sweetly fragrant. In keeping with the dainty scale of the flowers, the glossy, coarsely toothed leaves are also small.

Plants are moderate growers. Bushy and compact, they are ideal for smaller gardens and containers, and are also excellent for training as a standard. This rose is hardy and disease resistant.

'PIERRINE'

CLASSIFICATION: miniature

BLOOM PERIOD: spring to fall

HEIGHT: 15 to 18 inches

HARDINESS: Zones 5-10

ARS RATING: 9.4

DATE INTRODUCED: 1988

The high-centered double flowers of 'Pierrine' are colored medium salmon pink with a lighter reverse. Blossoms are borne singly, and each has about 40 petals. Their fragrance is reminiscent of damask roses. Leaves are medium green and semiglossy, with serrated edges; stems bear light green curved prickles. Hips are round, and range in color from green to orange-yellow.

This plant is a moderate grower with an upright habit. Its diminutive size makes it most useful as an edging or container specimen.

'PINKIE'

CLASSIFICATION: polyantha

BLOOM PERIOD: spring and fall

HEIGHT: 1½ to 3 feet

HARDINESS: Zones 5-10

ARS RATING: 7.9

DATE INTRODUCED: 1947

Flowers of 'Pinkie' have 14 to 16 petals that are rose pink with a salmon blush. These form a cup-shaped 1½- to 2½-inch semidouble blossom. The flowers occur in large clusters in spring and repeat in fall; they are heavily fragrant. Leaves are soft green and glossy.

'Pinkie' is small and bushy, with a width often equal to its height. Useful in the foreground of a bed or border, it also makes a fine container plant. This rose is tolerant of partial shade. A climbing sport, which grows 6 to 12 feet tall, has thornless canes that are easily trained on fences and trellises, although it can also be grown without support as a graceful shrub or hedge with cascading blooms. 'Pinkie' is an AARS winner.

'PLAYBOY'

CLASSIFICATION: floribunda

BLOOM PERIOD: spring to fall

HEIGHT: 3 feet

HARDINESS: Zones 4-10

ARS RATING: 8.1

DATE INTRODUCED: 1976

The burgundy-bronze buds of 'Playboy' open to display large flowers that are a vivid blend of orange, yellow, and scarlet. Each 3½-inch bloom has seven to 10 petals and a yellow eye. Borne in clusters, the flowers are delightfully fragrant and appear all season. In fall, spent blooms produce attractive hips. Foliage is dark and glossy.

'Playboy' is aggressive and easy to grow. The bushes are useful in beds and borders, and the flower sprays are long-lasting both in the garden and when cut for indoor arrangements. This rose is disease resistant and tolerates partial shade.

'PLUM DANDY'

CLASSIFICATION: miniature

BLOOM PERIOD: spring to fall

HEIGHT: 24 inches

HARDINESS: Zones 5-10

ARS RATING: 9.0

DATE INTRODUCED: 1991

The plump, pointed buds of 'Plum Dandy' open to cup-shaped medium lavender flowers that are a lighter shade toward the base of the petals; flowers fade to light lavender with age. Each very double bloom is 1½ to 2 inches across and bears a fruity fragrance. Foliage is medium green and semiglossy.

Plants are moderate growers. They are compact and bushy, with a somewhat spreading habit, and are useful for tucking into small places to add color to a shrub bed or perennial border. They are excellent for containers.

'PRISTINE'

CLASSIFICATION: hybrid tea

BLOOM PERIOD: summer

HEIGHT: 4 to 5 feet

HARDINESS: Zones 5-10

ARS RATING: 9.2

DATE INTRODUCED: 1978

Gardenia-like 'Pristine' blooms are lightly scented and colored a delicate ivory with a fragile pink blush. The long, spiraled buds open to 4- to 6-inch high-centered double flowers, each with 25 to 35 large petals. Flowers usually appear singly on stems but may be clustered; they bloom in midseason and repeat sparsely. Leaves are also large and are attractively colored a glossy reddish green.

Despite their daintily colored flowers, 'Pristine' plants are extremely vigorous, requiring greater space and more rigorous pruning than most other hybrid teas. They are well placed in a bed or border. For cutting, the flowers should be harvested when they are barely open to lengthen their vase life. Plants are tender and very disease resistant.

'PROSPERITY'

CLASSIFICATION: hybrid musk

BLOOM PERIOD: summer to fall

HEIGHT: 5 to 6 feet

HARDINESS: Zones 6-10

ARS RATING: 8.5

DATE INTRODUCED: 1919

The buds of 'Prosperity' are pale pink and open to reveal 1½-inch double ivory flowers that often display a pink blush. The blossoms are fragrant, appear all season in large, heavy clusters, and show off well against the abundant dark, glossy foliage.

This rose is a vigorous grower with an upright habit; its erect canes arch gracefully from the weight of the flowers. The bush can be as wide as it is tall and requires a large space in the garden. It makes a fine flowering hedge and tolerates partial shade.

'PROSPERO'

CLASSIFICATION: shrub

BLOOM PERIOD: spring to fall

HEIGHT: 2 to 2½ feet

HARDINESS: Zones 4-9

ARS RATING: 8.2

DATE INTRODUCED: 1983

The double gallica-like blooms of 'Prospero' open crimson with mauve shadings and mature to a rich purple. Flowers are flat, with small petals perfectly arranged in symmetrical rosettes, and exceptionally fragrant. They begin blooming in spring and repeat well throughout the season. Foliage is a dark matte green. This is a David Austin rose.

'Prospero' has an upright, bushy habit. Its compact size makes it appropriate for small gardens and containers, and the blooms are glorious in arrangements. A somewhat finicky plant, it requires exceptionally good soil for satisfactory growth.

'QUEEN ELIZABETH'

CLASSIFICATION: grandiflora

BLOOM PERIOD: summer to fall

HEIGHT: 4 to 7 feet

HARDINESS: Zones 4-9

ARS RATING: 9.0

DATE INTRODUCED: 1954

The 3½- to 4-inch double flowers of 'Queen Elizabeth' appear in a variety of soft pink shades in great abundance from summer to fall. They are borne singly or in clusters on extremely long stems, opening from pointed buds to lightly scented, cupped flowers. This was the first grandiflora rose introduced, and many consider it to be still the finest. Leaves are leathery, dark green, and glossy; stems are purplish brown and nearly thornless.

The tall, upright, vigorous plant is easy to grow and should not be overpruned. It can be effective planted either alone or in groups in beds or borders, or it may be used as a tall flowering hedge. The long-stemmed flowers are ideal for cutting and exhibition. Plants are disease resistant. This rose is an AARS winner.

'RAINBOW'S END'

CLASSIFICATION: miniature

BLOOM PERIOD: summer to fall

HEIGHT: 10 to 18 inches

HARDINESS: Zones 5-10

ARS RATING: 9.0

DATE INTRODUCED: 1984

'Rainbow's End' produces 1½-inch double flowers that are deep yellow with red petal edges. As the blooms age, they turn completely red. The flowers have the classic hybrid tea form and are nearly scentless. Leaves are small, dark, and glossy.

This miniature rose is upright and well branched, making it an excellent choice for edging a bed or walkway. It can also be incorporated into perennial borders and makes a fine container specimen, indoors or outside. Plants are hardy and disease resistant.

'RED CASCADE'

CLASSIFICATION: climbing miniature

BLOOM PERIOD: spring to fall

HEIGHT: 3 to 12 feet

HARDINESS: Zones 5-10

ARS RATING: 7.2

DATE INTRODUCED: 1976

This miniature climber produces a profusion of 1-inch blossoms that cover the entire length of the plant throughout the growing season. The flowers are double and deep red; petals are white at their base. Leaves are small and leathery, and canes have lots of prickles.

'Red Cascade' is vigorous and versatile. Unsupported, it makes an attractive spreading ground cover, and is very pretty cascading over a wall. Or it can be trained to climb on supports and will reach 12 feet in height in warm climates. This rose is also an excellent container plant, shown to its best advantage when spilling out of a hanging basket or when trained as a standard. It tolerates partial shade.

'REINE DES VIOLETTES'

CLASSIFICATION: hybrid perpetual

BLOOM PERIOD: summer

HEIGHT: 5 to 8 feet

HARDINESS: Zones 5-10

ARS RATING: 8.0

DATE INTRODUCED: 1860

The 3-inch flowers of this hybrid perpetual are very double, opening rosy purple and fading to violet. The undersides of the petals are lighter and silkier than the velvety upper surfaces. Petals are quartered and surround a button eye. The blossoms are borne singly or in small clusters and bear a strong, complex fragrance. Flowers fade quickly after they have fully matured. Foliage is sparse and silvery green; canes are nearly smooth.

This bushy plant grows tall and spreads wide; hard pruning is necessary to maintain a compact habit. The long, flexible canes can be trained to climb. The rose is particularly attractive grown on walls. It requires rich soil to perform at its best.

'REVE D'OR'

CLASSIFICATION: noisette

BLOOM PERIOD: spring to fall

HEIGHT: 8 to 12 feet

HARDINESS: Zones 6-10

ARS RATING: 8.1

DATE INTRODUCED: 1869

The pendulous, globe-shaped flowers of 'Rêve d'Or' are buff yellow with a hint of salmon. Flowers become lighter as they age; stamens are dark yellow. The blooms are loosely double and fragrant. Flowering begins in the spring and recurs intermittently throughout the season. In some areas, flowering is best in fall. Leaves are coppery when young, maturing to a glossy, rich green. Canes bear few prickles.

This rose is a vigorous grower, suitable for a warm, sunny spot in the garden. It has a climbing habit and is a good choice for training on a wall or pillar. It tolerates summer heat and humidity.

'RISE 'N' SHINE'

CLASSIFICATION: miniature

BLOOM PERIOD: summer to fall

HEIGHT: 12 to 16 inches

HARDINESS: Zones 5-10

ARS RATING: 9.1

DATE INTRODUCED: 1977

The 1½- to 2-inch blossoms of 'Rise 'n' Shine' are a bright, clear yellow, providing a dramatic contrast with foliage that is dark and glossy. The buds are long and pointed and open to high-centered flowers with 35 petals. Blossoms are borne singly or in clusters continuously throughout the summer, with a good repeat. They bear little fragrance.

Plants are upright and well branched, forming a short, rounded bush. They are perfect for edgings and containers and can easily be incorporated into beds or borders. They are easy to grow and disease resistant.

'ROBUSTA'

CLASSIFICATION: shrub

BLOOM PERIOD: spring to fall

HEIGHT: 5 to 6 feet

HARDINESS: Zones 6-10

ARS RATING: 8.9

DATE INTRODUCED: 1979

The 2½-inch single scarlet flowers of 'Robusta' are borne prolifically throughout the season on this aptly named plant. The blooms are pleasantly scented. Foliage is dense and very handsome, though also somewhat coarse. The dark green, leathery, glossy leaves provide a rich foil for the blooms. The thick canes are armed with nail-like prickles.

This vigorous rose has a full, bushy habit. It is ideal for use as an impenetrable hedge when plants are spaced 4 feet apart, and it is a good choice for a specimen shrub or for planting along a fence.

'ROGER LAMBELIN'

CLASSIFICATION: hybrid perpetual

BLOOM PERIOD: summer to fall

HEIGHT: 4 feet

HARDINESS: Zones 5-10

ARS RATING: 7.2

DATE INTRODUCED: 1890

The value of 'Roger Lambelin' is in the unique color pattern of its repeating double flowers: Petals are bright crimson edged and streaked with white, so that blooms appear to be wearing petticoats. As they age, the blooms fade to maroon. Each flower has about 30 fringed, velvety-textured petals. They are extremely fragrant.

This vigorous hybrid perpetual has a full, bushy habit. It is finicky, though, requiring very good soil, and is susceptible to both black spot and mildew. 'Baron Girod de l'Ain', a similar rose in this class, has flowers that are a little less richly colored but is a more reliable performer.

ROSA BANKSIAE BANKSIAE

CLASSIFICATION: species

BLOOM PERIOD: spring to early summer

HEIGHT: 12 to 25 feet

HARDINESS: Zones 8-10

ARS RATING: 8.6

DATE INTRODUCED: 1807

The double white flowers of *R. banksiae banksiae* appear in profusion in spring and continue for up to 6 weeks. The flowers cover the plant during this period. Each blossom is less than 1 inch across, pure white, and extremely fragrant with the scent of violets. Leaves are long, light green, and shiny, and the canes are nearly thornless.

Where it is hardy, this rose is a fast, vigorous grower and is quite long-lived. It grows well on a tree, wall, or trellis but may become rampant where the growth is not controlled. The related variety *R. banksiae lutea* bears pale to deep yellow double flowers and is slightly hardier and less fragrant; its ARS rating is 8.8. Both varieties are known as the Lady Banks' Rose.

ROSA EGLANTERIA

CLASSIFICATION: species

BLOOM PERIOD: late spring

HEIGHT: 8 to 14 feet

HARDINESS: Zones 5-10

ARS RATING: 8.6

DATE INTRODUCED: prior to 1551

R. eglanteria is commonly called the sweetbrier or eglantine rose. Its single blush pink flowers are 2 inches across, with petals surrounding golden stamens. They appear singly or in small clusters in late spring. Bright red hips follow the flowers. The leaves are tough and dark green and are distinctly apple scented, while flowers are sweetly fragrant. Canes bear abundant prickles.

This is a large, vigorous rose with a rambling habit. It has become naturalized in North America and can be found growing in pastures. In the garden, plants should be heavily pruned to contain them and to encourage new growth, which is especially fragrant.

ROSA FOETIDA BICOLOR

CLASSIFICATION: species

BLOOM PERIOD: late spring

HEIGHT: 4 to 8 feet

HARDINESS: Zones 5-9

ARS RATING: 8.1

DATE INTRODUCED: prior to 1590

This wild rose also goes by the name 'Austrian Copper'. It is a sport of the yellow species *R. foetida*. Its 2- to 3-inch flowers are orange to coppery red on the upper surface with a yellow reverse. Occasionally a branch spontaneously reverts to the species, resulting in both yellow and copper-colored flowers on the same bush. Foliage is small, neat, and light green; the prickly canes are chestnut brown.

Plants typically grow 4 to 5 feet with arching canes but can sometimes reach 8 feet. They usually require little pruning to maintain their attractive form. The plants are effective in beds or borders for a colorful spring flower display but should be kept apart from soft, pastel flowers, which do not blend well with the bold tones of this variety. This rose is hardy but susceptible to black spot.

ROSA GLAUCA

CLASSIFICATION: species

BLOOM PERIOD: late spring to early summer

HEIGHT: 6 to 7 feet

HARDINESS: Zones 4-9

ARS RATING: 8.9

DATE INTRODUCED: prior to 1830

R. glauca (sometimes listed as *R. rubrifolia*) is grown as much for its attractive foliage as for its flowers. The blooms are single with five medium pink petals with white bases surrounding bright yellow stamens. Leaves are gray-green with distinctive coppery and reddish overtones. Small scarlet hips follow the flowers. Canes are nearly thornless and purple-red.

This rose has a relaxed, rounded, arching habit and provides landscape interest over a very long season. It is useful in a shrub border and makes a fine hedge. Also, cuttings in flower arrangements provide foliage color contrast.

'ROSA MUNDI'

CLASSIFICATION: gallica

BLOOM PERIOD: summer

HEIGHT: 3 to 4 feet

HARDINESS: Zones 4-10

ARS RATING: 8.6

DATE INTRODUCED: prior to 1581

'Rosa Mundi' (*R. gallica versicolor*) is a sport of 'Apothecary's Rose' (*R. gallica officinalis*). Its 2- to 3-inch semidouble flowers are spectacularly striped crimson, pink, and deep pink over blush white. Borne singly or in small sprays, the very fragrant flowers open to wide and flattened cups. An occasional branch will revert to the deep-pink-colored flowers of its parent. Red hips appear in late summer. Leaves are a dark matte green, and stems are nearly smooth.

This upright, bushy rose is very hardy and tolerates summer heat and humidity. It is useful in beds or borders, and its flowers can be used for indoor arrangements and potpourri. This rose is somewhat prone to mildew.

ROSA PALUSTRIS

CLASSIFICATION: species

BLOOM PERIOD: summer

HEIGHT: 4 to 8 feet

HARDINESS: Zones 5-10

ARS RATING: not rated

DATE INTRODUCED: 1726

Also known as the swamp rose, *R. palustris* produces its single dark pink blooms intermittently throughout the summer, providing a longer flowering season than most species roses. Flowers are 2 inches across and are followed by oval hips. Foliage is medium to dark green; stems are reddish.

This rose has an erect, sparse form. Though typically about 4 feet tall, it may reach 8 feet in some areas. It prefers damp, swampy soil but also grows and flowers in poor, dry, sandy soil. It is tolerant of summer heat and humidity and can adapt to partial shade.

ROSA RUGOSA ALBA

CLASSIFICATION: species

BLOOM PERIOD: summer

HEIGHT: 4 to 6 feet

HARDINESS: Zones 3-8

ARS RATING: 9.0

DATE INTRODUCED: 1870

A color sport of *R. rugosa*, *R. rugosa alba* produces large single white flowers throughout the summer. Usually borne in clusters, each bloom is 2½ to 4 inches across and bears a strong clovelike fragrance. The flowers are followed by huge orange-red hips that stand out beautifully against the foliage, which turns from bright green to yellow in the fall. Another rugosa sport, *R. rugosa rubra*, bears magenta-purple flowers and red hips.

This vigorous and spreading rose may outgrow its space unless controlled. It is useful in shrub borders, as a hedge, or as a specimen shrub. An easy-to-grow rose, it thrives in sandy soil, is an excellent choice for seaside gardens, and is extremely hardy and resistant to diseases and insects.

'ROSE DE MEAUX'

CLASSIFICATION: centifolia

BLOOM PERIOD: summer

HEIGHT: 18 to 24 inches

HARDINESS: Zones 3-9

ARS RATING: 7.0

DATE INTRODUCED: 1789

This diminutive rose bears medium pink to light rose pompom-type double blooms in summer, with no repeat. The 1½-inch flowers have frilly petals and are very fragrant. Leaves are also small, in keeping with the overall size of the plant. Canes bear abundant straight prickles.

The plants have an upright, bushy, compact habit. They are useful for small gardens or for tucking into a small space, and are also a good choice for containers. 'Rose de Meaux' requires very good soil and can be somewhat temperamental; it is prone to black spot.

'ROSE DE RESCHT'

CLASSIFICATION: damask

BLOOM PERIOD: summer to fall

HEIGHT: 2 to 3 feet

HARDINESS: Zones 4-10

ARS RATING: 8.6

DATE INTRODUCED: unknown

The bright fuchsia-red blooms of 'Rose du Rescht' display lilac and purple tints and age to magenta-pink. Appearing abundantly in midseason and repeating well, each flower is 2 to 2½ inches across and very double, with about 100 petals. Blooms are borne in small, upright clusters and are intensely fragrant. The abundant medium green leaves have red margins when young.

This rose is short, with a compact and bushy habit. It provides a long season of color in beds or borders, but hard pruning of older plants is necessary to keep the flowers repeating. Plants are quite vigorous and tolerate heat well.

'ROSE DU ROI'

CLASSIFICATION: portland

BLOOM PERIOD: summer to fall

HEIGHT: 3 to 4 feet

HARDINESS: Zones 5-10

ARS RATING: 7.6

DATE INTRODUCED: 1815

The double flowers of 'Rose du Roi' are bright red mottled with violet and purple. Each loosely arranged bloom is 2½ inches across and is rich in fragrance. Flowers appear abundantly in midseason and repeat well. Foliage is pointed, small, and dark green.

Plants are short and spreading with a somewhat straggly form. They provide a long season of heavily perfumed blooms in beds and borders, and are particularly well suited to smaller gardens. 'Rose du Roi' is disease resistant and winter-hardy.

'ROSERAIE DE L'HAY'

CLASSIFICATION: hybrid rugosa

BLOOM PERIOD: spring to fall

HEIGHT: 4 to 6 feet

HARDINESS: Zones 3-8

ARS RATING: 8.1

DATE INTRODUCED: 1901

The long, pointed, scrolled buds of 'Roseraie de l'Hay' open to deep crimson blossoms with cream-colored stamens and age to a magenta pink. Flowers are 4½ to 5 inches across and semidouble, with loosely arranged, folded petals. The blooms are very fragrant. Few hips are produced. Foliage is dense and apple green, with vibrant color in the fall.

Like other hybrid rugosas, this vigorous rose is a tough plant with good disease resistance, and it tolerates a wide range of soils and seaside conditions. Its repeating blooms and attractive foliage make it an excellent choice for mixed-shrub plantings or hedges.

'RUGOSA MAGNIFICA'

CLASSIFICATION: hybrid rugosa

BLOOM PERIOD: spring to fall

HEIGHT: 4 to 6 feet

HARDINESS: Zones 3-9

ARS RATING: 8.3

DATE INTRODUCED: 1905

The deep red-purple to lavender petals of repeat-blooming 'Rugosa Magnifica' surround golden yellow stamens. The fragrant blooms are double and are followed by abundant large orange-red hips. The foliage is dense.

This shrub is a very vigorous grower with a wide-spreading habit. It is good in mixed-shrub plantings, as a specimen, or as a hedge. Like other hybrid rugosas, it is extremely hardy and disease resistant, adapts to a wide range of soils, and tolerates seaside conditions.

'SALLY HOLMES'

CLASSIFICATION: shrub

BLOOM PERIOD: early summer to fall

HEIGHT: 4 to 12 feet

HARDINESS: Zones 5-9

ARS RATING: 8.9

DATE INTRODUCED: 1976

The single blossoms of 'Sally Holmes' are borne in profusion in large, compact clusters. Buds are apricot, opening to creamy white 3½-inch blooms that turn pure white as they mature. Petals surround bright golden stamens. The flowers are delicately fragrant. Foliage is leathery, dark green, and shiny.

This robust rose can be grown as a large mounding shrub with a height of 4 to 6 feet and an equal spread. It makes a dramatic specimen or can be used in a large border. 'Sally Holmes' is also lovely trained as a climber, in which case it can reach 12 feet. Plants are disease resistant and tolerant of heat and partial shade. The blooms are exceptionally long-lasting in indoor flower arrangements.

'SEA FOAM'

CLASSIFICATION: shrub

BLOOM PERIOD: summer to fall

HEIGHT: 2½ to 3 feet

HARDINESS: Zones 4-9

ARS RATING: 8.0

DATE INTRODUCED: 1964

The creamy white flowers of 'Sea Foam' are 2 to 3 inches across and are borne in large clusters throughout the growing season. Buds are rounded, and open to cupped or flat blossoms with short petals that stand out well against the small, dark, glossy leaves. It has a slight fragrance.

The plant is exceptionally versatile, with a vigorous, semi-prostrate or trailing habit that, unless supported, generally does not exceed 2½ or 3 feet in height. Its long, arching canes, however, may spread 8 to 12 feet. 'Sea Foam' can be used in the landscape as a ground cover, a mounded shrub, or as a climber on pillars or walls. Its flowers are delightful for cutting. Plants are easy to grow and quite disease resistant.

'SEXY REXY'

CLASSIFICATION: floribunda

BLOOM PERIOD: spring to fall

HEIGHT: 3 feet

HARDINESS: Zones 4-10

ARS RATING: 9.0

DATE INTRODUCED: 1984

The 2½- to 3½-inch double flowers of 'Sexy Rexy' are carried in large clusters throughout the season. Each mildly fragrant blossom is composed of 40 or more medium to light pink petals. Flowers flatten as they mature. The abundant small leaves are light green and glossy.

This free-flowering rose is vigorous and bushy. It is effective in beds with perennials or in front of taller roses, where it can cover leggy stems. It also makes an attractive low hedge. Plants are very disease resistant.

'SHOWBIZ'

CLASSIFICATION: floribunda

BLOOM PERIOD: summer to fall

HEIGHT: 2½ to 3 feet

HARDINESS: Zones 4-10

ARS RATING: 8.6

DATE INTRODUCED: 1981

The short, pointed buds of 'Showbiz' open to 2½- to 3-inch scarlet flowers. Blooming in large sprays, they are double and loosely cupped, with ruffled petals and bright yellow stamens, and have a slight fragrance. The abundant leaves are dark green and glossy.

This rose is bushy, low, and compact. A fine contribution to beds and borders with its boldly colored blooms and rich foliage, it also can be planted in numbers as an attractive low hedge or mass planting. The flowers are good for cutting, and plants are disease resistant. 'Showbiz' is an AARS winner.

'SILVER MOON'

CLASSIFICATION: large-flowered climber

BLOOM PERIOD: summer

HEIGHT: 15 to 20 feet

HARDINESS: Zones 5-10

ARS RATING: 7.3

DATE INTRODUCED: 1910

The long, pointed yellow buds of 'Silver Moon' open to large creamy white single or semi-double flowers. Borne singly or in clusters, the flowers are 4½ inches across with up to 20 petals that surround golden amber stamens. Blooms do not repeat. Their fragrance is fruity. Foliage is large, dark, leathery, and glossy.

'Silver Moon' is a very vigorous and strong climber, and may reach beyond 20 feet. Effective on a trellis or other support, it is also an ideal rose for training into a tree. Though somewhat shy about flowering, the blooms it does produce are outstanding.

'SIMPLICITY'

CLASSIFICATION: floribunda

BLOOM PERIOD: summer to fall

HEIGHT: 3 to 6 feet

HARDINESS: Zones 4-10

ARS RATING: 8.1

DATE INTRODUCED: 1979

The 3- to 4-inch-wide semi-double flowers of 'Simplicity' are borne in clusters. Each blossom is cupped or flattened, with 18 medium pink petals surrounding yellow stamens that darken with age. Flowers bear little fragrance. Foliage is a fresh light to medium green and is semiglossy.

Bushy and dense with graceful, arching canes, 'Simplicity' is an excellent choice for a hedge; when first introduced it was even marketed as a "living fence." It also works well in beds and borders, and the flowers are good for cutting. Plants are disease resistant.

'SNOW BRIDE'

CLASSIFICATION: miniature

BLOOM PERIOD: summer to fall

HEIGHT: 15 to 18 inches

HARDINESS: Zones 5-10

ARS RATING: 9.3

DATE INTRODUCED: 1982

'Snow Bride' is a prolific bloomer with long, pointed, hybrid-tea-type buds opening to 1½-inch double flowers with high centers. Petals are white with just a hint of yellow, and they surround yellow stamens. Leaves are semiglossy and dark green.

This vigorous miniature is easy to grow. Compact and well branched, it may be used as an edging or incorporated with other plants into a bed or border. 'Snow Bride' is also a perfect container plant. The flowers are excellent for cutting and exhibition.

'SOMBREUIL'

CLASSIFICATION: climbing tea

BLOOM PERIOD: summer to fall

HEIGHT: 8 to 12 feet

HARDINESS: Zones 6-10

ARS RATING: 8.8

DATE INTRODUCED: 1850

The exquisite very double blooms of this rose are creamy white with pale blush tones, and they are deliciously fragrant. Borne in clusters on nodding stems, the blossoms are quartered, 3½ to 4 inches across, and saucer shaped. Unlike many old roses, 'Sombreuil' blooms throughout the growing season. Its leaves are light green and semiglossy, and its canes are thorny.

The plant is a moderately vigorous climber, with pliable canes that are easily trained on a trellis, fence, or wall. Its blooms, often pendulous, occur along the entire length of the cane, making it a good choice for an arbor where it can be viewed from below. Flowers are good for cutting. 'Sombreuil' likes to be fed frequently; it tolerates partial shade and hot summers.

'SOUVENIR DE LA MALMAISON'

CLASSIFICATION: bourbon

BLOOM PERIOD: summer to fall

HEIGHT: 3 feet

HARDINESS: Zones 5-9

ARS RATING: 8.4

DATE INTRODUCED: 1843

The delicate blush pink blossoms of 'Souvenir de la Malmaison' are slightly darker toward the center. They are cupped when they first open but gradually flatten into flowers that are 4 or 5 inches across. As the blooms age they fade slightly to almost white. Flowers are double and quartered, with a rich, spicy fragrance. Foliage is medium green and glossy.

This rose is a bit of a challenge to grow. It thrives in hot, dry weather but does poorly during wet periods, when buds may refuse to open. Dwarf, bushy, and rounded, it is lovely in beds and borders. A climbing form, rated 8.2 by the ARS, reaches 6 to 8 feet and is well suited to growing up a pillar.

'STARINA'

CLASSIFICATION: miniature

BLOOM PERIOD: summer to fall

HEIGHT: 12 to 15 inches

HARDINESS: Zones 6-10

ARS RATING: 9.0

DATE INTRODUCED: 1965

The lightly fragrant, bright orange-scarlet flowers of 'Starina' are touched with yellow at their base. They are double with a classic hybrid tea form; each is 1½ inches across and has about 35 petals. Blooms appear continuously during the season. Foliage is small and glossy.

Plants are upright, bushy, and compact, usually about a foot tall and wide. Exceptional as a uniform edging, they are also attractive in beds and borders with perennials and shrubs, and grow well as container plants.

'SUN FLARE'

CLASSIFICATION: floribunda

BLOOM PERIOD: summer to fall

HEIGHT: 2 to 3 feet

HARDINESS: Zones 4-10

ARS RATING: 8.1

DATE INTRODUCED: 1983

The small, pointed buds of 'Sun Flare' open to 3-inch flat, double blossoms. Colored bright lemon yellow, the flowers have 25 to 30 petals and a licorice fragrance. They are borne freely, mostly in large clusters but sometimes singly. The leaves are very glossy and deep green, providing a dramatic foil for the blooms.

Plants are vigorous, with a round, somewhat spreading-habit. Attractive landscape plants, they are well suited to many purposes, including beds, borders, and hedges. Flowers are good for cutting. 'Sun Flare' is highly disease resistant, a rare trait in a yellow rose. It's an AARS winner.

'SUNSPRITE'

CLASSIFICATION: floribunda

BLOOM PERIOD: spring to fall

HEIGHT: 2½ to 3 feet

HARDINESS: Zones 5-10

ARS RATING: 8.7

DATE INTRODUCED: 1977

The high-centered oval buds of 'Sunsprite' open to deep yellow flowers. Appearing in clusters of five or more, the blossoms are double, each with about 28 petals, and are richly scented. Flowers are borne continuously throughout the season. Foliage is light green and glossy.

This rose has a compact, upright habit. It is suitable for use in beds and borders, where its low growth neatly covers the base of taller, leggier plants. Its flowers are excellent for cutting and exhibition. 'Sunsprite' is disease resistant.

'TAUSENDSCHON'

CLASSIFICATION: rambler

BLOOM PERIOD: summer

HEIGHT: 8 to 12 feet

HARDINESS: Zones 5-10

ARS RATING: 8.5

DATE INTRODUCED: 1906

Produced in enormous loose clusters, the double flowers of 'Tausendschön' have wavy petals that are colored a deep rose pink with a white base. As they age, blooms fade to soft pink, lavender, blush, and white, and all colors may be present on the same cluster. Plants bloom once in the summer, and flowers are lightly fragrant. Leaves are light green and glossy; canes are smooth.

Although 'Tausendschön' grows tall, it is not as rampant as some ramblers. Its long, pliable canes are easily trained to a pillar or fence, but supports that don't allow plenty of air circulation—such as a wall—should be avoided because the rose is prone to mildew. Prune sparingly immediately after it flowers.

'THE FAIRY'

CLASSIFICATION: polyantha

BLOOM PERIOD: summer to fall

HEIGHT: 1½ to 3 feet

HARDINESS: Zones 4-9

ARS RATING: 8.7

DATE INTRODUCED: 1932

'The Fairy' produces large clusters of small buds that open to ruffled light pink blooms. The cupped, double flowers fade to almost white under the summer sun. They have no scent but are produced in abundance. Foliage is bright green and glossy.

This easy-to-grow, vigorous rose has a compact, spreading habit. Usually wider than it is tall, it is useful as a ground cover or in beds or borders in front of taller shrubs. Also, its nonstop bloom makes it a good choice for a low flowering hedge, and its small size is suitable for containers. Flowers are long-lasting when cut. The plant is extremely disease resistant and tolerates both heat and humidity. A climbing sport of this rose grows 8 to 12 feet high.

'THERESE BUGNET'

CLASSIFICATION: hybrid rugosa

BLOOM PERIOD: summer

HEIGHT: 5 to 6 feet

HARDINESS: Zones 3-9

ARS RATING: 8.2

DATE INTRODUCED: 1950

The long, lilac buds of 'Thérèse Bugnet' open to rose red flowers that fade to pale pink with age. Blooms are 4 inches across and double, with 35 petals, and have a moderately spicy scent. Foliage is gray-green with a quilted appearance; the leaves provide a particularly attractive foil for the colorful flowers.

This vigorous hybrid rugosa is large and shrubby—usually equal in height and width—and perfect for use as a tall, flowering hedge. It is disease resistant, hardy, and tolerant of seaside conditions.

'TIFFANY'

CLASSIFICATION: hybrid tea

BLOOM PERIOD: summer to fall

HEIGHT: 4½ feet

HARDINESS: Zones 5-10

ARS RATING: 8.3

DATE INTRODUCED: 1954

Long and pointed, the buds of 'Tiffany' have a beautiful, classic form; they open to 4- to 5-inch double blossoms whose soft rose pink petals blend to yellow at their base. Flowers are produced singly and in clusters over a long season; they are high centered and bear a strong, sweet, fruity fragrance. The foliage is dark green and glossy.

'Tiffany' is vigorous and easy to grow. Tall and upright in habit, it is effective in beds and borders and makes an exceptional, long-lasting cut flower. Performing best in warm climates, it is more disease resistant than most hybrid teas. This is an AARS winner.

'TOUCH OF CLASS'

CLASSIFICATION: hybrid tea

BLOOM PERIOD: summer to fall

HEIGHT: 4 feet

HARDINESS: Zones 5-10

ARS RATING: 9.5

DATE INTRODUCED: 1984

'Touch of Class' produces spiraled orange buds whose color takes on coral and cream shading as they open and eventually evolves to pink. Flowers are 4½ to 5½ inches across and double. They have little or no fragrance. Usually borne singly on long stems, the blooms are attractively set off against dark green, semiglossy foliage.

This rose has a tall, upright, bushy habit. It is well suited to beds and borders, where it produces its flowers over a lengthy season. The long-stemmed blooms are long-lasting in indoor arrangements. Foliage is prone to mildew. 'Touch of Class' is an AARS winner.

'TOURNAMENT OF ROSES'

CLASSIFICATION: grandiflora

BLOOM PERIOD: spring to fall

HEIGHT: 4 to 6 feet

HARDINESS: Zones 5-10

ARS RATING: 8.0

DATE INTRODUCED: 1989

The flowers of 'Tournament of Roses' are shades of pink and beige with a darker pink reverse that fades to coral pink with age. The double blooms are high centered, 4 inches across, and lightly fragrant. They usually appear in small sprays of three to six flowers. Leaves are large, glossy, and dark green, and canes bear large prickles.

This rose is moderately vigorous and has an upright habit. It performs best maintained as a 5-foot shrub, although it will grow taller if allowed, and is suitable for beds and borders. Flowers are borne freely and are long-lasting, but may not be ideal for cutting because stems can be short or weak. It is highly disease resistant. This is an AARS winner.

'TROPICANA'

CLASSIFICATION: hybrid tea

BLOOM PERIOD: summer to fall

HEIGHT: 4 to 5 feet

HARDINESS: Zones 5-10

ARS RATING: 7.9

DATE INTRODUCED: 1960

The 4- to 5-inch double flowers of 'Tropicana' are a bright orange-red and fruity with fragrance. Buds are very large and pointed. Borne singly, the blooms are high centered, becoming cup shaped as they mature. They appear over a lengthy season, and their color holds up well even in hot weather. Foliage is glossy and dark green.

Plants are vigorous, upright, and bushy. The vibrant color of its flowers can be stunning in beds and borders but is difficult to blend with soft pastel shades. The blooms are excellent for cutting. Plants are prone to mildew. 'Tropicana' is an AARS winner.

'TUSCANY'

CLASSIFICATION: gallica

BLOOM PERIOD: spring

HEIGHT: 3 to 4 feet

HARDINESS: Zones 4-10

ARS RATING: 7.7

DATE INTRODUCED: prior to 1820

The large semidouble flowers of 'Tuscany' are dark crimson to deep purple with a velvety texture. Petals are flat and are arranged around prominent yellow stamens, creating a dramatic contrast. Although very fragrant, the flowers are not as heavily scented as some gallicas. They appear in abundance in spring and do not repeat. Leaves are small and dark green.

The vigorous plants have a tidy, rounded form and are well suited to small gardens. The intense colors of the flowers make them spectacular in bloom. They are winter-hardy and tolerant of summer heat and humidity.

'UNCLE JOE'

CLASSIFICATION: hybrid tea

BLOOM PERIOD: summer to fall

HEIGHT: 5 feet

HARDINESS: Zones 5-10

ARS RATING: 7.7

DATE INTRODUCED: 1971

'Uncle Joe' (sometimes listed as 'Toro') bears its 6-inch-wide double blooms singly on long stems. The buds open slowly to become high-centered medium to dark red flowers with a strong fragrance. The large, leathery leaves are a glossy dark green.

Plants are vigorous growers with a tall, upright habit. Their stems are quite strong and amply able to hold up the huge blossoms. This rose is suitable for beds and borders and is excellent for cutting. Cool, damp weather may stunt the production of flowers.

'VARIEGATA DI BOLOGNA'

CLASSIFICATION: bourbon

BLOOM PERIOD: summer

HEIGHT: 5 to 8 feet

HARDINESS: Zones 5-9

ARS RATING: 7.6

DATE INTRODUCED: 1909

No two flowers of 'Variegata di Bologna' are exactly alike in coloration: Petals are white and individually striped with various shades of crimson and purple. The double blooms are 3 to 4 inches wide and globular, flattening and quartering with age. Borne in clusters of three to five, the blossoms bear a strong and long-lasting fragrance. They appear in abundance in midseason but repeat sparsely, if at all. Leaves are narrow and glossy; canes are nearly smooth.

The bushes are vigorous, upright, and slender, and are versatile in the landscape. Their long, flexible canes are easily trained to climb a fence, trellis, or pillar, or can be pegged. Heavy pruning will produce a more compact, 4- to 5-foot shrub suitable for borders. Flowers are good for cutting.

'VEILCHENBLAU'

CLASSIFICATION: rambler

BLOOM PERIOD: late spring

HEIGHT: 10 to 15 feet

HARDINESS: Zones 5-9

ARS RATING: 7.9

DATE INTRODUCED: 1909

'Veilchenblau' produces large clusters of cupped semidouble flowers whose violet color is about as close to blue as any rose has come; in fact, it is sometimes referred to as the blue rose. Petals are streaked with white, especially near the center, where golden stamens are prominent. As they age, the blooms fade to blue-gray. Their fragrance is long-lasting and fruity. In some areas flowers repeat in summer. Foliage is light green and glossy. Canes bear very few prickles.

This vigorous plant can be trained to climb a pillar, fence, or trellis for an outstanding display. It can also be pruned to maintain a loose, open shrub. It is drought resistant and tolerates partial shade. In partially shaded sites the flower color remains intense without fading.

'WHITE MEIDILAND'

CLASSIFICATION: shrub

BLOOM PERIOD: summer to fall

HEIGHT: 2 to 2½ feet

HARDINESS: Zones 4-9

ARS RATING: 8.3

DATE INTRODUCED: 1986

Clusters of small, double, pure white flowers cover the plant of 'White Meidiland' from early summer through fall. They are enhanced by a background of dark green, glossy leaves; canes are not visible through the dense foliage.

This rose is vigorous and very easy to grow. It has a low, spreading habit and is often twice as wide as it is tall, making it useful as a ground cover, especially on sunny banks. If used for this purpose, plants should be spaced 4 feet apart. 'White Meidiland' is hardy and pest and disease resistant, and requires little pruning.

'WHITE PET'

CLASSIFICATION: polyantha

BLOOM PERIOD: spring to fall

HEIGHT: 2 feet

HARDINESS: Zones 5-9

ARS RATING: 7.2

DATE INTRODUCED: 1879

'White Pet' is a profuse bloomer with small, creamy white buds touched with carmine that open to rosette-type double flowers. Appearing in large clusters, the flowers are borne continuously throughout the season and are well displayed against abundant dark green foliage.

Plants are small and round, up to 2 feet with an equal spread. Their neat form and free-flowering nature make them good candidates for edging or for incorporating into beds or borders. 'White Pet' is also perfectly suited to growing in containers and is a good source of flowers for cutting.

'WILLIAM BAFFIN'

CLASSIFICATION: shrub

BLOOM PERIOD: summer to fall

HEIGHT: 5 to 10 feet

HARDINESS: Zones 3-9

ARS RATING: 9.4

DATE INTRODUCED: 1983

This kordesii shrub, one of the Explorer series, produces clusters of up to 30 deep pink blooms over a lengthy season. Each loosely arranged, semidouble blossom is 2 to 3 inches across. Blooms have little or no fragrance. Foliage is medium green and glossy.

'William Baffin' is robust and upright, with arching canes. Versatile in the landscape, it can be grown as a climber with a spread equal to its height or as a stunning large hedge, or it can be pruned as a border shrub. The canes can also be trained to sprawl on the ground for use as a ground cover. One of the hardiest roses available, it is disease resistant as well.

'WILL SCARLET'

CLASSIFICATION: hybrid musk

BLOOM PERIOD: spring and fall

HEIGHT: 6 to 12 feet

HARDINESS: Zones 5-10

ARS RATING: 8.2

DATE INTRODUCED: 1947

The bright red buds of 'Will Scarlet' open to vivid rose red semidouble flowers that lighten in color toward the flower center. Hot weather tends to induce shades of lilac at the center, which makes an especially pleasing contrast with the flowers' numerous yellow stamens. The flowers are delicately scented. Plants bloom profusely in spring and again in fall. The blooms are followed by clusters of round orange hips.

This rose can be grown as a large shrub, best maintained at 6 to 7 feet with a nearly equal spread. It is also a fine climber, reaching up to 12 feet on a trellis or pillar. It has a graceful, arching form, and it tolerates partial shade.

'ZEPHIRINE DROUHIN'

CLASSIFICATION: bourbon

BLOOM PERIOD: spring to fall

HEIGHT: 8 to 20 feet

HARDINESS: Zones 5-10

ARS RATING: 7.9

DATE INTRODUCED: 1868

The semidouble cerise-pink flowers of 'Zéphirine Drouhin' are 3½ to 4 inches across and are loosely formed. Borne in profusion in spring, they continue to appear intermittently until fall, when the plant once again flowers heavily. Blooms are very sweetly scented. Young leaves are a coppery purple, maturing to dark green, and the canes are smooth.

'Zéphirine Drouhin' is a vigorous grower with an upright, semiclimbing habit. It can be pruned as a shrub placed in a large border or displayed as a specimen, and it makes a fine formal hedge. Or, train it as a climber on a trellis, fence, or porch, where it may grow as high as 20 feet. The lack of prickles makes it a good choice for planting near walkways or play areas.

Ground Covers and Vines

IN RECENT YEARS, MORE AND MORE GARDENERS are discovering that ground covers are the perfect alternative to traditional lawns. Once established, these creeping or low-growing plants demand little of our attention. And they work wonders in difficult sites where other plants perish, such as rocky slopes or shady spots under trees.

But ground covers do more than just cover the ground. A huge and diverse group ranging from colorful, ground-hugging perennials to spreading, low-growing evergreen shrubs, they can define or unify parts of the landscape. Even vines—commonly trained to climb trellises, arbors, or walls—make attractive ground covers. There's no end to the ways you can use these versatile plants to add beauty and interest to the garden. Using a combination of different ground covers and vines, you can create a stunning scene of varying heights, colors, and textures. The plant descriptions presented in this section will help you select the species that best match your plans and growing conditions.

Ajuga (a-JOO-ga)

BUGLEWEED

Ajuga reptans 'Burgundy Glow'

HARDINESS: Zones 3-9

PLANT TYPE: ground cover

HEIGHT: 3 to 12 inches

INTEREST: foliage, flowers

SOIL: well-drained

LIGHT: bright full shade to full sun

A reliable ground cover for areas where grass will not grow, bugleweed forms a thick mat of crinkled, often colorful foliage ideal for banks, bulb beds, rock gardens, and under trees. Flowers appear in spikes in spring or early summer.

Selected species and varieties
A. genevensis (Geneva bugle)—blue, pink, or white spring flowers on erect 6- to 12-inch stems atop green leaves; Zones 4-9. *A. pyramidalis* (pyramid bugle)—blue flowers 4 to 6 inches tall, less invasive than other species; Zones 3-9; 'Metallica Crispa' [also listed as 'Crispa'] has iridescent purplish bronze wrinkled leaves and blue flowers. *A. reptans* (carpet bugle)—a fast spreader 4 inches tall with 10-inch flower stems in spring; Zones 3-8; 'Bronze Beauty' has bronze-purple leaves and blue flowers; 'Burgundy Glow', green, white, and pink variegated leaves with blue or purple flowers in spring.

Growing conditions and maintenance
Bugleweed grows well in almost any soil. For complete cover in one growing season, plant *A. reptans* in well-drained acid loam about 6 inches apart. This species may become invasive.

Akebia (a-KEE-bee-a)

CHOCOLATE VINE

Akebia quinata

HARDINESS: Zones 4-8

PLANT TYPE: ground cover or vine

HEIGHT: 20 to 40 feet

INTEREST: foliage, fruit

SOIL: well-drained

LIGHT: full shade to full sun

Akebia is equally good at covering ground or walls, quickly twining around anything close at hand. With its semi-evergreen foliage, it offers multiseason interest to the landscape. Fruit pods, usually a bright, rich purple, dangle abundantly from the plant in fall; in the spring, small fragrant flowers peep out from the new foliage. A good choice for a trellis or pergola, akebia can also provide quick cover of an eyesore in the landscape.

Selected species and varieties
A. quinata (five-leaf akebia)—attractive, dark blue-green compound leaves with five leaflets, each to 3 inches long, nearly masking dark purple fragrant flower racemes that are hard to see from a distance, followed by purple fruit pods up to 4 inches long that ripen in late summer and leaves that usually hold their color until the first hard freeze.

Growing conditions and maintenance
A tough, vigorous plant, akebia tolerates nearly any growing conditions and can easily choke out other plants. Pruning is required to keep it under control.

Alchemilla (al-kem-ILL-a)

LADY'S-MANTLE

Alchemilla mollis

HARDINESS: Zones 3-8

PLANT TYPE: ground cover

HEIGHT: 4 to 18 inches

INTEREST: foliage

SOIL: moist, well-drained

LIGHT: partial shade to full sun

Lady's-mantle forms sprawling mats of round, deeply veined, cupped leaves with softly downy undersides that are attractive as a coarse-textured seasonal ground cover or at the front of the border. Frothy clusters of tiny flowers rise on stiff stalks in summer.

Selected species and varieties
A. alpina—dwarf species forms mats of silver-edged foliage only about 6 inches tall with inconspicuous spring-to-summer-blooming chartreuse flowers. *A. conjuncta*—has pale green ⅛-inch flowers and star-shaped green leaves edged with silver. *A. mollis*—mats of broad gray-green leaves grow up to 10 inches high with clusters of yellow flowers from spring to summer on stems to 18 inches tall.

Growing conditions and maintenance
Plant lady's-mantle 1½ feet apart and provide partial shade in hot climates. Propagate from seed, by division, or by transplanting self-sown seedlings.

Aristolochia (a-ris-to-LO-kee-a)

DUTCHMAN'S-PIPE

Aristolochia macrophylla

HARDINESS: Zones 4-8

PLANT TYPE: vine

HEIGHT: 30 feet

INTEREST: foliage

SOIL: moist, well-drained

LIGHT: partial to bright full shade

Dutchman's-pipe is a vigorous twining vine with glossy dark green heart-shaped deciduous leaves up to 10 inches long. Hidden in the overlapping foliage are dark flowers that look like small pipes with fluted edges. Valued for its fast growth, aristolochia has long been used for shading a porch, covering a trellis for privacy, or concealing an unsightly wall.

Selected species and varieties
A. macrophylla [also classified as *A. durior*] (pipe vine)—has 4- to 10-inch heart- or kidney-shaped leaves masking purplish brown, yellow-throated flowers in early summer.

Growing conditions and maintenance
Aristolochia does well in bright to medium or partial shade. It tolerates any average garden soil but performs with more vigor if compost is applied to its base in spring. Water during droughts. New plants need training during the first year.

Artemisia (ar-tem-IS-ee-a)

WORMWOOD, ARTEMISIA

Artemisia schmidtiana 'Silver Mound'

HARDINESS: Zones 3-7

PLANT TYPE: ground cover

HEIGHT: 4 to 18 inches

INTEREST: foliage

SOIL: well-drained to dry, poor

LIGHT: full sun

Artemisias are primarily grown for their aromatic, silvery gray foliage. The fine texture and subdued color of the foliage complement other plants in the border, and they are particularly useful for separating and blending colors. The lower-growing types are suited to rock gardens or the front of beds.

Selected species and varieties
A. schmidtiana—12 to 18 inches tall and wide with a neat, mounding habit and twice-divided fernlike foliage covered with silvery white hairs that give the plant a velvety texture. Flowers are inconspicuous; 'Silver Mound' grows 4 to 10 inches tall and 12 inches wide with silvery gray, aromatic leaves showing a blue-green undertone and is effectively planted near spring bulbs, where it develops as the bulb foliage dies back; Zones 3-7.

Growing conditions and maintenance
Space plants 1 foot apart in the garden. Humid conditions may cause them to rot; good drainage is critical, especially in winter. Trim just prior to flowering to encourage a compact habit, and remove flowers as they form to encourage abundant leaf growth.

Asarum (a-SAR-um)

WILD GINGER

Asarum europaeum

HARDINESS: Zones 4-8

PLANT TYPE: ground cover

HEIGHT: 5 to 10 inches

INTEREST: foliage, fragrance

SOIL: moist, fertile

LIGHT: full shade

The low-growing perennial wild gingers—particularly the evergreen forms—make good ground covers for medium to deep shade. The small, dark spring flowers are mostly insignificant, hidden beneath the foliage. Rhizomes and crushed leaves carry a ginger fragrance.

Selected species and varieties
A. canadense (snakeroot, Canadian wild ginger)—mat-forming, 7 or more inches tall, with heart-shaped 3- to 7-inch-wide deciduous leaves that are reddish hued in spring, then turn bronze-green. *A. europaeum* (European wild ginger)—5 to 10 inches tall, with evergreen leaves 2 to 3 inches wide; Zones 4-7. *A. hartwegii* (Sierra wild ginger)—marbled evergreen leaves 1½ to 5 inches long; hardy to Zone 5. *A. shuttleworthii* [also listed as *Hexastylis shuttleworthii*] (mottled wild ginger)—8 inches tall with evergreen leaves that are usually mottled with silver.

Growing conditions and maintenance
Wild ginger needs slightly acid, humus-rich soil and protection from direct sun. *A. canadense* can also grow in slightly calcareous or limy soils. Propagate by division or from root cuttings.

Astilbe *(a-STIL-bee)*

FALSE SPIREA

Astilbe chinensis 'Pumila'

HARDINESS: Zones 4-8

PLANT TYPE: ground cover

HEIGHT: 8 inches to 4 feet

INTEREST: flowers, foliage

SOIL: moist, well-drained, fertile

LIGHT: partial shade to full sun

Astilbe's feathery spikes appear on stiff stems above mounds of glossy, fernlike foliage. Astilbes are excellent as a border filler or massed as a ground cover in a partly shaded bed.

Selected species and varieties
A. x *arendsii* (garden spirea)—2- to 4-foot-tall flower spikes in white, pink, rose, red, coral, and lilac over clumps of foliage; 'Fanal' is an early bloomer, 24 inches tall, with deep red flowers and bronze leaves, and produces the darkest red of astilbe flowers. *A. chinensis* 'Pumila' (dwarf Chinese astilbe)—8 to 15 inches tall with spreading habit and mauve pink flowers in mid- to late summer; *A.* var. *taquetii* 'Purple Lance' (fall astilbe)—4 feet tall with purple-red blooms.

Growing conditions and maintenance
Plant astilbes 1½ to 2 feet apart in moist soil, preferably in a cool location. Water well and mulch if in full sun. Propagate by division every 3 or 4 years in spring or early summer.

Bergenia *(ber-JEN-ee-a)*

BERGENIA

Bergenia cordifolia

HARDINESS: Zones 3-8

PLANT TYPE: ground cover

HEIGHT: 12 to 18 inches

INTEREST: foliage, flowers

SOIL: moist, well-drained

LIGHT: full sun to partial shade

Striking foliage and flowers make bergenia a standout in perennial beds and edgings. Slowly creeping by rhizomes, it is effective when used to cover small areas or planted in masses along the edge of a stream. The cabbagelike leaves are evergreen in warmer climates and sometimes turn burgundy in winter.

Selected species and varieties
B. cordifolia (heartleaf bergenia, pig squeak)—deep pink, pale pink, or white flower racemes borne just above the 12- to 18-inch clump of puckered, leathery heart-shaped leaves, up to 12 inches long, with saw-toothed edges. *B. crassifolia* (leather bergenia, Siberian tea, winter begonia)—fleshy oval or spoon-shaped leaves, smaller than those of heartleaf bergenia, and spikes of lavender-pink flowers held well above the foliage, hardy to Zone 4; 'Redstar' produces rose-purple flowers and reddish winter foliage.

Growing conditions and maintenance
Bergenia tolerates any well-drained soil but maintains the best foliage color in poor soil. Provide afternoon shade in hot climates. After several years, divide plants in early spring to rejuvenate.

Bignonia *(big-NO-nee-a)*

CROSS VINE

Bignonia capreolata

HARDINESS: Zones 6-9

PLANT TYPE: vine

HEIGHT: 30 to 50 feet

INTEREST: flowers, foliage

SOIL: moist, well-drained

LIGHT: full sun to shade

A rapidly growing plant, cross vine is graced in the spring with clusters of large, trumpet-shaped flowers that are dark orange on the outside and yellow-orange on the inside. In summer, this Southeast native produces slender, 4- to 6-inch flattened fruit that turns from green to brown. Cross vine's attractive, 2- to 6-inch, dark green compound leaves are borne in pairs, along with clasping tendrils with which the vine attaches itself to trees, fences, trellises, or buildings.

Selected species and varieties
B. capreolata (cross vine, trumpet flower)—30 to 50 feet with lustrous, thinly spaced, semi-evergreen to evergreen leaves that turn reddish purple in cold weather. The flowers, borne in clusters of two to five, are 2 inches long and 1½ inches wide, and lightly mocha-scented; 'Atrosanguinea' has more narrow, dark purple-red flowers tinted with brown or orange-red, and longer, narrower leaves than the species.

Growing conditions and maintenance
Cross vine produces more abundant flowers and leaves in full sun. It thrives in all but excessively wet or dry soil. Propagate by seed or cuttings.

Brunnera (BRUN-er-a)

BRUNNERA

Brunnera macrophylla 'Variegata'

HARDINESS: Zones 4-9

PLANT TYPE: ground cover

HEIGHT: 1 to 2 feet

INTEREST: foliage, flowers

SOIL: moist, well-drained

LIGHT: light shade to full sun

Brunnera forms compact mounds of broad, heart-shaped leaves topped by frothy clusters of tiny flowers. The deeply textured foliage spreads into an informal ground cover beneath trees, among newly planted shrubs, or paired with spring bulbs.

Selected species and varieties
B. macrophylla (Siberian bugloss)—¼-inch deep blue spring-blooming flowers with prominent yellow eyes above deep green leaves; 'Langtrees' has silver-speckled foliage; 'Variegata', leaves edged in yellow or cream.

Growing conditions and maintenance
Plant brunnera in soils enriched with organic matter. Plants need constant moisture in full sun. Propagate from seed, by division in spring or fall, or by transplanting self-sown seedlings.

Calluna (ka-LOO-na)

HEATHER, LING

Calluna vulgaris 'Corbett's Red'

HARDINESS: Zones 4-7

PLANT TYPE: ground cover

HEIGHT: 24 inches

INTEREST: flowers, form

SOIL: moist, well-drained, acid, sandy

LIGHT: full sun to partial shade

Scotch heather produces a sea of wavy bloom when its tiny spikes of urn-shaped flowers begin blooming in midsummer. Minute, scalelike, evergreen leaves are closely pressed to dense colonies of floating stems and may turn bronze in winter. Let this fine-textured plant form a thick mat in sunny locations where ground cover is needed, or tuck it into rock gardens and edgings.

Selected species and varieties
C. vulgaris (Scotch heather)—variable height up to 2 feet, spreading 2 feet or more, and bearing purplish pink flower clusters up to 1 foot long until fall; 'Else Frye' has double white flowers and reaches 18 inches; 'H. E. Beale' grows 2 feet high with silvery pink flowers; 'Mrs. Ronald Gray', 4 inches high with reddish flowers.

Growing conditions and maintenance
Heathers grow best in loam of low fertility. Good drainage is critical. Plant in full sun for best flowering and protect from drying winds. Mulch to conserve moisture, and water during dry spells. Prune faded flowers and stem tips to reduce legginess.

Campanula (kam-PAN-ew-la)

BELLFLOWER

Campanula portenschlagiana

HARDINESS: Zones 3-9

PLANT TYPE: ground cover

HEIGHT: 4 to 12 inches

INTEREST: flowers, foliage

SOIL: moist, well-drained

LIGHT: full sun to partial shade

The Dalmatian and Serbian bellflowers, which are small with delicate blue flowers, are actually quite vigorous and well suited for rock gardens, dry walls, or the front of a border. They have a creeping, spreading habit and form attractive clumps of neat foliage. The flowers appear in sprays above the leaves.

Selected species and varieties
C. portenschlagiana (Dalmatian bellflower)—4 to 8 inches tall, spreading, with rounded, sharply serrated leaves and star-shaped, lilac-blue flowers blooming from late spring to early summer; hardy to Zone 5. *C. poscharskyana* (Serbian bellflower)—8 to 12 inches tall, up to 18 inches wide, with midsummer-blooming lilac flowers and roots that may become invasive; hardy to Zone 4.

Growing conditions and maintenance
Both species thrive when grown among rocks or cascading over walls. In warmer zones, they benefit from partial shade and supplemental moisture.

Cardiospermum (kar-dee-o-SPER-mum)

BALLOON VINE

Cardiospermum halicacabum

HARDINESS: Zones 9-11

PLANT TYPE: vine

HEIGHT: 8 to 12 feet

INTEREST: fruit, foliage

SOIL: light, well-drained

LIGHT: full sun

Native to India, Africa, and tropical America, balloon vine has become naturalized in parts of the southern United States. It produces tiny white summer flowers followed by green balloonlike seedpods that seem to float among the feathery leaves. Climbing by hooklike tendrils, it grows rapidly and is useful for providing a temporary screen or for covering a fence or trellis.

Selected species and varieties

C. halicacabum (balloon vine, love-in-a-puff, heart pea, winter cherry) produces attractive doubly compound leaves and ¼-inch white flowers with four petals and four sepals. Pods are green, 1 to 1½ inches across, and contain black pea-like seeds, each with a heart-shaped white spot.

Growing conditions and maintenance

Start seed indoors 6 weeks prior to the last frost; in Zones 8 and warmer plant often reseeds. Transplant outdoors in late spring, allowing 12 to 14 inches between plants. Plants thrive in warm weather and tolerate drought. Provide support for climbing; perennial in Zones 9 to 11.

Ceratostigma (ser-at-o-STIG-ma)

PLUMBAGO, LEADWORT

Ceratostigma plumbaginoides

HARDINESS: Zones 5-10

PLANT TYPE: ground cover

HEIGHT: 8 inches to 4 feet

INTEREST: foliage, flowers

SOIL: well-drained

LIGHT: full sun to partial shade

Plumbago is useful as a ground cover or a shrubby perennial at the back of a border. The plant will be covered with masses of flat 1-inch flowers over a long season of bloom. The foliage colors attractively in fall to contrast with the blossoms.

Selected species and varieties

C. plumbaginoides (common leadwort, dwarf plumbago)—blue flowers bloom from late summer through frost above 8- to 12-inch-tall tufts of glossy, nearly evergreen 3-inch leaves that color reddish bronze in fall in cooler climates. *C. willmottianum* (Chinese plumbago)—shrubby mounds of foliage up to 4 feet tall covered with deep blue, 1-inch-wide flowers from late summer through frost.

Growing conditions and maintenance

Plant plumbago 18 inches apart. It does not tolerate soggy soil or competition from tree roots. Mulch over winter in Zones 5 and 6. Shear before new spring growth begins to promote flowering. Propagate by division in spring every 2 to 4 years.

Chrysogonum (kris-AHG-o-num)

GOLDENSTAR

Chrysogonum virginianum var. virginianum

HARDINESS: Zones 5-9

PLANT TYPE: ground cover

HEIGHT: 4 to 9 inches

INTEREST: flowers, foliage

SOIL: moist, well-drained, fertile

LIGHT: dappled to bright full shade

Goldenstar produces bright yellow star-shaped flowers from spring to midsummer amid lush green foliage. Each bloom consists of five ray florets around a yellow disk. Spreading by means of leafy runners along the ground, goldenstar forms a low, dense carpet, making it useful as a ground cover, for edging, or in a rock garden.

Selected species and varieties

C. virginianum var. *virginianum* (green and gold)—grows 6 to 9 inches tall in a matlike habit with rich green, broadly serrated leaves that are triangular to oval, and 1- to 1½-inch-wide flowers that bloom well into summer in cooler zones, where there is sometimes a second flush before fall; var. *australe* is a rapidly spreading form 4 to 8 inches high.

Growing conditions and maintenance

Goldenstar grows well in average soil but benefits from the addition of organic matter such as leaf mold or peat moss. Once established, it tolerates occasional dryness. Site plants 1 foot apart for ground coverage. Mulch in colder zones to assist in overwintering. Propagate by division in spring.

VIRGIN'S BOWER

Clematis x jackmanii

HARDINESS: Zones 3-9

PLANT TYPE: vine

HEIGHT: 4 to 30 feet

INTEREST: flowers

SOIL: moist, well-drained, fertile

LIGHT: light shade to full sun

Clinging to supports, climbing through shrubs, or trailing along walls or fences, twining clematis offers attractive, sometimes evergreen foliage and billows of showy, flat-faced spring-, summer-, or fall-blooming flowers. Fluffy seeds develop for added fall interest.

Selected species and varieties

C. armandii (Armand clematis)—glossy evergreen, drooping leaflets and fragrant, shimmering white, 2-inch spring flowers on vines to 16 feet; 'Apple Blossom' produces cup-shaped flowers that emerge pink, fade to white; 'Farquhariana', pink flowers; 'Snowdrift', very fragrant waxy white flowers on drooping stems. *C. heracleifolia* var. *davidiana*—semiherbaceous subshrub 2 to 4 feet tall with dense clusters of fragrant, 1-inch-long tubular blue summer flowers. *C. x jackmanii* (Jackman hybrids)—summer-to-fall flowers up to 7 inches across with petals like pointed stars in single or double rows in white, soft pink, carmine, orchid, deep lavender, pale violet, mauve, purple, and rich shades of blue on 12- to 18-foot vines. *C. lanuginosa* (Lanuginosa hybrids)—6-inch spring-to-summer flowers on 6-foot vines; 'Crimson

King' grows abundant single and double crimson flowers; 'Fairy Queen', large pink blooms; 'Lady Northcliffe', large, deep lavender flowers; 'Nelly Moser', abundant, large pale mauve-pink flowers with a carmine bar down the sepals. *C. montana* var. *rubens*—2-inch rosy red spring flowers amid bronzy leaves on vigorous 25-foot vines. *C. paniculata* (sweet autumn clematis)—fragrant white 1¼-inch flowers in frothy profusion from summer through fall on rampant vines to 30 feet. *C. recta* 'Purpurea' (ground clematis)—fragrant 1-inch-wide white flower stars amid deep purple leaves from spring through summer on short 2- to 5-foot vines. *C. viticella* —2-inch midsummer flowers on 15-foot vines; 'Alba Luxurians' has white blooms with a mauve tint and purple anthers; 'Caerulea', violet flowers; 'Plena', double violet flowers; 'Rubra Grandiflora', large carmine flowers.

Growing conditions and maintenance

Plant clematis in a constantly moist soil. Mulch plants heavily in full sun to keep roots cool. Spring-blooming varieties bloom on the previous year's wood; summer- or fall-blooming kinds bloom on spring growth. Prune a month after flowering to shape plants and increase flowers the following year. Prune new plants severely for the first several years. Propagate from seed or cuttings.

Clematis viticella

CUP-AND-SAUCER VINE

Cobaea scandens

HARDINESS: Zones 9-11

PLANT TYPE: vine

HEIGHT: 10 to 25 feet

INTEREST: flowers

SOIL: well-drained, sandy

LIGHT: full sun

This extremely vigorous vine is native to Mexico. It derives its common name from showy, velvety blue cup-shaped flowers that are surrounded by a green saucerlike calyx. Technically a tender perennial, it is usually grown as an annual and can reach 25 feet in a single season. It provides a quick, temporary cover for a fence, a wall, an arbor, or a trellis.

Selected species and varieties

C. scandens, using branched tendrils, climbs easily on any support. Leaves are divided into two or three pairs of oblong leaflets. Flowers are green at first, turning deep violet or rose-purple as they mature; 'Alba' bears flowers in a pale shade of greenish white.

Growing conditions and maintenance

Start seeds indoors in individual peat pots 6 weeks prior to the last frost, first nicking the hard seed coat, and barely covering the seed. Transplant outdoors in late spring to a warm, sunny site, providing support for growth. Space plants 1 to 2 feet apart, and provide abundant water. In Zones 9 to 11, plant will become a woody vine and grow up to 40 feet.

Convallaria (kon-va-LAH-ree-a)

LILY OF THE VALLEY

Convallaria majalis

HARDINESS: Zones 2-7

PLANT TYPE: ground cover

HEIGHT: 8 to 10 inches

INTEREST: flowers, fragrance, foliage

SOIL: moist, well-drained, acid, fertile

LIGHT: full to partial shade

The incomparable fragrance and waxy, bell-shaped flowers of lily of the valley make this a springtime favorite for woodland settings, borders, and shady rock gardens. A natural spreader, lily of the valley makes an effective ground cover. The cut flowers are favored additions to arrangements and bridal bouquets.

Selected species and varieties
C. majalis—a vigorously growing species with five to 13 white flowers pendant from an 8-inch-tall wiry stalk that arises in late spring from a pair of tonguelike leaves 8 inches long and 1 to 3 inches wide that tend to look unkempt by late summer and die down early; 'Aureovariegata' has leaves with yellow stripes; 'Flore Pleno', double white flowers; var. *rosea*, dusty pink flowers.

Growing conditions and maintenance
Lily of the valley blooms best if it is not sited in dense shade. Plant pips—single rhizomes with growth buds—4 to 6 inches apart from early to midfall. Top-dress with compost or complete fertilizer after the first frost. Once established, though, plantings do fine with a minimum of attention.

Cotoneaster (ko-toe-nee-AS-ter)

COTONEASTER

Cotoneaster apiculatus

HARDINESS: Zones 4-7

PLANT TYPE: ground cover or shrub

HEIGHT: 18 inches to 6 feet

INTEREST: foliage, berries

SOIL: well-drained

LIGHT: full sun

Tiny deep green, sometimes evergreen leaves line stiff, spreading branches that grow in dense mounds as wide as or wider than their height. White or pink spring flowers are followed in fall by red berries persisting through winter. Cotoneasters make excellent ground covers or bank plants.

Selected species and varieties
C. adpressus (creeping cotoneaster)—prostrate plants 18 inches tall and 6 feet wide. *C. apiculatus* (cranberry cotoneaster)—tangle of branches 3 feet tall and 6 feet wide. *C. dammeri* 'Skogholmen' (bearberry cotoneaster)—1-foot-high branches trailing 3 feet with evergreen leaves. *C. divaricatus* (spreading cotoneaster)—mounds of arching branches 6 feet tall and as wide. *C. horizontalis* (rockspray cotoneaster)—scalelike leaves along twiggy ladders on shrubs to 3 feet tall and twice as wide or wider.

Growing conditions and maintenance
Although they prefer well-drained, fertile soil, cotoneasters will do well in virtually any soil. Propagate from softwood cuttings or by detaching rooted stem tips and carefully transplanting them.

Cucumis (KEW-kew-mis)

CUCUMIS

Cucumis melo

HARDINESS: tender

PLANT TYPE: vine

HEIGHT: 6 feet

INTEREST: fruit, flowers

SOIL: moist, fertile

LIGHT: full sun

This annual vine grows to 6 feet, producing rounded, arrow-shaped leaves and bright yellow flowers followed by small oval fruit no larger than an orange, with flattened ends. As the fruit matures it develops a sweet fragrance.

Selected species and varieties
C. melo, Dudaim Group (pomegranate melon, Queen Anne's pocket melon) is a relatively small member of this genus of generally coarse vines that includes numerous gourds and melons. When the fruit is young, it is green, but as it matures yellow stripes or marbling becomes evident and the background turns brown. Queen Anne supposedly carried one of these to fend off the less pleasant odors she was likely to encounter in her castle.

Growing conditions and maintenance
Start seed indoors in peat pots 4 weeks prior to the last frost, planting three seeds to a pot. Transplant outside after all danger of frost has passed, discarding the weaker two seedlings. Or sow directly in the garden when soil has warmed. To avoid mildew, do not wet the foliage late in the day.

Cucurbita (kew-KUR-bi-ta)

GOURD

Cucurbita pepo var. ovifera

HARDINESS: tender or Zones 9-11

PLANT TYPE: vine

HEIGHT: 5 to 12 feet

INTEREST: fruit, foliage

SOIL: well-drained, sandy

LIGHT: full sun

Plant these tropical squash and pumpkin vines on a trellis, a fence, or an arbor, and watch how quickly they will cover it with their lush foliage. Their fruit can be harvested for fall decorations.

Selected species and varieties

C. ficifolia (Malabar gourd, fig-leaf gourd) is a perennial in Zones 9 to 11 and is grown as an annual elsewhere. It climbs to 12 feet, producing smooth, rounded, white-striped green fruit up to 12 inches long. *C. maxima* (Hubbard squash) is an 8-foot annual vine bearing edible rounded or oblong furrowed fruit; the variety 'Turbaniformis' (Turk's-cap squash, Turban squash) produces 6- to 7-inch orange, white, and green fruit that looks as if it is made of two separate parts. Annual *C. pepo* var. *ovifera* (pumpkin gourd) grows 5 to 12 feet and produces small fruit in a wide range of shapes and colors.

Growing conditions and maintenance

Sow seed directly in the garden after the last frost, allowing 9 to 12 inches between plants. Or start indoors in individual peat pots 4 weeks before the last frost. Plants thrive in warm weather and grow best when given some support for climbing.

Dolichos (DO-li-kos)

HYACINTH BEAN

Dolichos lablab

HARDINESS: Zones 10-11

PLANT TYPE: vine

HEIGHT: 10 to 20 feet

INTEREST: flowers, foliage, fruit

SOIL: loose, well-drained

LIGHT: full sun

This lush, tropical twining vine produces purplish stems and purple-veined compound leaves. Attractive clusters of pink, purple, or white pea-like flowers appear in summer and are followed by showy red-purple seedpods. The seeds are edible and are an important food source in many parts of the world. As an ornamental, plants provide a colorful screen or covering for a fence, an arbor, or a trellis.

Selected species and varieties

D. lablab climbs to 20 feet in one season by twining stems. Leaves are composed of three heart-shaped leaflets, each 3 to 6 inches long. The loosely clustered flowers stand out against the deeply colored leaves. Pods are 1 to 3 inches long.

Growing conditions and maintenance

Start seed indoors in peat pots 4 to 6 weeks prior to the last frost, or sow directly in the garden after the soil has warmed. Space plants 12 to 24 inches apart and provide support for climbing. Hyacinth bean thrives in warm weather and is perennial in Zones 10 and 11.

Epimedium (ep-i-MEE-dee-um)

BARRENWORT

Epimedium x youngianum 'Roseum'

HARDINESS: Zones 4-8

PLANT TYPE: ground cover

HEIGHT: 8 to 12 inches

INTEREST: flowers, foliage

SOIL: moist, well-drained, fertile

LIGHT: partial to bright full shade

Epimedium produces sprays of spurred flowers and heart-shaped leaves. Leaves are red as they unfurl, light green in summer, bronzy red in fall. Its slow creeping habit makes it a good ground cover.

Selected species and varieties

E. grandiflorum (longspur epimedium)—1 foot tall with pink blooms; 'Rose Queen' has large deep pink flowers in late spring; 'White Queen', white flowers. *E. pinnatum* ssp. *colchicum* (Persian epimedium)—yellow flowers above evergreen leaves turning bronze in winter. *E. x rubrum* (red barrenwort)—broad clumps to 12 inches tall, bearing flowers with red sepals and yellow petals. *E. x versicolor* 'Sulphureum' (bicolored barrenwort)—spreading mounds to 12 inches tall with pale yellow flowers. *E. x youngianum* (Young's barrenwort)—low-growing species with usually white blooms; 'Niveum' has nearly double pure white flowers; 'Roseum' has mauve-pink flowers.

Growing conditions and maintenance

Add peat moss or leaf mold to the soil and plant 8 to 10 inches apart in spring or fall. Mulch well. Remove dead growth before new foliage appears in spring.

Erica (ER-i-ka)

HEATH

Erica carnea 'Winter Beauty'

HARDINESS: Zones 6-9

PLANT TYPE: ground cover

HEIGHT: to 16 inches

INTEREST: flowers, buds

SOIL: moist, well-drained

LIGHT: full sun to partial shade

Spring heath produces a mass of colorful flower spikes from winter to spring above a spreading evergreen carpet of bright green needlelike foliage. Use singly in rock gardens and flower beds, or plant in masses to cover a sunny slope or to edge a path.

Selected species and varieties

E. carnea (spring heath, snow heather)—prostrate branches with upright branchlets up to 16 inches high and spreading 2 to 6 feet wide bearing bell-shaped flowers of white, pink, rose, red, or purple in nodding clusters; 'Springwood Pink' grows 6 to 8 inches high with clear pink flowers; 'Springwood White', 6 to 8 inches high with pure white flowers and bronze new growth; 'Winter Beauty', to 5 inches high with a profusion of dark pink flowers.

Growing conditions and maintenance

Plant in sandy loam amended with peat moss or leaf mold. Heath usually fares poorly in heavy clay. Mulch to conserve moisture for the shallow roots, and water during dry periods. Spring heath prefers acid soil, but unlike many other heaths, tolerates slight alkalinity. Prune after flowering to encourage compactness.

Euonymus (yew-ON-i-mus)

SPINDLE TREE

Euonymus fortunei 'Emerald Charm'

HARDINESS: Zones 3-8

PLANT TYPE: ground cover, vine, or shrub

HEIGHT: 4 inches to 5 feet

INTEREST: foliage

SOIL: well-drained

LIGHT: full sun to shade

The genus includes evergreen ground covers and vines with a wide variety of white, cream, or yellow markings.

Selected species and varieties

E. fortunei (winter creeper euonymus)—evergreen ground cover or low hedge; 'Emerald Charm' is an erect 3-foot shrub; 'Longwood' produces low mats of ¼-inch leaves; var. *radicans* is a climber or trailer with 2-inch leaves; 'Gold Prince' grows in mounds 2 feet high with gold-tipped leaves that later turn all green; 'Vegetus' is a freely fruiting shrub or trailing vine to 5 feet.

Growing conditions and maintenance

Euonymus will grow in any soil, but dislikes both sogginess and drought.

Ficus (Fy-kus)

FIG

Ficus pumila

HARDINESS: Zones 9-10

PLANT TYPE: vine

HEIGHT: 20 to 60 feet

INTEREST: foliage

SOIL: moist, well-drained

LIGHT: full sun to partial shade

Related to the edible fig, creeping fig is grown for its foliage and rarely produces fruit. In warm climates or greenhouses, it will rapidly cover walls or unsightly objects and climb to great heights. It is particularly useful for covering masonry, because its small, clinging roots attach easily to brick, cement, or stucco. In cooler regions, creeping fig is grown as a houseplant.

Selected species and varieties

F. pumila (creeping fig, climbing fig)—numerous intertwined, slender stems that crisscross to form a dense mat on a support, rapidly growing 20 to 60 feet. The leaves are 1 inch long, heart-shaped, and evergreen. If allowed to develop, mature plants produce erect shoots with thickened 2- to 4-inch leaves and sometimes 2-inch, heart-shaped fruit; 'Variegata' bears white-mottled leaves.

Growing conditions and maintenance

Creeping fig thrives with abundant water during the growing season. To promote bushiness, pinch new shoots; to maintain a neat clinging habit, remove the mature branches that project outward from the support. In late fall or early spring, thin to reduce density and maintain vigor.

Gaultheria (gawl-THER-ee-a)

GAULTHERIA

Gaultheria shallon

HARDINESS: Zones 3-7

PLANT TYPE: ground cover or shrub

HEIGHT: 3 inches to 4 feet

INTEREST: foliage, fruit, fragrance

SOIL: moist, well-drained, acid

LIGHT: dappled to bright full shade

Gaultheria forms a lustrous evergreen carpet for shady areas. Small bell-shaped flowers appear in spring amid clustered leaves that release their scent when crushed. Mint-flavored bright red berries develop later and remain into spring.

Selected species and varieties
G. procumbens (wintergreen, checkerberry, teaberry, mountain tea)—spreading carpet 3 to 6 inches tall, with waxy flowers that are mostly hidden by the 1- to 2-inch leaves, prominent berries ¼ to ½ inch wide, and foliage that is red when new, green in summer, and bronze in the fall; Zones 3-7. *G. shallon* (salal, shallon)—variable habit, including ground cover to 2 feet tall or shrub to 4 feet tall in normal landscape conditions, but grows to 8 feet in the Pacific Northwest woods, bearing 5-inch clustered, conspicuous leaves that stay glossy green all year, urn-shaped flowers in late spring, and purple-black berries; hardy to Zone 5.

Growing conditions and maintenance
Gaultheria thrives in humus-rich soil; supplement the soil with leaf mold or peat moss before planting. Mulch to maintain moisture.

Gelsemium (jel-SEE-mee-um)

CAROLINA JASMINE

Gelsemium sempervirens

HARDINESS: Zones 6-9

PLANT TYPE: vine or ground cover

HEIGHT: to 20 feet

INTEREST: flowers, fragrance

SOIL: well-drained

LIGHT: bright full shade to full sun

The fragrant flowers of Carolina jasmine bloom in spring amid shiny green leaves that tend to be evergreen in the warmer zones. Although it can be allowed to scramble upon itself, forming a loose mounding shrub or ground cover, it is best used as a climbing vine for trellises, porches, and fences. *Caution:* All parts of the plant are poisonous.

Selected species and varieties
G. sempervirens (false jasmine, evening trumpet flower)—yellow flowers with a funnel-shaped corolla and five rounded lobes, clustered in the axils of leaves that are 2 to 4 inches long; 'Pride of Augusta' has double flowers that bloom more profusely and for a longer period than the species.

Growing conditions and maintenance
Carolina jasmine, which grows naturally in roadside meadows and open woodlands in the South, needs little special care. Although it prefers moist soils rich in organic matter, it adapts to other conditions. The foliage is denser and the flowers more abundant when the plant receives some direct sun. If the vine gets top-heavy, prune back severely.

Geranium (jer-AY-nee-um)

CRANESBILL

Geranium sanguineum 'Album'

HARDINESS: Zones 4-8

PLANT TYPE: ground cover

HEIGHT: 8 to 12 inches

INTEREST: flowers, foliage

SOIL: moist, well-drained

LIGHT: full sun to partial shade

Cranesbill is valued both for the profusion of flowers that appear in spring and summer, and for the mounds of lush green foliage that turns red or yellow in the fall.

Selected species and varieties
G. macrorrhizum—forms a wide-spreading mound 8 to 12 inches high, with aromatic leaves and magenta, pink, or white flowers that emerge in clusters in late spring and early summer; 'Ingwersen's Variety' has lilac-pink flowers; 'Spessart', pink flowers. *G. sanguineum*—bears magenta flowers and forms a deep green mound of foliage 9 to 12 inches tall and 24 inches across that turns red in fall; 'Album' has white flowers. *G. s.* var. *striatum* (also known as *G. s.* var. *lancastriense*)—light pink flowers with dark red veins.

Growing conditions and maintenance
In the warmer zones, cranesbill prefers partial shade. Do not overfertilize, as it will produce rank growth and weakened plants. Divide in spring when clumps show signs of crowding—approximately every 4 years.

Hedera (HED-er-a)

IVY

Hedera helix

HARDINESS: Zones 5-10

PLANT TYPE: vine

HEIGHT: 6 inches to 100 feet

INTEREST: foliage

SOIL: moist, well-drained

LIGHT: full shade to full sun

Ivies are perfect for carpeting shady banks and borders and, with their aerial roots, for climbing fences and posts. After climbing ceases at maturity, they produce yellowish green flowers 1½ to 2½ inches wide and poisonous black berries.

Selected species and varieties
H. canariensis (Algerian ivy, Canary ivy, Madeira ivy)—three- to seven-lobed dark green leathery leaves on dark red petioles; Zones 9-10; 'Variegata' has showy yellow or pale green streaks. *H. colchica* 'Dentata' (colchis ivy, fragrant ivy, Persian ivy)—a fast climber with slightly toothed leaves from 5 to 10 inches wide; hardy to Zone 6; 'Dentata-variegata' has creamy yellow margins. *H. helix* 'Cavendishii' (English ivy)—three- to five-lobed leaves 2 to 4 inches wide with creamy white margins; 'Gold Heart' has triangular leaves with a gold center; 'Needlepoint' is a very dense slow grower with dark green leaves ¼ to 1 inch wide.

Growing conditions and maintenance
Though ivy tolerates a wide variety of soil types, it benefits from a good start: Enrich the soil with organic matter and keep the plants moist until they are established.

Helianthemum (hee-lee-AN-the-mum)

SUN ROSE, ROCKROSE

Helianthemum nummularium

HARDINESS: Zones 5-7

PLANT TYPE: ground cover

HEIGHT: 6 to 12 inches

INTEREST: flowers

SOIL: dry, poor, well-drained, alkaline

LIGHT: full sun

Sun roses provide a colorful cover for dry, sunny slopes, look good tumbling out of a crevice in a rock wall, and brighten rock gardens. From late spring to early summer, flowers resembling wild roses with five crepe-paper-like petals cover a low-growing mound with trailing stems. Varieties come in yellow, orange, red, rose, pink, apricot, salmon, peach, white, bicolors, and in double flowers.

Selected species and varieties
H. nummularium (yellow sun rose)—a sprawling mound, 12 to 24 inches wide, with trailing stems that bear grayish green leaves 1 to 2 inches long with silvery undersides and 1-inch-wide flowers with broad petals and prominent stamens.

Growing conditions and maintenance
Sun roses like dry, poor, gravelly or sandy soils and do not grow well in fertile soils. Good drainage is essential. Prune in early spring to encourage dense growth, and prune again after flowering to get a second flush of bloom in late summer. Protect with mulch over the winter. Propagate by division in spring or by soft stem cuttings.

Hemerocallis (hem-er-o-KAL-is)

DAYLILY

Hemerocallis 'Stella de Oro'

HARDINESS: Zones 3-9

PLANT TYPE: ground cover

HEIGHT: 1 to 3 feet

INTEREST: flowers, foliage

SOIL: moist, well-drained

LIGHT: full sun to partial shade

Daylilies form dense clumps of arching, grasslike leaves that provide an attractive ground cover when the plants are massed. Branching stalks bear a succession of flower trumpets 2 to 6 inches across, often with frilled, spotted, or double petals.

Selected species and varieties
Hybrid daylilies provide flowers in yellow, orange, peach, melon, pink, red, lavender, maroon, and bronze. Cultivars bloom in spring, summer, or fall. Spring-blooming daylilies include 36-inch-tall, fragrant yellow 'Hyperion'; 28-inch fragrant golden apricot 'Ruffled Apricot'. Summer bloomers include 30-inch, pale orchid 'Catherine Woodbury'; 14-inch light yellow 'Eenie Weenie'; canary yellow, orange-throated, low-growing 'Stella de Oro'. Fall bloomers include 28-inch, lemon yellow 'Bountiful Valley'; 34-inch, carmine 'Oriental Ruby'.

Growing conditions and maintenance
Plant daylilies in soil that has been enriched with organic matter, spacing small varieties 18 to 24 inches apart, taller ones 2 to 3 feet apart. Propagate by division every 3 to 6 years.

Heuchera (HEW-ker-a)

ALUMROOT

Heuchera micrantha 'Palace Purple'

HARDINESS: Zones 3-9

PLANT TYPE: ground cover

HEIGHT: 1 to 2 feet

INTEREST: foliage, flowers

SOIL: moist, well-drained, fertile

LIGHT: full sun to partial shade

Alumroot's round, evergreen leaves with scalloped edges, often veined or tinted, form neat mounds that are attractive as edgings or fillers or massed as a ground cover. Wiry, branched flower stalks carry loose clusters of dainty flowers high above the foliage.

Selected species and varieties
H. micrantha 'Palace Purple'—pink flowers held on 18-inch stems above purplish green foliage. *H.* cultivars—long-lasting blossoms from spring to summer; 'Firebird' has deep scarlet blossoms on 18-inch stalks; 'June Bride', white flowers on 18-inch stems; 'Pluie de Feu', cherry red blossoms on 18-inch stems; 'Pewter Veil', purple-tinged silvery leaves; 'Scintillation', red flowers on 30-inch stems; 'Snowflake', white flowers.

Growing conditions and maintenance
Plant heuchera 12 to 18 inches apart in soil enriched with organic matter. Propagate from seed or by division every 3 years.

Hosta (HOS-ta)

PLANTAIN LILY, FUNKIA

Hosta sieboldiana 'Elegans'

HARDINESS: Zones 3-9

PLANT TYPE: ground cover

HEIGHT: 8 inches to 3 feet

INTEREST: foliage, flowers

SOIL: rich, moist, well-drained, acid

LIGHT: partial to dense shade

Grown primarily for their luxuriant foliage, hostas make ideal ground covers in woodland gardens or other shady areas.

Selected species and varieties
H. fortunei 'Albopicta'—15 inches tall, with leaves having yellow-green centers and dark green margins. *H. plantaginea*—forms a large mound of broad, bright green leaves, with fragrant white flowers on 2½-foot stems. *H.* 'Honeybells'—fragrant lavender flowers with blue stripes on 2-foot stems. *H. sieboldiana* 'Elegans'—large blue-gray leaves and white flowers; 'Frances Williams', large blue-green leaves with broad yellow margins; other fine varieties include 'Gold Standard', 'Blue Cadet', and 'Hyacintha'.

Growing conditions and maintenance
Hostas prefer shade, but will tolerate a sunny location in cooler areas with abundant moisture. Good drainage, especially during the winter, is critical.

Humulus (HEW-mew-lus)

HOPS

Humulus japonicus

HARDINESS: tender

PLANT TYPE: vine

HEIGHT: 10 to 20 feet

INTEREST: foliage

SOIL: moist, fertile

LIGHT: full sun

This fast-growing vine from Asia produces large deeply cut and coarsely toothed leaves. It is very useful for providing a quick screen over fences, arbors, trellises, or any unsightly object.

Selected species and varieties
H. japonicus (Japanese hopvine) climbs by twining its stems around its support. Leaves are broad, up to 8 inches across with five to seven deep lobes. Flowers are small and green and are often obscured by the foliage. Varieties with golden and variegated foliage are available.

Growing conditions and maintenance
Start seeds indoors 6 weeks prior to the last frost, or sow seed directly in the garden in midspring. Space plants 12 to 18 inches apart. Once established, they often self-seed, and may become invasive. Provide sturdy support for twining stems. Plants thrive in warm weather.

Hydrangea (hy-DRANE-jee-a)

HYDRANGEA

Hydrangea anomala ssp. petiolaris

HARDINESS: Zones 3-9

PLANT TYPE: vine or shrub

HEIGHT: 3 to 80 feet

INTEREST: flowers, foliage, bark

SOIL: moist, well-drained

LIGHT: full sun to light shade

Hydrangeas punctuate the garden with huge flower clusters above coarse, lustrous leaves that color attractively in fall. Older stems often have peeling bark, adding winter interest.

Selected species and varieties

H. anomala ssp. *petiolaris* (climbing hydrangea)—vine to 80 feet long with white spring-to-summer-blooming flower clusters as much as 10 inches across. *H. arborescens* 'Grandiflora' (hills-of-snow hydrangea)—white summer-to-fall flower clusters 6 to 8 inches across on shrubs to 5 feet. *H. macrophylla* (bigleaf hydrangea)—pink or blue summer flowers on shrubs 3 to 10 feet tall.

Growing conditions and maintenance

Plant hydrangeas in soil richly amended with organic matter. *H. arborescens* does better in partial shade. Propagate from cuttings.

Hypericum (hy-PER-i-kum)

ST.-JOHN'S-WORT

Hypericum calycinum

HARDINESS: Zones 5-9

PLANT TYPE: ground cover or shrub

HEIGHT: 1 to 3 feet

INTEREST: flowers

SOIL: average to poor

LIGHT: full sun to partial shade

St.-John's-wort bears brilliant yellow five-petaled flowers. Creeping St.-John's-wort spreads by stolons and rooting stems to create a thick carpet of dark green semi-evergreen leaves and is useful for covering difficult hillsides. Shrubbier forms are suited for borders and edgings.

Selected species and varieties

H. calycinum (creeping St.-John's-wort, Aaron's-beard)—18 inches tall and spreading to 2 feet wide, with rising and trailing stems bearing 3-inch flowers from midsummer to early autumn, when foliage turns purplish; Zones 5-8. *H.* 'Hidcote' —3 feet tall and wide, blooming profusely with fragrant 2- to 3-inch-wide flowers from early summer to fall; hardy to Zone 6. *H.* x *moseranum* (gold flower, Moser's St.-John's-wort)—12- to 24-inch-high mound with arching reddish branches bearing 2½-inch golden yellow flowers from midsummer to fall; hardy to Zone 7 and often grown as a perennial.

Growing conditions and maintenance

St.-John's-wort grows well in poor, sandy, or gravelly soils and requires little care. Cold winters often kill plant tops, but subsequent flowering is not affected.

Impatiens (im-PAY-shens)

BALSAM, JEWELWEED

Impatiens wallerana

HARDINESS: tender

PLANT TYPE: ground cover

HEIGHT: 6 to 36 inches

INTEREST: flowers

SOIL: moist, well-drained, fertile

LIGHT: partial to bright full shade

Easy-to-grow impatiens covers the ground in shady areas with a bevy of colors from spring until frost.

Selected species and varieties

I. balsamina (garden balsam)—10- to 36-inch mound, with usually double flowers in pink, salmon, red, purple, lavender, yellow, or white, borne along the stems or on top of the foliage, some very double; Camellia-Flowered Mixed 'Tom Thumb' has ruffled flowers at the top of 10- to 12-inch-high foliage. *I. wallerana* (busy Lizzy) —6- to 18-inch mounds with flat, five-petaled flowers 1 to 2 inches wide in salmon, orange, pink, white, red, rose, and violet, or bicolored with white borne directly over the foliage; Accent series grows 6 to 8 inches high with early-blooming single flowers; Dazzler series, 8-inch-high mounds with single flowers; Rosette mixture, 18 to 20 inches tall with single, semi-double, and double flowers.

Growing conditions and maintenance

Both species prefer loose, rich soil. Space according to eventual size and mulch to keep soil cool and moist; *I. wallerana* will grow taller with more water and fertilizer. Plants wilt in hot afternoon sun.

MORNING GLORY

Ipomoea purpurea

HARDINESS: tender

PLANT TYPE: vine

HEIGHT: 6 to 20 feet

INTEREST: flowers, foliage

SOIL: well-drained

LIGHT: full sun

Twining over trellises and fences or cascading over walls and banks, morning glories produce a new crop of trumpet-shaped blossoms each day from summer until frost. They are native to the American tropics and are generally easy to grow. They can be used to provide a screen or temporary ground cover, and are charming ramblers on a fence or porch.

Selected species and varieties

I. alba (moonflower) is a tender perennial that climbs as much as 20 feet. Its large heart-shaped leaves provide a lush foil for the white blooms that appear from midsummer to frost. Spiraled flower buds are 4 inches long and open before your eyes to reveal 5- to 6-inch beautiful, fragrant flowers. Buds open at night, scenting the evening air and attracting night pollinators, then close by midmorning the following day. *I. coccinea* (starflower) is an annual that grows to 10 feet with 6-inch heart-shaped leaves and 1½-inch scarlet flowers with yellow throats that appear throughout summer. Annual *I.* x *multifida* (cardinal climber, hearts-and-honey vine) grows 6 to 10 feet, producing feathery leaves and bright red 2-inch flowers with

white throats. *I. nil* (morning glory) grows to 10 feet with 6-inch shallowly divided leaves and 4-inch blooms that may be fluted or fringed. Flower colors include purple, pink, red, white, and blue; 'Chocolate' bears flowers that are pale chocolate brown; 'Scarlett O'Hara' produces 6-inch cherry red flowers. *I. purpurea* (common morning glory) is an annual native to Mexico that has naturalized in many parts of the United States. It grows 8 to 10 feet with 5-inch leaves. The 2- to 4-inch single or double flowers are trumpet shaped and come in shades of blue, purple, pink, and white. *I. quamoclit* (cypress vine, star-glory), also an annual, grows 10 to 20 feet with 2½- to 4-inch leaves that are finely divided into threadlike sections; its 1½-inch flowers are orange or scarlet.

Growing conditions and maintenance

Start seed indoors in individual peat pots 4 to 6 weeks prior to the last frost, or sow directly in the garden after all danger of frost has passed. To hasten germination, nick the hard seed coat and soak the seed overnight. Space plants 8 to 18 inches apart and provide support for climbing. Plants thrive in hot weather. Provide abundant water during dry periods. Do not overfertilize.

Ipomoea x multifida

JASMINE, JESSAMINE

Jasminum nudiflorum

HARDINESS: Zones 6-10

PLANT TYPE: vine or shrub

HEIGHT: shrub to 15 feet, vine to 40 feet

INTEREST: form, stems, flowers

SOIL: well-drained

LIGHT: partial shade to full sun

Jasmine forms a spreading mound of stiff, arching branches that remain green even in winter, sporadically producing yellow or white flowers. A good plant for slopes or for walls, jasmine can also be trained to climb a trellis or wall.

Selected species and varieties

J. mesnyi (Japanese jasmine)—spreading mound 5 to 6 feet high and greater in width with compound leaves of three leaflets and bright yellow tubular flowers that bloom periodically in early spring to midsummer; Zones 8-9. *J. nudiflorum* (winter jasmine) —3 to 4 feet high (to 15 feet on a trellis) and 4 to 7 feet wide with yellow flowers opening in winter; Zones 6-10. *J. officinale* 'Grandiflorum' (common white jasmine) —a deciduous or semi-evergreen shrub (10 to 15 feet tall) or climber (30 to 40 feet) with clusters of fragrant white star-shaped flowers blooming from summer to fall; Zones 8-10; reliably hardy to Zone 9 in the Southeast.

Growing conditions and maintenance

Jasmine grows well in poor soils and tolerates some drought. Flowers are produced on wood of the previous season; prune soon after flowering.

Juniperus (joo-NIP-er-us)

JUNIPER

Juniperus conferta 'Emerald Sea'

HARDINESS: Zones 3-9

PLANT TYPE: ground cover

HEIGHT: 4 inches to 8 feet

INTEREST: form, foliage, berries

SOIL: well-drained to dry

LIGHT: full sun

Junipers are extremely hardy plants producing fine-needled foliage in shades of green to blue-green, silvery blue, or gold in forms that suit a multitude of landscaping uses. Branches may trail over walls or among rocks, spread horizontally into dense ground covers, or droop gracefully into weeping forms. Fleshy blue-black berries develop on female plants. The species here offer choices for ground covers that anchor plantings of other evergreens, perennials, or bulbs by offering consistent year-round color, texture, and form.

Selected species and varieties

J. chinensis 'Gold Coast' (Chinese juniper)—compact ground cover mounding to 3 feet tall and spreading up to 5 feet with golden yellow foliage; 'Mint Julep' produces a loose fountain of bright green foliage 4 to 6 feet tall and slightly wider; var. *sargentii* (Sargent's juniper) has blue-green foliage on plants 18 to 24 inches tall and up to 10 feet wide. *J. conferta* 'Blue Pacific' (shore juniper)—9- to 12-inch plants with blue-green foliage on branches trailing up to 8 feet; 'Emerald Sea' grows slightly greener, salt-tolerant foliage. *J.*

horizontalis (creeping juniper)—scalelike needles coloring purplish in winter along feathery twigs; 'Bar Harbor' produces salt-tolerant blue-green foliage in tight mats 1 foot high and up to 8 feet wide; 'Blue Chip' has silvery blue foliage; 'Wiltonii' (blue rug juniper), trailing mats of intense silvery blue foliage only 4 to 6 inches high. *J. procumbens* 'Nana' (dwarf Japanese garden juniper)—spreading mounds of blue-green foliage up to 2 feet tall and 10 feet wide. *J. sabina* 'Broadmoor' (Savin juniper)—dark green foliage on plants spreading up to 10 feet wide from a central cushion of branches up to 3 feet tall.

Growing conditions and maintenance

Plant junipers in acid soil. If necessary, prune to shape plants in spring.

Juniperus procumbens 'Nana'

Lagenaria (la-jen-AIR-ee-a)

CALABASH GOURD

Lagenaria siceraria

HARDINESS: tender

PLANT TYPE: vine

HEIGHT: 10 to 30 feet

INTEREST: fruit, flowers

SOIL: well-drained, fertile

LIGHT: full sun

These annual vines require a great deal of space to accommodate their lush growth. They are grown for their fruit, which comes in a variety of sizes and shapes. Depending on the shape, the gourds can be used for containers, bird feeders, and autumn decoration.

Selected species and varieties

L. siceraria produces a hairy stem with branched tendrils and broad 6- to 12-inch leaves. The 5-inch white flowers open in the evening or on overcast days, and are sweetly fragrant. The fruit ranges from 3 to 36 inches in length and may be rounded or flattened, coiled, bottle shaped, or dumbbell shaped.

Growing conditions and maintenance

Start seed indoors in peat pots 6 to 8 weeks prior to the last frost. In areas with long growing seasons, seed can be planted directly in the garden after the last frost. Space plants 24 inches apart, and provide a sturdy support for climbing. Plants require a long season for fruit to mature, so allow gourds to remain on the vine as long as possible. Harvest before the first hard frost, and dry in an airy room.

Lamium (LAY-mee-um)

DEAD NETTLE

Lamium maculatum 'Beacon Silver'

HARDINESS: Zones 4-8

PLANT TYPE: ground cover

HEIGHT: 8 to 12 inches

INTEREST: foliage, flowers

SOIL: well-drained

LIGHT: partial to full shade

The spreading, trailing habit of dead nettle makes it useful as a ground cover among shrubs or trees, or in the front of a shady border. It helps hide the fading foliage of early-spring bulbs and fills in bare spots, and is also well suited for trailing over a stone wall or cascading from a container.

Selected species and varieties
L. maculatum 'Beacon Silver'—effective for brightening a shady part of the garden, silver 1- to 2-inch leaves with narrow green margins, pink flowers in late spring bloom in whorls at the stem tips; 'Chequers'—green leaves that sport a wide stripe down the center, pink flowers in late spring through summer.

Growing conditions and maintenance
Dead nettle tolerates a wide range of soils as long as they are well drained. Bare patches may appear if the plant is allowed to dry out too often. It prefers shade but will tolerate sun if sufficient moisture is supplied. To contain its aggressive, spreading habit and to promote compact growth, shear dead nettle in midsummer.

Lathyrus (LATH-er-us)

VETCHLING, WILD PEA

Lathyrus latifolius

HARDINESS: Zones 4-9 or half-hardy

PLANT TYPE: vine, ground cover, or shrub

HEIGHT: 6 inches to 9 feet

INTEREST: flowers

SOIL: well-drained

LIGHT: full sun to partial shade

Lathyrus bears flowers with puffy or furled petals on branching flower stalks. Use it as a trailing ground cover, a climbing vine for a screen or backdrop, or as a bushy accent among spring bulbs.

Selected species and varieties
L. latifolius (perennial pea)—twining vine to 9 feet tall with 1-inch-wide summer flowers. *L. odoratus* (sweet pea)—fragrant spring or summer flowers up to 2 inches wide on compact, 6-inch to 2½-foot-tall annual bushes or twining vines to 5 feet long or more. *L. vernus* (spring vetchling)—bushy, sprawling perennial 10 to 15 inches high with ferny foliage and profuse rose-violet spring flowers fading to greenish blue.

Growing conditions and maintenance
Plant lathyrus in well-drained garden loam. Propagate all species from seed, perennial pea and spring vetchling also by division. Remove spent flowers to prolong blooming season.

Liriope (li-RYE-o-pee)

LILYTURF

Liriope muscari 'Variegata'

HARDINESS: Zones 4-10

PLANT TYPE: ground cover

HEIGHT: 8 to 18 inches

INTEREST: foliage, flowers, fruit

SOIL: well-drained, fertile

LIGHT: deep full shade to full sun

The grasslike blades of liriope start out in tufts, gradually spreading until large clumps form. Ideal for use in edgings and rock gardens or as a ground cover, liriope also comes in variegated forms that provide textural accents. Flower spikes in purples or white bloom in late summer above the semi-evergreen foliage, followed by shiny black berries. In colder climates, the leaves look messy in winter.

Selected species and varieties
L. muscari (big blue lilyturf)—tufts of straplike leaves 18 inches tall and violet flowers; Zones 6-9; 'Gold Banded' is a compact form with wide, yellow-edged leaf blades; 'Monroe's White' grows 15 to 18 inches tall with narrower leaf blades than the species and white flowers; 'Variegata', 12 inches tall with creamy yellow leaf margins and lilac flowers; hardy to Zone 6. *L. spicata* (creeping lilyturf)—8 to 18 inches tall with leaves only ¼ inch wide and purplish white flowers; Zones 4-10.

Growing conditions and maintenance
Amend the soil with organic matter. Once established, liriope can tolerate dry shade. Shear or mow the old leaves before new growth begins in spring.

Lonicera (lon-ISS-er-a)

HONEYSUCKLE

Lonicera heckrottii

HARDINESS: Zones 4-9

PLANT TYPE: vine or shrub

HEIGHT: 4 to 20 feet

INTEREST: flowers, fruit, foliage

SOIL: moist to dry, average

LIGHT: partial shade to full sun

Honeysuckles produce abundant medium green foliage studded with fragrant flowers and berries often liked by birds.

Selected species and varieties

L. heckrottii (goldflame honeysuckle)—a climbing vine to 20 feet high, with buds opening to yellow inside, the outside slowly changing to pink, borne in terminal clusters, followed by sparse red fruit amid oval leaves that are evergreen in Zone 9. *L. nitida* 'Baggesen's Gold' (yellow box honeysuckle)—gold evergreen leaves on a 4- to 6-foot dense mound with white flowers and bluish fruits; hardy to Zone 7. *L. pileata* (privet honeysuckle)—an evergreen or semi-evergreen spreading shrub to 4 feet tall with horizontal branches bearing small yellowish white flowers and purple fruit amid narrow ½- to 1-inch-long leaves; Zones 6-8. *L. sempervirens* (trumpet honeysuckle)—unscented scarlet flowers with yellow-orange throats and red berries on a twining vine to 20 feet.

Growing conditions and maintenance

Honeysuckles are easy to grow in almost any soil. Provide vines with a support. Privet and box honeysuckles do well in seashore conditions.

Lysimachia (ly-sim-MAK-ee-a)

LOOSESTRIFE

Lysimachia nummularia 'Buttercup'

HARDINESS: Zones 4-8

PLANT TYPE: ground cover

HEIGHT: 2 to 6 inches

INTEREST: flowers, foliage

SOIL: moist, fertile loam

LIGHT: full sun to partial shade

Some loosestrifes make excellent ground covers, especially near a garden pond or at the edge of a moist woodland. The flowers, which bloom singly or in small spikes amid attractive foliage, present a fine summer display.

Selected species and varieties

L. congestiflora 'Eco Dark Satin'—4 to 6 inches tall, forming dense mats of oval leaves with clusters of ¾-inch red-throated yellow flowers in summer. *L. nummularia* (moneywort, creeping Jenny)—2- to 4-inch-tall creeper with ¾-inch yellow cup-shaped flowers appearing in late spring and sporadically through midsummer amid 1-inch deep green leaves; 'Aurea' has yellow leaves; 'Buttercup' bears intense yellow flowers.

Growing conditions and maintenance

Plant *L. congestiflora* 'Eco Dark Satin' in partial shade and *L. nummularia* in full sun or partial shade. Space plants 12 inches apart. *L. nummularia* will not thrive in a dry location. If planted in a border, loosestrife will need frequent division in spring or fall to contain its growth. Propagate by seed or division in spring.

Mandevilla (man-div-ILL-a)

MANDEVILLA

Mandevilla x amabilis

HARDINESS: Zones 8-10

PLANT TYPE: vine

HEIGHT: 10 to 20 feet

INTEREST: flowers, fragrance, foliage

SOIL: rich, moist, well-drained

LIGHT: partial shade

While hardy only in warm climates, mandevilla can be grown farther north as an annual or kept indoors over winter. The twining vine can be trained to a trellis, post, or arbor, where its pink or white trumpet-shaped flowers produce an elegant summer display set off by lush foliage.

Selected species and varieties

M. x amabilis—vigorous twining vine with evergreen leaves and abundant summer flowers opening pale blush pink and maturing to deep rose; Zone 10. *M. laxa* [also classified as *M. suaveolens*] (Chilean jasmine)—twining stems 15 to 20 feet long with oval, deciduous to semi-evergreen leaves and 2-inch fragrant white flowers in summer.

Growing conditions and maintenance

Plant mandevilla in spring after all danger of frost has passed. Provide abundant organic matter, and keep evenly moist throughout the growing season. Pinch shoots to encourage bushiness; remove faded flowers. Where it is hardy, mulch in fall. *M. x amabilis* thrives in containers, and can be cut back in fall and overwintered indoors. *M. laxa* can be planted as an annual in cooler regions.

Mazus (MAY-zus)

MAZUS

Mazus reptans

HARDINESS: Zones 6-9

PLANT TYPE: ground cover

HEIGHT: 2 inches

INTEREST: foliage, flowers, form

SOIL: moist, well-drained, slightly acid, fertile

LIGHT: partial shade to full sun

A true ground hugger, mazus forms a dense, prostrate carpet with medium green oval leaves and one-sided clusters of charming flowers in late spring. It works well in rock gardens and borders, and since it tolerates occasional foot traffic, it makes an ideal plant for tucking between steppingstones.

Selected species and varieties

M. reptans—procumbent stems bearing inch-long coarsely toothed leaves that hold well into late fall or early winter and ½-inch-long flowers gathered into profuse lavender to purplish blue clusters, usually spotted with white or yellow in the center; 'Alba' has snowy white flowers.

Growing conditions and maintenance

Although mazus is sometimes listed as hardy in Zone 5, it is often killed back. Set plants 12 to 15 inches apart in moisture-retentive soil amended with organic matter such as compost or peat moss. Because mazus roots all along its stems, it competes well with weeds and grass. Propagate by dividing.

Mina (MEE-na)

CRIMSON STARGLORY

Mina lobata

HARDINESS: Zones 8-11

PLANT TYPE: vine

HEIGHT: 15 to 20 feet

INTEREST: flowers

SOIL: moist, well-drained, fertile

LIGHT: full sun to partial shade

This vigorous, fast-growing vine is native to Mexico and climbs by twining its reddish stems around supports. Throughout the summer numerous red buds open to reveal tubular flowers that turn from orange to white as they mature. Plants provide an elegant light-textured screen or background for other flowers when grown on a trellis or fence. They can also be grown in containers.

Selected species and varieties

M. lobata produces attractive dark green three-lobed leaves along self-twining stems. The 1-inch flowers appear in showy long-stalked clusters, beginning as red boat-shaped buds that open orange, change to yellow, and eventually turn creamy white. All colors are present on a single cluster.

Growing conditions and maintenance

Start seed indoors in individual peat pots 6 weeks prior to the last frost or directly in the garden after danger of frost has passed. Keep plants well mulched and supplied with abundant water. Plants are hardy from Zone 8 south, but in warmer areas will benefit from midday shade.

Ophiopogon (o-fi-o-PO-gon)

LILYTURF

Ophiopogon japonicus 'Nana'

HARDINESS: Zones 6-10

PLANT TYPE: ground cover

HEIGHT: 2 to 14 inches

INTEREST: foliage, flowers, fruit

SOIL: moist, well-drained

LIGHT: full shade to full sun

Like liriope, with which it shares the common name lilyturf, *Ophiopogon* forms tufts of arching blades that spread to create a ground cover in any kind of light, including dense shade. Its flowers differ from those of liriope by appearing within the foliage, not above it. Clusters of small blue berries follow. Evergreen in the South, *Ophiopogon* is useful beneath trees and in borders and edgings.

Selected species and varieties

O. japonicus (dwarf lilyturf, dwarf mondo grass)—6 to 14 inches tall with dark green leaves ⅛ inch wide or less and up to several bluish violet flowers per stalk; 'Kyoto Dwarf' is only 2 inches tall with narrow, dark green leaves; 'Nana', roughly half as tall as the species; Zones 7-9. *O. planiscapus* 'Nigrescens' (black dragon)—purplish black foliage 6 inches tall, pink or lilac flowers and black berries; Zones 6-10.

Growing conditions and maintenance

Although lilyturf tolerates average garden soil, it grows best when peat moss or leaf mold has been added. In colder climates the foliage becomes shabby. Shear in early spring to promote new growth. Propagate by dividing in early spring.

Pachysandra (pak-i-SAN-dra)

SPURGE

Pachysandra terminalis

HARDINESS: Zones 4-9

PLANT TYPE: ground cover

HEIGHT: 4 to 12 inches

INTEREST: foliage, flowers

SOIL: moist, well-drained, acid, fertile

LIGHT: partial to dense full shade

Pachysandra forms an attractive, vigorous ground cover that thrives in shady areas where other plants may not survive. Japanese pachysandra tolerates dense shade and competes well with shallow-rooted trees.

Selected species and varieties
P. procumbens (Allegheny spurge)—flat gray-green or blue-green scalloped-edged deciduous to evergreen leaves, 2 to 4 inches long and 2 to 3 inches wide, sometimes mottled with brownish purple, that turn bronze in fall, and fragrant white or pinkish early-spring flower spikes 2 to 4 inches long. *P. terminalis* (Japanese pachysandra)—lustrous green toothed evergreen leaves, 2 to 4 inches long and 1 inch wide, in clusters at the end of unbranched stems 6 to 10 inches high, with 1- to 2-inch spikes of white flowers in spring and insignificant white berries in the fall; Zones 4-8; 'Green Carpet' has small, waxy green leaves and, at 4 inches, hugs the ground; Zones 4-9; 'Silver Edge' has green leaves edged with white.

Growing conditions and maintenance
Set the plants 12 inches apart in soil enriched with leaf mold or peat moss. Keep soil mulched until plants start to spread.

Parthenocissus (par-then-o-SIS-us)

WOODBINE

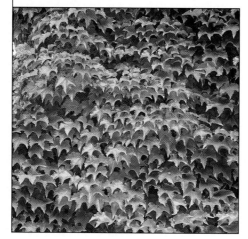

Parthenocissus tricuspidata

HARDINESS: Zones 3-9

PLANT TYPE: vine

HEIGHT: 50 feet or more

INTEREST: foliage

SOIL: average to poor

LIGHT: full shade to full sun

A tough, extremely fast climber that can easily scale 10 feet and more in a season, woodbine can make short work of covering walls, trellises, and slopes. Fastening itself to a structure with tendrils, it needs no support. Its dark green compound leaves turn purplish red to crimson in fall.

Selected species and varieties
P. henryana (silver-vein creeper)—leaves with five leaflets up to 2½ inches long that are bluish green veined with white when young, with purple undersides, and turn red to reddish purple in fall; Zones 7-8. *P. quinquefolia* (Virginia creeper, American ivy, five-leaved ivy)—five leaflets up to 4 inches long, opening reddish bronze then turning dark green, then purplish to crimson in the fall, with greenish white early-summer flowers and small blue-black berries visible after the leaves have fallen. *P. tricuspidata* (Japanese creeper, Boston ivy)—leaves are three-lobed, simple, and lustrous; Zones 4-8.

Growing conditions and maintenance
Woodbine tolerates almost any soil, polluted conditions, winds, and salt. Although it is prey to a number of pests, it usually needs little care.

Passiflora (pas-i-FLOR-a)

PASSIONFLOWER

Passiflora incarnata

HARDINESS: Zones 6-10

PLANT TYPE: vine

HEIGHT: to 25 feet

INTEREST: flowers, foliage, fruit

SOIL: well-drained

LIGHT: full sun to partial shade

The perennial passionflowers are herbaceous vines native to the eastern United States with showy flowers, lush, tropical-looking foliage, and edible fruit.

Selected species
P. incarnata (passionflower, maypop)—to 25 feet with white to lavender flowers 2 to 3 inches across followed by large apricot-colored fruit. The 4- to 6-inch leaves have three lobes and are dark green above and whitish below. *P. lutea* (passionflower)—to 15 feet with greenish yellow flowers and purple-black fruit. Its leaves turn yellow in autumn.

Growing conditions and maintenance
Grow passionflowers in well-drained soil. *P. incarnata* adapts to either sun or partial shade, while *P. lutea* prefers partial shade. Their abundant growth requires sturdy support. Pinch vines their first growing season to increase bushiness. Propagate by seed or cuttings, or separate suckers from the base of established plants.

Phaseolus (faz-ee-OH-lus)

BEAN

Phaseolus coccineus

HARDINESS: tender

PLANT TYPE: vine

HEIGHT: 6 to 10 feet

INTEREST: flowers, foliage, fruit

SOIL: moist, well-drained, fertile

LIGHT: full sun

This tender perennial twining vine from tropical America produces abundant dark green leaves that are a perfect foil for its brilliant scarlet flowers. The vine will grow quickly to cover a trellis or fence, or climb up a porch railing. It also forms a dense and dramatic backdrop for a flower border. The flowers attract hummingbirds.

Selected species and varieties
P. coccineus (scarlet runner bean) produces twining stems with 5-inch dark green leaves composed of three leaflets. Flowers are bright red and pea-like and appear in large clusters from early to midsummer, followed by flat 4- to 12-inch pods filled with black-and-red mottled seeds. Both flowers and beans are edible.

Growing conditions and maintenance
Plant seed outdoors in spring after danger of frost has passed. Thin to allow 2 to 4 inches between plants. Provide support for climbing, and water when dry.

Phlox (FLOCKS)

PHLOX

Phlox divaricata 'Fuller's White'

HARDINESS: Zones 3-9

PLANT TYPE: ground cover

HEIGHT: 5 to 14 inches

INTEREST: flowers

SOIL: moist, well-drained, acid, fertile

LIGHT: partial to bright full shade

Phlox and its flat, five-petaled flowers come in a variety of plant forms suitable for rock gardens, borders, retaining walls, and perennial beds. The flowers, borne singly or in loose clusters, sometimes bear a noticeable eye at the center.

Selected species and varieties
P. 'Chattahoochee'—1-inch-wide, deep violet flowers with purple eyes on a spreading tuft of stems to 12 inches tall; Zones 4-9. *P. divaricata* (wild sweet William, blue phlox, woodland phlox)—semi-evergreen oval leaves hug the ground beneath 1-foot-tall scapes topped with blue, purple, or white flowers; Zones 3-9; 'Dirigo Ice' reaches 14 inches with fragrant pale lavender flowers; 'Fuller's White' has white flowers. *P. stolonifera* (creeping phlox)—creeping 5- to 10-inch stems with evergreen leaves forming a mat with blue, pink, or white flowers; Zones 3-8; 'Blue Ridge' has pale blue flowers and lustrous foliage; 'Pink Ridge', pink flowers.

Growing conditions and maintenance
These species of phlox like humus-rich soil. Plant 1 to 1½ feet apart in soil well supplemented with leaf mold, peat moss, or compost. Propagate by division.

Polygonatum (po-lig-o-NAY-tum)

SOLOMON'S-SEAL

Polygonatum odoratum 'Variegatum'

HARDINESS: Zones 3-9

PLANT TYPE: ground cover

HEIGHT: 10 inches to 3 feet

INTEREST: flowers, fruit

SOIL: moist, well-drained, fertile

LIGHT: deep to bright full shade

Arching stems arise from rootstocks to bear 1½-inch-long greenish white bell-shaped flowers that dangle from the axils of parallel-veined green leaves in late spring. Black or blue fruits mature in fall. The plant spreads slowly by rhizomes to form a good ground cover for shade.

Selected species and varieties
P. biflorum (small Solomon's-seal)—to 3 feet tall or more, greenish white flowers with greenish lobes usually hang in pairs below the stem in late spring to early summer, followed by blue berries. *P. humile*—10 to 12 inches tall with heavily veined leaves; Zones 4-7. *P. multiflorum*—3 feet tall, white flowers with greenish apexes, in clusters of two to six usually on the bottom half of the stem; blue-black berries. *P. odoratum* 'Variegatum' (variegated Solomon's-seal)—1- to 3-foot-tall stems bearing leaves with white margins and tips, topped with fragrant white flowers having green spots in the throat, followed by blue-black berries; Zones 3-9.

Growing conditions and maintenance
Supplement soil with leaf mold, peat moss, or compost before planting. Propagate by division.

Pulmonaria (pul-mo-NAY-ree-a)

LUNGWORT

Pulmonaria saccharata 'Sissinghurst White'

HARDINESS: Zones 3-8

PLANT TYPE: ground cover

HEIGHT: 8 to 18 inches

INTEREST: flowers, foliage

SOIL: well-drained

LIGHT: light to full shade

Pulmonaria's clusters of spring flower trumpets nod at the tops of stems rising from clumps of broadly oval, hairy leaves spreading twice their height. They are effective when massed as a coarse ground cover or used as accent specimens.

Selected species and varieties
P. angustifolia (blue lungwort)—½-inch blue flower trumpets on 12-inch-tall stems in spring; ssp. *azurea* has sky blue blossoms. *P. saccharata* (Bethlehem sage)—pink flowers aging to blue on 18-inch stems above leaves mottled green and white; 'Janet Fiske' produces leaves marbled almost to white; 'Margery Fish', very large silvery leaf spots; 'Mrs. Moon', subdued silvery white leaf spots; 'Sissinghurst White', bears white flowers above speckled leaves.

Growing conditions and maintenance
Plant lungwort 1 to 1½ feet apart. Can be grown in sun but looks poor by midsummer. Propagate by division in fall.

Rhodochiton (ro-DOH-ki-ton)

RHODOCHITON

Rhodochiton atrosanguineum

HARDINESS: Zones 9-11

PLANT TYPE: vine

HEIGHT: 5 to 15 feet

INTEREST: flowers, foliage

SOIL: well-drained, fertile

LIGHT: full sun

Native to Mexico, where it is a perennial, the purple bell vine is grown as an annual north of Zone 9. It climbs by twisting its long petioles around any nearby support. From summer to frost, tubular deep purple flowers hang from thin stalks and are surrounded by a four-pointed fuchsia calyx. Plants make an attractive cover for a fence or trellis, or can be allowed to cascade from a hanging basket.

Selected species and varieties
R. atrosanguineum [also called *R. volubile*] (purple bell vine) grows to 15 feet in its native habitat but usually reaches 5 to 8 feet in temperate zones. Its thick-textured, heart-shaped leaves are tipped with purple. Elongated bell-shaped flowers are about an inch in length.

Growing conditions and maintenance
Start seed indoors in individual peat pots 3 to 4 months prior to the last frost. Place several seeds in each pot because germination may be spotty. Cut out all but the strongest seedling. Transplant to the garden after soil has warmed, allowing 1 foot between plants. They thrive in warm weather. Fertilize and water regularly.

Saxifraga (saks-IF-ra-ga)

SAXIFRAGE, ROCKFOIL

Saxifraga umbrosa

HARDINESS: Zones 7-9

PLANT TYPE: ground cover

HEIGHT: 4 to 24 inches

INTEREST: flowers, foliage

SOIL: moist, well-drained, neutral, fertile

LIGHT: full to dappled shade

An ideal plant for rock gardens, saxifrage's rosettes of leaves form a mat from which runners or stolons spread. The red threadlike runners of strawberry geranium, which is also grown as a houseplant, produce baby plants. Delicate flowers rise above the foliage in spring.

Selected species and varieties
S. stolonifera (strawberry geranium, beefsteak geranium)—18- to 24-inch branched stems bearing 1-inch-wide white flowers above 4-inch-tall clumps of round, hairy leaves with white veins and red undersides, up to 4 inches wide. *S. umbrosa* (Londonpride)—18-inch-high clumps of 2-inch-long oval leaves, pea green above and red beneath, with white, pink, rose, or bicolored flower sprays on 6-inch stems from late spring to early summer.

Growing conditions and maintenance
Saxifrages grow best in neutral, rocky soil but will tolerate other soils as long as they are very well drained but evenly moist. Generously enrich the soil with leaf mold or peat moss. Plant 8 to 10 inches apart in spring, and mulch lightly to overwinter. Apply an all-purpose fertilizer in spring. Propagate by dividing after flowering.

Sedum (SEE-dum)

SEDUM, STONECROP

Sedum spathulifolium

HARDINESS: Zones 3-10

PLANT TYPE: ground cover

HEIGHT: 2 to 8 inches

INTEREST: foliage, flowers

SOIL: well-drained

LIGHT: partial to full shade

Sedums are succulent plants commonly found growing on rocky outcrops or in woodlands. The following perennial species make attractive specimens for rock gardens or ground covers.

Selected species and varieties

S. rosea ssp. *integrifolium* (roseroot)—to 6 inches high with bright green rounded leaves topped by clusters of star-shaped red-purple flowers from spring to summer and showy red-purple seed pods; Alaska to California and Colorado; Zones 3-9. *S. spathulifolium* (common stonecrop)— 2- to 8-inch stems bearing clusters of yellow flowers in spring and summer above rosettes of green, blue-green, or white leaves; California to British Columbia; Zones 7-10. *S. ternatum* (wild stonecrop)—white flowers on 4- to 8-inch stalks above creeping stems with light green foliage; New York to Minnesota and south to Tennessee; Zones 5-10.

Growing conditions and maintenance

These sedums grow in well-drained soil in partial shade. *S. ternatum* also adapts to full shade. Propagate by seed, division, or cuttings.

Stachys (STAY-kis)

LAMB'S EARS

Stachys byzantina 'Silver Carpet'

HARDINESS: Zones 4-8

PLANT TYPE: ground cover

HEIGHT: 6 to 18 inches

INTEREST: foliage, flowers

SOIL: well-drained

LIGHT: full sun to light shade

Stachys foliage adds color and texture to the border. Mats of woolly, pointed leaves of low-growing species are ideal for ground covers or informal edgings. The large, corrugated leaves and fine-textured flowers of taller species fill spaces in the border.

Selected species and varieties

S. byzantina (lamb's ears, woolly betony) —dense 8-inch-high mats of velvety gray-green oval leaves to 6 inches and woolly, pinkish summer-blooming flower spikes up to 1½ feet tall; 'Silver Carpet' is a non-flowering cultivar. *S. macrantha* (big betony)—stems to 1½ feet, tipped with whorls of purple summer flowers above heart-shaped, rippled green leaves; 'Superba' has lavender pink flowers.

Growing conditions and maintenance

Plant stachys 12 to 18 inches apart in soil that is not overly fertile. Remove old leaves before new growth begins in the spring. Propagate by transplanting self-sown seedlings, from seed, or by division.

Thunbergia (thun-BER-jee-a)

CLOCK VINE

Thunbergia alata

HARDINESS: tender

PLANT TYPE: vine

HEIGHT: 3 to 6 feet

INTEREST: flowers

SOIL: moist, well-drained, fertile

LIGHT: full sun to partial shade

Thunbergia, native to South Africa, is a small climbing or trailing vine that produces a mass of neat, triangular leaves and trumpet-shaped flowers in shades of yellow, orange, and cream, usually with a very dark center, throughout the summer. Plants are attractive in window boxes and hanging baskets, and are excellent as a fast-growing screen on a trellis or fence.

Selected species and varieties

T. alata (black-eyed Susan vine) develops twining stems with 3-inch leaves with toothed margins and winged petioles. The solitary flowers are 1 to 2 inches across with 5 distinct, rounded petal segments, usually surrounding a black or dark purple center.

Growing conditions and maintenance

Start seed indoors 6 to 8 weeks prior to the last frost, or sow directly outdoors after danger of frost is past. Space plants 12 inches apart and provide support if you wish them to climb. Plants thrive where summer temperatures remain somewhat cool. Water during dry periods.

Tiarella (ty-a-REL-a)

FOAMFLOWER

Tiarella cordifolia

HARDINESS: Zones 3-9

PLANT TYPE: ground cover

HEIGHT: 6 to 12 inches

INTEREST: flowers, foliage

SOIL: moist, well-drained, rich

LIGHT: partial shade to shade

Foamflowers are low-growing perennials found in cool, moist woodlands and on the banks of streams. They are ideal ground covers or edgings along a woodland garden path and are also effective in a shady rock garden.

Selected species and varieties
T. cordifolia (foamflower)—eastern native with compact clusters of tiny star-shaped white flowers on 6- to 12-inch stalks above neat mounds of lobed leaves from midspring to early summer. Mature plants spread by runners; Zones 3-8. *T. unifoliata* (western foamflower, sugar scoop)—western native white bell-shaped flowers on 6- to 8-inch stalks from midspring to summer above rounded evergreen leaves. Flowers are followed by fruits shaped like sugar scoops; Zones 5-9.

Growing conditions and maintenance
Foamflowers thrive in full or partial shade and moist, rich, slightly acid soil with a high organic content. Water during dry spells. Propagate by seed or division.

Tropaeolum (tro-PEE-o-lum)

NASTURTIUM

Tropaeolum majus 'Whirlybird Bright Scarlet'

HARDINESS: tender

PLANT TYPE: vine or ground cover

HEIGHT: 6 inches to 8 feet

INTEREST: flowers, foliage

SOIL: poor, well-drained to dry

LIGHT: full sun

Nasturtiums bear brightly colored flowers from summer until frost and attractive, shieldlike leaves. Some selections are high-climbing vines; others have a trailing habit or are short and bushy. The flowers come in shades of yellow, orange, red, and white, and may be double or single. These fast-growing plants make excellent screens or bedding plants.

Selected species and varieties
T. majus (common nasturtium)—1 foot tall and twice as wide, with trailing stems 1 to 3 feet long, or climbing stems reaching 6 to 8 feet high. Leaves are round and 2 to 7 inches across, with long stems. The 2- to 3-inch flowers are red, yellow, white, or orange and may be spotted or streaked; 'Whirlybird Bright Scarlet' bears upturned flowers. *T. minus* (dwarf nasturtium)—6 to 12 inches tall with a bushy habit suitable for edgings or massing.

Growing conditions and maintenance
Sow seed directly outdoors after danger of frost has passed. Space dwarf types 8 to 12 inches apart; space vines 2 to 3 feet apart and provide support. Do not fertilize, or plants will produce lush foliage but few flowers.

Vinca (VING-ka)

PERIWINKLE, MYRTLE

Vinca minor

HARDINESS: Zones 3-9

PLANT TYPE: ground cover

HEIGHT: 3 to 6 inches

INTEREST: foliage, flowers

SOIL: moist, well-drained

LIGHT: full sun to full shade

Periwinkle is a wide-spreading evergreen ground cover that provides a dense carpet of leaves in a relatively short time. Its runners extend in all directions along the ground, rooting where they contact the soil. In spring, lilac-blue flowers appear in profusion and continue blooming sporadically into the summer.

Selected species and varieties
V. minor—3 to 6 inches tall, spreading indefinitely, fast-growing, mat-forming habit, leaves emerge yellow-green and mature to dark, glossy green, ½ to 1½ inches long, flowers are lilac-blue, 1 inch across, blooming mainly in the spring, effective ground cover under trees or in front of shrubs.

Growing conditions and maintenance
Periwinkle spreads quickly in moist, well-drained soil amended with organic matter. In warmer climates, it performs best in light to deep shade. Space plants to be used as ground cover 12 inches apart. Shear once a year after the main flowering season to promote dense growth.

Viola (vy-O-la)

VIOLET

Viola cucullata 'Freckles'

HARDINESS: Zones 3-9

PLANT TYPE: ground cover

HEIGHT: 3 to 8 inches

INTEREST: flowers, fragrance

SOIL: wet to dry, well-drained

LIGHT: bright full to dappled shade

Members of a huge genus, the violets below produce tufts of heart-shaped leaves and fall, winter, or spring flowers. Spreading quickly by surface runners or rhizomes, they are useful as ground covers or in rock gardens and edgings.

Selected species and varieties

V. cucullata [also listed as *V. obliqua*] (marsh blue violet)—6 inches tall with spring blooms; 'Freckles' has pale blue flowers with purple spots; 'White Czar', white flowers with a yellow eye. *V. labradorica* (Labrador violet)—blue to violet flowers in spring on 3-inch stems with purplish ¾-inch-wide green leaves; Zones 3-8. *V. odorata* (sweet violet)—8-inch stems rising in clumps from long runners, bearing 1- to 3-inch leaves; hybrids of the species offer fragrant single and double flowers in purple, blue, rose, or white, blooming in fall and winter in warm climates, spring in cold areas; Zones 6-9.

Growing conditions and maintenance

Mix organic matter into the soil. Marsh-blue violets do well in moist or wet sites; sweet violets need a moist soil; Labrador violets tolerate drier conditions. Marsh and Labrador violets self-seed freely.

Vitis (VY-tis)

GRAPE

Vitis vinifera 'Purpurea'

HARDINESS: Zones 5-8

PLANT TYPE: vine

HEIGHT: 20 to 50 feet

INTEREST: foliage, bark

SOIL: well-drained

LIGHT: full sun

With their twining tendrils, grapes quickly scramble over arbors and trellises to create almost instant screens, canopies, or arches. The broad leaves, attractively lobed and incised, color brilliantly in fall. Older stems have shredding, peeling bark.

Selected species and varieties

V. amurensis (Amur grape)—5- to 10-inch leaves coloring crimson to purple in fall. *V. coignetiae* (crimson glory vine)—extremely fast-growing vine, up to 50 feet per year, with 4- to 10-inch leaves turning scarlet in fall. *V. vinifera* 'Purpurea' (wine grape, common grape)—4- to 6-inch heart shaped leaves emerge reddish burgundy, then mature to purple.

Growing conditions and maintenance

Plant grapes in deeply cultivated soil enriched with organic matter. When growing for shade or an arbor, cut canes back in winter to control spread. Propagate from cuttings.

Wisteria (wis-TEE-ree-a)

WISTERIA

Wisteria sinensis

HARDINESS: Zones 4-9

PLANT TYPE: vine

HEIGHT: 30 feet

INTEREST: flowers

SOIL: moist, well-drained

LIGHT: full sun

Panicles of lavender flowers drip from this vigorous, twining vine. Lovely near patios and porches, where its bright green foliage provides dense shade for the rest of the growing season, wisteria needs a sturdy support, since the vines can eventually crush wood. It can also be trained into a tree form. Velvety green pods turn brown and persist into winter.

Selected species and varieties

W. floribunda (Japanese wisteria)—twines clockwise, bearing small, slightly fragrant, violet or violet-blue flowers in clusters 9 to 20 inches long in early to midspring just before the leaves emerge. *W. sinensis* (Chinese wisteria)—twines counterclockwise and produces blue-violet flowers, not as fragrant as those of Japanese wisteria, borne in dense, 6- to 12-inch-long clusters in mid- to late spring; cultivars include white, dark purple, double, and more fragrant varieties; Zones 5-8.

Growing conditions and maintenance

Amend soil to create a deep, well-drained loam, and add lime if soil is very acid. Prune roots before planting. Feed with superphosphate fertilizers; too much nitrogen creates excessive foliage.

Ornamental Grasses and Ferns

ORNAMENTAL GRASSES AND FERNS ARE AMONG THE most visually appealing plants in the gardener's palette. With their graceful foliage and soothing, earthy colors, they provide interest and beauty in the landscape, often when the rest of the garden is in the doldrums. And the majestic flower plumes of some grasses, or the tall feathery fronds of some ferns, add an exotic touch to any planting scheme.

There's more to recommend ornamental grasses and ferns than beauty and drama, however. Fast-growing and adaptable, most require little attention besides occasional pruning. And there are grasses and ferns to suit just about any garden condition, from full sun to deep shade, from wet conditions to dry, and from fertile to poor soil.

You can choose from a wide array of species and varieties, which vary in form, height, and foliage or flower color. On the following pages you'll find descriptions of some of the most popular grasses and ferns grown in American gardens today.

Ornamental Grasses

Andropogon (an-dro-PO-gon)

BLUESTEM

Andropogon gerardii

HARDINESS: Zones 3-9

PLANT TYPE: perennial

HEIGHT: 2 to 8 feet

SOIL: dry, sandy to moist

LIGHT: full sun

Bluestems are perennial bunch grasses found in prairies, open woods, and lowlands over much of the United States. The narrow leaves are blue-green in spring and summer and copper or maroon in fall.

Selected species and varieties

A. gerardii (big bluestem, turkeyfoot)—clumps 4 to 8 feet tall with purplish late-summer flowers in branched clusters resembling a turkey's foot. Leaves blue-green in summer and maroon to tan in fall; Zones 4-9. *A. glomeratus* (bushy bluestem)—clumps 2 to 5 feet tall with silvery green to pinkish flowers in bold feathery racemes surrounded by salmon sheaths in fall followed by fluffy white seed heads. Leaves and stems turn coppery after frost and remain attractive in winter; Zones 6-9.

Growing conditions and maintenance:

A. gerardii grows best in a sandy loam and withstands periodic flooding. *A. glomeratus* prefers a moist site. Both need full sun and should be cut or mowed to the ground in late winter or early spring. Propagate by seed or division.

Arundo (a-RUN-doh)

GIANT REED

Arundo donax

HARDINESS: Zones 7-10

PLANT TYPE: perennial

HEIGHT: 3 to 20 feet

SOIL: moist, well-drained

LIGHT: full sun

This tall perennial grass has an upright, arching habit and thick, hollow stems that bear wide leaves and large, silky plumes, which last from late summer into winter. Its large size makes it an excellent choice for use as a screen, specimen, or background plant. Giant reed is especially attractive alongside a stream or pond and is useful for erosion control.

Selected species and varieties

A. donax (giant reed)—12- to 20-foot-tall clumps of light green to blue-green, bamboolike leaves to 2 feet long; 'Variegata', striped giant reed, grows 3 to 8 feet tall and has green leaves with white stripes.

Growing conditions and maintenance

Giant reed does best in full sun and moist, well-drained soil. Cut branches to the ground before new growth begins in the spring. Propagate by division or seed.

Bambusa (bam-BOO-sa)

BAMBOO

Bambusa glaucescens 'Alphonse Karr'

HARDINESS: Zones 8-10

PLANT TYPE: perennial

HEIGHT: 8 to 50 feet

SOIL: moist, fertile

LIGHT: full sun or partial shade

A native of the tropics, bamboo forms dense clumps of hollow, shiny stems with prominent joints and lance-shaped leaves. It makes an outstanding accent plant, hedge, or screen. Some species, such as the hedge bamboo, may also be grown in containers.

Selected species and varieties

B. glaucescens [also listed as *B. multiplex*] (hedge bamboo)—forms 10- to 20-foot-tall clumps of slender yellow stems and narrow green leaves up to 6 inches long; 'Alphonse Karr' produces yellow stems with bright green stripes; 'Silverstripe' has white-striped leaves. *B. oldhamii* (giant timber bamboo)—large and vigorous, with thick green stems up to 50 feet tall and bright green leaves up to 1 foot long. *B. vulgaris* (common bamboo)—clumps of thick green stems that can reach 50 feet, with lance-shaped leaves to 10 inches long.

Growing conditions and maintenance

Grow hedge or common bamboo in full sun or partial shade; giant timber bamboo prefers full sun. Plants do best in moist, fertile soil. Propagate by division in spring.

Bouteloua (boo-te-LOO-a)

GRAMA

Bouteloua curtipendula

HARDINESS: Zones 3-10

PLANT TYPE: perennial

HEIGHT: 1 to 2 feet

SOIL: well-drained to dry

LIGHT: full sun

These clump-forming drought-tolerant grasses are found in prairies, open woodlands, and on rocky slopes throughout much of the United States. They are useful for meadow plantings or as accents in a rock garden.

Selected species and varieties
B. curtipendula (sideoats grama, mesquite grass)—wiry clumps 1 to 2 feet tall; small flowers arranged in numerous spikelets with downward-pointing tips along one side of each flower stem in summer; in fall the seed heads bleach to a tan color and foliage often turns red or purple. *B. gracilis* (blue grama)—1 to 1½ feet tall with narrow, fine-textured foliage; forms a dense sod when mowed, making it a good turf grass for dry climates.

Growing conditions and maintenance
Grama grasses require full sun and a well-drained to dry soil. Both are excellent plants for low-maintenance gardens. To propagate, collect seed in fall and sow immediately, or stratify and sow in spring. Plants can also be divided while dormant.

Briza (BRY-za)

QUAKING GRASS

Briza maxima

HARDINESS: tender

PLANT TYPE: annual

HEIGHT: 1 to 2 feet

SOIL: well-drained

LIGHT: full sun

While they are not appropriate for the formal garden, the arching leaves and nodding seed heads of quaking grass add grace and movement to an informal border or a garden path. They are also a good choice for the cutting garden because their wheat-like spikelets are outstanding for both fresh and dried arrangements. The spikelets dangle from thin stems and tremble when touched, hence the common name.

Selected species and varieties
B. maxima produces a tuft of leaves, each leaf 6 inches long and ¼ inch wide. In late spring and early summer, flower heads rise to 2 feet, producing 4-inch nodding panicles on threadlike stems. The flowers start out green and then turn straw colored as they dry.

Growing conditions and maintenance
Plant seed outdoors as soon as soil can be worked in spring. Thin to allow 9 to 12 inches between plants. Provide moisture when plants are young. Once established, plants usually self-seed. For use in winter arrangements, cut the seed heads before seeds ripen.

Calamagrostis (kal-a-ma-GROS-tis)

REED GRASS

Calamagrostis x acutiflora 'Karl Foerster'

HARDINESS: Zones 6-9

PLANT TYPE: perennial

HEIGHT: 4 to 7 feet

SOIL: well-drained, acid

LIGHT: full sun to partial shade

Reed grass has a slender, erect habit that provides a vertical accent in the border. As one of the first grasses to bloom, it offers a long season of interest.

Selected species and varieties
C. x *acutiflora* 'Karl Foerster'—4 to 6 feet tall, with pink flowers maturing to golden tan from early summer to fall; 'Stricta', 5 to 7 feet tall, with greenish pink flowers appearing about 2 weeks later than those of 'Karl Foerster' and lasting through fall.

Growing conditions and maintenance
Reed grass is adaptable to a wide range of conditions, tolerating both heavy soils and poor, dry soils. It withstands moist to wet areas as well as drought. It is effective used as a garden accent, as a specimen, or massed beside ponds or streams.

Carex (KAY-reks)

SEDGE

Carex morrowii 'Variegata'

HARDINESS: Zones 5-9

PLANT TYPE: perennial

HEIGHT: 1 to 3 feet

SOIL: moist, well-drained, fertile

LIGHT: bright full shade to full sun

The mounds of gracefully arching grasslike leaves make sedge useful in the foreground of edgings and in rock gardens, where, as a single specimen or in groups, it lends texture and fluidity to the shady landscape.

Selected species and varieties
C. buchananii (leatherleaf sedge, fox-red sedge)—dense clumps of very narrow reddish bronze leaves to 20 inches high; Zones 8-9. *C. morrowii* 'Variegata' (variegated Japanese sedge)—12 to 18 inches tall, gracefully swirling moplike mounds, with leathery evergreen cream-and-green leaves ¼ to ½ inch wide; Zones 6-9. *C. pendula* (drooping sedge, giant sedge, sedge grass) —mounds 2 to 3 feet high with bright green, furrowed, usually evergreen leaves ¾ inch wide and 18 inches long; Zones 5-9.

Growing conditions and maintenance
Unlike true ornamental grasses, sedge is a native of woodland environments and performs well in shade. Avoid exposing *C. pendula* to dry, sunny conditions, particularly in winter. Propagate by dividing in spring.

Chasmanthium (kaz-MAN-thee-um)

WILD OATS

Chasmanthium latifolium

HARDINESS: Zones 5-10

PLANT TYPE: perennial

HEIGHT: 2 to 4 feet

SOIL: moist, well-drained

LIGHT: full sun to partial shade

The genus *Chasmanthium* offers landscape interest during three seasons of the year. Its green flowers appear in drooping panicles in summer. In autumn the leaves turn a bright yellow-gold. The panicles turn bronze and persist throughout winter, providing color and graceful movement.

Selected species and varieties
C. latifolium (wild oats)—clump-forming perennial grass from the east and central United States; 2 to 4 feet in height with blue-green, bamboolike leaves; fall foliage most intense in full sun; oatlike spikelets of flowers on slender, arching stems in summer. This grass is effectively used in borders and beside pools and streams.

Growing conditions and maintenance
Unlike most ornamental grasses, chasmanthium adapts well to partial shade, where it has darker green foliage and tends to grow taller than it does in full sun. Propagate by division or seed. It may self-sow.

Coix (KO-ix)

JOB'S-TEARS

Coix lacryma-jobi

HARDINESS: tender

PLANT TYPE: annual

HEIGHT: 3 to 4 feet

SOIL: average, moist

LIGHT: full sun to light shade

Job's-tears produces long, narrow leaves clasping tall, jointed stems that create a lacy vertical accent as a border backdrop or temporary screen. It also does well as a container plant. In summer, the arching flower spikes rise like froth above the foliage, and female flowers, enclosed in hard, oval husks, hang decoratively in strings like dripping tears. Children enjoy stringing the small beads into bracelets and necklaces. Dry the stems for everlasting arrangements.

Selected species and varieties
C. lacryma-jobi (Job's-tears)—leaves 2 feet long and 1½ inches wide on stems to 4 feet tipped with spiky flower clusters, male at the end, female at the base, encased in hard green husks that turn pearly white, gray, or iridescent violet as they ripen.

Growing conditions and maintenance
Sow Job's-tears in spring when soil warms to 68° F; in colder climates, start seed indoors 2 to 3 months in advance. Keep soil constantly moist. Potted specimens do best in light shade. To dry, pick stems before seeds dry and shatter.

Cortaderia (kor-ta-DEER-ee-a)

PAMPAS GRASS

Cortaderia selloana

HARDINESS: Zones 7-10

PLANT TYPE: perennial

HEIGHT: 6 to 10 feet

SOIL: fertile, moist, well-drained

LIGHT: full sun to light shade

Popular for its majestic plumed flowers, pampas grass forms dense, upright clumps of long, narrow, sharp-edged leaves. This evergreen perennial makes a stunning lawn specimen and can be planted in groups to form hedges or windbreaks. It is especially attractive near water. The showy flowers are useful in both fresh and dried arrangements.

Selected species and varieties
C. selloana—8- to 10-foot-tall clumps of arching, gray to green foliage. Feathery silver plumes, up to 3 feet long, bloom in late summer atop erect stalks 2 feet or more above the foliage and persist into winter. 'Pumila', dwarf pampas grass, grows to 6 feet and bears a profusion of creamy white flowers. 'Rosea' features pale pink blooms. 'Sunningdale Silver' has large silver plumes.

Growing conditions and maintenance
Pampas grass prefers full sun and fertile, moist, well-drained soil. However, it will grow in partial shade and can withstand difficult conditions, including drought. When planting in groups, allow 10 feet between plants. Remove old flowers and foliage in spring. Propagate by division in spring.

Cymbopogon (sim-bo-PO-gon)

OIL GRASS

Cymbopogon citratus

HARDINESS: Zones 10-11

PLANT TYPE: perennial

HEIGHT: 2 to 6 feet

SOIL: well-drained, sandy, slightly acid

LIGHT: full sun to light shade

Lemon grass's fragrant leaves are a staple in Thai and Vietnamese cuisines. The tough stems are sliced and simmered to release their citrus flavor, then discarded before serving. Steep fresh or dried leaves for tea. Use clumps of lemon grass with its gracefully arching leaf blades in the middle of a border in warm-climate gardens. Elsewhere, grow as an annual and pot it to overwinter indoors.

Selected species and varieties
C. citratus (lemon grass, fever grass)—inch-wide aromatic evergreen leaves with sharp edges growing from bulbous stems in clumps to 6 feet tall and 3 feet wide.

Growing conditions and maintenance
Divisions of lemon grass should be planted in spring; space them 2 to 3 feet apart. Apply mulch both to conserve moisture in summer and to protect roots in winter. Where frost is a possibility, pot divisions in fall after cutting back to 3 inches and keep indoors over the winter, watering only sparingly to prevent root rot. Cut stems at ground level for fresh use, taking care when handling the leaf's sharp edges, and use the lower 3 to 4 inches for best flavor.

Deschampsia (des-SHAMP-see-ah)

HAIR GRASS

Deschampsia caespitosa

HARDINESS: Zones 4-9

PLANT TYPE: perennial

HEIGHT: 1 to 3 feet

SOIL: moist, fertile

LIGHT: partial shade

Found naturally in damp meadows and woods, hair grasses are good companions for hostas, ferns, and other plants that love moisture. They produce dense tufts of evergreen foliage and a profusion of delicate, airy flowers, which appear throughout summer. Hair grasses are useful as ground covers or flowering accents, and are suitable for borders, rock gardens, and moist sites such as stream banks.

Selected species and varieties
D. caespitosa (tufted hair grass)—pale green or yellow, purple-tinged flowers on long, delicate stems, creating a misty cloud above 1- to 3-foot-tall mounds of narrow, rough, dark green foliage; 'Bronzeschleier', bronze veil tufted hair grass, bears bronze-yellow flowers; 'Goldschleier', gold veil tufted hair grass, has bright yellow flowers; 'Tardiflora' is a late-blooming cultivar. *D. flexuosa* (crinkled hair grass)—shiny, bluish green leaves, to 8 inches long, forming a dense, 1- to 2-foot-tall clump. Silvery purple flowers appear in summer.

Growing conditions and maintenance
Hair grasses thrive in light shade, in moist, fertile soil; crinkled hair grass prefers soil on the acidic side. The plants dislike hot, dry conditions.

Erianthus (er-ee-AN-thus)

PLUME GRASS

Erianthus ravennae

HARDINESS: Zones 6-10

PLANT TYPE: perennial

HEIGHT: 6 to 12 feet

SOIL: moist, well-drained

LIGHT: full sun

Plume grasses are warm-season perennials with reedlike stems, long flat leaves, and large showy plumes. Flowers emerge in late summer, and foliage turns color in fall. Plume grass makes a dramatic specimen, an attractive screen, or an effective background plant in a border.

Selected species and varieties

E. officinarum 'Pele's Smoke' [also listed as *Saccharum officinarum* 'Pele's Smoke']—dense, 6-foot-tall clumps of arching purple foliage and glossy purple canes. Fluffy grayish white flowers rarely appear, except in tropical regions; Zones 9-10. *E. ravennae* (ravenna grass)—vigorous, densely tufted grass to 12 feet tall, with coarse, stiff leaves to 3 feet long. The gray-green foliage turns orange, brown, and purple in autumn. Silvery purple flowers appear atop 8- to 12-foot spikes, turn beige in fall, and remain throughout winter.

Growing conditions and maintenance

Grow plume grass in full sun, in moderately fertile, well-drained soil. Plants tolerate drought but do best in moist conditions. Provide protection from wind. Remove old flowers before new growth begins in spring. Propagate from seed or by division.

Fargesia (far-JEEZ-ee-a)

BAMBOO

Fargesia murielae

HARDINESS: Zones 5-9

PLANT TYPE: perennial

HEIGHT: 10 to 15 feet or more

SOIL: adaptable

LIGHT: partial shade

Narrow, tapered dark green leaves flutter from purplish sheaths on slender purplish gray culms, or canes, that arch as they mature and spread to form mounded clumps. Use as a dramatic color and vertical accent in ornamental beds. Cut canes make good garden stakes.

Selected species and varieties

F. murielae [also classified as *Thamnocalamus spathaceus*] (umbrella bamboo)—slender bright green canes to 12 feet tall, aging to yellow, bend at the top under the weight of rich green leaves 3 to 5 inches long that turn yellow in fall before dropping; hardy to Zone 6. *F. nitida* [also classified as *Sinarundinaria nitida*] (clump bamboo, hardy blue bamboo, fountain bamboo)—hollow dark purple canes ½ inch in diameter and 10 to 15 feet tall (reaching 20 feet under optimum conditions) are coated with a bluish white powder when young and, after the first year, produce leaves to 7 inches long with bristly margins on one side.

Growing conditions and maintenance

As clumps begin to develop above soil level, divide and replant. Clump bamboo is less invasive than umbrella bamboo.

Festuca (fes-TOO-ka)

FESCUE

Festuca amethystina

HARDINESS: Zones 4-9

PLANT TYPE: perennial

HEIGHT: 6 inches to 3 feet

SOIL: poor to average, well-drained

LIGHT: full sun

This large genus includes many species of clumping, evergreen, cool-season grasses that are valuable in the landscape. Foliage is generally fine-textured and lance-shaped, and ranges from gray- or blue-green to medium or dark green. Narrow flower spikes appear in spring or summer in shades of green, purple, and brown. Fescue makes an excellent specimen or accent plant; use the low-growing varieties as ground covers or edgings. Ideal in rock gardens and borders, the plants blend well with conifers, ferns, and hostas, as well as other types of fescues. Some are also suitable for growing in containers.

Selected species and varieties

F. amethystina (large blue fescue)—forms dense, upright, 1½-foot-tall tufts of soft, blue- to gray-green leaves and small greenish or purplish flowers that fade to whitish tan as they age. *F. gigantea* (giant fescue)—native woodland grass with medium green, upright, arching leaves up to 3 feet long and summer-blooming flowers that gradually turn a tannish color. *F. mairei* (Atlas fescue, Maire's fescue)—forms dense clumps of shiny, gray-green leaves to 3 feet long and gray-green flowers that bloom in early summer. *F. ovina* [also listed as *F.*

amethystina] (sheep fescue)—mounds of fine-textured, blue-green foliage to 1 foot tall, with purplish to greenish flower spikes that appear well above the foliage and gradually turn a gold to gray color as they dry. *F. ovina glauca* [also listed as *F. ovina* 'Glauca', *F. glauca*] (blue sheep fescue, blue fescue)—popular variety that grows 8 to 12 inches high and produces neat tufts of soft blue leaves; 'Elijah Blue' reaches 8 inches tall and has powder blue foliage; 'Sea Urchin' produces silvery gray-blue mounds 6 to 12 inches tall; 'Solling' grows to 8 inches tall, with grayish blue foliage that turns reddish brown in autumn.

Growing conditions and maintenance
Fescue grows best in full sun, in poor to average, well-drained soil. It does not tolerate soggy conditions or high temperatures. Cut back in early spring before new growth begins. For best color, divide clumps every 2 or 3 years. Propagate by seed or division.

Festuca ovina glauca 'Sea Urchin'

Glyceria (gli-SEER-ee-a)

MANNA GRASS

Glyceria maxima 'Variegata'

HARDINESS: Zones 5-10

PLANT TYPE: perennial

HEIGHT: 2 to 3 feet

SOIL: moist, fertile soil or shallow water

LIGHT: full sun

Manna grass is a perennial aquatic plant suitable for wet sites such as water gardens, ponds, and alongside streams. A vigorous spreader, it forms upright clumps of long, narrow leaves and airy, green to purple, summer-blooming flowers.

Selected species and varieties
G. maxima 'Variegata' (variegated manna grass, sweetgrass)—spreads to form dense, 2- to 3-foot-tall clumps of attractive variegated foliage. The leaves, up to 2 feet long, are pink when young, then turn green with white and creamy yellow stripes.

Growing conditions and maintenance
Manna grass prefers full sun and thrives in moist, fertile soil or in a few inches of water. It can also be grown in containers, which keeps its spread in check. Propagate by division in spring.

Hakonechloa (hah-kon-eh-KLO-a)

HAKONECHLOA

Hakonechloa macra 'Aureola'

HARDINESS: Zones 5-9

PLANT TYPE: perennial

HEIGHT: 12 to 18 inches

SOIL: moist, well-drained, fertile

LIGHT: partial to bright full shade

A slow-spreading deciduous ground cover, hakonechloa can also be used as an accent alone, in masses along walkways, or in borders and rock gardens. Breezes rustling through the foliage produce soft textural effects. Hakonechloa also makes a good container plant.

Selected species and varieties
H. macra 'Aureola' (golden variegated hakonechloa)—a 12- to 18-inch-high rhizomatous clump with arching habit, consisting of bamboolike stems that display 8-inch-long, tapering, cream-colored, bronzy-green-edged leaves that usually spill over in the same direction and become buff colored in fall, as well as inconspicuous open panicles of yellowish green flowers that appear in late summer or early autumn.

Growing conditions and maintenance
Hakonechloa needs shelter from hot afternoon sun. Amend the soil liberally with organic matter such as compost, leaf mold, or peat moss before planting, and space plants 12 to 15 inches apart.

Helictotrichon (he-lik-toh-TRY-kon)

BLUE OAT GRASS

Helictotrichon sempervirens

HARDINESS: Zones 4-8

PLANT TYPE: perennial

HEIGHT: 2 to 3 feet

SOIL: well-drained

LIGHT: full sun

Blue oat grass produces a dense clump of stiff, steel blue foliage and is a valuable addition to a rock garden or a herbaceous border for both color and form. It contrasts well with perennials having green or silvery white foliage. The color is also a lovely complement to the burgundy leaves of shrubs such as barberry 'Crimson Pigmy' or smoke bush 'Royal Purple'. The flowers are buff-colored and appear in graceful sprays above the leaves.

Selected species and varieties
H. sempervirens—forms a dense mound 2 to 3 feet high and wide, with light blue-gray leaves and flowers in drooping, one-sided, 4- to 6-inch clusters on slender stems held above the foliage.

Growing conditions and maintenance
Blue oat grass is easy to grow in most soils, including dry, infertile ones. It requires good air circulation to prevent disease. Cut back the foliage in early spring, before new growth begins.

Imperata (im-per-AY-ta)

JAPANESE BLOOD GRASS

Imperata cylindrica rubra

HARDINESS: Zones 6-9

PLANT TYPE: perennial

HEIGHT: 12 to 18 inches

SOIL: well-drained

LIGHT: full sun to partial shade

Japanese blood grass produces clumps of leaves whose top half turns a rich blood red. It is very effective planted in small groups or large masses at the front of a border. The flowers of this grass are ornamentally insignificant, but its vivid foliage, which provides color from summer through fall, makes it well worth including in a garden.

Selected species and varieties
I. cylindrica rubra 'Red Baron'—leaves are 12 to 18 inches long and ¼ inch wide, turning red in early summer; color increases in intensity in fall; outstanding for long-season color contrast.

Growing conditions and maintenance
Japanese blood grass grows in sun or partial shade in nearly any well-drained soil. It is particularly showy when viewed with the sun shining through the colorful leaves. It is completely dormant in the winter, and old leaves should be cut back before new growth emerges in spring. *Note:* If any part of 'Red Baron' reverts to green, it should be removed at once. The green form is highly aggressive and is listed in the United States as a noxious weed.

Lagurus (lag-YOU-rus)

RABBIT-GRASS

Lagurus ovatus

HARDINESS: tender

PLANT TYPE: annual

HEIGHT: 12 to 18 inches

SOIL: light, well-drained

LIGHT: full sun

This annual ornamental grass is native to the Mediterranean region but has naturalized in parts of the western United States. Its furry seed heads add interest and soft texture to a border or beside a walkway. Plants are effective in drifts or massed beds. Seed heads are attractive for both fresh and dried arrangements.

Selected species and varieties
L. ovatus (hare's-tail grass) produces narrow, hairy leaves and distinctive seed heads that are fuzzy and light green, turning creamy white as they mature. At 1½ to 2½ inches long, they resemble a rabbit's tail, hence the common name; 'Nanus' is a dwarf variety that grows to 6 inches.

Growing conditions and maintenance
Start seed indoors 8 weeks prior to the last frost or sow directly outdoors as soon as the soil can be worked. Allow 6 to 12 inches between plants. This grass tolerates heat very well.

Miscanthus (mis-KAN-thus)

EULALIA

Miscanthus sinensis 'Zebrinus'

HARDINESS: Zones 5-9

PLANT TYPE: perennial

HEIGHT: 3 to 10 feet

SOIL: well-drained

LIGHT: full sun

The tall flower plumes of eulalia arise in summer and add graceful movement and soft colors to the garden. Both the flowers and the foliage remain attractive throughout the winter. Eulalias are useful as specimens and screens, and add drama to rock gardens and herbaceous borders.

Selected species and varieties

M. sinensis—5 to 10 feet tall, narrow leaves 3 to 4 feet long with a prominent white midrib, flowers are feathery, fan-shaped, blooming in late summer to fall; 'Morning Light'—5 feet, variegated leaves with silver midrib and white margins, reddish bronze flowers; 'Purpurascens'—3 to 4 feet, orange-red in fall; 'Variegatus'—5 to 7 feet, leaves have cream-colored stripes; 'Yaku Jima'—3- to 4-foot dwarf; 'Zebrinus'—6 to 7 feet, horizontal yellow stripes on leaves.

Growing conditions and maintenance

Transplant eulalia in spring, selecting a sunny site. It tolerates nearly any well-drained soil. Cut back old foliage in late winter 2 to 6 inches above the ground.

Molinia (mo-LIN-ee-a)

MOOR GRASS

Molinia caerulea 'Variegata'

HARDINESS: Zones 5-9

PLANT TYPE: perennial

HEIGHT: 3 to 7 feet

SOIL: fertile, moist, acidic

LIGHT: full sun or light shade

Moor grass forms tufted clumps of soft, narrow, flat leaves that often show brilliant color in autumn. Tall, stiff stems carry graceful purple, summer-blooming flowers well above the foliage. This colorful perennial grass makes an excellent accent or specimen plant. Use the lower-growing plants as edgings or ground covers; taller ones are attractive at the back of a border.

Selected species and varieties

M. caerulea (purple moor grass)—upright, arching leaves, to 18 inches long, and purple flower spikes on 3-foot stems; 'Variegata', variegated purple moor grass, is more compact than the species and produces mounds of green leaves with creamy yellow stripes. *M. caerulea arundinacea* (tall purple moor grass)—larger leaves and taller flowers than those of the species. Flowers and foliage turn golden in autumn; 'Karl Foerster' has tall purple flowers that can reach 7 feet; 'Sky Racer' sports leaves that grow up to 3 feet long.

Growing conditions and maintenance

Moor grass grows well in full sun or partial shade. It prefers rich, moist, neutral to acid soil. Propagate by division in spring.

Muhlenbergia (myoo-len-BUR-jee-a)

MUHLY

Muhlenbergia capillaris

HARDINESS: Zones 6-10

PLANT TYPE: perennial

HEIGHT: 1½ to 4 feet

SOIL: moist, sandy to dry, rocky

LIGHT: full sun to partial shade

The graceful foliage and airy flowers of these clump-forming perennial grasses make them valuable for mass plantings or as garden accents. The softly colored seed heads that develop in fall remain attractive through winter.

Selected species and varieties

M. capillaris (pink muhly, hair grass)—1½ to 3 feet with narrow, wiry, nearly evergreen leaves; 8- to 20-inch clusters of soft pink flowers on branching stems in early fall followed by purplish seed heads; native to eastern half of United States. *M. lindheimeri* (Lindheimer muhly)—clumps of narrow blue-green leaves 18 inches long and purplish flower spikes on stalks up to 4 feet tall in fall, followed by silvery seed heads; Texas native; Zones 7-9.

Growing conditions and maintenance

Pink muhly needs full sun. It adapts to moist to dry, sandy to clayey soil and tolerates occasional flooding or drought. Lindheimer muhly prefers full sun and a moist, well-drained rocky soil, but it tolerates both drought and some shade. Cut muhly grasses to the ground in early spring before new growth begins. Propagate by seed.

Panicum (PAN-i-kum)

PANIC GRASS

Panicum virgatum 'Heavy Metal'

HARDINESS: Zones 5-9

PLANT TYPE: perennial

HEIGHT: 3 to 6 feet

SOIL: moist, well-drained

LIGHT: full sun

Branching stalks up to 6 feet tall bearing feathery clusters of tiny buff flowers rise from panicum's 3-foot-high clumps of arching, attractively colored leaves in fall. The seed heads that follow remain attractive through winter. Use panicum as a specimen or filler or at the edge of a woodland garden.

Selected species and varieties
P. virgatum (switch grass)—loose, open flower clusters above green leaves coloring yellow and red in fall before fading to winter brown; 'Haense Herms' has red summer foliage lasting until frost and grayish dried seed heads on 3- to 3½-foot stalks; 'Heavy Metal', 3- to 4-foot flower stalks above stiff, deep blue leaves that color yellow in fall; 'Strictum' has blue-green, more-erect foliage.

Growing conditions and maintenance
Switch grass thrives in moist soil but will tolerate much drier conditions, even drought, though it will spread more slowly. It will also tolerate salt spray and seaside conditions. Cut it back nearly to ground level in early spring, before new growth begins. Propagate by division.

Pennisetum (pen-i-SEE-tum)

FOUNTAIN GRASS

Pennisetum setaceum 'Rubrum'

HARDINESS: Zones 5-9 or tender

PLANT TYPE: perennial or annual

HEIGHT: 2 to 4 feet

SOIL: moist, well-drained

LIGHT: full sun

Perennial and annual fountain grasses produce narrow spikes of tiny, bristly summer flowers above dense mounds of arching leaves. The flowers last through fall, and the leaf clumps of perennial fountain grass remain effective through winter. Use fountain grass as a border specimen or massed as a backdrop.

Selected species and varieties
P. alopecuroides (perennial or Chinese fountain grass)—rosy silver flowers in 5- to 7-inch spikes above leaf mounds 3 to 4 feet tall and as wide; 'Hameln' is a fine-textured 2-foot dwarf. *P. setaceum* (annual fountain grass)—nodding foot-long flower spikes in shades of pink to purple above leaf mounds 2 to 4 feet tall and as wide until frost; 'Rubrum' has burgundy leaves and deep purple flowers.

Growing conditions and maintenance
Plant fountain grass 2 to 3 feet apart. Cut back to 6 inches before growth begins in spring. Propagate either species from seed, cultivars by division of clumps in the spring.

Phalaris (fa-LAR-is)

RIBBON GRASS

Phalaris arundinacea picta

HARDINESS: Zones 4-9

PLANT TYPE: perennial

HEIGHT: 2 to 5 feet

SOIL: dry, moist, or wet

LIGHT: partial shade

This mound-forming perennial grass bears flat leaves and greenish white flowers on stems up to 5 feet tall in summer. A fast spreader, it makes an excellent ground cover and is a good choice for controlling erosion on stream banks. Ribbon grass is also suitable as an accent plant in a border as long as its growth is kept in check.

Selected species and varieties
P. arundinacea picta (ribbon grass, gardeners' garters)—2- to 3-foot-tall mounds of foliage striped in green, creamy white, and sometimes pink. Leaves are pointed and up to 12 inches long. White or pale pink flowers appear in June.

Growing conditions and maintenance
Ribbon grass prefers partial shade; its colors fade in full sun. It tolerates a wide range of soil types and conditions, and will even grow in shallow water. Because plants can become invasive, choose sites carefully and plant in bottomless containers if necessary. Propagate by division.

Sasa (SASS-a)

BAMBOO

Sasa veitchii

HARDINESS: Zones 5-8

PLANT TYPE: perennial

HEIGHT: 2 to 8 feet

SOIL: moist, fertile

LIGHT: bright full shade to full sun

Bamboo displays long, green leaves that jut out from tall, cylindrical canes. A woody grass that develops rhizomes, running bamboo spreads rapidly, functioning as both a ground cover and, for the taller species, as a screen. It is evergreen except in the coldest climates.

Selected species and varieties
S. palmata (palm-leaf bamboo, palmate bamboo)—leaves up to 15 inches long and 4 inches wide, medium green above and bluish green beneath, arise from narrow canes up to 8 feet tall and slightly more than ¼ inch in diameter; hardy to Zone 5. *S. veitchii* (Kuma bamboo grass, Kuma zasa)—purplish canes 2 to 4 feet tall bear leaves up to 8 inches long and 2 inches wide that are dark green above and bluish gray below, developing straw-colored, dry leaf margins in fall; Zones 7-8.

Growing conditions and maintenance
Bamboo that is healthy and vigorous can quickly take over an area; restraints are essential. If foliage looks unkempt at the end of winter, prune plants to the ground. Propagate by division.

Schizachyrium (ski-ZAK-e-ree-um)

LITTLE BLUESTEM

Schizachyrium scoparium

HARDINESS: Zones 3-10

PLANT TYPE: perennial

HEIGHT: 2 to 5 feet

SOIL: well-drained to dry

LIGHT: full sun

This clump-forming perennial grass is native to prairies, rocky slopes, and open woodlands from Canada to the Gulf of Mexico and west to Idaho. Little bluestem can be massed as a ground cover, used in a meadow garden, or planted singly in a perennial border. Its flowers and seed heads are attractive in arrangements.

Selected species and varieties
S. scoparium (little bluestem, prairie beard grass)—narrow blue-green foliage in an upright clump, most often about 3 feet tall and to 8 inches in diameter. In fall the foliage turns mahogany brown. Loose clusters of tiny flowers on 2½-inch spikes open from late summer to fall and are followed by shiny white seed heads.

Growing conditions and maintenance
Little bluestem is adaptable and easy to grow, thriving in most dry or well-drained soils, including those of low fertility. It does not, however, tolerate wet conditions. Mow in early spring before new growth begins. Propagate by seed. Young plants can also be propagated by division.

Setaria (see-TAIR-ee-a)

BRISTLE GRASS

Setaria italica

HARDINESS: tender

PLANT TYPE: annual

HEIGHT: 2 to 5 feet

SOIL: well-drained

LIGHT: full sun

Setaria is an ornamental grass from Asia with narrow, linear leaves that have a pungent odor when crushed. Cylindrical seed heads appear in late summer to fall and are up to 12 inches long; they often bow down to the ground under the weight of the seed. Plants can be used as a background or summer hedge and are often cut for dried indoor arrangements.

Selected species and varieties
S. italica (foxtail millet) produces rough-textured leaves, each with a hairy basal sheath, and tall, dense flower spikes with green, purple, or brown bristles.

Growing conditions and maintenance
Setaria is easy to grow. Start seed indoors in individual peat pots, 4 to 6 weeks prior to the last frost, or sow directly outdoors in early spring. Allow 12 to 36 inches between plants. Once established, plants often self-seed and may become weedy.

Sorghastrum (sor-GAS-trum)

INDIAN GRASS

Sorghastrum avenaceum

HARDINESS: Zones 4-9

PLANT TYPE: perennial

HEIGHT: 3 to 5 feet

SOIL: moist, well-drained

LIGHT: full sun to partial shade

This clump-forming perennial grass is a native of the tallgrass prairie and makes an excellent screen, specimen, or background plant. Both the flowers and foliage of Indian grass turn bronze as the plants dry, adding interest to the garden in fall and winter. The feathery flowers are used in fresh and dried arrangements.

Selected species and varieties
S. avenaceum [also listed as *S. nutans*] (Indian grass)—3 to 5 feet tall, with narrow, 1-foot-long, light green to blue leaves and graceful, yellowish tan flower heads, up to 1 foot long, that appear on erect stems above the foliage in late summer; 'Sioux Blue' has bright blue-green to blue-gray foliage.

Growing conditions and maintenance
Indian grass thrives in full sun and moist, well-drained soil. It will tolerate light shade and poor soil, and can withstand drought conditions once established. Propagate by seed or division.

Spartina (spar-TEE-na)

CORD GRASS

Spartina pectinata 'Aureomarginata'

HARDINESS: Zones 4-9

PLANT TYPE: perennial

HEIGHT: 3 to 8 feet

SOIL: moist to wet

LIGHT: full sun or light shade

This graceful perennial grass has long, coarse, shiny green foliage and spreads rapidly by rhizomes. The erect stems are topped with one-sided, narrow, spikelike flowers in late summer. Prairie cord grass makes an attractive plant alongside a pond or stream, or in a bog garden. It is also effective at the back of a border.

Selected species and varieties
S. pectinata 'Aureomarginata' (prairie cord grass)—3 to 8 feet tall, bearing narrow, 2- to 4-foot-long, arching leaves with golden yellow margins. In autumn the foliage turns bright yellow before dropping from the plant.

Growing conditions and maintenance
Prairie cord grass will grow in light shade but prefers full sun. It does best in moist, fertile soil and tolerates both salt and fresh water; when grown in water, however, it can become invasive. Propagate by dividing the rhizomes.

Sporobolus (spor-OB-o-lus)

DROPSEED

Sporobolus heterolepis

HARDINESS: Zones 3-8

PLANT TYPE: perennial

HEIGHT: 2 feet

SOIL: dry, sandy

LIGHT: full sun

Native to the prairies of the central United States and Canada, this perennial grass forms a fountainlike clump of gracefully arching, fine-textured leaves. It is ideal for small and large meadow gardens, herbaceous borders, and as a ground cover in dry, sunny sites.

Selected species and varieties
S. heterolepis (northern prairie dropseed)—narrow rich green leaves 20 inches long in a clump 2 feet tall and 3 feet wide. Loose clusters of dark green flowers bloom in summer and fall. The entire plant, including the seed heads, turns an attractive tan-bronze in fall.

Growing conditions and maintenance
Northern prairie dropseed prefers dry, sandy soil and full sun, but it will tolerate a little shade. Plants require about 3 years to reach their mature size. Propagate by seed sown in fall or spring. The dense root system makes division difficult.

Stipa (STY-pa)

FEATHER GRASS

Stipa tenuissima

HARDINESS: Zones 7-10

PLANT TYPE: perennial

HEIGHT: 1½ to 4 feet

SOIL: fertile, well-drained

LIGHT: full sun

Named for its showy, feathery flowers, this perennial grass has narrow leaves and a dense, clump-forming habit. It makes an outstanding specimen or accent in flower gardens, and is shown to best advantage when backlit. Feather grass is also attractive in flower arrangements, both fresh and dried.

Selected species and varieties

S. gigantea (giant feather grass, golden oats)—cool-season evergreen forming a tufted mound, to 4 feet tall, of arching, gray- to mid-green foliage. Leaves are 1½ to 2 feet long and ⅛ inch wide. Showy golden flower spikes appear above the foliage in summer and persist into fall. *S. tenuissima*—1½- to 2-foot-tall deciduous perennial with narrow, needlelike, bright green leaves and feathery, summer-blooming, light green flowers that turn golden as they mature.

Growing conditions and maintenance

Feather grass requires full sun. It prefers well-drained, fertile soil and tolerates wind and coastal conditions. Avoid planting in wet, poorly drained sites. Propagate by division or seed.

Typha (TYE-fa)

CATTAIL

Typha latifolia

HARDINESS: Zones 3-10

PLANT TYPE: perennial

HEIGHT: 1 to 10 feet

SOIL: fertile soil covered by 6-12 inches of water

LIGHT: full sun

Cattails are aquatic perennials found in moist to wet sites worldwide. They bear long, slender leaves and soft brown flower spikes that resemble cigars. Some species, including *T. angustifolia* and *T. latifolia*, can become invasive and are suitable only for large ponds or water gardens. *T. minima* is a good choice for small to average-size pools. The flowers of cattails are attractive in dried arrangements.

Selected species and varieties

T. angustifolia (narrow-leaved cattail)—flat, ½-inch-wide leaves, to 5 feet tall, and brown flower spikes up to 10 inches long. *T. latifolia* (common cattail, bulrush)—flat, 1-inch-wide leaves that can reach 10 feet tall, and brown flower spikes up to 12 inches long. *T. minima* (dwarf Japanese cattail)—small version of the common cattail, with very slender, 1- to 2-foot-tall, grayish green leaves and reddish brown flower spikes to 3 inches long.

Growing conditions and maintenance

Cattails thrive in full sun and fertile soil covered with 6 to 12 inches of water. They tolerate partial shade as well as heat, wind, and all types of soils. To keep their spread in check, grow plants in sunken tubs.

Vetiveria (vet-i-VERR-ee-a)

VETIVER

Vetiveria zizanioides

HARDINESS: Zones 9-10

PLANT TYPE: perennial

HEIGHT: 6 to 9 feet

SOIL: average to rich, moist to wet

LIGHT: full sun

Vetiver forms fountains of narrow, rough-edged leaves. Because its fibrous roots grow 10 feet deep, it is often planted to hold soil along the edges of streams and rivers. Flowers, when they occur, develop as flat spikelets in plumes on tall stems above the leaf clumps. The fragrant roots, with a woodsy, resinous scent overlaid by violets, can be dried to scent sachets. In the Far East, roots are woven into mats, screens, and baskets whose fragrance is renewed by dampening to scent rooms. Vetiver also yields an oil prized in expensive perfumes, soaps, and cosmetics.

Selected species and varieties

V. zizanioides (vetiver, khus-khus)—leaves ⅓ inch wide and up to 3 feet long and foot-long flowering spikes on stalks to 9 feet.

Growing conditions and maintenance

Vetiver grows best from divisions. Space plants 2 to 3 feet apart. The complex roots form dense sods that crowd out weeds. Harvest roots and renew plants by lifting and dividing every 3 to 4 years. Scrub the roots and spread on racks or screens to dry slowly. Use dried roots as weaving material or crumble for potpourri and sachets.

Adiantum (ad-ee-AN-tum)

MAIDENHAIR FERN

Adiantum pedatum

HARDINESS: Zones 2-11

PLANT TYPE: perennial

HEIGHT: 8 inches to 3 feet

SOIL: moist, well-drained, fertile

LIGHT: dense to bright full shade

Maidenhair ferns add airiness and texture to rock gardens, shady borders, and naturalized areas, such as stream banks or the edge of woodlands. Black or chestnut stripes accent the delicately etched green fronds. Slowly creeping on rhizomes, these mostly deciduous ferns form colonies.

Selected species and varieties

A. capillus-veneris (common maidenhair, dudder grass)—1- to 2-foot-tall arching fronds; Zones 7-10. *A. caudatum* (trailing maidenhair fern, walking fern)—tender evergreen fern bearing pale greenish pink fronds, to 1½ feet long, that turn darker as they mature and often root at the tips; a good houseplant in colder regions; Zones 10-11. *A. hispidulum* (rosy maidenhair, Australian maidenhair)—erect, finely textured fronds, rosy as they unfurl, growing to 1 foot tall with hairy stripes; Zones 8-10. *A. pedatum* (northern maidenhair, five-fingered maidenhair)—slightly arching, branched and fan-shaped fronds, 10 to 18 inches tall, with chestnut brown stripes, spreading slowly; Zones 2-8. *A. venustum* (evergreen maidenhair)—lacy, arching fronds 8 to 12 inches long; Zones 5-8.

Growing conditions and maintenance

Like most ferns, maidenhairs do best in sites that mimic the moisture and shade of their native woodland settings. Amend soil with leaf mold or peat moss before planting, and top-dress with bone meal every year. *A. capillus-veneris* does best in alkaline soil. Remove dead fronds in early spring, before new growth begins. Propagate by dividing rhizomes in spring; root plantlets of *A. caudatum*.

Adiantum caudatum

Athyrium (a-THER-ee-um)

ATHYRIUM

Athyrium nipponicum 'Pictum'

HARDINESS: Zones 4-7

PLANT TYPE: perennial

HEIGHT: 1 to 3 feet

SOIL: moist, well-drained

LIGHT: full shade

Athyriums are deciduous woodland ferns that thrive in even the deepest shade. Arising in clumps, the light green fronds are finely divided and grow upright or gracefully arched. These delicately textured plants work well as accents, space fillers, background plants, or beside water. By late summer, the foliage tends to look worn before it dies back in the fall.

Selected species and varieties

A. filix-femina (lady fern)—2 to 3 feet tall, with reddish, brownish, or tan stalks and erect, twice-pinnate fronds 6 to 9 inches wide and often wider. *A. nipponicum* [also classified as *A. goeringianum*] 'Pictum' (painted lady fern)—12 to 18 inches tall with divided fronds, gray-green foliage flushed with maroon only on the upper half of maroon stems; hardy to Zone 4.

Growing conditions and maintenance

Although lady ferns perform best in the slightly acid, rich loam of their native woodland settings, they accept a wide range of soil types and are among the easiest of all ferns to grow. Locate them out of windy areas, as the fronds are easily broken. The painted lady fern needs less light than almost any other fern.

Cyrtomium (sir-TOH-mee-um)

CYRTOMIUM

Cyrtomium falcatum

HARDINESS: Zones 5-10

PLANT TYPE: perennial

HEIGHT: 1 to 2 feet

SOIL: moist, well-drained, fertile

LIGHT: bright full shade

Cyrtomium has toothy, hollylike, semievergreen fronds arranged in a circle and arching outward. Scattered amid rhododendrons or other evergreens, the fern's medium-fine, leathery, glossy foliage adds textural interest to the shady landscape. In the North, it is often grown as a houseplant.

Selected species and varieties

C. falcatum (Japanese holly fern)—1 to 2 feet tall, with leathery, dark green coarsely serrated fronds having four to 10 pairs of pinnae about 3 inches long. *C. fortunei*—erect fronds to 2 feet high and up to 10 inches wide with 12 to 26 pairs of pinnae that taper sharply and are a paler green and less lustrous than those of Japanese holly fern and not as serrated.

Growing conditions and maintenance

Good drainage is particularly important in winter, when the cyrtomium can be subject to rot. Work leaf mold, peat moss, or compost into the soil when planting. In marginal zones, provide a site that is sheltered from winter winds and hard frost, and mulch heavily.

Dennstaedtia (den-STET-ee-a)

CUP FERN

Dennstaedtia punctilobula

HARDINESS: Zones 3-8

PLANT TYPE: perennial

HEIGHT: 1½ to 3 feet

SOIL: dry to moist, well-drained, slightly acid

LIGHT: bright full shade to full sun

Hay-scented fern forms wide-ranging, dense mats of finely textured light green fronds that smell like fresh-mown hay when crushed. A moderately fast-growing ground cover, it is particularly useful for shady slopes and rocky areas that need filling in but are difficult to manage.

Selected species and varieties

D. punctilobula (hay-scented fern, boulder fern)—curved, pyramidal, very lacy fronds up to 36 inches long and 3 to 6 inches wide, covered with gland-tipped whitish hairs from which the scent emerges, the foliage turning yellow to brown in fall.

Growing conditions and maintenance

Although hay-scented fern grows best in slightly acid, loamy soils, it also tolerates a wide range of soil conditions and, once it is established, can withstand summer drought. Give the plants plenty of room, setting them 2 feet apart. It requires little care but enjoys a springtime application of bone meal to the soil surface at the rate of 1 ounce per square yard. It spreads by slender, underground rhizomes; divide by separating the rhizomatous mats in spring.

Dryopteris (dry-OP-te-ris)

WOOD FERN

Dryopteris erythrosora

HARDINESS: Zones 3-8

PLANT TYPE: perennial

HEIGHT: 1½ to 3½ feet

SOIL: moist to wet, well-drained, fertile

LIGHT: deep to bright full shade

Wood ferns are native to moist woodlands or swamps but are easily adapted to the home garden. They lend texture to rock gardens, shelter early bulbs, and provide a soft background in perennial beds.

Selected species and varieties

D. cristata (narrow swamp fern, crested wood fern, crested fern)—arching ferns 18 to 30 inches tall, bearing 3- to 6-inch-wide, dark green, brittle fronds whose pinnae bend at midstem if fertile and whose sori are large and rusty brown; evergreen in Zones 6-7, hardy to Zone 3. *D. dilatata* (broad wood fern, broad buckler fern)—deep green fronds 2 to 3½ feet long, erect to arching and deciduous. *D. erythrosora* (Japanese shield fern, copper shield fern, autumn fern)—arching evergreen fronds 30 inches long, 8 to 12 inches wide, coppery when new and turning deep glossy green as they mature; hardy to Zone 5. *D. filix-mas* (male fern)—deciduous fern to 3 feet tall, producing a large cluster of feathery, medium green fronds; 'Barnesii' forms longer, more narrow fronds than the species; 'Linearis Group' has more finely cut, delicate-looking fronds. *D. marginalis* (marginal shield fern, leather wood fern)—1½- to 2-foot-tall evergreen fern bearing 10-inch-long, dark gray-green to blue-green fronds with a leathery texture.

Growing conditions and maintenance

Once established in soil that has been well amended with organic matter, wood ferns need little care. *D. cristata* grows especially well in moist soil and flourishes alongside streams and ponds. Choose sites that are sheltered from the wind. Propagate by division in spring or fall.

Dryopteris marginalis

Matteuccia (ma-TOO-chee-a)

OSTRICH FERN

Matteuccia struthiopteris

HARDINESS:	Zones 4-7
PLANT TYPE:	perennial
HEIGHT:	2 to 6 feet
SOIL:	very moist, well-drained, fertile
LIGHT:	partial to bright full shade

Under average garden conditions, these magnificently feathery, medium green, deciduous ferns easily tower to 4 feet—and even more in wet soil—making them excellent background plants. Vase-shaped, they spread vigorously by way of stolons and can soon cover large areas. Fertile fronds are useful in dried arrangements.

Selected species and varieties

M. struthiopteris (shuttlecock fern)—upright plumelike vegetative fronds with 30 to 50 pairs of feathery leaflets surround 12- to 18-inch-tall fertile fronds, which are olive green at first, then change to light brown.

Growing conditions and maintenance

Ostrich ferns appreciate consistently moist locations and can tolerate full sun only in moisture-retentive soil in cool climates. They also grow in wet, but not waterlogged, soil. Easy to maintain and very vigorous, they can become invasive. Divide by cutting the stolons and digging up the new plants.

Osmunda (oz-MUN-da)

FLOWERING FERN

Osmunda cinnamomea

HARDINESS:	Zones 2-10
PLANT TYPE:	perennial
HEIGHT:	2 to 6 feet
SOIL:	moist to wet, acid, sandy loam
LIGHT:	bright full shade

These stately, deciduous ferns grow wild mostly in marshes and swamps, where they reach even greater heights, but they also adapt to the home garden. Spreading slowly on rhizomes, they make excellent background plantings in borders and rock gardens or against a wall. Cinnamon fern can be used to hide leggy shrubs.

Selected species and varieties

O. cinnamomea (cinnamon fern, fiddleheads, buckhorn)—a 2- to 4-foot-tall sterile frond that looks like a cinnamon stick rising above light green foliage changing to gold in late summer before finally turning brown; Zones 3-9. *O. claytoniana* (interrupted fern)—2 to 4 feet tall with tierlike new spring growth; Zones 2-8. *O. regalis* (royal fern)—has 3- to 6-foot-tall fronds opening wine red then turning green, with 2- to 3-inch-long feathery leaflets that turn bright yellow in fall.

Growing conditions and maintenance

Flowering ferns thrive in soil consisting of 1 part loam, 1 part sand, and 2 parts leaf mold or peat moss. The interrupted fern needs highly acid conditions. Cinnamon and royal ferns can tolerate part sun if the soil remains wet, as by a stream or pond.

Polystichum (po-LISS-ti-kum)

HOLLY FERN

Polystichum munitum

HARDINESS: Zones 3-9

PLANT TYPE: perennial

HEIGHT: 1 to 4 feet

SOIL: moist, well-drained, fertile

LIGHT: deep to bright full shade

The lustrous foliage of the holly fern provides evergreen beauty to rock gardens, borders, and edgings.

Selected species and varieties

P. acrostichoides (Christmas fern, canker brake)—18 to 24 inches tall, with dark green, once-divided arching fronds that are widest at the base, developing multiple crowns. *P. braunii* (shield fern, tassel fern) —has dark green, twice-divided fronds to 24 inches long, tapering to the base and arranged in a vaselike circle; Zones 3-8. *P. munitum* (western sword fern, giant holly fern)—2 to 3½ feet tall with long, narrow, once-divided fronds; Zones 6-9. *P. polyblepharum* (Japanese tassel fern)—2- to 2½-foot-tall evergreen fern producing glossy, dark green fronds to 2½ feet long, with yellow hairs and spiny-toothed edges; Zones 5-8. *P. setiferum* (soft shield fern, hedge fern, English hedge fern)—semievergreen, glossy, rich medium green, twice-divided fronds, 1½ to 4 feet long and soft to the touch; 'Divisilobum' has a very lacy habit with thrice-divided, leathery leaves; 'Multilobum' has thrice-divided fronds, but does not have a leathery texture and has less of a lacy look than 'Divisilobum'; 'Plumosumultilobum' bears fronds that

are divided four times, with overlapping leaflets; Zones 5-8.

Growing conditions and maintenance

Holly ferns grow well in cool, rich, moist soil, although Christmas fern is tolerant of dry periods. Crown rot can be a problem; take special care to make sure the soil is well drained. Remove old fronds in spring, before new growth starts. Propagate by division in spring.

Polystichum polyblepharum

Woodwardia (wood-WAR-dee-a)

CHAIN FERN

Woodwardia fimbriata

HARDINESS: Zones 3-10

PLANT TYPE: perennial

HEIGHT: 1 to 9 feet

SOIL: moist to wet, well-drained, fertile

LIGHT: bright full shade

Chain ferns come in distinctly different forms. The netted chain fern spreads vigorously on branching rhizomes to form a ground cover. Arising in a clump, the giant chain fern's spray of large, arching fronds makes a dramatic statement in the shade garden.

Selected species and varieties

W. areolata (netted chain fern)—erect, deciduous fronds rise 1 to 2 feet high from creeping rhizomes, the sterile fronds reddish green when new, turning glossy dark green with maturity, and bearing netted veins; Zones 3-9. *W. fimbriata* (giant chain fern)—arching, evergreen fronds to 9 feet high arise upright in clumps from woody rhizomes; Zones 8-10.

Growing conditions and maintenance

One of the easiest ferns to grow, the netted chain fern does best in soil that mimics its native habitat, the bogs and swamps of the East, although it tolerates drier conditions. The giant chain fern prefers consistently moist, shady settings.

Herbs

WHEN YOU PLANT LAVENDER IN YOUR GARDEN OR pot up a basil seedling for your kitchen window, you're part of a tradition as old as recorded history. Herbs—a class of plants distinguished by their wide range of practical uses—have played a role in the household, in commerce, and in religious life for thousands of years. Today they are used as seasoning in food, as teas, and as the active ingredients in medicines, cosmetics, perfumes, and even pesticides. And these hardworking plants have ornamental value as well.

On the following pages you'll find descriptions of a wide array of herbs suitable for borders, kitchen gardens, and containers. Each entry cites the herb's specific uses, along with the plant parts appropriate for each use. The medicinal use of an herb, often based on folklore or centuries-old tradition, is noted only when modern scientific evidence exists to support it. Where applicable, there are also cautionary notes indicating that an herb once considered therapeutic is now known to be toxic.

Achillea *(ak-il-EE-a)*

YARROW

Achillea millefolium 'Paprika'

HARDINESS: Zones 3-8

PLANT TYPE: perennial

HEIGHT: 1 to 3 feet

LIGHT: full sun

SOIL: average, well-drained

USES: landscaping, arrangements

Yarrow's broad, flat clusters of tiny summer-to-fall flowers on stems lined with soft, aromatic, ferny leaves are long-lasting in both fresh and dried arrangements. Yarrow spreads into dense, weed-suppressing mats good for covering difficult garden sites. Reminiscent of sage and somewhat bitter, the leaves are sometimes chopped into salads. Yarrow yields yellow and olive green dyes and has a long tradition in herbal medicine.

Selected species and varieties
A. millefolium (common yarrow, sanguinary, milfoil, thousand-seal, nosebleed)—gray-white to faded pink flowers on 2- to 3-foot stems; 'Cerise Queen' has deep pink flowers on stems 18 to 24 inches tall and is less invasive than the species; 'Paprika', long-lasting orange-red flowers on 12- to 18-inch plants.

Growing conditions and maintenance
Sow yarrow seeds or plant divisions in spring, setting them 12 inches apart. Gather leaves and flowers in late summer to dry; cut low to the ground to promote a second bloom. Hang in bunches to dry. Divide yarrow every 2 years in spring or fall to propagate or to control its spread.

Acorus *(AK-o-rus)*

SWEET FLAG

Acorus gramineus 'Variegatus'

HARDINESS: Zones 3-10

PLANT TYPE: perennial

HEIGHT: 1 to 5 feet

LIGHT: full sun to partial shade

SOIL: moist

USES: landscaping, potpourri

The creeping rhizomes of sweet flag thrive in wet soils along stream banks or in aquatic gardens. The grasslike leaves smell of tangerine; the rhizomes have a spicy cinnamon aroma prized in potpourri. Once used in herbal medicine, sweet flag is now considered hazardous. It is being researched as an insecticide.

Selected species and varieties
A. calamus (sweet flag)—sword-shaped ¾-inch-wide leaves up to 5 feet tall and tiny yellow-green summer flowers; Zones 3-10. *A. gramineus* (Japanese sweet flag)—narrow leaves up to 20 inches long and a 2- to 3-inch spadix in summer; 'Ogon' has 12-inch leaves striped golden green and cream; 'Variegatus', white-edged 1½-foot leaves only ¼ inch wide; Zones 7-10.

Growing conditions and maintenance
Plant sweet flag in a constantly moist site, even under as much as 2 inches of water. It can be propagated from seed, but the seed must not be allowed to dry out. Otherwise, divide rhizomes in spring or fall. Collect rhizomes that are at least 2 to 3 years old in spring, wash well, slice, and dry; do not peel them, as much of their aromatic oil is in the outer layers.

Adiantum *(ad-ee-AN-tum)*

MAIDENHAIR

Adiantum capillus-veneris

HARDINESS: Zones 7-10

PLANT TYPE: perennial

HEIGHT: 12 to 24 inches

LIGHT: partial to full shade

SOIL: moist, well-drained, acid

USES: landscaping, pot culture

Delicate maidenhair ferns provide a fine-textured embellishment to shade gardens when massed as ground covers, used as fillers among larger plants, or allowed to cascade over the edges of banks and walls. They also do well as container specimens for patio use. Native Americans and traditional herbalists use maidenhair fronds for medicinal purposes.

Selected species and varieties
A. capillus-veneris (southern maidenhair, Venus's-hair, common maidenhair, dudder grass)—deep green arching, branching deciduous fronds up to 2 feet long with glossy purple-black stems and several broad, triangular leaflets composed of tiny fan-shaped ¾-inch segments; Zones 7-10.

Growing conditions and maintenance
Sow maidenhair spores or set out divisions of the fern's slender rhizome in spring; spores take 6 weeks to germinate. For pot culture, set whole plants or divisions in a mixture of equal parts garden loam, leaf mold, peat moss, and sand. Keep ferns moist; plants that dry out completely may shed fronds, although these will regrow when moisture reaches normal levels.

Agastache (a-GAH-sta-kee)

GIANT HYSSOP

Agastache barberi 'Tutti-Frutti'

HARDINESS: Zones 4-9

PLANT TYPE: perennial

HEIGHT: 2 to 5 feet

LIGHT: full sun to light shade

SOIL: moist, well-drained

USES: landscaping, culinary, dried arrangements

Clumps of erect stems lined with fragrant leaves and tipped with spikes of colorful flowers make giant hyssop a bold border accent. The nectar-filled summer flowers are edible, attract bees, and dry well for everlasting arrangements. Scatter the leaves in salad or infuse them for teas.

Selected species and varieties
A. barberi—red-purple flowers with a long season of bloom on stems to 2 feet tall; 'Firebird' has copper orange blooms; 'Tutti-Frutti', raspberry pink to purple flavorful flowers; Zones 6-9. *A. foeniculum* (anise hyssop, blue giant hyssop, anise mint, licorice mint)—licorice-scented leaves and purple-blue flowers on 3-foot stems; 'Alba' has white blossoms; Zones 4-9. *A. rugosa* (Korean anise hyssop)—wrinkly, mint-scented leaves and small purple flower spikes on 5-foot stems; Zones 5-9.

Growing conditions and maintenance
Start seeds indoors 10 to 12 weeks before last frost, and set seedlings out 18 inches apart to bloom the first year. Mature plants self-sow; or propagate by division in spring or fall every 3 to 5 years. Hang flowers upside down in bunches to dry.

Alcea (al-SEE-a)

HOLLYHOCK

Alcea rosea

HARDINESS: Zones 2-9

PLANT TYPE: biennial (perennial to Zone 5)

HEIGHT: 4 to 9 feet

LIGHT: full sun

SOIL: well-drained

USES: landscaping

Hibiscus-like, 3- to 4-inch-wide flowers blooming in spires at the tips of hollyhock's erect stems make a bold statement in a summer border. The heart-shaped, rough-textured leaves lining the stems create an effective temporary screen or backdrop when the 2-foot-wide clumps are closely spaced. The cup-shaped blossoms yield a yellow dye and figure in herbal medicine.

Selected species and varieties
A. rosea (garden hollyhock)—single- or double-petaled flowers in shades of white, yellow, pink, or purple; 'Chater's Double' bears double-petaled flowers like small peonies in yellow, pink, or deep purple; 'Nigra', deep maroon-black single-petaled blooms.

Growing conditions and maintenance
Although hollyhocks are a short-lived perennial, they are most commonly grown as biennials. Sow seed in spring or late summer for bloom the second season. To coax a second bloom in fall from mature plantings, cut stems to the ground after plants bloom in summer and feed with any good garden fertilizer.

Alchemilla (al-kem-ILL-a)

LADY'S-MANTLE

Alchemilla mollis

HARDINESS: Zones 3-8

PLANT TYPE: perennial

HEIGHT: 4 to 18 inches

LIGHT: partial shade

SOIL: moist, well-drained

USES: landscaping, arrangements

Lady's-mantle carpets the ground with large cupped leaves that reveal silvery undersides when tipped by a breeze. Use the frothy clusters of tiny greenish flowers that rise above the semievergreen foliage in summer as fillers in fresh or dried arrangements. Young leaves are sometimes tossed with salads or added to tea; they also yield a green dye. Lady's-mantle was traditionally used in herbal remedies.

Selected species and varieties
A. alpina (Alpine lady's-mantle)—broad leaves composed of pointed, lobed leaflets arranged like fingers on a hand and clusters of green flowers on creeping plants 4 to 8 inches tall, ideal for informal edgings. *A. mollis*—scalloped, fan-shaped leaves up to 6 inches across and yellow-green flowers on plants to 18 inches tall.

Growing conditions and maintenance
Sow seeds of lady's-mantle in the spring; transplant divisions or the freely self-sown seedlings in spring or fall. Cut plants back hard to keep them compact; they recover readily. Plants can tolerate full sun in cool, moist northern areas. To dry, cut flowers just as they open and hang in bunches in a well-ventilated area.

ONION

Allium ampeloprasum var. ampeloprasum

HARDINESS: Zones 3-9	

PLANT TYPE: bulb

HEIGHT: 8 to 36 inches

LIGHT: full sun to partial shade

SOIL: rich, moist, well-drained

USES: culinary, landscaping, arrangements

Plants in this large genus produce round or domed umbels of white, blue, pink, or purple flowers amid grassy leaves from summer through fall. Depending on the species, edible underground bulbs, aerial bulbils, the flat or cylindrical leaves, or young flowers provide texture, color, and a range of flavors for culinary use. Some species are suited to the flower border, others add interest to winter bouquets, and still others figure in herbal medicine.

Selected species and varieties

A. ampeloprasum var. *ampeloprasum* (elephant garlic)—plants to 3 feet tall with several large, mildly sweet cloves forming bulbs 4 inches or more across that can be sliced for flavoring or prepared alone as a side dish. *A. cepa* var. *proliferum* (tree onion, Egyptian onion)—stiff stalks to 3 feet tall, tipped with small aerial bulbs or bulbils from late summer through fall, grown ornamentally or for the bulbils that are used whole for cooking or pickling. *A. fistulosum* (Welsh onion, Spanish onion, ciboule, two-bladed onion)—small, cylindrical bulbs elongating into pencil-thick blanched stems topped with pungent 12- to 36-inch leaves, all parts of which can be

sliced fresh for flavoring or garnish. *A. sativum* (garlic)—up to 15 pungently flavored small cloves in bulbs 2 to 3 inches across with edible pale violet flowers tipping stems up to 36 inches tall from late summer through fall; softneck artichoke varieties have three to five layers of cloves in lumpy bulbs; softneck silverskin varieties, uniform bulbs that are sometimes braided into decorative ropes for storage; hardneck varieties, coiled stalks and decorative seedpods that are prized in dried arrangements; all varieties are used for flavoring. *A. schoenoprasum* (chive)—clumps of slender foot-long leaves with mild onion flavor and stalks tipped with edible pale purple flowers from summer through fall, all varieties of which are used fresh, frozen, or dried as garnishes or flavoring

Allium sativum

or planted as border accents; 'Forescate' is a particularly vigorous variety with rose pink flowers on stalks to 18 inches. *A. scorodoprasum* (rocambole, Spanish garlic)—inch-wide bulbs with mild garlicky flavor and 3-foot stalks tipped with edible bulbils; both leaves and bulbils are used for flavoring. *A. tricoccum* (ramp, wild leek)—2-inch-wide arrow-shaped leaves that wither before white summer-to-fall flowers bloom on 12- to 18-inch stalks; the extremely pungent bulbs and leaves are used for flavoring, the flowers as ornamentals. *A. tuberosum* (garlic chive, Oriental garlic, Chinese leek)—scented white summer flowers on 1- to 1½-foot stalks grown ornamentally for fresh or dried bouquets; the summer flowers and mildly flavored flat leaves are used in cooking or salads.

Allium tuberosum

Growing conditions and maintenance

Sow allium seeds indoors 10 to 12 weeks before the last frost or outdoors in fall 8 to 12 weeks before the first frost; alliums require two growing seasons to produce eating-size bulbs from seed. For earlier harvest, plant sets of *A. fistulosum* or *A. schoenoprasum* in spring or plant the small aerial bulbils or cloves of other allium species in fall for harvest the following year; left unharvested, bulbils self-sow. Most alliums do best in moist but very well-drained organic soils; ramp prefers constantly moist soils and tolerates shade; rocambole tolerates drier soils. Set bulbs or cloves 1 to 3 inches deep. Space sets or cloves of smaller species such as *A. fistulosum* or *A. schoenoprasum* 4 to 6 inches apart, those of larger species such as *A. cepa* var. *proliferum*, *A. sativum*, or *A. ampeloprasum* var. *ampeloprasum* 8 to 10 inches apart. Wider spacing produces larger bulbs. Grow chives in containers and move indoors for harvest through the winter. Divide clumps of chives and garlic chives every 3 to 4 years to maintain vigor. Harvest allium leaves any time during the growing season; chives do best sheared close to the ground and allowed to regrow. Harvest flowers of garlic, chives, and garlic chives for salads and garnishes just after opening. Cut seed heads of garlic chives to prevent proliferation of seedlings. Pick aerial bulbils of tree onion and rocambole in fall. Dig allium bulbs for fresh use in fall as leaves begin to wither. To store elephant garlic or garlic for up to 10 months, allow skins to dry for several days, then either braid stems or cut them off 2 inches from bulb; store with good air circulation.

Aloe *(AL-oh)*

ALOE

Aloe vera

HARDINESS: tender or Zone 10

PLANT TYPE: annual

HEIGHT: 2 to 3 feet

LIGHT: full sun to light shade

SOIL: well-drained, sandy

USES: landscaping, houseplant

Aloes produce rosettes of fleshy, pointed leaves that twist and arch to create architectural border specimens. Where aloe can be grown outdoors, the plants produce a flower stalk in summer, but potted plants maintained indoors seldom bloom. Science has proved the truth of folklore and demonstrated that the sap inside aloe leaves soothes burns and skin irritations.

Selected species and varieties
A. vera [also classified as *A. barbadensis*] (medicinal aloe, Barbados aloe, unguentine cactus)—mottled gray-green leaves up to 3 feet long and 3- to 4-foot-tall flower stalks with dense clusters of 1-inch yellow to orange or red flowers.

Growing conditions and maintenance
Grow aloes from the small offsets produced by mature plants, removing 1-inch offsets for potted plants or 6- to 8-inch offsets for outdoor specimens. Allow offsets to harden 2 days before replanting outdoors or potting in a 50:50 mixture of compost and sand. Water aloes infrequently. To use the gel-like sap, split leaves lengthwise and rub the cut surface on the skin; fresh sap is best, as stored sap loses its healing properties.

Aloysia *(a-LOYZ-ee-a)*

LEMON VERBENA

Aloysia triphylla

HARDINESS: Zones 9-10

PLANT TYPE: deciduous shrub

HEIGHT: 2 to 8 feet

LIGHT: full sun

SOIL: average, well-drained

USES: potpourri, culinary, houseplant

The lemon-lime aroma of *Aloysia*'s narrow leaves perfumes the garden from spring through fall. Its fragrance is this shrub's primary attraction; where it can be grown outdoors, it is often pinched and pruned as an espalier or standard to give it shape. Use fresh leaves in cold drinks, salads, and fish or poultry dishes or infused in liquids to flavor baked goods and puddings. Steep fresh or dried leaves for tea. Dried leaves retain their fragrance for several years in potpourri.

Selected species and varieties
A. triphylla (lemon verbena, cidron, limonetto)—whorls of lemon-scented leaves along open, sprawling branches growing 6 to 8 feet outdoors, 2 to 4 feet as a potted plant, and loose clusters of tiny white to lilac late-summer flowers.

Growing conditions and maintenance
Sow lemon verbena seeds 3 feet apart in spring. Where frost is a possibility, cut stems to 6 to 12 inches in fall and provide protective winter mulch. Potted plants drop their leaves in winter and do best if moved outdoors during warmer months. Propagate lemon verbena from seed or from cuttings taken in summer.

Althaea *(al-THEE-a)*

MARSH MALLOW

Althaea officinalis

HARDINESS: Zones 3-9

PLANT TYPE: perennial

HEIGHT: 4 to 5 feet

LIGHT: full sun

SOIL: moist

USES: landscaping, culinary

Marsh mallows create colorful border backdrops as well as temporary screens in marshy, wet garden sites. Tender young leaves at the tips of stems and the cup-shaped flowers growing where leaves and stems join can be tossed in salads, as can the nutlike seeds contained in the plant's ring-shaped fruits, called cheeses. Steam leaves or fry roots after softening by boiling and serve as a side dish. Roots release a thick mucilage after long soaking, which was once an essential ingredient in the original marshmallow confection and is sometimes used in herbal medicine.

Selected species and varieties
A. officinalis (marsh mallow, white mallow)—clumps of stiffly erect 4- to 5-foot-tall stems lined with velvety triangular leaves and pink or white summer flowers.

Growing conditions and maintenance
Sow seeds of marsh mallow in spring or divisions in spring or fall, setting plants 2 feet apart. Keep marsh mallow's woody taproot constantly moist. Pick leaves and flowers just as the flowers reach their peak. Dig roots of plants at least 2 years old in fall, remove rootlets, peel bark, and dry whole or in slices.

Amaranthus (am-a-RAN-thus)

AMARANTH

Amaranthus hypochondriacus

HARDINESS: tender

PLANT TYPE: annual

HEIGHT: 4 to 6 feet

LIGHT: full sun

SOIL: dry, well-drained

USES: culinary, landscaping

Flowering spikes rise from amaranth's clumps of spinachlike leaves in late summer. While amaranth can be used in the border, its primary value is as a food crop. Young leaves are steamed or boiled as a side dish. The high-protein seeds are cooked as a cereal, popped like popcorn, or ground into flour. Seed heads can also be saved as a winter treat for birds.

Selected species and varieties
A. hypochondriacus [also listed as *A. hybridus* var. *erythrostachys*] (golden amaranth, prince's-feather)—purple-green or golden green 6-inch leaves and tiny long-lasting deep burgundy flowers on 4- to 6-foot-tall stalks followed by red-brown or golden bronze seeds.

Growing conditions and maintenance
Sow amaranth seeds ¼-inch deep in rows 2 to 3 feet apart and thin seedlings to stand 4 to 10 inches apart. Keep soil moist until seed germinates; plants tolerate dry conditions thereafter. Harvest seeds after frost. Thresh by walking on seed heads or pushing them through ½-inch hardware cloth, then through window screening. Winnow in front of an electric fan to remove chaff.

Anethum (a-NEE-thum)

DILL

Anethum graveolens

HARDINESS: tender

PLANT TYPE: annual

HEIGHT: 3 to 4 feet

LIGHT: full sun

SOIL: average to rich, well-drained

USES: culinary, dried arrangements

Dill's aromatic feathery leaves and flat, open clusters of yellow summer flowers add delicate texture to garden beds. Dill also thrives in window-sill gardens. Snippets of tangy, fresh leaves are a culinary staple in fish, egg, meat, and vegetable dishes; immature flower heads flavor cucumber pickles; and the flat, ribbed seeds season breads and sauces.

Selected species and varieties
A. graveolens (dill)—soft 3- to 4-foot stems lined with fine, threadlike foliage; 'Bouquet' is a compact cultivar that produces more leaves than flowers; 'Mammoth' is fast-growing with blue-green foliage.

Growing conditions and maintenance
Sow dill seed in the garden and thin seedlings to stand 8 to 10 inches apart. Plants may need staking. Dill self-sows readily; remove flower heads to prevent self-sowing and to encourage leaf production. Snip leaves and immature flower heads as needed. Harvest seed heads just before they turn brown and place in paper bags until seeds loosen and fall. Preserve leaves by freezing whole stems or drying in a microwave oven; dried conventionally, dill loses flavor.

Angelica (an-JEL-i-ka)

ANGELICA

Angelica gigas

HARDINESS: Zones 3-9

PLANT TYPE: biennial or short-lived perennial

HEIGHT: 3 to 8 feet

LIGHT: partial shade to full sun

SOIL: rich, moist

USES: landscaping, culinary, potpourri

Tall columns of coarse-textured, licorice-scented leaves make angelica a bold border specimen or backdrop. In their second year, plants produce broad, flat clusters of tiny summer flowers, then die. Fresh angelica leaves are used to flavor acidic fruits such as rhubarb, stems are steamed as a vegetable or candied for a garnish, and seeds add sweet zest to pastries. Dried leaves can be used to scent potpourri. Angelica can cause dermatitis. It should be eaten sparingly, as some herbalists believe it may be carcinogenic. Do not attempt to collect angelica in the wild, as it closely resembles poisonous water hemlock.

Selected species and varieties
A. archangelica (archangel, wild parsnip)—plants to 8 feet tall with 6-inch-wide clusters of greenish white flowers. *A. gigas*—specimens to 6 feet tall, with 8-inch clusters of burgundy flowers.

Growing conditions and maintenance
Sow very fresh angelica seed in the garden in spring or fall. Remove flower stalks to prolong the life of the plants. Angelica self-sows readily; transplant seedlings before taproots become established.

Anthemis (AN-them-is)

CHAMOMILE

Anthemis tinctoria

HARDINESS: Zones 3-7

PLANT TYPE: short-lived perennial

HEIGHT: 2 to 3 feet

LIGHT: full sun

SOIL: rich, moist, well-drained

USES: landscaping, arrangements

Chamomile forms mounds of lacy, pungent foliage ideal as a border filler. Masses of daisylike flowers on thin stalks that bloom from summer through late fall are long-lasting as cut flowers. The blossoms yield a range of dye colors from yellow through khaki; the finely cut foliage yields a pale green shade.

Selected species and varieties

A. tinctoria (dyer's chamomile, yellow chamomile, dyer's marguerite, golden marguerite)—has pale cream to deep gold petals rimming golden brown centers on 2-inch-wide blossoms.

Growing conditions and maintenance

Sow chamomile seeds in spring, and thin seedlings to stand 1 to 2 feet apart. Mulch to suppress weeds, and fertilize to prolong blooming period. Deadhead to shape plants and extend blooming. Stake plants if flowering stems become floppy. Divide yearly or every other year, discarding the dead center of each clump. To ensure flowers of a particular hue, propagate by rooting stem cuttings taken in summer. Dyer's chamomile self-sows freely and can be treated as a self-sown annual.

Anthriscus (an-THRIS-kus)

CHERVIL

Anthriscus cerefolium

HARDINESS: tender

PLANT TYPE: annual

HEIGHT: 1 to 2 feet

LIGHT: light to full shade

SOIL: average, well-drained

USES: culinary, containers, arrangements

One of the fines herbes of French cuisine, chervil's finely divided leaves resemble parsley with a hint of warm anise flavor. Chervil is an ideal outdoor container plant. Chop fresh chervil into fish, vegetable, egg, and meat dishes. Use flower stalks in fresh or dried arrangements, and add dried leaves to herbal potpourri.

Selected species and varieties

A. cerefolium (chervil, salad chervil)— mounds 1 to 2 feet tall of lacy bright green leaves topped by small, open clusters of tiny white flowers in summer.

Growing conditions and maintenance

Sow chervil seeds in the garden for harvestable leaves in 6 to 8 weeks. Make successive sowings for a continuous supply of fresh leaves; seeds sown in fall produce a spring crop. Remove flowers to encourage greater leaf production; alternatively, allow plants to go to seed and self-sow, producing both early- and late-summer crops. Pick leaves before flowers appear, starting when plants reach 4 inches in height, and preserve by freezing alone or mixed with butter. Flavor fades when leaves are dried. Hang flower stalks to dry for use in winter bouquets.

Apium (A-pee-um)

WILD CELERY

Apium graveolens

HARDINESS: hardy

PLANT TYPE: biennial

HEIGHT: 1 to 3 feet

LIGHT: full sun to light shade

SOIL: rich, moist, well-drained

USES: culinary

The ridged stems, parsleylike leaves, and tiny seeds of wild celery all share the scent of the cultivated vegetable beloved as an aromatic culinary staple. While their bitterness limits their use raw to a sprinkling in salads, fresh stems and fresh or dried leaves substitute for celery in soups, stews, and stuffings. Use wild celery sparingly, as it is toxic in large amounts. Proponents of herbal medicine include wild celery in various remedies.

Selected species and varieties

A. graveolens (wild celery, smallage)— rosettes of flat, fan-shaped leaflets with toothed edges the first year, followed by elongated, ridged, branching stems tipped with small clusters of greenish cream summer flowers the second year.

Growing conditions and maintenance

Sow wild celery seeds in sites sheltered from drying winds. Thin out the seedlings to stand 12 to 16 inches apart. Dry the leaves flat in a single layer in a shady, well-ventilated area. To obtain seed, pick flower heads as they begin to brown and store in paper bags until they dry and release seeds.

Arctostaphylos (ark-toh-STAF-i-los)

BEARBERRY

Arctostaphylos uva-ursi

HARDINESS: Zones 2-6

PLANT TYPE: ground cover

HEIGHT: 6 to 12 inches

LIGHT: full sun to light shade

SOIL: well-drained, acid, sandy or organic

USES: landscaping

Bearberry's long trailing stems lined with tiny dark green oval leaves root wherever they touch the soil. Spreading into low mats of evergreen foliage, bearberry makes an ideal ground cover to control erosion on difficult rocky or sandy banks. Dangling flower clusters lining the stems in spring are followed by bright red oval berries in fall. Native Americans used the berries for necklaces, in rattles, and as a survival food. Bearberry figures in herbal medicine, and its leaves, stems, and berries yield yellow, gray, and green dyes.

Selected species and varieties

A. uva-ursi (common bearberry, hog cranberry, bear's grape, mealberry, kinnikinnick, sandberry, mountain box, creashak, trailing manzanita)—has slender arching stems to 5 feet long, producing ¼-inch urn-shaped red-tinged white flowers.

Growing conditions and maintenance

Sow bearberry seeds or set out rooted cuttings in spring, spacing plants 1 to 2 feet apart. Bearberry will tolerate dry conditions as long as it receives periodic deep watering. Propagate bearberry from seed, from stem cuttings, or by layering stems and moving rooted runners.

Armoracia (ar-mo-RAH-kee-a)

HORSERADISH

Armoracia rusticana

HARDINESS: Zones 3-10

PLANT TYPE: perennial

HEIGHT: 2 to 4 feet

LIGHT: full sun to light shade

SOIL: moist, well-drained

USES: culinary

Spring clumps of oblong leaves with ruffled, wrinkled edges grow from horseradish's fleshy taproot, followed by clusters of tiny white summer flowers. The pungent bite of fresh horseradish root grated into vinegar, cream, or mayonnaise for sauces and dressings is enjoyed in German cuisine. Chop fresh young leaves and toss in salad. Horseradish was once used as a medicinal plant, and its dried leaves yield a yellow dye.

Selected species and varieties

A. rusticana (horseradish, red cole)—has thick, branching white-fleshed roots a foot long or longer with leaves to 2 feet and flower stalks to 4 feet; 'Variegata' has leaves streaked white.

Growing conditions and maintenance

Plant pieces of mature root at least 6 inches long in spring or fall. Set root pieces 3 to 4 inches deep and 1 to 2 feet apart. Dig roots in fall and store in dry sand; slice and dry for later grinding, or grate into white vinegar to preserve. Horseradish can be invasive, as new plants grow from any root pieces left in the garden.

Arnica (AR-ni-ka)

ARNICA

Arnica montana

HARDINESS: Zones 6-9

PLANT TYPE: perennial

HEIGHT: 6 to 24 inches

LIGHT: full sun

SOIL: well-drained, sandy, acid

USES: rock gardens, wildflower gardens

Slender flower stalks rise from arnica's rosettes of narrow aromatic leaves in summer, each with up to three daisylike flowers. Arnica once figured in herbal medicine but is now regarded as toxic when taken internally and is legally restricted in some countries. Arnica preparations for external use, however, are important homeopathic remedies, and ointments made from its flowers are used in Europe for sprains and bruises, though they may cause dermatitis in some.

Selected species and varieties

A. montana (leopard's-bane)—tufts of 2- to 5-inch-long blunt-tipped, finely toothed leaves and golden yellow 3-inch flowers composed of narrow petals surrounding a buttonlike center.

Growing conditions and maintenance

Sow arnica seeds in fall or divide mature plants in spring, setting divisions 6 to 8 inches apart. Arnica does not do well in hot, humid sites or where winters are wet. Flower stems become leggy and floppy in rich soils. For an aromatic muscle liniment, pick flowers when fully open, heat equal parts of flowers and oil or lard, then strain and cool.

WORMWOOD

Artemisia absinthium 'Lambrook Silver'

HARDINESS: hardy annual or Zones 3-10

PLANT TYPE: annual, perennial, or shrub

HEIGHT: 1 to 8 feet

LIGHT: full sun to partial shade

SOIL: average, dry to moist

USES: landscaping, culinary, dried arrangements

Artemisia's aromatic filigreed foliage in shades of green through gray-green to silver and almost white is prized as a border filler or background. The foliage dries well for use in arrangements and sachets. While most species bear inconspicuous flowers or none at all, a few produce airy sprays of tiny, fragrant, early- to late-summer blossoms useful as fillers in fresh bouquets. One variety is used as an ingredient in fines herbes, but some species are poisonous. Herbal tradition ascribes medicinal and insect repellent properties to wormwoods, and boiled stems yield a yellow dye.

Selected species and varieties
A. abrotanum (southernwood)—a deciduous subshrub or perennial 3 to 6 feet tall with gray-green camphor- or citrus-scented foliage; Zones 5-9. *A. absinthium* 'Lambrook Silver' (absinthe, common wormwood)—an evergreen shrub or perennial with filigreed silver gray foliage in neat 18- to 36-inch-high mounds; Zones 3-9. *A. annua* (sweet Annie)—an annual growing quickly into a pyramid of feathery foliage up to 8 feet tall accented by frothy clusters of tiny light green to yellow flowers in summer. *A. arborescens* (tree wormwood)—an evergreen or semievergreen shrub or perennial forming mounds 3 feet high and almost as wide of threadlike silver gray leaves, with loose sprays of tiny yellow flowers from summer through fall; Zones 8-9. *A. dracunculus* var. *sativa* (French tarragon, estragon)—a sprawling perennial to 2 feet high with glossy green leaves whose peppery anise flavor is prized in cooking and seasoning; Zones 4-7. *A. lactiflora* (white mugwort)—a perennial producing upright columns of narrow dark green leaves with pale gray undersides and branched clusters of tiny creamy white flowers on purple stems up to a foot long from summer through fall; Zones 4-8. *A. ludoviciana* 'Silver King' (western mugwort, white sage)—a bushy perennial with silvery white leaves in mounds up to 4 feet high and as wide; 'Silver Queen' grows to only 2 feet with silvery white leaves; Zones 5-9. *A. pontica* (Roman wormwood)—an upright perennial 1 to 4 feet tall with feath-

Artemisia arborescens

ery silver gray leaves used to flavor vermouth; Zones 5-9. *A.* x 'Powis Castle'—a perennial to 30 inches with mounds of woolly white stems and silvery fernlike foliage; Zones 6-9. *A. vulgaris* (mugwort)—an upright perennial to 5½ feet high and half as wide with lacy green white-speckled leaves having downy silver undersides; Zones 4-10.

Growing conditions and maintenance
Sow seeds of sweet Annie in the spring; plant rooted stem cuttings or divisions of other wormwoods 1 to 2 feet apart for low hedges, 3 to 4 feet apart as specimens or backdrop plantings, in spring or fall. Most wormwoods prefer dry, average to poor, well-drained soil, becoming leggy in fertile soils and rotting under hot, humid conditions. White mugwort, however, grows best in moist, rich soil. *A. absinthium* makes a poor companion plant, as

Artemisia x 'Powis Castle'

the substance absinthin flushed from its leaves by rain or watering acts as a growth inhibitor to nearby plants. All wormwoods grow in full sun; French tarragon, *A. absinthium* 'Lambrook Silver', white mugwort, and *A. vulgaris* 'Variegata' tolerate partial shade. Prune southernwood to control its size and shape, Roman wormwood to train as a hedge or curb its invasiveness. Propagate sweet Annie from seed or by replanting its self-sown seedlings; propagate shrubby 'Lambrook Silver', Roman wormwood, southernwood, and tree wormwood from rooted stem cuttings taken in spring or fall. Propagate all perennial wormwood species by division every 3 to 4 years in spring or fall. Grow French tarragon in patio containers, or pot divisions in fall, leaving them outdoors for 2 to 3 months to expose them to colder temperatures, then bringing indoors to pick fresh leaves for culinary use. Gather flowers of sweet Annie or white mugwort for filler; use the foliage of all wormwoods as an aromatic addition to fresh bouquets. Weave fresh foliage into wreaths or swags for drying, or hang foliage in bunches in a shady, warm location with good ventilation to dry. Use dried branches in arrangements or crumble leaves into herbal mixes for potpourri and sachets.

Asarum (AS-a-rum)

WILD GINGER

Asarum canadense

HARDINESS: Zones 3-8

PLANT TYPE: perennial

HEIGHT: 6 to 12 inches

LIGHT: full to light shade

SOIL: moist, well-drained, acid

USES: ground cover, rock gardens

Pairs of deciduous heart-shaped leaves on thin, arching stems hide wild ginger's bell-shaped spring flowers growing at ground level. The attractive foliage, resembling that of cyclamen, grows along creeping rhizomes that develop into ground-covering carpets. While the edible roots are seldom used, they can substitute for fresh or dried ground ginger. Young leaves add flavor to salads, though they may cause dermatitis. Wild ginger figures in traditional herbal medicine.

Selected species and varieties
A. canadense (Canadian wild ginger, snakeroot)—broad, hairy dark green leaves up to 7 inches across on 12-inch-tall stems with inch-wide brown to purple flowers.

Growing conditions and maintenance
Sow wild ginger seeds in spring, or plant divisions in spring or fall, cutting sections of rhizome with at least one pair of leaves. Set sections 1 inch deep in beds prepared with ample leaf mold or other organic amendments, and space plants 12 inches apart. Keep new beds evenly moist; once established, wild ginger becomes a low-maintenance, weed-suppressing ground cover.

Asclepias (as-KLEE-pee-as)

MILKWEED, SILKWEED

Asclepias tuberosa

HARDINESS: Zones 3-9

PLANT TYPE: perennial

HEIGHT: 1 to 2 feet

LIGHT: full sun

SOIL: dry, sandy

USES: landscaping, arrangements

In summer, milkweed's thick, stiff stems lined with willowy deep green leaves are tipped with broad domed clusters of tiny nectar-rich flowers attractive to bees and butterflies. The flowers are long-lasting in arrangements. Those left on plants are followed by boat-shaped pods, prized in dried arrangements, that burst to release tiny seeds with tufts of silky, downy hair. Milkweed's stems and leaves are thought to be poisonous to animals. The roots have figured in herbal medicine.

Selected species and varieties
A. tuberosa (butterfly weed, tuberroot, Indian paintbrush, chigger flower)—deep orange flower clusters throughout summer on thick stems filled with milky sap and lined with narrow 4-inch-long leaves.

Growing conditions and maintenance
Propagate milkweeds from seed or root cuttings in spring or fall, spacing plants 12 inches apart. Because of their long taproots, milkweeds resent division or transplanting. Once established, they often self-sow. For long-lasting arrangements of milkweed cut for fresh use, sear the stems. To dry pods, cut before the seeds are released and hang.

Atriplex (AT-ri-plex)

ORACH, SALTBUSH

Atriplex hortensis 'Rubra'

HARDINESS: hardy

PLANT TYPE: annual

HEIGHT: 2 to 6 feet

LIGHT: full sun

SOIL: rich, moist, organic

USES: culinary, landscaping, arrangements

Garden orach sends up stiff stems lined with arrowhead-shaped leaves that can be massed together as an effective seasonal screen. The leaves add color and a slightly salty tang to salads. Leaves and young shoots can be boiled like spinach. Use the colorful foliage as a filler in fresh arrangements. Orach was once used for medicinal purposes.

Selected species and varieties
A. hortensis (mountain spinach)—smooth deep green leaves and branching clusters of tiny yellow-green flowers tinged red in summer on stems to 6 feet; 'Rubra' (purple orach) has deep red leaves and stems.

Growing conditions and maintenance
Sow orach seeds in spring and thin plants to stand 8 to 12 inches apart. Orach will tolerate both saline soils and dry conditions but produces the most succulent leaves when kept constantly moist. Successive sowings every 2 weeks ensure a continuous supply of young salad leaves. Pinch out flower heads to encourage greater leaf production. Allowed to form seed, orach self-sows freely. Dip stem ends in boiling water to seal them before using in arrangements.

Borago (bor-RAY-go)

BORAGE

Borago officinalis

HARDINESS: hardy

PLANT TYPE: annual

HEIGHT: 1 to 3 feet

LIGHT: full sun

SOIL: rich, moist, well-drained

USES: culinary, houseplant, arrangements

Borage forms sprawling mounds of hairy, cucumber-scented oval leaves. Bees find the nodding clusters of star-shaped summer flowers with black stamens extremely attractive. Chop borage leaves into salads, soups, and dips for a cucumber flavor without gastric distress; brew leaves as tea, or sauté for a side dish. Toss flowers with salads for color, freeze them into ice cubes to garnish cool drinks, or candy them to decorate cakes and other sweets. Borage can be grown as a houseplant, and its flowers used in fresh arrangements.

Selected species and varieties
B. officinalis (talewort, cool-tankard)—leaves 6 to 8 inches long and deep blue flowers; 'Alba' has white blossoms.

Growing conditions and maintenance
Sow borage in the garden in spring and thin seedlings to stand 12 inches apart. Borage will tolerate dry soils but grows best with constant moisture. Plants will self-sow. Indoors, plant borage in large pots to accommodate its spreading roots. Pick rosettes of young leaves for fresh use; borage does not dry or freeze well but can be preserved in vinegar.

Brassica (BRASS-ik-a)

MUSTARD, COLE

Brassica juncea

HARDINESS: hardy

PLANT TYPE: annual

HEIGHT: 3 to 4 feet

LIGHT: full sun

SOIL: average, well-drained

USES: culinary

Mustard's pungent oval leaves add zest to salads and can be boiled or sautéed as a side dish. The four-petaled summer flowers are followed by pods filled with tiny round seeds used whole to flavor pickles and curries or ground to create mustard spread. Mustard can be grown in pots indoors for a continuous supply of young salad greens in winter.

Selected species and varieties
B. juncea (brown mustard, Chinese mustard, Indian mustard, mustard cabbage, mustard greens)—leaves 6 to 12 inches long, with open, branching clusters of pale yellow flowers followed by 1½-inch beaked pods filled with dark reddish brown seeds.

Growing conditions and maintenance
Sow mustard seeds ¼ inch deep in spring in rows 18 inches apart and thin plants to stand 8 inches apart. Use the thinnings in salads; young leaves are ready for salad picking in 8 to 10 days. Mustard self-sows freely for future crops. Harvest pods as they begin to brown, and finish drying them in paper bags to collect the ripening seed. Brown mustard develops its hottest flavor when ground and mixed with cold liquids.

Calamintha (kal-a-MIN-tha)

CALAMINT

Calamintha grandiflora 'Variegata'

HARDINESS: Zones 5-10

PLANT TYPE: perennial

HEIGHT: 12 to 24 inches

LIGHT: full sun to light shade

SOIL: average, well-drained, neutral to alkaline

USES: landscaping, culinary, potpourri

Calamint forms neat spreading clumps of erect stems lined with mint-scented oval leaves and tipped with spikes of tiny tubular flowers in summer. Ideal as a border edging, this herb also grows well in patio containers. Use fresh leaves to garnish summer drinks; steep fresh or dried leaves in boiling water for tea. Mix dried leaves into herbal potpourri.

Selected species and varieties
C. grandiflora (mountain balm, ornamental savory)—brown-fringed, slightly hairy deep green leaves on 12- to 18-inch-tall stems and pink flowers; 'Variegata' has a bushy habit and leaves flecked off-white. *C. nepeta* ssp. *nepeta* [also classified as *Satureja calamintha*] (lesser calamint)—shiny green leaves on 18- to 24-inch stems and pale lilac to white flowers.

Growing conditions and maintenance
Sow calamint seed in spring or fall or set out divisions in spring, spacing plants 12 inches apart. Cut stems back in fall and provide winter mulch in cooler climates. Calamint spreads by creeping rhizomes and self-sows as well. Dry the leaves on screens in a shady, well-ventilated area.

Calendula (kal-EN-dew-la)

MARIGOLD

Calendula officinalis

HARDINESS: hardy

PLANT TYPE: annual

HEIGHT: 18 to 24 inches

LIGHT: full sun

SOIL: average, well-drained

USES: landscaping, culinary, potpourri

Pot marigold's thick stems lined with hairy oval leaves each bear one or two blossoms resembling zinnias from spring through frost. Their long season of bloom makes them valuable in borders, and they also grow well in patio containers or as houseplants. Pot marigolds are long-lasting as cut flowers. Young leaves were once used like spinach in salads and stews. Use the fresh, slightly salty flower petals to add color to salads, soups, sandwiches, and pâtés. Dried and ground, the petals can substitute for saffron in rice dishes and baked goods. Mix dried petals into potpourri for color.

Selected species and varieties
C. officinalis (pot marigold, common marigold, Scotch marigold, ruddles)—coarse 2- to 3-inch leaves and 1½- to 4-inch-wide pale yellow to deep orange flowers.

Growing conditions and maintenance
Sow pot marigold seeds in early spring and thin plants to 10 inches apart. Deadhead to encourage flower production. To dry, pull petals and lay in a single layer on paper (the petals will stick to screens). Dry in a shady, well-ventilated area, and store in moisture-proof containers.

Capsicum (KAP-si-kum)

PEPPER

Capsicum frutescens 'Tabasco'

HARDINESS: tender or Zone 10

PLANT TYPE: annual or short-lived perennial

HEIGHT: 1 to 3 feet

LIGHT: full sun

SOIL: rich, moist, well-drained

USES: culinary, landscaping, containers

Pepper plants bear hundreds of small, colorful fruits from summer into fall, held above low clumps of narrow oval leaves. Use them as border edgings, massed in beds, or in patio containers. Chop the fiery fruits into salsa, chutneys, marinades, vinegar, salad dressings, and baked goods. The tiny peppers are even spicier when dried.

Selected species and varieties
C. annuum var. *annuum* 'Jalapeno' (chili pepper)—narrow, conical 2½- to 4-inch-long fruits ripening from green to red. *C. chinense* 'Habañero' (papaya chili)—extremely hot, bell-shaped 1- to 2-inch fruits ripening from green to yellow-orange. *C. frutescens* 'Tabasco' (tabasco pepper)—small, upright green fruits with a slightly smoky flavor ripening to red.

Growing conditions and maintenance
Start peppers indoors 8 to 10 weeks before the last frost and transplant to the garden when soil temperature reaches 65° F or more. Set plants 18 inches apart and mulch from midsummer on to prevent drying out. Harvest by cutting stems when green or ripe. To dry, string on a line or pull entire plants and hang.

Carthamus (KAR-tha-mus)

SAFFLOWER

Carthamus tinctorius

HARDINESS: tender

PLANT TYPE: annual

HEIGHT: 1 to 3 feet

LIGHT: full sun

SOIL: well-drained to dry

USES: landscaping, culinary, arrangements

Both safflower's stiff stems lined with spiny leaves and its thistlelike summer flowers add texture and color to seasonal borders. Surrounded by a cuff of spiny bracts, the blossoms make excellent cut flowers. Dried flower petals are ground and used as a substitute for saffron in sauces, soups, and other dishes. They also yield dyes for textiles and cosmetics in shades from yellow through red. The seeds are pressed for oil.

Selected species and varieties
C. tinctorius (safflower, saffron thistle, false saffron, bastard saffron)—yellow to yellow-orange tousled flowers up to 1 inch across followed by white seeds yielding polyunsaturated oil for cooking.

Growing conditions and maintenance
Sow safflower seeds in spring and thin seedlings to stand 6 inches apart. Safflowers grow best under dry conditions and are subject to disease in rainy or humid areas. Cut and dry the mature flowers, storing in airtight containers for up to a year to grind as food coloring. Alternately, carefully pluck petals from mature blossoms and allow the oily seeds to develop so that plants can self-sow.

Carum *(KAY-rum)*

CARAWAY

Carum carvi

HARDINESS: Zones 3-8

PLANT TYPE: biennial

HEIGHT: 2 feet

LIGHT: full sun to light shade

SOIL: rich, well-drained

USES: culinary

Carum's feathery, aromatic carrotlike leaves grow in loose clumps from thick branching roots. In late spring or early summer of their second year, plants send up branching flower stalks tipped with flat clusters of tiny flowers followed by flavorful seeds. Chop the leaves, which have a parsley-dill flavor, into salads, and cook the roots like carrots or parsnips. Use the anise-flavored seeds in breads and cakes; add them to meat, cabbage, and apple dishes; or crystallize them in sugar for an after-dinner candy to sweeten the breath and settle the stomach.

Selected species and varieties

C. carvi (caraway)—ferny leaves up to 10 inches long and white flowers followed by ¼-inch dark brown seeds.

Growing conditions and maintenance

Sow caraway in the garden in spring or fall and thin seedlings to stand 8 inches apart; once established, it self-sows. Snip leaves at any time. Harvest seeds as flower clusters turn brown but before the seed capsules shatter. Hang to dry over a tray or cloth, and store the seeds in airtight containers. Dig 2-year-old roots to serve as a side dish.

Catharanthus *(kath-ah-RAN-thus)*

PERIWINKLE

Catharanthus roseus

HARDINESS: tender or Zone 10

PLANT TYPE: annual

HEIGHT: 1 to 2 feet

LIGHT: full sun to light shade

SOIL: moist, well-drained

USES: landscaping, containers

Periwinkle's main stems divide into multiple erect branches lined with shiny, fleshy leaves and tipped with small clusters of flat-faced flowers. Perennial in tropical climates, it is often grown as an annual bedding plant elsewhere for its long season of bloom—which runs from spring through fall—and neat, compact habit. Madagascar periwinkle also makes a showy greenhouse specimen and is useful as a cut flower. It yields alkaloids used in cancer chemotherapy; the plants are highly toxic if eaten.

Selected species and varieties

C. roseus (Madagascar periwinkle, rose periwinkle, cayenne jasmine)—has 2-inch smooth, oval leaves with spiny tips and 1½-inch five-petaled pink flowers with darker pink centers in clusters of twos and threes.

Growing conditions and maintenance

In warm climates, sow Madagascar periwinkle outdoors in spring. Elsewhere, start seed indoors 3 to 4 months before the last frost or take fall cuttings of nonflowering stems and grow them through the winter for transplanting in spring. Space plants 10 to 12 inches apart. Pinch early growth to promote bushiness.

Cedronella *(see-dro-NEL-la)*

BALM-OF-GILEAD

Cedronella canariensis

HARDINESS: Zone 10

PLANT TYPE: perennial subshrub

HEIGHT: 5 feet

LIGHT: full sun

SOIL: organic, well-drained

USES: landscaping, houseplant, potpourri

Balm-of-Gilead's aromatic leaves scent the garden with a musky blend of cedar, camphor, and lemon. The pointed, oval leaves line square stems tipped with tufts of small tubular flowers from summer through fall. In frost-free gardens, train it against trellises or walls or grow it in patio containers where its fragrance can be enjoyed. Elsewhere, it grows as a houseplant. Brew the fresh leaves as tea alone or blended with other herbs. Dried leaves and flower buds add aroma to potpourri.

Selected species and varieties:

C. canariensis (balm-of-Gilead, canary balm)—toothed leaves up to 4 inches long and dense spikes of pink to lilac flowers.

Growing conditions and maintenance

Sow balm-of-Gilead seeds or plant divisions of mature plants in spring, spacing transplants or thinning seedlings to stand 18 inches apart. Prune in early spring and again in fall after flowering to encourage branching and bushiness. Pick leaves just before flowers open, or use leaves from pruned branches. Dry the leaves and buds in a single layer in a shady, well-ventilated area.

Centaurea (sen-TOR-ee-a)

KNAPWEED

Centaurea cyanus

HARDINESS: tender

PLANT TYPE: annual

HEIGHT: 8 to 36 inches

LIGHT: full sun

SOIL: well-drained

USES: landscaping, potpourri, arrangements

Cornflowers form colorful clumps of slender, branching stems with clinging gray-green foliage ideal for massing in a summer border. From summer through fall plants are crowned with buttonlike tufted flowers in bright hues. Both flowers and foliage are attractive in fresh arrangements. Toss flower petals into summer salads for color or dry them to add color to potpourri.

Selected species and varieties
C. cyanus (cornflower, bachelor's-button, blue bottle)—narrow leaves up to 6 inches long and single or double blue, sometimes purple, pink, or white flowers up to 1½ inches across.

Growing conditions and maintenance
Sow cornflower seeds in fall in mild winter areas, in spring elsewhere, and thin seedlings to stand 1 foot apart. Soil that is too rich or has too much fertilizer encourages foliage growth at the expense of flowers. Cornflower often self-sows. To dry for potpourri, cut flowers and dry whole blossoms or pull florets apart to dry. Cornflowers retain their bright colors when dried.

Centella (KEN-tel-a)

NAVELWORT

Centella asiatica

HARDINESS: Zones 8-10

PLANT TYPE: perennial

HEIGHT: 6 to 20 inches

LIGHT: light shade to full sun

SOIL: moist

USES: ground cover, containers, houseplant

Dainty cupped leaves with scalloped edges line centella's slender, trailing reddish green stems. Centella, designated by many authorities as *Hydrocotyle,* spreads to form mats of soft-textured ground cover as the leaf nodes root wherever they touch the ground to develop new plants. Tiny flowers hide beneath the leaves. Allow gotu kola *(C. asiatica)* to ramble, or confine it in patio containers or as a houseplant. Its colorful trailing stems make it an ideal basket plant. Gotu kola figures in Eastern herbal medicine, but its safety has recently been called into question.

Selected species and varieties
C. asiatica [also classified as *Hydrocotyle asiatica*] (gotu kola, tiger grass)—kidney-shaped 1- to 2-inch bright green leaves and white to pink flowers in summer.

Growing conditions and maintenance
Sow gotu kola seeds in spring or fall in moist, or even wet, sites. Plants grow best in light shade but will tolerate full sun if there is ample moisture. Alternately, cut rooted daughter plants from main stems and replant, spacing them 1 to 2 feet apart. Gotu kola can be invasive where conditions are favorable for its growth.

Chamaemelum (ka-mee-MAY-lum)

ROMAN CHAMOMILE

Chamaemelum nobile

HARDINESS: Zones 4-8

PLANT TYPE: perennial

HEIGHT: 1 to 6 inches

LIGHT: full sun to light shade

SOIL: dry, well-drained

USES: ground cover, lawn, potpourri, culinary

Roman chamomile's feathery leaves release an apple scent when crushed. The roots spread quickly into dense mats ideal as informal ground covers or as fillers among paving stones. Dry the leaves for potpourri. The flowers that bloom from late spring through early fall can be dried and steeped for a tea. Chamomile figures in many herbal remedies.

Selected species and varieties
C. nobile [formerly classified as *Anthemis nobilis*] (Roman chamomile)—lacy, ferny bright green leaves and 1-inch white flowers with golden centers; 'Flore Pleno' has double-petaled cream flowers on plants 6 inches high spreading 18 inches wide; 'Treneague' is a nonflowering cultivar that grows 1 to 2 inches tall and 18 inches wide.

Growing conditions and maintenance
Sow Roman chamomile seeds in spring or fall or plant divisions in spring; the species self-sows freely, but cultivars only come true from division. For lawns, space plants 4 to 6 inches apart and allow to spread before mowing. Harvest flowers as petals begin to fade, and dry on screens in a shady, well-ventilated area.

Chenopodium (ken-o-PO-dee-um)

GOOSEFOOT, PIGWEED

Chenopodium ambrosioides

HARDINESS: hardy

PLANT TYPE: annual

HEIGHT: 2 to 5 feet

LIGHT: full sun

SOIL: rich, well-drained

USES: culinary, arrangements, potpourri

Epazote's leaves are prized for flavoring beans, corn, and fish in Central American cuisines. They should be used sparingly, however, as the plant's oils are a potent, sometimes toxic vermifuge and insecticide. Both the fragrant foliage and plumy flower spikes of ambrosia are valued in both fresh and dried arrangements; leaves and seeds can be used in potpourri.

Selected species and varieties
C. ambrosioides (epazote)—spreading clumps of woody stems to 5 feet tall, lined with both broad, toothed, oval leaves and finely lacy leaves. *C. botrys* (ambrosia)—lobed ½- to 4-inch leaves that are deep green above and red below, and airy sprays of tiny yellow-green summer flowers without petals along arching 2-foot stems.

Growing conditions and maintenance
Sow epazote and ambrosia seeds in spring or fall, and thin seedlings to stand 12 inches apart. Pinch plants to keep them bushy. Both species self-sow freely and can become invasive weeds. Use epazote leaves either fresh or dried for cooking. For dried arrangements, hang ambrosia in a shady, well-ventilated area or stand stems in vases without water.

Cichorium (si-KOR-ee-um)

CHICORY

Cichorium intybus

HARDINESS: Zones 3-10

PLANT TYPE: perennial

HEIGHT: 1 to 5 feet

LIGHT: full sun

SOIL: poor to average, well-drained, slightly alkaline

USES: culinary, landscaping, potpourri

Chicory forms loose mounds of coarsely toothed leaves with a branching central flower stalk. Common chicory forms conical heads of young leaves called chicons. While it can be grown for ornament in a wildflower garden, chicory is most useful in the kitchen. Steam or braise young seedlings and roots. Toss bitter young leaves into salads. Roast and grind the young caramel-flavored roots to blend with coffee. Cultivars can be forced to produce blanched chicons ideal for salads or braising. Dried flowers add color to potpourri.

Selected species and varieties
C. intybus (common chicory, witloof, barbe-de-capuchin, succory)—daisylike 1- to 1½-inch sky blue—in rare cases white or pink—flowers the second year from seed.

Growing conditions and maintenance
Sow chicory seeds in spring and thin to 18 inches. Chicory self-sows freely. To roast, lift year-old roots in spring, slice and dry at 350° F. For blanched chicons, lift roots their first fall, cut back all but 1 inch of foliage and shorten root 1 inch; bury in moist, sandy compost and keep in total darkness at 50° F for 4 weeks.

Cimicifuga (si-mi-SIFF-yew-ga)

BUGBANE, RATTLETOP

Cimicifuga racemosa

HARDINESS: Zones 3-8

PLANT TYPE: perennial

HEIGHT: 3 to 8 feet

LIGHT: partial shade to full sun

SOIL: rich, moist, acid

USES: landscaping

Black cohosh produces lacy mounds of large leaves composed of many coarsely toothed, pointed leaflets. In summer, tall, wiry stems bear wands of fuzzy flowers to provide a vertical accent in shady borders. The creeping rhizomes by which the plants spread were once used by Native Americans for remedies, including snakebite antidote. The strong odor of the flowers is said to repel garden insects.

Selected species and varieties
C. racemosa (black cohosh, black snakeroot)—leaves to 1½ feet long in mounds up to 24 inches wide and small, creamy white flowers in elongated bottle-brush spikes to 3 feet long on stems to 8 feet tall.

Growing conditions and maintenance
Sow black cohosh seeds in fall to flower in 3 years, or divide mature clumps anytime, spacing plants 2 to 3 feet apart. Black cohosh grows best in light shade, particularly in hot climates, but will grow in full sun if given ample moisture; if late-summer weather turns leaves brown, cut plants back. Plants seldom need staking despite their height. Top-dress annually with aged manure or compost, and provide protective winter mulch.

Cinnamomum (sin-am-O-mum)

CINNAMON

Cinnamomum zeylanicum

HARDINESS: Zones 9-11

PLANT TYPE: tree

HEIGHT: to 100 feet

LIGHT: full sun

SOIL: rich, moist, well-drained

USES: specimen, houseplant, potpourri

Cinnamon and camphor tree have glossy evergreen leaves that are red, pink, or bronze when young. Use either species as a specimen tree, as their competitive roots crowd out other plants. Alternately, pot them for indoor enjoyment. Use camphor tree's foliage in potpourri or moth-repellent sachets. When cut and dried, the inner bark of cinnamon curls into sticks or quills, which can be used whole or powdered to flavor teas, baked goods, and fruit dishes and to scent potpourri.

Selected species and varieties
C. camphora (camphor tree)—trees to 100 feet and half as wide or wider with 3- to 6-inch oval leaves and yellow-green spring-to-summer flowers. *C. zeylanicum* (cinnamon, Ceylon cinnamon)—trees to 30 feet and half as wide with papery outer bark, leathery 7-inch leaves, and clusters of yellowish white summer flowers.

Growing conditions and maintenance
Sow camphor tree or cinnamon seeds in spring, or root cuttings of semiripe wood taken in spring or summer. Roots will rot if sites are not well drained. Pinch and prune potted specimens to a height of 6 to 8 feet.

Citrus (SIT-rus)

LEMON, ORANGE

Citrus aurantium

HARDINESS: Zones 9-11

PLANT TYPE: tree

HEIGHT: 8 to 30 feet

LIGHT: full sun

SOIL: rich, moist, well-drained

USES: landscaping, containers, culinary

Glossy evergreen foliage, fragrant white flowers, and juicy fruits with aromatic skins all recommend *Citrus* species as specimen trees. Space them closely for hedges or grow them in containers. Chop bitter (Seville) oranges for piquant marmalade or dry their peels for potpourri. Slice lemons for garnish, add slices to tea, squeeze the juice for cool drinks. Grate lemon peels for flavoring, candy them for garnishes, or dry them for potpourri.

Selected species and varieties
C. aurantium (bitter orange)—trees 30 feet tall and as wide with bright orange fruits. *C. limon* (lemon)—'Eureka' is a nearly thornless spreading tree to 20 feet tall; 'Meyer' is a cold-resistant 8- to 12-foot-tall dwarf with sweet yellow fruits; 'Ponderosa' has grapefruit-sized yellow fruits.

Growing conditions and maintenance
Sow lemon seeds in spring or propagate from cuttings of semiripe wood in summer. Choose sites protected from wind and frost. Keep plants constantly moist but ensure good drainage; mulch to conserve moisture. Grow potted citruses in containers 18 inches in diameter or larger, and prune both branches and roots.

Colchicum (KOL-chi-kum)

AUTUMN CROCUS

Colchicum autumnale 'Plenum'

HARDINESS: Zones 5-7

PLANT TYPE: bulb

HEIGHT: 1 foot

LIGHT: full sun to light shade

SOIL: moist, well-drained

USES: landscaping

Meadow saffron's broad, straplike spring leaves fade away by midsummer, but in early fall, clusters of stemless flowers in shades from white to pink-lavender or deep purple with prominent yellow anthers rise to brighten the landscape. Scatter meadow saffron under shrubs, in rock gardens, or in lawns for a splash of fall color or use them along the edges of perennial borders. Though it was used medicinally in ancient times, meadow saffron is now known to be extremely poisonous.

Selected species and varieties
C. autumnale (meadow saffron, mysteria, wonder bulb)—deep green 1- to 1½-inch-wide leaves up to 12 inches long and stemless flowers composed of petal-like pointed tepals 1¼ inch to 1¾ inch long; 'Plenum' has double lilac-pink blooms.

Growing conditions and maintenance
Propagate meadow saffron by lifting the corms in summer and removing and replanting the tiny offsets, setting them 2 to 3 inches deep and 3 to 9 inches apart. Meadow saffron can be grown from seed, but corms take 3 to 6 years to reach blooming size.

Comptonia (komp-TONE-ee-a)

SWEET FERN

Comptonia peregrina

HARDINESS: Zones 2-6

PLANT TYPE: shrub

HEIGHT: 3 to 5 feet

LIGHT: full sun to light shade

SOIL: well-drained, acid

USES: landscaping

In the morning and evening, sweet fern perfumes the air in the wildflower garden or perennial border, where it makes an ideal specimen planting. Sweet fern's lacy deciduous leaves covered with rusty brown hairs form mounds of foliage almost as wide as they are tall. The leaves were used by Native Americans for both herbal remedies and as a poison.

Selected species and varieties

C. peregrina—fans of narrow, pointed 5-inch leaves with red-brown dangling male catkins and smaller, round female flowers in summer followed by shiny conical brown nutlets in fall.

Growing conditions and maintenance

Sow ripe sweet fern seeds in fall, and over-winter in cold frames to transplant in spring. Otherwise, remove and transplant rooted suckers in spring or layer branches to develop rooted cuttings. Sweet fern can be difficult to transplant; to disturb roots as little as possible, dig up a large rootball when moving suckers or layered cuttings. Sweet fern grows best in loose, open soils and tolerates dry conditions.

Convallaria (kon-va-LAIR-ee-a)

LILY OF THE VALLEY

Convallaria majalis 'Albistriata'

HARDINESS: Zones 2-8

PLANT TYPE: perennial

HEIGHT: 9 to 12 inches

LIGHT: light to full shade

SOIL: rich, moist, organic

USES: ground cover, arrangements, pot culture

Lily of the valley's fragrant white flower bells are a welcome sight in spring planted beneath deciduous trees in shade or wildflower gardens. The tiny blossoms lining arching, square stems clasped by a pair of broad green leaves add fragrance to nosegays or small bouquets. Lily of the valley can be forced for indoor enjoyment. The plant is poisonous.

Selected species and varieties

C. majalis—deeply veined 9- to 12-inch-long leaves up to 4 inches across and five to 13 small flower bells followed by orange to red fall berries; 'Albistriata' [also called 'Striata'] has leaves veined white.

Growing conditions and maintenance

Plant lily of the valley pips in late fall, setting them 1 inch deep and 6 to 12 inches apart. In subsequent years, mulch with compost or aged manure in fall. *C. majalis* 'Albistriata' tends to lose its color in deep shade. To force lily of the valley, buy pre-chilled pips or hold pips in the refrigerator in a plastic bag for 8 weeks or more; pot with tips just below the surface and bring into a warm room to grow and flower. Propagate by division in fall.

Coriandrum (kor-ri-AND-rum)

CORIANDER

Coriandrum sativum

HARDINESS: tender

PLANT TYPE: annual

HEIGHT: 1 to 3 feet

LIGHT: full sun to light shade

SOIL: rich, well-drained

USES: culinary, potpourri

Coriander's pungent young leaves, commonly known as cilantro or Chinese parsley, are a staple in East Asian, Mexican, and Indian cuisines. With a hint of citrus, the round, ribbed seeds are used whole or ground in baked goods, curries, chutneys, and vegetable dishes. Add them to potpourri for a lingering lemon fragrance. The unpleasant odor of immature fruits earned coriander the nickname stinkplant; the characteristic agreeable fruity aroma develops as they ripen. Chop coriander roots into curries or steam them as a nutty vegetable.

Selected species and varieties

C. sativum—young leaves grow in small, scalloped fans resembling parsley; older leaves look ferny and threadlike, with flat, loose clusters of tiny white to mauve summer flowers; 'Long Standing' is a slow-to-bolt cultivar.

Growing conditions and maintenance

Sow coriander seed in spring and thin seedlings to stand 8 inches apart. Use fresh, immature leaves for best flavor; cilantro loses flavor if dried. To collect seed, mature seeds heads and dry in a paper bag to catch seeds. Dig roots in fall.

Crocus (KRO-kus)

CROCUS

Crocus sativus

HARDINESS: Zones 5-7

PLANT TYPE: bulb

HEIGHT: 6 to 12 inches

LIGHT: light shade to full sun

SOIL: well-drained

USES: landscaping, pot culture, culinary

In fall, saffron crocus's bright cups open to reveal three prominent red branching stigmas. Picked and dried as saffron, they can be used to color food and textiles a delicate yellow. It takes 5,000 flowers to yield an ounce of saffron, but a dozen or so produce enough for a single recipe. *Caution:* Be careful not to confuse saffron crocus with the poisonous meadow saffron *(Colchicum autumnale)*, which blooms at the same time. Mass saffron crocuses in rock gardens or scatter them in lawns. Force for indoor bloom.

Selected species and varieties
C. sativus (saffron crocus)—pale purple—though sometimes lavender, white, or reddish—1½- to 2-inch flowers and grassy leaves with a white midrib.

Growing conditions and maintenance
Remove cormels growing alongside mature saffron crocus corms in spring and replant 3 to 4 inches deep at 6-inch intervals. Divide corms every few years. Pick stigmas when flowers open, dry on paper, and store in airtight containers. To force, plant 12 to 18 corms in a 6-inch bulb pan. Refrigerate for at least 8 weeks, then put in a warm place to bloom.

Dianthus (dy-AN-thus)

PINK, CARNATION

Dianthus plumarius

HARDINESS: Zones 5-9

PLANT TYPE: perennial

HEIGHT: 4 to 20 inches

LIGHT: full sun to light shade

SOIL: moderately rich, well-drained, alkaline

USES: landscaping, arrangements, culinary

Pinks' clove-scented flowers add fragrance to borders, beds, and rock gardens, where their evergreen foliage fills in among other plants or sprawls into ground-covering mats. Petals are often fringed, doubled, and shaded in tones of white to pink, red, purple, and yellow. The long-lasting flowers can also be dried for potpourri. Toss petals into salad or use to flavor vinegar, fruit syrup, or wine.

Selected species and varieties
D. x *allwoodii* (Allwood pink)—tufted blue-green foliage on 4- to 20-inch stems and 1- to 2-inch flowers. *D. caryophyllus* (carnation)—compact border varieties to 14 inches with blue-green leaves along woody stems and 2- to 3-inch flowers. *D. plumarius* (cottage pink, grass pink)—loose mats of gray-green foliage with 1½-inch flowers on 10- to 18-inch stems.

Growing conditions and maintenance
Sow seed in spring or propagate hybrids by summer cuttings or division in fall. Space plants 12 to 18 inches apart and mulch in cooler climates. Pinch to promote bushier plants, remove side buds for larger flowers, and deadhead to prolong the bloom.

Dictamnus (dik-TAM-nus)

GAS PLANT

Dictamnus albus 'Purpureus'

HARDINESS: Zones 3-9

PLANT TYPE: perennial

HEIGHT: 2 to 3 feet

LIGHT: full sun to light shade

SOIL: moist, well-drained, slightly alkaline

USES: landscaping, arrangements

As a border specimen, gas plant offers open mounds of lemon-scented glossy foliage crowned in late spring to early summer with tall flower spikes. The flowers, attractive in fresh bouquets, are followed by star-shaped seed capsules that add interest to dried arrangements. Gas plant once figured in herbal medicine, but all parts of the plant are now considered potentially toxic. The plant causes dermatitis in susceptible individuals.

Selected species and varieties
D. albus (gas plant, fraxinella, white dittany)—leathery oval leaflets with finely toothed edges in mounds to 3 feet high and as wide with spikes of 1-inch white flowers on erect stems; 'Purpureus' has mauve-purple blossoms veined deeper purple; 'Ruber', rose pink flowers.

Growing conditions and maintenance
Sow gas plant seeds in soil amended with organic matter. Space plants 3 to 4 feet apart; transplanting or dividing plants often kills them. Plants grown from seed take 2 to 3 years to produce blossoms.

Digitalis (di-ji-TAL-us)

FOXGLOVE

Digitalis lanata

HARDINESS: hardy

PLANT TYPE: biennial

HEIGHT: 2 to 5 feet

LIGHT: light shade to full sun

SOIL: well-drained, acid

USES: landscaping, arrangements

Foxglove's towering spikes of funnel-shaped flowers make a dramatic backdrop in shady borders, in combination with roses, or along the edge of woodland gardens. Flowers open in sequence from bottom to top along one side of erect stems. Foxgloves are the source of several important medicines but are highly toxic if ingested.

Selected species and varieties
D. lanata (Grecian foxglove, woolly foxglove)—a single stem to 3 feet tall lined with narrow, pointed, hairy leaves and tipped with cream to beige 1-inch flowers veined purple and brown. *D. purpurea* (common foxglove, purple foxglove)—clumps of stems to 5 feet tall lined with oval pointed leaves and flowers in multiple hues, often spotted and with contrasting throats; 'Alba' has white blossoms.

Growing conditions and maintenance
Sow foxglove seeds in spring to produce a rosette of leaves the first year, flowers the second year. Foxgloves self-sow freely; transplant self-sown seedlings in fall. Remove spent flower stalks to force a second, smaller bloom. Protect year-old plants with a winter mulch.

Eruca (e-ROO-ka)

ROCKET, ARUGULA

Eruca vesicaria ssp. sativa

HARDINESS: hardy

PLANT TYPE: annual

HEIGHT: 2 to 3 feet

LIGHT: full sun to light shade

SOIL: rich, moist

USES: culinary

Arugula's tangy young leaves add biting zest to mixed green salads. An essential ingredient in mesclun blends of salad greens, it can also be chopped to flavor sauces or steamed as a side dish. Use the flowers, which have a slightly milder flavor than the leaves, as a salad garnish.

Selected species and varieties
E. vesicaria ssp. *sativa* (arugula, rocket, Italian cress, roquette)—has mustardlike leaves, rounded or arrowhead shaped at their tips, coarsely toothed along their midrib, and delicate purple-veined creamy late-summer-to-fall flowers followed by slender upright seedpods.

Growing conditions and maintenance
Make successive sowings of arugula seed from early spring through early summer, and thin plants to stand 6 to 8 inches apart. Leaves are ready to pick in 6 to 8 weeks. Plants develop their best flavor when they grow quickly in cool, moist soil; mature leaves or those grown in dry ground during hot weather become strong and bitter. Pull out maturing plants to make space for other sowings or allow a few plants to develop pods and self-sow for harvest the following spring.

Eucalyptus (yew-ka-LIP-tus)

EUCALYPTUS

Eucalyptus citriodora

HARDINESS: Zones 9-11

PLANT TYPE: tree

HEIGHT: 60 to 160 feet

LIGHT: full sun

SOIL: rich, organic

USES: landscaping, houseplant, potpourri

Eucalyptus is best known for its lemon-camphor-scented evergreen leaves, but the smooth bark on the bare, branching trunks also lends an architectural accent. The tree grows rapidly but can be pruned to remain a potted specimen for up to 6 years. Use dried leaves in potpourri, dried branches or seed capsules in arrangements. The oil derived from leaves, roots, and barks is toxic taken internally but has many medicinal uses as a respiratory aid and insect repellent.

Selected species and varieties
E. citriodora (lemon-scented gum) white, sometimes pink to red, bark on trees up to 160 feet tall and spreading half as wide with 3- to 7-inch golden green narrow leaves and clusters of tiny white winter blooms followed by ⅜-inch seed capsules.

Growing conditions and maintenance
Sow eucalyptus seeds in spring or fall. Choose planting sites carefully, as roots secrete toxins that inhibit the growth of nearby plants. Trees grow 10 to 15 feet per year. Prune in spring to contain size, encourage more juvenile foliage, and develop thicker trunks. Avoid summer pruning, as excess sap attracts insects.

Eupatorium (yew-pa-TOR-ee-um)

BONESET

Eupatorium perfoliatum

HARDINESS: Zones 3-10

PLANT TYPE: perennial

HEIGHT: 2 to 10 feet

LIGHT: full sun to light shade

SOIL: rich to average, moist

USES: landscaping, arrangements

Boneset and Joe-Pye weed bear broad clusters of summer-to-fall flowers atop stiff stems lined with narrow, pointed leaves. The leaves are pleasantly aromatic when crushed, and the blossoms make long-lasting cut flowers. Use boneset and Joe-Pye weed in moist meadow gardens or at the back of perennial borders. Once widely used as an herbal medicine, boneset is now considered ineffective and possibly damaging to the liver and kidneys.

Selected species and varieties
E. perfoliatum (common boneset)—clusters of white flowers on 2- to 5-foot stems lined with pairs of 8-inch wrinkled vanilla-scented leaves dotted with yellow resin; Zones 3-8. *E. purpureum* (Joe-Pye weed) —clusters of rose pink flowers up to 12 inches across on 4- to 10-foot purplish stems lined with whorls of purple-veined vanilla-scented leaves; Zones 4-9.

Growing conditions and maintenance
Grow both species from seed sown in spring or from divisions transplanted in the spring or early fall. Cut stems to the ground after flowering. The tough rhizomes can be invasive; spade around established clumps to control their spread.

Filipendula (fil-i-PEN-dew-la)

MEADOWSWEET

Filipendula ulmaria

HARDINESS: Zones 3-9

PLANT TYPE: perennial

HEIGHT: 2 to 6 feet

LIGHT: full sun to light shade

SOIL: rich, moist

USES: landscaping, arrangements, potpourri

Meadowsweet's billowy clusters of almond-scented flowers make long-lasting cut flowers especially prized in bridal bouquets. The feathery plumes open from summer through fall on erect stems lined with wintergreen-scented leaves. Meadowsweet grows well in moist meadows or along the edges of ponds and streams. Dry the leaves and flowers for potpourri. All parts of the plant yield various colors of dye, and the buds were the first recognized source of salicylic acid, the active ingredient in aspirin.

Selected species and varieties
F. ulmaria (queen-of-the-meadow)—has cream-colored flowers on stems to 6 feet tall above oval, pointed, wrinkled leaves; 'Flore Pleno' has double flowers on 2- to 4-foot stems; 'Variegata' produces leaves splashed yellow on 2-foot plants.

Growing conditions and maintenance
Sow meadowsweet seeds in spring or divide roots in fall. Thin out seedlings or space transplants to stand 2 to 3 feet apart. Mulch to conserve moisture. Gather young leaves for drying before flowers appear. Cut flowers just as buds begin to open for fresh bouquets, or hang to dry.

Foeniculum (fee-NIK-you-lum)

FENNEL

Foeniculum vulgare

HARDINESS: tender or Zones 9-10

PLANT TYPE: perennial or annual

HEIGHT: 4 to 6 feet

LIGHT: full sun

SOIL: organic, well-drained

USES: culinary, landscaping

Fennel forms spreading clumps of succulent stems lined with feathery foliage. Flat summer-to-fall flower clusters are followed by oval seeds. Stems, leaves, and seeds all taste of anise. Substitute fresh stems for celery, or steam as a vegetable. Leaves complement seafood or garnish salads. Add seeds to baked goods, chew to freshen breath, or sprout for salads.

Selected species and varieties
F. vulgare (fennel, sweet anise)—branching stems to 6 feet lined with soft needle-like foliage and tipped with yellow flowers; 'Purpurascens' (copper fennel) has pink, copper, or bronze young foliage.

Growing conditions and maintenance
Fennel, though a tender perennial, is usually grown as an annual. Sow seeds successively from spring through summer for a continuous supply of leaves and stems. Left to form seed, fennel readily self-sows in fall for a spring harvest. Harvest stems as they thicken. Snip leaves anytime and use them fresh or frozen; they lose flavor on drying. Collect seed heads as they turn from yellow-green to brown and store in a paper bag until the seeds drop. Store in airtight containers.

Galium (GAY-lee-um)

SWEET WOODRUFF

Galium odoratum

HARDINESS: Zones 4-8

PLANT TYPE: perennial

HEIGHT: 6 to 36 inches

LIGHT: full shade to full sun

SOIL: moist to dry

USES: landscaping, potpourri

Sweet woodruff spreads into ground-covering mats with small clusters of white spring flowers above ruffs of leaves that become vanilla scented as they dry. Yellow bedstraw bears plumes of honey-scented yellow flowers from summer to fall. Weave fresh sweet woodruff stems into wreaths to dry or add dried leaves to potpourri. Use the dried flowers of yellow bedstraw to stuff herbal pillows.

Selected species and varieties
G. odoratum (sweet woodruff)—has open clusters of ¼-inch flowers and shiny 1½-inch leaves on 6- to 8-inch stems. *G. verum* (yellow bedstraw, Our-Lady's bedstraw)—elongated clusters of ¼-inch flowers and needlelike leaves on 1- to 3-foot stems.

Growing conditions and maintenance
Sow woodruff seeds in late summer or divide roots after flowering, setting plants 6 to 9 inches apart in a shady, moist location enriched with organic matter. Sow bedstraw seeds or divide roots in spring, setting plants 9 to 12 inches apart in an average to dry location in sun or light shade; to control spread, set a can with the bottom removed in the soil; plant the seeds or divisions in the can.

Gaultheria (gawl-THER-ee-a)

WINTERGREEN

Gaultheria procumbens

HARDINESS: Zones 3-10

PLANT TYPE: shrub

HEIGHT: 4 to 6 inches

LIGHT: full to light shade

SOIL: moist, organic, acid

USES: ground cover, culinary

Wintergreen slowly creeps along to form low mats of glossy aromatic evergreen foliage ideal for ground cover and for use in rock gardens and wildflower gardens. Waxy summer flower bells dangle below the leaves, followed by fleshy red berries that remain on plants through the winter. Brew freshly chopped leaves or berries for a refreshing tea with hints of mint and camphor. Add a few berries to jams. Both yield an oil, now replaced by a synthetic formula, that was once used as a food flavoring and was applied externally to soothe sore muscles.

Selected species and varieties
G. procumbens (wintergreen, checkerberry, teaberry, ivry leaves)—leathery oval 2-inch leaves on short, erect stalks along trailing stems and ¼-inch white to pink flowers followed by edible red berries.

Growing conditions and maintenance
Propagate wintergreen from seeds sown or divisions made in spring, from rooted suckers in fall, or from cuttings taken in summer, and space plants 1 foot apart. Mulch with pine needles or leaf mold to conserve moisture. Harvest leaves anytime, berries when ripe.

Geranium (jer-AY-nee-um)

CRANESBILL

Geranium maculatum

HARDINESS: hardy or Zones 3-8

PLANT TYPE: perennial or annual

HEIGHT: 1 to 2½ feet

LIGHT: full sun to light shade

SOIL: organic, moist to well-drained

USES: landscaping, potpourri

Wild geranium forms loose clumps of deeply notched, hand-shaped leaves with spring flowers followed by long, beaked seed capsules. Herb Robert has finely divided lacy leaves along hairy red-tinged, somewhat malodorous, sprawling stems and paired flowers from summer through fall. Use both as border fillers or in a wildflower garden. Add dried flowers of wild geranium to potpourri.

Selected species and varieties
G. maculatum (wild geranium, spotted cranesbill, wild cranesbill)—inch-wide pink to rose, sometimes lavender, flowers on stems to 2 feet and leaves up to 8 inches across; Zones 3-8. *G. robertianum* (herb Robert)—an annual with 4½-inch-wide leaves and red-purple ¼-inch flowers.

Growing conditions and maintenance
Sow seeds of wild geranium or herb Robert in spring or fall or divide wild geranium's roots in fall. Both self-sow freely. Choose moist to wet sites for wild geranium; herb Robert prefers well-drained spots in the garden. Both will grow in light shade but are more compact or less sprawling in full sun. Remove spent flowers to prolong bloom period.

Glycyrrhiza (gly-ki-RY-za)

LICORICE

Glycyrrhiza glabra

HARDINESS: Zones 5-9

PLANT TYPE: perennial

HEIGHT: to 3 feet

LIGHT: full sun to light shade

SOIL: rich, moist

USES: landscaping, culinary

Licorice spreads in broad clumps of erect branching stems lined with long leaves composed of paired 1- to 2-inch sticky yellow-green leaflets. In summer, short flower spikes appear in the leaf axils. A branching taproot contains glycyrrhizin, a compound 50 times sweeter than sugar and a source of the food flavoring. Dry root pieces to chew, or boil dried roots to extract the flavoring. *Caution:* Some people are severely allergic to glycyrrhizin.

Selected species and varieties
G. glabra (licorice)—yellow-green leaflets and white to blue, sometimes violet, ½-inch flowers resembling tiny sweet peas on plants growing from a 4-foot or longer taproot branching into tangled mats.

Growing conditions and maintenance
Licorice grows very slowly from seed. More often, it is grown from division of the crowns, rooted suckers, or root cuttings at least 6 inches long with two to three eyes. Space plants 18 inches apart. Wait at least 3 years before harvesting roots; root pieces left behind will sprout the next year. Dry the roots in a shady location for up to 6 months and store in a cool location in airtight containers.

Hedeoma (hed-ee-O-ma)

AMERICAN PENNYROYAL

Hedeoma pulegioides

HARDINESS: hardy

PLANT TYPE: annual

HEIGHT: 4 to 12 inches

LIGHT: full sun to light shade

SOIL: rich, sandy

USES: landscaping, potpourri

With mint-scented leaves growing along erect, branching stems, American pennyroyal develops into low, bushy mounds. Tiny, insignificant flower clusters grow where leaves meet stems, emerging from summer through fall. Use American pennyroyal as an edging, ground cover, or filler plant in informal borders. Sow it into lawns for fragrance, or allow it to trail gracefully over the edges of hanging baskets. Add dried leaves and stems to herbal potpourri; they are widely used as an herbal repellent for fleas and weevils. Although it figures in herbal medicine, its oil can be toxic.

Selected species and varieties
H. pulegioides (American pennyroyal, mock pennyroyal)—1½-inch hairy oval leaves along square stems to 12 inches tall and ¼-inch blue to lavender flowers.

Growing conditions and maintenance
Start American pennyroyal seed indoors 6 weeks before the last frost or sow directly outdoors. Seed-grown plants take 2 years to reach flowering, but plants self-sow freely and seedlings transplant easily. To dry, pick stems while they are in flower and hang.

Helichrysum (hel-i-KRY-sum)

EVERLASTING

Helichrysum angustifolium

HARDINESS: Zones 9-10

PLANT TYPE: perennial

HEIGHT: 12 to 18 inches

LIGHT: full sun

SOIL: rich, well-drained to dry

USES: landscaping, culinary, potpourri

Curry plant's silvery needlelike evergreen foliage releases a sweet aroma reminiscent of curry spice when brushed or crushed, although it is not used in curry blends. Curry plants form tidy mounds ideal for formal edgings and can be grown in containers to bring indoors during winter in colder climates. Both the leaves and the small clusters of fragrant yellow gold summer flowers can be preserved for dried arrangements or added to potpourri.

Selected species and varieties
H. angustifolium [also classified as *H. italicum*] (curry plant, white-leaf everlasting)—woolly, erect stems to 18 inches long lined with narrow, inch-long leaves in compact mounds with flat flower clusters.

Growing conditions and maintenance
Grow curry plant from stem cuttings or divisions made in spring or fall. Space plants 12 to 18 inches apart. Protect plants from frost by burying in leaves or grow in containers to bring indoors when frost threatens. Pick leaves anytime, flowers as they mature.

Heuchera (HEW-ker-a)

ALUMROOT

Heuchera americana

HARDINESS: Zones 4-9

PLANT TYPE: perennial

HEIGHT: 6 to 36 inches

LIGHT: full to light shade

SOIL: organic, well-drained

USES: landscaping, arrangements

American alumroot forms neat clumps of evergreen foliage mottled gray-green or brown-green in spring, developing a reddish cast in summer through fall. Use it as edging or a ground cover in woodland gardens or under shrubs. In spring and summer, long stalks carry airy clusters of tiny flower bells, which make excellent fillers in fresh arrangements. The plant's roots have figured in herbal medicine.

Selected species and varieties

H. americana (American alumroot, rock geranium)—round or heart-shaped leathery leaves 2 to 5 inches across with finely toothed edges on long stalks, and plumy clusters of tiny green to white, sometimes pink, flower bells with protruding stamens on 2- to 3-foot stalks.

Growing conditions and maintenance

Sow American alumroot seed in spring or fall. Otherwise, divide plants in spring or fall and replant with crowns just at the soil surface. American alumroot tolerates full sun but grows best in somewhat dry soils in light shade.

Hibiscus (hy-BIS-kus)

MALLOW, ROSE MALLOW

Hibiscus sabdariffa

HARDINESS: tender or Zones 7-11

PLANT TYPE: perennial or annual

HEIGHT: 4 to 8 feet

LIGHT: full sun

SOIL: well-drained

USES: landscaping, culinary

Roselle develops round heads of broad leaves, sometimes deeply divided like the fingers on a hand, on woody stems. The dense foliage makes a handsome temporary screen. The showy flowers appearing in late summer through fall are surrounded by sepals that swell into succulent fleshy pseudofruits with a tart, acid flavor like that of cranberries. Fresh or cooked leaves taste like rhubarb. The fruits, which color dishes a deep burgundy, are used fresh or dried in herbal teas, jellies, jams, sauces, and curries. Steep leaves for tea, or roast the seeds for snacks.

Selected species and varieties

H. sabdariffa (roselle, sorrel, Jamaica sorrel, Indian sorrel, red sorrel)—leaves up to 6 inches across and 1½- to 2-inch-wide yellow flowers with red-purple throats on branching stems to 8 feet tall.

Growing conditions and maintenance

Sow roselle seeds outdoors after the soil warms in spring or start indoors 8 to 10 weeks before planting time. Space plants 1½ to 2 feet apart. Protect from frost, since blooms emerge only after the days begin to become shorter, and early frost will ruin fruits.

Humulus (HEW-mew-lus)

HOP

Humulus lupulus 'Aureus'

HARDINESS: Zones 3-8

PLANT TYPE: perennial vine

HEIGHT: 10 to 25 feet

LIGHT: full sun to light shade

SOIL: rich, moist, well-drained

USES: landscaping, culinary, crafts

Twining deciduous vines with coarse foliage like that of grapevines, hops quickly clamber over trellises to form dense, textured screens. In summer, female and male flowers appear on separate plants. Weave lengths of hopvine into wreaths or garlands for drying. Dry and stuff female flowers, used as a bitter flavoring for beer, into herbal pillows to promote sleep. Blanch young leaves to remove bitterness and add to soups or sauces. Cook young side shoots like asparagus.

Selected species and varieties

H. lupulus (common hop, European hop, bine)—heart-shaped lobed leaves up to 6 inches across and female plants with paired yellow-green flowers ripening to papery scales layered in puffy cones; 'Aureus' has golden green leaves.

Growing conditions and maintenance

Because female plants are more desirable than male ones and the gender of plants grown from seed is unknown for 3 years, it is best to grow hops from tip cuttings taken from female plants, divide their roots, or remove their rooted suckers in spring. Space plants 1½ to 3 feet apart. Cut hops to the ground at season's end.

Hydrastis (hy-DRAS-tis)

ORANGEROOT

Hydrastis canadensis

HARDINESS: Zones 3-8

PLANT TYPE: perennial

HEIGHT: 6 to 12 inches

LIGHT: full to light shade

SOIL: organic, moist, well-drained

USES: landscaping

Goldenseal sends up solitary stems, each with a few broad, coarse leaves, and very slowly spreads into mats in woodland gardens. Tiny spring flowers develop into inedible fruits resembling raspberries in fall. Indians used goldenseal for body paint, as an insect repellent, and in various herbal medicines. Modern herbalists now consider it toxic, especially in large doses. In the past, inflated claims for its medicinal powers led to overcollecting in the wild, and goldenseal is now endangered in many places.

Selected species and varieties
H. canadensis (goldenseal, turmeric)—deeply lobed, hand-shaped leaves up to 8 inches across, a single leaf at the base of each stem and one or two at the top, growing from thick, yellow-fleshed rhizomes with a licorice odor and petal-less ½-inch green-white flowers with fluffy stamens.

Growing conditions and maintenance
Grow goldenseal from pieces of rhizomes with leaf buds collected in spring or fall. Set pieces ½ inch deep and space them 8 inches apart. Protect with a winter mulch. Propagation from seed is difficult, as seeds need 18 months to germinate.

Hypericum (hy-PER-i-kum)

ST.-JOHN'S-WORT

Hypericum perforatum

HARDINESS: Zones 5-9

PLANT TYPE: perennial

HEIGHT: 2 to 3 feet

LIGHT: full sun to light shade

SOIL: average to poor, dry, well-drained

USES: landscaping

Aromatic St.-John's-wort's erect, branching stems lined with balsam-scented foliage are crowned in summer with flat, loose clusters of bright yellow lemon-scented flowers. Use St.-John's-wort as a fragrant filler in sunny borders or along the edges of woodland gardens. Flowers and stems provide both yellow and red dyes; petals exude a red pigment when pinched or crushed. Although once used in herbal medicine, St.-John's-wort in large amounts causes photosensitivity, with resulting sunburn and dermatitis.

Selected species and varieties
H. perforatum (common St.-John's-wort, perforate St.-John's-wort, Klamath weed)—pairs of inch-long oval leaves and inch-wide yellow flowers with black dots along their edges and fluffy golden stamens.

Growing conditions and maintenance
Start new plants from seeds in spring, from cuttings taken in midsummer, or from divisions in fall. Space plants 1 foot apart. Plants spread quickly by leafy runners but can be controlled by pulling unwanted stems.

Hyssopus (hiss-O-pus)

HYSSOP

Hyssopus officinalis

HARDINESS: Zones 3-8

PLANT TYPE: perennial

HEIGHT: 18 to 36 inches

LIGHT: full sun to light shade

SOIL: well-drained to dry

USES: landscaping, culinary

Hyssop's stems are lined with camphor-scented narrow leaves and tipped with thick spikes of tubular flowers having flared lips favored by bees and hummingbirds. Grow them as bushy specimens or plant them closely for low hedges. Add the flowers to salads, use the sagelike leaves to flavor poultry or stuffings. Use dried flowers and leaves in herbal teas or potpourri.

Selected species and varieties
H. officinalis (common hyssop, European hyssop)—willowlike ¾- to 1¼-inch leaves and ½-inch blue-violet flowers on plants to 3 feet; 'Albus' [also called 'Alb'] (white hyssop) has white flowers; ssp. *aristatus* (rock hyssop) produces fine leaves on 18- to 24-inch plants.

Growing conditions and maintenance
Sow hyssop from seed to bloom its second year. Otherwise, grow from stem cuttings in midsummer or from divisions taken in spring or fall. Remove spent flowers to prolong bloom. Prune mature plants to the ground in spring. Shear into formal hedges for knot gardens or for use as edgings in formal gardens. Hyssop is sometimes evergreen in milder climates.

Inula (IN-yew-la)

ELECAMPANE

Inula helenium

HARDINESS: Zones 3-9

PLANT TYPE: perennial

HEIGHT: 4 to 6 feet

LIGHT: partial shade to full sun

SOIL: moist, well-drained

USES: landscaping, dried arrangements

Elecampane's erect stems are lined with bold leaves and tipped with small clusters of sunflower-like blooms from summer through fall. The shaggy blossoms can be dried to add color to potpourri or allowed to form seed heads attractive in dried arrangements. Elecampane's sticky roots, with an aroma of bananas, were once sliced and crystallized for candies and also figured in herbal medicine.

Selected species and varieties
I. helenium (elecampane, wild sunflower)—has grooved stems lined with pointed, elliptical leaves up to 18 inches long with downy gray hairs on their undersides and 3- to 4-inch-wide flowers with narrow yellow to orange petals arranged around prominent yellow centers that mature to brown.

Growing conditions and maintenance
Sow elecampane seeds or plant divided roots in spring or fall, spacing plants 2 to 3 feet apart. Plants self-sow. While elecampane is not fussy about light, constantly moist but well-drained soil is essential for it to thrive. Cut flowers for drying just after they open, and dry them on screens in a shady location.

Iris (EYE-ris)

FLAG, FLEUR-DE-LIS

Iris x germanica var. florentina

HARDINESS: Zones 3-10

PLANT TYPE: perennial

HEIGHT: 20 to 40 inches

LIGHT: full sun

SOIL: rich, well-drained or moist to wet

USES: landscaping, potpourri

Growing on zigzag stems rising from tight fans of sword-shaped leaves, intricate iris flowers add drama to sunny borders with their arching petals, contrasting veining, and fuzzy beards. The thick roots of some species yield violet-scented orris, prized as a fixative in potpourri and sachets. Though irises once figured in herbal medicine, their fresh leaves and roots are now considered poisonous.

Selected species and varieties
I. x *germanica* var. *florentina* (orris)—pale blue or violet to iridescent white petals with prominent yellow beards on stems to 30 inches tall in spring; Zones 4-10. *I. versicolor* (blue flag, wild iris)—clusters of up to six yellow-veined beardless purple flowers on 20- to 40-inch stems in summer; Zones 3-8.

Growing conditions and maintenance
Divide irises after they flower, planting divisions 1 to 2 feet apart, pointing the leafless end of the root in the direction the plant is to grow. Choose well-drained sites for orris; blue flag prefers moist to wet soil. To dry orris, dig roots that are at least 2 years old in fall, peel, and cut into chunks.

Isatis (EYE-sat-is)

WOAD

Isatis tinctoria

HARDINESS: hardy or Zones 4-8

PLANT TYPE: biennial

HEIGHT: 2 to 4 feet

LIGHT: full sun

SOIL: rich, moist, well-drained

USES: landscaping, potpourri

Before the discovery of indigo, weavers used fermented leaves of dyer's woad to produce blue hues. Now dyer's woad is enjoyed as a specimen or border backdrop, where the clouds of tiny yellow spring flowers produced on 2-year-old plants contrast attractively with the blue-green foliage. Dangling fiddle-shaped black seeds decorate the plants in fall. Dry the flowers to add color to potpourri. Woad is considered toxic.

Selected species and varieties
I. tinctoria (dyer's woad, asp-of-Jerusalem)—rosettes of oval leaves the first year followed by tall flowering stalks the second year tipped with large, airy clusters of ¼-inch-wide, four-petaled yellow flowers on sprawling to erect stems lined with narrow leaves.

Growing conditions and maintenance
Sow dyer's woad in late summer for flowering the following year. Space plants 6 inches apart in deep soil that can accommodate their long taproots. Pick flowers just after opening and dry on screens in a well-ventilated area. Left to form seed, plants self-sow freely; transplant seedlings in spring.

Laurus (LAR-us)

LAUREL, SWEET BAY

Laurus nobilis

HARDINESS: Zones 8-10

PLANT TYPE: tree or shrub

HEIGHT: 4 to 40 feet

LIGHT: full sun to light shade

SOIL: well-drained

USES: culinary, landscaping, dried arrangements

In warm climates, evergreen bay laurel grows as a multistemmed shrub or tree to 40 feet; in colder climates, it reaches 4 to 6 feet as a container-grown standard. The glossy, leathery, aromatic leaves with intense flavor are prized by cooks and essential in bouquets garnis. Add leaves to potpourri, or dry branches for bouquets or wreaths. Bay laurel is a traditional medicinal and insect-repellent herb.

Selected species and varieties
L. nobilis (bay laurel, bay, bay tree, true laurel)—narrow, oval 2- to 4-inch gray-green leaves; 'Angustifolia' (willow-leaved bay) has extremely narrow leaves; 'Aurea', tapered golden yellow leaves.

Growing conditions and maintenance
Plant balled-and-burlapped or container-grown specimens to harvest leaves the first season. Choose sites protected from winds. To grow as standards, train plants to a single stem and prune frequently; bring the plants indoors before frost. Propagate from seed or hardwood cuttings. Dry the leaves in a single layer in a warm, dark place; weigh down with a board to dry them flat. Store in airtight containers.

Lavandula (lav-AN-dew-la)

LAVENDER

Lavandula angustifolia 'Hidcote'

HARDINESS: Zones 5-10

PLANT TYPE: perennial or small shrub

HEIGHT: 1 to 5 feet

LIGHT: full sun

SOIL: dry, well-drained, sandy, alkaline

USES: landscaping, culinary, arrangements

Dense spikes of intensely fragrant blue to purple, sometimes white, ¼- to ½-inch flowers bloom throughout summer on leafless stalks above cushions of gray-green foliage. Mounds of lavender make fragrant border specimens or can be used as low hedges. Aromatic oils permeate all parts of the plant but are concentrated in flowers. Use fresh flowers to flavor jellies, vinegars, and sauces, toss with salads, or crystallize as a garnish. Use fresh or dried flower stalks in bouquets, dried flowers in sachets and potpourri. Some species are reputed to have medicinal and insect-repellent properties.

Selected species and varieties
L. angustifolia [also listed as *L. officinalis, L. spica, L. vera*] (English lavender)—compact, broad mounds of aromatic foliage; 'Hidcote' is slow growing to 16 inches with sweetly scented deep purple flowers above silvery foliage; 'Jean Davis' has prolific pale pink flowers on 18-inch mounds; 'Munstead', early large purple flowers on compact 14-inch plants; Zones 5-9. *L. dentata* var. *candicans* (French lavender, fringed lavender)—2- to 3-foot stalks of blue flowers above pine-scented mounds of toothed leaves; Zones 9-10. *L.* x *intermedia* (lavandin)—robust, very fragrant hybrids ideal for landscaping; 'Alba' has white flower spikes on 3-foot stems; 'Dutch', very early dark violet flowers on 3-foot stems; 'Grosso', thick, 4- to 6-inch spikes of deep lavender flowers on 30-inch stems above compact 8-inch mounds of silvery foliage; 'Provence', very fragrant violet blossoms on 2-foot stems; 'Seal', pale violet flowers on vigorous plants to 5 feet tall; Zones 6-8. *L. lanata* (woolly lavender)—deep purple flowers on 5-foot stems above mounds of white woolly foliage spreading to 4 feet; Zones 7-9. *L. pinnata*—an almost ever-blooming species in mild zones with lavender to deep purple blossoms on 30-inch stems above ferny foliage; Zones 8-10. *L. stoechas* (Spanish lavender)—extremely fragrant magenta-purple flowers on 18- to 24-inch stems; Zones 6-9.

Growing conditions and maintenance
Plant rooted lavender cuttings or divisions in spring, spacing them 12 inches apart for hedges, up to 6 feet apart in borders. Poor soil intensifies fragrance. Protect fringed lavender and *L. pinnata* from frost, or grow in containers that you can move indoors. Pinch flowers the first year to encourage wider mounds. Stems become woody their second season; prune woody stems in fall, or shear entire plant to 8 to 12 inches tall. Pick lavender before the flowers are fully open, cutting early in the day before the sun dries volatile oils. Hang in bunches to dry, or remove flowers from stems and spread on screens. Store in airtight containers.

Lavandula lanata

Levisticum (le-VIS-ti-kum)

LOVAGE

Levisticum officinale

HARDINESS: Zones 3-8

PLANT TYPE: perennial

HEIGHT: 3 to 6 feet

LIGHT: full sun to light shade

SOIL: organic, moist, well-drained

USES: culinary, landscaping

With divided leaflets resembling flat pars-ley, lovage develops into towering clumps of greenish red stalks useful as specimens or to shade lower-growing herbs. Lovage's hollow stems, wedge-shaped leaves, thick roots, and ridged seeds all share an intense celery flavor and aroma. Chop leaves and stems or grate roots to garnish salads or flavor soups, potatoes, poultry, and other dishes. Steam stems as a side dish. Toss seeds into stuffings, dressings, and baked goods. Steep leaves for herbal tea.

Selected species and varieties
L. officinale (lovage)—deep green leaflets with toothed edges on branching stems to 6 feet topped with a flat cluster of tiny yellow-green spring-to-summer flowers.

Growing conditions and maintenance
Sow lovage seeds in fall or divide roots in spring or fall, spacing plants 2 feet apart. Top-dress annually with compost or aged manure and keep well watered during dry spells. Harvest leaves two or three times a season. Deadhead to encourage greater leaf production, or allow flowers to ripen for seeds. Dry leaves in bundles, or blanch and freeze.

Lindera (lin-DER-a)

SPICEBUSH

Lindera benzoin

HARDINESS: Zones 4-9

PLANT TYPE: shrub

HEIGHT: 6 to 15 feet

LIGHT: light shade

SOIL: moist, acid

USES: landscaping, culinary, potpourri

A round, dense deciduous shrub with erect branches, spicebush offers three-season in-terest, fragrance, and flavor as a specimen or in a shrub border. Flowers bloom along bare branches of both male and female plants in early spring, followed by spicy-scented leaves. On female plants, leaves color and drop in fall to reveal bright red fruits. Steep young twigs and fresh or dried leaves and berries for herbal tea. Add dried berries and leaves to woodsy potpourri, or grind dried berries as a substitute for all-spice.

Selected species and varieties
L. benzoin (spicebush, Benjamin bush)—fragrant, tiny yellow-green flowers in clus-ters emerge before the 2- to 5-inch point-ed, oval leaves, which turn deep gold in fall, and ½-inch oval red fruits.

Growing conditions and maintenance
Sow ripe spicebush seed in the fall before it dries out, or hold at least 4 months in the refrigerator and sow in spring. Otherwise, start new shrubs from softwood cuttings taken in summer. Collect twigs in spring, leaves throughout the growing season, and berries in fall, and use either fresh or dried.

Lippia (LIP-ee-a)

MEXICAN OREGANO

Lippia graveolens

HARDINESS: Zones 9-11

PLANT TYPE: shrub

HEIGHT: 3 to 6 feet

LIGHT: full sun

SOIL: organic, sandy, well-drained

USES: culinary, containers, landscaping

Mexican oregano's upright branches are lined with intensely aromatic wrinkled leaves used fresh or dried to flavor chili, seafood, and cheese dishes as well as toma-to and other vegetable dishes. Try adding them to salads and dressings, or steep them with other herbs for teas. In frost-free areas, Mexican oregano can be grown as a specimen plant or pruned into a hedge. Elsewhere, grow it as a container plant to move indoors for the winter.

Selected species and varieties
L. graveolens [also called *Poliomintha longiflora*] (Mexican oregano)—pointed, oval 1- to 2½-inch downy leaves and tiny yellow to white winter-to-spring flowers growing where leaves meet stems.

Growing conditions and maintenance
Sow Mexican oregano seeds anytime, or start new plants from softwood cuttings taken anytime. Keep plants slightly on the dry side. Remove deadwood in spring and prune severely to keep shrubs from sprawling. Pinch to promote branching and bushiness. Top prune, root prune, and repot container specimens as needed to maintain their size. Pick leaves anytime and dry in a single layer.

Marrubium (ma-ROO-bee-um)

HOREHOUND

Marrubium vulgare

HARDINESS: Zones 4-9

PLANT TYPE: perennial

HEIGHT: 18 to 24 inches

LIGHT: full sun

SOIL: poor, sandy, well-drained to dry

USES: landscaping, containers, culinary

Horehound's deeply puckered, aromatic gray-green leaves, woolly with white hairs, add texture and soft color as fillers or edgings. Horehound can also be pruned into container specimens. Flowers attract bees. Use the branching foliage as a filler in fresh or dried bouquets. Steep the fresh or dried leaves, which taste slightly of thyme and menthol, for a soothing tea or add seeds to cool drinks for flavor. Horehound is a staple for cough remedies in herbal medicine.

Selected species and varieties
M. vulgare (common horehound, white horehound)—pairs of 2-inch-long heart-shaped leaves with deeply scalloped edges along square stems, and whorls of tiny white spring-to-summer flowers.

Growing conditions and maintenance
Sow horehound seeds in spring, thinning seedlings to stand 1 foot apart. Horehound can also be grown from divisions in spring and from stem cuttings taken in summer. In addition, it self-sows so easily as to be invasive. Prune before or after flowering to keep edgings or container plants compact. Dry the leaves in a single layer and store in airtight containers.

Matricaria (mat-ri-KAY-ree-a)

GERMAN CHAMOMILE

Matricaria recutita

HARDINESS: tender

PLANT TYPE: annual

HEIGHT: 24 to 30 inches

LIGHT: full sun

SOIL: average to poor, well-drained

USES: landscaping, culinary, arrangements

German chamomile's erect stems lined with feathery, finely divided leaves are crowned with numerous daisylike, honey-scented flowers from late spring to early summer. The soft foliage is excellent as a filler, especially among plants reaching their maximum size in late summer, as German chamomile tends to disappear after flowering and setting seed. The plant makes an excellent filler in fresh or dried bouquets. Its flowers make a soothing tea with an aroma of apple or pineapple.

Selected species and varieties
M. recutita (German chamomile, sweet false chamomile, wild chamomile)—airy clumps of fine-textured leaves and inch-wide flowers with yellow centers fringed with drooping white petals.

Growing conditions and maintenance
Sow German chamomile in fall for early-spring flowers or in early spring for summer blossoms. Thin or transplant seedlings to stand 8 to 10 inches apart. Plants self-sow freely. Hang stems in bundles to dry. Flowers for tea are best if fresh or frozen, as they lose their flavorful oils on drying.

Melissa (mel-ISS-a)

BALM

Melissa officinalis 'All Gold'

HARDINESS: Zones 4-9

PLANT TYPE: perennial

HEIGHT: 12 to 24 inches

LIGHT: full sun to light shade

SOIL: moist, well-drained

USES: landscaping, culinary, potpourri

Lemon balm's highly aromatic foliage and small flowers growing where the paired leaves join the square stems attract bees and perfume the garden. Although the loosely branching plants can be somewhat floppy and coarse, cultivars with colorful foliage are often sheared as ground covers. The plant's fresh leaves add a citrusy tang to salads, poultry or fish dishes, marinades, and vinegar. Dried leaves and stems scent potpourri.

Selected species and varieties
M. officinalis (lemon balm, bee balm, sweet balm)—1- to 3-inch pointed, oval leaves puckered by deep veins and whorls of ½-inch white to yellow flowers in summer and fall; 'All Gold' has golden yellow foliage; 'Aurea', green-veined yellow leaves.

Growing conditions and maintenance
Sow lemon balm seeds or divide mature plants in spring or fall, spacing them 1 to 2 feet apart. Plant 'All Gold' in light shade to prevent leaf scorch, and shear 'Aurea' to prevent flower formation and greening of leaves. Lemon balm self-sows readily. Contain the creeping roots by planting in bottomless pots at least 10 inches deep. Dry the leaves on screens.

MINT

Mentha aquatica var. crispa

HARDINESS: Zones 3-10

PLANT TYPE: perennial

HEIGHT: 1 inch to 4 feet

LIGHT: full sun to light shade

SOIL: moist, well-drained

USES: landscaping, culinary, potpourri

Paired mint leaves line the characteristic square stems and lend a sharp, peppery, sweet fragrance to borders, beds, and rock gardens. Tiny white, pink, lilac, purple, or blue summer flowers appear in spiky tufts at stem tips or in whorls where leaves join stems. Mints thrive in containers and can be potted for indoor use. Low-growing species make good ground covers for potted shrubs and quickly fill niches among paving stones; mow sturdy species into an aromatic carpet. Cooks prize the hundreds of mint varieties, which vary greatly in leaf shape, size, and fragrance. Fresh leaves are the most intensely flavored, but mint can also be frozen or dried. Use sprigs of fresh mint to flavor iced drinks and accent vegetable dishes. Mint sauces and jellies are a traditional accompaniment for meats; mint syrups dress up desserts; and crystallized mint leaves make an edible garnish. Steep fresh or dried leaves in boiling water for tea, or allow the infusion to cool into a refreshing facial splash. Add to bathwater for an aromatic soak. Mix dried leaves into potpourri. Mints are a traditional herbal remedy, especially as a breath freshener and digestive aid. Pennyroyal is used for repelling insects but can be toxic if eaten.

Selected species and varieties

M. aquatica (water mint)—heart-shaped 2-inch leaves on 1- to 2-foot stems; var. *crispa* (curly mint) has decoratively frilled leaf edges; Zones 5-10. *M. arvensis* var. *piperescens* [also spelled *piperascens*] (Japanese mint)—has oval leaves with strong peppermint aroma; Zones 6-9. *M. x gracilis* (redmint, gingermint)—shiny red-tinged leaves and stems popular in Southeast Asian cuisine; Zones 3-9. *M. longifolia* (horsemint)—has narrow, pointed, oval leaves; Zones 3-9. *M. x piperita* (peppermint)—characteristic 1- to 2-foot purple stems lined with intensely menthol-flavored deep green leaves yielding commercially important peppermint oil; var. *citrata* (bergamot mint, orange bergamot mint, lemon mint, eau de Cologne mint) has lemon fragrance and flavor; other varieties have aromatic overtones ranging from citrus to floral to chocolate; Zones 5-9. *M. pulegium* (pennyroyal)—round leaves to 1 inch long on 6- to 12-inch stems; 'Cunningham' (creeping pennyroyal) is a dwarf growing only 2 to 4 inches tall; Zones 6-9. *M. requienii* (Corsican mint, creme-de-menthe plant diminutive creeper only an inch tall forming mosslike mats of extremely aromatic ⅜-inch bright green leaves; Zones 7-9. *M. x smithiana* (red raripila mint)—narrow red-tinged leaves on 2- to 4-foot stems; Zones 7-9. *M. spicata* (spearmint)—wrinkled, oval, pointed leaves 2 inches long with a sweet taste and fragrance lining 1- to 3-foot stems; Zones 3-9. *M. suaveolens* (apple mint, woolly mint)—hairy, wrinkled 2-inch leaves with a distinctly fruity aroma on 1- to 3-foot stems; 'Variegata' (pineapple mint, varie-

Mentha arvensis var. piperescens

gated apple mint) has creamy leaf edges and a pineapple scent; Zones 5-9.

Growing conditions and maintenance

Corsican mint and horsemint prefer very moist situations in partial shade. Give other mints a moist but well-drained location in full sun; they will grow in partial shade but they may be less fragrant. With the exception of pennyroyal, mints do not grow true from seed; plant divisions or rooted cuttings in spring or fall, setting them 8 to 12 inches apart. Provide Japanese mint, redmint, and apple mint with a protective

Mentha x piperita

winter mulch in colder zones. Restrain mint's aggressive spread by spading deeply around plants at least once annually or, more reliably, by confining plants in bottomless plastic or clay containers sunk with their rims projecting at least 2 inches above the soil and their sides at least 10 inches deep; pull out any stems that fall to the ground and root outside this barrier. Mints can also be restrained by growing them in patio containers. Established beds of pennyroyal, peppermint, horsemint, apple mint, and spearmint tolerate mowing. The leaves are most flavorful when cut before flowers appear; shear plants when buds first form to yield about 2 cups of leaves per plant, and continue to pinch or shear at 10-day intervals to prolong fresh leaf production. Dry the leaves flat on screens, or hang stems in bunches in a warm, well-ventilated area to dry, then rub the leaves from the stems. Crystallize leaves for garnishes by simmering gently in a heavy sugar syrup.

Monarda (mo-NAR-da)

WILD BERGAMOT

Monarda fistulosa

HARDINESS: tender or Zones 4-10

PLANT TYPE: annual or perennial

HEIGHT: 1 to 4 feet

LIGHT: full sun to light shade

SOIL: rich, moist or dry, slightly alkaline

USES: landscaping, arrangements, culinary

Monarda's tousled, spiky, fragrant flowers in a wide array of colors are attractive to gardeners, bees, and hummingbirds alike. The spreading clumps of erect, square stems are ideal as border fillers or background plants; vegetable gardeners plant bee balm to attract the bees that pollinate their crops. The ragged whorls of tiny tubular flowers atop each stem make long-lasting cut flowers. Fresh blooms add color to salads; dried blossoms retain their fragrance well in potpourri.

The pairs of fragrant, citrus-flavored gray-green leaves lining the stalks add their pungency to Earl Grey tea. Fresh leaves add flavor to fruit salads, preserves, fruit punches, and iced tea. Dried leaves are also used in tea and to scent potpourri.

Selected species and varieties

M. citriodora (lemon bergamot, lemon mint)—an annual to 2 feet with lemon-flavored leaves and showy purple to pink blossoms. *M. didyma* (bee balm, Oswego tea, red balm)—a perennial with deep scarlet blooms and bergamot-orange-scented leaves ideal for tea; 'Adam' grows especially prolific salmon red blossoms on 2- to 3-foot stems; 'Croftway Pink' has soft

rose pink blooms on 2½- to 4- foot stems; 'Mahogany', deep red-bronze blooms on 2- to 3-foot stems; 'Violet Queen', lavender to deep violet flowers on 2- to 3-foot plants; 'Snow White', pure white flowers on stems to 3 feet; Zones 4-10. *M. fistulosa* (lavender wild bergamot)—a perennial with lemon-oregano-scented leaves and lavender flowers on 4-foot plants; Zones 4-9. *M. punctata* (spotted bee balm, dotted mint, dotted horsemint)—a short-lived perennial with mint-thyme-scented leaves and purple-flecked yellow flowers on 1- to 3-foot stems; Zones 4-9.

Growing conditions and maintenance

Sow seed of annual or perennial monardas or set out divisions of perennials in spring, spacing or thinning to 2 feet; pinch flower heads from seed-grown perennials their first year to increase root vigor. Bee balm prefers moist, rich soil; plant other monardas in dry, well-drained sites. Monardas, particularly lavender wild bergamot, will fill in garden spaces quickly and can be invasive. Weed by hand to avoid damaging the shallow roots, and thin clumps to minimize powdery mildew. Cutting stems to within 2 inches of the soil just after the flowers bloom may force a second bloom. Harvest leaves as needed, stripping them from stems and drying in a single layer on screens in a shady, well-ventilated area. Cut plants back severely in fall, and provide a protective winter mulch. Propagate monardas from seed, by transplanting the self-sown seedlings of lavender wild bergamot, or by division every 3 or 4 years in early spring, discarding the inner portion of older, mature clumps.

Monarda punctata

Myrica (mi-RYE-ka)

BAYBERRY

Myrica cerifera

HARDINESS: Zones 1-9

PLANT TYPE: shrub

HEIGHT: 2 to 35 feet

LIGHT: full sun to light shade

SOIL: poor, moist to dry

USES: landscaping, dried arrangements

Southern wax myrtle and sweet gale have glossy leaves dotted underneath with fragrant resin. Both bear minute spring flowers in dangling catkins on separate male and female plants followed by waxy berries clinging to the stems of female plants. Boil berries to remove the waxy coating for candlemaking; one bushel of berries yields 4 pounds of wax. Allow berries to dry on branches for arranging.

Selected species and varieties

M. cerifera (southern wax myrtle, candleberry)—shrub to 35 feet high and as wide, with narrow 1½- to 3-inch evergreen leaves lining reddish stems and ⅛-inch fruits on previous season's growth; Zones 7-9. *M. gale* (sweet gale, bog myrtle)—oval 1½- to 2½-inch leaves on deciduous shrubs 2 to 4 feet tall and wide; Zones 1-9.

Growing conditions and maintenance

Sow seeds of both species in spring or fall or propagate from cuttings taken in summer. Plant southern wax myrtle 8 to 10 feet apart and shear into hedges or prune specimens as small trees. This salt-tolerant plant grows in poor, dry soil but does best in the moist, organically rich soil also preferred by sweet gale.

Myrrhis (MIR-ris)

SWEET CICELY, MYRRH

Myrrhis odorata

HARDINESS: Zones 3-8

PLANT TYPE: perennial

HEIGHT: 2 to 3 feet

LIGHT: partial shade to full sun

SOIL: rich, moist, organic

USES: landscaping, culinary, crafts

Sweet cicely's finely cut leaves perfume the garden with celery and anise when used as a filler. As flavorful as they are fragrant, the fresh leaves can be used as a sweetener for tart fruits to reduce the amount of sugar needed or to flavor salads, omelets, and soups. The spring-blooming flowers are followed by seeds that can be added either green or ripe to fruit dishes, salads, baked goods, and other dishes. The anise-scented taproot can be chopped into salads, served raw with dressing, or steamed and eaten as a vegetable.

Selected species and varieties

M. odorata (sweet cicely, myrrh)—fernlike leaflets along arching stems to 3 feet and flat clusters of tiny white flowers followed by ¾-inch upright, oblong, ridged green seeds ripening to brown-black.

Growing conditions and maintenance

Because sweet cicely germinates erratically, the most reliable way to grow it is to divide mature plants in fall and plant the divisions. Space seedlings or transplants 2 feet apart. Harvest fresh leaves anytime, seeds either green or ripe. Dry leaves lose their taste but can be used for crafts. Dig roots for culinary use in fall.

Myrtus (MIR-tus)

MYRTLE

Myrtus communis 'Variegata'

HARDINESS: Zones 7-11

PLANT TYPE: shrub

HEIGHT: 5 to 20 feet

LIGHT: full sun to light shade

SOIL: average, well-drained

USES: landscaping, containers, culinary

Myrtle's lustrous evergreen leaves, tiny flower buds, and white flowers with puffs of golden stamens share a spicy orange scent that has made the plant a favorite in wedding bouquets. Myrtle develops into upright specimens ideal for massing into hedges. Grown as container plants to move indoors when the weather turns cold, myrtle is often pruned into topiary. Weave fresh branches into wreaths. Toss fresh, peeled buds into salads. Use leaves and berries to flavor meats. Add dried flowers and leaves to potpourri.

Selected species and varieties:

M. communis (sweet myrtle, Greek myrtle)—pairs of 2-inch pointed, oval glossy leaves and creamy white ¾-inch flowers followed by blue-black berries; 'Flore Pleno' has doubled petals; 'Microphylla' is a dwarf ideal for containers; 'Variegata' has leaves marbled gray-green and cream.

Growing conditions and maintenance

Start myrtle from seed sown in spring or from half-ripe cuttings taken in summer; plant in sites protected from drying winds. Myrtle will grow in light shade but prefers full sun. It tolerates severe pruning to maintain its size in containers.

Nepeta (NEP-e-ta)

CATMINT

Nepeta x faassenii

HARDINESS: Zones 3-9

PLANT TYPE: perennial

HEIGHT: 12 to 36 inches

LIGHT: full sun to light shade

SOIL: well-drained, sandy

USES: landscaping, culinary

Catmints produce sprawling mounds of downy gray-green leaves along square stems tipped with spikes of tubular flowers attractive to bees. Catnip (*N. cataria*) is even more attractive to cats. Drawn by its musty, minty aroma, they go into ecstasies of rolling and rubbing. Use catmints as fillers or ground covers in an informal border. Steep dried leaves for tea or sew them into toys for a favored feline.

Selected species and varieties

N. cataria (catnip)—coarse 2- to 3-inch leaves and spikes of violet to white ¼- to ½-inch summer-to-fall flowers on 2- to 3-foot plants. *N. x faassenii* (Persian ground ivy)—sprawling 2-foot mounds of 1- to 1½-inch leaves and lavender-blue early summer flowers. *N. mussinii* 'Blue Wonder'—large 6-inch spikes of lavender-blue flowers that first emerge in spring on 12- to 18-inch plants.

Growing conditions and maintenance

Sow catmint seeds or divide mature plants in spring, spacing plants 12 to 18 inches apart. Shearing plants to remove dead flowers encourages a second bloom and keeps plants from becoming leggy. Catmint self-sows freely.

Nicotiana (ni-ko-she-AN-a)

TOBACCO

Nicotiana rustica

HARDINESS: tender

PLANT TYPE: annual

HEIGHT: 2 to 4 feet

LIGHT: full sun

SOIL: rich, organic

USES: landscaping

Indian tobacco's bold leaves alternating along sturdy stems and crowned with summer-to-fall flowers create a dramatic backdrop for borders large enough not to be overwhelmed by their size and coarse texture. Plants contain nicotine, a natural insecticide that is poisonous if taken internally or absorbed through the skin. Dry and powder the leaves for an insecticidal dust effective against both root- and leaf-chewing insects.

Selected species and varieties

N. rustica (Indian tobacco, wild tobacco)—pointed oval leaves 4 to 8 inches long covered with sticky hairs, and hundreds of ½-inch yellow-green flowers.

Growing conditions and maintenance

Sow Indian tobacco outdoors in warm soil or start indoors 6 to 8 weeks before the last frost. Space seedlings 18 to 24 inches apart. Harvest wearing protective rubber gloves, picking leaves individually as they begin to yellow. Hang to dry, then crumble, remove stems, and store in airtight containers. Wearing protective clothing and equipment, grind the dried leaves to a powder and dust on plants at least 1 month before harvest.

Nigella (nye-JELL-a)

FENNEL FLOWER

Nigella sativa

HARDINESS: tender

PLANT TYPE: annual

HEIGHT: 12 to 18 inches

LIGHT: full sun

SOIL: well-drained, slightly alkaline

USES: landscaping, culinary, potpourri

Black cumin forms neat clumps of erect stems lined with finely cut leaves and crowned with intricate flowers whose spidery centers are surrounded by flat, broad petals. The inflated seedpods that follow are prized in dried arrangements and yield triangular seeds with a pepper-nutmeg flavor used in curries, breads, and cakes as a substitute for caraway or cumin. It is one of the four spices included in the *quatre épices* of classic French cuisine. Black cumin is particularly effective as a specimen or edging plant in a blue garden.

Selected species and varieties

N. sativa (black cumin, nutmeg flower, Roman coriander)—has gray-green ferny leaves and 1½-inch-wide blue flowers in summer.

Growing conditions and maintenance

Sow black cumin in the garden in fall or spring and thin seedlings to stand 4 to 6 inches apart. Black cumin does not transplant well. Plants will grow in light shade, but with less intense flower color. Harvest seedpods on stems as they turn dark brown for dried arrangements. Crush pods open to collect seeds.

Ocimum (OS-si-mum)

BASIL

Ocimum 'African Blue'

HARDINESS: tender

PLANT TYPE: annual

HEIGHT: 6 inches to 3 feet

LIGHT: full sun

SOIL: rich, organic, well-drained

USES: culinary, landscaping, potpourri

Pointed, oval, slightly curved leaves with mixed scents of cinnamon, clove, anise, lemon, rose, orange, thyme, mint, or camphor make basil not only a classic culinary seasoning but also a choice fragrance planting. All species do well in containers, and most are ideal for window-sill pot culture throughout winter. Whorls of tiny flowers grow in spikes at the tips of stems from summer through fall. Add fresh or dried basil leaves to salads, sauces, soups, and vegetable dishes or steep them for tea. Use flowers as an edible garnish or in herbal bouquets. Add dried basil to herbal potpourri.

Selected species and varieties

O. 'African Blue'—resinous leaves tinged with purple-green on 3-foot stems tipped with purple flower spikes, valued as a border specimen and for fresh flowers. *O. basilicum* (common basil, sweet basil)—bushy 8- to 24-inch plants prized by cooks and ideal for garden edging, with fragrant 2- to 3-inch leaves lining stems tipped with white flowers; 'Anise' has purple-tinged licorice-scented leaves and pink flowers; 'Cinnamon', cinnamon-scented leaves especially good in tea; 'Dark Opal', deep purple leaves and pink flowers; 'Minimum' (bush basil, Greek basil) is a 6- to 12-inch dwarf with ½-inch leaves, ideal indoors; 'Minimum Purpurascens' (purple bush basil) has small purple leaves on 12-inch plants; 'Purple Ruffles', purple-black leaves whose edges are curled and frilled, excellent in pots. *O. sanctum* [also classified as *O. tenuiflorum*] (holy basil, clove basil, sri tulsi)—clove-scented 1½-inch leaves and branching spikes of tiny white flowers on stems 18 to 24 inches tall, primarily used in landscaping.

Growing conditions and maintenance

Sow basil indoors 8 to 12 weeks before the last frost or outdoors where it is to grow, spacing or thinning plants to 1 to 2 feet apart. Basil can be sown in pots for indoor culture year round. It can also be propagated from cuttings, which remain true to type. Basil needs soils 50° F or warmer to thrive. Provide mulch to keep roots from drying out and to keep leaves clean. Leaves are best picked before flowers appear; to delay flowering and encourage bushiness, pinch stems back to 4 sets of leaves as flower buds form. Avoid washing basil unless necessary as mold forms quickly on damp leaves. Preserve by blending fresh leaves into olive oil and refrigerating the oil or freezing it in small batches. Whole leaves can be layered in olive oil to preserve them, frozen flat on trays after first brushing both sides with olive oil, or layered in white vinegar; the leaves of purple bush basil give vinegar a burgundy tint. Basil can be hard to dry; lay the leaves in a single layer on trays between layers of paper towels so they don't turn black.

Ocimum basilicum 'Dark Opal'

MARJORAM

Origanum majorana

HARDINESS:	hardy or Zones 5-10
PLANT TYPE:	perennial or half-hardy annual
HEIGHT:	6 to 24 inches
LIGHT:	full sun
SOIL:	rich, dry, well-drained
USES:	culinary, landscaping, potpourri

Fragrantly spicy small, oval leaves and branching clusters of tiny flowers on mounding or sprawling plants make marjorams useful in kitchen gardens, where leaves can be snipped to flavor meat, vegetable, cheese, and fish dishes. They can also be used as border edgings or ground covers. Tender perennial species grow as annuals in cooler climates; marjorams also do well in containers both indoors and out. Use fresh or dried marjoram leaves in cooking, dried leaves and flowers in teas and herbal potpourri.

Selected species and varieties

O. dictamnus (dittany-of-Crete)—tiny woolly white leaves and loose, nodding clusters of tiny pink summer-to-fall flowers on sprawling 1-foot-high plants ideal in rock gardens or hanging baskets; Zones 8-9. *O. majorana* (sweet marjoram)—spicy 1¼-inch leaves, an essential seasoning in Greek cuisine and more intensely flavored than those of *O. vulgare*, along 2-foot stems tipped with white to pink blooms; Zones 9-10. *O. x majoricum* (hardy marjoram, Italian oregano)—a hybrid similar to sweet marjoram but slightly hardier; Zones 7-10. *O. onites* (Greek oregano, pot marjoram)—has very mildly thyme-flavored medium-green leaves used in bouquets garnis or laid across charcoal to flavor grilled foods, and mauve to white flowers from summer to fall on 24-inch plants; Zones 8-10. *O. vulgare* (oregano, pot marjoram, wild marjoram, organy)—mildly pepper-thyme-flavored green leaves on sprawling 2-foot stems, not the same plant used in commercial dried oregano

Origanum vulgare 'Aureum'

but used for flavoring and valued in landscaping for its branching clusters of white to red-purple summer flowers, Zones 5-9; 'Aureum' has golden leaves, Zones 6-9; 'Aureum Crispum', round, wrinkled ½-inch golden leaves on 1-foot plants, Zones 7-9; 'Nanum' is an 8-inch dwarf with purple flowers, Zones 6-9; 'White Anniversary' has green leaves edged in white on 6- to 10-inch plants; Zones 8-9.

Growing conditions and maintenance

Sow marjoram seeds or plant divisions in spring or fall, spacing or thinning plants to 12 to 18 inches apart. Give golden-leaved cultivars light shade. Pinch stems to promote bushiness and delay flowering. Cut perennial marjorams back to two-thirds of their height before winter. *O. vulgare* can be invasive. Indoors, pot up divisions or sow seeds in pots where they are to grow. Propagate marjorams from seed, from early-summer stem cuttings, or by division in spring or fall. For best flavor, harvest leaves just as flower buds begin to open. Mash leaves in oil to preserve them, layer with vinegar, or freeze. Dry leaves or flowers in a single layer in a shady, well-ventilated area.

Panax (PAN-ax)

GINSENG

Panax quinquefolius

HARDINESS: Zones 3-8

PLANT TYPE: perennial

HEIGHT: 6 to 36 inches

LIGHT: light to full shade

SOIL: organic, moist, well-drained

USES: landscaping, culinary

Ginseng's thick roots send up a single thin stalk with leaves composed of several pointed leaflets arranged like the fingers on a hand. In late spring or summer, a short flower stalk carries a cluster of tiny yellow-green flowers above the foliage, followed by red berries. In woodland gardens, ginseng slowly spreads to form a lacy ground cover. Ginseng's Greek name means "all ills," reflecting its root's fame as an herbal tonic in Oriental medicine. Roots are also used in herbal teas.

Selected species and varieties
P. pseudoginseng [also classified as *P. ginseng*]—stems 2 to 3 feet tall with two to six leaves composed of toothed leaflets growing from a carrotlike root. *P. quinquefolius* (American ginseng)—stems 6 to 20 inches tall with leaves composed of 6-inch leaflets growing from a cigar-shaped root.

Growing conditions and maintenance
You can sow ginseng seeds in spring or fall, but division and replanting of roots in spring is often more successful as the seeds take a year to germinate. Provide organic mulch annually. When roots are at least 6 years old, dig them up in fall to use fresh or dried for teas.

Papaver (pa-PAY-ver)

POPPY

Papaver rhoeas

HARDINESS: tender

PLANT TYPE: annual

HEIGHT: 8 to 36 inches

LIGHT: full sun

SOIL: well-drained

USES: landscaping, culinary, dried arrangements

Corn poppies decorate borders with brilliantly colored flower cups composed of crepey petals on slender stalks lined with hairy gray-green foliage. Mass them for showy display, then harvest their bulbous seedpods to collect the tiny blue-gray seeds. The seeds add a nutty flavor to breads and cakes. Add seed heads, with interesting flat caps, to dried arrangements.

Selected species and varieties
P. rhoeas (corn poppy, Flanders poppy, Shirley poppy)—branching stems lined with lobed leaves carrying red to reddish purple 2- to 4-inch blossoms, sometimes double petaled, with purplish filaments and dark throats; 'Shirley Single Mixed' has a single rim of petals in shades of red, pink, salmon, orange, white, or bicolors.

Growing conditions and maintenance
Sow corn poppies in spring or fall, just pressing the seeds into the soil. Thin plants to stand 12 inches apart. Make successive sowings and deadhead plants to prolong the blooming season. Pick seed heads just before fully ripe; allowed to ripen, poppies self-sow freely.

Pelargonium (pel-ar-GO-nee-um)

GERANIUM, STORKSBILL

Pelargonium capitatum

HARDINESS: tender or Zone 10

PLANT TYPE: annual, perennial, or shrub

HEIGHT: 12 inches to 6 feet

LIGHT: full sun to light shade

SOIL: rich, moist, well-drained

USES: landscaping, culinary, potpourri

When brushed or rubbed, the foliage of scented geraniums emits a citrusy, floral, minty, or resinous perfume depending on the species or cultivar. The kidney-shaped or broad, triangular leaves are wrinkled, lobed, frilled, or filigreed to add texture to the border. Loose, open clusters of small white, pink, mauve, or lilac flowers on branching stalks add color in spring or summer. Outdoors year round where they can be protected from frost, taller species grow as border specimens or background shrubs or can be pruned into standards; sprawling types can be used as ground covers or trained against trellises. Elsewhere, scented geraniums are treated like summer bedding plants or grown in containers or hanging baskets; they also do well year round as houseplants. Use fresh leaves of citrus, floral, or mint-scented geraniums in teas and to flavor baked goods, jam, jelly, vinegar, syrup, or sugar; use resinous leaves to flavor pâté and sausage. Toss flowers into salads for color. Add dried leaves to floral or herbal potpourri.

Selected species and varieties
P. capitatum (wild rose geranium, rose-scented geranium)—a spreading plant 1 to

2 feet tall and up to 5 feet wide with crinkled, velvety 2-inch rose-scented leaves and mauve to pink summer flowers. *P. citronellum*—lemon-scented 3½-inch-wide leaves with pointed lobes and pink summer flowers streaked purple on upright shrubs to 6 feet tall and half as wide. *P. crispum* (lemon geranium)—strongly lemon-scented, kidney-shaped ½-inch leaves and pink to lavender flowers in spring and summer on plants 2 feet tall and half as wide, whose leaves are traditionally used in finger bowls; 'Variegatum' has cream-colored leaf edges. *P.* 'Fair Ellen'—finely textured lacy leaves with a balsam aroma and pale mauve summer flowers marked with pink on compact plants 1 to 2 feet tall and up to 3 feet wide. *P.* x *fragrans* 'Variegatum' (nutmeg geranium)—small, downy gray-green leaves smelling of nutmeg and pine, and white spring-to-summer flowers lined with red on compact plants 12 to 16 inches tall and as wide. *P. graveolens* (rose geranium)—

Pelargonium 'Fair Ellen'

filigreed, strongly rose-scented gray-green leaves and pale pink spring-to-summer flowers spotted purple on upright shrubs to 3 feet tall and as wide. *P.* 'Lady Plymouth'—lacy leaves with creamy edges and a rose-lemon scent with minty overtones on shrubs to 5 feet tall and as wide. *P. odoratissimum* (apple geranium)—a spreading plant 1 foot tall and twice as wide with small kidney-shaped, velvety, intensely apple-scented leaves and red-veined white spring and summer flowers on trailing flower stalks. *P.* 'Old Spice'—a compact mound 1½ to 2 feet tall and as wide with a piny aroma. *P. quercifolium* (oak-leaved

geranium)—round, lobed 2- to 4-inch leaves with a resinous balsam odor and pink-purple spring-to-summer flowers on upright shrubs 1½ to 4 feet tall and up to 3 feet wide. *P.* 'Rober's Lemon Rose'—gray-green 2-inch leaves with an intense rose-lemon scent and pink summer flowers on shrubs to 5 feet tall and almost as wide. *P. tomentosum* (peppermint geranium)—a spreading plant to 3 feet tall and twice as wide with 4- to 5-inch peppermint-scented leaves and white spring-to-summer flowers.

Growing conditions and maintenance
Sow seeds of scented geraniums indoors 10 to 12 weeks before the last frost. While all scented geraniums do best in full sun, lemon geranium, apple geranium, and peppermint geranium will tolerate light shade. Too-rich soil tends to minimize fragrance. Remove faded flowers to encourage further blooming. In containers, scented geraniums do best when slightly potbound; repot only into the next larger size pot. Indoors, provide daytime temperatures of 65° to 70°F, about 10° cooler at night, with at least 5 hours of direct sunlight daily. Keep potted plants from becoming leggy by pruning them hard after blooming or in very early spring, then feeding with any complete houseplant fertilizer. To propagate scented geraniums, cut a branch tip at least 3 inches long just below a leaf node, dip into rooting hormone, and place in clean, moist sand to root; transplant into potting soil after 2 weeks. Pick scented geranium leaves for drying anytime and lay in a single layer on screens in a shady location.

Pelargonium 'Lady Plymouth'

PERILLA

Perilla frutescens 'Atropurpurea'

HARDINESS:	tender
PLANT TYPE:	annual
HEIGHT:	12 to 36 inches
LIGHT:	full sun to light shade
SOIL:	average to rich, sandy
USES:	landscaping, culinary, dried arrangements

Perilla forms mounds of wrinkled burgundy leaves that contrast nicely when used as a filler among gray or white foliage in an herb garden or border. The leaves and seeds, with a fragrance and flavor blending mint with cinnamon and an oil 2,000 times sweeter than sugar, are staples in Japanese cuisine. Fresh or pickled, they are used to garnish sushi and to flavor bean curd. Spikes of flower buds may be batter-fried for tempura. Leaves are used to color vinegar and fruit preserves. Add the dried seed heads to herbal wreaths.

Selected species and varieties
P. frutescens 'Atropurpurea' (black nettle)—pairs of wrinkled oval leaves up to 5 inches long on square stems tipped with spikes of tiny white summer flower in whorls, followed by brown nutlets.

Growing conditions and maintenance
Sow perilla seed in spring, and thin seedlings to stand 1 foot apart. Harvest leaves anytime, harvest flowers for tempura just as buds form. Pinch off spikes of flower buds to encourage bushier growth. Allowed to form seed, perilla self-sows freely.

Petroselinum (pet-ro-se-LEE-num)

PARSLEY

Petroselinum crispum var. neapolitanum

HARDINESS: hardy or Zones 6-9

PLANT TYPE: biennial

HEIGHT: 12 to 24 inches

LIGHT: full sun

SOIL: rich, moist, well-drained

USES: culinary, landscaping, containers

Bundled into a classic bouquet garni or chopped for use in sauces, eggs, vegetables, stuffings, and herb butters, parsley's deep green curly or flat leaves blend well with many flavors. Vitamin-rich parsley also freshens breath. Cooks consider flatleaf types more strongly flavored than curly varieties. A biennial flowering its second year, parsley is usually grown as an annual in an herb garden, as an edging plant, or in containers indoors or out.

Selected species and varieties

P. crispum var. *crispum* (curly parsley, French parsley)—highly frilled leaves on plants 12 to 18 inches tall. *P. crispum* var. *neapolitanum* (Italian parsley, flatleaf parsley)—flat, deeply lobed celery-like leaves on plants to 24 inches.

Growing conditions and maintenance

Soak parsley seed overnight to speed germination. Sow seed ¼ inch deep in soil warmed to at least 50° F. Thin seedlings to stand 4 to 6 inches apart. Begin harvesting leaves when plants are 6 inches tall. Dry Italian parsley in the shade, oven, or microwave. Chop curly parsley and freeze in ice cubes for best flavor.

Plectranthus (plec-TRAN-thus)

INDIAN BORAGE

Plectranthus amboinicus 'Variegata'

HARDINESS: tender or Zones 10-11

PLANT TYPE: annual

HEIGHT: 12 to 36 inches

LIGHT: full sun to light shade

SOIL: rich, well-drained

USES: landscaping, culinary, containers

The fleshy lemon-scented leaves of Indian borage have a flavor reminiscent of thyme, oregano, and savory. In tropical areas where those herbs fail to thrive, cooks grow the plant as an attractive ground cover. Elsewhere, grow it as a houseplant or a patio plant to move indoors when frost threatens. The leaves trail attractively from hanging baskets. Use fresh leaves to complement beans, meats, and other strong-flavored dishes.

Selected species and varieties

P. amboinicus (Indian borage, Spanish thyme, French thyme, soup mint, Mexican mint, Indian mint, country borage)—round gray-green leaves up to 4 inches across in pairs along thick stems, and whorls of tiny mintlike blue summer flowers in spikes up to 16 inches long; 'Variegata' has gray-green leaves edged in cream.

Growing conditions and maintenance

Start Indian borage from tip cuttings or divisions in spring or summer. Plants stop growing at temperatures below 50° F and are quickly killed by even light frost. Pinch tips to keep plants bushy and contain their spread. Cut leggy plants back in spring. Feed potted plants monthly.

Pogostemon (po-go-STAY-mon)

PATCHOULI

Pogostemon cablin

HARDINESS: tender or Zones 10-11

PLANT TYPE: perennial

HEIGHT: 3 to 4 feet

LIGHT: full sun to light shade

SOIL: rich, moist

USES: landscaping, containers, potpourri

Patchouli's hairy triangular leaves contain a minty, cedar-scented oil valued in the making of perfume. Dried leaves gradually develop the scent and retain it for long periods in potpourri. In tropical gardens, patchouli forms mounds of fragrant foliage; elsewhere it is grown in containers to bring indoors when frost threatens.

Selected species and varieties

P. cablin [also classified as *P. patchouli*] (patchouli)—lightly scalloped leaves up to 5 inches long and half as wide in pairs along square stems tipped with 5- to 6-inch spikes of violet-tinged white flowers with violet filaments in fall.

Growing conditions and maintenance

Patchouli rarely sets seed. Start new plants from tip cuttings or divisions in fall or spring. Outdoors where patchouli is not hardy, start tip cuttings to overwinter and treat plants as annuals, or grow in containers to move indoors. Feed potted plants weekly during spring and summer. Young leaves develop the best fragrance. Pinch plants two or three times each year to harvest young leaves and keep plants bushy. Dry leaves in a shady, well-ventilated area.

Polygonum (po-LIG-o-num)

KNOTWEED

Polygonum odoratum

HARDINESS: Zones 8-9

PLANT TYPE: perennial

HEIGHT: 1 to 1½ feet

LIGHT: light shade

SOIL: moist

USES: culinary, containers, landscaping

Vietnamese coriander's pointed dark green leaves have a lemony, cilantro-like aroma and flavor prized in Asian cuisine, particularly in poultry and meat dishes. Where short growing seasons prevent plants from blooming and setting seed, Vietnamese coriander can be grown as a fragrant, rambling annual ground cover. Elsewhere, it is grown in indoor or outdoor containers.

Selected species and varieties

P. odoratum (Vietnamese coriander, Vietnamese mint)—green leaves up to 3 inches long with darker green triangular blotches along jointed 1- to 1½-foot stems that root wherever they touch the ground and, rarely, small clusters of tiny pink flowers in autumn.

Growing conditions and maintenance

Start new Vietnamese coriander plants from tip cuttings taken in summer and rooted in water. In cooler climates, grow as an annual and take cuttings to root over-winter as houseplants for the following year's planting outdoors. Keep plants well watered, even constantly moist, and provide winter protection where they remain outdoors year round.

Poterium (po-TEER-ee-um)

SALAD BURNET

Poterium sanguisorba

HARDINESS: Zones 3-9

PLANT TYPE: perennial

HEIGHT: 12 to 36 inches

LIGHT: full sun

SOIL: well-drained

USES: landscaping, culinary

Burnet forms round mounds of delicate blue-green foliage ideal for soft, colorful edgings. In summer, tall flower stalks carry thimble-shaped clusters of tiny flowers well above the hummocks of leaves. Add the cucumber-flavored young leaves to salads, cole-slaw, soups, vegetables, and cool summer drinks. Preserve them in vinegar for tasty dressings.

Selected species and varieties

P. sanguisorba [also classified as *Sanguisorba minor*] (burnet, garden burnet, salad burnet)—¾-inch oval leaflets with deeply scalloped edges paired along the flexible leafstalks to 1 foot and dense ½-inch heads of minute greenish flowers tinged pink on stems to 3 feet.

Growing conditions and maintenance

Sow burnet seeds in spring or fall or divide young plants before taproots become well established. Space plants 8 to 12 inches apart. Established plants self-sow. Burnet is evergreen in milder climates; elsewhere, shear old foliage to the ground in late fall or early spring. Leaves are most flavorful when picked in early spring or late fall.

Primula (PRIM-yew-la)

PRIMROSE

Primula veris

HARDINESS: Zones 3-8

PLANT TYPE: perennial

HEIGHT: 6 to 12 inches

LIGHT: partial to full shade

SOIL: organic, moist, well-drained

USES: landscaping, culinary, arrangements

Cowslip and common primrose both produce fragrant, very early spring flowers above rosettes of oblong leaves. Use cowslip's nectar-rich flowers in jams or dry them for tea and potpourri; add the leaves to salads. Gather common primrose's flowers into posies, crystallize for decorations, add to salads, and dry for potpourri; boil the leaves as a vegetable, and add dried, powdered roots to potpourri. Both species make fine edging plants. Cowslip thrives as a houseplant.

Selected species and varieties

P. veris (cowslip)—clusters of tubular yellow 1- to 1½-inch-long flowers marked with orange on stalks to 12 inches above blue-green 2- to 8-inch leaves. *P. vulgaris* (common primrose)—single, flat-faced ½-inch-wide yellow, purple, or blue flowers with notched petals on 6-inch stems among 1- to 10-inch yellow-green leaves.

Growing conditions and maintenance

Sow seed when ripe in fall or divide plants after blooming, spacing them 6 to 12 inches apart. Where conditions are ideal, plants may rebloom in fall. Pick young leaves and flowers just after opening. Dig and dry roots in fall.

Prunella (pru-NELL-a)

SELF-HEAL

Prunella vulgaris

HARDINESS: Zones 4-9

PLANT TYPE: perennial

HEIGHT: 12 to 20 inches

LIGHT: light shade to full sun

SOIL: average to dry, well-drained

USES: landscaping

Common self-heal slowly creeps via underground runners and rooting stems into dense mats that are useful as ground covers, especially in difficult areas such as under shrubs. From summer through fall, small spikes of hooded flowers rise decoratively above the foliage, attracting bees and butterflies with their sweet nectar. Common self-heal's leaves and flowers have figured in herbal medicine.

Selected species and varieties
P. vulgaris (common self-heal, heal-all)—pairs of 1- to 2-inch oval or diamond-shaped leaves along square stems and dense 1- to 2-inch spikes of ½-inch-long purple to pale violet and sometimes pink flowers with flared upper lips overhanging lower ones like a small hood.

Growing conditions and maintenance
Sow common self-heal seeds in fall while ripe, or divide the underground runners in spring. Floppy stems root wherever they touch the ground, and plants self-sow freely. Common self-heal survives in dry, average soils but can be very invasive in moist, rich soils, particularly when planted at the edges of lawns.

Pulmonaria (pul-mo-NAY-ree-a)

LUNGWORT

Pulmonaria saccharata 'Mrs. Moon'

HARDINESS: Zones 3-8

PLANT TYPE: perennial

HEIGHT: 6 to 18 inches

LIGHT: light to full shade

SOIL: moist, well-drained

USES: landscaping

Lungworts produce low mounds of attractive silver-mottled hairy green leaves that remain evergreen in milder climates. In spring, clusters of flared tubular flowers bloom in soft pastel shades, then age to a second color. Use lungworts as foliage specimens or mass them as ground covers under deciduous trees and shrubs. As its name implies, lungwort once figured in herbal medicine but is now suspected to be toxic.

Selected species and varieties
P. officinalis (common lungwort, Jerusalem sage)—leaves up to 3 inches long and deep pink flowers aging to blue-purple; 'Sissinghurst White' has white blooms. *P. saccharata* (Bethlehem sage)—6-inch-long leaves in mounds 18 inches high and twice as wide; 'Mrs. Moon' has pink buds aging to blue; the vigorous 'Roy Davidson' has light blue flowers aging to pink.

Growing conditions and maintenance
Sow lungwort seeds in spring, or divide mature plants in late fall, spacing plants 1 to 1½ feet apart. Plants will grow in full sun, but foliage becomes unattractive by midsummer. Cut fading foliage back in fall in cooler climates.

Punica (PEW-nik-a)

POMEGRANATE

Punica granatum var. nana

HARDINESS: Zones 7-10

PLANT TYPE: tree or shrub

HEIGHT: 2 to 20 feet

LIGHT: full sun

SOIL: well-drained

USES: landscaping, culinary, containers

In spring, brilliantly colored fragrant blossoms with crepey pointed petals crown pomegranate's glossy deciduous foliage. In warm climates, plants produce shiny fruits filled with tangy-sweet juicy pulp and sour seeds. Pomegranate juice is used to flavor sorbets, fruit salad, and ice cream and to produce the cordial grenadine. Pulp and seeds can be boiled with sugar for a flavorful syrup. Pomegranates make excellent container specimens.

Selected species and varieties
P. granatum (pomegranate)—light green oval leaves turning yellow in fall along spiny branches with inch-wide red to red-orange blossoms and apple-sized yellow, orange, or red fruits with leathery skins; var. *nana* (dwarf pomegranate) is only 2 to 3 feet high with proportionally smaller foliage, making it ideal for containers or bonsai.

Growing conditions and maintenance
Sow pomegranate seeds in spring or root semiripe cuttings taken in summer. Fruits seldom develop except in warm climates with long summers. Remove root suckers that appear, or transplant them in fall for new plants.

Pycnanthemum (pik-NAN-thee-mum)

MOUNTAIN MINT

Pycnanthemum virginianum

HARDINESS: Zones 4-8

PLANT TYPE: perennial

HEIGHT: 2 to 3 feet

LIGHT: full sun to light shade

SOIL: moist, well-drained

USES: landscaping, culinary, dried arrangements

A sharp, peppery aroma fills gardens wherever Virginia mountain mint grows. The square stems lined with whorls of very narrow, pointed leaves branch into loose mounds. In the summer, tufts of flowers growing at stem tips attract bees and butterflies where the plant grows in wildflower or meadow gardens. As intensely flavored as it is fragrant, Virginia mountain mint is an excellent culinary substitute for true mint. Dry the dense flower heads for arrangements, or add dried leaves and flowers to potpourri.

Selected species and varieties

P. virginianum (Virginia mountain mint, wild basil, prairie hyssop)—smooth or slightly toothed, pointed, very narrow 1- to 1½-inch leaves and tiny white to lilac flowers in very dense, flat heads.

Growing conditions and maintenance

Virginia mountain mint grows best from cuttings or divisions of mature plants. Set plants out in spring or fall, spacing them 8 to 12 inches apart. Restrain their spread by spading around plants annually or by planting them in bottomless tubs.

Ricinus (RISS-i-nus)

CASTOR BEAN

Ricinus communis 'Carmencita'

HARDINESS: tender

PLANT TYPE: annual

HEIGHT: 4 to 15 feet

LIGHT: full sun

SOIL: organic, well-drained

USES: landscaping, containers

Castor bean grows rapidly into a coarse-textured border backdrop or temporary screen composed of glossy leaves up to 3 feet across. Each colorful leaf is composed of numerous toothed, pointed leaflets. Insignificant summer flower spikes precede seeds enclosed in burrlike cases. The source of medicinal castor oil, which is safe when extracted commercially, these seeds are extremely poisonous, as are all other parts of the plant.

Selected species and varieties

R. communis (castor bean)—purple-tinged young leaves maturing to gray-green or purple-green and white flowers on plants to 15 feet; 'Carmencita' has deep mahogany leaves and red flowers on plants to 5 feet; 'Impala', red-maroon young leaves and creamy yellow blooms on plants to 4 feet tall.

Growing conditions and maintenance

In tropical climates, castor bean grows as a tree to 40 feet; elsewhere, grow it as an annual. Sow seeds indoors 6 to 8 weeks before the last frost or outdoors after the last frost, spacing plants 4 feet apart. Mulch to conserve moisture. If grown in containers, plants should not be pruned.

Rosa (RO-za)

ROSE

Rosa canina

HARDINESS: Zones 2-10

PLANT TYPE: shrub

HEIGHT: 3 to 10 feet

LIGHT: full sun

SOIL: organic, well-drained

USES: landscaping, arrangements, potpourri

Besides using roses in arrangements, try adding the petals to salads or crystalliz-ing them as a garnish. Dry the buds and petals for potpourri. Use the fruit, or hips, for tea or jam.

Selected species and varieties

R. canina (dog rose, brier rose)—10-foot canes with white or pink 2-inch blooms, ¾-inch hips; Zones 4-9. *R. damascena* (damask rose)—has very fragrant 3-inch blooms on 6-foot canes; 'Autumn Damask' is a double pink; 'Madame Hardy', a double white; Zones 5-9. *R. gallica* (French rose)—2- to 3-inch blooms on 3- to 4-foot plants; 'Officinalis' (apothecary rose) is a semidouble deep pink; 'Versicolor' (rosa mundi) is a semidouble pink- or red-striped white, red, or pink; Zones 4-10. *R. rugosa* (Japanese rose)—crimson 3½-inch blossoms and 1-inch hips; 'Alba' is white; 'Rubra', burgundy red; Zones 3-8.

Growing conditions and maintenance

Sow rose seeds, root hardwood cuttings, or plant commercial rootstock in fall. Mulch to conserve moisture. Prune dead or damaged wood in late winter, avoiding the previous season's growth, on which this season's flowers grow.

Rosmarinus (rose-ma-RY-nus)

ROSEMARY

Rosmarinus officinalis 'Prostratus'

HARDINESS: Zones 7-10

PLANT TYPE: perennial

HEIGHT: 6 inches to 7 feet

LIGHT: full sun

SOIL: well-drained, alkaline

USES: landscaping, culinary, potpourri

Rosemary's branching, stiff stems are lined with resinous, aromatic needlelike leaves. Small flowers cluster along the woody stems in winter. Grown as a ground cover or shrub in warm climates, rosemary is pot grown elsewhere. Use the piny leaves, fresh or dried, to flavor meats, sauces, vinegar, herb butter, and breads. Toss sprigs on coals for aromatic grilling or weave into wreaths. Add leaves to potpourri.

Selected species and varieties
R. officinalis (garden rosemary)—gray-green ⅓- to 1½-inch leaves along branches to 6 feet outdoors, 4 feet indoors, and ½-inch blue flowers; 'Arp' is very hardy, with lemon-scented leaves; 'Miss Jessup's Upright' has vertical branches; 'Prostratus' is almost everblooming, with twisting 6-inch-high, 36-inch-long branches; 'Tuscan Blue' is fast growing, with large deep blue leaves on branches to 7 feet.

Growing conditions and maintenance
Sow rosemary seed in spring, or start from summer cuttings, spacing plants 3 feet apart. Prune after flowering to encourage bushiness, removing no more than 20 percent of the plant at a time.

Rubia (ROO-bee-a)

MADDER

Rubia tinctorum

HARDINESS: Zones 4-10

PLANT TYPE: perennial

HEIGHT: 10 to 36 inches

LIGHT: full sun

SOIL: rich, well-drained

USES: dyes

Madder's jointed, prickly stems ramble along the ground or climb weakly over other plants. Leathery leaves grow in whorls at each joint, and in summer and fall a light froth of tiny pale flowers blooms among the foliage. Madder forms mats of pencil-thick, red-fleshed roots up to 3 feet long, which yield red dye valued by textile craftspeople or, with various mordants, shades of pink, lilac, brown, orange, or black.

Selected species and varieties
R. tinctorum (madder)—2-inch oblong, pointed leaves in whorls of four to eight and ⅒-inch pale yellow or white open flower bells in airy clusters on plants 3 years old or older, followed by ⅛-inch reddish brown fruits, which turn black.

Growing conditions and maintenance
Sow madder seeds while ripe in fall, divide plants anytime between spring and fall, or start new plants from cuttings. Plants root wherever joints touch the ground. Provide supports to control madder's spread and give plants structure. Dig roots of plants that are at least 3 years old in fall.

Rumex (ROO-mex)

SORREL, DOCK

Rumex crispus

HARDINESS: Zones 3-8

PLANT TYPE: perennial

HEIGHT: 6 inches to 5 feet

LIGHT: full sun to light shade

SOIL: well-drained

USES: culinary, dried arrangements

Sorrel's slightly sour, lemony, arrowhead-shaped leaves add zest to salads and accent soups and sauces. Use fresh leaves sparingly, as the high oxalic acid content can aggravate conditions such as gout. Boil leaves for a spinachlike vegetable, changing the water once to reduce the acid content. Birds love the tiny seeds produced at the tips of the stalks.

Selected species and varieties
R. acetosa (garden sorrel, sour dock)—narrow 5- to 8-inch leaves on clumps of 3-foot stems. *R. crispus* (curled dock)—extremely wavy, curly 12-inch leaves on plants 1 to 5 feet tall. *R. scutatus* (French sorrel)—thick, broad, shield-shaped leaves 1 to 2 inches long on trailing stems growing into mats 6 to 20 inches high and twice as wide.

Growing conditions and maintenance
Sow sorrel indoors 6 to 8 weeks before the last frost, outdoors after the last frost, or divide mature plants and space 8 inches apart. Leaves become bitter in hot weather, but flavor returns with cooler temperatures. Pinch out flowering stalks to encourage leaf production and control invasive self-sowing.

Ruta (ROO-ta)

RUE

Ruta graveolens

HARDINESS: Zones 5-9

PLANT TYPE: perennial

HEIGHT: 12 to 36 inches

LIGHT: full sun

SOIL: well-drained

USES: landscaping, dried arrangements

Common rue forms clumps of lacy, aromatic evergreen foliage that makes an attractive filler or low hedge in a perennial border. For several weeks in summer, frilly, spidery flowers bloom atop the foliage. The inflated lobed seed capsules that follow are attractive in dried arrangements. Once used in herbal medicine, rue is now considered poisonous. Sensitive individuals develop a blistering dermatitis after touching the leaves.

Selected species and varieties
R. graveolens (common rue)—upright stems lined with oblong leaflets and ½-inch yellow flowers in loose, open clusters; 'Jackman's Blue' is a compact, nonflowering cultivar with waxy blue foliage; 'Variegata' has leaves splashed with cream.

Growing conditions and maintenance
Start rue seeds indoors 8 to 10 weeks before the last frost, sow outdoors after the last frost, plant cuttings taken in summer, or divide mature plants in spring or fall. *R. graveolens* 'Variegata' comes true from seed, but 'Jackman's Blue' must be grown from cuttings or divisions. Wearing gloves, prune back hard to force new growth and to keep plants compact.

Salvia (SAL-vee-a)

SAGE

Salvia officinalis 'Purpurea'

HARDINESS: hardy or Zones 4-11

PLANT TYPE: annual, biennial, perennial, or shrub

HEIGHT: 1 to 4 feet

LIGHT: full sun

SOIL: average to alkaline, dry, well-drained

USES: landscaping, culinary, potpourri

Puckered by a network of pronounced veins and colored a distinct gray-green hue, sage leaves bring both interesting texture and an aroma reminiscent of pine or rosemary to the border or kitchen garden. The leaves, largest at the base of the stems, are of gradually diminished size toward the spikes of tiny white, blue, lilac, magenta, or pink flowers at the tips. There are sages useful as edgings or throughout the border, and many do well as container plants or houseplants. Those suitable only for mild winter climates are often grown as half-hardy annuals in cooler zones. Add sage leaves and flowers to salads, or steep them for tea. Use fresh or dried leaves to flavor meat, cheese, or vegetable dishes and sausages and stuffings; the dried herb is stronger than the fresh. Mix dried leaves into potpourri. Use sage in the water for a facial steam, add to the bath, or use an infusion of sage in water as a slightly astringent facial splash or aftershave or as a hair rinse. Sage is reputed to repel insects and also figures in herbal medicine; used in excess or for long periods, however, this herb can be toxic.

Selected species and varieties
S. clevelandii (blue sage, Jim sage)—an evergreen shrub with wrinkled 1-inch leaves on downy stems 2 to 3 feet tall and as wide tipped with violet or white spring-to-summer flowers, recommended for containers or as a houseplant; Zones 9-10. *S. coccinea* (Texas sage, scarlet sage)—a perennial or subshrub grown as an annual, with 2-inch heart-shaped leaves having wavy, indented edges on 3-foot stems tipped with branched spikes of red or white summer flowers that are valued in landscaping. *S. dorisiana* (fruit-scented sage)—an evergreen perennial with sweetly scented, velvety oval leaves 4 inches wide and up to 7 inches long on stems to 4 feet tall tipped with 6-inch spikes of 2-inch magenta to pink flowers in fall and winter; Zones 10-11. *S. elegans* (pineapple sage)—an evergreen perennial with fruit-scented, red-edged 3½-inch oval leaves lining 3- to 4-foot red stems tipped with late-summer red to pink 8-inch flower spikes used in cold drinks and fruit salads; Zones 8-10. *S. fruticosa* (Greek sage)—an evergreen shrub to 4½ feet with lavender-scented leaves and loose, 8-inch clusters of mauve to pink spring-to-summer flowers; Zones 8-9. *S. lavandulifolia* (Spanish sage, narrow-leaved sage)—a spreading evergreen shrub 12 to 20 inches tall with 1-inch white woolly leaves having a piny lavender aroma and red-violet summer flowers; Zones 7-9. *S. officinalis* (common sage, garden sage)—an evergreen shrub in mild climates with 2-inch velvety leaves on branching 2- to 3-foot stems tipped with edible violet to purple flower spikes in summer; 'Berggarten' is a compact 18-inch

Salvia coccinea

cultivar with almost round leaves and blue-purple flowers; 'Icterina', a dwarf cultivar with yellow-splotched leaves; 'Nana', a compact cultivar with small, narrow leaves; 'Purpurea', an 18-inch plant with purple leaves; all are good for indoor winter pot culture; Zones 4-9. *S. sclarea* var. *turkestaniana* (clary sage)—a biennial producing rosettes of 6- to 9-inch oval leaves on pink stems its first year and branching 3- to 4-foot flower stalks the second year tipped with pink-and-white flowers used in tea and salads. *S. viridis* (bluebeard, painted sage)—an annual with narrow, pointed, oval leaves on erect 18-inch stems with inconspicuous summer flowers.

Growing conditions and maintenance

Sow sage seed in spring or set divisions out in spring or fall, spacing them 18 to 24 inches apart. Avoid hot, humid locations or those with too-rich soils. Provide a protective winter mulch in cooler climates. Prune sage heavily in spring to remove winter-killed stems and encourage bushy growth; cut back again immediately after flowering. Perennial sages are short-lived; renew plantings every 4 or 5 years. Propagate by division or by rooting 4-inch stem cuttings taken in summer to plant in fall. Seedlings or rooted cuttings take 2 years to reach maturity for picking. Fresh leaves can be harvested anytime but are most flavorful before flowers appear. Dry leaves slowly to prevent a musty odor, laying them in a single layer on a screen or cloth; refrigerate or freeze the dried leaves. To make an infusion for an aftershave or a hair rinse, steep leaves in boiling water, cool, and strain.

Salvia sclarea var. turkestaniana

Sanguinaria (sang-gwi-NAR-ee-a)

BLOODROOT

Sanguinaria canadensis

HARDINESS:	Zones 3-9
PLANT TYPE:	perennial
HEIGHT:	3 to 8 inches
LIGHT:	partial to full shade
SOIL:	rich, moist, well-drained
USES:	landscaping

Bloodroot's very early spring flowers emerge tightly clasped within kidney-shaped leaves. The waxy leaves, with deep lobes and scalloped edges, slowly unfurl to reveal a single flower resembling a tiny water lily. Allow the creeping rhizomes to spread slowly in woodland and rock gardens or under the shade of shrubs. The red-orange juice flowing in stems and roots was once used in herbal medicine but is now thought to be toxic.

Selected species and varieties

S. canadensis (red puccoon)—grayish green leaves up to a foot across marked with radiating veins and 1½- to 2-inch flowers composed of a whorl of white waxy, pointed petals raised above leaves on 8-inch red stalks; 'Flore Pleno' [also called 'Multiplex'] has double whorls of petals.

Growing conditions and maintenance

Sow seeds of the species in spring or fall or divide roots immediately after flowering, spacing plants 6 to 8 inches apart and incorporating leaf mold into the soil. *S. canadensis* 'Flore Pleno' must be grown from divisions, as it does not come true from seed.

Santolina (san-to-LEE-na)

LAVENDER COTTON

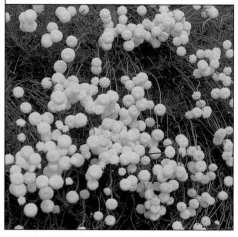

Santolina virens

HARDINESS:	Zones 6-8
PLANT TYPE:	subshrub
HEIGHT:	1 to 2 feet
LIGHT:	full sun
SOIL:	well-drained
USES:	landscaping, dried arrangements

Gray lavender cotton forms stiff cushions of aromatic gray-white finely divided foliage. A favorite in Victorian knot gardens, it is often sheared into low hedges, but its feathery light-colored foliage contrasts well with darker plants as a border specimen. Dry the musky leaves for potpourri or add the leaves and buttonlike flowers to dried arrangements. Herbalists consider lavender cotton a moth repellent.

Selected species and varieties

S. chamaecyparissus (gray lavender cotton)—dainty, hairy leaves only ⅟₁₆ inch wide and ½- to ¾-inch yellow summer flowers like felted domes. *S. virens* (green lavender cotton)—spreading plants to 24 inches tall with fine-textured green leaves strongly scented of pine and ⅜-inch yellow summer flowers.

Growing conditions and maintenance

Sow santolina seeds in spring, start cuttings in spring, or divide in spring or fall, spacing plants 12 to 18 inches apart. Renew the brittle, woody stems by pruning back severely in early spring. Deadhead plants in fall, but do not prune. Pick leaves to dry anytime. Hang flowers to dry in midsummer.

Saponaria (sap-o-NAR-ee-a)

SOAPWORT

Saponaria officinalis 'Rubra Plena'

HARDINESS:	Zones 3-8
PLANT TYPE:	perennial
HEIGHT:	1 to 2 feet
LIGHT:	full sun to light shade
SOIL:	average to poor
USES:	landscaping, potpourri

Bouncing Bet produces clusters of clove-raspberry-scented summer flowers atop clumps of erect stems. The flowers resemble ruffled funnels during the day, then open fully at night into shaggy, open bells. Toss flowers into salads or dry them for potpourri. Leaves, stems, and roots boiled in rainwater produce a soapy liquid prized for cleaning antique textiles. Soapwort once figured in herbal medicine but is now considered toxic.

Selected species and varieties

S. officinalis (bouncing Bet)—pointed, oval leaves paired along sturdy stems and 1- to 1½-inch-wide pink flowers with single or double rows of petals; 'Rubra Plena' has double red petals that fade to pink.

Growing conditions and maintenance

Sow bouncing Bet in spring or fall, or divide mature plants in late fall or early spring. Avoid planting near ponds, as root secretions are toxic to fish. Plants self-sow invasively. Shear spent flowers to prevent seed formation and control spread. Shearing sometimes produces a second bloom. For liquid soap, boil sliced roots, stems, and leaves in lime-free water for 30 minutes and strain.

Satureja (sat-yew-REE-jia)

SAVORY

Satureja hortensis

HARDINESS:	hardy or Zones 5-9
PLANT TYPE:	annual or perennial
HEIGHT:	3 to 18 inches
LIGHT:	full sun
SOIL:	well-drained, slightly alkaline
USES:	landscaping, culinary

Savory's aromatic needlelike leaves line erect stems tipped with whorls of tiny blossoms from summer through fall. Plant savories as border edgings, in kitchen or rock gardens, or in pots for the window sill. Use leaves fresh, dried, or frozen as fines herbes. Savory also figures in traditional herbal medicine.

Selected species and varieties

S. hortensis (summer savory)—a hardy annual to 18 inches tall with pink flowers. *S. montana* 'Nana' (pygmy winter savory)—6-inch plants with peppery leaves, white or lilac blooms; Zones 5-8. *S. spicigera* (creeping savory)—evergreen mats of 3-inch stems with white flowers; Zones 7-8. *S. thymbra* (goat thyme)—16-inch stems with pink blossoms; Zones 8-9.

Growing conditions and maintenance

Sow savory seeds outdoors in spring or transplant divisions of perennials in spring or fall. Pinch early growth to delay blooming, as fresh leaves are best picked before flowers emerge. For window sills, sow summer savory in fall or pot divisions of winter savory after cutting top growth back by half. Hang branches in bunches to dry, then rub leaves from stems.

Sesamum (SES-am-um)

SESAME

Sesamum indicum

HARDINESS:	tender
PLANT TYPE:	perennial
HEIGHT:	18 to 36 inches
LIGHT:	full sun
SOIL:	well-drained
USES:	culinary

Each of sesame's bell-shaped flowers, which grow where leaves join the stem, produces an upright, pointed, oval capsule that bursts when ripe to release tiny nutty-tasting oily seeds, prized in Middle Eastern cuisines. The seeds are used whole in baked goods and candies and to garnish vegetables and salads. They can also be ground into dips, spreads, and sauces and pressed for cooking oil.

Selected species and varieties

S. indicum (sesame, benne, gingili)—square, sticky stems lined with oval, pointed 3- to 5-inch leaves and 1-inch white flowers tinged pink, yellow, or red.

Growing conditions and maintenance

Sow sesame seeds ¼-inch deep once nighttime low temperatures climb to 60° F, or start plants indoors 6 to 8 weeks in advance of this time. Space plants 6 to 8 inches apart. Plants need at least 120 days of hot weather to set seed. Harvest just as oldest pods begin to dry, cutting stems off at ground level, and hold them in a paper bag until pods dry and release seeds. Each seed that grows produces a single stem yielding approximately 1 tablespoon of seeds.

Solidago (sol-i-DAY-go)

GOLDENROD

Solidago odora

HARDINESS: Zones 3-9

PLANT TYPE: perennial

HEIGHT: 3 to 4 feet

LIGHT: full sun

SOIL: average to poor, dry

USES: landscaping, culinary, arrangements

From late summer into fall, sweet goldenrod produces enormous clusters of tiny yellow flowers. The plant will quickly spread through a meadow garden, or you can confine it in a container as a specimen. Although folk wisdom has long held its pollen to be allergenic—the troublemaker is actually *Ambrosia* (ragweed)—the flower clusters can safely be used in fresh or dried arrangements. Brew the fresh or dried anise-scented leaves for tea. The flowers yield yellow dye.

Selected species and varieties
S. odora (sweet goldenrod)—single stems lined with glossy, narrow 2- to 4-inch leaves and tipped with one-sided 8- to 12-inch plumes of ¼-inch yellow flowers.

Growing conditions and maintenance
Sow sweet goldenrod seeds or divide mature plants in early spring, spacing seedlings or divisions 12 to 15 inches apart. Plants begin blooming their second year and self-sow freely. Contain growth by planting in large containers or in the garden in bottomless pots, and remove spent flowers before they set seed. Shear plants to the ground in late winter or early spring, before new growth begins.

Stachys (STAY-kis)

LAMB'S EARS, BETONY

Stachys officinalis

HARDINESS: Zones 4-8

PLANT TYPE: perennial

HEIGHT: 1 to 3 feet

LIGHT: full sun to light shade

SOIL: average, moist, well-drained

USES: landscaping, culinary

Lamb's ears forms low rosettes of heart-shaped leaves with tall flower stems carrying short, dense spikes of small tubular flowers above them. A few sparser flowers often grow where leaves meet the square flower stems. Betony gradually spreads into low mats that provide a colorful filler in the perennial border when plants are blooming. Use the flowers in fresh bouquets. Steep the fresh or dried leaves for tea. Betony once figured prominently in herbal medicine but is now considered largely ineffective.

Selected species and varieties
S. officinalis (lamb's ears)—4- to 5-inch wrinkled, coarsely toothed basal leaves, with 1-inch leaves along flower stems, and whorls of ½- to ¾-inch purple, pink, or white flowers in 1- to 3-inch spikes.

Growing conditions and maintenance
Sow lamb's ears seed in early spring, and thin seedlings to stand 12 to 18 inches apart. Betony benefits from division every 3 or 4 years in early spring or late fall. The plants self-sow but are not invasive.

Symphytum (SIM-fit-um)

COMFREY

Symphytum officinale

HARDINESS: Zones 3-9

PLANT TYPE: perennial

HEIGHT: 3 to 5 feet

LIGHT: full sun to light shade

SOIL: rich, moist

USES: landscaping, toiletries

Comfrey forms bold clumps of coarse, hairy oval leaves useful as a backdrop in large borders or meadow gardens. From spring through fall, drooping clusters of funnel-shaped flowers decorate plants. Rich in nutrients, comfrey once figured prominently in herbal medicine but is now a suspected carcinogen and is recommended only for external use. Add dried and crumbled leaves to a bath as a skin softener. Steep leaves for liquid fertilizer, or add to the compost heap.

Selected species and varieties
S. officinale (common comfrey)—deep green rough-textured 10- to 20-inch basal leaves and ½-inch blue, white, purple, or rose tubular blossoms. *S.* x *uplandicum* (Russian comfrey)—free-flowering with blue or purple blossoms; 'Variegatum' has leaves marbled cream and green.

Growing conditions and maintenance
Grow comfrey from root cuttings containing a growing tip, setting these divisions 6 to 8 inches deep and 2 to 3 feet apart. Choose sites carefully, as comfrey is difficult to eradicate once established. To control its spread, grow in large containers removed from other garden sites.

Tagetes (ta-GEE-teez)

MARIGOLD

Tagetes patula

HARDINESS: tender or Zones 8-9

PLANT TYPE: annual or perennial

HEIGHT: 6 to 36 inches

LIGHT: full sun

SOIL: organic, well-drained

USES: landscaping, culinary, potpourri

Primarily grown as bedding plants for their ferny, pungent foliage and clusters of flat flowers, marigolds are also valued for their root chemicals, which repel nematodes and inhibit weeds. Use leaves and flowers of some species as seasonings or to make tea; dried flower petals add color to potpourri.

Selected species and varieties

T. lucida (sweet mace)—a perennial to 30 inches tall with anise-scented leaves that can substitute for tarragon, and ½-inch yellow flowers; both leaves and flowers can be dried for tea; Zones 8-9. *T. minuta* (muster-John-Henry)—an annual to 3 feet with leaves lending an apple flavor; pale yellow flowers. *T. patula* (French marigold)—an annual 6 to 18 inches tall with yellow, orange, or brown flowers.

Growing conditions and maintenance

Sow annual marigold seeds indoors 4 to 6 weeks before the last frost or outdoors when the soil temperature reaches 60°F; transplant or thin to 12 inches. Deadhead to prolong bloom. Separate flower petals, and lay leaves flat to dry. Propagate sweet mace by division in spring in mild climates; grow as an annual elsewhere.

Tanacetum (tan-a-SEE-tum)

TANSY

Tanacetum vulgare var. crispum

HARDINESS: Zones 4-9

PLANT TYPE: perennial

HEIGHT: 8 inches to 4 feet

LIGHT: full sun to light shade

SOIL: average to poor, dry, well-drained

USES: landscaping, potpourri, arrangements

Tansy bears dainty flowers with conspicuous yellow button-shaped centers surrounded by a fringe of narrow, often inconspicuous white or yellow petals. Singly or in clusters, the flowers grow on branching stalks above pungent foliage that is semievergreen in milder climates. Smaller cultivars make informal border edgings, while others provide midborder fillers. Add the fresh flowers to rustic bouquets, or dry the branched flower stalks to accent dried arrangements. Insect-repellent properties are ascribed to all tanacetums, and some species are used in cosmetics and dyes. Traditional herbalists prescribed several species in medicines and teas, but these uses are no longer recommended, as the active chemicals can be toxic.

Selected species and varieties

T. balsamita [formerly classified as *Chrysanthemum balsamita*] (costmary)—has pointed, oval, spearmint-scented leaves and clusters of tiny late-summer flowers on shrubby plants to 3 feet tall and 2 feet wide; Zones 4-8. *T. cinerariifolium* [formerly classified as *Pyrethrum cinerariifolium* and *Chrysanthemum cinerariifolium*] (pyrethrum)—loose columns of foliage 18 to 24 inches tall and 12 inches wide with narrow filigreed leaves and almost petalless summer-through-fall flowers borne singly or in sparse clusters that are the source of the relatively nontoxic insecticide pyrethrum; Zones 4-9. *T. parthenium* [formerly classified as *Pyrethrum parthenium* and *Chrysanthemum parthenium*] (feverfew)—cushions 1 to 3 feet tall and as wide of lacy leaves and clusters of ¾-inch summer flowers ideal for fresh or dried bouquets ; 'Aureum' (golden-feather) has golden green leaves on 12-inch mounds; 'Golden Ball', double rows of yellow petals on plants to 18 inches; 'White Bonnet', double-petaled white flowers on stems to 2 feet; Zones 4-9. *T. vulgare* var. *crispum* (fern-leaved tansy)—leaves like small fern fronds in mounds to 4 feet high and flowers with yellow centers surrounded by insignificant petals; Zones 4-9.

Growing conditions and maintenance

Sow tanacetum seeds or transplant divisions in spring or fall, spacing them 1 to 4 feet apart. While tanacetums grow best in full sun, costmary and fern-leaved tansy tolerate partial shade. Rich soils produce floppy stems; trim plants back to prevent legginess. Provide a winter mulch in colder zones. Pick branching flower stalks just as blossoms open, and dry hanging upside down in bunches. Store dried tanacetums in tightly sealed containers to prevent their odor from penetrating other herbs. Propagate from seed, by vegetative cuttings taken in summer, or by division in spring or fall. All tanacetums self-sow, and feverfew and fern-leaved tansy can become invasive weeds.

Tanacetum parthenium

Teucrium (TEWK-ree-um)

GERMANDER

Teucrium chamaedrys

HARDINESS: Zones 5-9

PLANT TYPE: shrub

HEIGHT: 6 to 15 inches

LIGHT: full sun to light shade

SOIL: well-drained, slightly acid

USES: landscaping, dried arrangements

Wall germander's spreading mounds of shiny evergreen foliage are covered from early to midsummer with spikes of small, lipped flowers. Allow a specimen to spread in a rock garden, or plant closely and clip into a low hedge resembling a miniature boxwood. The scalloped, oval leaves release a faintly garlicky odor when disturbed. Weave the branches into dried wreaths. Wall germander once figured in herbal medicine but has fallen out of use.

Selected species and varieties

T. chamaedrys (wall germander)—square stems that trail, then turn up to stand 10 to 15 inches high lined with pairs of oval- to wedge-shaped ¼- to 1-inch leaves and tipped with whorls of ¾-inch white-dotted purple-pink flowers; 'Prostratum' has stems 6 to 8 inches tall spreading to 3 feet and pink flowers; 'Variegatum' has green leaves splotched white, cream, or yellow.

Growing conditions and maintenance

Grow wall germander from seed, from spring cuttings, or by division, setting plants 1 foot part. Prune to shape in spring and deadhead to encourage bushiness. Provide protection from drying winter winds.

Thymus (TY-mus)

THYME

Thymus x citriodorus 'Aureus'

HARDINESS: Zones 4-9

PLANT TYPE: evergreen perennial or shrub

HEIGHT: 2 to 18 inches

LIGHT: full sun

SOIL: average to poor, dry, well-drained, alkaline

USES: landscaping, culinary, potpourri

Thyme adds pungent aroma, fine texture, and soft color to borders, rock gardens, and garden paths. Shrubby species with erect branches can be grown as specimens or low hedges. Creeping types fill niches among rocks or between paving stones, drape over walls, and sprawl into ground-covering mats. Thyme also grows well on window sills. Small clusters of ¼-inch nectar-filled summer-long flowers in a variety of shades are attractive to bees. Fresh or dried, the tiny ¼- to ½-inch-long narrow green to gray-green, sometimes variegated, leaves are used as a basic ingredient in bouquets garnis and fines herbes and are used to make tea. Both leaves and flowers are used in potpourris and toiletries. Herbalists use thyme as an insect repellent, medicinal plant, household disinfectant, and preservative.

Selected species and varieties

T. caespititius [formerly classified as *T. azoricus*] (tufted thyme, Azores thyme)—a subshrub forming 6-inch-high mats of twiggy branches lined with sticky, resinous leaves and tipped with white, pink, or lilac flowers; 'Aureus' has deep yellow-green leaves and pink flowers; Zones 8-9. *T. capitatus* (conehead thyme)—upright bushy plants 10 inches tall and as wide with gray leaves and pink flowers crowded into cone-shaped tufts at the tips of branches; Zone 9. *T. cilicicus* (Cilician thyme)—deep green lemon-scented leaves and clusters of pale mauve to lilac blossoms on 6-inch stems; Zones 6-8. *T. x citriodorus* (lemon thyme)—forms a shrubby carpet up to 2 feet wide of foot-tall branches with tiny lemon-scented leaves; 'Aureus' (golden lemon thyme) has gold-edged leaves; 'Silver Queen', leaves marbled cream and silver gray; Zones 5-9. *T. herba-barona* (caraway thyme)—a fast-growing subshrub forming mats 4 inches tall and 2 feet across with leaf flavors reminiscent of caraway, nutmeg, or lemon, and loose clusters of rose flowers; Zones 4-8. *T. mastichina* (mastic thyme)—an erect or sprawling shrub with 6- to 12-inch branches lined with gray-green eucalyptus-scented leaves; Zones 7-9. *T. praecox* ssp. *arcticus* [often sold under the name *T. serpyllum*] (creeping thyme, English wild thyme, nutmeg thyme)—2- to 3-inch-high carpets up to

Thymus herba-barona

18-inches wide with especially flavorful leaves and mauve to purple flowers; 'Coccineus' (crimson creeping thyme) has striking deep red blossoms; Zones 4-9. *T. pulegioides* [often sold under the name *T. serpyllum*] (broad-leaved thyme)—a shrub with large oval leaves lining 10-inch stems tipped with pink to purple flowers in broad mats; Zones 4-8. *T. serpyllum* (mother-of-thyme, wild thyme)—creeping stems only 2 to 3 inches tall in 3-foot-wide mats with cultivars in many shades of green or yellow, sometimes variegated; Zones 4-8. *T. vulgaris* (common thyme)—bushy shrubs 12 inches tall and as wide or wider with gray-green leaves used in cooking; 'Orange Balsam' has a scent recalling pine and citrus; Zones 4-8.

Growing conditions and maintenance

Plant thyme in spring, spacing transplants 12 to 24 inches apart. Select sites with average to poor soil and incorporate a small amount of bone meal at planting time; rich or wet soils invite fungus and winter kill. To shape plants and encourage branching, prune hard in early spring before flowering or lightly after blooms appear. Remove green shoots of variegated cultivars to prevent them from reverting. Leaves are most pungent when picked while plants are in bloom and used while fresh; dried leaves are more flavorful than fresh winter leaves. Add leaves to meat dishes, stuffings, pâtés, salad dressings, vegetable dishes, herb butter, vinegars, and mayonnaise. To dry, hang bundles of branches upside down in a shady, warm, well-ventilated location, then crumble or strip fresh leaves from stems and dry on screens; store in airtight containers for use in cooking or sachets. To propagate thyme, root softwood cuttings taken in late spring or early summer or divide mature plants in early spring or late summer. Propagate from seed by sowing thickly in pots 6 to 8 weeks before the last frost, then set 4- to 6-inch seedlings out in clumps. Start thyme for a window-sill garden from seed, or pot divisions in late summer to bring indoors in late fall.

Thymus praecox ssp. arcticus

Tropaeolum *(tro-PEE-o-lum)*

NASTURTIUM

Tropaeolum majus

HARDINESS: tender

PLANT TYPE: annual

HEIGHT: 15 inches to 6 feet

LIGHT: full sun to light shade

SOIL: average, well-drained, sandy

USES: landscaping, culinary, containers

Nasturtiums bear funnel-like flowers with irregularly shaped petals from summer through frost. The flowers appear along mounding or trailing stems amid saucer-shaped leaves on twining stalks. Use dwarf, mounding nasturtiums as fillers, as houseplants, or among paving stones. Allow the trailing or vining types to ramble as ground covers, cascade over walls, or trail from hanging baskets. Both the leaves and the flowers have a peppery flavor that adds zest to salads and sandwiches. Add flowers to vinegar. Substitute unripe seeds, fresh or pickled, for capers.

Selected species and varieties

T. majus (common nasturtium, Indian cress)—dwarf varieties to 15 inches tall, vining to 6 feet, with leaves to 6 inches wide and 2½-inch yellow, orange, red, or mahogany flowers; 'Empress of India' has vermilion flowers and blue-green leaves.

Growing conditions and maintenance

Sow nasturtium seeds ½ to ¾ inch deep in very early spring, spacing dwarf varieties 6 inches apart, vining types 12 inches apart. Plants growing in shade or rich soil produce more foliage and fewer flowers. Nasturtiums often self-sow.

Tulbaghia *(tul-BAJ-ee-a)*

SOCIETY GARLIC

Tulbaghia violacea

HARDINESS: Zones 9-10

PLANT TYPE: bulb

HEIGHT: 1 to 2½ feet

LIGHT: full sun to light shade

SOIL: average, moist, well-drained

USES: landscaping, arrangements, culinary

In summer, society garlic carries large clusters of starry flowers on tall stalks above clumps of grassy evergreen leaves. Use society garlic's neat mounds as a specimen in the perennial border, or grow the plant as an edging for garden beds or walkways. In cooler climates, society garlic grows well as a potted plant and can be wintered on a sunny window sill. Use the flowers in fresh bouquets. The leaves, with an onion or garlic aroma and a mild taste that does not linger on the breath, can be chopped and used like garlic chives as a garnish flavoring for salads, vegetables, and sauces.

Selected species and varieties

T. violacea (society garlic)—flat, grassy 8- to 12-inch leaves and ¾-inch white or violet flowers in clusters of eight to 16 blossoms on 1- to 2½-foot stalks; 'Silver Streak' has leaves striped cream and green.

Growing conditions and maintenance

Propagate society garlic by removing and replanting the small bulblets growing alongside mature bulbs in spring or fall. Space plants 1 foot apart. For indoor culture, plant one bulb per 6- to 8-inch pot.

Valeriana (va-leer-ee-AY-na)

VALERIAN

Valeriana officinalis

HARDINESS: Zones 3-9

PLANT TYPE: perennial

HEIGHT: 3 to 5 feet

LIGHT: full sun to light shade

SOIL: average, moist, well-drained

USES: landscaping, arrangements, potpourri

Valerian carries small flat-topped tufts of tiny flowers in summer in an open, branching cluster above a rosette of lacy leaves composed of narrow, paired leaflets. Both cats and butterflies find the plants attractive. The flowers, scented of honey and vanilla, are good in fresh bouquets. While some gardeners find the odor of the dried roots agreeable and add them to potpourri, others compare it to dirty socks. The roots yield a sedative compound used in herbal medicine. Add the mineral-rich leaves to compost.

Selected species and varieties:
V. officinalis (common valerian, garden heliotrope)—erect, hairy stems lined with light green ferny leaves and flower stalks to 5 feet with tubular white, pink, red, or lavender-blue flowers in clusters up to 4 inches wide.

Growing conditions and maintenance
Sow common valerian seeds in spring, or divide the creeping roots in spring or fall. Space plants 2 feet apart, and mulch to conserve moisture. Valerian can be invasive; contain its spread by growing it in bottomless pots and removing flower heads before they form seed.

Verbascum (ver-BAS-cum)

MULLEIN

Verbascum thapsus

HARDINESS: hardy or Zones 3-10

PLANT TYPE: biennial

HEIGHT: 4 to 6 feet

LIGHT: full sun

SOIL: dry, well-drained

USES: landscaping, arrangements, potpourri

Mullein forms broad, low rosettes of gray-green velvety leaves its first year, followed by dramatic, tall flower spikes the second. Woolly leaves clasp each thick stalk, crowded at its tip with large green buds that open into small flowers with prominent stamens. Great mullein is one of the few gray plants that tolerate heat and humidity, making it a back-of-the-border specimen particularly well suited to warmer climates. Use the thick spikes in arrangements, or dry the honey-scented flowers, attractive to bees, for potpourri. Herbalists have used great mullein in medicines as well as for bandaging material. It has also been used for tinder, torches, and to reinforce shoe soles.

Selected species and varieties
V. thapsus (great mullein, common mullein, flannel plant, Aaron's rod)—thick, woolly leaves 6 to 18 inches long and spreading 3 feet wide, and ¾- to 1-inch-wide yellow flowers with orange stamens.

Growing conditions and maintenance
Sow great mullein seeds in fall or spring and space seedlings 2 to 2½ feet apart. Plants die after flowering but reseed themselves if flowers remain on plants.

Viola (vy-O-la)

VIOLET

Viola odorata

HARDINESS: Zones 3-10

PLANT TYPE: perennial or hardy annual

HEIGHT: 6 to 12 inches

LIGHT: partial shade to full sun

SOIL: moist, well-drained

USES: landscaping, culinary, potpourri

Clumps of violets with five-petaled blossoms resembling tiny faces are a staple in old-fashioned gardens as fillers among taller perennials, as edgings for beds and walkways, or in containers. Available in a wide range of shades, the small blossoms add cheer and fragrance to nosegays of fresh flowers. Their soft colors and faintly wintergreen taste accent salads, jams, and jellies. Candied violets garnish cakes, puddings, and other desserts. Violet water enhances baked goods, ices, and chilled soups, and can be used as a mouthwash or facial rinse. Add dried blossoms to potpourri. Add the slightly tangy leaves, high in vitamins A and C, to salads, or use them to perfume water for a facial steam. The flowers, leaves, and roots all figure in herbal medicine.

Selected species and varieties
V. odorata (sweet violet, florist's violet, English violet)—a perennial with sweetly scented deep purple or white, sometimes yellow, 1- to 1½-inch blossoms having prominent yellow centers on 6- to 8-inch stems amid quilted heart-shaped leaves in late winter to early spring in mild climates, from late spring through summer else-

where; 'Alba' bears quantities of snow white flowers; 'Royal Robe' has extremely fragrant deep purple blossoms on 8-inch stems; Parma violets produce double rows of petals; Zones 3-10 for most except Parma violets, which are hardy only to Zone 6. *V. tricolor* (Johnny-jump-up, miniature pansy)—hardy annual or short-lived perennial with small, inch-wide, purple-white-and-yellow blossoms on 6- to 8-inch stems amid clumps of scalloped leaves in spring and summer.

Growing conditions and maintenance

Sow violet seeds directly in the garden in late summer or early spring, or start indoors 8 to 12 weeks before the last frost. Sweet violet grows best in partial shade, Johnny-jump-up in full sun, but either tolerates less than ideal light. Johnny-jump-up self-sows readily and behaves like a perennial in locations that favor its growth; treat sweet violet as an annual in regions with mild winters. Provide sweet violets, which spread by underground runners, with a light winter mulch. For more prolific flowering, feed violets in very early spring and remove faded flowers; shear sweet violets in late fall and remove excess runners. Divide sweet violets in fall, and space transplants 6 to 12 inches apart. For fresh use, pick flowers early in the day, leaves while still young. Candy the blossoms by dipping them in a heavy sugar syrup, then laying them flat to dry. Pour 3 ounces of boiling water over 2 ounces of leaves and petals and allow to steep for use in baking or as a cosmetic. Dry blossoms slowly in a shaded location to retain their delicate color.

Viola tricolor

Vitex (VY-tex)

CHASTE TREE

Vitex agnus-castus

HARDINESS:	Zones 7-10
PLANT TYPE:	shrub or tree
HEIGHT:	6 to 15 feet
LIGHT:	full sun
SOIL:	average, moist to dry
USES:	landscaping

Chaste tree's aromatic gray-green leaves are composed of narrow, pointed leaflets arranged like the fingers on a hand. Usually growing as a multitrunked shrub in a shrub border, it can be pruned as an umbrella-shaped tree to serve as a lawn specimen. In summer and sporadically in fall, chaste tree produces large flower spikes followed by fleshy fruits. The tiny fruits have a peppery flavor and are sometimes dried and ground as a condiment.

Selected species and varieties

V. agnus-castus (chaste tree, hemp tree)—shrubs up to 15 feet tall and as wide with lacy, fan-shaped leaves up to 6 inches across, dark green above and gray below, and 7-inch spikes of tiny lavender-blue flowers followed by red-black berries.

Growing conditions and maintenance

Sow chaste tree seed in spring or fall, or start new plants from softwood cuttings in spring or from semiripe cuttings in summer. Plants bloom on the current season's growth. Cut dead or damaged branches back to 2 inches in very early spring to renew older shrubs or those touched by frost. Collect and dry fruits in fall.

Zingiber (ZIN-ji-ber)

GINGER

Zingiber officinale

HARDINESS:	Zones 9-11
PLANT TYPE:	perennial
HEIGHT:	3 to 4 feet
LIGHT:	light shade
SOIL:	rich, moist, well-drained
USES:	containers, culinary

Ginger's aromatic branching roots with a spicy, citrusy bite have been prized by cooks for centuries. Fresh grated or dried ground ginger flavors baked goods, marinades, curries, chutneys, beverages, syrups, vegetables, fruit dishes, and more. Grow ginger outdoors in hot, humid regions or as a container plant elsewhere.

Selected species and varieties

Z. officinale (common ginger)—2- to 4-foot-long flat leaves composed of pointed leaflets lining reedlike stems and, rarely, yellow-petaled summer flowers with yellow-streaked purple lips in conical spikes.

Growing conditions and maintenance

Purchase gingerroot from a nursery or grocery store. Pot a section with large growth buds just below the surface in equal parts of sand, loam, peat moss, and compost. Plants grow best in warm temperatures with constant humidity and soil moisture. After 8 to 10 months, harvest the roots, retaining a small section to replant. Refrigerated, roots keep 2 to 3 months wrapped in a damp towel and plastic film. Alternatively, peel the roots, slice into a jar of sherry, and refrigerate indefinitely.

Vegetables

IF YOU'RE A VEGETABLE GARDENER, YOU KNOW that nothing tastes better than something you've grown in your own garden. And if you raise your vegetables organically, you know they are as healthful as they can be, free of contamination from synthetic chemical pesticides and other substances that may be harmful.

With all the varieties of vegetables and fruits available, deciding which crops to grow can seem like a daunting task. And it takes careful planning if you want your garden to be productive all season. Presented here is a selection of delicious season-spanning vegetables, along with several fruits, all of which can be grown in the home garden. As you create your "wish list" of plants, check the hardiness information at the top of each entry, and refer to the frost maps on page 467 to find out when you can expect the last hard spring frost and the first hard fall frost in your area. Each entry also lists the relative days to maturity so you'll know when the crop will be ready for harvesting and when you can plant a successive crop in its place.

ARTICHOKES

'Green Globe'

HARDINESS: Zones 8-11; warm-season annual

PLANTING METHOD: direct sowing; rooted cuttings

PLANT SPACING: 2 to 4 feet

LIGHT: full sun to light shade

Large, edible flower buds 4 to 6 inches across. Grown as perennials, artichokes are harvested in the spring; as annuals, they are harvested in the fall. Artichokes can be grown as container plants.

Selected varieties

'Green Globe'—very prolific with buds in 100 days. 'Imperial Star'—spineless buds; performs well as an annual. 'Purple Sensation'—bronze-tinted buds.

Growing conditions

Artichokes need cool, moist summers and loose, constantly moist, well-drained soil enriched with manure. When grown as annuals, they need at least 100 frost-free days. Plant cuttings 6 to 8 inches deep and 2 to 4 feet apart in spring if grown as an annual; where perennial, plant in spring or fall. To grow from seed as a perennial, sow seed outdoors ½ inch deep. Thin young plants to 6 inches, then thin again to stand 2 to 4 feet apart. For annual artichokes, start seed indoors 4 to 6 weeks before last frost date and transplant when the soil temperature reaches 70° F. Renew a perennial planting every 3 to 4 years. Plants yield six to 12 buds.

ARUGULA, ROCKET

Arugula

HARDINESS: cool-season annual

PLANTING METHOD: direct sowing

PLANT SPACING: 6 inches

LIGHT: full sun to light shade

Peppery young leaves in spring or fall provide leafy salad greens or a zesty garnish for pasta or other dishes. Add the spicy flowers of bolting plants to salads for color and flavor.

Selected varieties

No named varieties; sold as arugula. Rosettes of broad oval leaves are ready in 35 to 45 days.

Growing conditions

Plant seeds ½ inch deep in wide rows in early spring and again in fall 4 to 8 weeks before the first frost date. Arugula can be grown outdoors in winter where temperatures do not go below 25° F. The heat and short nights of summer cause plants to bolt and leaves to become bitter. Pick outer leaves when they are 2 to 4 inches long to encourage new growth, or harvest entire plant; small weekly sowings prolong harvest. Handpick snails and slugs or use baited traps. Interplant arugula with taller cool-season vegetables such as peas or broccoli, and fill spaces left after a spring planting is harvested with warm-season crops such as green beans or eggplant.

ASPARAGUS

'Jersey Giant'

HARDINESS: winter-hardy Zones 3-8

PLANTING METHOD: crowns; transplants

PLANT SPACING: 15 to 18 inches

LIGHT: full sun

Succulent shoots ½ inch or more in diameter tipped with tight, tender buds rise from perennial rootstocks in spring. When the year's harvest ends, allow shoots to develop into 4- to 6-foot-tall stems with ferny leaves. Plant lettuce or other low-growing cool-season crops where asparagus foliage will shade them.

Selected varieties

'Argenteuil'—stems especially good for blanching white. 'Jersey Giant'—a hybrid with very high yields of large spears with purplish tips; resists rust and tolerates fusarium wilt, root rot, and crown rot. 'Jersey Knight'—high-yielding hybrid adaptable to many soil types; resistant to rust and tolerant of fusarium wilt, root rot, and crown rot. 'Mary Washington'—widely available rust-resistant variety producing crisp, deep green spears over a long season. 'UC157'—a hybrid especially suited to areas with mild winters; produces clumps of three to five uniform spears with some tolerance of root rot and fusarium wilt.

Growing conditions

Plant crowns in spring when the soil temperature reaches 50° F or more, or in fall. Set crowns in trenches 1 foot deep lined with 3 to 4 inches of well-rotted manure or compost. When new shoots appear, cover them with 2 to 3 inches of a mixture of equal parts of soil and compost. As the shoots elongate, continue adding more of the mixture until the trench is filled in. Mulch heavily with compost to suppress weeds. Although planting from crowns is the easiest method, asparagus can be started outdoors or indoors from seed that has been soaked for 2 days in tepid water before sowing. Seedlings started indoors are transplanted to the garden when 10 to 12 weeks old, after all danger of frost is past. To sow outdoors, plant seed ½ inch deep when the soil reaches 70° F or more. Asparagus takes 2 years to reach full production from roots and 3 years to reach picking size from seed. Harvest about one-third of the new shoots the first year after planting roots. Harvest established beds once or twice daily, cutting or snapping off 6- to 8-inch spears just above the soil line. Pick 2- to 3-year-old beds over 4 weeks and older beds for as long as 10 weeks. To produce white spears, blanch shoots as they emerge by covering them with 8 to 10 inches of soil or straw and harvesting when the tips peek through. Asparagus beds remain productive for 20 years or more. Control asparagus beetles and spotted asparagus beetles by handpicking them or shaking them onto a sheet and destroying them; by releasing beneficial insects such as ladybeetles or parasitic wasps; and by cleaning up garden debris in fall. Asparagus is susceptible to crown or root rot, fusarium wilt, and rust; remove and destroy affected plants. Mature plants yield 15 to 25 spears each.

'Mary Washington'

BEANS, DRY

'Jacob's Cattle'

HARDINESS: warm-season annual

PLANTING METHOD: direct sowing

PLANT SPACING: 3 to 6 inches

LIGHT: full sun

Also known as shelling beans. Successive plantings of bush or vining beans yield pods filled with ¼- to ¾-inch beans from summer through fall that are high in fiber and protein. Shell mature beans and use them fresh in side dishes, casseroles, and soups, or preserve them by freezing or canning. Alternatively, let pods dry on the plant, then shell and store beans. Soak dry beans to rehydrate and use like mature fresh beans.

Selected varieties
'Adzuki'—small, dark red dry beans on 2-foot bushy plants in 118 days. 'Black Turtle'—bush variety with small black dry beans with a nutty flavor in 98 to 103 days. 'Cannellini'—vining pole bean with mildly flavored white to greenish white shelling beans in 50 to 60 days or dry beans in 80 days. 'French Horticultural'—18-inch heirloom, disease-resistant bush bean producing dry beans in 90 days. 'Great Northern'—prolific bush bean with oval, white dry beans in 85 days. 'Hutterite Soup'—heirloom bush bean with thick, yellowish white beans in 75 to 85 days. 'Jacob's Cattle', also called 'Dalmatian Bean'—heirloom 24-inch bush bean producing meaty, kidney-shaped white beans with maroon speckles, for shelling in 65 days or dry beans in 80 to 100 days. 'Pinto'—pole bean producing kidney-shaped maroon-and-white-speckled dry beans in 90 days. 'Soldier'—18-inch heirloom bush bean tolerant of both cool temperatures and drought, with slender white dry beans splotched in brown in 85 days. 'Swedish Brown'—extremely hardy 15-inch heirloom bush bean producing quantities of small oval red-brown shelling beans with a small white eye in 65 days or dry beans in 85 days. 'Tongues of Fire'—ivory pods streaked with red producing shelling beans in 70 days. 'Vermont Cranberry'—heirloom bush bean producing plump, white shelling beans swirled with maroon in 60

'Cannellini'

days and dry beans in 75 to 98 days. 'Yellow Eye'—prolific heirloom bush bean bearing white beans spotted with yellowish or tan eyes, good for shelling or for dry beans.

Growing conditions
Plant seeds outdoors after the soil temperature has reached 65° F or more and all danger of frost is past, setting them 1 to 1½ inches deep after pretreating with a bacterial legume inoculant. Make several successive weekly plantings to prolong harvest. Provide trellises or other tall supports for vining pole beans. Mulch to suppress weeds and conserve moisture, which is essential while plants are flowering and seeds are developing in the pods. To harvest beans for shelling and using fresh or for freezing or canning, pick as seeds reach maturity and fill out the pods. Continuous picking of mature pods is essential for further pod production for shelling beans;

plants stop producing as soon as even a few pods become overmature. To harvest dry beans, stop watering. When at least 90 percent of the leaves have fallen and at least two-thirds of the beans are dry, pull plants and spread them on tarpaulins or hang in a well-ventilated area to finish drying. When seeds can no longer be dented when bitten, they are ready to thresh; do this by flailing them in a cloth bag. Screen or winnow to remove pod debris. Remove and discard broken beans, freeze the remainder for several hours to destroy bean weevil larvae, then store in airtight containers for up to 3 years.

'Tongues of Fire'

BEANS, FAVA

'Broad Windsor Longpod'

HARDINESS: cool-season annual

PLANTING METHOD: direct sowing

PLANT SPACING: 4 to 6 inches

LIGHT: full sun

Also called broad beans. Large, meaty seeds mature in long pods on erect bushy plants in late spring. Shell mature fava beans for fresh use, or allow beans to dry for long-term storage.

Selected varieties
'Aquadulce'—16-inch pods up to 2 inches wide filled with seven or eight large white beans in 85 days. 'Broad Windsor Longpod'—up to seven light green beans in 8-inch pods on heat-tolerant 3-foot plants in 85 days. 'Imperial Green Longpod'—20-inch pods in 84 days.

Growing conditions
Fava beans tolerate frost and grow best where spring weather remains cool for a long time. In hot weather, flowers will not set pods. Plant seed outdoors 4 to 6 weeks before the last spring frost, setting seeds 1 to 1½ inches deep after pretreating with a bacterial legume inoculant. Seeds may be broadcast or grown in wide rows. Provide twiggy branches or other supports among plants. Mulch to keep plants cool, suppress weeds, and conserve moisture. Continuous picking of mature pods encourages further production; plants stop producing as soon as even a few pods become overmature.

BEANS, FILET

'Tavera'

HARDINESS: warm-season annual

PLANTING METHOD: direct sowing

PLANT SPACING: 2 to 6 inches

LIGHT: full sun

Heavy crops of long, straight, elegantly thin green beans for fresh use in late spring through summer on upright, bushy plants.

Selected varieties
'Astral'—miniature 3- to 4-inch beans on disease-resistant plants in 60 days. 'Finaud'—very thin 6- to 8-inch beans. 'Fin des Bagnols'—high yields of 7- to 8-inch beans. 'Tavera'—very thin, stringless 4- to 5-inch beans in 54 days. 'Triumph de Farcy'—straight 5- to 6-inch dark green beans in 48 days.

Growing conditions
Plant outdoors after all danger of frost is past and the soil temperature has reached 65° F, setting seeds 1 to 1½ inches deep. Mulch to conserve moisture and suppress weeds. Filet beans are best when they are ⅛ to ¼ inch in diameter. Pick every other day in hot weather and at least every 5 days, but preferably more frequently, in cool weather to prolong harvest over several weeks.

BEANS, GREEN

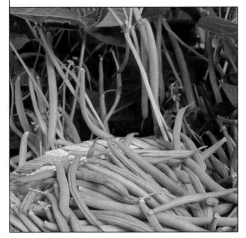

'Derby'

HARDINESS: warm-season annual

PLANTING METHOD: direct sowing

PLANT SPACING: 2 to 4 inches

LIGHT: full sun

Also called snap beans. Clusters of pods on compact 1- to 2-foot bushes can be harvested from early summer into fall when seed is sown in succession. Use green beans fresh, or freeze or can them.

Selected varieties

'Blue Lake Bush'—6½-inch-long cylindrical pods produced all at once on disease-resistant plants in 58 days. 'Derby'—continuously produced cylindrical pods 7 inches long on vigorous bushes starting in 57 days over several weeks. 'Greencrop'—early crops of flat, stringless pods in 52 days. 'Harvester'—large crop of 5- to 6-inch curved, stringless pods on disease-resistant plants in 60 days. 'Jade'—large crop of straight 5- to 7-inch pods in 60 days. 'Provider'—early crop of 6-inch oval pods in 50 days on plants that resist disease, heat, and drought. 'Slenderette'—thin, stringless 5-inch pods in 53 days on plants that resist disease. 'Stringless Greenpod'—stringless 6-inch cylindrical pods in 50 days. 'Tendercrop'—cylindrical 6-inch stringless pods on disease-resistant plants in 50 days. 'Tendergreen'—6-inch stringless pods on heat-tolerant plants.

Growing conditions

Plant outdoors after all danger of frost is past and the soil temperature has reached 65° F, setting seeds 1 to 1½ inches deep after pretreating with a bacterial legume inoculant purchased from a seed supplier. The bacteria live in nodules on the roots of the plants and extract nitrogen from the air that helps the beans grow. The shallow roots of beans are easily damaged by cultivation, so control weeds by keeping the plants well mulched. Spacing plants closely also helps to suppress weeds.

Most varieties produce a single crop all at once, so plant weekly for a month to ensure successive harvests. Harvest green beans when pods snap crisply but before seeds start to form. Continuous picking of the pods encourages further production; plants stop producing flowers as soon as even a few pods go to seed.

'Provider'

BEANS, LIMA

'Burpee's Improved Bush'

HARDINESS: warm-season annual

PLANTING METHOD: direct sowing

PLANT SPACING: 2 to 4 inches

LIGHT: full sun

Starchy, delicately flavored beans on 1½- to 2-foot bushy plants or 7- to 12-foot vining plants from early summer into fall with successive plantings. Shell lima beans for using fresh or allow them to dry on plants for long-term storage.

Selected varieties

'Baby Fordhook'—an early baby lima bush variety with three or four small light green beans in 3-inch pods in 70 days. 'Burpee's Best'—a high-yielding pole variety with three to five beans per pod in 92 days. 'Burpee's Improved Bush'—bush variety with four or five large beans in easily shelled 5½-inch pods in 75 days. 'Fordhook 242'—midseason bush variety with three or four very large, uniform beans per pod on heat-tolerant plants in 74 days. 'Henderson's Bush'—early baby lima bush variety with three or four small white beans per pod in 65 days. 'King of the Garden'—a vining pole variety with four or five creamy white or pale green beans per pod in 88 days, good for drying.

Growing conditions

Plant outdoors after all danger of frost is past and the soil temperature has reached at least 65° F and preferably 75° F, setting seeds 1 to 1½ inches deep after pretreating with a bacterial legume inoculant, which can be purchased from most seed suppliers. Make several successive weekly plantings to prolong harvesting. Plant bush lima beans in double rows and provide supports among the plants to keep leaves and pods off the ground. Provide trellises or other tall supports for vining pole varieties. If the supports have been used previously for bean crops, treat them with a mixture of 10 parts water to 1 part household bleach to kill any disease organisms that may have overwintered. Mulch plants well and keep soil moist, especially while plants are flowering and beans are developing in the pods. Continuous picking of mature pods encourages further production for shelling beans; plants stop producing as soon as even a few pods become overmature and begin to dry.

To harvest dry beans, withhold water and allow at least two-thirds of the beans to dry, then pull out plants and spread on tarps or hang in a well-ventilated area to finish drying. When seeds can no longer be dented when bitten, thresh by flailing them in a cloth bag. Screen or winnow to remove pod debris, freeze for several hours to destroy bean weevil larvae, and store in airtight containers for up to 3 years.

'Fordhook 242'

BEANS, POLE

'Trionfo Violetto'

HARDINESS: warm-season annual

PLANTING METHOD: direct sowing

PLANT SPACING: 3 to 6 inches

LIGHT: full sun

Vines up to 12 feet long produce green, yellow, or purple pods from summer into fall with successive plantings. Pole beans produce almost twice as many beans as green bush beans, which makes them an ideal choice for small spaces and intensive gardening.

Selected varieties
'Blue Lake'—early-maturing variety with straight, round, stringless 5½-inch pods in 66 days. 'Emerite'—early, very slender stringless pods on very productive vines in 55 days. 'Kentucky Wonder'—flavorful beans, with good texture for freezing, in 65 days; can also be left on vine longer for dry beans. 'Kwintus'—long, flat pods that stay tender even when mature. 'Merchant of Venice', also called 'Meraviglia di Venezia'—flat, stringless golden yellow 3-inch pods filled with black seeds in 75 days. 'Trionfo Violetto'—an heirloom variety with attractive purple flowers that make it a good landscaping plant, followed by deep purple stringless beans in 62 days.

Growing conditions
Plant outdoors after all danger of frost is past and the soil temperature has reached 65° F, setting seeds 1 to 1½ inches deep after pretreating them with a bacterial inoculant, which can be purchased from most

seed suppliers. The bacteria live in nodules on the roots of the plants and extract nitrogen from the air that helps the beans grow. Provide wooden or wire trellises, netting, tepee poles, or other supports for pole beans to climb. Disease organisms can overwinter on supports; reuse supports that beans have grown on in previous years only after sterilizing them with a mixture of 10 parts water to 1 part household bleach.

Beans have shallow roots that can easily be damaged by cultivation, so keep them well mulched to control weeds. It is important to keep plants well watered, especially when they are flowering and pods are developing. Harvest beans when pods snap crisply when broken but before seeds start to form. Continuous picking of mature pods encourages further pod production; plants stop producing flowers as soon as even a few pods go to seed. For dry beans, allow pods to mature and dry on plants in the garden. Thresh seeds from pods by flailing them in a cloth bag when seeds can no longer be dented when bitten.

'Kentucky Wonder'

BEANS, PURPLE

'Royal Burgundy'

HARDINESS: warm-season annual

PLANTING METHOD: direct sowing

PLANT SPACING: 3 to 6 inches

LIGHT: full sun

Produced from early summer to fall if sown successively, the colorful pods are easy to find among the foliage. Use purple-podded beans raw to add color to salads or hors d'oeuvres; they turn green when cooked.

Selected varieties

'Royal Burgundy'—an insect-resistant variety with deep purple stringless, slightly curved 5½-inch pods in 54 days. 'Royalty'—bright purple, curving pods in 53 days. 'Sequoia'—flat purple pods filled with large, meaty seeds.

Growing conditions

Plant outdoors after the last spring frost, setting seeds 1 to 1½ inches deep. Make successive plantings over a month's time to extend the harvest into fall. Provide supports among the plants to keep beans up off the ground. Continuous picking of mature pods encourages further production; plants stop producing as soon as even a few pods become overmature.

BEANS, RUNNER

'Scarlet Runner'

HARDINESS: Zones 7-9; cool-season annual

PLANTING METHOD: direct sowing

PLANT SPACING: 3 to 6 inches

LIGHT: full sun

Long, flat fuzzy pods filled with colorful seeds develop from large, brilliantly colored flowers on long vines in summer and fall. Plants are perennial where winters are mild. Use immature runner bean pods fresh and mature pods as shell beans. Train runner bean vines on a trellis as a flowering screen.

Selected varieties

'Painted Lady'—red-and-white flowers followed by 12-inch pods in 90 days; 'Scarlet Emperor'—red flowers followed by tender pods in 75 days; seeds mature more slowly than other varieties. 'Scarlet Runner'—edible red flowers in clusters of 20 to 40 blossoms, followed by long, meaty pods filled with black-purple seeds in 90 days. Pods can also be picked before seeds mature and eaten fresh.

Growing conditions

Plant seeds 1 to 1½ inches deep after the last spring frost and make successive bi-weekly sowings to prolong harvest. Provide a trellis or other support for vines to climb, and keep mulched. Continuous picking of mature pods encourages further production; plants stop producing flowers as soon as even a few pods become overmature. Mulch heavily over winter to protect roots in Zones 7-9.

BEANS, YARDLONG

'Green-Pod Yardlong'

HARDINESS: warm-season annual

PLANTING METHOD: direct sowing

PLANT SPACING: 8 to 12 inches

LIGHT: full sun

Also called asparagus beans. Quantities of extremely long, thin pods on vining plants in late summer and fall. Yardlong beans can grow as long as their name suggests but are the most tender when they are about 10 to 12 inches long. Eat raw or cooked.

Selected varieties

'Green-Pod Yardlong'—2- to 3-foot, pencil-thin green beans in 75 days. 'Orient Wonder'—stringless 15- to 20-inch pods in 60 days. 'Purple-Pod Yardlong'—2- to 3-foot, very slender purple pods ready for harvest in 75 days.

Growing conditions

Yardlong beans require both a long growing season and warm temperatures. Plant seeds outdoors after the last spring frost, setting them 1 to 1½ inches deep. Provide tall trellises or other supports for the vines to climb. Mulch to conserve moisture and suppress weeds. Continuous picking of the pods encourages further production; plants stop producing flowers when any pods become overmature.

BEANS, YELLOW OR WAX

'Pencil Pod Wax'

HARDINESS: warm-season annual

PLANTING METHOD: direct sowing

PLANT SPACING: 3 to 6 inches

LIGHT: full sun

Delicately flavored, buttery yellow pods develop on bushy plants from summer into fall with successive plantings. Use the colorful pods raw or cooked to brighten salads and side dishes, or preserve them by freezing.

Selected varieties

'Brittle Wax'—heavy crop of crisp 7-inch pods in 52 days. 'Cherokee'—heavy crop of stringless pods on disease-resistant plants in 50 days. 'Dorabel'—small 4- to 5-inch pods ready to pick in 57 to 60 days. 'Golden Rocky'—deep yellow 7-inch pods on cold-tolerant plants in 63 days. 'Goldenrod'—round, straight 6-inch pods with small seeds in 55 days. 'Pencil Pod Wax'—round, very crisp, slender 7-inch stringless pods in 55 days. 'Roc d'Or'—round, straight, buttery tender pods on disease-resistant plants in 57 days. 'Roma Gold'—flat, stringless pods with plump seeds in 55 days. 'Wax Romano'—broad, flat beans with meaty seeds in 59 days.

Growing conditions:

Plant wax beans outdoors after all danger of frost is past and the soil temperature has reached 65° F, setting seeds 1 to 1½ inches deep. Continuous picking of mature pods encourages further production.

BEETS

'Early Wonder'

HARDINESS: cool-season annual

PLANTING METHOD: direct sowing

PLANT SPACING: 2 to 4 inches

LIGHT: full sun

Sweet, tender red, yellow, or white roots and tangy greens are harvested from summer through fall. Varieties may be globe shaped or cylindrical. Both roots and greens can be used raw or cooked. The pigment in red beets is drawn out during cooking to color dishes.

Selected varieties

'Albina Vereduna'—globe variety with mild white flesh and wavy greens in 60 days. 'Big Red'—globe variety with fine-textured roots and disease-resistant greens in 55 days. 'Burpee's Golden'—globe variety with reddish gold roots of excellent keeping quality in 55 days. 'Chioggia'—globe variety with rosy pink skin and white flesh marked with bright pink concentric rings, and especially tasty greens. 'Cylindra'—cylindrical variety with long, 5- to 7-inch roots ideal for uniform slicing in 55 days. 'Detroit Dark Red'—globe variety with dark red roots in 60 days that store well. 'Early Wonder'—a globe variety with fine-grained 3-inch roots in 50 days. 'Formanova'—cylindrical variety with roots 6 to 8 inches long and 2½ inches in diameter in 50 days. 'Golden'—sweet, nonbleeding variety with deep yellow-orange flesh in 60 days. 'Long Season'—tapered variety with large roots and excellent storage qualities

in 78 days. 'Lutz Green Leaf', also called 'Winter Keeper'—tapered variety with succulent glossy greens with white stems and very sweet dark red roots with excellent keeping quality in 80 days. 'Red Ace'—vigorous, fast-growing globe variety with exceptionally sweet, deep red roots in 53 days. 'Ruby Queen'—globe variety with smooth, deep red roots of uniform size in 54 days.

Growing conditions

Beets can be sown outdoors as soon as the soil can be worked. Soak seeds for 24 hours in warm water before setting them ½ inch deep in a loose, well-tilled soil rich in organic matter to allow growth of the long taproots. Fertilize at planting with a 5-10-10 organic fertilizer or well-rotted manure. Mark rows of slow-germinating beets with quick-growing radishes for intensive cropping. Cover with floating row covers to help warm the soil and speed germination; row covers will also control insect pests on greens. Mulch to help provide the even moisture needed to produce sweet beets. Thin seedlings twice, first to stand 2 inches apart and later to stand 4 inches apart. Beets can be harvested anytime after they are half grown. For a fall crop, sow seed in mid- to late summer. Beet roots toughen when the temperature is 80° F or more. To avoid root rot, rotate beets with nonroot crops.

'Golden'

BLACKBERRIES

'Ebony King' Blackberry

HARDINESS: winter-hardy Zones 5-10

PLANTING METHOD: bare root; containers

PLANT SPACING: 3 to 5 feet

LIGHT: full sun

Juicy, sweet-tart berries 1 to 2 inches long in midsummer and sometimes again in fall on erect or trailing canes. Except for a handful of varieties, blackberries and the closely related boysenberries, loganberries, and youngberries are notorious for the sharp thorns that line the canes. Both trailing and erect types produce canes that grow one year, then bear fruit and die the second year. The berries can be enjoyed fresh from the garden, baked into pies and other desserts, frozen, or made into preserves or wine. Blackberries and their relatives are long lived, often remaining productive for as long as 20 years.

Selected varieties

Trailing blackberries include: 'Boysen'—drought-resistant canes that bear very large 1½-inch, deep red to purple-black berries with a whitish bloom. 'Logan'—deep red to dusky maroon berries 1½ inches long on semierect canes; best suited to the West Coast. 'Lucretia'—early-ripening, medium to large, jet black fruit. 'Thornless Boysen'—very large, almost seedless, black-purple berries on thornless canes. 'Young'—large, round, wine-colored berries with exceptional juiciness and sweetness; performs well on both the West Coast and the Gulf Coast. All of the

trailing varieties are hardy in Zones 7-10.

Upright blackberry varieties include: 'Comanche'—midseason crop of very large, glossy black berries. 'Darrow'—with early- to midseason crops of firm, inch-long fruits on virus-free, winter-hardy canes; Zones 5-10. 'Ebony King'—rust-resistant 3- to 4-foot canes bearing early-ripening purple-black fruits; Zones 5-10. 'Ranger'—with very early, very large yields of sweet berries ideal for fresh eating or winemaking. 'Thornfree'—late-ripening, medium to large fruits on thornless 7- to 8-foot canes; Zones 7-10.

Growing conditions

Plant certified disease-free bare-root or container-grown plants in deep, fertile, moist but well-drained loam with a pH between 5.5 and 7.5, setting the top of the roots just below the soil line. From Zone 5 north, set plants out in early spring, as soon as the soil can be worked. From Zone 6 south, set plants out in fall, winter, or spring. Plant upright types 3 feet apart in rows spaced 6 feet apart; trailing types should be planted 5 feet apart in rows 8 feet apart. For both types, cut the canes of newly planted bushes back to 6 inches from the ground. Water regularly and provide a deep mulch to suppress grass and weeds. For established erect varieties, prune the side branches of canes produced the previous year back to about 18 inches in early spring to encourage heavy fruit production in the coming season; the side branches of trailing varieties should be cut back to 12 inches. For both newly planted and established bushes, pinch off the tips of any new canes that are produced during

'Thornless Boysen'

the current season when they are about 3½ feet tall; pinching is important because it stimulates the canes to produce side branches and thus helps ensure heavy production the following year.

When the fruiting season is over, cut out all the canes that produced berries. Trailing types are most productive if their canes are trained in a fan shape on a support of horizontal wires. Harvest blackberries after fruits turn from pink to red and finally deep glossy black-purple; the berries should be so ripe that they drop off at the slightest touch. Leave berries that are still firmly attached to ripen fully; otherwise, they will be sour. A single plant yields 4 to 8 quarts of fruit.

'Logan'

BLACK-EYED PEAS

'California Blackeye #5'

HARDINESS: warm-season annual

PLANTING METHOD: direct sowing

PLANT SPACING: 2 to 4 inches

LIGHT: full sun

Also called cowpeas. White, cream, or tan ⅜- to ½-inch seeds with a dark spot, or eye, fill long clusters of pods at the top of bushy or semivining plants in summer through early fall. Harvest immature pods and cook like green beans; shell mature pods and use the peas fresh; or allow pods to dry on plants, then shell and store the beans.

Selected varieties
'California Blackeye #5'—large seeds in pods up to 12 inch-es long on nematode- and wilt-resistant plants in 75 to 95 days. 'Mississippi Silver' —bears easy-to-shell cowpeas with 6-inch pods in 65 days. 'Pinkeye Purple Hull'—purple-eyed white cowpeas in 6- to 7-inch pods in 65 days; usually produces two crops a season.

Growing conditions
Plant after all danger of frost is past and the soil temperature reaches 70° F, sowing seeds ½ to 1 inch deep; seeds germinate in 10 to 14 days. Extend the harvest time with successive plantings. Fertilize soil before planting with phosphorus and potassium; adding nitrogen isn't necessary. Anthracnose, blight, powdery mildew, aphids, bean beetles, leafhoppers, mites, and nematodes may all damage black-eyed peas.

BLUEBERRIES

Vaccinium corymbosum

HARDINESS: Zones 2-8

PLANTING METHOD: transplants

PLANT SPACING: 3 to 8 feet

LIGHT: full sun to partial shade

The blue-green summer leaves of blueberries become a riot of color in fall. Delicate spring flowers and edible, delicious berries add to the landscape value of this native shrub.

Selected species
V. corymbosum (highbush blueberry)—6 to 12 feet tall, 8 to 12 feet wide, multiple-stemmed shrub with rounded, upright habit, leaves are 1 to 3½ inches long, blue-green in summer, turning red, orange, yellow, and bronze in fall, flowers are white, urn-shaped, ½ inch long, fruit is blue-black, ¼ to ½ inch across; Zones 3-8. *V. angustifolium* (lowbush blueberry)—6 inches to 2 feet tall, 2 feet wide, low spreading habit, leaves are ⅓ to ¾ inch long, blue-green in summer, turning red to bronze in fall, flowers are white with red tinge, delicious fruit is blue-black and ¼ to ½ inch across; Zones 2-6.

Growing conditions
Plant blueberries in moist, well-drained soil with a pH of 4.5 to 5.5. Set highbush varieties 6 to 8 feet apart; allow 3 feet between lowbush blueberries. Add generous amounts of organic matter prior to planting. Mulch to preserve moisture. Prune after fruiting.

BROCCOLI

'Green Comet'

HARDINESS: warm-season annual

PLANTING METHOD: direct sowing; transplants

PLANT SPACING: 12 to 24 inches

LIGHT: full sun

Tiny flowers packed into green or blue-green heads on thick, upright stalks in summer or fall. Some broccoli varieties tend to produce a single, large central head, while others develop a smaller central head and multiple side shoots.

Selected varieties
'Bonanza'—large central heads and many side shoots. 'De Cicco'—a very early, disease-resistant, highly productive variety with many side shoots. 'Emperor'—a heat- and disease-tolerant variety good for close spacing with dense 6- to 8-inch single heads. 'Green Comet'—a disease-resistant, very fast-maturing variety with firm blue-green central heads and abundant side shoots. 'Green Valiant'—a cold-tolerant, disease-resistant variety. 'Oktal'—early variety with large, open heads and plentiful side shoots. 'Premium Crop'—a slow-to-bolt, disease-resistant variety with a central blue-green head and no side shoots. 'Romanesco Minaret'—pale green conical heads. 'Super Dome'—very productive compact plants ideal for close spacing. 'Waltham 29'—heat-tolerant, compact variety with a single head, good for close spacing and growing in fall.

Growing conditions

Start broccoli indoors 6 to 8 weeks before the last frost and transplant to the garden 3 weeks before the last frost; otherwise, sow directly in the garden 1 to 2 weeks before the last frost. Sow fall crops 3 to 4 months before the first fall frost. Set seeds ¼ to ½ inch deep in a constantly moist but not wet soil enriched with compost or other organic matter. Cold snaps while heads are forming may cause production of small buttons of buds instead of large heads, and temperatures above 80° F may cause plants to bolt. Single-head varieties are generally best for summer harvest and side-shoot types for fall.

Fertilize at planting and again as heads begin forming with fish emulsion or a balanced 10-10-10 organic fertilizer. Mulch to retain soil moisture. Use paper collars to foil cutworms and floating row covers or parasitic wasps to thwart cabbageworms, flea beetles, cabbage loopers, and other insect pests. Remove plant tops and roots in fall to control soil-borne diseases and wait 3 years before replanting broccoli in the same location.

To harvest, cut the large central head first to encourage production of a second crop of smaller side shoots. Soak heads in warm water with a small amount of added vinegar and salt to dislodge insects among the buds. One plant yields 1 to 2 pounds of broccoli.

'Premium Crop'

BROCCOLI RABE

Broccoli Rabe

HARDINESS: cool-season annual

PLANTING METHOD: direct sowing

PLANT SPACING: 4 to 8 inches

LIGHT: full sun

Also called rapini. Tender greens with a mustardy tang and 1-inch broccoli-like florets in early summer or fall; a good choice for the winter garden in mild climates. Use the greens and florets raw in salads or cooked as a side dish.

Selected varieties

None. Ruffled leaves and small florets on slender stalks ready to harvest in 40 days. Cut entire plant just as the flower buds are about to open.

Growing conditions

Start seed indoors 6 weeks before last frost or sow ½ inch deep outside in early spring; young plants tolerate light frost. Where summers are cool, plant in late summer or early fall for a late-fall crop. In milder climates, plant in late fall for a winter crop. Water generously and fertilize 2 to 3 weeks after plants are well established. In windy locations, protect stems from damage by mounding soil around the base of plants or tying plants to stakes. Broccoli rabe is a heavy feeder; rotate with legumes such as peas or beans and renew the soil with compost before planting. Harvest leaves when they are 4 to 6 inches long and cut florets with 2 to 3 inches of stem. A 10-foot row will produce about 3 pounds of greens over a 2- to 4-week period.

BRUSSELS SPROUTS

'Jade Cross'

HARDINESS: cool-season annual

PLANTING METHOD: transplants; direct sowing

PLANT SPACING: 18 to 24 inches

LIGHT: full sun

Firm, blue-green flower buds resembling miniature cabbages growing in a spiral up tall stalks in mid- to late fall in northern gardens and from late fall through winter in milder climates. Use them fresh or frozen cooked as a side dish.

Selected varieties

'Jade Cross'—extremely cold-tolerant variety with abundant, closely spaced sprouts in 115 days. 'Prince Marvel'—very early crop of small, sweet sprouts with creamy white centers in 95 days. 'Rubine'—a late crop of tiny red sprouts in 130 days.

Growing conditions:

Brussels sprouts are best harvested after the first fall frost. Plants started indoors from seed will be ready to plant outside in 4 to 8 weeks. For direct sowing, plant seed ½ inch deep in soil enriched with compost, and mulch plants to conserve moisture. Do not plant where other members of the cabbage family have grown for at least 3 years. Harvest sprouts from the bottom of the stalk upward when they are 1 inch or more across. Fresh sprouts will keep for several weeks if the entire plant is pulled up and stored in a cool location. One plant produces 50 to 100 sprouts.

'Stonehead'

HARDINESS: cool-season annual

PLANTING METHOD: transplants; direct sowing

PLANT SPACING: 12 to 24 inches

LIGHT: full sun or filtered sun

Common cabbage has firm, dense heads of succulent green or red leaves in spring, summer, or fall. Plant early varieties for spring crops of small to medium 3- to 4-pound heads; midseason varieties with medium to large heads weighing 5 to 8 pounds for spring or fall crops; or slow-maturing late varieties with large heads weighing up to 12 pounds or more for fall crops. Savoy cabbage has crinkled leaves that are more tender and milder in flavor than the common cabbage varieties.

Selected varieties
Green-leaved varieties include: 'Copenhagen Market'—midseason variety with heads in 72 days that last well in the garden. 'Danish Ballhead'—late-season variety with 6- to 8-pound heads that store well in 105 days. 'Earliana'—very early variety with 2-pound heads in 60 days. 'Early Flat Dutch'—midseason variety with split-resistant, flattened heads in 85 days. 'Early Jersey Wakefield'—disease-resistant early variety with small conical heads that tolerate close spacing in 63 days. 'Emerald Cross Hybrid'—early variety with round heads with blue-green outer leaves and creamy centers in 63 days. 'Golden Acre'—early disease-resistant variety with round

light green heads in 64 days. 'Late Flat Dutch'—late variety with flat 10- to 12-pound heads in 100 days. 'Stonehead'—early variety with blue-green leaves packed into extremely dense 3-pound heads that keep well in the garden in 60 to 70 days. 'Wisconsin All Seasons'—disease-resistant late variety with excellent storage quality in 94 days.

Red-leaved varieties include: 'Crimson'—midseason variety that stores well in the garden in 82 days. 'Lasso'—early variety with solid 2- to 4-pound heads in 70 days. 'Red Acre'—insect-tolerant, split-resistant midseason variety with 3- to 4-pound heads on compact plants in 76 days. 'Ruby Ball'—midseason variety with round 3- to 4-pound heads that keep well in the garden in 68 days. 'Ruby Perfection'—split-resistant midseason variety with solid, round red heads in 85 days.

Savoy varieties include: 'Chieftain Savoy'—midseason variety with round, 4- to 5-pound heads of crinkled leaves. 'Julius'—late variety with blue-green leaves in 3- to 5-pound heads with sweet flavor in 90 days. 'Savoy Ace'—midseason variety with delicately flavored leaves in 78 days.

Growing conditions
Start early cabbages for spring crops indoors 4 to 8 weeks before the last frost, planting seeds ¼ to ½ inch deep. Transplant to garden soil enriched with compost after all danger of frost is past and mulch to conserve moisture. Direct-sow midseason cabbages as soon as all danger of frost is past. For fall crops, direct-sow late cabbages at least 100 days before the first fall frost. Plant spring varieties with small

'Ruby Ball'

heads 12 to 15 inches apart, medium-sized midseason varieties 15 to 24 inches, and large fall varieties 24 inches apart. Close spacing produces smaller heads and may cause mature heads to split.

Keep cabbages constantly moist but not soggy, and fertilize every 2 to 3 weeks with fish emulsion or other organic fertilizer with at least 10 percent nitrogen. Use paper collars to foil cutworms, water sprays to remove aphids. Use Bt, handpicking, floating row covers, or parasitic wasps to thwart cabbageworms, flea beetles, cab-

'Chieftain Savoy'

bage loopers, and other insect pests. To minimize clubroot and other soil-borne diseases, do not plant cabbages where other cabbage-family members have been planted for at least 3 years.

Harvest cabbages anytime after heads form. Root-pruning on one side of the plant will delay splitting and prolong garden storage; in addition, growth is slowed. Harvesting spring varieties when the heads are softball-sized while leaving five or six large outer leaves attached to the stalk stimulates plants to produce a second crop of small heads in fall. Cabbage tolerates light frost. Heads harvested in fall will keep several weeks or more in a cool, humid place. Common green cabbages store better than red or savoy.

CABBAGE, CHINESE

'Blues'

HARDINESS: cool-season annual

PLANTING METHOD: transplants; direct sowing

PLANT SPACING: 10 to 18 inches

LIGHT: full sun

Also called celery cabbage. Vase-shaped heads of crinkly leaves with succulent ribs and mild, sweet flavor in early summer or fall. Use Chinese cabbage in salads, soups, or steamed as a side dish.

Selected varieties
'Blues'—small disease-resistant, slow-to-bolt heads in 50 days, especially good for spring planting. 'Jade Pagoda'—disease-resistant hybrid with upright green heads with yellow hearts in 68 days. 'Monument'—tall, dense heads with creamy white centers in 80 days. 'Orient Express' —a very early, heat-resistant variety with crisp, peppery flavor in 43 days. 'Two Seasons Hybrid'—oval, slow-to-bolt heads in 62 days, good for spring or fall crops.

Growing conditions
Start Chinese cabbage indoors 8 to 10 weeks before the last frost, setting seed ½ inch deep in peat pots to transplant directly into the garden. Choose locations where cabbage-family members have not grown for at least 3 years and mulch to conserve moisture. Harvest heads before the increasing length of summer days causes plants to bolt. For fall crops, sow seed for leafy varieties 7 weeks and heading varieties 10 to 12 weeks before the first frost.

CARDOON

Cardoon

HARDINESS: Zones 5-9

PLANTING METHOD: direct sowing; transplants

PLANT SPACING: 1½ to 2 feet

LIGHT: full sun

Crunchy roots and thick, succulent leaf midribs in fall on perennial thistlelike plants that can also be grown as annuals. Use the mature midribs or cubed roots blanched and marinated in salads and antipasto and parboiled or battered and fried as a side dish.

Selected varieties
Usually sold without a variety name; silver-gray foliage on plants to 8 feet tall in 120 to 150 days.

Growing conditions
Start cardoon indoors 10 weeks before the last frost or sow directly in the garden 1 to 2 weeks before the last frost in a rich, constantly moist but well-drained loam. Space transplants or thin seedlings to stand 1½ to 2 feet apart. Approximately a month before first frost, when plants are 3 feet tall or more, blanch stalks by tying them together with twine and wrapping with paper or burlap; leaves will blanch in 3 to 4 weeks. Harvest by cutting stems just below the crown. Discard tough outer leaves and trim leaves from the thick midribs before cooking. Plants will grow taller and stronger the second year. If grown as an annual, pull up the whole plant and use the roots as well as the midribs for cooking.

CARROTS

'Gold Pak'

HARDINESS: cool-season annual

PLANTING METHOD: direct sowing

PLANT SPACING: 2 to 4 inches

LIGHT: full sun

Sweet, crisp red-orange roots with fine-textured flesh surrounding a pithier core from late spring through fall and into winter with successive plantings. The deeper the color, the higher the vitamin content. Choose among several carrot shapes and sizes according to soil type. Imperator types with long, slender roots need deeply tilled, loose soils. Cylindrical Nantes types and thick, blocky Chantenay and Danvers types will grow where soils are heavy or rocky. Use the very short ball-shaped and baby varieties in extremely heavy soils. The short Nantes, Chantenay, and Danvers types can be grown in pots. Plant carrots in a border among ornamental annuals or perennials, where the lacy foliage will be an attractive filler. It also makes a pretty addition to bouquets.

Selected varieties
Long varieties include: 'Gold Pak'—pencil-thin tapered roots up to 10 inches long in 76 days. 'Imperator'—slender, tapering 8-inch roots in 77 days. 'Sweetness II'—very sweet and juicy 6- to 8-inch cylindrical roots in 73 days; 'Tendersweet'—slender, coreless roots 7 inches or longer produced in 75 days.

Medium varieties include: 'Artist'—thick, blunt 7- to 8-inch roots in 65 days that retain exceptional sweetness even through winter storage. 'Coreless Nantes' —almost coreless, blunt-tipped, 6-inch roots in 65 days; 'Danvers Half Long'— crisp, cylindrical 6- to 7-inch roots that

'Danvers Half Long'

will grow in heavy soils in 75 days, good for canning and storing; 'Nantes'—small-cored cylinders of sweet flesh 1½ inches thick and 6 to 7 inches long in 65 days; 'Nantes Half Long'—slim, blunt-tipped 6- to 7-inch cylindrical roots with small cores in 70 days; 'Napoli'—with early-maturing, slim blunt 7-inch roots that tolerate crowding in 66 days. 'Red Cored Chantenay', also called 'Goldinhart'—stocky, blunt-tipped 4- to 5-inch roots up to 2½ inches wide in 65 days that are good for canning and freezing and grow well in heavy soils. 'Royal Chantenay'—produces thick, tapering roots that are deep red-orange in color and up to 8 inches long in 70 days. 'Scarlet Nantes'—bright red-orange cylindrical roots with dependably sweet flavor and very small cores in 68 days. 'Touchon'—a very sweet Nantes-type carrot up to 7 inches long with high moisture content, ideal for juicing.

Ball-shaped carrot varieties include: 'Parmex'—very early ½- to 1-inch roots with exceptionally good flavor in 50 days. 'Planet'—deep orange 1½-inch roots in 55 days. 'Thumbelina'—roots ½ to 1½ inches in diameter with sweet flesh and thin skin that needs no peeling in 60 to 70 days.

Finger carrot varieties include: 'Baby Spike'—early-maturing tapered roots only 3 to 4 inches long and ½ inch in diameter in 52 days. 'Little Finger'—3½-inch roots 1 inch in diameter in 60 days. 'Minicor'—

sweet, very slender, blunt-tipped 6- to 7-inch roots in 55 days.

Growing conditions

Sow carrots ¼ to ½ inch deep in well-tilled, loose loam. Begin sowing 2 to 4 weeks before the last frost, making successive sowings every 2 to 3 weeks until midsummer for continuous harvesting. To speed germination, soak seed for 24 hours, then freeze for 1 week before sowing. Mix the tiny seeds with sand for easier handling. Thin seedlings to stand 2 to 3 inches apart in blocks or rows. Use thinnings in soups or stews. Carrots can be harvested young or allowed to mature. Keep dirt mounded around shoulders to prevent them from turning green. Forked roots indicate injury by stones, hairy carrots indicate an over-fertile soil, and twisted roots indicate inadequate thinning. Excessive moisture from heavy rains or heavy watering after a period of drought can cause roots to crack. Store carrots in the garden through the winter by covering them with a deep mulch of straw or leaves anchored with black plastic to keep the ground from freezing. A 10-foot row yields 10 to 15 pounds of carrots.

'Thumbelina'

CAULIFLOWER

'Snow Crown'

HARDINESS: cool-season annual

PLANTING METHOD: transplants; direct sowing

PLANT SPACING: 18 to 36 inches

LIGHT: full sun

Mounds of immature white or purplish flower buds called curds packed tightly into broad, domed heads on upright plants in early summer or fall. Use cauliflower raw for crudités or in salads. Purple cauliflower makes a colorful raw garnish but loses its tint when cooked.

Selected varieties

'Early Snowball'—medium-sized heads on compact plants in 60 days. 'Early White Hybrid'—early-maturing variety with tight outer leaves that naturally blanch curds in 52 days. 'Green Goddess'—easy-to-grow variety with yellow-green curds that do not need to be blanched. 'Self-Blanche'—tight outer leaves ensure naturally creamy white curds for fall crops in 71 days. 'Snow Ball'—early-maturing variety with medium-sized heads in 55 days. 'Snow Crown'—early-maturing, vigorous variety for spring or fall crops in 50 days. 'Violet Queen'—looser, broccoli-like purple heads with milder flavor for fall harvest in 54 days.

Growing conditions

Plant heat-sensitive cauliflower for early-spring or late-fall crops when it will have the cool daytime temperatures between 57° and 68° F it requires to produce heads.

For spring crops, start transplants indoors 6 to 8 weeks before the last frost date and move outdoors into a rich garden soil amended with compost or other organic matter around the time of the last frost. Light frost does not harm transplants, but after a hard frost they may produce "buttons," immature heads only an inch or two across. Mulch the plants to conserve moisture. For a late-fall or early-winter crop, sow seeds ½ inch deep 10 to 15 weeks before the first frost.

Keep cauliflower constantly moist but not soggy, and fertilize every 2 to 3 weeks with fish emulsion or other organic fertilizer with at least 10 percent nitrogen. Use paper collars to foil cutworms, water sprays to remove aphids. Use Bt, handpicking, floating row covers, or parasitic wasps to thwart cabbageworms, flea beetles, cabbage loopers, and other insect pests. To minimize clubroot and other soil-borne diseases, do not plant cauliflower where other members of the cabbage family have been planted for at least 3 years.

Exposure to sun will discolor the curds. When the heads of varieties that are not self-blanching reach softball size, pull the outer leaves together over the curds and secure them with a rubber band or string; this covering will blanch the curds and keep them tender. The leaves of self-blanching varieties may need to be tied over the curds if heat wilts them. Harvest as soon as heads are full and firm; overmature heads become coarse or discolored. Each cauliflower plant produces a 1- to 2-pound head. A 10-foot row produces four to seven heads, depending on spacing.

'Snow Ball'

CELERIAC

'Brilliant'

HARDINESS: warm-season annual

PLANTING METHOD: transplants

PLANT SPACING: 12 inches

LIGHT: light shade to full sun

Also called celery root. Ball-shaped roots with a nutty flavor that are harvested in fall when they are 2 to 4 inches in diameter. Shred celeriac raw for salads or cook like celery, which is a close relative.

Selected varieties
'Brilliant'—smooth 3- to 4-inch roots with a creamy white interior in 110 days. 'Large Smooth Prague'—buff-colored roots in 110 days.

Growing conditions
Sow celeriac seeds ⅛ inch deep indoors 6 to 8 weeks before the last frost and keep them covered with a damp cloth until seedlings emerge. Transplant after all danger of frost is past into a constantly moist but well-drained soil enriched with compost, setting seedlings 12 inches apart. Feed at planting time and during the growing season with a balanced organic 5-10-10 fertilizer. Celeriac requires constant, even moisture and daytime temperatures between 55° and 85° F to grow. Harvest celeriac when roots are between 2 and 4 inches in diameter. Trim leaves and stems close to roots and discard. Roots keep well in the garden under heavy mulch for up to a month after the first frost. Or store in damp sand at 40° F in a root cellar. A 10-foot row yields 6 to 10 pounds of celeriac.

CELERY

'Utah'

HARDINESS: warm-season annual

PLANTING METHOD: transplants

PLANT SPACING: 6 to 9 inches

LIGHT: full sun to light shade

Crisp, succulent stalks enclosing a pale, leafy heart in early summer or fall. Use celery in salads, for hors d'oeuvres, as a side dish, and as an aromatic flavoring in soups and stews.

Selected varieties
'Fordhook Giant'—stocky 15- to 18-inch plants ready to harvest in 120 days. 'Giant Pascal'—thick stalks, creamy hearts, and dark green foliage on 2-foot plants in 125 days. 'Golden Self-Blanching'—very early variety with golden yellow, almost stringless 2-foot stalks in 85 days. 'Utah 52-70 R Improved'—dark green stalks with excellent keeping quality on 26-inch disease-resistant plants in 105 days.

Growing conditions
Sow celery seeds ¼ inch deep indoors 6 to 8 weeks before last frost. When seedlings are about 4 inches tall and all danger of frost is past, transplant them to a constantly moist but well-drained garden soil enriched with compost; a pH between 5.8 and 6.7 is ideal. Set seedlings 6 to 9 inches apart. Sow seed directly in the garden in late spring for a fall crop. Feed at planting and about once a month during the growing season with a balanced 5-10-10 organic fertilizer. Celery requires daytime temperatures between 55° and 85° F to grow.

CELTUCE

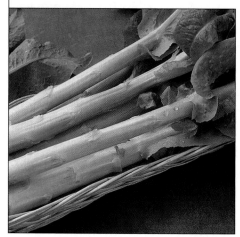

Celtuce

HARDINESS: cool-season annual

PLANTING METHOD: direct sowing; transplants

PLANT SPACING: 12 inches

LIGHT: full sun to light shade

Tender spring leaves and succulent midribs on mature leaves in late spring to early summer. Use the tasty young leaves in salads or cook them as spring greens. Midribs have a consistency like that of artichoke hearts. Peel and eat them raw or cooked; they can be substituted in recipes calling for celery or asparagus. In frost-free areas, grow celtuce as a winter green.

Selected varieties
Sold only as celtuce; has rosettes of puckered, lobed leaves ready to eat in 45 days; the midribs are ready to harvest in 90 days.

Growing conditions
Start celtuce seeds indoors 4 weeks before the desired transplanting date, setting seeds ½ inch deep. Transplant outdoors as early as 4 weeks before the last frost, in time for the crop to mature before hot weather arrives. Celtuce prefers a loose soil amended with compost or other organic matter. Celtuce can also be sown directly outdoors 4 to 6 weeks before last frost for spring crops and 8 weeks before first frost for fall crops. Sow seed in wide bands and thin when seedlings are 2 inches tall. Provide ample water to keep the leaves from becoming bitter and to keep the midribs succulent.

CHARD, SWISS CHARD

'Rhubarb'

HARDINESS: warm-season annual

PLANTING METHOD: direct sowing

PLANT SPACING: 6 to 12 inches

LIGHT: full sun to light shade

Smooth or crinkled broad leaves with thick, crunchy midribs from late spring to fall. Actually a type of beet that lacks an edible root, chard is heat tolerant and provides a reliable crop of vitamin-rich greens throughout the summer, when many other greens bolt. Leaves have a flavor reminiscent of spinach, while the midribs are prepared like celery or asparagus. Some varieties may overwinter as perennials in milder climates. Plant chard in containers in a kitchen garden and use red-ribbed varieties in an edible landscape with carrots, nasturtiums, and other attractive vegetables and herbs.

Selected varieties
'Fordhook Giant'—fleshy leaves with creamy white midribs up to 2½ inches across in 60 days. 'Large White Ribbed'—wide white midribs and veins on deep green, smooth leaves in 60 days. 'Lucullus'—pale green leaves and white stems in 60 days. 'Perpetual Spinach'—early variety with smooth, dark green leaves and very little midrib, ideal for cooking greens, in 50 days. 'Rhubarb'—thick, reddish green leaves and brilliant ruby red midribs and veins in 60 days. 'Swiss Chard of Geneva'—winter-hardy variety with large, celery-like midribs in 60 days.

Growing conditions
Sow chard outdoors just after the last frost, setting seeds ½ inch deep in well-drained soil enriched with organic matter; chard does not transplant well. It can be planted at any time throughout spring and summer up until 8 weeks before the first fall frost and is ideal for succeeding spring crops such as peas. Thin seedlings to stand 6 to 12 inches apart and use thinnings in salads and soups. Maintain a constant moisture level for the sweetest, most succulent leaves and midribs. Pick outer leaves continuously to keep new young leaves coming on, or cut entire plants 2 inches above the crown when leaves reach 6 inches or taller; plants will regrow from the deep, strong roots in 3 to 4 weeks for harvesting again. Cutting plants back whenever leaves become too tough or coarse will stimulate them to produce tender young leaves. A 10-foot row yields approximately 5 pounds of chard.

'Lucullus'

CHAYOTE

Chayote

HARDINESS: Zones 8-10

PLANTING METHOD: direct sowing

PLANT SPACING: 10 to 15 feet

LIGHT: full sun

Also called vegetable pear. A member of the squash family with furrowed, pear-shaped green fruits on climbing vines in late summer to fall. Grow as a hot-season annual north of Zone 8. Use the mature fruits like winter squashes and the mild-flavored young fruits like summer squashes. The single large seed has a nutty flavor. Harvest young shoots of established plants and prepare like asparagus or dig the large roots and use like potatoes. Also called mirliton or christophene.

Selected varieties

There are no named varieties; sold as chayote. Young fruits ready to harvest in 90 days and ½- to 1-pound mature fruits ready in 180 days.

Growing conditions

For each vine, plant an entire fruit, laying it at an angle with the stem end slightly exposed above the soil level. Ideal soil pH is between 5.5 and 6.5. Plant in pairs to ensure pollination needed for fruit set and provide a trellis, wall, or other support for the fast-growing vines to climb. Keep well watered. Begin harvesting when young fruits are 4 to 6 inches in length. Chayote can be stored in a cool location for up to 2 to 3 months. A well-grown vine typically bears about 35 fruits.

COLLARDS

'Georgia'

HARDINESS: cool-season annual

PLANTING METHOD: direct sowing

PLANT SPACING: 12 to 18 inches

LIGHT: full sun

Tall rosettes of thick blue-green leaves with a mild cabbagelike flavor in summer or fall. Frost sweetens the flavor. Cook collards as a side dish or use in soups.

Selected varieties

'Georgia'—heat-tolerant variety with loose rosettes of white-veined leaves in 70 to 80 days. 'Vates'—thick, broad leaves on compact, bolt-resistant plants in 75 days.

Growing conditions

A member of the cabbage family, collards tolerate heat better than kale and are more cold tolerant than cabbage, two closely related vegetables. Plant seed ½ inch deep outdoors 3 to 4 weeks before the last frost for harvesting from spring through summer, or in midsummer for a fall crop. Collards may overwinter in mild climates.

Keep collards constantly moist but not soggy, and fertilize every 2 to 3 weeks with fish emulsion or other organic fertilizer with at least 10 percent nitrogen. To minimize soil-borne diseases, do not plant collards where other members of the cabbage family have been planted for at least 3 years. Young leaves are ready to pick in 40 days. Twelve plants will supply a family of four with summer and fall greens.

CORN

'Silver Queen'

HARDINESS: hot-season annual

PLANTING METHOD: direct sowing

PLANT SPACING: 12 to 14 inches

LIGHT: full sun

Sweet, juicy yellow, white, or bicolored starchy kernels lining cylindrical cobs on stalks up to 9 feet tall in mid- to late summer. Plant breeders have improved both the taste and the keeping quality of sweet corn by manipulating the gene that makes sweet corn sweet to produce "sugar-enhanced" varieties that have a higher initial sugar content and a storage life 3 to 5 days longer than standard varieties. Also the result of breeding programs are "supersweet" varieties that have twice the sugar content of standard varieties and a storage life up to 10 days longer. Choose early, midseason, and late-maturing varieties of sweet corn for a continuous harvest through the end of summer. Sweet corn freezes well for long-term storage. Popcorn varieties are higher in starch and lower in sugar than sweet corn; the ears are harvested after the stalks have dried.

Selected varieties

Sweet corn varieties include: 'Burgundy Delight'—a midseason variety with bicolored kernels on 8-inch ears wrapped in burgundy-colored husks in 80 days. 'Butter and Sugar'—early variety with bicolored kernels on 7½-inch ears in 70 days. 'Earlivee'—early yellow variety with ears in 63 days, making it a good choice for short-season gardens or a succession planting to follow spring crops such as peas or spinach. 'Golden Cross Bantam'—popular yellow hybrid with 8-inch ears in 85 days. 'Platinum Lady'—drought-resistant midseason variety with white kernels on 8-inch ears in 78 days. 'Silver Queen'—extremely sweet and tender late-season, blight- and wilt-resistant variety bearing white kernels on 9-inch ears in 92 days.

Sugar-enhanced varieties include: 'Bodacious'—midseason variety with yellow

'Lancelot'

kernels on 8-inch ears in 80 days. 'Clockwork'—vigorous midseason variety that will germinate in cool soil with bicolored kernels on 8-inch ears in 78 days. 'Double Gem'—early variety that will germinate in cool soil with tender, bicolored kernels on blocky, 8-inch ears in 70 days. 'Duet'—midseason variety with bicolored kernels on 9-inch ears wrapped in burgundy-tinged husks in 74 days. 'Lancelot'—wilt-resistant, drought-tolerant bicolored variety with 9-inch ears in 80 days. 'Miracle'—late season, rust-resistant variety with yellow kernels on large 9½-inch ears in 84 days. 'Pristine'—midseason variety with very sweet white kernels on 8½-inch ears in 76 days. 'Seneca Starshine'—early white variety with 8½-inch ears of exceptional keeping quality in 70 days. 'Sugar Buns'—early hybrid with creamy yellow kernels on 7½-inch ears in 70 days. 'Tuxedo'—wilt-resistant and drought-tolerant, midseason yellow variety with 8½-inch ears in 74 days.

Supersweet varieties include: 'Early Xtra Sweet'—early yellow hybrid with 9-inch ears in 70 days. 'How Sweet It Is'—midseason white variety with 8-inch ears

in 88 days. 'Northern Xtra Sweet'—early variety with yellow kernels on 7½-inch ears in 67 days. 'Skyline'—early bicolored variety that germinates in cool soil with very sweet kernels on 8-inch ears in 70 days. 'Starstruck'—late-maturing variety that yields bicolored kernels on 8- to 9-inch ears in 92 days.

Popcorn varieties include: 'Giant Yellow'—tender yellow kernels in 105 days. 'Mini-Blue'—stubby 2- to 4-inch ears with tiny blue kernels for decorative use or popping in 100 days. 'Robust 20-70'—late-maturing yellow variety with high popping volume in 98 days. 'White Cloud'—late white variety with 5-inch ears in 95 days. 'Yellow Hybrid'—deep yellow kernels in 89 days.

Growing conditions

Corn needs a long, hot summer for good growth; days to maturity are a less reliable measure of when a variety will ripen than the number of hot days. Plant seeds 1 to 2 inches deep when the temperature of the soil is at least 60° F, in late spring to early summer; supersweet varieties need very warm, moist soil to germinate well. Row covers help to speed the germination and growth of early varieties in cool soil. Since corn is pollinated by the wind, sow seed in blocks of at least four rows to ensure good pollination. If you are planting more than one variety, choose varieties with maturity dates at least 14 days apart to avoid cross-pollination. If space allows, you can also prevent cross-pollination by planting different varieties at least 250 feet apart.

Thin plants to stand 12 to 14 inches apart; closer spacing lowers yields and en-

'Early Xtra Sweet'

courages fungal diseases. When the first sowing is knee high, plant a second variety to extend the harvest season. To ensure that ears on the edges of the blocks get pollinated, strip pollen from the tassels and sprinkle it on the silks. Provide ample water throughout the growing season and feed corn with a balanced 5-10-10 organic fertilizer when stalks are knee high and again when silks become visible at the tips of the ears. Rotate corn with other crops to control both pests and diseases.

Harvest sweet corn 3 weeks after silks appear; the highest ear on the stalk ripens first. Allow popcorn stalks to dry, then harvest ears, pull husks back, and hang in a well-ventilated area to finish drying. Sweet corn and popcorn produce one or two ears per stalk.

'How Sweet It Is'

CORN SALAD, MACHE

'Vit'

HARDINESS: winter-hardy Zones 5-9

PLANTING METHOD: direct sowing

PLANT SPACING: 2 inches

LIGHT: full sun

Mounded rosettes of tender smooth greens with a mild nutty flavor prized for salads in spring or fall in northern gardens and throughout the winter in mild regions. Also called lamb's lettuce.

Selected varieties

'Big Seed', also called 'Grosse Graine'—smooth, round, bright green leaves in 45 days. 'Coquille'—cold-tolerant variety with spoon-shaped, cupped leaves in 45 days. 'D'Etampes'—prominently veined, smooth, round leaves on compact, cold-tolerant plants good for overwintering. 'Elan'—has short, smooth shiny upright leaves; especially suitable for fall and winter crops where the weather is cold and wet because of its mildew resistance. 'Verte des Cambrai'—pest-resistant and very cold-tolerant compact rosettes of 3- to 4-inch flat round leaves in 60 days. 'Vit'—vigorous with long, glossy leaves and a minty flavor, good for overwintering.

Growing conditions

Plant corn salad ½ inch deep in very early spring 2 to 4 weeks before the last frost or in late summer to early fall; corn salad grows best at temperatures below 75° F. Keep constantly moist. Mulch fall crops lightly after frost to keep them growing into winter.

CRESS

Watercress

HARDINESS: Zones 6-9; cool-season annual

PLANTING METHOD: transplants; direct sowing

PLANT SPACING: 4 inches

LIGHT: full sun to light shade

Plants of three different species that go by the same common name because their leaves have a similar peppery flavor. Two of these cresses grow in ordinary garden soil, while the third is an aquatic plant that requires constant moisture. Use any of the cresses for garnishes, add to sandwiches for a crunchy bite, and add to salads to complement the blander taste of tender lettuces. Sprout cress seeds for use in salads as well as sandwiches, stir-fry dishes, and casseroles.

Selected species

Curly cress, also called broadleaf cress, garden cress, mountain grass, peppergrass *(Lepidium sativum)*—cool-season annual with finely cut, tightly frilled leaves in 10 to 21 days; seeds are especially recommended for sprouting. Watercress *(Nasturtium officinale)*—aquatic perennial with broad, mildly pungent leaves and succulent stems in 60 days. Winter cress, upland cress *(Barbarea verna)*—hardy biennial grown as a cool-season annual bearing smooth leaves on 6- to 8-inch stalks in 60 days.

Growing conditions

Plant curly cress 4 to 6 weeks before the last frost. Make successive sowings every 2 weeks until 2 weeks after the last frost for a continuous supply of fresh greens until plants bolt in summer heat. Sow fall crop starting 2 to 4 weeks before the first frost; plants will tolerate severe frost. Harvest by snipping stems about an inch above the plant's base; the plant will send up new growth two or three times. Indoors, sprout seeds on wet paper towels, cover with glass, and keep warm until seeds sprout, then allow to grow to about 4 inches tall, keeping towels constantly moist.

Sow winter cress ¼ inch deep in full sun to light shade in late fall or winter. Keep soil constantly moist but not wet. Thin to 4 inches. Harvest leaves from winter until late spring or early summer, when they become bitter. Seed can also be sown in early spring for harvest in 7 weeks.

Sow watercress indoors in containers, pressing seeds into the soil and covering containers with glass or plastic until seeds germinate. Transplant seedlings to individual pots, then transplant to constantly moist soil on bank of a pond or stream in full sun 2 to 4 weeks before the last frost; weight roots down with pebbles until they anchor themselves. Pinch plants back when they are 6 inches tall. Alternatively, grow watercress indoors in a container set in a saucer of water that is changed daily; when grown in soil, watercress needs indirect light to keep from becoming bitter. Pinch flower buds off; leaves become bitter if plants are allowed to bloom.

Upland Cress

CUCUMBERS

'Marketmore 76'

HARDINESS: warm-season annual

PLANTING METHOD: transplants; direct sowing

PLANT SPACING: 12 inches

LIGHT: full sun

Oblong, cylindrical, mildly flavored succulent fruits with green skins on climbing vines or low bushy plants. Use juicy 8- to 10-inch slicing cucumbers fresh in salads and as a garnish. Crisp, stubby varieties, including dwarf cornichon types, have been specially bred for making pickles and relishes. Dwarf bush cucumbers require only one-third the space of vining types and are ideal for small garden plots or containers. Allow cucumber vines to sprawl in the garden among cornstalks or train vines on trellises or fences for edible landscaping. Gynecious varieties, which bear only female flowers, are noted for their very high yields. To ensure pollination and fruit production of gynecious cucumbers, plant at least one monoecious variety (a type that bears both male and female flowers).

Selected varieties

Cornichon cucumbers include: 'Verte de Massy'—with very slim, 4-inch, bumpy fruits.Bush types include: 'Bush Pickle'—heavy crop of early-maturing 4- to 5-inch fruits on compact 24-inch plants in 45 days. 'Salad Bush'—disease- and wilt-resistant plants with 8-inch fruits in 58 days. 'Spacemaster'—7- to 8-inch cucumbers in 62 days on compact, mosaic-re-sistant plants suitable for containers or hanging baskets.

Pickling types include: 'Boston'—extremely prolific vines with early crop of smooth 6- to 7-inch tapered fruits in 58 days. 'Early Green Cluster'—large crop of deep green, 5- to 6-inch fruits suitable for pickling or slicing in 55 days. 'Gherkin'—2- to 3-inch fruits ideal for sweet pickles in 60 days. 'Little Leaf'—high-yielding, very disease-resistant vines with small fruits in 70 days. 'Miss Pickler'—gynecious variety producing a large crop of uniform fruits. 'Saladin'—large crop of knobby, crisp 4- to 5-inch fruits on mildew- and disease-resistant gynecious vines in 55 days.

Slicing types include: 'Burpee Hybrid II'—gynecious plants producing straight 8-inch fruits in 55 days. 'Burpless'—somewhat disease-tolerant hybrid with 10- to 12-inch fruits that are more easily digested than those of other varieties, in 62 days. 'Early Pride'—large crop of 8½-inch fruits on mildew- and mosaic-resistant vines in 55 days. 'Early Surecrop'—vigorous, mildew-resistant variety with 8- to 9½-inch fruits in 58 days. 'Fanfare Hybrid'—disease- and mildew-resistant semidwarf with slender, 8- to 9-inch fruits in 63 days. 'Marketmore 76'—vines with exceptional disease resistance producing 8-inch fruits in 67 days. 'Poinsett 76'—early to midseason variety with wilt and mildew resistance bearing 7½-inch fruits in 63 days. 'Slicemaster'—an early crop of 8-inch fruits on disease- and wilt-resistant gynecious vines in 55 days. 'Straight Eight'—slightly striped 8-inch fruits in 63 days. 'Sweet Slice'—very mild burpless 10- to 12-inch

'Salad Bush'

fruits on disease- and mildew-resistant vines in 63 days. 'Sweet Success'—mildew-resistant vines bearing seedless, burpless 14-inch fruits in 54 days.

Growing conditions

Start cucumbers indoors 4 to 6 weeks before the last frost or direct-sow 2 to 3 weeks after last frost, setting seed 1 inch deep in rows and thinning plants to stand

'Burpless'

12 inches apart. Alternatively, plant five or six seeds in hills spaced 6 feet apart and thin to two or three plants. If you have planted a gynecious (female) variety with a monoecious pollinator, be sure to mark the pollinator so it is not accidentally thinned out. Monoecious cucumbers have green seeds, and gynecious types have beige seeds. There should be 1 pollinator plant for every 5 or 6 female plants. Provide ample water. Mulch to conserve moisture and reduce fruit rot. Plant varieties that are resistant to disease; remove and destroy any infected plants.

Pick cucumbers often to keep vines productive. They are ready to harvest when the flower falls off the blossom end. For best flavor and texture, pick them promptly, before seeds enlarge and toughen; a yellowish tinge at the blossom end signals an overmature fruit. Use a sharp knife to cut cucumbers from the vine to avoid injury to stems. Twenty-five plants yield about 30 pounds of cucumbers.

EGGPLANT

'White Egg'

HARDINESS: warm-season annual

PLANTING METHOD: transplants; direct sowing

PLANT SPACING: 18 to 24 inches

LIGHT: full sun

Glossy, smooth-skinned, shiny deep purple to lavender or white fruits with mild-flavored, soft flesh. Depending on the variety, fruits range in size from 1 to 12 inches or more. The low-growing, small-fruited varieties make excellent container plants. All parts of the plant except the fruits are poisonous.

Selected varieties

'Bambino'—extremely heavy yields of rounded purple fruits only 1 to 2 inches in diameter on disease-resistant foot-high plants 60 days after transplanting. 'Black Beauty'—very heavy yield of glossy black-purple, almost round fruits 80 days after transplanting. 'Classic'—long, slim, glossy black-purple fruits on vigorous plants 76 days after transplanting. 'Ichiban'—slender fruits 12 inches long and 1½ inches in diameter 58 days after transplanting on bushy 3-foot plants ideal for small gardens. 'Neon'—large yield of cylindrical, dark pink fruits completely free of bitterness 60 days from transplanting. 'Slim Jim'—slender 4- to 6-inch lavender to deep purple fruits on compact plants with handsome lavender-tinged foliage 75 days after transplanting, suitable for containers. 'Violette di Firenze'—large oblong to round, deep lavender fruits, sometimes with white stripes. 'White Egg', also called 'Osterei' or 'Easter Egg'—clusters of 2- to 3-inch oval white fruits 52 days after transplanting on bushy 2-foot plants ideal for containers.

Growing conditions

Eggplant requires long, warm seasons to mature. In areas with a long growing season, sow seed ¼ to ½ inch deep directly in the garden when soil temperature is 70° F. Elsewhere, start indoors 8 to 10 weeks before last frost and set plants out about 2 to 3 weeks after the last frost, when night temperatures will remain above 50° F. Space plants 18 to 24 inches apart in rows 3 feet apart and stake to keep fruits growing straight. Use floating row covers to speed the growth of transplants and control insects. Feed biweekly with a side dressing of fish emulsion or manure tea and water well, especially from flowering through harvest. To control verticillium wilt, do not plant eggplant where tomatoes, peppers, or strawberries have grown the year before. Avoid working among plants after smoking to prevent introduction of tobacco mosaic virus. Harvest eggplant before the skin loses its shine; an overmature eggplant is dull and likely to be bitter. Cut the stem with shears or a knife and clip eggplant from stems; pick continuously to keep plants producing. A 10-foot row yields 7 to 8 pounds of eggplant.

'Black Beauty'

ENDIVE AND ESCAROLE

'Batavian'

HARDINESS: cool-season annuals

PLANTING METHOD: direct sowing

PLANT SPACING: 8 to 12 inches

LIGHT: full sun to light shade

Tender, piquant greens with distinctively different leaf shapes. Endive has rather slender, curly, finely cut leaves in loose, flat rosettes, while the broad, somewhat twisted or ruffled leaves of escarole form open, upright heads. Endive and escarole are most often used in salads but are also delicious cooked as side dishes or in soups. The gourmet vegetable called Belgian endive is actually not an endive but a type of chicory.

Selected varieties

Endive types include: 'Green Curled Ruffec'—a cold-tolerant endive good for fall planting with lacy dark green outer leaves and a creamy white heart in prostrate rosettes 15 to 17 inches across in 95 days. 'Salad King'—vigorous endive variety with deeply cut, curly dark green leaves with a pale green heart in spreading 2-foot plants that withstand light frost and are heat resistant and slow to bolt in 100 days. 'Tres Fin', also called 'Fine Curled'—lacy dark green leaves with a white midrib and a creamy blanched heart in 60 to 70 days on spreading 10- to 12-inch plants that are slow to bolt.

Broad-leaved escarole types include: 'Batavian'—crumpled yellow-green outer leaves with fleshy, white midribs surrounding creamy white hearts in 85 days. 'Cornet d'Anjou'—loose head of very broad leaves with fan-shaped midribs in spring or fall that can be blanched to mellow its flavor.

Growing conditions

Plant endive and escarole for spring or fall crops; in summer leaves become bitter and plants go to seed. Sow spring crops outdoors 4 weeks before the last frost, setting seed ¼ inch deep; sow fall crops in midsummer. Space the plants that will be blanched 8 inches apart; otherwise, allow 12 inches between plants. Overcrowding encourages rot. Interplant escarole and endive among herbs and lettuce or in the shade of tomatoes. Keep the soil constantly moist and side-dress biweekly with weak manure tea or fish emulsion. In warm weather, escarole types are prone to bitterness, which can be prevented by blanching. To blanch, tie the outer leaves together around the inner heart for 2 to 3 weeks. In humid climates blanching may cause plants to rot.

To harvest, pick individual leaves or cut entire plant at the soil line. If only the central core of leaves is removed and outer leaves are left in place, plants will sprout a new, smaller center in 3 to 4 weeks.

'Salad King'

GARLIC

'California Silverskin'

HARDINESS: Zones 3-8

PLANTING METHOD: cloves

PLANT SPACING: 3 to 6 inches

LIGHT: full sun to light shade

Plump, pungently aromatic bulbs composed of wedge-shaped cloves in midsummer. Softneck garlic varieties produce medium-sized, intensely flavored cloves surrounding several overlapping inner layers of small bulbs. These varieties have good keeping quality and are excellent for braiding. Stiffneck garlic, the most cold-hardy type, produces both underground bulbs, composed of four to six mildly flavored, easy-to-peel cloves with no inner layer, and clusters of tiny bulblets atop coiled stalks called scapes; save the bulblets for planting the next year's crop. Elephant garlic has very large, mild bulbs that are delicious raw or baked whole. Use spring greens like chives and cut blossoms for flower bouquets.

Selected varieties

'California Silverskin' —softneck garlic with pearly white, sometimes yellow-veined bulbs composed of up to 20 cloves; excellent keeping quality. 'Elephant Garlic'—large 2½- to 3-inch bulbs composed of four to six enormous cloves. 'German Red'—stiffneck type with bright purple ¼-pound bulbs composed of up to 12 yellow-fleshed cloves. 'German White Stiffneck'— a stiffneck type with five or six plump cloves forming large bulbs. 'Italian Pur-

ple'—stiffneck garlic producing medium-sized bulbs striped with purple; biting flavor. 'New York Strains'—very cold-hardy softneck garlic with a purple blush on papery white skins. 'Rocambole'—stiffneck garlic type with fat, mild-flavored bulbs. 'Spanish Roja Garlic'— softneck type with a particularly sharp, biting flavor. Spring plantings of all types mature in 120 to 150 days; fall plantings mature the following summer.

Growing conditions

Separate the garlic cloves and plant them with the pointed tip up about 1½ to 2 inches deep in compost-enriched soil starting 6 weeks before first frost and continuing until early winter; alternatively, plant in early to midspring. Mulch to prevent heaving. Garlic will grow in light shade, producing smaller bulbs than it does when grown in full sun. Spring-planted crops also yield smaller bulbs. Pinch the coiled scapes of stiffneck garlic as they appear, to produce larger bulbs instead of a dual crop of bulbs and bulblets. Harvest by forking out of ground in summer when tops begin to yellow. Use bruised bulbs immediately or freeze. Cure unblemished bulbs for several days on screens in a well-ventilated place, then braid them, hang in bunches, or put in mesh bags and store in a dry, cool area until needed.

'German White Stiffneck'

JERUSALEM ARTICHOKES

'French Mammoth White'

HARDINESS: Zones 6-9

PLANTING METHOD: root cuttings

PLANT SPACING: 12 to 24 inches

LIGHT: full sun

Small, knobby, round tubers with a nutty flavor and crunchy texture from late summer through fall. Peel Jerusalem artichokes and slice raw for salads, use like water chestnuts, or prepare like potatoes. During the growing season the tall foliage can serve as a screen for the vegetable garden.

Selected varieties
'French Mammoth White'—clumps of egg-sized tubers in 110 to 150 days and stout 6- to 10-foot stalks bearing 3-inch yellow blossoms resembling sunflowers.

Growing conditions
Plant small whole tubers or pieces of Jerusalem artichoke with two or three eyes each 4 to 6 inches deep in spring, allowing 3 feet between rows. Jerusalem artichoke thrives in a dry, infertile soil, so water and fertilize sparingly. Remove flower buds as they form to encourage greater root growth. Dig tubers as needed or store in sand in a cool location. They can also be mulched and stored in the ground over the winter. Jerusalem artichoke sprouts readily from tubers or pieces left in the ground and can become invasive.

JICAMA

Jicama

HARDINESS: hot-season annual

PLANTING METHOD: transplants

PLANT SPACING: 1 to 2 feet

LIGHT: full sun

Large, round tubers with crispy, sweet white flesh resembling water chestnuts in fall. Slice jicama into fruit or vegetable salads, use in place of crackers for hors d'oeuvres, or fry like potatoes. Leaves, flowers, and seeds and ripe seedpods are all poisonous.

Selected varieties
Sold only as jicama, a climbing vine with large, heart-shaped leaves, pealike purple flowers, and a single rounded to heart-shaped tuber up to 6 inches in diameter with smooth, brown-gray skin in 120 to 180 days.

Growing conditions
Start jicama seeds indoors 8 to 10 weeks before last frost and set transplants outdoors into a loose, fertile soil enriched with compost as soon as soil warms; soak seeds for best germination. Provide a trellis or other support for vines. Pinch growing tips when vines reach 3 feet and remove all flower buds to produce the largest tubers. Dig tubers before the first frost. Jicama requires a 9-month growing season to reach full size; roots grown in a shorter growing season will be proportionally smaller.

KALE

'Dwarf Blue Curled Scotch Vates'

HARDINESS: cool-season annual

PLANTING METHOD: direct sowing; transplants

PLANT SPACING: 8 to 12 inches

LIGHT: full sun to light shade

Dense rosettes of ruffled and curled succulent leaves in multiple shades of green and blue-green with a mild cabbage flavor in spring or fall; tastes best in the fall, when a touch of frost sweetens flavor. Greens can even be harvested beneath a blanket of snow for a fresh winter vegetable. Use spring thinnings and crunchy young kale leaves in salads or as a garnish. Cook greens in soups, side dishes, and casseroles, making sure to discard the tough midrib before preparing. The bold rosettes are attractive accents in beds and borders as well as containers.

Selected varieties:
'Blue Siberian'—a dwarf variety with ruffled blue-green leaves in open rosettes up to 2 feet across in 70 days. 'Dwarf Blue Curled Scotch Vates'—very early variety with tightly curled leaves on low-spreading 12- to 14-inch plants from seed in 55 days; not as cold tolerant as other varieties. 'Red Russian', also called 'Ragged Jack'—heirloom variety with wavy, oaklike leaves on tall plants that turn from blue-green to deep purple-red when touched by frost in 48 days. 'Winterbor'—very cold-tolerant variety with curly green leaves in 60 days on large plants 3 feet tall and 2 feet wide

that regrow vigorously when picked for a continuous harvest.

Growing conditions

For spring crops, plant seed outdoors 4 to 6 weeks before the last frost, setting seeds ½ inch deep in rows 2 to 3 feet apart. Make successive sowings that will mature before hot weather induces semidormancy and leaves become bitter and tough. For fall and winter crops, make successive sowings starting 6 to 8 weeks before the first frost. Plant kale in moist, well-drained fertile loam enriched with compost and use mulch to retain moisture. Feed growing plants every 2 weeks with fish emulsion or any other balanced organic fertilizer that provides ample nitrogen to support leaf growth. To minimize clubroot and other soil-borne diseases, do not plant kale where other members of the cabbage family have been planted for at least 3 years.

To harvest, remove outer leaves for a continuous supply of greens or cut whole plant at the soil line. Kale can be stored over winter in the garden and harvested as needed. It will keep for several weeks after cutting if refrigerated. A 10-foot row produces about 5 pounds of kale.

'Red Russian'

KOHLRABI

'Early Purple Vienna'

HARDINESS: cool-season annual

PLANTING METHOD: transplants; direct sowing

PLANT SPACING: 4 to 6 inches

LIGHT: full sun to light shade

Pale green or purplish bulbs with a very mild cabbagelike flavor in late spring or fall. Eat young kohlrabi raw out of hand like apples, slice into salads, or steam or parboil for side dishes.

Selected varieties

'Early Purple Vienna'—greenish white flesh beneath purple skin in 60 days, recommended for fall planting. 'Early White Vienna'—an especially cold-tolerant variety with 2-inch pale green bulbs in 55 days, recommended for fall planting. 'Grand Duke'—small bulbs with crisp, tender white flesh on compact plants in 45 days, recommended for spring planting.

Growing conditions

For a spring crop, sow seed indoors in peat pots 6 to 8 weeks before setting outdoors—anytime from 5 weeks before the last frost until 2 weeks after—in soil enriched with compost. For a fall crop, sow seeds ½ inch deep outdoors in mid- to late summer; light frost improves flavor. Harvest when bulbs are 2 inches across; older bulbs become woody and fibrous. Kohlrabi can be grown in light shade but if so produces elongated, rather than round, bulbs that aren't as crisp in texture. A 10-foot row yields 5 to 8 pounds of bulbs.

LEEKS

'Large American Flag'

HARDINESS: cool-season annual

PLANTING METHOD: transplants; direct sowing

PLANT SPACING: 4 to 6 inches

LIGHT: full sun to light shade

Thick white stems and broad, flat green leaves with a mild onion flavor in fall and winter. Use like onions for flavoring, garnishes, salads, soups, and side dishes.

Selected varieties

'Alaska'—thick, sweet stems, good for overwintering, in 125 days. 'Blue Solaise' —short 4- to 6-inch stems in 140 days. 'King Richard'—early variety maturing in 75 days; will withstand frost to 20° F but is not winter hardy. 'Large American Flag', also called 'Broad London'—stems 1 to 1½ inches thick, very cold tolerant and excellent for overwintering, in 120 days. 'Winter Giant'—very tall, thick stems, good for overwintering.

Growing conditions

For fall harvest, sow leeks ¼ inch deep indoors 8 to 12 weeks before the last frost date. Bury transplants up to their leaf joints in a narrow trench 8 to 12 inches deep. As leeks grow, gradually fill trench in to develop thick, blanched stalks. For a winter or early-spring crop, sow seed of cold-hardy varieties outdoors from late spring to early summer. Where winter temperatures fall below 20° F, mulch with 12 to 18 inches of straw or leaves. A 10-foot row can yield 30 pounds of leeks.

LETTUCE

'Buttercrunch'

HARDINESS: cool-season annual

PLANTING METHOD: direct sowing; transplants

PLANT SPACING: 4 to 14 inches

LIGHT: full sun to light shade

Loose rosettes or firm heads of delectable leaves from spring to early summer and again from early to late fall when a succession of different varieties is planted. Crisphead varieties have tight, firm heads that are blanched at the center. They require a very long growing season and are lowest in nutrients of all lettuce types. Butterhead or Boston varieties have tender, easily bruised leaves folded into loose heads with creamy blanched centers; they contain vitamins A and C as well as calcium and iron. Leaf or bunching varieties form open rosettes of curly, puckered leaves that are easy to grow, mature quickly, and are very nutritious, with high levels of vitamins A and C, and calcium. The stiff, erect leaves of romaine or cos varieties fold into upright heads that blanch at their centers; more heat tolerant than other types, they are similar nutritionally to leaf varieties.

Lettuce reigns as the supreme green in salads. Sauté lettuce alone or with other greens as a side dish, add whole or shredded leaves to soups, tuck into sandwiches, or use as a garnish.

Selected varieties
Crisphead varieties, also called Batavian or iceberg lettuces, include: 'Great Lakes'—a cold-tolerant, slow-to-bolt variety with crisp, juicy leaves in 82 to 90 days. 'Iceberg'—creamy blanched centers and deep green outer leaves in 85 days. 'Ithaca'—bolt-resistant variety best for spring crops in 72 days. 'Red Grenoble'—slow-to-bolt spring lettuce with wine red leaves, to cut as needed when young or allow to develop into heads. 'Rosy'—slow-to-bolt variety with burgundy-tinged leaves in small heads. 'Summertime'—heads of crisp leaves ready for harvest in 68 days.

Butterhead or Boston lettuce varieties include: 'Bibb'—3½-inch heads of deep green leaves in 75 days. 'Buttercrunch'—thick, dark green leaves in firm heads with buttery yellow centers on heat-resistant plants in 53 to 65 days. 'Dark Green Boston'—tight heads of deep green leaves in 70 days. 'Four Seasons', also called 'Merveille des Quatre Saisons'—large 16-inch heads, outer leaves tinged with bronze around a tender, pale green inner heart in

'Green Ice'

49 to 65 days; best for spring planting because of its tendency to bolt. 'Tom Thumb'—firm miniature heads of medium green leaves ideal as an individual serving in 52 to 60 days.

Leaf or bunching lettuce varieties include: 'Black-Seeded Simpson'—fast-growing, heat-tolerant variety with crisp, highly frilled leaves in 45 days. 'Green Ice'—very slow-to-bolt rosettes of sweet, deep green, crinkled leaves in 45 days. 'Oakleaf'—deeply lobed, tender leaves on slow-to-bolt plants in 45 to 55 days. 'Prizehead'—frilly red-tinged leaves in large, loose heads in 48 days. 'Red Sails'—bolt-resistant variety with large crumpled leaves fringed with red in broad, open heads up to a foot across in 45 days. 'Ruby'—heat-tolerant variety with frilled, curly leaves shading from deep burgundy to pale green in 47 days. 'Salad Bowl'—rosettes of bright green, frilly leaves ready for harvest in 60 days in cool weather, ideal for spring planting.

'Oakleaf'

Romaine or cos lettuce varieties include: 'Cimarron Red'—compact heads with crinkled, red-tinged leaves in 58 days. 'Little Gem', also called 'Diamond Gem'—crisp miniature heads 4 inches across and 6 inches tall with creamy blanched centers in 45 to 56 days. 'Paris Island Cos'—thick-ribbed, dense 12-inch-tall heads with blanched hearts in 65 days. 'Rosalita'—thick-ribbed summer lettuce with oval, curly leaves in dense heads in 62 days. 'Rouge d'Hiver'—has very large heads of broad, deep red leaves enfolding crisp hearts, best for fall planting, in 60 days. 'Winter Density'—extremely frost-tolerant cross between cos and butterhead types, good for fall planting in 65 days.

Growing conditions
Plant lettuce seeds ¼ to ½ inch deep outdoors in a moisture-retentive, compost-enriched soil as soon as the ground can be worked in spring. In areas where the cool growing season is short, start seeds of long-season crisphead, butterhead, and romaine crops 4 to 6 weeks before the last frost date. Lettuce is very shallow rooted; keep soil evenly moist for continuous growth and sweetest flavor. Loosehead and butterhead varieties tolerate light shade, especially as summer heat approaches. Let-

tuce grows best in cool soil at cool temperatures. Make small successive sowings of different varieties for a continuous supply of lettuce until summer temperatures of 85° F cause plants to bolt and leaves to become bitter. Sow again in early fall when daytime temperatures become cool again. Proper thinning of lettuce is critical to success; thin crisphead or butterhead varieties to stand 12 to 14 inches apart, leaf or romaine varieties to stand 4 to 6 inches at first and later to 6 to 10 inches apart depending on the variety. Use thinnings in salads or transplant to another spot for a later harvest. To harvest, pull up the entire head of crisphead or butterhead varieties. Pick outer leaves of loosehead or cos varieties as they mature, or cut entire plant off at the base; it will regrow a second, smaller crop of leaves. A 10-foot row yields 10 heads of head lettuce or 9 pounds of leaf lettuce.

'Red Sails'

MELONS

'Earlisweet' Muskmelon

HARDINESS: warm-season annual

PLANTING METHOD: transplants; direct sowing

PLANT SPACING: 18 to 36 inches

LIGHT: full sun

Round or oval fruits with sweet, juicy, often aromatic flesh enclosed in a hard rind on sprawling vines. Muskmelons, sometimes incorrectly called cantaloupes, have a deeply ribbed, heavily netted rind and orange flesh with a musky aroma. Charentais-type cantaloupes, or true cantaloupes, are small, round orange-fleshed melons with smooth rinds and no netting. Honeydew, Crenshaw, and casaba melons are large, smooth-skinned melons with pale green or orange flesh that has a fruity aroma rather than a musky one. Oval or round, smooth-skinned watermelons have deliciously sweet and exceptionally juicy, crisp red or yellow flesh with seeds scattered throughout rather than in the central seed cavity found in other types of melons.

Selected varieties

Netted muskmelon types include: 'Alaska'—with very early oval melons with deep salmon flesh in 72 days. 'Ambrosia'—3- to 5-pound melons with thick peach-colored flesh and small seed cavities on disease-resistant vines in 86 days. 'Casablanca'—mildew-resistant vines bearing 4-pound melons with soft-textured, juicy, creamy white flesh tinged with pink in 85 days. 'Earlisweet'—very early-maturing 5-inch fruits with deep salmon flesh in 70 days, resistant to fusarium wilt. 'Hale's Best Jumbo'—4-pound melons with thick salmon flesh on drought-tolerant vines in 86 days. 'Hearts of Gold'—an extremely sweet salmon-fleshed variety with small seed cavities in 90 days. 'Musketeer'—compact vines only 2½ to 3 feet long bearing 3-pound fruits with fragrant, light orange flesh in 90 days. 'Super Market'—wilt- and mildew-resistant vines bearing 4-pound melons with thick, bruise-resistant rinds and juicy orange flesh in 84 days. 'Sweet Bush'—very compact vines ideal for small gardens bearing 2-pound melons in 74 days. 'Topmark'—wilt-resistant oval melons with orange flesh and a small seed cavity in 90 days.

Charentais-type cantaloupes include: 'Alienor'—round, 2-pound fruits with pale, smooth skins and deep orange flesh in 90 days or sooner if vines are pruned to force earlier maturity. 'Charentais'—exceptionally sweet heirloom variety from France that ripens in 75 to 85 days even in cool areas. 'Pancha'—wilt- and mildew-resistant vines bearing 2-pound fruits with aromatic flesh in 80 days. 'Savor'—2½-pound melons with pale gray-green skin and deliciously aromatic flesh on disease-resistant vines in 78 days.

Honeydew melons include: 'Earlidew'—vigorous, disease-tolerant vines recommended for gardens in the East and the Midwest, with fruits that have aromatic, pale yellow-green flesh in 75 to 80 days. 'Orange Flesh'—late-maturing 4- to 6-pound round melons with sweet salmon-colored flesh in 90 days; 'Venus'—with

'Alaska' Muskmelon

heavy crops of 5½-inch oval fruits with a golden yellow rind enclosing bright green sweet flesh in 88 days.

Watermelon varieties include: 'Black Diamond'—enormous round melons up to 50 pounds each with dark green skins and bright red flesh in 90 days. 'Bush Baby II'—very compact, space-saving vines bearing round 10-pound melons in 80 to 90 days. 'Charleston Gray'—wilt-resistant and drought-tolerant vines with 28- to 35-pound melons that store well in 90 days. 'Crimson Sweet'—round 25-pound melons with skin striped light and dark green and firm, deep red flesh in 80 days on disease-resistant vines. 'Redball Seedless'—round 12-pound melons with glossy green skin and only a few white, edible

'Orange Flesh' Honeydew Melon

seeds in 80 days. 'Sugar Baby'—10-inch round fruits with red flesh in 80 days. 'Yellow Baby'—small melons up to 7 inches in diameter with crisp yellow flesh in 80 days.

Miscellaneous melons include: 'Casaba Golden Beauty'—7- to 8-pound oval melon with wrinkled golden skin, white flesh, and a small seed cavity in 110 days. 'Crenshaw'—large, oval melons up to 14 pounds each with very tender peach-colored flesh and a small seed cavity in 90 days. 'Galia'—a tropical melon with pale green, very sweet flesh and a flavor reminiscent of banana in 75 days. 'Jaune des Canaries'—oval melon with slightly wrinkled green skin turning yellow when ripe and whitish green flesh in 100 to 110 days. 'Passport'—3½- to 4-pound tropical melon with thick, juicy pale green flesh with a banana-like aroma in 70 to 78 days.

Growing conditions

Start melons indoors 4 to 6 weeks before the last frost or direct-sow 2 to 3 weeks after the last frost, setting seed ½ inch deep in rows and thinning plants to stand 18 to 36 inches apart. Allow 4 to 6 feet between rows. For direct sowing, plant five or six seeds in hills spaced 6 feet apart after the soil has warmed and thin to two or three plants. Choose compact bush-type vines for small gardens.

Melons grow best when the soil temperature is 70° F or more and need hot, dry weather in late summer and early fall to produce good fruit; air or soil temperatures below 50° F cause damage. Use black plastic mulch to warm soil and keep fruits clean. Water well during early stages of growth and when plants are blooming and pollinating. Use floating row covers to protect young plants from insect pests, but remove row covers when plants blossom so flowers will be pollinated. After fruit sets, withhold water in order to concentrate sugars in the fruits, which need 2 to 3 weeks to ripen.

Powdery mildew attacks melon seedlings and vines with heavy fruit set in cool, damp weather; once leaves become mildewed, fruit will not ripen. Melons do not ripen off the vine.

Thumb pressure at the blossom end causes ripe cantaloupes to slip from their vines. Harvest tropical melons as the deep green skin changes to buff-yellow. Watermelons are ripe when the tendril closest to the fruit stem on the vine browns or when the part of the rind resting on the ground turns yellow. Each vine produces two to four fruits.

'Crimson Sweet' Watermelon

MUSTARD GREENS

'Florida Broadleaf'

HARDINESS: cool-season annual

PLANTING METHOD: direct sowing

PLANT SPACING: 4 to 6 inches

LIGHT: full sun

Smooth or highly frilled leaves with a pungent flavor in early spring or late fall. Pick young leaves to add zest and crunch to salads; parboil mature leaves for side dishes or use as a garnish.

Selected varieties

'Florida Broadleaf'—smooth, lobed oval leaves with a white midrib in 45 days. 'Fordhook Fancy'—heat-tolerant variety with rather mild-flavored, deeply curled and fringed leaves in 40 days. 'Green Wave'—bright green leaves with tightly frilled edges in 45 days. 'Osaka Purple'—mild-flavored, broad dark purple leaves with white veins in 40 days, extremely slow to bolt. 'Red Giant'—red and green crinkled leaves up to 18 inches tall on very productive plants in 45 days. 'Southern Giant Curled'—light green leaves with frilly edges in 45 to 50 days, cold tolerant and resistant to bolting.

Growing conditions

Sow mustard seeds outdoors ¼ to ½ inch deep in a compost-enriched soil as soon as the ground can be worked in spring. In mild-winter areas, sow a second crop 6 to 8 weeks before the first fall frost. For tender leaves, keep evenly moist and harvest while young, cutting them as needed. A 10-foot row yields 10 pounds of greens.

OKRA

'Annie Oakley'

HARDINESS: hot-season annual

PLANTING METHOD: direct sowing; transplants

PLANT SPACING: 18 to 24 inches

LIGHT: full sun

Smooth or ribbed pods, often with spines, on erect bushy plants. The pods thicken soups, gumbos, and stews and are delicious served as a side dish.

Selected varieties
'Annie Oakley'—large crop of pods on dwarf 3- to 4-foot plants in 55 days. 'Burgundy'—plants to 4 feet with ornamental red-veined leaves and burgundy-colored pods in 60 days that retain their color after cooking. 'Clemson Spineless'—with spineless pods on 5-foot plants in 56 to 65 days.

Growing conditions
Sow okra seed ½ inch deep outdoors after soil temperatures reach 60° F; presoaking improves their germination rate. Thin dwarf plants to stand 18 inches apart, others to 24 inches. Okra grows best at temperatures between 70° and 85° F; where the warm growing season is short, start okra seeds indoors 4 to 6 weeks before setting outdoors, and mulch with black plastic to warm the soil. Feed regularly and keep constantly moist for succulent pods. Wear gloves and a long-sleeved shirt while snipping pods from plants. Pick young, tender pods 3 to 4 inches long every 2 or 3 days to keep plants producing. A single plant produces 50 to 200 pods.

ONIONS

'Granex Yellow'

HARDINESS: Zones 3-9

PLANTING METHOD: direct sowing; transplants; sets

PLANT SPACING: 2 to 3 inches

LIGHT: full sun

Pungently sweet, crisp bulbs, thickened stems, and piquant hollow greens in summer or fall depending on the type. Onion bulb formation is sensitive to day length. Plant short-day varieties as a winter bulb crop in mild-winter areas or for small pickling onions farther north. Grow long-day varieties for bulb crops in northern gardens or for bunching onions in milder areas. Delicately flavored chives grow as a perennial in Zones 3-9. Egyptian onions form small bulbs at the tips of their stems rather than underground. Bunching onions have either very small bulbs or no bulb at all and are perennials in Zones 3-9.

Onions are the soul of many dishes. Use them as flavorings or as cases for stuffings. Cream, fry, scallop, boil, steam, or glaze them for side dishes. Slice them raw for salads, sandwiches, crudités, and garnishes. Pickle small onions or freeze chopped or whole small onions. Grow chives in pots indoors or out.

Selected varieties
Short-day varieties include: 'Granex Yellow'—very mild bulbs in 162 days. 'Red Granex'—slow-to-bolt bulbs with mild red flesh in 162 days. 'Red Hamburger'—has slightly flattened bulbs with red-and-white flesh, excellent eaten raw, in 95 days. 'Texas Early Grano'—sweet jumbo bulbs best for fresh use in 175 days. 'Texas Grano'—large disease-resistant bulbs with thick rings of soft, white flesh in 168 days. 'Texas Grano 1015Y', also called 'Texas Supersweet'—a heat- and drought-tolerant variety with very sweet softball-sized bulbs in 175 days. 'Yellow Bermuda'—sweet white flesh in thick rings in 92 days.

Long-day varieties include: 'Ailsa Craig'—exceptionally large, early bulbs with pale yellow skins in 110 days. 'Early Yellow Globe'—uniform yellow onions that store well in 100 days. 'Northern Oak'—white flesh and heavy, dark brown skins with good keeping quality in 108 days. 'Sweet Sandwich'—large globes 3½ inches across with sweet yellow flesh in 112 days. 'Walla Walla'—mildly flavored, sweet jumbo bulbs in 110 to 120 days spring seeded, 300 days fall seeded. 'White Sweet Spanish'—very mild, sweet white bulbs with good

'Walla Walla'

keeping quality in 110 days. 'Yellow Sweet Spanish'—very mild, sweet yellow-fleshed bulbs up to a pound each in 110 days.

Egyptian onions—very cold-hardy perennials that form small bulbs at the tips of the thick, hollow stems in lieu of flowers and a smaller number of bulbs underground in 180 days.

Green onion varieties, also called scallions or bunching onions, include: 'Beltsville Bunching'—very hardy variety for spring or fall planting in 65 days. 'Evergreen Long White', also called 'Nebuka'—good for overwintering in 60 days. 'Ishikura'—bulbless, long white stems and blue-green tops in 66 days.

Growing conditions

Grow onions from seeds, transplants, or sets, depending on the length of the growing season and the type of onions desired. Plant short-day varieties in fall to produce bulbs the following summer; plant long-day varieties in spring for onions in fall. Plant bunching onions in spring or fall for use throughout the season. Plant perennial Egyptian onions in spring or fall; divide clumps every 3 or 4 years to maintain vigor. Sow seeds of bunching onions or long-day onions ½ inch deep in a fertile, moisture-retentive soil enriched with compost or manure 4 to 6 weeks before last frost, as soon as the ground can be worked in spring. Thin to stand 2 to 3 inches apart in rows 1 to 2 feet apart. For larger bulbs in a shorter time, start seeds indoors 12 weeks before setting out; transplants can be moved outdoors up to a month before the last frost. Small, dry onions called sets are the most reliable way to produce large bulbs, particularly for long-day varieties. Plant sets in early spring.

Harvest bulb onions by pulling them when half of their tops have fallen over. When the tops are completely wilted, snip them off 1½ inches above the bulbs, wipe off dirt and any loose skins, and continue to dry for 2 weeks or more in a dry area with good ventilation. Store the dry onions at 35° to 50° F. Harvest Egyptian onions when the tops begin to wilt and dry; dry for storage, pickle, or freeze. Bulb and bunching onions yield about 10 pounds per 10-foot row.

'Ishikura'

ORACH

'Green Orach'

HARDINESS: cool-season annual

PLANTING METHOD: direct sowing

PLANT SPACING: 6 to 10 inches

LIGHT: full sun

Also called mountain spinach. Arrow-shaped leaves with a mild spinachy flavor in erect 1- to 4-foot clumps from spring into summer. Slower to bolt than spinach, orach is a good warm-weather alternative. Use tender young orach leaves in mesclun mixtures of young greens, and older leaves cooked or as a salad green mixed with lettuces; the red and yellow cultivars retain their tints when cooked. The seed heads are attractive in floral arrangements.

Selected varieties

'Green Orach'—sweet, juicy leaves that do not become bitter as they age. 'Red Orach'—red-tinted stems and leaves. 'Yellow Orach'—golden leaves. All varieties ready to pick in 40 days.

Growing conditions

Sow orach seeds outdoors ½ inch deep when the soil temperature reaches 50° to 60° F. Keep soil moist. Make successive sowings throughout spring for a continuous supply of mesclun greens. Pick 6-inch leaves for mesclun; use leaves a foot or longer for summer salads or for cooking. Pinch out flower heads as they appear to encourage continued leaf growth. Orach tolerates both light frost and summer heat.

PAK-CHOI OR BOK CHOY

'Mei Quing Choi'

HARDINESS: cool-season annual

PLANTING METHOD: direct sowing

PLANT SPACING: 8 to 12 inches

LIGHT: full sun

Broad rosettes of upright leaves with thick, succulent stalks that have a mildly pungent flavor. Pak-choi is essential in stir-fry dishes. Uncooked, the crisp stalks can be used like celery or carrots with dips and sauces.

Selected varieties

'Lei Choi'—heat-tolerant variety with crunchy, celery-like white 8- to 10-inch stalks and deep green leaves in 47 days. 'Mei Quing Choi'—baby pak-choi with very tender, pale green 6- to 8-inch stalks and leaves in 45 days; frost tolerant, heat tolerant, and slow to bolt.

Growing conditions

Sow pak-choi seeds outdoors as soon as ground can be worked in spring, setting seeds ½ inch deep and thinning plants to stand 8 to 12 inches apart. Pak-choi needs cool temperatures for best growth and goes to seed as days lengthen and weather warms. Plant a second crop in fall 50 to 60 days before first frost. Pak-choi will tolerate light frost. Harvest by cutting stems just above the soil line.

PARSNIPS

'Hollow Crown'

HARDINESS: cool-season annual

PLANTING METHOD: direct sowing

PLANT SPACING: 2 to 3 inches

LIGHT: full sun

Tapering white roots resembling carrots with a fine texture and sweet, nutty flavor that mature in late fall and can be stored in the garden through winter. Parsnips can be baked, steamed, grilled, sautéed, or prepared in many of the same ways as carrots or potatoes. Parboiling, however, dissolves and draws out the sugars in the roots, leaving them bland tasting.

Selected varieties

'Harris Early Model'—short, stocky 12-inch roots with wide shoulders in 120 days. 'Hollow Crown'—exceptionally sweet, fine-grained roots up to 18 inches long in 125 days.

Growing conditions

Sow parsnip seeds in very early spring as soon as the ground can be worked. Soak seeds for 24 hours before setting them ½ to 1 inch deep in soil that has been tilled to a depth of 12 to 18 inches. Mulch to conserve moisture; lack of water causes roots to toughen. Begin harvesting after the first hard fall frost has sweetened the flavor. Store parsnips in the garden over the winter under a 12-inch mulch of hay or leaves anchored under black plastic. Harvest the previous season's parsnips by early spring. A 10-foot row yields about 8 pounds of parsnips.

PEANUTS

'Early Spanish'

HARDINESS: hot-season annual

PLANTING METHOD: direct sowing; transplants

PLANT SPACING: 12 inches

LIGHT: full sun

Pods or shells filled with richly flavored kernels under bushy plants. Each fertilized female flower develops a peg, or stem, that grows downward and into the soil; the pods are produced underground on the pegs. Eat shelled peanuts raw, roasted, or boiled or grind them for nut butter.

Selected varieties

'Early Spanish'—heavy-yielding plants with early-maturing pods with two or three kernels in 105 days. 'Jumbo Virginia'—many pods with one or two large kernels on 18-inch plants in 120 to 135 days.

Growing conditions

Pretreat pods or individual peanuts with skins intact with a bacterial inoculant, and plant 1 inch deep in a heavy soil or 2 or more inches deep in a loose, sandy soil after it has warmed in the spring. Where growing seasons are short, start peanuts indoors in individual peat pots and plant out after all danger of frost is past in soil prewarmed under black plastic mulch; remove the plastic mulch to allow pegs access to the soil. Thin plants to 12 inches apart. Harvest after foliage turns yellow but before first frost, pulling plants up and hanging by roots to dry before removing pods. One plant yields 40 to 50 pods.

PEAS

'Sugar Snap'

HARDINESS: cool-season annual

PLANTING METHOD: direct sowing

PLANT SPACING: 1 inch

LIGHT: full sun

Plump, sweet, round green seeds in long pods that are edible in some varieties, on vining or bushy plants in early spring or late fall. Garden or shelling peas have thick, stringy, inedible pods that contain long rows of up to 11 large peas. Snow peas are raised primarily for their thin, succulent edible pods. Exceptionally sweet sugar snap peas offer both plump seeds and thick-walled, edible pods. Among the first fruits of the spring garden, fresh garden peas are a tonic eaten raw out of hand or in salads; they are delicious parboiled or steamed for use in side dishes, soups, and stews. Use snow peas in Oriental cuisine or as an hors d'oeuvre. Prepare sugar snap peas like garden peas or snow peas. Freeze surplus peas for long-term storage.

Selected varieties

Garden or shelling pea varieties include: 'Alaska'—the earliest garden pea with a heavy yield of 2½-inch pods containing six to eight peas on 2-foot plants in 56 days. 'Alderman', or 'Tall Telephone'—late-maturing 5- to 6-foot vine with large peas in easy-to-shell pods in 76 days. 'Green Arrow'—large crop of 4-inch pods with up to 11 peas each on disease-resistant plants in 70 days. 'Lincoln'—vigorous 2-foot vines with 3½-inch pods filled with up to nine plump peas excellent for freezing in 67 days. 'Little Marvel'—dependable crop of very early 3-inch pods on 18-inch plants in 63 days. 'Petit Provencal'—heavy crop of 2½-inch pods filled with six or seven tiny, sweet peas, or *petit pois,* on bushy plants in 60 days. 'Progress No. 9'—4-inch pods containing up to seven peas each on short,

'Green Arrow'

15-inch vines in 62 days. 'Wando'—both heat and cold tolerant with very heavy crop of 3-inch pods containing seven or eight peas in 67 days, ideal for late-season crops in northern gardens. 'Waverex'—semiclimbing 18-inch vines bearing pods filled with seven or eight tiny, sweet peas, or *petit pois.*

Snow or sugar pea varieties include: 'Carouby de Maussane'—vigorous 5-foot vines with long, flat 5½-inch pods up to an inch wide in 65 days. 'Dwarf Gray Sugar'—pale green 2½- to 3-inch pods on 2½-foot vines in 63 days. 'Mammoth Melting Sugar'—disease-resistant 4-foot vines with broad pods in 72 days. 'Oregon Giant'—disease-resistant compact plants with broad, inch-wide pods up to 5 inches long filled with large, sweet peas in 70 days. 'Oregon Sugar Pod II'—heavy yields of crisp 4- to 5-inch pods, often in pairs, on nonclimbing dwarf vines in 70 days.

Sugar snap pea varieties include: 'Cascadia'—3-inch, thick-walled, juicy pods filled with sweet peas on compact plants in 58 days. 'Sugar Ann'—bushy, early-maturing variety bearing succulent 2½-inch pods on nonclimbing dwarf vines in 52 days. 'Sugar Bon'—disease-resistant, compact 2-foot plants with 3-inch pods in 56 days. 'Sugar Daddy'—stringless sugar

snap peas on compact bushy 2-foot plants in 65 days. 'Sugar Snap'—3-inch pods on climbing 6-foot vines in 62 days. 'Super Sugar Mel'—thick 4-inch pods on 3-foot vines in 68 days.

Growing conditions

Sow peas ½ to 1 inch deep and 1 inch apart in spring 6 weeks before the last frost date or in fall 6 weeks before the first frost date. Sprinkle planting holes or trenches with a bacterial legume inoculant. Peas are a cool-weather crop that will tolerate temperatures as low as 25° F without protection and even lower temperatures when started under floating row covers. They grow best at daytime temperatures between 50° and 60° F. Do not thin; peas grow best in crowded stands. Provide trellises, netting, or other supports for vines to climb, or lay twiggy brush among bush types to support plants and keep pods off the ground. Weed carefully, as disturbing roots causes flowers and pods to drop.

Harvest garden peas when pods are bulging and before there is any sign of yellowing or shriveling. Pick snow peas and sugar snap peas just as seeds begin to form; overmature pods become fibrous and tough. Pick daily to encourage vining peas to continue producing; the pods of most bush varieties mature all at once for a single picking. For a continuous harvest, select varieties with different maturity dates. A 10-foot row yields approximately 5 to 10 pounds of peas.

'Little Marvel'

PEPPERS

'Golden Bell'

HARDINESS: hot-season annual

PLANTING METHOD: transplants; direct sowing

PLANT SPACING: 18 to 24 inches

LIGHT: full sun

Succulent, fleshy fruits with thin skin, some mild and sweet, others hot, on bushy plants in late summer. Mildly flavored bell peppers are usually harvested at their immature green stage but can be left on plants to ripen to yellow, red, or purple and become even sweeter; use bell peppers as edible food cases, sliced raw in salads, or sautéed or parboiled as a flavoring. Most hot, or chili, peppers are picked after they ripen to red or yellow; use them in ethnic dishes. Surplus peppers can be chopped and frozen, dried, or pickled for long-term storage. The days to maturity for the peppers described below are counted from the date transplants are set out in the garden.

Selected varieties

Sweet bell pepper varieties include: 'Bell Boy'—a disease-resistant hybrid with thick-walled, glossy green fruits 3½ inches in diameter in 70 days that ripen to red. 'California Wonder'—thick-walled pepper 3 inches in diameter in 75 days. 'Cherry Sweet', also called 'Red Cherry'—1½-inch, slightly tapered peppers in 78 days especially recommended for pickling. 'Chocolate Belle'—blocky 4-inch fruits with chocolate brown skin and red flesh in 75 days. 'Cubanelle'—slender, tapering 6-inch-long pale green peppers 2½ inches wide at the shoulders in 65 days. 'Golden Bell'—blocky three- or four-lobed peppers in 70 days that ripen to a deep gold. 'Gypsy'—a disease-resistant variety with wedge-shaped 5-inch fruits in 65 days that mature from pale green to deep yellow. 'New Ace'—4-inch fruits in 62 days for short-season regions. 'Purple Beauty'—blocky

'Anaheim'

fruits with deep purple skin in 70 days, ripening to red. 'Whopper Improved'—disease-resistant, almost square 4-inch peppers in 71 days. 'Yolo Wonder'—disease-resistant plants with 4-inch squarish peppers in 75 days.

Chili, or hot, pepper varieties include: 'Anaheim TMR 23'—with tapering, flat peppers 8 inches long by 1½ inches wide in 77 days, milder flavored than most chilies and usually picked while still green. 'Ancho', also called 'Poblano'—relatively mild with 5- to 6-inch dark green to red peppers in 65 to 75 days. 'Habañero'—extremely hot, dark green peppers 1 to 2 inches long ripening to pinkish orange in 85 to 95 days. 'Hungarian Wax'—tapering, three-lobed 6-inch-by-2-inch peppers that mature from pale yellow to bright red with a medium-hot flavor, 65 to 75 days. 'Jalapeño'—tiny, extremely hot cone-shaped peppers 3 inches long in 70 to 80 days that are usually picked green before they ripen to red. 'Large Hot Cherry'—heavy crop of hot, slightly conical 1½-inch fruits ripening from green to red in 75 days, recommended for pickling. 'Numex Big Jim'—medium-hot 10-inch red peppers in 80 days. 'Serrano Chile'—extremely hot conical peppers 2½ inches long and ½ inch

across in 75 days that turn from green to red. 'Super Cayenne'—very hot, slim 4-inch peppers in 70 days that turn from green to red. 'Super Chili'—very hot, conical pale green fruits growing upright on bushes and maturing to orange then red in 70 days. 'Thai Hot'—very compact plants with extremely hot, ¾- to 1-inch green fruits that ripen to red in 75 days.

Growing conditions

Start pepper plants indoors 8 to 10 weeks before night temperatures stay reliably above 55° F, setting seeds ½ inch deep; in areas with a long growing season, peppers can be sown directly in the garden. For disease prevention, avoid planting where other peppers, eggplant, or tomatoes have grown in the past 3 years. Peppers grow best when night temperatures are 62° F or more and daytime temperatures are 75° F or less. Temperatures below 55° F or above 85° F will cause blossoms to drop; although plants will recover, the crop will be smaller. Chili peppers require warmer soil for germination and growth than bell peppers; warm soil with black plastic before setting plants out in spring.

Pick bell peppers while still green and immature, while they are changing color, or when they have fully ripened to yellow, red, or purple. Fully ripe bell peppers have more sweetness and flavor than green ones. With a few exceptions, most chilies are left on plants to ripen fully before being snipped from plants. Continuous picking encourages further fruiting.

'Hungarian Wax'

POTATOES

'Red La Soda'

HARDINESS: warm-season annual

PLANTING METHOD: seed potatoes

PLANT SPACING: 10 to 14 inches

LIGHT: full sun

Round or oblong firm-textured tubers, sometimes with colorful skins or flesh, from early summer to fall with successive planting of different varieties. Early-season varieties mature with thin skins tender enough to rub off when the potatoes are first harvested. Midseason and late-season or storage potatoes can be dug as thin-skinned "new" potatoes for immediate use or allowed to mature in the ground until their skins are fully set and cannot be rubbed off, then stored for fresh use over several months. Baby new potatoes are excellent boiled in their skins to eat whole or to slice into salads. Mature potatoes can be boiled, baked, fried, mashed, and scalloped in a myriad of flavorful ways. Home gardeners can enjoy potatoes with colorful yellow, blue, or purple flesh seldom available except in markets offering gourmet vegetables.

Selected varieties

Early-season varieties include: 'Irish Cobbler'—very early oblong tubers with smooth white skins and creamy white flesh in 65 days. 'Norgold Russet'—scab-resistant smooth, oblong, brown-skinned tubers with golden netting and flaky, moist flesh excellent for baking in 65 days. 'Red Norland'—scab-tolerant round potatoes with thin red skins and crisp white interiors in 65 days. 'Yukon Gold'—scab-resistant round or slightly oval potatoes with yellow skins and flavorful, buttery golden yellow flesh in 65 days with good keeping quality.

Midseason varieties include: 'Beltsville'—vigorous plants resistant to nematodes, scab, and wilt with white flesh and excellent keeping quality. 'Katahdin'—scab-resistant plants adapted to varied climate and soil conditions, producing round tubers with tan skins and white flesh. 'Kennebec'—blight-resistant plants with heavy yields of smooth-textured, round all-purpose potatoes in 80 days. 'Purple Marker'—disease-resistant plants producing medium-sized oval potatoes with deep purple-blue skins and flesh in 80 days. 'Red La Soda'—heat- and drought-tolerant round to oblong tubers with bright red skins and firm white flesh ideal for boiling in 80 days. 'Russet Burbank', also called 'Idaho Russet'—long, cylindrical, slightly flattened tubers with heavily netted brown skins and dry, flaky white flesh in 80 days. 'Russian Banana'—disease-resistant plants producing small to medium-sized fingerling potatoes with yellow skins and waxy pale yellow flesh. 'Viking Purple'—dark purple skins mottled red or pink over smooth-textured white flesh good for boiling in 80 days.

Late-season varieties include: 'Purple Peruvian'—long, narrow ½- to ¾-pound fingerling potatoes with deep purple skins, purple flesh, and purple-tinted foliage. 'Red Pontiac'—thin red skins over firm, white flesh with a light waxy texture good

'Irish Cobbler'

for boiling, midseason to late; excellent storage quality and also good harvested early for new potatoes.

Growing conditions

Use certified virus-free seed potatoes to plant a crop. An acidic soil inhibits the growth of the potato scab virus. Early varieties are planted out 6 to 8 weeks before

'Purple Peruvian'

the last frost date, as soon as the ground can be worked in spring. Before planting, the seed potatoes should be sprouted, or "chitted." About 2 weeks before the date they will be set out, put them in a single layer in a shallow box with the eyes facing up. Set the box in a cool, frost-free room in indirect light until the potatoes produce short, stubby 1-inch sprouts. Plant whole seed potatoes the size of an egg or cut larger ones into egg-sized sections at least a day in advance so the cut surfaces can dry and are more resistant to rot. Set the seed potatoes 10 to 14 inches apart in trenches 6 to 8 inches deep; rows should be 2 feet apart. Cover the seed potatoes with no more than 4 inches of soil. Keep soil evenly moist. When stems are 8 inches high, hill more soil around plants, leaving 4 inches of the stems exposed. Hill twice more at 2-week intervals. Hilling in this fashion is essential because the tubers form on underground stolons produced along the stems.

Plant mid- and late-season potatoes directly in the garden, without sprouting, or chitting, 1 to 4 weeks before the last frost. Set them 3 to 4 inches deep in rows 2 feet apart. Hill the soil as described above.

Where soil is hard or rocky, potatoes can be grown under mulch. Place seed

potatoes in shallow trenches and cover with a loose layer of straw, leaves, or dried grass clippings 6 to 10 inches deep; as stems elongate and plants emerge through mulch, add more mulch as though hilling soil as described above, taking care that tubers are covered at all times. Alternatively, grow potatoes in tall bottomless boxes, wooden cribs, barrels, or wire cages. Plant seed potatoes 6 to 8 inches apart and cover with 4 inches of soil; as plants grow taller, hill soil, compost, or mulch around the stems at 2-week intervals as described above.

Harvest potatoes anytime for new potatoes, carefully digging into soil to find small potatoes up to 2 inches in diameter. To harvest main-crop potatoes, cut off vines, then wait 2 weeks before digging. To dig, use a garden fork, carefully lifting soil starting 1½ to 2 feet out from the plant's crown and taking care not to spear tubers. Use cut or bruised tubers immediately. Allow intact, unbruised tubers to dry for 1 to 2 weeks in a dark, well-ventilated area at 60° F, then store at 40° F in wooden boxes, burlap bags, or other well-ventilated containers. Check occasionally and remove any rotting potatoes. One plant yields between 2 and 10 pounds of potatoes.

'Red Pontiac'

PUMPKINS

'Big Max'

HARDINESS: warm-season annual

PLANTING METHOD: transplants; direct sowing

PLANT SPACING: 2 to 4 feet

LIGHT: full sun

Globe-shaped fruits filled with deep orange, firm-textured flesh and edible seeds on strong, sprawling vines. The large varieties are ideal for Halloween jack-o'-lanterns; the medium-sized ones, for side dishes, soups, and pies. Hollow out miniature pumpkins as containers for soups or stuffings or try using them like decorative gourds in arrangements. Roasted pumpkin seeds, particularly the hull-less varieties, make a nutritious snack.

Selected varieties

'Atlantic Giant'—has huge, deeply ribbed fruits weighing up to several hundred pounds in 125 days. 'Baby Bear'—disease-resistant vines with small, slightly flattened fruits only 6 inches across and 3½ to 4 inches tall with fine-textured flesh and hull-less seeds in 105 days. 'Big Max'—enormous 50- to 100-pound fruits with thick orange flesh in 120 days, excellent for carving. 'Connecticut Field'—large 20- to 25-pound fruits with dark orange skins and slightly flattened shapes, good for carving. 'Jack Be Little'—six or seven miniature fruits only 3 inches across and 2 inches high on each vine in 95 days, ideal for decorations. 'Jack O' Lantern'—medium-sized, tall 7- to 9-pound pumpkins up to 9 inches across in 100 days. 'Lumina'—10- to 12-pound fruits up to 10 inches in diameter with creamy white skin and orange flesh in 110 days. 'Small Sugar Pie', also called 'New England Pie', 'Early Small Sugar'—5- to 6-pound fruits with very sweet, fine-textured yellow-orange flesh, excellent for pies, in 100 days.

Growing conditions

Plant pumpkin seeds outdoors after the last frost, setting seeds ½ to 1 inch deep, and thin to stand 2 to 3 feet apart in rows 4 to 6 feet apart for bush types and 3 to 4 feet apart in rows 8 to 12 feet apart for vining types. Alternatively, plant five or six seeds in hills spaced 4 feet apart for bush types and 8 feet apart for vining types and thin to two or three plants. Pumpkin seeds can be started indoors 4 to 5 weeks before the last frost date in peat pots that are planted directly in the garden. Mulch with black plastic to warm the soil and conserve water. Water well during early growth and fruit set; standing water on maturing fruits invites rot. Ensure good pollination by transferring pollen from male to female (with swollen stems just below the blossoms) flowers with a soft brush. When vines are 2 to 3 feet long and fruits are just beginning to develop, pinch shoots to stimulate larger fruit growth. For large exhibition pumpkins, allow only one fruit to develop per vine. Raise maturing pumpkins off the ground on boards to prevent rot. Harvest pumpkins when their skins harden or after frost has killed the vines. Pumpkins will store well for up to a year if skins are undamaged.

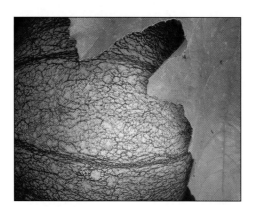

'Small Sugar Pie'

RADICCHIO

'Castelfranco'

HARDINESS: cool-season annual

PLANTING METHOD: direct sowing

PLANT SPACING: 12 inches

LIGHT: full sun

A type of chicory with loose rosettes or small heads of green or red, slightly bitter leaves in spring, summer, or fall, depending on the region. Use as a garnish and to add color and flavor to salads.

Selected varieties

'Augusto'—deep burgundy frost-resistant and bolt-resistant heads in 70 days. 'Castelfranco'—heirloom variety with loose red-and-white-marbled heads in 85 days. 'Early Treviso'—deep burgundy heads with white veins in 80 days. 'Giulio'—white-veined burgundy heads in 80 days. 'Red Verona'—heirloom variety with red heads veined in white in 100 days.

Growing conditions

Sow radicchio outdoors, setting seed ½ inch deep and thinning plants to 12 inches. In Zones 3-7, plant radicchio in spring. Harvest leaves as needed during summer, then cut plants back to an inch or so above the ground in late summer or early fall to stimulate roots to produce small heads in 4 to 6 weeks. Where winter temperatures do not go below 10° F, sow seed for leaves in early spring, followed by heads in early summer. 'Castelfranco' and 'Giulio' form heads without cutting back, and 'Early Treviso' often does. Sow seed from mid-summer to early fall for a fall crop.

RADISHES

'Easter Egg'

HARDINESS: cool-season annual

PLANTING METHOD: direct sowing

PLANT SPACING: 1 to 6 inches

LIGHT: full sun

Zesty roots in spring or fall. The large winter radishes, which are ready to harvest in fall, are stronger in taste and keep longer than spring varieties. Use as garnishes, hors d'oeuvres, or sliced in salads.

Selected varieties
Spring varieties include: 'Champion'—red, cold tolerant. 'Cherry Bell'—crisp red globes. 'Giant White Globe'—white, mildly flavored. 'Early Scarlet Globe'—very early, mildly flavored red globes. 'Easter Egg'—red, white, and purple roots. 'French Breakfast'—thick, cylindrical red roots with white tips. 'Plum Purple'—purple cylinders. 'White Icicle'—tapered white roots. All in 25 to 30 days.

Winter varieties include: 'Misato Rose' —sweet pink flesh. 'Munich Bier'—pungent white cylinders. 'Round Black Spanish'—black exterior, white flesh. 'Tokinashi'—strongly flavored white roots 8 or more inches long. All in 50 to 60 days.

Growing conditions
Sow seed ½ inch deep in fertile, moisture-retentive soil. Sow spring radishes successively from 5 weeks before the last frost until 4 weeks after; thin plants to 1 to 2 inches apart. Sow winter radishes from midsummer until 8 weeks before the first frost; thin to 4 to 6 inches apart.

RASPBERRIES

'Fall Red'

HARDINESS: Zones 4-7

PLANTING METHOD: bare root; containers

PLANT SPACING: 4 to 6 feet

LIGHT: full sun to light shade

Juicy, plump red, pink, golden, or black-purple berries on arching biennial canes growing from perennial rootstocks. Select varieties with maturity dates that provide fruit from early summer through frost. Standard red raspberries produce a single crop of fruit on 2-year-old canes; ever-bearing red raspberry canes bear fruit twice, once in the fall of their first year and again in the spring of their second year. Extremely fragile, delicately flavored yellow raspberries may be golden to pale pink. Black raspberries have a distinctly musky flavor and scent. Raspberries will spread rapidly via suckers along an underground network of rootlike stems.

Highly perishable, raspberries are most delectable straight from the garden. They can be frozen for long-term storage, although the berries become mushy when thawed. Use berries in pies, desserts, jams, and jellies. Besides producing fruit, Japanese wineberry is a handsome ornamental for winter color.

Selected varieties
Red and yellow raspberry varieties include: 'Canby'—standard variety with midsummer crop of fleshy, deliciously flavored red berries on thornless canes. 'Chief'—very early crop of small red fruits, recommend-

ed for the Midwest. 'Fall Gold'—very hardy plants with golden yellow berries that have a high sugar content. 'Fall Red'—everbearing variety with large, extremely sweet berries, producing a larger crop in fall than in summer; good for areas with a short growing season. 'Heritage'—everbearing variety with firm, conical bright red berries, producing a larger crop in summer than in fall. 'Latham'—medium-sized red fruits on very hardy, adaptable plants. 'Newburgh'—standard disease-resistant variety with firm, large red berries in midsummer on short plants that need no support. 'Taylor'—standard variety with conical, somewhat tart red berries on vigorous plants that sucker freely. 'Viking'—heavy crop of red berries on very tall canes.

Black raspberry varieties include: 'Allen'—heavy crop of large, firm, very sweet berries all at once in midsummer. 'Black Hawk'—late midseason crop of large, firm, glossy berries on plants resistant to drought and disease. 'Bristol'—large, very flavorful, nearly seedless berries on mosaic-resistant plants. 'John Robertson'—plump, juicy large berries on very hardy plants.

Hybrids include: Wineberry, also called Japanese wineberry—raspberry-blackberry hybrid with small, mildly flavored cherry red berries on attractive arching canes lined with soft red bristles that provide welcome color in the winter garden.

Growing conditions
Use only certified disease-free plants and never dig plants from the wild, since they may introduce viruses into the garden.

'Heritage'

Raspberries prefer deep, fertile loam enriched with compost. Plant rootstock with the top of the roots just below the soil line. Space plants 4 to 6 feet apart in rows 6 to 7 feet apart. Water regularly and provide a deep mulch to suppress grass and weeds. For the largest yields and easier picking, provide 3-foot-high wire trellises for vines to trail over. Cover canes with coarse ¾- to 1-inch netting to protect ripening berries from birds.

Remove spent fruiting canes of standard red or yellow raspberry varieties after ber-ries are harvested; prune the summer-fruiting canes of everbearing varieties after harvest. Remove weak suckers, leaving only two or three strong canes for every foot of row.

To prune black and purple raspberries, remove old or weak canes, leaving three or four strong canes per foot of row. Prune lateral branches on the previous year's canes back to about 6 inches for black raspberries or 10 inches for purple raspberries in late winter to early spring to encourage heavy fruit production later in the season. Pinch tips of new shoots when they are 18 to 24 inches tall to encourage lateral branching for next season's crop.

Harvest raspberries when the fruits soften and pull away easily from the stem. Use or process immediately, as fruits are highly perishable. A mature plant yields about 1½ quarts of berries.

'Bristol'

RHUBARB

'Cherry Red'

HARDINESS: Zones 3-8

PLANTING METHOD: root divisions

PLANT SPACING: 2 to 3 feet

LIGHT: full sun

Tart, juicy leafstalks in clumps in spring. Also called the pie plant, rhubarb is one of the earliest spring fruits for pies, cobblers, jams, and jellies. The foliage is very toxic; strip off when harvesting the stalks.

Selected varieties

'Cherry Red'—heavy yields of stalks that are cherry red outside, green inside. 'Valentine'—thick 12- to 24-inch stalks that retain their red color when cooked.

Growing conditions

Rhubarb needs at least 2 months of freezing weather and does not tolerate temperatures higher than 90° F. Start plants from root divisions purchased from suppliers or taken from plants at least 3 years old in late fall or very early spring; each division should have at least two eyes, or large buds. Set divisions 2 inches deep and space them 3 feet apart. Rhubarb can also be started from seed, but plants are usually not of the same quality and take a year longer to mature. Allow roots to become established the first year; harvest no more than 20 percent of the stalks the second year. Harvest stalks 1 inch or more in width from plants 3 years old or more over a 6- to 8-week period; do not remove more than half of the plant's stalks at one time. Each plant yields 10 to 20 stalks.

RUTABAGAS

'Improved Purple Top Yellow'

HARDINESS: cool-season annual

PLANTING METHOD: direct sowing

PLANT SPACING: 6 to 8 inches

LIGHT: full sun

Also called Swedish turnips. Large globe-shaped, 2- to 3-pound roots with mild, sweet, fine-grained yellow flesh and pungent leaves from fall into winter. Serve rutabaga roots mashed, baked, or fried, and boil or steam the greens.

Selected varieties

'American Purple Top'—5- to 6-inch-beige-yellow roots with purple crowns in 90 days. 'Improved Purple Top Yellow'—round to oblong roots that store well in 90 days. 'Laurentian'—round roots with pale yellow crowns that store well in 105 days.

Growing conditions

Sow rutabagas ½ inch deep 12 to 14 weeks before the first fall frost and thin seedlings to stand 6 to 8 inches apart. To control soil-borne diseases, don't plant rutabagas where they or any other members of the cabbage family have been grown within 3 years. Keep soil constantly moist but not soggy. Harvest rutabagas after several frosts have sweetened the roots, cutting off all but 1 inch of the leaves. To store roots, dip them in melted paraffin floating on top of warm water to prevent wrinkling. Store in a root cellar at 40° F. Rutabagas can also be overwintered in the garden under a thick layer of mulch. A 10-foot row yields about 10 pounds of roots.

SALSIFY

'Mammoth Sandwich Island'

HARDINESS: cool-season annual

PLANTING METHOD: direct sowing

PLANT SPACING: 2 to 4 inches

LIGHT: full sun

Also known as the oyster plant. Tapering white roots resembling parsnips from fall through winter. Salsify, which has a mild flavor reminiscent of oysters, can be boiled and mashed, fried, or added to soups.

Selected varieties
'Mammoth Sandwich Island'—roots 8 or more inches in length and about 1½ inches in diameter in 120 days.

Growing conditions
Sow salsify ¼ to ½ inch deep in spring in loose, well-tilled soil with all stones removed. Do not use manure when preparing salsify beds because the high nitrogen content results in hairy roots. Scratching wood ashes into the soil or watering with seaweed emulsion while roots are forming encourages thicker roots. Thin seedlings to 2 to 4 inches apart and mulch to keep soil evenly moist. Frost improves the flavor of salsify. Dig roots with a garden fork or shovel and store in moist peat or sand in a root cellar at 40° F. Alternatively, store salsify roots in the garden, covering them with a 12-inch mulch of straw or leaves. Harvest all roots by the following spring before new growth begins. A 10-foot row yields 10 to 20 pounds of salsify.

SHALLOTS

'Success'

HARDINESS: Zones 6-9; cool-season annual

PLANTING METHOD: sets

PLANT SPACING: 6 inches

LIGHT: full sun

Small, round bulbs with a delicate onion flavor from summer through fall or tender scallions in spring. Shallots are prized for the unique, mild accent they add to many gourmet dishes.

Selected varieties
'Atlantic'—clumps of plump bulbs with yellow-tan skins. 'Success'—small bulbs with reddish brown skins. Both in 120 to 150 days.

Growing conditions
Grow shallots from tiny bulbs called sets, setting them out in fall in mild climates or as soon as the ground can be worked in spring elsewhere. Place sets with their tips barely above the soil in a rich, deep garden loam enriched with compost, and keep evenly moist. Young shallots can be pulled and used like scallions. If allowed to mature, sets multiply into clusters of small bulbs each up to an inch across. When tops begin to yellow and wither in fall, pull shallots and allow to dry in a well-ventilated area. Remove dirt and loose skins, clip stems an inch above the bulbs, and store dried bulbs for up to a year. Each set produces eight to 12 shallots.

SOYBEANS

'Prize'

HARDINESS: warm-season annual

PLANTING METHOD: direct sowing

PLANT SPACING: 3 to 6 inches

LIGHT: full sun

Small, fuzzy pods in heavy clusters on bushy, erect plants in late summer. Shell mature soybeans and use them fresh or for canning or freezing. Pods can also be allowed to dry, then shelled for long-term storage. Dry soybeans are used in cooking like other dry beans and are also sprouted for salads, stir-frying, and stuffings.

Selected varieties
'Edible Early Hakucho'—early-maturing variety 1 foot tall for fresh use in 65 days. 'Prize'—large pod clusters with two to four beans per pod, suitable for fresh use in 85 days or dried in 100 days.

Growing conditions
Dry soybeans require a long growing season, but early varieties are suitable for shelling beans in northern gardens. After all danger of frost is past and the soil temperature is 65° F or more, plant seed that has been treated with a bacterial inoculant 1 inch deep. Plant in double rows, keep well watered, and mulch to conserve moisture. In windy areas, provide supports among plants. Harvest shelling beans before seeds turn from green to yellow. Harvest dry soybeans before pods shatter and release their seeds, then thresh like other dry beans.

SPINACH

'Tyee'

HARDINESS: cool-season annual

PLANTING METHOD: direct sowing

PLANT SPACING: 2 to 3 inches

LIGHT: full sun to light shade

Smooth or crinkled leaves in upright clumps from early to late spring or in fall. Use spinach in salads or for soups, side dishes, and stuffings.

Selected varieties

'Bloomsdale Long Standing'—thick, deeply crinkled leaves on slow-to-bolt plants. 'Imperial Spring'—smooth leaves on fast-growing, upright plants resistant to mildew. 'Indian Summer'—crinkled leaves on slow-to-bolt, disease-resistant plants. 'Melody'—thick, somewhat crinkled leaves that are resistant to both mold and blight. 'Space'—slow-to-bolt hybrid with smooth, deep green leaves on upright plants that are resistant to viruses and mildew. 'Tyee' —deeply crinkled leaves on upright, extremely bolt-resistant plants tolerant of mildew. All in 35 to 40 days.

Growing conditions

Sow spinach ½ inch deep outdoors in early spring, repeating every 10 days for an extended supply of greens. Keep well watered. Plant 4 to 6 weeks before the first frost for a fall crop. In mild areas it will winter over and produce a very early spring crop. Plants go to seed as weather warms; site later sowings in the shade of taller plants. A 10-foot row produces 4 to 6 pounds of spinach.

SPINACH, MALABAR

'Alba'

HARDINESS: warm-season annual

PLANTING METHOD: transplants; direct sowing

PLANT SPACING: 12 inches

LIGHT: full sun

Mild-flavored 4- to 6-inch leaves on 6- to 10-foot vines throughout summer. Use Malabar spinach leaves fresh in salads, cooked like spinach, or as a thickening agent in soups or sauces. Use the handsome vines in an edible landscape, either trained on a trellis or fence or cascading from hanging baskets.

Selected varieties

'Alba'—thick, dark green leaves. 'Rubra'— dark green leaves with red stems and veins. Both in 70 to 100 days.

Growing conditions

Start Malabar spinach indoors 8 weeks before the last frost or sow directly in the garden in late spring to early summer after the soil has warmed to at least 65° F. Plant seeds 1 inch deep in humus-enriched soil, and keep soil moist. Thin plants to 12 inches apart and provide supports for vines to climb. Malabar spinach requires warm temperatures to grow and will not bolt in hot weather like spinach. Begin picking young leaves for salads before vines reach maturity. Pinch tips to encourage branching, and remove any flower blossoms to prolong leaf production.

SPINACH, NEW ZEALAND

New Zealand Spinach

HARDINESS: Zones 9-11; warm-season annual

PLANTING METHOD: direct sowing; transplants

PLANT SPACING: 12 inches

LIGHT: full sun

Small clumps of thick, succulent leaves with a flavor reminiscent of spinach on trailing heat-resistant vines in summer and fall. Use New Zealand spinach fresh in salads or cooked as a hot-weather substitute for spinach. The plants are an attractive addition to an edible landscape. Use them as a ground cover, train on trellises, or plant in hanging baskets.

Selected varieties

No named varieties; sold as New Zealand spinach—mildly flavored triangular leaves on pest-free plants in 55 to 70 days.

Growing conditions

Soak seeds overnight before planting ½ to 1 inch deep. In Zones 9-11, seeds should also be chilled for 1 to 2 days before sowing directly outdoors. From Zone 8 north, sow seed outdoors 2 weeks before the last frost. For transplants, sow seed in peat pots and set them directly in the garden to minimize transplant shock, after all danger of frost is past. Pick leaves when they are young, harvesting frequently to encourage continued growth. In warm climates plants often seed themselves. A 10-foot row yields about 5 pounds of New Zealand spinach.

SQUASH, SUMMER

'Early Golden Summer'

HARDINESS: warm-season annual

PLANTING METHOD: direct sowing; transplants

PLANT SPACING: 18 inches to 7 feet

LIGHT: full sun

Mild-tasting, tender-skinned fruits on sprawling vines or compact, bushy plants ideal for small gardens. Summer squashes are grouped according to their shape. The crookneck summer squashes have bumpy surfaces and narrow, curved necks. The flat, round, scallop squashes have pretty fluted edges. Straightneck varieties have narrow stem ends and bulbous blossom ends. The zucchini squashes are uniform cylinders and are often speckled and slightly ribbed.

Summer squashes, especially the scallop varieties, are delectable harvested as baby vegetables, before seeds enlarge and harden. Whether half-grown or larger, the mild flavor of summer squashes mingles well with other vegetables in salads or hors d'oeuvres, soups, or side dishes. Use hollowed-out squashes as edible casings for a variety of meat or vegetable dishes.

Selected varieties

Crookneck squashes include: 'Crescent'—vigorous, adaptable vines bearing early-maturing bright yellow fruits in 45 days. 'Early Golden Summer'—vining variety producing a large crop of bumpy yellow fruits that freeze well in 53 days. 'Sundance'—creamy yellow, miniature oval fruits on compact, bushy plants, ready in 50 days. 'Yellow Crookneck'—bumpy-skinned, deep yellow fruits with buttery flavor and firm flesh beginning in 58 days and continuing over a long season when picked often.

Scallop varieties include: 'Early White Bush', also called 'White Patty Pan'—flattened, creamy white fruits in 60 days. 'Patty Green Tint'—a very early variety with pale green fruits on bushy plants in 52 days, exceptionally tender if picked when about 2 to 3 inches across. 'Scallopini'—extremely productive compact, bushy plants that bear early-maturing small, round dark green fruits with a nutty flavor in 50 days. 'Sunburst'—compact, bushy plants with numerous flat golden yellow fruits with a green sunburst pattern at the stem and blossom ends in 48 days.

Straightneck varieties include: 'Early Prolific'—heavy yield of yellow fruits in 50 days, best picked when about 6 inches long. 'Park's Creamy Hybrid'—compact plants only 18 inches across with heavy yields of creamy yellow 6- to 8-inch fruits in 48 days and throughout the summer. 'Seneca'—high yield of cylindrical, bright yellow fruits in 51 days. 'Sundrops'—smooth-skinned golden fruits in 50 days, best harvested when 2 inches across.

Zucchini varieties include: 'Black Eagle'—very dark green, slender fruits with creamy flesh in 53 days. 'Cocozelle'—very prolific vines bearing fruits attractively striped in pale and dark green in 55 days. 'Condor'—early crop of glossy deep green fruits flecked with pale green on bushy plants in 48 days. 'Gold Rush'—bushy plants with bright yellow fruits in 50 days.

'Sunburst'

'Greyzini'—slightly tapered light green fruits in 50 days. 'Milano'—bushy plants bearing dark green fruits ready to harvest in 42 days. 'Raven'—very early crop of deep green fruits in 42 days with delicate flesh even in more mature fruits.

Growing conditions

Plant seed outdoors 1 inch deep after all danger of frost is past and when soil has

'Black Eagle'

warmed to 70° F. Thin bush types to stand 18 to 36 inches apart and vining types to stand 3 to 7 feet apart. Alternatively, plant five or six seeds in hills 3 to 4 feet apart and thin to two or three plants. Summer squash can also be started indoors 3 to 4 weeks before the last frost. For a fall crop, sow seeds 8 to 10 weeks before the first frost. To save space, train vining varieties against trellises or fences.

Pick summer squashes while still immature for fine-textured flesh with tender seeds; mature fruits become pithy and have woody seeds that must be removed before cooking. Keep vines picked clean to encourage greater fruit production. Three or four vigorous summer squash plants may produce 60 to 75 pounds of summer squash over the season.

'Cream of the Crop'

HARDINESS: warm-season annual

PLANTING METHOD: direct sowing; transplants

PLANT SPACING: 18 inches to 7 feet

LIGHT: full sun

Hard-skinned fruits with firm-textured flesh around a large seed cavity in an array of colors, shapes, and sizes. Acorn squash has heart-shaped, deeply ribbed fruits with sweet, somewhat dry orange flesh. Butternut squash fruits have bulbous blossom ends with small seed cavities and long, fleshy necks. Hubbard squash has teardrop- or pear-shaped fruits with rough, ribbed blue-gray skin and yellow-orange flesh. The light yellow flesh of spaghetti squash is composed of moist, slightly crunchy strands that can be served like pasta. Sweet-potato squashes have extremely sweet, fine-grained flesh. Turban squashes are flattened globes, sometimes with contrasting splotches of color and buttonlike protrusions at the ends of their blossoms.

Bake or parboil as a side dish; hollow out smaller fruits to use as containers for a variety of dishes; or add to soups and stews. Winter squash stores well if the skin is undamaged; the cooked flesh freezes well. The colorful varieties make attractive decorations.

Selected varieties
Acorn squash varieties include: 'Bush Table'—bushy plants only 3 feet across bearing deeply ribbed, dark green 5-inch fruits with fine-textured orange flesh in 80 days. 'Cream of the Crop'—compact, bushy vines with 2-pound cream-colored fruits with a nutty flavor in 82 days. 'Table Ace'—compact plants with a very early crop of deep green fruits in 70 days. 'Table Queen'—large vines with deep green, almost black 1½-pound fruits with yellow flesh in 80 days.

Butternut varieties include: 'Butterbush'—thin-skinned fruits with deep red-orange flesh on compact, bushy plants 4 feet in diameter in 75 days. 'Early Butternut'—very productive vines with thick-necked, light tan fruits in 85 days. 'Ponca'—long-necked tan fruits with very small seed cavities in 83 days. 'Waltham'—fruits with sweet, dry flesh in 85 days.

Hubbard varieties include: 'Blue Hubbard'—12- to 20-pound pear-shaped blue-gray fruits with rough-textured, ribbed skin and fine-grained yellow-orange flesh in 120 days. 'Golden Hubbard'—oval, 10-pound, orange-skinned fruits in 105 days. Spaghetti squash varieties include: 'Tivoli'—cream-colored fruits on compact, bushy plants in 100 days. 'Vegetable Spaghetti'—oblong 2- to 3-pound fruits in 100 days that store well.

Sweet-potato squash varieties include: 'Delicata'—short vines with slender, oblong 1½- to 2-pound cream-colored fruits marked with green stripes and filled with very sweet orange flesh in 100 days, good for baking, stuffing, and storage. 'Sweet Dumpling'—medium-length vines bearing small 4-inch, slightly flattened fruits with very sweet, tender flesh in 100 days.

Turban squash varieties include: 'But-

'Early Butternut'

tercup'—flattened, blocky, deep green 3- to 5-pound fruits with a gray button at the blossom end and with sweet, fine-textured deep orange flesh in 105 days. 'Turk's Turban'—turban-shaped, bright orange fruits streaked green and white in 100 days.

Growing conditions
Plant winter squash outdoors after the last frost, setting seeds ½ to 1 inch deep. Thin bush types to stand 18 to 36 inches apart and vining types to stand 3 to 7 feet apart. Alternatively, plant five or six seeds in hills spaced 4 feet apart; thin each hill to two or three plants. Winter squash can also be started indoors 3 to 4 weeks before the last frost date. Mulch with black plastic to

'Sweet Dumpling'

warm the soil and conserve water. Water well during early growth and fruit set. When vines are 2 to 3 feet long and fruits are just beginning to develop, pinch shoots to stimulate the production of large fruits. Harvest winter squashes when the skin hardens to the point where it is difficult to nick with a fingernail; leave several inches of stem attached to prevent the fruit from rotting during storage. Acorn, hubbard, and turban squashes bear two to four fruits per plant; spaghetti squash bears five to nine fruits per plant.

STRAWBERRIES

'Chandler'

HARDINESS: Zones 4-7

PLANTING METHOD: direct sowing; runners

PLANT SPACING: 15 inches

LIGHT: full sun

Juicy, fragrant, conical or wedge-shaped red berries in late spring, summer, or fall. Alpine strawberries form neat mounds of toothed foliage and are ideal for edging a vegetable garden or an ornamental border. Garden varieties, which send out plentiful runners that quickly spread into large mats, are categorized according to the time they set fruit. June-bearing varieties produce a single large crop of late-spring or early-summer berries. Everbearing varieties produce two crops, one in summer and another in fall; usually one crop is heavier than the other. Because they are not influenced by day length, the "day-neutral" varieties produce a continuous supply of berries from summer through autumn.

Strawberries are at their best eaten fresh from the garden and are the basis of innumerable delicious desserts including shortcakes, pies, and tortes. Excess berries can be frozen or made into jams and jellies. Plant garden strawberries in containers and hanging baskets.

Selected varieties

Alpine strawberry varieties include: 'Alexandria'—inch-long, very sweet conical berries, somewhat larger than other alpine strawberries. 'Frais de Bois'—tiny golden, red, or deep crimson fruits with a fruity perfume on very cold-hardy plants. 'Reugen Improved'—slim, elongated, very fragrant fruits continuously from early summer through fall, with the heaviest crop in autumn.

Garden varieties include: 'Big Red'—June-bearing variety with glossy conical fruits that are a deep red throughout. 'Chandler'—an everbearing variety with flat, wedge-shaped berries on plants that produce numerous runners. 'Earliglow'—June-bearing variety producing a large, very early spring crop of medium to large, deep red berries. 'Ever Red'—everbearing variety with large conical fruits that are deep red throughout. 'Ozark Beauty'—an everbearing variety with large, rich red, exceptionally sweet berries. 'Picnic'—everbearing strawberry that produces sweet, medium-sized fruits in just 4 months from seed. 'September Sweet'—disease-resistant day-neutral variety with very sweet, medium-sized berries from June through September, with the heaviest yield in fall. 'Serenata'—an everbearing variety with deep pink rather than the typical white flowers, followed by glossy red berries. 'Sparkle'—a single, large, late-summer crop of firm, flavorful berries on hardy plants that are resistant to disease. 'Sure Crop'—June-bearing, drought-tolerant, disease-resistant variety with a reliably heavy yield of very large berries. 'Tribute'—day-neutral variety steadily producing plump, slightly acidic fruits with excellent flavor on disease-resistant plants. 'Tristar'—day-neutral variety with firm, sweet red berries on wilt- and mildew-resistant plants; ideal for hanging baskets.

'Sparkle'

Growing conditions

Select virus-free strawberry plants and set them out in spring or fall in a loose, fertile soil enriched with organic matter. Plant in raised beds where soils are heavy or clayey. Set bare-rooted stock in the ground with the soil line where the roots and crown meet; plants set with their crowns below the soil line will rot, and those set too shallow will die because their roots are exposed. Mulch plants to control weeds and reduce rot. Alpine strawberries and some garden strawberries can also be started from seed sown indoors 2 to 3 months before the last frost, then planted outdoors.

Grow strawberries in mats or hills. For mats, set plants out 15 inches apart in rows 3 to 4 feet apart. Allow the runners to fill the area but keep a pathway open between

'Sure Crop'

rows for access. For hills, set plants 1 foot apart in double or triple rows spaced 12 inches apart; keep a pathway between each group of rows. Cut off all runners produced the first summer.

Remove old plants and renew strawberry beds when berry production slows. Everbearing varieties usually need renewing every year or every other year. June-bearing strawberries may remain productive for as long as 5 years.

SUNFLOWER

'Mammoth Russian'

HARDINESS: warm-season annual

PLANTING METHOD: direct sowing

PLANT SPACING: 18 inches

LIGHT: full sun

Tasty, oil- and protein-rich seeds from late summer to fall in heavy seed heads that follow attractive white or yellow flowers on tall stalks. Eat raw or roasted seeds as a snack, or add them to salads and breads.

Selected varieties
'Aztec Gold'—early-maturing variety with seed heads up to 11 inches across on 6-foot plants in 68 days. 'Grey Stripe', also called 'Giant Grey Stripe'—20-inch seed heads filled with large, thin-shelled seeds on 8- to 12-foot stalks in 85 days. 'Mammoth'— seed heads crammed with thin-shelled, meaty seeds on 6- to 12-foot stalks in 80 days. 'Mammoth Russian'—disease-resist- ant 8- to 12-foot plants with 12-inch heads filled with large, richly flavored, striped seeds in 80 days.

Growing conditions
Plant seeds outdoors after all danger of frost is past, setting them ½ inch deep and thinning them to 18 inches apart. Tall stalks may need staking. Cover seed heads with cheesecloth to protect ripening seeds from birds and animals. Harvest when the back of the head dries or frost has killed foliage. Cut with 1 foot of the stalk at- tached and hang or lay on newspaper to finish drying in a well-ventilated area. Store seeds in airtight containers.

SWEET POTATOES

'Centennial'

HARDINESS: warm-season annual

PLANTING METHOD: plants

PLANT SPACING: 12 inches

LIGHT: full sun

Tapered tubers with sweet, moist, highly nutritious orange or red-orange flesh in fall. Enjoy baked or parboiled for side dishes, casseroles, and pies.

Selected varieties
'Centennial'—fast-maturing variety with baby tubers ready to harvest in 90 to 100 days. 'Georgia Jet'—large red-skinned potatoes in 90 to 100 days. 'Jewell'—pro- lific variety with coppery red skins and fine-textured flesh in 100 days. 'Var- daman'—potatoes with deep orange flesh on compact, bushy plants in 100 days.

Growing conditions
Sweet potatoes are heat- and drought-re- sistant and need to grow where night tem- peratures will not drop below 60° F. Set certified virus-free plants out after all dan- ger of frost is past and the soil is warm. Plant them in mounds of loose soil 6 to 10 inches high. Harvest sweet potatoes when vines yellow in fall. If an unseasonable frost is predicted before harvest, protect plants with floating row covers. Tubers must be harvested immediately if plants are nipped by frost. Cure tubers in a warm, humid, well-ventilated area for 8 to 10 days, then store at 55° to 60° F. A 10-foot row yields about 10 pounds of tubers.

TAMPALA

Tampala

HARDINESS: hot-season annual

PLANTING METHOD: direct sowing

PLANT SPACING: 6 inches

LIGHT: full sun

Tangy red- or green-leaved vegetable that resembles spinach but thrives in hot weather and can be sown successfully for harvesting all summer. Use tender young tampala leaves in salads, soups, and side dishes, either alone or combined with oth- er greens.

Selected varieties
No named varieties; sold only as tampala. Heart-shaped 4-inch leaves ready to cut in 40 to 55 days on drought-tolerant, bushy plants.

Growing conditions
Sow tampala seeds ¼ inch deep after all danger of frost is past in a well-drained garden soil, working a balanced 5-10-5 organic fertilizer into the soil before plant- ing. Tampala requires warm soil and high temperatures for best growth. When seed- lings are 4 inches tall, thin to stand 6 inch- es apart; use thinnings in salads and soups. When plants reach 6 to 8 inches in height, harvest by cutting the entire plant at the soil line. For a continuous harvest of young, tender leaves, make successive sow- ings every 2 weeks until a month before the first frost date.

TOMATILLOES

Tomatillo

HARDINESS: warm-season annual

PLANTING METHOD: transplants

PLANT SPACING: 18 to 24 inches

LIGHT: full sun

Also called Mexican ground cherries. Round fruits encased in thin, papery husks on broad, bushy plants up to 4 feet tall. Tomatilloes are piquant when picked green and tangy-sweet when they ripen and turn yellow. A staple in Mexican cuisine, tomatilloes are used fresh, depending on their degree of ripeness, for savory sauces and dishes such as salsa verde or for dessert toppings, jams, and preserves. Cooked tomatilloes freeze well.

Selected varieties

'Goldie', also called 'Golden'—¾-inch berries ripening in 75 days. 'Toma Verde'—firm-textured, 1½-inch, pale green sweet-sour berries in 60 to 80 days.

Growing conditions

Start tomatillo seeds indoors 3 to 6 weeks before the last frost, setting seeds ½ inch deep in peat pots. Transplant seedlings in their peat pots to the garden after the soil has warmed and all danger of frost is past, spacing them 18 to 24 inches apart. For firm, tart fruits, harvest when the husks turn from green to tan. For sweet, ripe fruits, wait until the fruits drop off the plant. Tomatilloes will keep well in the refrigerator.

TOMATOES

'Better Boy'

HARDINESS: warm-season annual

PLANTING METHOD: transplants; direct sowing

PLANT SPACING: 3 to 4 feet

LIGHT: full sun

Juicy, meaty, red, yellow, pink, purple, or white fruits ranging from bite-sized miniatures to 2-pounders. All tomato varieties belong to one of two groups, based on the type of vine they have. The indeterminate tomatoes have tall, lanky vines and bear fruit over a long period, while the determinate tomatoes tend to be compact and bushy and to produce the season's crop all at once. Varieties mature at markedly different times. Early tomatoes set fruit in about 55 to 65 days from the time seedlings started indoors are set out in the garden, or a total of 85 to 90 days from seed; midseason tomatoes set fruit in about 65 to 75 days from the transplanting date, or 95 to 105 days from seed; and late-season tomatoes begin fruiting in 80 to 100 days after the transplanting date, or 110 to 130 days from seed.

The largest fruits are the enormous beefsteak varieties, which have a high proportion of seeds and juice to flesh. Large and medium-sized slicing tomatoes also have a high proportion of juice to pulp. Slice or chop them fresh for use in salads, sandwiches, and garnishes; stuff them, or bake, simmer, or sauté them for main or side dishes. The paste tomatoes are smaller and have a higher proportion of flesh to

seeds and juice. Ideal for cooked relishes, salsa, and sauces, they can be dried for long-term storage. Small-fruited tomato varieties have grapelike clusters of tiny sweet fruits that are good raw or cooked.

Selected varieties

Large-fruited varieties include: 'Ace 55'—broad, smooth fruits in 75 days on disease-resistant determinate vines. 'Beefmaster'—extremely large, somewhat flattened fruits in midseason on vigorous, disease-resistant indeterminate vines in 80 days. 'Beefsteak', also called 'Crimson Cushion' or 'Red Ponderosa'—meaty, thick-ribbed tomatoes weighing 2 pounds or more on indeterminate vines in 90 days. 'Better Boy'—round fruits that weigh up to a pound on strong, disease-resistant indeterminate vines in 72 days. 'Big Boy'—firm, thick-walled, aromatic fruits weighing a pound or more on indeterminate vines in 78 days. 'Big Early'—½- to 1-pound fruits with thick walls on indeterminate vines in 62 days. 'Big Girl'—large, crack-resistant fruit weighing a pound or more on disease-resistant indeterminate vines in 78 days. 'Burpee's VF'—thick-walled, crack-

'Early Girl'

resistant medium-sized fruits on indeterminate vines in 72 days. 'Celebrity'—crack-resistant ½-pound fruits on compact disease-resistant determinate vines in 75 days. 'Delicious'—record-setting fruits weighing up to 3 pounds or more each with excellent flavor on indeterminate vines in 77 days. 'Early Cascade'—large clusters of early-ripening 1½- to 2-inch heart-shaped tomatoes on disease-resistant indeterminate vines in 55 days. 'Early

'Quick Pic'

Girl'—offers clusters of early-ripening small, meaty, deep red fruits on indeterminate vines in 54 days. 'Fantastic'—smooth 3- to 5-inch tomatoes in 70 days on indeterminate vines. 'First Lady'—flavorful, early-ripening 4- to 6-ounce fruits on compact, indeterminate vines in 60 days. 'Heatwave'—medium-sized fruits on compact, disease-resistant determinate vines that will set fruit at temperatures above 90° F in 68 days. 'Heinz 1350'—crack-resistant 6-ounce fruits ideal for canning on determinate vines in 75 days. 'Heinz 1439'—meaty 6-ounce fruits good for sauces and canning on compact determinate vines in 72 days. 'Jubilee'—mild-flavored medium-sized yellow fruits on disease-resistant indeterminate vines in 80 days. 'Lady Luck'—large meaty fruits weighing up to a pound on adaptable, disease-resistant indeterminate vines in 78 days. 'Long-Keeper'—light red-orange fruits on indeterminate vines in 78 days; stores well for up to 12 weeks or more at 60° to 70° F. 'Marglobe Improved'—fruits ideal for canning on determinate vines in 75 days. 'Mountain Delight'—medium-sized fruits in clusters of three or four on disease-resistant determinate vines in 75 days. 'Northern Exposure'—half-pound flavorful fruits on compact semideterminate vines bred for cool seasons in 67 days. 'Oregon Spring'—early 4-inch tomatoes on disease-resistant, somewhat cold-tolerant determinate vines in 58 days. 'Patio'—medium to large firm, flavorful fruits on compact dwarf determinate vines suited for container growing in 60 days. 'Pilgrim'—small clusters of 7-ounce fruits on determinate vines in 65 days. 'President'—

large, smooth red fruits on disease-resistant determinate vines in 68 days. 'Quick Pic'—early variety with medium-sized fruits on indeterminate vines starting in 68 days. 'Spring Giant'—large fruits with thick walls and small cores on determinate vines adaptable to many climate conditions in 65 days. 'Super Bush'—meaty fruits starting in 85 days and continuing over a long season on bushy determinate plants 38 inches tall and wide that require no pruning, staking, or caging and are ideal for containers and small gardens. 'Wonder Boy'—meaty 8-ounce fruits on vigorous indeterminate vines in 80 days.

Small-fruited varieties include: 'Florida Basket'—1- to 2-inch fruits in 70 days on very short determinate vines about 6 inches long, ideal for hanging baskets. 'Gardener's Delight', also called 'Sugar Lump' —clusters of up to a dozen bite-sized, sweet bright red fruits ripening early on indeterminate vines in 65 days. 'Red Cherry Large'—clusters of sweet, deep red 1½-inch round fruits ripening in midseason on vigorously branching indeterminate vines good for hanging baskets in 75 days. 'Sun Gold'—early apricot-colored fruits in grapelike clusters of up to 20 fruits on vigorous, disease-resistant indeterminate vines in 60 days. 'Sweet Million'—very sweet, crack-resistant 1- to 1¼-inch fruits in clusters on highly disease-resistant vines starting in 60 days and continuing for a long period. 'Sweet 100'—large elongated clusters of cherry-sized sweet tomatoes throughout the summer on indeterminate vines in 60 days. 'Tiny Tim'—very early variety with bite-sized tomatoes on compact 15-inch determinate vines in 45 days.

'Gardener's Delight'

'Toy Boy'—early crop of 1½-inch fruits on 14-inch determinate vines in 58 days.

Paste tomato varieties include: 'Italian Gold'—firm, thick-walled golden-orange fruits on determinate vines in 82 days. 'La Roma'—very large crop of meaty 3- to 4-ounce fruits ideal for canning on determinate vines in 62 days. 'La Rossa'—pear-shaped 3½-inch fruits with thick flesh and thin skins in 75 days, ideal for fresh use as well as for cooking. 'Mama Mia'—heavy crop of small pear-shaped fruits on determinate disease-resistant vines in 62 days. 'Roma VF'—heavy crop of meaty, medium-sized, pear-shaped fruits on disease-resistant determinate vines in 75 days. 'San Marzano'—large crop of elongated, pear-

'Sweet Million'

shaped 3½-inch tomatoes in 80 days on indeterminate vines. 'Viva Italia'—sweet, meaty 3-ounce fruits that can be stored for 2 to 3 weeks, on vigorous, heat-tolerant, disease-resistant vines in 80 days.

Yellow tomato varieties include: 'Golden Boy'—large, mildly flavored golden yellow fruits on indeterminate vines in 80 days. 'Husky Gold'—half-pound deep yellow fruits on compact 4½-foot disease-resistant indeterminate vines that require no pinching or pruning in 70 days. 'Lemon Boy'—lemon yellow, low-acid 6- to 7-ounce fruits on disease-resistant indeterminate vines in 72 days. 'Yellow Canary'—clusters of bite-sized golden fruits on compact branching determinate vines only 6 inches long, ideal for containers and hanging baskets, in 63 days. 'Yellow Pear'—long clusters of tiny pear-shaped yellow fruits 2 inches long and an inch across, ideal for salads and relishes, on bushy, indeterminate vines good for container culture in 112 days.

White tomato varieties include: 'White Wonder'—medium-sized, 6- to 8-ounce, very low-acid fruits with creamy white flesh and skin on indeterminate vines in 115 days.

'Sweet 100'

Growing conditions

Tomatoes can be directly sown when the soil temperature reaches 50° F or more, but they do best when started indoors 4 to 6 weeks before the last frost and transplanted into compost-enriched garden loam about a week after the last frost, when soil has warmed. Set transplants deeply, burying the lower portion of the stem to stimulate it to form new roots. Cover with plant caps or cloches if frost threatens. Tomatoes set fruit best when nighttime temperatures are 76° F or higher and daytime temperatures are below 90° F. If nighttime temperatures drop below 50° F or daytime temperatures rise above 90° F, vines will not set fruit.

Plant bushy determinate varieties 24 inches apart. Plant indeterminate varieties that will be allowed to sprawl on the ground 4 feet apart. Allow 18 inches between plants that will be staked and 2½ to 3 feet between plants that will be supported with cages. Indeterminate vines that sprawl tend to produce more but smaller fruits, while those that are supported produce larger but fewer fruits.

Fertilize tomato plants when they are set out, and again when the fruits begin to set, with a balanced 5-10-10 organic fertilizer or manure tea. Foliar sprays of fish emulsion increase yields. Periods of wet or dry weather can stunt growth and cause blossom end rot. Mulch to maintain constant moisture levels, to suppress weeds, and to help keep the fruits of sprawling vines clean and free of decay. If you grow indeterminate tomatoes in cages or tied to stakes, you may want to pinch off the suckers that grow at the junction of stems and side branches. Removing the suckers hastens fruiting, encourages sturdier vines, and forces more uniform ripening of larger fruits.

Use floating row covers to protect young plants from flea beetles. Use Bt to ward off tomato hornworms. Rotate tomato planting sites every 3 years to avoid nematode damage; when planning crop rotation, group tomatoes with eggplant, peppers, and potatoes, and follow them with a legume such as peas or beans. To prevent disease problems, choose disease-resistant varieties, prune lower branches to increase air circulation, and remove and destroy all garden debris at the end of the season.

Harvest tomatoes when they are fully ripe if the temperature is under 90° F. When the temperature is higher, pick tomatoes just before they reach full ripeness and finish the ripening process indoors at temperatures of 70° F or more. Allow tomatoes to ripen fully before refrigerating for short-term storage. Dry or can tomatoes or cook and freeze them for long-term storage; because of their high water content, tomatoes become mushy if frozen fresh. Save the seed of open-pollinated varieties for planting the following season. Hybrid varieties do not breed true.

'Lemon Boy'

TURNIP

'Purple-Top White Globe'

HARDINESS: cool-season annual

PLANTING METHOD: direct sowing

PLANT SPACING: 3 to 5 inches

LIGHT: full sun

Rumpled leaves and globe-shaped roots with a mild, sweet flavor in spring and fall. Enjoy turnip roots raw, cooked in side dishes, or cubed in stews. Cook the greens as you would spinach or collards.

Selected varieties

'Purple-Top White Globe'—3- to 4-inch white globes with purple shoulders, fine-textured flesh, and dark green leaves in 55 days. 'Royal Crown'—early variety with deep purple shoulders and deep green tops in 52 days. 'Tokyo Cross'—disease-resistant variety with white 2- to 6-inch roots and glossy green tops in 40 days.

Growing conditions

For a late-spring crop, sow seed ¼ to ½ inch deep in spring as soon as the ground can be worked. Sow again in late summer for a fall crop. Frost increases sweetness. Keep turnips constantly moist but not soggy. Use floating row covers or parasitic wasps to prevent damage from pests. To minimize soil-borne diseases, do not plant turnips where other brassicas have grown for at least 3 years. For tender turnip greens, pick when they are small, no more than 12 inches in height. Roots can be harvested when they are an inch or more in diameter. A 10-foot row of turnips yields 30 to 40 pounds.

Trees and Shrubs

WHAT WOULD A GARDEN BE WITHOUT TREES AND shrubs? Architectural linchpins, they are what give shape to a landscape and hold an entire planting scheme together. But that's not all. These workhorses also create shade, provide backdrops, accent focal points, block the wind, and screen out unwanted views. They provide nesting sites for birds and sheltered places for other plants. And they add four-season beauty that often lasts for generations.

Selecting the right shrubs and trees for your garden is one of the most important landscaping decisions you will make. To help you make the right choices, presented here is a sampling of trees and shrubs to suit a wide range of conditions and landscape designs. Because these plants will most likely be permanent features, be sure to consider their eventual size as you make your final selections.

Abelia (a-BEE-li-a)

ABELIA

Abelia x 'Edward Goucher'

HARDINESS: Zones 6-10

PLANT TYPE: shrub

HEIGHT: 3 to 6 feet

INTEREST: form, flowers, foliage

SOIL: moist, well-drained, acid

LIGHT: partial shade to full sun

Abelia's fountainlike sprays of glimmering foliage lend airy grace and fine texture to borders and hedges. Tiny bell-shaped or tubular flowers bloom from early summer to frost. The small, pointed, richly green leaves are bronze when young and often turn bronze or bronzy purple again in fall. In the northern parts of its range, abelia is semievergreen.

Selected species and varieties
A. x *grandiflora* (glossy abelia)—rounded shrub 3 to 6 feet high (to 8 feet in the South) and equally wide, with small pinkish white flowers. *A.* x 'Edward Goucher', the result of a cross between *A.* x *grandiflora* and *A. schumannii*, forms a 4- to 5-foot-tall shrub with equal spread bearing pinkish lavender flowers. *A. schumannii*—mauve-pink flowers amid downy, blunt-pointed leaves; hardy to Zone 7.

Growing conditions and maintenance
Abelia flowers best when provided with at least a half-day of sunlight each day. It tolerates less-than-ideal soil. Prune in late winter or early spring; flowers are borne on new growth.

Abies (AY-beez)

FIR

Abies concolor

HARDINESS: Zones 3-7

PLANT TYPE: tree

HEIGHT: 30 to 50 feet or more

INTEREST: form, foliage

SOIL: moist to dry, well-drained

LIGHT: full sun

White fir develops into a grand evergreen pyramid ideal as a specimen, screen, or vertical accent. The upper branches are upright in habit; the middle and lower, horizontal to descending. The trees bear flat, aromatic needles that have blunt tips and a glaucous coating. Greenish or purplish cones, up to 6 inches long, mature to a brown hue and fall apart when ripe.

Selected species and varieties
A. concolor (white fir, Colorado fir)—30 to 50 feet high (but reaching 100 feet under ideal conditions) by 15 to 30 feet wide, having a central trunk with whorled branches and producing bluish green, grayish green, or silvery blue needles up to 2½ inches long; 'Compacta' is a densely branched dwarf usually 3 feet high, with 1½-inch blue needles, acquiring an attractively irregular form as it matures.

Growing conditions and maintenance
Although white firs accept dry, rocky soils, they grow better in deep, sandy or gravelly loams. They withstand drought, heat, cold, and air pollution better than other firs. They tolerate light shade but fare best in full sun. Mulch well with shredded bark, woodchips, or leaves.

Acacia (a-KAY-sha)

ACACIA, WATTLE

Acacia dealbata

HARDINESS: Zones 9-10

PLANT TYPE: tree

HEIGHT: 20 to 60 feet

INTEREST: foliage, flowers, fragrance

SOIL: well-drained to dry

LIGHT: full sun

Acacias are grown in Southern California and Arizona, where they provide some of the earliest flowers of the season. Each flower is typically composed of a mass of stamens that form a dense cluster. Though not long-lived, these natives of Australia are remarkably fast growers and may reach 30 feet in only 5 years.

Selected species and varieties
A. baileyana (cootamundra wattle)—20 to 40 feet tall, with a wide canopy of fernlike leaves and tiny yellow flowers in winter; Zone 10. *A. dealbata* (silver wattle)—30 to 60 feet tall, with silvery green leaves, silvery bark, and extremely fragrant yellow flowers; less drought tolerant than cootamundra wattle.

Growing conditions and maintenance
Acacias require warm temperatures and, once established, tolerate both drought and seaside conditions. Though generally trouble-free, their rapid growth results in weak wood that is subject to wind damage. Plant container-grown specimens and stake them until roots are well established. Water infrequently and thoroughly to encourage deep roots. Thin plants to reduce wind damage.

Acanthopanax (a-kan-tho-PAN-aks)

FIVE-LEAF ARALIA

Acanthopanax sieboldianus 'Variegatus'

HARDINESS: Zones 4-8

PLANT TYPE: deciduous shrub

HEIGHT: 8 to 10 feet

INTEREST: foliage

SOIL: well-drained

LIGHT: full sun to full shade

Acanthopanax is an excellent plant for difficult sites. The arching, wide-spreading stems form a broad, rounded shrub, but it can be sheared to produce a dense hedge. Its bright green compound leaves appear in early spring and persist into fall. Slender prickles along the stems make acanthopanax an effective barrier.

Selected species and varieties
A. sieboldianus—an erect shrub with arching branches, five to seven leaflets per leaf, and light brown stems with slender prickles; 'Variegatus' stands 6 to 8 feet tall and has leaves with creamy white margins.

Growing conditions and maintenance
Acanthopanax is easy to transplant and adapts to nearly every site. It tolerates a wide range of soil types, from acid to alkaline and from sandy to clay, and it stands up well to air pollution and drought. As a hedge, it can be heavily pruned or sheared to encourage compact growth and maintain the desired height. In an informal, mixed planting, little pruning is necessary.

Acer (AY-ser)

MAPLE

Acer griseum

HARDINESS: Zones 2-9

PLANT TYPE: shrub or tree

HEIGHT: 6 to 75 feet

INTEREST: foliage, form, fruit

SOIL: moist, well-drained

LIGHT: full sun to partial shade

The genus *Acer* includes a diverse group of deciduous plants ranging from towering trees with brilliant fall foliage to small, picturesque specimens ideal as centerpieces for ornamental beds. The mid-size maples included here are good specimen or patio trees. Flowers are usually inconspicuous, followed by winged seeds.

Selected species and varieties
A. ginnala (Amur maple, fire maple)—15 to 25 feet tall, usually branched close to the ground, with a canopy wider than its height, bearing serrated medium to dark green three-lobed leaves 1½ to 3 inches long that unfurl early in spring along with small, fragrant, yellowish white flower panicles, followed by winged fruits, often red, that persist to late fall; Zones 2-8. *A. griseum* (paperbark maple)—oval- to round-crowned tree 20 to 30 feet tall with up to an equal spread, clad in exfoliating reddish brown bark and producing dark green to blue-green leaves with three leaflets that may turn red in fall; Zones 4-8. *A. macrophyllum* (bigleaf maple, Oregon maple)—three- to five-lobed leaves 8 to 12 inches wide that turn yellow to orange in fall on a wide-crowned, 45- to 75-foot-tall

tree with fragrant greenish yellow flowers in nodding clusters that appear with the leaves in spring; hardy to Zone 5. *A. nigrum* [also classified as *A. saccharum* ssp. *nigrum*] (black maple)—a 60- to 75-foot-tall tree closely related to the sugar maple with drooping lobed leaves 3 to 6 inches wide that turn a brilliant yellow in fall; Zones 4-8. *A. palmatum* (Japanese maple)—slow-growing tree or multistemmed shrub 15 to 25 feet tall and at least as wide, with deeply cut leaves having five, seven, or nine lobes, and young stems that are reddish purple to green and become gray with age, Zones 5-8; 'Bloodgood' grows upright to 15 to 20 feet with maroon or reddish purple leaves that turn scarlet in fall, blackish red bark, and attractive red fruit; 'Dissectum' (threadleaf Japanese maple) is a small, pendulous, lacy shrub usually 6 to 8 feet tall, with drooping green-barked branches that bear very finely divided pale green leaves with up to 11 lobes that turn yellow in fall; 'Dissectum

Acer palmatum 'Dissectum'

Atropurpureum' has a moundlike appearance similar to 'Dissectum', with lacy purple-red new leaves that fade to green or purple-green and turn crimson or burnt orange in fall, as well as tortuous branching that is most apparent in winter. *A. rubrum* (red maple, scarlet maple, Canadian maple)—a medium- to fast-growing tree to 60 feet tall, and sometimes much taller, with ascending branches forming an irregular, oval to rounded crown 20 feet wide and with reddish twigs bearing red 1-inch flowers in early spring followed by red winged seeds, then small, shiny, three- to five-lobed green leaves yielding a dazzling fall color that is unreliable in the species but consistent among cultivars; 'Autumn Blaze' [*A. x freemanii*] is a fast-growing cultivar reaching 50 feet tall by 40 feet wide exhibiting superb orange-red fall color on its dense, oval to rounded crown, hardy to Zone 4; 'October Glory' has a round crown and vivid bright orange to red foliage in midfall, holding late into the season and coloring well in the South. *A. saccharum* (sugar maple, rock maple)—60 to 75 feet tall with a spread about two-thirds the height in a symmetrical crown bearing greenish yellow flowers in spring and three- or five-lobed medium to dark green leaves that turn yellow, burnt orange, or reddish in fall; Zones 3-8.

Growing conditions and maintenance
Most maples can withstand occasional drought; red maples grow naturally in wet soil. Bigleaf maples prefer a cool, moist climate like that of their native Pacific Northwest. Sugar and red maples prefer slight acidity but tolerate other soil types. *A. rubrum* 'Autumn Blaze' is said to be slightly more drought tolerant than true red maple cultivars. Amur and paperbark maples tolerate a wide range of acid and alkaline soils. Japanese maples need highly organic loam; amend the soil with peat moss or leaf mold before planting. The finely divided foliage of threadleaf maples often shows leaf burn in hot, dry climates; find a spot sheltered from strong winds, late spring frosts, and searing sun. Amur and sugar maples tolerate some shade. Large maples have extensive, fibrous root systems, making it difficult to sustain significant plantings beneath them.

Acer rubrum 'October Glory'

Aesculus (ES-kew-lus)

BUCKEYE

Aesculus glabra

HARDINESS: Zones 3-7

PLANT TYPE: tree

HEIGHT: 20 to 40 feet

INTEREST: foliage, form, buds

SOIL: moist, well-drained, slightly acid

LIGHT: full sun to partial shade

One of the first trees to leaf out in spring, the buckeye (also called horse chestnut) is a low-branched, round-topped tree with deep green five-fingered compound leaves that turn a vibrant orange in fall. Its large greenish yellow spring flowers are usually lost amid the foliage. The fruit is a brown seed capsule with a prickly cover, considered by some to be a good-luck charm. Buckeyes cast deep shade, discouraging grass below. Plant them in a naturalized area or a mulched bed where leaf, flower, and fruit litter will not be a nuisance. The seeds are poisonous.

Selected species and varieties
A. glabra (Ohio buckeye, fetid buckeye)—20 to 40 feet tall with an equal spread, bearing medium to dark green leaflets 3 to 6 inches long that open bright green, followed by flower panicles up to 7 inches long, and later 1- to 2-inch oval fruit.

Growing conditions and maintenance
A native of rich bottomlands and riverbanks, the Ohio buckeye prefers deep loam. Mulch well to conserve moisture; dry soil causes leaf scorch. Prune in the early spring.

Agonis (a-GO-nis)

PEPPERMINT TREE

Agonis flexuosa

HARDINESS: Zone 10

PLANT TYPE: evergreen tree

HEIGHT: 25 to 35 feet

INTEREST: foliage, bark, flowers

SOIL: well-drained to dry

LIGHT: full sun to partial shade

The peppermint tree is a fast-growing evergreen for warm climates. Its leaves are willowlike and are borne on graceful, arching branches. It is a good choice for a wide-spreading lawn tree, street tree, or large container plant.

Selected species and varieties
A. flexuosa—to 35 feet, with an equal spread of deep green leaves that grow 3 to 6 inches long and are aromatic when crushed; small white, fragrant flowers appear in early summer, followed by woody capsules; has attractive reddish brown, vertically fissured bark.

Growing conditions and maintenance
The peppermint tree requires a nearly frost-free location; it will die back to the ground if temperatures fall below 25° F. It thrives in warm coastal locations and is tolerant of most soil types and moisture conditions.

Amelanchier (am-el-ANG-kee-er)

SERVICEBERRY

Amelanchier alnifolia

HARDINESS: Zones 4-9

PLANT TYPE: large shrub or tree

HEIGHT: 15 to 40 feet

INTEREST: foliage, flowers, fruit, bark

SOIL: moist, well-drained, acid

LIGHT: full sun to partial shade

Serviceberry provides year-round landscape interest. White flower clusters appear in early spring; leaves emerge purplish gray and change to deep green in summer and to shades of yellow to apricot and red in fall. The smooth gray bark is attractive all winter.

Selected species and varieties
A. arborea—30 to 40 feet in the wild, rarely above 20 feet in cultivation; leaves grow 1 to 3 inches long, flowers form 2- to 4-inch pendulous clusters, and fruit is blueberry-like and attracts birds; it is useful in naturalized areas and woodland gardens as well as mixed-shrub borders.

Growing conditions and maintenance
Serviceberry is often found growing wild beside stream banks, at the edge of woodlands, or along fence rows. In the garden, it tolerates a broad range of moisture conditions. Pruning is generally not necessary except to remove damaged wood.

Arbutus (ar-BEW-tus)

STRAWBERRY TREE

Arbutus unedo

HARDINESS: Zones 7-9

PLANT TYPE: large shrub or small tree

HEIGHT: 8 to 12 feet

INTEREST: foliage, bark, flowers, fruit

SOIL: well-drained, acid

LIGHT: full sun to partial shade

The strawberry tree provides interest in both southern and West Coast gardens throughout the year. The leaves are evergreen, the bark is deep reddish brown and exfoliates, and the branches become attractively gnarled with age. Small urn-shaped flowers grow in 2-inch clusters in the fall, and the orange-red berrylike fruit ripens the following season.

Selected species and varieties
A. unedo 'Compacta'—a slow-growing dwarf variety that eventually reaches 8 to 12 feet in height, it produces flowers, fruit, and dark green leaves almost continuously; useful as a hedge, as a specimen, or in a mixed-shrub border.

Growing conditions and maintenance
Plant where leaves will be protected from drying winds. The strawberry tree tolerates a wide range of soil conditions as long as drainage is good. It requires watering only during periods of drought. It is also tolerant of seaside conditions.

Arctostaphylos (ark-toh-STAF-i-los)

BEARBERRY

Arctostaphylos densiflora

HARDINESS: Zones 2-10

PLANT TYPE: ground cover or shrub

HEIGHT: 6 inches to 8 feet

INTEREST: foliage, flowers, fruit, bark

SOIL: poor, sandy, acid

LIGHT: full sun to partial shade

Bearberry is an evergreen bearing tiny urn-shaped, spring-blooming flowers.

Selected species and varieties
A. uva-ursi—a ground cover that grows 6 to 12 inches high, with trailing stems up to 15 feet long and leathery, dark green leaves; it produces white flowers with a pink blush and, in late summer, bright red fruit that attracts birds; Zones 2-7. *A. densiflora*—grows 4 to 6 feet tall and equally as wide, with mahogany red bark and pink or white flowers in early spring; it is useful in a mixed-shrub border or as a specimen; Zones 7-10.

Growing conditions and maintenance
Both species require well-drained soil. They are drought resistant, though periodic deep watering is suggested during droughts. They are difficult to transplant except from containers. *A. uva-ursi* requires no pruning. *A. densiflora* is primarily grown on the West Coast. It may be pruned to reveal attractive bark and a branching habit.

ARDISIA

Ardisia crenata

HARDINESS: Zones 7-10

PLANT TYPE: small shrub or ground cover

HEIGHT: 8 inches to 6 feet

INTEREST: foliage, flowers, fruit

SOIL: moist, well-drained, acid, fertile

LIGHT: bright full shade

A lovely low evergreen for shady areas, ardisia has glossy dark green serrated leaves that are tapered at both ends and clustered at the ends of stems. Small star-shaped flowers are borne in racemes in summer, followed by berries that persist into winter.

Selected species and varieties
A. crenata (Christmas berry, coralberry, spiceberry)—shrublike growth to 6 feet tall with lustrous foliage and bright red berries; Zones 7-10. *A. japonica* (marlberry)—mat-forming ground cover, 8 to 12 inches tall bearing lustrous dark green toothed leaves, 1½ to 3½ inches long, that are pink when new, white flowers in summer and red berries in the fall; variably hardy to Zone 5 but best in Zones 7-9; 'Hakuokan' is one of the largest cultivars and has broad, white leaf margins; 'Ito Fukurin', light, silvery green leaves thinly edged in white; 'Nishiki', rosy pink leaf margins that turn yellow with age.

Growing conditions and maintenance
Amend soil with leaf mold, peat moss, or compost. Provide protection from harsh winter winds. Variegated forms are less cold hardy than the green ones.

CHOKEBERRY

Aronia melanocarpa

HARDINESS: Zones 4-9

PLANT TYPE: shrub

HEIGHT: 3 to 10 feet

INTEREST: fruit, foliage, flowers

SOIL: well-drained

LIGHT: full sun to partial shade

Chokeberry produces a profusion of tiny white flowers that develop into shiny black or red berries in hanging clusters that persist into winter. Glossy, dark green oval leaves turn bright scarlet in the fall. Chokeberry's upright colonies look best when massed.

Selected species and varieties
A. arbutifolia 'Brilliantissima'—6 to 10 feet tall and 3 to 5 feet wide with an upright habit and 1- to 1½-inch clusters of white to reddish spring flowers, followed by abundant clusters of dark red ¼-inch berries in fall. *A. melanocarpa* (black chokeberry)—3 to 5 feet tall with similar spread, white spring flowers followed by purplish black berries; suckers profusely.

Growing conditions and maintenance
Easy to transplant and tolerant of almost any soil, it flowers and fruits more heavily and produces better fall color in full sun than in shade. Base suckers may become a nuisance. Propagate by digging up suckers, taking softwood cuttings, or layering.

AUCUBA

Aucuba japonica 'Picturata'

HARDINESS: Zones 7-10

PLANT TYPE: shrub

HEIGHT: 6 to 10 feet

INTEREST: leaves, berries

SOIL: moist, well-drained

LIGHT: partial shade to shade

Aucuba's glossy, evergreen, pointed leaves line tidy clumps of stems. The plant softens the landscape beneath tall trees, provides a transition between heavily wooded areas and garden borders, and can be massed as a screen.

Selected species and varieties
A. japonica (spotted laurel)—erect or arching 6- to 10-foot-tall stems with open clusters of purple spring-blooming flowers on male plants, followed by ½-inch red fruits on female plants in fall through winter; 'Variegata' (gold dust plant) has yellow-speckled leaves; 'Nana' grows 3 to 5 feet tall with abundant, prominent berries; 'Picturata' has yellow markings on each leaf surrounded by flecks of yellow.

Growing conditions and maintenance
Aucuba grows best in locations with year-round shade and soil enriched with organic matter. Young leaves blacken if exposed to strong sun. The shrubs tolerate urban pollution well. Pollination from a male bush nearby is essential for female shrubs to set berries.

Berberis (BER-ber-is)

BARBERRY

Berberis x gladwynensis 'William Penn'

HARDINESS: Zones 4-8

PLANT TYPE: shrub

HEIGHT: 18 inches to 8 feet

INTEREST: foliage, fruit

SOIL: well-drained

LIGHT: full sun to light shade

Barberries are dense, somewhat stiff-limbed shrubs that produce bright yellow flowers in spring and red, blue, or black fruit. All are more or less thorny, with spines occurring along their stems, and some leaves also have spiny margins. Deciduous forms exhibit bright fall foliage and colorful berries that persist through winter. Barberries are useful as hedges, barriers, foundation plants, or specimens. Varieties with red or yellow leaves provide dramatic contrast in green landscapes and work especially well in combination with low-growing junipers.

Selected species and varieties

B. buxifolia var. *nana* (dwarf Magellan barberry)—spiny leaves up to 1 inch long on an evergreen shrub 18 inches tall and 24 inches wide, usually bearing orange-yellow flowers and purple berries; hardy to Zone 5. *B. x gladwynensis* 'William Penn' —mounded evergreen 4 feet high and wide, with showy flowers and lustrous dark green foliage that turns bronze in winter; hardy to Zone 6, but deciduous north of Zone 8. *B. julianae* (wintergreen barberry)—evergreen mound with upright habit, 6 to 8 feet high and wide, with often light-colored stems bearing spines up to 1 inch long and narrow, spiny leaves 2 to 3 inches long that may turn bronze or dark reddish in color in winter, profuse bloom in spring, and ⅓-inch bluish black berries that may linger into fall; hardy to Zone 5. *B. thunbergii* (Japanese barberry)—multibranched deciduous shrub, 3 to 6 feet tall and 4 to 7 feet wide, producing bright green leaves that appear early to hide small flower clusters and turn orange, red, and reddish purple in fall as ⅓-inch bright red berries form; 'Aurea' grows 3 to 4 feet tall, with vivid yellow leaves in the growing season but relatively few flowers and fruit; var. *atropurpurea* 'Crimson Pygmy' [sometimes referred to as 'Little Gem', 'Little Beauty', 'Little Favorite', or 'Atropurpurea Nana'] has maroon to purplish red summer foliage and grows to 2 feet tall and 3 feet wide; var. *atropurpurea* 'Rose Glow' reaches 5 to 6 feet tall and produces foliage opening rosy pink with splotches of darker red-purple changing to solid red-purple.

Growing conditions and maintenance

Evergreen barberries grow best in moist, slightly acid soil in sites that are protected from drying winds and strong sun. Deciduous barberries adapt to almost any soil and are tolerant of drought and urban pollution. They show their best fall color in full sun. The red and yellow forms revert to green in shade. Pruning is usually not necessary. Although *B. vulgaris* (common barberry) serves as an alternate host for black stem rust, a destructive disease of wheat, all of the varieties listed here are safe to grow.

Berberis thunbergii

Betula (BET-u-la)

BIRCH

Betula nigra

HARDINESS: Zones 2-9

PLANT TYPE: tree

HEIGHT: 40 to 70 feet

INTEREST: bark, form, foliage

SOIL: moist, acid

LIGHT: full sun

Birches grace the landscape with trunks of decorative bark and airy canopies of medium to dark green finely toothed leaves that flutter in the slightest breeze and turn yellow in fall before dropping. Male and female flowers, called catkins, are borne on the same tree. Birches create a light dappled shade and are lovely in groups or singly as specimens.

Selected species and varieties

B. nigra (river birch, red birch, black birch) —40 to 70 feet tall with a spread almost equal to its height, usually multitrunked, with cinnamon brown bark, peeling when young and becoming deeply furrowed into irregular plates with age, and nearly triangular leaves to 3½ inches long that often show brief fall color; Zones 4-9. *B. papyrifera* (paper birch, canoe birch, white birch, cluster birch)—a low-branched tree with reddish brown bark when young, aging to creamy white and peeling thinly to reveal reddish orange tissue beneath, growing 50 to 70 feet tall by 25 to 45 feet in spread, and bearing 2- to 4-inch roundish, wedge-shaped leaves turning a lovely yellow in fall; Zones 2-7. *B. pendula* (European white birch, warty birch, silver birch, common birch)—has graceful, drooping branches on a 40- to 50-foot-tall by 20- to 35-foot-wide tree with the bark on trunk and main limbs changing gradually from whitish to mostly black-on-white with age, golden brown twigs and slender branches bearing serrated, almost diamond-shaped leaves 1 to 3 inches long that hold later in the fall than do the other species but often show little fall color, Zones 2-7; 'Dalecarlica' (cut-leaf weeping birch, Swedish birch) has pendulous branches that arc to touch the ground and dangling, deeply lobed and sharply toothed leaves.

Growing conditions and maintenance
Give birches optimum growing conditions and keep a sharp eye out for insects or disease. Although river birches can thrive in periodic flooding, most species need good drainage and grow best in loose, rich, acid loams. Paper birch and European white birch tolerate neutral soils, but river birch must have acid soil. Amend soil with peat moss, leaf mold, or finished compost. Add sand if the soil is heavy. Mulch to retain moisture and to protect from lawn-mower damage. All birches bleed heavily in late winter or early spring; prune in summer or fall. Bottom branches on paper birch can easily be removed to create a high-branched specimen tree. Although river birch and paper birch are resistant to the bronze birch borer, European white birch is quite susceptible and may succumb if a routine spraying program is not followed. Most birches live about 50 years.

Betula papyrifera

BUTTERFLY BUSH

Buddleia davidii 'Empire Blue'

HARDINESS: Zones 5-9

PLANT TYPE: shrub

HEIGHT: 6 to 20 feet

INTEREST: flowers, texture

SOIL: well-drained, fertile

LIGHT: full sun

Its arching stems lined with narrow, gray-green leaves, the butterfly bush is effective massed at the edge of a border or lawn. Elongated clusters of fragrant flowers with contrasting centers bloom in spring and summer.

Selected species and varieties
B. alternifolia 'Argentea'—4-inch leaves with silky hairs and soft purple flowers on plants to 20 feet tall. *B. davidii* (summer lilac)—leaves to 10 inches long on shrubs to 10 feet; 'Black Knight' has deep purple blooms; 'Dubonnet', long sprays of dark purple flowers; 'Empire Blue', violet flowers; 'Royal Red', 20-inch-long red-purple flower clusters.

Growing conditions and maintenance
Remove spent flowers to prolong bloom. In northern zones, grow *B. davidii* as a perennial, cutting to the ground in fall for flowers on new shoots in spring. *B. alternifolia* 'Argentea' flowers on the previous year's growth.

BOX, BOXWOOD

Buxus microphylla 'Wintergreen'

HARDINESS: Zones 4-9

PLANT TYPE: evergreen shrub

HEIGHT: 2 to 20 feet

INTEREST: foliage

SOIL: moist, well-drained

LIGHT: bright full shade to full sun

These long-lived shrubs are widely used for hedges and foundation plantings.

Selected species and varieties
B. microphylla (littleleaf boxwood)—very slow growing mound, 3 to 4 feet tall with an equal spread, producing medium green ⅓- to 1-inch-long leaves in summer that become yellowish to green-brown in winter; Zones 6-9; 'Tide Hill' grows slowly to 2 feet tall and 5 feet wide, with foliage that stays green all winter; Zones 4-9; 'Wintergreen' has small, light green leaves; Zones 4-9. *B. sempervirens* (common boxwood) —leaves ½ to 1 inch long on a slow-growing shrub, 15 to 20 feet in height with an equal or greater spread; Zones 5-8; 'Suffruticosa' is very slow growing, dense and compact, reaching 4 to 5 feet, with fragrant leaves; 'Vardar Valley' has a flat-topped habit, growing 2 to 3 feet tall with 4- to 5-foot spread and dark blue-green foliage; Zones 4-8.

Growing conditions and maintenance
Plant in wind-protected areas and mulch to keep roots cool and moist. Shade helps protect boxwoods from leaf burn in winter. Boxwoods do best in climates that do not have extreme heat or cold.

Callicarpa (kal-i-CAR-pa)

BEAUTYBERRY

Callicarpa americana

HARDINESS: Zones 5-10

PLANT TYPE: shrub

HEIGHT: 3 to 8 feet

INTEREST: fruit

SOIL: well-drained

LIGHT: full sun to light shade

Clusters of colorful ⅛-inch berries dangle from the tips of beautyberry's arching stems for several weeks after the leaves have fallen in autumn. The oval, pointed leaves, arranged like ladders on either side of the stems, turn yellowish, sometimes pinkish, before dropping.

Selected species and varieties

C. americana (American beautyberry)— inconspicuous lavender summer flowers followed by magenta fruit clusters encircling stem tips; var. *lactea* produces white berries, Zones 7-10. *C. japonica*—violet to metallic purple berries; 'Leucocarpa' grows white berries after inconspicuous pink or white summer flowers, Zones 5-8.

Growing conditions and maintenance

Pruning to within 4 to 6 inches of the ground in early spring will create new shoots; only these produce flowers and fruit. Callicarpas are easy to grow from softwood cuttings or seed and are easily transplanted.

Calycanthus (kal-i-KAN-thus)

SWEET SHRUB

Calycanthus floridus 'Athens'

HARDINESS: Zones 4-9

PLANT TYPE: shrub

HEIGHT: 6 to 9 feet

INTEREST: flowers, fragrance

SOIL: moist, well-drained

LIGHT: full sun to partial shade

Sweet shrub is an adaptable plant that blends well with other shrubs in many garden settings. Its summer flowers are unusual looking and produce a delightfully fruity fragrance.

Selected species and varieties

C. floridus—6 to 9 feet tall and up to 12 feet wide, with long, dark green aromatic leaves that are deciduous but persist late into fall; rounded, fragrant, dark burgundy flowers with spreading, straplike petals blooming from late spring through early summer; and urn-shaped fruit persisting into winter; 'Athens' is a cultivar with highly fragrant yellow flowers.

Growing conditions and maintenance

Although it prefers moist, deep, well-drained soil, sweet shrub tolerates other soil conditions. It is easily transplanted. Suckers sometimes present a problem in garden beds.

Camellia (kah-MEEL-ee-a)

CAMELLIA

Camellia japonica

HARDINESS: Zones 8-10

PLANT TYPE: shrub or small tree

HEIGHT: 6 to 25 feet

INTEREST: flowers, foliage

SOIL: moist, well-drained, acid

LIGHT: partial shade

Camellias are dense evergreens that produce very showy flowers in shades of pink, rose, white, and red. The flowers bloom from fall through spring and may be single, semidouble, or double.

Selected species and varieties

C. japonica (Japanese camellia)—grows 10 to 25 feet tall as a large shrub or a small tree, with a dense, upright habit, dark glossy evergreen leaves, and flowers 3 to 5 inches across from late winter through spring. *C. sasanqua* (sasanqua camellia)— 6 to 10 feet tall, with a pyramidal habit, dark glossy evergreen leaves, and flowers 2 to 3 inches across blooming from fall to winter; varieties with increased cold hardiness include 'Polar Ice', 'Snow Flurry', 'Winter's Charm', 'Winter's Dream', 'Winter's Hope', 'Winter's Interlude', 'Winter's Rose', 'Winter's Star', as well as 'Winter's Waterlily'.

Growing conditions and maintenance

Camellias require protection from winter winds. They benefit from the addition of generous amounts of organic matter to the soil. Keep them continuously mulched, and do not overfertilize.

Carpinus *(car-PY-nis)*

HORNBEAM

Carpinus betulus 'Fastigiata'

HARDINESS: Zones 4-7

PLANT TYPE: tree

HEIGHT: 30 to 60 feet

INTEREST: foliage, form, bark

SOIL: well-drained

LIGHT: full sun to partial shade

A deciduous tree with crisp summer foliage, smooth gray bark, and a well-contoured winter silhouette, hornbeam (also called ironwood) makes a handsome specimen tree. Because it has dense foliage that takes well to pruning, however, it is often used as a hedge or screen. The dark green leaves may turn yellow or brown in fall. Hornbeam has extremely hard wood that was once used to make ox yokes.

Selected species and varieties
C. betulus (European hornbeam, common hornbeam)—pyramidal when young, maturing to a rounded crown, 40 to 60 feet tall under average conditions with a spread of 30 to 40 feet, bearing sharply toothed leaves 2½ to 5 inches long and 1 to 2 inches wide that remain unusually pest free; 'Columnaris' has a densely branched, steeple-shaped outline; 'Fastigiata' grows 30 to 40 feet tall with a spread of 20 to 30 feet, an oval to vaselike shape, and a forked trunk.

Growing conditions and maintenance
A highly adaptable and trouble-free plant, European hornbeam tolerates a wide range of soil conditions.

Caryopteris *(kar-ee-OP-ter-is)*

BLUEBEARD

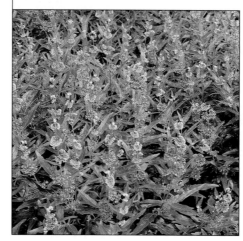

Caryopteris x clandonensis 'Dark Knight'

HARDINESS: Zones 6-9

PLANT TYPE: shrub

HEIGHT: 1½ to 4 feet

INTEREST: flowers, foliage

SOIL: light, well-drained

LIGHT: full sun

Bluebeard is a small deciduous shrub with pleasantly aromatic flowers, stems, and leaves. The slender, upright stems form a rounded mound of gray-green foliage that is topped with blue flowers from mid to late summer.

Selected species and varieties
C. x *clandonensis* 'Blue Mist'—2 feet tall, with powder blue flowers; 'Dark Knight', 2 feet tall, deep purple flowers; 'Longwood Blue', 1½ to 2 feet tall, violet-blue flowers with dark stamens.

Growing conditions and maintenance
Although it produces woody stems, bluebeard is best treated as a herbaceous perennial; cut it back to the ground in the winter. When flower production wanes in the summer, a light pruning will often stimulate a second flush of blooms.

Ceanothus *(see-a-NO-thus)*

WILD LILAC, REDROOT

Ceanothus arboreus

HARDINESS: Zones 7-11

PLANT TYPE: tree, shrub, or ground cover

HEIGHT: 18 inches to 25 feet

INTEREST: flowers

SOIL: well-drained to dry

LIGHT: full sun

Wild lilacs are widely used on slopes and in masses in West Coast gardens. They improve the soil by fixing nitrogen. Evergreen forms bloom in spring.

Selected species and varieties
C. arboreus (Catalina mountain lilac, felt-leaf ceanothus)—blue plumes on a 25-foot-tall shrub or tree with 4-inch evergreen leaves; Zones 9-10. *C.* x *delilianus*—3-foot deciduous shrub with 4- to 6-inch blue flowers in summer and fall and dark green leaves 3 inches long; 'Gloire de Versailles' grows 6 feet tall with fragrant lavender-blue flowers; hardy to Zone 7. *C. griseus* var. *horizontalis* (Carmel creeper)—18 to 30 inches tall and 5 to 15 feet wide with light blue flower clusters 1 inch wide and glossy 2-inch-long evergreen leaves; hardy to Zone 8. *C. thyrsiflorus* 'Skylark' (blueblossom)—dark blue spikes bloom on a broad 3- to 6-foot-tall shrub with 2-inch-long evergreen leaves; hardy to Zone 8.

Growing conditions and maintenance
Wild lilacs thrive on rocky slopes that usually stay dry all summer. Plant them in light, sandy soil, and water only during their first season. Fast drainage is a must.

Cedrus (SEE-drus)

CEDAR

Cedrus deodora

HARDINESS: Zones 6-9

PLANT TYPE: evergreen tree

HEIGHT: 100 to 150 feet

INTEREST: form, foliage

SOIL: well-drained

LIGHT: full sun

Cedars grow into magnificent specimen trees, their sweeping branches and great height best displayed on broad lawns.

Selected species and varieties

C. atlantica (Atlas cedar)—slowly reaches more than 100 feet tall and two-thirds as wide, appearing open and spindly when young but maturing into a flat-topped shape with bluish green or sometimes green to silvery blue inch-long needles and 3-inch-long cones that take 2 years to mature; 'Glauca' (blue Atlas cedar) has rich blue needles. *C. deodara* (deodar cedar)— pyramidal and more attractive when young than Atlas cedar, becoming flat topped and broad with age, growing 40 to 70 feet tall with a nearly equal spread but sometimes reaching 150 feet, with light blue to grayish green needles up to 1½ inches long, a gracefully drooping habit, and 3- to 4-inch cones; Zones 7-8.

Growing conditions and maintenance

Give both species ample room to develop in a site protected from strong winds. Atlas cedar grows best in moist, deep loam but will tolerate other soils as long as they are well drained. A moderately dry site is best for deodar cedar.

Cercis (SER-sis)

REDBUD, JUDAS TREE

Cercis canadensis 'Forest Pansy'

HARDINESS: Zones 4-9

PLANT TYPE: large shrub or small tree

HEIGHT: 8 to 30 feet

INTEREST: flowers, fruit

SOIL: moist, well-drained

LIGHT: bright full shade to full sun

An early and prolific spring bloomer, redbud is a good accent tree for shady areas. Large heart-shaped leaves appear after the flowers, and long green seed pods turn brown and persist into winter.

Selected species and varieties

C. canadensis (eastern redbud)—a small tree with a spreading crown 20 to 30 feet tall, bearing 5-inch-wide leaves that turn a subdued yellow in fall; 'Alba' has white flowers; 'Forest Pansy', red-purple leaves and pink-lavender flowers; hardy to Zone 7. *C. chinensis* (Chinese redbud)—a multi-trunked shrub or tree 8 to 12 feet tall with upright growth and rose-purple flowers; Zones 6-9; 'Avondale' grows to 9 feet, with deep rose-purple flowers that bloom profusely. *C. reniformis*—usually 15 to 20 feet tall with glossy dark green leaves 2 to 4 inches wide and pale pink flowers; Zones 7-9; 'Oklahoma' has glossy leaves and wine red flowers.

Growing conditions and maintenance

Eastern redbud needs some sun in late winter and early spring for the the best flower production. In Zones 5-7, plant in spring; farther south, plant at any time from fall to spring.

Chaenomeles (kee-NOM-e-lees)

FLOWERING QUINCE

Chaenomeles speciosa 'Texas Scarlet'

HARDINESS: Zones 4-8

PLANT TYPE: deciduous shrub

HEIGHT: 3 to 10 feet

INTEREST: flowers

SOIL: moist to dry, acid

LIGHT: full sun

A thorny, rounded, spreading shrub, flowering quince's best attribute is its showy profusion of early-spring flowers before the foliage appears. The small, yellowish green quincelike fruits that ripen in fall can be used for jams and jellies but cannot be eaten raw. The shrub's dense, twiggy branching makes a coarse winter silhouette. Budded stems can be used for late-winter arrangements.

Selected species and varieties

C. speciosa (common flowering quince, Japanese quince)—6 to 10 feet tall with equal or greater width, usually with red or scarlet, but sometimes pink or white, flowers and lustrous dark green leaves that open bronzy red; 'Cameo' has peachy pink double flowers; 'Nivalis', white flowers; 'Texas Scarlet', profuse tomato red flowers on a 3- to 5-foot plant.

Growing conditions and maintenance

Flowering quince adapts to most soils except the very alkaline. Full sun produces the best bloom. Restore vigor and improve flowering by cutting out older branches. Leaf spot and too much spring rain can cause a loss of foliage, but some leaf drop by midsummer is normal.

Chamaecyparis (kam-ee-SIP-a-ris)

FALSE CYPRESS

Chamaecyparis obtusa

HARDINESS: Zones 4-8

PLANT TYPE: shrub or tree

HEIGHT: 4 to 75 feet

INTEREST: form, foliage

SOIL: well-drained, fertile, acid to neutral

LIGHT: full sun to partial shade

False cypresses are coniferous evergreen specimen trees with fan-shaped, flattened branch tips and scalelike foliage.

Selected species and varieties

C. lawsoniana (Lawson false cypress, Lawson cypress, Port Orford cedar)—40- to 60-foot columnar tree with massive central trunk, short ascending branches with drooping tips, and glaucous green to dark green foliage, Zones 5-7; 'Allumii' grows a narrow silvery blue spire to 30 feet. *C. obtusa* (hinoki false cypress, hinoki cypress)—dark green slender pyramid growing 50 to 75 feet tall; 'Crippsii' forms a broad pyramid with drooping golden yellow branch tips; 'Gracilis' takes a narrow conical form, 6 to 10 feet tall; 'Nana Gracilis' is 4 to 6 feet tall and 3 to 4 feet wide, and has very dark green foliage arranged in slightly curved sprays.

Growing conditions and maintenance

Although hinoki false cypress is moderately tolerant of light shade and drier climates, most other species prefer full sun in cool, moist climates. Provide partial shade in hot regions and protect from drying wind. Amend soil with peat moss or leaf mold to hold moisture.

Chilopsis (kill-OP-sis)

DESERT WILLOW

Chilopsis linearis

HARDINESS: Zones 8-10

PLANT TYPE: shrub or tree

HEIGHT: 10 to 25 feet

INTEREST: flowers, foliage

SOIL: dry, sandy

LIGHT: full sun

Showy, trumpet-shaped spring flowers resembling snapdragons bloom in clusters at the tips of desert willow's branches in spring and often sporadically until fall. Its open, branching and willowlike leaves, evergreen in milder climates, lend an airy appearance. A heavy crop of thin, foot-long pods persists through winter. Desert willow can be trained into a graceful specimen for dry gardens.

Selected species and varieties

C. linearis (desert catalpa, flowering willow)—shrubby habit, 10 to 25 feet tall and 10 to 15 feet wide, with twisted branches bearing narrow 6- to 12-inch-long leaves and fragrant lilac, rosy pink, purple, or white flowers with curled lobes and white or yellow markings.

Growing conditions and maintenance

Native to arid lands of the Southwest, desert willow enjoys light soil that is very well drained. Prune to develop a tree form or to eliminate shagginess.

Cistus (SIS-tus)

ROCKROSE

Cistus x purpureus

HARDINESS: Zones 9-10

PLANT TYPE: shrub

HEIGHT: 18 inches to 4 feet

INTEREST: flowers, foliage

SOIL: dry to well-drained

LIGHT: full sun

Rockrose is well suited to dry areas of the West Coast. It adds a long season of color to mixed-shrub borders, rock gardens, and dry banks. Its leaves are aromatic and nearly evergreen. The flowers, which resemble roses, last only one day but are prolific; flowering continues over several weeks in the spring and early summer.

Selected species and varieties

C. x purpureus—3 to 4 feet tall and equally as wide, with attractive 2-inch-long leaves that are dark green on top, gray-green below, and reddish purple flowers with a red spot at the base in early summer. *C. salviifolius*—18 to 24 inches tall and up to 6 feet wide, with gray-green textured leaves and white flowers with a yellow spot at the base in late spring.

Growing conditions and maintenance

Rockroses grow well in dry, windy areas, tolerating drought, seaside conditions, and poor soil. These plants are useful as fire retardants.

Cladrastis (cla-DRAS-tis)

YELLOWWOOD

Cladrastis kentukea

HARDINESS: Zones 4-8

PLANT TYPE: tree

HEIGHT: 30 to 50 feet

INTEREST: flowers, foliage, form, bark

SOIL: well-drained

LIGHT: full sun

An excellent deciduous shade tree for small landscapes, yellowwood produces long, hanging panicles of fragrant flowers in mid- to late spring and a broad canopy of bright green foliage that turns yellow in fall. The bark is smooth and gray. Open, delicate, zigzag branching creates an airy form. The color of the interior wood gives the tree its name. Flowering is best every second or third year.

Selected species and varieties
C. kentukea [formerly called *C. lutea*] (American yellowwood, Kentucky yellow-wood, virgilia)—low-branching habit with a rounded crown 40 to 55 feet wide, producing 3- to 4-inch-long compound leaves opening bright yellowish green before darkening slightly later, with flower clusters up to 14 inches long, and thin brown seedpods 4 to 5 inches long in fall.

Growing conditions and maintenance
Although it occurs naturally on rich, limestone soils, American yellowwood adapts to a wide range of soil types from acid to alkaline and is remarkably pest free. Once established, it is drought tolerant. Prune only in summer to prevent heavy sap bleeding.

Clethra (KLETH-ra)

SUMMER-SWEET

Clethra barbinervis

HARDINESS: Zones 3-9

PLANT TYPE: shrub

HEIGHT: 3 to 20 feet

INTEREST: flowers, fragrance, foliage

SOIL: moist, acid

LIGHT: full sun to full shade

Summer-sweet is well named; its pink or white flowers appear in midsummer and are delightfully fragrant. Tolerant of most growing conditions, this deciduous shrub can easily be sited in any mixed border or moist woodland garden.

Selected species and varieties
C. alnifolia—3 to 8 feet tall and 4 to 6 feet wide, it produces deep green leaves that turn gold in the fall and very fragrant white flowers in 2- to 6-inch-long clusters; 'Hummingbird' grows to 4 feet with a dense habit; 'Pink Spires' has deep pink buds that open to soft pink flowers. *C. barbinervis*—10 to 20 feet tall, with dark green leaves in clusters at branch tips, fragrant white late-summer flowers in 4- to 6-inch-long clusters, and beautiful gray to brown, smooth, exfoliating bark; Zones 5-8.

Growing conditions and maintenance
Summer-sweet tolerates most soil types as well as coastal conditions. It thrives in both sun and shade. Incorporate organic matter into the soil prior to planting. Prune in early spring.

Cornus (KOR-nus)

DOGWOOD

Cornus florida

HARDINESS: Zones 3-9

PLANT TYPE: large shrub or small tree

HEIGHT: 15 to 30 feet

INTEREST: flowers, foliage, fruit, form, bark

SOIL: well-drained

LIGHT: bright shade to full sun

Dogwoods can turn the spring landscape into a fairyland and in fall provide bright red fruit for birds. They may also offer red to reddish purple fall foliage, colorful bark, and low, layered branching for an attractive winter silhouette.

Selected species and varieties
C. alternifolia (pagoda dogwood, green osier)—strongly fragrant yellowish white flowers borne in flat clusters 1½ to 2½ inches wide on a horizontally branched tree growing 15 to 25 feet tall with a greater spread and tierlike habit, also bearing fruit that matures from green to red to blue-black; Zones 3-7. *C. florida* (flowering dogwood)—small tree with broad crown, usually 20 to 30 feet tall with an equal or greater spread, producing white flowerlike bracts lasting 10 to 14 days in spring before the leaves emerge, followed in fall by small glossy red fruits borne in clusters of at least three to four; Zones 5-9. *C. kousa* (kousa dogwood)—large shrub or small tree 20 to 30 feet tall and wide with exfoliating gray, tan, and brown bark and tiered branching, flowering in late spring after the leaves appear and lasting for up to 6 weeks, followed by pink to red

fruit up to 1 inch wide in late summer to fall, when the leaves turn reddish purple or scarlet, Zones 5-8; var. *chinensis* (Chinese dogwood)—grows to 30 feet and has larger bracts than the species. *C. mas* (cornelian cherry, sorbet)—multistemmed shrub or small, oval to round tree 20 to 25 feet tall and 15 to 20 feet wide, branching nearly to the ground with attractive exfoliating gray to brown bark, bearing small clusters of yellow flowers for 3 weeks in early spring and bright red fruit in midsummer that is partly hidden by the lustrous dark green leaves, 2 to 4 inches long; usually shows little fall color; Zones 4-8.

Growing conditions and maintenance

Give flowering and pagoda dogwoods a moist, acid soil enriched with leaf mold, peat moss, or compost. Partial shade is best in hotter areas. Mulch to keep soil cool and prevent lawn-mower damage, which invites invasion by dogwood borers. Kousa dogwood prefers loose, sandy, acid soil, rich with organic matter, in sunny locations. It is more drought tolerant than flowering dogwood. Although adaptable to a wide range of soil types, cornelian cherry prefers moist, rich sites in sun or partial shade and is probably the best performer of the dogwoods for the Midwest. Susceptible to the usually fatal anthracnose, which has killed many dogwoods on the East Coast, flowering dogwood has a better chance of staying healthy if stress is reduced. For colder climates, the best bud hardiness in flowering dogwoods occurs in trees native to those regions.

Cornus mas

Corylopsis (kor-ee-LOP-sis)

WINTER HAZEL

Corylopsis pauciflora

HARDINESS:	Zones 5-8
PLANT TYPE:	deciduous shrub
HEIGHT:	4 to 15 feet
INTEREST:	flowers, fragrance, foliage
SOIL:	moist, well-drained, acid
LIGHT:	bright full shade to full sun

One of the first shrubs to flower in spring and one of the best for thick summer foliage, winter hazel is useful against bare walls or in informal shrub borders. Drooping panicles of fragrant yellow bell-shaped flowers appear before the leaves in April.

Selected species and varieties

C. glabrescens (fragrant winter hazel)—8 to 15 feet tall with similar spread, followed by oval, pointed, toothy leaves 2 to 4 inches long; Zones 5-8. *C. pauciflora* (buttercup winter hazel)—4 to 6 feet tall, with flowers in clusters of only 2 or 3, and leaves 1½ to 3 inches long; Zones 6-8. *C. sinensis* (Chinese winter hazel)—5 to 8 feet tall but may grow to 15 feet, bearing blue-green downy leaves 2 to 5 inches long and flowers in 2-inch drooping clusters.

Growing conditions and maintenance

Winter hazels grow best in light shade, but they need some sun in early spring to promote flowering. Protect from winter winds, sudden temperature dips, and spring frosts that can easily kill flower buds. Work leaf mold, peat moss, or compost liberally into the soil before planting. There is usually no need to fertilize.

Cotinus (ko-TYE-nus)

SMOKE TREE

Cotinus coggygria 'Velvet Cloak'

HARDINESS:	Zones 5-9
PLANT TYPE:	shrub
HEIGHT:	10 to 15 feet
INTEREST:	fruiting panicles
SOIL:	well-drained
LIGHT:	full sun

For most of the summer and early fall, smokebush almost explodes with puffy, smoky pink plumes, actually hairs arising from the 6- to 8-inch fruiting stalks as the tiny yellowish flowers fade. A striking accent plant that often has colorful fall foliage, smokebush also works well in borders and groupings.

Selected species and varieties

C. coggygria (common smokebush, smoke plant, Venetian sumac, wig tree)—a loose and open multistemmed deciduous shrub, 10 to 15 feet wide, bearing 1½- to 3-inch-long leaves that unfurl pink-bronze in midspring, mature to medium blue-green, and sometimes show yellow-red-purple fall color and branched puffs changing to gray; 'Royal Purple' has purplish maroon leaves with scarlet margins, eventually turning scarlet all over; 'Velvet Cloak', purple plumes and velvety dark purple leaves throughout the summer before changing to reddish purple in fall.

Growing conditions and maintenance

Tolerant of a wide range of soils, smokebush demands only that a site be well drained. Too-rich or too-moist soil reduces bloom and subdues leaf color.

COTONEASTER

Cotoneaster microphyllus

HARDINESS: Zones 5-8

PLANT TYPE: evergreen shrub or ground cover

HEIGHT: 1 to 15 feet

INTEREST: foliage, fruit, form

SOIL: well-drained

LIGHT: full sun to partial shade

Red berries decorate the stiff, spreading branches of cotoneasters in fall and winter, and the tiny, deep green leaves lend a fine texture to the garden in all seasons. White or pink flowers, often quite small, appear in spring. Usually spreading at least as wide as their height, cotoneasters are used as fast-growing ground covers that are ideal for slopes, rock gardens, and walls; in masses; or as shrubs good for borders and screens. Cotoneasters can also be trained into espaliers.

Selected species and varieties

C. dammeri (bearberry cotoneaster)—prostrate form, 12 to 18 inches high, an excellent ground cover because it roots wherever its branches touch the soil and spreads quickly to 6 feet wide, with white flowers up to ½ inch wide, a light crop of red berries, and narrow, 1-inch-long, lustrous dark green leaves that may become tinged with red-purple in winter, Zones 5-8; 'Skogholm' grows vigorously to 1½ to 3 feet high, spreading several feet each year. *C. lacteus* (red cluster-berry, parney cotoneaster)—a 6- to 10-foot shrub with a handsome fruit display persisting through winter and 2- to 3-inch-wide white flower clusters in spring, sometimes partly hidden by the foliage; Zones 6-8. *C. microphyllus* (littleleaf cotoneaster, rockspray cotoneaster)—a nearly prostrate shrub, usually 24 inches high or less, spreading up to 10 feet wide with ¼- to ½-inch-long glossy leaves, tiny white flowers, and red fruit; Zones 5-8. *C. salicifolius* (willowleaf cotoneaster)—a shrub with an arching habit, growing 10 to 15 feet tall with a smaller spread and producing narrow, willowlike leaves 1½ to 3½ inches long that are lustrous dark green in summer becoming plum-purple in winter, flat 2-inch-wide white flower heads often masked by the foliage, and tiny, long-lasting bright red fruit, Zones 6-8; 'Autumn Fire' forms a 2- to 3-foot-high ground cover with 1½- to 2-inch very glossy leaves turning reddish purple in winter and scarlet fruit; 'Repens' has lustrous 1-inch leaves on a prostrate ground cover to 12 inches tall.

Growing conditions and maintenance

Bearberry cotoneaster is tolerant of most well-drained soils and is easily grown. Willowleaf and parney cotoneasters need moist, well-drained, acid to nearly neutral soil. Mature plants will tolerate drought, seashore conditions, and wind; dry or poor soil often produces the best fruiting. Cotoneaster is susceptible to fire blight, a blackened die-off of branch tips which, if not treated, is fatal to the plant; littleleaf cotoneaster may be more susceptible in the South. Other pests are borers, red spiders, and lace bugs. Prune only to control the plant's shape.

Cotoneaster salicifolius

HAWTHORN

Crataegus viridis 'Winter King'

HARDINESS: Zones 4-7

PLANT TYPE: tree or shrub

HEIGHT: 20 to 35 feet

INTEREST: flowers, berries

SOIL: well-drained

LIGHT: full sun

Hawthorns develop neat, round crowns of lobed, triangular leaves with finely toothed edges that give them a delicate texture as a specimen tree or in a shrub border. The foliage has a reddish cast when young, turns green through the summer, then colors attractively in fall. Clusters of small white spring flowers produce bright red berries that persist through winter. Long thorns along its woody branches are a drawback.

Selected species and varieties

C. phaenopyrum (Washington hawthorn)—multiple-stemmed shrub or tree to 30 feet with foliage that turns scarlet in fall. *C. viridis* 'Winter King' (green hawthorn)—round to vase-shaped tree to 35 feet tall with lustrous green foliage coloring purple or red in fall.

Growing conditions and maintenance

Plant hawthorns in loose, slightly alkaline soil. Thorns make pruning or shearing difficult, so allow room for the tree or shrub's mature spread. Propagate from seed.

x Cupressocyparis

LEYLAND CYPRESS

x Cupressocyparis leylandii 'Silver Dust'

HARDINESS: Zones 6-10

PLANT TYPE: evergreen tree

HEIGHT: 60 to 70 feet

INTEREST: foliage, form

SOIL: adaptable

LIGHT: full sun

A dense, towering, columnar or pyramidal tree when left unchecked, x *Cupressocyparis*—a hybrid of *Cupressus* and *Chamaecyparis*—produces some of the fastest-growing and finest-textured screen or hedge plants available. The fanlike arrangement of bluish green scalelike needles appears soft and feathery.

Selected species and varieties
x *C. leylandii* (Leyland cypress)—a cross between *Cupressus macrocarpa* (Monterey cypress) and *Chamaecyparis nootkatensis* (Alaska cedar) that grows 3 feet a year or more to 70 feet tall and usually 10 to 18 feet wide, with reddish brown scaly bark; cultivars include silvery green, variegated, and golden yellow forms; 'Silver Dust' has creamy white markings on green foliage.

Growing conditions and maintenance
Leyland cypress grows best in moist, well-drained, moderately fertile loams but is very tolerant of almost any soil. Provide protection from drying winter winds. It is best transplanted from a container; field-grown plants are hard to ball and burlap. Unaffected by serious pests, it also resists sea winds and cold damage.

Cupressus (kew-PRESS-us)

CYPRESS

Cupressus sempervirens

HARDINESS: Zones 7-9

PLANT TYPE: evergreen tree

HEIGHT: 30 to 40 feet

INTEREST: form, foliage, bark

SOIL: dry to well-drained

LIGHT: full sun

These graceful, fine-textured trees make handsome specimens, screens, or windbreaks. Their aromatic foliage consists of scalelike leaves closely pressed on braided-cord stems. Reddish brown exfoliating bark becomes dark brown and furrowed with age. Cones with shieldlike scales are 1 inch across.

Selected species and varieties
C. glabra [sometimes labeled by nurseries as *C. arizonica*, which is actually a separate species] (smooth-barked Arizona cypress) —a dense, bushy pyramid 30 to 40 feet tall and 15 to 20 feet wide with soft green, gray-green, or blue-green foliage. *C. sempervirens* (Italian cypress, Mediterranean cypress)—a slender column 30 or more feet tall, with horizontal branches and dark green foliage; cultivars include bright green, gold, and blue forms.

Growing conditions and maintenance
Best suited to the West and the Southwest, cypress enjoys mild to hot, dry climates and needs no supplemental water once established. Soil must be perfectly drained. When grown in its natural habitat, cypress is generally insect and disease free. It is short-lived in the Southeast.

Cytisus (SIT-is-us)

BROOM

Cytisus scoparius

HARDINESS: Zones 5-10

PLANT TYPE: shrub

HEIGHT: 3 to 6 feet

INTEREST: foliage, flowers, stems

SOIL: well-drained to dry

LIGHT: full sun

Brooms are fast-growing shrubs that brighten the spring border with masses of pealike flowers that are typically yellow, but may be pink, red, purple, or white. Their small leaves line arching stems that remain green all year, adding interest during winter months.

Selected species and varieties
C. x praecox (Warminster broom)—3 to 6 feet tall with a similar spread and graceful, slender cascading stems that produce lemon yellow blooms in early spring; 'Albus' is slightly smaller with white flowers. *C. scoparius* (Scotch broom)—4 to 6 feet with a broad, rounded habit and erect green stems with distinct ridges and bright yellow, 1-inch blooms in late spring to early summer.

Growing conditions and maintenance
Brooms are most easily established in the garden by planting small container-grown specimens in spring. Prune immediately after flowering by cutting back stems by two-thirds. Propagate by cuttings or layering in spring.

Danae (DAY-nah-ee)

ALEXANDRIAN LAUREL

Danae racemosa

HARDINESS: Zones 8-9

PLANT TYPE: evergreen shrub

HEIGHT: 2 to 4 feet

INTEREST: foliage, fruit, form

SOIL: moist, well-drained

LIGHT: dappled to bright full shade

The lustrous rich green leaves of Alexandrian laurel and its gracefully arching habit lend elegance and texture throughout the seasons. Related to butcher's-broom, this laurel arises bamboolike into sheaves of stems and leaves. Orange-red berries appear in the fall. The branches make long-lasting cuttings for indoor arrangements.

Selected species and varieties
D. racemosa—2 to 4 feet high and equally as wide, with long, pointed, rich green "leaves" that are actually flattened stems 1½ to 4 inches long and ¼ to 1½ inches wide, inconspicuous greenish yellow flowers, and showy berries that are ¼ to ⅜ inch in diameter.

Growing conditions and maintenance
Alexandrian laurel prefers light, open shade; direct hot sun can discolor leaves or, in winter, produce leaf burn. Supplement the soil with organic matter such as leaf mold. Propagate by dividing.

Daphne (DAF-nee)

DAPHNE

Daphne x burkwoodii 'Carol Mackie'

HARDINESS: Zones 4-9

PLANT TYPE: shrub

HEIGHT: 3 to 5 feet

INTEREST: flowers, fragrance, fruit, foliage

SOIL: moist, well-drained, near neutral

LIGHT: partial to bright full shade

Daphnes are temperamental plants, but their intensely fragrant late-winter or early-spring flowers make them worthwhile. They can be either deciduous or evergreen. Birds love the red berries that appear in summer. *Caution:* All parts of the plant are poisonous to humans.

Selected species and varieties
D. x *burkwoodii* (Burkwood daphne)—3 to 4 feet high with an equal spread, producing clusters of fragrant, creamy white to pinkish spring flowers and semievergreen foliage; Zones 4-8; 'Carol Mackie' has leaves with creamy margins. *D. mezereum* (February daphne, mezereum)—3 to 5 feet high and wide, with lavender to rosy purple flowers that emerge in late winter to early spring before the semievergreen to deciduous leaves; Zones 4-8. *D. odora* (winter daphne)—3 feet high, densely branched, and evergreen, growing extremely fragrant rosy purple flowers in late winter to early spring; Zones 7-9.

Growing conditions and maintenance
Consider eventual spread; daphnes do not withstand transplanting. Despite the best care, however, daphnes may suddenly die for unknown reasons.

Deutzia (DEWT-see-a)

SLENDER DEUTZIA

Deutzia gracilis

HARDINESS: Zones 4-8

PLANT TYPE: shrub

HEIGHT: 2 to 5 feet

INTEREST: flowers

SOIL: moist, well-drained

LIGHT: full sun to partial shade

Slender deutzia is a graceful deciduous shrub bearing pure white flowers in midspring. Like forsythia, it has a relatively short season of interest but is easy to grow and adaptable to most sites. Deutzia can be effectively used as a hedge or as a background for perennials, or in a mixed-shrub border.

Selected species and varieties
D. gracilis—to 5 feet tall and an equal width, with slender arching stems in a broad mounding habit, serrated leaves 1 to 3 inches long, and white flowers in erect clusters in spring that are effective for 2 weeks; 'Nikko'—compact cultivar 2 feet tall and 5 feet wide, with leaves that turn burgundy in fall.

Growing conditions and maintenance
Planted in spring, deutzia is easy to transplant and grow and is tolerant of most soils. Encourage vigorous growth and abundant flowers by cutting the oldest stems back to the ground after flowering.

Elaeagnus (e-lee-AG-nus)

OLEASTER

Elaeagnus angustifolia

HARDINESS: Zones 2-9

PLANT TYPE: shrub or tree

HEIGHT: 12 to 20 feet

INTEREST: foliage, flowers, fruit, fragrance

SOIL: well-drained

LIGHT: full sun

Often found along roadsides, oleaster is extremely adaptable in difficult sites. Usually grown as large shrubs with multiple stems, the species described here can be pruned to a single trunk to form a small tree. Use as windbreaks, hedges, accents in a shrub border, or specimens.

Selected species and varieties

E. angustifolia (Russian olive)—usually a 12- to 15-foot-tall shrub with an equal or greater spread, but may grow to 20 feet as a single-trunk tree. The inconspicuous but very fragrant flowers are followed in late summer and fall by yellow fruit coated with silvery scales. *E. umbellata* (autumn olive)—large shrub growing 12 to 18 feet tall with a wide-spreading habit, sometimes reaching 30 feet across. Tiny, fragrant, yellowish white flowers are followed by silvery brown fruit that ripens to scarlet; Zones 3-8.

Growing conditions and maintenance

Plants adapt to a wide range of soil types but prefer a light, sandy loam. They tolerate wind, drought, alkaline soil, and seaside conditions. They grow rapidly, transplant easily, and respond well to shearing. For a hedge, plant shrubs 3 to 5 feet apart.

Enkianthus (en-kee-AN-thus)

ENKIANTHUS

Enkianthus campanulatus

HARDINESS: Zones 4-7

PLANT TYPE: shrub or small tree

HEIGHT: 6 to 30 feet

INTEREST: foliage, flowers

SOIL: moist, well-drained, acid, organic

LIGHT: full sun to partial shade

Pendulous clusters of dainty flowers in spring and brilliant fall foliage make this deciduous shrub a stand-alone specimen or a welcome addition to groups of acid-loving rhododendrons and azaleas.

Selected species and varieties

E. campanulatus (redvein enkianthus)—narrow, upright habit, 6 to 8 feet tall in cold areas, to 30 feet in warmer climates, with layered branches bearing at their tips tufts of 1- to 3-inch-long medium green leaves that turn bright red to orange and yellow in fall, and producing long-stalked clusters of pale yellow or light orange bell-shaped flowers with red veins in late spring as the leaves develop, the blooms sometimes persisting for several weeks; hardy to parts of Zone 4. *E. perulatus* (white enkianthus)—6 feet high and wide, with white urn-shaped flower clusters in midspring before the foliage appears, the bright green 1- to 2-inch-long leaves turning scarlet in fall; hardy to Zone 5.

Growing conditions and maintenance

Mix peat moss or leaf mold into the soil before planting. Mulch to retain moisture. Pruning is rarely necessary.

Eriobotrya (air-ee-o-BOT-ree-a)

LOQUAT

Eriobotrya japonica

HARDINESS: Zones 8-10

PLANT TYPE: shrub or tree

HEIGHT: 15 to 25 feet

INTEREST: foliage, fruit, fragrance

SOIL: moist, well-drained

LIGHT: full sun to partial shade

Lustrous wrinkled evergreen leaves that are sometimes a foot long create interesting textural effects in the landscape. Stiff panicles of fragrant, but not showy, woolly flowers form in fall or winter, and by late spring edible yellow-orange fruits are ready to be picked in the Deep South. Loquat can be used as an accent, or it can be trained into a patio tree or espalier.

Selected species and varieties

E. japonica (Chinese loquat, Japanese plum, Japanese medlar)—a tree or rounded multistemmed shrub 15 to 25 feet tall and wide, with supple branches bearing heavily veined 6- to 12-inch-long toothy leaves that are deep green above and a rust color on the undersides, with five-petaled dull white ½-inch-wide flowers borne in 6-inch clusters and covered with brown fuzz, and pear-shaped fruit almost 2 inches long in the southern half of its range.

Growing conditions and maintenance

Loquat prefers moist loam but tolerates moderately alkaline soils and occasional drought. Provide protection from wind. Feed only lightly; rampant new growth is subject to fire blight.

Escallonia (es-ka-LOAN-ee-a)

ESCALLONIA

Escallonia x langleyensis 'Apple Blossom'

HARDINESS: Zones 8-10

PLANT TYPE: evergreen shrub

HEIGHT: 3 to 5 feet

INTEREST: flowers, foliage, fragrance

SOIL: well-drained

LIGHT: full sun

Escallonia produces short clusters of pink, white, or red funnel-shaped flowers amid glossy, often sweetly fragrant foliage over a long blooming season. A good choice for coastal gardens, it is often used for hedges or screens and in masses.

Selected species and varieties

E. x *langleyensis* 'Apple Blossom'—a dense, sprawling shrub 3 to 5 feet high, with arching branches bearing large leaves and pink buds opening to pinkish white flowers throughout the warm months. *E.* 'Pride of Donard'—dense, broad-spreading habit with rosy pink flowers throughout the year in mild climates. *E. rubra* 'C. F. Ball' (red escallonia)—a compact, upright shrub to 5 feet tall, good for hedging, with very glossy leaves and bright red flowers in 1- to 3-inch clusters blooming freely during warm seasons.

Growing conditions and maintenance

A native of Chile, escallonia thrives in salt spray and coastal winds. *E.* x *langleyensis* 'Apple Blossom', however, does not do well in fully exposed locations. Escallonia likes average soils and withstands some drought but is intolerant of high alkalinity. Pinch back or prune after flowers fade.

Euonymus (yew-ON-i-mus)

SPINDLE TREE

Euonymus alata 'Compacta'

HARDINESS: Zones 4-9

PLANT TYPE: shrub, ground cover, or vine

HEIGHT: 4 inches to 70 feet

INTEREST: foliage, form

SOIL: well-drained

LIGHT: full sun to deep shade

This broad genus includes deciduous shrubs that produce dazzling fall foliage and a cleanly defined winter silhouette as well as evergreen ground covers, shrubs, and clinging vines. Inconspicuous flowers form in spring, and hidden pink to red fruit capsules, which are usually hidden, split to expose orange seeds in fall, attracting birds. In its varied forms, euonymus provides structure to the garden. Use burning bush *(E. alata)* for hedges that need no trimming or for massing. Japanese euonymus is suitable for hedges and tall foundation plants. Winter creeper euonymus can be trained to climb a brick wall or cover a bank.

Selected species and varieties

E. alata [also listed as *E. alatus*] (winged spindle tree, winged euonymus, burning bush)—a slow-growing, wide-spreading, flat-topped shrub of variable height, usually 15 to 20 feet tall and wide, with soft green leaves 1 to 3 inches long that turn brilliant red in fall, yellow-green flowers in spring, and small red fruits borne under the leaves, Zones 4-8; 'Compacta' [also listed as 'Compactus'] (dwarf burning bush) grows 10 feet tall, its slender branch-

es exhibiting less prominent corky ridges and forming a denser, more rounded outline; hardy to Zone 5. *E. fortunei* (winter creeper euonymus)—an evergreen ground cover 4 to 6 inches high or a climbing vine 40 to 70 feet high, with lustrous dark green, silvery veined, vaguely serrated inch-long oval leaves; 'Colorata' [also listed as 'Coloratus'] is a ground cover with glossy leaves lacking silver veins and turning plum-purple in winter; 'Emerald Gaiety' leaves have irregular white margins that turn pink in winter on a mounding, loosely erect shrub to 5 feet tall, or vine if near a structure. *E. japonica* [also listed as *E. japonicus*] (Japanese spindle tree, Japanese euonymus)—dark green, leathery, waxy leaves 1 to 3 inches long and slightly toothed on a dense, oval evergreen shrub usually 5 to 10 feet tall and half as wide, with greenish white flowers in early summer and ineffective pinkish fruits, Zones 7-9; 'Albo-marginata' [also listed as 'Albo-marginatus'] bears leaves with narrow white margins.

Growing conditions and maintenance

Euonymus does well in all except very wet soils and accepts severe pruning. Although burning bush shows fall color in full shade, brighter hues seem to develop in full sun. Winter creeper euonymus needs snow cover or shade to withstand Zone 4 winters; it is used as a substitute for ivy in semiarid climates. Japanese euonymus shows great tolerance for salt spray and seaside conditions. All except burning bush are susceptible to scale, a destructive insect.

Euonymus fortunei 'Emerald Gaiety'

Exochorda (ex-o-KORD-a)

PEARLBUSH

Exochorda x macrantha 'The Bride'

HARDINESS: Zones 5-9

PLANT TYPE: shrub

HEIGHT: 3 to 15 feet

INTEREST: flowers, foliage

SOIL: well-drained

LIGHT: full sun to partial shade

The pearlbush derives its common name from the pearl-like chains of round flower buds that appear in clusters along the previous season's stems. Open in mid- to late spring, the 1½- to 2-inch white flowers cover the shrub in white for a period of 1 to 2 weeks. The attractive foliage provides a fine backdrop at other times.

Selected species and varieties
E. x macrantha—up to 10 feet high and wide and bearing snow white flowers; 'The Bride' is 3 to 6 feet tall with a mounded, compact habit and flowers to 2 inches across. *E. racemosa* (common pearlbush) —upright habit reaching 10 to 15 feet tall with an equal spread, and 1¼-inch flowers.

Growing conditions and maintenance
Pearlbush tolerates most soils as long as they are well drained. Plant in early spring. Prune immediately after flowering by removing old, twiggy branches. Propagate by cuttings taken in late spring or early summer, or by layering.

Fagus (FAY-gus)

BEECH

Fagus sylvatica 'Atropunicea'

HARDINESS: Zones 3-9

PLANT TYPE: tree

HEIGHT: 50 to 70 feet or more

INTEREST: form, foliage

SOIL: moist, well-drained, acid

LIGHT: full sun to dappled shade

Long-lived beeches have massive trunks clad in smooth gray bark. In spring, as inconspicuous flowers form, silky leaves unfurl, turning bronze or ochre in the fall. Nuts are small but edible. Shallow rooted, often with branches sweeping the ground, beeches usually inhibit grass.

Selected species and varieties
F. grandifolia (American beech)—50 to 70 feet tall and almost as wide, with light gray bark and toothy leaves 2 to 5 inches long, dark green above and light green below. *F. sylvatica* (common beech, European beech, red beech)—usually 50 to 60 feet tall and 35 to 45 feet wide, with elephant-hide bark, branching close to the ground, Zones 4-7; 'Atropunicea' ['Atropurpurea'] (purple beech, copper beech) has black-red new leaves that turn purple-green; 'Aurea Pendula' is a weeping form with yellow new leaves aging to yellow-green; 'Dawyck Purple' grows in a narrow column with deep purple leaves.

Growing conditions and maintenance
Although both species listed here enjoy acid soil, European beech adapts to most soils. Best growth occurs in full sun.

Fatsia (FAT-see-a)

FATSIA

Fatsia japonica

HARDINESS: Zones 8-10

PLANT TYPE: evergreen shrub

HEIGHT: 6 to 10 feet

INTEREST: foliage, flowers, fruit

SOIL: moist, slightly acid, fertile

LIGHT: medium to bright full shade

Fatsia produces a broad, rounded shrub whose huge, finger-shaped dark green leaves lend a tropical effect to the shade garden. Panicles of white flowers appear in fall, followed by black berries. Interesting for its textural effects, fatsia makes a good backdrop for smaller shrubs. In the North, fatsia is used as a houseplant.

Selected species and varieties
F. japonica (Formosa rice tree, Japanese fatsia, glossy-leaved paper plant)—6 to 10 feet high with equal spread, bearing seven- to nine-lobed leaves 6 to 14 inches across and white flowers; inconsistently hardy to Zone 8. x *Fatshedera lizei*—the result of a cross between fatsia and English ivy, a semiclimbing shrub or vine with five-lobed leaves 4 to 10 inches across and pale green flowers; hardy to Zone 8.

Growing conditions and maintenance
Fatsia's leaves may become brown if exposed to full sun or winter winds. At the northern limits of hardiness, site in a courtyard or against a wall for increased protection. Although it tolerates a wide range of soils, fatsia grows best in soil high in organic matter. Allow it plenty of room, and prune to discourage legginess.

Forsythia (for-SITH-ee-a)

FORSYTHIA

Forsythia x intermedia 'Lynwood'

HARDINESS: Zones 5-8

PLANT TYPE: shrub

HEIGHT: 1 to 10 feet

INTEREST: flowers

SOIL: loose, well-drained

LIGHT: full sun

The bright yellow flowers of forsythia mark the onset of spring in many areas. Flowers are arranged along the entire length of the arching stems that grow from the base.

Selected species and varieties

F. x intermedia 'Spectabilis'—8 to 10 feet tall and wide, with leaves 3 to 4 inches long and bright yellow, tapered flowers 1½ inches across; 'Lynwood' has lighter yellow flowers than 'Spectabilis' and grows 6 to 7 feet tall, with a more upright habit, making it useful for mixed-shrub borders, massed on sunny banks, or in small groupings. *F. viridissima* 'Bronxensis'—12 inches tall with a 2- to 3-foot spread, compact and flat-topped; it has bright green stems and yellow flowers that bloom slightly later and are less showy than those of other species.

Growing conditions and maintenance

Forsythias can adapt to partial shade, although flowering will be reduced. Immediately after flowering, prune by removing the oldest stems back to the ground. Do not shear.

Fothergilla (faw-ther-GIL-a)

FOTHERGILLA

Fothergilla major

HARDINESS: Zones 4-8

PLANT TYPE: shrub

HEIGHT: 2 to 10 feet

INTEREST: flowers, foliage

SOIL: moist, well-drained, acid

LIGHT: full sun to partial shade

Fothergilla is a deciduous shrub that provides two seasons of garden interest. In spring, it is covered with small, fragrant, white bottlebrush-type flowers, and in fall the leaves turn shades of yellow, orange, and scarlet; all colors may appear on a single leaf. It is a useful shrub for a mixed border, a mass planting, or a small grouping. It makes an attractive companion to azaleas and rhododendrons.

Selected species and varieties

F. gardenii—2 to 3 feet tall with an equal or greater spread, dark blue-green leaves 1 to 2½ inches long, and petalless flowers with a showy stamen growing in 1- to 2-inch-long clusters in spring. *F. major*—6 to 10 feet tall with a slightly smaller spread and leaves 2 to 4 inches long, but otherwise similar to *F. gardenii*.

Growing conditions and maintenance

Fothergilla is easy to grow in soil amended with generous amounts of organic matter.

Fraxinus (FRAK-si-nus)

ASH

Fraxinus pennsylvanica

HARDINESS: Zones 2-9

PLANT TYPE: tree

HEIGHT: 45 to 80 feet

INTEREST: foliage

SOIL: wet to dry

LIGHT: full sun

Ashes are moderate- to fast-growing trees that give light shade. In fall, the leaves may crumble after they drop, requiring little if any raking. Small greenish yellow flowers are borne on separate male and female trees in spring. Paddle-shaped winged seeds on female trees germinate easily and may become a nuisance. Select a male clone or a seedless variety.

Selected species and varieties

F. americana (white ash)—to 80 feet tall with an open, rounded crown, with compound leaves, dark green above and pale below, that turn a rich yellow, then maroon to purple in fall, hardy to Zone 3; 'Champaign County', to 45 feet, with a dense canopy of leaves. *F. pennsylvanica* (red ash, green ash)—50 to 60 feet tall with an irregular crown half as wide, bearing shiny green leaves that may turn yellow in fall, to Zone 3; 'Patmore', a seedless form, grows 45 feet tall, with a symmetrical, upright-branching crown; to Zone 2.

Growing conditions and maintenance

Though ashes prefer moist, well-drained soil, white ash tolerates dry and moderately alkaline soils, and green ash adapts to wet and dry soils and high salt.

Gardenia *(gar-DEE-ni-a)*

GARDENIA

Gardenia augusta

HARDINESS: Zones 8-10

PLANT TYPE: shrub

HEIGHT: 1 to 6 feet

INTEREST: flowers, foliage, fragrance

SOIL: moist, well-drained, acid

LIGHT: full sun to partial shade

Each intensely fragrant, double, camellia-like flower is creamy white, and is attractively displayed against the dark evergreen leaves in spring and summer. While hardy only to Zone 8 this shrub is worth the effort to grow wherever conditions allow. Where it is not hardy, it can be grown as a container plant.

Selected species and varieties
G. augusta [formerly *G. jasminoides*]—evergreen shrub, 3 to 6 feet tall and wide with a dense, rounded habit, with 3- to 4-inch glossy, oval leaves and double blooms up to 5 inches across; 'August Beauty' grows 4 to 6 feet tall with abundant 4- to 5-inch blooms; 'Radicans', to 1 foot tall and 3 feet wide with smaller foliage and flowers than the species.

Growing conditions and maintenance
Plant gardenias in acid soil enriched with organic matter. It thrives in hot weather, and requires monthly fertilizing during the growing season. Mulch to keep soil moist and protect shallow roots. Propagate by cuttings.

Ginkgo *(GINK-o)*

MAIDENHAIR TREE

Ginkgo biloba

HARDINESS: Zones 4-8

PLANT TYPE: tree

HEIGHT: 30 to 80 feet

INTEREST: foliage, form

SOIL: moist, well-drained, slightly acid

LIGHT: full sun to partial shade

A native of China, this deciduous tree is now extinct in the wild. It has an irregular form and bears clusters of exotic-looking, fan-shaped leaves on short branchlets. Ginkgos provide dappled shade and make excellent specimen trees.

Selected species and varieties
G. biloba (maidenhair tree)—30 to 80 feet tall and 30 to 40 feet wide, with gray-brown, furrowed bark and mid-green foliage that turns bright yellow in autumn. Male and female flowers are produced on separate trees; the fruit of female trees has an unpleasant odor. 'Autumn Gold' is a male cultivar with a broadly conical form and golden yellow color in fall; Zones 5-8. 'Fastigiata' (sentry ginkgo) is male and narrowly pyramidal.

Growing conditions and maintenance
Ginkgo will grow in full sun or partial shade. It does best in moist, well-drained soil that is slightly acid. Ginkgos are tolerant of air pollution and are trouble-free in general.

Gleditsia *(gle-DIT-see-a)*

HONEY LOCUST

Gleditsia triacanthos

HARDINESS: Zones 3-9

PLANT TYPE: tree

HEIGHT: to 70 feet

INTEREST: foliage, form

SOIL: well-drained

LIGHT: full sun

Leafing late in spring on a wide-spreading canopy of arching branches, honey locust produces bright green ferny foliage, creating light to dappled shade during a short season. Inconspicuous fragrant flowers in late spring are followed by 12- to 18-inch reddish brown to brown strap-shaped pods, usually viewed as a nuisance. When the leaves turn yellow and fall in early autumn, they crumble into the grass and mostly disappear.

Selected species and varieties
G. triacanthos var. *inermis* (thornless honey locust, sweet locust)—highly variable size, from 30 to 70 feet tall and equally wide ranging in spread, with a short trunk and an open crown bearing doubly compound leaves with oblong leaflets ⅓ to 1½ inches long and greenish yellow flowers; 'Imperial' [also called 'Impcole'] is a seedless version that grows to 35 feet high and wide; Zones 4-7.

Growing conditions and maintenance
Honey locusts grow best in moist, rich loam but tolerate acid and alkaline soils, drought, and salt. Under average conditions, they grow 2 feet per year or more but may be insect and disease prone.

Grevillea (gre-VIL-ee-a)

GREVILLEA

Grevillea rosmarinifolia

HARDINESS: Zones 10-11

PLANT TYPE: shrub

HEIGHT: 4 to 6 feet

INTEREST: flowers, foliage

SOIL: well-drained, acid

LIGHT: full sun

Rosemary grevillea is a tender evergreen shrub with dark, needle-shaped leaves. It produces dense clusters of red-and-cream flowers that cover the entire plant. The flowers attract hummingbirds.

Selected species and varieties

G. rosmarinifolia—has a rounded, well-branched form, 1-inch-long narrow leaves that are dark green on top and white below with silky hairs, and flowers 1 inch across.

Growing conditions and maintenance

Rosemary grevillea can withstand heat, drought, and wind. It can be grown in containers and moved indoors in areas where it is not hardy. Water container-grown plants sparingly in winter.

Halesia (ha-LEE-zhi-a)

SILVER BELL

Halesia monticola

HARDINESS: Zones 4-8

PLANT TYPE: deciduous tree

HEIGHT: 25 to 80 feet

INTEREST: flowers, bark, fruit

SOIL: moist, well-drained, acid, fertile

LIGHT: bright full shade to full sun

Silver bell's dangling clusters of white bell-shaped flowers in spring appear before or with the dark yellow-green leaves, which hold their color until they turn yellow early in the fall. Green to brown four-winged fruits remain after the leaves have fallen. The furrowed and plated bark is gray, brown, and black. Silver bell serves well as an understory tree but can also be used to create shade for other plants.

Selected species and varieties

H. monticola (mountain silver bell)—60 to 80 feet tall with a usually conical habit displaying 1-inch-long flowers in two- to five-flowered clusters as the 3- to 6½-inch-long leaves begin to develop; 'Rosea' has pale rose-colored flowers. *H. tetraptera* [also classified as *H. carolina*] (Carolina silver bell, opossumwood)—a smaller, low-branched version of mountain silver bell 25 to 40 feet tall with a rounded crown 20 to 35 feet wide consisting of ascending branches with 2- to 4-inch leaves, flowers ½ to ¾ inch long, and fruits 1½ inches long.

Growing conditions and maintenance

Silver bells do best in soil supplemented with organic matter. They are pest resistant and require little maintenance.

Hamamelis (ha-ma-MEL-lis)

WITCH HAZEL

Hamamelis japonica 'Zuccariniana'

HARDINESS: Zones 3-8

PLANT TYPE: large shrub or small tree

HEIGHT: 6 to 20 feet

INTEREST: flowers, foliage, fragrance

SOIL: well-drained to moist

LIGHT: bright full shade to full sun

Witch hazels brighten the fall and winter landscape with heavily fragrant yellow to red flowers on angular branches, sometimes appearing long after their colorful fall foliage has fallen. The two-valved, dry fruit capsules explode, propelling the black seeds many feet away.

Selected species and varieties

H. x *intermedia* 'Arnold Promise'—to 20 feet tall and wide with 1½-inch primrose yellow flowers in winter to early spring and gray-green foliage that becomes yellow, orange, or red in fall; 'Diane' grows 14 to 20 feet tall, bearing slightly fragrant orange-red flowers with purple-red calyxes and yellow-orange to red autumn foliage; 'Jelena' [sometimes called 'Copper Beauty'] bears copper-colored flowers and orange-red fall foliage; 'Primavera', very fragrant prolific clear yellow flowers borne later than the species; 'Ruby Glow', coppery red to reddish brown flowers and orange-red fall foliage; all *H.* x *intermedia* are hardy to Zone 5. *H. japonica* 'Sulphurea' (Japanense witch hazel)—10 to 15 feet high and wide with open, flat-topped habit, producing yellow flowers with red calyx cups in late winter and lustrous green leaves that turn yellow, red, and purplish in fall; hardy to Zone 5; 'Zuccariniana' has rich yellow flowers with a hint of green inside the calyx; hardy to Zone 5. *H. mollis* 'Goldcrest' (Chinese witch hazel)—an oval, broadly open large shrub or small tree 10 to 15 feet tall and wide with medium green leaves in summer that turn a vivid yellow to yellow-orange in fall and fragrant yellow flowers with red-brown calyx cups blooming for a long period in winter; reliably hardy to Zone 6; 'Pallida' has a spreading habit and lustrous leaves, with yellow flowers suffused with a blush of chartreuse in late winter; hardy to Zone 5. *H. vernalis* (American witch hazel)—multistemmed, broad rounded outline 6 to 10 feet tall with a greater spread and very fragrant yellow to red flowers from late winter to early spring and medium to dark green foliage in summer turning golden yellow in fall; hardy to Zone 4; 'Carnea' has richly colored flowers with a red calyx and petals that are red at the base blending to orange at the tip. *H. virginiana* (common witch hazel)—large shrub to small tree 20 feet tall and equally wide with angular spreading branches and fragrant yellow flowers that emerge in mid- to late fall, sometimes just as its 4- to 6-inch-long leaves have turned yellow; hardy to Zone 3.

Growing conditions and maintenance
Common and American witch hazel can tolerate heavy, poorly drained clay. Give Chinese and Japanese witch hazels well-drained acid soil to which organic matter has been added. Prune *H. x intermedia* to encourage dense branching.

Hamamelis mollis

HEBE

Hebe buxifolia 'Patty's Purple'

HARDINESS:	Zones 8-10
PLANT TYPE:	shrub
HEIGHT:	2 to 5 feet
INTEREST:	flowers, foliage, form
SOIL:	well-drained
LIGHT:	full sun to partial shade

Native to New Zealand, hebes are rounded, leathery-leaved evergreen shrubs that produce spikes of white, pink, red, lavender, or purple flowers 2 to 4 inches long at the ends of the branches. Their small, glossy leaves, densely arranged on stems, make these fine-textured spreading shrubs good candidates for shrub borders, hedges, edgings, rock gardens, and perennial beds.

Selected species and varieties
H. 'Autumn Glory'—a mounding form 2 to 3 feet high and 2 feet wide, with glossy dark green leaves 1½ inches long tinged with red when young, and dark lavender-blue flower spikes, 2 inches long and sometimes branched, blooming profusely from midsummer through fall. *H. buxifolia* 'Patty's Purple' (boxleaf veronica)—1-inch-long purple clusters and leaves scarcely ½ inch long, growing to 5 feet.

Growing conditions and maintenance
Hebes need good drainage and prefer either acid or alkaline soil of average fertility. They thrive in cool coastal gardens, and need partial shade where summers are hot. Prune after flowering to avoid legginess. They are tolerant of salt spray.

CALIFORNIA HOLLY

Heteromeles arbutifolia

HARDINESS:	Zones 8-10
PLANT TYPE:	shrub or small tree
HEIGHT:	12 to 25 feet
INTEREST:	foliage, fruit
SOIL:	well-drained
LIGHT:	full sun to partial shade

The California holly has glossy, dark, evergreen leaves. In late summer it produces large clusters of orange-to-red berries that attract birds and other wildlife to the garden. Cut the berry clusters for indoor arrangements and holiday decorations.

Selected species and varieties
H. arbutifolia—to 25 feet tall and equally as wide, with leathery, sharply toothed leaves and inconspicuous white flowers that bloom in spring and are followed by showy clusters of fruit.

Growing conditions and maintenance
Although California holly prefers a fertile, well-drained soil and full sun, it tolerates a wide range of conditions, including partial shade and drought. The plants can be pruned to reveal their attractive branching habit.

Hibiscus (hy-BIS-kus)

MALLOW

Hibiscus syriacus 'Diana'

HARDINESS: Zones 5-9

PLANT TYPE: perennial or shrub

HEIGHT: 5 to 12 feet

INTEREST: flowers

SOIL: moist, well-drained

LIGHT: full sun to light shade

The genus *Hibiscus* includes both woody shrubs and herbaceous perennials. Their showy flowers add color and a tropical appearance to borders or beds from summer to frost.

Selected species and varieties
H. coccineus (scarlet rose mallow)—a 5- to 8-foot-tall perennial with 6-inch-wide scarlet blooms from mid- to late summer; Zones 5-9. *H.* x 'Lady Baltimore'—crimson-eyed pink flowers. *H. syriacus* (rose of Sharon)—6- to 12-foot shrub with stiffly upright branches and 2½- to 4-inch flowers in shades of pink, red, purple, and white in late summer and fall; 'Diana' grows to 8 feet and bears 4- to 6-inch-wide single white blooms; Zones 5-8.

Growing conditions and maintenance
Both *H. coccineus* and *H.* hybrids are good choices for wet spots in the garden. Space 3 feet apart. Propagate by seed, cuttings, or division. *H. syriacus* requires well-drained soil. Allow 6 to 8 feet between the plants and propagate by softwood cuttings in summer.

Hydrangea (hy-DRAN-jee-a)

HYDRANGEA

Hydrangea arborescens 'Annabelle'

HARDINESS: Zones 3-9

PLANT TYPE: shrub, tree, or vine

HEIGHT: 3 to 80 feet

INTEREST: flowers, foliage, bark

SOIL: moist, well-drained

LIGHT: full sun to partial shade

Hydrangeas are valued for their large clusters of summer flowers. The genus includes deciduous shrubs that go well in mixed borders or mass plantings, small trees that make excellent specimens, and a climbing vine that can grow to 80 feet or more if supported. All have relatively coarse leaves, are easy to grow, and produce long-lasting blossoms that are used in both fresh and dried arrangements.

Selected species and varieties
H. anomala ssp. *petiolaris* (climbing hydrangea)—a vine capable of reaching 60 to 80 feet in height but maintainable at a much lower height with pruning; it has very attractive cinnamon brown bark in winter, glossy dark green leaves 2 to 4 inches long, and white flowers in 6- to 10-inch flat-topped clusters emerging early to midsummer; excellent for growing on brick or stone walls, arbors, trellises, or trees; Zones 4-7. *H. arborescens* 'Grandiflora' (hills-of-snow hydrangea)—3 feet tall and equally as wide, with 6- to 8-inch clusters of white flowers in mid to late summer, useful as a foundation planting or an informal hedge, Zones 3-9; 'Annabelle' produces flower clusters up to 10 inches

across that bloom about 2 weeks later than those of 'Grandiflora'. *H. paniculata*—10 to 25 feet tall, 10 to 20 feet wide, an upright, spreading, large shrub or small tree with dark green leaves 3 to 6 inches long and white flowers maturing to dusty pink in grapelike clusters 6 to 8 inches long in midsummer, Zones 3-8; 'Grandiflora' (peegee hydrangea) bears flower clusters up to 18 inches long and makes a spectacular specimen. *H. quercifolia* (oakleaf hydrangea)—4 to 6 feet tall and more than 6 feet wide, with coarse, deeply lobed leaves 3 to 8 inches long that are deep green in summer and turn a brilliant dark reddish bronze in fall and white flowers turning dusty pink, then brown, in erect clusters up to 12 inches long, Zones 5-9; 'Snowflake' grows flowers in clusters to 15 inches long with layered bracts that give the flowers the appearance of double blooms; 'Snow Queen' has wine red fall leaf color and flowers larger and denser than those of the species.

Growing conditions and maintenance
Hydrangeas thrive in fertile soil; incorporate abundant amounts of organic matter into the soil before planting. *H. arborescens* prefers partial shade; other species adapt well to sun or light shade. Climbing hydrangea requires several years to adjust after transplanting, but once established will grow rapidly.

Hydrangea quercifolia

Hypericum (hy-PER-i-kum)

ST.-JOHN'S-WORT

Hypericum calycinum

HARDINESS: Zones 3-9

PLANT TYPE: shrub or ground cover

HEIGHT: 1 to 4 feet

INTEREST: flowers, fruit

SOIL: poor, well-drained to dry

LIGHT: bright full shade to full sun

St.-John's-wort has bright yellow flowers over a long period in summer. Dry three-winged fruit capsules persist all winter.

Selected species and varieties

H. calycinum (creeping St.-John's-wort)—12 to 18 inches high, spreading by stolons to 2 feet wide, with very bright yellow, 3-inch-wide flowers all summer and semi-evergreen dark green leaves; Zones 5-8. *H. frondosum* (golden St.-John's-wort)—shrubby habit, 3 to 4 feet tall and wide, with reddish brown exfoliating bark, bluish green leaves 1 to 2 inches long and 1- to 2-inch-wide flowers from early to midsummer; Zones 5-8. *H.* 'Hidcote'—3 feet high and wide, blooming with 2½- to 3-inch-wide flowers in late spring to midsummer over dark green leaves; Zones 6-9. *H. prolificum* (shrubby St.-John's-wort, broombrush)—1 to 4 feet high and wide, with light brown exfoliating bark, dark to bluish green, narrow, oblong leaves up to 3 inches long and ¾- to 1-inch-wide flowers in summer; Zones 3-8.

Growing conditions and maintenance

A good plant for gravelly, limy soils; may be short-lived in poorly drained soils and high humidity. Prune in early spring.

Ilex (EYE-lex)

HOLLY

Ilex aquifolium 'Argenteo-marginata'

HARDINESS: Zones 4-10

PLANT TYPE: shrub or tree

HEIGHT: 2 to 50 feet

INTEREST: foliage, fruit, form

SOIL: moist, well-drained

LIGHT: full sun to partial shade

The genus produces a broad range of mostly evergreen plants in all sizes and shapes. Dense, lustrous foliage and a neat habit make shrub hollies ideal foundation plants, hedges, and background plants. The taller hollies make lovely specimen plants and effective screens. Tiny, sometimes fragrant spring flowers are inconspicuous. In most species, a female plant must be within 100 feet of a male to set fruit.

Selected species and varieties

I. x *altaclarensis* 'Wilsonii' (Altaclara holly)—a 30-foot-tall tree with spiny leaves up to 5 inches long and 3 inches wide and red fruit; Zones 7-9. *I. aquifolium* (common holly, English holly)—30 to 50 feet tall, bearing fragrant whitish flowers in spring, wavy leaves with spines, and red berries, Zones 6-9; 'Argenteo-marginata', a female, has dark green leaves edged with white; 'Boulder Creek', also a female, glossy black-green leaves. *I.* x *attenuata* 'Fosteri' (Foster Hybrids)—small pyramidal trees 10 to 25 feet high with small red berries; Zones 6-9. *I. cornuta* (Chinese holly, horned holly)—a dense, rounded shrub 8 to 10 feet tall, with spiny rectangular leaves up to 4 inches long, small, fragrant spring flowers, and bright red berries lasting until late winter, Zones 7-9; 'Berries Jubilee' has large berry clusters and grows 6 to 10 feet tall; 'Carissa' is 3 to 4 feet tall and up to 6 feet wide, bearing oval leaves with only one spine; 'Needlepoint' has narrow, twisted leaves and a single spine. *I. crenata* (Japanese holly, box-leaved holly)—a dense, multibranched rounded shrub that grows slowly to 5 to 10 feet high and wide, with lustrous oval leaves ½ to 1 inch long and small black berries hidden under the foliage, Zones 5-8; 'Convexa' is a very dense cultivar that eventually grows to 9 feet tall and more than twice as wide, with ½-inch-long curved leaves and heavy fruit; 'Green Island' has an open habit, growing to 4 feet tall and 6 feet wide; 'Helleri' is 2 to 3 feet tall by 5 feet wide with ½-inch dull, very dark green leaves; 'Microphylla' has an upright habit and leaves smaller than the species. *I. decidua* (possum haw, winterberry)—deciduous shrub or small tree up to 15 feet tall, with glossy green leaves turning yellow in fall and orange to red berries that linger until the next spring; Zones 5-9. *I. glabra* (Appalachian tea, inkberry)—an upright, multibranched rounded shrub 6 to 8 feet tall by 8 to 10 feet wide, becoming open with age, with narrow-oval leaves 1 to 2 inches long and bearing small black berries, partly hidden by the leaves, from fall to the following spring, Zones 4-9; 'Compacta', a female, is a more tightly branched form 4 to 6 feet tall. *I.* x *meserveae* (Meserve Hybrids)—a group of dense, bushy shrubs 8 to 12 feet tall, with lustrous dark green or

Ilex cornuta

bluish green leaves on deep purple stems, hardy to Zone 4; 'Blue Prince', a male, forms a broad pyramid; 'Blue Princess', known to grow as much as 15 feet high and 10 feet wide, has dark blue-green leaves and red berries. *I. opaca* (American holly)—a 40- to 50-foot tree, pyramidal when young, becoming open and irregular over time, with dull to dark yellow-green leaves and bright red berries persisting into winter; Zones 5-9. *I. pedunculosa* (long-stalked holly)—a moderately dense, large shrub or small tree, 15 to 20 feet tall, with dark green leaves, 1 to 3 inches long, and red berries borne on long stems in fall, usually not lasting into winter; Zones 5-8. *I.* x 'Sparkleberry'—forms a narrow column, with small red berries that persist well into winter and nearly black bark. *I. vomitoria* (yaupon, cassina)—15 to 20 feet tall and less in width, with attractively irregular branches, gray to white bark, and a heavy fruit crop lasting till spring, Zones 7-10; 'Nana' grows 5 feet high and wide, with fruit often hidden by the foliage.

Growing conditions and maintenance
Although hollies tolerate partial shade, they prefer full sun. Most evergreen hollies do not endure hot, windy, or dry climates. For best results, provide a loose, well-drained loam. Chinese holly tolerates most soils and withstands drought. Japanese holly prefers moist, slightly acid soils. Inkberry, found naturally in swamps, thrives in wet, acid soils. American holly needs very well-drained, acid loam in wind-protected areas. Long-stalked holly tolerates heavy soils and drying wind. Yaupon withstands dry to wet sites and tolerates alkalinity.

Ilex pedunculosa

Illicium (ill-ISS-ee-um)

ANISE TREE

Illicium anisatum

HARDINESS: Zones 7-9

PLANT TYPE: evergreen shrub or tree

HEIGHT: 6 to 25 feet

INTEREST: fragrance, flowers, fruit

SOIL: moist, well-drained, fertile

LIGHT: full shade to full sun

The spicy aroma of the anise tree comes not from its flowers but from its broad, evergreen leaves. Small, star-shaped fruit clusters are decorative. *Note:* The species listed here may be poisonous.

Selected species and varieties
I. anisatum (star anise)—broad pyramidal shrub or small tree 8 to 25 feet high with fragrant, yellow-green to white flowers emerging in early spring; Zones 7-9. *I. floridanum* (Florida anise tree, purple anise)—multistemmed shrub 6 to 10 feet high, with dark green leaves 2 to 6 inches long and smelly but showy dark red flowers to 2 inches wide in spring. *I. parviflorum* (small anise tree)—8 to 20 feet tall, bearing 2- to 4-inch olive green leaves that emit some of the best anise odor of the genus. The yellow-green flowers appearing in late spring carry no odor.

Growing conditions and maintenance
Of these species, only *I. parviflorum* is adaptable to dry soil; it will succeed in very moist soil as well. Add peat moss or compost to the soil; maintain moisture. *I. anisatum* needs partial shade; *I. parviflorum*, partial shade to full sun; *I. floridanum* tolerates deep shade to full sun.

Itea (IT-ee-a)

SWEETSPIRE

Itea virginica

HARDINESS: Zones 5-9

PLANT TYPE: shrub

HEIGHT: 2 to 5 feet

INTEREST: flowers, foliage

SOIL: fertile, moist

LIGHT: full sun to partial shade

Sweetspire offers a fine garden display in both summer and fall. Its flowers appear in midsummer, well after most shrubs have finished blooming. In fall its leaves put on a show, turning reddish purple to scarlet and persisting for several weeks.

Selected species and varieties
I. japonica 'Beppu'—2 to 5 feet tall with spreading, moundlike habit, plants spread by suckers, leaves are rich green in summer, red in fall, flowers are white and fragrant, useful as a ground cover. *I. virginica* 'Henry's Garnet'—3 to 4 feet tall, 4 to 6 feet wide, green leaves turn purple-red in fall, fragrant white flowers in clusters up to 6 inches long, excellent addition to mixed-shrub border.

Growing conditions and maintenance
Sweetspire is easily transplanted, and new plants can be obtained by dividing an existing specimen. It prefers a rich, moist to wet site. In mild climates it is semievergreen.

Juniperus (joo-NIP-er-us)

JUNIPER

Juniperus conferta

HARDINESS: Zones 2-9

PLANT TYPE: tree, shrub, or ground cover

HEIGHT: 6 inches to 60 feet

INTEREST: foliage, form

SOIL: light, well-drained

LIGHT: full sun

Junipers vary from wide, flat mats that hug the ground to tall, thin spires good for accents or corner plantings. Their scalelike evergreen foliage ranges in color from green to silvery blue to yellow and sometimes a different shade in winter. Female plants produce small blue berries. Tall forms make good screens or windbreaks.

Selected species and varieties
J. chinensis (Chinese juniper)—usually a narrow, conical tree 50 to 60 feet high with green to bluish to gray-green foliage, Zones 3-9; 'Mint Julep' is a fountain-shaped shrub 4 to 6 feet tall with greater spread, bearing arching branches and bright green foliage; 'Old Gold' has ascending branches with bronze-gold foliage and grows to 3 feet tall by 4 feet wide; 'Pfitzeriana Glauca' has bluish foliage becoming purplish blue in winter, normally 5 feet high by 10 feet wide but often larger. *J. conferta* (shore juniper)—shrub that spreads 6 to 9 feet and 1 to 1½ feet high with soft, needlelike bluish green foliage in summer turning bronzy or yellow-green in winter; Zones 6-9. *J. horizontalis* (creeping juniper, creeping savin)—1 to 2 feet high by 4 to 8 feet wide, with trailing branches

bearing glaucous green, blue-green, or blue plumelike foliage turning plum-purple in winter, Zones 3-9; 'Wiltonii' (blue rug juniper) forms a flat mat less than 6 inches high, spreading up to 8 feet, with grayish blue foliage. *J. occidentalis* (Sierra juniper, California juniper)—shrub or tree to 40 feet, with glaucous green foliage; hardy to Zone 5. *J. procumbens* [sometimes classified as *J. chinensis* var. *procumbens*] (Japanese garden juniper)—1 to 2 feet high and 10 to 15 feet wide, with bluish green to gray-green foliage; 'Nana', a dwarf of the species, forms a low, rounded, compact mat 6 to 12 inches high and spreading up to 12 feet, with overlapping branches of bluish green foliage turning purplish in winter. *J. sabina* (savin)—a vase-shaped shrub 4 to 6 feet high by 5 to 10 feet wide, with dark green foliage turning a drab green tinged with yellow in winter; 'Broadmoor' grows 2 to 3 feet high with a 10-foot spread, bearing soft gray-green foliage in short upright sprays; hardy to Zone 4. *J. scopulorum* (Rocky Mountain juniper, Colorado red cedar)—a narrow pyramidal tree growing 30 to 40 feet high and 3 to 15 feet wide, with foliage ranging from light green to dark blue-green; 'Skyrocket' forms a narrow spire, 10 to 15 feet tall, with bluish foliage.

Growing conditions and maintenance
Tolerant of almost any soil as long as it is well drained, junipers do best in moist, light soils. Loosen heavy soils with sand. Most junipers tolerate drought and pollution. Shore junipers grow well in seaside gardens. Savin and Chinese junipers accept limestone soils.

Juniperus horizontalis 'Wiltonii'

Kalmia (KAL-mee-a)

MOUNTAIN LAUREL

Kalmia latifolia 'Ostbo Red'

HARDINESS: Zones 4-9

PLANT TYPE: shrub

HEIGHT: 7 to 15 feet

INTEREST: flowers, foliage

SOIL: moist, well-drained, acid

LIGHT: full sun to full shade

In early summer, mountain laurel bears white, pink, or rose-colored blossoms, set off by a background of dark, leathery leaves. It is equally at home as a foundation plant, in a mixed-shrub border, or in a naturalized, woodland garden.

Selected species and varieties
K. latifolia—variable height, usually to 15 feet with equal spread, leaves 2 to 5 inches long, evergreen, flower buds are deep pink or red and crimped, flowers are ¾ to 1 inch across in 4- to 6-inch rounded, terminal clusters; 'Nipmuck'—red buds, flowers are creamy white to light pink on inside and dark pink on outside; 'Ostbo Red'—red buds, soft pink flowers; 'Pink Charm'—deep pink buds, pink flowers with red ring on inside near base.

Growing conditions and maintenance
Mountain laurel is easy to grow and virtually maintenance free as long as its cultural conditions are met. While it adapts to sun or shade, it requires a moist, acid soil; add generous amounts of organic matter. Mulch to retain moisture.

Kerria (KER-ee-a)

JAPANESE KERRIA

Kerria japonica 'Pleniflora'

HARDINESS: Zones 4-9

PLANT TYPE: shrub

HEIGHT: 3 to 8 feet

INTEREST: flowers, stems

SOIL: fertile, loamy, well-drained

LIGHT: partial to full shade

Japanese kerria produces masses of bright yellow spring flowers on arched, lime green stems. It is a lively addition to the mixed-shrub border or a woodland garden. Its green stems add color to the winter landscape.

Selected species and varieties
K. japonica—3 to 6 feet tall, spreading to 9 feet across, arching green stems zigzag from one node to the next, deciduous, bright green leaves are 1½ to 4 inches long, bright yellow five-petaled flowers, 1½ inches across; 'Picta'—leaves with attractive white margin; 'Pleniflora'—up to 8 feet, habit more erect than species, flowers are double, rounded, golden yellow.

Growing conditions and maintenance
Japanese kerria performs better with some shade; too much sun causes the flowers to fade quickly. Prune to remove any dead branches whenever they appear, and remove green shoots that arise among the variegated foliage of 'Picta'. Do not overfertilize, as this causes rank growth and reduces flowering.

Koelreuteria (kol-roo-TEER-ee-a)

GOLDEN-RAIN TREE

Koelreuteria paniculata 'September'

HARDINESS: Zones 5-9

PLANT TYPE: tree

HEIGHT: 30 to 40 feet

INTEREST: flowers, foliage, form

SOIL: well-drained

LIGHT: partial shade to full sun

A delightful small tree to shade a garden bench or patio, the golden-rain tree produces airy sprays of yellow flowers in early summer on wide-spreading branches. Greenish balloon-shaped seed capsules turn yellow, then brown and papery in fall; the color change takes about 2 months. The dense canopy consists of large compound leaves that are medium bright green, changing to yellow before dropping in fall. Sparse branching gives the tree a coarse look in winter.

Selected species and varieties
K. paniculata (golden-rain tree, varnish tree)—rounded crown with spread equal to or greater than its height, bearing 6- to 18-inch-long leaves composed of seven to 15 toothed and lobed leaflets 1 to 3 inches long, purplish red when opening, and flower clusters 12 to 15 inches long and wide; 'September' flowers in late summer and is less hardy than the species.

Growing conditions and maintenance
Golden-rain tree tolerates a wide variety of conditions including drought. It grows best—about 1½ feet per year—in soil well amended with peat moss or leaf mold. Provide shelter from wind.

Lagerstroemia (la-gur-STREE-mee-a)

CRAPE MYRTLE

Lagerstroemia indica 'Seminole'

HARDINESS: Zones 7-9

PLANT TYPE: shrub or tree

HEIGHT: 7 to 25 feet

INTEREST: flowers, bark

SOIL: moist, well-drained

LIGHT: full sun

Crape myrtle's large clusters of crinkly flowers in pink, white, rose, or purple come in late summer at a time when little else may be in bloom. In fall, the dark green leaves turn red, orange, and yellow, all on the same plant. As the light gray bark ages, it exfoliates, revealing dark gray and brown underbark. Crape myrtle is often grown as a specimen.

Selected species and varieties
L. indica (common crape myrtle)—a fast-growing multistemmed shrub or tree 15 to 25 feet tall, with flower clusters 6 to 8 inches long; 'Natchez' reaches 20 feet tall and wide, with cinnamon brown exfoliating bark and white flower clusters 6 to 12 inches long from early summer to fall, when glossy dark green leaves turn orange and red; 'Seminole' bears medium pink flowers for 6 to 8 weeks beginning in midsummer on a 7- to 8-foot shrub.

Growing conditions and maintenance
Amend soil with peat moss or leaf mold. At its northern limits, crape myrtle is grown as a herbaceous perennial; when severe cold kills the plant to the ground, it returns the next spring with abundant, lush new growth.

Lantana (lan-TAN-a)

LANTANA

Lantana montevidensis

HARDINESS: Zones 9-10

PLANT TYPE: annual or tender shrub

HEIGHT: 12 inches to 6 feet

INTEREST: flower, foliage, fragrance

SOIL: well-drained

LIGHT: full sun

Lantanas have somewhat stiff branches and a trailing habit that is particularly effective when stems cascade over the walls of raised beds or containers. The 1- to 2-inch flower clusters in shades of yellow, white, orange, red, lavender, and bicolors appear throughout the summer. The flowers and leaves have a slightly pungent fragrance.

Selected species and varieties

L. camara (yellow sage)—2- to 6-foot shrub with dark, hairy leaves and flat-topped clusters of tiny flowers that start yellow and turn orange-red; 'Confetti' bears white, pink, and red flowers all on the same plant. *L. montevidensis* [also listed as *L. sellowiana*] (weeping lantana)—to 30 inches with a greater spread, mounding habit, dark green wrinkled leaves and flower clusters similar to *L. camara*.

Growing conditions and maintenance

Space plants 18 inches apart. They can be trained to standards, and are easily dug and potted in fall for indoor winter flowering. Propagate from cuttings.

Laurus (LAR-us)

LAUREL, SWEET BAY

Laurus nobilis

HARDINESS: Zones 8-10

PLANT TYPE: large shrub or small tree

HEIGHT: 30 to 40 feet

INTEREST: fragrance, form

SOIL: well-drained

LIGHT: partial shade to full sun

Laurel is valued for its aromatic evergreen foliage, the same leaves that were used to fashion wreaths and crowns in ancient times and that are used for seasoning today. The berries yield an oil that is a perfume ingredient. Easily sheared, laurel is often kept in planters and trained into odd shapes. In the North, it can be brought inside to overwinter.

Selected species and varieties

L. nobilis (true laurel, bay laurel, bay tree)—grows very slowly with a pyramidal habit to 40 feet and has dark green elliptical or lance-shaped leaves to 4 inches long with small, inconspicuous yellowish green flowers in late spring or early summer followed by purple or black berries in the fall.

Growing conditions and maintenance

Laurel grows well in ordinary garden soil. A native of the Mediterranean region, it can endure dry spells once it is well established. In very hot regions, provide it with afternoon shade.

Lavandula (lav-AN-dew-la)

LAVENDER

Lavandula angustifolia 'Hidcote'

HARDINESS: Zones 5-10

PLANT TYPE: shrub

HEIGHT: 1 to 4 feet

INTEREST: form, fragrance, flowers

SOIL: well-drained to dry, neutral to alkaline

LIGHT: full sun

The gray-green woolly foliage of lavender, prized for its fragrance, contrasts well with both dark green and blue plants in the landscape. Dainty flower spikes top tightly packed upright stems in late spring to summer. Lavender is used in edgings, rock gardens, and perennial beds, and its fine-textured evergreen foliage softens the landscape. In addition, the species can be trimmed into a low hedge.

Selected species and varieties

L. angustifolia (English lavender, common lavender)—blue-violet flowers in whorls 2 to 3 inches tall bloom at the top of 1- to 2-foot (occasionally 4-foot) stems that are lined with narrow 1- to 2-inch leaves, Zones 5-9; 'Hidcote', 12 to 15 inches tall, has dense deep purple spikes and silvery leaves. *L. stoechas* (Spanish lavender)—1½ to 3 feet tall with 1-inch leaves and short dark purple spikes topped with tufts of petal-like bracts; Zones 8-10.

Growing conditions and maintenance

Fast drainage is essential; loosen heavy soils with sand, and do not fertilize. Set plants 12 to 18 inches apart. Cut back in early spring to encourage dense growth. Propagate by division in spring.

Leptospermum (lep-toh-SPER-mum)

NEW ZEALAND TEA TREE

Leptospermum scoparium

HARDINESS: Zones 9-10

PLANT TYPE: shrub

HEIGHT: 6 to 10 feet

INTEREST: flowers, foliage

SOIL: fertile, moist, well-drained, acid

LIGHT: full sun to light shade

The New Zealand tea tree is a fine-textured evergreen shrub with a dense branching habit and small leaves. Its flowers are borne in winter, spring, or summer, and though blossoms of the species are white, varieties are available with pink or red flowers.

Selected species and varieties

L. scoparium—6 to 10 feet, slightly smaller in spread, rounded form, compact, leaves are dark gray-green and aromatic, profuse white flowers are ½ inch across.

Growing conditions and maintenance

The New Zealand tea tree is easy to grow in mild climates in a well-drained acid to neutral soil. It prefers full sun, except in hot, dry areas, where it benefits from partial shade. It thrives under humid coastal conditions. Though it is somewhat tolerant of drought, supplemental water should be given, especially where the climate is hot. Prune in early spring.

Lespedeza (les-ped-EE-za)

BUSH CLOVER

Lespedeza thunbergii 'White Fountain'

HARDINESS: Zones 4-8

PLANT TYPE: shrub

HEIGHT: 3 to 10 feet

INTEREST: flowers

SOIL: well-drained to sandy, dry

LIGHT: full sun

Bush clovers are deciduous shrubs valued for their late-season flowers. They are most attractive when massed or mixed in a sunny shrub border.

Selected species and varieties

L. bicolor (shrub bush clover)—6 to 10 feet, with trifoliate leaves along arching stems, and rosy purple flowers in 2- to 5-inch-long clusters arising from the current season's growth from mid- to late summer; Zones 4-8. *L. thunbergii* [also listed as *L. sieboldii*] (purple bush clover)—to 6 feet tall and 10 feet wide with slender arching stems that become weighted down by the 8-inch-long dark purple flower clusters from late summer to fall; 'White Fountain' has white flowers; Zones 5-8.

Growing conditions and maintenance

Because bush clovers tend toward legginess if allowed to grow unpruned, cut stems to the ground in early spring before growth begins. New stems will reach 3 to 4 feet by flowering time. Propagate by seed or stem cuttings.

Leucothoe (loo-KO-tho-ee)

FETTERBUSH

Leucothoe fontanesiana 'Rainbow'

HARDINESS: Zones 4-9

PLANT TYPE: evergreen shrub

HEIGHT: 2 to 6 feet

INTEREST: foliage, flowers, form

SOIL: moist, well-drained, acid, fertile

LIGHT: partial to bright full shade

With its clusters of creamy, urn-shaped flowers, lustrous green leaves, arching branches, and spreading, broad-mounded habit, leucothoe looks stunning in the garden either as a specimen plant or planted in masses. The low forms make elegant ground covers.

Selected species and varieties

L. davisiae (Sierra laurel)—to 5 feet high with nodding upright panicles of flowers up to 6 inches long, borne above 1- to 3-inch leaves in late spring or early summer. *L. fontanesiana* (dog-hobble, drooping leucothoe)—3 to 6 feet high and wide, with arching branches of dark green, pointed, 2- to 5-inch-long leaves that turn red-bronze for fall and winter and fragrant 2- to 3-inch flower clusters protruding from beneath the foliage in spring; 'Rainbow' [also called 'Girard's Rainbow'] has leaves variegated in pink, yellow, cream, and green; 'Nana' is a dwarf 2 feet tall spreading to 6 feet; Zones 4-6.

Growing conditions and maintenance

Add peat moss, leaf mold, or dried compost liberally to soil when planting, and mulch to keep roots cool, particularly if exposed to sun. Prune after flowering.

Ligustrum (li-GUS-trum)

PRIVET, HEDGE PLANT

Ligustrum japonicum

HARDINESS: Zones 6-10

PLANT TYPE: shrub

HEIGHT: 6 to 15 feet

INTEREST: foliage, flowers, fruit

SOIL: adaptable

LIGHT: full sun or shade

Privet is grown primarily for its dense habit and lustrous foliage, which is highly amenable to heavy shearing. Usually used for hedges, screens, and foundation plants, privet can also be tailored into topiary specimens. White flowers, often considered malodorous, bloom in late spring or early summer, followed by black or blue-black berries.

Selected species and varieties
L. japonicum (Japanese privet, waxleaf privet, waxleaf ligustrum)—an upright, dense evergreen shrub 6 to 12 feet tall and up to 8 feet wide with 2- to 6-inch-high pyramidal flower clusters offsetting very dark green leaves 1½ to 4 inches long; Zones 7-10. *L. ovalifolium* 'Aureum' (California privet)—has yellow leaves with a green spot in the center when planted in sun, heavily scented flower clusters 2 to 4 inches wide in summer, and shiny black berries on 10- to 15-foot densely arranged upright stems, semievergreen to evergreen in warmer climates.

Growing conditions and maintenance
Easily grown and undisturbed by insects or disease, privet adapts to almost any soil except those that are constantly wet.

Liquidambar (li-kwid-AM-bar)

SWEET GUM

Liquidambar styraciflua

HARDINESS: Zones 5-9

PLANT TYPE: tree

HEIGHT: 60 to 120 feet

INTEREST: foliage

SOIL: moist, slightly acid

LIGHT: full sun

The sweet gum is a neatly conical tree whose star-shaped leaves linger till late fall and turn lovely shades of yellow, purple, and scarlet. Its name is derived from the fragrant, gummy sap, used in making perfume. The bark is deeply furrowed and resembles cork. Spiny globe-shaped fruits drop from late fall to early spring, a liability for patios, walkways, and barefoot walks in the grass.

Selected species and varieties
L. styraciflua (American sweet gum, red gum, bilsted)—narrow-pyramidal when young, then changing to a semirounded crown with a spread two-thirds the height, the branches edged with corky wings and bearing glossy rich medium green leaves 4 to 7½ inches long and wide, with five to seven finely serrated, pointed lobes.

Growing conditions and maintenance
Although native to rich, moist bottomlands, sweet gum is tolerant of poor soils if they are neutral to slightly acid and reasonably moist. The roots need plenty of room to develop. Plant in spring in soil amended with peat moss or leaf mold. Sweet gum usually takes 2 to 5 years to become established. Prune in winter.

Liriodendron (lir-ee-o-DEN-dron)

TULIP TREE

Liriodendron tulipifera

HARDINESS: Zones 4-9

PLANT TYPE: tree

HEIGHT: 70 to 100 feet or more

INTEREST: foliage, form

SOIL: moist, well-drained, slightly acid

LIGHT: full sun

A giant suitable only for large areas, the tulip tree is a columnar to oval deciduous tree with distinctive bright green foliage that turns golden yellow in fall. In mid- to late spring, tuliplike greenish white flowers with a deep orange blotch at the base of the petals appear high on the tree after the foliage unfurls. The conelike clusters of winged fruit persist into winter.

Selected species and varieties
L. tulipifera (yellow poplar, tulip magnolia, tulip poplar, whitewood)—fast growing with a spread of 35 to 50 feet and the potential of topping 100 feet tall, pyramidal when young, bearing lobed leaves up to 8 inches wide and long opening early in spring, and cup-shaped flowers 2½ inches wide with six petals, borne singly at or near branch tips.

Growing conditions and maintenance
Give tulip trees a moist, deep loam with plenty of room to grow. They prefer slightly acid soils but will tolerate neutral to slightly alkaline soils. Leaves occasionally turn black with a mold that grows on the sweet, sticky substance secreted by scale and aphids. In ideal soil, tulip trees may grow 2½ to 3 feet per year.

MAGNOLIA

Magnolia virginiana

HARDINESS: Zones 5-9

PLANT TYPE: tree or shrub

HEIGHT: 10 to 80 feet

INTEREST: flowers, foliage, fruit

SOIL: moist, well-drained, loamy, acid

LIGHT: full sun to partial shade

Magnolias include both deciduous and evergreen shrubs and trees. They vary greatly in size and form, but all produce large, lovely flowers in shades from pink and purple to pure white. The fruit of magnolias is a conelike pod, which splits to reveal bright pink or red seeds.

Selected species and varieties

M. grandiflora (southern magnolia)—60 to 80 feet tall, 30 to 50 feet wide, low-branching, pyramidal, evergreen or semi-evergreen to deciduous, leaves are 5 to 10 inches long, tops are dark green and shiny, undersides are light green, brown, or rust-colored, flowers are creamy white and richly textured, 8 to 12 inches across, blooming in late spring and sporadically throughout summer, 3- to 5-inch cone-shaped fruit pods open to reveal scarlet seeds in fall; Zones 6-9. 'Bracken's Brown Beauty'—up to 30 feet, compact habit, small leaves are 6 inches long and dark brown on undersides, flowers are 5 to 6 inches; 'Edith Bogue'—tight pyramidal form, leaves are narrow and deep green, flowers are large and fragrant, probably the hardiest southern magnolia variety; 'Goliath'—large flowers up to 12 inches

across; 'Little Gem'—10 to 20 feet tall, shrublike habit, small leaves are 4 inches with bronze undersides, flowers bloom in spring and fall, well suited for small landscapes; 'St. Mary'—20 feet tall with equal spread, compact habit, produces flowers at a young age. *M.* x 'Galaxy'—30- to 40-foot deciduous tree with stout branches, pyramidal habit, medium green leaves, reddish purple flowers up to 10 inches in diameter; Zones 5-9. *M.* x 'Nimbus'—up to 40 feet, single- or multiple-trunk tree, leaves are dark and shiny green, flowers are creamy white, very fragrant, blooming in late spring; Zones 5-9. Several hybrids have been developed from crosses of *M. liliiflora* (lily magnolia) and *M. stellata* 'Rosea': They are deciduous with a shrublike habit, 10 to 15 feet tall at maturity, bark is light gray, flower buds are furry and attractive in winter, flowers appear before leaves in spring but later than star magnolia's, so they are less susceptible to damage by late frosts, flowering continues sporadically through summer, Zones 5-9; 'Ann'—10 feet tall with equal or greater spread, blooms earliest among these hybrids, deep purple-red flowers; 'Judy'—10 to 15 feet tall, erect habit, flowers are deep purple-red on outside, white on inside; 'Randy'—narrow habit to 15 feet, flowers are purple outside, white inside; 'Ricky'—similar to 'Randy', with flowers deep purple on outside and white to purple on inside. *M. virginiana* (sweet bay or swamp magnolia)—size and form vary with growing conditions, 10 to 20 feet tall, large multiple-stemmed deciduous shrub in colder zones, in warmer climates may reach 60 feet as semievergreen to evergreen pyramidal

Magnolia grandiflora 'Little Gem'

tree, 3- to 5-inch-long dark green leaves, creamy white flowers, 2 to 3 inches across, blooms late spring and early summer and continues sporadically until fall, the 2-inch fruit opens to show bright red seeds; Zones 5-9.

Growing conditions and maintenance

Transplant magnolias in early spring. The southern magnolia often drops many of its leaves when it is transplanted but usually recovers quickly. All require moist, rich, acid soils and grow well in woodland areas with the protection of nearby trees, as long as they are not too close. The southern magnolia prefers a well-drained, sandy soil, while the hybrids and sweet bay magnolias tolerate heavier, poorly drained soils; the sweet bay magnolia thrives even in swampy conditions. The southern magnolia, with its broad evergreen leaves, requires protection from winter winds and sun, especially in colder areas; leaves exposed to winter stress look ragged and scorched. Deciduous magnolia flowers can be damaged by late-spring frosts. Give plants a northern exposure to delay flowering, thus reducing possible frost damage.

Magnolia 'Ricky'

Mahonia (ma-HO-nee-a)

MAHONIA

Mahonia bealei

HARDINESS: Zones 4-9

PLANT TYPE: shrub

HEIGHT: 3 to 12 feet

INTEREST: foliage, flowers, fruit

SOIL: moist, well-drained, acid

LIGHT: partial shade

Mahonias bear large clusters of yellow flowers in spring, followed by showy blue berries. They are attractive year round as foundation plants and border shrubs, or in a woodland garden.

Selected species and varieties
M. aquifolium (Oregon grape)—3 to 6 feet tall, 3 to 5 feet wide, spreads by suckers, compound leaves are evergreen, 6 to 12 inches long, each hollylike leaflet is dark green, turning purplish in winter, flowers are yellow in terminal clusters in early spring, grapelike berries are dark blue in late summer; Zones 4-8. *M. bealei* (leatherleaf mahonia)—6 to 12 feet, upright habit, compound leaves are evergreen and leathery, blue-green leaflets have prominent spines, fragrant yellow flowers in showy clusters in very early spring, steel blue berries appear midsummer; Zones 6-9.

Growing conditions and maintenance
Mahonias prefer partial shade. They perform well under trees but tolerate full sun if adequate moisture is supplied. Protect them from drying winter winds.

Malus (MAY-lus)

CRAB APPLE

Malus sargentii

HARDINESS: Zones 4-8

PLANT TYPE: tree or shrub

HEIGHT: 6 to 20 feet

INTEREST: flowers, fruit

SOIL: moist, well-drained, acid

LIGHT: full sun

Crab apples are small deciduous trees or large shrubs that bear many flowers in spring before the leaves are fully expanded. In summer and fall, the small, brightly colored fruits provide color and interest.

Selected species and varieties
M. x 'Donald Wyman'—20 feet tall, 25 feet wide, wide-spreading and rounded tree, lustrous dark green leaves, pink buds open to white, single flowers, fruit is bright red, ⅜ inch in diameter, persists into winter. *M. sargentii*—6 to 8 feet tall, 8 to 16 feet wide, densely branched, mounded shrub form, red flower buds open to white, single flowers, fruit is bright red, ¼ inch in diameter, attracts birds.

Growing conditions and maintenance
Crab apples tolerate a wide range of soil conditions. They are easy to transplant and should be pruned while young to establish the desired shape and to remove suckers. Prune lightly to avoid the development of water sprouts. Pruning should be done immediately after flowering.

Myrica (mi-RYE-ka)

BAYBERRY, WAX MYRTLE

Myrica cerifera

HARDINESS: Zones 2-9

PLANT TYPE: shrub or tree

HEIGHT: 5 to 25 feet

INTEREST: foliage, fruit

SOIL: adaptable

LIGHT: full sun to partial shade

Bayberries are irregularly shaped shrubs or small trees that serve well as hedges or foundation plants. Their blue-gray fruit, borne on female plants only, is covered with a waxy coating that is used to make bayberry candles.

Selected species and varieties
M. californica (California bayberry)—15 to 35 feet tall, 15 feet wide, bronze-colored evergreen leaves, purple fruit in fall and winter; Zones 7-8. *M. cerifera* (southern wax myrtle)—10 to 20 feet tall, equally wide, leaves are semievergreen or evergreen and aromatic, gray fruit clusters along stems of previous season's growth; Zones 7-9. *M. pensylvanica* (northern bayberry)—5 to 12 feet tall with equal spread, suckers help form dense thickets, aromatic deciduous or semievergreen leaves, gray fruit; Zones 2-6.

Growing conditions and maintenance
Bayberries adapt to a wide range of soil conditions. They thrive in sandy, sterile soil and tolerate heavy clay soils. They take pruning well and make attractive, dense hedges.

Nandina (nan-DEE-na)

HEAVENLY BAMBOO

Nandina domestica

HARDINESS: Zones 6-9

PLANT TYPE: evergreen shrub

HEIGHT: 2 to 8 feet

INTEREST: foliage, fruit, flowers, form

SOIL: moist, fertile

LIGHT: full shade to full sun

Nandina's fine-textured bluish green foliage, emerging pink or coppery and often turning red to reddish purple in fall and winter, splays out from bamboolike canes. In late spring or early summer, panicles of creamy flowers appear, followed by spectacular clusters of red berries that persist through winter. Nandina is suited for foundations or borders, in masses, or as a specimen.

Selected species and varieties
N. domestica (sacred bamboo)—erect habit, 6 to 8 feet tall, with compound leaves having sharply tapered leaflets, each 1½ to 4 inches long and half as wide, 8- to 15-inch-long clusters of tiny white flowers with yellow anthers, and heavy panicles of ⅓-inch berries; 'Harbour Dwarf' grows to 2 to 3 feet, forming a graceful mound.

Growing conditions and maintenance
Although nandina grows best in acid loam, it tolerates a wide range of other soils and withstands drought. Winter sun helps redden foliage. Plant in groups to improve berrying. If left unpruned, it becomes leggy; remove old canes or cut canes to various lengths to create a dense plant. Canes cannot be forced to branch.

Nerium (NEE-ree-um)

OLEANDER

Nerium oleander

HARDINESS: Zones 8-10

PLANT TYPE: shrub

HEIGHT: 6 to 20 feet

INTEREST: flowers, foliage

SOIL: moist, well-drained

LIGHT: full sun to partial shade

Oleander is a tough, easy-to-grow evergreen for warm climates. It bears attractive leaves that resemble those of bamboo, as well as clusters of fragrant flowers from spring through fall. All parts of the oleander are poisonous.

Selected species and varieties
N. oleander—usually 6 to 12 feet with equal spread, may reach 20 feet, upright stems, bushy, rounded form, leaves are 3 to 5 inches long, leathery, and dark green throughout the year, fragrant flowers form in terminal clusters, are pink, white, or red and very showy, long blooming season; 'Casablanca'—3 to 4 feet, single white flowers; 'Little Red'—red flowers; 'Mrs. Roeddling'—6 feet, smaller leaves result in finer texture, flowers are double and salmon-pink.

Growing conditions and maintenance
Oleanders prefer a moist, well-drained soil but adapt to drier conditions. They tolerate drought, wind, salt spray, and air pollution. Prune in early spring to the desired height and shape and to maintain a dense habit.

Osmanthus (oz-MAN-thus)

DEVILWOOD

Osmanthus fragrans

HARDINESS: Zones 7-10

PLANT TYPE: evergreen shrub

HEIGHT: 8 to 30 feet

INTEREST: fragrance, foliage

SOIL: moist, well-drained, acid, fertile

LIGHT: bright full shade to full sun

Devilwood's clusters of tiny white four-petaled fall flowers may be mostly hidden by its foliage, but its fragrance is spectacular. Some species have hollylike leaves with spines that are gradually lost as the plant ages; because of their density, these shrubs make good barrier plants. Others are useful as foundation plants, in borders, and as screens, but are especially valuable near walkways.

Selected species and varieties
O. x fortunei (Fortune's osmanthus)—oval habit, 15 to 20 feet tall, with white flowers in the fall; Zones 8-10. *O. fragrans* (fragrant olive, tea olive)—the most fragrant form, a 15- to 30-foot shrub or tree that sometimes produces a spring bloom as well, with lustrous dark green spineless leaves; reliably hardy only in Zones 9-10. *O. heterophyllus* 'Gulftide' (holly olive, Chinese holly, false holly)—dense, upright form 8 to 15 feet high with glossy green leaves and prominent spines; 'Variegatus' slowly grows to 8 feet or so, with white margins on the leaves; Zones 7-9.

Growing conditions and maintenance
Devilwood weathers pollution, is relatively pest free, and can be heavily pruned.

Oxydendrum (ok-si-DEN-drum)

SORREL TREE

Oxydendrum arboreum

HARDINESS: Zones 5-9

PLANT TYPE: tree

HEIGHT: 25 to 30 feet

INTEREST: foliage, flowers

SOIL: moist, well-drained, acid

LIGHT: full sun to partial shade

The sorrel tree provides landscape interest throughout the year. In spring its leaves emerge a lustrous dark green. White, urn-shaped flowers hang in clusters from slender branches in midsummer. The pendulous, light green fruit appears in fall, creating a stunning display against the leaves, which turn a brilliant scarlet. The fruit turns brown and persists into winter.

Selected species and varieties
O. arboreum—25 to 30 feet tall and 20 feet wide in cultivation, pyramidal tree with rounded crown and drooping branches, leaves 3 to 8 inches long, fragrant white flowers form in drooping clusters 4 to 10 inches long.

Growing conditions and maintenance
Incorporate generous amounts of organic matter into the soil prior to planting. The trees are slow growing but attractive even when young. Although they thrive in sun or partial shade, plants grown in the sun produce more flowers and better fall color.

Paeonia (pee-O-nee-a)

TREE PEONY

Paeonia suffruticosa

HARDINESS: Zones 5-8

PLANT TYPE: shrub

HEIGHT: 3 to 5 feet

INTEREST: flowers, foliage

SOIL: fertile, well-drained

LIGHT: full sun to light shade

Tree peonies bear spectacular blooms, up to 8 inches across, amid graceful, bronze-green to blue-green, compound leaves. The flowers range in color from white, yellow, and orange to pink, lavender, and red.

Selected species and varieties
P. suffruticosa (tree peony)—slow-growing deciduous shrub, 3 to 5 feet tall with an equal or greater spread, producing richly colored, 10- to 12-inch leaves with irregularly toothed leaflets and spherical flower buds that open to reveal blooms in many colors; 'Age of Gold' bears ruffled, semidouble flowers of creamy yellow, sporting a golden center and a touch of red at the base; 'Banquet' produces cut-leaf foliage and red semidouble blooms; 'Chromatella' bears orange buds opening to huge double yellow blossoms; 'Reine Elizabeth' offers delicate pink double flowers; 'Silver Sails' has single pale yellow blossoms.

Growing conditions and maintenance
Protect tree peonies from wind; prolific bloomers may require staking. Prune in spring to remove dead branches. Cut stems to the ground in fall to rejuvenate old, misshapen plants.

Parrotia (pa-ROTE-ee-a)

IRONWOOD

Parrotia persica

HARDINESS: Zones 4-8

PLANT TYPE: shrub or tree

HEIGHT: 20 to 40 feet

INTEREST: foliage, bark

SOIL: well-drained

LIGHT: full sun

Parrotia's trunk and horizontal branches are covered with flaky bark that peels away to give the plant an attractive, mottled green-gray-and-brown texture. Tiny, inconspicuous flowers with red stamens bloom along young branches before the leaves emerge in spring. The oval foliage colors attractively in fall. Use parrotia as a specimen tree or part of a shrub border.

Selected species and varieties
P. persica (Persian parrotia)—grows to 30 feet tall with a spread as wide or wider and with 3- to 4-inch-long lustrous green leaves in brilliant shades of yellow and orange turning rosy pink and scarlet in fall.

Growing conditions and maintenance
Plant Persian parrotia in slightly acidic soil, leaving space for its mature spread. Allow young plants to develop as multi-stemmed shrubs or prune to a single trunk. Propagate from seed or cuttings.

Phellodendron (fell-o-DEN-dron)

CORK TREE

Phellodendron amurense

HARDINESS: Zones 3-8

PLANT TYPE: tree

HEIGHT: 30 to 45 feet

INTEREST: bark

SOIL: adaptable

LIGHT: full sun

Cork tree is valued for the ridged and furrowed gray-brown bark, resembling cork, that cloaks the few wide-spreading horizontal main branches on old trees. Inconspicuous yellowish green flowers bloom in late spring, followed by small clusters of black berries in late fall on female trees. Both the flowers and fruit have a turpentine-like odor when they are bruised. Lustrous green compound leaves, like those of black walnut, cast a light shade and sometimes turn yellow in fall, lingering on the tree only briefly.

Selected species and varieties
P. amurense (Amur cork tree)—30 to 45 feet tall with equal or greater spread, with orange-yellow stems bearing glossy dark green leaflets to 4 inches long, and corky bark developing in old age. *P. chinense* (Chinese cork tree)—grows 30 feet tall, with dark yellow-green leaflets to 5 inches long on red-brown stems; hardy to Zone 5.

Growing conditions and maintenance
Cork tree tolerates drought, pollution, and a wide variety of soil types. It is easily transplanted and is usually pest free. Prune in winter.

Philadelphus (fill-a-DEL-fus)

MOCK ORANGE

Philadelphus coronarius

HARDINESS: Zones 4-9

PLANT TYPE: shrub

HEIGHT: 4 to 12 feet

INTEREST: flowers, fragrance

SOIL: moist to dry, well-drained

LIGHT: full sun to light shade

Mock orange is an old-fashioned shrub that bears fragrant blooms reminiscent of orange blossoms in early summer. Because of its somewhat gangly habit, it is best planted with other flowering plants in a mixed shrub border.

Selected species and varieties
P. coronarius (sweet mock orange)—large, vigorous, rounded shrub with ascending, arching branches, growing 10 to 12 feet tall and equally wide and often becoming leggy with age. It has exfoliating orange-brown bark and 1½- to 3-inch-long, pointed, oval leaves with a slightly quilted texture. The flowers, borne in small clusters on wood formed the previous year, are single, white, and extremely fragrant. 'Aureus' has foliage that emerges bright yellow in spring and turns yellow-green by midsummer; 'Nanus' is double-flowered and grows to only 4 feet; 'Variegatus' bears leaves with white margins.

Growing conditions and maintenance
Mock orange is fast-growing and tolerates a wide range of conditions. Prune immediately after flowering to control size; increase bushiness by cutting back stems that have borne flowers to a strong bud.

Picea (PYE-see-a)

SPRUCE

Picea abies 'Nidiformis'

HARDINESS: Zones 4-9

PLANT TYPE: shrub

HEIGHT: 4 to 12 feet

INTEREST: flowers, fragrance

SOIL: moist to dry, well-drained

LIGHT: full sun to light shade

These needled evergreens form towering pyramids useful as windbreaks, screens, or single specimens. Smaller forms are good as accents or in groups.

Selected species and varieties
P. abies (Norway spruce)—a fast-growing pyramid with drooping branches, 40 to 60 feet tall (can reach 150 feet) and 25 to 30 feet wide, its medium green foliage maturing to dark green, bearing 4- to 6-inch cylindrical cones and often losing its form in old age; 'Nidiformis' (bird's-nest spruce) is a 3- to 6-foot-tall spreading mound. *P. glauca* (white spruce)—a tree aging to a narrow, dense spire 40 to 60 feet tall by 10 to 20 feet wide, with ascending branches, Zones 2-6; 'Conica' (dwarf Alberta spruce) is a neat, very slow growing (to 10 feet in 25 years) cone-shaped plant with light green foliage.

Growing conditions and maintenance
Spruces prefer moist, acid, deep loam but tolerate other soils with adequate moisture, especially in the first few years. They prefer sunny sites in cold climates. White spruce withstands heat and drought better than many other species.

Pieris (PYE-er-is)

PIERIS

Pieris japonica 'Deep Pink'

HARDINESS: Zones 5-8

PLANT TYPE: shrub

HEIGHT: 2 to 12 feet

INTEREST: foliage, flowers, buds

SOIL: moist, well-drained, acid

LIGHT: full sun to partial shade

Pieris provides beauty all year long. It makes an outstanding specimen, foundation, border, or woodland shrub.

Selected species and varieties

P. floribunda—2 to 6 feet tall and wide, bushy, low habit, evergreen leaves 1 to 3 inches long, fragrant white flowers bloom in 2- to 4-inch upright clusters in midspring. *P. japonica* (Japanese andromeda)—9 to 12 feet tall, 6 to 8 feet wide, leaves emerge bronze-pink in spring, become dark green in summer, evergreen, 1½ to 3½ inches long, flowers are white, urn-shaped, in pendulous 3- to 6-inch clusters in early to midspring, flower buds form in late summer in attractive, drooping chains; 'Dorothy Wyckoff'—compact form, red buds open to pale pink flowers; 'Flamingo'—deep rose-red flowers; 'Valley Rose' —tall, open habit, pink flowers; 'White Cascade'—heavy flowering, white flowers, long-lasting.

Growing conditions and maintenance

Grow pieris in well-drained soil supplemented with organic matter. Provide protection from heavy winds.

Pinus (PYE-nus)

PINE

Pinus strobus

HARDINESS: Zones 2-10

PLANT TYPE: evergreen tree

HEIGHT: 6 to 90 feet

INTEREST: foliage, form, fruit

SOIL: wet to dry

LIGHT: full sun

This diverse genus of needle-leaved evergreen conifers includes picturesque specimen and accent plants, towering screens, and lovely single shade trees.

Selected species and varieties

P. arisata (bristlecone pine)—a very slow grower, some examples of which are, at over 4,000 years old, the oldest living things on earth, reaching 8 to 20 feet tall with bluish white to dark green needles; Zones 4-7. *P. contorta* var. *contorta* (shore pine)—a 25- to 30-foot-tall tree with twisted trunk and branches; hardy to Zone 7. *P. densiflora* 'Umbraculifera' (Japanese umbrella pine)—upright-spreading, with umbrella-like crown to 9 feet tall or more, with exfoliating orange bark and bright to dark green needles; Zones 3-7. *P. edulis* [also classified as *P. cembroides* var. *edulis*] (pinyon, nut pine)—slow growing, 10 to 20 feet tall, with horizontal branches and an often flat crown, and dark green needles; hardy to Zone 5. *P. eldarica* (Afghanistan pine)—fast growing, 30 to 80 feet tall, with dark green needles to 6 inches long; hardy to Zone 7. *P. mugo* (mountain pine, mugo pine)—a broad pyramid to 20 feet tall or a low, broad, bushy shrub,

with usually medium green foliage; Zones 2-7. *P. nigra* (Austrian pine)—pyramidal shape broadening to a flat top with heavy, spreading branches, 50 to 60 feet tall by 20 to 40 foot wide, with dark green needles; Zones 4-7. *P. palustris* (longleaf pine, southern yellow pine, pitch pine)— a sparsely branched tree 55 to 90 feet tall, bearing needles to 9 inches long on mature trees and 10-inch cones; Zones 7-10. *P. strobus* (white pine)—a low-branched tree growing 50 to 80 feet tall and half as wide, pyramidal when young but becoming broad crowned with age, producing a dense growth of bluish green needles; Zones 3-8. *P. thunbergiana* (Japanese black pine)—an irregular pyramid usually 20 to 40 feet tall, with sometimes drooping, wide-spreading branches bearing dark green, crowded, twisted needles 2½ to 7 inches long and 1½- to 2½-inch cones; Zones 5-7.

Growing conditions and maintenance

Bristlecone pine does well in poor, dry soils but suffers in drying winds or pollution. Shore pine grows naturally in boggy areas. Japanese umbrella pine prefers well-drained, slightly acid soil. Afghanistan pine and pinyon thrive in desert conditions; the former also tolerates salt spray. Mountain pine needs moist, deep loam. Austrian pine tolerates alkaline soils, moderate drought, salt, and urban pollution but grows best is moist soil. White pine grows best in moist loams but is also found on dry, shallow soils and wet bogs; it is intolerant of air pollutants, salt, and alkaline soil. Japanese black pine prefers moist loams but tolerates sand and salt.

Pinus thunbergiana

Pistacia (pis-TAY-shee-a)

PISTACHIO

Pistacia chinensis

HARDINESS: Zones 6-9

PLANT TYPE: tree

HEIGHT: 30 to 35 feet

INTEREST: foliage, fruit

SOIL: adaptable

LIGHT: full sun

One of the best deciduous trees for fall foliage in the South, Chinese pistache has lustrous dark green compound leaves that turn a brilliant orange to orange-red even in semidesert conditions. Tiny inedible fruits begin red and mature to robin's-egg blue. Chinese pistache is usually the rootstock onto which the pistachio-nut tree is grafted. In the tree's native China, young shoots are eaten as a vegetable.

Selected species and varieties
P. chinensis (Chinese pistache)—30 to 35 feet high with equal spread, rather awkward in youth, eventually oval to rounded, bearing 10 to 12 leaflets 2 to 4 inches long per leaf, and inconspicuous male and female flowers on separate trees.

Growing conditions and maintenance
Chinese pistache grows best in moist, well-drained soil, where it may achieve 2 to 3 feet per year, but it tolerates other soil types and drought. Young trees develop multiple leaders and may not have straight trunks; stake trees early. Once corrective pruning is done, Chinese pistache usually needs little other special attention and is disease and insect free.

Pittosporum (pit-o-SPO-rum)

PITTOSPORUM

Pittosporum tobira

HARDINESS: Zones 8-10

PLANT TYPE: evergreen shrub

HEIGHT: 10 to 12 feet

INTEREST: foliage, fragrance, form

SOIL: well-drained

LIGHT: full sun to full shade

A dense, impenetrable evergreen shrub whose insignificant flowers carry the scent of orange blossoms, Japanese pittosporum is useful for foundation beds, drifts, barriers, hedges, and windbreaks. The round-tipped leaves are borne in rosettes at the ends of branches, lending a soft, clean appearance to the slow-growing, symmetrical mound. A variegated form works well as a bright accent. Japanese pittosporums may be left unsheared or pruned into formal shapes.

Selected species and varieties
P. tobira (Japanese pittosporum, mock orange)—10 to 12 feet high and nearly twice as wide, with leathery dark green leaves 1½ to 4 inches long and up to 1½ inches wide, and tiny, five-petaled creamy white flowers in 2- to 3-inch clusters in spring, turning yellow with age and eventually becoming green to brown pods that split to expose orange seeds in fall.

Growing conditions and maintenance
Japanese pittosporums tolerate soil from dry and sandy to moist clay, requiring only that the soil be well drained. They withstand salt spray and thrive in hot, humid climates and exposed locations.

Platanus (PLAT-a-nus)

SYCAMORE, PLANE TREE

Platanus x acerifolia

HARDINESS: Zones 5-9

PLANT TYPE: tree

HEIGHT: 75 to 100 feet

INTEREST: bark, form

SOIL: moist, well-drained

LIGHT: full sun

These large deciduous shade trees are both tall and wide, with massive trunks and crooked branches. They have large lobed leaves, distinctive flaking bark, and round fruits. Because of their imposing size, they are best suited for large properties.

Selected species and varieties
P. x *acerifolia* (London plane tree)—similar to sycamore but more columnar and more adaptable to difficult conditions; Zones 6-9. *P. occidentalis* (American sycamore, buttonwood)—wide-spreading, with attractive grayish brown bark that flakes off to reveal patches of cream. The leaves are 4 to 9 inches wide, three-lobed, and coarsely toothed. The spiny round fruits hang singly from long stalks and often persist through winter.

Growing conditions and maintenance
Plane trees prefer full sun and moist, well-drained soil, but will grow almost anywhere. Extremely adaptable, they can tolerate air pollution, compacted soil, and other conditions that are commonly found in cities.

Plumbago (plum-BAY-go)

CAPE PLUMBAGO

Plumbago auriculata

HARDINESS: Zones 9-11

PLANT TYPE: shrub

HEIGHT: 6 to 8 feet

INTEREST: flowers, foliage

SOIL: well-drained

LIGHT: full sun to partial shade

Cape plumbago is a large evergreen shrub that develops a mounded habit with long vinelike branches. Flowers are azure blue or white, and under ideal conditions they will appear year round.

Selected species and varieties
P. auriculata—6 to 8 feet tall, spreading 8 to 12 feet or more, leaves are 1 to 2 inches long, medium to light green, evergreen, flowers are 1 inch across in 3- to 4-inch clusters, blue or white, main blooming season is from early spring through fall.

Growing conditions and maintenance
Cape plumbago is a mounding shrub and can be maintained through pruning as a dense, low hedge or foundation plant. If trained it will climb a trellis or wall, and it is also well suited as a tall ground cover for large, well-drained slopes. Cape plumbago thrives in full sun but tolerates light shade in hot areas; it tolerates coastal conditions as well, but is sensitive to frost. Prune the oldest canes to the ground each year in early spring, and pinch new growth to encourage branching.

Populus (POP-yew-lus)

POPLAR, ASPEN

Populus tremuloides

HARDINESS: Zones 1-7

PLANT TYPE: tree

HEIGHT: 40 to 90 feet

INTEREST: form, foliage, bark

SOIL: adaptable

LIGHT: full sun

Quaking aspen is a fast-growing slender deciduous tree whose lustrous dark green leaves, turning yellow in the fall, quiver with the slightest breeze. The bark is smooth, creamy to greenish white, becoming dark and furrowed on old trees. Quaking aspens are best planted in groups rather than as single specimens. Invasive root systems also make them good for erosion control.

Selected species and varieties
P. tremuloides (quaking aspen, trembling aspen, quiverleaf)—slender and pyramidal in youth, developing a slightly more rounded crown with age, usually high branched and spreading 20 to 30 feet, with pointed, roundish, finely serrated leaves 1½ to 3 inches long and wide that turn medium yellow in fall.

Growing conditions and maintenance
The most widely distributed tree in North America, quaking aspen grows in almost any site except soggy soils. Best growth occurs, however, in moist, deep, well-drained soil. The wood is weak and easily broken by storms. Quaking aspens usually live less than 50 years. They tolerate salt spray, drought, and urban pollution.

Potentilla (po-ten-TILL-a)

BUSH CINQUEFOIL

Potentilla fruticosa

HARDINESS: Zones 2-7

PLANT TYPE: shrub

HEIGHT: 1 to 4 feet

INTEREST: flowers, foliage

SOIL: adaptable

LIGHT: full sun to partial shade

Bush cinquefoil is a low-growing shrub with neat foliage and a long flowering season. It has many landscape uses, serving as a low hedge, foundation planting, or edging; it can also be combined with other shrubs or perennials in a mixed border.

Selected species and varieties
P. fruticosa—1 to 4 feet tall and 2 to 4 feet wide, compound leaves, new leaves are gray-green, turning dark green, flowers are 1 inch across, bright yellow, from early summer to late fall; 'Abbotswood'—2 feet with white flowers and dark bluish green leaves; 'Coronation Triumph'—3 to 4 feet, gracefully arching habit, lemon yellow cuplike flowers; 'Primrose Beauty'—3 feet, primrose flowers with deeper colored centers; 'Tangerine'—2 to 4 feet, flowers are yellow flushed with orange-copper tones.

Growing conditions and maintenance
The bush cinquefoil thrives in moist, well-drained soil but tolerates poor, dry soil as well. It produces more flowers in full sun but grows well in partial shade. Prune a third of the oldest stems back to the ground in late winter.

Prunus (PROO-nus)

CHERRY, APRICOT

Prunus subhirtella var. pendula

HARDINESS: Zones 4-10

PLANT TYPE: shrub or tree

HEIGHT: 3 to 50 feet

INTEREST: flowers, foliage, fruit

SOIL: moist, well-drained

LIGHT: full sun to partial shade

This huge genus ranges from shrubs and small to mid-size deciduous trees valued for their spring flowers to robust broad-leaved evergreens used for screens, foundation plants, and hedges. None of the species listed here have edible fruits.

Selected species and varieties

P. caroliniana (Carolina cherry laurel, mock orange)—an evergreen oval-pyramidal shrub or tree, 20 to 30 feet high and 15 to 25 feet wide, with lustrous dark green, sharply tapered, sometimes spiny leaves 2 to 3 inches long and 1 inch wide hiding black fruits, and heavily scented white flower clusters to 3 inches long in early spring, Zones 7-10; 'Bright 'n' Tight' has smooth-edged leaves smaller than the species on a tightly branched pyramid growing to 20 feet tall. *P. laurocerasus* (common cherry laurel, English laurel)—lustrous medium to dark green leaves 2 to 6 inches long and one-third as wide, slightly toothed and borne on green stems tightly branched on a broad 10- to 18-foot-tall evergreen shrub that produces heavily fragrant flowers in racemes 2 to 5 inches long, and purple to black fruit masked by the leaves, hardy to Zone 6; 'Otto Luyken' is a compact form 3 to 4 feet tall and 6 to 8 feet wide that blooms profusely and has dark green leaves 4 inches long and 1 inch wide; 'Schipkaensis' has shorter, slightly narrower, smooth-edged leaves, to 5 feet high; hardy to Zone 5. *P. lusitanica* (Portugal laurel, Portuguese cherry laurel)—fragrant white clusters 6 to 10 inches long in late spring and dark purple cone-shaped fruits on a bushy shrub or tree 10 to 20 feet high with evergreen leaves 2½ to 5 inches long; Zones 7-9. *P. mume* (Japanese flowering apricot)—pale rose flowers in winter, after which shiny green leaves and yellowish fruit appear on a tree to 20 feet; Zones 6-9 (to Zone 10 in California). *P. subhirtella* var. *pendula* (weeping Higan cherry)—pink single flowers appear before the leaves on graceful, weeping branches on a 20- to 40-foot tree, followed by black fruit; Zones 4-9. *P.* x *yedoensis* (Japanese flowering cherry)—40- to 50-foot tree that bears pink or white flowers in spring before or as the leaves appear, black fruit, Zones 5-8; 'Akebono' has pink double flowers on a tree 25 feet high and wide.

Growing conditions and maintenance

As a rule, plant flowering fruit trees in full sun in well-worked loam; add sand to loosen heavy clay. Prune cherries only when necessary, removing crossed or ungainly branches. Laurels can thrive in full sun to partial shade in soil enriched with organic matter, usually enduring drought once established. In warmer climates, provide afternoon shade for Carolina cherry laurel, even in winter. Common cherry laurel is tolerant of wind and salt spray. Laurels take pruning well.

Prunus x yedoensis

Pseudotsuga (soo-doe-SOO-ga)

DOUGLAS FIR

Pseudotsuga menziesii

HARDINESS: Zones 4-7

PLANT TYPE: evergreen tree

HEIGHT: 40 to 80 feet

INTEREST: foliage, form, fruit

SOIL: moist, well-drained, acid to neutral

LIGHT: full sun

Douglas fir is a tall evergreen conifer with an attractive conical to pyramidal shape. Single trees make spectacular specimens.

Selected species and varieties

P. menziesii (Douglas fir)—pyramidal tree that can reach 80 feet tall. The branches are wide-spreading; the upper branches ascend while the lower ones droop. The blunt, 1- to 1½-inch-long needles are dark green on the upper side and banded in white on the underside. Cones are oval-shaped, 2 to 4 inches long, and purplish when young, turning yellow-brown as they mature; Zones 4-6. *P. menziesii glauca* (Rocky Mountain Douglas fir) is slower-growing and more compact, with bluish green needles; Zones 4-7.

Growing conditions and maintenance

Douglas fir requires full sun and moist, well-drained soil that is acid to neutral. Protect from strong winds; the roots are shallow, and the trees are easily uprooted.

Punica (PEW-ni-ka)

PUNICA

Punica granatum

HARDINESS: Zones 8-10

PLANT TYPE: shrub or small tree

HEIGHT: 12 to 20 feet

INTEREST: flowers, fruit

SOIL: moist, well-drained

LIGHT: full sun to partial shade

Small, carnation-like flowers with crumpled petals in red, orange, pink, white, or yellow adorn this multistemmed rounded deciduous shrub from early summer and sometimes into fall. Juicy yellow edible fruits up to 3 inches across, sporting thick, leathery skins, develop a reddish flush and are ready to be picked by early to midfall. Use pomegranates in shrub borders and groups, or grow in containers for a handsome small patio specimen.

Selected species and varieties
P. granatum (pomegranate)—12 to 20 feet high, with equal or less spread, bearing lustrous dark green leaves 1 to 3 inches long and 1 inch or less wide that unfurl bronzy and turn yellow in fall, and producing red flowers 1 inch wide; 'Legrellei' has double flowers with salmon pink petals variegated with white.

Growing conditions and maintenance
Easily cultivated, pomegranate grows best in rich, moist loam but is adaptable to a range of other soils if they are well drained. Prune after flowering.

Pyracantha (py-ra-KAN-tha)

FIRETHORN

Pyracantha coccinea 'Mohave'

HARDINESS: Zones 6-9

PLANT TYPE: shrub

HEIGHT: 2 to 16 feet

INTEREST: foliage, flowers, berries

SOIL: well-drained

LIGHT: full sun

Firethorn's shiny, dark brown branches are lined with ½-inch thorns and evergreen or semievergreen leaves. Clusters of tiny white spring flowers are followed by bright berries. Use massed as informal hedges, or espaliered against walls or trellises.

Selected species and varieties
P. coccinea (scarlet firethorn)—1- to 1½-inch oval leaves and red-orange fall berries; 'Apache' grows bright red berries on shrubs to 5 feet tall and as wide or wider; 'Mohave' is a cold-hardy, heavily berried, evergreen shrub to 12 feet tall and as wide; 'Navajo' has red-orange fruit on dense, 6-foot-round mounds of branches; 'Teton' grows narrow columns of branches 16 feet tall and half as wide with yellow-orange berries.

Growing conditions and maintenance
Firethorns can grow in light shade but flower much less. Prune anytime to shape plants. Propagate from seed or cuttings.

Pyrus (PY-rus)

CALLERY PEAR

Pyrus calleryana

HARDINESS: Zones 5-8

PLANT TYPE: tree

HEIGHT: 40 feet

INTEREST: flowers, foliage

SOIL: well-drained

LIGHT: full sun

Callery pears are showy, spring-flowering, deciduous trees with glossy green summer leaves that turn deep red to purple in the fall. The small, round, russet-colored fruit provides winter food for birds.

Selected species and varieties
P. calleryana 'Capital'—40 feet tall with 12-foot spread, distinctly columnar form with strongly ascending branching pattern, leaves are dark green in summer, red to red-purple in early fall, remaining on tree late, off-white flowers are profuse in early spring, useful as a tall screen or windbreak; 'Whitehouse'—40 feet tall, 18 feet wide, pyramidal form, leaves are long and pointed, glossy green, turning wine red in fall, white flowers in spring, useful where space is limited.

Growing conditions and maintenance
Plant callery pears in late winter or early spring while they are still dormant. They adapt to nearly any well-drained soil and tolerate dryness and pollution. Prune while dormant. 'Capital' may be susceptible to fire blight.

Quercus (KWER-kus)

OAK

Quercus ilex

HARDINESS: Zones 2-9

PLANT TYPE: tree

HEIGHT: 40 to 100 feet or more

INTEREST: form, foliage

SOIL: light to heavy, well-drained

LIGHT: full sun

Deciduous or evergreen trees that can provide the dominant structure and framework for the landscape, oaks have a central main trunk and usually stout horizontal branches supporting a broad canopy of dark green foliage. The leaves of deciduous forms often remain into winter. Small flowers form in spring, followed by acorns in late summer to fall.

Selected species and varieties
Q. ilex (holly oak, holm oak, evergreen oak)—reaching 40 to 70 feet high and wide, with leathery evergreen leaves, sometimes toothed and usually 1½ to 3 inches long, deep green above and yellowish to gray below; hardy to Zone 5. *Q. macrocarpa* (bur oak, mossy-cup oak)—spreading crown of heavy branches, usually 70 to 80 feet tall and at least as wide but has been known to top 100 feet, with 4- to 10-inch-long leaves, lobed near the stem, dark green above and whitish below, showing greenish yellow to yellow-brown fall color, and acorns, usually fringed, up to 1½ inches long; Zones 2-8. *Q. phellos* (willow oak)—narrow, slightly wavy, willowlike leaves up to 5½ inches long, turning yellow, yellow-brown, and reddish in fall, on an oval crown 40 to 60 feet high and two-thirds as wide; Zones 5-9. *Q. robur* (English oak, truffle oak, common oak, pedunculate oak)—a short trunk leads to a broad, fairly open crown, 40 to 60 feet tall with equal spread under average landscape conditions (but can reach 100 feet tall), with 2- to 5-inch-long rounded-lobed leaves that are dark green above and pale blue-green below, showing no fall color, and oblong acorns; Zones 4-8. *Q. shumardii* (Shumard's oak, Shumard red oak)—grows 40 to 60 feet tall and wide, pyramidal when young but maturing to a spreading crown, with russet-red to red fall color on deeply lobed and sharply pointed leaves 4 to 6 inches long and 3 to 4 inches wide; Zones 5-9. *Q. suber* (cork oak)—trunk and main limbs clad in thick, corky bark on an evergreen tree 60 feet high and equally wide, bearing coarsely toothed 3-inch lobeless leaves that are dark green above, fuzzy gray below; Zones 7-9.

Growing conditions and maintenance
Oaks grow best in moist, deep soil, but most species fare well in a wide range of soil types as long as there is no hardpan present. Although oaks tolerate partial shade, they grow best, and stay healthier, in full sun. Holly oak can withstand inland drought and salt spray, but may become shrubby in exposed, seaside locations. Shumard oak tolerates either wet or dry sites. A good oak for desert conditions, cork oak needs well-drained soil and is drought resistant once established; its leaves yellow in alkaline soil. Do not compact or change the elevation of soil within the oak's root zone, which usually extends far beyond the canopy's reach.

Quercus robur

Raphiolepis (raf-ee-O-le-pis)

INDIAN HAWTHORN

Raphiolepis indica

HARDINESS: Zones 8-10

PLANT TYPE: shrub

HEIGHT: 3 to 6 feet

INTEREST: foliage, flowers

SOIL: moist, well-drained

LIGHT: full sun

Indian hawthorn is a medium-size evergreen shrub that produces showy white or pink flowers in early spring. It is useful for massing or growing in containers, and is attractive as an unpruned hedge in southern gardens.

Selected species and varieties
R. indica—3 to 6 feet, equally wide, dense, rounded form, leaves are dark, leathery, evergreen, 2 to 3 inches long, flowers are white, pink, or rose-red, blooming in early spring, followed by clusters of purple-black berries that persist through winter; 'Charisma'—3 to 4 feet, light pink double flowers; 'Snow White'—4 feet, white flowers; 'Springtime'—up to 6 feet, deep pink flowers, prolific bloom.

Growing conditions and maintenance
Indian hawthorn thrives in moist, well-drained soils but adapts to drier conditions, and established plants will withstand drought. Plants tolerate the salt spray of coastal conditions. They are well suited to growing in containers and rarely need pruning.

AZALEA

Rhododendron occidentale

HARDINESS: Zones 3-8

PLANT TYPE: shrub

HEIGHT: 2 to 12 feet

INTEREST: flowers, foliage

SOIL: moist, well-drained, acid, fertile

LIGHT: partial to bright full shade

Members of the genus *Rhododendron*, azaleas differ from rhododendrons in a number of ways, some of them rather technical. Among the visible differences, azaleas are more likely to be deciduous (though there are many exceptions), while rhododendrons are mostly evergreen; azalea flowers are usually funnel shaped, rhododendrons bell shaped; azaleas have five stamens, rhododendrons 10. Azalea is one of the most popular blooming shrubs for shade and is available in a range of colors, sizes, and hardiness.

Selected species and varieties
Deciduous: Exbury and Knap Hill azaleas—upright-growing, 8 to 12 feet tall and nearly as wide, with medium green leaves that turn yellow, orange, or red in fall, and flowers in pink, yellow, orange, rose, red, cream, and off-white; Zones 5-7; 'Gibraltar' has extra large, brilliant orange, ruffled flowers and orangish fall foliage; Zones 4-8. Ghent azaleas (*R. x gandavense*)—shrubby habit 6 to 10 feet tall, with single or double flowers in yellow, white, pink, orange, red, and combination colors; generally hardy to Zone 5; 'Daviesi' has fragrant white flowers with yellow centers on

a wide-growing, multistemmed plant; 'Narcissiflora', fragrant, double yellow, hose-in-hose blooms. Northern Lights azaleas—6 to 7 feet high and wide, with showy 1½-inch-long flowers in clusters of up to 12 that open before the leaves appear; hardy to Zone 3; 'Golden Lights' has fragrant yellow flowers; 'Rosy Lights', fragrant dark pink blooms brushed with rosy red; 'White Lights', pale pink buds that open to fragrant off-white flowers with yellow centers. *R. atlanticum* (coast azalea, dwarf azalea)—3 to 6 feet high and wide, producing pinkish white flowers opening with or before blue-green leaves; hardy to Zone 6. *R. calendulaceum* (flame azalea, yellow azalea)—open habit, 4 to 8 feet tall and wide, with flowers in a multitude of yellows, pinks, oranges, peach, and red, and medium green leaves changing to a quiet yellow or red in fall; Zones 5-7. *R. occidentale* (western azalea)—a native of the West Coast, with white or pinkish flowers, 1½ to 2 inches wide, in late spring and red or yellow fall foliage; Zones 6-7. *R. prinophyllum* [also known as *R. roseum*] (roseshell azalea, early azalea)—2 to 8 feet tall with densely branched, spreading habit, bright green foliage that turns bronze in fall, and bright pink flowers that smell like cloves; Zones 3-8. *R. schlippenbachii* (royal azalea)—6 feet tall with equal spread in a rounded upright habit, bearing large, fragrant, light to rose pink flowers that open with bronze foliage that turns yellow, orange, or red in fall; Zones 4-7. *R. vaseyi* (pink-shell azalea)—upright form to 8 feet with rose-colored, bell-shaped flowers appearing before medium green summer foliage that turns red in fall; Zones 5-8. Ever-

Rhododendron schlippenbachii

green: Gable Hybrids—2 to 4 feet high and wide with glossy dark green 1-inch-long leaves and pink, red, lavender, and other colors; Zone 5; 'Caroline Gable' has large wavy-edged leaves and large lavender flowers; 'Louise Gable', a round, dense form to 4 feet tall with deep salmon pink double flowers with dark blotches; 'Purple Splendor', purple hose-in-hose flowers;

Rhododendron Gumpo Group

'Rosebud', 4 feet high and wide with hose-in-hose double flowers similar to miniature roses in silvery deep pink. Girard Evergreen Hybrids—very showy plants with large flowers and profuse bloom, good for colder climates, with buds hardy to Zone 6; 'Girard Border Gem' has deep rose pink flowers that blanket the dwarf plant, hiding the ½-inch glossy dark green leaves, which turn red in winter; 'Girard Crimson', 2½-inch-wide bright red flowers and large, glossy green leaves; 'Girard Fuchsia', ruffled reddish purple flowers and dark green glossy leaves; hardy to Zone 6. Glenn Dale Hybrids—developed for the mid-Atlantic region, with large flowers whose buds are reliably hardy to Zone 7; 'Martha Hitchcock' has white flowers with purple edges. Kurume Hybrid azaleas—single or double flowers, usually pinks and reds, on a compact plant with small leaves; hardy to Zone 7; 'Coral Bells' bears 1½-inch-wide coral pink hose-in-hose flowers on a 3-by-4-foot plant; 'Hershey's Red', bright red flowers 2 inches wide, blooming early and hardy to Zone 6; 'Sherwoodii' [also known as 'Sherwood Orchid'], single reddish violet blooms with a darker blotch. North Tisbury Hybrids—'Joseph Hill' bears bright red flowers, 2

RHODODENDRON

inches wide, in a dense, large mound; hardy to Zone 6. Satsuki Hybrids—dwarf, spreading, evergreen shrubs with many flower types and color combinations; 'Amagasa' has deep pink flowers, 3½ inches wide; 'Beni-Kirishima' has double orange-red flowers; Gumpos come in a rainbow of colors on small, compact plants, including pink, rose, salmon, lavender, coral, white, and bicolors. *R. kaempferi* (torch azalea)—upright habit to 10 feet with deciduous or semi-evergreen foliage and orange-red to pink flowers; hardy to Zone 6. *R. obtusum* 'Amoenum' (Hiryu azalea, Kirishima azalea)—double magenta flowers on a semi-evergreen shrub to 3 feet; hardy to Zone 6. *R. yedoense* (Yodogawa azalea)—5 feet tall with double purple flowers and deciduous to semi-evergreen leaves, 1 to 3 inches long, that turn reddish purple in fall; hardy to Zone 6; var. *poukhanense* (Korean azalea) grows to 6 feet tall, with 1⅞-inch-wide, lavender flowers, and loses most of its leaves in winter; hardy to Zone 4.

Rhododendron 'Purple Splendor'

Growing conditions and maintenance

Find a site protected from hot afternoon suns and cold winter winds. Add peat moss, leaf mold, or compost to soil. Unlike other azaleas, the royal and rose-shell types tolerate near neutral soils. For the acid-loving majority, maintain the soil's acidity if planting near a foundation; lime can leach out of building materials and raise the soil's pH. Keep soil moist and water deeply in dry periods. Mulch to keep soil cool and conserve moisture; azaleas root near the surface. Prune in early spring after blooming; cut back to a bud or shoot.

Rhododendron 'Yaku Princess'

HARDINESS: Zones 4-9

PLANT TYPE: shrub or tree

HEIGHT: 3 to 30 feet

INTEREST: flowers, foliage

SOIL: moist, well-drained, acid, fertile

LIGHT: bright full shade to full sun

If ever there was a magnificent flowering shrub for the shade garden, it is the rhododendron. Its showy bell-shaped flowers are usually borne in clusters at the end of branches in spring or early summer. Its large, dark green leaves and rotund nature accentuate the lavish displays of white, pink, lavender, purple, or red.

Selected species and varieties

Catawbiense cultivars and hybrids—6 to 10 feet tall and slightly less in spread, with flower colors ranging from lilac to purplish rose with touches of yellowish brown or green and leaves 3 to 6 inches long; Zones 4-8; 'Album Elegans' has white flowers; hardy to Zone 6; 'Lee's Dark Purple', a broad, compact habit with dark purple buds opening to medium purple flowers and wavy leaves; hardy to Zone 5; 'Mrs. C. S. Sargent', red-rose flowers spotted yellow; 'Nova Zembla', red flowers, heat resistant and hardy to Zone 5. Dexter hybrids—large plants with mixed parentage, resembling *R. fortunei*, with dense foliage; hardy to Zone 6; 'Scintillation' is a heat-tolerant cultivar that grows to 6 feet tall with compact form and has lovely, luminous pink flowers with amber throats.

R. yakusimanum selections and hybrids—usually compact shrubs, 3 to 4 feet high; hardy to Zone 6; 'Anna H. Hall' has rich pink buds opening to white flowers on a semidwarf plant; Zones 5-9; 'Centennial Celebration', fragrant, deeply frilled white flowers brushed with lilac-pink on a 4-foot-high plant; Zones 5-8; 'Yaku Princess', 3 to 4 feet tall and slightly wider, with ball-shaped trusses of two-tone pink spotted with green; Zones 4-8. Other cultivars of various strains: 'Baden-Baden' is a broad semidwarf with rich red, waxy flowers and slightly twisted foliage; reliably hardy to Zone 6; 'Ben Mosely' is lightly frilled and yields bright pink flowers with darker margins and dark red throats on a 4- to 6-foot plant; hardy to Zone 6; 'Blue Peter' is of variable size to 8 feet tall with frilled blue-violet and purple flowers; Zones 6-8; 'Boule de Neige' has a compact, rounded form, 5 feet tall by 8 feet wide, with white flowers; hardy to Zone 5; 'Chionoides', white flowers on a 5-foot plant; hardy to Zone 6; 'Dolly Madison', white flowers blooming early on an 8- to 10-foot plant; hardy to Zone 5; 'Janet Blair', 4 to 6 feet high, producing lavender-pink flowers with greenish throats; hardy to Zone 6; 'Vulcan's Flame' is a sun-tolerant variety, 4 to 6 feet tall, producing red flowers on red stems; hardy to Zone 6. Other species: *R. augustinii*—compact, upright habit to 10 feet with large, light gray-blue, pink, or mauve flowers with green spots and long, narrow leaves; hardy to Zone 7. *R. carolinianum* (Carolina rhododendron)—3 to 6 feet tall and wide, with leaves 2 to 3 inches long on red to purplish red stems, which bear clusters of white,

Rhododendron 'Nova Zembla'

pink, or lilac flowers; Zones 5-8; var. *album* has white flowers. *R. fortunei* (Fortune's rhododendron)—fragrant pale pink, lilac, or white flowers and large dark green leaves on a large shrub or small tree 20 to 30 feet tall; hardy to Zone 6. *R. williamsianum*—pale rose flowers 2¼ inches wide on a low and spreading shrub to 5 feet; hardy to Zone 7.

Growing conditions and maintenance
Catawbiense and Yakusimanum hybrids can tolerate full sun in cool areas, where they are also reliably hardy. The other species and cultivars listed here prefer partial shade and accept bright full shade. Apply liberal amounts of organic matter such as peat moss, leaf mold, or compost to the soil. Make sure the site is very well-drained and there is no hardpan; poor drainage is usually the chief reason for rhododendron failure. If soil is heavy clay, amend it with sharp sand and peat moss or leaf mold as required, position the plant so that the top of the rootball is several inches above the soil level, and mulch thickly around the base of the shrub. If the plant has been container grown and is potbound, make vertical slits down the outside of the root mass before planting. Water deeply during dry periods, and mulch to keep the root zone cool and moist. Pinching off faded flowers will help to improve bloom the next year.

Rhododendron 'Scintillation'

Rhus (RUSS)

SUMAC

Rhus typhina 'Laciniata'

HARDINESS:	Zones 3-9
PLANT TYPE:	shrub
HEIGHT:	2 to 30 feet
INTEREST:	foliage, flowers, fruit
SOIL:	well-drained to dry
LIGHT:	full sun to partial shade

Shrubby sumacs are fast-growing, rather weak-wooded plants that are useful for covering large areas of poor soil. They spread rapidly to form dense thickets on steep banks and along roadsides. Low-growing types are useful as ground covers or for fronting taller shrubs in a mixed border; taller types are best suited to large-scale plantings. These plants offer colorful fall foliage and bright red fruit.

Selected species and varieties
R. aromatica (fragrant sumac)—3 to 6 feet tall and 6 to 10 feet wide, with glossy green trifoliate leaves that turn red to reddish purple in fall, and red fruit on female plants; 'Gro-Low' reaches only 2 to 4 feet in height and has lovely orange-red fall color. *R. typhina* (staghorn sumac)—15- to 30-foot-tall shrub with equal or greater spread, an open habit, and pinnately compound leaves that turn orange to scarlet in autumn. Four- to 8-inch-long flower clusters in early spring are followed by crimson fruit in fall; 'Laciniata' (cut-leaf staghorn sumac) bears deeply dissected leaves.

Growing conditions and maintenance
Sumacs prefer acid soil and do not tolerate wet sites. They need minimal care.

Rosa (RO-za)

ROSE

Rosa hybrid tea rose 'Chicago Peace'

HARDINESS:	Zones 2-10
PLANT TYPE:	shrub
HEIGHT:	3 inches to 20 feet
INTEREST:	flowers
SOIL:	well-drained
LIGHT:	full sun

Roses offer limitless choices for landscaping, from formal gardens to informal rock garden or border plantings. They can be cultivated as specimens, massed as hedges, pegged as ground covers, or trained against fences and trellises. Velvety petals surround fluffy stamens in flat single rows, in double-petaled cups, or in overlapping rows that create rounded forms, rosettes, and pompoms. The often fragrant flowers bloom singly or in clusters on arching or stiff woody stems lined with small thorns, sometimes appearing in a single flush, sometimes one at a time from summer through fall. Roses are extensively hybridized, and cultivars bloom in almost every color of the rainbow. For detailed descriptions of some of the roses that are available, see pages 170-223.

Selected species and varieties
Bush roses—large-flowered varieties [also called hybrid tea roses] blooming singly over the season on 2- to 6-foot-tall shrubs; cluster-flowered roses [also called floribunda roses] have small clusters of blossoms blooming over the season on plants to 10 feet. Shrub roses—English roses with large flowers in old-fashioned rosettes on

plants to 8 feet; hybrid musk roses have heavily fragrant, almost everblooming clusters on shrubs to 8 feet; hybrid rugosa roses, single- or double-petaled fragrant flowers on arching canes; unclassified modern shrub roses are a variable group with flowers on spreading mounds or upright bushes. Climbing roses—a single flush or repeating blooms along canes to 20 feet; large-flowered climbing roses have single flowers like hybrid tea roses; cluster-flowered climbing roses, smaller blossoms in multiples. Miniature roses—tiny versions of hybrid tea and floribunda roses only 3 to 18 inches tall. Old garden roses—moss roses with a single flush of flowers on soft, floppy stems; hybrid perpetual roses have fragrant rosettes up to 7 inches across on plants to 8 feet or more; climbing tea roses, large single flowers on stiff, arching canes to 10 feet. Wild roses—arching stems with a flush of single-petaled, often fragrant flowers.

Growing conditions and maintenance

Plant roses in sites with good air circulation and a slightly acidic soil enriched with organic matter. Mulch to suppress weeds and protect roots in winter. Pruning to remove old canes and shape plants is essential to maintain vigor and promote flowering. Propagate species from seed or by dividing rooted suckers, cultivars and species from softwood cuttings.

Rosa climbing rose 'American Pillar'

Rosmarinus (rose-ma-RY-nus)

ROSEMARY

Rosmarinus officinalis

HARDINESS:	Zones 7-10
PLANT TYPE:	evergreen shrub
HEIGHT:	2 to 6 feet or more
INTEREST:	foliage, fragrance, flowers
SOIL:	moist to dry, well-drained
LIGHT:	full sun to partial shade

Rosemary is a culinary herb and sachet ingredient that can also spice up the shrub border. Its gray-green needlelike foliage, aromatic when bruised, and its loose, irregular habit contrast well with dark green plants of formal shapes. Tiny blue flowers are borne in the leaf axils from fall to spring. Shrub varieties can be pruned into hedges. The trailing forms work well as ground covers, in rock gardens, and in window boxes.

Selected species and varieties

R. officinalis—a dense shrub with many erect stems, usually growing 2 to 4 feet tall and wide in free form, but topping 6 feet if conditions are favorable, and bearing closely spaced leathery leaves and ½-inch light blue flowers; 'Lockwood de Forest' grows 2 feet high with a 3- to 8-foot spread and has trailing stems with lighter green leaves and bluer flowers than the species.

Growing conditions and maintenance

Rosemary needs at least 4 hours of midday sun but grows best in full sun. It is intolerant of wet soils but performs well in seaside gardens.

Salix (SAY-liks)

WILLOW

Salix babylonica

HARDINESS:	Zones 2-9
PLANT TYPE:	tree
HEIGHT:	30 to 75 feet
INTEREST:	form, foliage, flowers
SOIL:	moist to wet, well-drained
LIGHT:	full sun

Willow trees grow to 75 feet tall, with graceful, arched branches that sweep the ground. They bear long, narrow leaves and small flowers in dense catkins. Willows make lovely specimen or accent trees, especially when they are sited near a pond or other body of water.

Selected species and varieties

S. alba 'Tristis' (golden weeping willow)—grows 50 to 75 feet tall and wide, with pendulous golden branchlets and narrow leaves; Zones 2-8. *S. babylonica* (Babylon weeping willow)—30- to 40-foot tree at maturity, with a short, stout trunk and a rounded crown. Leaves emerge pale green in spring and turn dull green in summer and yellow in autumn. Light green catkins appear among the leaves in the spring; Zones 7-9.

Growing conditions and maintenance

Willows are generally fast-growing, especially in sunny sites that are well supplied with water. Avoid planting near underground pipes, which can be damaged by the vigorous roots.

Sapindus (SAP-in-dus)

SOAPBERRY

Sapindus drummondii

HARDINESS: Zones 5-9

PLANT TYPE: tree

HEIGHT: 25 to 50 feet

INTEREST: flowers, foliage, fruit, bark

SOIL: dry to adaptable

LIGHT: full sun to light shade

Panicles of yellowish white flowers 6 to 10 inches long bloom in late spring on this graceful deciduous shade tree. The strong-wooded, rounded crown bears medium green compound leaves that turn gold in fall. Small yellow-orange berries, supposedly used by American Indians to make soap, emerge in fall and persist through winter, finally turning black. Scaly bark flakes off to expose gray, orange-brown, and reddish brown tissue.

Selected species and varieties
S. drummondii (western soapberry, wild China tree)—either single stemmed or low branched, 25 to 50 feet tall with an equal spread, producing 8 to 18 tapered, slightly curved leaflets, each 1½ to 3½ inches long, per 10- to 15-inch leaf, glossy above and fuzzy below, and sometimes abundant crops of ½-inch berries.

Growing conditions and maintenance
Soapberry is tolerant of most soils but is especially at home in the poor, dry soils of its native Southwest. It is also tolerant of urban pollution and is insect and disease resistant. Easy to cultivate, soapberry needs little special attention and usually hangs on to its branches in storms.

Sarcococca (sar-ko-KO-ka)

SWEET BOX

Sarcococca hookerana var. humilis

HARDINESS: Zones 5-8

PLANT TYPE: evergreen shrub

HEIGHT: 18 inches to 5 feet

INTEREST: foliage, fragrance, fruit

SOIL: moist, well-drained, fertile

LIGHT: partial to bright full shade

A handsome plant with year-round ornamental value, sarcococca has shiny, narrow leaves on its roundly mounded shape. In late winter to early spring, inconspicuous but fragrant white flowers bloom, to be replaced by shiny black or red berries that linger into fall. Sarcococca spreads slowly by suckers; the low form makes a good ground cover.

Selected species and varieties
S. confusa—leaves to 2 inches long and ¾ inch wide on a densely branched shrub growing 3 to 5 feet tall and wide; Zones 7-8. *S. hookerana* var. *humilis* (Himalayan sarcococca)—18 to 24 inches tall and wide, blooming in early spring under 2- to 3½-inch-long and ½-inch-wide leaves; Zones 5-8. *S. ruscifolia* (fragrant sarcococca, fragrant sweet box)—very fragrant flowers and red fruits on a 3-foot-high-and-wide mound; Zones 7-8.

Growing conditions and maintenance
Best grown in Zone 8 in the South and along the Pacific Coast, *S. confusa* and *S. ruscifolia* need shelter in Zone 7. Protect from winter winds. Add leaf mold or peat moss to the soil to improve drainage. Mulch to conserve moisture.

Skimmia (SKIM-ee-a)

SKIMMIA

Skimmia japonica

HARDINESS: Zones 7-9

PLANT TYPE: evergreen shrub

HEIGHT: 3 to 4 feet

INTEREST: flowers, fruit, foliage

SOIL: moist, well-drained, acid

LIGHT: partial to bright full shade

Skimmia forms a low mound of leathery leaves decorated in spring with clusters of flowers and in fall with bright berries that remain into the next spring. In order for a female bush to produce berries, a male bush, which produces larger flowers that are also fragrant, has to be located within 100 feet. Skimmia is beautiful in foundation plantings and in masses.

Selected species and varieties
S. japonica (Japanese skimmia)—a rounded, densely branched habit, slow growing to 3 to 4 feet tall and slightly wider, bearing bright green leaves, 2½ to 5 inches long, that are tightly spaced at the end of branches, and producing 2- to 3-inch clusters of red buds that open to creamy white flowers on reddish purple stems.

Growing conditions and maintenance
Japanese skimmia may be planted in Zone 9 on the West Coast and north to Zone 7 on the East Coast if given a protected location. In hot climates, site it out of afternoon sun. Foliage may discolor in winter sun. Add 1 part peat moss or leaf mold to every 2 parts of soil to improve drainage. Fertilizing and pruning are not usually necessary.

Spiraea (spy-REE-a)

BRIDAL WREATH

Spiraea x bumalda 'Anthony Waterer'

HARDINESS: Zones 3-8

PLANT TYPE: shrub

HEIGHT: 2 to 8 feet

INTEREST: flowers, foliage

SOIL: well-drained

LIGHT: full sun to partial shade

Rugged and hardy deciduous shrubs, spireas produce showy clusters of dainty flowers in spring or summer.

Selected species and varieties

S. x *bumalda* (Bumald spirea)—a flat-topped shrub, 2 to 3 feet tall and 3 to 5 feet wide, with 4- to 6-inch white to deep pink clusters in summer, and leaves that are pinkish when young, aging to blue-green and turning subdued bronzy red or purplish in fall; 'Anthony Waterer' is 3 to 4 feet tall and 4 to 5 feet wide, with brownish red new foliage and pink flowers; 'Gold Flame' has reddish orange new leaves that turn yellow-green in summer and bright red-orange in fall, with pinkish blooms. *S. japonica* 'Little Princess' (Japanese spirea)—pink flowers and blue-green leaves tinted red in fall on a 30-inch plant; hardy to Zone 4. *S.* x *vanhouttei* (Vanhoutte spirea)—vase- or fountain-shaped 6 to 8 feet tall by 10 to 12 feet wide, with 1- to 2-inch white clusters in spring; hardy to Zone 4.

Growing conditions and maintenance

Spireas are easy to grow in any garden soil. Prune summer bloomers in late winter, spring bloomers after flowering.

Stephanandra (stef-a-NAN-dra)

LACE SHRUB

Stephanandra incisa 'Crispa'

HARDINESS: Zones 3-8

PLANT TYPE: shrub

HEIGHT: 1½ to 3 feet

INTEREST: foliage

SOIL: moist, well-drained, acid

LIGHT: full sun to light shade

Lace shrub is a tidy plant with a gracefully mounding habit. It can be grown on banks to prevent erosion or used as a low hedge or tall ground cover. Its dense foliage and low habit make it well suited to growing under low windows or among tall, leggy shrubs in a mixed border.

Selected species and varieties

S. incisa 'Crispa'—1½ to 3 feet tall, 4 feet wide, spreads by arching branches rooting readily when they touch the ground, leaves are 1 to 2 inches long, deeply lobed, bright green, turning reddish purple or red-orange in the fall, inconspicuous pale yellow flowers appear in early summer.

Growing conditions and maintenance

Plant lace shrub in moist, acid soil in full sun or light shade. Add generous amounts of organic matter to the soil prior to planting to help retain moisture. Plants require little pruning other than removing winter-damaged tips in early spring.

Stewartia (stew-AR-tee-a)

STEWARTIA

Stewartia pseudocamellia

HARDINESS: Zones 5-9

PLANT TYPE: shrub or tree

HEIGHT: 10 to 40 feet

INTEREST: flowers, foliage, bark

SOIL: moist, well-drained, acid, organic

LIGHT: partial shade to full sun

Stewartia has camellia-like summer flowers and colorful fall foliage. A fine specimen tree, Japanese stewartia has exfoliating bark in cream, rusty red, and gray.

Selected species and varieties

S. ovata (mountain stewartia, mountain camellia)—creamy white flowers 2½ to 3 inches wide and oval leaves 2 to 5 inches long that turn orange to red in fall on spreading branches of a bushy shrub or small tree 10 to 15 feet tall and wide, with bark not as showy as that of Japanese stewartia. *S. pseudocamellia* (Japanese stewartia)—20 to 40 feet tall with open, spreading branches, producing white 2- to 2½-inch flowers with white filaments and orange anthers amid 1½- to 3½-inch leaves that turn vibrant yellow, red, and reddish purple in fall; Zones 5-7.

Growing conditions and maintenance

Stewartia is difficult to transplant and should be put into the ground as a 4- to 5-foot-tall balled-and-burlapped plant and not moved again. Dig a large hole and amend the soil liberally with peat moss, leaf mold, or compost. In warmer climates, provide some afternoon shade. Stewartias rarely need pruning.

Styrax (STY-racks)

SNOWBELL, STORAX

Styrax obassia

HARDINESS: Zones 5-8

PLANT TYPE: tree

HEIGHT: to 30 feet

INTEREST: flowers, form

SOIL: moist, well-drained, acid, fertile

LIGHT: partial shade to full sun

White flowers appear in late spring or early summer on this lovely specimen tree for lawn or patio. The Japanese snowbell has zigzag stems and smooth gray-brown bark with irregular orange-brown fissures. Sinewy gray branches twist and turn on the fragrant snowbell. Both forms create an attractive winter effect. If the deciduous leaves escape an early fall freeze, they turn reddish or yellow.

Selected species and varieties
S. japonicus (Japanese snowbell, snowdrop tree)—grows 20 to 30 feet high with wide-spreading branches to 30 feet or more, bearing fine leaves held aloft and clusters of ¾-inch wide, bell-shaped flowers with yellow stamens, and gray-brown smooth bark with irregular orange-brown fissures; 'Kusan' is more compact than the species, growing to about 12 feet. *S. obassia* (fragrant snowbell)—has drooping, fragrant racemes up to 8 inches long on a 20- to 30-foot tree with ascending branches bearing large, heart-shaped leaves.

Growing conditions and maintenance
Snowbells need a soil rich in organic matter. Transplant into the garden while still young. Prune in the winter.

Syringa (si-RING-ga)

LILAC

Syringa reticulata

HARDINESS: Zones 3-8

PLANT TYPE: tree or shrub

HEIGHT: 3 to 30 feet

INTEREST: flowers, fragrance

SOIL: moist, well-drained

LIGHT: full sun

Deciduous staples of gardens past, lilacs produce fat, highly scented flower clusters after their dark green pointed-oval leaves have appeared.

Selected species and varieties
S. patula [formerly classified as *S. velutina*] 'Miss Kim' (Manchurian lilac)—fragrant 4- to 6-inch-long icy blue bloom clusters open from purple buds in late spring to early summer on a 3- to 6-foot-tall shrub. *S. reticulata* [formerly classified as *S. amurensis* var. *japonica*] (Japanese tree lilac)—20 to 30 feet tall, with branches spread stiffly 15 to 25 feet before becoming more arching and graceful with age, with an oval to round crown and creamy white, privet-scented terminal flower clusters 6 to 12 inches long and wide for 2 weeks in early summer, and reddish brown cherrylike bark; Zones 3-7.

Growing conditions and maintenance
Lilacs grow best in loose, slightly acid loam, but they adjust to both acid or slightly alkaline soil. Prune after flowering and remove crowded branches; lilacs need good air circulation. Japanese tree lilac is pest free and resistant to mildew.

Taxodium (taks-ODE-ee-um)

CYPRESS

Taxodium distichum

HARDINESS: Zones 4-9

PLANT TYPE: tree

HEIGHT: 50 to 70 feet or more

INTEREST: form, foliage, bark

SOIL: moist, sandy, acid

LIGHT: full sun

These stately deciduous conifers have sage green needlelike foliage that turns bright orange-brown in fall. In swampy areas or along the edge of a lake, the shaggy reddish brown main trunk is flanked by narrow root projections that reach out of the water in kneelike bends to collect oxygen for the tree. Inconspicuous flowers bloom in spring, and fragrant green to purple cones 1 inch across mature to brown. Use common bald cypress as a dramatic fine-textured vertical accent in the garden, or plant in groups along the edge of a pond.

Selected species and varieties
T. distichum (swamp cypress, common bald cypress, tidewater red cypress)—new foliage opens bright yellow-green in graceful sprays amid short, ascending branches on a slender pyramid 50 to 70 feet high or more by 20 to 30 feet wide.

Growing conditions and maintenance
Although common bald cypress makes its best growth in moist to wet deep, sandy loams, it is surprisingly tolerant of dry soil and low fertility. It is also very resistant to strong winds, and is seldom seriously bothered by disease or insects.

Taxus (TAKS-us)

YEW

Taxus cuspidata 'Capitata'

HARDINESS: Zones 4-7

PLANT TYPE: shrub or tree

HEIGHT: 4 to 50 feet

INTEREST: foliage

SOIL: moist, well-drained, fertile

LIGHT: full sun to light shade

Fine-needled evergreen plants, yews are employed as ground covers, shrubbery backdrops, hedges, screens, or specimen plantings.

Selected species and varieties

T. baccata (English yew)—dense, wide-spreading branches with dark green needles to 50 feet tall; 'Adpressa', very short needles on bushes to 30 feet; 'Fastigiata', stiff, upright branches in columns to 30 feet tall and 8 feet wide; 'Repandens', a dwarf to 4 feet tall and up to 15 feet wide. *T. cuspidata* (Japanese yew)—medium-textured species cultivated in many forms of shrub or tree; 'Capitata', pyramids of branches to 50 feet; 'Densa', a dwarf spreading to twice its 4-foot height; 'Thay-erae', branches angled slightly upward into flat-topped shrubs 8 feet tall and twice as wide. *T. x media* (Anglo-Japanese yew)—medium-size pyramidal shrub or tree; 'Hatfieldii' grows to 12 feet tall; 'Hicksii' forms a narrow column to 20 feet.

Growing conditions and maintenance

Yews must have excellent drainage and should be protected from drying winds. They take well to pruning and shearing. Propagate from cuttings.

Ternstroemia (tern-STRO-mee-a)

TERNSTROEMIA

Ternstroemia gymnanthera

HARDINESS: Zones 7-10

PLANT TYPE: evergreen shrub

HEIGHT: to 20 feet

INTEREST: foliage, flowers, fruit

SOIL: moist, well-drained, organic

LIGHT: full to partial shade

Leathery leaves that open brownish red and mature to rich, glossy green clothe gracefully arching branches. In early summer, small clusters of fragrant creamy white flowers put on a modest display. Small red berries turn black and last through winter. Primarily grown for its foliage, ternstroemia works well as a foundation plant or hedge; it can also be trained into a small tree.

Selected species and varieties

T. gymnanthera [sometimes confused with *Cleyera japonica*] (Japanese ternstroemia) —6 to 15 feet tall and wide, with elliptic to oblong 2- to 6-inch-long leaves often arranged in whorls on the ends of branches and ½-inch flowers produced in clusters on the previous year's growth, with bloom and berries occurring only on mature plants.

Growing conditions and maintenance

Although Japanese ternstroemia grows best in rich, slightly acid soil that stays moist, it tolerates occasional drought. Good drainage is essential. Given suitable conditions, the species is usually problem free. Prune after flowering. Propagate by stem cuttings.

Thuja (THOO-ya)

ARBORVITAE

Thuja occidentalis 'Hetz Midget'

HARDINESS: Zones 2-9

PLANT TYPE: tree or shrub

HEIGHT: 3 to 30 feet

INTEREST: foliage

SOIL: moist, well-drained, fertile

LIGHT: full sun to light shade

Arborvitae's fine-textured evergreen foliage develops along dense pyramids of branches in shades of green, yellow-green, and blue-green. Use them as specimens, in shrub borders, or planted into screens or hedges.

Selected species and varieties

T. occidentalis (American or eastern arborvitae, white cedar)—shiny green needles that turn brown in winter; 'Hetz Midget' is a dense 3- to 4-foot globe; 'Lutea' forms a golden yellow pyramid to 30 feet; 'Nigra' has dark green foliage on trees 20 feet high and 4 feet wide; 'Rheingold', deep gold foliage on oval shrubs to 5 feet. *T. orientalis* [also called *Platycladus orientalis*] (Oriental arborvitae)—bright green or yellow-green young foliage maturing to dark green and holding its color through winter.

Growing conditions and maintenance

Arborvitaes located in shade will grow loose and open. Plants can be transplanted year round from containers or in balled-and-burlapped form. *T. orientalis* is less cold tolerant than American arborvitae; plant only to Zone 5 or 6. Propagate from cuttings.

Tsuga (TSOO-ga)

HEMLOCK

Tsuga canadensis

HARDINESS: Zones 3-8

PLANT TYPE: shrub or tree

HEIGHT: 40 to 70 feet

INTEREST: foliage

SOIL: moist, well-drained, acid

LIGHT: deep full shade to full sun

Hemlocks are softly pyramidal evergreens whose graceful, drooping branches and small needles lend a fine texture to the shade garden. Canadian hemlock makes a beautiful, fine-textured hedge, screen, or accent plant.

Selected species and varieties
T. canadensis (Canadian hemlock, eastern hemlock)—tapering trunk 65 feet or more tall, bearing medium green needles ¼ to ⅔ inch long and oval ½- to 1-inch cones. *T. caroliniana* (Carolina hemlock)—45 to 60 feet tall, a species more tolerant of urban conditions, with darker green needles than those of Canadian hemlock and with a stiffer form.

Growing conditions and maintenance
Unlike many other conifers, hemlocks tolerate shade well. They are shallow-rooted plants that are intolerant of wind, drought, and heat; add organic matter to sandy soils to aid in moisture retention, and mulch to keep soil moist and cool. Sunscald occurs at 95°F and above. Canadian hemlocks can be kept at 3 to 5 feet with shearing. Host to a number of pests, the hemlock has been besieged in parts of the East by the woolly adelgid.

Ulmus (UL-mus)

ELM

Ulmus parvifolia

HARDINESS: Zones 4-9

PLANT TYPE: tree

HEIGHT: 40 to 70 feet

INTEREST: bark, form, foliage

SOIL: moist, well-drained

LIGHT: full sun

Exfoliating, mottled gray, green, orange, or brown bark is this graceful, durable shade tree's most outstanding feature. Lacebark elm has a spreading, rounded crown of medium fine, lustrous dark green foliage that holds late into fall, when it turns yellow to reddish purple.

Selected species and varieties
U. parvifolia (lacebark elm, Chinese elm, evergreen elm)—40 to 50 feet high and wide in most situations, usually with a forked trunk and drooping branches, bearing leathery, saw-toothed elliptical leaves ¾ to 2½ inches long and inconspicuous flower clusters hidden by the foliage in late summer to early fall, followed by ⅓-inch-wide winged fruits.

Growing conditions and maintenance
Lacebark elm grows best in moist, well-drained loams but adapts well to poor, dry soils, both acid and alkaline. Soil should be deep to accommodate the extensive root system. Growth averages 1½ feet per year. Prune to remove weak, narrow crotches. Although it is not immune to Dutch elm disease, it shows considerable resistance.

Viburnum (vy-BUR-num)

ARROWWOOD

Viburnum carlesii

HARDINESS: Zones 4-9

PLANT TYPE: shrub

HEIGHT: 3 to 12 feet

INTEREST: flowers, fruit, foliage

SOIL: moist, well-drained

LIGHT: full sun to partial shade

The mostly deciduous, highly ornamental viburnums listed here offer snowy clouds of flowers in spring and often colorful berries that may persist well into winter. Others are valued for their fragrance, reddish fall foliage, or branching patterns. Viburnums are useful in shrub borders, as screens, or as specimens.

Selected species and varieties
V. carlesii (Koreanspice viburnum)—pink buds open to white, domelike, enchantingly fragrant flower clusters 2 to 3 inches wide on a rounded, dense shrub 4 to 8 feet tall and wide, followed by ineffective black fruit in late summer; Zones 4-8. *V. davidii* (David viburnum)—turquoise blue fruits on an evergreen mound 3 to 5 feet high that also produces dull white flower clusters 2 to 3 inches wide; Zones 8-9. *V. dilatatum* (linden viburnum)—8 to 10 feet tall and 6 to 8 feet wide, bearing flat, creamy white clusters to 5 inches wide in late spring, bright red or scarlet berries that ripen in fall and persist into winter, and semilustrous dark green leaves 2 to 5 inches long, sometimes turning russet-red in fall, Zones 5-7; 'Catskill' is a dwarf form 5 to 6 feet tall and 8 feet wide with dark

green leaves that turn yellow, orange, and red in fall, and dark red fruit clusters that ripen in late summer and linger until midwinter. *V. plicatum* var. *tomentosum* (doublefile viburnum)—layered, tierlike, horizontal branches on a plant 8 to 10 feet tall and wide. Flat, pure white flower clusters 2 to 4 inches wide on 2-inch stems consisting of fertile nonshowy flowers rimmed by a ring of showy sterile flowers, followed by red berries that turn black in summer. Coarsely toothed, prominently veined leaves 2 to 4 inches long that turn reddish purple in fall, Zones 5-8; 'Mariesii' has larger sterile flowers and slightly longer flower stems; 'Shasta' grows 6 feet tall and 10 to 12 feet wide, with 4- to 6-inch wide-spreading flower clusters that obscure the leaves. *V. setigerum* (tea viburnum)—a multistemmed shrub 8 to 12 feet tall and 6 to 8 feet wide, with 3- to 6-inch-long bluegreen leaves, once used to make tea, and unremarkable 1- to 2-inch white flower clusters but with a profuse crop of bright red berries in fall; Zones 5-7.

Growing conditions and maintenance
Viburnums grow best in slightly acid loam but tolerate slightly alkaline soils. Amend the soil with peat moss or leaf mold to increase moisture retention, and add sand if soil is poorly drained. Allow enough lateral room for the plant to fully develop; prune if necessary after flowering.

Viburnum setigerum

Vitex (VY-tex)

VITEX

Vitex agnus-castus

HARDINESS: Zones 6-9

PLANT TYPE: shrub or tree

HEIGHT: to 20 feet

INTEREST: flowers, fragrance

SOIL: moist, well-drained, neutral

LIGHT: full sun

A vase-shaped shrub or small tree with an airy, open habit and leaves that are aromatic when bruised, chaste tree produces fragrant lilac or pale violet flowers in foot-long mounded clusters of 3- to 6-inch spikes on new wood. Let chaste tree provide late-summer color for the shrub border, or prune high to create a specimen.

Selected species and varieties
V. agnus-castus (chaste tree, hemp tree, sage tree, Indian-spice, monk's pepper tree, wild pepper)—multistemmed, 8 to 10 feet tall, and reaching to 20 feet in the southern part of its range, with deciduous compound leaves composed of leaflets arranged in maple-leaf fashion, gray-green above and fuzzy gray below, showing no fall color, and showy flower panicles from midsummer to autumn; 'Rosea' bears pink flowers.

Growing conditions and maintenance
Chaste tree is marginally hardy in Zone 6, where it is usually killed to the ground in winter but revives in spring. Fast growing, it can often achieve 5 or 6 feet in the next season. Too much fertilizer creates paler flowers. Chaste tree has no significant pests.

Zelkova (zel-KOH-va)

ZELKOVA

Zelkova serrata

HARDINESS: Zones 5-8

PLANT TYPE: tree

HEIGHT: 50 to 80 feet

INTEREST: foliage, form, bark

SOIL: moist, well-drained

LIGHT: full sun

Japanese zelkova is an elmlike deciduous tree resistant to Dutch elm disease. Vase shaped and often multistemmed, it frequently develops attractive exfoliating bark as it ages. Sharply toothed dark green leaves turn yellow or russet in fall.

Selected species and varieties
Z. serrata (Japanese zelkova)—a tree that grows 50 to 80 feet high and wide, with ascending branches bearing 2- to 5-inch-long pointed oval leaves, somewhat rough with prominent veins, the smaller ones located on upper branches, insignificant male and female flowers in spring, and bark that is smooth, gray, and beechlike in youth, eventually flaking to expose patches of orange; 'Green Vase' is a vigorous, extremely fast-growing tree 60 to 70 feet tall with arching branches bearing orange-brown to bronze-red fall foliage.

Growing conditions and maintenance
Japanese zelkova grows best in deep, moist, fertile soil and adjusts to either alkalinity or acidity. Mulch to conserve moisture when the tree is young and to prevent mower damage. Once established, the tree tolerates wind, drought, and air pollution.

Beneficials, Pests, and Diseases

THIS SECTION WILL HELP YOU RECOGNIZE THE many beneficial insects that inhabit your garden and some of the most common pests and diseases that afflict gardens in the continental United States and southern Canada. Each entry includes a choice of measures designed to prevent problems or to control them if they appear in your garden.

This section is divided into three parts—Beneficials, Pests, and Diseases. The first (pages 420-426), presents 18 kinds of beneficials—beetles, spiders, and other small creatures that feed on pests and serve as natural controls. In the part devoted to pests (pages 426-449), some of the 55 entries cover a single species of pest, while others cover several different pests that are closely related or that inflict similar damage. The last part (pages 449-465) provides clues for diagnosing 49 infectious and deficiency diseases.

AMBUSH BUGS

RANGE: throughout North America; most prevalent in the West

GENERATIONS PER YEAR: multiple

TYPE: predator

Ambush bugs are stout bugs that look as if they were wearing armor. They conceal themselves in flowers and wait to attack any unwary insects that come along.

Description and life cycle

Adult ambush bugs have uniquely thickened front legs, equipped for grasping and holding their prey. Most of the several species are small—less than a half-inch long—and are yellowish brown to yellowish green with darker markings. Their coloring provides effective camouflage while they await their prey. The females lay their eggs on plants; nymphs resemble adults but are smaller and wingless.

Beneficial effects

Although small, ambush bugs capture and kill insects considerably bigger than themselves. Both nymphs and adults are predaceous. They prefer to hide in the flowers of goldenrod and boneset. When a bee, wasp, fly, or butterfly visits the flower, the ambush bug uses its strong forelegs to grasp the prey, then sucks out the contents of its body. Ambush bugs do not bite humans.

How to attract

Avoid using pesticides. Grow goldenrod and boneset.

ASSASSIN BUGS

RANGE: many species found throughout North America

GENERATIONS PER YEAR: usually 1

TYPE: predator

There are more than 100 native species of assassin bugs in North America. Some attack humans and other animals and can inflict painful bites, but many are voracious predators of insects and are helpful in reducing populations of a wide array of plant pests.

Description and life cycle

Depending on the species, these predators overwinter as larvae, adults, or eggs. Adults are usually flat, brown or black, and a half-inch long. They have long, narrow heads and curved beaks that are folded back under their bodies; many have a hoodlike structure behind their head. Nymphs resemble the adults but are smaller and wingless; some are brightly colored. Eggs are laid in sheltered locations. Once hatched, the nymphs begin feeding on insects and undergo several molts before becoming adults. Most species complete their life cycle in a single year, but some require several years.

Beneficial effects

Adults and nymphs feed on many plant-eating insects, including beetles, caterpillars, aphids, and leafhoppers. They also feed on mosquitoes, bees, and flies.

How to attract

Assassin bugs occur naturally in most gardens. Avoid the use of pesticides.

BIG-EYED BUGS

RANGE: throughout western parts of North America

GENERATIONS PER YEAR: 2 or 3

TYPE: predator

Big-eyed bugs resemble tarnished plant bugs and may be mistaken for that pest. However, this small beneficial insect feeds on many troublesome pests, both as a nymph and as an adult.

Description and life cycle

Adult big-eyed bugs overwinter in plant debris or other protected sites. Adults are $\frac{1}{8}$ to $\frac{1}{4}$ inch long and black or yellow-green, with spots on the head and thorax. They emerge in spring, and females lay eggs on plant stems and the undersides of leaves. Nymphs develop for 4 to 6 weeks, then molt to become adults and repeat the process. The nymphs look like the adults, but are smaller and wingless. Both adults and nymphs move about very rapidly, and both have large, prominent eyes.

Beneficial effects

Big-eyed bugs prey on aphids, leafhoppers, plant bugs, spider mites, and small caterpillars, and feed on the eggs of mites and insects. When pests are scarce, big-eyed bugs feed on flower nectar.

How to attract

Grow goldenrod and tolerate some pigweed, which big-eyed bugs prefer for egg laying. Avoid the use of pesticides.

BRACONID WASPS

RANGE: widespread throughout North America

GENERATIONS PER YEAR: several

TYPE: parasitoid

More than 2,000 species of braconid wasps are native to North America. Some are raised and sold commercially.

Description and life cycle
Depending on the species, adult braconid wasps are between $\frac{1}{10}$ and $\frac{1}{2}$ inch long. Slender, with a distinctly pinched waist, they may be brown, black, yellow, or red. Adults feed on nectar and pollen. Females inject eggs into a susceptible host. The eggs hatch as white, wormlike larvae that parasitize the host by feeding from within, eventually killing it. Some species feed externally as well. The larvae pupate near, on, or in a host, in white or brown cocoons. The life cycle is short and yields several generations per year. Wasps overwinter as larvae or pupae inside their hosts.

Beneficial effects
Braconid wasp larvae help control a wide range of insect pests, including codling moths, cabbage worms, armyworms, elm bark beetles, hornworms, and aphids.

How to attract
Some species are commercially available, but it is best to encourage native populations. Grow dill, fennel, parsley, and yarrow to sustain adult wasps. Avoid killing caterpillars bearing brown cocoons. Avoid the use of pesticides.

CHALCID WASPS

RANGE: widespread throughout North America

GENERATIONS PER YEAR: several

TYPE: parasitoid

Worldwide, there are more than 100,000 species of chalcid wasps. These include both the trichogramma wasp and *Encarsia formosa,* two highly effective parasitoids of plant pests. Chalcid wasps feed on eggs, larvae, and pupae of their prey; species vary in host preference.

Description and life cycle
Adults are tiny, often only $\frac{1}{100}$ inch long, and may be black or golden brown. They feed on plant nectar and on honeydew excreted by insect hosts. The females often feed on insect fluids seeping from wounds they make as they lay their eggs. Inserting eggs into a host's body, or under a scale insect's shell-like covering, they often paralyze the host. Larvae develop and feed within the host, eventually killing it; they pupate in or near the host's body. These wasps produce several generations per year; many species overwinter as larvae in hosts.

Beneficial effects
Chalcid wasps are parasitoids of many plant pests, including scale insects, aphids, mealybugs, and tussock moths. One species, *Encarsia formosa,* controls whiteflies.

How to attract
Avoid using pesticides, including sulfur fungicides.

FLOWER FLIES

RANGE: many species found throughout North America

GENERATIONS PER YEAR: 3 to 7

TYPE: predator

Flower flies, or syrphid flies, are often called hover flies, for their helicopter-like flying habits. There are more than 800 species native to North America.

Description and life cycle
Adults are $\frac{1}{3}$ to $\frac{1}{2}$ inch long and black with yellow or white stripes. They resemble honeybees or hornets in appearance and in their attraction to flowers, but unlike bees, they have only a single pair of wings, large eyes, and no stinger. Flower flies overwinter in the soil as pupae; adults emerge in early spring to feed on flower nectar. Females lay small white, pitted eggs singly among colonies of aphids. The hatching larvae are sluglike, and can be mottled in color, or green, brown, or gray. They feed voraciously on aphids for about 2 weeks, then drop to the soil to pupate. Adults emerge in 2 weeks to repeat the cycle.

Beneficial effects
One larva can consume 400 aphids. Larvae may also feed on mealybugs, mites, scale crawlers, and other small insects.

How to attract
Include daisy-flowered plants that provide abundant nectar and pollen, such as cosmos and coreopsis. Stagger plantings to ensure continuous bloom. Avoid pesticide use.

ICHNEUMON WASPS

RANGE: widespread throughout North America

GENERATIONS PER YEAR: 1 to 10

TYPE: predator, parasitoid

Both larval and adult ichneumon wasps (sometimes called ichneumon flies) help control insect pests. Some species have a very narrow host range; others attack a wide variety of insects.

Description and life cycle
Adults vary in size from ¹⁄₁₀ to 1½ inches, and are slender and dark colored. They typically are wide ranging and often feed on nectar or pollen. Females have a long, threadlike ovipositor for inserting eggs into the host eggs or larvae. The larvae generally develop and feed within the host, killing it in the process. Larvae are white grubs, tapered at both ends. In some species, adults kill hosts by stinging them and consuming the body fluids. Most species overwinter as mature larvae in cocoons, or as adult females.

Beneficial effects
Larvae feed within host eggs, larvae, or pupae, providing natural control for a wide range of plant pests. Hosts include sawflies, spruce budworms, tent caterpillars, pine tip moths, European corn borers, and woodborer beetles.

How to attract
Include flowers in the garden to attract and maintain adults. Avoid pesticide use.

LACEWINGS

RANGE: widespread throughout North America

GENERATIONS PER YEAR: 3 to 6

TYPE: predator

Hundreds of species of lacewings are found in North America. Sometimes called aphid lions, and broadly grouped as green or brown lacewings, they are widely distributed and highly beneficial.

Description and life cycle
Lacewings overwinter as adults or pupae. In spring, they emerge as adults, ½ to ¾ inch long with elongated lacy, transparent wings, to feed on pollen and nectar and lay eggs. Green lacewings lay their eggs on the end of a silk thread, while brown lacewings lay eggs directly on leaves. Eggs hatch in less than a week. The larvae are mottled yellow or brown and spindle shaped, with large jaws. They feed for about 3 weeks, pupate for 5 to 7 days, and emerge as adults to repeat the cycle.

Beneficial effects
While lacewing larvae prefer aphids, they also feed on thrips, mealybugs, scales, moth eggs, small caterpillars, other soft-bodied insects, and mites. Adults are rarely predaceous.

How to attract
Grow plants that offer plenty of pollen and nectar, such as dill, fennel, clover, and cosmos. Provide a source of water in dry weather. Buy lacewing eggs from an insectary and distribute them throughout the garden. Avoid use of dormant oil sprays.

LADYBIRD BEETLES

RANGE: widespread throughout North America

GENERATIONS PER YEAR: 2 to 4

TYPE: predator

Ladybird beetles, also called lady beetles or ladybugs, are probably the best known of all beneficial insects. Of some 4,000 species worldwide, about 400 are native to North America. Some common beneficial species include the convergent ladybird beetle, the twice-stabbed ladybird beetle, and the two-spotted ladybird beetle.

Description and life cycle
Adult ladybird beetles are shiny, round, and about ¼ inch long. They may be gray, yellow, or orange-red, with or without black spots; some are solid black, others black with red spots. Larvae are spindle shaped, wrinkled, and up to ⅜ inch long; when young, they are dark and look like tiny alligators. As the larvae mature, they develop conspicuous yellow, red, or white markings. Pupae are reddish black with red markings and are usually attached to the upper leaf surface.

Ladybird beetles overwinter as adults in garden debris. They emerge in spring to feed and lay eggs in clusters among aphids or other potential prey. Once hatched, the larvae feed for about 3 weeks, then pupate, emerging as adults about a week later to repeat the cycle.

The convergent ladybird beetle, the most common species in North America, is red-orange with black spots; it is distinguished by two converging white lines on its thorax. This species migrates, flying hundreds of miles to overwintering sites and returning in spring. The twice-stabbed ladybird beetle is shiny black with two bright red spots, while the two-spotted ladybird beetle is red with two black spots and a black head.

Beneficial effects

Both larvae and adults feed on many soft-bodied insect pests, including aphids, mealybugs, scales, psyllids, whiteflies, and spider mites; they also eat insect eggs. One larva can eat up to 300 aphids before it molts; then, as an adult beetle, it can eat another 300 to 400 aphids.

Food preferences vary with the species. Convergent ladybird beetles feed mainly on aphids; twice-stabbed ladybird beetles prefer scales; and two-spotted ladybird beetles devour both scales and aphids. A related species known as the mealybug destroyer has a strong preference for mealybugs but also eats aphids and scales. The vedalia ladybird beetle, a red-bodied beetle with black marks, prefers soft scales; the red-mite destroyer feeds on spider mites. Adults also feed on pollen and nectar.

How to attract

Grow dill and tansy to lure adults with pollen and nectar. If you buy convergent ladybird beetles or mealybug destroyers, note that they tend to fly away when released. In a greenhouse, first close all vents; in a garden, first water well, then free the beetles at night, when they are less active.

Two-Spotted Ladybird Beetles

PIRATE BUGS

RANGE: widespread throughout North America

GENERATIONS PER YEAR: 2 to 4

TYPE: predator

Also called minute pirate bugs for their tiny size, pirate bugs are voracious predators, attacking most small insects. Not all of their victims are pests, but their overall effect is beneficial.

Description and life cycle

Pirate bugs overwinter as mated adult females, emerging in spring to insert their eggs into plant stems or leaves. Adults are quick fliers, ¼ inch long, and black with white patches on their wings. Eggs hatch in 3 to 5 days; nymphs are oval, ⅕ inch long, and may be yellow, orange, or brown. Nymphs feed for 2 to 3 weeks on the insects they find on leaves and in flowers, then molt to become adults and repeat the cycle.

Beneficial effects

Both nymphs and adults consume large numbers of insect pests such as thrips, small caterpillars, leafhopper nymphs, spider mites, and insect eggs. They are especially adept at finding prey in flowers and are therefore particularly good at controlling flower thrips.

How to attract

Include goldenrod, daisies, and yarrow; adults feed on their pollen. In fall, collect pirate bugs on wild goldenrod and release them in your garden. In a greenhouse, release one pirate bug for every five plants.

PRAYING MANTISES

RANGE: various species throughout North America

GENERATIONS PER YEAR: usually 1

TYPE: predator

Of the 20-odd praying mantis species found in North America, several are imports from Europe and China. All are aggressive predators of other insects.

Description and life cycle

Praying mantises overwinter as clusters of 50 to 400 eggs in an egg case of hardened froth stuck to a plant. In early spring, nymphs emerge and begin to feed, taking ever-larger insect prey as they grow—including other praying mantises. After mating, the female often devours the male before laying eggs. Adults are 2 to 4 inches long and green or brown, with large eyes, long hind legs, and powerful front legs adapted for grasping prey. Nymphs resemble adults but are smaller and wingless.

Beneficial effects

Praying mantises feed on both pests and beneficial insects, including aphids, beetles, bugs, leafhoppers, caterpillars, butterflies, flies, bees, and wasps. Adults feed on larger insects that usually are not pests.

How to attract

Provide sites for overwintering eggs by including shrubs and other permanent plantings. Do not release purchased praying mantises, because they may destroy native populations of bees and butterflies. Instead, protect egg cases found in your yard. Avoid pesticide use.

PREDATORY MITES

RANGE: widespread throughout North America

GENERATIONS PER YEAR: multiple

TYPE: predator

Predatory mites look like plant-feeding mites, but are less hairy and quicker.

Description and life cycle
Adult predatory mites are tiny, about 1/50 inch long. They are usually tan, beige, or red. Nymphs are similar, but even smaller and usually translucent. Females overwinter in soil, crevices in bark, or plant debris. In spring they lay their eggs on leaves near plant-feeding mites. Nymphs hatch in 3 to 4 days and begin to feed. They molt to become adults within 5 to 10 days, and repeat the cycle. There are many overlapping generations each year.

Beneficial effects
Predatory mites have varying preferences in their prey. The phytoseiid mite eats several spider-mite species, and controls that pest well by reproducing twice as fast. Other predator-mite species feed on thrips, other mite pests, and pollen.

How to attract
Grow cattails and dandelions for their pollen. Mist plants to encourage predaceous mites and discourage spider mites. Buy and release commercially available predatory mites. Avoid pesticide use.

ROBBER FLIES

RANGE: various species throughout North America

GENERATIONS PER YEAR: 1- to 2-year life cycle

TYPE: predator

Robber flies are fast-flying, loud-buzzing insects that snatch their prey in flight. Once a victim is caught, the robber fly inserts its proboscis into the prey and sucks the juices.

Description and life cycle
Adult robber flies resemble wasps or bees but are usually gray, although some species may be yellow or black. Most are 1/2 to 3/4 inch long and hairy, with a long, narrow abdomen. They are equipped with a long, horny proboscis for piercing prey. Females lay their eggs on the ground, and most species overwinter as larvae in the soil. Larvae are white, slightly flattened, distinctly segmented grubs, and feed on a variety of soil-borne insects. Adults prefer sunny sites such as open fields or woodland edges. Many species have a life cycle of 2 years.

Beneficial effects
Robber flies are fairly indiscriminate predators, but are generally beneficial. Larvae eat a wide variety of white grubs, grasshopper eggs, beetle pupae, and caterpillars. Adults catch and consume many flying insects, including beetles, leafhoppers, butterflies, flies, bugs, and bees.

How to attract
Avoid pesticide use.

ROVE BEETLES

RANGE: widespread throughout North America

GENERATIONS PER YEAR: 1

TYPE: predator, parasite, parasitoid

Of the nearly 30,000 rove beetle species worldwide, about 3,000 occur in North America. They differ in geographic ranges and food preferences. Some are predators of plant pests; some parasitize ants, termites, and fleas; and some feed on decaying organic matter.

Description and life cycle
Rove beetles overwinter as adults, emerging in spring to mate and lay eggs in the soil. Adults are slender, 1/10 to 1 inch long, and may be black, brown, or yellow, often with spots. When disturbed, a rove beetle raises the tip of its abdomen in a menacing, combative pose. Most are active at night. The larvae look like wingless adults.

Beneficial effects
Rove beetle species vary in their food preferences. Pests they help control include snails, slugs, aphids, springtails, mites, flies, nematodes, and root maggots. Rove beetles also help decompose organic matter in the soil.

How to attract
Provide permanent beds to help rove beetle populations develop. Provide daytime shelter with organic mulches and living mulches. Avoid the use of pesticides.

SOLDIER BEETLES

RANGE: several species throughout most of the United States

GENERATIONS PER YEAR: 1 or 2

TYPE: predator

Soldier beetles, often called leatherwings, resemble lightning bugs without the light. Both larvae and adults are believed to be predaceous, feeding on a wide variety of insects.

Description and life cycle
Soldier beetles overwinter in a late larval stage, in the soil or under tree bark. Larvae are grublike, hairy or velvety, and may be brown, purple, or black. In spring they pupate and emerge as adult beetles, usually less than ½ inch long, and dark with orange, yellow, or red markings. Beetles are often found on flowering plants such as goldenrod, milkweed, and hydrangea. Many species include pollen and nectar in their diet. Females lay eggs in masses in the soil or other sheltered sites.

Beneficial effects
The Pennsylvania leatherwing, found east of the Rocky Mountains, feeds on locust eggs, cucumber beetles, corn ear worms, and European corn borers. The downy leatherwing occurs in most of the United States and eats all kinds of aphids. Other species feed on grasshopper eggs and various caterpillars and grubs.

How to attract
Avoid the use of pesticides. Grow goldenrod, hydrangea, and milkweed.

SPIDERS

RANGE: widespread throughout North America

GENERATIONS PER YEAR: 1 to many

TYPE: predator

All of the 35,000 known species of spiders are natural predators of insects. Spiders themselves are not insects but arachnids, in the same family as mites and scorpions; spiders have four pairs of legs and only two body segments. Species most helpful to gardeners include the crab spider and the wolf spider.

Description and life cycle
Spiders lay their eggs in a silk cocoon. The young resemble adults but undergo several molts before becoming adults. Spiders inject captured victims with paralyzing venom and eat them, or wrap them in silk for a later meal.

Spiders are either hunters or trappers. The wolf spider is a hunter that pounces on its prey. Wolf spiders are ground dwellers, ½ to 1⅜ inches long, and active at night. The crab spider is a trapper, spinning a web and waiting for prey to wander in; it often lies in wait near flowers visited by insects.

Beneficial effects
Feeding almost exclusively on the insects they hunt and trap, spiders are highly beneficial in the garden. Most spiders eat a wide variety of insects but avoid wasps, hornets, ants, and hard-shelled beetles.

How to attract
Avoid pesticide use. Do not disturb webs.

SPINED SOLDIER BUGS

RANGE: widespread throughout North America

GENERATIONS PER YEAR: 1 or 2

TYPE: predator

Spined soldier bugs are common in every part of the United States. The nymphs are voracious predators of some of the most damaging garden and forest pests.

Description and life cycle
Spined soldier bugs overwinter as adults, emerging in spring to lay eggs on plant leaves. One female may lay up to 1,000 eggs. Adults are about ½ inch long and shield shaped. They are pale brown or yellow with black specks and have spined, or pointed, shoulders. Nymphs resemble adults but have no wings. They feed briefly on plant sap, but after their first molt, they eat only insects for 6 to 8 weeks before becoming adults.

Beneficial effects
Nymphs eat a wide variety of caterpillars, including gypsy moths and tent caterpillars. They also feed on the larval stages of fall armyworms, sawflies, Colorado potato beetles, and Mexican bean beetles.

How to attract
Maintain permanent perennial beds to provide shelter for native populations of spined soldier bugs. Avoid pesticide use. If you buy spined soldier bugs commercially, release them at the rate of two to five nymphs per square yard of garden. Pheromone lures are also available.

TACHINID FLIES

RANGE: widespread throughout North America

GENERATIONS PER YEAR: 1 to 3

TYPE: parasitoid

There are more than 1,200 native species of tachinid flies. The adult flies live on nectar and honeydew, but the larvae parasitize many serious plant pests.

Description and life cycle
Tachinid fly larvae overwinter inside a host insect. These tiny white maggots feed on the host from the inside out, eventually killing it. The larvae pupate in or near the host's carcass; adult flies emerge and mate. Adults are ⅓ to ½ inch long, gray, brown, or black in color, and look like big, bristly houseflies but have only two wings. Females lay eggs on young host larvae or on leaves where potential hosts are feeding. Eggs or nymphs may be eaten by the host insect, or the nymphs may bore into the host, then feed and develop there.

Beneficial effects
Tachinid fly larvae kill the larvae of many harmful species, including armyworms, cutworms, tent caterpillars, cabbage loopers, ear worms, gypsy moths, hornworms, and codling moths. Some species also infest sawflies, squash bugs, and grasshoppers.

How to attract
Grow dill, parsley, and sweet clover; their flowers attract adult tachinid flies. Avoid killing caterpillars with white eggs on their backs. Avoid pesticide use.

APHIDS

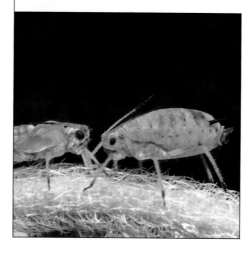

RANGE: most of the United States and southern Canada

GENERATIONS PER YEAR: 20 or more

HOST(S): most ornamentals and vegetables

More than 4,000 species of aphids are known; most plants are susceptible to at least one.

Description and life cycle
Aphids overwinter as eggs. During the growing season, they feed on soft plant tissues and produce several generations each year. Adult aphids are pear shaped, less than ⅕ inch long, and may be green, yellow, black, brownish, or gray. The nymphs are smaller versions of the adult.

Damage and detection
Feeding in large groups, aphids suck plant sap, leaving leaves wilted and yellow and flowers deformed. They secrete a sticky substance called honeydew, which drops onto plants. Honeydew serves as a growing medium for sooty mold, an unsightly black fungus that further damages plants by blocking light. Aphids also spread certain viral diseases.

Control
PHYSICAL—Knock aphids off affected plants with a jet of water; use reflective mulch and sticky traps; cut off heavily infested leaves. BIOLOGICAL—Convergent ladybird beetle; green lacewing; syrphid fly; aphid midge. CHEMICAL—Horticultural oil; insecticidal soap; pyrethrins; rotenone.

ARMYWORMS

RANGE: east of the Rocky Mountains; Arizona, New Mexico, California

GENERATIONS PER YEAR: 2 to 6

HOST(S): turf grasses and vegetables

The armyworm is a serious pest of grasses and vegetable crops. Its favorite hosts include corn and grasses.

Description and life cycle
Larvae are 1 to 2 inches long and pale green to greenish brown, with yellow or white stripes; they overwinter in plant debris or in soil. Adults are grayish brown moths, with a wingspan of 1 to 2 inches, and are active only at night. Moths lay eggs on the lower leaves of plants and produce as many as six generations per year, depending on the species and the climate.

Damage and detection
Larvae hide during the day in protected areas and feed at night on leaves, stems, and buds. Large numbers can defoliate plants overnight.

Control
PHYSICAL—Handpick worms. CULTURAL—Keep weed growth down; till soil to expose pupae to predators. BIOLOGICAL—Beneficial nematodes; birds; Bt; ground beetles; toads; trichogramma wasps. CHEMICAL—Horticultural oil in July to control second generation; neem.

BAGWORMS

RANGE: east of the Rocky Mountains

GENERATIONS PER YEAR: 1

HOST(S): trees and shrubs

The bagworm feeds on the leaves of many deciduous and evergreen trees and shrubs, especially juniper and arborvitae.

Description and life cycle
Bagworms overwinter as eggs inside small bags, hatching in late spring or early summer. Each dark brown larva spins a silken bag some 2 inches long around itself and covers it with bits of plant debris. In late summer, the larva attaches its bag to a twig and pupates. In a few days, adult males emerge from their bags as black, clear-winged moths and fly off in search of adult females, which remain inside their bags. Females lay 500 to 1,000 eggs after mating, and then both sexes die.

Damage and detection
Larvae feed on a host's leaves, often stripping twigs bare and giving the plant a ragged look. Heavy infestations may defoliate entire trees. The bags are easy to spot.

Control
PHYSICAL—Handpick and destroy bags in winter or early spring, before eggs hatch; set pheromone traps. BIOLOGICAL—Bt when larvae begin to feed; parasitic wasps. CHEMICAL—Rotenone applied when bags are small, usually in June.

BARK BEETLES

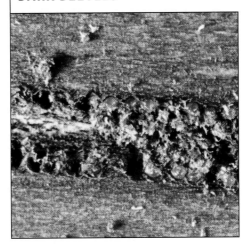

RANGE: most of the United States and southern Canada

GENERATIONS PER YEAR: 1 to 3

HOST(S): deciduous and coniferous trees

Bark beetles include many species of minute or small beetles that are typically stout and cylindrical in shape; the scientific name of the family to which all the species belong means "cut short" in Greek. These pests tunnel into tree bark to lay their eggs. They attack various hosts, but most evergreen and many deciduous trees are susceptible to one or more species. Some of the most destructive bark beetles include the ambrosia beetle *(Corthylus punctatissimus)*, the elm bark beetles *(Scolytus multistriatus* and *Hylurgopinus rufipes)*, the pine engraver *(Ips pini)*, the shothole borer *(Scolytus rugulosus)*, and the Southern pine beetle *(Dendroctonus frontalis)*.

Description and life cycle
Adults are commonly black or brown and less than ¼ inch long; they have short snouts and are covered with fine hairs or bristles. The adult beetle—in some species the male and in others the female—bores into the bark of a living or rotting tree to make a tunnel in which the female deposits her eggs. When the eggs hatch, the larvae begin to feed on the wood, creating tunnels, or galleries, beneath the bark, usually at right angles to the original tunnel bored by the male. The adult male ambrosia beetle carries fruiting bodies of a fungus into the tunnels to serve as food for the larvae. At the ends of the galleries, the larvae pupate, then emerge as adults to mate and repeat the process for a total of two or three generations a year, depending on the species and location. Beetles overwinter in a dormant state in the galleries.

Damage and detection
Evidence of bark beetle infestation includes holes in the bark that frequently ooze sap. Sawdust from the hole may be found at the base of the tree. Shothole borer holes are numerous and small, giving the tree the appearance of having been hit with buckshot. Tunneling by feeding larvae destroys tissue in the cambium—the layer that produces new growth—and can eventually kill the infested tree. Those not killed by beetle damage are susceptible to invasion by pathogens. In the case of the elm bark beetle, it spreads the fungus responsible for Dutch elm disease. The adult elm bark beetle tunnels and lays eggs in weakened or diseased elm wood, which is often infected with Dutch elm disease. When the new adults emerge, they fly to healthy leaves of nearby elms and spread the disease as they feed.

Control
PHYSICAL—Remove and destroy infested trees; prune and destroy infested branches; set pheromone traps. CULTURAL—Plant species that are resistant to Dutch elm disease. BIOLOGICAL—Beneficial nematodes; braconid wasps.

BILLBUGS

RANGE: United States and southern Canada in grassland regions and lawns

GENERATIONS PER YEAR: 1

HOST(S): grasses

Billbugs are named for the adult's peculiar bill-like, elongated snout. The larvae do most of the damage to lawns.

Description and life cycle
Billbugs overwinter as adults in the soil. They are ¼ to ½ inch long and may be gray, brown, or black. They emerge in spring to feed and lay their eggs on the leaf sheaths of grass. The hatching larvae—white, legless, and very small—begin feeding on stems, then move into the soil to feed on grass roots.

Damage and detection
Symptoms of billbug damage include yellow or brown patches in the lawn, which show up first during periods of drought, especially near driveways or sidewalks, where soil tends to be driest. Sawdustlike material around grass stems may also indicate billbug feeding. Infested areas of turf are easy to pull up because the roots have been eaten.

Control
CULTURAL—Plant grass varieties that are resistant to billbugs. PHYSICAL—Dethatch lawn if thatch layer is more than ¾ inch thick. BIOLOGICAL—Beneficial nematodes. CHEMICAL—Neem.

BLISTER BEETLES

RANGE: most of the United States and southern Canada

GENERATIONS PER YEAR: 1

HOST(S): many ornamentals and vegetables

Most common east of the Rocky Mountains, blister beetles feed on the flowers and foliage of many ornamentals, vegetables, and fruits; members of the tomato family are favorite hosts. When crushed, they emit a liquid that causes blisters on the skin; hence their common name.

Description and life cycle
Larvae of the blister beetle overwinter in the soil. They pupate and emerge as adults in midsummer. The adults have an elongated body, less than ¾ inch long, and may be black, brown, gray, blue, or striped. Females lay their eggs in grasshopper burrows, and when the larvae hatch, they feed on grasshopper egg masses.

Damage and detection
Large numbers of beetles can defoliate plants very rapidly. Only the adult is damaging; the larva is considered beneficial because it serves to control grasshoppers.

Control
PHYSICAL—Handpick the beetles, wearing gloves to protect skin; cover all valuable plants with cheesecloth. BIOLOGICAL—Beneficial nematodes. CHEMICAL—Pyrethrins; rotenone.

BORERS/CLEARWING MOTHS

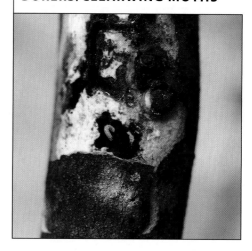

RANGE: throughout the United States and southern Canada

GENERATIONS PER YEAR: 1

HOST(S): many ornamentals and vegetables

There are numerous species of clearwing moths. The larvae, or caterpillars, cause serious injury to a wide variety of woody and herbaceous plants by boring into stems, twigs, or trunks and feeding on interior plant tissues. Some of the most destructive are the dogwood borer, greater peach tree borer, lilac borer, and rhododendron borer.

Description and life cycle
Most clearwing moths overwinter as larvae in host tissue. They are ⅛ to 1 inch long and yellow or white with dark heads. In spring the larvae pupate and emerge as adult moths, swift fliers that resemble wasps. The wings are at least somewhat transparent; the bodies are often striped with yellow, brown, or orange bands. Females lay eggs on bark or stems of susceptible host plants, especially near wounds.

After hatching, the larvae enter their host by way of wounds, scars, or twig crotches. The dogwood borer (known in the South as the pecan borer) infests many hardwood trees, including cherry, apple, hickory, willow, birch, and oak. It afflicts cultivated dogwoods more often than those growing in the wild. The greater peach tree borer infests stone fruits, birch trees, and several species of ornamental shrubs. It enters plants near the base of the trunk and sometimes invades the surface roots. The lilac borer attacks not only lilacs but also privet and ash trees. It generally enters a host within 3 feet of the soil line. The rhododendron borer, the smallest of the clearwing moths, is most serious in the mid-Atlantic region. It attacks mountain laurel, azaleas, and rhododendrons.

Damage and detection

Symptoms of borer infestation include wilted leaves; loose, sloughing, or cracking bark; and dieback of branches. Any evident holes are usually the exit holes, since entry holes are so tiny they go undetected. The borer feeds on and destroys the cambium—a layer of tissue that produces girth-increasing growth—and often girdles the plant. Branches above the site of infection usually die. If borers invade the host near the soil line, the whole plant dies.

Control

PHYSICAL—Remove infested branches and badly infested plants; encircle peach trees with a 4- to 6-inch ring of tobacco dust in spring; set pheromone traps. CULTURAL—Keep trees and shrubs healthy and vigorous, and avoid mechanical injuries, since borers generally enter through wounds or scars. BIOLOGICAL—Bt; parasitic wasps. CHEMICAL—Horticultural oil.

Lilac Borer

CABBAGE LOOPERS

RANGE: throughout the United States and southern Canada

GENERATIONS PER YEAR: 2 to 7

HOST(S): many ornamentals and vegetables

Cabbage loopers feed on members of the cabbage family and other vegetables, as well as many herbaceous ornamentals including carnations, chrysanthemums, nasturtiums, and geraniums. Cabbage loopers closely resemble the imported cabbage worm in appearance and in the damage they cause.

Description and life cycle

Cabbage loopers overwinter as pupae on plant leaves or stems. Adults emerge in spring as brown moths with a silver spot on each forewing, and a wingspan of 1½ to 2 inches. Eggs are laid on host plants, where they hatch in about a week. The caterpillars are green, with white stripes down their back. They feed for 2 to 4 weeks before pupating.

Damage and detection

The larvae chew large, irregular holes in leaves. While their color provides an effective camouflage, their damage is easily spotted.

Control

PHYSICAL—Handpick larvae and destroy greenish white eggs; use row covers. BIOLOGICAL—Apply Bt at 2-week intervals; lacewings; trichogramma wasps; birds. CHEMICAL—Pyrethrins; rotenone; sabadilla.

CANKERWORMS

RANGE: Maine to North Carolina, west to Missouri; Colorado, Utah, California

GENERATIONS PER YEAR: 1

HOST(S): deciduous trees and shrubs

Cankerworms are often referred to as inchworms or measuring worms because of the way they arch their backs as they move. They feed on the leaves and buds of many deciduous plants; beech, cherry, elm, maple, and oak are favorite hosts.

Description and life cycle

Fall cankerworms overwinter as eggs, hatching in spring when trees and shrubs are putting out new leaves. The slender caterpillars may be green, brown, or black, with white stripes; they grow to 1 inch in length. They feed for 3 to 4 weeks, then crawl into the soil to pupate. The adults emerge in late fall to lay their eggs on the bark of trees. Spring cankerworms are similar but overwinter as moths that emerge in spring.

Damage and detection

The leaves are chewed up to the midrib. Heavily infested plants are defoliated.

Control

PHYSICAL—Wrap sticky bands around the trunks of susceptible trees before egg laying occurs; destroy egg masses. CULTURAL—Till the soil to expose pupae. BIOLOGICAL—Bt; spined soldier bugs; trichogramma wasps. CHEMICAL—Horticultural oil; neem.

CHINCH BUGS

RANGE: throughout the United States, southern Canada, and Mexico

GENERATIONS PER YEAR: 2 or 3

HOST(S): grasses

Chinch bugs are found throughout North America but are most prevalent in the Mississippi, Ohio, and Missouri river valleys, as well as Texas and Oklahoma.

Description and life cycle
Chinch bugs overwinter under plant debris as adults, which are about ⅓ inch long and have a black body and white wings. In spring the females lay eggs over a period of 3 weeks. Young nymphs are bright red with a white band across the back; older nymphs are black with white spots.

Damage and detection
The nymphs are the most damaging stage. They feed on both the roots and stems of grasses, sucking juices and secreting toxic salivary fluids. Infested turf turns yellow and often dies in patches. Injury resembles that of Japanese beetle grubs and is most serious during hot, dry periods.

Control
PHYSICAL—Dethatch heavily thatched lawn. CULTURAL—Plant resistant varieties; reduce nitrogen fertilizer. BIOLOGICAL—Big-eyed bugs; lacewings; ladybird beetles; pirate bugs. CHEMICAL—Flood an infested area with soapy water and cover with a light-colored flannel sheet; the bugs will crawl onto the underside to escape the soap. Kill them by dipping the sheet in hot, soapy water; neem; pyrethrins; soap sprays.

CICADAS

RANGE: eastern United States, west to Texas and Oklahoma

GENERATIONS PER YEAR: variable

HOST(S): deciduous trees and shrubs

The periodical cicadas live either 13 or 17 years, but because generations overlap, almost every year brings at least a few periodical cicadas. The dog-day cicada is also known as the annual cicada—erroneously, since it has a 2- to 4-year cycle. Its generations also overlap.

Description and life cycle
These pests spend most of their lives as nymphs underground, feeding on plant roots. They emerge and climb into trees for their last molt. The adults are 1 to 2 inches long. Within weeks they mate, lay eggs, and then die. The eggs hatch in about 2 months, becoming new nymphs.

Damage and detection
Although adult cicadas suck sap from young twigs, they do their greatest harm laying eggs. The female cuts into the bark of twigs and splinters the sapwood as she deposits her eggs. One female may make 20 separate egg pockets, each of which can cause twig dieback and make the host vulnerable to infection.

Control
PHYSICAL—Apply sticky bands to the tree trunks; remove injured twigs before eggs hatch; cover shrubs with netting. CULTURAL—Avoid planting young trees when major outbreaks are expected. BIOLOGICAL—Beneficial nematodes.

COLORADO POTATO BEETLES

RANGE: throughout the United States except the South and the Pacific Northwest

GENERATIONS PER YEAR: 1 to 3

HOST(S): many solanum family members

The Colorado potato beetle is a serious garden pest in most parts of the country. In addition to potato plants, eggplants, peppers, tomatoes, and petunias are often attacked.

Description and life cycle
The Colorado potato beetle overwinters as an adult. It is oval, ⅓ inch long, with yellow-and-black-striped wing covers. Beetles emerge in spring, feed, and lay eggs that hatch in about a week. The plump larvae are orange-red with black spots. They feed, reenter the soil to pupate, and emerge as adults in 1 to 2 weeks.

Damage and detection
Adults and larvae alike decimate the foliage and stems of potatoes, tomatoes, and related plants, reducing yields in both quantity and quality. Heavy infestations can be fatal, especially to young plants. While feeding, beetles leave highly visible black excrement on leaves and stems.

Control
PHYSICAL—Use a thick organic mulch to inhibit migrating larvae; handpick beetles, larvae, and eggs. CULTURAL—Rotate crops; plant resistant varieties. BIOLOGICAL—Bt San Diego strain; ladybird beetles; spined soldier bugs. CHEMICAL—Neem; pyrethrins; rotenone.

CONIFER SAWFLIES

RANGE: eastern United States to the Mississippi River, southeastern Canada

GENERATIONS PER YEAR: 1 to 5

HOST(S): coniferous trees and shrubs

Conifer sawflies are among the most damaging insect pests of pine, spruce, and hemlock. There are several species, each with its own range of host plants.

Description and life cycle
With sawlike egg-laying organs, females slit needles and deposit eggs in the slits. Depending on the species, sawflies overwinter as eggs or as cocooned pupae in soil or on lower tree bark. Larvae are as much as 1 inch long and gray, green, yellow, or tan, with dark brown or red heads and black dots along their bodies. The adults are less than ½ inch long and stout, with translucent wings.

Damage and detection
Hundreds of larvae feed together on the current season's needles, devouring an entire shoot before moving on to the next. Their color blends with the foliage, so they often do serious damage before they are detected. Left untreated, they can defoliate and even kill the host.

Control
PHYSICAL—Spread flannel dropcloths under trees, shake limbs to dislodge larvae, and destroy them in a soap solution. CULTURAL—Keep trees healthy and vigorous. BIOLOGICAL—Parasitic wasps; predaceous beetles; shrews; tachinid flies. CHEMICAL—Horticultural oil; soap sprays.

CORN EAR WORMS

RANGE: throughout the United States, especially southern and central states

GENERATIONS PER YEAR: 2 to 7

HOST(S): corn and tomato

The corn ear worm is also known as the tomato fruit worm, depending on the host it infests. It may also attack potatoes, beans, peas, peppers, and squash.

Description and life cycle
Corn ear worms overwinter as pupae in the soil. In spring the gray-green or brown moths emerge and lay eggs on corn silk or the undersides of leaves; the eggs hatch within in a few days. The larvae, ½ inch long, are green, yellow, or white caterpillars with black longitudinal stripes. They feed for 3 to 4 weeks, then return to the soil to pupate. In the North, they usually produce two generations each year; in the South, as many as seven.

Damage and detection
Larvae feed on corn silk, leaves, and fruit, inhibiting pollination, disfiguring ears, and opening them to invasion by other insects or pathogens. Similar damage occurs with other hosts.

Control
CULTURAL—Till vegetable garden in fall to expose the pupae. PHYSICAL—Handpick worms. BIOLOGICAL—Larvae are cannibalistic and help control their own numbers; Bt; tachinid flies; trichogramma wasps. CHEMICAL—Neem; ryania.

CRICKETS AND GRASSHOPPERS

RANGE: widespread throughout North America

GENERATIONS PER YEAR: 1 to 3

HOST(S): most ornamentals and vegetables

Crickets and grasshoppers are common pests that attack almost all cultivated plants. Although they usually cause only minor damage to crops, populations may build up, and migrating swarms devour nearly all vegetation in their path. Such attacks are infrequent in North America, but the common name of one species, the Mormon cricket, is a reminder of the swarm that attacked the crops of Mormon settlers in Utah in 1848. This pest, which is actually a grasshopper and not a true cricket, ranges from California to Minnesota and Kansas. Including the Mormon cricket, there are only five North American grasshopper species that become numerous enough to damage crops significantly. Weather conditions play an important role in determining the size of grasshopper populations in any given year. They are smaller in years with a cool, wet spring and summer, but a long, hot, dry season can cause the populations to rise dramatically. True crickets are less destructive than grasshoppers. They damage seedlings and are also household pests, feeding on clothing, paper, and foods such as fruit and potatoes.

Description and life cycle
The many species of grasshoppers differ in appearance, range, and preferred host. Most species produce one generation per

year, although in the South, a few produce two. Like other grasshoppers, the Mormon cricket overwinters in soil as eggs that hatch the following spring. The nymphs go through seven molts before taking on their final adult form, some 2 to 3 months after hatching. The nymphs feed on any available plant material, exhausting one food source completely before moving on to another. In late summer adult females, which are about 1 inch in length, deposit tiny sacs or packets—holding up to 100 or so eggs—in soil. Female and male adults continue to feed until they are killed by cold weather.

Crickets produce one to three generations per year, overwintering in the South as nymphs or adults and in cooler climates as eggs. After hatching, the nymphs go through 8 to 12 molts before emerging as full-size adults that are ¾ to 1 inch long and dark brown or black, with wiry antennae. They often have large hind legs and flat, folded wings, although some species are wingless. Males of species common to the United States make a loud, chirping noise by rubbing together parts of their forewings. Most crickets are nocturnal and seek shelter during the day, some in vegetation and others in the ground. Females lay their eggs in soil or in plant stems in late summer or early fall. In winter, adult crickets frequently seek shelter indoors.

Damage and detection
Among the most damaging of all grasshopper species is the migratory grasshopper, which causes significant crop losses in the western United States and southwestern Canada. It feeds in swarms, stripping

Mormon Cricket

away the leaves and stems of nearly all vegetation in areas of up to several square miles. Migratory grasshoppers prefer grasses but in their absence will feed on virtually any other kind of plants. The swarm then migrates to another feeding ground. Other species feed in a similar manner but may have a narrower range of hosts.

Crickets, like grasshoppers, are not a serious problem until they are present in large numbers. Masses of field crickets damage plantings of tomatoes, peas, beans, cucumbers, and squash by consuming seeds or seedlings. Further damage occurs when adults and nymphs chew on the foliage and flowers of vegetable crops. Tree crickets injure stems of trees or shrubs by inserting their eggs into the plant tissue.

Control
CULTURAL—Cultivate soil in fall to expose overwintering eggs. PHYSICAL—Use row covers; trap the pests in jars buried to the brim and containing a mixture of 1 part molasses to 9 parts water. BIOLOGICAL—The pathogen *Nosema locustae* is effective for long-term control over large areas; beneficial nematodes; blister beetle larvae; praying mantises; predatory flies. CHEMICAL—Insecticidal soap.

CUCUMBER BEETLES

RANGE: United States and Canada, east of the Rocky Mountains

GENERATIONS PER YEAR: 1 to 4

HOST(S): many vegetables and ornamentals

Widespread east of the Rockies, cucumber beetles are most damaging in the South, where they often produce four generations a year. They attack cucumbers, melons, squash, and other members of the cucumber family. Ornamentals commonly infested include chrysanthemums, cosmos, dahlias, roses, zinnias, and grasses.

Description and life cycle
Adults are ¼ inch long and yellowish green with black spots or stripes. They overwinter in garden debris, emerging in spring to lay eggs at the base of host plants. The eggs hatch in about 10 days, and slender, white larvae, which reach ½ inch in length, burrow into the soil to feed on plant roots and pupate. Emerging adults feed on leaves, flowers, and fruit, and repeat the cycle.

Damage and detection
Larvae feeding on roots stunt and may kill plants. Adults chew holes in leaves and flowers; some species also eat fruit. Adults and larvae can carry cucumber mosaic virus and cucumber wilt.

Control
PHYSICAL—Handpick beetles; use row covers. CULTURAL—Plant varieties resistant to the diseases carried by cucumber beetles. BIOLOGICAL—Beneficial nematodes; braconid wasps; tachinid flies. CHEMICAL—Rotenone; sabadilla.

CUTWORMS

RANGE: various species throughout North America

GENERATIONS PER YEAR: 1 to 5

HOST(S): most herbaceous plants

The roughly 3,000 species of cutworms in North America can be grouped according to their feeding habits as tunnelers, climbers, and subterraneans.

Description and life cycle
Most cutworms overwinter as larvae or pupae. The soft, gray-brown larvae, 1 to 2 inches long, feed at night, burrow into the soil during the day, and curl into a C-shape when disturbed. They pupate in the soil and emerge as night-flying adult moths, brown or gray, with a 1½-inch wingspan. Females lay their eggs on leaves and stems; eggs hatch in 2 to 10 days.

Damage and detection
Tunneling cutworms chew on seedlings near the soil surface, making them topple and die. Climbing cutworms feed on leaves and flowers of vegetables and herbaceous ornamental plants. The subterranean cutworms feed on roots and underground stems, causing wilting and stunting.

Control
PHYSICAL—Use plant collars around seedlings. CULTURAL—Till soil in fall to expose the larvae or pupae; till again in early spring and wait 2 weeks before planting. BIOLOGICAL—Beneficial nematodes; braconid wasps; Bt; tachinid flies; trichogramma wasps.

ELM LEAF BEETLES

RANGE: throughout North America wherever elms grow

GENERATIONS PER YEAR: 1 to 4

HOST(S): elm, zelkova

Both adults and larvae of the elm leaf beetle cause serious damage to elms, especially in California, where there are three or four generations each year.

Description and life cycle
Adult elm leaf beetles overwinter in protected places such as the crevices in tree bark, garages, or sheds. The beetle is yellow or dull green and ¼ inch long. In spring, as tree leaves unfurl, beetles fly to elms to feed and mate. Females lay eggs in clusters on the leaves. Larvae are up to ½ inch long and yellow-green with black stripes and head. They feed on the undersides of leaves for several weeks, then move down the tree to pupate on the trunk or on the ground. In about 2 weeks adults emerge to repeat the cycle.

Damage and detection
Adults chew roughly round holes in leaves; larvae skeletonize foliage, leaving only veins. Leaves turn brown and drop prematurely, often to be replaced by a new flush of foliage just in time for the next generation of beetles. Repeated defoliations can weaken a tree, making it vulnerable to Dutch elm disease.

Control
PHYSICAL—Handpick adults; apply sticky bands. BIOLOGICAL—Bt San Diego strain; chalcid wasps; tachinid flies.

EUROPEAN CORN BORERS

RANGE: north and central United States and southern Canada

GENERATIONS PER YEAR: 1 to 3

HOST(S): many herbaceous plants

Although the European corn borer, as its name suggests, is primarily a pest of corn, it also attacks other plants, such as tomato, celosia, sunflowers, cosmos, hollyhocks, chrysanthemums, asters, and dahlias.

Description and life cycle
The European corn borer overwinters as larvae in plant debris and pupates in early spring. Adult moths are pale brown, with dark markings on their wings and a 1-inch wingspan. Females lay masses of eggs on the undersides of leaves. Eggs hatch in about a week and the larvae begin to feed. Larvae are 1 inch long when fully grown, and beige with brown spots and dark heads. They feed for 3 to 4 weeks, pupate, and repeat the cycle.

Damage and detection
Larvae bore into corn ears at either end to feed on kernels. They also feed on tassels and leaves. On other plants, the larvae tunnel into stems and fruits.

Control
PHYSICAL—Remove and destroy plant debris. CULTURAL—Plant varieties resistant to borers; time plantings to avoid peak periods of borer infestation. BIOLOGICAL—Bt, applied before the larvae enter the stems or ears; braconid wasps; ladybird beetles; tachinid flies. CHEMICAL—Pyrethrins; ryania; sabadilla.

FLEA BEETLES

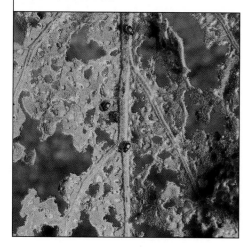

RANGE: several species throughout North America

GENERATIONS PER YEAR: 2 to 4

HOST(S): most herbaceous plants

Flea beetles, common garden pests, attack most herbaceous ornamentals and vegetables. They are especially troublesome on members of the cabbage family and the solanum family, which includes eggplant, peppers, potatoes, and tomatoes. The beetles get their name from the way they jump when disturbed.

Description and life cycle
Flea beetles overwinter as adults near the soil surface, emerging in spring to feed and mate. Beetles are small—1/10 inch long—and black, brown, or bronze; they lay eggs in the soil near hosts. The larvae, 1/4-inch, legless white grubs with brown heads, eat plant roots, pupate, and emerge as adults to repeat the cycle.

Damage and detection
Adults chew tiny round holes in leaves. Seedlings are weakened or may be killed by a heavy infestation. Larvae weaken plants with their root feeding. Flea beetles carry several viral diseases.

Control
PHYSICAL—Use row covers; spray with jets of water; ring plants with diatomaceous earth or wood ashes. CULTURAL—Cultivate soil often to expose eggs and larvae. BIOLOGICAL—Beneficial nematodes; braconid wasps; tachinid flies. CHEMICAL—Pyrethrins; rotenone; sabadilla.

GALL MITES

RANGE: various species throughout North America

GENERATIONS PER YEAR: many

HOST(S): many trees and shrubs

Mites are not insects; they belong to the arachnid class, which includes spiders. There are many species of mites, each with its own range of host plants. Some of the most common mites are the maple bladder gall mite, the maple spindle gall mite, and the hickory bladder gall mite. Other mite species cause galls on beech, cherry, elm, linden, and poplar.

Description and life cycle
Most mites are too small for the unaided eye to see, and their life cycles are poorly understood. Maple gall mites overwinter as adults in maple bark. In early spring, individual mites enter leaves, injecting a toxin that stimulates the leaf to develop an enlarged growth called a gall. Each mite feeds inside its gall, and the females lay eggs in their galls; when the eggs hatch, the resident adults move to new leaves. There is often a new generation every 2 to 3 weeks.

Damage and detection
The maple bladder gall mite causes wartlike growths on the upper sides of maple leaves. The maple spindle gall mite causes narrow, spindlelike projections. Numerous galls may distort leaves, but the damage is rarely serious.

Control
BIOLOGICAL—Predatory mites. CHEMICAL—Dormant lime-sulfur spray.

GALL WASPS

RANGE: various species throughout the United States and Canada

GENERATIONS PER YEAR: 2

HOST(S): oak, rose, and thistle families

Gall wasps stimulate host plants to form enlarged growths called galls on leaves, twigs, or stems. There are hundreds of species of gall wasps, which have specific host ranges and produce characteristic galls. Most of these galls, while unsightly, do little harm to the host.

Description and life cycle
Adult gall wasps overwinter in the gall and emerge in spring. Females lay eggs on the host; after hatching, the larvae begin to feed. Where each one feeds, it stimulates the host to form a new gall, then uses this mass of plant tissue as food and as shelter during pupation. Adults emerge in summer to produce a second brood; this generation overwinters as adults in new galls.

Damage and detection
Galls may form on leaves or stems of host plants. They are often high in tannins and have been used in the past to make ink. While the galls may be somewhat unsightly, they rarely injure or even weaken a plant.

Control
PHYSICAL—Prune and destroy overwintering galls to reduce gall wasp population.

GYPSY MOTHS

RANGE: eastern and central United States; sometimes the Pacific Northwest

GENERATIONS PER YEAR: 1

HOST(S): many trees and shrubs

The gypsy moth was introduced to Massachusetts from Europe in 1869 in an effort to improve American silk production. Accidentally released, it spread rapidly throughout New England, feeding on a wide variety of deciduous and evergreen trees and shrubs. Among the moth's preferred hosts are oak, apple, alder, hawthorn, poplar, and willow. Its spread has continued throughout the eastern and central United States and southeastern Canada. In the West, there are occasional outbreaks in Washington, Oregon, and California. A closely related Asian species has appeared on the West Coast; it is attacking an even wider range of plants than gypsy moths.

Description and life cycle
Gypsy moths overwinter as eggs, which hatch in April or early May. The larvae are gray caterpillars that grow up to 2 inches in length and have tufts of brown hairs on the sides of their bodies. They are easy to identify because of the distinctive markings on their backs—five pairs of blue tubercles or dots, followed by six pairs of red dots. At first, larvae feed at night on leaves of trees and shrubs, and take shelter under fallen leaves, in woodpiles, or in other dark or shady places during the day. As the larvae grow larger, they begin to feed during the day as well as at night.

When a tree suffers a heavy infestation, the larvae's excrement rustles like a gentle rain, as it falls accumulating in a visible layer of tiny tan pellets on the ground. After approximately 7 weeks of feeding, each caterpillar finds a protected spot, such as a crevice in the bark, in which to pupate. Adult moths emerge from mid- to late summer.

The moths are an inch long, with a 2-inch wingspan. Wings are gray-brown in the male, off-white in the female, with dark wavy markings in both. The males fly freely, but the females do not fly until after mating. The females lay their eggs in fuzzy, chamois-colored masses of 100 to 1,000 on any hard surface. Gypsy moth egg masses are often found attached to vehicles or camping gear and may be inadvertently transported over great distances by such means. Checking infested trees and nearby buildings for these egg masses and eliminating them when found is one way to reduce future infestations.

Damage and detection
Gypsy moths defoliate plants, leaving only the midrib of each leaf. Infested plants are left weakened and susceptible to disease. Deciduous trees often die if defoliated two or three consecutive seasons, and evergreens may die after a single defoliation.

Control
PHYSICAL—Handpick egg masses; paint egg cases with creosote; apply tree bands and sticky bands around trees; set pheromone traps. CULTURAL—Plant resistant varieties. BIOLOGICAL—Bt; chalcid wasps; ground beetles; tachinid flies; trichogramma wasps. CHEMICAL—Neem; pyrethrins; ryania.

Gypsy Moth Caterpillar

HEMLOCK WOOLLY ADELGIDS

RANGE: eastern United States from North Carolina to Connecticut

GENERATIONS PER YEAR: 2 or 3

HOST(S): eastern hemlock, spruce

The hemlock woolly adelgid is an extremely destructive pest of eastern hemlock (*Tsuga canadensis*). It also occurs in the Pacific Northwest but is not as serious a problem there because western hemlocks are somewhat resistant.

Description and life cycle
The hemlock woolly adelgid overwinters as a tiny adult covered with a protective white, cottony sac about ¼ inch long. From February to June, the female lays 50 to 300 eggs inside her sac. Chocolate-colored, oval nymphs hatch in spring and early summer, then crawl away from the egg sac and settle into their own feeding sites. Some of the nymphs mature into wingless females and stay on the same hemlock, where they produce another generation. Other nymphs mature into winged adults that spend part of their life cycle on spruce trees.

Damage and detection
The woolly egg sacs are easy to see at the base of needles. Needles turn yellow, then brown, and drop off. The adelgids suck sap and weaken trees. If left untreated, an infested tree generally dies in 4 years. If severely infested, it may die within a year.

Control
CHEMICAL—Horticultural oil or insecticidal soap; apply as soon as problem is detected.

HORNWORMS

RANGE: widespread throughout North America

GENERATIONS PER YEAR: 1 to 4

HOST(S): tomato, pepper, eggplant

The hornworm, which is the larva of the sphinx moth, is large and eats voraciously; even a single hornworm feeding on a plant can cause significant damage.

Description and life cycle
Hornworms spend the winter in the soil as brown, 2-inch pupae. These emerge in summer as mottled gray moths with yellow-spotted abdomens and a 4- to 5-inch wingspan, and lay eggs on the undersides of leaves. When the eggs hatch, the emerging larvae are bright green caterpillars 3 to 4 inches long, with diagonal white side bars and a black, green, or red horn at the tail end. The caterpillars eat leaves for 3 to 4 weeks before entering the soil to pupate. Damage and detection: Hornworms eat large holes in leaves and fruit. Their color camouflages them well in foliage, but the sudden appearance of leafless stems gives away their presence, as do greenish black droppings on the leaves.

Control
CULTURAL—Cultivate soil in fall. PHYSICAL—Handpick caterpillars, unless their backs bear the white cocoons of braconid wasps, a natural predator. BIOLOGICAL—Braconid wasps; lacewings; ladybird beetles; trichogramma wasps. CHEMICAL—Bt; pyrethrins; rotenone.

IMPORTED CABBAGE WORMS

RANGE: widespread throughout North America

GENERATIONS PER YEAR: 3 to 6

HOST(S): members of the cabbage family

Brought from Europe in the late 19th century, the cabbage worm is now a common pest in gardens throughout the United States. The larva of the cabbage butterfly, it attacks ornamental kale along with its edible relatives.

Description and life cycle
Cabbage worms overwinter as pupae in garden debris. The adults emerge in early spring as day-flying, white or pale yellow butterflies, with dark gray or black wing tips and a 1½-inch wingspan. Eggs are laid on the underside of hosts' leaves, and hatch in 4 to 8 days. Each larva—1¼ inches long, velvety green, with one yellow stripe along its back—feeds for 2 to 3 weeks, then pupates on or near its host. A new generation of adults emerges in 2 to 3 weeks. Generations overlap, so infestations may appear continuous.

Damage and detection
Larvae chew large, ragged holes in leaves; tunnel into heads of cabbage, kale, and cauliflower; and eat broccoli florets. They leave green-black droppings.

Control
PHYSICAL—Handpick larvae; use row covers. BIOLOGICAL—Bt at 1- to 2-week intervals; green lacewings; spined soldier bugs; trichogramma wasps. CHEMICAL—Neem; rotenone; sabadilla.

IRIS BORERS

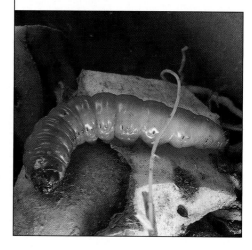

RANGE: eastern North America, west to Iowa, north to Ontario, and south to Georgia

GENERATIONS PER YEAR: 1

HOST(S): iris

In its geographic range, this larva is the most serious insect pest of the iris. The night-flying miller moth is the adult stage. Description and life cycle: Iris borers overwinter as eggs on old leaves. They hatch in midspring as green larvae that mature to dusky pink with brown heads; the backs bear a light stripe and rows of black dots. Fat and up to 2 inches long, the larvae tunnel into iris foliage to feed for several weeks, then pupate in the soil near the iris rhizomes. The adult miller moths emerge in late summer; they have brown forewings, yellow hind wings, and a 2-inch wingspan. They lay eggs on leaves and flower stalks.

Damage and detection
Larvae tunnel through leaves and crowns and into rhizomes as they feed; infested leaves develop ragged edges and areas that appear water soaked. Infested rhizomes are extremely vulnerable to bacterial soft rots.

Control
PHYSICAL—Remove and destroy leaves and stems in late fall to eliminate eggs; dig up infested rhizomes and either discard them or poke a wire into visible borer holes to kill pests; dust with sulfur before planting.

JAPANESE BEETLES

RANGE: eastern United States, southeastern Canada, occasionally California

GENERATIONS PER YEAR: 1

HOST(S): more than 275 species of plants

Natives of the Far East, Japanese beetles were brought to the United States around 1916. They first appeared in New Jersey but have gradually spread north to Nova Scotia and Ontario, west to the Mississippi River, and south to the Gulf of Mexico, and are occasionally found in California. They cause serious damage to a wide variety of plants in both the larval (grub) stage and the adult (beetle) stage. Among their preferred hosts are rose, grape, willow, hibiscus, apple, hydrangea, linden, raspberry, and grasses. They are particularly destructive in nurseries and orchards, and on golf courses.

Description and life cycle
Japanese beetles overwinter as partially grown grubs in the soil below the frostline. Grayish white with dark heads, grubs are fat and up to ¾ inch long; they are usually found curled in a C-shape. They feed on the roots of grasses before pupating in late spring or early summer, and emerge as adults in May, June, and July.

The beetles are ½ inch long, with shiny, metallic blue or green bodies and copper-colored wings. Their bodies are covered with grayish hairs, with tufts of white hairs on the abdomen. Beetles fly only during the day and prefer feeding in sunny locations. When they find a suitable host plant, they release feeding and sex pheromones that attract many other Japanese beetles. They feed for 30 to 45 days, then the females lay as many as 60 eggs each, in clusters of one to four, several inches deep in the soil. Females prefer to lay eggs in loose, acid soils in sunny sites; the heaviest infestations usually occur in soils with a pH of 5.3 or lower. Grubs hatch in about 2 weeks and feed on grass roots until cold weather forces them to burrow below the frostline. In spring, grubs migrate back to the soil surface and resume feeding on roots.

Damage and detection
Grub damage begins as patches of turf that grows poorly and starts to turn yellow. These patches get larger and gradually turn brown. To check such a patch for Japanese beetle grubs, peel back the turf and examine the root zone; severely damaged turf has lost most of its roots and can be rolled up like carpet to reveal the grubs. Unnoticed and untreated, an infestation of grubs can do irreversible damage, even kill an entire lawn. Adult beetles ignore grasses, preferring to attack woody and herbaceous ornamentals as well as vegetables and fruits. Feeding in groups in daytime, they chew away leaf tissue between the veins, skeletonizing foliage; they may cause defoliation. They also feed on buds and flowers, causing disfiguration.

Control for adults
PHYSICAL—Handpick beetles in the early morning while they are sluggish; knock beetles off foliage onto a sheet spread under infested plants; collect beetles with hand-held vacuum, then immerse them in soapy water. CHEMICAL—Neem as a repellent; pyrethrins; rotenone.

Control for grubs
CULTURAL—Check lawn for grubs in early spring or fall by selecting four or five different areas, marking off a square foot, and peeling back the sod. Control is warranted if you find more than 10 grubs per square foot. BIOLOGICAL—Beneficial nematodes; milky spore; parasitic wasps; tachinid flies. CHEMICAL—Neem.

LACE BUGS

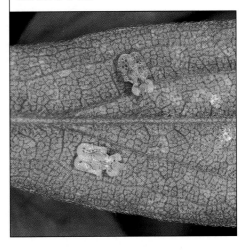

RANGE: various species throughout North America

GENERATIONS PER YEAR: 2 to 5

HOST(S): many woody and herbaceous plants

Lace bugs are sucking insects that feed primarily on woody ornamentals such as rhododendron, hawthorn, pyracantha, and azalea. One species infests chrysanthemums and asters. Species vary in both geographic range and host preference.

Description and life cycle
Lace bugs overwinter as eggs or adults in garden debris. Nymphs undergo five molts in as little as 2 to 3 weeks to become adults. They are tiny and dark; many are covered with spines. Adults are ⅛ inch long, with lacy wings that are nearly transparent. Adults lay black eggs on the undersides of leaves, along the midrib, usually near the tops of plants.

Damage and detection
Both nymphs and adults feed in clusters and suck the plant's juices, leaving the upper sides of leaves stippled or blanched. Plants lose color, become unsightly, and bloom poorly. Nymphs feeding on the undersides of leaves excrete distinctive brown, sticky droppings. Repeated infestations can weaken and kill plants.

Control
PHYSICAL—Spray with water. CULTURAL—Maintain vigor and health of plants. CHEMICAL—Horticultural oil; insecticidal soap; neem; pyrethrins; rotenone; sabadilla.

LEAFHOPPERS

RANGE: widespread throughout North America

GENERATIONS PER YEAR: 2 to 5

HOST(S): most ornamentals and vegetables

There are more than 2,700 leafhopper species in North America. They especially favor calendula, marigold, and other members of the composite family, but also attack other herbaceous and woody ornamentals, vegetables, and fruits.

Description and life cycle

Adult leafhoppers overwinter on host plants. In spring the females insert eggs into leaf or stem tissue. Adults are wedge shaped, $\frac{1}{10}$ to $\frac{1}{2}$ inch long; most are green, brown, or yellow, with colorful spots or bands. Nymphs are smaller, often wingless versions of adults. Each generation lives only a few weeks.

Damage and detection

Nymphs and adults feed on the undersides of leaves, sucking sap and injecting their toxic saliva into the plant. Heavy infestations can stunt, bleach, or mottle leaves; leaves may brown at the margins and drop prematurely. Leafhoppers also carry serious plant diseases such as aster yellows and curly top virus.

Control

PHYSICAL—Use row covers; strong streams of water. CULTURAL—Till soil in fall. BIOLOGICAL—Big-eyed bugs; lacewing larvae. CHEMICAL—Horticultural oil; insecticidal soap; rotenone; sabadilla; systemic pesticide.

LEAF MINERS

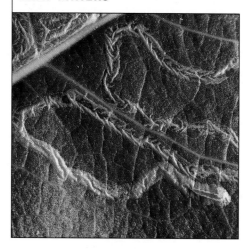

RANGE: throughout North America

GENERATIONS PER YEAR: variable

HOST(S): many ornamentals and vegetables

Leaf miners are the larvae of different species of beetles, flies, sawflies, and moths, and feed between the upper and lower surfaces of leaves. They disfigure plants such as azalea, birch, boxwood, chrysanthemum, holly, and delphinium.

Description and life cycle

Birch leaf miners, which also infest elms, overwinter as larvae in cocoons in the soil and pupate in spring. The adults, which are black with transparent wings, emerge in spring, mate, and lay eggs in leaves. The hatching larvae feed inside the leaves, then pupate. This species has up to four generations a year. The boxwood miner has only one generation per year. Eggs are laid in leaves in midspring; the larvae overwinter in leaves and pupate the following year. Adults are very small, gnatlike flies. They emerge in midspring and mate, lay eggs, and die in a few days.

Damage and detection

Larvae feeding inside leaves make blotches, blisters, or winding tunnels. These mines weaken plants and are very unsightly.

Control

PHYSICAL—Use row covers; destroy damaged leaves; remove such weed hosts as lamb's-quarters and dock. CULTURAL—Rotate crops. BIOLOGICAL—Lacewings; birds. CHEMICAL—Horticultural oil; neem.

LOCUST LEAF MINER BEETLES

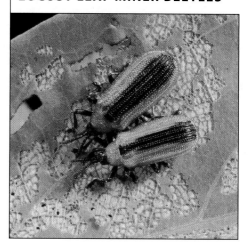

RANGE: eastern United States, west to the Mississippi River

GENERATIONS PER YEAR: 1 or 2

HOST(S): primarily black locust

The locust leaf miner beetle feeds on black locust trees, making them extremely unsightly. It also feeds on a number of other hosts in the legume family, such as sophora and American yellowwood, but rarely does much damage.

Description and life cycle

The adult beetle overwinters in a sheltered site, then emerges in spring to feed on the margins of growing leaves of black locust. The $\frac{1}{4}$-inch adult is orange-yellow, with a wide black stripe along the back. Females lay eggs in clusters of three to five on the undersides of leaves. Larvae are flattened and yellow-white with dark heads; upon hatching, they tunnel into leaves, feed for a month, and pupate. There is often a second generation.

Damage and detection

Feeding at the margins of leaves, adults cause little damage, but larvae tunnel into leaves to form mines that create irregular blotches, spreading back from the leaf tip. Leaves turn brown and drop prematurely. Sometimes trees produce a second set of leaves, which are often infested with the second generation of leaf miner beetles. Repeated infestations can weaken trees.

Control

BIOLOGICAL—Wheel bugs; trichogramma wasps.

MAY/JUNE BEETLES

RANGE: throughout the United States; most troublesome in the South and Midwest

GENERATIONS PER YEAR: 1- to 4-year life cycles

HOST(S): many ornamentals; lawn grasses

The adult stage of this pest is known as May beetle, June beetle, or daw bug; the larva is often called a white grub. Both the adults and the larvae cause plant damage.

Description and life cycle
May beetles overwinter as larvae in the soil, feeding on roots, especially those of lawn grasses. The grubs are ½ to 1½ inches long and white with dark heads. Depending on the species, they stay in the larval stage for 1 to 3 years. Then they pupate, emerging in late spring as 1-inch black, brown, or green beetles. Active at night, the beetles eat the foliage of trees and shrubs, vegetables, and flowers. By day, they hide in debris or foliage. Eggs are laid in the soil and hatch in about 3 weeks.

Damage and detection
Grubs eat roots of grasses and other plants such as potato and strawberry, giving them a wilted, stunted look. Where grubs dig out dime-size holes in turf, grass turns brown. Adults chew ragged holes in leaves.

Control
PHYSICAL—Handpick beetles. CULTURAL—Cultivate soil in fall to kill larvae. BIOLOGICAL—Beneficial nematodes; milky spore; vertebrate predators of grubs, including birds, skunks, and moles. CHEMICAL—Pyrethrins; neem.

MITES

RANGE: widespread throughout North America

GENERATIONS PER YEAR: many

HOST(S): many ornamentals and vegetables

Mites are not insects but belong to the class of animals called arachnids, which includes ticks and spiders. Of the hundreds of mite species, most benefit gardeners by feeding on pests. Other species, however, are parasites of plants or animals. Among the most damaging to plants are the two-spotted spider mites, cyclamen mites, and rust mites.

Description and life cycle
Mites have short life cycles; in warm climates, homes, and greenhouses, reproduction is continuous. Uncontrolled populations of mites can build rapidly, resulting in serious plant infestations and losses.

Outdoors, most plant-feeding mites overwinter as adults or eggs, in garden debris or on the bark of trees or shrubs. Mites are barely visible to the naked eye; a spider mite is about the size of a grain of salt, less than 1/50 inch long. Magnification through a hand lens shows that the adult spider mites have 8 legs and hairy, oval-shaped bodies. They may be brown, green, red, or yellow; their color varies, to a large degree, according to their diet. Nymphs are similar to adults but smaller, and early stages have only 6 legs.

Cyclamen or rust mites, about one-fourth the size of adult spider mites, are hardly visible without a hand lens that magnifies at least 15x. Adult cyclamen mites are pinkish orange; nymphs are translucent. Rust mites have only 4 legs, are wedge shaped, and are usually pinkish white or yellow.

Mites emerge in spring to feed and mate. Eggs are laid on the host plant and usually hatch in less than a week. The new generation reaches maturity in 5 to 10 days. New broods are produced continuously until cold weather sets in.

Damage and detection
In both nymph and adult forms, mites feed on plants by sucking the cell sap, generally feeding in large colonies. Because of their minute size, however, their damage tends to go unnoticed until long after they have become established in a planting.

Spider mites cause leaves to become stippled, bleached, yellow, or brown. The leaves often drop prematurely, weakening plants and stunting fruit. A heavy spider mite infestation may cover affected plant parts with a fine webbing, spun by the mites as they feed. Damage is most severe in the hot, dry, and dusty conditions that accelerate their reproduction rate.

Cyclamen mites generally infest new, unfolding leaves. As the leaves continue to develop, they appear crinkled and deformed; stems may fail to elongate normally. Cyclamen mites also attack young flowers, causing growth distortions. On strawberries, they feed on the fruit, stunting its development and making it look dry and shriveled. Rust mites damage the surfaces of the leaves on which they feed, disrupting the chlorophyll and turning leaves brown or rust colored.

Control
PHYSICAL—Remove and destroy heavily infested leaves, branches, or entire plants; spray with water. BIOLOGICAL—Lacewings; ladybird beetles; predatory mites. CHEMICAL—Use insecticides only as a last resort, as they may harm predators and result in a greater mite problem; horticultural oil; insecticidal soap; neem; pyrethrins.

PINE TIP MOTHS

RANGE: various species throughout
North America

GENERATIONS PER YEAR: 1 to 5

HOST(S): pine trees

Seven species of pine tip or pine shoot moths occur in different parts of the United States. Although they have different hosts among the many species of pine, the damage they do is similar.

Description and life cycle
Pine tip moths hibernate as larvae or pupae in the tips of shoots or in buds. Adults are night-flying moths, reddish brown to gray, with a wingspan up to ¾ inch. Females lay their eggs at the tips of host branches. Larvae are about ½ inch long, and may be brown, reddish brown, or yellow; they tunnel into the bases of needles and buds to feed. They pupate in these hollows or near the base of the tree. Most species produce one generation each year. The Nantucket pine tip moth, however, may produce as many as five.

Damage and detection
Larvae kill the host's shoot tips, leaving them brown and dry. Pine resin and insect excrement accumulate near the feeding site. Buds are blasted, and growth is stunted or produces a tuft of thin, weak twigs. Heavy infestations can kill young trees.

Control
PHYSICAL—Prune and destroy any infested branches in early spring. BIOLOGICAL—Braconid wasps; predatory spiders. CHEMICAL—Systemic pesticide.

PLANT BUGS

RANGE: widespread throughout
North America

GENERATIONS PER YEAR: 1 to 5

HOST(S): many ornamentals and vegetables

The plant bugs are a large family of insects that includes predaceous and beneficial species as well as several serious pests. Among the most common pests are the four-lined plant bug and the tarnished plant bug, or lygus bug. The four-lined plant bug feeds on more than 250 plant species. Its geographic range is east of the Rocky Mountains. Most of its hosts are herbaceous ornamentals, such as aster, chrysanthemum, dahlia, phlox, and zinnia. It also infests such ornamental trees and shrubs as azalea, dogwood, forsythia, rose, and viburnum.

The more common tarnished plant bug, found throughout North America, is probably the most damaging member of this family. It attacks over 385 plant species, including most vegetables and fruits as well as numerous woody and herbaceous ornamentals.

Description and life cycle
Four-lined plant bugs overwinter as eggs in young plant shoots. The egg clusters, protruding from slits made across the stem, are easy to see in fall after the leaves have dropped. They hatch in spring, and the nymphs feed for about a month before their final molt to become adults. Nymphs are bright red, yellow, or orange with black spots. Adults are ¼ to ⅓ inch long and greenish yellow, with 4 black stripes and yellow or bright green forewings. There is one generation per year.

Tarnished plant bugs overwinter as adults under bark or in garden debris, emerging in early spring to attack opening buds. Females lay eggs in the stems and flowers of herbaceous host plants. Adults are ¼ inch long, oval, and mottled brown and tan; each forewing has a black-tipped yellow triangle. Eggs hatch in about 10 days. The yellow-green nymphs resemble the adults but are wingless. They feed for 3 to 4 weeks, then molt to become adults, and repeat the cycle. There are as many as five generations per year.

Damage and detection
Plant bugs injure their host by sucking plant sap in both nymph and adult stages. Four-lined plant bugs feed on leaves, removing the chlorophyll and causing spots that lose color or turn brown or black. The injured area may fall out, or the entire leaf may fall prematurely. The tarnished plant bug feeds on leaves, stems, buds, fruit, and flowers. Adults feeding on buds in spring often kill the growing tip of a twig. As a consequence, lateral shoots develop, giving the plant a bushy, often stunted appearance. Besides sucking sap, the tarnished plant bug injects a toxin that disrupts plant growth.

Control
PHYSICAL—Use row covers; remove plant debris where eggs or adults may be overwintering; set white sticky traps. BIOLOGICAL—Big-eyed bugs; braconid wasps; chalcid wasps; damsel bugs; pirate bugs. CHEMICAL—Insecticidal soap; rotenone; sabadilla; apply sprays in early morning.

Tarnished Plant Bug

PLANTHOPPERS

RANGE: throughout the United States and southern Canada

GENERATIONS PER YEAR: 1

HOST(S): ornamentals, vegetables, and fruits

Planthoppers infest a broad range of trees, shrubs, and woody vines, and a few herbaceous ornamentals, as well as vegetables and fruits. Some of the more common plants attacked include boxwood, viburnum, magnolia, maple, oak, and many fruit trees. Although various species are found throughout the United States, planthoppers are most troublesome in the South.

Description and life cycle
Planthoppers overwinter as eggs in the twigs of host plants. Hatching in late spring, the nymphs are white or yellow-green. They cover themselves with a white, cottony material and suck plant sap from leaves or shoots. In about 9 weeks, nymphs molt to become adults up to ⅓ inch long that are brown, gray, green, white, or yellow. Females slit the bark of twigs and lay eggs in the slits.

Damage and detection
The white cottony covering of planthoppers detracts from the appearance of ornamentals. The egg laying may cause some dieback in twigs, but planthoppers seldom do other harm. In fruit trees, however, the loss of sap injures fruit and foliage.

Control
PHYSICAL—Spray with water. CHEMICAL—Pyrethrins.

PSYLLIDS

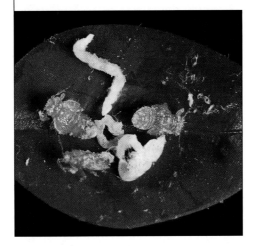

RANGE: widespread throughout North America

GENERATIONS PER YEAR: 1 to 5

HOST(S): many ornamentals and vegetables

Each of the many psyllid species has its own preferred host. The boxwood psyllid and the pear psyllid are two of the most damaging species.

Description and life cycle
Boxwood psyllids overwinter as eggs that hatch in spring. The nymphs feed on new leaves, secreting a waxy material for their own protection. After several weeks, the nymphs become gray-green adults, with transparent wings ⅛ inch across. Females insert eggs in the base of buds; there is one generation per year. Pear psyllids hibernate in bark crevices or plant debris as tiny brown adults with transparent wings. In early spring they fly to pear trees, mate, and lay eggs; nymphs suck sap. There are three to five generations per year.

Damage and detection
The nymphs harm plants by sucking sap. Some cause gall formation; others spread serious plant diseases. Boxwood psyllids distort new leaves and stunt twig growth. Pear psyllids turn leaves yellow, carry the pear-decline virus, and secrete honeydew, which supports sooty mold fungus.

Control
PHYSICAL—To discourage feeding, remove any water sprouts that appear. BIOLOGICAL—Chalcid wasps; lacewings; pirate bugs. CHEMICAL—Horticultural oil.

ROSE CHAFERS

RANGE: widespread throughout North America

GENERATIONS PER YEAR: 1

HOST(S): many

Because the rose chafer prefers a light, sandy soil, its range is somewhat limited. Where it is found, it feeds on bramble fruit, grape, peony, hollyhock, rose, strawberry, and many other fruit, vegetable, and ornamental plants.

Description and life cycle
Larvae, or grubs, overwinter in the soil, pupating and emerging as adults in spring. They often appear suddenly in swarms to feed on leaves, flowers, and fruit. Adults are ½-inch, reddish brown beetles with spiny legs. They feed for 4 to 6 weeks, then females lay eggs in clusters in the soil. Eggs hatch in about 2 weeks. The larvae are ¾-inch white grubs with brown heads; they feed on the roots of grasses.

Damage and detection
Adults eat flowers and fruit, skeletonize leaves, and soil other plant parts with black excrement. The larvae do minor root damage. Rose chafers are poisonous to many birds.

Control
PHYSICAL—Handpick beetles; use row covers; set white sticky traps. CULTURAL—Cultivate soil to destroy larvae and pupae. BIOLOGICAL—Beneficial nematodes for grubs. CHEMICAL—Pyrethrins; rotenone.

SAWFLIES

RANGE: various species throughout North America

GENERATIONS PER YEAR: 1 to 6

HOST(S): many trees and shrubs

Although the hundreds of species of sawflies look similar and cause similar damage, each has particular host preferences. Sawflies are common pests of azaleas, birches, dogwoods, roses, and many other trees and shrubs.

Description and life cycle

Most sawflies hibernate as larvae or pupae in cocoons in the soil. Some species may remain in this state for two or more seasons. Emerging in spring and summer, adults resemble clearwing wasps, which belong to the same family. Instead of a stinger, however, females have a sawlike organ for inserting eggs into leaves or needles. Newly hatched larvae are wormlike and are usually green, yellow, or brown. They feed in colonies until mature, then drop to the ground to pupate.

Damage and detection

Larvae eat their host's leaves. They feed in masses, completely defoliating one branch before moving on to the next, and sometimes stripping an entire tree. Some sawfly species mine leaves, bore into fruit, or stimulate galls.

Control

CULTURAL—Remove garden debris. PHYSICAL—Spray the plants with water. BIOLOGICAL—Parasitic wasps. CHEMICAL—Horticultural oil; ryania.

SCALE INSECTS

RANGE: widespread throughout North America

GENERATIONS PER YEAR: 1 to 6

HOST(S): many

The roughly 200 species of these piercing-sucking insects can be divided into two major groups: armored scales and soft scales. The armored scales bear a hard, scalelike shell that entirely covers the insect's body and can be separated from it. The soft scales have a waxy covering that does not quite enclose the body and cannot be separated from it. Scales attack many trees and shrubs and can be troublesome on houseplants and in greenhouses, where their reproduction is continuous. Scale species differ in both geographic ranges and hosts.

Description and life cycle

Scales may overwinter as eggs, nymphs, or adults. In many species, female adults look significantly different from males; they may lay eggs or give birth to live nymphs. Called crawlers, young nymphs are soft bodied and about ⅒ to ⅟₁₆ inch long. They crawl out of the shell to feed, sucking plant sap. They may remain on the same plant or be carried by wind to infest a new plant. The crawler stage may last for a few hours or a few days. The female nymph then settles onto one spot and secretes her protective shell. She pupates within the shell, matures, and then lays her eggs there. Male crawlers pupate to become winged adults.

Common armored species include: *Euonymus scale*—which attacks numerous

species of bittersweet, citrus, euonymus, lilac, and pachysandra. Mature females overwinter on branches under their protective brown, shell-like scales; males overwinter under narrow, white scales. The pale yellow crawlers begin to appear in late spring. There are one to three generations per year.

Juniper scale—which infests arborvitae, cypress, incense cedar, and juniper. The insects overwinter as fertilized females under round white scales with yellow centers. Crawlers appear in early summer. Males have slender white bodies. There is one generation per year.

Obscure scale—most troublesome in the South. It infests shade trees and is a serious pest of pecan. The insects overwinter as fertilized females, and crawlers are present throughout the summer. The shell is gray and roughly circular. One generation is produced each year.

Oystershell scale—which is very widespread in its geographic range but most common in the northern parts of the United States. This pest can occur in such large numbers that the shells cover all of the bark of a host plant. While oystershell scale attacks many deciduous trees and shrubs, it is most troublesome on apple, ash, lilac, pear, poplar, and willow. The insects overwinter as eggs under the female's grayish brown, oyster-shaped shell. The male shell is smaller and oval. These scales infest only the bark of their host, and do not feed on leaves. Nymphs appear in late spring and move about as crawlers only a few hours before settling permanently to feed and produce their shells. There are one or two generations per year.

Wax Scale

San Jose scale—which is found throughout the United States and southern Canada. It infests many ornamental trees and shrubs but is most serious on deciduous fruit trees. Partially grown nymphs overwinter under their scale coverings and resume their feeding and development in late spring. Young scales are light in color but become gray-black and crusty at maturity. Nymphs are yellow. San Jose scale usually occurs in large numbers, making fruit and bark look as if they were covered with ashes. Female scales are round; males are smaller and oval. Generations overlap, and there are as many as five per year.

Oystershell Scale

Common soft species include: *Hemispherical scale*—a tropical pest common in southern California and Florida, where it infests a number of ornamental plants and citrus trees. Hemispherical scales are also common pests in greenhouses and of houseplants nearly everywhere, favoring ferns as a host. Young hemispherical scales are oval in shape. The shell of mature females is a nearly perfect hemisphere, shiny and brown. There are one or two generations per year, but they overlap, so all stages may be present at any time.

Wax scale—which is distinguished from other species of scale by its waxy white covering. Most common in the South, wax scales feed on many hosts, including barberry, boxwood, camellia, euonymus, flowering quince, hemlock, holly, pyracantha, and spiraea. They also attack plants in greenhouses. Most overwintering individuals are adult females, which begin egg laying in midspring. The eggs hatch in late spring or summer, and after a short period

of mobility, the crawlers settle to feed and secrete their waxy covering. Some wax scale species settle on leaves, others on stems. There are one or two generations per year.

Damage and detection
Because of their generally dull color and limited mobility, scales often remain unnoticed until damage to the host has occurred. As piercing-sucking insects that feed on plant sap, many scales settle on stems, others on foliage, often on the undersides of leaves, along the major veins. Leaves of infested plants turn yellow and may drop prematurely; plants lose vigor. Many scales, especially soft scales, secrete honeydew, a sugary, sticky substance that serves as a growing medium for sooty mold. This dark fungus blocks light from the leaf surface, reducing photosynthesis, causing further yellowing, and seriously reducing a plant's ornamental value.

Control
PHYSICAL—Remove scales with a cotton-tipped swab or soft toothbrush dipped in soapy water or a solution of rubbing alcohol and water; prune and destroy any infested branches. BIOLOGICAL—Ladybird beetles; parasitic wasps; soldier beetles. CHEMICAL—Horticultural oil.

Euonymus Scale

SLUGS AND SNAILS

RANGE: widespread throughout North America

GENERATIONS PER YEAR: may live for years

HOST(S): most ornamentals and vegetables

Among the hundreds of species of slugs and snails, only a few are significant pests of plants. The difference between a slug and a snail is a shell: A snail has one, a slug does not. Both are mollusks, related to clams and oysters. They need moist conditions and prefer cool, dark places because they dry out easily. For this reason, they are primarily night feeders, although they may come out of their dark hiding places on cloudy or rainy days. Both secrete slimy mucus as they slither along, leaving a narrow, shiny trail in their wake. They are common pests, infesting nearly every garden moist enough to support them.

Description and life cycle
Slugs and snails pass the winter in sheltered locations—often in garden debris, under boards, or in soil. Some species overwinter only as eggs, although most will survive at any stage. In warmer regions and in greenhouses, these pests are active year round.

Each slug and snail is hermaphroditic, having both male and female sex organs. They breed during the warm parts of the year. Adults lay eggs in clusters of 25 or more in moist soil or garden debris. Clear to white and up to ⅛ inch across, eggs hatch in about a month. Slugs can be gray, black, brown, pink, or beige, and some have spots. Snails are usually brown or gray. Both have eyes at the tips of protruding tentacles; two other tentacles bear smelling organs.

Slugs range from ½ to 8 inches long; a snail's body is rarely larger than 3 inches. Snail shells are spiral shaped and usually between ½ and 1½ inches across. Because of their shells, snails are more protected than slugs, and if conditions become too dry, snails can retreat into their shells and live in dormancy for up to 4 years. Young slugs and snails look like adults but are smaller. Depending on conditions, they take several months or years to mature.

Damage and detection
Slugs and snails have file-like mouth parts, with which they tear fleshy leaves, especially those near the ground. Because they feed at night, they are rarely seen, but their damage is plain. They make tender seedlings disappear overnight. They eat large ragged holes in the middle and along the edges of leaves on mature plants, and defoliate favorite hosts. They also feed on fleshy fruit and vegetables. The slimy trails they leave behind are a telltale sign of a slug or snail infestation.

Control
CULTURAL—Cultivate soil in early spring to expose eggs, juveniles, and adults. PHYSICAL—Handpick at night by flashlight until damage ceases; use copper barriers; set board traps, checking them each morning and destroying pests; bury a shallow pan filled with beer to attract and drown slugs and snails; spread sand or cinders around plants. BIOLOGICAL—Decollate snails. CHEMICAL—Spread diatomaceous earth on the ground around plants.

Snail

SOD WEBWORMS

RANGE: widespread throughout the United States and southern Canada

GENERATIONS PER YEAR: 2 or 3

HOST(S): turf grasses

The sod webworm feeds on many lawn turf grasses, including bent grass, fescues, Kentucky bluegrass, perennial ryegrass, and zoysia. It also attacks corn.

Description and life cycle
Sod webworms hibernate as larvae in tunnels near the soil surface. The ¾-inch larvae are light brown with dark spots. In spring they feed briefly, pupate, and emerge as adults, which are 1-inch-long, dull gray or brown moths with spotted wings. They fly at night in a zigzag fashion, laying eggs near the base of grass stems. Upon hatching, the larvae feed on grass blades and form tunnels near the soil surface. Pupation occurs in the tunnel. There are usually two or three generations per year, although in warm areas reproduction is continuous.

Damage and detection
Blades are chewed off at the base, creating small brown patches in the lawn. To test for sod webworms, soak damaged lawn areas with a mild detergent solution; if there are more than two webworms per square foot, treatment is recommended.

Control
CULTURAL—Plant turf grass containing endophytic fungi; dethatch in fall. BIOLOGICAL—Beneficial nematodes; birds; Bt; parasitic wasps. CHEMICAL—Insecticidal soap.

SPITTLEBUGS

RANGE: widely distributed throughout North America

GENERATIONS PER YEAR: 1 or 2

HOST(S): many ornamentals and vegetables

Although spittlebugs have inhabited most of North America for a long time, only in the past two to three decades have their populations increased enough to make them significant plant pests. Sometimes called froghoppers, spittlebugs are related to cicadas and aphids. The several spittlebug species have different hosts and geographic ranges. One of the most destructive species is the Saratoga spittlebug, which infests pines throughout the United States. The most abundant and widely distributed species, the meadow spittlebug, eats many kinds of herbaceous plants.

Some spittlebugs complete their entire life cycle on one plant, feeding on the same plant on which the egg was laid. Others feed first on low-growing, herbaceous plants, then they migrate to taller, woody plants. Many spittlebugs are a problem in high-humidity areas like the Northeast and the Pacific Northwest. Commonly infested hosts include strawberry, legumes, corn, clover, and pines.

Description and life cycle
Spittlebugs overwinter as eggs in grasses or weeds, or on host plants, and hatch in midspring. The nymphs are tiny, wingless, and yellow or green. They produce drops of clear liquid that, when mixed with air, forms a froth around their bodies, protecting them from sun and predators. The

nymphs keep hidden under this mass of bubbles, usually in groups of three or four, and feed for 6 to 7 weeks. When adults emerge, they continue to feed, but since they do not create spittle, they can walk, hop, or fly. They move quickly when disturbed and may migrate to other hosts. Adults are usually tan and mottled brown or black, often with stripes or bands on their wings. Bluntly wedge shaped, with sharp spines studding their hind legs, they resemble leafhoppers but are somewhat stouter and ¼ to ⅓ inch long, depending on the species. Females lay rows of white or beige eggs on or near hosts.

Damage and detection
The bubbly froth formed by the feeding nymphs is the best evidence of spittlebugs' presence. Both nymph and adult spittlebugs feed on tender stems and leaves, by sucking plant sap. A few spittlebugs on a plant rarely cause significant damage, but when their populations are large, they can cause stunting, loss of vigor, and reduced yields. Heavy infestations of spittlebugs can reduce growth of the trees' twigs, and make needles lose color and die. Twigs die back from their tips, diminishing the plant's ornamental value.

Control
(only when significant numbers are present)
CULTURAL—In fall, remove and destroy plant debris that can harbor overwintering eggs. PHYSICAL—Spray with water; prune and destroy parts of plants where spittle is present; use row covers. CHEMICAL—Insecticidal soap.

SPRUCE BUDWORMS

RANGE: northern half of the United States and most of Canada

GENERATIONS PER YEAR: 1

HOST(S): conifers

Spruce budworms are the most serious defoliators of coniferous plants in the United States. They prefer to feed on spruce and balsam fir, but they also attack larch, pine, and hemlock.

Description and life cycle
Spruce budworms overwinter as larvae in cocoonlike shelters on twigs of the host tree. In spring they emerge to feed on buds, flowers, and new needles for 3 to 4 weeks. When mature, each of the thick, dark brown, 1-inch-long larvae ties young shoots together with silk threads, forming a shelter in which to pupate. The adult moths that emerge less than 2 weeks later are capable of migrating long distances. Females lay their eggs on hosts in a series of elongated, overlapping clusters, each of which contains as many as 60 eggs. Larvae hatch in about 10 days and feed until they prepare their winter cocoons.

Damage and detection
Spruce budworms mine needles and buds, and defoliate trees. Heavy infestations often kill hosts in 3 to 5 years. Surviving trees are weakened and susceptible to further insect or disease damage.

Control
BIOLOGICAL—Bt; parasitic wasps.

TENT CATERPILLARS

RANGE: two species, one in eastern and the other in western North America

GENERATIONS PER YEAR: 1

HOST(S): most deciduous trees and shrubs

Tent caterpillars spin silk tents in the crotches of trees and shrubs. Plants most commonly infested are apple, aspen, crab apple, and wild cherry.

Description and life cycle
Tent caterpillars overwinter as eggs on host twigs. Eggs hatch in early spring, and the larvae move to the nearest crotch and spin a silk tent. They feed at night and return to the protection afforded by the tent by day. The 2- to 2½-inch caterpillars are hairy and black, with white stripes and blue or red side markings. After 5 to 8 weeks, they pupate, emerging about 10 days later as adult moths, tan or brown with striped forewings and a 1- to 1½-inch wingspan. Females lay a black, lumpy ring of eggs around host twigs.

Damage and detection
This pest's large tent is easy to spot. Larvae eat leaves and can cause total defoliation. Trees may produce a second flush of leaves but are weakened and stunted.

Control
PHYSICAL—Handpick pests; prune and destroy infested branches; use sticky bands on trees; remove egg masses in winter. BIOLOGICAL—Bt; parasitic flies; parasitic wasps; spined soldier bugs. CHEMICAL—Insecticidal soap.

THRIPS

RANGE: widespread throughout North America

GENERATIONS PER YEAR: 5 to 15

HOST(S): most ornamentals and vegetables

Thrips are tiny insects that feed on a wide range of plants. Some of their favorite hosts are roses, peonies, gladiolus, daylilies, and onions.

Description and life cycle
With a life cycle of about 3 weeks, thrips produce many generations per year, especially in warm climates. They overwinter as adults or eggs. Adults have bristly wings, are yellow, brown, or black, and are only ⅟₅₀ to ⅟₂₅ inch long. Nymphs are even smaller and light green or yellow.

Damage and detection
Thrips usually feed in groups, scraping host tissue with their specialized mouthparts and sucking the released sap. They cause silvery speckling on leaves; infested plants may be deformed or stunted, with buds that turn brown without opening. Some thrips also spread viral diseases.

Control
PHYSICAL—Remove infested buds and flowers; spray with water; use sticky yellow traps. CULTURAL—Remove garden debris to eliminate overwintering adults or eggs; rotate crops. BIOLOGICAL—Green lacewings; ladybird beetles; pirate bugs; predatory mites. CHEMICAL—Horticultural oil; insecticidal soap; rotenone.

TREEHOPPERS

RANGE: widespread throughout North America

GENERATIONS PER YEAR: 1

HOST(S): many woody and herbaceous plants

Treehoppers are unusual-looking insects that infest herbaceous plants as nymphs and trees as adults.

Description and life cycle
Treehoppers overwinter as eggs on bark. In spring the hatching nymphs, green with a humped back, drop to the ground and feed on low-growing herbaceous plants for about 6 weeks. After molting to become adults, they return to trees to continue feeding and to lay eggs.

Damage and detection
In both nymph and adult stages, treehoppers pierce stems and leaves with their mouthparts and suck the sap. The worst damage is done when females slit the bark of twigs and deposit their eggs in the slits. Twigs may dry out and die above the point where the eggs are laid, and they may also be invaded by fungi or bacteria.

Control
CULTURAL—Cultivate soil under fruit trees to eliminate nymph feeding sites. CHEMICAL—Dust the plants with diatomaceous earth; horticultural oil.

WEBWORMS

RANGE: throughout the United States and southern Canada

GENERATIONS PER YEAR: 1 to 4

HOST(S): many ornamentals and vegetables

The several species of webworms differ mainly in their preferred hosts. Fall webworms feed on a wide range of deciduous trees and shrubs. Garden webworms feed on many vegetables and strawberries. Juniper webworms attack juniper.

Description and life cycle
Fall webworms overwinter as pupae on tree bark or in plant debris. In spring the adults, 2-inch white moths with brown spots, lay eggs in masses on the undersides of leaves. The hatching larvae spin a web and feed inside it for 4 to 6 weeks. The larvae are about 1 inch long, hairy, and pale green or yellow. When fully grown, they leave the web and pupate on the bark or in plant debris. Garden webworms have a similar life cycle. Larvae are ¾ inch long, hairy, and green to black, often with a stripe. Adults are ¾-inch brown moths with gold and gray wing markings.

Damage and detection
As larvae chew on the leaves, they spin a conspicuous web around the host. Webworms can completely defoliate hosts.

Control
PHYSICAL—Handpick larvae; prune and destroy branches with webs; rake up and dispose of plant debris in fall. BIOLOGICAL—Bt; trichogramma wasps. CHEMICAL—Pyrethrins; rotenone.

WEEVILS

RANGE: widespread throughout North America

GENERATIONS PER YEAR: 1 or 2

HOST(S): many ornamentals and vegetables

Weevils that attack plants in the garden include Asiatic and black vine weevils. They are particularly damaging to azalea, bramble fruit, camellia, mountain laurel, rhododendron, strawberry, and yew.

Description and life cycle
Most adult weevils have a long, jaw-tipped snout. They are nocturnal and winged but flightless; most are black or brown and are less than ½ inch long. Most weevils overwinter in the soil or in plant debris as pale, legless larvae that feed on roots. In spring they pupate and emerge as adults to feed on a wide range of hosts. Females lay eggs in soil or debris near hosts.

Damage and detection
Larvae feeding on roots cause stunting and wilting, and may kill heavily infested plants. Adults cut large holes or notches along leaf margins or eat leaves to the midrib.

Control
PHYSICAL—Use row covers; handpick the adults; CULTURAL—Cultivate soil to expose overwintering larvae; destroy infested plants; remove and dispose of plant debris in fall; rotate garden crops; use sticky traps. BIOLOGICAL—Beneficial nematodes; birds. CHEMICAL—Pyrethrins; rotenone; sabadilla.

WHITEFLIES

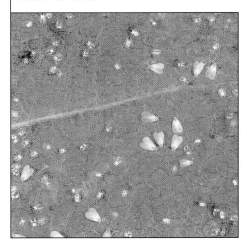

RANGE: southern United States and West Coast

GENERATIONS PER YEAR: many

HOST(S): many ornamentals and vegetables

The 200 or so species of whiteflies are primarily tropical pests. In warm climates they reproduce year round. In cooler regions, they infest greenhouses and feed on houseplants. They may be transported to temperate gardens in the spring on greenhouse-grown stock, but most species will not survive a cold winter. Indoors or out, whiteflies spread fast to nearby plants, and a short life cycle allows them to build up destructive populations in weeks. Whiteflies attack many different plants, which include citrus, gerbera, lantana, poinsettia, and salvia. The ash whitefly is a serious pest in California, where it attacks many ornamental trees and shrubs.

Description and life cycle
Most whiteflies complete their life cycle in about a month; generations overlap and reproduction is continuous. Females lay a circle of black cone-shaped eggs on the undersides of older leaves. Eggs usually hatch in less than a week, and the active, young nymphs move about and begin to feed. Once established in a feeding spot, they undergo their first molt and lose their legs to become immobile. Translucent or light green, tiny and flat, the nymphs are hard to see without a hand lens. They molt into white, mothlike adults, ⅟20 to ⅟10 inch long. The wings of adult whiteflies are covered with a fine, powdery wax.

Damage and detection
Although whiteflies are small, they are usually easy to detect because they occur in large numbers and feed in groups. When an infested plant is disturbed, they rise in a cloud, then quickly resettle. Both nymphs and adults suck plant sap, usually feeding on the youngest leaves. Nymphs feed from the undersides of leaves, which yellow and drop prematurely. Feeding whiteflies secrete honeydew, a sweet liquid that sticks to plants. Honeydew supports sooty mold, a fungus that blocks light, reduces photosynthesis, and further weakens plants. The ash whitefly's generous secretions of honeydew drip from host trees onto cars, outdoor furniture, and walkways, creating a sticky mess and attracting ants and wasps. Whiteflies transmit several viral diseases.

Control
PHYSICAL—Rinse plants to remove larvae and adults; wipe off larvae from the undersides of tender leaves with a gloved hand; destroy eggs on the undersides of older leaves; set sticky yellow traps. BIOLOGICAL—Lacewings; parasitic wasps. CHEMICAL—Horticultural oil; insecticidal soap.

Garden Whitefly

WHITE-FRINGED BEETLES

RANGE: eastern United States from New Jersey to Florida, west to Arkansas

GENERATIONS PER YEAR: 1 to 4

HOST(S): most herbaceous plants

A South American native first spotted in Florida in 1936, the white-fringed beetle has spread throughout the southern states and as far north as New Jersey. It feeds on many herbaceous ornamentals, including aster and goldenrod, and on vegetables such as beans, okra, peas, and potatoes.

Description and life cycle
White-fringed beetles overwinter as ½-inch, legless white larvae, often 9 to 12 inches deep in the soil. Pupating in late spring and early summer, they emerge as adults that are ½ inch long, brownish gray, and hairy, with broad snouts. They have white-banded wings but do not fly. They feed in large numbers and lay eggs for up to 2 months, depositing them on host plants, near the soil. The larvae hatch in about 17 days and enter the soil to feed.

Damage and detection
Adult white-fringed beetles feed on lower stems, often severing them from the roots. The larvae feed on roots and tubers. Infested plants wilt and die.

Control
PHYSICAL—Dig ditches 1 foot deep around the vegetable garden to trap and destroy the flightless beetles. CULTURAL—Spade deeply in early spring to expose larvae.

WHITE-MARKED TUSSOCK MOTHS

RANGE: eastern United States and Canada, west to Colorado and British Columbia

GENERATIONS PER YEAR: 1 to 3

HOST(S): deciduous trees and shrubs

Tussock moths are feeders of ornamental deciduous trees and shrubs and may seriously weaken them.

Description and life cycle
Tussock moths overwinter as eggs, which hatch in spring. The larvae are caterpillars, 1¼ inches long, with distinctive tufts of long black and shorter white hairs. Caterpillars feed for several weeks, then pupate. In 2 to 4 weeks, adults emerge. Males are gray with dark wing markings; females are lighter and nearly wingless. Females lay eggs in masses covered with a white, frothy material that hardens as it dries. The number of generations per year varies with the climate.

Damage and detection
Tussock moths are leaf feeders. They skeletonize leaves and defoliate plants.

Control
PHYSICAL—Remove egg masses or paint with creosote. BIOLOGICAL—Bt; trichogramma wasps. CHEMICAL—Horticultural oil.

WIREWORMS

RANGE: widespread throughout North America

GENERATIONS PER YEAR: 1- to 6-year life cycle

HOST(S): many

Wireworms are tough-skinned larvae of the various species of click beetles. These larvae live in the soil, where they feed on the underground parts of a wide range of plants, including herbaceous ornamentals and vegetables.

Description and life cycle
Some wireworm species complete their life cycle in 1 year; others take as long as 6 years. Adult click beetles overwinter in the soil, coming to the surface in spring. They are about ½ inch long, narrow, and black or brown. Females lay their eggs 1 to 6 inches below the surface. Larvae hatch within a few weeks and begin to feed, continuing for up to 6 years. Gray, creamy, or dark brown, they are ½ to 1½ inches long, jointed, and have shiny, tough skin. Pupation occurs in late summer.

Damage and detection
Wireworms feed on seeds and bore into the corms, roots, and other underground plant parts, opening the plants to decay-causing bacteria and fungi.

Control
PHYSICAL—Bury pieces of potato or carrot to trap wireworms, then dig and destroy the pests. CULTURAL—Cultivate soil often to expose the larvae. BIOLOGICAL—Beneficial nematodes.

WOODBORER BEETLES

RANGE: various species throughout the United States and southern Canada

GENERATIONS PER YEAR: 1- to 3-year life cycle

HOST(S): many deciduous trees

The many species of woodborer beetles differ in their geographic ranges and preferred hosts. They are broadly classified as flatheaded or roundheaded borers, according to the shape of the larva's head. Among the numerous destructive species are the bronze birch borer, the lurid flatheaded borer, the flatheaded apple tree borer, and the two-lined chestnut borer.

Bronze birch borers attack birch, cottonwood, poplar, and willow. They are found throughout the northern parts of the United States, south to Virginia and in Arizona, New Mexico, and southern Canada. The lurid flatheaded borer infests hickory and alder trees throughout the eastern part of North America. The flatheaded apple tree borer attacks most deciduous shade and fruit trees and is found throughout the United States and southern Canada. The two-lined chestnut borer occurs east of the Rocky Mountains and sometimes in California; its preferred hosts include beech, chestnut, and oak.

Description and life cycle
Most borers spend the greater part of their lives as larvae, and it is during this stage that they inflict the most serious damage. Borers overwinter as larvae in their host. In the spring they feed and pupate, then emerge in the summer as beetles. Females lay their eggs in bark crevices, especially near wounds. Soon the larvae hatch and bore into the tree, where they feed on the bark, the sapwood (the layer of young tissue that includes the plant's food- and water-conducting layer), or the older heartwood. The larvae stay in the tree for 1 to 2 years.

The adult stage of the bronze birch borer is a beetle resembling the lightning bug, ¼ to ½ inch long, with a green-black body and a bronze head. The larvae are creamy white, slender, and flattened and are ½ inch long when fully grown. Adult lurid flatheaded borers are shiny, dark brown beetles about ¾ inch long. The flatheaded apple tree borer adults are flat, dark brown, and ½ inch long; larvae are white with flat, brown heads, and grow to 1¼ inches in length. The two-lined chestnut borer adult is dark green or bluish black with yellow or bronze stripes, and is about ¼ inch long; the larva is cream colored and grows to about ½ inch in length. This species usually requires 2 years to complete its life cycle.

Damage and detection
The adults feed to some extent on the host's foliage, but their damage is insignificant compared to the often lethal mining done by the larvae. By the time this internal borer damage is noticed, it is usually too late to save the tree. The larvae tunnel through the young sapwood, cutting off the flow of water and nutrients up and down the tree. Leaves turn yellow and branches die back. As the upper branches die, the tree sends up many shoots from the crown. Most trees that do survive borer infestations display swollen areas on their trunks where new tissue has grown and healed around the damage. Borers are most often attracted to trees that have been damaged by other insects or that have sustained mechanical injuries.

Control
PHYSICAL—Remove damaged limbs. CULTURAL—Avoid mechanical injuries to trees; feed and water trees to minimize stress and keep them healthy and vigorous; plant resistant species, such as the black birch and river birch. BIOLOGICAL—Parasitic wasps; woodpeckers.

Diseases

ANTHRACNOSE, COLLETOTRICHUM

TYPE OF DISEASE: fungal

HOST(S): many herbaceous plants

The term *anthracnose* is derived from the Greek word for ulcer and refers to the ulcerlike lesions that appear on leaves, stems, and fruit. There are many species of *Colletotrichum,* and each has a specific group of hosts. Herbaceous plants are more susceptible, although some woody plants are also attacked. Commonly infected ornamental plants include orchids, hollyhocks, pansies, foxgloves, and turf grasses.

Symptoms
Infected fruit, stems, or leaves develop small sunken spots with a water-soaked appearance. Spots often enlarge and may coalesce into irregular dark areas. Sometimes leaf spots turn black; the blackened tissue then falls out to leave ragged holes. In damp weather, pinkish spore masses ooze from the center of the lesions. Infected fruit darkens and rots.

Transmission
The fungus overwinters in seeds and in garden debris. Spores are spread by splashing water, insects, and garden tools.

Control
PHYSICAL—Prune infected stems; remove and destroy severely infected plants and fallen leaves. CULTURAL—Plant resistant varieties; use certified, disease-free seed; rotate crops; avoid handling plants when they are wet.

ANTHRACNOSE OF DOGWOOD

TYPE OF DISEASE: fungal

HOST(S): flowering dogwood, Pacific dogwood

Discula anthracnose of dogwood, which is caused by the *Discula destructiva* fungus, was first discovered in the early 1970s. In the eastern part of the United States, the disease affects the native flowering dogwood *(Cornus florida)*; on the West Coast, it attacks the Pacific dogwood.

Symptoms
In late spring, tan spots with purple margins appear on leaves. Blighted leaves remain attached to the trees. Small, uniformly spaced brown dots—the spore-producing structures—appear on spotted leaves and twigs. As the infection progresses, branches die. Trees may produce numerous water sprouts. Cankers form on the trunk. When the cankers girdle the trunk, the entire tree dies.

Transmission
This fungus thrives in cool, moist conditions. Spores are spread by rain and dew.

Control
PHYSICAL—Prune water sprouts in summer. CULTURAL—Plant resistant species and varieties; plant trees in open areas with at least a half-day of sun; keep them mulched and water them deeply during dry spells but avoid wetting leaves. CHEMICAL—Spray infected trees with a fungicide containing propiconazole or chlorothalonil every 2 weeks from the time new leaves emerge until day temperatures are above 80° F.

ANTHRACNOSE OF SYCAMORE

TYPE OF DISEASE: fungal

HOST(S): sycamore

Anthracnose of sycamore trees is a conspicuous cosmetic disease but is seldom fatal. Caused by one species of fungus, it develops in cool, damp spring weather. A number of closely related fungi cause anthracnose in other kinds of trees, including ash, elm, oak, walnut, hickory, and maple.

Symptoms
There are three distinct phases of sycamore anthracnose, each affecting different portions of the plant. In the shoot-blight phase, new leaves and shoots turn brown and die rapidly; they look as if they have been killed by frost. In the leaf-blight phase, large irregular brown areas develop along the veins. Trees look tattered and may defoliate completely; repeated defoliations weaken the tree. In the third phase, twig cankers develop and girdle and kill branches. However, when the weather warms up, the fungus recedes and a new set of leaves restores the tree's vigor.

Transmission
The fungus overwinters in twig cankers and on fallen leaves. Its growth is favored by cool, damp conditions. It is spread by wind and rain.

Control
PHYSICAL—Gather and destroy all fallen leaves and twigs in fall; fertilize trees to maintain their vigor; prune branches with cankers. CULTURAL—Replace sycamores with London plane trees.

BLACK KNOT OF PRUNUS

TYPE OF DISEASE: fungal

HOST(S): many Prunus species

Black knot is a serious disease of more than 20 species of *Prunus,* including cherry, plum, flowering almond, chokecherry, peach, and apricot. It occurs throughout moist, humid regions of the United States and Canada, wherever susceptible plants are grown.

Symptoms
Rough, black, spindle-shaped swellings or knots develop on small branches over a 2-year period. The first sign of infection emerges in spring, when the bark ruptures and an olive green fungal mass appears. It can grow to 12 inches in length and may be two to four times as thick as the branch. This growth eventually hardens and turns black and knotty. As the infection progresses, branches become girdled and die. Trees are stunted and unattractive, and varieties planted for fruit are unproductive.

Transmission
Spores of this fungus are spread by wind in early spring.

Control
PHYSICAL—Prune any infected branches at least 4 inches behind any visible damage in winter or early spring, disinfecting the pruners after each cut in a 10-percent bleach solution; eradicate or prune any wild cherries or plums in the vicinity as a preventive measure.

BLACK SPOT

TYPE OF DISEASE: fungal

HOST(S): roses

While black spot of rose occurs wherever roses are grown, it is severe only in humid climates. It is especially troublesome east of the Mississippi River and on the West Coast. Rose varieties differ in their susceptibility. Those with yellow or gold flowers are generally more susceptible than varieties with red or pink flowers.

Symptoms
Round black spots with fringed margins appear on the upper surfaces of leaves and on young canes in spring. At the center of the spots are tiny blisterlike, spore-producing structures that are visible with a hand lens.

Transmission
The black spot fungus survives the winter in a dormant state on infected canes and fallen leaves. In greenhouses, it is active year round. It is spread by splashing water and by the gardener's hands, tools, and clothing.

Control
PHYSICAL—Prune to increase air circulation; remove and destroy infected leaves and canes. CULTURAL—Grow resistant varieties; avoid wetting foliage when watering. CHEMICAL—Spray dormant plants with lime-sulfur; during the growing season, spray with a fungicidal soap or a fungicide that contains triforine, mancozeb, or chlorothalonil.

BLIGHT, BOTRYTIS

TYPE OF DISEASE: fungal

HOST(S): many

Various *Botrytis* species cause blighting on a wide range of herbaceous and woody ornamentals, soft fruits, and vegetables. Certain species such as *B. cinerea,* which causes gray mold blight, have a broad host range. Common hosts include poinsettia, chrysanthemum, and rhododendron. Others such as *B. tulipae,* which causes a blight on tulips, and *B. paeoniae,* which causes blight on peonies, are very host specific. All species produce similar symptoms and are favored by cool, moist conditions.

Symptoms
Leaves and flowers of infected plants develop irregularly shaped, water-soaked spots that dry and turn tan or brown. Similar spots on stems form cankers that girdle stems, causing dieback. Seedlings are often killed. Infected fruit turns soft and mushy. In humid conditions, a fuzzy gray mold develops on the surface of infected tissue.

Transmission
Botrytis is spread by splashing rain and wind. The fungus persists in infected tissue and in soil.

Control
PHYSICAL—Remove and destroy any fading blossoms and infected plants or plant parts. CULTURAL—Space plants to promote air circulation; avoid wetting foliage; use healthy plants and bulbs for propagation. CHEMICAL—Spray with a fungicide containing chlorothalonil or mancozeb.

BLIGHT, CERCOSPORA LEAF

TYPE OF DISEASE: fungal

HOST(S): many

There are hundreds of *Cercospora* species, which attack leaves and shoots of trees, shrubs, vegetables, and herbaceous ornamentals. Most species attack one plant or a few closely related plants. Often infected are arborvitae, azalea, cryptomeria, cypress, dahlia, geranium, mountain laurel, and red cedar.

Symptoms
Leaves or needles of infected plants develop spots that often enlarge and coalesce. On carrot, celery, geranium, and many other hosts, the spots are yellowish at first, then turn ash gray and become paper-thin as they enlarge. Entire leaves die, and in severe cases all of the foliage dies. A fine gray mold develops on infected tissue. Leaf spots may be bordered by a dark purple margin. On cypress and arborvitae, needles and branchlets turn brown or purplish and drop off.

Transmission
Leaf-blight fungus overwinters in or on seed or on infected leaves or needles. Warm, humid weather favors its spread. Spores are spread by wind and rain.

Control
PHYSICAL—Prune out infected stems or branches, and rake up and destroy infected leaves or needles. CULTURAL—Plant disease-free seed. CHEMICAL—Spray plants with Bordeaux mixture or a fungicide containing chlorothalonil.

BLIGHT, DIPLODIA TIP

TYPE OF DISEASE: fungal

HOST(S): 2- and 3-needle pines

Diplodia tip blight infects older pines. Most often attacked are Scotch, Austrian, mugo, ponderosa, red, scrub, and Japanese black pines.

Symptoms
The first symptom usually noted is the browning of new needles, particularly on branches near the base of the tree. The dead needles remain attached to the tree; infected branches ooze resin. Close observation reveals small black spore-producing structures embedded under the needle sheath and in dead needles, on old cones, and in bark. After several seasons of repeated infection, the branches take on a clubbed appearance and eventually die.

Transmission
Spores are produced from early spring to late fall, especially during periods of wet weather. They are spread by splashing rain, insects, birds, and pruning tools. The fungus invades the tree through young needles, buds, and shoots or through wounds. It persists over winter on infected trees and on the ground nearby.

Control
PHYSICAL—Prune and destroy dead branches in fall; collect and destroy infected needles and twigs on the ground. CHEMICAL—Spray with a fixed-copper fungicide, thiophanate-methyl, or Bordeaux mixture when new needles begin to emerge from the candles and again 10 days later.

BLIGHT, FIRE

TYPE OF DISEASE: bacterial

HOST(S): members of the rose family

Fire blight occurs only in plants belonging to the rose family. Landscape plants often damaged include crab apple, cotoneaster, flowering quince, hawthorn, mountain ash, pear, and pyracantha.

Symptoms
In early spring, bees and other pollinators carry bacteria into flowers, which turn brown and shrivel. The bacteria then invade twigs, producing cankers. Bacteria oozing from cankers can be blown or splashed onto young shoots and leaves. The shoots turn dark brown or black, and the leaves turn black and remain on the tree, which looks as if it has been scorched by fire. In highly susceptible plants, cankers form on the trunk and large branches.

Transmission
The bacteria overwinter in branch and trunk cankers. In humid weather, bacteria-laden ooze is produced along the edges of cankers. Insects feeding on the ooze carry the bacteria to flowers. Throughout the growing season, bacteria may be spread from blighted shoots, and cankers may be spread by wind. Fire blight is most severe in regions of warm, humid weather.

Control
PHYSICAL—During winter or dry weather, prune out all of the visible cankers; avoid wounding plants. CULTURAL—Plant resistant cultivars; avoid excessive nitrogen fertilization.

BLIGHT, SOUTHERN

TYPE OF DISEASE: fungal

HOST(S): many

Southern blight occurs in the eastern United States from New York south but is most serious in the Southeast, because it is a disease of hot, humid weather. It infects hundreds of herbaceous and woody plants and is particularly hard on ajuga, artemisia, chrysanthemum, lamb's ears, lavender, santolina, sage, thyme, and tomato and legume family members.

Symptoms
The southern blight fungus can be recognized by the sclerotia—small tan lumps about the size of a mustard seed—that appear on the blighted plant and the surrounding soil or mulch. Infection starts from these "mustard seed" sclerotia in soil or mulch. Plants rapidly yellow, wilt, and die. Infected bulbs and fleshy roots rot. Look for a white cottony growth on stems and surrounding soil.

Transmission
The fungus survives in the soil for many years as sclerotia. Its growth is favored by hot, wet weather and acidic soils. It is spread by running water as well as infested tools, soil, mulch, or compost.

Control
PHYSICAL—Remove and destroy any diseased plants and the white, cottony fungal growth around them. CULTURAL—Solarize the soil of a new bed; thin perennials to improve air circulation; mulch plants with a thin layer of sterile sharp sand.

CANKER AND DIEBACK

TYPE OF DISEASE: fungal

HOST(S): many woody plants

Botryosphaeria dothidea infects over 50 species of woody plants, including apple, azalea, eucalyptus, fig, forsythia, pecan, pyracantha, quince, rhododendron, rose, sequoia, sweet gum, and willow. This fungus is also responsible for the most destructive canker disease of redbud.

Symptoms
On redbud, the cankers begin as small, sunken, oval spots that enlarge and girdle branches, causing wilting and dieback above the canker. The canker turns black at the center and cracks at the margins. Similar symptoms occur on forsythia. On roses, leaves turn brown and die but remain on the plant. On rhododendron, watery spots occur on leaves and twigs, followed by twig dieback. Cankers on the trunks of willows are generally fatal in a few years. Apple trees develop watery lesions on the bark, and vigor gradually declines. When an infected branch or stem is cut crosswise, there is usually a pie-shaped section of discolored tissue.

Transmission
Canker and dieback fungi are spread by wind, rain, insects, and pruning tools.

Control
PHYSICAL—Cut infected branches to wood that is not discolored and destroy, disinfecting pruners with a 10-percent bleach solution after each cut. CULTURAL—Water plants during periods of drought.

CANKER, CYTOSPORA

TYPE OF DISEASE: fungal

HOST(S): many trees and shrubs

Many species of fungi cause cankers on trees and shrubs; most have a narrow host range. Cytospora canker is especially troublesome on Norway spruce, Colorado blue spruce, and *Prunus* species. It also attacks maple, cottonwood, black cherry, willow, and poplar.

Symptoms
On spruce, the cankers most often form on branches near the ground and enlarge to girdle the branches. Needles dry up and the branches die back. Infected areas ooze an amber-colored sap that turns white as it dries. On poplar, cankers form on the trunk and the larger branches, discoloring the bark and causing dieback. Weakened trees often die.

Transmission
These fungi survive the winter on infected plant parts. They are spread by splashing rain, insects, and pruning tools. Damaged or weakened trees are more likely to be infected.

Control
PHYSICAL—Remove and destroy infected branches when the weather is dry, making pruning cuts at least 6 inches below the canker and disinfecting pruners with a 10-percent bleach solution after each cut. CULTURAL—Keep plants vigorous; avoid wounding and excessive use of nitrogen fertilizer; do only essential pruning.

CANKER, NECTRIA

TYPE OF DISEASE: fungal

HOST(S): many trees and shrubs

Coral spot nectria canker, tubercularia canker, and perennial nectria canker are common in landscape plants, including apple, beech, boxwood, elm, honey locust, magnolia, maple, and zelkova.

Symptoms
Coral spot and tubercularia cankers are usually noticed in late spring, when shoots or entire branches wilt and die. At the base of the diseased branch are peach-colored to orange-red fruiting bodies emerging through openings or wounds in the bark.

Perennial nectria cankers, which persist for years, begin as small sunken areas, often surrounding a twig stub or a wound. As they grow they develop a series of concentric ridges of bark around the original spot; in time the ridges can become quite large. Bright red-orange fruiting bodies are produced on the bark ridges and on exposed wood in the canker's center from fall through spring.

Transmission
Nectria fungi produce spores that are spread by wind, rain, insects, and animals.

Control
PHYSICAL—Prune out infected branches in late spring through summer. CULTURAL—Avoid wounding plants; select species that are well adapted to your climate; fertilize properly and water during drought to maintain plant vigor.

CANKER OF STONE FRUIT

TYPE OF DISEASE: bacterial

HOST(S): fruits, shrubs, and vegetables

Different forms of the bacterium *Pseudomonas syringae* are responsible for canker of stone fruit, infecting many hosts and causing a variety of symptoms. Ornamental plants affected include flowering stock, lilac, oleander, rose, and sweet pea.

Symptoms

All parts of peach, plum, apricot, and other stone fruit trees are subject to infection, but the most destructive symptoms are the gummy cankers on the branches and the trunk, which exude a foul-smelling secretion. Flower buds may be killed while they are still dormant or after they have emerged; leaves may wilt or die. On lilacs, leaves and shoots display brown, water-soaked spots, and flower buds turn black. Infected oleanders develop oozing, bacteria laden galls on branches, leaves, and flowers.

Transmission

The bacteria responsible for these diseases are spread by water. Mild, wet weather favors their growth and development.

Control

PHYSICAL—Prune and destroy infected branches, disinfecting pruners after each cut. CULTURAL—Thin plants to encourage good air circulation; avoid the use of high-nitrogen fertilizers.

DAMPING-OFF

TYPE OF DISEASE: fungal

HOST(S): most seedlings

Damping-off is a disease of seedlings caused by a variety of different fungi, including species of *Pythium* and *Rhizoctonia*. These fungi may also attack seeds or older plants.

Symptoms

When these fungi attack seeds, the disease is known as preemergent damping-off; the seeds rot without germinating. Called postemergent damping-off when seedlings are infected, the disease usually occurs at or just below the soil line. The stem turns soft and brown, and the seedling topples over and dies. When the fungi attack older plants, brown lesions form on the stem or roots. When abundant, these lesions cause stunting, wilting, and sometimes death.

Transmission

The fungi responsible for damping-off are found in soil and water throughout the world. They survive on dead organic matter when they have no living host.

Control

CULTURAL—Use a soilless growing medium for seedling propagation; promote rapid growth with optimum light and temperature levels, and provide good drainage and air circulation; rotate crops in the vegetable garden. CHEMICAL—Buy pretreated seeds or treat seeds with captan.

DECLINE

TYPE OF DISEASE: infectious/environmental

HOST(S): trees and shrubs

Decline is a general loss of health that is not attributable to a single pathogen or pest. Rather, it is the result of stress that can arise from a variety of factors, usually over a period of years. Both infectious agents and environmental conditions may be involved. They may act on the plant at the same time or in sequence.

Symptoms

Symptoms of decline vary among plant species. Generally, yellowing and wilting of leaves, dieback of branches, and stunted or distorted growth are seen. Declining trees exhibit reduced twig growth, and in advanced decline, the dead branches, or stag heads, protrude from the healthy canopy. Eventually the plant may die, although this may take years. Some of the factors often associated with decline are repeated insect infestations, infectious disease, soil compaction, root damage, injury to the trunk, an inappropriate site, girdling roots, a chronic water deficit, and poorly drained soil. Plants weakened by adverse cultural conditions may be especially vulnerable to pathogens and are very attractive to wood-boring insects.

Control

Once decline has become obvious, it is often too late to save the plant. However, it is important to identify the source of stress so you can try to prevent decline in new plants installed in the same area.

DEFICIENCY, IRON

TYPE OF DISEASE: nutritional

HOST(S): all plants

While iron is rarely deficient in soils, it may be unavailable to plants because it exists in an insoluble form. This is a common problem for acid-loving plants growing in neutral or alkaline soils, which have a pH of 7 or higher. In some cases, iron becomes chemically bound and unavailable to plants when large amounts of phosphate fertilizers have been added to the soil. Plants growing in sandy soils in cold, wet conditions are more likely to experience iron deficiency.

Symptoms

Iron is essential for chlorophyll synthesis, and when it is deficient, young leaves are yellow with green veins, a symptom called interveinal chlorosis. Leaves are smaller than normal, and their margins often turn brown. If the deficiency is severe, leaves turn reddish brown and drop prematurely. Overall growth of the plant is stunted.

Control

CULTURAL—Avoid liming turf near acid-loving trees and shrubs; apply iron sulfate to soil to supply iron and acidify soil; replace acid-loving species and varieties with plants that tolerate a higher soil pH.

DEFICIENCY, MAGNESIUM

TYPE OF DISEASE: nutritional

HOST(S): all plants

Magnesium is required for healthy plant growth and development because it is a constituent part of the chlorophyll molecule. This element is also essential for various processes controlled by enzymes. It may be naturally deficient in soils, as is common on the Atlantic and Gulf coasts, or it may have been removed by heavy cropping or constant leaching by rain. This deficiency is common in very acid soils and in gardens to which excessive amounts of potassium fertilizers have been applied.

Symptoms

Deficiency symptoms show up first on older growth. The tip and margins of an affected leaf typically turn yellow, then brown, though in some plants the discoloration is reddish. The abnormal color spreads between the veins to the center and base of the leaves, which often drop prematurely. On some plants the leaves become puckered. In the case of conifers, needles that are 2 years old or older turn yellow. Continued magnesium deficiency causes stunting.

Control

CULTURAL—Apply Epsom salts, which contain magnesium; till in dolomitic limestone, which contains magnesium and also raises the pH; use balanced fertilizers that contain magnesium; do not use wood ashes, which have a high potassium content.

DEFICIENCY, NITROGEN

TYPE OF DISEASE: nutritional

HOST(S): all plants

Nitrogen is essential for healthy vegetative growth, protein synthesis, and other critical plant functions. A lack of available nitrogen in the soil, which is more common in unusually cold, wet conditions, results in poor growth and weakened plants.

Symptoms

A plant's oldest leaves are the first to show signs of nitrogen deficiency: They turn yellow, then brown, and drop off. New leaves are smaller than normal and lighter in color because of the decreased synthesis of plant proteins. Leaf margins may turn brown. The plant grows slowly, and its stems are slender and weak. Fruit and vegetable yields are reduced.

Control

CULTURAL—Apply nitrogen-rich fertilizers such as blood meal, soybean meal, fish emulsion, or urea to the soil; incorporate well-rotted manure or compost into the soil every year; do not apply fresh organic matter such as uncomposted woodchips, leaves, or sawdust, because soil microbes will tie up available nitrogen as they attack the cellulose in these materials.

DEFICIENCY, POTASSIUM

TYPE OF DISEASE: nutritional

HOST(S): all plants

Potassium is essential to such processes as nitrogen metabolism and water uptake and movement. It acts as a catalyst for numerous other reactions, especially in growing points—buds, shoot tips, and root tips.

Symptoms
Potassium moves easily within a plant. Because it tends to move to the youngest growth, older plant parts are the first to show signs of deficiency. Leaf margins turn yellow or brown, and the discoloration then moves into the leaf between the veins. Some leaves turn reddish purple rather than brown. Dead areas along leaf margins may drop out, giving leaves a ragged edge. Growth slows, and leaves may drop prematurely. Flowering and fruiting are reduced. Plants are more subject to damage by freezing and a variety of pathogens.

Control
CULTURAL—Apply a potassium-rich fertilizer such as kelp meal; apply wood ashes in small quantities; if the soil is very sandy, allowing potassium to leach out quickly, incorporate organic matter to increase the soil's water-holding capacity; incorporate vermiculite, a good source of slow-release potassium, into the soil.

DODDER

TYPE OF DISEASE: parasitic

HOST(S): many plants

Dodders are stringy, leafless plants that lack roots and chlorophyll and parasitize a wide range of plants to obtain water and nutrients. They are particularly troublesome in areas where clover and alfalfa, two favorite hosts, are grown.

Symptoms
Dodder seed germinates and produces a slender stem that curls around the nearest plant. The stem develops "feeding pegs," which invade the host and absorb juices. As it continues to grow, the tangled mass of yellow to orange spaghetti-like stems increases while the host plant loses color and vigor and may die. Other common names for this parasitic plant include devil's hair, gold thread, strangle weed, pull down, and hell-bind.

Transmission
Dodder is transmitted as seed in mulch, humus, compost, and soil, where it can survive for up to 5 years. Dodder seed may also contaminate commercial seed lots.

Control
PHYSICAL—Thoroughly clean tools and other equipment after use in a dodder-infested area; remove and burn all dodder and its host plants before the dodder produces seed. CULTURAL—Use dodder-free seed and nursery plants. CHEMICAL—Treat the infested area with a preemergent herbicide; kill germinating dodder seeds.

DUTCH ELM DISEASE

TYPE OF DISEASE: fungal

HOST(S): elms

Dutch elm disease (DED) has caused a devastating loss of elms since its introduction to the United States around 1930. Although DED affects many species of elm, the American elm is especially susceptible and nearly always dies.

Symptoms
The fungus grows in the vascular system, producing toxins and clogging the flow of water and nutrients. Symptoms generally begin with the sudden, severe wilting of leaves on a single branch. Leaves curl, turn yellow and then brown, and may fall or stay attached to the branch. The infection can spread rapidly, causing death within a year, or it can spread slowly, causing the tree to die over several years' time.

Transmission
Dutch elm disease overwinters in the bark of dead or diseased elm trees and is carried by elm bark beetles, which introduce it into healthy trees as they feed. The fungus is also transmitted through natural root grafts occurring between an infected and a healthy tree.

Control
PHYSICAL—Remove dead elms; prune wilting branches 12 inches below wood showing symptoms, disinfecting pruners between cuts. BIOLOGICAL—Control elm bark beetles with beneficial nematodes or braconid wasps. CULTURAL—Plant elms that are DED resistant.

GALL, AZALEA LEAF

TYPE OF DISEASE: fungal

HOST(S): many plants of the heath family

Though seldom a serious threat, azalea leaf gall is unattractive. It is a fairly common problem with azaleas, especially in the South. Other susceptible plants include Japanese andromeda, blueberry, mountain laurel, and rhododendron.

Symptoms
Symptoms vary somewhat depending on the host. On azalea, bladder-shaped galls form on all or part of a leaf or flower. The galls are soft when they are young, eventually hardening and darkening with age. As a gall develops, a white velvety layer that produces spores appears on its surface.

Transmission
This fungus overwinters in infected tissue and rapidly spreads during periods of warm, wet weather, particularly in shade. Galls do not appear until the following spring.

Control
PHYSICAL—Handpick and destroy galls, preferably before the white spore-producing layer appears. CULTURAL—Make sure susceptible plants have good air circulation; avoid watering with a sprinkler in spring, when mature galls produce spores —wet foliage increases the chance of spreading the infection.

GALL, CROWN

TYPE OF DISEASE: bacterial

HOST(S): many plants

Crown gall is caused by a bacterium that lives in the soil. It has one of the broadest host ranges of any bacterial plant pathogen. Common ornamental hosts include aster, chrysanthemum, euonymus, flowering quince, forsythia, honeysuckle, and willow.

Symptoms
Rounded corky galls develop on roots, on stems near the soil line or, in the case of grafted plants, near the graft union. At first the gall is soft and either white or flesh colored. It darkens and its surface becomes rough as it grows, sometimes to several inches in diameter. Infected plants may be stunted and weakened and more susceptible to environmental stress.

Transmission
The bacterium responsible for crown gall can persist in the soil for several years. It spreads from one region to another in shipments of infected nursery stock. The bacterium enters plants through wounds.

Control
PHYSICAL—Remove and destroy infected plants. CULTURAL—Plant disease-free stock; avoid wounding plants, especially near the soil line.

LEAF BLISTER AND LEAF CURL

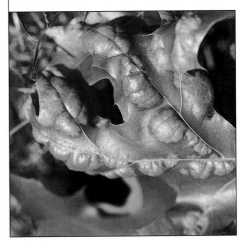

TYPE OF DISEASE: fungal

HOST(S): fruit and ornamental trees

Several species of *Taphrina* are responsible for leaf blister and leaf curl. Ornamental trees commonly infected include birch, elm, flowering cherry, maple, oak, ornamental plum, and poplar.

Symptoms
Symptoms of leaf blister and leaf curl vary somewhat depending on the plant. In the case of cherry leaf curl, which infects both ornamental and edible cherry, peach, and plum trees, portions of the leaves pucker, thicken, and turn yellow or reddish brown. Leaves drop prematurely. Twigs develop knobby swellings from which a cluster of new shoots, called a witch's broom, arises. These twigs often die over winter. Oak leaf blister often begins as raised, cup-shaped areas that range from a quarter inch to several inches in diameter and are silver-gray on the lower leaf surface and yellow above. As with cherries, the leaves drop prematurely. Similar symptoms occur on maple, poplar, elm, and birch.

Transmission
The fungus overwinters on the bark, twigs, and buds of infected trees. The spores are spread by rain and infect the young tissues only.

Control
CULTURAL—Plant resistant varieties; prune to promote good air circulation. CHEMICAL—Apply lime-sulfur to commonly infected plants while they are dormant.

LEAF SCORCH, BACTERIAL

TYPE OF DISEASE: bacterial

HOST(S): black oak, elm, maple, sycamore

The bacterium *Xylella fastidiosa* causes leaf scorch on a variety of landscape trees. It is common on American elm, species in the black oak group, mulberry, sycamore, and some maples. Unlike leaf scorch that is caused by drought, drying winds, or root damage, bacterial leaf scorch is unevenly distributed in the tree canopy and on individual leaves.

Symptoms
Bacterial leaf scorch appears in midsummer as irregular brown or reddish brown areas along the leaf margin. These areas are typically bordered by a yellow halo. As the scorch progresses toward the midrib, the leaves curl and drop prematurely. Infections recur from year to year, slowing growth and causing dieback of branches. On sycamore, mulberry, and red maple, the leaves develop patterns of light brown and reddish brown that are bordered by a yellow halo. Plants may be infected with the leaf-scorch bacterium yet display few symptoms.

Transmission
Leafhoppers and spittlebugs carry the leaf-scorch bacterium from plant to plant.

Control
PHYSICAL—If only a few branches are infected, cut them back to a point well below leaves showing symptoms. CULTURAL—Remove diseased, failing trees and replace them with less susceptible varieties.

LEAF SPOT, ALTERNARIA

TYPE OF DISEASE: fungal

HOST(S): many woody and herbaceous plants

A number of *Alternaria* species cause leaf spot on a wide variety of plants, including fruits, vegetables, herbaceous perennials, and woody ornamentals, among them carnation, catalpa, chrysanthemum, flowering tobacco, geranium, hibiscus, magnolia, marigold, Shasta daisy, stock, and zinnia.

Symptoms
Leaves develop small dark brown to black spots. Often numerous, the spots first appear on the plant's lowest leaves and progress upward. As spots enlarge, they develop concentric rings like a bull's-eye target. Stems may have sunken lesions that girdle and kill them, and fruit and tubers may be spotted. In moist weather the spots on fruit are sometimes covered with fuzzy black structures that produce spores.

Transmission
Alternaria fungi overwinter in infected plant debris or on seeds. Spores are spread by wind, rain, and tools.

Control
PHYSICAL—Remove and destroy infected plant debris. CULTURAL—Plant resistant varieties; use disease-free or treated seed; rotate crops. CHEMICAL—Treat infected plants with chlorothalonil.

LEAF SPOT, BACTERIAL

TYPE OF DISEASE: bacterial

HOST(S): many

Species of two different genera of bacteria, *Pseudomonas* and *Xanthomonas,* are responsible for leaf spots on an extremely wide range of plants. Ornamental plants susceptible to bacterial leaf spot include begonia, California laurel, English ivy, geranium, and gladiolus.

Symptoms
The spots are usually brown and are often surrounded by a yellow halo; they may appear on stems and fruit as well as on leaves. Some of the spots are round, while others are elongated streaks bounded by leaf veins running parallel to one another. A branching or fish-bone vein pattern gives spots a triangular outline. As a spot enlarges, the damaged tissue may drop out, making "shot holes" in the leaf. Spots can also coalesce and cover the entire leaf. Leaves often drop prematurely; bacterial spot of English ivy, for instance, can temporarily defoliate a planting.

Transmission
The bacteria are transmitted by water, tools, and infested soil. They overwinter in infected plant parts, on seeds, and in soil.

Control
PHYSICAL—Remove and destroy infected plants and debris. CULTURAL—Plant resistant varieties; use pathogen-free seed; rotate crops. CHEMICAL—Treat infected plants with a fungicide that contains copper.

LEAF SPOT, SEPTORIA

TYPE OF DISEASE: fungal

HOST(S): many

There are many species of *Septoria* responsible for leaf-spot and blight diseases on a wide range of plants. Common ornamental hosts include azalea, aster, chrysanthemum, dogwood, poplar, and tomato.

Symptoms
Like alternaria leaf spot, the symptoms of septoria leaf spot arise first on lower leaves and progress upward on the plant. The typical spot is angular, small, and initially yellow, later turning brown, with black spore-producing bodies scattered over the surface. On some plants the spots have purple margins. Diseased leaves often turn yellow and drop prematurely. When a tomato plant loses a substantial portion of its foliage, the fruit exposed to the sun may be ruined by sunscald.

Transmission
The spores of septoria are spread by rain, irrigation water, tools, and animals. The fungi overwinter in or on seeds and in plant debris.

Control
PHYSICAL—Remove and destroy debris. CULTURAL—Plant resistant varieties; use disease-free or treated seed; rotate crops. CHEMICAL—Spray with a fungicide such as Bordeaux mixture or chlorothalonil.

MILDEW, DOWNY

TYPE OF DISEASE: fungal

HOST(S): many

There are seven genera of fungi that cause downy mildew. Most of these fungi have a narrow host range. Some of the most common ornamental plants attacked are Boston ivy, grape, pansy, redbud, rose, snapdragon, sunflower, and viburnum.

Symptoms
The first visible symptom of this fungal infection is the development of angular yellow spots on the upper leaf surface. These areas gradually turn brown, while corresponding spots on the underside of the leaf develop a white, tan, gray, or purple downy growth that can be seen in early morning during humid weather. Fruit and young stems may also be covered with the downy fungal growth. The plants may be stunted, and grapes and other susceptible crops are often completely ruined. Most downy mildews are favored by cool weather, and all require moist conditions.

Transmission
The spores of the fungi are spread by wind, rain, insects, and infected seed.

Control
PHYSICAL—Remove and destroy plant debris and infected plants; space plants widely to provide good air circulation. CULTURAL—Use resistant varieties; rotate crops. CHEMICAL—Spray with a copper fungicide, sulfur, Bordeaux mixture, mancozeb, or chlorothalonil.

MILDEW, POWDERY

TYPE OF DISEASE: fungal

HOST(S): many

Powdery mildews are caused by more than 100 species of fungi. They occur worldwide, attacking over 7,000 kinds of plants. Ornamental hosts include begonia, chrysanthemum, euonymus, gardenia, hawthorn, hydrangea, lilac, phlox, rose, sycamore, turf grasses, and zinnia.

Symptoms
The white, powdery growth that appears on leaves and buds and occasionally on shoots makes powdery mildew easy to identify. Most species of powdery mildew fungi spread rapidly when the weather is dry and days are warm and nights cool. The fungi are also favored by poor air circulation. Infected leaves turn yellow and may drop, and growth is stunted and often distorted. Plants are weakened or killed. In fall, fruiting bodies form on the mildew, starting out as tan-yellow specks before turning dark brown-black.

Transmission
Spores are spread by wind. They thrive in shade and overwinter on infected plants.

Control
PHYSICAL—Spray plants daily with water, which kills spores; remove and destroy badly infected plant parts or entire plants. CULTURAL—Plant resistant varieties; allow adequate room between plants and thin overcrowded growth. CHEMICAL—Apply a summer oil or a fungicide that contains propiconazole, triadimefon, or triforine.

MOLD, SOOTY

TYPE OF DISEASE: fungal

HOST(S): many

Several genera of fungi are responsible for the disorder known as sooty mold. These fungi do not attack plants directly. Instead, they feed on the sugary secretions, or honeydew, produced by sucking insects such as aphids, leafhoppers, mealybugs, psyllids, scales, and whiteflies. Besides being unsightly, a heavy growth of sooty mold can slow plant growth by shading the leaf surface and reducing photosynthesis.

Symptoms
A black growth appears on leaves and twigs that may be fine and sootlike or lumpy or crusty with spiky protuberances. The mold can be scraped off the plant.

Transmission
Cool, moist conditions favor the growth of sooty mold. Its spores are spread by rain and wind.

Control
PHYSICAL—If the plant is small, wipe off the mold with a damp cloth. BIOLOGICAL OR CHEMICAL—Identify the insect pest responsible for producing the honeydew, and choose an appropriate control measure. If you cannot find honeydew-producing insects on a plant with sooty mold, the honeydew may be dripping down from an infested overhanging plant.

MOSAIC

TYPE OF DISEASE: viral

HOST(S): many

There are several viruses that cause mosaic disease, some with a narrow host range and others capable of infecting many different hosts. The tobacco mosaic virus is common in gardens and greenhouses, attacking such ornamental hosts as ash, episcia, flowering tobacco, gloxinia, petunia, and streptocarpus. Other mosaics occur on such hosts as birch, canna, carnation, coleus, horse chestnut, and rose.

Symptoms
A mottling of leaves is the most obvious symptom of a mosaic infection. The irregular patches or streaks of abnormal color range from light to dark green and yellow. The leaves are often distorted, and growth is almost always stunted.

Transmission
Some mosaic viruses are transmitted by insects such as aphids. Many are spread from an infected plant to healthy ones on a tool or on the gardener's hands, as is the case with the tobacco mosaic virus. It can persist for years in dried tobacco.

Control
PHYSICAL—Remove and destroy infected plants; smokers should wash hands before handling plants. CULTURAL—Plant resistant varieties. BIOLOGICAL—Use beneficial predators to control insects that carry the viruses. CHEMICAL—Use organic pesticides on insects that spread the viruses.

NEEDLE CAST

TYPE OF DISEASE: fungal

HOST(S): conifers

A variety of different species of fungi are responsible for needle cast, a name shared by several diseases in which a conifer sheds a large portion of its needles prematurely. Some species are common only in the Northwest, while others are largely limited to the Southeast and the Gulf Coast region. There are also a number of species that occur throughout the United States. Many needle-cast fungi attack a single species or a few closely related species. Common hosts include Douglas fir (*Pseudotsuga*), fir (*Abies*), pine, and spruce.

Symptoms
Mottled yellow spots on needles are the earliest sign of disease, appearing from spring through fall. Separate at first, they tend to form bands around the needles as the disease progresses. The needles turn brown and are often shed 6 months to a year after the first spots appear. Young trees are particularly susceptible and may be killed by repeated defoliation.

Transmission
Spores are spread locally by rain and over great distances by wind. There must be an extended period of wet weather for needles to become infected.

Control
PHYSICAL—Clean up and destroy fallen needles. CULTURAL—Plant resistant species; allow enough space around plants for good air circulation.

NEMATODES, FOLIAR

TYPE OF DISEASE: parasitic

HOST(S): many herbaceous ornamentals

Foliar nematodes infect the leaves and buds of a variety of herbaceous plants, including African violet, anemone, begonia, chrysanthemum, cyclamen, ferns, hosta, iris, lily, primrose, and orchids. They are most destructive in areas with humid summers; the nematodes move through the film of water on a wet plant from one leaf to another. These tiny roundworms enter leaves through their pores.

Symptoms
New shoots may be stunted, twisted, and misshapen. Abnormally colored areas of pale green, yellow, or red-purple appear on the leaves. These spots are bounded by the veins and are roughly triangular in plants with branching veins; in plants that have parallel veins, such as hosta and lily, they are elongated stripes. The leaves turn brown or black and die.

Transmission
Foliar nematodes can survive for up to 3 or more years in the soil, compost, and plant debris. They are common in woodland plants and are usually introduced into the garden by infected but healthy-looking plants. They are spread from plant to plant by these materials or by splashing water.

Control
PHYSICAL—Remove and destroy seriously infected plants; pick and destroy all leaves showing symptoms. CULTURAL—Purchase disease-free plants.

NEMATODES, PINEWOOD

TYPE OF DISEASE: parasitic

HOST(S): pines

Pinewood nematodes are indigenous to the United States. Native pine species are resistant to infection but become vulnerable when subjected to drought, poor soil, or other environmental stresses. Exotic species such as Austrian, Japanese black, and Scotch pines are highly susceptible.

Symptoms
Needles turn yellow, then turn brown and wilt but remain on the tree. An infestation may kill branches or the entire tree.

Transmission
Pinewood nematodes are spread by the flying long-horned or cerambycid beetle, which feeds on growing branch tips. As the insect feeds, it releases nematodes that enter the plant through wounds. Inside, they multiply rapidly and spread through the trunk and branches. One beetle may carry as many as 20,000 nematodes.

Control
PHYSICAL—Remove and destroy infected trees promptly.

NEMATODES, ROOT KNOT

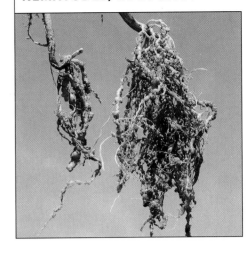

TYPE OF DISEASE: parasitic

HOST(S): many woody and herbaceous plants

Root knot nematodes are the most common plant parasitic nematode, infecting over 2,000 plant species. There are more than 50 species, which vary in their geographic ranges and attack different kinds of plants, among them boxwood, geranium, gladiolus, grape hyacinth, pachysandra, peony, rose, and hibiscus.

Symptoms
Galls form on the roots of infected plants. These galls are part of the root and cannot easily be rubbed off. Symptoms aboveground include stunting, yellowing, wilting during hot weather, and death. Infected plants are more susceptible to wilts, root rots, and crown gall.

Transmission
The nematodes overwinter in infected roots or soil and are spread by soil, transplants, and tools. They invade root tissue to feed and reproduce. A generation takes about 21 days. Each female nematode produces 200 to 500 eggs in a mass that protrudes from the galls. After the eggs hatch, the larvae move through the soil and invade the roots of other plants.

Control
CULTURAL—Plant resistant varieties; add organic matter to the soil; do not plant susceptible plants in infested soil; solarize soil to kill nematodes; rotate susceptible and nonsusceptible plants.

ROT, BLOSSOM-END

TYPE OF DISEASE: environmental

HOST(S): tomatoes and other vegetables

Blossom-end rot is a disease caused by a deficiency of calcium at the blossom end of susceptible fruit. Plants frequently affected include tomato, pepper, watermelon, and squash. While there may be a substantial supply of calcium in the soil, it may not reach rapidly growing fruit when the weather is hot and dry and irrigation is irregular or inadequate. Another common factor is overzealous nitrogen fertilization.

Symptoms
Blossom-end rot first appears as a brown discoloration at the blossom end of a tomato or other susceptible fruit. The spot enlarges and darkens, eventually becoming sunken and leathery. This tissue may cover the bottom third to one-half of the fruit and is subject to invasion by pathogens.

Control
CULTURAL—Apply limestone or gypsum to provide adequate calcium (a soil test can determine how much to apply); mulch to keep soil evenly moist; provide additional water during drought; avoid excessive nitrogen fertilization.

ROT, BROWN

TYPE OF DISEASE: fungal

HOST(S): stone fruit and some ornamentals

Brown rot occurs worldwide, wherever peaches, plums, cherries, and other stone fruits are grown, and is particularly troublesome in warm, humid regions. It also attacks a number of ornamentals, including flowering quince, chokeberry, western sand cherry, and flowering almond.

Symptoms
The first symptom to appear is brown spots on blossoms. The spots spread rapidly to cover the entire flower and stem. During humid weather, a brown fuzz covers infected parts. As the disease progresses, cankers develop on twigs near the flower stem and sometimes cause girdling and dieback. Next, ripe fruit develops watersoaked, brown spots that enlarge and expand rapidly. Rotted flowers and fruit shrivel and may remain on the plant for a long time. Fuzzy gray mold appears on the bark.

Transmission
Spores are spread by wind, rain, and insects. The fungus overwinters in the dry, shriveled fruit, called mummies, and on twig cankers.

Control
PHYSICAL—Dispose of all fruit mummies and prune out twigs with cankers. CHEMICAL—Protect fruit with a fungicide spray such as propiconazole or triadimefon.

ROT, MUSHROOM ROOT

TYPE OF DISEASE: fungal

HOST(S): many

Mushroom root rot, also known as armillaria root rot, oak-root fungus, and shoestring root rot, occurs throughout the United States. It infects a wide range of trees and shrubs; herbaceous plants are occasionally infected. Particularly susceptible are azalea, boxwood, oak, pine, rhododendron, rose, spruce, and sycamore.

Symptoms
Plants may suffer a mild infection for years with no symptoms. Then, when they are subjected to stress from drought, defoliation by insects, or another disease, the symptoms of mushroom root rot begin to appear. Among these are yellowing; wilting; premature dropping of leaves; dark, spongy bark; dieback of branches; tough, fan-shaped growths under the bark; and, in fall and winter, clusters of honey brown mushrooms at the base of the plant.

Transmission
The fungus spreads underground from infected to healthy plants by the black or brown cordlike structures, or shoestrings, it produces. In addition, airborne spores from the mushrooms can enter plants through wounds to start new colonies.

Control
PHYSICAL—Remove and destroy infected plants, including stumps and roots; remove soil from around rotted stumps. CULTURAL—Plant resistant species.

ROT, PHYTOPHTHORA ROOT

TYPE OF DISEASE: fungal

HOST(S): many

Several *Phytophthora* species with different geographical ranges and different hosts cause root rots in a wide range of trees, shrubs, and herbaceous plants. Ornamentals often infected include azalea, calla lily, camellia, eucalyptus, Fraser fir, oak, periwinkle, pine, rhododendron, rose, snapdragon, and yew. Wet soils and cool temperatures favor the fungus.

Symptoms
Small feeder roots die back, and brown lesions appear on larger roots. Because of this damage, roots cannot take up adequate amounts of water and nutrients. The symptoms produced vary in different hosts. Wilting is common, growth is frequently stunted, and twigs may suffer dieback. Foliage may be sparse, yellowed, abnormally small, or misshapen. Infected plants are especially vulnerable to environmental stresses and to other diseases. Established plants may survive for years; seedlings may die within days.

Transmission
Phytophthora root rot fungi overwinter in infected roots or soil. Spores are spread by infested soil and water, or by seed.

Control
PHYSICAL—Remove and destroy seriously infected plants. CULTURAL—Plant resistant species or varieties; incorporate composted tree bark into the soil to suppress fungus growth; improve soil drainage.

RUST

TYPE OF DISEASE: fungal

HOST(S): many

Some 4,000 species of rust fungi are known to cause diseases on plants. Many of these fungi require two different kinds of plants in order to complete their life cycle, while a smaller number infect only one kind of plant. Commonly infected ornamentals include carnation, crab apple, hollyhock, red cedar, rose, snapdragon, spruce, and white pine.

Symptoms
Crusty rust-colored, orange, dark brown, or purplish spots dot the undersides of leaves and stems. The upper surfaces of infected leaves become mottled with yellow. On a severely infected plant, leaves shrivel but remain attached. Plants are weakened, and their growth is often stunted.

Transmission
Rust fungi overwinter on infected hosts and in plant debris. Spores are spread by wind and splashing water and by infected nursery plants or cuttings.

Control
PHYSICAL—Remove and destroy infected plant parts in fall and again in spring. CULTURAL—Plant only resistant varieties. CHEMICAL—Spray with sulfur, lime-sulfur, Bordeaux mixture, propiconazole, triadimefon, or triforine during the growing season.

RUST, CEDAR-APPLE

TYPE OF DISEASE: fungal

HOST(S): red cedar, apple, and crab apple

The cedar-apple rust fungus requires both an apple and a cedar host to complete its life cycle. Spores produced on red cedars (*Juniperus virginiana*) infect apple trees and ornamental crab apples, and spores produced on apples infect red cedars. This disease is common from the Mississippi Valley eastward.

Symptoms
In early spring, orange gelatinous tendrils emerge from spherical leaf galls 1 to 2 inches in diameter on red cedar; the galls reach this stage 18 months after the tree is infected. In early to midsummer, bright yellow spots with orange-red margins appear on apple and crab apple leaves. The spots are ⅛ to ½ inch in diameter. Spotted leaves may turn yellow and fall prematurely. Fruit may have sunken brown spots and be lumpy and deformed.

Transmission
The cedar-apple rust fungus overwinters on the cedar host as immature galls. Spores are spread by wind to the alternate host.

Control
CULTURAL—Plant resistant apple or crab apple cultivars; do not plant red cedars within 500 yards of apples.

SCAB, APPLE

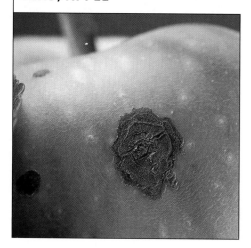

TYPE OF DISEASE: fungal

HOST(S): apple and crab apple

Apple scab is the most important disease of apples and ornamental crab apples and can cause severe injury from defoliation. This disease is most troublesome in areas with frequent rainfall, high humidity, and mild temperatures in spring and summer.

Symptoms
Dull olive green spots ¼ inch or more in diameter with a velvety surface appear in the spring on leaves, flowers, shoots, and young fruit. The spots are slightly raised on fruit and become dark, scabby, and cracked. Leaves and fruit are deformed, and if the plant is highly susceptible, they fall prematurely.

Transmission
The apple-scab fungus overwinters on fallen leaves. In early spring it develops fruiting bodies that release spores spread by wind. During the growing season, spores are washed down by rain from leaf and fruit spots to infect other leaves and fruits.

Control
PHYSICAL—Rake and destroy fallen leaves and fruit. CULTURAL—Plant varieties resistant to apple scab.

WILT, CUCUMBER

TYPE OF DISEASE: bacterial

HOST(S): most cucumber family members

Bacterial wilt of cucumber is a vascular disease carried by striped and spotted cucumber beetles. It occurs throughout the United States but is most prevalent east of the Rocky Mountains, especially north of Tennessee. Hosts include cucumbers, squash, muskmelons, and pumpkins.

Symptoms
At first, one or more leaves on a vine droop as if they needed watering. Soon all the leaves droop, and the vine's stem collapses. Wilted leaves shrivel and dry. When the vine is cut in two and squeezed, a viscous white liquid collects in droplets on the cut ends. When the two cut ends are put together, then pulled apart, delicate, mucuslike threads stretch between the cut ends. This symptom confirms that the plant's problem is bacterial wilt. The liquid may ooze from cracks in diseased vines.

Transmission
The cucumber-wilt bacterium survives the winter in the intestines of the striped and spotted cucumber beetle. These beetles spread the disease as they feed on susceptible plants. Other insects such as flea beetles and grasshoppers may further spread the disease during the growing season.

Control
PHYSICAL—Use row covers; remove and destroy infected plants. BIOLOGICAL—Control with beneficial nematodes or tachinid flies. CHEMICAL—Use rotenone or sabadilla.

WILT, FUSARIUM

TYPE OF DISEASE: fungal

HOST(S): many

Numerous strains and species of *Fusarium* cause wilt diseases on herbaceous ornamentals and vegetables. Most strains are highly host specific. Common ornamental hosts include China aster, carnation, cattleya orchid, chrysanthemum, cyclamen, and gladiolus.

Symptoms
Leaves of infected plants turn yellow and droop. Brown patches appear on leaves, often spreading to cover the entire leaf. Lower leaves are usually affected first, and symptoms may initially occur on only one side of the plant. Plants may be permanently stunted or may wither and die. This is one of the most serious diseases of China asters, causing plants to wilt and die at any stage of growth; leaves turn straw yellow and curl. Leaves and flower spikes of infected gladiolus are stunted, and flowers are small and faded. The stems may split, revealing brown streaks in the conductive tissues.

Transmission
Fusarium is a soil-borne pathogen that is spread in infested soil and by infected seeds and plants. Resistant varieties may become susceptible if they are injured by insects or nematodes.

Control
CULTURAL—Plant only resistant varieties; purchase disease-free plants; solarize infested soil.

WILT, OAK

TYPE OF DISEASE: fungal

HOST(S): many oak species

This lethal disease of oaks occurs east of the Rocky Mountains but is most troublesome in Texas and the Great Lakes area. Many species of red oaks are particularly susceptible. Also infected, though usually less severely, are species in the white oak group. One non-oak, the Chinese chestnut, is also susceptible.

Symptoms
Symptoms vary with the host. Red oaks display wilting first at the tops of trees. Leaves turn brown along their margins and yellow or brown along their veins. These symptoms progress downward and inward until all leaves are affected. Leaves fall prematurely, often before they turn brown. Total defoliation occurs within several days to several weeks. Branches die back, and trees typically die within the year. Symptoms on white oaks are similar but progress more slowly. Trees may survive for several years after infection.

Transmission
The oak-wilt fungus overwinters in infected trees. It is spread by oak bark beetles and nitidulid beetles and by natural root grafts occurring between a diseased tree and a healthy one.

Control
PHYSICAL—Remove and destroy infected trees, including stumps; prune susceptible species only when they are dormant and the carrier beetles are inactive.

WILT, VERTICILLIUM

TYPE OF DISEASE: fungal

HOST(S): many

Widely occurring verticillium wilt is most troublesome in the temperate zones, attacking over 200 species of plants. Some strains are highly host specific; others attack a broad range of plants. Susceptible ornamentals include aster, azalea, barberry, catalpa, chrysanthemum, dahlia, daphne, magnolia, maple, nandina, peony, photinia, privet, and snapdragon.

Symptoms
Symptoms usually appear first on the infected plant's lower or outer leaves. Leaves develop a yellowish tinge and droop, then turn brown and die. On herbaceous plants, the leaves shrivel and remain attached to the stem for some time. Individual stems or the entire plant dies, and vascular tissue in the stems is streaked with brown. On woody plants, symptoms include elongated cankers, wilting, premature defoliation, and dieback. The symptoms may be acute, spreading within a few weeks, or chronic, progressing over several seasons.

Transmission
This soil-borne pathogen enters a plant through its feeder roots or wounds. It can survive in soil for as long as 20 years.

Control
CULTURAL—Plant resistant species such as conifers and ginkgos; purchase disease-free plants; solarize infested soil; keep plants vigorous and protect them from drought stress.

YELLOWS, ASTER

TYPE OF DISEASE: bacterial

HOST(S): many herbaceous plants

The bacteria that cause aster yellows infect more than 40 different families of plants. Ornamentals often attacked include asters, gladiolus, calendulas, cosmos, delphiniums, flax, hydrangeas, phlox, strawflowers, and zinnias.

Symptoms
Symptoms of aster yellows vary somewhat depending on the host, but infected plants generally develop spindly stems and clear veins. The internodes of stems are short and sometimes curled, giving the plant a dwarfed, bushy appearance. Flowers and leaves are frequently deformed. On asters, leaves turn yellow and flowers are green and dwarfed, if they appear at all. Gladiolus and zinnias are dramatically dwarfed.

Transmission
Aster yellows is transmitted from infected to healthy plants by leafhoppers, which pick up bacteria while feeding. The pathogens overwinter in infected perennials, including common weeds such as thistle, wild chicory, dandelion, wild carrot, and wide-leaf plantain.

Control
PHYSICAL—Eradicate potential weed hosts; remove and destroy infected plants; use row covers to protect vegetables from leafhoppers.

Zone and Frost Maps

To determine if a plant will flourish in your climate, first locate your zone on the map below and check it against the zone information given in the encyclopedia entries that begin on page 10 or in the Plant Selection Guide that begins on page 496. For annuals and biennials, planting dates depend on when frosts occur: Hardy annuals can be safely sown 6 weeks before the last spring frost, whereas tender annuals should be sown only after all danger of frost is past. Also, while cool-season annuals can withstand some frost, warm-season plants can be grown without protection only in the frost-free period between the last and first frosts. Used together, the zone map and the frost-date maps shown opposite will help you select plants suited to your area and determine when to plant them. Frost dates vary widely within each region, however, so check with your weather service or Cooperative Extension Service for more precise figures, and record the temperatures in your own garden from year to year.

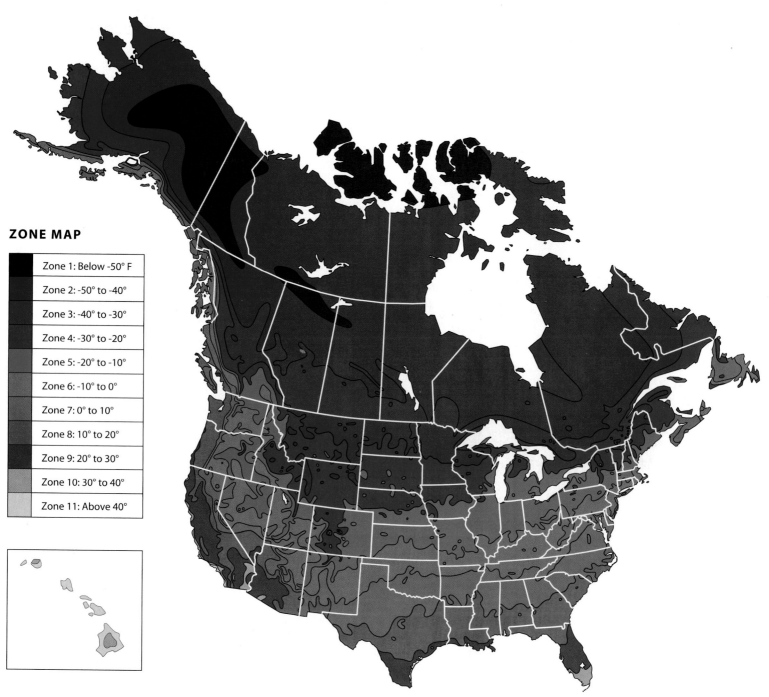

ZONE MAP

	Zone 1: Below -50° F
	Zone 2: -50° to -40°
	Zone 3: -40° to -30°
	Zone 4: -30° to -20°
	Zone 5: -20° to -10°
	Zone 6: -10° to 0°
	Zone 7: 0° to 10°
	Zone 8: 10° to 20°
	Zone 9: 20° to 30°
	Zone 10: 30° to 40°
	Zone 11: Above 40°

**AVERAGE DATES OF
LAST SPRING FROST**

	June
	May
	April
	March
	February
	January

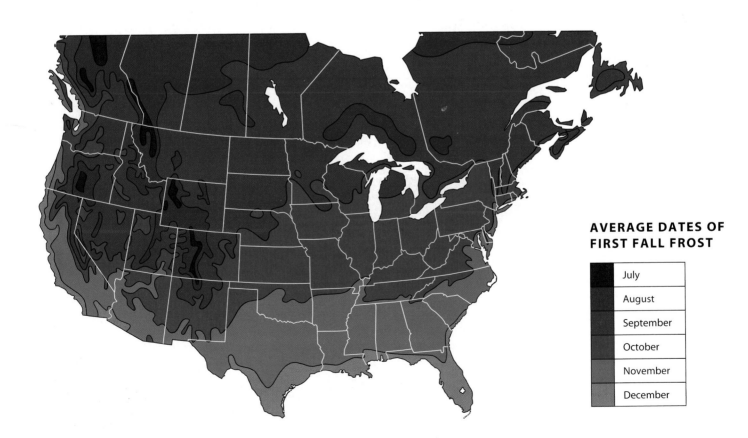

**AVERAGE DATES OF
FIRST FALL FROST**

	July
	August
	September
	October
	November
	December

Answers to Common Questions

One side of our patio is quite open to view from several neighbors' yards, and we'd like more privacy. The patio is screened off with shrubs on the other open sides, but I was wondering if there are any annuals that could function as **screening?**

Annual vines such as *Humulus japonicus* (Japanese hopvine) and *Lagenaria siceraria* (calabash gourd) can be grown on 2-by-3-inch wood poles set in the ground and strung with durable twine or plastic fishline for plant supports. These plants, which can be grown in pots that are set on the edge of the patio, have dense enough foliage to block the view from outside.

My favorite kind of foundation planting is an annual border, but I know from soil testing that the foundation of my house leaches limestone into the soil, keeping it on the alkaline side. What annuals are best for **alkaline soil?**

Within reasonable limits—say, a pH of no more than 8—you can confidently expect the following annuals to adapt comfortably to the soil around your foundation: *Calendula officinalis* (pot marigold), *Catharanthus roseus* (Madagascar periwinkle), *Dianthus barbatus* (sweet William), *Gaillardia pulchella* (Indian blanket), *Gypsophila elegans* (baby's-breath), *Iberis umbellata* (globe candytuft), *Lathyrus odoratus* (sweet pea), *Papaver rhoeas* (corn poppy), *Pelargonium* (geranium), *Phlox drummondii* (annual phlox), *Scabiosa atropurpurea* (pincushion flower), *Senecio cineraria* (dusty-miller), *Tropaeolum majus* (garden nasturtium), *Verbena* x *hybrida* (vervain), and *Zinnia elegans* (common zinnia).

I have a little rill running through a corner of my property that I can see from my kitchen window, and I would like to brighten up its banks with annuals. Can you recommend some that will adapt to **damp sites?**

The versatile clan of annuals includes species that will be right at home in very boggy conditions, including *Limnanthes douglasii* (meadow foam), *Mimulus* x *hybridus* (monkey flower), and *Myosotis sylvatica* (forget-me-not). In soil that is not boggy but is generally moist, you can grow *Caladium* x *hortulanum* (fancy-leaved caladium), *Catharanthus roseus* (Madagascar periwinkle), *Cleome hasslerana* (spider flower), *Coleus* x *hybridus* (coleus), *Exacum affine* (Persian violet), *Impatiens, Torenia fournieri* (blue-wings), and *Viola* x *wittrockiana* (garden pansy).

Because we can almost never find time to tend our **garden** except for a bit **on weekends,** we're looking for flowers that can get along pretty well on their own. Are there any annuals that will bloom nicely from spring to frost without assistance?

Once you've gotten them off to a good start in well-prepared soil, you can expect self-sufficient performance from *Begonia* x *semperflorens-cultorum* (wax begonia), *Catharanthus roseus* (Madagascar periwinkle), *Heliotropium arborescens* (cherry pie), *Pentas lanceolata* (Egyptian star-cluster), *Petunia* x *hybrida* (common garden petunia), and *Salvia splendens* (scarlet sage).

I buy annuals at the home and garden center, and they look great, but when I plant them, they soon **stop blooming.** Am I doing something wrong?

To entice buyers, home and garden centers and roadside stands often display lushly blooming annuals—particularly tender annuals—several weeks before the ground is warm enough to accommodate them. Many of these plants have been forced into early bloom and may also have had extra applications of chemical fertilizers. Plants that have been raised like this are liable to suffer severe transplant shock when set out in the garden, especially if it's done too early in the season. To avoid this kind of frustration, buy plants that are not yet in full bloom and safeguard them under cover or in a cold frame until it is safe to set them out.

There's a patch of ground out near my property line facing the road with rather **infertile, dry, and sandy soil.** I'd like to dress up the area a bit, but without putting in a lot of effort. Are there any annuals that would work in such soil?

Happily, a wide variety of annuals will do well in these unpromising conditions. You can choose from *Arctotis* (African daisy), *Calendula officinalis* (pot marigold), *Callistephus chinensis* (China aster), *Clarkia amoena* (farewell-to-spring), *Coreopsis tinctoria* (tickseed), *Dyssodia tenuiloba* (Dahlberg daisy), *Euphorbia marginata* (snow-on-the-mountain), *Gaillardia pulchella* (Indian blanket), *Kochia scoparia* (burning bush, summer cypress), *Lobularia maritima* (sweet alyssum), *Phlox drummondii* (annual phlox), *Portulaca grandiflora* (moss rose), *Tithonia rotundifolia* (Mexican sunflower), and *Verbena* x *hybrida* (vervain).

We own a seaside cabin where we spend our summers, and I'd like to put several beds of annuals around it. What plants will do best in the conditions found **at the beach?**

Even in this trying environment of wind and salt-laden air, a fairly large variety of annuals will succeed. You can choose with confidence from among *Ageratum houstonianum* (flossflower), *Antirrhinum majus* (common snapdragon), *Calendula officinalis* (pot marigold), *Dimorphotheca* (Cape marigold), *Lavatera trimestris* (tree mallow), *Lobelia erinus* (edging lobelia), *Lobularia maritima* (sweet alyssum), *Pelargonium* (geranium), *Phlox drummondii* (annual phlox), *Portulaca grandiflora* (moss rose), *Salvia argentea* (silver sage), *Senecio cineraria* (dusty-miller), *Tagetes patula* (French marigold), and *Verbena* (vervain).

One of my great joys is **attracting wildlife** to my garden. What are the most alluring annuals for butterflies and hummingbirds? Do any annuals produce seed that birds can feed on over the winter?

Of the long list of annuals on the butterfly hit parade, the best are *Cosmos bipinnatus* (garden cosmos), *Gaillardia pulchella* (Indian blanket), *Helianthus* (sunflower), *Heliotropium arborescens* (cherry pie), *Hesperis matronalis* (dame's rocket), *Limonium sinuatum* (notchleaf statice), *Rudbeckia hirta* (black-eyed Susan), *Tithonia rotundifolia* (Mexican sunflower), *Verbena* (vervain), and *Zinnia elegans* (common zinnia). Hummingbirds will flock to *Alcea rosea* (hollyhock), *Antirrhinum majus* (common snapdragon), *Dianthus barbatus* (sweet William), *Digitalis purpurea* (common foxglove), *Ipomopsis aggregata* (scarlet gilia), and *Salvia* (sage). For seed heads that will feed a variety of birds during the cold months, plant *Amaranthus* (amaranth), *Coreopsis* (tickseed), *Cosmos*, *Gomphrena*, *Helianthus annuus* (common sunflower), *Rudbeckia hirta*, and *Verbena bonariensis* (Brazilian verbena).

I have a perennial border with lots of **bold colors** like red, orange, and yellow. These colors are compatible, but my garden seems to lack continuity. What can I do?

Tie your bold colors together by introducing perennials with blue flowers. Leadwort (*Ceratostigma*), globe thistle (*Echinops*), flax (*Linum*), Siberian iris (*Iris sibirica*), Russian sage (*Perovskia*), false indigo (*Baptisia*), and blue cultivars of moss phlox (*Phlox subulata*) are a few of the best. You may also want to try plants with silver or gray foliage, such as lavender (*Lavandula angustifolia*), lamb's ears (*Stachys byzantina*), or *Artemisia* 'Silver Mound'. For best results, repeat your selections along the length of the border, and remember to mass blue-flowered plants as much as possible because blue is a receding color.

My perennial bed gets 6 hours of morning sun. Will my plants thrive with this amount of **light?**

Plant requirements for sun are determined by the intensity and duration of sunlight. For sun-loving perennials, 6 hours of sun is adequate only when it occurs at midday or in the afternoon. In other words, when picking plants for a garden with morning sun and afternoon shade, you should opt for shade plants. If, on the other hand, your garden is shaded all morning but gets afternoon sun, pick plants that require full sun.

What is the **longest-blooming** perennial I can plant in my shade garden?

In all but the hottest, driest parts of the country, the plant you seek is undoubtedly *Corydalis lutea*. It starts to bloom fairly early in spring and continues producing its small clusters of pendant, tubular yellow flowers until the onset of hard frost.

A lot of perennials in my garden need **staking** in late summer. This requires a good bit of work on my part, and the result looks rather artificial. Is there any way to avoid this tedious task?

First of all, if you know that a favorite plant is going to need support, put a protective hoop around it or make a frame of stakes and string as the plant is coming up; the developing foliage will soon hide the supports. Second, perennials require less staking if you select cultivars that are naturally more compact; if you space your plants far enough apart so that sunlight and circulating air reach all the foliage; and if you feed them a low-nitrogen organic fertilizer. Pinching back your unruly plants also helps.

I have tried unsuccessfully over the years to grow **delphiniums** in my garden. Plants that I purchase from nurseries will flourish for the summer and then fail to return the following year. Are delphiniums really perennials?

Most gardeners plant various forms of the Pacific Coast hybrids. Members of this strain do exceptionally well in climates where cold winters and cool summers prevail. But they do not do well in areas where winter temperatures fluctuate above and below freezing and where summer temperatures are hot. If you live in a less-than-perfect delphinium climate, you might try *Delphinium bellamosa*, *D. belladonna*, or *D. chinense* and their cultivars, which are more forgiving.

I'm having trouble establishing **Oriental poppies** despite planting them the recommended 2 inches deep and in ideal growing conditions. Any suggestions?

Most Oriental poppies prefer the colder regions (Zones 5-7). Where winter temperatures fluctuate, poppies may break dormancy during warm periods, only to be struck down a few days later by a frost. Winter mulching can sometimes protect them, but don't mulch during the rest of the year, or you'll invite crown rot. Also, poppies hate wet feet during their late-summer dormant period, so don't water them in late spring when their foliage begins to brown.

WILDFLOWERS

I have a **traditional landscape** that includes an evergreen foundation planting, a number of specimen shrubs, and a large lawn. Is there some way I can incorporate wildflowers into existing plantings, or will I need to tear them out and start from scratch?

You don't need to do anything drastic to incorporate wildflowers into your garden. Many of them are perfectly appropriate in a traditional garden that has a large proportion of nonnative plants. Your major concern will be to choose plants whose moisture, light, and soil requirements match the conditions of your site.

One of my gardening goals is to have **color throughout the year.** Is that possible with wildflowers?

With careful planning, year-round color is certainly possible. Just be sure to pick species with bloom periods that overlap each other; as one species completes its life cycle, another species will begin to bloom and will take its place. Also, be sure to plant a mix of perennials and annuals. The annuals will bloom for many weeks or even all season, providing continuous color and interest to fill any intervals between waves of perennial flowers. In fall and winter, foliage, fruits, and seed pods will offer a beauty unique to those seasons.

How can I get my wildflowers to **bloom for a longer period?**

Deadheading—that is, removing blossoms that are past their prime—encourages wildflowers to bloom longer and more profusely, and it also keeps the plants looking fresh and tidy. However, this practice isn't appropriate if you want to collect seed from your wildflower garden for propagating, because it prevents seed production.

Four years ago I planted a small **meadow of wildflowers** and native grasses from a commercial seed mix. It's beautiful, but some of the plants that bloomed heavily the first season aren't as dominant anymore. Is it normal for a meadow to change like this from year to year?

Yes. A wildflower meadow is a complex, interactive plant community that evolves over time. Annuals are its main source of color until the slower-developing perennials mature. Also, the species that are best adapted to a particular site will eventually come to dominate. In time the balance of species will tend to stabilize, but there will always be differences from year to year because of weather conditions such as a mild winter or a wet summer.

Which wildflowers are suited to an exposed spot in a **desert garden** that is in full sun almost all day in summer?

Southwestern verbena, desert marigold, and desert mallow are just three of the many attractive wildflowers that will thrive in this hot, dry microhabitat.

Water drains from several neighboring properties into my backyard, so the soil is often damp and the lawn is growing poorly. Are wildflowers a sensible **alternative to turf grass?**

Although the majority of wildflowers would do no better than your lawn, some tolerate or even demand the soggy conditions you describe, including such fine ornamentals as sweet flag, swamp milkweed, rose mallow, blue flag, and cardinal flower.

My family enjoys watching the **birds** that visit our garden, and we also value them as a natural means of pest control. We already have a number of trees and shrubs with fruits that attract birds and would like to plant some wildflowers that would increase the food supply. What are some especially good choices for this purpose?

You can attract a variety of birds with an array of different seed- or fruit-producing annuals, perennials, and grasses, such as asters, compass plant, fire pink, goat's-rue, goldenrod, jack-in-the-pulpit, mountain mint, partridgeberry, pickerelweed, purple coneflower, rudbeckia, Rocky Mountain bee plant, sideoats grama, spikenard, sunflowers, switch grass, tickseed, and wild geranium. Hummingbirds are attracted to nectar-producing flowers such as bee balm, cardinal flower, copper iris, columbine, lupine, monkshood, penstemon, fire pink, sage, spider lily, spigelia, verbena, wild four-o'clocks, wild hyssop, and yucca.

My yard is rather small, and it's already so full of plants that I'm not sure I can fit in any wildflowers. Is it worth trying to grow some in pots or in **window boxes?**

Growing wildflowers in containers is a wonderful way to enjoy the benefits of native plants where space is at a premium, and they are just as appropriate as other annuals and perennials. They provide concentrated splashes of color and can be moved as light conditions change or retired to an unobtrusive spot when their blooming season ends. They are also a great way to introduce children to the pleasures of growing plants. Among the many attractive natives for container plantings are baby-blue-eyes, bitterroot, clarkia, common stonecrop and wild stone crop, California poppy, Drummond phlox, mealy blue sage, purple saxifrage, and Tahoka daisy. Water plants suited to container gardening include fragrant water lily and pickerelweed.

BULBS

I would like to grow bulbs in partial shade, but I understand they don't do well under some trees. Which kinds of **trees** should I avoid?

Maples, beeches, and other trees with shallow, fibrous roots are the ones to avoid. Bulbs and most other kinds of plants have a hard time competing with them for nutrients, water, and growing space. Also avoid evergreens and other trees with low canopies that prevent at least a half-day of filtered light from getting through.

I have more bulbs than I need for this fall. Can I **save bulbs** to plant next fall?	Unlike some seeds, bulbs cannot be held from one year to the next, because the moisture in their tissues will dry out and they will die.
We have had a mild winter so far, and my daffodils and tulips are coming up too early. Now we are expecting some **hard freezes.** How do I protect my bulbs?	The surprisingly tough foliage of these plants can take temperatures down to around 15° F. Below that point, the leaves may be "burned"—dried out by the cold—unless you cover or surround the plants with a light mulch. Even if the foliage is damaged, however, it doesn't seem to greatly affect later bloom and overall plant performance.
I think my newly planted bulbs must have frozen, because we had a very cold winter and they didn't come up this spring. When I dug them, they were **soft and mushy.** How can I keep this from happening again?	You can do several things: Plant your bulbs early, and at a depth at least 3 times their height; water well after planting to initiate root growth, because well-rooted bulbs resist frost damage better; mulch after planting to keep the soil temperature stable while the bulbs are rooting; and make sure the area is well drained, because soil that holds too much moisture is more likely to freeze and to encourage rot.
My double daffodils send up nice big fat **buds that never open.** What is the problem?	Your plants are experiencing "blasting." Double daffodils are especially susceptible to blasting, which happens when the plump buds are subjected to sudden freezing, high temperatures, or insufficient moisture. Protect buds from temperature extremes and water well. Some new cultivars have been developed that are blast resistant.
My bulb **foliage gets too long** and flops over, leaving an unsightly mess in my garden. How can I keep my plants from getting so tall?	Plants grow too tall and leggy when they do not have enough light. Most bulbs that do not get at least a half-day of sun not only flop over but also have sparse blooms. Transplant the bulbs to a sunnier location; fertilize and water well; and thin out overhanging vegetation to let in more light. For future plantings on this site, choose cultivars that are more shade tolerant.
How can I figure out where to put down **fertilizer** for my bulbs in fall when there is no remaining foliage to guide me?	Plant *Muscari* (grape hyacinth) bulbs around the edges of your other bulbs; the foliage will emerge in the fall and show you where to fertilize. Or place markers such as vinyl plant labels or even golf tees around the edge of your planting in the spring; they will stay around to show you the way. Finally, you could take photographs of your plot in the spring and use them as a guide.

I use **bone meal** to fertilize my bulbs, as the old gardening books advise. But the bulbs just aren't blooming well. What's going wrong?

Bone meal is not a complete fertilizer; it supplies only phosphorus and calcium. Bulbs also need nitrogen, potash, and trace elements. If you wish to fully fertilize your bulbs using only organic nutrient sources, you must add blood meal or cottonseed meal for nitrogen and "New Jersey Greensand" or wood ashes for potash and trace elements. Or you can use a ready-formulated fertilizer made just for bulbs. A 9-9-6 slow-release formula is best for tulips and members of the lily family but can be used for all bulbs. A 5-10-20 slow-release formula with trace elements is best for daffodils and members of the amaryllis family.

Many of my bulbs have **stopped blooming,** and others aren't blooming as well as they used to. Do I need to dig them up and divide them?

That is one solution, but perhaps an easier and more efficient way would be to fertilize the clumps to resupply the nutrients the bulbs have used up as they multiplied over the years. Once they have enough nutrients, along with moisture and sunshine, most of those old clumps will bloom gloriously.

Something is eating my tulip and crocus bulbs underground. Could it be **moles,** and how do I deal with this problem?

Moles are carnivorous and do not eat plants. The underground bulb monster is more than likely a vole, also known as a field mouse. One way to protect your bulbs is to plant them a bit deeper than normal; voles work in the top 3 to 4 inches of soil. Another is to put a handful of sharp-edged, crushed gravel—pieces about the size of a fingernail—around each bulb; voles do not like to dig through or move around in gravelly soil.

ROSES

We have a summer place right **on the ocean** in Massachusetts. Are there any roses that will grow in this setting?

Any of the rugosa species and most hybrid rugosas, such as 'Blanc Double de Coubert' or 'Belle Poitevine', will grow and bloom in your situation. Rugosas tolerate salt spray and will grow in sand dunes unattended. In fact, the Japanese native species has naturalized on beaches in the northeastern and northwestern United States.

My yard has a lot of **shade.** Are there any roses that will grow in it?

Roses need sun to perform well. The best ones to try under your conditions would be the modern hybrid musks, such as 'Ballerina', 'Belinda', 'Buff Beauty', or 'Prosperity'. If they don't grow and bloom there, no rose will.

I get **black spot** on my roses every year. I really don't want to use chemical fungicides, but I'm getting desperate. Is there any way I can keep the disease from ruining my plants without adding toxic chemicals to the garden?

Try this year-round preventive program that uses nonharmful products: Before the first frost, spray your roses with a commercial antidesiccant, according to label directions, to keep any fungus spores off the leaves during the winter. Then, while the plants are still dormant in the spring, spray them with wettable or liquid sulfur fungicide, followed by a thorough spray of dormant oil. Keep applying the sulfur periodically until frost—every week to 10 days at most. Don't spray sulfur, though, when the temperature is 85° F or higher, because it may burn the foliage, and keep it away from rugosa roses and their hybrids altogether; rugosas are damaged by sulfur—but they're immune to most fungi in the first place. This treatment will control not only black spot but also rust and powdery mildew, as well as infestations of aphids, thrips, and mites.

Are there any roses that **deer** do not eat?

Probably not. Try planting companions that deer dislike, such as rosemary or artemisia. Sometimes people put wire and fencing around their roses to keep deer from browsing, but this defeats the purpose of roses beautifying the garden. Instead, lay wire mesh on the ground near and in the rose bed, and plant ground covers such as ivy, phlox, or dianthus, making the mesh invisible. Deer will not step into these areas.

GROUND COVERS AND VINES

I built a shaded flagstone terrace where the roots of a nearby maple restricted my gardening efforts. Now I spend too much time pulling weeds **between the stones.** Can I plant anything in these spaces to reduce maintenance and add interest?

Plant the narrowest crevices with *Sagina subulata* (Corsican pearlwort), a fine plant for paving areas with its creeping, mossy evergreen foliage and tiny white spring flowers. In wider spaces you can establish *Mentha requienii* (Corsican mint), with ground-hugging leaves that emit a delicious fragrance of peppermint when trod upon occasionally, and *Mazus reptans,* a creeper with purple-blue to white flowers. For extra interest, but not to be walked on, consider *Lysimachia nummularia* 'Aurea' (creeping Jenny), with rounded yellow leaves and yellow blossoms in summer, or one of the several cultivars of *Ajuga,* with colored or variegated foliage.

The back of my lot slopes down so steeply from my house that the **soil is washing away.** I want to terrace the land for planters, but I'm concerned because the area is large and I might be creating a monster in terms of maintenance. What do you suggest?

Why not terrace the upper portion closest to your house and clothe the lower part in shrubs and ground covers? Plants with dense root systems, such as cotoneaster, *Hypericum calycinum* (St.-John's-wort), or juniper, will help prevent erosion. You would be well advised to call a landscape architect to prepare a plan for the terraced portion. A professional can help you select the most cost-effective material for a retaining wall and can engineer the wall to stand up to the force of soil and water pushing against it.

Are there any **wildflowers** that I could use **as a ground cover** to control soil erosion on a slope in my side yard?

New England aster, lanceleaf coreopsis, Indian blanket, and Rocky Mountain penstemon are all excellent choices for solving this problem.

I've had no luck luring **hummingbirds** to my shade garden. Most plants recommended for this purpose seem to be sun lovers, and others bloom only briefly. Do you have any suggestions?

One of the best plants for attracting hummingbirds is *Lonicera sempervirens* (trumpet or coral honeysuckle). It is also one of the most beautiful and longest-flowering vines you can bring into the garden. Train it up a trellis, where it will grow 10 to 15 feet high. The 2-inch-long blossoms are scarlet with orange throats and appear in great numbers from midspring to fall. The plant succeeds in partial shade, although it will blossom better in full sun. It is hardy to Zone 4.

I have a **tiny city garden** that is walled in on all sides with almost no planting space around the patio. How can I make it a year-round garden that is full of plants that bloom in succession?

If you can't go outward go up: Plant the space thickly with climbers. Combine vines so that when one is finished, another will bloom—for example, a planting of *Clematis montana*, 'New Dawn' climbing roses, and *Clematis paniculata (C. maximowicziana)* to cover spring, summer, and fall. Use bold foliage plants like *Yucca filamentosa* and *Mahonia bealei* for accents. Make a dense evergreen background by planting ivies or *Clematis armandii*. On the patio, set pots of annuals and bulbs in groups, or arrange them on a baker's rack for even more planting space.

SHADE GARDENING

The **potted plants** I grow on my shaded terrace never have that lush, overflowing look that I see in pictures in books and magazines. What am I doing wrong?

The secret is to be *very* generous initially with the number of plants used in each pot; regularly pinch back new buds on plants that require it to promote bushy growth; never let the soil dry out completely; and use a freely draining potting mix that contains a slow-release fertilizer. After 2 months, start applying a liquid fertilizer every 10 to 14 days. By early to midsummer your containers should be spilling over with lush growth.

My outside sitting area is shaded by day, but I enjoy it the most at **night** during the hot summer months. How can I add horticultural interest for this very special time?

A few wonderful shade garden plants are perfect for these conditions. The pure white lilylike flowers of *Hosta plantaginea* open fully at night to release a honey-scented fragrance. Nicotianas are also fragrant at night. If you have a spot nearby that receives several hours of sun, be sure to put in the hauntingly fragrant *Ipomoea alba* (moonflower) vine, with its enormous white blossoms that open around sunset and glow in the moonlight. Look also for new *Hemerocallis* cultivars called nocturnal bloomers, which keep their blossoms open into evening, and extended bloomers, whose flowers stay open for up to 2 days.

What can I plant to give me lots of fragrance in my shade garden?

You should rely upon a succession of plants through the seasons and avoid the many species that are fragrant only at close range. From late winter to early spring, cultivars of *Hamamelis mollis* and *H.* x *intermedia* waft their enticing fragrance over the awakening landscape. As spring progresses, *Viburnum carlesii* (Koreanspice viburnum) will add its own tangy scent. Few plants are more fragrant from midspring to early summer than azaleas. One of the best is *Rhododendron arborescens* (sweet azalea). In summer, mass plantings of night-fragrant *Hosta plantaginea* and annuals such as *Lobularia maritima* (sweet alyssum) and the night-fragrant nicotianas are very effective. Finish up in autumn with another native, *Hamamelis virginiana*.

My shade garden really goes into the doldrums in summer. Although I plant drifts of impatiens and begonias, I miss the individuality and charm of blooming perennials and shrubs at this time. What can I plant to enliven the scene?

In addition to the unlimited potential of daylilies, here are a dozen stalwart perennials to bridge your early-to-late-summer flower gap: *Aconitum napellus*, *Astilbe* x *arendsii* cultivars, Chelone *lyonii* (pink turtlehead), *Chrysogonum virginianum*, *Cimicifuga racemosa* (black cohosh) and *C. americana* (American bugbane), *Dicentra eximia* cultivars and hybrids, hosta, *Ligularia dentata* 'Desdemona', Lilium (lily), *Physostegia virginiana* (false dragonhead) cultivars, *Stokesia laevis* (Stokes' aster), and *Thalictrum rochebrunianum* (lavender mist meadow rue). Two very hardy native shrubs for outstanding blossoms in July are *Aesculus parviflora* (bottlebrush buckeye) and *Rhododendron prunifolium* (plum-leaved azalea), a real beauty with blossoms of glowing orange-red.

I'm starting a woodland shade garden, but the site has lots of poison ivy. How should I get rid of it?

Use great caution when removing this plant; even people who have always been immune to it can develop a sensitivity. Avoid direct contact, contaminated clothing or pet fur, and even smoke from burning plants. With a long-handled hoe, uproot small plants as soon as you notice them. Spray larger plants with the herbicide glyphosate; repeat if necessary. If the poison ivy has ascended a tree, cut its stems near the base with a long-handled pole saw and treat the basal portions with herbicide. Wearing washable cloth gloves or a double layer of disposable latex gloves, dig a hole about 2 feet deep and bury all pruned and dead plant parts. If you are particularly sensitive or if the infestation is large, seek professional help to eradicate the plants.

HERBS

I love to grow roses and wonder if I can plant my herbs with them.

Absolutely. Roses and herbs make ideal companions. Plant sun-loving herbs such as lavender, rosemary, thyme, and sage near roses to highlight their blooms. But be sure to space the plants generously to give roses good air circulation.

A cottage garden would fit in perfectly outside my kitchen door. How can I achieve the look of **lush informality** using herbs?

Herbs are particularly well suited to a cottage garden design. But don't let the seemingly random nature of a cottage garden fool you; it takes careful planning to achieve the casual effect. Begin by listing the plants and combinations you want to include. When you plant, place herbs, annuals, and perennials close together so that bare soil is covered quickly. If some plants die or simply don't look good together, remove them and experiment until the planting pleases you. Try arranging foliage and flowers in specific color combinations such as gray and red or blue and gold. Or plant freely and see what pairings of foliage, plant shape, and flower form and color arise.

I've always wanted a **knot garden,** but I don't have a big yard. Any suggestions?

Create a miniature knot garden in a container. Select herbs that take well to container culture, such as basil, thyme, chamomile, and rosemary, and keep them neatly pruned. Devise a knot pattern that looks good when viewed from above—star shapes and figure eights are only two of the possibilities. If you can't overwinter the miniature knot garden, harvest the herbs at the end of the growing season and start over in the spring.

What's the **best way to start herbs**—from seed or from plants?

Sow fast-growing, short-lived annuals such as dill, coriander, and nasturtium directly in your garden. Many biennials, including angelica and clary sage, also take best to direct-sowing. Perennial herbs can be grown from seed, division, cuttings, or layering. The method will vary depending on the plant. For example, thyme, lavender, rosemary, and mint hybridize freely and are best grown from cuttings. Other perennials such as lovage are best propagated by division.

I would like to **harvest seeds** from my herbs, but I don't know when or how to harvest them.

Seeds are ripe when they have just turned brown. Cut the seed heads on a dry day and place them in a brown bag. Let the seeds dry for 1 to 2 weeks, and when they are completely dry, store them in airtight jars.

When I order new herb plants, how do I know if they are **correctly labeled?**

First check the plants in the herbs section starting on page 268. If you believe a plant is labeled incorrectly but can't identify it yourself, cut a stem of the plant when it is in bloom and take both leaves and flowers to a nursery or garden center for identification. You can also press the specimen and have it identified at a later date. If there is a chance the herb in question is poisonous, be sure not to ingest it.

Are there any culinary herbs that will grow in a shady container?

Sweet cicely (*Myrrhis odorata*) and chervil (*Anthriscus cerefolium*) prefer shade; mint, angelica, and lovage grow well in light shade. Although you can grow sun-loving herbs in light shade, their flavor will be less intense and often they will not flower. In hot climates, some gardeners plant herbs in a location that gets midday shade to prevent them from being scorched by the summer sun.

Can I have a productive herb garden indoors?

Herbs generally grow best in the garden, where they can enjoy full sun, fresh air, and plenty of soil. If you want to cultivate herbs indoors, they will perform better under commercial plant lights. During warm seasons, the herbs will need more water, but take care not to overwater them in winter.

Is it true that herbs have better flavor if they are grown in poor soil?

No. Herbs have the fullest flavor when planted in moderately fertile soil that encourages healthy, strong growth. Soil that is too rich or too poor will result in herbs with compromised flavor and a greater susceptibility to disease.

Will the flavor of an herb decrease if I fertilize it? Should I limit the amount of compost applied to the soil?

Using moderate amounts of fertilizer will not diminish an herb's flavor. However, heavy fertilization will encourage weak and unhealthy growth, particularly in culinary herbs. Compost is a great soil amendment for herbs, but again, don't overdo it.

When should I pinch back my herbs to make them bushier?

It varies with the life cycle of each herb. Rosemary, for example, benefits from an early, low pinching to encourage side branching. Most perennial herbs respond well to a midspring pinching back to stimulate dense growth. Annual herbs with a short life cycle, such as dill and coriander, do not require any pinching. When harvesting them, take the entire plant. Annual herbs whose leaves you plan to harvest throughout the growing season, such as basil and chervil, should be pinched back in early summer to encourage bushiness. Removing their flower buds whenever they appear will hasten the growth of new foliage.

I want to rejuvenate an established lavender plant that has grown leggy and produces few blooms. Will pruning it do the job?

Yes. Prune your lavender in early spring just as new growth emerges. To rejuvenate an old plant, cut it back close to the base instead of pruning it lightly. Although you may lose the plant completely if it has grown weak and feeble, more likely it will return stronger and healthier than before.

How do you make an herb tea?

Herb teas can be made with either fresh or dried herbs, but fresh herbs result in a more pungent brew. Place the shredded leaves, seeds, or chopped root or bark in a teapot, using about 3 teaspoons of fresh or 1 heaping teaspoon of dried ingredients per cup. Add boiling water, let the tea steep for 3 to 5 minutes, strain, and serve. If you like strong tea, use a larger quantity of herbs; brewing the tea more than 5 minutes may result in an off taste.

Which herbs should I grow for tea?

Delicious herb teas are made from pungent herbs such as lemon verbena, which has a tart, lemon flavor; chamomile, which is fragrant and relaxing; sage, which tastes best in the cold months because it has a warming quality; and anise seed, which possesses a warm and wonderful licorice flavor. Create blends to suit your own taste. For example, peppermint combined with spearmint makes a soothing tea.

Is there any trick to preparing herbal vinegars?

No, they are easy to make. To quickly extract herbal essences, warm up any type of vinegar—wine vinegar is a good choice—and pour it into a sterile bottle filled with your favorite culinary herbs. Avoid using metal utensils, which may react with the vinegar, producing an unpleasant taste. You can also make flavored vinegar by adding herbs to a bottle of vinegar and setting it in the sun for 2 weeks. Strain the vinegar and replace the herbs with attractive fresh ones if you plan to display the vinegar or give it as a gift. Choice herbs used to flavor vinegars include tarragon, lemon verbena, basil, garlic, and chili peppers.

Is there a fun way to teach children about the life cycle of plants from seed to harvest using herbs?

Try making a salad farm using edible herbs that grow easily from seed. As they tend the miniature farm, children will learn about seed germination, a seedling's growth cycle, plant care, and when and how to harvest. If you have seeds that were collected from the garden, show children how to separate the ripe seeds from the rest of the plant. Sow the seed in rows and label each row. Watch the plants grow, and harvest them for salads. Some of the best plants to grow from seed are coriander, corn salad, dill, lettuce, nasturtium, purple hyacinth bean, arugula, and sweet fennel.

VEGETABLES

Is companion planting—for example, putting beans and onions side by side because they like each other— a valid organic technique or an old wives' tale?

Companion planting is a valid technique, but not because plants "like" each other. It works for one of several reasons: because the companions have different needs and thus don't compete with one another for nutrients; because their root zones are at different levels and their roots don't compete for space; or because one of the companions helps protect the other from predatory insects.

My father planted his vegetable garden in rows with good results, and I'm inclined to do the same thing. But nowadays everyone talks about **raised beds.** What are the advantages of raised beds?

The main advantages are that they are more productive and take less work than conventional row gardening. Because you prepare the soil intensively with organic matter and fertilizers, you can plant vegetables very closely, getting more crops from far less space than row gardening requires. As the leaves of the vegetables touch, they shade the soil and slow weed growth. Paths don't take up as much space in a raised-bed garden as they do when vegetables are planted in rows, so you don't have to spend as much time weeding and maintaining them.

I'm building a deck and have **pressure-treated scrap wood** left over. Can I use it as an edging material for raised beds, or would the chemicals used in the pressure treatment contaminate vegetables grown in the beds?

The chemicals used to pressure-treat wood are quite toxic and might very well contaminate your crops. For raised beds, use ordinary wood scrap or cheap grades of redwood, black locust, or other rot-resistant wood for longevity. You can also make raised beds without constructing edges. They really aren't needed except to improve appearance, although they may cut down on grasses creeping into the beds.

Is **rooting hormone**—the kind you use to stimulate root formation on cuttings—organic?

Yes. Rooting hormones are naturally occurring plant substances and are perfectly safe to use in an organic garden. Cuttings from sweet potato vines should be dipped in rooting hormone before planting, and you can also dip root cuttings from small bush fruits such as currants to stimulate rooting. Gardeners in areas with long growing seasons can also use the hormone to root stem cuttings of their early eggplant, tomato, and pepper crops for subsequent plantings.

TREES AND SHRUBS

Are there any **shrubs** that don't have to be **pruned?**

Unfortunately, no. You can start by buying shrub cultivars that have been selected specifically for their compact growth form and neat branching habits. But in any event, the conscientious gardener should follow the three Ds of pruning: Remove dead, diseased, and deformed branches at any time in a plant's life. To reduce the amount of pruning that you have to do, plant shrubs in a space large enough to allow them to achieve their mature dimensions without becoming obstacles. Also, try to remove no more than a third of the top growth at any time; this will limit the amount of suckering that occurs. Also, let shrubs assume their natural shape rather than pruning them into geometric globes and boxes.

Some of my **rhododendrons** have become **overgrown.** Can I cut them back? If so, when can I do this?

Rhododendrons usually need little or no pruning unless they get out of bounds, or if the growth becomes sparse, with long stretches of stem devoid of leaves. Then they will require drastic action. Cut back entire branches to within 2 feet of the ground, all at one time, just after the flowers have faded. You should see new sprouts from previously dormant buds on the old stems in about 4 to 8 weeks, but sometimes resprouting does not occur and the entire plant is lost. If this causes concern with a choice cultivar, you can take a more conservative approach by removing one-third of the branches at a time over a 3-year period.

How can I prevent **winter damage** to my broadleaf evergreens—rhododendrons, azaleas, and hollies—and also to evergreen perennials such as bergenia and Christmas and Lenten roses?

Sun and wind are usually the culprits in winter injury to evergreen plants. Leaves are most susceptible to damage when the plant becomes dehydrated, and drought conditions can often exist in the winter garden. Even though your neighbors may think you're crazy, water your evergreen plants in winter to help prevent injury to leaves and tender twigs. If you know that a plant is susceptible to winter damage, select a sheltered site that will provide some protection from wind and afternoon sun, such as against the north wall of the house or on the shady side of a tall hedge.

One spot in my **lawn stays wet,** and I am always getting my riding lawn mower stuck in it. Is there anything I can do short of putting in a tile drain?

There are many trees that thrive in wet areas, where they take up lots of water, thus drying the area. Some members of the willow family—pussy willow (*Salix discolor*), weeping willow (*S. babylonica*), and the corkscrew willow (*S. matsudana* 'Tortuosa')—are good choices. Be sure, though, that there are no walkways, terraces, or drainfields close by; willow roots are extremely invasive and can damage them.

What are some good **trees** to plant in front of a new two-story townhouse **on a very small lot?**

Choose deep-rooted species; avoid such trees as sweet gum and Norway maple, which have greedy, shallow roots that compete with nearby shrubbery and make it impossible to grow grass. In the past few years nurseries have introduced several narrow-crowned, upright selections of familiar shade trees suitable for use in small gardens and as street plantings. Trees with less than a 15-foot spread include *Pyrus calleryana* 'Chanticleer' (Callery pear), pyramidal *Carpinus betulus* 'Fastigiata' (European hornbeam), *Quercus robur* 'Fastigiata' (English oak), and one of the several red maples selected for upright form, such as *Acer rubrum* 'Armstrong'.

GARDEN DESIGN

I have many garden ideas for different parts of my property, but I have a **hard time visualizing** how they might all fit together. How can I work them out?

Go out into the landscape and try them. Place tall stakes where you think you would like trees; use hose, string, or powdered lime to define lawn shapes, paths, and beds; string up lines to represent fencing; spread out sheets or blankets where you might like a small paved area. Set outdoor furniture in places where you might want seating. Then look at these elements from different angles and keep making adjustments until you feel satisfied.

When I try to **copy planting schemes** I see in garden books, they don't always look right in my own garden. Why?

Apart from incompatible cultural requirements among plants, the most common cause for an unsuccessful duplication of a garden scheme in another location is the difference in scale, proportion, and conformation of the surrounding space. When you see a design that you like, check to determine whether the setting of the locale where you want to duplicate it is similar to that of the original. You're almost certain to be disappointed, for example, if you pick out an arrangement set against a fenced-in corner for reproduction at the edge of a lawn opening onto woods.

Many design books emphasize the importance of **shape and mass** in planting design, but I can't seem to get past the flower colors when I am making plant arrangements. How can I begin to see plants the way designers see them?

To see shape only, first try to look at your plant groupings as if they were all one color. Use a black-and-white photocopy of a garden view and trace an outline of trees, shrubs, and groups of smaller plants in the picture. Don't try to follow the outline shape in detail; generalize as much as possible, so that you end up with a diagram of circles, ovals, cones, horizontal lines, and so on. If the diagram turns out to be a series of boring circles, try adding vertical spikes or a taller cone shape to vary the composition. Once you have hit upon a pleasing combination of shapes, use this as the basis for working out a detailed planting plan that will include texture and color.

I've recently bought an older home with a rather boring landscape. I can't afford to redo the entire property at once. How can I **develop the garden gradually** over a period of, say, 5 years? In what order should I proceed?

Spend the first year getting to know your garden. Keep a notebook to record such data as when the plants bloom and how the sun strikes different areas throughout the day and in different seasons. Test the soil, and begin correcting any deficiencies. Bring in an arborist to evaluate the trees. The autumn and winter of the first year is a good time for removing diseased or poorly placed trees and planting new ones. The second year, put your money into "hardscape" items—an irrigation system, if needed, and patios, walkways, retaining walls, and fences. Protect trees during the construction process by surrounding the root zone with temporary fencing. During the third year, concentrate on shrubbery— thinning, transplanting, and adding color and texture. Use the fourth year to establish herbaceous beds. By the fifth year you should be ready to add the finishing touches—a sundial, perhaps, or garden art to serve as focal points.

Plant choices aside, are there certain garden designs that are more **maintenance free** than others?

Garden styles definitely affect maintenance requirements. In general, the more formal your design, the more upkeep the garden will need, because formality requires balance, symmetry, and exactness, which means more pruning and trimming of shrubs and trees. Informal designs, on the other hand, allow plants more freedom to follow natural growth patterns.

What designs would you advise for someone who has a **limited budget** as well as a **limited amount of time?**

After you decide which low-maintenance trees, shrubs, and evergreens you like, repeat them throughout your garden. The same holds true for herbaceous perennials: Limit the types of plants you choose, and plant more of them. However, you'll want to have a certain amount of plant diversity so that if disease strikes, you won't lose everything. Select and site your plants carefully to ensure against cultural, disease, or insect problems.

I have planted different gardens in our large suburban lot over the years, but now I don't have the time to keep up all the areas as well as I would like to. How can I revamp the gardens so they will look good with **less maintenance?**

Categorize the different garden areas according to the levels of maintenance needed to keep each looking good: intensive, moderate, or casual. Are the intensive areas too many, too scattered, and too far away to be noticed or enjoyed? If so, concentrate your efforts where they matter. Let the farther reaches revert to woodland. Turn a mixed border into a low-maintenance shrub border. Replace a struggling woodland garden with a hardy ground cover. Put your main effort into pruning a few key specimen trees and shrubs for shape and intensively maintaining a close-in flower border.

Along the foundation of my house I have combinations of evergreens, both needled and broadleaf, that tend to look like big lumps of green rather than a **designed grouping.** How can I create a more dramatic effect?

Select the most interesting evergreens as the basis for a revamped design—that is, the ones with the most distinct shape, foliage texture, or colors—and transplant to other areas the shrubs that have less character. If the open space is appealing, either keep it open and cover it with a mulch or plant it with a low ground cover whose color contrasts with the evergreens around it. If the open space calls for a plant, consider a deciduous one with twisting, sinuous trunks or branches, or one whose form or texture strongly contrasts with the plants around it.

I have a spot on a rise where the sun sets—a perfect place for **backlighting** plants with the late afternoon sun. What plants would look good with backlight?

The Japanese maple *Acer palmatum* with *Imperata cylindrica* 'Rubra' (Japanese blood grass) in front makes a great combination for backlighting, especially in fall, when the maple is turning color. Grapevines, black locust, and many other thin-leaved plants are also beautiful when the sun shines through them.

I try to put together perennials and annuals with matched flower colors, but the effect is rather haphazard. What's the secret to making good-looking **color combinations?**

The problem you describe is usually caused by too few plants in the combination. Single plants tend to recede to mere points of color when viewed from even a short distance. Try using drifts rather than just one, two, or three plants. A drift is a group of five to nine plants, all of the same variety, usually arranged in a shape with tapered ends. Drifts will give you broad swaths of color that can be combined by weaving their tapered ends into one another. These generous areas of color will have much more impact than the spotty color afforded by single plants.

Most days I get to enjoy my garden only in the evening, after work, when the light is low and failing. Are there any plants that I can combine to add interest to the **evening garden?**

As daylight fails, the cones, or color-sensing cells in the eye, begin to stop functioning in favor of the rods, or light-sensing cells. Colors on the red end of the spectrum appear to darken first, and eventually red looks black. The violet- and lavender-sensing cones are the last to lose their function in the dimming light. Thus, planting lavender or violet flowers will give you a startlingly fluorescent display as this shift occurs in the eye. Among perennials, a combination of *Platycodon grandiflorus* 'Blue' (balloon flower), *Adenophora confusa* (ladybells), and *Linum perenne* (blue flax) is an excellent choice for an evening garden.

I've tried lots of **plant combinations** but am still not satisfied that I've hit on one with exquisite beauty. How do I get beyond pretty to truly beautiful?

The foremost quality of any beautiful plant combination is simplicity. You may be using too many different plants or arranging them in a way that makes them hard to read visually. Some of the best ways to achieve simplicity include limiting your palette to just two or three kinds of plants (although you may use several of each kind in a massed effect); limiting your flower colors to variations on a single color theme; and planting them so that there is open space around or between them, even when they grow to full, mature size. Simple, beautiful combinations possess restraint, yet enough contrast in form, foliage, and color to stir the viewer's interest.

PLANTING AND MAINTENANCE

What's the easiest way to tackle the job of planting a **steep bank?**

Soil preparation is a must, since most banks have inadequate soil. For each plant, dig a deep hole and add amendments to the soil; stagger the placement of the holes to achieve a less linear effect. To control the growth of weeds on a slope, lay down landscape fabric and put the plants into the ground through slits cut in the fabric. Spread pine needles or shredded bark on top of the fabric; these materials tend to stay in place, whereas a chunky mulch like pine bark nuggets will slide off a steep slope. Terracing with landscape timbers or stone reduces potential erosion and increases moisture retention but requires a bigger investment of both labor and money.

What is the least time-consuming way to fertilize a garden?

Blended organic fertilizers are the backbone of any fertilizing program for low maintenance. They contain a great variety of mineral nutrients and organic molecules that are released slowly into the soil. Gardeners can also turn to timed-release fertilizer pellets; when applied in late winter, the pellets deliver nitrogen, phosphorus, and potassium evenly over an entire growing season.

What is manure tea and how do I use it?

Manure tea is one of the secrets to success in an organic garden. Put 1 gallon of fresh, rotted, or dried farm-animal manure or manure-based compost in a burlap or muslin bag and close it securely (use poultry, goat, horse, or cow manure only). Put the bag in a 5-gallon bucket and fill it with water. Let the manure steep for 3 days to a week. Spray this manure tea onto growing plants every 3 to 4 days. It is especially helpful when they are growing rapidly or setting flowers or fruit. You'll be amazed at how well plants respond.

I know some organic gardeners who swear by foliar seaweed spray. Is there any value in this?

Yes. Foliar seaweed spray is an extract of seaweed containing many trace elements that are essential for vigorous growth in many plants. These nutrients can be absorbed through a plant's leaves as well as its roots, so regular applications of foliar seaweed spray are certainly beneficial.

I'm a person who hates to weed. What can I do to keep weeding to a minimum?

It is much easier to remove a tiny weed seedling than a full-grown weed that has had time to develop long, tough roots. By weeding when the plants are young, you also remove them before they have a chance to go to seed, a situation that makes your weeding problems even worse.

Is one kind of mulch better than another?

Organic gardeners use all sorts of materials to cover bare soil— black plastic, cardboard, leaves, shredded bark, compost, grass clippings that are free of pesticides and herbicides, farm-animal bedding, and spoiled hay are just a few of the possibilities. Even stones can serve as mulch if they cover the surface of the soil completely. For most situations, it is best to use an organic mulch because it offers multiple benefits: suppressing weeds, conserving soil moisture, acting as a fertilizer, and decomposing into soil-conditioning humus.

Should I mulch my herbs? Which mulches do you recommend?

Like all plants, herbs should be mulched for weed control and in soils where moisture retention is a problem. But be sure to use a mulch that does not hold in too much moisture, and keep the mulch away from the crown of the plant to prevent rot. Mediterranean herbs such as rosemary, thyme, and oregano are especially prone to rotting if a heavy mulch is used. Gravel, sand, and poultry grit are good choices for herbs that like good drainage. Other options include cocoa hulls, fine pine chips, and pine needles, all of which add a handsome finish of color and texture to the garden.

When is the **best time to mulch** all of my plants—trees, shrubs, and flower beds?

Mulching after a recent rainfall would be ideal, and the best months are those during which the garden is dormant. Mulching later may bury and damage young bulb and perennial foliage. If you wait until the garden is actively growing to mulch, you'll spend a lot of extra time and effort working around your growing foliage so that you can apply the mulch evenly. The ground should be weed free before mulch is applied.

COMPOSTING AND SOIL CONDITIONING

I've tried making **compost,** but it doesn't heat up, and it **smells bad.** What's the problem?

It probably doesn't heat up because the pile doesn't have enough nitrogen-rich material such as fresh farm-animal manure. A pile that's layered with 3 or 4 parts plant debris to 1 part fresh manure and that's kept moist but not sopping wet will heat up. Your compost smells bad because little or no air is getting into the pile, and anaerobic bacteria are decomposing it. Rebuild it, adding manure and layering in straw, pine needles, or other coarse materials to get air into the pile. Aerobic bacteria will continue to decompose the pile, but it will not smell bad.

What is **sheet composting?**

It's a fancy name for covering the soil with the same kinds of organic matter used in a compost pile and letting them decay slowly, without turning or watering. Sheet composting has two advantages: It adds organic matter that conditions the soil as it decays, and it acts as a mulch to keep weed growth down and the soil moist. Make sure the material contains no weed seeds or other kinds of seeds; it won't be massive enough to heat up, so seeds will remain viable. On the downside, sheet-composted material may provide a breeding ground for slugs, pill bugs, earwigs, and other unwanted insects. It may also deplete the soil of nitrogen unless high-nitrogen materials such as farmyard manure are included.

I have tried to garden organically, and I compost all my plant debris—trimmings, old foliage, and weeds that I hoe from the garden—but it seems I have more weeds, disease, and insects every year. Why is **composting making things worse?**

You are probably composting weeds that have seeds, giving them a fertile place to germinate before returning them to the garden to grow strong. Instead, put weeds that have gone to seed into the trash. Also, take care not to compost any diseased plant foliage. Many disease-causing organisms have resistant spores or go through resting stages that can survive the rigors of the composting process, particularly if your pile doesn't heat up sufficiently. Lacing your compost with 5-10-5 fertilizer or a compost activator, and turning it so that the outer, cooler portions are moved inward will help generate the heat necessary to kill insect larvae and disease organisms that may find their way into your compost pile.

Are there **things that shouldn't go into a compost pile?**

Yes. Don't use domestic pet or human waste, since it may carry dangerous diseases or parasites. Don't use meat or meat scraps, which attract vermin and cause a stench as they decay. Don't compost diseased portions of plants that you've cut away; dispose of them with the household trash or by burning, if that is permitted in your area. Don't use coal ashes, as these contain toxic wastes; wood ashes in moderation are fine. Don't add any synthetic materials or chemicals or any plants that have been treated with herbicides or pesticides. And don't compost weeds that have set seed, or you'll spread them around the garden when you use the compost. Manures, vegetable and fruit kitchen waste, and nonseedy plant debris are all fine.

I've had problems with **animals disturbing the compost pile.**

An easy solution is to keep special garbage-eating worms called red wigglers in a container that marauding animals can't get into, and let them turn your kitchen scraps into compost. A sturdy wood box with a lid and a hardware-cloth bottom will serve nicely, or you can buy a plastic worm bin from a mail-order garden supply company, along with red wigglers.

Where's the **best place to build a compost pile**—in the shade or in the sun? And should I cover it with black plastic?

The best place for the pile is close to the garden so the hose reaches it and you don't have to carry the finished compost very far. A shady spot is probably best because the composting organic matter won't dry out as fast as it would in sun. Covering the pile with black plastic holds in moisture and keeps the temperature in the pile higher, so it decays faster. The plastic will also prevent hard rains from dissolving and leaching nutrients from the pile.

My **soil is very acid,** and I need to raise its pH from 5 to at least 6.5. What's the organic way to do this?

Two substances that are especially good at raising a soil's pH are leached wood ashes and ground limestone. Wood ashes work faster, but ground limestone sweetens the soil over a longer period of time. Use 10 pounds of limestone or 2 pounds of wood ashes per 100 square feet, worked into the top 6 inches of soil, to raise the pH 1 point. Don't raise it more than 1 point per year. If you use 10 pounds per 100 square feet this year and 5 pounds next year, your soil pH should increase 1.5 points to reach your target level.

How do I **prepare soil** in the different sections of my garden **to accommodate various perennials** I want to plant? It seems that some species like more acid soil and some like more alkaline soil.

Of the thousands of perennials to select from, only a few have pH requirements that fall outside the average range for most garden soils. Maintain a pH between 6 and 7, and almost any perennial will do well. For those plants that require more alkalinity, dig dolomitic limestone into the soil at the planting location; it won't leach out into the surrounding soil. In the case of acid-loving plants, try adding peat moss to the planting site.

My soil is a **heavy clay.** What amendments should I add to improve the structure of my soil?

Your first impulse might be to add sand, but while sand will loosen your heavy clay, it is not enough to transform it into a good garden soil. You will need to add lots of organic matter as well. Compost is an excellent choice; you can also use peat moss, leaf mold, bark chips or ground bark, sawdust, or well-rotted animal manure.

What is **poultry grit?** Why should I add it to the soil in which I grow herbs?

Poultry grit is finely crushed rock—usually granite—given to chickens and other poultry to aid their digestion. It is available in three sizes and can be purchased at a farm-supply store. Medium-sized poultry grit added to soil improves drainage best and increases aeration around plant roots. In heavy clay soils it works better than sand because its particles are larger than grains of sand. Since poultry grit is inorganic and does not break down over time, add it to the soil only once. Herb gardeners can also use poultry grit as a mulch, spreading a 3-inch layer over the soil surface.

PESTS AND DISEASES

How can I attract **beneficial insects** to my garden?

Reserve a portion of the garden for whatever weeds happen to appear there. Beneficial insects are adapted to the local flora, using it as a source of food, as hunting grounds for prey, and for shelter. Also, make sure you plant a number of umbelliferous plants— such as fennel, carrot, and dill—in your garden. These are nectar sources for several beneficials, including green lacewings. Finally, don't use pesticides. Beneficial insects are more susceptible to pesticides than pests and will be the first to be killed off.

I understand that **rotenone, ryania, and sabadilla** are all organically acceptable pesticides. Should I dust the garden routinely with them as a preventive?

No. Although these pesticides are derived from plants and are active for a comparatively short time, each of them kills a broad spectrum of insects and can do the same kind of ecological damage as chemical pesticides. The goal is not a garden free of pests—you simply want to keep their numbers to a manageable level. Try beneficial insects, physical controls such as traps, and other, less toxic methods of organic insect control before reaching for these pesticides. They should be used only as a last resort.

I've heard that organic gardeners use **homemade sprays** containing hot chili peppers, garlic, or tobacco on their vegetables to ward off pests. Do they work?

Yes. Many insects won't go near a plant sprayed with these substances. But never use a tobacco spray on any vegetables of the nightshade family, which includes tomatoes, potatoes, and eggplant; tobacco is also a member of the nightshade family and harbors a mosaic virus that can be spread to these crops by spraying.

Do you recommend using **traps** to catch insects like Japanese beetles?

Insect traps today are quite improved over the ones on the market a few years ago. Be sure not to place them directly in the garden, however, because you will only attract insects from outside areas to the very plants you are trying to protect.

Some of my **herbs die out** in summer when the weather gets hot and humid. What is the problem and what can I do about it?

In regions of the country with extended periods of hot, humid weather, the branches of herbs may turn brown and die as a result of diseases caused by soil fungi. These disease organisms are activated when plants are stressed and the weather is humid. Removing all the diseased portions of the plant will help to revive it, but if the herb is severely infected, dispose of it entirely. Then try a new plant in a different location in soil that has been amended with poultry grit, which enhances air circulation at the root zone.

Most years my strawberry plants get **powdery mildew** on their leaves. How can I prevent this organically?

Thin your plants to increase the flow of air between them, and pick off and destroy infected foliage. You can apply lime sulfur, available at garden centers, as directed on the package, or spray plants with a solution of 1 tablespoon of baking soda in a gallon of water; adding ⅛ to ¼ teaspoon of insecticidal soap will help the spray stick to the leaves. Don't increase the proportion of baking soda, as a higher concentration can damage leaves.

How can I prevent **red spider infestations** on my astilbes? A miticide I used killed most of the foliage.

Moisture-retentive soil and an inch of water a week during drought are essential for astilbes, especially in warm climates. Dryness and sun are an open invitation to red spider infestations. If dull green leaves and characteristic webbing show that an infestation has occurred, spray the undersides of the leaves often with a forceful stream of water to knock off the pests.

One of my perennials has **yellow, stunted foliage.** When I dug it up, it had **nodules all over the roots.** What is the problem?

More than likely your plant has root knot nematodes. You can control this pest by using a nontoxic material made from ground crab shells that is available at better garden centers.

The branches of my **bay tree** (*Laurus nobilis*) are often **covered with a brown crust.** What is the problem and what is the best way for me to get rid of it?

Piercing-sucking scale insects—shiny brown and shell-like in appearance—are a common problem on bay trees. Left untreated, scales will spread to the foliage of a bay tree and eventually kill it. To control a small infestation, try scrubbing them off with a cotton-tipped swab or soft toothbrush dipped in soapy water or a solution of 1 part each of rubbing alcohol and water. For a larger infestation, spray on a horticultural oil; once this is done, however, you must refrain from using the leaves for culinary purposes.

I have a bed of irises that is overrun with **iris borer.** What should I do?

First, establish a new iris bed in another location. Then dig up and divide irises from your infested bed in mid to late summer, selecting only healthy, young rhizomes. Throw away all the old rhizomes and plant debris. Dip the transplants in a solution of 1 part chlorine bleach to 9 parts water, and let them dry in the shade before planting. Keep the new bed clear of decaying foliage to discourage the adult moths from laying their eggs in the vicinity.

My **peonies** have petals that are **brown all over,** and they don't open properly. What is wrong and how can I correct it?

One of three things could be happening. First, your flower buds could be suffering from excessive heat—more than 85° F—at bloom time (called bullheading). Second, your peonies could have a fungal disease called botrytis blight. Third, the damage you describe could be caused by tiny sucking insects called thrips.

Here in the West, **gophers** are an awful problem. They burrow through the soil, eating the roots off many plants, even pulling whole plants down into their burrows. What can I do to control them?

A king snake, black snake, or gopher snake is a great boon where gophers are a problem, and some cats are avid gopher hunters. But lacking these predators, you might try mechanical gopher traps.

Common Garden Weeds

Amaranthus retroflexus (Redroot Pigweed)

This annual produces as many as 200,000 seeds per plant. Some western pigweeds break loose from their roots and roll like tumbleweeds across the land, scattering their seeds as they go. Control pigweed by uprooting young plants or cutting the stems off at ground level.

Ambrosia artemisiifolia (Common Ragweed)

Although the seed is a favorite food of birds, ragweed pollen is the bane of hay fever sufferers. The seeds need light for germination, so a layer of mulch is a good preventive. The shade cast by larger plants will also discourage growth. Mow or cut plants down before they go to seed.

Brassica kaber (Wild Mustard)

Introduced to the Americas as a seasoning, wild mustard has spread to become a pest species. Dig out or cut plants to the ground before they flower to prevent seeds from forming. The seeds are numerous and remain viable for years.

Cenchrus species (Sandbur)

The spiny seeds of these annual or biennial grasses are painful for humans and animals alike and, if plentiful enough, can make a yard unusable. As the name implies, sandburs prefer sandy soils. When they invade a lawn, their blades are camouflaged and hard to see. Hand pull or dig, taking care not to touch the seeds.

Centaurea solstitialis (Star Thistle)

Fast becoming a serious pest in California, Washington, and Oregon, star thistle usually grows as an annual but sometimes acts like a biennial. Cut it down before the flowers form; the bracts around the flowers bear sharp spines.

Cerastium arvense (Field Chickweed)

This perennial weed grows in gardens throughout the United States. Destroy it with shallow cultivation before it can flower and go to seed. Gather up all the stems you've cut, since each one can form roots and develop into a new plant.

Chenopodium album (Lamb's-Quarters)

An annual that appears early in the season, lamb's-quarters grows in gardens all over the United States. Mulch beds to discourage germination, and pull out or cut down any plants that appear before they flower.

Cirsium arvense (Canada Thistle)

Despite its name, this perennial weed is a Eurasian native. A single plant can extend its root system over a large area, sending up numerous stems to create a massive stand. Cut stems down but don't hoe the plants, since root pieces start new plants. Treat persistent stands with a systemic herbicide.

Convolvulus arvensis (Field Bindweed)

This perennial has a huge root system that makes an established plant almost impossible to get rid of. Avoid tilling near the roots; severed pieces will produce new plants. Control with regular hoeing. Never allow plants to go to seed. Thick mulches help suppress germination.

Cyperus esculentus (Nut Sedge, Nut Grass)

Nut sedge, a perennial, is usually found in moist or poorly drained soil. Its roots send up new shoots whenever the main stem is cut. Dig up the roots or cut off new growth as it appears; this will eventually kill the plants. Use landscape fabric, not wood-chips or other organic mulches, to block the foliage.

Datura stramonium (Jimson Weed)

All parts of this annual are poisonous, so remove it as soon as you see it. Most herbicides don't affect it; hoe it or hand pull it, wearing gloves to protect against the spines that form on the flower capsules. Because of its poisons, jimson weed should be disposed of according to local ordinances for plant debris.

Digitaria ischaemum, D. sanguinalis (Crab Grass)

Crab grass, an annual, is well known for its sprawling presence in lawns, especially in places where the soil is compacted. Aerate the lawn and let turf grass grow taller than usual to shade out crab grass. In flower beds, dig it out before it sets seed; mulch to prevent seeds from sprouting.

Eleusine indica (Goose Grass)

Goose grass is an annual that commonly takes hold in a sparse lawn growing in compacted, nutrient-poor soil. Aerating the soil, fertilizing, and mowing the lawn higher all help to control the weed. Remove plants from the lawn by hand before they flower, and mulch beds to discourage seedlings.

Oxalis stricta (Wood Sorrel, Sourgrass)

This annual weed and its look-alike relative, the perennial *O. corniculata*, have seed capsules that explode and shoot seeds as far as 6 feet from the mother plant. Mulch to smother seeds or dig out the taproots.

Euphorbia maculata (Spotted Spurge)

This annual, which often takes root in pavement cracks, grows so low that the blades of a lawn mower pass above it, leaving the weed intact. Pull it out by the roots before it produces its tiny, pink-white flowers and thousands of seeds.

Phytolacca americana (Pokeweed)

Most pokeweed plants are seeded by birds, which relish pokeberries. If you can dig up this perennial's long taproot, do so. Otherwise, keep the stems cut to the ground; this will eventually starve out the plant.

Hordeum jubatum (Foxtail Barley, Wild Barley)

Foxtail barley grows to 2 feet and has sharp awns (bristles) on its seed heads that pose a danger to animals, since they can lodge in the ears, mouth, and eyes or be drawn into the lungs. Mow this perennial low or dig it out. Don't compost it; awns may not decompose completely.

Polygonum perfoliatum (Mile-a-Minute)

A native of Asia, this fast-spreading vine thrives in many different habitats in the United States. If you discover no more than a plant or two in your garden, dig them out, taking care to avoid the sharp thorns. If the vines are more numerous, treat them with a systemic herbicide.

Portulaca oleracea (Purslane)

Because purslane lives on a very compressed schedule, there are often several generations of this drought-tolerant annual in a single growing season. Hoe regularly to destroy new plants, or pull them up by hand. Dispose of purslane promptly; left lying on the ground, it can go to seed or re-root weeks later.

Rhus diversiloba (Poison Oak)

This West Coast native produces an oil that causes a bad rash in most people. It may grow as a shrub or a vine. Dig out by the roots or use a systemic herbicide if the site allows, following the precautions recommended for poison ivy *(right)*. Handle eastern poison oak *(R. toxicodendron)* in the same way.

Rhus radicans (Poison Ivy)

Another cause of nasty rashes, poison ivy varies in form but generally has leaves arranged in threes. Dig out the roots or use a systemic herbicide if the site allows. Wear protective clothing, and wash it and tools well afterward. Never compost or burn poison oak or poison ivy; inhaling the smoke is dangerous.

Rosa multiflora (Multiflora Rose)

Once sold as a decorative hedge plant, this tough perennial spreads by seeds and rooting stems, and takes hold in uncultivated areas. Dig small plants up by the roots. Cut larger ones to the ground and treat the stubs with a systemic herbicide.

Rubus species (Wild Bramble)

In time, the thorny canes of brambles such as raspberry, dewberry, and blackberry create impassable thickets. If you get at a plant when it is still young, however, digging out as much of the roots as you can and cutting new shoots to the ground, it will eventually die. This may take more than a year.

Taraxacum officinale (Dandelion)

The long taproots of dandelion nourish it through many a beheading, so for effective removal, dig out the root. Try to get it all: New shoots spring from root pieces left in the ground.

Plant Selection Guide

Organized by plant types and flower colors, these charts provide information on select species and varieties that will thrive in the particular conditions of your garden.

	ZONES	SOIL			LIGHT			BLOOM SEASON				PLANT HEIGHT					NOTED FOR			
		Dry	Well-drained	Moist	Full sun	Partial shade	Shade	Spring	Summer	Fall	Winter	Under 1 ft.	1–3 ft.	3–6 ft.	6–10 ft.	Over 10 ft.	Flowers	Foliage	Fruit/seeds	Fragrance
HERBACEOUS PLANTS																				
Achillea ptarmica 'The Pearl'	4–9		✓		✓				✓				✓				✓	✓		
Ageratum houstonianum 'Summer Snow' [2]			✓	✓	✓				✓	✓		✓					✓	✓		
Anemone x hybrida 'Honorine Jobert'	4–9		✓	✓	✓	✓			✓	✓			✓	✓			✓	✓		
Aruncus dioicus	4–9			✓		✓			✓					✓			✓	✓		
Chrysanthemum parthenium	4–9		✓		✓				✓	✓			✓				✓	✓		✓
Crambe cordifolia	5–9		✓		✓			✓	✓					✓			✓	✓		✓
Datura metel 'Alba' [1]			✓	✓	✓	✓			✓					✓			✓	✓		✓
Dicentra spectabilis f. alba	4–8		✓			✓		✓	✓				✓				✓	✓		
Galanthus nivalis	3–8		✓	✓		✓		✓				✓					✓			
Gaura lindheimeri	6–9		✓		✓				✓					✓			✓			
Helianthus annuus 'Italian White' [1]			✓	✓	✓				✓	✓				✓			✓			
Helleborus niger	4–8		✓	✓	✓		✓				✓		✓				✓	✓		
Ipomoea alba [4]	9–10		✓		✓				✓	✓						✓	✓	✓		✓
Leucojum vernum	4–8			✓		✓	✓					✓					✓			
Lysimachia clethroides	4–8		✓	✓	✓				✓				✓				✓	✓		
Mandevilla laxa	8–10		✓	✓		✓			✓							✓	✓	✓		✓
Phlox stolonifera 'Bruce's White'	3–8		✓	✓	✓	✓	✓	✓				✓					✓	✓		
Polygonatum commutatum	3–9			✓		✓	✓	✓							✓			✓	✓	✓	
Tiarella cordifolia	3–8		✓	✓		✓	✓	✓	✓			✓					✓	✓		
Yucca glauca	4–8	✓	✓		✓				✓				✓	✓			✓	✓		
Acanthus spinosus	7–10	✓	✓		✓	✓			✓				✓	✓			✓	✓		
Antirrhinum majus 'Pink Rocket' [4]	8–11		✓		✓	✓			✓				✓	✓			✓			
Bergenia 'Abendglut'	4–8		✓	✓	✓	✓		✓					✓				✓	✓		
Bergenia cordifolia	3–8			✓	✓	✓		✓					✓				✓	✓		
Chrysanthemum coccineum 'Helen'	3–7		✓		✓			✓	✓				✓				✓	✓		

(Left-margin color groupings: **WHITE** = *Achillea ptarmica* through *Yucca glauca*; **PINK** = *Acanthus spinosus* through *Chrysanthemum coccineum 'Helen'*.)

[1] Tender annual   [2] Half-hardy annual   [3] Hardy annual   [4] Tender perennial grown as an annual in colder zones

Plant	Zones	Dry	Well-drained	Moist	Full sun	Partial shade	Shade	Spring	Summer	Fall	Winter	Under 1 ft.	1–3 ft.	3–6 ft.	6–10 ft.	Over 10 ft.	Flowers	Foliage	Fruit/seeds	Fragrance
PINK																				
Fuchsia x hybrida 'Pink Chiffon' [4]	9–11		✓	✓		✓			✓				✓				✓			
Geranium cinereum	4–9	✓	✓	✓	✓	✓			✓			✓					✓	✓		
Gypsophila paniculata 'Pink Fairy'	4–9		✓	✓	✓				✓				✓				✓			
Origanum vulgare	3–10	✓	✓		✓				✓	✓			✓				✓	✓		✓
Sedum sieboldii	5–9	✓	✓		✓					✓		✓					✓	✓		
MIXED/MULTICOLOR																				
Alcea rosea 'Chater's Double'	3–9		✓		✓				✓						✓		✓			
Anemone coronaria 'de Caen'	7–9		✓	✓	✓	✓		✓				✓					✓	✓		
Antirrhinum majus 'Tahiti' [4]	8–11		✓		✓	✓			✓	✓		✓					✓			
Aristolochia macrophylla	4–8		✓	✓	✓	✓			✓							✓	✓	✓		
Cosmos bipinnatus 'Candy Stripe' [1]		✓	✓		✓	✓			✓	✓			✓				✓	✓		
Impatiens wallerana 'Shady Lady' [4]	10		✓	✓		✓	✓		✓	✓			✓				✓	✓		
Lathyrus odoratus 'Royal Family' [3]			✓	✓	✓	✓		✓	✓					✓			✓	✓		✓
Nicotiana alata 'Domino Hybrids' [1]			✓	✓					✓	✓			✓				✓	✓		
Papaver rhoeas 'Fairy Wings' [3]		✓	✓		✓	✓		✓	✓				✓				✓			
Tagetes patula [1]			✓		✓				✓	✓		✓	✓				✓	✓		
YELLOW																				
Achillea 'Moonshine'	3–8	✓	✓		✓				✓	✓			✓				✓	✓		✓
Alchemilla mollis	3–7		✓	✓	✓	✓		✓	✓				✓				✓	✓		
Allium moly 'Jeannine'	3–9		✓	✓	✓	✓		✓				✓					✓	✓		
Arum italicum	5–9		✓	✓		✓	✓	✓					✓				✓	✓	✓	
Caltha palustris	3–8			✓	✓	✓		✓					✓				✓	✓		
Digitalis grandiflora	3–9		✓	✓		✓		✓	✓				✓				✓	✓		
Doronicum 'Harper Crewe'	4–8		✓	✓	✓	✓		✓						✓			✓			
Helianthus angustifolius	6–9			✓	✓				✓	✓			✓	✓			✓	✓		
Lysimachia punctata	4–8			✓	✓	✓			✓				✓				✓	✓		
Rudbeckia fulgida var. sullivantii 'Goldsturm'	4–9		✓		✓	✓			✓	✓			✓				✓			
Rudbeckia nitida 'Herbstsonne'	4–9		✓		✓	✓			✓	✓					✓		✓			
Tanacetum vulgare	3–9		✓		✓	✓			✓				✓	✓			✓	✓		✓
Tropaeolum peregrinum [1]		✓	✓		✓				✓						✓		✓	✓		
ORANGE																				
Asclepias tuberosa	4–9		✓		✓				✓				✓				✓			
Calendula officinalis 'Geisha Girl' [3]			✓		✓			✓	✓	✓			✓				✓			
Cosmos sulphureus 'Diablo' [1]		✓	✓		✓	✓			✓	✓			✓				✓			
Euphorbia griffithii 'Fireglow'	4–9		✓		✓				✓				✓				✓			

[1] Tender annual   [2] Half-hardy annual   [3] Hardy annual   [4] Tender perennial grown as an annual in colder zones

	ZONES	SOIL			LIGHT			BLOOM SEASON				PLANT HEIGHT					NOTED FOR			
		Dry	Well-drained	Moist	Full sun	Partial shade	Shade	Spring	Summer	Fall	Winter	Under 1 ft.	1–3 ft.	3–6 ft.	6–10 ft.	Over 10 ft.	Flowers	Foliage	Fruit/seeds	Fragrance
ORANGE																				
Helenium 'Moerheim Beauty'	4–8		✔		✔					✔			✔				✔			
Hemerocallis fulva	3–9		✔	✔	✔	✔			✔				✔				✔	✔		
Sphaeralcea ambigua	9–10		✔		✔				✔				✔				✔	✔		
Thunbergia alata 'Aurantiaca'[4]	10–11		✔	✔	✔	✔			✔					✔			✔			
Tithonia rotundifolia 'Torch'[1]			✔		✔				✔	✔			✔				✔			
RED																				
Achillea millefolium 'Red Beauty'	3–8	✔	✔		✔				✔	✔			✔				✔	✔		✔
Astilbe 'Fanal'	5–9			✔		✔			✔				✔				✔	✔		
Centranthus ruber	5–9		✔		✔			✔	✔	✔			✔				✔	✔		
Dianthus deltoides 'Flashing Light'	4–7		✔	✔	✔	✔		✔				✔					✔	✔		
Hemerocallis 'Anzac'	3–9		✔	✔	✔	✔			✔				✔				✔	✔		
Heuchera sanguinea	4–8			✔	✔	✔			✔				✔					✔		
Knautia macedonica	5–9		✔		✔				✔				✔				✔			
Lobelia 'Queen Victoria'	3–8			✔	✔				✔	✔			✔				✔	✔		
Lychnis chalcedonica	4–9		✔	✔	✔	✔		✔	✔				✔				✔	✔		
Monarda didyma 'Cambridge Scarlet'	4–8		✔	✔	✔				✔				✔				✔	✔		
Pelargonium x hortorum 'Ringo Scarlet'[4]	9–10		✔	✔	✔			✔	✔	✔		✔	✔				✔	✔		
Penstemon 'Garnet'	4–9		✔		✔				✔	✔			✔				✔	✔		
Phaseolus coccineus[4]	9–10		✔	✔	✔			✔	✔	✔							✔			
Potentilla nepalensis 'Miss Wilmott'	5–7	✔		✔	✔	✔			✔				✔				✔	✔		
Primula japonica 'Miller's Crimson'	6–8			✔		✔	✔	✔	✔				✔				✔			
Rheum palmatum 'Atrosanguineum'	5–9		✔		✔				✔						✔		✔	✔		
Salvia splendens[4]	10–11		✔		✔	✔			✔	✔		✔	✔				✔	✔		
Thymus praecox 'Coccineus'	4–9	✔	✔		✔			✔				✔					✔	✔		✔
PURPLE																				
Ageratum houstonianum 'North Sea'[2]			✔	✔	✔				✔	✔		✔					✔	✔		
Allium giganteum	5–8		✔	✔	✔				✔					✔			✔			
Campanula glomerata 'Superba'	3–8		✔	✔	✔	✔			✔				✔				✔			
Centaurea montana	3–8		✔		✔				✔				✔				✔	✔		
Cleome hasslerana 'Purple Queen'[1]			✔	✔	✔	✔			✔	✔				✔			✔		✔	
Cynara cardunculus	9–10		✔		✔				✔						✔		✔	✔		
Hosta 'Krossa Regal'	3–9			✔		✔	✔		✔					✔				✔		
Lavandula dentata[4]	8–9		✔		✔				✔				✔				✔	✔		✔
Linaria triornithophora	6–9		✔		✔				✔				✔				✔	✔		

[1] Tender annual   [2] Half-hardy annual   [3] Hardy annual   [4] Tender perennial grown as an annual in colder zones

	ZONES	SOIL			LIGHT			BLOOM SEASON				PLANT HEIGHT					NOTED FOR			
		Dry	Well-drained	Moist	Full sun	Partial shade	Shade	Spring	Summer	Fall	Winter	Under 1 ft.	1–3 ft.	3–6 ft.	6–10 ft.	Over 10 ft.	Flowers	Foliage	Fruit/seeds	Fragrance
PURPLE																				
Liriope muscari	6–10	✓	✓	✓	✓	✓	✓		✓	✓			✓				✓	✓	✓	
Mentha spicata	4–9			✓	✓	✓			✓				✓				✓	✓		✓
Pelargonium peltatum 'Amethyst' [4]	9–10		✓	✓	✓			✓	✓	✓		✓					✓	✓		
Petunia x hybrida 'Heavenly Lavender' [1]			✓		✓				✓	✓		✓					✓			
Platycodon grandiflorus	4–9		✓		✓				✓				✓				✓	✓		
Salvia x superba 'East Friesland'	5–8		✓		✓	✓		✓	✓				✓				✓	✓		
Teucrium chamaedrys	5–10		✓		✓	✓			✓				✓				✓	✓		
Veronica longifolia 'Romiley Purple'	4–8		✓		✓				✓					✓			✓	✓		
BLUE																				
Agapanthus africanus	8–10		✓	✓	✓				✓	✓		✓	✓				✓	✓		
Ajuga reptans 'Bronze Beauty'	3–9	✓	✓	✓	✓	✓		✓	✓			✓					✓	✓		
Allium azureum	4–10		✓		✓				✓				✓				✓			
Aquilegia flabellata	3–9		✓	✓	✓	✓		✓	✓			✓					✓	✓		
Borago officinalis [3]			✓		✓				✓	✓			✓				✓			
Campanula latifolia	4–8		✓	✓	✓	✓			✓					✓			✓			
Cyananthus microphyllus	5–7		✓			✓			✓			✓					✓	✓		
Echinops bannaticus	8–10		✓		✓				✓					✓			✓			
Gentiana sino-ornata	5–7			✓		✓				✓		✓					✓			
Geranium x 'Johnson's Blue'	5–8	✓	✓	✓	✓	✓		✓	✓				✓				✓	✓		
Iris sibirica 'Caesar's Brother'	3–9		✓	✓	✓				✓					✓			✓	✓		
Ixiolirion tataricum	7–10		✓		✓			✓	✓			✓					✓			
Lobelia erinus 'Crystal Palace' [3]			✓		✓				✓	✓		✓					✓	✓		
Meconopsis betonicifolia	8			✓			✓	✓	✓				✓				✓			
Mertensia virginica	3–8		✓	✓		✓	✓	✓					✓				✓	✓		
Nepeta x faassenii	4–8		✓		✓			✓	✓				✓				✓	✓		✓
Perovskia atriplicifolia	5–9		✓		✓			✓	✓					✓			✓	✓		✓
Polygala calcarea	5–7		✓		✓			✓	✓			✓					✓			
Rosmarinus officinalis	7–10	✓	✓	✓	✓	✓			✓	✓	✓		✓	✓			✓	✓		✓
Scabiosa caucasica 'Fama'	4–9		✓		✓				✓				✓				✓			
Scilla siberica 'Atrocoerulea'	1–8		✓		✓			✓				✓					✓			
Sisyrinchium angustifolium	3–10			✓	✓	✓		✓	✓				✓				✓	✓		
Veronica longifolia	4–8		✓		✓	✓			✓	✓			✓	✓			✓	✓		
Vinca major [4]	7–9		✓	✓	✓	✓	✓	✓				✓					✓	✓		

[1] Tender annual [2] Half-hardy annual [3] Hardy annual [4] Tender perennial grown as an annual in colder zones

WHITE

Name	Zones	Partial shade	Diseases	Heat	Seaside conditions	Spring	Summer	Fall	Single	Semidouble	Double	Very double	Miniature	Bush/shrub <3'	Bush/shrub 3–6'	Shrub >6'	Climber/rambler	Fragrance	Cut flowers	Hips
'Alba Semi-plena'	4–10	✓	✓				✓			✓					✓	✓		✓		✓
'Blanc Double de Coubert'	3–10		✓		✓	✓	✓	✓		✓					✓			✓		✓
'Boule de Neige'	5–10		✓				✓	✓			✓				✓			✓		
'Candeur Lyonnaise'	5–10					✓	✓	✓			✓				✓				✓	
'City of York'	5–10	✓					✓			✓							✓	✓		
'Fair Bianca'	4–10						✓	✓				✓		✓				✓		
'Frau Karl Druschki'	5–10						✓	✓			✓					✓				
'French Lace'	4–9		✓				✓	✓			✓				✓				✓	
'Great Maiden's Blush'	4–10						✓				✓				✓			✓		
'Handel'	5–9	✓					✓	✓			✓						✓			
'Henry Hudson'	3–10		✓		✓	✓	✓	✓		✓					✓			✓		
'Iceberg'	4–9		✓				✓	✓			✓				✓			✓	✓	
'Irresistible'	5–10					✓	✓	✓			✓		✓						✓	✓
'Koricole'	4–9					✓	✓	✓			✓			✓						
'Lamarque'	7–10			✓			✓	✓					✓				✓	✓	✓	✓
'Madame Alfred Carriere'	6–9	✓		✓			✓	✓			✓						✓	✓	✓	
'Madame Hardy'	4–9		✓			✓	✓					✓			✓			✓	✓	
'Madame Legras de St. Germain'	4–9	✓	✓				✓					✓					✓	✓	✓	✓
'Madame Plantier'	4–10	✓	✓				✓					✓			✓			✓	✓	
'Marie Pavie'	4–9					✓	✓	✓			✓			✓				✓		
'Nastarana'	6–10	✓		✓			✓	✓		✓					✓			✓		
'Pristine'	5–10		✓				✓				✓				✓				✓	
'Prosperity'	6–10	✓					✓	✓			✓				✓			✓		
Rosa banksiae banksiae	8–10					✓	✓				✓						✓	✓		
Rosa rugosa alba	3–8		✓		✓		✓		✓						✓			✓		✓
'Sally Holmes'	5–9	✓	✓	✓			✓	✓		✓					✓			✓	✓	
'Sea Foam'	4–9		✓				✓	✓			✓			✓				✓	✓	
'Silver Moon'	5–10						✓		✓							✓	✓	✓		
'Snow Bride'	5–10						✓	✓			✓		✓						✓	
'Sombreuil'	5–10	✓		✓			✓	✓				✓					✓	✓	✓	
'White Meidiland'	4–9		✓				✓	✓			✓			✓						
'White Pet'	5–9					✓	✓	✓			✓			✓					✓	

	Zones	Partial shade	Diseases	Heat	Seaside conditions	Spring	Summer	Fall	Single	Semidouble	Double	Very double	Miniature	Bush/shrub <3'	Bush/shrub 3-6'	Shrub >6'	Climber/rambler	Fragrance	Cut flowers	Hips
YELLOW																				
'Alberic Barbier'	5–10	✔	✔	✔			✔			✔							✔	✔		
'Alchymist'	5–10						✔					✔					✔	✔	✔		
'Celine Forestier'	6–10			✔			✔	✔					✔			✔		✔	✔		
'Elina'	5–10						✔	✔				✔			✔					✔	
'Garden Party'	5–10						✔	✔				✔				✔			✔	✔	
'Golden Showers'	5–9	✔	✔				✔	✔				✔					✔	✔	✔	✔	
'Golden Wings'	4–10					✔	✔	✔	✔			✔				✔			✔	✔	✔
'Gold Medal'	5–10		✔				✔	✔				✔				✔			✔	✔	
'Graham Thomas'	4–10			✔			✔	✔				✔				✔		✔	✔		
'Granada'	5–10						✔	✔				✔				✔			✔	✔	
'Lafter'	5–10		✔				✔	✔		✔						✔					
'Mrs. Dudley Cross'	7–10		✔	✔		✔	✔	✔				✔				✔			✔	✔	
'Mutabilis'	7–10			✔			✔	✔	✔							✔	✔		✔		
'Party Girl'	5–10		✔				✔	✔				✔		✔					✔	✔	
'Peace'	5–10		✔				✔	✔				✔				✔				✔	
'Rainbow's End'	5–10						✔	✔				✔		✔							
'Reve d'Or'	6–10			✔		✔	✔	✔				✔						✔	✔		
'Rise 'n' Shine'	5–10		✔				✔	✔				✔		✔							
'Sun Flare'	4–10		✔				✔	✔				✔			✔				✔	✔	
'Sunsprite'	5–10		✔			✔	✔	✔				✔			✔				✔	✔	
ORANGE/APRICOT																				
'Albertine'	5–10						✔					✔					✔	✔	✔		
'America'	5–10		✔				✔	✔				✔						✔	✔	✔	
'Apricot Nectar'	4–10						✔	✔				✔			✔				✔		
'Buff Beauty'	5–10						✔	✔				✔				✔			✔	✔	
'Cherish'	4–9		✔				✔	✔				✔			✔					✔	
'First Edition'	4–10		✔				✔	✔				✔				✔				✔	
'Folklore'	5–10		✔				✔	✔				✔				✔			✔	✔	
'Jean Kenneally'	5–10		✔				✔	✔				✔		✔							
'Just Joey'	5–10						✔					✔			✔				✔	✔	
'Leander'	4–10		✔			✔	✔						✔				✔		✔		
'Loving Touch'	5–10					✔	✔	✔				✔		✔						✔	✔
'Margo Koster'	5–9		✔				✔	✔				✔			✔						
'Pierrine'	5–10					✔	✔	✔				✔		✔						✔	✔

		ZONES	TOLERATES				BLOOM SEASON			BLOOM TYPE				PLANT HEIGHT					NOTED FOR		
			Partial shade	Diseases	Heat	Seaside conditions	Spring	Summer	Fall	Single	Semidouble	Double	Very double	Miniature	Bush/shrub <3'	Bush/shrub 3-6'	Shrub >6'	Climber/rambler	Fragrance	Cut flowers	Hips
ORANGE/APRICOT	'Playboy'	4–10	✓	✓			✓	✓	✓	✓						✓			✓	✓	✓
	Rosa foetida bicolor	5–9					✓			✓						✓	✓				
	'Starina'	6–10						✓	✓			✓		✓							
	'Touch of Class'	5–10						✓	✓			✓				✓				✓	
	'Tropicana'	5–10			✓			✓	✓			✓				✓				✓	✓	
PINK	'Aquarius'	5–10		✓			✓	✓	✓			✓				✓				✓	
	'Autumn Damask'	4–10					✓	✓	✓			✓				✓			✓		
	'Ballerina'	5–10	✓	✓				✓	✓	✓					✓	✓				✓	
	'Baronne Prevost'	5–10		✓				✓	✓				✓			✓			✓		
	'Belinda'	5–10	✓	✓				✓	✓		✓					✓	✓	✓			
	'Belle Poitevine'	3–10		✓		✓		✓	✓		✓					✓			✓		✓
	'Belle Story'	4–10						✓	✓		✓					✓			✓		
	'Betty Prior'	4–10		✓				✓	✓	✓					✓	✓					
	'Bonica'	4–9	✓	✓				✓				✓				✓					✓
	'Bride's Dream'	5–10						✓	✓			✓				✓				✓	
	'Cabbage Rose'	4–10						✓					✓			✓			✓		
	'Carefree Beauty'	4–10		✓				✓	✓		✓					✓			✓		
	'Cecile Brunner'	4–9	✓				✓	✓	✓			✓				✓			✓	✓	
	'Celestial'	4–10	✓					✓			✓					✓			✓		
	'Celsiana'	4–10		✓				✓			✓					✓			✓		
	'Communis'	4–10		✓				✓				✓				✓			✓		
	'Complicata'	4–10			✓			✓		✓						✓	✓	✓			✓
	'Constance Spry'	4–10						✓				✓					✓	✓	✓		
	'Crested Moss'	4–10		✓				✓					✓			✓			✓		
	'Dainty Bess'	5–10		✓	✓			✓		✓						✓			✓	✓	
	'Duchesse de Brabant'	7–10		✓	✓		✓	✓	✓			✓				✓			✓		
	'Felicite Parmentier'	4–10	✓	✓	✓			✓					✓			✓			✓		
	'Frau Dagmar Hartopp'	3–10		✓		✓	✓	✓	✓	✓					✓				✓	✓	✓
	'Gartendirektor Otto Linne'	4–10		✓				✓	✓			✓				✓			✓	✓	
	'Gruss an Aachen'	4–10	✓	✓			✓	✓	✓			✓			✓				✓		
	'Heritage'	4–10						✓				✓				✓			✓	✓	
	'Ispahan'	4–10		✓			✓	✓				✓				✓			✓	✓	
	'Jeanne Lajoie'	5–10					✓	✓	✓			✓					✓		✓		✓

	ZONES	Partial shade	Diseases	Heat	Seaside conditions	Spring	Summer	Fall	Single	Semidouble	Double	Very double	Miniature	Bush/shrub <3'	Bush/shrub 3-6'	Shrub >6'	Climber/rambler	Fragrance	Cut flowers	Hips
'Jens Munk'	3–10		✔		✔	✔	✔	✔			✔				✔			✔		
'La Marne'	5–10					✔	✔	✔		✔					✔			✔		
'Louise Odier'	5–9		✔				✔	✔				✔				✔		✔	✔		
'Madame Isaac Pereire'	5–9						✔	✔			✔					✔	✔	✔	✔	✔	
'Marchesa Boccella'	5–10					✔	✔	✔				✔				✔					
'Minnie Pearl'	5–10		✔				✔	✔			✔		✔							✔	
'Mrs. B. R. Cant'	7–10			✔		✔	✔	✔				✔			✔	✔			✔	✔	
'New Dawn'	5–10	✔	✔				✔			✔							✔	✔	✔		
'Old Blush'	6–10		✔	✔			✔	✔			✔					✔			✔		
'Paulii Rosea'	4–10						✔		✔						✔				✔		
'Penelope'	5–10	✔	✔				✔	✔		✔						✔			✔		✔
'Queen Elizabeth'	4–9		✔				✔	✔			✔					✔				✔	
Rosa glauca	4–9					✔	✔		✔								✔			✔	✔
'Rosa Mundi'	4–10			✔			✔			✔						✔			✔	✔	✔
Rosa palustris	5–10	✔		✔			✔		✔							✔	✔				✔
'Souvenir de la Malmaison'	5–9			✔			✔	✔			✔				✔				✔		
'The Fairy'	4–9		✔	✔			✔	✔			✔				✔					✔	
'Tiffany'	5–10		✔				✔	✔			✔					✔			✔	✔	
'William Baffin'	3–9		✔				✔	✔		✔						✔	✔	✔			
'Zephirine Drouhin'	5–10					✔	✔	✔		✔							✔	✔	✔		
'Altissimo'	5–9		✔	✔			✔	✔	✔								✔	✔			
'Archduke Charles'	6–10			✔			✔	✔			✔			✔							
'Blaze'	5–10			✔		✔	✔	✔		✔								✔			
'Champlain'	4–10		✔				✔	✔			✔					✔					
'Chrysler Imperial'	5–10			✔			✔	✔			✔					✔			✔	✔	
'Country Dancer'	4–10						✔	✔			✔				✔		✔	✔	✔		
'Crimson Glory'	5–10			✔			✔	✔			✔					✔			✔		
'Don Juan'	5–10		✔			✔	✔	✔			✔							✔	✔	✔	
'Dortmund'	4–10	✔	✔				✔	✔	✔								✔	✔			✔
'Double Delight'	5–10						✔	✔			✔					✔			✔	✔	
'Dreamglo'	5–10		✔				✔	✔			✔		✔								
'Dublin Bay'	5–10		✔			✔	✔	✔			✔							✔	✔		
'Europeana'	4–10		✔				✔	✔			✔				✔				✔		

PINK

RED

	ZONES	Partial shade	Diseases	Heat	Seaside conditions	Spring	Summer	Fall	Single	Semidouble	Double	Very double	Miniature	Bush/shrub <3'	Bush/shrub 3-6'	Shrub >6'	Climber/rambler	Fragrance	Cut flowers	Hips
RED																				
'F. J. Grootendorst'	3–10		✔		✔		✔	✔			✔				✔					
'Fragrant Cloud'	5–10						✔	✔			✔				✔			✔	✔	
'Hansa'	3–8		✔		✔	✔	✔	✔			✔				✔			✔		✔
'Hurdy Gurdy'	5–10		✔	✔		✔	✔	✔			✔		✔							
'John Cabot'	3–10		✔				✔	✔			✔					✔	✔			
'John Franklin'	5–10		✔	✔		✔	✔	✔		✔						✔			✔	
'Linda Campbell'	3–8		✔	✔	✔		✔	✔		✔						✔				
'Louis Philippe'	7–10		✔	✔		✔	✔	✔			✔					✔			✔	
'Magic Carrousel'	5–10		✔				✔	✔		✔				✔						✔
'Mister Lincoln'	5–10		✔				✔				✔					✔			✔	✔
'Olympiad'	5–10						✔	✔			✔					✔				✔
'Red Cascade'	5–10	✔				✔	✔	✔			✔				✔					
'Robusta'	6–10					✔	✔	✔	✔							✔			✔	
'Roger Lambelin'	5–10						✔	✔			✔					✔			✔	
'Roseraie de l'Hay'	3–8		✔		✔	✔	✔	✔		✔						✔			✔	
'Showbiz'	4–10		✔				✔	✔			✔			✔						✔
'Therese Bugnet'	3–9		✔		✔		✔				✔					✔			✔	
'Uncle Joe'	5–10						✔	✔				✔				✔			✔	✔
'Variegata di Bologna'	5–9						✔					✔				✔		✔	✔	✔
'Will Scarlet'	5–10	✔				✔		✔		✔						✔	✔	✔		✔
MAUVE/PURPLE																				
'Angel Face'	4–9						✔	✔			✔			✔					✔	✔
'Camaieux'	4–10			✔		✔					✔					✔			✔		✔
'Cardinal de Richelieu'	4–10			✔		✔					✔					✔			✔	
'Celina'	4–10			✔		✔			✔							✔			✔	
'Delicata'	3–10		✔		✔	✔	✔	✔	✔				✔					✔		✔
'Escapade'	4–10						✔	✔		✔				✔					✔	
'Lavender Lassie'	5–10	✔	✔				✔	✔			✔					✔	✔	✔	✔	
'Paradise'	5–10						✔	✔			✔					✔			✔	✔
'Plum Dandy'	5–10					✔	✔	✔				✔	✔						✔	
'Reine des Violettes'	5–10					✔						✔				✔	✔	✔	✔	
'Rugosa Magnifica'	3–9		✔		✔	✔	✔	✔			✔					✔			✔	✔
'Tuscany'	4–10			✔		✔				✔						✔			✔	
'Veilchenblau'	5–9	✔				✔				✔							✔	✔	✔	

	Zones	Dry	Moist	Full sun	Partial shade	Shade	Spring	Summer	Fall	Winter	Under 3 ft.	3–6 ft.	6–10 ft.	10–20 ft.	Over 20 ft.	Form	Foliage	Flowers	Fruits/seeds	Bark/twigs
GROUND COVERS																				
Calluna vulgaris 'Mrs. Ronald Gray'	4–7		✓	✓	✓			✓			✓					✓	✓	✓		
Ceanothus griseus var. *horizontalis*	8–10	✓		✓				✓			✓							✓		
Cotoneaster dammeri 'Skogholm'	5–8	✓	✓	✓	✓		✓				✓					✓	✓			
Erica carnea 'Springwood Pink'	6–9		✓	✓	✓					✓	✓							✓		
Euonymus fortunei 'Colorata'	4–9	✓	✓	✓	✓	✓					✓						✓			
Hypericum calycinum	5–9	✓		✓	✓			✓	✓		✓						✓			
Juniperus horizontalis 'Wiltonii'	3–9	✓	✓	✓							✓					✓	✓			
Juniperus procumbens	3–9	✓	✓	✓							✓						✓			
Liriope muscari 'Variegata'	7–10	✓	✓	✓	✓	✓		✓			✓						✓	✓	✓	
Mahonia repens	5–10		✓		✓	✓					✓						✓	✓	✓	
Pachysandra terminalis 'Green Carpet'	4–9		✓		✓	✓					✓					✓	✓	✓		
VINES																				
Akebia quinata	4–8	✓	✓	✓	✓	✓	✓							✓			✓	✓	✓	
Clematis armandii	7–9		✓	✓	✓		✓							✓			✓	✓		
Clematis paniculata	5–8		✓	✓	✓				✓						✓			✓		
Gelsemium sempervirens	6–9		✓	✓	✓		✓							✓				✓		
Hedera helix 'Needlepoint'	5–10		✓	✓	✓	✓									✓		✓			
Hydrangea anomala ssp. *petiolaris*	4–7		✓	✓	✓	✓		✓							✓			✓		✓
Ipomoea alba	10			✓				✓	✓						✓			✓		
Jasminum officinale	8–10	✓		✓				✓	✓						✓			✓		
Lonicera heckrottii	4–9	✓	✓	✓	✓			✓						✓				✓		
Vitis coignetiae	5–8	✓		✓					✓						✓		✓			✓
Wisteria floribunda	4–9	✓	✓	✓			✓								✓			✓		
GRASSES																				
Andropogon glomertatus	6–9		✓	✓				✓	✓		✓						✓		✓	
Bouteloua curtipendula	3–10	✓		✓				✓	✓		✓						✓		✓	
Calamagrostis x acutiflora 'Stricta'	6–9	✓	✓	✓				✓					✓				✓	✓		
Carex morrowii 'Variegata'	6–9		✓	✓	✓	✓					✓					✓	✓			
Fargesia murielae	5–9	✓	✓		✓									✓		✓	✓			
Imperata cylindrica rubra	5–9		✓	✓				✓			✓						✓			
Miscanthus sinensis 'Zebrinus'	5–9		✓	✓					✓				✓			✓	✓	✓		
Muhlenbergia lindheimeri	6–10		✓	✓	✓				✓			✓					✓		✓	

	ZONES	SOIL		LIGHT			BLOOM SEASON				PLANT HEIGHT					NOTED FOR				
		Dry	Moist	Full sun	Partial shade	Shade	Spring	Summer	Fall	Winter	Under 3 ft	3–6 ft	6–10 ft	10–20 ft	Over 20 ft	Form	Foliage	Flowers	Fruits/seeds	Bark/twigs
Panicum virgatum 'Haense Herms'	5–9		✔	✔				✔	✔		✔						✔	✔	✔	
Pennisetum setaceum 'Rubrum'	8–10	✔	✔	✔				✔			✔					✔	✔	✔		
Schizachyrium scoparium	3–10	✔		✔				✔	✔			✔					✔			
FERNS																				
Adiantum hispidulum	8–10		✔			✔					✔					✔	✔			
Athyrium nipponicum 'Pictum'	5–8		✔			✔					✔					✔	✔			
Cyrtomium falcatum	6–10		✔			✔					✔					✔	✔			
Dennstaedtia punctilobula	3–8	✔		✔	✔	✔					✔					✔	✔			
Dryopteris erythrosora	5–8		✔			✔					✔					✔	✔			
Matteuccia struthiopteris	3–6		✔		✔	✔						✔				✔	✔			
Osmunda cinnamomea	3–9		✔			✔					✔					✔	✔			
Polystichum setiferum 'Divisilobum'	5–8		✔			✔						✔				✔	✔			
Woodwardia fimbriata	8–10		✔			✔						✔				✔	✔			
DECIDUOUS SHRUBS																				
Abelia x 'Edward Goucher'	6–10		✔	✔	✔			✔	✔			✔					✔	✔		
Acer palmatum 'Dissectum'	5–8		✔	✔	✔		✔						✔			✔	✔			✔
Aronia arbutifolia 'Brilliantissima'	3–9	✔	✔	✔	✔		✔						✔					✔	✔	
Berberis thunbergii 'Crimson Pygmy'	4–8	✔	✔	✔			✔				✔						✔		✔	
Buddleia alternifolia 'Argentea'	5–9	✔		✔			✔	✔						✔		✔	✔	✔		
Callicarpa japonica	5–8	✔		✔	✔			✔					✔						✔	
Chaenomeles speciosa 'Cameo'	4–8	✔	✔	✔			✔					✔						✔	✔	
Cotinus coggygria 'Velvet Cloak'	5–8	✔	✔	✔				✔						✔			✔	✔	✔	
Enkianthus campanulatus	4–7		✔	✔	✔		✔						✔				✔	✔		
Euonymus alata 'Compacta'	5–8	✔	✔	✔	✔	✔	✔						✔				✔		✔	✔
Forsythia x intermedia 'Spectabilis'	6–9	✔	✔	✔			✔						✔			✔		✔		
Fothergilla major	4–8	✔	✔	✔	✔		✔						✔				✔	✔		
Hamamelis x intermedia 'Arnold Promise'	5–8		✔	✔	✔					✔				✔			✔	✔		
Hydrangea arborescens 'Annabelle'	3–9		✔	✔	✔	✔		✔				✔						✔		
Jasminum nudiflorum	6–10	✔	✔	✔	✔					✔		✔				✔		✔		✔
Kerria japonica 'Pleniflora'	4–9	✔	✔	✔	✔		✔						✔			✔		✔		✔
Lagerstroemia indica 'Seminole'	7–10		✔	✔				✔					✔				✔	✔		✔
Ligustrum ovalifolium 'Aureum'	5–10	✔	✔	✔	✔		✔							✔			✔	✔	✔	
Myrica pensylvanica	3–7	✔	✔	✔	✔		✔						✔				✔		✔	

Plant	Zones	Dry	Moist	Full sun	Partial shade	Shade	Spring	Summer	Fall	Winter	Under 3 ft	3–6 ft	6–10 ft	10–20 ft	Over 20 ft	Form	Foliage	Flowers	Fruits/seeds	Bark/twigs
Potentilla fruticosa 'Klondike'	3–7	✔	✔	✔	✔			✔	✔		✔						✔	✔		
Punica granatum 'Legrellei'	8–10		✔	✔	✔			✔					✔					✔	✔	
Rhododendron mucronulatum	4–7		✔		✔					✔	✔	✔					✔	✔		
Rhododendron schlippenbachii	4–7		✔		✔		✔						✔				✔	✔		
Spiraea x bumalda 'Gold Flame'	3–8		✔	✔	✔			✔			✔						✔	✔		
Stewartia ovata	5–9		✔	✔	✔			✔							✔			✔	✔		✔
Syringa patula 'Miss Kim'	3–8		✔	✔			✔						✔					✔	✔		
Viburnum plicatum var. *tomentosum*	5–8		✔	✔	✔		✔							✔			✔	✔	✔	✔	
Vitex agnus-castus 'Rosea'	7–9		✔	✔				✔	✔				✔	✔					✔		
EVERGREEN SHRUBS																				
Ardisia crenata	7–10		✔		✔							✔						✔		✔	
Aucuba japonica 'Variegata'	7–10		✔		✔	✔	✔						✔					✔		✔	
Berberis buxifolia var. *nana*	5–8		✔	✔	✔	✔	✔					✔						✔	✔	✔	
Berberis julianae	5–8		✔	✔	✔	✔	✔						✔					✔	✔	✔	
Buxus microphylla 'Tide Hill'	4–9		✔	✔	✔							✔						✔			
Camellia japonica	7–9		✔		✔			✔	✔					✔					✔		
Chamaecyparis obtusa 'Nana Gracilis'	4–8		✔	✔	✔								✔				✔	✔			
Cistus x hybridus	8–10	✔		✔			✔						✔					✔	✔		
Cistus x purpureus	8–10	✔		✔				✔					✔						✔		
Cotoneaster salicifolius	6–8		✔	✔	✔		✔							✔			✔	✔		✔	
Daphne odora	7–9		✔		✔	✔	✔				✔	✔						✔	✔		
Eriobotrya japonica	8–10		✔	✔	✔				✔					✔	✔			✔		✔	
Escallonia x langleyensis 'Apple Blossom'	8–10	✔	✔	✔			✔	✔	✔				✔					✔	✔		
Euonymus fortunei 'Emerald Gaiety'	5–9	✔	✔	✔	✔	✔	✔						✔				✔	✔			
Fatsia japonica	8–10		✔			✔			✔					✔				✔	✔	✔	
Hebe 'Autumn Glory'	8–10	✔		✔				✔	✔		✔							✔	✔		
Ilex cornuta 'Berries Jubilee'	7–9		✔	✔	✔		✔						✔					✔		✔	
Juniperus chinensis 'Mint Julep'	3–9	✔	✔	✔									✔				✔	✔			
Ligustrum japonicum	7–10	✔	✔	✔	✔	✔	✔							✔	✔		✔	✔	✔		
Mahonia bealei	7–10		✔		✔						✔		✔					✔	✔	✔	
Nandina domestica 'Harbour Dwarf'	6–9		✔	✔	✔	✔			✔			✔					✔	✔	✔	✔	
Picea abies 'Nidiformis'	3–7		✔	✔	✔								✔				✔	✔			
Pieris japonica 'Variegata'	5–8		✔	✔	✔	✔	✔						✔	✔			✔	✔	✔		

	ZONES	SOIL		LIGHT			BLOOM SEASON				PLANT HEIGHT					NOTED FOR				
		Dry	Moist	Full sun	Partial shade	Shade	Spring	Summer	Fall	Winter	Under 3 ft.	3–6 ft.	6–10 ft.	10–20 ft.	Over 20 ft.	Form	Foliage	Flowers	Fruits/seeds	Bark/twigs
Pittosporum tobira	8–10	✔	✔	✔	✔	✔	✔						✔				✔			
Prunus laurocerasus 'Otto Luyken'	6–10		✔	✔	✔		✔					✔					✔	✔		
Pyracantha coccinea 'Mohave'	6–9	✔		✔			✔						✔					✔	✔	
Raphiolepis indica	9–10		✔	✔			✔					✔					✔	✔		
Rhododendron catawbiense	4–8	✔	✔		✔	✔	✔						✔				✔	✔		
Rhododendron 'Scarlet Wonder'	6–8		✔		✔	✔	✔			✔							✔	✔		
Sarcococca confusa	7–8		✔		✔	✔			✔		✔					✔	✔		✔	
Skimmia japonica	7–8		✔		✔	✔					✔						✔	✔	✔	
Taxus cuspidata 'Thayerae'	5–7	✔	✔	✔							✔					✔	✔		✔	
Thuja occidentalis 'Rheingold'	3–8	✔		✔	✔							✔				✔	✔			
Thuja orientalis	4–8	✔		✔	✔						✔					✔	✔			
Viburnum davidii	8–9		✔	✔	✔		✔				✔						✔	✔	✔	
DECIDUOUS TREES																				
Acer griseum	4–8		✔	✔	✔		✔							✔			✔			✔
Acer palmatum 'Senkaki'	3–8	✔		✔	✔		✔						✔			✔				✔
Acer rubrum 'October Glory'	3–9		✔	✔	✔		✔								✔		✔			✔
Betula nigra	4–9		✔	✔	✔		✔								✔	✔				✔
Carpinus betulus 'Columnaris'	4–7	✔	✔	✔	✔		✔								✔	✔	✔			✔
Cercis canadensis	3–9	✔		✔	✔		✔								✔		✔	✔		
Chilopsis linearis	8–10	✔		✔			✔						✔	✔		✔	✔			
Cladrastis kentukea	4–8	✔	✔	✔			✔								✔	✔	✔	✔		✔
Cornus alternifolia	3–7		✔	✔	✔		✔						✔	✔		✔		✔	✔	
Cornus kousa var. *chinensis*	5–8		✔	✔	✔		✔	✔						✔		✔	✔	✔	✔	✔
Crataegus phaenopyrum	4–7	✔		✔			✔							✔		✔	✔	✔	✔	
Fagus sylvatica 'Aurea Pendula'	4–7		✔	✔	✔		✔								✔	✔	✔			✔
Fraxinus americana 'Champaign County'	3–9	✔	✔	✔			✔								✔		✔			
Gleditsia triacanthos var. *inermis 'Imperial'*	4–7	✔	✔	✔			✔								✔		✔			
Halesia tetraptera	4–8		✔	✔	✔	✔	✔								✔	✔		✔	✔	✔
Koelreuteria paniculata	5–9	✔	✔	✔	✔			✔							✔	✔	✔	✔	✔	
Lagerstroemia indica 'Natchez'	7–10		✔	✔				✔	✔				✔				✔	✔		✔
Liriodendron tulipifera	4–9		✔	✔			✔								✔	✔	✔	✔		
Magnolia stellata 'Royal Star'	4–8		✔	✔	✔					✔			✔				✔	✔		
Magnolia virginiana	5–9		✔	✔	✔		✔							✔	✔	✔	✔	✔	✔	

	ZONES	SOIL		LIGHT			BLOOM SEASON				PLANT HEIGHT					NOTED FOR				
		Dry	Moist	Full sun	Partial shade	Shade	Spring	Summer	Fall	Winter	Under 3 ft.	3–6 ft.	6–10 ft.	10–20 ft.	Over 20 ft.	Form	Foliage	Flowers	Fruits/seeds	Bark/twigs
Malus 'Red Jade'	4–8		✓	✓			✓							✓		✓		✓	✓	
Oxydendrum arboreum	5–9		✓	✓	✓		✓								✓	✓	✓	✓		
Parrotia persica	4–8	✓		✓			✓								✓	✓	✓			✓
Phellodendron amurense	3–8	✓	✓	✓			✓								✓	✓				✓
Pistacia chinensis	6–9	✓	✓	✓			✓								✓	✓	✓		✓	
Populus tremuloides	3–7	✓	✓	✓			✓								✓	✓	✓			✓
Prunus mume	6–9		✓	✓	✓					✓				✓			✓	✓		
Pyrus calleryana 'Chanticleer'	5–8	✓	✓	✓			✓								✓	✓	✓	✓		
Quercus shumardii	5–9	✓	✓	✓			✓								✓	✓	✓			
Sapindus drummondii	6–9	✓		✓	✓		✓								✓		✓	✓	✓	✓
Stewartia pseudocamellia	5–7		✓	✓	✓			✓							✓		✓	✓		✓
Styrax japonicus	5–8		✓	✓	✓		✓								✓		✓		✓	✓
Styrax obassia	5–8		✓	✓	✓		✓	✓						✓		✓	✓	✓		
Syringa reticulata	3–7		✓	✓				✓							✓			✓		
Taxodium distichum	4–9		✓	✓			✓								✓	✓	✓			✓
Ulmus parvifolia	4–9		✓	✓				✓							✓	✓	✓			✓
Zelkova serrata 'Green Vase'	5–8		✓	✓			✓								✓	✓	✓			✓
EVERGREEN TREES																				
Abies concolor	3–7	✓	✓	✓											✓	✓	✓			
Cedrus deodara	7–8	✓	✓	✓											✓	✓	✓			
Chamaecyparis lawsoniana	5–7		✓	✓											✓	✓	✓			✓
x Cupressocyparis leylandii 'Silver Dust'	6–10	✓	✓	✓											✓	✓	✓			
Cupressus sempervirens	7–9	✓		✓											✓	✓	✓			✓
Ilex opaca	5–9		✓	✓	✓		✓								✓		✓		✓	
Ilex vomitoria	7–10	✓	✓	✓	✓		✓							✓			✓		✓	✓
Osmanthus fragrans	9–10		✓	✓	✓	✓	✓	✓						✓				✓		
Picea glauca	3–6		✓	✓	✓										✓	✓	✓			
Pinus contorta var. contorta	7–10		✓	✓											✓	✓	✓			
Pinus nigra	4–7	✓	✓	✓											✓	✓	✓			
Prunus caroliniana	7–10		✓	✓	✓	✓	✓							✓		✓	✓	✓		
Taxus baccata	6–7		✓	✓	✓										✓	✓	✓		✓	
Taxus x media 'Hicksii'	4–7	✓	✓	✓	✓								✓			✓	✓		✓	
Tsuga canadensis	3–7		✓	✓	✓	✓									✓	✓	✓			

	HARDINESS			HEIGHT				LIGHT			SOIL			BLOOM SEASON				PARTS USED				
	Hardy	Half-hardy	Tender	Under 1 ft.	1–3 ft.	3–5 ft.	Over 5 ft.	Full sun	Light shade	Shade	Dry	Well-drained	Moist	Spring	Summer	Fall	Winter	Leaves	Flowers	Root/bulb	Seeds/fruit	Stems/bark
HERBS—Annuals and Biennials																						
Aloe vera			✔	✔				✔	✔			✔			✔			✔				
Amaranthus hypochondriacus		✔						✔	✔		✔	✔			✔			✔			✔	
Anethum graveolens 'Mammoth'		✔			✔			✔				✔			✔			✔			✔	
Angelica archangelica*	✔							✔	✔	✔			✔		✔			✔			✔	
Angelica gigas*	✔							✔	✔	✔			✔		✔			✔			✔	
Anthriscus cerefolium		✔		✔					✔	✔		✔			✔			✔	✔			
Apium graveolens*	✔				✔			✔	✔			✔	✔		✔			✔			✔	
Artemisia annua	✔					✔		✔			✔	✔			✔			✔	✔			
Atriplex hortensis	✔						✔	✔				✔	✔		✔			✔				
Borago officinalis 'Alba'	✔				✔			✔				✔	✔		✔			✔	✔			
Brassica juncea	✔					✔		✔				✔			✔			✔			✔	
Calendula officinalis	✔				✔			✔				✔		✔	✔	✔			✔			
Capsicum annuum var. annuum			✔		✔			✔				✔	✔	✔							✔	
Capsicum chinense 'Habanero'			✔		✔			✔				✔	✔	✔							✔	
Capsicum frutescens 'Tabasco'			✔		✔			✔				✔	✔								✔	
Carthamus tinctorius			✔		✔			✔			✔	✔			✔				✔		✔	
Carum carvi*	✔				✔			✔	✔			✔		✔	✔			✔		✔	✔	
Catharanthus roseus			✔		✔			✔	✔			✔	✔	✔	✔	✔			✔			
Centaurea cyanus			✔		✔			✔				✔			✔	✔		✔	✔			
Chenopodium ambrosioides	✔					✔		✔				✔			✔			✔	✔		✔	
Chenopodium botrys	✔				✔			✔				✔			✔			✔	✔		✔	
Coix lacryma-jobi		✔					✔	✔	✔				✔		✔			✔			✔	
Coriandrum sativum			✔		✔			✔	✔			✔			✔			✔		✔	✔	
Digitalis lanata*	✔				✔			✔	✔			✔			✔				✔			
Digitalis purpurea*	✔					✔		✔	✔			✔			✔				✔			
Eruca vesicaria ssp. sativa	✔				✔			✔	✔				✔	✔	✔			✔	✔			
Foeniculum vulgare 'Purpurascens'		✔					✔	✔				✔			✔	✔		✔		✔	✔	✔
Hedeoma pulegioides	✔			✔				✔	✔			✔			✔	✔		✔				
Hibiscus sabdariffa		✔					✔	✔	✔			✔			✔	✔		✔			✔	
Isatis tinctoria*	✔					✔		✔				✔	✔	✔					✔			
Matricaria recutita		✔		✔				✔				✔		✔	✔			✔	✔			

*Biennial

	HARDINESS			HEIGHT				LIGHT			SOIL			BLOOM SEASON				PARTS USED				
	Hardy	Half-hardy	Tender	Under 1 ft.	1–3 ft.	3–5 ft.	Over 5 ft.	Full sun	Light shade	Shade	Dry	Well-drained	Moist	Spring	Summer	Fall	Winter	Leaves	Flowers	Root/bulb	Seeds/fruit	Stems/bark
Monarda citriodora			✔		✔			✔	✔			✔			✔			✔	✔			
Nicotiana rustica			✔			✔		✔				✔			✔	✔		✔	✔			
Nigella sativa			✔		✔			✔				✔			✔						✔	
Ocimum 'African Blue'			✔			✔		✔				✔			✔	✔		✔	✔			
Ocimum basilicum 'Cinnamon'			✔		✔			✔				✔			✔	✔		✔	✔			
Ocimum basilicum 'Dark Opal'			✔		✔			✔				✔			✔	✔		✔	✔			
Ocimum basilicum 'Minimum'			✔	✔				✔				✔			✔	✔		✔	✔			
Ocimum sanctum			✔		✔			✔				✔			✔	✔		✔	✔			
Ocimum tenuiflorum			✔		✔			✔				✔			✔			✔				
Origanum dictamnus		✔			✔				✔			✔			✔	✔		✔	✔			
Origanum majorana		✔			✔			✔				✔			✔			✔	✔			
Origanum x majoricum		✔			✔			✔				✔			✔	✔		✔	✔			
Origanum onites		✔		✔				✔				✔			✔	✔		✔	✔			
Papaver rhoeas			✔	✔				✔				✔		✔	✔				✔		✔	
Pelargonium capitatum			✔	✔				✔				✔			✔			✔	✔			
Pelargonium x fragrans 'Variegatum'			✔	✔				✔				✔			✔			✔	✔			
Pelargonium odoratissimum			✔	✔				✔	✔			✔		✔	✔			✔	✔			
Pelargonium quercifolium			✔			✔		✔				✔		✔	✔			✔	✔			
Pelargonium tomentosum			✔		✔			✔	✔			✔		✔	✔			✔	✔			
Perilla frutescens 'Atropurpurea'			✔		✔			✔	✔			✔			✔			✔	✔		✔	
Petroselinum crispum var. *crispum**	✔				✔			✔				✔			✔			✔				
Petroselinum crispum var. *neapolitanum**	✔				✔			✔				✔			✔			✔				
Plectranthus amboinicus			✔		✔			✔	✔			✔			✔			✔				
Ricinus communis 'Carmencita'			✔				✔	✔				✔			✔			✔				
Salvia coccinea	✔				✔			✔			✔	✔			✔			✔	✔			
*Salvia viridis**	✔				✔			✔			✔	✔			✔			✔	✔			
Satureja hortensis	✔				✔			✔				✔			✔	✔		✔				
Tagetes lucida			✔		✔			✔				✔			✔	✔		✔	✔			
Tagetes minuta			✔		✔			✔				✔			✔	✔		✔	✔			
Tagetes patula			✔	✔				✔				✔			✔	✔			✔			
Tropaeolum majus			✔	✔	✔	✔		✔	✔			✔			✔	✔		✔	✔		✔	
*Verbascum thapsus**	✔						✔	✔				✔			✔	✔		✔	✔			

* Biennial

HERBS—Perennials, Ferns, and Bulbs

	Zones	Under 1 ft.	1–3 ft.	3–5 ft.	Over 5 ft.	Full sun	Light Shade	Shade	Dry	Well-drained	Moist	Spring	Summer	Fall	Winter	Leaves	Flowers	Root/bulb	Seeds/fruit	Stems/bark
Achillea millefolium	3–8		✔			✔				✔			✔	✔		✔	✔			
Acorus calamus	3–10				✔	✔					✔		✔			✔		✔		
Adiantum capillus-veneris	7–10		✔				✔	✔		✔	✔					✔				
Agastache foeniculum	5–9		✔			✔	✔			✔	✔		✔			✔	✔			
Alcea rosea	3–9				✔	✔				✔			✔				✔			
Alchemilla alpina	3–8		✔			✔	✔			✔	✔		✔			✔	✔			
Allium ampeloprasum var. *ampeloprasum*	4–9		✔			✔	✔			✔	✔		✔	✔		✔		✔		
Allium sativum	4–9		✔			✔	✔			✔			✔	✔		✔	✔	✔	✔	✔
Allium schoenoprasum	3–9	✔				✔	✔			✔	✔		✔	✔		✔	✔			
Allium tuberosum	3–9		✔			✔	✔			✔			✔	✔		✔	✔	✔	✔	
Althaea officinalis	3–9			✔		✔					✔		✔			✔		✔	✔	
Anthemis tinctoria	3–10		✔			✔				✔	✔		✔	✔		✔	✔			
Arctostaphylos uva-ursi	3–10	✔				✔	✔			✔		✔							✔	
Armoracia rusticana	3–10			✔		✔	✔			✔	✔		✔			✔		✔		
Arnica montana	6–9		✔			✔				✔			✔				✔			
Artemisia absinthium 'Lambrook Silver'	3–9		✔			✔	✔		✔	✔						✔				
Artemisia arborescens	8–9		✔			✔			✔	✔			✔	✔		✔				
Artemisia dracunculus var. *sativa*	4–7		✔			✔	✔		✔	✔						✔				
Artemisia ludoviciana 'Silver King'	5–9			✔		✔			✔	✔						✔				
Asarum canadense	3–8	✔					✔	✔	✔	✔	✔	✔				✔		✔		
Asclepias tuberosa	3–9		✔			✔			✔				✔				✔		✔	
Calamintha grandiflora	5–10		✔			✔	✔			✔			✔			✔				
Centella asiatica	8–10		✔			✔	✔				✔		✔			✔	✔			
Chamaemelum nobile	4–8	✔				✔	✔					✔	✔	✔		✔				
Cichorium intybus	3–10			✔		✔				✔		✔	✔	✔		✔	✔	✔		
Cimicifuga racemosa	3–8				✔	✔	✔				✔		✔					✔		
Colchicum autumnale	5–8	✔				✔	✔			✔				✔				✔		
Convallaria majalis	3–9	✔					✔	✔		✔	✔	✔					✔			
Crocus sativus	5–7	✔				✔	✔			✔				✔			✔			
Cymbopogon citratus	8–10		✔			✔	✔			✔						✔				
Dianthus x allwoodii	5–9		✔			✔	✔			✔		✔	✔	✔			✔			
Dianthus caryophyllus	5–9		✔			✔	✔			✔		✔	✔	✔			✔			

	Zones	Under 1 ft.	1–3 ft.	3–5 ft.	Over 5 ft.	Full sun	Light Shade	Shade	Dry	Well-drained	Moist	Spring	Summer	Fall	Winter	Leaves	Flowers	Root/bulb	Seeds/fruit	Stems/bark
Dianthus plumarius	5–9		✔			✔	✔			✔		✔	✔				✔			
Dictamnus albus	3–9		✔			✔	✔			✔	✔	✔	✔				✔		✔	
Eupatorium purpureum	3–10			✔		✔	✔				✔		✔	✔			✔			
Filipendula ulmaria	3–9				✔	✔	✔				✔		✔	✔		✔	✔			
Galium odoratum	3–8		✔			✔	✔	✔	✔		✔	✔					✔	✔		
Geranium maculatum	3–8		✔			✔	✔		✔		✔	✔					✔			
Geranium robertianum	3–8		✔			✔	✔		✔		✔			✔	✔		✔			
Glycyrrhiza glabra	7–9			✔		✔	✔				✔			✔					✔	
Helichrysum angustifolium	8–10		✔			✔			✔	✔				✔			✔	✔		
Heuchera americana	4–9		✔				✔	✔	✔	✔		✔	✔				✔			
Hierochloe odorata	3–9		✔			✔	✔			✔	✔	✔					✔			
Humulus lupulus	3–8				✔	✔	✔			✔	✔		✔				✔	✔		
Hydrastis canadensis	4–8	✔					✔	✔		✔	✔	✔					✔			
Hypericum perforatum	5–9		✔			✔	✔				✔			✔				✔			
Hyssopus officinalis	3–8		✔			✔	✔		✔	✔		✔	✔	✔			✔	✔			
Inula helenium	3–9				✔	✔	✔			✔	✔		✔	✔			✔	✔		
Iris germanica var. *florentina*	4–10		✔			✔				✔	✔	✔						✔		
Iris versicolor	3–8		✔			✔					✔		✔					✔		
Lavandula angustifolia	5–8		✔			✔				✔			✔				✔	✔		
Lavandula lanata	7–9			✔		✔				✔			✔				✔	✔		
Lavandula stoechas	8–10		✔			✔				✔			✔				✔	✔		
Levisticum officinale	3–8				✔	✔	✔			✔	✔	✔	✔				✔			✔
Marrubium vulgare	4–8		✔			✔			✔	✔		✔	✔				✔			
Melissa officinalis	4–9		✔			✔	✔			✔	✔		✔	✔			✔			
Mentha x piperita	4–9		✔			✔	✔			✔	✔		✔				✔			
Mentha pulegium	6–9	✔				✔	✔			✔	✔		✔				✔			
Mentha requienii	7–9	✔					✔				✔		✔				✔			
Mentha spicata	3–9		✔			✔	✔			✔	✔		✔				✔			
Monarda didyma	4–10			✔		✔	✔				✔		✔	✔			✔	✔		
Monarda fistulosa	3–9			✔		✔	✔		✔				✔	✔			✔	✔		
Myrrhis odorata	3–8		✔			✔	✔			✔	✔						✔	✔	✔	
Nepeta cataria	3–9		✔			✔	✔			✔		✔	✔	✔			✔	✔		
Origanum onites	8–10		✔			✔			✔	✔			✔	✔			✔	✔		

Plant	Zones	Under 1 ft.	1–3 ft.	3–5 ft.	Over 5 ft.	Full sun	Light Shade	Shade	Dry	Well-drained	Moist	Spring	Summer	Fall	Winter	Leaves	Flowers	Root/bulb	Seeds/fruit	Stems/bark
Origanum vulgare	5–9		✓			✓			✓	✓			✓			✓	✓			
Panax pseudoginseng	4–8		✓				✓	✓		✓	✓	✓	✓					✓		
Pogostemon cablin	10			✓		✓	✓			✓				✓		✓				
Polygonum odoratum	8–9		✓			✓				✓				✓		✓				
Poterium sanguisorba	3–9		✓			✓				✓			✓			✓				
Primula veris	3–8	✓				✓				✓	✓	✓				✓	✓			
Primula vulgaris	3–8	✓				✓				✓	✓	✓				✓	✓			
Prunella vulgaris	4–9		✓			✓	✓			✓			✓	✓		✓	✓			
Pulmonaria saccharata	3–8		✓				✓	✓		✓	✓	✓				✓	✓			
Pycnanthemum virginianum	4–8		✓			✓	✓			✓	✓		✓			✓	✓			
Rosmarinus officinalis	7–10				✓	✓				✓					✓	✓				
Rubia tinctorum	6–10		✓			✓				✓			✓	✓				✓		
Rumex acetosa	4–8		✓			✓	✓			✓			✓			✓				
Rumex scutatus	4–8		✓			✓	✓			✓			✓			✓				
Ruta graveolens	4–9		✓			✓				✓			✓			✓			✓	
Salvia clevelandii	9–10		✓			✓			✓	✓		✓	✓			✓	✓			
Salvia dorisiana	10			✓		✓			✓	✓				✓	✓	✓	✓			
Salvia lavandulifolia	7–9					✓			✓	✓			✓			✓	✓			
Salvia officinalis	4–9			✓		✓			✓	✓			✓			✓	✓			
Sanguinaria canadensis	3–9	✓					✓	✓		✓	✓	✓				✓	✓			
Santolina chamaecyparissus	6–8		✓			✓				✓			✓			✓	✓			
Saponaria officinalis	3–8		✓			✓	✓			✓			✓			✓	✓	✓		✓
Satureja montana 'Nana'	5–8	✓				✓				✓			✓	✓		✓				
Satureja thymbra	8–9		✓			✓				✓			✓	✓		✓				
Sesamum indicum	10		✓			✓				✓			✓						✓	
Solidago odora	3–9			✓		✓			✓				✓	✓		✓	✓			
Stachys officinalis	4–9		✓			✓	✓			✓	✓		✓			✓	✓			
Symphytum officinale	3–9			✓		✓	✓			✓	✓	✓	✓			✓				
Tanacetum balsamita	4–8			✓		✓	✓		✓	✓			✓			✓	✓			
Tanacetum cinerariifolium	4–9		✓			✓	✓		✓	✓			✓	✓		✓	✓			
Tanacetum parthenium	4–9		✓	✓		✓	✓		✓	✓			✓			✓	✓			
Thymus capitatus	9	✓				✓			✓	✓			✓			✓	✓			
Thymus x citriodorus	5–9	✓				✓			✓	✓			✓			✓	✓			

	ZONES	HEIGHT				LIGHT			SOIL			BLOOM SEASON				PARTS USED				
		Under 1 ft.	1–3 ft.	3–5 ft.	Over 5 ft.	Full sun	Light Shade	Shade	Dry	Well-drained	Moist	Spring	Summer	Fall	Winter	Leaves	Flowers	Root/bulb	Seeds/fruit	Stems/bark
Thymus serpyllum	4–8	✔				✔			✔	✔			✔			✔	✔			
Thymus vulgaris	4–8	✔				✔			✔	✔			✔			✔	✔			
Tulbaghia violacea	9–10		✔			✔	✔			✔	✔		✔			✔	✔			
Valeriana officinalis	4–9			✔		✔	✔			✔	✔		✔				✔	✔		
Vetiveria zizanioides	9–10				✔	✔				✔	✔		✔					✔		
Viola odorata	3–10	✔				✔	✔			✔	✔	✔	✔		✔	✔	✔			
Viola tricolor	3–10	✔				✔	✔			✔	✔	✔	✔			✔	✔			
Zingiber officinale	9–10		✔			✔				✔	✔		✔					✔		
HERBS—Shrubs and Trees																				
Aloysia triphylla	9–10				✔	✔				✔			✔			✔	✔			
Artemisia abrotanum	6–10			✔		✔			✔	✔			✔			✔				
Cedronella canariensis	10			✔		✔				✔			✔	✔		✔	✔			
Cinnamomum camphora	8–10				✔	✔				✔	✔	✔	✔			✔				
Cinnamomum zeylanicum	9–10				✔	✔				✔	✔		✔							✔
Citrus aurantium	9–10				✔	✔				✔	✔	✔	✔				✔		✔	
Citrus limon	9–10				✔	✔				✔	✔	✔	✔				✔		✔	
Comptonia peregrina	3–7			✔		✔	✔			✔			✔			✔				
Eucalyptus citriodora	9–10				✔	✔				✔					✔	✔		✔	✔	✔
Gaultheria procumbens	3–10	✔					✔	✔	✔	✔			✔			✔			✔	
Laurus nobilis 'Aurea'	8–10				✔	✔	✔			✔		✔				✔				
Lindera benzoin	4–9				✔		✔			✔	✔	✔				✔			✔	✔
Lippia graveolens	9–10				✔	✔				✔		✔				✔				
Myrica cerifera	7–9				✔				✔	✔	✔								✔	
Myrica gale	3–9			✔						✔	✔								✔	
Myrtus communis 'Flore Pleno'	9–10				✔	✔	✔			✔		✔	✔			✔	✔		✔	
Punica granatum var. *nana*	7–10		✔			✔				✔		✔					✔		✔	
Rosa canina	3–9				✔	✔				✔		✔	✔				✔		✔	
Rosa damascena	5–9				✔	✔				✔			✔	✔			✔		✔	
Rosa gallica 'Officinalis'	4–9		✔			✔				✔			✔	✔			✔		✔	
Rosa rugosa	3–9				✔	✔				✔		✔	✔				✔		✔	
Teucrium chamaedrys	5–9		✔			✔	✔			✔			✔	✔		✔				
Thymus pulegioides	4–8	✔				✔			✔	✔			✔			✔	✔			
Vitex agnus-castus	7–10				✔	✔			✔		✔		✔	✔					✔	

Column groups: **HARDINESS** (Cool-season annual, Warm-season annual, Hot-season annual, Winter-hardy) · **LIGHT** (Sun, Partial shade) · **PLANTING DEPTH** (<½ in., ½–2 in., >2 in.) · **PLANT SPACING** (<1 ft., 1–2 ft., >2 ft.) · **ROW SPACING** (1–2 ft., 2–4 ft., >4 ft.) · **DAYS TO MATURITY** (<70 days, 70–100 days, 100–130 days, >130 days) · **WAYS TO USE** (Fresh, Frozen, Canned, Pickled, Jam/preserves, Dried, Containers, Landscaping)

VEGETABLES

	Cool-season annual	Warm-season annual	Hot-season annual	Winter-hardy	Sun	Partial shade	<½ in.	½–2 in.	>2 in.	<1 ft.	1–2 ft.	>2 ft.	1–2 ft.	2–4 ft.	>4 ft.	<70 days	70–100 days	100–130 days	>130 days	Fresh	Frozen	Canned	Pickled	Jam/preserves	Dried	Containers	Landscaping
Artichoke 'Green Globe'		✔		✔	✔	✔		✔			✔				✔			✔		✔	✔		✔			✔	✔
Arugula	✔				✔	✔	✔			✔			✔			✔				✔							
Asparagus 'Jersey Knight'			✔		✔				✔		✔			✔						✔	✔						✔
Basil 'Spicy Globe'		✔			✔		✔			✔			✔							✔	✔				✔	✔	✔
Bean, Dry 'Black Turtle'		✔			✔			✔		✔			✔					✔		✔		✔			✔		
Bean, Dry 'French Horticultural'		✔			✔			✔		✔			✔					✔		✔	✔	✔			✔		
Bean, Fava 'Aquadulce'	✔				✔			✔		✔			✔					✔		✔	✔				✔		
Bean, Filet 'Tavera'		✔			✔			✔		✔			✔			✔				✔							
Bean, Green 'Provider'		✔			✔			✔		✔						✔				✔							
Bean, Green 'Tendercrop'		✔			✔			✔		✔			✔			✔				✔	✔	✔					
Bean, Lima 'Fordhook 242'		✔			✔			✔		✔			✔					✔		✔	✔	✔			✔		
Bean, Pole 'Emerite'		✔			✔			✔		✔			✔			✔				✔	✔						
Bean, Pole 'Trionfo Violetto'		✔			✔			✔		✔			✔			✔				✔	✔						
Bean, Purple 'Royal Burgundy'		✔			✔			✔		✔			✔			✔				✔	✔						
Bean, Runner 'Scarlet Runner'	✔				✔			✔		✔			✔					✔		✔					✔		✔
Bean, Yardlong 'Green Pod'		✔			✔			✔		✔			✔					✔		✔	✔						
Bean, Yellow 'Dorabel'		✔			✔			✔		✔			✔			✔				✔	✔						
Beet 'Detroit Dark Red'	✔				✔			✔		✔			✔			✔				✔	✔	✔	✔				
Beet 'Golden'	✔				✔			✔		✔			✔			✔				✔	✔	✔	✔				
Blackberry 'Ranger'				✔	✔				✔		✔			✔						✔	✔			✔			
Blackberry 'Thornfree'				✔	✔				✔			✔			✔					✔	✔				✔		
Blackberry 'Young'				✔	✔				✔			✔			✔					✔	✔				✔		
Black-Eyed Pea 'Mississippi Silver'		✔			✔			✔		✔			✔			✔				✔	✔	✔			✔		
Broccoli 'Emperor'		✔			✔	✔		✔			✔							✔		✔	✔						
Broccoli Rabe	✔				✔			✔		✔				✔						✔	✔						
Brussels Sprout 'Prince Marvel'	✔				✔			✔			✔		✔					✔		✔	✔						
Cabbage 'Early Jersey Wakefield'	✔				✔	✔		✔			✔		✔			✔				✔			✔				
Cabbage 'Wisconsin All Seasons'	✔				✔	✔		✔			✔		✔					✔		✔			✔				
Cabbage, Chinese 'Two Seasons Hybrid'		✔			✔			✔			✔		✔							✔							
Cardoon			✔		✔			✔			✔		✔							✔	✔						
Carrot 'Little Finger'	✔				✔		✔			✔			✔				✔			✔	✔	✔	✔			✔	✔
Carrot 'Napoli'	✔				✔		✔			✔			✔			✔				✔	✔	✔				✔	✔

	HARDINESS				LIGHT		PLANTING DEPTH			PLANT SPACING			ROW SPACING			DAYS TO MATURITY				WAYS TO USE							
	Cool-season annual	Warm-season annual	Hot-season annual	Winter-hardy	Sun	Partial shade	< ½ in.	½–2 in.	> 2 in.	< 1 ft.	1–2 ft.	> 2 ft.	1–2 ft.	2–4 ft.	> 4 ft.	< 70 days	70–100 days	100–130 days	> 130 days	Fresh	Frozen	Canned	Pickled	Jam/preserves	Dried	Containers	Landscaping
Carrot 'Tendersweet'	✔				✔		✔			✔			✔			✔				✔	✔	✔				✔	✔
Cauliflower 'Early White Hybrid'	✔				✔			✔			✔			✔		✔				✔	✔		✔				
Celeriac 'Brilliant'		✔			✔	✔	✔				✔			✔				✔		✔							
Celery 'Utah 52-70R'		✔			✔		✔			✔			✔					✔		✔					✔		
Celtuce	✔				✔	✔	✔			✔			✔				✔			✔							
Chard 'Rhubarb Chard'		✔			✔	✔	✔			✔			✔			✔				✔	✔					✔	✔
Chayote			✔		✔	✔					✔		✔						✔	✔							
Chicory 'Ceriolo'	✔				✔	✔				✔			✔				✔			✔							
Collard 'Georgia'	✔				✔			✔			✔			✔		✔				✔	✔						
Corn 'Earlivee'		✔			✔			✔			✔			✔		✔				✔	✔	✔		✔			
Corn 'Seneca Starshine'		✔			✔			✔			✔			✔			✔			✔	✔	✔		✔			
Corn 'Starstruck'		✔			✔			✔			✔			✔			✔			✔	✔	✔		✔			
Corn Salad 'Coquille'				✔	✔			✔		✔			✔				✔			✔							
Cress 'Winter Cress'	✔				✔	✔	✔			✔			✔			✔				✔							
Cucumber 'Burpless'		✔			✔			✔			✔				✔	✔				✔			✔				
Cucumber 'Saladin'		✔			✔			✔			✔				✔	✔				✔			✔				✔
Cucumber 'Spacemaster'		✔			✔			✔			✔				✔	✔				✔			✔			✔	
Eggplant 'Ichiban'		✔			✔	✔					✔			✔			✔			✔							
Endive 'Tres Fin'	✔				✔	✔				✔			✔				✔			✔							
Fennel 'Zefa Fino'	✔				✔	✔				✔			✔				✔			✔							
Garlic 'Elephant Garlic'			✔	✔	✔			✔	✔	✔								✔		✔					✔		
Garlic 'Spanish Roja Garlic'			✔	✔	✔		✔	✔		✔								✔		✔					✔		
Horseradish 'Maliner Kren'			✔	✔	✔					✔			✔					✔		✔	✔						
Jerusalem Artichoke 'French Mammoth White'			✔	✔	✔			✔		✔			✔					✔		✔	✔						✔
Jicama		✔			✔			✔		✔			✔					✔		✔	✔						
Kale 'Winterbor'	✔				✔	✔		✔			✔		✔			✔				✔	✔					✔	✔
Kohlrabi 'Grand Duke'	✔				✔	✔		✔		✔			✔			✔				✔							
Leek 'Broad London'	✔				✔	✔	✔			✔								✔		✔							
Lettuce 'Little Gem'		✔			✔	✔	✔			✔						✔				✔							
Lettuce 'Ruby'		✔			✔	✔	✔			✔						✔				✔						✔	
Lettuce 'Summertime'		✔			✔	✔	✔			✔						✔				✔							
Lettuce 'Tom Thumb'		✔			✔	✔	✔			✔						✔				✔							
Melon 'Casablanca'		✔			✔				✔			✔		✔			✔			✔	✔						

	HARDINESS				LIGHT		PLANTING DEPTH			PLANT SPACING			ROW SPACING			DAYS TO MATURITY				WAYS TO USE							
	Cool-season annual	Warm-season annual	Hot-season annual	Winter-hardy	Sun	Partial shade	<½ in.	½–2 in.	>2 in.	<1 ft.	1–2 ft.	>2 ft.	1–2 ft.	2–4 ft.	>4 ft.	<70 days	70–100 days	100–130 days	>130 days	Fresh	Frozen	Canned	Pickled	Jam/preserves	Dried	Containers	Landscaping
Melon 'Pancha'		✔			✔			✔			✔			✔		✔				✔	✔						
Melon 'Venus'		✔			✔			✔			✔			✔			✔			✔	✔						
Mustard Greens 'Southern Giant Curled'	✔				✔		✔			✔			✔			✔				✔							
Nasturtium 'Tip Top Mix'	✔				✔	✔		✔		✔			✔							✔					✔	✔	✔
Okra 'Clemson Spineless'			✔		✔				✔	✔	✔		✔							✔							
Onion 'Ishikura'	✔				✔			✔		✔			✔			✔				✔	✔						
Onion 'Northern Oak'	✔		✔	✔	✔			✔		✔			✔					✔		✔	✔				✔		
Onion 'Texas Grano 1015Y'	✔		✔	✔	✔			✔		✔			✔						✔	✔					✔		
Orach 'Red Orach'	✔				✔			✔		✔			✔			✔				✔							
Pak-Choi 'Mei-Quing Choi'	✔				✔			✔		✔			✔			✔				✔							
Parsley 'Moss Curled Forest Green'	✔		✔	✔	✔	✔	✔			✔			✔							✔						✔	✔
Parsnip 'Hollow Crown'	✔				✔			✔		✔			✔					✔		✔							
Pea, Garden 'Little Marvel'	✔				✔			✔		✔			✔			✔				✔	✔	✔					
Pea, Snow 'Oregon Sugar Pod II'	✔				✔			✔		✔			✔				✔			✔	✔						
Pea, Sugar Snap 'Sugar Daddy'	✔				✔			✔		✔			✔			✔				✔	✔						
Peanut 'Jumbo Virginia'			✔		✔			✔			✔		✔					✔		✔							
Pepper, Chili 'Large Hot Cherry'			✔		✔			✔			✔		✔					✔		✔				✔			
Pepper, Sweet 'California Wonder'			✔		✔			✔			✔		✔					✔		✔	✔						
Pepper, Sweet 'Gypsy'			✔		✔			✔			✔		✔				✔			✔							✔
Potato 'Norgold Russet'		✔			✔				✔	✔			✔			✔				✔	✔					✔	
Potato 'Red la Soda'		✔			✔				✔	✔			✔				✔			✔	✔					✔	
Potato 'Russet Burbank'		✔			✔				✔	✔			✔					✔		✔	✔					✔	
Pumpkin 'Connecticut Field'		✔			✔				✔			✔		✔				✔		✔	✔						
Pumpkin 'Jack Be Little'		✔			✔				✔		✔			✔				✔		✔	✔						
Radicchio 'Castelfranco'		✔			✔				✔	✔			✔					✔		✔							
Radish 'French Breakfast'	✔				✔		✔	✔		✔			✔			✔				✔							
Raspberry 'Black Hawk'			✔	✔	✔			✔			✔									✔	✔			✔			
Raspberry 'Newburgh'			✔	✔	✔			✔			✔		✔							✔	✔			✔			
Raspberry 'Wineberry'			✔	✔	✔			✔			✔		✔							✔	✔			✔			✔
Rhubarb 'Cherry Red'				✔	✔			✔			✔		✔							✔	✔			✔			
Rutabaga 'Improved Purple Top Yellow'	✔				✔			✔		✔			✔					✔		✔	✔						
Salsify 'Mammoth Sandwich Island'	✔				✔		✔			✔			✔					✔		✔	✔						
Shallot 'Success'	✔			✔	✔			✔		✔			✔						✔	✔							

	Hardiness				Light		Planting Depth			Plant Spacing			Row Spacing			Days to Maturity				Ways to Use							
Plant	Cool-season annual	Warm-season annual	Hot-season annual	Winter-hardy	Sun	Partial shade	< ½ in.	½–2 in.	> 2 in.	< 1 ft.	1–2 ft.	> 2 ft.	1–2 ft.	2–4 ft.	> 4 ft.	< 70 days	70–100 days	100–130 days	> 130 days	Fresh	Frozen	Canned	Pickled	Jam/preserves	Dried	Containers	Landscaping
Sorrel				✔	✔	✔	✔			✔			✔				✔			✔	✔					✔	
Soybean 'Prize'		✔			✔			✔		✔			✔				✔			✔	✔				✔		
Spinach 'Melody'	✔				✔	✔	✔			✔			✔				✔			✔	✔						
Spinach, Malabar 'Alba'		✔			✔		✔				✔		✔				✔			✔						✔	✔
Spinach, New Zealand		✔	✔		✔		✔			✔			✔				✔			✔	✔					✔	
Squash, Summer 'Park's Creamy Hybrid'		✔			✔			✔			✔		✔							✔	✔						
Squash, Summer 'Raven'		✔			✔			✔			✔		✔							✔	✔						
Squash, Summer 'Scaloppini'		✔			✔			✔			✔		✔							✔	✔						
Squash, Summer 'Sundance'		✔			✔			✔			✔		✔							✔	✔						
Squash, Winter 'Butterbush'		✔			✔			✔			✔						✔			✔	✔						
Squash, Winter 'Cream of the Crop'		✔			✔			✔			✔							✔		✔	✔						
Squash, Winter 'Sweet Dumpling'		✔			✔			✔			✔							✔		✔	✔						
Squash, Winter 'Turk's Turban'		✔			✔			✔			✔							✔		✔	✔						
Strawberry 'Alexandria'		✔		✔				✔		✔			✔						✔	✔	✔			✔		✔	✔
Strawberry 'Picnic'		✔		✔				✔		✔			✔					✔		✔	✔			✔		✔	
Sunflower 'Mammoth'		✔			✔			✔			✔		✔				✔			✔							✔
Sweet Potato 'Centennial'			✔		✔		✔			✔				✔			✔			✔	✔						
Tampala		✔			✔		✔			✔			✔				✔			✔							
Tomatillo 'Toma Verde'		✔			✔		✔				✔		✔				✔			✔							
Tomato 'Big Girl'		✔			✔		✔				✔		✔					✔		✔		✔					
Tomato 'Early Cascade'		✔			✔		✔				✔		✔				✔			✔	✔						
Tomato 'Heinz 1439'		✔			✔		✔				✔							✔		✔		✔					
Tomato 'Sugar Lump'		✔			✔		✔				✔		✔				✔			✔							
Tomato 'Viva Italia'		✔			✔		✔				✔		✔					✔		✔		✔		✔			
Tomato 'Yellow Canary'		✔			✔		✔				✔		✔				✔			✔					✔		
Turnip 'Tokyo Cross'	✔				✔		✔			✔			✔			✔				✔	✔	✔					

Picture Credits

The sources for the illustrations that appear in this book are listed below. Credits from left to right are separated by semicolons; credits from top to bottom are separated by dashes.

Cover: © Gene Ahrens/Bruce Coleman, Inc. 2: Catriona Tudor Erler. 10-11: Jerry Pavia. 12: © Cynthia Woodyard; Eric Crichton, London; Jerry Pavia. 13: Jerry Pavia; Thomas E. Eltzroth; Jerry Pavia. 14: © Cynthia Woodyard; Thomas E. Eltzroth; Jerry Pavia. 15: © Cynthia Woodyard; © Mark Turner; Jerry Pavia. 16: © Cynthia Woodyard; Jerry Pavia (2). 17: Jerry Pavia. 18: © Richard Shiell; Jerry Pavia; © Walter Chandoha. 19: Rosalind Creasy; Jerry Pavia (2). 20: Rosalind Creasy; Joanne Pavia; Jerry Pavia. 21: David Cavagnaro; Joanne Pavia; Virginia R. Weiler. 22: Jerry Pavia (2); © Cynthia Woodyard. 23: Joanne Pavia; Jerry Pavia (2). 24: Photos Horticultural, Ipswich, Suffolk, U.K.; Jerry Pavia; © Cynthia Woodyard. 25: Joanne Pavia; Jerry Pavia; © Michael S. Thompson. 26: Thomas E. Eltzroth; Jerry Pavia; Thomas E. Eltzroth. 27: Thomas E. Eltzroth; Jerry Pavia (2). 28: Jerry Pavia (2); Thomas E. Eltzroth. 29: Jerry Pavia; Thomas E. Eltzroth (2). 30: Jerry Pavia (2); Steven Still. 31: Steven Still; Jerry Pavia (2). 32: Thomas E. Eltzroth (2); Jerry Pavia. 33: © Richard Shiell; © Walter Chandoha; Joanne Pavia. 34: W. D. Bransford/National Wildflower Research Center; Jerry Pavia (2). 35: Jerry Pavia. 36: Jerry Pavia; Robert S. Hebb; Jerry Pavia. 37: Jerry Pavia; Joanne Pavia; Jerry Pavia. 38: Jerry Pavia. 39: © R. Todd Davis; Thomas E. Eltzroth;

Jerry Pavia. 40: © Cynthia Woodyard; Jerry Pavia; M. W. Carlton/National Wildflower Research Center. 41: Jerry Pavia; Thomas E. Eltzroth; Jerry Pavia. 42: © Walter Chandoha (2); Jerry Pavia. 43: Thomas E. Eltzroth; Jerry Pavia (2). 44: Jerry Pavia. 45: Photos Horticultural, Ipswich, Suffolk, U.K.; © Walter Chandoha; © Charles Mann. 46: © Cynthia Woodyard; Jerry Pavia (2). 47: Thomas E. Eltzroth; © Cynthia Woodyard; Jerry Pavia. 48: © Walter Chandoha; Thomas E. Eltzroth; Jerry Pavia. 49: Thomas E. Eltzroth; Peter Loewer (2). 50: © Christi Carter/Grant Heilman Photography, Lititz, Pa.; Jerry Pavia (2). 51, 52: Jerry Pavia. 53: Thomas E. Eltzroth; Jerry Pavia (2). 54, 55, 56, 57: Jerry Pavia. 58-59: Jerry Pavia. 60: Jerry Pavia (2); © Michael S. Thompson. 61: Joanne Pavia; Jerry Pavia; Joanne Pavia. 62: Jerry Pavia (2); © R. Todd Davis. 63: Jerry Pavia. 64: Steven Still (2); Joanne Pavia. 65: Jerry Pavia. 66: Steven Still; C. Colston Burrell; Jerry Pavia. 67: Joanne Pavia; Jerry Pavia; Steven Still. 68: Joanne Pavia (2); Jerry Pavia. 69: Jerry Pavia. 70: Steven Still; Jerry Pavia; Joanne Pavia. 71: Jerry Pavia. 72. Steven Still; Jerry Pavia; Joanne Pavia. 73: Jerry Pavia (2); Steven Still. 74: Thomas E. Eltzroth; John A. Lynch; Jerry Pavia. 75: Jerry Pavia. 76: John A. Lynch; Steven Still; © Richard Day/Daybreak Imagery. 77: Steven Still; Jerry Pavia; Joanne Pavia. 78: Jerry Pavia; © Michael S. Thompson; Michael Dirr. 79: © Richard Shiell; Joanne Pavia; Jerry Pavia. 80: Jerry Pavia (2); © Richard Shiell. 81: Jerry Pavia (2); Joanne

Pavia. 82: Jerry Pavia (2); © R. Todd Davis. 83: Jerry Pavia; Michael Dirr; Jerry Pavia. 84: Joanne Pavia; Jerry Pavia; David Cavagnaro. 85: © Richard Shiell; © Carole Ottesen; Joanne Pavia. 86: John A. Lynch; Jerry Pavia (2). 87: Steven Still; Jerry Pavia. 88: Jerry Pavia; Steven Still; Michael Dirr. 89: Mark Kane; © R. Todd Davis; Jerry Pavia. 90: Joanne Pavia; Jerry Pavia (2). 91: Jerry Pavia; Joanne Pavia; © Carole Ottesen. 92: Jerry Pavia. 93: Steven Still; Jerry Pavia (2). 94: Jerry Pavia; Joanne Pavia (2). 95: Jerry Pavia; André Viette; © R. Todd Davis. 96: Steven Still; Jerry Pavia; Michael Dirr. 97: Joanne Pavia (2); © R. Todd Davis. 98: © R. Todd Davis; Roger Foley/design by Sheela Lampietti, Landscape Designer; Jerry Pavia. 99: Virginia R. Weiler; Jerry Pavia; W. D. Bransford/National Wildflower Research Center. 100: Joanne Pavia; Jerry Pavia; Joanne Pavia. 101: Jerry Pavia; Michael Dirr; Joanne Pavia. 102: Jerry Pavia (2); Joanne Pavia. 103: Robert S. Hebb; Jerry Pavia; John A. Lynch. 104: Jerry Pavia; Joanne Pavia; Jerry Pavia. 105: Jerry Pavia. 106: © Carole Ottesen; Jerry Pavia (2). 107: Jerry Pavia. 108: Jerry Pavia (2); C. Colston Burrell. 109: Jerry Pavia; © Richard Shiell; © R. Todd Davis. 110: Virginia R. Weiler; Jerry Pavia; Joanne Pavia. 111: Jerry Pavia; Catriona Tudor Erler; John A. Lynch. 112: Steven Still; Jerry Pavia (2). 113: Joanne Pavia; © Carole Ottesen; © Saxon Holt. 114: Joanne Pavia; Jerry Pavia (2). 115: Jerry Pavia (2); Joanne Pavia. 116: Robert S. Hebb; Joanne Pavia (2). 117: John A. Lynch; © R.

Todd Davis; Jerry Pavia. 118: © Michael S. Thompson; C. Colston Burrell; © R. Todd Davis. 119: Joseph Strauch; Jerry Pavia (2). 120: Steven Still; © Michael S. Thompson; Jerry Pavia. 121: © Carole Ottesen; Jerry Pavia; Andy Wasowski. 122-123: Brent Heath. 124: Brent Heath; Photos Horticultural, Ipswich, Suffolk, U.K.; Jerry Pavia. 125: Joanne Pavia; Jerry Pavia (2). 126: Thomas E. Eltzroth; © Saxon Holt. 127: Jerry Pavia; © Alan L. Detrick; Joanne Pavia. 128: Jerry Pavia (2); Robert E. Lyons. 129: Robert E. Lyons (2); © R. Todd Davis. 130: Robert E. Lyons; © Michael S. Thompson; Photos Horticultural, Ipswich, Suffolk, U.K. 131: Brent Heath; Jerry Pavia; Brent Heath. 132: Jerry Pavia; © Michael S. Thompson; Jerry Pavia. 133: © Michael S. Thompson (2); Photos Horticultural, Ipswich, Suffolk, U.K. 134: Rosalind Creasy; © Michael S. Thompson (2). 135: © Michael S. Thompson (2); Brent Heath. 136: Jerry Pavia; © J. S. Sira/Garden Picture Library, London; © Michael S. Thompson. 137: C. Colston Burrell; © Michael S. Thompson (2). 138: © Richard Shiell; © Michael S. Thompson; Brent Heath. 139: Joanne Pavia; Leonard G. Phillips; Jerry Pavia. 140: Jerry Pavia. 141: C. Colston Burrell; Joanne Pavia; Brent Heath. 142: Steven Still; Joanne Pavia; Jerry Pavia. 143: Eric Crichton Photos, London; Robert E. Lyons (2). 144: © Richard Shiell; Joanne Pavia (2). 145: Joanne Pavia (2); PhotoSynthesis™. 146: Jerry Pavia; © Michael S. Thompson. 147: © Richard Shiell; Jerry Pavia; Photos Horticultural,

Ipswich, Suffolk, U.K. 148: Jerry Pavia; Joseph G. Strauch Jr.; Jerry Pavia. 149: Jerry Pavia; Brent Heath; © Michael S. Thompson. 150: Joanne Pavia (2); Jerry Pavia. 151: Jerry Pavia (2); Richard L. Doutt. 152: Brent Heath; Joanne Pavia; © J. S. Sira/Garden Picture Library, London. 153: © Alan L. Detrick; © Richard Shiell; Jerry Pavia. 154: Jerry Pavia (2); Joanne Pavia. 155: Robert E. Lyons; C. Colston Burrell. 156: Joanne Pavia; © Michael S. Thompson; Joseph G. Strauch Jr. 157: Joanne Pavia; Jerry Pavia (2). 158: Joanne Pavia; Jerry Pavia (2). 159: Brent Heath; Thomas E. Eltzroth; Brent Heath. 160: © Michael S. Thompson; Brent Heath; Andrew Lawson, Charlbury, Oxfordshire, U.K. 161: © Richard Shiell; Jerry Pavia (2). 162: Jerry Pavia; Photos Horticultural, Ipswich, Suffolk, U.K.; Joanne Pavia. 163: Brent Heath; © Michael S. Thompson (2). 164: Brent Heath; Joanne Pavia; Thomas E. Eltzroth. 165: Brent Heath; © Richard Shiell; Brent Heath. 166: Eric Crichton Photos, London; Jerry Pavia (2). 167: Joanne Pavia; Photos Horticultural, Ipswich, Suffolk, U.K. 168: C. Colston Burrell; Jerry Pavia; © Saxon Holt. 169: Jerry Pavia (2); © Richard Shiell. 170-171: Jerry Pavia. 172: Peter Haring; Mike Shoup (2); Peter Haring. 173: © Alan L. Detrick; Peter Haring (2); Jerry Pavia. 174: Jerry Pavia; Michael M. Smith; © Cheryl R. Richter; Peter Haring. 175: Peter Haring (3); Jerry Pavia. 176: Peter Haring; © Alan L. Detrick; Peter Haring; Jerry Pavia. 177: Peter Haring; Jerry Pavia (2); Peter Haring. 178: Jerry Pavia (2); © Priscilla Connell/Photo/Nats Inc.; Peter Haring. 179: Roses of Yesterday and Today; Mike Shoup; Peter Haring; Jerry Pavia. 180: Peter Haring. 181: Peter Haring; Jerry Pavia; © Alan L. Detrick; Jerry

Pavia. 182: Jerry Pavia; Mike Shoup; © Alan L. Detrick; Peter Haring. 183: Peter Haring; Jerry Pavia (2); Peter Haring. 184: Peter Haring; © Alan L. Detrick; Peter Haring (2). 185: Peter Haring; Jerry Pavia; Peter Haring (2). 186: Peter Haring (3); Jerry Pavia. 187: Joanne Pavia; Peter Haring (3). 188: Peter Haring; Jerry Pavia; Peter Haring; © Alan L. Detrick. 189: Peter Haring; © Cheryl R. Richter; Peter Haring; Jerry Pavia. 190: Joanne Pavia; Mike Shoup; Michael M. Smith; Peter Haring. 191: Jerry Pavia; © Alan L. Detrick (2); Peter Haring. 192: © Alan L. Detrick; Peter Haring (2); Jerry Pavia. 193: Peter Haring; Jerry Pavia; Mike Shoup; © Alan L. Detrick. 194: Jerry Pavia; Peter Haring (2); Jerry Pavia. 195: Photos Horticultural, Ipswich, Suffolk, U.K.; Peter Haring; Jerry Pavia; Peter Haring. 196: Jerry Pavia; Peter Haring (2); Mike Shoup. 197: Jerry Pavia (2); Peter Haring (2). 198: © Alan L. Detrick; Peter Haring (2); Mike Shoup. 199: Jerry Pavia; Peter Haring; © Alan L. Detrick; Peter Haring. 200: Jerry Pavia; Peter Haring (3). 201: © Alan L. Detrick; Peter Haring (3). 202: Peter Haring. 203: © Alan L. Detrick; Mike Shoup; Jerry Pavia; Peter Haring. 204: Peter Haring; © Alan L. Detrick (2); Mike Shoup. 205: Peter Haring; © Cheryl R. Richter; Peter Haring (2). 206: Peter Haring (2); Jerry Pavia (2). 207: Peter Haring; Photos Horticultural, Ipswich, Suffolk, U.K.; © Alan L. Detrick; © Cheryl R. Richter. 208: © Carole Ottesen; © Cheryl R. Richter; Peter Haring; John Glover, Churt, Surrey, U.K. 209: Jerry Pavia; © Alan L. Detrick; Peter Haring; Mike Shoup. 210: © Alan L. Detrick; Peter Haring (2); Jerry Pavia. 211: Jackson & Perkins (photographer: Goodman); Peter Haring (3). 212: Jerry Pavia; Peter Haring (2); © Alan L. Detrick. 213: Peter Haring; Jerry

Pavia; Photos Horticultural, Ipswich, Suffolk, U.K.; Peter Haring. 214: Peter Haring (2); © Alan L. Detrick (2). 215: Jerry Pavia; Mike Shoup (2); Peter Haring. 216: Peter Haring (2); Photos Horticultural, Ipswich, Suffolk, U.K.; Peter Haring. 217: Peter Haring (2); Jerry Pavia (2). 218: Peter Haring; Jerry Pavia; Peter Haring (2). 219: Jerry Pavia; Peter Haring (3). 220: © Alan L. Detrick (2); Peter Haring (2). 221: Jerry Pavia; Peter Haring; © Alan L. Detrick; Peter Haring. 222: Jerry Pavia (2); Mike Shoup; Peter Haring. 223: Peter Haring; Mike Shoup (2); Peter Haring. 224-225: Catriona Tudor Erler. 226: Joanne Pavia; © Michael S. Thompson; Joanne Pavia. 227: © Richard Shiell; Joseph Strauch; Jerry Pavia. 228: Jerry Pavia; Michael Dirr; © Roger Foley. 229: Robert S. Hebb; Jerry Pavia; David Cavagnaro. 230: Peter Loewer; Jerry Pavia (2). 231: Michael Dirr; Jerry Pavia; Thomas E. Eltzroth. 232: © R. Todd Davis; Jerry Pavia; © Dr. David Darom. 233: Thomas E. Eltzroth; Jerry Pavia (2). 234: © Dency Kane; © R. Todd Davis; Jerry Pavia. 235: Jerry Pavia; Thomas E. Eltzroth, Jerry Pavia. 236: Jerry Pavia (2); Joanne Pavia. 237: Michael Dirr; Steven Still; Andrew Lawson, Charlbury, Oxfordshire, U.K. 238: Jerry Pavia; © Dency Kane; Jerry Pavia. 239: © Walter Chandoha; Thomas E. Eltzroth; © Michael S. Thompson. 240: Jerry Pavia (2); Photos Horticultural, Ipswich, Suffolk, U.K. 241: Steven Still; Michael Dirr; Jerry Pavia. 242: Jerry Pavia (2); © Richard Shiell. 243: © Michael S. Thompson; © Richard Shiell (2). 244: Jerry Pavia (2); © Dency Kane. 245: Jerry Pavia; Joanne Pavia; Jerry Pavia. 246: Michael Dirr; Jerry Pavia (2). 247: Jerry Pavia; Michael Dirr; © Walter Chandoha. 248: Joseph Strauch; © Richard Shiell; Joanne Pavia.

249: © judywhite; Mark Lovejoy; © Richard Shiell. 250-251: Jerry Pavia. 252: © Richard Day/Daybreak Imagery; Jerry Pavia (2). 253: C. Colston Burrell; © Cynthia Woodyard; Steven Still. 254: Jerry Pavia (2); Holly H. Shimizu. 255: Jerry Pavia; © Richard Shiell; Jerry Pavia. 256: Jerry Pavia; Michael Dirr; Jerry Pavia. 257: Jerry Pavia (2); © Robert E. Lyons. 258: Jerry Pavia; © Richard Shiell; © Michael S. Thompson. 259: Jerry Pavia (2); © Carole Ottesen. 260: Michael Dirr; Jerry Pavia (2). 261: © Michael S. Thompson; © Richard Day/Daybreak Imagery; © Michael S. Thompson. 262: Jerry Pavia (2); © Carole Ottesen. 263, 264, 265, 266: Jerry Pavia. 267: Joanne Pavia; Jerry Pavia; © Michael S. Thompson. 268-269: Jerry Pavia. 270: Joanne Pavia; Jerry Pavia (2). 271: Jerry Pavia; Holly H. Shimizu; Joanne Pavia. 272: Jerry Pavia; Joanne Pavia; Jerry Pavia. 273: © Dency Kane; Thomas E. Eltzroth; Holly H. Shimizu. 274: © Walter Chandoha; Thomas E. Eltzroth; Jerry Pavia. 275: Joanne Pavia; Holly H. Shimizu; Jerry Pavia. 276: Joanne Pavia; Jerry Pavia; © 1996 Steven Foster. 277: Jerry Pavia. 278: Jerry Pavia (2); Joanne Pavia. 279: Jerry Pavia; © Dency Kane; Jerry Pavia. 280: Joanne Pavia; Catriona Tudor Erler; © William H. Allen Jr. 281: © Dency Kane; Jerry Pavia; Holly H. Shimizu. 282: © Dency Kane; Catriona Tudor Erler; Jerry Pavia. 283: © Dency Kane; Jerry Pavia; Joanne Pavia. 284: Holly H. Shimizu; Thomas E. Eltzroth; Jerry Pavia. 285: Jerry Pavia; © Deni Bown/Oxford Scientific Films, Long Hanborough, Oxfordshire, U.K.; © Richard Shiell. 286: © Carole Ottesen; Jerry Pavia (2). 287: © Deni Bown/Oxford Scientific Films, Long Hanborough, Oxfordshire, U.K.; Holly H. Shimizu (2). 288, 289: Jerry Pavia. 290:

Jerry Pavia; Holly H. Shimizu (2). 291: Holly H. Shimizu (2); Jerry Pavia. 292: Rita Buchanan; Jerry Pavia (2). 293: Jerry Pavia. 294: Jerry Pavia (2); Catriona Tudor Erler. 295: Joanne Pavia; © Walter Chandoha; Jerry Pavia. 296: Joanne Pavia; Jerry Pavia (2). 297: Jerry Pavia; © Dency Kane; Jerry Pavia. 298: Jerry Pavia (2); © Walter Chandoha. 299: Joanne Pavia; Jerry Pavia; © Richard Shiell. 300: Holly H. Shimizu; Jerry Pavia; © Dency Kane. 301: © Richard Shiell (2); Jerry Pavia. 302: © Tom Ulrich/Oxford Scientific Films, Long Hanborough, Oxfordshire, U.K.; Jerry Pavia; © Dency Kane. 303: © Dency Kane; Joanne Pavia; Jerry Pavia. 304: Jerry Pavia; © Dency Kane; Rita Buchanan. 305: © Dency Kane; © Richard Shiell; Joanne Pavia. 306: Jerry Pavia (2); Andrew Lawson, Charlbury, Oxfordshire, U.K. 307: Catriona Tudor Erler; Jerry Pavia (2). 308: Jerry Pavia; Rita Buchanan; Joanne Pavia. 309: Jerry Pavia (2); Joanne Pavia. 310: Jerry Pavia; Joanne Pavia; Jerry Pavia. 311: Jerry Pavia; Thomas E. Eltzroth; Holly H. Shimizu. 312: Jerry Pavia (2); Joanne Pavia. 313: Jerry Pavia (2); Holly H. Shimizu. 314: Jerry Pavia; © Richard Shiell; Joanne Pavia. 315: Jerry Pavia. 316: Harry Smith Horticultural Photographic Collection, Chelmsford, Essex, U.K.; Joanne Pavia; Holly H. Shimizu. 317: Jerry Pavia; Holly H. Shimizu; Jerry Pavia. 318-319: Jerry Pavia. 320: Jerry Pavia; Thomas E. Eltzroth; © Walter Chandoha. 321: © Walter Chandoha; Thomas E. Eltzroth; © Dwight R. Kuhn. 322: © Dwight R. Kuhn; Thomas E. Eltzroth; © Dwight R. Kuhn. 323: Thomas E. Eltzroth; © Dwight R. Kuhn; Thomas E. Eltzroth. 324: Thomas E. Eltzroth; © Walter Chandoha; Thomas E. Eltzroth. 325: Thomas E. Eltzroth; © Walter Chandoha; Thomas E. Eltzroth.

326: Thomas E. Eltzroth (2); Joanne Pavia. 327: © Walter Chandoha; Thomas E. Eltzroth (2). 328: Thomas E. Eltzroth; Jerry Pavia; © Walter Chandoha. 329: Thomas E. Eltzroth. 330: Thomas E. Eltzroth (2); Jerry Pavia. 331: Jerry Pavia; © Walter Chandoha; Thomas E. Eltzroth. 332: John Marshall; Thomas E. Eltzroth (2). 333: Joanne Pavia; Jerry Pavia; Joanne Pavia. 334: Thomas E. Eltzroth. 335: Thomas E. Eltzroth; © Walter Chandoha (2). 336: © Dwight R. Kuhn; Thomas E. Eltzroth (2). 337: © Walter Chandoha; Thomas E. Eltzroth; © Dwight R. Kuhn. 338: Thomas E. Eltzroth. 339: Thomas E. Eltzroth (2); Jerry Pavia. 340: Jerry Pavia; Thomas E. Eltzroth (2). 341: Thomas E. Eltzroth. 342: Thomas E. Eltzroth; Jerry Pavia; Thomas E. Eltzroth. 343: Thomas E. Eltzroth; Joanne Pavia; Jerry Pavia. 344: Joanne Pavia; Thomas E. Eltzroth (2). 345: Thomas E. Eltzroth (2); Jerry Pavia. 346: Thomas E. Eltzroth (2); Jerry Pavia. 347: Thomas E. Eltzroth; © David Cavagnaro; Jerry Pavia. 348: Thomas E. Eltzroth (2); © Walter Chandoha. 349: Joanne Pavia; Thomas E. Eltzroth; © David Cavagnaro. 350: Jerry Pavia (2); Thomas E. Eltzroth. 351: Thomas E. Eltzroth; © Walter Chandoha; Thomas E.Eltzroth. 352: Thomas E. Eltzroth; Joanne Pavia; Thomas E. Eltzroth. 353: Joanne Pavia; Thomas E. Eltzroth (2). 354: © Walter Chandoha (2); Thomas E. Eltzroth. 355: Thomas E. Eltzroth. 356: Jerry Pavia; Thomas E. Eltzroth; Jerry Pavia. 357: Thomas E. Eltzroth (2); Joanne Pavia. 358: Thomas E. Eltzroth. 359: Thomas E. Eltzroth; © Walter Chandoha; © Dwight R. Kuhn. 360, 361: Thomas E. Eltzroth. 362: Jerry Pavia; Thomas E. Eltzroth (2). 363: Leonard G. Phillips; Thomas E. Eltzroth (2). 364-365: Jerry Pavia. 366:

© Richard Shiell; Jerry Pavia; Thomas E. Eltzroth. 367: Michael Dirr; Jerry Pavia (2). 368: © Richard Shiell (2); Thomas E. Eltzroth. 369: Monrovia; Michael Dirr; Thomas E. Eltzroth. 370: Jerry Pavia. 371: Jerry Pavia (2); © Alan and Linda Detrick. 372: © Hal H. Harrison/Grant Heilman Photography, Lititz, Pa.; Michael Dirr; Jerry Pavia. 373: Michael Dirr (2); Jerry Pavia. 374: Thomas E. Eltzroth; Jerry Pavia; © Saxon Holt. 375: Jerry Pavia; Joanne Pavia; © Richard Shiell. 376: © Dency Kane; © Richard Shiell; Thomas E. Eltzroth. 377: © Jane Grushow/Grant Heilman Photography, Lititz, Pa.; Steven Still; Jerry Pavia. 378: Jerry Pavia. 379: Jerry Pavia (2); Michael Dirr. 380: Jerry Pavia; Thomas E. Eltzroth; Jerry Pavia. 381: Michael Dirr; Jerry Pavia (2). 382: © Richard Shiell; Jerry Pavia; © Richard Shiell. 383: Michael Dirr; © Richard Shiell; © Dency Kane. 384: Jerry Pavia (2); Joanne Pavia. 385: © Richard Shiell; Jerry Pavia; Michael Dirr. 386: Derek Fell; Jerry Pavia (2). 387: Michael Dirr; © Robert E. Lyons; © Michael S. Thompson. 388: Jerry Pavia; © Richard Shiell (2). 389: Jerry Pavia; © Richard Shiell (2). 390: © Robert E. Lyons; Jerry Pavia (2). 391: © Dency Kane; Michael Dirr; © R. Todd Davis. 392: Jerry Pavia; Thomas E. Eltzroth; Jerry Pavia. 393: Jerry Pavia (2); © R. Todd Davis. 394: Jerry Pavia (2); Joanne Pavia. 395: Thomas E. Eltzroth; Anita Sabarese; Jerry Pavia. 396: Jerry Pavia; © Richard Shiell; © R. Todd Davis. 397: Michael Dirr (2); © Richard Shiell. 398: Jerry Pavia; Thomas E. Eltzroth; Michael Dirr. 399: Jerry Pavia; Michael Dirr; Jerry Pavia. 400: © Dency Kane; Jerry Pavia (2). 401: © R. Todd Davis; Jerry Pavia (2). 402: Monrovia; Jerry Pavia (2). 403: © Richard Shiell (2); Jerry Pavia. 404:

© Richard Shiell; © Grant Heilman/Grant Heilman Photography, Lititz, Pa.; Jerry Pavia. 405: Jerry Pavia. 406: © Richard Shiell; Jerry Pavia (2). 407: Jerry Pavia. 408: Jerry Pavia; © Michael S. Thompson; Jerry Pavia. 409: Jerry Pavia; © Michael S. Thompson; © R. Todd Davis. 410: Jerry Pavia; © Richard Shiell; Jerry Pavia. 411: Jerry Pavia; © Richard Shiell; Jerry Pavia. 412: Michael Dirr; Jerry Pavia (2). 413: © Alan and Linda Detrick; Steven Still; Joanne Pavia. 414: Jerry Pavia. 415: Jerry Pavia; Thomas E. Eltzroth; Jerry Pavia. 416: Jerry Pavia; Thomas E. Eltzroth; Jerry Pavia. 417: © Dency Kane; © Jane Grushow/Grant Heilman Photography, Lititz, Pa.; © Runk/Schoenberger/Grant Heilman Photography, Lititz, Pa. 418-419: © Dwight R. Kuhn. 420: © Dwight R. Kuhn; © J. Alcock/Visuals Unlimited; Agricultural Research Service-USDA. 421: © Dwight R. Kuhn. 422: © Dwight R. Kuhn (2); © Robin Mitchell, All Rights Reserved. 423: Animals Animals © 1995 G. A. MACLEAN/Oxford Scientific Films; © Ron West; © Dwight R. Kuhn. 424: Jan Taylor/Bruce Coleman Ltd., Uxbridge, Middlesex, U.K.; © Gregory K. Scott/Nature Photos; © Ron West. 425: © July Hile/Unicorn Stock Photos; © Dwight R. Kuhn; © Ron West. 426: © J. Alcock/Visuals Unlimited; © Dwight R. Kuhn; © Grant Heilman/Grant Heilman Photography, Lititz, Pa. 427: © Dwight R. Kuhn; © Science VU/Visuals Unlimited. 428: David J. Shetlar; © Bill Beatty/Visuals Unlimited; Scott Aker. 429: © Science VU/Visuals Unlimited; Agricultural Research Service-USDA; E. R. Degginger. 430: © Ray Kriner/Grant Heilman Photography, Lititz, Pa.; © Richard Thom/Visuals Unlimited; © Dwight R. Kuhn. 431: Scott Aker; © Dwight R. Kuhn (2). 432: © Breck P. Kent;

© Dwight R. Kuhn. 433: E. R. Degginger; Scott Aker; E. R. Degginger. 434: © Kenneth D. Whitney/Visuals Unlimited; © K.G. Preston-Mafham/Premaphotos Wildlife, Bodmin, Cornwall, U.K.; © Ron West. 435: © Dwight R. Kuhn (2); Mark S. McClure. 436: © Breck P. Kent; © Runk/Schoenberger/Grant Heilman Photography, Lititz, Pa.; © Grant Heilman/Grant Heilman Photography, Lititz, Pa. 437: © Dwight R. Kuhn; Animals Animals © 1995 D. R. Specker. 438: © Dwight R. Kuhn (2); David J. Shetlar. 439: © Dwight R. Kuhn; Animals Animals © 1995 Richard Shiell. 440: David J. Shetlar; E. R. Degginger; © Runk/Schoenberger/Grant Heilman Photography, Lititz, Pa. 441: © Ron West; © Grant Heilman/Grant Heilman Photography, Lititz, Pa.; © Glenn Oliver, Visuals Unlimited. 442: © Bill Beatty/Visuals Unlimited; © Runk/Schoenberger/Grant Heilman Photography, Lititz, Pa.; © Grant Heilman/Grant Heilman

Photography, Lititz, Pa. 443: © Ron West; Scott Aker; © Dwight R. Kuhn. 444: © Dwight R. Kuhn; © Grant Heilman/Grant Heilman Photography, Lititz, Pa.; © Dwight R. Kuhn. 445: © Douglas C. Allen; © Dwight R. Kuhn. 446: © Runk/Schoenberger/Grant Heilman Photography, Lititz, Pa. (2); E. R. Degginger. 447: Animals Animals © 1995 D. R. Specker; © Ron West; © Dwight R. Kuhn. 448: Arlyn W. Evans; © Jeffrey Howe/Visuals Unlimited; © Ron West. 449: Animals Animals © 1995 Richard Shiell; Ethel Dutky. 450: Anne Bird Sindermann; E. R. Degginger; Katharine D. Widin. 451: © Alan L. Detrick; Ethel Dutky (2). 452: Ethel Dutky; Agricultural Research Service-USDA; Anne Bird Sindermann. 453: Ron Jones; Cooperative Extension Service, North Carolina State University; Ethel Dutky (2). 454: Ethel Dutky; Ron Jones/Cooperative Extension Service, North Carolina State University; Scott Aker. 455: Ann F. Rhoads;

© John Colwell/Grant Heilman Photography, Lititz, Pa.; © Runk/Schoenberger/Grant Heilman Photography, Lititz, Pa. 456: Potash & Phosphate Institute; E. R. Degginger; © Runk/Schoenberger/Grant Heilman Photography, Lititz, Pa. 457: Ethel Dutky; E. R. Degginger; Ethel Dutky. 458: George W. Hudler; © Grant Heilman/Grant Heilman Photography, Lititz, Pa.; Ethel Dutky. 459: Arlyn W. Evans; G. David Lewis/E. R. Degginger (2). 460: Scott Aker; Ethel Dutky (2). 461: Ethel Dutky (2); James G. Kantzes. 462: © John Colwell/Grant Heilman Photography, Lititz, Pa.; © Larry Lefever/Grant Heilman Photography, Lititz, Pa.; Ann F. Rhoads. 463: Anne Bird Sindermann; Scott Aker; © Alan L. Detrick. 464: Runk/Schoenberger/Grant Heilman Photography, Lititz, Pa.; James Dill; E. R. Degginger. 465: © Robert & Linda Mitchell; Ethel Dutky (2). 466-467: Maps by John Drummond, Time-Life Books,

Inc. 492: © William J. Weber/Visuals Unlimited (2); © Larry Lefever/Grant Heilman Photography, Lititz, Pa.— © John D. Cunningham/Visuals Unlimited; Barbara H. Emerson; Science VU/Visuals Unlimited. 493: © Ted Rose/Unicorn Stock Photos; John Gerlach/Visuals Unlimited; © Walt Anderson/Visuals Unlimited— © John Colwell/Grant Heilman Photography, Lititz, Pa.; © Jane Grushow/Grant Heilman Photography, Lititz, Pa.; © Grant Heilman/Grant Heilman Photography, Lititz, Pa. 494: © Jane Grushow/Grant Heilman Photography, Lititz, Pa.; © Alan L. Detrick; John D. Cunningham/Visuals Unlimited— © Jim Strawser/Grant Heilman Photography, Lititz, Pa.; © A. Gurmankin/Unicorn Stock Photos; © Liz Ball. 495: © Alan L. Detrick; © Mark E. Gibson; © R. J. Matthews/Unicorn Stock Photos— © William J. Weber/Visuals Unlimited; © Mark E. Gibson; © Alan L. Detrick.

Index

Canary creeper: 55
Candleberry: *298*
Candytuft: *36, 93;* fragrant, 36; globe, *36*, 468; rocket, 36
Canker brake: 267
Cankerworms: *429*
Canna, canna lily (*Canna*): *19, 132;* diseases of, 460; x *generalis, 19, 132*
Cantaloupes: 344
Canterbury bells: *19*
Cape Coast lily: *136*
Cape cowslip: *152*
Cape marigold: *29*, 469
Cape plumbago: *404*
Cape tulip: 147
Capsicum: 19, 280, chart 510
Caraway: *281*
Cardinal climber: *239*
Cardinal flower: *97*, 472
Cardiocrinum: 133; giganteum, 133
Cardiospermum: 230; halicacabum, 230
Cardoon: 26, *331, chart* 516
Carex: 254, chart 505
Carmel creeper: 374
Carnation: *79-80*, 286; diseases of, 458, 460, 463, 464; insect pests of, *429*
Carpet bugle: 226
Carpinus: 374, chart 508; *betulus,* 482
Carrots: *331-332, chart* 516, *chart* 517; and beneficial insects, 489; wild, *28*
Carthamus: 20, 280, chart 510
Carum: 281; carvi, 281, chart 510
Caryopteris: 374; x *clandonensis, 374*
Cassina: 391
Caster-oil plant: *50*
Castor bean: *50*, 307
Catalpa (*Catalpa*): diseases of, 458, 465
Catalpa (*Chilopsis*): desert, *376*
Catchfly (*Lychnis*): *97;* German, 97
Catchfly (*Silene*): *53*, 114; drooping, 53; fire-pink, 114; sweet William, 53
Caterpillars: predators of, *420, 422, 423, 424, 425*
Catharanthus: 20, 281, 468, *chart* 510

Catherine-wheel: *147*
Catmint: *100, 299;* blue, 100; Persian, *100*
Catnip: 299
Cattail: *263;* and beneficial insects, 424
Cauliflower: *332-333, chart* 517; insect pests of, *436*
Ceanothus (*Ceanothus*): *374, chart* 505
Cedar: insect pests of incense, 442
Cedar (*Cedrus*): *375;* Atlas, 375; blue Atlas, 375; deodar, *375*
Cedar (*Chamaecyparis*): Port Orford, 376
Cedar (*Juniperus*): Colorado red, 392; diseases of red, 451, 463
Cedar (*Thuja*): white, 415
Cedronella: 281; canariensis, 281, chart 515
Cedrus: 375; atlantica, 375; deodara, 375, chart 509
Celandine: tree, *98*
Celeriac: *333, chart* 517
Celery: *333, chart* 517; wild, *275*
Celery cabbage: *331*
Celery root: *333*
Celosia (*Celosia*): *20;* insect pests of, *433*
Celsia (*Celsia*): *21;* Cretan, *21; cretica, 21*
Celtuce: *334, chart* 517
Cenchrus species: *492*
Centaurea (*Centaurea*): *21, 73, 282; americana,* 21; *cyanus, 21, 282, chart* 510; *dealbata,* 73; globe, 73; *hypoleuca,* 73; *macrocephala,* 73; *montana, 73, chart* 498; *moschata,* 21; Persian, 73; ruthenian, 73; *ruthenica,* 73; *solstitialis, 492*
Centella: 282; asiatica, 282, chart 512
Centranthus: 73; ruber, 73, chart 498
Century plant: *62*
Ceonothus (*Ceonothus*): *chart* 505
Cerastium: arvense, 492
Ceratostigma: 74, 230, 470
Cercis: 375; canadensis, 375, chart 508; *chinensis,* 375; *reniformis,* 375
Chaenomeles: 375, chart 506

Chamaecrista: 21
Chamaecyparis: 376, chart 507, *chart* 509
Chamaemelum: 282; nobile, 282, chart 512
Chamomile: 478; teas of, 480
Chamomile (*Anthemis*): *65, 275;* dyer's, *275;* St. John's, 65; yellow, *275*
Chamomile (*Chamaemelum*): garden, *282;* Roman, *282*
Chamomile (*Matricaria*): German, *296;* sweet false, *296;* wild, *296*
Chard: *334, chart* 517
Chasmanthium: 254; latifolium, 254
Chaste tree: *317,* 417
Chayote: *335, chart* 517
Checkerberry: 235, 289
Checkerbloom: *113*
Checkered lily: *144*
Checkermallow: *113*
Cheiranthus: 22; allionii. See Erysimum; cheiri, 22
Chelone: 74, 477
Chenopodium: 283, 493, chart 510
Cherry (*Cardiospermum*): winter, *230*
Cherry laurel (*Prunus*): Carolina, 405; common, 405; Portuguese, 405
Cherry pie: *35*, 468, 469
Cherry (*Prunus*): *405;* diseases of, 450, 453, 457, 462; insect pests of, *428, 429,* 434, 445; Japanese flowering, *405;* weeping Higan, *405*
Chervil: *275*, 479; salad, *275*
Chestnut: diseases of Chinese, 465; insect pests of, *449*
Chickweed: field, *492*
Chicory: *283, chart* 517; common, *283*
Chigger flower: *278*
Chilopsis: 376, chart 508
China aster: *18,* 469; diseases of, 464
Chinch bugs: *430*
Chincherinchee: 160; giant, 160
Chinese cabbage: *331, chart* 516
Chinese forget-me-not: 26
Chinese houses: *24*
Chinese lantern lily: *162*

Chinese parsley: *See Coriandrum*
Chionodoxa: 133; luciliae, 133; sardensis, 133
Chives: 272; drumstick, *63, 125;* garlic, *272*
Chlidanthus: 133; fragrans, 133
Chocolate vine: 226
Chokeberry: *370;* diseases of, 462
Chokecherry: diseases of, 450
Christmas berry: *370*
Christmas rose: *90;* winter damage and, 482
Chrysanthemum (*Chrysanthemum*): *22, 74-75;* annual, *22; balsamita. See Tanacetum; carinatum,* 22; *cinerariifolium. See Tanacetum; coccineum, 74, chart* 496; *coronarium,* 22; diseases of, 451, 452, 457, 458, 459, 461, 464, 465; florist's, *74-75; frutescens,* 74; garland, *22;* hardy, *74-75;* insect pests of, *429, 432, 433, 437, 438,* 440; *leucanthemum,* 74; x *morifolium, 74-75; nipponicum,* 75; *parthenium,* 75, *chart* 496. *See also Tanacetum;* x *superbum,* 75; tricolor, 22
Chrysogonum: 75, 230; virginianum, 230, 477; *virginianum* var. *australe,* 75; *virginianum* var. *virginianum,* 75, 230
Chrysopsis: 76
Ciboule: 272
Cicadas: *430*
Cichorium: 283; intybus, 283, chart 512
Cidron: *273*
Cigar plant: *26;* Mexican, *26*
Cilantro: *See Coriandrum*
Cimicifuga: 76, 283; americana, 76, 477; *racemosa, 283,* 477, *chart* 512; *ramosa,* 76; *simplex,* 76
Cinnamomum: 284; camphora, 284, chart 515; *zeylanicum, 284, chart* 515
Cinnamon: *284;* Ceylon, *284*
Cinquefoil: *107;* bush, *404;* Himalayan, 107; Nepal, *107;* ruby, 107; spring, 107; staghorn, 107; wineleaf, 107
Cirsium: 22, 493
Cistus: 376; x *hybridus, chart* 507; x *purpureus, 376, chart* 507; *salvi-*

Snails: 443-444; predators of, *424*
Snakeroot (*Asarum*): 68, 227, *278*
Snakeroot (*Cimicifuga*): black, *283*
Snake's-head iris: *147*
Snakeweed: *107*
Snakewort: button, *153*
Snapdragon: *14;* common, 469; diseases of, *459, 463, 465*
Sneezeweed: *88;* common, *88*
Snowbell: fragrant, *414;* Japanese, 414
Snowdrop: *145;* common, *145;* giant, 145
Snowdrops windflower: 65
Snowdrop tree: 414
Snowflake (*Leucojum*): *153;* giant, *153;* spring, 153; summer, *153*
Snowflake (*Ornithogalum*): summer, *160*
Snow-on-the-mountain: *31,* 469
Soapberry: *412;* western, *412*
Soapweed: 121
Soapwort: *111, 311;* rock, *111*
Society garlic: *315*
Sod webworms: *444*
Soil: acid, 489; adjusting pH of, 489; amendments, 489; conditioning, 489; improving clay, 489; preventing erosion of, 475, 476
Solanum family: insect pests of, *434*
Solidago: 115, 312, chart 514
Solomon's-seal (*Polygonatum*): *106,* 245; great, 106; small, *106,* 245; variegated, *245*
Solomon's-seal (*Smilacina*): false, *114;* false starry, 114
Sophora: insect pests of, *438*
Sorbet: *378*
Sorghastrum: 262
Sorrel (*Hibiscus*): *291;* Indian, *291;* Jamaica, *291;* red, *291*
Sorrel (*Oxalis*): wood, *160*
Sorrel (*Rumex*): *308, chart* 519; French, *308;* garden, 308
Sorrel tree: *400*
Soup mint: *304*
Sourgrass: *494*
Southern pine beetle: 427
Southernwood: 277
Soybeans: *355, chart* 519
Sparaxis: 164

Spartina: 262; pectinata, 262
Spearmint: 297; teas of, 480
Specialized gardens: children's, 480; city gardens, 476; cottage gardens, 478; evening gardens, 476, 485; fragrance, 476, 477; low-maintenance gardens, 468, 484; seaside gardens, 469, 474; small gardens, 476, 482. *See also* Shade gardens
Speedwell: *119;* long-leaf, 119; silver, 119; spike, 119; woolly, 119
Sphaeralcea: 115, chart 498
Spiceberry: *370*
Spicebush: *295*
Spider flower: *23,* 468
Spider lily: 472
Spider lily (*Crinum*): *136*
Spider lily (*Hymenocallis*): *149*
Spider lily (*Lycoris*): 155; golden, 155; red, 155
Spider mites: 423, 439; predators of, *420, 423, 424*
Spiderwort: *117*
Spigelia (*Spigelia*): *116,* 472
Spikenard: 472
Spikenard (*Aralia*): 66
Spikenard (*Smilacina*): false, 114
Spinach: *356, chart* 519; Malabar, *356, chart* 519; New Zealand, *356, chart* 519
Spinach (*Atriplex*): mountain, *16,* *278, 347*
Spindle tree: *234,* 383; Japanese, 383; winged, *383*
Spiraea, spirea (*Spiraea*): *413;* Bumald, *413;* x *bumalda, 413, chart* 507; insect pests of, *442,* 443; Japanese, 413; *japonica,* 413; Vanhoutte, 413; x *vanhouttei,* 413
Spirea (*Astilbe*): false, *228;* garden, 228; perennial, 69
Spittlebugs: 444-445
Sporobolus: 262; heterolepis, 262
Spotted dog: 108
Spotted laurel: *370*
Sprekelia (*Sprekelia*): *164*
Spring beauty: 76
Spring starflower: *150*
Springtails: predators of, *424*
Spruce: *401;* diseases of, 453, 460, 462, 463; dwarf Alberta, 401; in-

sect pests of, *431, 445;* Norway, *401;* white, 401
Spruce budworms: *445;* predators of, *422*
Spurge (*Euphorbia*): *84;* cushion, *84;* flowering, *84;* spotted, *494*
Spurge (*Pachysandra*): *244;* Allegheny, 101, 244
Squash: diseases of, 462, 464; insect pests of, *431, 432, 432;* summer, *357, chart* 519; winter, 233, *358, chart* 519
Squash bugs: predators of, *426*
Squawroot: 118
Squill (*Puschkinia*): striped, 161
Squill (*Scilla*): 163; Chinese, 164; meadow, 163; Siberian, 164; twinleaf, 163, *164*
Squill (*Urginea*): sea, 167
Sri tulsi: 301
St. James's lily: *164*
St.-John's-wort: *238, 292, 390, 475;* common, *292;* creeping, *238, 390;* golden, 390; Moser's, *238;* perforate, *292;* shrubby, 390
Stachys: 116, 247; byzantina, 116, *247,* 470; *macrantha, 247; officinalis, 312, chart* 514
Star anise: *391*
Starflower: 239
Star-glory: 239
Star-of-Bethlehem (*Eucharis*): 143
Star-of-Bethlehem (*Ornithogalum*): 160; nodding
Stars-of-Persia: 63, *125*
Statice: *38;* notchleaf, *38,* 469; Russian, 38
Stephanandra: 413; incisa, 413
Sternbergia: 165; lutea, 165
Stewartia (*Stewartia*): *413;* Japanese, *413;* mountain, 413; *ovata,* 413, *chart* 507; *pseudocamellia,* *413, chart* 509
Stipa: 263
Stock: *41;* diseases of, 458; evening, 41; night-scented, 41
Stokes' aster (*Stokesia*): 116, 477; *laevis,* 477
Stonecrop: *112-113, 247;* Aizoon, 112; common, *247,* 472; great, 112; orange, *112;* showy, 112; Siebold, 112; two-row, *112-113;* wild, 247, 472

Storax: *414*
Storksbill: *302-303*
Strawberries: *359, chart* 519; insect pests of, *439, 441, 444, 446, 447*
Strawberry geranium: 246
Strawberry tree: *369*
Strawflower: *35;* diseases of, 465
Streptocarpus: diseases of, 460
Styrax: 414, chart 509
Succory: *283*
Sugar scoop: 248
Sumac (*Cotinus*): Venetian, *378*
Sumac (*Rhus*): *410;* cut-leaf staghorn, *410;* fragrant, 410; staghorn, 410
Summer cypress: *37,* 469
Summer hyacinth: *145*
Summer lilac: *372*
Summer snowflake (*Leucojum*): *153*
Summer snowflake (*Ornithogalum*): *160*
Summer-sweet: *377*
Sundrop: *100;* common, *100;* Ozark, 100
Sunflower (*Balsamorhiza*): Oregon, *70*
Sunflower (*Helianthus*): *35, 360,* 469, 472, *chart* 519; common, *35,* 469; diseases of, *459;* insect pests of, *433*
Sunflower (*Heliopsis*): *89;* false, *89*
Sunflower (*Inula*): wild, *293*
Sunflower (*Tithonia*): Mexican, *54,* 469
Sun plant: *49*
Sun rose: *236;* yellow, *236*
Swamp lily: long-neck, *136;* Powell's, *136*
Swan River daisy: *17*
Sweet alyssum: *39,* 469, 477
Sweet anise: *288*
Sweet Annie: 277
Sweet balm: *296*
Sweet bay (*Laurus*): 294, 394
Sweet bay (*Magnolia*): 397
Sweet box: *412*
Sweet cicely: *299,* 479
Sweet clover: and beneficial insects, 426
Sweet flag: *270,* 472
Sweet gale: 298
Sweetgrass: *257*